MORE BOOKS KIDS WILL SIT STILL FOR

MORE BOOKS KIDS WILL SIT STILL FOR™

A Read-Aloud Guide

Judy Freeman

R. R. Bowker®
A Reed Reference Publishing Company
New Providence, New Jersey

Published by R. R. Bowker,
a Reed Reference Publishing Company
Copyright © 1995 by Reed Elsevier Inc.
All rights reserved

PRINTED AND BOUND IN THE UNITED STATES OF AMERICA

The following has been reprinted with permission of
the publishers:

A passage from *Junie B. Jones and a Little Monkey
Business* by Barbara Park. Copyright © 1993 by Barbara
Park. Reprinted by permission of Random House, Inc.

Quote from "Books on Top," by E. Annie Proulx, May
26, 1994. Copyright © 1994 by The New York Times
Company. Reprinted by permission.

"Quiet," from THE MALIBU AND OTHER POEMS by
Myra Cohn Livingston. Copyright © 1972 by Myra
Cohn Livingston. Reprinted by permission of Marian
Reiner for the author.

Library of Congress Cataloging-in-Publication Data

Freeman, Judy.
    More books kids will sit still for : a read-aloud guide / Judy
Freeman.
        p. cm.
    Includes bibliographical references and index.
    ISBN 0-8352-3520-3   0-8352-3731-1 (pbk.)
    1. Children—United States—Books and reading. 2. Children's
literature—Bibliography. 3. Oral reading. 4. School libraries—
Activity programs—United States. I. Title.
Z1037.F848 1995
[PN1009.A1]
028.1'62—dc20
                                                    95-36760
                                                         CIP

ISBN 0 - 8352 - 3520 - 3

9 780835 235204

Once more to Izzy, the nicest person I know,
with whom I gratefully share my wavelengths

CONTENTS

List of Illustrations   ix
Foreword   xi
Acknowledgments   xv

MAKING THE MOST OF CHILDREN'S LITERATURE

Looking for Read-Alouds   3

A Few Good Books   4
New Trends   6
50 Ways to Recognize a Read-Aloud   7
Freeman's Favorites   23
Books That Bomb   25
Reassessing Books   26
Kid-Testing   29
The Caldecott Project   31
Authors and Illustrators   33
A List of Memorable Authors
    and Illustrators   34

Reading with Expression   37

Finding Your Voice   38
Literature-Based Teaching   42
Welcome Back   44
Do You Get It?   46
Planning Literature Lessons   50
Making Connections   52

Reader's Theater and Creative
    Drama   62
Fantasy Versus Realistic Fiction   64
Fiction Versus Nonfiction   65
Fact for the Day   66
Evaluating Readability   67

The Importance of a School
Library/Media Center Program   71

The Role of the School Librarian   72
Thoughts on Flexible Scheduling   74
A Sampling of Library Skills   76
Book Care Lessons   78
Book Location Lessons
    for Grades 1–6   80
Orientation Games for Grades 3–6   83
Mucking About in the Card Catalog   87
Discipline and Rewards   93
The Van Holten Library Curriculum
    in Progress, Grades K–5   95
Books and Technology   100

ANNOTATED READ-ALOUD LISTS

How to Get the Most Out of
the Booklists   105

Fiction for Preschool   109

Fiction for Preschool–
Kindergarten   125

Fiction for Kindergarten–Grade 1   165

Fiction for Grades 1–2   215

Fiction for Grades 2–3   269

Fiction for Grades 3–4   303

Fiction for Grades 4–5   321

Fiction for Grades 5–6   335

Folk & Fairy Tales, Myths
& Legends: Single Stories   351

Folk & Fairy Tales, Myths
& Legends: Collections   411

Nonfiction and Biography   425

Poetry, Nonsense, and Language-
Oriented Nonfiction   473

BIBLIOGRAPHY AND INDEXES

Professional Bibliography   521
Author Index   545
Title Index   589
Illustrator Index   633
Subject Index   675
About the Author   869

LIST OF ILLUSTRATIONS

Charles Dickens: The Man Who Had Great Expectations by Diane Stanley
and Peter Vennema. Illustration by Diane Stanley. — xvi

Lives of the Writers: Comedies, Tragedies (and What the Neighbors Thought) by Kathleen Krull.
Illustration by Kathryn Hewitt. — 2

Martha Speaks by Susan Meddaugh. Illustration by Susan Meddaugh. — 36

Pete's Chicken by Harriet Ziefert. Illustration by Laura Rader. — 70

Attaboy, Sam! by Lois Lowry. Illustration by Diane de Groat. — 102

Frog Medicine by Mark Teague. Illustration by Mark Teague. — 104

A Zooful of Animals by William Cole. Illustration by Lynn Munsinger. — 108

Owen by Kevin Henkes. Illustration by Kevin Henkes. — 124

Bootsie Barker Bites by Barbara Bottner. Illustration by Peggy Rathmann. — 164

Stellaluna by Jannell Cannon. Illustration by Jannell Cannon. — 213

When Cats Dream by Dav Pilkey. Illustration by Dav Pilkey. — 214

The Widow's Broom by Chris Van Allsburg. Illustration by Chris Van Allsburg. — 302

Wanted . . . Mud Blossom by Betsy Byars. Illustration by Jacqueline Rogers. — 320

The Daydreamer by Ian McEwan. Illustration by Anthony Browne. — 334

American Tall Tales by Mary Pope Osborne. Illustration by Michael McCurdy. — 423

Antics! An Alphabetical Anthology by Cathi Hepworth. Illustration by Cathi Hepworth. — 424

Junie B. Jones and the Stupid Smelly Bus by Barbara Park. Illustration by Denise Brunkus. — 518

Making Friends with Frankenstein: A Book of Monstrous Poems and Pictures by
Colin McNaughton. Illustration by Colin McNaughton. — 520

The Summer I Shrank My Grandmother by Elvira Woodruff. Illustration by Katherine Coville. — 544

The Stinky Sneakers Contest by Julie Anne Peters. Illustration by Cat Bowman Smith. — 632

The Houdini Box by Brian Selznick. Illustration by Brian Selznick. — 674

The Knights of the Kitchen Table by Jon Scieszka. Illustration by Lane Smith. — 868

FOREWORD

I'VE TOLD THIS STORY BEFORE. IT'S ABOUT A LITERARY SOIREE. IT WAS meet-the-authors night at the bookstore in the mall. All the writers in the county were there, the flying saucer man, the lady who writes mysteries, the chef who wrote the cookbook, a couple who wrote a book about refinishing furniture, a novelist who writes about the seamy side of life in Poughkeepsie, and me, the children's author.

As each of us authors arrived we were given a card, with adhesive on the back, to stick to ourselves. The card had the author's name and the title of his or her book.

Then we all stood around, drinking cider and munching cookies and talking to each other, and members of the public, and autographing books. I did fairly brisk business. I must have signed twenty books, the royalties on which would probably cover the tacos I had eaten at the other end of the mall, before walking over to join the literati.

The people were nice. The cider was cold. I had a pretty good time. One family was particularly pleasant—an academic-looking mother and father—a middle size kid, maybe ten, and a diminutive, elf-like kid, a girl, eight years old, tops. They talked about *The Worms of Kukumlima*, a book of mine, long out of print because too many people were unable to read and pronounce the made-up Swahili word, "Kukumlima," in the title. This bunch was able to say it.

About an hour passed. My admirers began to thin out.

Then there was this tiny person standing before me. It was the little girl from the well-spoken family.

"You again!" I said, giving her my best, most avuncular smile.

"I came to say good-bye," she said.

"That's very nice of you," I said, crouching down a little, and emanating warmth and good-humor.

The kid stood there. She had a complicated expression. It was clear something was eluding me.

"No," she said. "You see . . ."

She started to reach out a hand and then withdrew it.

I took her hand.

"You see . . . you're my favorite author."

She stared up at me. *Now* did I understand that this was not an ordinary moment?

"That's very pleasant to hear," I told her. "Thank you very much. You know, I've written about seventy books. I'll bet there are some you haven't found yet."

"I've read thirty-five," she said.

"Really? Thirty-five? Are you sure?"

She fixed me with a steely stare. She reeled off the titles of a dozen or so of the novels, the harder ones. Then she searched my face, clearly praying for me to say something that wasn't stupid—almost moving her lips—staring at mine.

"You know," I told her, "It's an honor to have a reader like you."

Her expression conveyed, "Well, finally! That took forever, you oaf," combined with a dawning realization that her favorite author was, in person, just that—an oaf. What was more, I was a fatuous oaf, and a non-listening oaf. I know that she suppressed these observations of my oafishness. She suppressed them because she needed not to know that the guy who wrote the books that meant so much to her was condescending and insincere with children, and didn't even know it.

Having finally managed to get her point across—namely that the stuff I write had become very important to her—the little girl spun on her heel and ran out of the bookstore, not giving me a chance to say anything else that she'd have to work at overlooking.

My purpose in telling this is not to show that I am thick-witted and clumsy. In fact, as authors go, I am probably of about average alertness and comprehension—better than average, actually, because I am honest about it, and able to improve by tiny increments.

People who make children's books are not necessarily child experts, or thoughtful, well-adjusted, or even bright. We are, one hopes, more or less talented folks, who have found a pleasant way to capitalize on our gifts. Not many started out with this particular career in mind. We might have been mainstream novelists, or screenwriters, or advertising people, had our luck broken a different way. This is fine. Lots of folks drift into a field of endeavor, only to discover they like it.

The man who raises pigs for market may know his business, but have little to offer in the way of serving suggestions, or tips for chefs. It's enough to produce the raw material. Someone else must have skills to exercise before the pork chops are presented at the table.

So it is with writers of children's books. Within the limitations imposed by publishers, we make what we make. What it means, what it can do, what use it has, and what value it has may have less to do with the author than the manner in which a book is presented, or made available, to the intended readers.

Most of us were, and still are, introduced to the realm of the written word, entirely or in part, through contact with professionals, into whose care books, and our minds, are entrusted. Retail sales of children's books do not amount to enough to make a difference, and too few parents are in a position to be of help in developing reading habits, and appreciation. It's teachers who do it, and librarians.

I have had a fair amount of contact with teachers and librarians, and I have no illusions about some of them. While these professions include some of the most dedicated and valuable people in our society, there are also some—too many—who are undereducated and unmotivated. I have received my share of fan-mail written by kids and sent on by a professional who did not know enough to include a return address, letters from those same professionals with not a sentence intact, and words misspelled. And I've visited schools where the faculty clearly regarded an author visit as nothing more than time off for them. I'm not going to characterize these depressing experiences of mine as representative of a tiny minority—because they're not.

I am not suggesting for a moment that there are not thousands and thousands of committed parents, teachers, and librarians, constantly searching for ways to make sure that children like my little friend at the bookstore will be able to find thirty-five books to love. I have to say that every disappointing experience I have is balanced, or outweighed, by shining examples of understanding and helpfulness—this bibliography being one.

I'd be the last person on earth to foreshadow the end of culture, and the final disintegration of society, because education is sinking into the swamp. I couldn't, because every day my mail contains proofs that kids are smarter than ever, and that the luckiest ones are getting high-quality help.

There is always plenty of reason to hope, if not rejoice. Packed with those shocking cover letters have been letters from kids who were clearly taking hold, had seen the possibilities of language, and wanted to experiment with it. It's in the nature of kids to be determined and serious people, busily gnawing away at whatever fare they're offered, trying to get a few useful calories.

The book you hold in your hands is a menu of elegant and satisfying fare. These are the memorable dishes that you can serve to your readers that will have them coming back for more. It doesn't take much. A single encounter, a single conversation, a single book can be enough to open a door, reveal a direction, save a life. How much better then to actively address the possibilities, seek the connections, and allow people new to the experience of reading to feel welcome and entitled.

DANIEL PINKWATER

ACKNOWLEDGMENTS

THE BOOK IS FINALLY FINISHED, THANKS TO THE PATIENT PEOPLE below who put up with two years of my compulsive reading and writing:

The wild and crazy crew in the children's room of the Somerset County Library, the best public library I know, who let me crash in their office weekly for a year while I plowed through their books, and offered me Tootsie Roll® Pops and their cheerful opinions.

Jane Scherer, the best high school librarian Plainfield ever had, who gave up far too many Saturdays to go through hundreds of "read cards" and hunt for titles with me in the Somerset County Library, and possessed the stamina to edit my never-ending text and annotations.

My brother Richard Freeman and the indefatigable Vivian Lottie Chideckel Klein for their meticulous copy editing.

The Somerset County Library Wednesday Night Children's Book Writers Group, who helped whip the chapters into shape.

Sharon Kalter, who never groaned when I brought in new boxes of books to process or lists of titles I needed yesterday, and always shared her jellybeans and chocolate covered pretzels, and her husband Bruce Kalter, for their astute analysis of my text.

Pauline Adamides, my fairy godmother, who alphabetized everything in sight, found a hundred typos, and wrote out a million review cards.

The students, staff, and Principal Ernie Shuba at Van Holten School in Bridgewater, New Jersey, for always being eager to try out my stash of new titles, and for supporting their library.

Steve Hynes, Dawn Sheppard, Debbie DiBlasi, Nancy Ghilarducci, and the other kind folks at Follett Library Resources who lent me hundreds of books each year and helped make each of my yearly Rutgers "Winners" Conferences such a success, and the many marketing and publicity people from all the children's book publishers who made sure the new titles I requested kept coming.

My parents, Bob and Gladys Freeman, brother Richard, sister Sharron, friends Lois and Mort Farrah, Carol and John Shields, Craig Horowitz and Marta Smith, Jill Schneider, and Cathy Darby, for phone calls, meals away from the computer, and lots of good laughs.

Sam and Margaret Feldman and family, who provided me with far more than just a writing home away from home.

Alice H. Yucht, my fellow presenter and book whiz partner.

The peripatetic Caroline Feller Bauer who traded titles and funny stories.

Dr. Dorothy S. Strickland, State of New Jersey Professor of Reading at Rutgers University, who asked me to speak at her conferences twice a year for four years running, for forcing me to think deeply about my profession, books, and kids as I composed each speech.

My editor Catherine Barr for her unflagging interest and support.

Editor Robert L. Chapman's *Roget's International Thesaurus, 5th edition* (HarperCollins, 1992), which not only helped me glide through hundreds of tough spots but gave me great pleasure each time I rambled through a new entry in pursuit of a better word.

Illustration from CHARLES DICKENS: THE MAN WHO HAD
GREAT EXPECTATIONS, by Diane Stanley and Peter Vennema,
illustrated by Diane Stanley.
Reprinted by permission of Morrow Junior Books,
a division of William Morrow & Company, Inc.

MAKING THE MOST OF CHILDREN'S LITERATURE

Illustration from
LIVES OF THE WRITERS: COMEDIES, TRAGEDIES (AND WHAT THE
NEIGHBORS THOUGHT) by Kathleen Krull, illustrations copyright © 1994 by
Kathryn Hewitt, reproduced by permission of Harcourt Brace & Company.

LOOKING FOR READ-ALOUDS

MORE BOOKS KIDS WILL SIT STILL FOR TAKES UP WHERE ITS COMPANion book, *Books Kids Will Sit Still For,* left off in 1990. Both are manuals of ways to use children's books, plus a series of graded, annotated lists with a combined total of over 3,500 of my favorite books to read aloud. All titles have been kid-tested to ensure that it's not just the grownups who are satisfied with the selections. I culled these books by first reading every recommended title for kids I could put my hands on.

Unlike the preparations for my last book, this time I didn't need to spend the bulk of my time scouting the shelves of the Somerset County Library for new books. Since I took on writing the monthly "Learning with Literature" column for *Instructor* magazine, publishers deliver boxes of books to my doorstep daily; millions and billions of them—actually, upward of 3,000 books a year. My cousin Ezra climbed up to my garret one day when I was working on my computer. He picked his way over the boxes and stacks of books, folders, catalogs, and papers, fell into my reading chair and exclaimed, "This place is amazing. It looks like the inside of your brain!"

The titles in this volume cover the years 1990–1995, plus titles from 1989 and before that I didn't discover until recently. Some, but certainly not all, spring 1995 titles are included, with the bulk to be part of the next volume, five years down the road. It was not possible to get my hands on every book I wanted to read, and if I've left off some of your favorites please send me a note and let me know.

In *Books Kids Will Sit Still For,* the first hundred pages comprised a manual on reading aloud, booktalking, creative drama, storytelling, using poetry and nonsense, and nonfiction and biography, and detailed 101 ways to celebrate books. I thought I had said it all, but in the intervening five years I've done a lot of thinking and learning and speaking about children's literature, whole language classrooms, book selection criteria, libraries, and the changing role of the school librarian. In *More Books Kids Will Sit Still For,* I've written an all-new text that further explores these issues for teachers, school and public librarians, parents, and anyone who works with children in preschool through sixth grade. My focus is unabashedly the school library, for that is my professional home, though teachers and parents and anyone else who spends time with children and books will find it a simple matter to recycle my library-based ideas to best fit their own needs.

When *Books Kids Will Sit Still For* came out in 1990, my publisher R. R. Bowker invited me to the American Library Association Annual Conference in Atlanta for an autographing session at their booth, a most enjoyable experience for an author. One woman approached me warily, saying, "Before I buy this, are there any offensive titles in here?" I guess it depends on what offends you. It is my hope instead that the more than 1,400 books included in this new volume will prove stimulating, provocative, hilarious, sobering, and memorable to both you and the children who are clamoring for a good read.

A survey by the National Assessment of Educational Progress in 1992 found that though students spent little time reading for pleasure or homework, they did manage to find the time to watch television three or more hours per day. We have our work cut out for us.

Back to school after an unprecedented five straight snow days in 1994, one of Lois Thompson's kindergarteners met her at the classroom door. "I forgot everything," he announced cheerfully. During Library that morning, I asked the class what they did during that cold and icy week off. "Played Nintendo"or "watched TV" were the most common responses.

"Don't you know if you watch too much TV and play too many computer games your brain will turn into mashed potatoes?" I asked. They giggled. "There is one known cure for mashed-potato brains, however. Do you know what you can do to get your brains back again?"

"Read books!" one boy shouted.

"Exactly right," I told him, and we do just that every day.

A FEW GOOD BOOKS

People ask me, "How do you decide which books are the best ones to read aloud to kids?" There's no simple answer. I could say I know one when I read one, but that's not always true. I test them on my students, on my Rutgers graduate classes, on my teachers at school. My school library classes have been my guinea pigs through a vast number of titles, and older children have tried out books on younger ones. I can't know for sure that a book will work until I read it aloud. Many books I like don't pass that test and get knocked out of my database.

As an adult reader of children's books, I have quirky tastes and will try out any type of book. I can suspend disbelief with the best of them. What's hard is figuring out which books will send kids reeling. Adults tend to read books with a critical standard so high that we sometimes overestimate a book's child appeal without considering its true audience. Many lovely, lyrically written, elegant stories are disdained by young readers, who deem acceptable books we aesthetes dismiss as fluff.

One librarian told me, "I never read mysteries or fantasy. I don't care for them." If we want to eliminate categories from our adult reading, fine; but to skip any genre while selecting books for our students to read is to deny them our expertise. We are duty bound to learn to appreciate all types of children's books if we expect to tap into and nurture our children's tastes.

Invaluable children's book review journals and sources including *Book Links*, *Booklist*, *Bulletin of the Center for Children's Books*, *Hornbook*, *Library Talk*, *The New Advocate*, *Reading Teacher*, *School Library Journal*, and the *New York Times Book Review* help me find out what other professionals think, and my own instincts, combined with the opinions of other teacher and librarian friends "in the business," help me compile my final lists.

The good part is reading all of those great new books. The bad part is that of the 5,000 children's books published each year so many are less than memorable. Many books start out wonderfully only to become dull halfway through. Others don't get started until the kids have already lost interest. Many are preachy or boring or garish or overdone or lack child appeal.

Plenty of books are marvelous for one-on-one sharing, or for children to read themselves, including controlled vocabulary readers, like many of the I Can Read series. Many picture books have illustrations too small to be seen in a group setting. There are informational nonfiction books great for reports and individual browsing, but not great when read aloud from cover to cover. Some otherwise delectable fiction books are too personal to read aloud—Phyllis Reynolds Naylor's Alice books, for example, which are great stories, but with too much pondering about sex to go over in a classroom without the kids going wild or sniggering.

In my search, I'm looking for books a teacher or librarian can read aloud, some for sheer pleasure and some to use in tandem with the curriculum, and I search specifically for books that will enthrall a whole class. My success rate seems to average out at one read-aloud per every four books read. For instance, of the 300 new spring 1994 books I read in May and June 1994, I found 40 easy fiction/picture books, 11 folk or fairy tales, eight poetry or joke books, ten new fiction books, and six nonfictions to add to my lists as read-alouds. That makes 75 new read-alouds out of the 300 I read. I donated to my school library an additional 100 other books that were appealing or useful but not read-alouds, and rejected 125 others as not meeting our needs or standards.

Publishers are starting to cut back now, after the boom of the past ten years when it seemed as though anything could end up in print. There are still too many lovely mood-piece books that are nice but don't break any new ground, and a crush of mass-market TV-based gimmick books; but according to rumor it's becoming a lot harder to get published.

Some books are amusingly bad for kids, like Kevin O'Malley's new version of "Froggie Went a-Courtin'." I've always loved the folk song, and the illustrations were terrific, but O'Malley decided to set it in a frog gangster gambling den, 1930's style. My husband looked at it and said, "Oh look—Miss Mousie seems to be a hooker." Next.

If many of my own students did not come to school conditioned on supermarket-quality kids' books, I would think *The Candyland Mystery* was a joke. Remember the swell game Candyland? Under the heading "It's Scent-sational!" comes the following listing in a mainstream children's book catalog: "In this storybook with scent patches based on the all-time best-selling board game, wicked Lord Licorice has cast a spell, hiding King Kandy and his Candy Castle, too! Children and candy lovers can help the Candy Land Kids solve the mystery by sniffing out the castle's cinnamon scent to find the King! Along the way, they'll scratch and sniff gingerbread, peppermint, orange gumdrops, and more—until they finally uncover King Kandy, in a most unexpected place!" I shudder to imagine where.

NEW TRENDS

Several cheering advances have changed the children's book field. First is the increase in outstanding titles with ethnically diverse characters. When *Books Kids Will Sit Still For* was published in 1990, one reviewer chided me for not having more minority representation among the 2,100 titles I had chosen. Alarmed, I searched through the literature to see what titles I might have missed, and came up empty. Just because a book has a multicultural bent does not mean it makes a suitable read-aloud, and I cannot include titles that kids will find dull, slight, or confusing just because they fill a one-dimensional need. The book has to work with kids. Period.

In the intervening five years, the number of new multicultural titles has been reassuring and very welcome. While the first volume contained less than 9 percent multicultural titles, *More Books Kids Will Sit Still For* contains almost 20 percent, reflecting the astonishing proliferation of quality multiethnic titles. Small publishers like Lee & Low and Children's Book Press are nurturing new minority authors and making a big impact with their books, while mainstream companies are more tuned in to cultural diversity than ever. I still await the publication of books about Indian and Pakistani children so my students from those countries will have characters with whom they can identify. The number of Latino titles is also far too low.

It's a pleasure to see how many new books include a matter-of-fact mix of races and sexes in their illustrations without making a fuss. My hope is to see more multicultural books that deal with current children in everyday situations instead of always being enmeshed in societal crises or problems from history.

One truth emerged as I plowed through the thousands of new books: far greater care is still spent publishing magnificent and groundbreaking picture books than fiction books, especially chapter books for children in grades three to six. While read-alones have proliferated, I have been hard pressed to identify a sufficient number of outstanding read-alouds for upper-grade children. So the fiction lists are far smaller than the picture books, but not for lack of looking.

Series are extremely popular right now, from the beautifully packaged American Girls books, a welcome way to get children interested in historical fiction; to the Goosebumps books by R. L. Stine, which are too mindlessly scary and formulaic to read aloud as examples of good thrillers; to the various everlasting Choose Your Own Adventure series. It's not that there's anything wrong with the Sweet Valley books—"Training bras for Harlequin romances," as Professor Janice Antczak calls them—and other mass-market series, but there's often nothing outstanding or memorable about them either. I call them "potato-chip books," since it's easy to go through quantities of them. Formula books do have a valuable place in a child's reading development in that they're easy going down, and, if we play our cards right, can lead kids to better examples of contemporary literature—e.g., such authors as Lois Lowry, Betsy Byars, Gordon Korman, Phyllis Reynolds Naylor, or Gary Paulsen.

Just ten years back, children graduating to chapter books had to make a large leap from Nate the Great and other I Can Read-style chapter books to writers like Beverly Cleary and Johanna Hurwitz. There were few middle-ground chapter books to bridge the gap from easy readers to 100-page fiction books. Patricia Reilly Giff's short, easy-to-read Polk Street School series started a much-welcome trend for first-, second-, and third-graders not yet ready to tackle longer fiction. Other publishers have followed suit with many middle-range series that children have loved, including Stepping Stone books from Random House, Redfeather Books from Henry Holt, and Springboards from Little, Brown.

50 WAYS TO RECOGNIZE A READ-ALOUD

Sometimes, when reading a book for the first time, I realize I'm living the book in my head as I go. I can hear the characters speaking the dialogue, each in his distinct voice, instead of just seeing words on the page. The story becomes so clear, I inhabit its space.

Then the phone rings or the cat meows and I blink, look up at my usual surroundings, and come back to my senses. I envy each author who can pull off the miracle of such a story that invites you to step into a new world, sometimes familiar as in contemporary fiction, sometimes alien as in fantasy. In a successful book, we, the readers, must be able to put ourselves into that world as comfortably as if we were born there, without anyone preaching or boring us along the way.

What makes a book memorable for me? Here are the 50 standards and selection criteria I've compiled over the years for great read-alouds, some of which I apply as I read a new book to myself, and some of which come into play when I test the book with children, with examples taken from some of my very favorites among the more than 1,400 titles listed in the bibliographies in this book. Obviously, one would not expect one book to fit every criterion, though looking at all the possibilities makes me wonder how authors and illustrators manage to create so many innovative, exciting, and successful new books each year.

1. **The book has a universal plot that relates to children's lives and speaks to them.**

All children can identify with the mouse in *Chrysanthemum* who is teased at school for having such a long name, or *Owen* who has no intention of giving up his treasured blanket even though he is about to start school. Author/illustrator Kevin Henkes may portray his characters as mice, but we know they are really us.

2. **The plot pulls us into the story and keeps us involved, entertained, and always interested to see what will happen next.**

"Just one more chapter," the kids beg, and you know they're hooked. In *Forest* by Janet Taylor Lisle, we witness humans from squirrels' eyes and squirrels from humans' eyes, and we root both for Amber who has run away from home again after fighting with her dictatorial father and for Woodbine and Brown Nut, two squirrels who buck the unyielding new power authority to protect her. The chapters alternate from Upper Forest to Lower Forest, and the struggle between good and power keeps us turning those pages.

3. The book takes a fresh and unhackneyed approach to a familiar theme.

Many times I'll turn down a new title just because it's been done so many times before. It's not that there's anything particularly wrong with it, but there's nothing special about it either. I want a story that will make kids say "WOW!"

In Margaret Mahy's never-dull picture book *The Rattlebang Picnic*, the McTavish family, with all seven kids and granny in tow, heads off on a picnic in their old car. But what a picnic! With bits and pieces dropping off the jalopy as they drive up the steep road to Mount Fogg, we fear for the family's safety. Granny's pizza, baked at a low temperature for an hour and a half, may be too tough to eat, but when Mount Fogg erupts and the family sets off in a mad race to outpace the lava, and a wheel falls off the rattlebang, it is just the ticket for a spare tire. Steven Kellogg's detailed watercolors have never been fresher or funnier.

4. The author takes a common plot, makes it seem new again, and breaks new ground.

Louis Sachar unexpectedly blends hilarious and sad scenes in his easy-to-read chapter book *Marvin Redpost: Alone in His Teacher's House*. Asked to take care of his teacher's old dog Waldo for a week, third-grader Marvin does his best, but the dog refuses to eat and in a surprise scene Marvin finds Waldo dead. What is so extraordinary is the trust the author has in his readers to forgo a pat or predictable episode where the dog recovers just in time, and instead allow them to experience such complex emotions as guilt, sorrow, and panic, as Marvin wonders how he will explain the tragedy to his teacher, copes with a substitute teacher who has taken a dislike to him, and takes in the disparaging comments of his classmates.

5. The story surprises us with the unexpected because it's unlike anything else we've ever read.

I had no idea what my students would think of Laurence Yep's *Ghost Fox*, a fictionalized classic Chinese ghost story about a young boy whose father goes away on business leaving him and his mother at the mercy of a vengeful ghost fox who tries to steal his mother's soul. It was one of those stories that I needed to test on children before I could decide on its suitability. My third-graders sat rapt through both sittings, and though they decided it was a story that depended on being read aloud or they might not have understood it, they rated it very highly, as did I.

6. It generates memories and recognition of common threads from our own lives.

When I read aloud Donald Hall's sly and wise prose poem *I Am the Dog, I Am the Cat*, with its alternating lifelike prose and watercolor portraits of a contented rottweiler and a self-satisfied tabby, my fifth-graders could have talked about their own pets for the rest of the day. Every reflection on life posed by cat and dog brought knowing nods and many hands waving frantically to add an observation.

7. It introduces unforgettable, colorful, and believable characters worth knowing.

In *Amazing Grace* by Mary Hoffman, the resolute look on Grace's face when she decides to try out for the part of Peter Pan, even if he is a boy and even if he isn't black, as her classmate reminds her, will fill your listeners with courage to overcome obstacles and never give up. This radiant kindergarten child who acts out stories and loves to pretend has a face you'll want to study, thanks to Caroline Binch's superb illustrations.

Every character in Susan Shreve's short novel *The Gift of the Girl Who Couldn't Hear* is quirky and real. Narrator Eliza desperately wants to audition for the lead in *Annie*, this year's seventh-grade musical, but feels weighted down by a severe case of mood-swinging puberty. Her best friend Lucy, who is deaf, intends to try out for the role of an orphan despite not knowing how to sing. Here's Mr. Blake, the director of the musical, elfin and with gray beard and gray hair to his shoulders and a way with students, as described by Eliza:

> He is always asking, "Would you care for a cigarette, or a glass of red wine, or chocolate milk mixed with cyanide?" as if it's the most natural conversation in the world to have with a seventh grader.

> "Yes, please," I say. He offers me an imaginary cigarette, lights it, and we both pretend to smoke while I tell him about Lucy.

His gentle irreverence combined with his understanding of Eliza's problem made me think back to offbeat teachers I admired who knew how to talk to kids and gain their trust.

8. It lets us in on personal secrets about the author or the characters so we feel as if we really do know them.

Reading books by Betsy Byars, I always feel her characters are my good friends because of all the telling details she includes about each one. Giving us invaluable literary advice on writing, her autobiographical *The Moon and I* reveals where she gets her ideas for favorite books like *Cracker Jackson* and the Blossom series, many of which came from her own life. It becomes clear that she and her characters have an awful lot in common.

Shelley A. Barre's *Chive*, about a boy whose farm family loses everything during hard times, is an involving novel that depends on alternating sequential flashback and current-day chapters to build up to the full force of the tragedy that has befallen Chive's family over several harrowing years. Gradually we get to know Chive both through his own words and those of Terry, the middle-class boy whose mother comes across Chive in the supermarket parking lot, where he helps her load her car, and brings him home for a good meal.

9. The story is told from an unusual or unexpected point of view.

We've accepted as narrators talking animals, adults looking back to their childhoods, and little kids like Junie B. Jones in the Barbara Park series. When it's handled in a believable manner, with the children not sounding too adult or the adults sounding too childlike, we can buy it and like it. *A Teeny Tiny Baby* by Amy Schwartz is told by the title character, who happens to be a newborn child, and from his vast experience tells us what a person of his age likes, wants, and gets, where he's been, who he's met, what he eats, and how he sleeps: "I like to sleep on my quilt or in my swing or on the sofa (though once I fell off), or in the car or on my sheepskin rug, on my right side or my left side or on my belly or on my back." The illustrations are from the point of view of the limited omniscient narrator; we see his weary but pleased parents and grandparents, but the baby is the focus of every picture.

10. The setting allows us to experience a new and different environment unlike the place where we live.

During the miserable New Jersey winter of 1994, when my school district called 12 snow days and the ice and snow didn't melt until spring, I shivered through Kirkpatrick Hill's *Winter Camp*, an Alaskan survival story of two children who undergo two months in a cabin where the temperature drops to 65 below, and felt like a wimp for ever complaining about our temperate climate. Then there's Joanna Cole and Bruce Degen's brilliant Magic School Bus series that has allowed us to see the planets, the ocean floor, and even go back in time to see the dinosaurs.

11. There is at least one memorable scene that you remember long after the book is finished.

Reading so many books, one tends to forget plots, characters, and endings, until just a vague memory remains, and too often one book blurs into another similar one. "Have you read this?" a student will inquire, and I'll say, "I remember reading it, and I remember liking it, but I don't remember enough to tell you about." For a read-aloud, there is usually at least one scene that sticks in your mind.

Upon first reading Jack Ziegler's picture book *Mr. Knocky*, about an eccentric old guy who drives the neighborhood kids crazy with his constant rambling storytelling, I wasn't sure the children would like it as much as I did. There's one amazing scene, where the kids are having the first-of-the-season snowball fight in Deep Dene, their private play area, and Mr. Knocky comes along, "singing some stupid song about how hard it is to fit an airplane into a breadbox." All the children ignore him, until he is accidentally creamed with a snowball by Yip Yakima and he falls down, out cold. Yip is panicked, and runs over to him, yelling, "DON'T DIE, MR. KNOCKY. I DIDN'T MEAN IT! IT WAS AN ACCIDENT. IT WAS JUST SNOW. PLEASE, MR. KNOCKY, DON'T DIE!" The large letters on the page, coupled with the abrupt mood switch as all the children gather around the old man, convey the terror of the situation, which is broken seconds later when the irrepressible Mr. Knocky comes to. I thought it was such an effective way to get kids thinking about the people around them whom they take for granted and don't appreciate. Apparently, my students were affected as well, as they still ask for the book by name a year later.

12. The language flows well when read aloud.

This does not necessarily mean that the language is flowery and esoteric, but that it feels right and appropriate to the story. You don't have to edit or stumble over awkward phrases (which is not to say it's simplistic, just well-paced), and you have a sense of satisfaction as you read.

Gary Paulsen is usually such a physical writer, with in-your-face descriptions of survival and outdoors catastrophes, that when you pick up one of his quieter novels like *The Cookcamp* it's a surprise. I had only one 40-minute period to read aloud his *A Christmas Sonata* to a fifth-grade class, but figured we could make it. I wasn't sure how they'd react to the long descriptive passages the narrator lays out with the grace of an artist, but the vision of a young boy in his recollection of the Christmas week he spent with his dying cousin Matthew held them rapt. The writing has a poetic sense of wonder with touches of humor and a child's matter-of-factness that makes it exhilarating to read aloud, and not that much happens until the end, when Santa Claus comes to the house, fulfilling Matthew's one wish: that Santa is real. When I finished, feeling like I had run an emotional Iditarod, my fifth-graders let out a collective sigh. "That was wonderful!" one girl said, and many agreed. They knew they were hearing something special, and had the patience to let themselves listen to the rhythm of the story.

13. **Every time you read the book aloud to a new group, it is an instant hit with your listeners.**

Children love books with a gimmick, and sometimes those gimmicks give equal pleasure to the adult reader. Ed Emberley's *Go Away, Big Green Monster!*, with its overlaid die-cut pages that uncover the monster's two big yellow eyes, scraggly purple hair, and sharp white teeth, and then allow us to make him disappear, piece by piece, delights children from preschool on up through grownup. My fifth-graders loved the design; my kindergarteners delighted in commanding, "Go away, big green monster, and don't come back . . . until I say so!"

Aside from the fact that Phyllis Reynolds Naylor's *The Boys Start the War* is a very funny book, it contains a number of ingredients that make it a class read-aloud favorite. There's the rivalry between the four Hartford brothers and their new neighbors the three Malloy sisters, played out through a series of escalating pranks that fan the flames of male-female rivalry but ultimately show how we can't do without one another. You'll find dialogue that sizzles, parents who seem to be unaware of the intrigue swirling about their kids, and a varied cast of characters who keep the plot bubbling. There are sequels for readers who want more, and even the cover is great. Can't go wrong here.

14. **The book gives you great pleasure every time you read it aloud, even after repeated readings.**

I usually get tired of doing a book aloud after four readings or so, and go looking for a new thrill. On my list of books that continue to enthrall and entertain is Susan Meddaugh's *Martha Speaks* in which Martha, the darling dumpy dog who also appears in *The Witches' Supermarket* and *Martha Calling*, gains the ability to speak, thanks to a bowl of alphabet soup that works cerebrally instead of nutritionally. This mouthy mutt recalls details from her puppyhood, she orders extra food from the meat market over the phone, and like an unrefined toddler embarrasses the family by blurting out whatever she observes at inopportune times. There's a wonderful full page of Martha's liberated stream-of-consciousness monologue that cascades across the page and is a delight to read aloud. When the underappreciated Martha defeats the burglar, her family says "Good dog, Martha," to which Martha replies, "You're so right." Each time I read her dialogue, I feel vindicated for her.

Certain books have true staying power, and certainly Donna Jo Napoli's *The Prince of the Pond: Otherwise Known as De Fawg Pin* is at the top of my list. Pin, who was a prince until the witch turned him into a frog, is bewildered and out of his depth until narrator frog Jade steps in to teach him how to eat bugs, stay alive, and he in return teaches her about love. The dialogue crackles, and I always want to cry at the end when Pin leaves his adoring tadpoles and becomes a prince again. Books like this don't get old, they get better.

15. **The story makes children laugh.**

Books that make kids laugh often don't make the best books lists, which are more often composed of serious titles that list-makers find more meaningful or inspirational. Most students want to hear stories that make them laugh out loud, but they're not so easy to find. Because of this, I await each new Barbara Park book as a possible howler, and she rarely lets me down. When I think of the three misfits, brought together for the first time in the principal's office, cutting out and hiding together in the big green garbage dumpster in *Maxie, Rosie, and Earl—Partners in Grime*, I laugh. What's even better, so do my students.

Other authors who consistently make children laugh uproariously include Judy Blume, Betsy Byars, Bruce Coville, Roald Dahl, Gery Greer and Bob Ruddick, Johanna Hurwitz, Dick King-Smith, Suzy Kline, Gordon Korman, Lois Lowry, Stephen Manes, James Marshall, Dav Pilkey, Daniel Pinkwater, Barbara Robinson, Louis Sachar, Jon Scieszka, and Jerry Spinelli.

16. It helps children develop and stretch their senses of humor.

There are books kids find uproarious, and books that adults laugh over, and the two don't necessarily coincide. Children will read a book that you found hilarious, and tell you, "I don't know why you said this book was so funny. I didn't laugh at all." With contemporary fiction, sometimes it's because the situation mirrors a child's own experience, and he or she is still too close to it to see the humor. Children understand slapstick best, while exaggeration, irony, and satire may fly right over their heads.

Dav Pilkey has been writing hilarious satires and sendups of old movies, filled with puns that will make you groan with glee but which many younger children may not "get." Read *Dogzilla, Kat Kong,* and *Dog Breath: The Horrible Trouble with Hally Tosis* first for the general laughs, but then go back and unobtrusively ask listeners to explain the puns just in case. In *Kat Kong*, in order to bring the cat monster back to civilization, the mice truss it up in a burlap sack, taking great care "not to let the cat out of the bag." In *Dogzilla*, when the mouse leader chases menacing pooch, we cheer as "The Big Cheese tried to catch up to the hot dog with all the relish he could muster." And in *Dog Breath*, even the painting of the Mona Lisa holds her nose when Hally, the Tosis family dog, comes into the room.

17. The use of language and fantastical situations acts to strengthen and expand children's imaginations.

I asked my fourth-grade students to tell about their dreams, whether any of their dreams had ever come true, if they believed their dreams could predict the future, and if they ever had recurring dreams they couldn't forget. It was startling to hear how violent their dreams were, and how full of guns and consumer goods. When I start to wonder if children are losing their spontaneity, I think about my nephew Charlie, now 16 and over six feet tall, who admitted at dinner one night that when he was five years old his goal in life was to be corn—"Not just a kernel or an ear, but the whole cornstalk!"

The creativity is still there, but the older children get the harder we need to work to get it flowing. Each day, after Linda Forte read her fourth-graders a new chapter of Ian McEwan's *The Daydreamer*, she'd meet me in the lunchroom with an update: "Peter made his family disappear with vanishing cream today. We all loved that one." Title character Peter spends a fair amount of his time observing people and things around him and then getting into their skins. We are prepared to believe him each time he trades places with a new character, becoming the cat, the baby, and even the grown-up, for his observations are so real. In the most poignant chapter, he unzips the skin of his family's old cat, William Boy, and switches bodies, then fights and wins one last garden battle for the tired tom before it succumbs to its 17 years. Children will see the people around them with new eyes after a book like this.

18. **The story enables us to put in effect our willing suspension of disbelief.**

In Kathleen Leverich's *Hilary and the Troublemakers*, we know that it's probably Hilary's overstimulated imagination that causes a giant owl to eat her fractions homework, but we are perfectly willing to believe in each outrageous situation. And in the strange but hilariously sensible *The Kooken* by Julia Lebentritt and Richard Ploetz, we can accept first that Johanna's aunt's Doberman would eat her valuable cello, and then that the dog would allow the girl to play him as a substitute instrument, like a giant Stradivarius. He has a fabulous tone, too, and saves the day at Johanna's debut concert at Carnegie Hall when she gets stage fright with a real cello.

19. **All of the supporting details are just right, so that plot, characters, and setting work together believably and harmoniously without the unintentional loose ends that can cause a good story to fall apart midstream.**

In a chance encounter at the grocery store, narrator Vernon, a seventh-grader who has eagerly participated with his friends in tormenting almost-bag lady Maxine and her retarded son Ronald, suddenly sees her as a person and in time gets to know and help the two of them. Jane Lesley Conley's *Crazy Lady!* is unpredictable and unforgettable, with unlikely characters you come to care about, a gritty Baltimore neighborhood setting, and a bittersweet but realistic ending that makes sense and stays with you.

20. **The ending is logical and/or satisfying and/or boffo, as compelling as the rest of the story.**

Have you noticed that many children will read the first half of a book and then return it unfinished? You'd think they don't like it, and that's often the case, though sometimes a child will tell you he liked a book because he doesn't want to disappoint you. What's odd is the number of children who let themselves lose interest in a book midstream. Is it because they are used to clicking channels when the TV show gets boring? Perhaps. "Didn't you want to find out what happened to the character?" I ask, and the child shrugs and smiles, "No, not really." By reading aloud books with exciting or satisfying endings, you may be able to reverse that trend. What a pleasure it is to read aloud a good ending, and then sigh and close the book reluctantly.

When fifth-grade teacher Pat Stabile was reading aloud Vaunda M. Nelson's *Mayfield Crossing*, about seven children who start a new school and encounter racial prejudice, she came into lunch 15 minutes late. We only get 30 minutes, so we asked what had kept her. "My kids made me finish the book. They said they couldn't eat until they knew what happened at the final baseball game in the story. It was worth it."

21. **The ending takes us by surprise.**

If you know what you're looking for, you'll spot plenty of clues as to the identity of the title heroine of Jacqueline K. Ogburn's sly and naughty picture book *Scarlett Angelina Wolverton-Manning*, about a toothy, bug-eyed wealthy little girl who is kidnapped from the family estate. Why is it so imperative she be home by dark? And what happened to kidnapper Ralph's parrot, goldfish, and kitty? My second-graders gasped in delight at the ending, where the family's true identity becomes known with the rising of the full moon. The last line from the little girl ("Grrr.") had them howling with laughter. Did they predict the ending? No, but they loved going back to search for foreshadowing (a word we learned when we read *Dog Breath* by Dav Pilkey), and figuring out the meaning of the title. Next time they should be more savvy in their predictions of outcomes, too.

22. The special experience of hearing this book read aloud causes children to want to continue reading on their own.

Cimorene, a convention-defying princess who hates the insipid princes her parents want her to marry, runs away to become chef to a large dragon in *Dealing with Dragons* by Patricia Wrede, the first of four grand fantasies in her Enchanted Forest Chronicles. I thought my fifth-graders would find the subsequent volumes too challenging or arcane, but they devoured each one. They are drawn the same way to Lloyd Alexander's Chronicles of Prydain series and Brian Jacques's *Redwall* and all its 400-page sequels, which they read ragged every year.

When I started David McPhail's *Santa's Book of Names* with a kindergarten class, several reacted to Edward's not being able to read, saying, "Hey, we can't read yet either."

"You know some words and letters, don't you?" I queried.

"Oh sure, we know that."

They're anxious to be able to tackle whole books, and hearing how Edward received the gift of reading from Santa one Christmas Eve gave them great satisfaction and hope for their own reading futures.

23. The story works to broaden children's literary knowledge and experience and lead them to other books of the same genre or theme.

Readers may tell you they don't like historical fiction, but that's before you read a book like *Weasel* by Cynthia deFelice with its life-and-death fight against evil. In the 1839 Ohio frontier, siblings Nathan and Molly become the new target of a dangerous man named Weasel. You can kill several genres with one book: historical fiction, adventure, and suspense, an unbeatable combination, especially when people complain there aren't enough books that appeal to boys.

24. The author takes risks and does not underestimate his or her audience.

Modern-day survival novel *Monkey Island* by Paula Fox allows us behind the labels of homeless and runaways and welfare. With a mere $28.00 in his pocket, left behind by his mother who has abandoned him at their welfare hotel, Clay Garrity takes to the New York streets. He spends weeks living with other homeless people in a small park, under the protection of Buddy, a young black man who has lost his job and his apartment, and Calvin, an alcoholic former teacher. We feel the winter cold, the indignity of being a shadow and an outcast to the more fortunate people around them, the danger of attack by tormenters, and the illness brought on by exposure.

Fifth-grade teacher Lois DuFour stopped me in the school office to tell me how her kids were hanging on every word of Berlie Doherty's bleak but gripping *Street Child*, a Dickensian story based on the actual life of a destitute orphan who escaped the workhouse only to end up slaving without respite on Grimy Nick's boat loading coal.

25. The story provides a sense of history and connection to times past.

My international melange of fourth-graders listened to *Grandfather's Journey* by Allen Say in pensive silence and then launched into a spirited, free-ranging discussion about their own family origins, migrations to America, and Ellis Island. In a very different kind of grandfather story, *The Great Pumpkin Switch* by Megan McDonald, a cozy and congenial Grampa regales his grandkids with a story from his boyhood, a long time ago, when he managed to squeeze out of trouble after accidentally breaking his sister's prized, home-grown pumpkin. Though times change, children can see that their grandparents were also children once, with the same host of joys and problems.

26. **The story introduces people of other races, cultures, and communities, and encourages children to make connections to their own lives and broaden their own views of the world.**

We learn how tamales are made as Mexican American child Maria kneads the *masa* or corn meal dough in Gary Soto's Christmas story *Too Many Tamales*. What we also learn is that all of us sometimes do things we shouldn't and then have to come clean and admit our mistakes, as Maria does when, after trying on her mother's diamond ring, she realizes she must have dropped it in the masa and enlists her visiting cousins to eat every tamale to find it. We all breathe a sigh of relief when we spot the ring on her mother's finger, cringe for Maria as she confesses her irresponsibility, and smile when the family works together to make a new batch of tamales. Guilt, remorse, and forgiveness are universal.

On the other hand, so are intolerance and bigotry, which is why Yunmi is worried when her best friends volunteer her Korean-speaking grandmother, newly arrived in New York City, to chaperone the annual class picnic in Central Park in Sook Nyul Choi's *Halmoni and the Picnic*. What if children mock Halmoni's pointed rubber shoes and long Korean dress or refuse to eat the kimbap or drink the barley tea she brings? Listeners will be relieved for Yunmi to see that her fears are unfounded. Stories like these allow children to discuss differences and take pride in their own and other cultures.

27. **The narrative does not stoop to stereotypes or clichés.**

These days, every professional magazine I read has an article explaining why this or that book is all wrong. Characters of that ethnic group would never behave that way, or wear those clothes, or talk like that. This is a tough issue, when purists insist Native American stories can only be told by Native Americans of that region, or only African American writers can write about slavery. This perfectionism sets such a tough standard; it's a wonder anyone ever gets it right. "Write about what you know" takes on new meaning if everyone is limited to his or her own ethnic group and experience. Yes, we need to pay close attention to possibly offensive stereotypes, but not go overboard in condemning innocent oversights.

Author/illustrator Patricia Polacco's autobiographical *Chicken Sunday* introduces Miss Eula, the large and soulful grandmother of the author's two best friends from childhood, African American brothers Stewart and Winston, and old Mr. Kodinski, a Russian Jewish immigrant shopkeeper who, we adults know from the number tattooed on his forearm, is a concentration camp survivor. Both are characters who could be caricatured as Mammy or Shylock, but Polacco's skilled portraits help us understand and respect them both.

28. **The book provokes interesting discussions and allows kids to reevaluate their opinions and prejudices.**

General Pinch and his skinny wife brook no opposition to their way of running the neighborhood in *The Araboolies of Liberty Street* by Sam Swope. Children are afraid to play outside at the risk of incurring their wrath. "I'll call in the army!" bellows the General at every infraction of his rules. But when the extended Araboolie family moves in, with family members whose skin color changes daily and pets no one has ever seen before, Pinch declares war.

Fortunately the plucky neighborhood children come to the rescue, painting the exterior of every house in colorful colors Araboolie-style, except the General's, and when the army moves in, following orders, it's Pinch and his spouse who get hauled off the street for being different. Children who hear adults speak disparagingly of others whose skin color, customs, and way of dress are outside of their experience will find themselves rooting for and admiring the "weirdos."

29. **The text fosters intolerance to injustice and helps children develop empathy, a sense of fairness, and a social conscience.**

In 1942, the U.S. government, at war with Japan, moved people of Japanese descent, including American citizens, to internment camps. This shocking and tragic event is difficult to explain to children, but author Ken Mochizuki, whose own parents spent the war in a camp in Idaho, has brought it down to issues that all can grasp in *Baseball Saved Us*. A young boy recounts the conditions in camp, where there's always a man with a rifle watching them from the guardhouse tower. Faced with living in horse-stall barracks, with frequent dust storms and no meaningful work or recreation available, the parents build a baseball field, sew uniforms, and organize teams. Everybody plays, and the boy hits one treasured home run. Back home after the war, people still call him "Jap" and once again he proves his worth on the baseball field. Magnificent sepia-toned illustrations take us from desperation to triumph in a story that will get children talking about why people discriminate against those who are different.

30. **The issues raised allow readers to get beneath surface emotions and issues.**

How would it feel to have a debilitating disease or condition? Most children can imagine themselves stoically withstanding every trial as they undergo pain and suffering without complaint. The reality can be quite different, as David Getz makes clear in his brilliantly funny and scathing *Fresh Air*, where we get to live the plight of Jacob, a chronically and dangerously asthmatic sixth-grader who fights to get away from anyone's pity and be considered normal.

31. **It exposes children to, and lays out or makes sense of, difficult and sensitive issues.**

There are ways to explain tragedies and other impossible problems to children, as in Eve Bunting's Caldecott Medal picture book *Smoky Night*, based on the Los Angeles riots of 1992, as witnessed by a young boy, and Jeanne Moutoussamy-Ashe's *Daddy and Me: A Photo Story of Arthur Ashe and His Daughter Camera*, a matter-of-fact description of the tennis star's last year before he succumbed to AIDS.

I booktalked fiction and nonfiction books about the two World Wars to one fifth grade and then read them Michael Foreman's *War Game*, which is dedicated to the memory of his four relatives who died in World War I and is based on an actual episode where British and German troops fraternized and played soccer in No-Man's Land on Christmas Day in 1914 before they had to get back to the business of killing each other. Foreman's watercolors plus the many reproductions of period memorabilia hit home with the students, and even the war-loving types were jolted and sobered by the story, which they mulled over at length.

32. **The story encourages children to wrestle with and make decisions about personal ethics.**

Phyllis Reynolds Naylor's *Shiloh* makes readers ponder both sides of a tough issue. If Marty doesn't take in the mistreated beagle, its owner Judd might even kill it, as Marty believes the man has done to another of his dogs. At the very least, Marty knows Judd mistreats his dogs and seeing him kick Shiloh confirms Marty's fears. Then again, taking in and caring for Shiloh and keeping him hidden means Marty must lie to everyone who trusts him.

What's more important: finding work to support your family or telling the truth? One depends on the other, as we learn in Eve Bunting's picture book *A Day's Work*. Waiting to be hired for day work one Saturday are young Francisco and his grandfather, who is newly arrived from Mexico and speaks no English. A man pulls up in his truck looking for a worker to do some gardening, and even though Abuelo tells his grandson he was a carpenter in a city, Francisco is sure they can manage. They do, spending the day in the hot sun, pulling out what look like weeds, but when the man returns he is aghast to discover the two have pulled out his ice plants and left all the chickweed. Abuelo is angry, and when Francisco reminds him they needed a day's work, he replies, "We do not lie for work," and offers to return the next day to make right what they have done. Ben, their employer, impressed, offers them future work, saying, "The important things your grandfather knows already. And I can teach him gardening."

In books like these, children can examine both sides of the issue and decide what their own courses of action would be.

33. The story is so provocative, it demands debate on issues raised.

In a society built on prejudice and fear that excludes all but Certified Purebred humans, where the blue hunters search out and imprison or destroy any animal they catch hobnobbing with humans, the narrator hides the fact that his absent father is an ox. *The Oxboy* by Anne Mazer is a stark and compelling allegory that will stimulate comparisons with modern-day practices of discrimination and oppression. Reviewers seemed to either love or hate it, and I couldn't get it out of my mind, even after reading it three times; nor could the students in one fifth-grade class whose teacher read it aloud, who were still talking about it months later.

34. It allows children to identify with fictional characters and feel vicariously a range of emotions—anger, jealousy, grief, fear, joy—that help them learn to cope with similar problems in their own lives.

"Lucille did it. She took Rosie's ribbon. I know she did," declared many first-graders as I read them Paula DePaolo's Christopher Medal winner *Rosie & the Yellow Ribbon*. The evidence does seem to point to Rosie's best friend, who proclaims her innocence, and listeners were taken aback and then relieved to discover a nest-building bird and not Lucille was the culprit. "Did you ever get blamed for something you didn't do, and the more you said you didn't do it, the more convinced everyone was that you did?" is one side of the issue. "Did you ever blame someone for something they said they didn't do?" is the other. "What did you do about it? How do you think you could have handled the situation better or differently?"

DePaolo's story led us to some deep conversation, and then one boy remarked, "Well, I think the reason they had a fight was that Rosie's black and Lucille's white. Everyone knows black and white people can't get along."

"No, I wasn't aware of that," I said to his bombshell comment from the blue, "for all of us get along right here at Van Holten just fine, and Rosie and Lucille were best friends in the story." We then talked over the validity of the child's theory, obviously a gift from home, and concluded that while some black and white people might not get along, there was no reason for us not to be friends with people of all colors, backgrounds, and countries. (The book I read to them after that was Chris Raschka's *Yo! Yes?*)

Marion Dane Bauer's *A Question of Trust* is a serious book that tackles a painful subject with sensitivity without sugar-coating it. Twelve-year-old Brad is furious that his mother has moved out, saying she wanted a life of her own. To get her to come back to him and his eight-year-old brother Charlie, Brad decides the two should refuse to speak to her on the phone until she becomes so miserable that she returns. Finding a homely orange-and-black cat who makes a nest for herself in their old shed, the boys decide to care for her and keep her secret from their preoccupied father. Through the cat's giving birth and the trauma of finding one kitten dead and half-eaten, the boys work through their rage at their mother for abandoning them, not realizing until it's almost too late that the cat and their mother both care about one thing: protecting and caring for their children.

35. The author plays with language in an enticing way and makes us want to join in.

Books like Bernard Most's *Hippopotamus Hunt* that makes sentences using words from the letters that spell hippopotamus and *Can You Find It?*, a selection of riddles with one-word answers containing the letters "it" ("You can look for **it** if you like music. You'll find **it** in a guitar!"), entice children to fool around with words. In Jon Agee's *Go Hang a Salami! I'm a Lasagna Hog! And Other Palindromes* incredulous fifth-graders painstakingly read each example from left to right and then right to left, like "I MADAM, I MADE RADIO! SO I DARED! AM I MAD, AM I?!"

Children cite Shel Silverstein and Jack Prelutsky as their witty-poem gurus, but there are many other inventive poets out there for them to discover, including word-play masters Douglas Florian in *Bing Bang Boing* and Jeff Moss in *The Butterfly Jar*.

36. The rhythm of the language is infectious and unforgettable.

To read aloud Caroline Stutson's *By the Light of the Halloween Moon* one needs good breath control and concentration. Children can tap out the rhythm with their hands or feet as they chant the refrain, "By the light," (tap, tap), "by the light," (tap, tap), "by the silvery light of the Halloween moon." *Earl's Too Cool for Me* by Leah Komaiko has the title refrain for listeners to chant, and I can just envision actor/comedian Steve Martin reading this with abandon and a bit of drum brush-on-cymbals background percussion.

37. Repeated refrains encourage listeners to join in and take part in the storytelling.

Along with Linda Williams's now-classic *The Little Old Woman Who Was Not Afraid of Anything*, there's now Erica Silverman's *Big Pumpkin*, a romp through Halloween with a witch, ghost, vampire, mummy, and bat, none of whom can manage to pull the pumpkin off the vine. Refrains like "It's big and it's mine, but it's stuck on the vine, and Halloween's just hours away" are rhythmic and fabulously silly to read with children, who can repeat each character's "Humph!" and "Drat!" in an appropriate voice.

38. The story is ideal for acting out for creative drama or Reader's Theater.

One boy, black and self-assured, encounters another, white and withdrawn, and offers his friendship. Chris Raschka's *Yo! Yes?* is an upbeat and innovative

34-word, two-character study, told entirely in exclamatory dialogue and the body language that's depicted in the watercolor and smudgy charcoal pencil illustrations. Fourth-grade friends Tommy Gallo and Ryan Kane read this picture book for all ages and identified with it so strongly that instead of simply reading it aloud to first-graders as planned, they spontaneously acted it out for them instead. The effect was mesmerizing, and before long dozens of children had acted out the story in pairs.

When I read it to first-grade classes (and to large groups of adults during workshops), I divided the audience in half so they could act out the story after I read it through. The dialogue on each page is in print large enough to read from a fair distance, and actors assumed the same expressions and poses as the book characters. We tried it a second time from a standing position so we could jump in the air with the final "Yow!"

Reader's Theater depends on having a set script, which you can borrow from other sources, such as Suzy Kline's appealing *The Herbie Jones Reader's Theater: Funny Scenes to Read Aloud*, or write yourself. One third-grade class was so taken with the Herbie Jones scripts they had just performed in class, they quoted many of their favorite lines aloud for me with obvious delight.

39. The illustrations are eyecatching and dynamic.

The 13 translated haiku in Sylvia Cassedy and Kunihiro Suetake's *Red Dragonfly on My Shoulder* are illustrated by Molly Bang, who used a collage of fabrics, household articles, and items from nature to form each of the animals described in the poems. Readers love to puzzle out how she did each one. There's a praying mantis made of clothespins, a clock key, saw blades, wire, and ribbon, all painted green. The illustrator's note on the last page lists materials used for each illustration.

40. The illustrations strengthen and extend the story.

The illustrations for Anne Isaacs's original tall tale *Swamp Angel* were painted on wood veneer in a folk art style that is old-fashioned American primitive and instantly appealing. As we read about Angelica Longrider's five-day wrestling match with gargantuan bear Thundering Tarnation that kicked up so much dust it created the Great Smoky Mountains, Paul O. Zelinsky's gorgeously funny oversized paintings show the tussle, with arms and legs, both girl's and bear's, poking out of the thick white clouds throughout the page. Visual jokes abound. Held underwater by the bear, Swamp Angel drinks the lake dry to keep from drowning. We follow a fisherman in a rowboat and see his astonishment when he finds himself no longer on the water but in the mud of the lake bottom. All through the story we examine each page to locate the eagle hovering near our heroine and in her huge straw hat. On the back cover we finally realize why: the eagle has built a nest in that hat and the babies have hatched. Every time you read this masterpiece, you'll find a detail in the paintings that you never noticed before.

41. In a biography or nonfiction book, the narrative and presentation of facts flows so smoothly and interestingly, it feels as if you are reading fiction.

Kathleen Krull knows how to tell a great story. In both *Lives of the Musicians: Good Times, Bad Times (And What the Neighbors Thought)* and *Lives of the Writers*, she regales us with the anecdotes, inspirations, and oddities of more than three dozen famous folks, with our most common interjection being "Wow!" every time she unearths another strange peccadillo. We get to know these eccentric artists and care about them enough to feel sorrowful at the end of each chapter when we find out how he or she died.

42. The book educates as it entertains us, and/or entertains us as it educates us.

In Robert E. Wells's nonfiction picture book *Is a Blue Whale the Biggest Thing There Is?* we find out that at 100 feet long and 150 tons, the blue whale is the biggest animal that ever lived, that "100 Mount Everests, stacked one on top of the other, would be a mere whisker on the face of the Earth," and that more than one million Earths would fit inside the sun. The watercolors are entertaining, the information is astonishing to contemplate, and the book will lead listeners to seek out more specialized titles about mountains, whales, stars, and the solar system. (One interesting fact to note: While researching what's known about Seismosaurus, the biggest dinosaur ever, one of my third-graders raced over to show me what he had found in a book: that scientists estimate the dinosaur's size at 120–150 feet. After reading *Is a Blue Whale the Biggest Thing There Is?*, present these new findings as a way to demonstrate how information changes as we learn more.)

43. The text encourages curiosity.

In Rudyard Kipling's *The Elephant's Child*, the snub-nosed little elephant kept getting spanked when he asked too many questions. In both library and classroom, we need to help unleash our children's "satiable curtiosity" when reading aloud nonfiction thrillers like Betsy Maestro's *Take a Look at Snakes* by making sure there are many more snake books available for them to dig into when we finish.

Among children, there are always specialists. Kelvin, my first-grade bat expert, after reading every bat book in the library, decided to write to Laurence Pringle, author of *Batman: Exploring the World of Bats* (Scribner, 1991), a fascinating book about bat expert Merlin Tuttle. He burst into the library one day clutching his personal reply from Mr. Pringle, amazed that the author would acknowledge him.

Third-grader Lauren asked me, "Do you have a book on the blue bobby?"

"You mean the blue-footed booby?"

"That's the one. I have a bird flash card set and wanted to find out more."

A quick jaunt to the catalog revealed a new book on the Galapagos Islands, replete with color photos and a whole section on our bird plus other odd and exotic creatures. I told her, "Just think. You'll probably end up becoming an environmental scientist who visits the Galapagos Islands one day, and all because of a flash card." Never underestimate the power of curiosity.

44. It invites an analysis of similarities and differences in comparison with other stories.

Children are always taken with the Brothers Grimm folktale "Rumpelstiltskin," where the miller's daughter is commissioned to spin straw into gold, which she does with the help of a little man who wants her firstborn child in exchange. Barry Moser updated the story to what looks like a Depression-era southern mining town in *Tucker Pfeffercorn: An Old Story Retold*. It's not a parody, but a sophisticated reworking. Bessie Grace Kinzelow is no shy maiden, but a self-assured young woman who will do what she must to get her child back from the greedy mine owner who wants his cotton turned to gold. Listeners can compare the characters, setting, plot, and ending to the traditional tale as retold by Alison Sage or Paul O. Zelinsky, and Margot Zemach's lighthearted English variant, *Duffy and the Devil*.

Parodies of fairy tales continue to be popular, and when cleverly constructed, are much enjoyed by children. Look at Ellen Jackson's *Cinder Edna*, about Cinderella's sensible next-door-neighbor who doesn't wait for a pumpkin coach to whisk her to the ball. She takes the bus. Girls who have learned from fairy tales that Prince Charming will show up someday get a welcome dose of reality when they see that a passive personality won't necessarily bring them bliss. The comparisons to be made by students after reading *Cinder Edna* could have far-reaching effects.

45. It has the power to perplex children and challenges them to think deeply and analyze a situation.

Chris Van Allsburg's books drip with irony and malice, and *The Sweetest Fig*—with nasty dentist Monsieur Bibot and his hapless dog Marcel, two figs that will make your dreams come true, and the Eiffel Tower twisted like a candy cane—is one of his most wicked. When dog eats fig and dreams he is Bibot, the man becomes the dog. Is this permanent? Will dog/man be as unfeeling to man/dog as Bibot was to Marcel? All of these questions spouted forth from my fourth-graders who had to present their opinions and defend them with supporting details.

Children like to have their brains tweaked, and George Shannon's *Stories to Solve: Fifteen Folktales from Around the World* and *More Stories to Solve* serve them well. Each folktale ends with a question, and listeners must puzzle out the ending. I like to have them pose yes-and-no questions to help them narrow down the possibilities and practice using questioning and deductive reasoning skills.

Other books don't come with answers. In each chapter of Lois Lowry's groundbreaking *The Giver*, we come to doubt whether Jonas's perfect society is all so desirable. Twelve-year-old Jonas is given the lifetime job as Receiver of Memory, and with it come emotions and concepts his regimented community has never known: joy, laughter, pain, sorrow, war, and death. Listeners will need to discuss issues such as: Is our society perfect? What would make it so for us? What would you do with people who don't fit in? Would you fit in? Readers have debated the ending, though most of my fifth-graders have decided Jonas will end up safe. This is one of those books that is more chilling and eye-opening the second time you read it, and the compelling images in the story never leave you.

46. The contents enhance the school curriculum.

What better role model could a librarian find than Eratosthenes, the brilliant and inquisitive astronomer and geographer who was also chief librarian at the famed library in Alexandria, Egypt, in the third century B.C.? Children studying the Earth will be eager to puzzle out his technique for measuring distance and calculating accurately the circumference of the world, as described in Kathryn Lasky's outstanding picture book biography *The Librarian Who Measured the Earth*, which will also give great pleasure to teachers who can integrate science, math, and social studies into their follow-ups.

47. Writing possibilities spawn meaningful literature extension activities.

A book like Anne Lindbergh's *Travel Far, Pay No Fare* is a natural for spawning writing, creative drama, and booktalking. Owen and his cousin Parsley use a magical library Summer Reading Club bookmark to enter into the plots of *Alice's Adventures in Wonderland, Little Women,* and *The Yearling,* where they interact with the characters and bring home souvenir animals, including the fawn Flag, whom they try to save from that book's fate. "What if" possibilities abound, as students can contemplate different books they'd enter, rewrite dialogues with characters, and act them out. Aside from leading children to titles they may otherwise have passed over, Lindbergh's book can get them started reading other classics as well.

48. The book wins a major award or widespread recognition.

Just because a book wins a big award like the Newbery or the Caldecott does not guarantee your children will like it. Some of these are stinkers too. However, when a book wins the Newbery or the Caldecott, it behooves us to take a careful look. If David Macaulay's *Black and White* hadn't garnered a Caldecott, I might never have picked it up again. If Jerry Spinelli's provocative *Maniac Magee* had not won the Newbery, would it have gotten the attention it deserves from teachers who are now using the book with classes with great success? Winning such an award gives a book instant status, and the psychological effect of that gold circle on the cover means that children will be willing to take it more seriously instead of giving up if the story seems difficult or rejecting an unusual style of illustration.

49. Other readers whose opinions you trust highly recommend the book.

For some unfathomable reason Gloria Houston's lovely biographical picture book *My Great Aunt Arizona* never made it onto any official "best books" lists in 1992, though it remains a favorite of mine. "Miz Shoes," as she was called by her students when she married and became Mrs. Hughes, was a teacher for 57 years, and Houston's lyrical text is an inspiration especially to teachers who know what it means to influence the lives of children. This is an uplifting book that teachers pass around to their colleagues when they wonder if they've made the right career decision.

50. It has the power to expand children's personal lifetime expectations or even change their lives.

After constant and overwhelming exposure to male composers, inventors, scientists, explorers, and presidents, a girl can get paranoid about what her role in society can be. There is token mention of women's achievements in school, but girls and boys both internalize the overriding message that women were never talented enough or smart enough or tough enough to make it big in the real world. Luckily, there are books out there that exemplify women of achievement who were never recognized by the male establishment and give today's children insights into our less-than-equitable past to prepare them for facing their own futures.

Sheila Cole's *The Dragon in the Cliff,* a fictionalized life of Mary Anning, the English girl who was the first person to discover and uncover the fossil of a dinosaur-like creature in 1811 (before the existence of dinosaurs was even known), will inspire girls and make them angry, too. The accomplishments of a poor self-educated girl who toiled in such an "unladylike" field as geology were co-opted by wealthier men who established their own scientific reputations by taking credit for the many fossils she found and restored.

Adults all know of Charles Lindbergh, but what a lift to read aloud a book like *Ruth Law Thrills a Nation* by Don Brown, which describes her attempt in 1916 to fly nonstop in one day from Chicago to New York City. Bundled up against the frigid weather, she made it as far as Binghamton in her "baby plane" before the 53 gallons of gas in the tank ran out; but those 590 miles set a record that wasn't broken until a year later—by pilot Katherine Simpson.

Tomie dePaola knew he wanted to be an artist when he was in kindergarten, as he relates in *The Art Lesson*. For children who love to draw but are told it is not a valued activity in comparison to more academic pursuits, a book like *Talking with Artists*, compiled by children's book author/illustrator Pat Cummings, is a revelation and an inspiration. Cummings interviewed 14 well-known children's book illustrators about the influences on their work since childhood and includes for each a reproduction of one piece of art the artist created as a child and one done as a famous adult. How many of your students will become artists and writers because of the influence of all the outstanding and innovative books in their school and public libraries?

FREEMAN'S FAVORITES

Since *Books Kids Will Sit Still For* and *More Books Kids Will Sit Still For* are collections of read-aloud lists, I decided to apply my own 50-item selection criteria, go through all of my lists of best books for the past 11 years, 1984–1994, and select my very favorite picture book, fiction, and nonfiction read-aloud book from each of those years. Looking to single out books that I had found most successful / provocative / fresh / kid-loved and still pleasurable to read aloud, I found it an instructive and amusing exercise, though coming up with just one book per category can be agonizing. You can tell a lot about a person by the books she loves.

Your own list would most likely be vastly different, and I urge you to try it for yourself and then ask your students to come up with lists of their past favorite books for each grade.

My choices are as follows:

1984:
Picture Book: *How My Parents Learned to Eat* by Ina R. Friedman, illus. by Allen Say
Fiction: *The War with Grandpa* by Robert Kimmell Smith
Nonfiction: *The New Kid on the Block* by Jack Prelutsky

1985:
Picture Book: *Foolish Rabbit's Big Mistake* by Rafe Martin, illus. by Ed Young
Fiction: *Cracker Jackson* by Betsy Byars
Nonfiction: *How Much Is a Million?* by David M. Schwartz, illus. by Steven Kellogg

1986:
Picture Book: *The Little Old Lady Who Was Not Afraid of Anything* by Linda Williams, illus. by Megan Lloyd
Fiction: *The Not-Just-Anybody Family* by Betsy Byars

Nonfiction: *Giants of the Land, Sea and Air, Past and Present* by David Peters (Knopf. Grades: All ages. Though it's not on my read-aloud lists, as you would not read it straight through, this oversized book of animals both alive and extinct, with pages that fold out to accommodate smashing illustrations of the biggest creatures like the blue whale showing their relative size to humans, is riveting for all children and adults.)

1987:
Picture Book: *Mufaro's Beautiful Daughters* by John Steptoe
Fiction: *Redwall* by Brian Jacques
Nonfiction: *Lincoln: A Photobiography* by Russell Freedman

1988:
Picture Book: *The Boy of the Three-Year Nap* by Dianne Snyder, illus. by Allen Say
Fiction: *All About Sam* by Lois Lowry
Nonfiction: *The Weighty Word Book* by Paul Levitt, Douglas A. Burger, and Elissa Guralnick, illus. by Janet Stevens

1989:
Picture Book: *The True Story of the 3 Little Pigs* by Jon Scieszka
Fiction: *Number the Stars* by Lois Lowry
Nonfiction: *The Magic School Bus Inside the Human Body* by Joanna Cole

1990:
Picture Book: *Black and White* by David Macaulay
Fiction: *Maniac Magee* by Jerry Spinelli
Nonfiction: *My Hiroshima* by Junko Morimoto

1991:
Picture Book: *Chrysanthemum* by Kevin Henkes
Fiction: *Shiloh* by Phyllis Reynolds Naylor
Nonfiction: *Flight: The Journey of Charles Lindbergh* by Robert Burleigh

1992:
Picture Book: *The Stinky Cheese Man and Other Fairly Stupid Tales* by Jon Scieszka, illus. by Lane Smith
Fiction: *The Prince of the Pond* by Donna Jo Napoli
Nonfiction: *Go Hang a Salami! I'm a Lasagna Hog! And Other Palindromes* by Jon Agee

1993:
Picture Book: *Baseball Saved Us* by Ken Mochizuki, illus. by Dom Lee
Fiction: *The Giver* by Lois Lowry
Nonfiction: *Lives of the Musicians* by Kathleen Krull

1994:
Picture Book: *Swamp Angel* by Anne Isaacs, illus. by Paul O. Zelinsky

Fiction: *The Daydreamer* by Ian McEwan
Nonfiction: *Bing Bang Boing* by Douglas Florian

If I had to pick one favorite book from the above list, it would have to be Jon Scieszka's *The Stinky Cheese Man and Other Fairly Stupid Tales*, an irreverent, smart-mouthed book that always makes me laugh out loud and offers so many possibilities for varying one's reading voice, inflection, and style of delivery. It is endlessly inventive and innovative in text, illustrations, and design, and appeals to an audience from kindergarten children, who miss most of the humor but who love it anyway, through adults, who have been known to give it to other adults as a gift. I gave a copy to my nephew Charlie, then 15, hoping he wouldn't think I'd lost my mind, sending him a picture book. He called to thank me and tell me what a cool book it was. His friends at school all read his copy and loved it too. From the price on the flap copy ("ONLY $16.00! 56 action-packed pages. 75% more than those old 32-page 'Brand X' books.") to the Little Red Hen running her mouth on the back cover (". . . blah, blah, blah, blah . . ."), this is my kind of book.

BOOKS THAT BOMB

What kinds of books do I reject? I cast a wary eye on the following:
1. Characters who sound phony, such as children who talk like world-wise adults for no apparent reason, or adults who are too good to be true.
2. Heart-tugging, emotionally wrenching stories that are manipulative in lieu of being real. I try to save my tears for worthy books, like Patricia Polacco's *Pink and Say*.
3. Stories written for adults instead of children, making one wonder what children would want to read them and how they could understand them. Often these books are lavishly produced and illustrated, making them the equivalent of coffee-table books. Maurice Sendak's *We Are All in the Dumps with Jack and Guy* (HarperCollins, 1993) is breathtaking to behold, but I have yet to find a child who understands it.
4. Books that preach a truth or value that is deemed good for children and hit them over the head with it. *Leo the Lop* and all the other titles in Stephen Cosgrove's Serendipity series are very sweet and insistent and make me gag.
5. Plots with loose ends that are never tied up or that end abruptly or disappointingly, as if the author couldn't figure out a more satisfying resolution and settled for the obvious.
6. Stories where the author seems to be intent on hearing his or her own voice more than is necessary and fills the narrative with long, flowery descriptions. Mark Helprin's *Swan Lake* (Houghton Mifflin, 1989) contains the most long-winded, convoluted prose I can recall, and its sheer verbosity makes it unintentionally hilarious to read aloud.
7. Circus clowns as characters. Personally, I detest clowns. Every reader has at least one theme or subject that makes him cringe or recoil, and a book needs to be awfully good to overcome that aversion. (Lisa Campbell Ernst's *Ginger Jumps* was a superb clown/circus story that I loved in spite of my own longstanding prejudice.)

8. Books that take longer than 25 pages to crack. My mother always said to give a book 40 pages before deciding whether to keep on with it, but children's books are shorter these days, and if it hasn't gotten good by page 25, most children will lose interest.

9. Books you can't recall even though you just read them. Sometimes I'll be halfway through a book before I remember having read it before.

10. Books that put you to sleep every night, even though you read just a few pages. I keep at least one of these on my bedside table at all times, and when I'm too keyed up to close my eyes, one or two new pages are all I need to render me unconscious. My friend Alice Yucht keeps a certain less-than-riveting Newbery Award book next to her bed and claims she never gets past page 11 before conking out.

REASSESSING BOOKS

Great books are usually easy to spot. You read it, you love it, the kids are crazy about it—easy. The truly awful books are also no problem to recognize. As book evaluators, it's the ones in the middle that are tough. Is it good enough to use with children? Is this a book only grownups will like? Is this worth investing school or library time on? Is it for the special reader?

Several experiences have taught me that in order to fully appreciate some books, we must try them out on children. Reviews can only take us so far. Often I'll read a book review and think, "That reviewer has no contact with real children. She's basing her opinion on a purely adult aesthetic." Books I've loved on my first reading have bombed with kids. And sometimes children's reactions make me reevaluate my own opinion.

Some books take time to grow on you. The first two times I read John Burningham's *Harvey Slumfenburger's Christmas Present*, about Santa's ordeal in making it to the top of the Roly Poly Mountain to deliver a forgotten present, I thought the story was too slight. Then I tried it out on a kindergarten. Magic. It's often how you present a book that makes it work. First we compiled an oral list of all the types of transportation we knew. In the story, every available means of transport Santa employs fizzles out in the snow and ice, and each time Santa asks someone new for help, he makes the same little speech, which we also recited each time.

My original disappointment was over the ending, where Santa finally delivers the present, Harvey picks up the box, and the narrator ends with, "I wonder what it was." At first I thought that ending was a cop-out, but on reading it aloud, saw that the journey was the important part of the story. When I finished reading it aloud, I held out an invisible box to the class. "In this box is the one thing you want the most. What is it?" We shook our boxes to see if we would hear anything. Then we unwrapped them and looked inside. Each child held up his invisible treasure and explained what it was.

I loved Angela Johnson's picture book *Julius* the first time I read it. Maya's Granddaddy brings her a gift from Alaska to teach her fun and sharing: an Alaskan pig named Julius who slurps his coffee, rolls in flour when he wants cookies, stays up late watching old movies, and teaches Maya how to dance to jazz records. I loved the exuberance of the two pals, the knock-out colors of the fabric-bordered acrylic and watercolors, and the expressive face of Maya, the African American child who loves her pig, her disapproving parents notwithstanding. The problem? When I read it aloud to a kindergarten and a first-grade class they all loved the illustrations, but I could hear the story go thud. Children were polite but unimpressed. There's no real climax, no conflict or problem, just a series of loosely connected descriptions of their adventures, so it feels unfocused. As a read-alone, it's dynamic and fun. As a story, it lacks plot. Reluctantly, I took it off my list.

Not everybody likes the same thing, either. When I read *Max Makes a Million* by Maira Kalman, about a dog who yearns to go to Paris to be a poet, one class hated it. They couldn't understand the new-wave art and the pun-laced stream-of-consciousness writing style, and it made them cranky. I gave it to Carol Shields to read to her eccentric and avant-garde third-graders, and it was one of their favorite books of the year. Why? Don't ask me. I love it too, but I can see where it isn't everyone's cuppa. Her kids quoted from it for the rest of the year.

Black and White

The most dramatic case of mind-changing came with David Macaulay's *Black and White*. I loathed this book the first ten times I read it as I pored over the four-paneled pages, trying to make sense of the recurrent cows, newspapers, and trains. It seemed dumb, the writing was stiff, and it felt too gimmicky. Then it won the Caldecott Medal, and I decided to read it aloud to several first- through third-grade classes who unlocked the magic for me.

First I had to figure out how to read it aloud. After exhibiting the title page, where the robber makes his escape, I read aloud the story titles: first the top left ("Seeing Things"), then bottom left ("Problem Parents"), then top right ("A Waiting Game"), and bottom right ("Udder Chaos"). I urged each class to look for any connecting threads in the illustrations, then showed them each page without reading it. The stories involve a boy on a train, a boy and dog playing with a model train, a train station of newspaper-folding commuters, and an escaping robber camouflaged by Holstein cows. Students grew animated, then frenzied as their observations mounted. They spotted dozens of sly visual jokes and coincidences that I had missed.

Finally, I went back to the beginning and read each page aloud, top to bottom, and the discussion continued as children found still more connections. It is easy to spend a fast-flying hour on the first read-through, as the children will howl with disappointment if you turn any page too soon. I have never seen a book provoke such a response, and listeners will discuss the story sequence for days afterward.

Black and White is the ultimate cooperative learning book. Kids who read the story alone think it's dumb and don't "get it." Every time I have introduced it to a class, the response has been magnetic, with children coming up with new and fascinating observations. During one session, a first-grade boy said, "I think the whole story is in the boy's imagination. He pretends he's the robber and the boy on the train, and his dog plays the part of all the cows." He may be right.

Since the book came out in 1990, I have encountered my original reaction among numerous teachers, librarians, and parents, who are simply baffled by it,

TEACHER & DATE: _DuFour   9/22/93_

READ-ALOUD SURVEY

> This book is being considered as a possible Read-Aloud title to include in Miss Freeman's new book, *More Books Kids Will Sit Still For*. Please help her decide if it is good enough to include or not. Some points to consider: Is the story interesting / different / appealing /attention-holding / worth finishing? Could you see the illustrations clearly, and were they worth seeing? (Use the back of this page if you need more space.)

AUTHOR _Lowry_

TITLE _The Giver_

GRADE LEVELS _5_

STUDENT &/OR TEACHER OPINIONS OF THIS BOOK AS A READ-ALOUD CHOICE:
Would you recommend this book as a Read-Aloud for other teachers and/or students? Why or why not? (BE VERY HONEST)

Yes, at fifth grade level it should be read by the teacher. In middle school students could handle it. My students were all mesmerized as I read this to them. We did a great deal of predicting what would happen next at the end of each reading. The story was appealing to all even those who did not especially like science fiction fantasy stories.

TIE-INS (Follow up activities, discussion points, related titles, etc.)

We discussed what we thought happened to Jonas + Gabriel, the Giver, the family he left behind.
It reminded one child of the movie Willow. We are reading All About Sam (the whole class) and next we'll read Number the Stars next. We'll then compare Lois Lowry's different forms of writing.

and have urged them to try it with children and chronicle their reactions. It is now one of my favorite books to read aloud.

I was fortunate to attend the 1991 Newbery/Caldecott Awards dinner at the American Library Association Conference in Atlanta. At each place setting was a copy of a special two-page newspaper, and author Macaulay, before delivering a most engrossing and thought-challenging speech, led all thousand of us in a riotous mass-folding and modeling of paper hats just like those in the book. It was perfect.

KID-TESTING

The teachers at Van Holten School where I am the librarian are always eager to field-test new books on their kids. Over the past two years I have asked teachers to fill in a Read-Aloud Survey form to record their comments and their children's reactions when they finished reading a new book that I needed tested. These forms are one way for me to determine if my designation of a book as a read-aloud is on target.

In September of 1993 I came to school with Lois Lowry's new book, *The Giver*, and told Lois DuFour, fifth-grade teacher, "I think this will win the Newbery this year. It's very odd and chilling, and it's probably too much for fifth-graders to understand completely, but I'd love you to try it out with your kids later on."

Mrs. DuFour loves problem books, so I try to give her odd and unusual titles her students can discuss. She loves touchy-feely books and her kids always develop empathy for characters and each other this way. Not about to wait for some later date, she grabbed the book and hooked her kids on the story of Jonah and his perfect society that falls apart for him when he starts to learn what the world was like before. The children were riveted, and, of course, shocked, as the story unfolded.

Early one January morning, I received a phone call with the just-announced Newbery and Caldecott winners, and I bounced into the library to greet Lois's class as they filed in for their weekly session. "I just found out the award winners!" I yelled. "Did *The Giver* win?" they yelled back. "You bet!" I told them, and they cheered.

I enlist my students in book evaluation at all levels. For third, fourth, and fifth grade I bring in boxes of new picture books and spread them across the library tables. I have the children work in pairs to select one book that looks tempting, and then read it aloud to each other. They examine the illustrations, and listen to see how the language sounds. Then they write up a critique of their reactions on a Winners and Losers sheet.

We discuss their opinions, and each pair booktalks and shows illustrations from their titles to the rest of the class. When the first-graders and kindergarteners come to the library, I invite the older kids to come too, and they pair off with the little ones, find a cozy spot in the room (often under the tables), and test the books out on them. Sometimes I ask the readers to record the comments and opinions of the younger children on their sheets so we can compare their reactions.

Two fourth-grade girls were sharing Kathy Jakobsen's *My New York* with two first-grade boys, and one of the girls enthusiastically explained how on almost every minutely detailed page you could find three things. After locating the first two—narrator Becky and an orange-and-white cat—they eagerly searched each double-page spread, where they found Becky and the cat in and

Your Name & Room # *Jenny C. Ashley T. B-4*

WINNERS & LOSERS 1992~~3~~

The "Experts" liked this book a lot. They are grown-ups. You are a kid. Kids are the ones who are going to read this book. The "Experts" are not always right. Sometimes they forget or misjudge what kids will like. I'd like you to read this book and give me an honest opinion of what *you* think.

AUTHOR *Liz Rosenberg   and   Stephen Gammel*

TITLE *Monster Mama*

After completing your book, write a paragraph or more explaining exactly what you thought of it. You do not need to give a summary of the plot. I have already read this book. Instead, consider these points:
THE ILLUSTRATIONS
THE STORY
TO WHOM WOULD YOU RECOMMEND THIS? WHY?
DOES THIS BOOK DESERVE TO BE CONSIDERED A "WINNER" OR A "LOSER"? EXPLAIN WHY.
BE VERY HONEST.

girls thinking Mother
We liked the illustration in the book. We would reccomend this to 1st-~~2nd~~ 5th grade. A winner because its well writen its cute and it has great suspence. But We've read a book just like it by Rosemary Wells other than that it's great. One thing we think is that the Monster Mama's face should not be shown in the begining. It should be shown at the end, to keep the kids in great suspence. On one page there is a picture of the kid who looks like Chuckie in Childs play. The mother looks like she is melting. We also think that the people look like they are staring at us and it is scary.

atop the Empire State Building and even at the dinosaur exhibit in the Museum of Natural History.

"What else can we find?" the two demanded.

"It's not on every page, but you can sometimes find two people kissing," the older girls explained.

I was across the room at the time, but I heard a small commotion and looked up to see the two little boys clutching their stomachs as one exploded, "Euchhh. Kissing! I'm going to throw up!" They took great glee in finding each pair of kissers, and every time they found an example he would cry out anew as the rest of us laughed.

You don't need to have all the latest titles to try out this most enjoyable book-evaluation exercise. Use new books from the library when they arrive, or pick out titles that look appealing, telling children you need to gauge their opinions before anyone else reads the books.

THE CALDECOTT PROJECT

My first- and second-graders engage in an eight-week Caldecott Project in late winter or early spring. After I read aloud and booktalk a slew of past Caldecott Award winners, children pair off to look through other past Caldecotts, finding their copyright dates to see how old they are, and selecting a favorite illustration to show to the rest of the class.

They present their findings as follows: "The title of our book is *The Polar Express*. Chris Van Allsburg wrote the story and illustrated it. It was published in 1985. Here is our favorite illustration. We thought this book was great because it shows the North Pole and we liked the train ride." (Note: Not all opinions are so favorable. With some books, children tell why they didn't like it.)

The following session, I select six new picture books for each table, giving us a starting pool of 24 books, one of which has just won the gold medal, and one or more of which has won the silver. (At this point in the year, I already know which books have garnered the awards, a piece of information I withhold from my students until our project is completed.) Each group must examine all six books at their table, talk over which illustrations they like the best, and come up with two nominated books out of the six. That gives us a total of eight nominated books, to which I add two choices of my own. If the groups do not select the award winners, I do.

Now we have ten books to read and evaluate. For the next several weeks, I read the ten nominated books aloud while children keep a written record on their "Top Secret Committee Book Rating Sheet and Secret Ballot for the Van Holten/Caldecott Medal." Since each class has selected its own ten books, the choices often differ from class to class, so I make a personalized rating sheet for each class and run copies for each student. Each time I finish reading a book aloud, listeners fill in their ratings (1–10, with 1 being "terrible" and 10 being "terrific; the best") and a several-word comment. Comments for one book can range wildly. Comments for David Wiesner's *Tuesday* included: cool, very funny, terrific, totally awesome, and stupid.

Finally, after we've been through all ten books, it's time to vote. On the school's button-making machine, I make up Caldecott Medal Committee buttons, running the Caldecott logo on bright yellow paper. Each child receives a button to wear while voting and to keep as a souvenir. I display the books on book wires on the tables, and the children spend the period reevaluating every title to see if they've changed their minds about any of their favorites. Up till now they've been rating books. Now we talk over how to rank the books, with each

NAME & ROOM # *Allison Kirchner A-5*

TOP SECRET

COMMITTEE BOOK RATING SHEET
AND SECRET BALLOT FOR

THE VAN HOLTEN / CALDECOTT MEDAL
FOR 1992

RATINGS:

1	TERRIBLE
2	PRETTY BAD
3, 4	NOT SO GOOD
5	OK; AVERAGE
6, 7	PRETTY GOOD
8	VERY GOOD
9	EXCELLENT
10	TERRIFIC; THE BEST!

	TITLE	AUTHOR	ILLUSTRATOR	YOUR RATING #	COMMENTS	FINAL VOTE
1	ABUELA	Arthur Dorros	Elisa Kleven	8 = eight	I learned spanish	2
2	BEAR	John Schoenherr	John Schoenherr	2 = Two	I didn't really like it	1
3	BERLIOZ THE BEAR	Jan Brett	Jan Brett	10 = Ten	I liked the pictures	3
4	HIGH-WIRE HENRY	Mary Calhoun	Erick Ingraham	6+7=seven	Pictures were good	5
5	MUCKY MOOSE	Jonathan Allen	Jonathan Allen	5 = five	It was ok	4
6	OLD MOTHER HUBBARD & HER WONDERFUL DOG	James Marshall	James Marshall	10 = Ten	It's excelent	9
7	TAR BEACH	Faith Ringgold	Faith Ringgold	Ten = 10	I like the picture	6
8	TIGRESS	Helen Cowcher	Helen Cowcher	10 = Ten	I loved it	10
9	TUESDAY	David Wiesner	David Wiesner	Nine = 9	Very funny	8
10	WITCH HAZEL	Alice Schertle	Margot Tomes	1 = one	It's Awful	7

A-5

getting a number from least favorite (1) to best (10). They take their ranking utterly seriously, reexamining each book, and figuring which number to give it on the "Final Vote" section of their ballot.

"I can't think. This is tough. I can't decide which to give a ten."

"I know what I'm giving this one."

Max's Dragon Shirt. That was pretty good, but not the best."

I watch them as they decide and marvel how kids that young can articulate their opinions so well. When all the papers are ranked, I collect them and tally the winners. There are many ways to do this including adding up the numbers for each title to see which one gets the highest score, or just tallying up the books with 10s to decide on first place and runners up. I announce the official results over the school public-address system the following morning, and then I announce the books that won the real Caldecotts.

In 1992, we had a problem in one first-grade class. The four groups were busy looking through their six books, debating over which two they should pick as having the best pictures, and I was sitting in on one group's discussion, when a student from another group came to get me. "Miss Freeman, help. Robbie's crying!"

Moving over to that table, I found Robbie sobbing noisily. "What! What happened! Talk to me!"

"They don't like the book I want for first choice. It's the best one and no one will believe me!" he said.

"Which book did you like?"

					RATINGS (on a scale of 1 to 5 , with 5 being best)				
VOTES		AUTHOR	TITLE		Story	Illus.	Cover	Title	Comments
	1.								
	2.								
	3.								
	4.								
	5.								
	6.								
	7.								
	8.								
	9.								
	10.								
	11.								
	12.								
	13.								

Valley View Library — Gr.___ Year ___ — LITTLE WILDCATS **BEST BOOK** SURVEY — PICTURE BOOKS (Category)

"*Tuesday*. But no one else thinks it's any good and I know it's the best."

I tried not to laugh. "Robbie, old man, I agree with you completely. As a matter of fact, it doesn't matter if they pick *Tuesday* for the table's choice, because I was already planning to choose that as one of my two nominated books if no one else did."

You know the rest. *Tuesday* by David Wiesner had won the 1992 Caldecott, and Robbie felt wonderfully smug when I announced the official results. (I tell the kids that story, and say, "Stick to your guns, folks, when you believe in something that strongly. Don't let people change your mind for no good reason.")

Of the three first-grade classes, *Tuesday* won the silver medal in two, and came in fourth in the other. *Swan Lake* by Rachel Isadora; *High-Wire Henry* by Mary Calhoun, illustrated by Erick Ingraham; and *Not the Piano, Mrs. Medley!* by Evan Levine, illustrated by S. D. Schindler each won one gold; and *Old Mother Hubbard and Her Wonderful Dog* by James Marshall received a silver.

If you do not have access to the newest books, use last year's for this project. Are there medals on these books already? Tape a two-and-a-half-inch square construction-paper patch on each book over any medals, or where a medal might be. Since all of your titles will now have patches on the front cover, your listeners can judge each book equally, without bias. When it's time to announce the winners, make a big show of removing the patches one by one, leaving the silver and gold medal winners for last. Librarian Cathy Darby expanded on the ballot idea, adding extra ratings columns for story, illustrations, cover, and title.

AUTHORS AND ILLUSTRATORS

Preparing to turn a giant cardboard appliance box into a cozy reading house (complete with skylight, carpeting, and a flashlight) for her kindergarteners,

Cindy Williams decided to have her children draw pictures of their favorite book characters to decorate the outside. As an introduction, during our library class I asked them to list their choices. Their responses were disappointing but not surprising: Bugs Bunny, the Ninja Turtles, the Power Rangers, Belle from *Beauty and the Beast*, Mickey Mouse, and Batman, along with Joanna Cole's Miss Frizzle, Katharine Holabird's Angelina Ballerina, and Dr. Seuss's immortal Cat in the Hat. I had assembled beside me a stack of books and proceeded to introduce a slew of literary main characters including Cynthia Rylant's Henry and Mudge, Harry Allard's Miss Nelson, Steven Kellogg's Pinkerton, Rosemary Wells's Max, and Marc Brown's Arthur. The children's resulting check-out frenzy was heartening. Back in the classroom, Cindy continued the lesson. When the children set to work on their illustrations, she was pleased to note that they passed over the TV and movie heroes in favor of book heroes. Parents, teachers, and librarians can counter the effects of pop TV and movie culture by exposing children to noteworthy book characters as role models.

A LIST OF MEMORABLE AUTHORS AND ILLUSTRATORS

Every time you open a new book and start to read, you are making an investment in a new situation, a new set of characters to get to know, a new place, and a new set of problems. If the book is worthwhile, your time will have been well spent, and it may lead you to its sequel or another book by its author.

In *Books Kids Will Sit Still For*, I drew up a list of authors and illustrators who had made a lasting contribution to children's literature and had accumulated a significant body of work. I broke them into suggested grade levels to assist teachers and librarians who wanted to institute monthly or weekly author/illustrator studies, either for reading aloud or having students familiarize themselves with an author's books. I have expanded this list, adding new names from the past five years, and while it is in no way comprehensive I hope professionals will also use it as a way to familiarize themselves with some of the best in the children's literature field and to introduce new and worthy characters to their media-dazed students.

(Key: Authors = A, Illustrators = I, Author/Illustrators = A/I)

Preschool Through Kindergarten

Frank Asch (A/I), Eric Carle (A/I), Donald Crews (A/I), Lois Ehlert (A/I), Denise Fleming (A/I), Don Freeman (A/I), Dick Gackenbach (A/I), Kevin Henkes (A/I), Shirley Hughes (A/I), Pat Hutchins (A/I), Keiko Kasza (A/I), Helen Lester and Lynn Munsinger (A/I), Suse MacDonald (A/I), Bill Martin, Jr. (A), Bruce McMillan (A/I), David McPhail (A/I), Margaret Miller (A/I), Mother Goose (A), Mwenye Hadithi and Adrienne Kennaway (A/I), Helen Oxenbury (A/I), Maurice Sendak (A/I), Martin Waddell (A/I), Eileen Stoll Walsh (A/I), Nicki Weiss (A/I), Rosemary Wells (A/I), Nadine Bernard Westcott (A/I).

Grade 1

Jose Aruego and Ariane Dewey (A/I), Lorna Balian (A/I), Jan Brett (A/I), Norman Bridwell (A/I), Marc Brown (A/I), Nancy Carlson (A/I), Judith Caseley

(A/I), Denys Cazet (A/I), Eileen Christelow (A/I), Demi (A/I), Arthur Dorros (A/I), Ruth Heller (A/I), Syd Hoff (A/I), Dolores Johnson (A), Ann Jonas (A/I), Ezra Jack Keats (A/I), Holly Keller (A/I), Eric A. Kimmel (A), Loreen Leedy (A/I), Leo Lionni (A/I), Arnold and Anita Lobel (A/I), Jonathan London (A), James Marshall (A/I), Mercer Mayer (A/I), Gerald McDermott (A/I), Patricia C. McKissack (A), Bernard Most (A/I), Robert Munsch (A), Dav Pilkey (A/I), Daniel Pinkwater (A/I), Beatrix Potter (A/I), Marisabina Russo (A/I), Amy Schwartz (A/I), Nancy Shaw (A/I), Janet Stevens (A/I), Jean Van Leeuwen (A), David Wiesner (A/I), Vera B. Williams (A/I), Audrey and Don Wood (A/I), Ed Young (A/I), Harriet Ziefert (A).

Grade 2

Verna Aardema (A), Aesop (A), Mary Jane Auch (A/I), Durga Bernhard (I) and Emery Bernhard (A), Eve Bunting (A), Carol (A) and Donald Carrick (I), Lynne Cherry (A/I), Joanna Cole (A), Barbara Cooney (A/I), Pat Cummings (A/I), Bruce Degen (I), Tomie dePaola (A/I), Lisa Campbell Ernst (A/I), Stephen Gammell (I), Gail Gibbons (A/I), Patricia Reilly Giff (A), James Howe (A), Tony Johnston (A), William Joyce (A/I), Steven Kellogg (A/I), Elizabeth Levy and Mordicai Gerstein (A/I), Thomas Locker (A/I), Betsy and Giulio Maestro (A/I), Margaret Mahy (A), Emily Arnold McCully (A/I), Susan Meddaugh (A/I), Eve Merriam (A), Tololwa M. Mollel (A), Lilian Moore (A), Peggy Parish (A), Barbara Park (A), Bill Peet (A/I), Brian Pinkney (I), Jerry Pinkney (I), Patricia Polacco (A/I), Robin Pulver (A), Gloria (A) and Ted Rand (I), Mary Rayner (A/I), Joanne Ryder (A), Allen Say (A/I), S. D. Schindler (I), Jon Scieszka (A), Dr. Seuss (A/I), Marjorie Weinman Sharmat (A), Lane Smith (A/I), William Steig (A/I), James Stevenson (A/I), Marc Teague (A/I), Chris Van Allsburg (A/I), Judith Viorst (A), Bernard Waber (A/I), Jane Yolen (A), Paul O. Zelinsky (A/I).

Grade 3 (All A Unless Noted)

David A. Adler, Hans Christian Andersen, Franklyn M. Branley, Ann Cameron, Beverly Cleary, Eth Clifford, Ellen Conford, Barbara Dillon, Betsy Duffey, Margaret Early (A/I), Barbara Juster Esbensen, Douglas Florian (A/I), Paul Goble (A/I), Jacob and William Grimm, Natalie Honeycutt, Lee Bennett Hopkins, Johanna Hurwitz, Trina Schart Hyman (A/I), Charles Keller, Rudyard Kipling, Suzy Kline, Patricia Lauber, Kathleen Leverich, J. Patrick Lewis, A. A. Milne, P. J. Petersen, Jack Prelutsky, Louis Sachar, Robert D. San Souci, Diane Siebert, Shel Silverstein, Peter Sis (A/I), Gennady Spirin (A/I), David Wisniewski (A/I).

Grade 4 (All A Unless Noted)

Caroline Arnold, Michael Bond, Joseph Bruchac, Roald Dahl, Leonard Everett Fisher (A/I), John D. Fitzgerald, Jean Fritz, Sheila Greenwald (A/I), E. W. Hildick, James Howe, X. J. Kennedy, Dick King-Smith, Patricia Lauber, Julius Lester, Jean Little, Myra Cohn Livingston, Ann Martin, Marianna Mayer (A/I), Barbara Park, Robert Newton Peck, Daniel Pinkwater (A/I), Joseph Rosenbloom, Alvin Schwartz, Jon Scieszka, Seymour Simon, Alfred Slote, Robert Kimmel Smith, Donald J. Sobol, Diane Stanley (A/I), Marvin Terban, Jean Van Leeuwen, E. B. White, Laura Ingalls Wilder, Elvira Woodruff.

Grades 5 and 6 (All A)

Lloyd Alexander, Avi, Natalie Babbitt, Lynne Reid Banks, Marion Dane Bauer, Rhoda Blumberg, Bill Brittain, Eve Bunting, Betsy Byars, Jane Leslie Conley, Bruce Coville, Cynthia deFelice, Paul Fleischman, Sid Fleischman, Russell Freedman, Jean Craighead George, Mary Downing Hahn, Patricia Hermes, Karen Hesse, Gordon Korman, Janet Taylor Lisle, Lois Lowry, Phyllis Reynolds Naylor, Katherine Paterson, Gary Paulsen, Cynthia Rylant, Marilyn Sachs, Jan Slepian, Jerry Spinelli, Mary Stolz, Mildred Taylor, Valerie Worth, Betty Ren Wright, Laurence Yep.

From MARTHA SPEAKS. Copyright © 1992 by Susan Meddaugh.
Reprinted by permission of Houghton Mifflin Co. All rights reserved.

READING WITH EXPRESSION

QUIET

it says

in the library

QUIET

and what I want to know is

what's quiet

inside the books

with all those

ideas and words

SHOUTING?

("Quiet" from *The Malibu and Other Poems* by Myra Cohn Livingston. Copyright © 1972 by Myra Cohn Livingston. Reprinted by permission of Marian Reiner for the author.)

"Always read with expression!" That's what my mother told me when I first learned to read, and of all the advice I have received over the years her words have most influenced my career and my life. How we read aloud to children makes a difference in how they will read to their kids. Kids pattern themselves on us, the adults who influence their lives.

A 1984 study sponsored by the Center for the Book in Washington, D.C., confirmed what we all know: that parents who read have a higher chance of raising readers than parents who don't. We also know that the more parents, teachers, and librarians read aloud to their children, the better off we'll all be.

This is in sharp contrast to what my friend Alice overheard at Toys "Я" Us during Christmas rush. Two ladies were pushing a toy-stuffed cart. One said, "I don't know what else to get him."

"Why don't you get him a book?" the other one asked.

"A book? I got him one last year. Besides, if I get him a book, I'll have to read it to him. I don't have time for that."

If there's time to watch TV at night, there's time to read or tell a story to your children. In school, if there's time to show a video, there's time to read. If we want our children to be readers, the choice is clear.

Kids need read-aloud role models if we expect them to keep their future spouses and children entertained in later years, and if we want them to raise a new generation of readers. The way we read aloud has a definite correlation to the way we present ourselves to the world. Through reading aloud, we infiltrate the thoughts and postures of many character types, and we become actors and imitators of styles of speech. The more dynamic, confident, and expressive the reader, the better that person tends to be at communicating with others, giving speeches, dealing with the public in a work-related situation, or just interacting with peers.

One week in the library, the fifth-graders were asked to decide which book they'd take with them to a desert isle and why, and pick out a passage that exemplified their choice to read aloud to the rest of the class the following week. I advised each class to practice their passages and to return to the library dressed for the beach.

The next week, the students arrived at the library to find the tables decked out like a tropical isle, replete with plants, beach umbrella, towels, sunglasses, and seashells. When I met one class at the door, dressed in my finest beach hat, lei, and shades, they said, "She wasn't kidding!" In another class, the children believed me and arrived clad in beach wear; two girls even wore hula skirts, including Abby, whose skirt ended up shedding grass all over the floor. They settled into a big circle we call Readers Roundtable and began to read aloud their selections.

It was then I made an astonishing discovery. Most of our teachers read aloud to their classes on a regular basis. The kids whose teachers read aloud in an animated, interesting way read aloud with verve. Those whose teachers read aloud in a monotone read with little or no inflection. Children need prodding and encouragement to use their voices as a tool to interest other people in what they are reading or saying.

Since then, I have included at least one library session per year per grade that involves children reading aloud, starting with second grade, when most children start to read with a fair degree of fluidity. Kindergarteners and first-graders join in on chantable refrains, retellings, and acting out stories with limited improvised drama to get them ready and willing to perform in front of a group. Starting in second grade, and on up till fifth, we continue acting out stories, but include several Reader's Theater plays where children read from prepared scripts. We stress reading with expression, finding the voice of the character, and using the voice to hold an audience in thrall.

FINDING YOUR VOICE

I have always loved to tell the story "Sody Saleratus" from Richard Chase's classic collection of Appalachian folktales, *Grandfather Tales*. In the story, a little boy is sent to the store to buy some sody saleratus (baking soda) so the old woman can bake biscuits, and though he obeys her orders not to dawdle on the way, he's waylaid and eaten by an audacious bear. Sent out to find Little Boy, the three other family members become the bear's snack as well, until their pet squirrel with the big bushy tail outwits the bear and saves the day. When I tell "Sody Saleratus," my students clutch each other and shriek every time the bear leaps

DON'T FORGET YOUR LIBRARY HOMEWORK!

Select one fabulous book by your favorite author. Pick a *SHORT* passage to read aloud to the class. (Two pages *TOPS*, and shorter if possible!) This passage should make clear to us why your author is such a great one.

Practice your passage OUT LOUD, and bring the book to the library for our DESERT ISLAND READ.

Bring your hula skirts, coconuts, and any other desert island items so we can get in the mood for being marooned with some good books!

out from under the bridge and roars. They sing along with me on the "Sody, sody, sody saleratus" refrain in the voices of the little boy and girl, the timid old man, the angry old woman, and the chattering squirrel. The next time we get together, second- and third-graders retell the story's sequence, and we cast parts and act it out.

Variants of this "swallowing" story include Paul Galdone's *The Greedy Old Fat Man*, Jack Kent's *The Fat Cat*, and Jack Prelutsky's narrative poem *The Terrible Tiger*. When Ken Kesey's *Little Tricker the Squirrel Meets Big Double the Bear* came out, I was entranced by the complex language and pacing of his literary variant and read it through several times to gauge how it would sound aloud. There's a riotous refrain by the bad-boy "grizzerly" bear that echoes and extends the one in "Sody Saleratus": "I'm BIG DOUBLE from the high wild ridges, and I'm DOUBLE BIG and I'm DOUBLE BAD and I'm *DOUBLE DOUBLE HONGRY a-ROARRR!*" After Big Double scarfs down several of the forest creatures, he goes after jaunty Little Tricker, who orchestrates the bear's downfall.

Folktales are usually straightforward, without much description, as each story plays out its details in the listeners' heads. But the Kesey book is stuffed with down-home details, from bucolic daybreak at Topple's Bottom to the scarifying rampages of the Ozark bully bear, and the dialogue is just plain funny, with good bits the kids can chime in on.

When I read it aloud to a class of entranced third-graders, it left me breathless by the end. One boy came up to me afterward and asked, "Miss Freeman, how did you know how to read that book aloud? There were some parts you read real fast, and the bear was so growly, and Little Tricker was so funny. How did you know how it all should sound? Are there directions in the book?"

I've thought about that question a lot over the past few years, for in the answer is the key to reading aloud. It's not enough to read aloud a story with expression and feigned interest. What works is to relive the story in your head as you read it aloud.

When I was growing up, I'd often hear comedians such as George Burns or Jack Benny discuss their timing in interviews. I couldn't figure out what they meant until I became a librarian and teacher. Now I know that timing is everything. It's how you hold a class in thrall when telling or reading a story or introducing a new lesson, pausing at dramatic moments, stopping for a beat before a punch line. The next time you see a great actor, analyze how he says his lines and what makes his dialogue so effective. Then steal like crazy.

In preparing a new read-aloud, read parts of the story out loud, including interesting dialogue, to yourself. Read dialogue aloud at least three different ways, experimenting with the tone of your voice, your inflection, and your pace to see which sounds most appropriate. Listen to the words of your story and try to work out how each character should sound, and how the story paces itself. Does the character remind you of someone you know? Borrow that person's cadences and accent for the dialogue.

Breath control is important, and so is your tone. Listen for the rhythm in the words. Let the story talk to you. Experiment with it, reading it differently each time until, like an actor trying out a new role, you find its center.

If it's a slow-moving story, draw out your words. Speed it up for tales set in the city. A book like Robert Burleigh's *Flight: The Journey of Charles Lindbergh* asks for a serious voice that emphasizes both the poetry and terse seriousness of the you-are-there narrative. You don't have to put on a Tennessee accent to read Anne Isaac's tall tale *Swamp Angel*, but the tone and pace of the narrative should make you settle into at least a slight drawl and an ironic but matter-of-fact tone of voice.

In Daniel Pinkwater's *Wempires,* when the vampires visit Jonathan Harker's bedroom and say, "Hallo, sonny boy! . . . How's by you?", I hear this in a Yiddish accent with just a touch of Transylvania and read their dialogue the way my Polish Grandma Rose used to talk. When Jonathan's mother comes into the kitchen in her bathrobe and says, "What's this? Vampires in my kitchen in the middle of the night?" I think of the shrill, hysterical voices of George Costanza's parents on the TV sitcom "Seinfeld."

Barbara Park's five-year-old narrator, the title character in the chapter book *Junie B. Jones and a Little Monkey Business,* is a pistol. Listen to her think up a new name for the dumb, stupid baby her mother is going to have:

> "Hey! I know one!" I said very excited. "It's the cafeteria lady at my school. And her name is Mrs. Gutzman!"
>
> Mother frowned a little bit. And so maybe she didn't hear me, I think.
>
> "MRS. GUTZMAN!" I hollered. "That's a cute name, don't you think? And I remembered it, too! Even after I heard it one time, Mrs. Gutzman sticked right in my head!"
>
> Mother took a big breath. "Yes, honey. But I'm not sure that Mrs. Gutzman is a good name for a tiny baby."
>
> And so then I scrunched my face up. And I thought and thought all over again.
>
> "How 'bout Teeny?" I said. "Teeny would be good."
>
> Mother smiled. "Well, Teeny might be cute while the baby was little. But what would we call him when he grows up?"
>
> "Big Teeny!" I called out very happy.
>
> Then Mother said, "We'll see."
>
> Which means no Big Teeny.

Whenever I read aloud in Junie B.'s earnest and out-of-breath voice, I think of Lisa and Michelle, identical twins in my school who are an unending source of questions, anecdotes, and priceless comments, like a double Junie B. in the flesh. (One typical day, Lisa announced, "Before I was born, when my parents lived in a department, their house was all yellow. But then they painted it peach," followed with, "I like your pin. I love jewelry. My aunt says when she dies, I can have all her jewelry!") Students in grades one to five are all crazy about Junie B. because her voice speaks to them and reminds them of the days when they were gullible and reckless, and they laugh out loud over the crazy things she says.

I went to hear Jon Scieszka speak to an audience of children and parents at the Highland Park Public Library one Sunday to hear how he read his own books aloud. I especially wanted to see if he shared my vision of the wolf's narration of *The True Story of the 3 Little Pigs.* "I'm the wolf. Alexander T. Wolf. You can call me Al. I don't know how this whole Big Bad Wolf thing got started, but it's all wrong . . . The real story is about a sneeze and a cup of sugar."

What I hear in the wolf's brilliant defense testimony is a Brooklyn accent, somewhere between John Gotti and Sylvester Stallone, and have always read it thus. Scieszka read it in a perfectly modulated, reasonable, and normal way. He read it in his own voice. It worked fine, but I craved more sparkle.

His *The Stinky Cheese Man and Other Fairly Stupid Tales* is an actor's dream. There's Jack, a normal guy, surrounded by that yenta The Little Red Hen, a dimbulbed giant, and of course, that lovable blob the title character, who chants, "Run, run, run, as fast as you can, you can't catch me, I'm the Stinky Cheese Man." Reading the whole book aloud is exhausting but worth it—a true test of your ability to adapt yourself to a book's characters and make them come alive.

Ever wonder why it is your listeners will clamor to borrow a book you just finished reading? It's because they love to reread the words you just read and hear your voice as they go. You owe it to your children to be their reading role model.

Every classroom and every library needs a reading corner where the group can sit together and enjoy a good story. If there's a meeting taking over the library, I'll relocate to the classroom and ask where the class sits for stories. "Oh, they just sit at their desks," some teachers have told me, "and I sit at mine." This is not adequate. Being read to is a shared activity. Children's book author Penny Pollock told me, "When I was in sixth grade in Swarthmore, Pa., our teacher stayed behind her desk all day long except for the most wonderful time of day when she emerged and joined us to read to us. It was so powerful."

LITERATURE-BASED TEACHING

An astonishing reading revolution has hit our schools over the past five years. Teachers who used to be self-sufficient with their basals by their sides are now venturing cautiously into literature-based teaching. While many of us have been teaching with children's books for years, this kind of curriculum has hit others like a new brick. Teachers are thrilled at the enthusiastic response of their students, but overwhelmed by the amount of work required to develop a whole new style of teaching.

With reading programs being handed back to the classroom teachers to devise, many teachers are in a state of panic, terrified they might do something wrong and the kids might miss an essential part of their education. My advice to everyone going through Whole Language Angst—a recent syndrome in my school system—is not to forget to have fun. For the first time in ages, the administrators are telling teachers it's OK to use their own talents to develop a cohesive reading curriculum. Librarians feel vindicated, for we've always advocated literature-based teaching.

One major aspect of whole language that frightens many teachers is the fact that if you plan to run a literature-based program you need to know books. They don't come all tidy in an anthology the way the basals did, and for upper-grade teachers it takes a fair amount of effort just to read titles that are recommended. Many teachers have formed monthly book-discussion groups to read and discuss children's novels.

There is no way for anyone to ever be "caught up" with all the good books out there. No matter how many hundreds you read, there are always thousands more waiting on the shelves. Working together, teachers and librarians need to plan which books their students are going to read together as a whole class, and in small groups. The lists in this book and its companion, *Books Kids Will Sit Still For*, should serve you well in compiling titles you want your children to know.

I find teachers and librarians often have different approaches to children's books. Librarians look for the aesthetic, while teachers look to see how they can use different books in their teaching. There needs to be a merging of ideas, a truce, or a union between the two camps that used to be so distinct but now appear to be recognizing each other.

Librarians need to find new ways to tell teachers about books, and look for ways to introduce children's literature into the school curriculum. And teachers need to read aloud more books for the sheer pleasure they bring, not just to teach this skill or introduce that curriculum project. We all need to expand our outlooks.

School and public librarians need to get together and discuss how their programs can complement each other. Public librarians often pay most of their attention to developing programming for the youngest children, figuring perhaps that the school librarians are taking care of the upper-grade students. School librarians often don't know about all the marvelous programs the public children's librarians offer. The object is for all librarians and teachers to join forces to bring children a few choice words on books and reading.

Fourth-grade teacher Linda Forte, who has always nabbed every loose minute in her school day to read aloud and pursue literary activities with her book-psyched students, confided gleefully, "I'm so excited about whole language. For years I kept quiet about all the book stuff my class did, since it wasn't in the teacher's manual. Now they're telling me reading aloud and literature-extension activities are a required component of the reading program. I've become legal!"

One problem—and it's a serious one—is that teachers are now expected to use children's books in a big way, and many teachers have either never had a children's literature class or took one 20 years back. Of course, taking a course doesn't always help either.

I've heard too many true-life stories of mis-teaching children's literature, with professors who don't know their Aesop from their elbows. There was the children's literature course at a local college that passed around the English department and bestowed on the low man on the totem pole each time it was offered. The professors there taught the course from an unillustrated anthology of children's literature.

A reliable source described one instructor who planned to base his entire course on *Alice in Wonderland*, the only children's book he knew. In still another course, students were assigned to read only one Newbery and one Caldecott award book, but they were required to write and illustrate their own picture books as their final projects. This is no way to teach teachers about existing children's books.

The daughter of a co-worker called me from her college in Pennsylvania where she was an education major. She was in a panic. Seems her professor's major assignment in her children's literature course—upon which the bulk of her grade would be based—was a project whereby each person was to select one subject area of interest and read 100 children's books on that subject. She had chosen bears. She was to find 100 bear books, both fiction and nonfiction, write up a spate of projects and activities on each one, and stash each one in a separate folder. (I don't know if the professor owned stock in the folder company.) Imagine coming out of a children's literature course an expert on bears. God forbid your new students like aardvarks or anacondas.

If your experiences mirror these, then it's up to you to educate yourself in kids' books so you can be a source of inspiration to your students. The only way to become well-rounded in the children's literature field is to keep reading.

"Which books are best?" you ponder. "What else can I do with this story? How do I put together a themed unit? How can I get my kids to read a better quality of books?"

First stop—the Library Media Center, that gold mine of materials.

WELCOME BACK

First-grade teacher Mr. Barbosa—heavily into kids' books and always eager for new titles—comes into my library the first day of school. "We're starting the week with a watermelon theme. I'm bringing in a whole one tomorrow. Do you have any good stories about watermelons?"

Whew! In 17 years, no one's ever asked me that one before. Think. THINK. Fruit, fruit salad, plums. I know lots of books on plums. Apples—they're easy. Every writer has at least one apple book in him. Watermelons? Cantaloupes, honeydews, cranshaws? Aaaahhhhh! Yes! John Gantos's *Greedy Greeny*. Perfect! A monster gets sick from eating too much watermelon.

That first week of September, the questions come fast and frantic:

"What science fiction book can I read to my fifth-graders that's short and funny?" I hand Pat Stabile *Aliens for Breakfast* by Jonathan Etra and Stephanie Spinner, about the perfect kid in class who turns out to be an evil alien.

The note reads, "Do you have 25 funny books to start the kids reading?" I send fifth-grade teacher Joan Bukavich 30. Using the example of a baker's dozen, I always try to give teachers more than they ask for, more than they knew I had, more than they knew existed.

Lois Thompson pops into my office. "I need everything you have on butterflies. The kindergarten monarch butterfly chrysalis should be opening tomorrow." No problem. Our insect section is first rate.

"We're doing trees," says second-grade teacher Julie Kotcho. "Identifying leaves and all that. I found some good ones in the 582s." Ah, but she hasn't seen Lisa Campbell Ernst's story *Squirrel Park*, or the picture book of Harry Behn's poem, *Trees*, and she missed George Ella Lyon's beautiful alphabet picture book *A B Cedar*. The beginning of the year, before the kids start borrowing, is so satisfying. Everything I look for is still on the shelves. I whip up a pile. She leaves happy.

At lunch, fourth-grade teacher Linda Forte asks, "Do you know of any books about things people treasure, the way *Miss Rumphius* loved her lupines? I want my kids to choose something in their lives that they treasure and write about it."

"And bring in a tangible object that symbolizes it?" I ask.

"Ooohh. Yeah! That's great."

I send her Tomie dePaola's *The Art Lesson*, Sherry Garland's *The Lotus Seed*, and Gail E. Haley's *Dream Peddler*.

Here we go again. Another year of trying to turn kids into book fanatics. What we do with our students makes a profound difference in their lives. I tell my students, "Every time you pick out a new book to read, you are making decisions about your future. With every book you read, you get a little smarter.

Books have the power to stretch the way you think and the way you look at the world."

Look at Morris Dees, who planned to become a publisher. Stuck in an airport during a snowstorm, he picked up a copy of Clarence Darrow's autobiography. "It changed my life," states Dees, now a famed civil rights lawyer in Alabama.

Books have the power to change all our lives. Kids are responsible for their own education—we all are—but they won't believe you if you just tell them. Ask your students to think back on a remarkable book that changed their lives or thinking in some way, one that they feel strongly about, that stayed with them a long time, that their peers will not want to miss, and give each child time to present his or her findings, which may surprise you all. If early on you make books and libraries an essential factor in their lives, they will reap the benefits all their lives.

One of the advantages of making children's books such a cohesive part of every curricular area is that books become natural and necessary to children throughout the school day. In basal readers, stories are abridged or excerpted, and children miss out on the full flavor of a book. Used to be, I'd recommend a good chapter book to a reader, and he'd say, "I already read that. It was in my reading book." No matter that he'd read but one episode, the fact that he'd already been exposed to it cut him off from the desire for further contact. Now that children are reading and discussing a variety of whole books in the classroom, they come into the library anxious to find other books by that author or in that genre. The library is not just a place where they venture to find books for reading and reports; it's the everyday brains of the school.

Teachers at my school know that when they request two books from the library, they'll probably get five. I'll attach a Post-it Note (one of the great inventions of the 20th century along with the personal computer, the microwave, and clumping kitty litter) with an idea or two for each book to get them started.

Librarians need ESP. On the whole, teachers will not remember to consult you before they begin a new unit. Sometimes they come into the library for books and assume they know all the best ones, and don't ask for any assistance. I try to keep my ears open. One teacher was halfway through a unit on Pueblo Indians, but I didn't know it until a crew of third-graders came in with their projects to display in the library. I quickly scanned the shelves, and seeing that the teacher had not borrowed any Native American folktales, pulled several good ones and sent them to her room with a note. She was delighted, and so were her students when she read the stories aloud.

Every time I finish processing a major book or AV order, I send the staff an invitation to come browse through them in the library before I make them available for students to borrow. I arrange everything by subject area (picture books, fiction, science and health, social studies, math, the arts, other interests), displaying them on every library table and shelf top. When a teacher comes in, she grabs a pencil and a pad of small Post-it Notes to flag every book she wants right away.

Children love the displays as well, and they are encouraged to fill out Post-it Notes too, though I tell them teachers get first dibs. Teachers love the chance to examine the shiny new books, and many make lists of other titles they'll want to request later on.

At the end of the two-day display, my aide Sharon Kalter and I deliver requested books to the teachers. If several teachers sign one Post-it, I attach it to the sign-out card so I can easily route it to the next person on the list when the book is returned. (Now that we've gotten our computerized circulation and cataloguing system set up, reserving books for kids and teachers will become easier and far more efficient.)

How to get even the most reluctant and book-phobic teachers into the library to look around? It's called baking (or buying, depending on your schedule). I bring in cakes or cookies, lemonade or cider, and even the most harried teacher will sneak in. Guilt causes them to look at the new books before they nosh, and I make sure to show them titles I know will fit into their teaching. It's as much fun to match teachers to good books as it is with children.

Often teachers will select a batch of read-alouds from the displays of new materials. One teacher used several of these picture books with her class with less-than-inspiring results. We discussed this, and she said, "I guess it's not enough to pick any random book to read aloud cold. There needs to be a reason to read a book to kids. It might be to tie in to a lesson, or to get them thinking about a new idea, but I think we need to plan how to use each book with kids, and not just take a new book and plow through it." Touché!

The varied read-alouds you select should reflect your children's mood, sense of humor, interests, and needs, or a subject area to be explored. It's not sufficient to say, "I need to read aloud today" with no further consideration.

Another important consideration is diversity. Some teachers select only humorous fiction chapter books or adventure stories to read aloud. We all need to present, on an ongoing basis, every type of book: all the genres of fiction, including both picture books and chapter books; biography; all areas of nonfiction; folklore; and all manner of poetry. Children who read only dinosaur books need to see what else is out there. Your children's reading tastes evolve every time you choose a new book to share.

A librarian asked me, "What do we do when our teachers come in waving book lists from the backs of teacher manuals, and want to know why we don't have all of them? Half are out of print; the others are plain dreadful. I try to explain that I can give them even better books, but some would rather believe a list made up by who-knows-whom than believe me."

"Don't give up," I told her. "Quality will triumph."

First-grade teacher Roni Sawin told me, "I was always happy using my own books from home until you started feeding me all those picture books from the library. Now I can see how most of those old books were not so great. In fact, some were just awful. Now that I have good books to compare them with, I don't need to use that many of my old ones anymore."

It's true. Once you've eaten in Paris, McDonald's will no longer satisfy you.

DO YOU GET IT?

Often we assume that children understand what we tell them, what they hear on television, and what they read. My advice is to assume nothing. Remember Ramona's interpretation of the National Anthem, that song about the "dawnzer lee light" in Beverly Cleary's *Ramona the Pest* and Shirley Temple Wong's reciting "I pledge a lesson to the frog" in Betty Bao Lord's *In the Year of the Boar and Jackie Robinson* (HarperCollins, 1984)?

CALLING ALL STAFF!!!

YOUR LIBRARY

HAS JUST FINISHED BARCODING

400 BRAND NEW BOOKS,

MOST OF THEM FICTION, AND VIDEOS, TOO.

COME TAKE A LOOK AT

THIS YEAR'S BEST READ-ALOUDS

TODAY AND TOMORROW

AND CHECK SOME OUT!!!

THURSDAY, NOVEMBER 17, AND

FRIDAY, NOVEMBER 18, 1994

(REFRESHMENTS WILL BE SERVED, OF COURSE)

True anecdote 1: Danielle, a third-grader, handed her teacher a doctor's note stating she couldn't go to gym—she was allergic to cold. "That's interesting," Mrs. Balunis said. "What are you going to do? Move to the equator?" "What's that?" Danielle asked.

True anecdote 2: Mark was doing an explorer report for his fifth-grade teacher. He read, "Magellan worked as a page under the queen." He asked, "Does that mean he was a writer?"

True anecdote 3: Elvira Woodruff, author of such kid-friendly books as *The Summer I Shrank My Grandmother* and *George Washington's Socks*, visited Van Holten School one day and spoke to my fourth- and fifth-graders about the ingredients she puts in her books. Naturally, they asked her about how much money you make for writing a book. She told them she makes about a dollar a book. One of my kids was aghast. "All that work for one dollar!" he exclaimed. "That seems like an awful lot of work for just one dollar." She had to explain how royalties work: it's a dollar for each book sold, not each book written. "Ohhh," he said, "That's more like it."

True anecdote 4: It was almost holiday time and third-grade teacher Carol Shields was having her students write word problems. She wrote on the board: REINDEER; SANTA CLAUS; ELVES, and told the class they needed to compose word problems using the numbers 4 and 6. Out of 21 children in the class, six wrote problems about elves that were a bit off the mark, including the following:

- Elves had 4 girlfriends. Each girlfriend had 6 pictures of him. How many pictures did they have in all?
- There are 4 Elves imitators. Each of them is wearing six bells. How many bells are they wearing in all?
- Elves Presley made 6 records. Each record had 4 songs. How many songs in all?

All of the above happened in my school, and we can laugh about it, but there is an underlying message here as well. Children are innocent and gullible and will often interpret information in strange ways. With nonfiction, they'll misinterpret facts or make erroneous assumptions about what they see in a book or on the tube. During a discussion on stars and planets, one child will say, "This guy, he was driving in his car, and these space aliens kidnapped him. It's true. I saw it on TV." Children read novels and return them saying, "I liked it but I didn't understand the ending" or they'll ask a question about the book, and you realize they missed the entire point of the story.

Just because children are reading good books doesn't mean they're understanding them, which is why, when we present sophisticated or unfamiliar concepts, we need to reinforce their comprehension skills with leading questions, discussions, and an introduction to the concept of rereading.

I read to a fourth-grade class Barbara Dugan's hilarious and touching *Loop the Loop* about young Anne's friendship with the elderly-but-indomitable Mrs. Simpson, who shouts from her wheelchair, "I'm Methuselah, and I'm nine hundred and sixty-nine years old." The two spend the summer together, but when Mrs. Simpson tries to get up from her wheelchair and walk, she falls, ending up in the hospital. Anne visits her and the old woman no longer recognizes her.

My fourth-graders loved the story, but our discussion afterward brought up an interesting point. They didn't understand how and why Mrs. Simpson had lost her memory when Anne went to see her. They assumed something happened to her—physically—when she fell, making her forget. "Maybe she hit her head," was one typical response. Finally, one child theorized that perhaps she lost her bearings from being lonely and in the hospital. As adults, we read the story and cry at the bittersweet ending, but children, without prior knowledge of hospitals or (as my mother-in-law puts it) "old-age people," will need some background.

View each new book you read aloud for the first time as a learning experience in the best way to present it the next time. I read the picture book *Appointment*, adapted by Alan Benjamin from a piece by W. Somerset Maugham, about a man who tries to run away from death. My fifth-graders didn't understand so many things—what a crone was, how death could be an old woman at the marketplace, whether the servant was a man or woman, why the servant wanted to go to Samarra, what was Samarra, why did the old woman have an appointment with him, what was the appointment for? Several children seemed to understand some of the nuances, but most seemed baffled, especially by the ending, when we realize the man has not escaped his fate but ridden right into it. After some discussion, I read the story again, and this time the children found it tantalizingly horrifying.

With the next class, we talked first about predetermination and how in some cultures people believe your life is preordained and you can't change your fate, using the wonderfully gruesome and titillating story of Oedipus as an example. This time, more children seemed to understand the story the first time, and our subsequent discussions were more fruitful. Hearing it read a second time helped them better see the structure of the story and make sense of the wonderful twist ending.

The best gift we teachers and parents can give our kids is the ability to laugh. An important step in developing language skills is nurturing a good sense of humor through nonsense and wordplay, which you can facilitate by telling your kids dumb jokes, tongue twisters, and poems. A book like *Appointment* exposes them to irony, which by fifth grade is often tied in to humor. One of my students culled this from a joke book: "What is it? The person who makes it doesn't keep it. The person who buys it doesn't use it. The person who uses it doesn't know it." Let them try to puzzle it out for a while before revealing the answer: a coffin.

It's only after they've built up a foundation of stories and nonsense that they can understand the nuances in parody, satire, and poetry. A book like Maryann Kovalski's *Pizza for Breakfast* is fun on its own, but much more satisfying if kids can make the connection to the Grimm fairy tale "The Fisherman and His Wife" upon which it was based.

Then again, sometimes children understand only too well. A *New York Times* editorial on September 15, 1993, "Regarding Barney," noted an amusing but telling revisionist rendition that children were heard singing about purple TV dinosaur Barney. The original theme song "I love you/ You love me/ We're a happy fam-i-lee/ With a great big kiss and a hug from me to you/ Won't you say you love me too?" has apparently evolved, modern nursery-rhyme style, into "I hate you/ You hate me/ Let's go out and kill Barney/ And a shot rang out and Barney hit the floor/ No more purple dinosaur."

The late Alvin Schwartz, the famed collector of children's rhymes and chants, would have gotten a chuckle out of that. In his *And the Green Grass Grew*

All Around: Folk Poetry from Everyone, which is filled with irreverent kid ditties, he included "Row row row your boat gently down the stream/ Throw your teacher overboard and you will hear her scream."

Children love to play with words, but now there's evidence that poetry can offer more than simple pleasure. A new study of reading disorders by Dr. Sally E. Shaywitz, a behavioral scientist at the Yale University School of Medicine, finds definitive evidence that men and women use their brains differently when decoding rhyming nonsense words. This could lead to new findings to help children deal with and overcome reading disabilities. One way to help dyslexic children, as suggested by Dr. Reid Lyon of the National Institute for Child Health and Human Development in Bethesda, Maryland, is to play rhyming games and read them books written in rhyme.

PLANNING LITERATURE LESSONS

Many of the literature-based ideas we generate to use with kids come from common sense and practice. The experts who have written all the teachers' manuals are not smarter or more clever than we are. In fact, many haven't been around actual children and classrooms for a while. Here's a new catalog I received from the Teacher Book Club: Literature-Based Whole Language Sets with a sample worksheet from Peggy Parish's *Amelia Bedelia*:

Change the Towels!

1. Amelia is told to change the towels in the green bathroom.

2. Color these towels the right color.

3. Use scissors to cut them out and change them the way Amelia does.

Innovative, eh?

Often you'll plan what seems like it will be the perfect lesson, only to realize halfway through that you've forgotten an essential ingredient. You're in the middle of reading *Stellaluna* by Jannell Cannon to an attentive kindergarten and suddenly remember the bat puppet you have stashed in your puppet cabinet. Or you remember the puppet, but forget to tie the fiction story into nonfiction books on bats. You then need either to dash across the library and pounce on the books in 599.4 (if you're a librarian and have all that material close at hand), or tell the children these books exist in the library.

In *Regina's Big Mistake* by Marissa Moss, a young schoolgirl makes a mistake on her wonderful drawing, but she turns the dented sun into a lovely moon and saves her picture. This is the "make lemonade" approach to art and life. If things don't turn out just the way you planned, then turn your errors into advantages.

How often have we chided ourselves for a lesson run amok, a story that bombs, or a class session that left us feeling we should have done better. Often novice librarians and teachers will say to me after a workshop, "It's all easy for you. You know how to take all these books and put them together, but we don't know all the perfect books."

First off, since when do we teachers have to be perfect? The world doesn't end if we read aloud a book the kids find boring or teach a lesson that doesn't fly. Each time we ponder how to make it better, we revise our teaching strategies until we get it right.

I Blew It

Friends say, "What do you mean, you had to stay at school late to write your lesson plans? Can't you just do the same ones every year? What's the difference?" I suppose I could, but boredom is not one of my more treasured emotions. To stay the same is to stagnate. I like to get a little smarter each year, and help my students do the same.

The teachers I know who are unhappy in their jobs are the ones who are resistant to all change, who don't want to try anything new. We need to build on our existing knowledge to refine what we do, and sometimes be prepared to give our teaching styles an overhaul.

Good teaching means that even the same lesson can be improved, tightened, strengthened. The kids may not know the difference, but we do. Perfect? Certainly not. What we all aim for is that feeling of personal satisfaction when a class catches on and is with you each step of the way, eagerly anticipating your next move. That feels wonderful, but if it doesn't happen there's always the next time. Our jobs are about knowledge. Ed Young put it perfectly in his Caldecott Honor Book, *Seven Blind Mice*: "Knowing in part may make a fine tale, but wisdom comes from seeing the whole."

Recently, to fulfill a course assignment, a Rutgers graduate student requested to sit in on a fifth grade to observe how I booktalked and read aloud to my students. I had just purchased a huge, perfect pomegranate to use with a fourth-grade class in a lesson I present every couple of years or so, and decided to do it with that fifth grade instead for the grad student's benefit. I had gathered up Chris Waldherr's lovely *Persephone and the Pomegranate*, along with several other versions of the tale, plus a sampling of collections of Greek and Roman myths from the 292s.

The fifth-graders came in, settled cozily onto the "story rug," and, when asked why the seasons changed each year, provided a nice bit of scientific explanation. I pulled out the pomegranate and said, "Here's why winter is coming." One third of the class responded with, "That's right. Persephone. You read that to us last year!"

Ever want to crawl under the rug and scream? I had no memory of doing the lesson the year before, though I keep careful records of everything I do, but obviously I had. With younger kids, you can say, "Well, this is such a great story it's worth hearing the second time." Older kids are not so easy.

"Don't you remember, Miss Freeman?" they asked cheerily. "Mrs. Forte wanted to do a lesson on myths and asked you to read the new Persephone book to us to get her started." Yup, now I remembered. Drat. "You can do it again. We liked it a lot."

The other two thirds of the class started agreeing. "We never heard it. Read it anyway."

Classic dilemma. What to do? Gut the lesson and give a booktalk on the new books in my office? Read aloud other myths? Not enough time to make it good. The solution? Make lemonade, of course. I introduced the Greek myths, booktalking and handing out books to enthusiastic readers, encouraged discussion of gods and goddesses they knew, and read the book a different way, by alternating pages with Penelope Proddow's elegant version, *Demeter and Persephone*, to compare the differences between the style, illustrations, and complexity of the two stories. We ended up cutting open the pomegranate and feasting on the seeds.

Grad student happy, librarian reasonably satisfied she had presented an old lesson in a new and interesting way, and kids content to stain their fingers with pomegranate juice.

Sometimes stories we read aloud to teach children a moral or behavioral lesson have the opposite effect from what we intended. I read aloud Helen Lester's charming *Me First* to a class of kindergarteners, thinking it would influence them to be more considerate of each other. After a congenial time spent giggling over the story, in which pushy Pinkerton the pig's insistence on always being first lands him in hot water with a demanding Sandwitch, the kids lined up to go back to class, all of them merrily trilling, "Me first!" as they pushed their way into line. Not quite the lesson the author or I had intended, somehow.

Allow yourself the satisfaction of doing it all right sometimes, and keep a record of your most successful activities for next time. Often, a teacher will come into the library and say, "I did a unit on similes last year, and you gave me some picture books that were just perfect. Do you remember what they were?" If they're lucky, I'll be able to ferret out just which books they used, but how much easier it would be for teachers to keep their own running logs of those titles worth using again. Build up a repertoire of those titles that best serve your curriculum, being careful to search out new and fresh titles each year.

Wonderful tie-in ideas will occur during or after a lesson, and you'll be annoyed with yourself for overlooking the obvious. Literature lessons offer many possibilities for creative extensions, to which you must remain receptive. Looking for other than the obvious ways to use a book can open up a new lesson.

Sometimes small, spur-of-the-moment ideas can work well. During a presentation of summer books with a first grade, I led off with Bruce McMillan's color photo-illustrated *One Sun: A Book of Terse Verse*, intending to whip through the book. While the class looked at the cover, I decided instead to cover each page's two-word rhyming poem for them to guess, which they greatly enjoyed. For a photo of a drenched dog, the page read "WET PET." One child guessed, "SOGGY DOGGY." Afterward, we made up new rhyming word couples. The tone of the lesson changed slightly, but for the better, I thought.

Children add their own imprints to what they hear. The chantable refrain in Martin Waddell's *Farmer Duck* is "How goes the work?" with a response of "Quack." One kindergarten class was so taken with the chant, they kept it up over the next several weeks after being read the story. They'd be browsing for books in the library and one voice would pipe up "How goes the work?" and the rest of the children would answer "Quack." One day I called out, "How goes the book?" There was quiet for a second as they pondered the new question, and then one child drawled, "We're reeeeading!"

MAKING CONNECTIONS

On the opposite end of curriculum integration is overkill. I recall hearing about a teacher who spent weeks teaching math, science, and language arts lessons related to the book *Everybody Needs a Rock* by Byrd Baylor. Too much time spent on one story leads to glazed children. The follow-up activities you select need to fulfill your objective for the lesson and allow you to segue into other avenues without beating the book to death.

Story setup can ensure the success of your readings. It shouldn't take too terribly long, or you'll have exasperated children asking "When are you going to read us the story?" (the adult translation of which is "Can't you cut the small talk and get to the point already?"). Ask yourself what the children need to know before a story, and how you can best introduce it. (This can be called the anticipatory set if you're fond of educational jargon.)

Anansi and the Moss-Covered Rock

When I read aloud *Anansi and the Moss-Covered Rock* by Eric Kimmel, instead of reading the story straight out I first asked my kindergarteners what a yam is. None knew. I gave hints: It grows in the ground, and you can bake it in the oven and eat it with butter. "Potato!" they shouted. "Almost. It tastes very sweet, and it's a different color than a potato." After a bit of speculation, several children guessed it was a sweet potato. I pulled a yam out of my pocket to show them and cut it in half so they could see the orange color. Next, pulling out a large loop of orange yarn, I told them the marvelous string story "The Farmer and His Yams" from Anne Pellowski's indispensable *The Story Vine*. I wore my spider pin (thank you, The Nature Company, for much of my animal jewelry), and told them a bit about the African trickster, Anansi, who appears as a spider or a man. By the time I read the story, my children knew about yams, knew what a trickster was, and had described the properties of moss. All of my introductions took about ten minutes, and when we started the story we were all ready to laugh at that unrepentant spider.

Making story connections is the next step in planning. After the Anansi story session, I could have followed up the next week in so many ways: by reading aloud another Anansi story, such as *Anansi Goes Fishing* or *Anansi and the Talking Melon* retold by Eric A. Kimmel, or another trickster tale, like *Coyote Steals the Blanket* by Janet Stevens, or a nonfiction spider book, or a fiction one to which we could compare the folktale. Then there's the wonderful Ashanti story "Talk," collected by Harold Courlander in his book *The Cow-Tail Switch and Other West African Stories*, about a talking yam, an old Pete Seeger song about cooking sweet potatoes, and even a Raffi song about Anansi the Spider. We could retell and act out the story, draw a picture of the main characters, write a group sequel where Anansi finds another rock with new magical properties, read William Steig's *Sylvester and the Magic Pebble* where the donkey turns into a rock, or examine moss. Every time you select a book to read aloud there are many connections you could choose to make, depending on the time available, your stated objective, and your students' needs and interests.

Earthlets

Lessons should be carefully planned but not scripted, allowing for unexpected occurrences both welcome and not. *Earthlets: As Explained by Professor Xargle* by Jean Willis was in full swing. The third-graders were analyzing the alien professor's lecture to his audience of aliens, containing as it did so many farcical, erroneous conclusions about the behavior of human earth babies. At that moment, a mom carrying her red-headed baby walked in. "Look everyone!" cried one student, "it's a real Earthlet!" The class laughed and applauded.

"Look at that funny white ring dangling from its feeding place," I said, pointing to its pacifier. "What would Professor Xargle make of that?"

The two most plausible answers were: an energy computer that keeps the earthlet charged up and a lip stopper to keep its teeth from exploding out of its mouth.

A teachable moment like that happens frequently in every classroom and library. Seizing the advantage, a resourceful teacher might ask students to come up with new explanations of baby lingo, and then work together to write for the misled professor a new lecture on other earth phenomena such as school, eating, pets, or sports, and present it to the class, which will identify the many mistaken notions.

Ginger Jumps

In Lisa Campbell Ernst's charming *Ginger Jumps*, circus pup Ginger dreams about becoming a dog with a real family, with a little girl who will love her and play with her. She envisions that little girl as always happy and laughing and starts her search in the circus, watching the children as they enter the tent each night. She finds her dream girl after saving the show when backbiting Prunella, that Precious Poodle of Precision, stumbles and Ginger takes her place, leaping from the impossibly high staircase onto the tiny trampoline below and becoming an instant star.

Putting ourselves in Ginger's place, first-graders discussed the qualities that made up a perfect dog owner. Then we switched gears when I asked, "Did you ever find the pet of *your* dreams? Tell us about it." On the board we listed the varying qualities of the ideal pet.

The following session, we read *Emma's Pet* by David McPhail in which bear Emma can't find a pet that has all her ideal criteria until she takes a good look at her soft, cuddly, friendly dad. I handed out white paper which I had folded so two flaps met in the middle like double doors. On the left side, children all wrote "The pet of my dreams is . . ." and on the right side, they listed their criteria with three adjectives or descriptive phrases such as "friendly, loyal, and always there when I call."

As ever, children used invented spelling for their words, writing them first on sentence strips, and when they needed respellings, I wrote the word over on the bottom of the strip so they could copy it correctly onto their good copies. Invented spelling is great for young children just starting out, but when we're writing something to be displayed for others to read, we correct our mistakes for the good copies.

Opening up both flaps, each child drew a large picture of that ideal pet. The following week, after first guessing all the animals in Tana Hoban's *A Children's Zoo*, each child had a turn to stand up, read his or her "doors," and ask the class to guess their pets. Then, with a flourish, each child opened the flaps, revealing the rabbit or cat or snake within.

Away from Home

Away from Home by Anita Lobel became the focus for a several-session exploration of the world for two first-grade classes. In the book, 26 boys assemble on stage for an alliterative tableau performance featuring cities around the world. "Adam arrived in Amsterdam," reads the first page, and we see him, suitcases in hand, beside a canal. "Bernard ballooned in Barcelona" shows him in his basket landing his hot air balloon beside a cathedral designed by Gaudi. Children guessed the country where each city is located as I read each page, giving them location clues as needed, and then showing the site on our globe. Notes on the last page further describe each city.

At our next meeting, children picked a city or country or state that started with the first letter of their names. They used atlases and country books to both select their places and find out more about them. Next they wrote a sentence using an action verb. With the information they had discovered, they drew pictures of their places, adding details as to its location, such as mountains, a river, buildings, and other background scenery, and a picture of themselves performing in the foreground. I loved "Kyle kicked in Kenya," showing him kicking the ankle of a very large elephant, and "Ryan ran in Rwanda," where Ryan is running from one of the mountain gorillas that lives there.

For the third session, we started off with *How to Make an Apple Pie and See the World* by Marjorie Priceman, following the young narrator as she assembled her ingredients, including semolina from Italy, cinnamon from Sri Lanka, sugar from Jamaica, and apples from Vermont. Again, we pinpointed each place on the globe.

We got our aerobic exercise with the song "Oh, My Aunt Came Back" (to the tune of "Old Hogan's Goat"), a call-and-response song in which children repeat each line and add motions until they are swaying and rocking like tipsy gymnasts. I added some verses to the song to make it more international.

OH, MY AUNT CAME BACK

Oh my aunt came back (Oh my aunt came back)

From old Japan (From old Japan),

And brought with her (and brought with her)

A hand-held fan (a hand-held fan). *(children fan selves)*

Oh my aunt came back from the Sydney fair,

And brought with her a rocking chair. *(add rocking motion)*

Oh my aunt came back from the London piers,

And brought with her a pinking shears. *(add cutting motion with fingers)*

Oh my aunt came back from cold Nepal,

And brought with her a crying doll. *(add crying face)*

Oh my aunt came back from the South Pole loop,

And brought with her a hula hoop. *(stand and add hip motion)*

Oh my aunt came back from the New York Zoo,

And brought with her a nut like you! *(point to singers)*

Now that we were all standing, each child found a "space" on our story rug and we acted out *Away from Home*, with children pantomiming the actions of each of the book's 26 travellers as I read it aloud.

Finally we formed into a circle, and each child read aloud his or her own alliterative sentence and showed the accompanying picture. I collected all the pictures and once again we stood up for some creative drama, this time acting out their sentences as I reread them aloud.

The pictures went up on a large bulletin board with a world map in the center, so other students could locate the places.

Zoodles

What's a Zoodle? In Bernard Most's book of the same title, he joins together two animals whose names overlap, posing a riddle to identify the new portmanteau. "What do you call an iguana that hogs all the food? A piguana." "What do you call a kangaroo that wakes you up every day? A kangarooster." After two second-grade classes guessed Most's riddles, they were raring to try some of their own. First we figured out the process of creating a Zoodle. The first two or last two letters of the animal's name must coincide with those of another animal. Not all animal names will work, of course, but one that did was ostrich, which we turned into an ostrichicken, ostricheetah, ostrichickadee, and ostrichinchilla. Then there were our tigermine, bearmadillo, and dodog.

Once we came up with the two animals, the next step was to write the riddle which would name one animal and give a short but on-target description of the other. Some we composed together were: "What do you call an ostrich that clucks?" "What do you call an armadillo that sleeps all winter and growls?" "What do you call a dumb dog that's extinct?"

Now the children understood how the words needed to be joined, and they worked in pairs to create a new creature, with the support of the library's many animal books. Indexes of animal encyclopedias were helpful for kids who were stumped and needed suggestions, and they were soon whizzing up and down the alphabet, muttering, "Is there an animal that starts with an 'MA'?"

Their perseverance was remarkable, and some of their animal combos and riddles were inspired: "What do you call a jaguar that lives in Texas and has a striped shell? A jaguarmadillo." What do you call a leopard that lives in the water? A whaleopard." "What do you call an octopus that meows? An octo-pussycat." "What do you call a llama with a trunk? A llamammoth." "What do you call a mongoose that balances balls on his nose? A mongooseal." "What do you call a narwhal that lives in a swamp? A narwhalligator." "What do you call a sheep that lives underwater and can't breathe air? A fisheep."

During our next session, they drew the illustrations, referring to animal books when unsure of how an animal should look. We folded white paper in half so they could draw the first animal asking the riddle, which was encircled in a speech balloon. (Our rule of thumb: Write the question first, and *then* draw the speech balloon around it!) Unfolding the paper, they then drew the other animal speaking the answer, patterned after Most's format.

Week three had them reading aloud their riddles for the rest of the class to figure out and laughing a lot.

My Hiroshima

Sandy Vitale, fourth-grade teacher, came into the library looking for information on Hiroshima for her tenth-grade daughter who was working on a report. In addition to the usual nonfiction titles I found for her, I gave her Junko Morimoto's *My Hiroshima*, a moving picture book memoir of "the day of the Thunderbolt," when the author was a child. Sandy was so taken with the book, she shared it with her class, and came back to say, "I never realized you could convey so much important information in a picture book."

I gave her Eleanor Coerr's *Sadako*, a picture book based on the life of Sadako Sasaki who died of bomb-related leukemia when she was 12 and we discussed other picture books that make profound and memorable statements.

She said, "I've always used picture books with my kids to demonstrate how a story is set up—characters, setting, plot—but for years I felt guilty when I used one, like I was teaching them with materials meant for little kids or something, but I loved those books so much. I used to make sure nobody was around so I wouldn't get 'caught' reading baby books aloud. Now, with all this whole language, it's acceptable and I feel like I've been allowed out of the closet!"

Sandy's feelings are echoed by teachers everywhere. An eighth-grade English teacher called me at work to tell me he'd read my article in *Teacher* magazine and wanted to know if I really thought it was advisable to read picture books to students at that level. I told him that my fellow librarian and book maven Alice Yucht had a whole picture book section in her middle-school library, and she used them constantly with her eighth-graders as did her teachers.

While upper-grade teachers can pass over many picture books intended mainly for very young children, they will howl with laughter or even cry over many of the picture books listed in the subject index under "Picture Books for All Ages."

Pink and Say

Patricia Polacco's *Pink and Say* is a case in point. The heartbreaking but uplifting Civil War story about Sheldon "Say" Curtis, a wounded 16-year-old white soldier who is rescued by Pincus "Pink" Aylee, a young black soldier, is one that made me sob on first reading. And second reading. By the time I had read the book to myself several more times, and written several book reviews about it, I felt "hardened" enough to read it to a class of fifth-graders. We talked about the causes of the Civil War, I booktalked a batch of related books, and then launched into Polacco's family story, written about her great-great-grandfather.

Midway through the story, when Pink's mother, Moe Moe Bay, is shot and killed by Confederate marauders, my throat got tight. I don't know how I got through the rest of the book, but sniffled and cried along with my students, and made my voice keep working until I whispered the last page. The book is a masterpiece, and any teacher who thinks she's "covered" the Civil War is leaving a huge gap in her curriculum unless she includes it.

To put together a thematic unit on a subject such as prejudice or immigration or war, picture books are indispensable and provide a quick window to introduce a new topic and draw a class together. With *Pink and Say* a teacher can launch a Civil War unit, but then expand the focus to encompass the prejudice endured by Japanese Americans during World War II in Ken Mochizuki's *Baseball Saved Us* or the hatred and mistrust left by war as in Daisaku Ikeda's allegorical *Over the Deep Blue Sea*. Show how war displaces people with Sherry Garland's *The Lotus Seed*, a somber picture book about a woman who leaves war-torn Vietnam and tries to make a new life for herself and her family in America. As students tackle longer fiction books on these themes, bring in nonfiction books to research the causes of war or prejudice. Compare Eleanor Coerr's picture book *Sadako* with her longer chapter book biography *Sadako and the Thousand Paper Cranes*, and after reading *Grandfather's Journey*, discuss how author Allen Say's life was different because of World War II. Children will chime in with war stories of their relatives, so ask them to verify some of these memories by interviewing their families on audio or video tape.

Antics

In the realm of language arts, *Antics* by Kathi Hepworth looks like an alphabet book for young children, but a closer inspection reveals it to be a clever vocabulary-enhancing collection of words that contain in them the letters "ANT," starting with full pages devoted to *ant*ique, brilli*ant*, ch*ant*, and devi*ant*. Each word is defined by the illustration, which features ants in all the character parts. Fifth-graders pored over each page, with their objective being to define each word in a sentence using the context clues of the illustration.

For K*ant*, they guessed the bewigged 18th-century German philosopher was a Revolutionary War hero, a writer, a poet, an old dead guy, and a big thinker.

We pulled out the encyclopedia to find out more. They assumed Rembr*ant* was a painter, and I showed examples of his paintings.

Most of the words were definable until we came to one that stumped me: xanthophile. In the illustration, there's an ant sunning herself atop a large bunch of bananas. A banana-lover? A sun-worshipper? The unabridged dictionary shed some light: it's a person who loves the color yellow.

The students then each selected an alphabet letter, rummaged through dictionaries to find a new "ant" word beginning with that letter, pored over nonfiction ant books to see how to draw them, and created marvelous ant-wise illustrations that defined their words in context. My favorites: ignor*ant*, with one ant saying to another, "You anteater," and fr*ant*ic, with a tear-faced mother ant crying, "Where's my little baby?" and the tyke hiding behind a tree saying, "Ha! Ha!"

Yo! Yes? Again

When I presented a workshop for teachers in my district on using children's literature in the classroom, I invited students Tommy Gallo and Ryan Kane to present their inspired version of Chris Raschka's *Yo! Yes?* for the 60 teachers assembled, and I explained the recent work the fourth-graders had done evaluating picture books with the first-graders. Two weeks later I received an enthusiastic note from Hillside Middle School teacher Pru Fletcher that said in part, "We had a great time with *Yo! Yes?* The kids adored it, and after dramatizing we did cartoon stories." Enclosed in the envelope was a sample of one boy's work. Ahmad's uplifting drawing was right on the mark.

READER'S THEATER AND CREATIVE DRAMA

My introduction to the educational values and pure fun of Reader's Theater came right before the winter vacation one year when a bad case of laryngitis rendered me incapable of telling holiday stories or singing songs with my third- and fourth-grade classes. I arrived at school and ran to the 812 section of nonfiction to see if we had any plays the children could read to me and found a clever one involving all the nursery-rhyme characters and the gifts Santa brings them. After a quick trip to the copying machine, we were ready to act. Sitting in a big circle, the class read the play aloud while I listened. The children adored it, and we've done more and more Reader's Theater each year since then. It's one of the most far-reaching components of our library program now, and each year children reminisce over their former roles.

Josh, a special education student who was mainstreamed with a third-grade class for library each week, became panicked when he realized we were going to be reading a play. He rushed over and whispered, "But Miss Freeman, I can't read. What can I do?"

"I've given you the best part," I told him. "Dog Tray is everybody's favorite, and all he has to say is 'Arf.' Sit next to me so I can give you your cue and you'll be great." He was. In our play, narrators read all of the stage directions aloud as well, so Josh knew how he should say each line. He later asked me several times when we were going to do that play again so he could be the dog.

In the past several years we've acted out whole plays and also broken into groups, with each group practicing a different play to put on for the rest of the class. During the first session, we look over the play or plays, assign parts, and have a first reading. If you're short on time, that can be it. If you're game to continue, the children benefit most from one or two additional practice sessions before presenting a final performance, scripts in hand.

Loretta Ark's second-grade class surprised me by not only memorizing their parts and practicing their plays back in their classroom, but by showing up to library in full costume. One girl who was playing a rich lady even wore a suitably dramatic pink feather boa. Their rise in self-esteem was remarkable that year. Otherwise-shy children had a chance to shine and be recognized, and their oral reading skills improved drastically. Monotonal voices changed to ones with verve and expression, in part prodded by the children who'd say, "Try that line like this," and then proceed to demonstrate a more vivacious style of delivery.

Carry Reader's Theater even further by presenting the play for an assembly, but remember: sometimes keeping it simple is just as effective as getting into a whole production. On the other hand, don't you remember your lines and parts from your class plays in elementary school? An optimal situation would be if each class or grade could mount one major school production per year, in addition to several in-class productions. There's no better way to carry out the principles of whole language than to involve children in living a story.

A good source for plays is the popular monthly magazine *Plays*, which children love to borrow so they can continue to put on skits with their friends at home. *Presenting Reader's Theater: Plays and Poems to Read Aloud* by Caroline Feller Bauer, *Stories on Stage: Scripts for Reader's Theater* by Aaron Shepard, and *Fantastic Theater: Puppets and Plays for Young Performers and Young Audiences* by Judy Sierra are all great time-savers for teachers who want to get started without fuss, as are the more narrowly focused *Show Time at the Polk Street School: Plays You Can Do Yourself or in the Classroom* by Patricia Reilly Giff and *The Herbie Jones Reader's Theater: Funny Scenes to Read Aloud* by Suzy Kline.

"The Travels of a Fox"

I tell an old English folktale called "The Travels of a Fox" to my first-graders in the spring. In it, a fox catches a bumblebee and stuffs it in his sack. At each house along his way, he knocks on the door and asks the woman of the house, "May I leave my bag here while I go to Squintums?" She says yes, and before he leaves, he warns her, "Be careful not to open the bag." As soon as he's gone, the woman of the house says, "I wonder what that fellow has in his bag that he's so careful about. I'll just take a little peek and see. It can't do any harm, for I shall tie it right up again."

Of course, as soon as each woman in turn unloosens the string, the bumblebee or rooster or pig or ox jumps out, giving the fox reason to take from her the animal responsible for the demise of whatever creature was in the bag. Putting a little boy in his bag proves the fox's undoing. Paul Galdone did a picture-book version called *What's in Fox's Sack?* and Jennifer Westwood did one called *Going to Squintums*, but I like the original Joseph Jacobs telling best, since it gives us no inkling of what Squintums is, and I like to listen to my kids' speculations.

Usually, the week after I tell the story, the kids act the whole thing out in sequence, but the last time I told it I decided to interview the listeners and ask them to give answers from different characters' points of view. At the last minute, as the class arrived at the door, I ran for the tape recorder and grabbed a small hand mike, figuring perhaps we could try this as an Oprah-type interview. I've interviewed students before, but never bothered with an external microphone as my tape recorder has one built in. The response to the extended microphone was incredible. Kids fell right into their roles and assumed new poses and voices to answer the questions put to them. Even Natalie, who never said boo to anyone, and was usually barely audible when she spoke, got into her bumblebee character and chattered away into the mike.

I asked them simple one-word response questions ("Is it true, Bumblebee, that you were caught by Mr. Fox?") to warm up each interviewee, then factual comprehension questions ("What were you doing when he caught you?"), then interpretive questions ("What were you thinking about when you were all tied up in that bag?"), and finally questions requiring synthesis ("What will you do, little boy, now that you're free again?") and evaluation ("Do you feel the fox deserved to die for what he did?").

While characters in folktales are by definition one-dimensional, that day my first-graders explored every aspect of that story with an extraordinary supply of insight, and they could have kept the interview going for far longer than the 40 minutes we have for our weekly library time. Put people in front of a mike and they'll sing like canaries. They took the resulting tape back to the classroom so they could hear themselves being interviewed. Step one in teaching children how dialogue works and how it can sound aloud, it succeeds equally well with upper-grade children.

FANTASY VERSUS REALISTIC FICTION

In grades three to five, when children are starting to sink their teeth into fiction, I do booktalks in many genres to introduce them to realistic fiction and fantasy literature. In my introductory lesson, we make two columns on my trusty white erasable marker board. First we list the components of both fantasy and realistic fiction, as I booktalk examples and hand out the books to eager readers. Here's a sample list to use with a third- or fourth-grade class, along with a couple of titles that could be used to demonstrate each concept.

Fantasy	Realistic Fiction
Animals talk: *The Grand Escape* (Phyllis Reynolds Naylor) *The Cuckoo Child* (Dick King-Smith)	**We don't find out what animals are thinking:** *Sable* (Karen Hesse) *Mary Marony and the Snake* (Suzy Kline)
People or animals have special powers: *The Adventures of King Midas* (Lynne Reid Banks) *The Magic Hare* (Lynne Reid Banks)	**People and animals behave as they do in real life:** *Gopher Takes Heart* (Virginia Scribner) *Dog Days* (Colby Rodowsky)
Magic occurs: *The Summer I Shrank My Grandmother* (Elvira Woodruff) *Your Mother Was a Neanderthal* (Jon Scieszka)	**Is true to life; Science happens:** *Grandfather's Day* (Ingrid Tomey) *The Gadget War* (Betsy Duffey)
There are made-up creatures: *Backyard Dragon* (Betsy & Samuel Sterman) *Shape-Changer* (Bill Brittain)	**All human and animal creatures are real:** *Juliet Fisher and the Foolproof Plan* (Natalie Honeycutt) *One Dog Day* (J. Patrick Lewis)
Characters travel into past or future: *Time Out* (Helen Cresswell) *Friends in Time* (Grace Chetwin)	**Characters live in the past or now:** *Hannah* (Gloria Whelan) *Rosy Cole Discovers America* (Sheila Greenwald)
Some events couldn't happen in real life: *The Tiny Parents* (Ellen Weiss and Mel Friedman) *Drummond: The Search for Sarah* (Sally Farrell Odgers)	**All events could or did happen in real life:** *The Stinky Sneakers Contest* (Julie Anne Peters) *Mayfield Crossing* (Vaunda Micheaux Nelson)

Can take place on other worlds:
Wizard's Hall (Jane Yolen)
Ned Feldman, Space Pirate
(Daniel Pinkwater)

Takes place on Earth:
Seven Treasure Hunts (Betsy Byars)
Class President (Johanna Hurwitz)

The following week, I arrange an assortment of 40 tempting fiction books on the tables, selecting an equal number of fantasy and realistic books in all genres, and making sure to select books children would want to check out and read independently. Students work in pairs, look over the tables, and select one book that looks good to them. Pairs then have five minutes to look through the book, read the blurb or flap, decide if their book is realistic or fantasy, and select one short paragraph to read aloud that corroborates their conclusion.

Back together as a group, we hand out two 3-by-5-inch flashcards to each child. The yellow ones say FANTASY, and the blue ones REALISTIC. Each pair presents its book's title and author and reads aloud the one-paragraph selection. On the count of three, the rest of the group identifies the book as realistic or fantasy by holding up the applicable card.

FICTION VERSUS NONFICTION

Amended, with a different set of books and flashcards that say FICTION and NONFICTION, the above lesson also works for a presentation of fiction versus nonfiction books for second- or third-grade students. For third- or fourth-graders, I hand out to each student a set of four 2-by-7-inch laminated flashcard strips, color-coded and labeled in large letters: FICTION, NONFICTION, REFERENCE, and BIOGRAPHY. On a cart at the front of the room is a stack of many books selected for child appeal and to stimulate interest in reading. Dividing the class into two teams, and alternating teams, I hold up a book, read the title, and say, "One, two, three, SHOW!" at which second all players on the one team must hold up the strip that best corresponds to the book. If I show *Witch-Cat* by Joan Carris, the team should wave the blue fiction strips in the air. I can see at a glance who has put up the wrong card, such as the yellow nonfiction one, and review the differences between fiction and nonfiction accordingly if too many children continue to put up the wrong cards each time. I score the team's correct responses on the board, and then hold up a new book for the other team. Over the course of the game, I showcase more than 20 varied books, so the game doubles as a type of book review and a booktalking session.

For first-graders, each child reaches into a basket and pulls out a pink card with the name and sketch of an animal on it. First, each must make the noise of that animal and locate the one partner in the room who has a copy of the same card and is also mooing or oinking or hissing. Once the pairs link up, they examine the 30 or so books scattered across the tables until they find the two about their animal. The duo finds a cozy place to sit, looks through both books, reads the titles, and decides which book is true and which is a story. Back together as a class, each pair stands up, shows both books, reads the titles aloud, and calls on one of the other children to state which is fiction and nonfiction and how he or she could tell.

FACT FOR THE DAY

What have you learned today? Every day, I tell my students, a person should learn at least one new thing. "Fact for the Day" I call it, and working in a library surrounded by every possible type of book it's hard not to come across something new.

"You are standing in a room of knowledge," I exhort. "Let your curiosity guide you. Find something unusual and astounding every day. Your brain depends on you to nurture it and keep it healthy. If you just eat junk food, your body will grow weak and flabby. Your brain works the same way, and it craves a steady, challenging diet of books to keep it stimulated."

It all started when I read Esther Quesada Tyrrell's *Hummingbirds: Jewels in the Sky* with photos by her husband, Robert A. Tyrrell. The two have studied hummingbirds for almost 20 years, but this was their first children's book. The title page was the first of many revelations. There we see a close-up of a bee hummingbird, wings outstretched, holding a 1979 Lincoln penny in its tiny claws. The penny is only slightly smaller than the hummingbird's body. On the next page, the bird is perched on a yellow plastic ruler, and we measure its wingspan at a mere three inches. The facts in the text are equally arresting. Did you know there are over 300 different kinds? That they can fly backward and upside down? That their wings can beat up to 200 times a second?

When I read this remarkable fact aloud to a third-grade class, we stopped and tried an experiment. They flapped their hands while I timed them for one second. We topped out at five fast flaps. "Do you think the Tyrrells knew when they were your age that they wanted to study birds? What subjects fascinate you?" I asked the class. So started my first "Fact for the Day" project, designed to stimulate curiosity in the strange ways of the world.

When the class returned to the library the following week, they discovered several dozen nonfiction books spread across the tables. Working alone or with a partner, their task was to peruse the books until finding one or more that looked tempting, find a cozy place to read, and see if they could ferret out some facts that they never knew before. Each group received a half-page pink sheet to record its best fact, along with the title, author, and call number of the book they used.

We discussed how to put a statement into our own words instead of copying from the book, a concept alien to some children but one we need to introduce early and reinforce often. The facts they found were indeed tantalizing and sometimes unnerving: "Did you know . . . that people thought Albert Einstein was stupid when he was a kid and he didn't talk until he was three?" "Did you know . . . that black widows have a habit of spinning their webs across a toilet seat?" "Did you know . . . that when Mount Tambora blew up the ash went into the air and blocked the sun in the New England states and caused six inches of snow in June, 1816?"

The following week, children presented their facts to the class, showing illustrations from their books to buttress their presentations. They added illustrations to good copies of their fact sheets, and we displayed the fruits of their research on the hall bulletin board so all could get curious. The fact searching continued for weeks as children dug through our nonfiction shelves for more books with good trivia. The animal section especially got a good workout.

FACT FOR THE DAY

DID YOU KNOW....

that when Mount Tambora blew up the ash went into the air and blocked the sun in the New England states and caused 6 inches of snow in June, 1816 **?**

(This fact was discovered by Stephanie Ciotta **in Room** B-6 **.**

You can find this fact in the following book:

Title: Volcanoes

Author: Franklyn M. Branley

Call number: 551.2 B

Nonfiction books to read aloud to introduce the "Fact for the Day" project include Nancy Milton's *The Giraffe That Walked to Paris*, about the first giraffe to reach France in 1826, and Robert Burleigh's *Flight*, about Charles Lindbergh's first transatlantic flight. What amazes me about the Burleigh book is that few fourth-grade children recognized Lindbergh's name. Burleigh's stunning paintings and his terse, heartstopping account, based in part on Lindbergh's own journal kept during the historic 1927 flight from New York to Paris, pull listeners into the tiny cockpit of the *Spirit of St. Louis*.

One book that always causes a commotion is Faith Ringgold's *Aunt Harriet's Underground Railroad in the Sky*, an impressive combination of fact and fiction about Harriet Tubman as seen through the eyes of modern African American child Cassie, who relives the journey slaves took to escape north via the Underground Railway before the Civil War. Ringgold uses the realistic fantasy segments to lead us into the chilling facts, making them understandable to my second-graders, who scramble for Harriet Tubman biographies afterward.

EVALUATING READABILITY

I want my students to realize they can depend on each other and themselves when it comes to selecting books to read. Children need to know they have resources of their own to employ. In kindergarten and first grade, parents occasionally phone or stop in to complain about a book their child has taken out of the library that week. "Why did you let him take such a hard/technical/inappropriate/dumb book?" they'll ask.

Obviously, I don't walk around the room recommending inappropriate and unwieldy books to my kids ("Here, David, let's try *War and Peace!*"), but when a kindergartener is clutching a much-too-complex title about dinosaurs or electricity or a fiction book that's way over his head, it's not always easy to disengage it. "That book's a little hard for you, don't you think?" is met by a suspicious glare; "Nah. My mom will read it to me." I don't forbid my students to take out books. I try to dissuade them sometimes, showing alternate titles I think they'll enjoy more, but if a kid has his heart set on a book, the worst thing that will happen is he'll find out it's not so great and exchange it for another. No great catastrophe there.

Parents are always encouraged to visit our library and take out books for their kids, so if someone is bringing home the same book each week and mom's having a fit, it's easily fixable. Some young children like big books because they make them feel more mature. Others take them out as a defense against reading. Teachers, librarians, and parents need to work together to assist children in their selections, but some final choices should be the child's. I request of my kindergarteners that at least one of the three books they check out at a time must be a story their parents can read to them. Once children begin to read independently, some teachers expect their children to borrow at least one or two books they can read on their own, and that's certainly fair as well.

With kindergarten and first grade, I present several lessons on how to pick out a wonderful book. It's almost an abbreviated version of what I do with the older students (see "Ten Ways to Pick a Great Book" Talk, page 47 of *Books Kids Will Sit Still For*, 2nd ed.). We brainstorm a list of ways kids can find great books, which usually include:

- The cover makes me want to look inside.
- My friend told me I'd like it.
- It was on display, so Miss Freeman thought it was great.
- I like books on that subject.
- I read other books by that author.
- The pictures inside look good to me.

I write each of their suggestions on my white board. (Those erasable color markers are an inspirational touch for teachers, making former chalkboard scribblings look so dated and dull. It's easy to draw pictures as you write, and children love to watch the message unfold.) Then I demonstrate each principle using an irresistible assortment of picture books, which I hand out to those who ask for them.

Listing selection techniques in such a concrete way empowers children to think about the choices they make. I show some books that look great on the outside but are far too dull or difficult once we open them, and some that look blah but aren't. We have "Be Kind to Bottom Shelf Day" for kindergarten and first-grade classes, where we pick the fullest bottom picture book shelf, and the children help me empty it out onto the tables. All spread out across four big tables, the books look so inviting, and children can see what they may have been missing. And each year, children begin to consider their selections instead of grabbing the first available book. If they do choose something they don't like, I remind them that the school library is open all day except Saturdays, Sundays, and when it's dark outside. They are always free to return the offensive title and go for another one.

The Test

By second grade most children are reading more fluidly, but many are still intimidated by longer books, not realizing that they now can handle some of them. Many children are reluctant to move from picture books to chapter books, and with the spectacular picture books on the market nowadays I can't blame them. So I suggest a blend. And that's when I teach classes how to do the Fist Test. Our school district, Bridgewater-Raritan, has always recommended the Fist Test to enable students to become independent evaluators of readability, and it truly works. A child selects a book, opens it to the first full page, puts out a fist, and reads that page. Every time he can't figure out a word, he puts out one finger. If he runs out of fingers before the end of the page, the book's too hard, and will be a struggle all the way through. If he has no fingers, the book's either too easy, or he's a good reader and can handle anything. One to four fingers means the book will be fine.

I demonstrate the Fist Test with a very simple three-words-on-a-page book, a very difficult book, and one in the middle, telling children, "This is a test for you to take any time you're not sure a book is for you. It will tell you honestly if the book is too hard, too easy, or just right, so you can pick books that fit you better." I scatter 50 appealing titles from very simple to longer chapter books on the tables and ask the children to pick one or two that catch their eye, and then sit down at a table and practice the Fist Test with those books. The classroom teacher, Sharon Kalter (my fabulous library aide), whatever parents are in the library volunteering, and I go from child to child listening to them try out their page on us and announce their evaluation. If the book is far too hard or easy, they select another and try again, until they've found something that's just right. From then on, whenever students undertake a longer book, they can judge for themselves if it's readable.

Cover illustration from PETE'S CHICKEN by Harriet Ziefert,
illustrated by Laura Rader. Illustration copyright © 1994 by Laura Rader.
Reprinted by permission of Tambourine Books.

THE IMPORTANCE OF A SCHOOL LIBRARY/MEDIA CENTER PROGRAM

"WHAT DOES THIS CHAPTER HAVE TO DO WITH CHILDREN'S LITERA-ture?" you may find yourself asking. Everything. A 1994 vision statement of the long-range planning committee of the American Association of School Librarians, a branch of the American Library Association, states:

"In five years, all schools will have library media specialists who are recognized as leaders in restructuring the total educational program, participating as active partners in the teaching/learning process, connecting learners with information and ideas, and preparing students for literacy and lifelong learning."

As part of my own vision, I'd like to share some of my thoughts and worries about the state of my chosen profession and offer concrete suggestions for practicing what I preach: the integration of library and literature skills.

One of my former students, just graduated from high school, came back to visit me. Jeremy was a rough-and-tumble kid who drove some of his teachers crazy, but I loved him. He often found himself in hot water for his boisterous behavior in fifth grade, but my best memory of him is how he would carry his baby sister up and down the hall, talking to her and tickling her, and showing her that he was crazy about her. "That boy's going to be all right," I thought.

So into the library comes a tall, handsome guy, who walks over to me and says, "Remember me?" and, glory be, I did. He was about to enter college, and had been living near Chicago since eighth grade, but stopped in to visit old friends in Bridgewater.

He looked around the room in delight. "I remember everything we ever did in here," he said. "The stories you told, the songs we sang, playing the Reference Game and the In What Book Game in fifth grade. I remember all the books I read. In first grade I used to check out *Where the Wild Things Are* every week. I loved that book. And in fifth grade, I read all the Gordon Korman books."

He strode around the room, stopping to pull familiar books off the shelves, laughing when he saw an old toy he recognized. He pointed to a chair. "I was sitting at that table right there when Mr. Shuba came on the loudspeaker and told us that the Challenger blew up. I'll never forget how terrible I felt."

We talked some more, and then he said, "When I left here, I thought this was what libraries were like everywhere. But my high school in Illinois had a tiny library with no librarian and no books. How do they expect people to like reading if there aren't any books? I never read books for fun all through high school. Just classics, and most of them were so bad."

My own personal need is to show all those Jeremys out there that libraries are the key to their success, and that librarians are nice, friendly, and slightly off-beat people who are passionate about books and reading. His total recall and still-obvious love for books were just what I needed after a long, hard, but satisfying year.

THE ROLE OF THE SCHOOL LIBRARIAN

The library should be the most important room in the school. It should be the mecca of every teacher and the pride of every administrator. Yet, in too many school districts, this is not the case. What are librarians for? We need to answer this question because of an alarming trend running rampant through the United States and possibly coming soon to districts near you. Proposition 13 in California and 2½ in Massachusetts are terrifying for schools, because the first thing that seems to happen is that schools lose everything that makes them so remarkable in the first place. School boards desperate to cut out funds think, "Who needs art, music, nurses, gym, and, of course, *librarians?*"

In California between 1980 and 1994, half of the state's school libraries were closed. According to an article by Universal Press Syndicate columnist Richard Reeves in December 1993 New Jersey's librarian-student ratio was then "1 to 8,512, compared with the national average of one librarian for every 826 students." Public library funding was slashed drastically as well, leading to massive cutbacks. An earlier article by Reeves revealed the not-so-surprising figures that in standardized national reading tests, California's public schools, "once a golden place where children were offered the best education in the world for free," tied with Mississippi for last place.

Recently the teachers in my district hosted educator Leanna Traill, who talked about the advanced educational programs in New Zealand, and while I thought she had some fascinating insights I gave an involuntary shudder when she explained how they made do with classes of over 30 students, no arts teachers, and, of course, no librarians. Do we aspire to that? I hope not, but I worry.

Administrators looking to save money can be convinced that libraries don't matter, that they're a source of fat in the budget, an unnecessary "frill." In the next breath, they'll tell you their district believes in the whole-language philosophy. Without a librarian to provide the materials and services to teachers, every whole-language classroom suffers. Librarians need to be considered master teachers as well as professionals who maintain a valuable facility of books and media. In my home state of New Jersey, state education officials decided in 1995 that librarians should be categorized as non-teaching administrative personnel, which could affect a school district's state funding status, thus encouraging administrators to eliminate library positions. Fortunately, after widespread protests, mostly through letters to the state's education commissioner, this proclamation was withdrawn.

If your school has resigned itself to enduring an underfunded library, a dated collection, or the lack of a professional to keep things humming, it's up to you to wake up and do something about it. Many schools don't miss having a good library because they don't know just what it is they're missing: a professional librarian who keeps up on all the thousands of new books published each year, orders materials that fit and extend the school's varied curricula and interests, knows what children like to read and has techniques to expand their tastes and knowledge base while keeping them interested and motivated, presents a coherent library skills program linking reading and the search for information, and creates an inviting and stimulating environment in the library that makes students, staff, and parents want to come back. Libraries are a last bastion of hope, knowledge, and aid whether times are tough or not.

I've been teaching at the Rutgers School of Communication, Information, and Library Studies for more than a dozen years now, teaching professional development courses on developing library skills and literature programs, and I've heard every horror story out there: librarians who teach in the gym because the library has been turned into a computer lab, librarians with three schools and a yearly budget of under $1,000, librarians who attempt to cycle through 30 or more classes a week. I attempt to help them cope and overcome such disasters, but it's no simple task.

What do school librarians need? They need full-time clerical help, and volunteers, too. They need budgets large enough to accommodate books and media purchases to support all the curriculum changes that leap up every three years, plus the ability to satisfy the reading interests of all students. They need to catch up to the technology that is transforming our society and revolutionizing our libraries' information retrieval capabilities, which means they need money, support, and training for computerization. They need the opportunity to advance themselves professionally, through regular district librarian meetings and sharing sessions, and ongoing in-service and out-of-district courses. They need the understanding of teachers and administrators that the library is not a place to dump kids and run, and that teacher and librarian need to work together on an ongoing basis to plan important instructional units. One librarian cannot satisfy the reading requests of an entire class—she needs the teacher working alongside recommending books, monitoring student reading, and acting as a role model for readers.

When there's a class in the library, the literary mood can be infectious. If we are excited and exciting, then so will our students be. Every minute we see them is precious, for a non-reader can be seduced by books at any given moment. Seeing them every week, all year, years in a row, helps develop a reading bond.

At the core is the question we all ask about people with jobs different than ours: "Just what does she do all day, anyway?"

So in case you've been wondering, here's a rundown of why we're here. Naturally, none of us runs a library in exactly the same way, just as no two teachers teach the same way, but here's how I view my job.

Depending on the year's student population, I see 17 to 21 classes of kids a week, in grades K–5. I want them every week so I can work with the teacher to turn them into readers. The classroom teacher can't do it all alone any more than I can. We depend on each other.

I see myself as the tester. All of those marvelous new books we get every year come to me first. I figure out the best ways to use them with kids and we try them out. I read aloud and tell stories, we act out stories, try out writing activities, retell stories, evaluate books for the year's "Best Books" lists, and investigate every nook and corner of the library.

I nurture their curiosity, exposing kids to literature genres, styles, and authors through booktalks, browsing sessions, and integrated library skills that tie in with the books in the library, and guide them in learning new reference and research techniques. In my weekly library lessons with each class, I also try to weave in new titles, odd facts, a new chant or song, something to stimulate both the intellect and the imagination.

We dive into each activity, with real books being used at every turn. There's no "Let's fill out this nice worksheet to see if you can alphabetize or use the card catalog." We get our hands dirty. We dig into the card catalog, find real books, file real cards above the rod, play Stump the Librarian, race to find books during "Two-Minute Search," and end up, in fifth grade, competing with other classes playing The Reference Game and The In What Book Game (see page 110 of *Books Kids Will Sit Still For*, 2nd ed. for a brief description). One celebrates information; the other, literature.

Often I help defuse a crisis. A second-grade teacher received this note:

> Dear Mrs. Fredericks:
>
> If you have the opportunity, will you ask Miss Freeman if she has any info on bobcats? Kyle has decided that the bobcat seen in our area is going to eat him, and no amount of reading we've done with him has convinced him otherwise. Oh yes, also he only eats children at bedtime. Thanks.

We sent home books on big cats and their feeding habits, and helped Kyle get over his fear. To date, no bobcat has messed with him.

The library is the most important resource in any school, a huge non-fattening candy store that allows kids to sample new interests while nurturing old ones. We try string games, explore poetry, crack jokes and riddles, investigate animals, poke into people's lives through biography, and share what we've discovered.

The library is the place of ever-expanding life learning. It needs to be home to kids. That's why I want them in here every week, for a dose of inspiration, a change from the teacher's voice, a new outlook on literature, and a chance to uncover something new. A library without a full library program shortchanges our kids and our teachers.

The librarian is a supplement to every classroom, often working with teachers on a new unit, and helping to provide children with the necessary study, library, and life skills to access information and literature skills that lead to a love of reading and learning. We need their warm little bodies in the library on a weekly or at least bi-weekly basis to provide the book-lovers with new supplies and to convert the skeptics and book-phobics who say they hate to read.

THOUGHTS ON FLEXIBLE SCHEDULING

Across the United States, one of the latest library buzz words is "flexible scheduling," where classes are not scheduled into the library on a regular weekly basis but according to their needs. If a school has more than 20 classes, this makes sense, as there is no way for a librarian to do the rest of her job effectively—selecting, ordering, weeding out the old stuff, processing new materials, becoming familiar with new books, filmstrips, videos, magazines, and computer software, acting as a teacher resource for whole-language curriculums, maintaining the library facility—if she is tied in to that many classes each week, especially if she does not have the minimum assistance necessary to function—specifically, a full-time library aide to run the desk, shelve books, type orders, and more.

Many school libraries are woefully understaffed, and librarians are expected to provide teacher prep time and teach more than 30 classes a week. This is inhumane, and any administrator who expects a quality program to come out of this kind of abuse of a professional is unrealistic and needs to reassess priorities. If the librarian is a dedicated, caring professional, as most are, he or she should be scanning the want ads for a school system that will better appreciate her talents. Some principals say, "But you have planning time, just like the rest of the staff." This is true, and this is time we need to plan our lessons. Then we need time to run our libraries and help the multitudes of teachers asking for materials, students working on reports, parents needing book guidance, and administrators who request our book and media expertise.

I know one librarian who saw 28 classes a week, had daily lunchroom and after-school playground duty, supervised the safety squad and saw them—all 75 on the squad—for one period a week, and had an aide all of 1½ days a week. This is madness, and a waste of money for the school system that squandered her immense talents on baby-sitting work. Realizing it was never going to get better, she found another job. Unfortunately, this situation is all too typical.

Flexible-scheduling proponents feel it is not necessary to set aside a weekly time for each class, but that teachers and librarian should cooperatively schedule and plan library time as needed for whole-class instruction, small-group and individual use. If a teacher needs several visits in one week to work on a class project, the library will be free to accommodate her. Instead of teaching weekly library lessons, the librarian will instead work with each teacher to jointly plan library skills instruction that will integrate with the classroom program. The library will now be available for any teacher who signs up or spontaneously wants to bring her students for research.

On the other hand, if a librarian has a reasonable class load of under 20 classes per week, then she owes it to students and staff to provide a weekly library period that students will be eager to experience. It is unrealistic to assume that all teachers will be willing to take the time and effort to work with us on cooperatively planned lessons. We are teachers as well as librarians, and should not need to depend on classroom teachers to consult with us on everything we plan to present to their classes.

When we can tie our teaching into the classroom curriculum, all to the good, but teachers also enjoy the fact that we can provide their students with a variety of extracurricular experiences as well as cocurricular. Many of the skills we teach are ongoing process skills that children need regardless of the class curriculum, such as locating materials or figuring out the most effective way to tackle a new reference source.

One aspect of the flexible-scheduling program that makes real sense is to stop using the librarian as teacher prep-time coverage. If the library is part of the school curriculum, teachers need to work with the librarian—although even mandating that teachers participate during library time does not ensure that they will.

It bothers me that flexible scheduling is promoted as a way to make the library more accessible when there are always teachers who will not take the time to come on a regular basis unless they have a compelling reason. One librarian I know is having a great time with her fourth-, fifth-, and sixth-graders, but sees the seventh- and eighth-graders far too infrequently. Those teachers tell her they are too busy with their curriculum to visit. In another library, sixth-graders complain that they rarely are allotted time even to exchange books. A regularly scheduled library period for each class ensures equal access for all children.

Children look forward to their 40-minute time each week at Van Holten, and are also encouraged to come in throughout the day for browsing, research, or quiet-reading time. If they arrive while I am teaching a class, they know to direct their questions to library aide Mrs. Kalter or a parent volunteer. My room is on the small side, the equivalent of one-and-a-half classrooms plus an office, but we regularly have wall to wall children and staff. During my open times, usually from 11:00 A.M. to 1:00 P.M., teachers can bring in their classes or send in groups for special projects. We deal with a daily onslaught of requests for books and AV to support thematic units, locate answers to thorny reference problems, provide a refuge for children who need a respite and a place to read, and consult with teachers who need a sounding board for curriculum planning.

Flexible scheduling is a creative way to alleviate the burdens of overscheduled professionals, and as such is worth considering. For us, a structured schedule of a weekly library-skills and/or literature lesson incorporating a book-exchange period for each class and several hours daily of open time, allows us to combine the best of both formats. Other librarians compromise by seeing one grade on a regular schedule for a block of weeks and then rotating with another grade, plus scheduling weekly book-change times for all classes, thus circumventing those teachers who might never show up otherwise. Ultimately, each librarian needs to work out a program that works for him or her.

A SAMPLING OF LIBRARY SKILLS

In this section is a sampling of children's literature-based information management lessons I've incorporated into my teaching of grades K–5 over the past 20-odd years. Many ideas have been borrowed/revised/lifted from other sources and I no longer know where they originated. All good teaching is like that, imitation being the sincerest form of flattery. Though these are lessons I present in the library, classroom teachers will surely find ideas here they can adopt or adapt into their own teaching, especially in schools that have the misfortune of having no librarians. I've left out the units we do on reference books and skills in favor of ones that tie more directly into books, from the basics of book care to book-location skills.

The library curriculum is one that needs to be covered in the library on an ongoing basis. We want children to become lifelong learners and library fanatics. As adults, we assume responsibility for the knowledge we choose to pursue, and we can choose to stagnate or to grow. The library is our source of information, not just through college but for always.

Some librarians groan, "I hate teaching the card catalog. It's so boring." If that means handing out worksheets from library skills books and having children fill in answers, then I agree, but what may be boring is not the theme of the lesson but the manner in which it is being taught.

If you think that library skills are dull to teach, it's time to reexamine the lessons you have developed to support your library curriculum. In most cases, a curriculum is merely a sequential listing of skills to be taught. Unlike teachers, who may depend on a teacher's manual to plan their lessons, librarians are wholly responsible for the way we set up and implement each unit. If our children seem bored, we must accept the blame for not challenging them and piquing their interests.

Most new librarians are overwhelmed when they realize that not only must they maintain their library collections, they must also develop literature-based library skills lessons for classes as well. When I started working fresh out of graduate school at the blushing age of 23, I spent countless weekends poring over library skills manuals, muttering, "What am I going to do with my classes next week?" Library school spent little time on preparing us to be master teachers. Instead, they assumed we could figure that part out; that it was more important to serve the needs of the classroom teachers than to worry about our own curricula.

I came to believe that there was a body of knowledge out there that needed to be presented in an orderly, sequential fashion if my students were going to become independent life-long library users. Over the last 20 years, through much trial and even more error, I have continued to build up my repertoire of library lessons to provide my students with an intensive, enjoyable, and illuminating indoctrination into the delights of the library. Now my problem is not what to teach, but how to fit in all the material and literature I want to present.

It is not sufficient to give our students a one-, two-, or three-lesson unit on a subject and then consider it taught, expecting them to retain the information forever. We each need to develop our own organized, creative, and innovative library curricula that expand and reinforce library, literature, critical thinking, and research skills year by year, building on prior knowledge, with a goal of our children being independent, comfortable, and competent in any library.

Librarians say, "But we can't teach library skills in isolation. We must teach our skills with the classroom teacher and plan the lesson together." Naturally, some of our lessons are more compelling and effective when tied in to other disciplines, but there is no reason to sit around waiting for some kind teacher to declare, "Man the card catalog (or the computer)! They need to look up a book!" before we show them what's in those mysterious little drawers or on the screen. Most teachers do not have the time to sit down with their librarian every week and plan a unit together. Many of the teacher/librarian contacts are on the fly, and the teacher trusts the librarian to develop a stimulating and useful curriculum that fulfills the children's needs.

Sure, if we teach library skills as a cut-and-dried subject, with lots of prepackaged worksheets and plenty of talky "How-to-Use-Your-Library-Good" filmstrips and videos, I guarantee the students will consider library the big snore.

Our topic is tricky. We want our students to be able to locate any and all needed information from fiction, nonfiction, biography, and reference. That, however, is not and must not be the only component of our curriculum. Teach in isolation? We have no reason to attempt to do that. Look around your library and what do you see: Biographies / Fiction / Folklore / Languages / Science Experiments / Space / Geology / Animals / Cooking / Codes and Ciphers / Drawing / Songs / Jokes and Riddles / Magic / Sports / Poetry / Plays / Disasters / History. The room is packed with literature, and the skills we teach are a means to locate and celebrate those treasures and provide our kids with the necessary skills to enjoy reading.

Kids admire us, their school book experts. One third-grade girl said to me, "I'm going to be a librarian when I grow up!"

"That's wonderful." I told her.

"Yeah," she said, "and then I'm going to take over your job!"

BOOK CARE LESSONS

If we expect children to develop a love and respect for all books, they first need to know how to treat them with care; turning pages from the corners instead of the bottom of the page (which causes all those tiny rips in the paper), using bookmarks, and keeping them safe from liquids, siblings, and pets. Children can be hard on books until it is made clear to them that mistreatment of books is undesirable and unacceptable. An entertaining reminder lesson at the beginning of each year helps them stay aware of their responsibility to the library and other readers.

Nesting Boxes

When I was a child, my sister Sharron once gave me a birthday present, wrapped in a huge box. Undoing the wrapping and ribbons, I opened the lid and found . . . another box. Tearing open that box, what did I discover but . . . another box! I can't recall the actual present, but the concept of nesting boxes stayed with me. When my kindergarteners are ready to check out their first books of the year, we talk about the importance of good book care, see an ancient filmstrip they love called "Glad Book, Sad Book," and I bring out a large wrapped gift box.

"I found this on my chair, but I don't know who left it here. There's no card, either. It's not my birthday, but it looks like a big present. Do you know anything about this?" I ask them innocently.

Naturally, no one does. "What do think could be in it?"

After a bit of speculation, I say, "Well, I guess we'll just have to open it up," and call up a child to undo the ribbon and lift the lid. They are always first delighted and then incredulous to find another box within, as one by one, they undo each smaller box, predicting all the while what will be inside. When we get to the smallest box, about three inches square, we finally reach the treasure—a tiny alphabet book by Edward Lear. (Any miniature book will do.) I announce, "I love presents like jewelry and chocolate, but there's no better present than a good book!"

No, No, Never, Never

Greeting my first-graders at the door, I am holding another box. On each side is written a word in large, fancy, purple letters, and I turn the box slowly so all can see it. "No, no, never, never," the children read.

"Ah, yes. It's the No, No, Never, Never Box," I announce, as we settle in on the story rug. "I'm going to ask two people to come up at a time, look inside my box, and pick one item to show you. Inside this box are all the awful things that can happen to books if we're not careful!"

In the box are a pair of scissors, a crayon, a magic marker, a roll of tape, an empty soda can, one Hershey's Kiss or a tiny chocolate bar, a stick of gum, a tiny jar of jam, a thumb-sized bathtub, a miniature doll baby, a toy dog, and a paper umbrella. As each pair comes up and selects an item, they whisper together to make up a sentence explaining what not to do, starting with "No no never never," which they then recite for the class, such as, ""No, no, never, never drop your book in the tub while you're taking a bath." The rest of the group then chimes in dramatically on the refrain, "No, no, never, never; no, no, a thousand times no!"

The Book Doctor

Thanks to first-grade teacher Matt Barbosa's white lab coat, all stained with markers and paint (book blood, I tell the kids), school nurse Kathy Staropoli's old stethoscope and first aid kit, and a huge old satchel that looks like a doctor's bag, I greet my second-graders at the door as . . . The Book Doctor.

First I show them the contents of the first aid kit: blank spine labels, special tapes and glues for broken spines and hurt pages, needle and thread for when a book needs stitches, a miniature dust jacket cover for when a book needs plastic surgery, and even crayons for when a dust jacket has lost its color.

I describe the Van Holten Book Hospital (actually a bottom shelf near the circulation desk) and how Doctors Freeman and Kalter can perform medical miracles and bring almost any wounded or ailing book back to health if we catch it in time. And then I show the unfortunate patients in my satchel; books that are too far gone from water damage, scribbling, and destroyed bindings for even the best surgeon to save them. Students are aghast to see these pathetic book victims, especially the poor *World Book Encyclopedia* volume that was thoroughly gnawed by a German shepherd.

"If your library book is feeling poorly—a rip in its page, a wobble in its spine—never try to fix it yourself. Bring it to . . . The Book Doctors! . . . before it's too late." And they do. For weeks afterward, they bring in patients for my library aide and me to heal.

Of course, it's not always the children's fault when books die. Children's books are made poorly these days, with many guaranteed to fall to pieces within several circulations. At $15.00 a pop, we do what we can to ensure our collection stays in top-notch shape, reinforcing scores of bad bindings with tape and glue when the new books arrive, covering paperbacks and cardboard covers of new books without dust jackets with high quality contact paper (Vistafoil Recovers), and replacing Mylar dust jacket covers to make old books look gorgeous.

Children are not wild about reading dilapidated and unattractive books. Just as we strive to keep our bookshelves orderly and neat to attract browsers, we make sure the books look as appealing as possible.

The Book Care Tape

What can you do to remind older children of the importance of proper book care? Have them record a Book Care Skits tape, ostensibly for reinforcing book manners for the younger kids, but also providing many trickle-down benefits for the third- through sixth-grade stars acting and producing the cassette.

Making an audio or video tape can take many forms. Depending on the time you wish to invest, you can have children devise their own book-related situations and compose skits; give each group one book care rule and have them develop a skit around it; give the group a brief script you've written and have them elaborate on it, adding dialogue and sound effects; or hand them finished scripts either you or your students have written to act out as a Reader's Theater production.

Every couple of years I enlist the fifth-graders to make a new tape. I hand out a skit outline for each situation such as: dog eats library book, little brother or sister scribbles in book, child puts book away on wrong shelf and other child looking for that book can't find it, or student rips page out of magazine. In the first session students work in groups of three to five making their skits amusing and understandable, figuring out pertinent sound effects to enhance our audio cassette, and rehearsing. The next week we record each 30-second to one-minute spot, and then play back our results for the whole class to enjoy.

When listening to each amusing episode, classes of kindergarteners to second-graders carefully analyze each dialogue and describe what has happened that's "bad for books." I prefer the audio cassette-tape format so children can use their imaginations to envision each situation, but a video would also be fun to do.

BOOK LOCATION LESSONS FOR GRADES 1–6

Mnemonic Devices

For starters, there are five major sections in any children's library: easy fiction, fiction, nonfiction, biography, and reference. Children often can't remember the difference between them. They get very confused with the designations "fiction" and "nonfiction." They'll tell you that nonfiction means not true. They think biography and bibliography mean the same thing. Then we make them even crazier when we categorize fiction into genres. Ask your students the opposite of fiction, and one child will always volunteer "science fiction."

Over the years, I've written many songs, chants, poems, and other mnemonic devices that deal with books and the library, on the theory that it's easier to recall information when it has a tune or rhythm to it. We accompany each chant with hand motions we made up. At the start of a lesson or as a reminder midway, chants and songs are an effortless way to impart information while giving students a change of pace.

There's:

Fiction, Fiction, it's a made-up story from the author's brain.

(We do this one as if we are dancing the Charleston.)

Next we do:

Nonfiction books have facts, that's true.

(The left hand scissors over the right hand, then right hand over left; whirl hands around each other in a circle, and clap on the last word "true.")

This one always works:

Bio-gra-phies (snap fingers after each syllable) / **They're in alphabetical order** (clap, clap) / **By the famous person's last name** / **Not the author!** (point accusingly at person next to you) / **They're in alphabetical order** (clap, clap) / **By the famous person's last name** / **Not the author!** (point again)

Putting the sections of the room together, we sing:

IT'S JUST THE LIBRARY
(Words and music by Judy Freeman, ©1995)

Some call it the Media Center or the Instructional Materials Room;
It's all the same, it's just a name, or so I would assume;
From easy fiction to novels to informational books,
Tapes, magazines, computer screens
In all the crannies and nooks.

(Chorus)
It's just the Library, that's where I long to be,
Finding all those fascinating stories to take home with me;
Browse through the fiction and the nonfiction and biography,
And select some books to borrow and take home for free.

If you want to read some fiction, there are so many kinds to choose,
Like fantasy and mystery, where I love to dig for clues;
I read science fiction for travel, for leaving the planet Earth;
Humor tickles me, the laughs are free,
Read fiction for what it's worth.

For facts go straight to nonfiction, there's a number on every spine;
They start at zero hundred, and go through nine ninety-nine.
520s are stars and planets, myths and legends 292;
States, plays, and bats, cars, songs, and cats;
Nonfiction is tried and true.

When you're curious about people, maybe heroes from history,
Inventor or star, a name that's gone far, then try biography;
They're in alphabetical order by the famous person's last name;
Choose one you admire: Artist, athlete, or flier,
And read about fortune and fame.

Finding Easy Fiction Books: Grades 1–2

Easy fiction books are the hardest books for children to find. They're in alphabetical order, but often the spine is so thin that the author's name is left off or hard to read. Children need to be encouraged to browse with gusto, pulling books off the shelves to investigate what's there. If books are not to their liking, they put them in an empty space on the end of the shelf so they can be shelved correctly later.

In first grade, with the children's teachers stressing a variety of authors, I instruct my classes on how to find a series book by a given author. First I introduce several different characters, such as Jill, Gwen, and languid-tongued Fletcher the dog in the Something Queer series by Elizabeth Levy; Joe, Spud, and Mary Frances in The Cut-Ups books by James Marshall; and straight-arrow kid detective from the Nate the Great series by Marjorie Weinman Sharmat. On the white board, children draw spine labels for each author, with an "E" on top for easy fiction, and the first letter of the author's last name underneath, and we figure out how to locate that author's books on the shelves.

Working in pairs, the children pick one new book from my pile, and after reading the author's name and the spine label, go to the shelves and search for other books from that series. As soon as they locate the books on the shelf, they select two additional titles from the shelf, and sit in a circle on the story rug. Each pair then holds up the three books, identifies the author, tells who the series is about, and either opts to check them out or hands them over to other interested classmates. During browsing time, if someone wants another in the Commander Toad series, he or she asks the pair who found the Jane Yolen books to show where they are located.

By second and third grades, students are used to asking who wrote a particular easy fiction or fiction book and looking it up on the shelves by the author's last name. They particularly like fiction and biography books where the three letters on the spine label spell a word. Donald J. Sobol (SOB), Lilian Moore (MOO), and biographies about Daniel Boone (BOO) always bring a smile.

Locating Nonfiction Books: Grades 1–3

Using a large, heavy plastic, red box embossed with dinosaur silhouettes (from The Nature Company, of course), I demonstrate for the second-graders how nonfiction books are arranged. Focusing on the 590s, I pull out different animals from the box, write their numbers on the board, and pull books about them from the shelves. Children see how each subject has its own number as out of the box jump such toy creatures as a fly (insects=595.7), shark (fish=597), turtle (reptiles=597.9), goose (birds=598); kangaroo (marsupials=599.2), and a Curious George doll (monkeys=599.8).

Next, each pair receives a laminated task card with a Dewey number on it. I demonstrate how to look for the number, using the guide numbers at the top of each shelf, and then read the titles of all the books with that same number to determine the subject. When the two investigators go to the shelves, they must find the two most interesting books with their number, show them to me and whisper what subject their number represents, and then sit down at the tables.

Once all the groups have found their books, we go around the room and each stands up to announce, "Our number is ___ , and our subject is ___ ," holding up both books for all to see. As ever, the books they find are often hot items, and anyone wanting to know where to find more planet or cooking or ballet or sign-language books asks the experts who just found them.

Once the second-graders know how to locate books in nonfiction, I no longer have to show them where things are. They love to come up and say, "What's the number for science experiments?" and then find the books themselves. What freedom!

Finding Books Fast: Grades 3–6

To get a quick inkling as to students' proficiency in locating books quickly, we play Two-Minute Search. After a quick review of the five types of books and how they're arranged, we divide into two teams. Each player on the first team is issued a spine card made from a bookmark-sized oaktag strip to which I've affixed a spine label for a first-rate fiction or nonfiction book on our shelves.

At the signal, we start the timer ("GO!") and each player runs to the appropriate shelf, finds a book that corresponds to the spine label on the card, and lines up to be checked. If she has found a book with the correct call number, I take the spine card, place the book on the pile, and hand her another card for a different location. If the book is not on the shelf, an assistant checker (teacher, aide, parent) makes sure the child is indeed looking at the correct area. If so, the checker calls to me to count that child's card. Most children find two or three books. The assistant checker keeps an eye out for those who get lost or frustrated and helps them get back on track. At the end of two (or three) minutes, I call "FREEZE!" Children with books in their hands can be checked; the rest return their spine cards and are seated. Now team two has a turn in the same fashion. When team two is seated, we count each team's cards and announce the winner.

Hold on. The game's not over yet. Now we play Three-Minute Return. Each child takes a minimum of one or two books to return to the shelves properly. As each book is shelved, the child puts a finger on the book and a hand in the air and waits to be checked. If necessary, children can use place-holder strips to mark their places as they play the game. This makes reshelving a bit easier. Of course, since many of the books they've found look awfully good, students always have the option of signing them out instead of shelving them.

ORIENTATION GAMES FOR GRADES 3–6

Below are two of the library-orientation games I play with my students to ease them back into the library routine at the beginning of the school year or to review what they have learned. They are both relatively easy to organize and play, though the baseball game requires you to make question cards in advance (laminate these, and you'll be set for years to come). Both games are written out as formal, detailed lesson plans.

Library Tic-Tac-Toe Game

Skills Area: Orientation / Review of Library Terminology / Location Skills
Grade Level(s): 3–6
Objective: To review and reinforce library terminology, location skills, procedures, and behavior.
Materials and Setup:

- Child-sized (6-foot square) tic-tac-toe grid mapped out on the floor with masking or colored tape (make sure a child can fit comfortably, cross-legged, in each square).
- X's and O's—One of either for each child; can be made out of two large pipe cleaners twisted together.
- Scoreboard/question board and markers or chalk.
- A list of library-related questions or key words (e.g., circulation desk, fiction, atlas, etc.) around which you can make up questions on the spot.
- Rearrange library furniture so both teams can sit on chairs around the periphery of the game board.

Procedure

1. Introduction
   Divide class into two teams as children come into the library. (Counting off usually ends up with a fair distribution, and helps to split up cliques.) When they are seated, welcome them to "Human Tic-Tac-Toe, Library Style." Explain the rules: no calling out answers, encouragement, or discouragement for any questions not directed to you; good sportsmanship is expected; one point will be awarded for each game won. Students will not be permitted to berate each other for wrong answers or faulty tic-tac-toe strategy. Explain that if anyone forgets this rule, the other team will automatically receive that game point.

2. Development
   Ask one question of the first player on the X (or O) team. If the student answers the question correctly, hand him a large pipe cleaner X (or O) to put on his head. (If you bend the pipe cleaner-constructed X's and O's, they will perch quite nicely on students' heads, where all can see them easily.) The student then decides where to position himself on the game board, and sits there, legs crossed.

   If the answer is incorrect, go on to the next person on the same team, and repeat the question. Students may not join the board unless their answers are correct. Once a team member answers the question correctly, it becomes the other team's turn for a new question. The game depends on two strategies: supplying correct answers for questions dealing with library matters, and playing a defensive game of tic-tac-toe.

   Questions should incorporate definitions of library terminology ("What do you call the person who writes a book?"), location skills ("How are fiction books arranged?"), and library procedures ("How do you sign out a magazine?"). Consider questions about the following vocabulary: author, title, illustrator, publisher, copyright date, spine, spine label, call numbers, dust jacket, easy fiction, fiction, nonfiction, biography, reference, encyclopedia, volume, guide words, topics, almanac, atlas, dictionary, index, glossary, table of contents, circulation desk, librarian, renew, reserve, and card catalog.

With older children, this game is an enjoyable way to review the parts of a catalog card (hold up oversized catalog cards and ask children questions about them). Write call numbers on the board and ask children to identify their components. Be heedful of each player's level of knowledge, and attempt to ask the hardest questions of children who can best handle them. If a child has missed one question in the previous go-round, try to see that he'll get the next one right. Your purpose is to review a large body of material quickly and painlessly, while allowing children to have a rousing good time.

3. Culmination

Each time a team wins, give them a point; then clear the board and start another round until your time limit is up. Announce the final score; lead each team in a rousing "silent cheer" for the other team.

Evaluation and follow-ups

By the conclusion of the game, you will have asked students every possible question about library use, and in every possible format (e.g., What is an illustrator? What do you call the person who does the artwork in a book?). By the number of correct versus incorrect answers, you should be able to ascertain in what areas students need reinforcement.

Since this lesson works well as an introductory lesson, every library skills lesson you present in subsequent weeks will be a follow-up lesson. Concentrate on hands-on lessons, such as locating specific books of fiction, nonfiction, and biography given the call numbers, or using the card catalog to find materials on the shelves.

If you feel the class needs more practice in defining library and book-related terms, play "Headbands": One at a time, children come up to front of room and sit on a high stool or chair facing the rest of the class. Place a mystery headband on their heads. (Make headbands out of stapled construction paper or oaktag strips, each with a word printed on it in large letters (e.g., "ATLAS"). Children in the audience can see the word to be defined, and have up to three chances to give clues as to its meaning without using the actual word. ("It's a big book that has all kinds of maps in it.") The player then guesses the word, and takes a bow while all applaud. If the player cannot guess the word after three clues, he or she takes off the headband and reads the word aloud. (Note: In many schools head lice are a recurring problem, so you may need to make a fresh set of disposable headbands and pipe cleaner X's and O's for each class.)

Library Baseball Game

Skills Area: Orientation / Review of Library Terminology / Location Skills
Grade Level(s): 3–6
Purpose: To review and reinforce library terminology, location skills, procedures, and behavior.
Materials and Setup:

- Four sets of questions, with ten questions per set, with set one being the simplest and set four the most challenging. I typed my questions onto oak-tag cards, then labeled the other sides with the level (Single, Double, Triple, Home Run) so children can see the level as I read each card.
- Scoreboard with markers or chalk
- Four diamond-shaped bases made from oaktag or cardboard; labeled 1, 2, 3, and Home Plate.
- Set up room, rearranging chairs and tables as needed so two teams can fit comfortably, and position the bases around the perimeter of your seating area, making sure children will have access to each as they walk the outline of the baseball diamond in the course of the game. We position the bases in wire book racks so they stand upright with no fuss.

Procedure

1. Introduction

   In September, when baseball and the upcoming World Series is on children's minds, Library Baseball is another diverting way to review library arrangement, procedures, and materials. Divide the class into two teams as children come into the library. When they are seated with their teams, explain the rules: no calling out answers for any questions not directed to you; good sportsmanship is expected; one point will be awarded for each run earned. Students will not be permitted to berate each other for wrong or uncompleted answers. Explain that if anyone forgets this rule, the other team will automatically receive that game point.

2. Development

   Toss a coin to see which team "bats" first. I place a high stool at Home Plate that each child sits upon as I ask his or her question. (You might want to bring in a tiny bat for them to hold when up at bat.) Each team is up until one player gets an Out (because of a question answered incorrectly or not completed in time), at which point players on base retire and the other team is up.

   At bat, the child may ask for a Single, Double, Triple, or Home Run question. For Singles and Doubles, the player has up to 30 seconds to give a correct response; for Triples and Homers, they have 60 seconds and may need to go and find a book on the shelf or a card in the catalog.

   Questions can incorporate definitions of library terminology ("What do you call the company that puts a book together?"), location skills ("Find a fiction book by Barbara Park"), reference skills ("Find a picture of the Empire State Building"), or literature trivia (In Louis

Sachar's *Wayside School Is Falling Down*, why does Mrs. Jewls push a computer out of the 30th story window?). Prepare your questions carefully to reflect the knowledge you want your class to demonstrate. You would want to make a different set of questions for third-graders as opposed to fifth- or sixth-graders.

When a student answers a question correctly, he or she advances to the appropriate base. If there's a runner on second and the next player correctly fields a Double, that player walks past first base to second, forcing the first runner to third. If the next player answers a Triple, the two on base will be forced home, and you'll record the score on the scoreboard.

Children decide which level of question they want to try, but if you run out of one set of questions they must pick from the remaining three sets. If you have a timid group that wants all singles, this forces them to toughen up a bit and try for harder questions.

3. Culmination
Each time a team retires with an out, lead the teams in a rousing "silent cheer" for a round well played. If you want to get fancy, make a tape of baseball organ music to play, and sing "Take Me Out to the Ball Game" as a warm-up or grand finale. Be sure to point out the 796 (sports) section of the library, booktalk a few baseball fiction books by Alfred Slote or Matt Christopher, Barbara Cohen's *Thank You, Jackie Robinson*, and Barbara Park's *Skinnybones*, and try out a few riddles from Joseph Rosenbloom's *The World's Best Sports Riddles and Jokes* and poems from Lee Bennett Hopkins's *Extra Innings* or Lillian Morrison's *At the Crack of the Bat*. As in all library lessons, you need to link the information with the literature.

Evaluation and follow-ups
By the conclusion of the game, you will have asked all students to demonstrate their familiarity with library terms, location, and arrangement. Take note of what kinds of questions gave them pause for future reinforcement.

This lesson works well as an introductory lesson or review of what children already know. Follow up with hands-on lessons, such as locating specific books of fiction, nonfiction, and biography given the call numbers, or using the card catalog to find materials on the shelves.

MUCKING ABOUT IN THE CARD CATALOG

I enjoy encouraging children's curiosity about the card catalog. At the start of every year at least one kindergartener or first-grader runs over to me to report, "Someone's looking in those drawers!"

"That's good," I reply. "In those drawers are cards for every book our library owns. It tells where all the books are."

"Can I look in there, too?"

"Sounds good to me."

THE CARD CATALOG SONG (OR CHANT)

(Words and music by Judy Freeman ©1984)

CHORUS: In the catalog, in the catalog, in the card card catalog,
Just take a look, you can find any book in the card card catalog.

The author card has the author on top,
Last name first, comma, first name after that,
You'll find there's one card for each book written by
That author, if you really try.

The title card has the title on top,
Title underneath, author in the middle;
It's a certain kind of sandwich we
Titled the bologna.

The subject card has the subject on top,
In capital letters; it's so different from the title,
'Cause it tells you what that book's about;
Now find that book and sign it out.

When you want the address of a book,
Just look up the author, or the subject, or the title;
Find the call number on the upper left side;
The card catalog is your guide.

Looking for a way to explain the three types of catalog cards to my third-graders, I wrote that song in my car on the way to work one day. It works well as a chant, with students chiming in on the refrain after each verse. (Now that our library is fully automated, I'll need to change the chorus a bit: "In the catalog, in the catalog, in the computerized catalog," and figure out how to rewrite the verses, based on the configuration of the computer screen "card.")

About the "bologna sandwich" business in the second verse: When I am teaching my students how to recognize each type of catalog card, I tell them the author's name is juggled, with a comma after the last name; the subject card has capital letters on top because it thinks it's so important; and the title card looks like a bologna sandwich.

The Mini Card Catalog

The card catalog is the brains of the library, whether you use a computer or let your fingers dance through those wonderful old cards. Many libraries have tossed out their lovely old-timey card catalogs in favor of the far more efficient computer terminals, and I suppose we'll do the same one year soon. Card catalog skills are still part of standardized tests, so we'll need to hold on to them for a bit longer as a backup to the computer. In the meantime, I'll continue to enjoy our card-catalog library lessons.

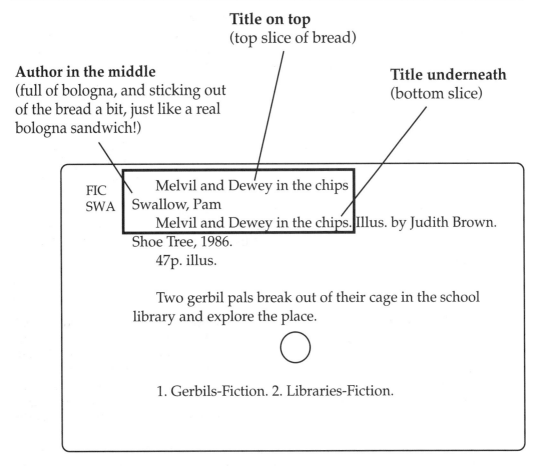

Title on top
(top slice of bread)

Author in the middle
(full of bologna, and sticking out
of the bread a bit, just like a real
bologna sandwich!)

Title underneath
(bottom slice)

FIC
SWA   Melvil and Dewey in the chips
       Swallow, Pam
       Melvil and Dewey in the chips. Illus. by Judith Brown.
Shoe Tree, 1986.
47p. illus.

Two gerbil pals break out of their cage in the school
library and explore the place.

1. Gerbils-Fiction. 2. Libraries-Fiction.

I remind students to ask me when they need an opinion of a book, but to ask "The Brain" where a book is located or who wrote it. Introducing the contents of the card catalog has become sheer pleasure and delight since I put together our Mini Card Catalog Box.

I was teaching a library skills course at Rutgers one summer, and during our final class participants were presenting their final projects. Librarian Joanne Schwartz brought a 30-drawer tool kit to the front of the room and proceeded to wow us with her Mini Card Catalog, an idea she had lifted from another librarian at a conference somewhere. She had gathered together a plethora of irresistible miniature objects and placed them alphabetically in the lettered drawers for children (and us) to identify. Each tiny object (dinosaur, football, car) corresponded to a subject one could locate in the card catalog and find on the library shelves.

Entranced, I went straight to my local hardware discount store, bought a nifty box, and started collecting. Finding objects is no problem. Raid old toy boxes, ask your students for things they are throwing away, comb flea markets, and you can find tiny animals, erasers shaped like watermelons, mini sports equipment, or found objects: a stone, leaf, or piece of popcorn. For the X–Y–Z drawer, which is admittedly tricky, I asked my dentist to donate a small x-ray, which she was only too happy to do. Keep an alphabetical list of what you have and what you still want, as your students will offer to donate many treasures. To date I have over 200 objects, all keyed into subjects about which we own books.

The mini-catalog can expose students to more than just subject access. Selecting scores of my favorite books from all areas of the library, I photocopied and reduced in size the title page for each book until it was small enough to cut up into its component parts. Each title or author's name was then glued onto a sturdy one-by-three-inch cardboard card, which I then painted with an art fixative to protect it. (You could laminate them, but the kids will peel them.) I made 100 different cards, 50 with an author's name, 50 with a title, with several for each alphabet letter. Each card looks wonderful, as it matches the print of its book. Making the tiny cards takes some time, but I've been using my catalog for many years and it hasn't worn out yet.

Once you find several subject items for each drawer and make your title and author cards, you'll have a representative card catalog to use starting with second grade to teach the ins and outs of the "brains" of the library. Now the fun begins.

Digging In: Grade 2–3

Many years back I purchased an indispensable story apron from Upstart Library Promotionals. Made of virgin polyester, it has proved indestructible, refusing even to wrinkle. Of course, they don't carry this item any more, though far handier folk than I have claimed to make them from plain butcher's aprons. Mine has six pockets below the waistband, each a different color, with the two center pockets large enough to hold picture books, and one pocket on top. I stash story-related props in each pocket, and even use it to coordinate a World Almanac Mystery lesson with my fifth-graders.

Each year, when the time comes to indoctrinate my second-graders into the delights and intricacies of the card catalog, I load up my story apron pockets with items from the mini-catalog, selecting one item per drawer. Wearing my colorful apron, I greet the class, and show them a real catalog drawer. "The real catalog is too huge and heavy for me to bring over here, but I know some magic, so I shrank it," I announce, and present the miniature version.

Two children at a time come in front of the class. One decides on the best pocket; the other reaches in that pocket and pulls out an item. Holding the trinket so the whole class can see, the pair announces what it is, what letter it begins with, and then removes its matching drawer from the mini-catalog. One by one, they hold up items from the drawer to show what types of subjects we have in our full-sized catalog. Children are mesmerized by the variety of objects. The mini-catalog's BA–BI drawer alone holds the following: a bear, bicycle, balloon, ballet dancer, baby, bathtub, beetle, baseball, basketball, and bird (I'm still on the lookout for a bee, a bat, a badger, and a bed). Then we read the title and author cards that can also be found in the drawer, such as *Be a Perfect Person in Just Three Days, Beans on the Roof*, Tom Birdseye, and Molly Bang).

The following week, children pair up and each receives one mini-drawer to investigate along with the full-sized drawer. At the tables, their mission is to identify each item in the mini-drawer, and then walk through the real drawer to see if they can locate any of the subjects, authors or titles. Each time they find something, they place a construction paper bookmark to mark its place. This is an open-ended browsing activity to get them to feel comfortable poking through the cards. We talk over how to locate a book using a catalog card, I demonstrate how it works using an oversized catalog card, and they are encouraged to find one of the books from their drawer on the library shelves.

Subject Cards, Grades 3–6

Take one object from each drawer of the mini-catalog and place it in a box, basket, or hat so children can reach in and take one, sight unseen. (Younger children can work in pairs or trios; grades five and six can work solo except for those who need a partner for support. Also pair up older children if you are working with a large class and don't have enough adults—aide, parent, another teacher—to help you check each child's findings.) Select your items carefully. The object of this lesson is for children to investigate the range of materials you have on a given subject. Animals work well, but don't pick uncommon ones.

Children will look up their topics and see how many books the library has, and find up to five different types of books. For example, if a child pulls out a tiger, by looking through the subject cards under TIGER, he or she should be able to find a nonfiction book in the 599.7s, a folktale in 398.2, an easy fiction, and a fiction book. Perhaps there will be a poetry book or a joke book as well. The child then jots down the title, author, and call number for each and goes to the shelves to find all of the books. Back together as a group, children can briefly show what they have found.

If time is a problem, omit the writing down of information, and tell children they will have 10 minutes to see how many different kinds of books they can locate. Races are effective, as they motivate dawdlers to work quickly and efficiently.

Title Cards, Grades 3–6

With third- or fourth-graders, place one to two dozen mini-title cards in a basket or interesting-looking box. (Be sure to check the shelves to ensure each title is there before you hand out its card.) Children working solo or in pairs select a title (make sure you don't use two cards starting with the same letter), bring the correct catalog drawer to their tables, look up that title, write down the author and call number, and then find the book on the shelf. When all have finished they can present their titles and authors for others to see and check out. Sometimes we put them in a large treasure box from which I pull the books one at a time, give a one-sentence booktalk, and hand them out to interested students.

Card-catalog lessons must link up the books to the children. Just teaching children the parts of a catalog card is busywork, unless they see how it helps them locate the books they want and need. The catalog will not usually tell us why a book is good, but only where it is on the shelf. We need other people— teachers, librarians, parents, and, most important of all, other kids—to spread the word on books worth reading.

With this in mind, in one lesson I paired up my fourth-graders and asked them to go to the shelves alone and, considering their partner's interests and tastes, find one terrific book that they thought their partners had not read and would love. Keeping the titles and locations a secret, they surreptitiously wrote down the titles and, back at their tables, traded papers with their partners. Each then had to look up his new title in the card catalog, write down the author and call number, find the book on the shelves, and bring it back to his or her partner. Each was then to take one minute to sell his or her book to the partner, and book-talk the plot, explaining why that title was chosen and why it was a perfect match.

Children came away with many new books to read that day, and were advised to keep their partners posted on their reactions. As a follow-up the next week, we talked about differences in reading preferences, and children related times they successfully and unsuccessfully recommended a favorite title. I advised them to keep a sharp eye open for readers who mirror their interests in books, for books are always better when shared with a sympathetic reader.

Author Cards, Grades 3–6

Hand out one mini-author card to children working in pairs or trios. The group first mentally juggles the author's name, looks up the last name in the catalog, and counts how many books he or she has written. Going to the shelves, the group then finds at least five of the author's books, and goes through them, reading the flap copy, reading the author blurb, paging through the books. Each group prepares a short presentation describing its author and the kinds of books he or she writes. Groups can either talk over what they have found and give a brief report the same period, or take notes on their findings and deliver a more formal presentation the following week, after which they can hand out that author's books to interested readers.

Stump! Grades 3–6

My fifth-graders love this game. I think children need to have time to wander through the card catalog and explore. Computers are starting to take over for cards in many libraries, including mine, but there's something satisfying about finger-walking through the cards, a tactile sense of history the computer lacks. There are so many interesting treasures in there.

To play Stump!, students in pairs select one drawer of the catalog and take it with them back to their seats. For each category, they have one minute to browse through the drawer and, using their fingers as placeholders, find the best possible card. Using oversized catalog cards I have made for appealing books in our library, I review with the class the location of all parts of the card. I demonstrate how to look through the cards, not one at a time, but in chunks, to find, say, the longest title. Then we start our rounds:

- Find the book with the most pages. (Players are searching only for page numbers, knowing that "unp." means unpaged.)
- Find the oldest book you can. (Players are searching only for copyright dates.)
- Find the most books by one author. (To find a goodly number, players are looking for author cards—all grouped together, with the author's name juggled on the top line—which they will then count.)

- Find the most books on one subject. (Players know to look for subject cards, with capital letters on the top line.)

At the end of each round, children read aloud their answers, including the title and author's name (unjuggled) and the type of book it is. We are thus reviewing all the parts of the card and general location skills in a most painless and laugh-filled manner. For oldest book, I ask them to respond by decade ("Who found a book from the 1970s?") so we move in sequence down to the group that has found the oldest title. I also play each round, with a drawer on my lap, so they have to stump my card as well.

Then we play Superstump! Early in the school year, I describe to my fifth-graders the In What Book Game we play every spring, in which each student writes a plot statement question for each of two fiction books of his or her choice, and tries to stump the other classes with it. (Example: In what book did a boy use a magic marker to play connect-the-dots with his chicken pox while his older sister was supposed to be taking care of him? *Anastasia on Her Own* by Lois Lowry.) I remind them to keep a running title-and-author list of all the books they read that year, and discuss the importance of getting to know different authors. In that game, students receive a bonus point each time they know the author in addition to the title. (See *Books Kids Will Sit Still For*, 2nd ed., page 110, for a longer description of the In What Book Game.) Superstump! gets them psyched up for the In What Book Game.

To bring home the fun of recalling titles and authors, I have each pair select from their drawers two titles of fiction books they think I won't know. They are to read aloud the title, and I must supply the author's first and last names. (Naturally, if you are not familiar with your fiction collection, do not attempt Superstump! You will lose. Your students will snicker at you. Fortunately, I remember lots of titles and authors, as do many of you. It is our job.) I tell them they get two points if I can't identify the first and last name, we split the points if I know only one or the other, and I get two points for each correct answer.

Students are aghast when they start reading titles, for I know most of the answers, and they cheer when I miss one. While I am goading and teasing them, I answer their questions like this: "Hmm. Who wrote *There's a Boy in the Girls' Bathroom*? Let's see. It's the guy who wrote *Marvin Redpost: Alone in His Teacher's House* and all the Wayside School books. He was a lawyer before he started writing kids' books. Let me think. Could it be . . . Louis Sachar?" So while I am supplying authors right and left, I am booktalking and getting them interested in those authors to investigate when they check out their books.

When the game is over, we've tallied the score (Fabulous Freeman 36, Class of Brilliant Bukavich 8), and the kids are roaming the shelves for an armload of readables, they continue to try to stump me with the books they've selected. "Have you read every book in this library?" they demand, a question dear to my heart. "I'm still working on it," I tell them, and I am.

DISCIPLINE AND REWARDS

In the library, where children sit in three rows on the "story rug," I was always reminding children to sit up straight, cross their legs, and make sure their bottoms were touching the rug, so children sitting in back of them could see. Turning it into a game, I freed myself from nagging and discovered an instant way to get children's attention.

In kindergarten, I teach them the magic words: BTR (Bottoms Touching Rug), SUS (Sit Up Straight), and CYL (Cross Your Legs). We trace the giant letters in the air using our sharpened fingers as pencils, as we go over what each letter stands for. I tell them to "sit sloppy," which they do without a hitch as I remind them, "No arms, legs, hands, feet, heads, or any other part touching anybody else." Then I say the magic acronyms: BTR, SUS, CYL, as fast as I can.

Instantly, the children sit perfectly, giggling happily to themselves. I tell them none of the other teachers know how these magic words work, and that it's our little secret. Each week, after everyone is settled on the rug ("Row two, unsquish. You look like a can of sardines. We don't want any sardines around here!"), I make a great pretense of forgetting something important—a book, my guitar, a tissue—and the kids hiss to each other, "Get sloppy!"

Two seconds later I return. "What? They're sitting sloppy again? I'm shocked. Shocked! Whatever am I going to do? I know: I'll tell their teacher."

"Won't work," one child mutters.

"I'll tell my mother on you," I declare. More giggles. "I'll . . . BTR, SUS, CYL!" Instant perfection. We vary the dialogue each time, but the end result is always the same. The class is ready to begin. Children of all grades are so conditioned to the words that I just have to say BTR if they start to get fidgety and they perk up instantly. I've tried it at all-school assemblies to get students ready, and the whole school straightens up fast. When we're sitting at desks or tables, the command changes to: BTC (Bottoms Touching Chair), SUS, FOF (Feet On Floor)!

My guiding principle is to use humor whenever possible, and never sarcasm. When children are working in the library and the noise level escalates too high, I'll call out, "FREEZE!" That usually stops everyone dead in their tracks, but if they're not listening, I yell it again, adding, "You can breathe, you can blink, the blood can circulate from your heart to your veins and through your arteries back to your heart, but you are frozen. You can't even twitch." It works wonders; afterward, I tell them to defrost or unfreeze, and they pretend to melt.

Yelling at children only works in an emergency. Kids are used to yelling from teachers, parents, and other authority figures, so instead try weaving a spell with your voice, getting quieter instead of louder. Reward good behavior with praise and occasional treats. I advise students never to ask that awful question "What do we get if we win/finish first/do a good job?" or they can expect nothing.

When my fifth-graders completed solving an almanac mystery, I rewarded them with hard cash: two hundred dollars each. One bill was the size of a thumbnail, and the other over twice the size of a real hundred. The tiny bills I found in my local drug store in the party-favor section; the large ones I photocopied and enlarged on green paper from a replica of a hundred-dollar bill I bought as a bookmark in the bookstore.

I bought a jelly bean/gum machine—the kind with a glass globe on top, a slot for a coin, and a handle to turn. When a class has completed a spectacular job, sometimes I give each child a penny to spend on jelly beans. They take great pleasure in turning the handle and counting out their seven jelly beans, which I tell them are reading beans, one for each day of the week, that will increase their appetites for books. It's such a simple reward, with the only pitfall being that I am now addicted to gourmet jelly beans, with which I reward myself every time an odious task is completed.

Prizes and favors for games won, work completed, or just as a tie-in to a good story don't need to be elaborate. Buttons, pencils, stickers, and bookmarks are always appreciated. Food, including pretzels and cookies, is never shunned. I gave out tiny plastic ants to one class after we read Beverly Allinson's *Effie*, about a loud-mouthed ant. I look for inexpensive and amusing prizes whenever I find a novelty store. If you offer to buy a large quantity and tell them you are a teacher, many stores will offer you a better price.

Third-graders received the Freeman Handshake after completing a card catalog exercise. It's a silly handshake I made up on the spot one day when I thought the kids needed a reward, and as each child finished, I delivered the shake while making eye contact, causing the recipient to grin and feel special. That's what teaching is all about.

THE VAN HOLTEN LIBRARY CURRICULUM IN PROGRESS, GRADES K–5

Over the years, my own curriculum has grown, and with the advent of computers in the library I expect it will continue to evolve. I tell students my aim is for them to feel at home in any library in North America and be able to locate whatever information they seek.

Below is the current and always evolving list of skills I use as a framework for my teaching over the course of the year. Many skills are ongoing, becoming more complex as the children move up the grades. They're separated into Information Management (including reference, research, and library skills) and Literature skills here, but the two are interdependent.

Kindergarten

Information Management Skills Covered

> What is a Library?
> Library Procedures: Browsing, selecting, and signing out books
> Proper Book Care: Including *Glad Book, Sad Book* (filmstrip)
> Parts of a Book: Author, illustrator, title, cover, dust jacket, spine, spine label, sign-out card, pocket
> Book Selection Skills: Evaluating cover, illustrations, subject

Literature Skills Covered

> *Listening and Comprehension Skills:*
> Listening to and sharing stories
> Predicting outcomes, drawing conclusions, making inferences, listening for details
> Sequencing: Recalling and retelling stories
> Interpreting illustrations
> Identifying and describing plot, setting, main characters

Relating personal experiences to stories

Participation in Storytelling, Singing Songs, Poetry, and Fingerplays

Creative Drama: Acting out stories in narrative pantomime and with improvised dialogue

Concepts: Including colors, shapes, sizes, opposites, following directions using prepositional phrases, days of the week, months, seasons

Introduction to Variety of Authors and Illustrators

Grade 1

Information Management Skills Covered

Review of Library Procedures: Browsing, selecting, and signing out books

Review of Proper Book Care

Parts of a Book: Author, illustrator, title, cover, dust jacket, spine, spine label, sign-out card, pocket, title page, publisher, copyright date

Book Selection Skills: Evaluating cover, illustrations, subject, contents, difficulty

How a Book Is Made: From writing to publishing

Arrangement of Easy Fiction: Finding books by a given author

Fiction vs. Nonfiction: Comparing and contrasting

Literature Skills Covered

Listening and Comprehension Skills:

Listening to and sharing stories

Predicting outcomes, drawing conclusions, making inferences, listening for details

Sequencing: Recalling and retelling stories

Interpreting illustrations

Identifying and describing plot, setting, main characters

Relating personal experiences to stories

Participation in Storytelling, Singing Songs, and Fingerplays

Introduction to Folklore (398.2): Comparing and contrasting like stories

Creative Drama: Acting out stories in narrative pantomime and with improvised dialogue

Writing and Illustrating: Composing spin-offs from predictable and pattern books

Introduction to Variety of Authors and Illustrators

Evaluating Caldecott Medal Books: The Caldecott Project

Introduction to Poets, Poetry, and Songs: Composing new verses

Grade 2

Information Management Skills Covered

> Review of Library Procedures: Browsing, selecting, and signing out books
>
> Review of Proper Book Care
>
> Reinforce and Review Parts of a Book: Author, illustrator, title, cover, dust jacket, spine, spine label, title page, publisher, copyright date, call numbers, call letters, place of publication
>
> Book Selection Skills: Evaluating cover, illustrations, subject, contents, difficulty
>
> Determining Readability: The Fist Test
>
> How a Book Is Made; From Writer to Reader: Composing a manuscript, illustrating, the role of the editor; dummies, galleys, proofs, printing press, signatures, folded and gathered sheets, binding
>
> Library Arrangement: Introduction to location and arrangement of easy fiction, fiction, nonfiction, biography and reference
>
> Review Arrangement of Easy Fiction: Finding books by a given author
>
> Arrangement of Fiction: Finding books given author's name
>
> Arrangement of Nonfiction: Finding books given the call number; determining subjects with a given call number
>
> Fiction vs. Nonfiction: Comparing and contrasting using title, cover, spine label, and examination of contents
>
> Introduction to Card Catalog: Identifying three types of cards; Locating a book by author, title, and subject
>
> Introduction to Encyclopedias: Arrangement; Finding topics

Literature Skills Covered

> *Listening and Comprehension Skills:*
>
> Listening to and sharing stories
>
> Predicting outcomes, drawing conclusions, making inferences, listening for details
>
> Sequencing: Recalling and retelling stories
>
> Interpreting illustrations
>
> Identifying and describing plot, setting, main characters, point of view
>
> Relating personal experiences to stories
>
> Comparing and contrasting two books or stories with a similar theme
>
> Participation in Storytelling
>
> Introduction to Folktales and Fables (398.2): Comparing and contrasting like stories; Tracing variants; Exposure to other countries and cultures through folktales
>
> Creative Drama: Acting out stories in narrative pantomime and with improvised dialogue; Reader's Theater (scripted plays)
>
> Writing and Illustrating: Composing spin-offs from predictable and pattern books
>
> Introduction to Variety of Authors and Illustrators
>
> Evaluating New Books for Content, Illustrations, and Child Appeal
>
> Continued Exposure to Poets, Poetry, and Songs: Composing new verses

Grade 3

Information Management Skills Covered

Reinforce and Review Parts of a Book as Needed: Author, illustrator, title, cover, dust jacket, spine, spine label, title page, publisher, copyright date, call number, call letters, place of publication, dedication, table of contents, index, glossary

Library Arrangement: Locating and defining all areas of library such as easy fiction, fiction, nonfiction, biography, reference, card catalog, circulation desk, paperbacks, AV, magazines, folklore

Fiction, Nonfiction, Biography, and Reference: Finding books given author's name and/or call numbers or letters; Differentiating between types of books using title, cover, spine label, and contents

Introduction to the Dewey Decimal System's Ten Classes; Categorizing nonfiction subject areas, given a Dewey number

Exploring Nonfiction: Fact for the Day Project

Reintroduction to Card Catalog: Identifying contents of three types of cards; Locating books given an author, title, or subject; The Card Catalog Song

Using Encyclopedias: Arrangement; Finding topics; Comparing sets; Answering simple reference questions after selecting the key word; Completing simple research reports

Literature Skills Covered

Reading Enrichment and Encouragement: Booktalks; Oral reading; Storytelling; Creative writing; Creative drama; Reader's Theater; Reading guidance

Comprehension Skills: Analysis of plot, setting, characters, point of view, style

Fiction Genres: Comparing and contrasting realistic fiction and fantasy

Evaluating New Books for Content, Illustrations, and Child Appeal

Continued Exposure to Poets, Poetry, and Songs

Oral Reading Skills: Selecting and reading aloud appealing poems and passages

Storytelling

Investigation of Folktales and Fables (398.2): Comparing and contrasting like stories; Tracing variants; Exposure to other countries and cultures through folktales

Magazines: Introduction to all titles in library

Grade 4

Information Management Skills Covered

Reinforce and Review Parts of a Book as Needed: Author, illustrator, title, cover, dust jacket, spine, spine label, title page, publisher, copyright date, call number, call letters, place of publication, dedication, table of contents, index, glossary

Library Arrangement: Locating and defining on a map all areas of library such as easy fiction, fiction, nonfiction, biography, reference, card catalog, circulation desk, paperbacks, AV, magazines

Review Arrangement and Definition of Fiction, Nonfiction, Biography, and Reference: Finding books given author's name and/or call numbers or letters; Differentiating between types of books from title, cover, spine label, and contents

Alphabetizing Skills: Fiction and Biography

Dewey Decimal System's Ten Classes: Review and reinforce; Categorizing titles and subjects into classes

Exploring Nonfiction: Dewey Browse Project

Overview of the History of Books and Libraries: Presentation tracing development of hieroglyphics, the Rosetta Stone, illuminated manuscripts, and Gutenberg's printing press, up to computers

Card Catalog Review: Identifying contents of three types of cards; Locating books given an author, title, or subject; Using the catalog to answer reference questions about books, first selecting the key word

Using Encyclopedias: Review of vocabulary; Locating topics; Selecting the key word or words; Comparing and evaluating sets and information found when answering simple reference questions; Compiling simple reports and presentations using more than one set of encyclopedias (Sport Reports)

Literature Skills Covered

Reading Enrichment and Encouragement: Booktalks; Oral reading; Storytelling; Creative writing; Creative drama; Reader's Theater; Reading guidance

Comprehension Skills: Analyzing plot, setting, characters, point of view, style

Fiction Genres: Comparing and contrasting genres of realistic fiction and fantasy

Oral Reading Skills: Selecting and reading aloud appealing poems and passages

Continued Investigation of Folktales and Fables (398.2): Comparing and contrasting like stories; Tracing variants; Exposure to other countries and cultures through folktales

Evaluating New Books for Content, Illustrations, and Child Appeal

Continued Exposure to Poets and Poetry

Grade 5

Information Management Skills Covered

Library Arrangement and Content Review Through Orientation Games: Library Baseball; Library Tic-Tac-Toe; Library Treasure Hunt

Review Arrangement and Definition of Fiction, Nonfiction, Biography, and Reference: Finding books given author's name and/or call numbers or letters; Differentiating between types of books from title, cover, spine label, and contents

Card Catalog Review: Identifying contents of three types of cards; Locating books given an author, title, or subject; Using the catalog to answer reference questions about books using the key word and locating materials

Using Encyclopedias: Review of vocabulary; Locating topics; Selecting the key word or words; Comparing and evaluating different encyclopedia sets and information found when answering reference questions; Researching a topic, taking notes, and compiling a brief presentation

World Almanac: Using the Index; Selecting stated and unstated key words; Locating information; Answering reference questions

Choosing and Using Reference Materials: Arrangement and use of basic sources including *National Geographic Index, Bartlett's Familiar Quotations*, specialized dictionaries and encyclopedias, and *Something About the Author* to answer reference questions

Choosing Proper Reference Sources to Answer Reference Questions and Locate Information: The Library Reference Game

Using Reference Materials for Report Research

Literature Skills Covered

Reading Enrichment and Encouragement: Booktalks; Oral reading; Storytelling; Creative writing; Creative drama; Reader's Theater; Reading guidance

Comprehension Skills: Analyzing plot, setting, characters, point of view, style; making inferences

Identifying Fiction Genres: Fantasy, science fiction, historical and biographical fiction, humorous fiction, animal stories, suspense and horror, adventure, ghost stories, realistic, contemporary, and problem fiction

Oral Reading Skills: Selecting and reading aloud appealing poems and passages

The In What Book Game: Composing plot statements; Identifying titles and authors given a one-sentence plot summary

Continued Investigation of Folktales and Fables (398.2): Comparing and contrasting like stories; Tracing variants; Exposure to other countries and cultures through folktales

Evaluating New Books for Content, Illustrations, and Child Appeal

Continued Exposure to Poets and Poetry

BOOKS AND TECHNOLOGY

My next goal as a librarian and teacher is to explore and experiment with teaching skills involving technology and telecommunications for information retrieval. As our libraries move into modern times and become computerized and networked with classrooms and other schools and libraries, our children need to know how to use all the latest tools for locating and managing information: electronic library catalogs, magazine indexes, dictionaries, encyclopedias, atlases, almanacs, and other reference searching tools on CD-ROM and computer databases. The look of libraries will change, but the books will continue to entertain, inform, and inspire.

Many school libraries use the term "media center," which is fine, but I have always loved that word "library," and I am proud to be known as a Librarian. To me, a Media Specialist sounds like someone who knows how to fix lots of machines, and while I can troubleshoot my equipment just fine I'd far rather be recognized for my book expertise as I travel the Internet and blaze new trails down the Information Superhighway. Other media supplement the books, but as yet don't supercede them.

Writer E. Annie Proulx, in "Books on Top," a May 26, 1994 *New York Times* Op Ed piece adapted from a talk she gave at the PEN/Faulkner awards ceremony, said it just right:

> Those who say the book is moribund often cite the computer as the asp on the mat. But the electronic highway is for bulletin boards on esoteric subjects, reference works, lists and news—timely, utilitarian information, efficiently pulled through the wires. Nobody is going to sit down and read a novel on a twitchy little screen. Ever.

> In a curious way the computer emphasizes the unique virtues of the book:

> The book is small, lightweight and durable, and can be stuffed in a coat pocket, read in the waiting room, on the plane. What are planes but flying reading rooms?

> Books give esthetic and tactile pleasure, from the dust jacket art, to the binding, paper, typography and text design, from the moment of purchase until the last page is turned.

> Books speak even when they stand unopened on the shelf. If you would know a man or woman, look at their books, not their software.

I was on bus duty early one morning, greeting all the troops as they marched into the school building, when a grinning first-grader approached me, dragging her overloaded bookbag. "Books, books, books!" she exclaimed, hoisting the bag onto her back. She sighed dramatically. "Reading—it's my life!"

And now, on to the booklists!

Illustration by Diane de Groat from ATTABOY, SAM! Copyright © 1992 by Lois
Lowry. Reprinted by permission of Houghton Mifflin Co. All rights reserved.

Annotated
Read-Aloud Lists

From FROG MEDICINE by Mark Teague. Copyright © 1991 by Mark Teague.
Reprinted by permission of Scholastic Inc.

HOW TO GET THE MOST OUT OF
THE BOOKLISTS

Most of the more than 1,400 children's books in the following lists were published between 1990 and 1995.

Here's what you'll find on a typical page:

Hurwitz, Johanna. *Class President.* **Illus. by Sheila Hamanaka. Morrow, 1990. ISBN 0-688-09114-8**

[8 chapters, 85p.] Though fifth-grader Julio Sanchez would secretly love to be elected president, he promises to be best friend Lucas Cott's campaign manager instead, a promise that proves impossible to keep. Introduce your class to the other humorous books in Hurwitz's on-target series: *Class Clown, Teacher's Pet* (1988), *School's Out* (1991), and *School Spirit*. Claudia Mills's *Dinah for President* and Barbara Park's *Rosie Swanson: Fourth-Grade Geek for President* put other spins on the campaign process. ELECTIONS. HISPANIC AMERICANS. MULTICULTURAL STORIES. SCHOOLS.

Each entry consists of the author(s), complete title, illustrator, publisher, copyright date, ISBN number if the book is in print, annotation, and up to seven subject headings under which the book is listed in the Subject Index. Where applicable, the number of pages, chapters, stories, and/or number of sittings required to read the book aloud are also included.

Each entry's annotation includes first a simple plot statement. Next come practical ideas for sharing the books with children to develop comprehension skills and creativity. These tie into a variety of subject areas including language arts, library skills, science, social studies, math, health, art, music, and physical education.

A majority of the annotations also cite related titles that fit in as companions, follow-ups, or extensions on that subject or theme. Most of these related titles also appear as main entries in this book or in the companion volume, *Books Kids Will Sit Still For*, 2nd ed. (R. R. Bowker, 1990), with their own annotations that provide still more relevant activities and titles. The Author, Title, Illustrator, and Subject indexes in this volume, which cite titles by entry numbers, also include the 2,117 entries from the Read-Aloud Lists in *Books Kids Will Sit Still For*. Entry numbers from *Books Kids Will Sit Still For* appear in regular type, while entry numbers from this volume appear in boldface type. When a related title in an annotation does not have its own entry in either book, the publisher and copyright date are noted in parentheses. For additional tie-ins, check the extensive cumulative Subject Index at the back of the book.

FICTION LISTS

Lists are arranged alphabetically by author. Fiction chapters overlap in terms of recommended grade levels and are set up as follows: PRE, PRE–K, K–1, 1–2, 2–3, 3–4, 4–5, and 5–6. My aim has been to peg each fiction book to the two grades I have found to be most suited to it, in terms of the literal comprehension and the maturity levels of children. Depending on the needs of your children, you should refer to the adjacent lists as well. Titles on all the nonfiction lists, including folklore and poetry, have a broader grade-level interest span.

All of the fiction lists include both "fiction" and "easy fiction/picture book" titles, as the two categories overlap. Chapter books are usually found on the fiction shelves of the library, whereas stories that can be finished in one sitting are most often in "easy fiction," though there are many exceptions to these rules.

FOLK AND FAIRY TALES LISTS

Folk and fairy tales are split into two separate chapters. The first—"Folk & Fairy Tales, Myths & Legends: Single Stories"—consists of single, illustrated versions of tales, most in picture-book format, which can be read aloud in one sitting. The second—"Folk & Fairy Tales, Myths & Legends: Collections"—contains folktale collections in which three to over four dozen stories are compiled into a single volume, from which you can chose to read all or some.

The authors listed in the two folklore chapters are actually retellers, since no one knows who originally composed the stories, some of which are hundreds of years old. Translators' names are also included where applicable. In the interests of easy access, all the German folktales collected by the brothers Jacob and Wilhelm Grimm are listed under "Grimm, Jacob," and the myriad editions of Aesop's fables are grouped under Aesop, regardless of how they were listed on the books' title pages. Likewise, nursery rhyme collections are listed under Mother Goose instead of the collectors or illustrators.

POETRY LISTS

On the poetry list, note that "comp." for compiler is written after many of the authors' names. This indicates that the author listed did not write the poems, but collected and edited them from other sources. In the subject index, check the heading POETRY–SINGLE AUTHOR for a complete list of collections by any one poet. Because so many picture books are told in rhyme, I decided to move single, picture-book renditions of narrative poems, such as Edward Lear's *The Owl and the Pussycat* and Ogden Nash's *The Adventures of Isabel*, in with the fiction grade-level lists instead of keeping them in the poetry chapter. You will find them all in the Subject Index, listed under "NARRATIVE POETRY."

PAPERBACKS

Although many titles on my lists are available in paperback editions, these editions are not usually noted here as they go in and out of print even faster than hardbacks. Then again, if you can't find a book in hardback, check in *Books in Print* (R. R. Bowker) at your library or bookstore to see if it's at least obtainable in paperback.

A NEW CHAPTER: FICTION FOR PRESCHOOL

After coming across scores of stories that seemed too basic for kindergarten but too good to omit, I decided to add a new chapter—"Fiction for Preschool"— to the bibliography section, listing books for preschoolers, ages three to four. These are stories with uncomplicated plots, usually very short, brightly illustrated, and simple to follow. Kindergarteners will still enjoy many of these books too, though they may consider some of the stories too "babyish," so choose accordingly.

PROFESSIONAL BIBLIOGRAPHY

In the intervening five years since I compiled the Professional Bibliography for *Books Kids Will Sit Still For*, the number of professional books for teachers and librarians has mushroomed. In my school, use of our extensive professional book collection, which sat virtually untouched for years, has soared as teachers clamor to find out more about literature-based teaching. Publishers, responding to the demand for literature-based teaching ideas, have given us innumerable treasures. We owe a debt of gratitude to astute publishers including the American Library Association, R. R. Bowker, H. W. Wilson, Heinemann, Libraries Unlimited and Teacher Ideas Press, Oryx, and Richard C. Owen. The real thanks must go to the authors, of course, who have anticipated our every need and written so eloquently about the state of children's literature and whole language. In particular, Caroline Feller Bauer, Mildred Laughlin, Margaret MacDonald, Sharron L. McElmeel, Laura Robb, Regie Routman, and Judy Sierra, all of whom have provided us with many rousing hours of professional guidance, continue to break new ground. The cumulative, updated professional bibliography now lists more than 150 of my favorite titles, double the number listed in *Books Kids Will Sit Still For*.

USING THE INDEXES

The four indexes at the back of the book (Author, Title, Illustrator, and Subject) should help you in your search for the perfect read-aloud. The Subject Index is extensive, listing not only author and title, but grade level as well, helping you make even more connections between similarly themed books, and frequent "see" and "see also" cross-references.

The Subject Index contains more than 600 topics, and though most use standard subject headings, I added several of my own that seemed pertinent, including: Alliteration, Autobiography, Biography, Caldecott Medal, Call-and-Response Stories, Cause and Effect, Chantable Refrain, Creative Drama, Creative Writing, Cumulative Stories, Days of the Week, Exaggeration, Fairy Tales–Satire, Fingerplays, Knock-Knock Jokes, Literary Fairy Tales, Narrative Poetry, Newbery Medal, Parodies, Picture Books for All Ages, Pourquoi Tales, Self-Esteem, Sequence Stories, Sound Effects, Stories to Tell, Stories with Songs, Tongue Twisters, Transformations, Trickster Tales, and Visual Perception.

Illustration from A ZOOFUL OF ANIMALS by William Cole.
Illustrations copyright © 1992 by Lynn Munsinger.
Reprinted by permission of Houghton Mifflin Co. All rights reserved.

FICTION FOR PRESCHOOL

1   **Abercrombie, Barbara.** *Michael and the Cats.* **Illus. by Mark Graham. McElderry, 1993. ISBN 0-689-50543-4**

Visiting his aunt and uncle for the week, Michael yearns to be friends with their large long-furred cats. As he learns how the cats like to be treated, they become more accepting of him until, on the last night, they snuggle up next to him in bed and purr. The soft-colored expressive oil paintings will make your listeners long to cuddle a pet, so hand out stuffed animals and discuss the rules of proper pet care. Continue with Dav Pilkey's impressionistic *When Cats Dream* to find out what goes on in their minds when they're asleep. CATS. PETS.

2   **Alborough, Jez.** *Where's My Teddy?* **Illus. by the author. Candlewick, 1992. ISBN 1-56402-048-7**

Eddie has lost his teddy in the woods, and when he finds an enormous one, it belongs to a giant bear who has found Eddie's. The simple funny rhyme and the oversized watercolors will hearten children with the fact the big bear is scared of the boy as well as vice versa. For another bear who's worse for wear, read *My Old Teddy* by Don Mansell. Lost toys loom large in V. H. Drummond's *Phewtus the Squirrel*, James Flora's *Sherwood Walks Home*, Sarah Hayes's *This Is the Bear* and *This Is the Bear and the Scary Night*, and Shirley Hughes's *Dogger*. BEARS. LOST. STORIES IN RHYME. TEDDY BEARS.

3   **Anholt, Catherine, and Laurence Anholt.** *All About You.* **Illus. by the author. Viking, 1992. ISBN 0-670-84488-8**

Readers are asked to identify their special feelings, clothes, activities, and likes through a series of questions and rhyming answers. Use with Crockett Johnson's *Is This You?* and have your children make a book of their illustrated responses. Also see the authors' *Kids* and *What Makes Me Happy?* CHILDREN. INDIVIDUALITY. QUESTIONS AND ANSWERS. STORIES IN RHYME. VOCABULARY.

4   **Baker, Keith.** *Big Fat Hen.* **Illus. by the author. Harcourt, 1994. ISBN 0-15-292869-3**

An oversized, colorful interpretation of the old nursery rhyme, "One, two, buckle my shoe" will keep kids counting as chicks hatch, bees buzz, and a big fat hen oversees all. Add *One Red Rooster* by Kathleen Sullivan Carroll, *Five Little Ducks* by Raffi, and *Over in the Meadow: An Old Counting Rhyme* by Olive A. Wadsworth for a simple math lesson. Next, act out the action verbs in *Count!* by Denise Fleming and *2 Is for Dancing: A 1 2 3 of Actions* by Woodleigh Hubbard. Michael Jay Katz's *Ten Potatoes in a Pot and Other Counting Rhymes* will bring you up to number 12. CHICKENS. COUNTING BOOKS. EGGS. NURSERY RHYMES. STORIES IN RHYME.

5   Bennett, David. *One Cow Moo Moo!* Illus. by Andy Cooke. Henry Holt, 1990. ISBN 0-8050-1416-0

In a rollicking cumulative counting story filled with frenzied animal noises, a boy wonders why all the panicked farm animals are chasing each other, only to discover the reason is a growling monstrous purple creature on the run. Follow the chain reactions in *Look Out, Bird!* by Marilyn Janovitz, *What's for Lunch?* by John Schindel, and Béatrice Tanaka's Native American folktale *The Chase*. Keep up the farm-based counting with *One Red Rooster* by Kathleen Sullivan Carroll, *Count!* by Denise Fleming, *2 Is for Dancing: A 1 2 3 of Actions* by Woodleigh Hubbard, *One Cow Coughs: A Counting Book for the Sick and Miserable* by Christine Loomis, and *Over in the Meadow: An Old Counting Rhyme* by Olive A. Wadsworth, with other versions by Paul Galdone, John Langstaff, and Louise Voce. *Go Away, Big Green Monster* by Ed Emberley and *One Hungry Monster: A Counting Book in Rhyme* by Susan Heyboer O'Keefe will appeal to creature-lovers. ANIMALS. CAUSE-AND-EFFECT. CHANTABLE REFRAIN. COUNTING BOOKS. CUMULATIVE STORIES. MONSTERS. SOUND EFFECTS.

6   Boland, Janice. *Annabel.* Illus. by Megan Halsey. Dial, 1993. ISBN 0-8037-1255-3

A little pig wants to be important so she helps the horse plow, the dog guard, and the hen keep her eggs warm, but it's her mother who lets her know that being herself is just as wonderful. Others who learn that they are special without all the trappings can be found in *The Mixed-Up Chameleon* by Eric Carle, *I Wish I Were a Butterfly* by James Howe, *The Pigs' Picnic* by Keiko Kasza, *I Wish That I Had Duck Feet* by Theo LeSieg, *Fish Is Fish* by Leo Lionni, *"You Look Ridiculous," Said the Rhinoceros to the Hippopotamus,* by Bernard Waber, and *Wriggles the Little Wishing Pig* by Pauline Watson. The young pigs in Charlotte Pomerantz's *The Piggy in the Puddle* and Valerie Reddix's *Millie and the Mud Hole* learn all about wallowing. DOMESTIC ANIMALS. INDIVIDUALITY. PIGS. SELF-ESTEEM.

7   Carroll, Kathleen Sullivan. *One Red Rooster.* Illus. by Suzette Barbier. Houghton Mifflin, 1992. ISBN 0-395-60195-9

"One red rooster went cock-a-doodle-doo/ Two black cows went moo moo moo." And so on, up to ten pigs fast asleep. Bright bordered illustrations give us ten farm animals, and encourage us to make all the usual noises, as do Denise Fleming's *Barnyard Banter* and Wendy Cheyette Lewison's lovely *Going to Sleep on the Farm*. Add another math experience with Denise Fleming's *Count!*, and prolong the country noises with Lorinda Bryan Cauley's, Nancy Hellen's, Carol Jones's, Tracey Campbell Pearson's, or Glen Rounds's *Old Macdonald Had a Farm*, or Gus Clarke's *EIEIO: The Story of Old MacDonald, Who Had a Farm*, Dee Dee Duffy's *Barnyard Tracks*, and Jill Runcie's *Cock-a-Doodle-Doo!* Mix up some noises with Charles Causley's *"Quack!" said the Billy Goat*, Victoria Forrester's *The Magnificent Moo*, and Andrea Zimmerman and David Clemesha's *The Cow Buzzed*. Flora McDonnell's *I Love Animals* features great amiable farm animal paintings. ANIMALS. COUNTING BOOKS. DOMESTIC ANIMALS. SOUND EFFECTS. STORIES IN RHYME.

8   **Cooke, Trish. *So Much*. Illus. by Helen Oxenbury. Candlewick, 1994. ISBN 1-56402-344-3**

"They weren't doing anything, Mom and the baby, nothing really . . . Then, DING DONG!" Each time the doorbell rings, it's another doting relative who wants to squeeze the baby, or kiss him, or eat him, or fight him, and all that love leaves the baby beside himself with pleasure. The extended African American family is brought to life in great big gaudy gouache paintings, and you'll want to pinch that precious baby, too. Lisa Kopper's *Daisy Thinks She Is a Baby*, Tom Paxton's *Where's the Baby?*, James Stevenson's *Rolling Rose*, Vera B. Williams's *"More More More," Said the Baby*, and Frieda Wishinsky's *Oonga Boonga* are also full of huggable little ones. BABIES. LOVE. MULTICULTURAL STORIES.

9   **Dodds, Siobhan. *Grandpa Bud*. Illus. by the author. Candlewick, 1993. ISBN 1-56402-175-0**

Planning to spend the night, Polly calls Grandpa Bud on the phone to request favorite snacks for herself and her friends. Children can chant the "Quick, quick, quick!" refrain and recall the goodies Polly requests for each of her stuffed animals. Bring in an old phone so children can act out the story and pretend they're talking to their grandparents. CHANTABLE REFRAIN. FOOD. GRANDFATHERS. STUFFED ANIMALS. TELEPHONE.

10   **Duffy, Dee Dee. *Barnyard Tracks*. Illus. by Janet Marshall. Bell Books/Boyds Mills Press, 1992. ISBN 1-878093-66-5**

"Look! I see some animal tracks. Listen! I hear oink! oink! Who's there?" Across the page run black tracks, and listeners will call out, "It's a pig!" before you can turn the page and show the picture. Why is it—along with the rooster, cat, ducks, and cow—making noises? The fox is coming, just like in Mem Fox's *Hattie and the Fox*. Guess more animals in Beatrice Schenk de Regniers's *It Does Not Say Meow and Other Animal Riddle Rhymes*, Stephanie Calmenson's *What Am I? Very First Riddles*, and Deborah Guarino's *Is Your Mama a Llama? One Red Rooster* by Kathleen Sullivan Carroll, *Barnyard Banter* by Denise Fleming, *Going to Sleep on the Farm* by Wendy Cheyette Lewison, and *I Love Animals* by Flora McDonnell are also farm-based stories. DOMESTIC ANIMALS. SOUND EFFECTS.

11   **Falwell, Cathryn. *Feast for 10*. Illus. by the author. Clarion, 1993. ISBN 0-395-62037-6**

An African American family shops for groceries and makes dinner in this simple but stunning one-to-ten rhyming counting book with cut paper collage illustrations. Ask your listeners how they get ready for dinnertime with their families. Other warm family descriptions include Melrose Cooper's rhyming *I Got a Family* and Laurence Pringle's *Octopus Hug*. AFRICAN AMERICANS. COUNTING BOOKS. FAMILY LIFE. SHOPPING. STORIES IN RHYME.

12   Fleming, Denise. *Barnyard Banter*. Illus. by the author. Henry Holt, 1994. ISBN 0-8050-1957-X

A raucous rhyming catalog of barnyard noises and animals is accompanied by the white goose who children will find lurking on every page. Assign animal noises to your listeners so you can act out the glorious cacophony on the final pages. Encourage sharp-eyed viewers to describe the location of the goose each time (e.g., behind the peacock, or beside the cow) instead of pointing. Versions of *Old MacDonald Had a Farm* by Cauley, Hellen, Jones, Pearson, and Rounds are always fun, along with Gus Clarke's *EIEIO: The Story of Old MacDonald, Who Had a Farm*, Dee Dee Duffy's *Barnyard Tracks*, Kathy Parkinson's and Mary Maki Rae's versions of *The Farmer in the Dell*, Martin Waddell's *The Pig in the Pond*, and Nadine Bernard Westcott's *Skip to My Lou*. Charles Causley's *"Quack!" said the Billy Goat*, Victoria Forrester's *The Magnificent Moo*, and Andrea Zimmerman and David Clemesha's *The Cow Buzzed* are nice and noisy too. DOMESTIC ANIMALS. GEESE. SOUND EFFECTS. STORIES IN RHYME.

13   Fleming, Denise. *Count!* Illus. by the author. Henry Holt, 1992. ISBN 0-8050-1595-7

Two zebras jump, four kangaroos bounce, and other animals up to number ten cavort across this counting book, which also counts by tens up to 50. Starting with one child, and then adding on, you can act out each animal's actions. This also works with Woodleigh Hubbard's *2 Is for Dancing: A 1 2 3 of Actions*. Jim Aylesworth's *One Crow: A Counting Rhyme*, Keith Baker's *Big Fat Hen*, David Bennett's *One Cow Moo Moo!*, Kathleen Sullivan Carroll's *One Red Rooster*, Lois Ehlert's *Fish Eyes: A Book You Can Count On*, Loreen Leedy's *A Number of Dragons*, and Ellen Stoll Walsh's *Mouse Count* are just a few of the splendid animal-based beginning counting books out there. ANIMALS. COUNTING BOOKS. CREATIVE DRAMA.

14   Fleming, Denise. *Lunch*. Illus. by the author. Henry Holt, 1992. ISBN 0-8050-1636-8

An exuberant gray mouse is so hungry he gorges on a colorful assortment of fruits and vegetables. Children will love guessing mouse's next course from the visual clue on each bright handmade paper illustration, and if you bring in the accompanying foods, they can have a colorful and healthful tasting party. Sample more food and colors in N. N. Charles's *What Am I? Looking Through Shapes at Apples and Grapes*, Dayle Ann Dodds's *The Color Box*, and Bruce McMillan's photo-illustrated *Growing Colors*, and top it off with a chorus of Eric Carle's food song, "Today Is Monday." Play mouse games with Martin Waddell's *Squeak-a-Lot*, and go voling with his *Sam Vole and His Brothers*; then share a berry with Don and Audrey Wood's *The Little Mouse, the Red Ripe Strawberry, and the Big Hungry Bear*. COLOR. FOOD. MICE.

15   Ford, Miela. *Little Elephant*. Photos by Tana Hoban. Greenwillow, 1994. ISBN 0-688-13141-7

Clear, close-up color photographs show an adorable baby elephant as she plays in the water and has trouble getting back on land. The simple story is just a ploy to let us fall in love with the pachyderm, though your goal may be to show other large mammals, such as those in Bruce McMillan's *Going on a Whale Watch*. Sarah Josepha Buell Hale's *Mary Had a Little Lamb* with photos by Bruce McMillan, and McMillan's own *Kitten Can* both feature simple texts and lovely pictures, while Tana Hoban's *A Children's Zoo* and Hope Ryden's *Wild Animals of America ABC* give a range of photogenic creatures. ELEPHANTS.

16   Gackenbach, Dick. *Claude Has a Picnic*. Illus. by the author. Clarion, 1993. ISBN 0-395-61161-X

In this sequel to *What's Claude Doing?*, the helpful hound gets his disaffected neighbors talking again, and enjoys himself at the ensuing neighborhood barbecue. Just as one nice action can influence more to occur, show how one nasty action can have the opposite effect in Byron Barton's farm story, *Buzz Buzz Buzz*. Get ready for a traditional summer picnic with Holly Keller's *Henry's Fourth of July*. CAUSE AND EFFECT. DOGS. HELPFULNESS. NEIGHBORS. PICNICS.

17   Garland, Michael. *My Cousin Katie*. Illus. by the author. Crowell, 1989. ISBN 0-690-04740-1

Katie lives on a farm where she helps gather eggs, watches the animals, weeds the lettuce patch and picks apples, and goes for picnics by the pond with her mother. The descriptions are basic, and the double-page paintings panoramic. To fill in more details of what happens on a farm, read Jennifer A. Ericsson's *No Milk!* and Martin Waddell's *Farmer Duck* and *The Pig in the Pond*. COUSINS. FARM LIFE.

18   Hall, Zoe. *It's Pumpkin Time!* Illus. by Shari Halpern. Blue Sky Press, 1994. ISBN 0-590-47833-8

A girl describes step-by-step how she and her brother get ready for Halloween each summer by planting and tending a big pumpkin patch. Huge and vibrant painted paper collages are child-friendly. Make a classroom jack-o'-lantern and toast the seeds. Look at veggies close up with *Growing Vegetable Soup* by Lois Ehlert, *The Carrot Seed* by Ruth Krauss, and *Growing Colors* by Bruce McMillan. *Bean and Plant* by Christine Back is a color photo-essay that shows how a bean seed matures. Linda Williams's *The Little Old Lady Who Was Not Afraid of Anything* and Erica Silverman's *Big Pumpkin* will get everyone into a festive mood. HALLOWEEN. PLANTS. PUMPKINS. VEGETABLES.

19   Hayes, Sarah. *This Is the Bear and the Scary Night*. Illus. by Helen Craig. Little, Brown, 1992. ISBN 0-316-35250-0

The teddy from Hayes's *This Is the Bear* is left behind in the park by his boy and spends a bad night in the pond after an owl picks him up and can't hold on. The stuffed animals in *Where's My Teddy?* by Jez Alborough, *Phewtus the Squirrel* by V. H. Drummond, *Beady Bear* by Don Freeman, *Sherwood Walks Home* by James

Flora, and *Dogger* by Shirley Hughes all are first lost and then found. LOST. STORIES IN RHYME. TEDDY BEARS.

20   **Hellen, Nancy.** *Old MacDonald Had a Farm.* **Illus. by the author. Orchard, 1990. ISBN 0-531-05872-7**

This cheerful and cleverly designed book sports die-cut overlays on each heavy-stock page, so as you turn each page, another animal appears standing next to the farmer along with each new verse of the song. Compare with other versions by Carol Jones, Tracey Campbell Pearson, and Glen Rounds, and Gus Clarke's *EIEIO: The Story of Old MacDonald, Who Had a Farm.* Lois Ehlert's *Color Farm* is another creatively designed animal book. Go for a romp in the country with Dee Dee Duffy's *Barnyard Tracks*, Denise Fleming's *Barnyard Banter*, Wendy Cheyette Lewison's lovely *Going to Sleep on the Farm*, Christine Loomis's *One Cow Coughs*, both Kathy Parkinson's and Mary Maki Rae's versions of *The Farmer in the Dell*, Jill Runcie's *Cock-a-Doodle-Doo!*, Martin Waddell's *The Pig in the Pond*, Nadine Bernard Westcott's *Skip to My Lou*, and Andrea Zimmerman and David Clemesha's *The Cow Buzzed.* CHANTABLE REFRAIN. DOMESTIC ANIMALS. FARM LIFE. FOLK SONGS. SOUND EFFECTS. TOY AND MOVABLE BOOKS.

21   **Hennessy, B. G.** *Sleep Tight.* **Illus. by Anthony Carnabuci. Viking, 1992. ISBN 0-670-83567-6**

After "Night time/ Quiet time/ Read our favorite book time," a brother and sister go to bed amid a sweet rhyming description of who is sleeping and where, from the animals outside to the toys in the bedroom. Margaret Wise Brown's *Goodnight, Moon* is the reigning classic, and Denise Fleming's *Barnyard Banter* and Wendy Cheyette Lewison's *Going to Sleep on the Farm* are also nice. BEDTIME STORIES. SLEEP. STORIES IN RHYME.

22   **Hughes, Shirley.** *Giving.* **Illus. by the author. Candlewick, 1993. ISBN 1-56402-129-7**

Accompanied by her baby brother, a little girl demonstrates the many different meanings of the verb "to give": She gives her mom a birthday present, dad gives her a shoulder ride, she gives an angry look and a big smile, gives up a seat on the bus, and her cat gives her a scratch. Explore multiple meanings of other words such as take, put, or try. For more action verbs, look at *Kitten Can* by Bruce McMillan and *Jiggle Wiggle Prance* by Sally Noll. Comparison words take us through a school day in *Super Super Superwords* by Bruce McMillan. GENEROSITY. GIFTS. VOCABULARY.

23   **Hutchins, Pat.** *My Best Friend.* **Illus. by the author. Greenwillow, 1993. ISBN 0-688-11486-5**

A little girl's best friend comes over to spend the night, and even though her friend can run faster, climb higher, and stay neater, when nighttime noises prove scary, the first little girl knows just how to reassure her that it's just the wind.

Use this simple story with its large gouache paintings to define friendship. Go around the group and have each person tell what's important in a best friend. Deal with more complex issues of friendship such as how to make friends, keep them, and overcome conflicts with Juanita Havill's *Jamaica and Brianna*, Amy MacDonald's *Little Beaver and the Echo*, Jane Thayer's *The Popcorn Dragon*, and Yoriko Tsutsui's *Anna's Secret Friend*. AFRICAN AMERICANS. FRIENDSHIP. MULTICULTURAL STORIES.

24   **Hutchins, Pat. *Silly Billy!* Illus. by the author. Greenwillow, 1992. ISBN 0-688-10818-0**

Monster sister Hazel uses reverse psychology to get her little brother to stop playing with her toys and go to sleep. Third in a quartet of tales that also includes *The Very Worst Monster, Where's the Baby?*, and *Three-Star Billy*. BROTHERS AND SISTERS. MONSTERS. SIBLING RIVALRY. TOYS.

25   **Jonas, Ann. *Where Can It Be?* Illus. by the author. Greenwillow, 1986. ISBN 0-688-05246-0**

A child searches her house without success to locate an unnamed treasure, but it's not until her friend Deborah comes over, bearing the missing item, that we find out what it is: her blanket. Pages open up to reveal what's in the closet, cupboards, and refrigerator, and children will try to guess what the child is searching for. Blanket-lovers will feel calmer with Kevin Henkes's *Owen* and John Prater's *Tim and the Blanket Thief*. Those trying to give up the habit will find sympathy in Nancy Evans Cooney's *The Blanket That Had to Go*, Shirley Hughes's *Alfie Gives a Hand*, Holly Keller's *Geraldine's Blanket*, and Deborah Robinson's *Bye-Bye, Old Buddy*. BLANKETS. LOST.

26   **Keller, Holly. *Henry's Fourth of July*. Illus. by the author. Greenwillow, 1985. ISBN 0-688-04013-6**

On the Fourth, a young opossum has a fine time at his family's annual picnic, watches the parade, participates in a potato sack race, goes swimming, and stays up to see the fireworks. A friendly dog gets the whole neighborhood together in *Claude Has a Picnic* by Dick Gackenbach, and a mouse family sets off on an outing in the wordless *Picnic* by Emily Arnold McCully. FOURTH OF JULY. HOLIDAYS. OPOSSUMS. PICNICS.

27   **Kopper, Lisa. *Daisy Thinks She Is a Baby*. Illus. by the author. Knopf, 1994. ISBN 0-679-94723-X**

The real baby doesn't like it when bull terrier Daisy sits in her high chair and stroller, naps with her blanket, and plays with her toys, but likes it fine when Daisy becomes a mommy. Simple as can be, with adorable colored-pencil illustrations, this will complement Alexandra Day's charming Carl series including *Good Dog, Carl* (Simon & Schuster, 1991). BABIES. DOGS. JEALOUSY.

28   Lewison, Wendy Cheyette. *Going to Sleep on the Farm*. Illus. by Juan Wijngaard. Dial, 1992. ISBN 0-8037-1097-6

As boy and dad lie on the floor playing with miniature toy animals, dad answers the boy's questions about how each animal sleeps. Children will chant the refrains and help make the appropriate animal noises. Captivating watercolors contrast with the bold colors of Kathleen Sullivan Carroll's *One Red Rooster*, another farm animal sleep story, and mesh with the detailed paintings in Jane Howard's *When I'm Sleepy*, where a girl dozes vicariously with a sampling of animals in the wild. Say good-night with *Sleep Tight* by B. G. Hennessy, wake up with *Cock-a-Doodle-Doo!* by Jill Runcie, and have a closer look at farm life with *I Love Animals* by Flora McDonnell. BEDTIME STORIES. DOMESTIC ANIMALS. FATHERS AND SONS. SLEEP. STORIES IN RHYME.

29   Lewison, Wendy Cheyette. *The Princess and the Potty*. Illus. by Rick Brown. Simon & Schuster, 1994. ISBN 0-671-87284-2

"Who ever heard of a princess who wouldn't use her potty? What would the neighbors say in the kingdom next door?" None of the potties brought into the palace please the picky princess, until she takes a shine to the idea of wearing pretty pantalettes, and that does the trick. Using humor, charming ink-and-watercolor illustrations, and an absorbing story line, Lewison has written the quintessential potty book that preschool teachers as well as parents will enjoy reading. PRINCES AND PRINCESSES. TOILET TRAINING.

30   McDonnell, Flora. *I Love Animals*. Illus. by the author. Candlewick, 1994. ISBN 1-56402-387-7

Huge acrylic and gouache paintings show a dog, waddling ducks, hopping hens, a racing goat, a braying donkey, and other eager-faced farm animals that the little girl narrator says she loves. Animal stories don't get more elemental than this. Explore the farm with Janice Boland's *Annabel*, Dee Dee Duffy's *Barnyard Tracks*, Lois Ehlert's *Color Farm*, Denise Fleming's *Barnyard Banter*, Wendy Cheyette Lewison's *Going to Sleep on the Farm*, Valerie Reddix's *Millie and the Mud Hole*, Jill Runcie's *Cock-a-Doodle-Doo!*, and Martin Waddell's *The Pig in the Pond*. There's also a version of *Old MacDonald Had a Farm* for every taste, such as those by Lorinda Bryan Cauley, Nancy Hellen, Carol Jones, Tracey Campbell Pearson, and Gus Clarke's *EIEIO: The Story of Old MacDonald, Who Had a Farm*. DOMESTIC ANIMALS.

31   McMillan, Bruce. *One, Two, One Pair!* Photos by the author. Scholastic, 1991. ISBN 0-590-43767-4

Two eyes make a pair, as do two feet, socks, shoes, and skates. It's not until the last page that you realize the child photographed getting dressed for ice skating is a pair too: twins! Children can point out other pairs, and move up to trios or quartets. Suzanne Aker's *What Comes in 2's, 3's & 4's?* and Rick Walton's *How Many, How Many, How Many* are additional number identification books. For more twins, read Beverly Cleary's *The Growing-Up Feet*. COUNTING BOOKS. TWINS.

32   Mansell, Dom. *My Old Teddy.* Illus. by the author. Candlewick, 1992. ISBN 1-56402-035-5

A little girl's mother is the teddy doctor, and she makes the shopworn bear better each time another of his limbs is pulled off. Kids who identify with the girl's attachment to her bedraggled toy will repeat the "Poor old teddy" refrain. Great with Jez Alborough's *Where's My Teddy?* Another worn-out bear gets fixed up in Barbara Douglas's *Good as New,* and a stuffed elephant in Nicola Smee's *The Tusk Fairy.* CHANTABLE REFRAIN. TEDDY BEARS.

33   Miller, Margaret. *Can You Guess?* Photos by the author. Greenwillow, 1993. ISBN 0-688-11181-5

For each question asked about objects children use, viewers are given four possible answers, all of them ridiculous, shown in a four-paneled page of color photos. The next full page shows the correct answer. Miller's *Guess Who?* and *Where Does It Go?,* plus Niki Yektai's *What's Missing?* and *What's Silly?* all get children laughing and talking. MULTICULTURAL STORIES. QUESTIONS AND ANSWERS. VOCABULARY.

34   Miller, Virginia. *Eat Your Dinner!* Illus. by the author. Candlewick, 1992. ISBN 1-56402-121-1

Bear George wants Bartholomew to eat dinner, but the little bear just says "NAH!"—until he learns there will be no dessert—a familiar scenario for all those kids who are tempted enough by the vision of dessert to clean their plates too. Chris L. Demarest's *No Peas for Nellie,* Dr. Seuss's *Green Eggs and Ham,* and Mitchell Sharmat's *Gregory the Terrible Eater* will appeal to picky eaters, while Cheryl Chapman's *Pass the Fritters, Critters* will teach a few manners. BEARS. FOOD.

35   Mother Goose. *Little Robin Redbreast: A Mother Goose Rhyme.* Illus. by Shari Halpern. North-South, 1994. ISBN 1-55858-248-7

Calico cat chases robin, but the bird gets away. This simplest of Mother Goose rhymes—actually one of the first ever published, circa 1800—features charming, oversized cut-paper collages. Put together some paper springtime flowers with your kids, a petal at a time. Kay Chorao's *Mother Goose Magic* has six more extended illustrated rhymes. Lois Ehlert's *Feathers for Lunch* features another hungry bird-chasing cat. BIRDS–POETRY. CATS–POETRY. NURSERY RHYMES.

36   Mueller, Virginia. *Monster's Birthday Hiccups.* Illus. by Lynn Munsinger. Albert Whitman, 1991. ISBN 0-8075-5267-4

Everyone offers a cure when Monster gets hiccups at his birthday party, but wishing on his cake candles finally cures him. Children can chant his "Hic! Hic!" refrain, and think up new solutions for this absurd condition. BIRTHDAYS. HICCUPS. MONSTERS. PARTIES.

37   Mwenye Hadithi. *Baby Baboon.* Illus. by Adrienne Kennaway. Little, Brown, 1993. ISBN 0-316-33729-3

Chased and caught by a hungry leopard, Baby Baboon is released thanks to the quick thinking of Velvet Monkey. Eileen Christelow's *Five Little Monkeys Sitting in a Tree* and Paul Galdone's folktale *The Monkey and the Crocodile* will keep kids in a jungle mood. BABOONS. HARES. LEOPARDS. TRICKSTER TALES.

38   Paxton, Tom. *Where's the Baby?* Illus. by Mark Graham. Morrow, 1993. ISBN 0-688-10693-5

We follow a tow-headed toddler as she gets ready for bed, first eating dinner, playing with cans in the kitchen, doing a jigsaw, reading a story with dad, and having a bath. What's fun is that the baby is always one step ahead of the rhyme, and children will love answering each page of questions with an emphatic "No" and then asking again, "Where's the baby?" Spot other feisty babies in Trish Cooke's *So Much,* Jeffie Ross Gordon's *Two Badd Babies,* Pat Hutchins's monster-themed *Where's the Baby?,* James Stevenson's *Rolling Rose,* and Vera B. Williams's *"More More More," Said the Baby: Three Love Stories,* and see how Daniel gets his baby sister to stop crying in Frieda Wishinsky's *Oonga Boonga.* BABIES. BEDTIME STORIES. CALL-AND-RESPONSE STORIES. CHANTABLE REFRAIN. STORIES IN RHYME.

39   Raffi. *Five Little Ducks.* Illus. by Jose Aruego and Ariane Dewey. Crown, 1988. ISBN 0-517-56945-0

The music to this old children's song is on the last page so you can sing this sad story about Mother Duck's brood who leave her one by one, but reappear in the end with their own new ducklings in tow. Two more favorite subtraction chants include Eileen Christelow's *Five Little Monkeys Jumping on the Bed* and *Five Little Monkeys Sitting in a Tree,* and *Ten Pink Piglets: Garth Pig's Wall Song* by Mary Rayner is another one you'll sing again and again. Count up again with Keith Baker's nursery rhyme *Big Fat Hen.* See how ducklings spend their first night away from the nest in *All Night Near the Water* by Jim Arnosky, and help Little Duck find a good place to swim in *Too Much* by Dorothy Stott. COUNTING BOOKS. DUCKS. SONGS. SUBTRACTION.

40   Reiser, Lynn. *Any Kind of Dog.* Illus. by the author. Greenwillow, 1992. ISBN 0-688-10915-2

Richard's mother says a dog is too much trouble, so she gives him a spate of animals—stuffed, as it turns out—that look a little like dogs, from a caterpillar to a lion, until she breaks down and gives him what he wants. Children will be able to chant the entire patterned story with you, and will identify each new animal before you say its name. From the 636.7 shelf in the library, find a nice big book with color photographs that show each breed of dog. Children can decide which dog they'd choose. Livingston Taylor's *Can I Be Good?* shows how much trouble and fun a dog can be. CHANTABLE REFRAIN. DOGS. PETS.

41   Runcie, Jill. *Cock-a-Doodle-Doo!* Illus. by Lee Lorenz. Simon & Schuster, 1991. ISBN 0-671-72602-1

Though Farmer Jones depends on the rooster to wake him up each morning, it's actually the owl that hoots and wakes the woodpecker who pecks and wakes the duck who quacks and wakes the frog who croaks and wakes the pig, and so on until the dog wakes the rooster who crows, finally. The zany watercolors will make everyone laugh and ask to see it again. Assign parts and act out this story in a long line, with each creature waking up in turn and waking up the next one. Farmer Bill's rooster won't crow in Patricia Brennan Demuth's *The Ornery Morning*. Jim Aylesworth's *Hush Up* and Byron Barton's *Buzz Buzz Buzz* are farm tales that come full circle. Go to bed with Kathleen Sullivan Carroll's *One Red Rooster* and Wendy Cheyette Lewison's *Going to Sleep on the Farm*. Denise Fleming's *Barnyard Banter*, Martin Waddell's *The Pig in the Pond*, and Andrea Zimmerman and David Clemesha's *The Cow Buzzed* are good for making noise. CAUSE AND EFFECT. CREATIVE DRAMA. DOMESTIC ANIMALS. FARM LIFE.

42 **Rydell, Katy. *Wind Says Good Night*. Illus. by David Jorgensen. Houghton Mifflin, 1994. ISBN 0-395-60474-5**

The night wind asks cloud to "cover the earth so Moon will stop shining so Moth will stop dancing so Frog will stop strumming so Cricket will stop playing so Mockingbird will stop singing so the child can go to sleep." The gentle pencil drawings and sweet cumulative story will make everyone long for a snooze, though it's also a fine one to act out. *Can't You Sleep, Little Bear?* by Martin Waddell is another reassuring bedtime tale. BEDTIME STORIES. CREATIVE DRAMA. CUMULATIVE STORIES. NIGHT.

43 **Shapiro, Arnold L. *Who Says That?* Illus. by Monica Wellington. Dutton, 1991. ISBN 0-525-44698-2**

"Monkeys chatter. Cats purr. Lions roar. Hummingbirds whir . . . But girls and boys make different noise!" Twenty more animal noises accompany attractive and colorful illustrations, and everyone will want to join right in. Wear out your voices with *Polar Bear, Polar Bear, What Do You Hear?* by Bill Martin, Jr., *Do Bunnies Talk?* by Dayle-Ann Dodds, and *The Listening Walk* by Paul Showers, and find out how these animals sound in different languages with *Who Says a Dog Goes Bow-Wow?* by Hank De Zutter and Marc Robinson's *Cock-a-Doodle-Doo! What Does It Sound Like to You?* ANIMALS. CHANTABLE REFRAIN. NOISE. SOUND EFFECTS. STORIES IN RHYME.

44 **Sheppard, Jeff. *Splash, Splash*. Illus. by Dennis Panek. Macmillan, 1994. ISBN 0-02-782455-1**

One at a time, a bee, mouse, pig, dog, cow, duck, cat, and frog fall into the water with a splash and a buzz or squeak or oink or another predictable animal exclamation. Children will love chanting each splashy refrain, and can compose new verses to chant about other clumsy creatures. Stay wet with Charlotte Pomerantz's *The Piggy in the Puddle*. Kathleen Sullivan Carroll's *One Red Rooster*, Charles Causley's *"Quack!" said the Billy Goat*, and Andrea Zimmerman and David Clemesha's *The Cow Buzzed* are also nice and noisy. ANIMALS. SOUND EFFECTS. STORIES IN RHYME.

45 Smee, Nicola. *The Tusk Fairy*. Illus. by the author. BridgeWater, 1994. ISBN 0-8167-3312-0

Lizzie's beloved knitted elephant that Grandma gave her on the day she was born begins to unravel until all that is left is the two tusks, which she puts under her pillow. The next day (after Grandma's all-night knitting marathon), there's a new elephant with a nice green trunk (the gray wool ran out), and, as in Barbara Douglas's *Good as New* and Dom Mansell's *My Old Teddy*, all's right with the world again. Children can bring in their oldest toy animals to admire. ELEPHANTS. GRANDMOTHERS. STUFFED ANIMALS. TOOTH FAIRY.

46 Stevenson, James. *Rolling Rose*. Illus. by the author. Greenwillow, 1992. ISBN 0-688-10675-7

In rhythmic prose that reads like poetry, we cheer for the baby in her rolling stroller, the "Rosemobile," when she rolls out the door too fast to catch and spearheads a parade of 85 babies rolling like thunder down a country lane. Watch more babies act up in Trish Cooke's *So Much*, Jeffie Ross Gordon's *Two Badd Babies*, Pat Hutchins's monster-themed *Where's the Baby?*, Kevin Henkes's *Julius, the Baby of the World*, Barbro Lindgren's *The Wild Baby*, Tom Paxton's *Where's the Baby?*, James Stevenson's *Worse Than Willy*, Vera B. Williams's *"More More More," Said the Baby: Three Love Stories*, and Frieda Wishinsky's *Oonga Boonga*. BABIES.

47 Stott, Dorothy. *Too Much*. Illus. by the author. Dutton, 1990. ISBN 0-525-44569-2

There's something unsuitable about all the comical places Little Duck tries to swim, such as in a pickle jar and in the dishes-filled sink, until he ends up in the pond. Ask your listeners to name other liquids where Little Duck might swim, and use a "describing word" to tell you what's wrong with them (Syrup? Too sticky. Apple juice? Too sweet.) What a sneaky way to teach about adjectives! Wander a bit more with *All Night Near the Water* by Jim Arnosky, *The Chick and the Duckling* by Mirra Ginsburg, *The Hungry Fox and the Foxy Duck* by Kathleen Leverich, *Five Little Ducks* by Raffi, and *Three Ducks Went Wandering* by Ron Roy. DUCKS. ENGLISH LANGUAGE–GRAMMAR. SWIMMING.

48 Waddell, Martin. *The Happy Hedgehog Band*. Illus. by Jill Barton. Candlewick, 1992. ISBN 1-56402-011-8

Harry Hedgehog's drum makes such a nice noise that three other hedgehogs make drums and play together in the woods. Divide children into four drum-noise groups: Tum-tum-te-tum, Diddle-dum-dum, Ratta-tat-tat, and BOOM. Keep the band going with Pamela Allen's *Bertie and the Bear*, David Kherdian's *The Cat's Midsummer Jamboree*, and Al Perkins's *Hand, Hand, Fingers, Thumb*. In *Hedgehog for Breakfast* by Ann Turner, there's a misunderstanding when a fox family invites Mrs. Hedgehog for a meal. ANIMALS. CHANTABLE REFRAIN. HEDGEHOGS. MUSIC. SOUND EFFECTS.

49 Waddell, Martin. *Owl Babies*. Illus. by Patrick Benson. Candlewick, 1992. ISBN 1-56402-101-7

When Owl Mother goes out hunting and doesn't come back, her three worried baby owls perch together on a branch and await her return. Large, stunning crosshatched illustrations portray perfectly their fear and anxiety. Children traumatized at being left behind will find comfort here and with Linda Wagner Tyler's *Waiting for Mom*. MOTHERS. NIGHT. OWLS. SEPARATION ANXIETY.

50 **Waddell, Martin.** *The Pig in the Pond.* **Illus. by Jill Barton. Candlewick, 1992. ISBN 1-56402-050-9**

To the accompaniment of the quacking ducks and honking geese, old farmer Nelligan's pig gets so hot he jumps in the pond, and so do the rest of the animals and Nelligan too. Examine more un-piglike behavior in Arthur Getz's *Humphrey the Dancing Pig*, Daniel Pinkwater's *Three Big Hogs*, Charlotte Pomerantz's *The Piggy in the Puddle*, and Valerie Reddix's *Millie and the Mud Hole*. All the animals get in the act in John Burningham's *Mr. Gumpy's Outing* too, while Dee Dee Duffy's *Barnyard Tracks*, Denise Fleming's *Barnyard Banter* and Jill Runcie's *Cock-a-Doodle-Doo!* are also noisy. DOMESTIC ANIMALS. FARM LIFE. PIGS. SOUND EFFECTS. SWIMMING.

51 **Waddell, Martin.** *Sam Vole and His Brothers.* **Illus. by Barbara Firth. Candlewick, 1992. ISBN 1-56402-082-7**

Much to his annoyance, every time Sam Vole tries to go out voling by himself for nuts, grass, or daisies, his two brothers join him and bring home more than he does. But when he finally gets out on his own, he finds it's more fun to vole with them. Take the class out for playtime and pretend you're voling. Play mouse games with Waddell's *Squeak-a-Lot* and Denise Fleming's *Lunch*. BROTHERS. LONELINESS. VOLES.

52 **Waddell, Martin.** *Squeak-a-Lot.* **Illus. by Virginia Miller. Greenwillow, 1991. ISBN 0-688-10245-X**

A small mouse looking for a playmate plays Buzz-a-lot with a bee, Woof-a-lot with a bassett hound, Cluck-a-lot with a chicken, and WHAM! BAM! SCRAM! with a cat before he finds other mouse companions to whom he teaches his new games, ending up with Sleep-a-lot. Children will love making all the animal noises with the winsome gray mouse, and thinking up new animals he could play with. Enjoy the company of mice with *Lunch* by Denise Fleming, *Thump and Plunk* by Janice May Udry, *Mouse Count* and *Mouse Paint* by Ellen Stoll Walsh, and *The Little Mouse, the Red Ripe Strawberry, and the Big Hungry Bear* by Don and Audrey Wood. Voles are fun too, as we see in Waddell's *Sam Vole and His Brothers*. ANIMALS. MICE. PLAY. SOUND EFFECTS.

53 **Walsh, Ellen Stoll.** *Hop Jump.* **Illus. by the author. Harcourt, 1993. ISBN 0-15-292871-5**

"No room for dancing," the green frogs tell blue frog Betsy, but she shows them there's room for dancing and hopping. Act this one out to music and invent some new moves along with the normal leaping, turning, and twisting. Keep moving with Rachel Isadora's *Max* and George Shannon's *Dance Away*. Another animal who does the unexpected is *The Pig in the Pond* by Martin Waddell. And more personable frogs cavort through Catherine Bancroft and Hannah Coale Gruenberg's *Felix's Hat* and Robert Kalan's *Jump, Frog, Jump*. CREATIVE DRAMA. DANCING. FROGS. INDIVIDUALITY.

54   Walsh, Ellen Stoll. *Mouse Count.* **Illus. by the author. Harcourt, 1991. ISBN 0-15-256023-8**

While ten sleepy mice nap in the meadow, a hungry snake captures them in his glass jar, counting as he adds each one. Get yourself a glass jar and ten toy mice so children can act out the story, "uncounting" each mouse as they rock the jar to escape. Stories like this are also heaven-sent for flannelboards. Count up and back again with Loreen Leedy's *A Number of Dragons*. In Libba Moore Gray's *Small Green Snake* and Faith McNulty's *A Snake in the House* it's the snake that gets captured and escapes. Keith Baker's *Big Fat Hen*, Kathleen Sullivan Carroll's *One Red Rooster*, Denise Fleming's *Count!*, and Woodleigh Hubbard's *2 Is for Dancing: A 1 2 3 of Actions* are all beginning counting books. COUNTING BOOKS. MICE. SNAKES.

55   Wellington, Monica. *Mr. Cookie Baker.* **Illus. by the author. Dutton, 1992. ISBN 0-525-44965-5**

Early every morning, Mr. Cookie Baker mixes his dough, cuts out shapes with cookie cutters, and bakes up delicious browned batches for his hungry young customers. The simplest of texts coupled with sturdy and colorful gouache illustrations make it a natural for acting out as you read. There's a nice frosted sugar cookie recipe at the back in case you can't resist baking with the kids. *If You Give a Mouse a Cookie* by Laura Joffe Numeroff is an obvious treat as well. COOKERY. CREATIVE DRAMA. FOOD.

56   Whybrow, Ian. *Quacky Quack-Quack!* **Illus. by Russell Ayto. Four Winds, 1991. ISBN 0-02-792741-5**

Ducks quack and geese honk when a baby starts to eat the bread his mommy gave him for the birds, and the noises escalate, with the band tooting, donkeys ee-aw-ing, dogs woofing, snakes sss-ssss-ing, and the whole zoo in an uproar, until the baby's big brother intervenes. Get ready for some loud sounds. *Bertie and the Bear* by Pamela Allen, *All the Way Home* by Lore Segal, and *Squeak-a-Lot* by Martin Waddell are all good noisy stories that are also fun to tell. ANIMALS. BABIES. DUCKS. SOUND EFFECTS. STORIES TO TELL.

57   Williams, Sue. *I Went Walking.* **Illus. by Julie Vivas. Gulliver/Harcourt, 1990. ISBN 0-15-200471-8**

"I went walking. What did you see? I saw a black cat looking at me." Large, soft watercolors take us on a spiky-headed child's animal walk. Though very similar in scope to Bill Martin, Jr.'s *Brown Bear, Brown Bear, What Do You See?*, this will indeed prove popular to act out with children, who can recall the sequence and add new animals and colors. Other simple animal color stories to consider include Dayle Ann Dodds's *The Color Box*, Lois Ehlert's *Color Farm* and *Color Zoo*, Merle Peek's *Mary Wore Her Red Dress and Henry Wore His Green Sneakers*, Mary Serfozo's *Who Said Red?*, and Ellen Stoll Walsh's *Mouse Paint*. ANIMALS. CALL-AND-RESPONSE STORIES. CHANTABLE REFRAIN. COLOR. STORIES IN RHYME.

58   Williams, Vera B. *"More More More," Said the Baby: Three Love Stories.* Illus. by the author. Greenwillow, 1990. ISBN 0-688-09174-1

In a multicultural gem about a white, a black, and an Asian child, there are three short charming tales of toddlers and the grownups who love them, illustrated with primitive gouache paintings and hand-lettering. Deliver more affection and tickles with Laurence Pringle's *Octopus Hug* and fall in love with the babies in Trish Cooke's *So Much*, Pat Hutchins's monster-ish *Where's the Baby?*, Tom Paxton's *Where's the Baby?*, James Stevenson's *Rolling Rose*, and Frieda Wishinsky's *Oonga Boonga*. BABIES. BEDTIME STORIES. FAMILY LIFE. LOVE. MULTICULTURAL STORIES.

59   Wood, Don, and Audrey Wood. *Piggies.* Illus. by Don Wood. Harcourt, 1991. ISBN 0-15-256341-5

In a new chant that might just usurp "This Little Piggie Went to Market," we meet the fat, smart, long, silly, and wee piggies that are sometimes hot, cold, dirty, clean, and good as they dance on fingers and toes. The huge vibrant paintings are uproarious, and children will want to hear the story more than once as they fool with their own fingers. This one would be fun to do with finger puppets. For more fingerplay, delve into Marc Brown's *Hand Rhymes* and *Finger Rhymes* and Joanna Cole and Stephanie Calmenson's *The Eentsy, Weentsy Spider: Fingerplays and Action Rhymes.* Meet some messy porcines in Charlotte Pomerantz's *The Piggy in the Puddle*, and Valerie Reddix's *Millie and the Mud Hole.* BEDTIME STORIES. FINGER-PLAYS. GAMES. PIGS.

60   Wood, Don, and Audrey Wood. *The Little Mouse, the Red Ripe Strawberry, and the Big Hungry Bear.* Illus. by Don Wood. Child's Play, 1990. ISBN 0-685-56131-3

An unseen narrator addresses a mouse as it ventures forth with a ladder to pick a strawberry, warning him about the big, hungry bear who can smell a just-picked strawberry a mile away, no matter where or how it's hidden. Bring in a basket of strawberries and do just as the mouse does: cut each in two and share. Dine and play with mice in *Mouse in the House* by Patricia Baehr, *Lunch* by Denise Fleming and *Squeak-a-Lot* by Martin Waddell. FRUIT. MICE.

61   Young, Ruth. *Who Says Moo?* Illus. by Lisa Campbell Ernst. Viking, 1994. ISBN 0-670-85162-0

An elemental animal identification story in rhyme, this one will charm children into calling out the names of the 24 animals described and pictured in the sweet-tempered watercolors. Read this twice—once for the animals, and once for the rhyme. More animals await identification in Stephanie Calmenson's *It Begins with an A* and *What Am I?*, Beatrice Schenk de Regniers's *It Does Not Say Meow and*

Other Animal Riddle Rhymes, and Deborah Guarino's *Is Your Mama a Llama?* Children can each select and draw a secret animal and think of a "who" question for others to guess. ANIMALS. QUESTIONS AND ANSWERS. STORIES IN RHYME.

From OWEN by Kevin Henkes. Copyright © 1993 by Kevin Henkes.
Reprinted by permission of Greenwillow Books,
a division of William Morrow & Company, Inc.

FICTION FOR PRESCHOOL–KINDERGARTEN

---

62 Aker, Suzanne. *What Comes in 2's, 3's & 4's?* Illus. by Bernie Karlin. Simon & Schuster, 1990. ISBN 0-671-67173-1

Using concrete examples, clear illustrations, and a simply stated text, Aker connects the numbers two, three, and four to everyday situations and observations; e.g., "You have 2 eyes, 2 ears, 2 arms . . ." or "Birds have 2 wings. And so do airplanes." *Mother Earth's Counting Book* by Andrew Clements, *Count* by Denise Fleming, *Only One* by Marc Harshman, *Ten Potatoes in a Pot and Other Counting Rhymes* by Michael Jay Katz, and *How Many, How Many, How Many* by Rick Walton are all practical counting books. Children can continue the format story by coming up with sets of five, six, and higher and illustrating each. COUNTING BOOKS.

63 Alborough, Jez. *It's the Bear!* Illus. by the author. Candlewick, 1994. ISBN 1-56402-486-5

In the sequel to *Where's My Teddy?*, Eddie is reluctant to follow Mom into the woods for a picnic because he's scared of the great big bear that lives there. Mom runs back to get the forgotten blueberry pie, and when the ravenous bear and his teddy stride onto the page, Eddie hides in the picnic basket. The huge bear illustrations and the rhyming text make for pure delight at storytime. Compare the berry-loving bear and Eddie with the cub and tot in Robert McCloskey's classic *Blueberries for Sal.* Chase away a few bears and assuage your listeners' fears with *Cully Cully and the Bear* by Wilson Gage, *We're Going on a Bear Hunt* by Michael Rosen, *I'm Going on a Bear Hunt* by Sandra Stroner Sivulich, and the Goldilocks turnabout *Deep in the Forest* by Brinton Turkle. BEARS. FEAR. PICNICS. STORIES IN RHYME. TEDDY BEARS.

64 Anholt, Catherine, and Laurence Anholt. *Kids.* Illus. by the authors. Candlewick, 1992. ISBN 0-56402-097-5

A rhyming description of what kids are really like, what they do, where they hide, what's in their pockets, what scares them, and what they dream of. Surely your kids will have more to add as they ponder their own kid-hoods. Also read their *All About You* and *What Makes Me Happy?* CHILDREN. INDIVIDUALITY. MULTICULTURAL STORIES. STORIES IN RHYME.

65   Anholt, Catherine, and Laurence Anholt. *What Makes Me Happy?* Illus. by Catherine and Laurence Anholt. Candlewick, 1995. ISBN 1-56402-482-2

As in the Anholts' *All About You* and *Kids*, we meet a varied crew of children and find out what makes them tick. Each child provides a list of what makes him or her laugh, cry, bored, proud, jealous, scared, sad, excited, shy, mad, and, finally, happy. Woodleigh Hubbard's *C Is for Curious: An ABC of Feelings* and Jeanne Modesitt's *Sometimes I Feel Like a Mouse: A Book About Feelings* will help you extend your discussion of children's emotions and why they feel the way they do. EMOTIONS. MULTICULTURAL STORIES. STORIES IN RHYME.

66   Appelt, Kathi. *Elephants Aloft.* Illus. by Keith Baker. Harcourt, 1993. ISBN 0-15-225384-X

After receiving a letter from Auntie Rwanda, elephants Rama and Raja cast off in their hot-air balloon and travel above the town, through the clouds, behind a waterfall, and across an ocean to visit her. The story is told through the large, cheerful paintings, with but a single preposition on each page. Children will need to use each word to describe the action, and then act out each situation. Use with Stan and Jan Berenstain's *Inside, Outside, Upside Down*, Cheryl Chapman's *Snow on Snow on Snow*, and Margaret Miller's *Where Does It Go?* and *Where's Jenna?* CREATIVE DRAMA. ELEPHANTS. ENGLISH LANGUAGE–PREPOSITIONS. VOCABULARY.

67   Arnosky, Jim. *All Night Near the Water.* Illus. by the author. Putnam, 1994. ISBN 0-399-22629-X

As evening falls, mother mallard leads her dozen ducklings from their nest in the meadow grass to the lake where they spend their first night observing the other animals before falling asleep. Luminous closeup watercolors make this a memorable slice of nature. See what the other animals are up to in *In the Small, Small Pond* by Denise Fleming and *Box Turtle at Long Pond* by William T. George. Sing the disappearing duckling song *Five Little Ducks* by Raffi and giggle with one duckling's search for swimmable substances in *Too Much* by Dorothy Stott. DUCKS. POND LIFE.

68   Baehr, Patricia. *Mouse in the House.* Illus. by Laura Lydecker. Holiday House, 1994. ISBN 0-8234-1102-8

Contented with her nightly routine of a good book, a cup of spice tea, and a slice of chocolate cake, Mrs. Teapot overreacts when she sees a mouse chewing her pages, nibbling her cake, and sipping her tea. As in Joanna Cole's *It's Too Noisy!*, Julia Donaldson's *A Squash and a Squeeze*, and Ann McGovern's *Too Much Noise*, she brings in other, messier animals before settling for life with mouse. After introducing Mrs. Teapot's problem, ask for suggestion from your listeners on how they'd solve it. *Lunch* by Denise Fleming, *If You Give a Mouse a Cookie* by Laura Numeroff, and *The Little Mouse, the Red Ripe Strawberry, and the Big Hungry Bear* by Don and Audrey Wood feature more mice with appetites. MICE. PETS.

69   Ballard, Robin. *Good-bye, House.* Illus. by the author. Greenwillow, 1994. ISBN 0-688-12526-3

A little girl takes us through her house as she says good-bye before she moves away, recalling in words and wistful watercolors her good memories of each room. Children having a hard time leaving will appreciate this tribute to a beloved house. Similar in scope to Frank Asch's *Goodbye House*, this also works with others on the same wavelength such as *Maggie Doesn't Want to Move* by Elizabeth Lee O'Donnell, *Moving* by Michael Rosen, and *Anna's Secret Friend* by Yuriko Tsutsui. HOUSES. MOVING, HOUSEHOLD.

70 **Bancroft, Catherine, and Hannah Coale Gruenberg.** *Felix's Hat.* **Illus. by Hannah Coale Gruenberg. Four Winds, 1993. ISBN 0-02-708325-X**

The rest of Felix's frog family tries to make it up to him when he loses his favorite orange hat at the beach, but it's not until his brother comes up with a new red hat that he's content again. Use with Shirley Hughes's *Dogger*. Frog fans will appreciate Jonathan London's *Froggy Gets Dressed* and *Let's Go, Froggy*, while hat losers will want to hear Joan L. Nodset's *Who Took the Farmer's Hat?*, Howie Schneider's *Uncle Lester's Hat*, and, naturally, Esphyr Slobodkina's *Caps for Sale*. BROTHERS AND SISTERS. FROGS. HATS. LOST. SEASHORE.

71 **Brown, Marc.** *D.W. Thinks Big.* **Illus. by the author. Joy Street / Little, Brown, 1993. ISBN 0-316-11305-0**

Arthur's feisty little sister D.W. ends up in her Aunt Lucy's wedding after all when ring-bearer Arthur drops the ring down a heating grate on the way down the aisle and D.W. retrieves it. Some of your children will have wedding experiences they can relate. Introduce all to the series of books about both Arthur and D.W. BROTHERS AND SISTERS. SIZE. WEDDINGS.

72 **Bunting, Eve.** *Flower Garden.* **Illus. by Kathryn Hewitt. Harcourt, 1994. ISBN 0-15-228776-0**

A little girl describes in simple rhyme how she and Dad buy plants at the market, bring them home by bus, and plant a beautiful flowering windowbox for Mom's birthday surprise. Work this into a Mother's Day planting project with seedlings, and plant a classroom windowbox to brighten everyone's mood. Once you're in the planting frame of mind, continue with Zoe Hall's *It's Pumpkin Time*, Anita Lobel's *Alison's Zinnia*, which matches flowers with girls' names, and Arnold Lobel's *The Rose in My Garden*, a cumulative tale of various blooms. *Bean and Plant* by Christine Back, *From Seed to Plant* by Gail Gibbons, and *The Reason for a Flower* by Ruth Heller provide some basic facts. Guess what Rachel has planned for a present in *Tomorrow Is Daddy's Birthday* by Ginger Wadsworth. AFRICAN AMERICANS. BIRTHDAYS. CITIES AND TOWNS. GARDENING. STORIES IN RHYME.

73 **Calmenson, Stephanie.** *Dinner at the Panda Palace.* **Illus. by Nadine Bernard Westcott. HarperCollins, 1991. ISBN 0-06-021011-7**

Animal diners in parties of one to ten arrive at Mr. Panda's restaurant, and somehow he accommodates all 55 of them, and even one more, in this delightful rhyming story. As each group arrives, count them, using physical and pictorial models such as flannel board pieces to represent the numbers. Children can think up fitting main courses for each set of animals. Keep feeding with *One Hungry Monster: A Counting Book in Rhyme* by Susan Heyboer O'Keefe. The hungry diners in Nancy Shaw's rhyming *Sheep Out to Eat* don't have as much luck in their tea room visit. ANIMALS. COUNTING BOOKS. PANDAS. RESTAURANTS. STORIES IN RHYME.

74   **Calmenson, Stephanie. *It Begins with an A*. Illus. by Marisabina Russo. Hyperion, 1993. ISBN 1-56282-123-7**

"This red rubber toy begins with a B./ It's round. It bounces. You throw it to me." Each page of this alphabet book guessing game contains a four-paneled illustration with a rhyming clue as to what each object is, and ending with the question "What is it?" The last two pages list and picture each object. See how many your class can recall without looking. Other rhyming riddle books include Beatrice Schenk de Regniers's *It Does Not Say Meow and Other Animal Riddle Rhymes*, Robin Michal Koontz's *I See Something You Don't See*, Bonnie Larkin Nims's *Just Beyond Reach and Other Riddle Poems*, and Ruth Young's *Who Says Moo?* Calmenson's *What Am I? Very First Riddles* is also easy to solve. ALPHABET BOOKS. RIDDLES. STORIES IN RHYME.

75   **Carle, Eric. *The Very Quiet Cricket*. Illus. by the author. Philomel, 1990. ISBN 0-399-21885-8**

Though he rubs his wings together to greet all the insects who wish him a good day, the little cricket can't make a sound until he encounters a quiet female cricket. As in Carle's *Papa, Please Get the Moon for Me, The Very Grouchy Ladybug, The Very Busy Spider,* and *The Very Hungry Caterpillar,* this is as simple as a story could be, with lots of repetitions that kids can recite, and a gimmick. When you open to the last page, the book chirps, thanks to a little black plastic device glued in the back cover. Meet insects close up in *"Leave That Cricket Be, Alan Lee"* by Barbara Ann Porte and *Mary Ann* by Betsy James. CHANTABLE REFRAIN. CRICKETS. INSECTS. SOUND EFFECTS.

76   **Carlstrom, Nancy White. *How Do You Say It Today, Jesse Bear?* Illus. by Bruce Degen. Macmillan, 1992. ISBN 0-02-717276-7**

A joyous rhyming description of how the young bear says "I love you" to his parents at each month and major holiday of the year. Pour on the good feelings with *Koala Lou* by Mem Fox and *Little Monster* by Barrie Wade. Review the holidays with *December Twenty-Fourth* by Denys Cazet, and enjoy each month with *Jump for Joy: A Book of Months* by Megan Halsey. BEARS. HOLIDAYS. LOVE. MONTHS. STORIES IN RHYME.

77   **Caseley, Judith. *Sophie and Sammy's Library Sleepover*. Illus. by the author. Greenwillow, 1993. ISBN 0-688-10616-1**

Sophie adores the nighttime library storytime with librarian Mrs. Terry, and feels guilty about her little brother Sammy staying home until she plans a special bedroom program just for him. Play Tom Chapins's wonderful "Library Song" from his

Family Tree album. Reinforce how terrific books and libraries are with Caroline Feller Bauer's *Too Many Books*, Crosby Bonsall's *Tell Me Some More*, Sue Felt's *Rosa-Too-Little*, Barbara A. Huff's *Once Inside the Library*, and Julia L. Sauer's *Mike's House*. BEDTIME STORIES. BOOKS AND READING. BROTHERS AND SISTERS. LIBRARIES.

78   Cauley, Lorinda Bryan. *Old MacDonald Had a Farm*. Illus. by the author. Putnam, 1989. ISBN 0-399-21628-6

In this version, the plump and contented farmer and his wife go through a typical animal-filled farm day, ending up with baby kittens and mama cat nestled on MacDonald's easy chair. See also the versions by Nancy Hellen, Carol Jones, Tracey Campbell Pearson, and Glen Rounds, and Gus Clarke's *EIEIO: The Story of Old MacDonald, Who Had a Farm*. Identify the animals in Lois Ehlert's *Color Farm*. Good country cousins include Denise Fleming's *Barnyard Banter*, Kathy Parkinson's and Mary Maki Rae's versions of *The Farmer in the Dell*, Martin Waddell's *The Pig in the Pond*, and Nadine Bernard Westcott's *Skip to My Lou*. Demonstrate the noises animals make in other countries with Hank De Zutter's *Who Says a Dog Goes Bow-Wow?* CHANTABLE REFRAIN. DOMESTIC ANIMALS. FARM LIFE. FOLK SONGS. SOUND EFFECTS.

79   Cauley, Lorinda Bryan. *Treasure Hunt*. Illus. by the author. Putnam, 1994. ISBN 0-399-22447-5

At Bear's house, a group of ten kids and animals congregate to read and solve a series of rhyming clues, which lead them through the house and outside into a clearing where Bear awaits them with a picnic treat. Eric Carle's *The Secret Birthday Message* and Ann Jonas's *The 13th Clue* provide more clues to follow, while Linda Bourke's *Eye Spy*, Ruth Brown's *If at First You Do Not See*, Tana Hoban's *Look Again!* and *Look! Look! Look!*, and Tomi Ungerer's *One, Two, Where's My Shoe?* will strengthen viewers' visual perception skills. Set up a series of rebus messages for your class to examine and follow, leading to their own treat. Tuck in a couple of birthday poems from *Birthday Rhymes, Special Times* selected by Bobbye S. Goldstein and *Happy Birthday*, selected by Lee Bennett Hopkins. PICNICS. STORIES IN RHYME. VISUAL PERCEPTION. WORD GAMES.

80   Cazet, Denys. "*I'm Not Sleepy*." Illus. by the author. Orchard, 1992. ISBN 0-531-08498-1

Father tells Alex his "no-matter-how-wide-awake-you-are-I-can-make-you-sleepy sleepy story" about a little boy exploring the boily, boily jungle. Ask children to share the stories their parents tell at bedtime, like Papa Mouse does in Arnold Lobel's *Mouse Tales*. Encourage them to make up their own bedtime stories, like the title characters in *Petey's Bedtime Story* by Beverly Cleary and *Posy* by Charlotte Pomerantz. BEDTIME STORIES. FATHERS AND SONS. SLEEP. STORYTELLING.

81   Chadwick, Tim. *Cabbage Moon*. Illus. by Piers Harper. Orchard, 1994. ISBN 0-531-06827-7

Albert, a curious bunny who won't eat his cabbage, wonders how the moon changes its shape until he slides up there on a moonbeam one night and discovers it is made of cabbage, nibbled away nightly by zealous rabbits until it becomes a crescent. In the month before reading the story, ask your children to observe the moon each night and describe how it changes, and ask them to speculate on what's happening up there. Frank Asch's *Happy Birthday, Moon* and *Moongame*, Eric Carle's *Papa, Please Get the Moon for Me*, and Edna Mitchell Preston's *Squawk to the Moon, Little Goose* will encourage further bursts of imagination. In Lois Ehlert's Peruvian folktale *Moon Rope*, Fox and Mole climb to the moon, as does Rabbit in Tony Johnston's *The Tale of Rabbit and Coyote*. Don't forget to balance the fun with interesting facts and photos from nonfiction moon books. BEDTIME STORIES. FOOD. IMAGINATION. MOON. RABBITS.

82   Chapman, Cheryl. *Pass the Fritters, Critters*. Illus. by Susan L. Roth. Four Winds, 1993. ISBN 0-02-717975-3

In this simply worded rhyming story, Bunny refuses to pass the honey, Bear declines to pass an éclair, and Parrot denies a request for a carrot, until the little boy learns to say please and thank you. Manners-learning listeners can dish up food requests and make similar-styled collage cut-outs of other animals. Keep rhyming with animals and/or food in Polly Cameron's *"I Can't," Said the Ant*, Katie Evans's *Hunky Dory Ate It*, Christine Loomis's *In the Diner*, Bill Morrison's *Squeeze a Sneeze*, Miriam Nerlove's *I Made a Mistake*, Raffi's *Down by the Bay*, Anne Shelby's alliterative *Potluck*, and John Stadler's *Cat Is Back at Bat*. ANIMALS. ETIQUETTE. FOOD. STORIES IN RHYME.

83   Chapman, Cheryl. *Snow on Snow on Snow*. Illus. by Synthia Saint James. Dial, 1994. ISBN 0-8037-1457-2

Waking up one winter day "under blankets under blankets under blankets," an African American child pulls on "clothes over clothes over clothes" and takes his shaggy dog sled riding in the snow. The repeating prepositions create a winter mood, and your students can imitate the pattern as they describe their daily fun. Prepare for snowy weather with Louise Borden's *Caps, Hats, Socks, and Mittens*, Jan Brett's *The Mitten* and *Trouble with Trolls*, Shirley Nietzel's *The Jacket I Wear in the Snow*, Eve Rice's *Oh, Lewis!*, Jean Rogers's *Runaway Mittens*, and Jonathan London's *Froggy Gets Dressed*. Kathi Appelt's *Elephants Aloft*, Stan and Jan Berenstain's *Inside, Outside, Upside Down*, and Margaret Miller's *Where Does It Go?* and *Where's Jenna?* all offer examples of prepositions. AFRICAN AMERICANS. DOGS. ENGLISH LANGUAGE–PREPOSITIONS. MULTICULTURAL STORIES. SLEDS. SNOW. WINTER.

84   Charles, N. N. *What Am I? Looking Through Shapes at Apples and Grapes*. Illus. by Leo and Diane Dillon. Blue Sky Press, 1994. ISBN 0-590-47891-5

In a handsome and sturdy format, here is a rhyming guessing game of fruits that introduces colors and shapes as well. On the page for the color yellow is a die-cut diamond shape through which we can see part of the answer to the riddle, "I'm yellow, I'm thin, you peel my skin. What am I?" After children have guessed, turn the page to reveal the banana and the plant from which it comes, both painted large and luscious. There's a red apple, orange, green avocado, blueberry, and purple grape, ending with a rainbow. Dayle Ann Dodds's *The Color Box*, Lois

Ehlert's *Color Farm* and *Color Zoo*, Ann Jonas's *Color Dance*, Bruce McMillan's photo-illustrated *Growing Colors*, Merle Peek's *Mary Wore Her Red Dress and Henry Wore His Green Sneakers*, Mary Serfozo's *Who Said Red?*, and Ellen Stoll Walsh's *Mouse Paint* will help you in the color wars. COLOR. FRUIT. SHAPES. TOY AND MOVABLE BOOKS.

85   **Christelow, Eileen.** *Five Little Monkeys Sitting in a Tree.* **Illus. by the author. Clarion, 1991. ISBN 0-395-54434-3**

In a chantable follow-up to *Five Little Monkeys Jumping on the Bed*, the rambunctious monkeys tease Mr. Crocodile and disappear one by one, much to the dismay of their cautious Mama. Paul Galdone's folktale *The Monkey and the Crocodile* and Mwenye Hadithi's *Baby Baboon* bring us more tricky simians in danger. Jump in the water with the counting fools in *Five Silly Fishermen*, an old folktale retold by Roberta Edwards, and count down to zero with *Ten Pink Piglets: Garth Pig's Wall Song* by Mary Rayner. CHANTABLE REFRAIN. COUNTING BOOKS. CROCODILES. MONKEYS. STORIES IN RHYME.

86   **Clarke, Gus.** *EIEIO: The Story of Old MacDonald, Who Had a Farm.* **Illus. by the author. Lothrop, 1993. ISBN 0-688-12215-9**

Here's a cheery version of the old song, with each animal adding its quack, oink, moo, cluck, baa, honk, or woof in cartoon-style balloons, until it gets so noisy the farmer says, "Enough!" In a surprise ending, he sells the lot to farmer McTavish, and now the old guy is perfectly content running a camping site. Other traditional versions include *Old MacDonald Had a Farm* by Lorinda Bryan Cauley, Nancy Hellen, Carol Jones, Tracey Campbell Pearson, and Glen Rounds. Kathy Parkinson's and Mary Maki Rae's versions of *The Farmer in the Dell*, Martin Waddell's *The Pig in the Pond*, and Nadine Bernard Westcott's *Skip to My Lou* will supplement your noisy farm unit, which you can skew a bit with Charles Causley's *"Quack!" said the Billy Goat*, Victoria Forrester's *The Magnificent Moo*, and Andrea Zimmerman and David Clemesha's *The Cow Buzzed*. CHANTABLE REFRAIN. DOMESTIC ANIMALS. FARM LIFE. FOLK SONGS. SOUND EFFECTS.

87   **Cooney, Nancy Evans.** *Chatterbox Jamie.* **Illus. by Marylin Hafner. Putnam, 1993. ISBN 0-399-22208-1**

The usually talkative Jamie won't say a word in his new preschool class until another child's mother brings a new baby to school, which gives him something to talk about. If you have a child who will not speak aloud, this gentle story might help. Other books on a similar topic include Wendy Cheyette Lewison's *Shy Vi* and Rosemary Wells's *Shy Charles*. Dolores Johnson's winning *What Will Mommy Do When I'm at School?* helps take the sting out of leaving home for the classroom. BABIES. MUTISM, ELECTIVE. SCHOOLS. SEPARATION ANXIETY. SHYNESS.

88   **Cooney, Nancy Evans.** *Go Away Monsters, Lickety Split.* **Illus. by Maxie Chambliss. Putnam, 1990. ISBN 0-399-21935-8**

A new kitten, Lickety, helps Jeffrey transcend the need for night-light, flashlight, and hall light at night in his shadow-filled new house. Mary Jane Auch's *Monster Brother*, Eve Bunting's *Ghost's Hour, Spook's Hour*, Eileen Christelow's *Henry and the Dragon*, and Mercer Mayer's *There's Something in My Attic* cover similar ground, and provide a nice contrast. BEDTIME STORIES. CATS. FEAR. NIGHT.

89   **Cowen-Fletcher, Jane.** *Mama Zooms.* **Illus. by the author. Scholastic, 1993. ISBN 0-590-45774-8**

A little boy describes how his mother zooms him everywhere on her lap as she steers her zooming machine (wheelchair). Other stories dealing with wheelchairs include Nancy Carlson's *Arnie and the New Kid*, Liz Damrell's *With the Wind*, Audrey Osofsky's *My Buddy*, Berniece Rabe's *The Balancing Girl*, and Marisabina Russo's *Alec Is My Friend*. HANDICAPS. MOTHERS AND SONS. PHYSICAL DISABILITY. WHEELCHAIRS.

90   **Cummings, Phil.** *Goodness Gracious!* **Illus. by Craig Smith. Orchard, 1992. ISBN 0-531-08567-8**

"Goodness gracious! Look at my faces! scary starey BOLD or hairy" is the first page of this review of other body parts, such as hair, peepers, mouth, arms, muscles, fingers, legs, knees, feet, culminating in a look at ME (or you, too). Kids can show their own corresponding body parts and repeat each line after you. Explore your psyches with Catherine and Laurence Anholt's *All About You* and *Kids*, and your faces and emotions with William Cole's *Frances Face-Maker*. BODY, HUMAN. STORIES IN RHYME.

91   **Cushman, Doug.** *Possum Stew.* **Illus. by the author. Dutton, 1990. ISBN 0-525-44566-8**

Claiming that he can help catch Old Catfish, hungry Old Possum tricks both Gator and Bear by tying both of their fishing lines together and running off with their baskets of fresh-caught fish. As in all good trickster tales, the two outwit Possum by pretending they are preparing possum stew. Keep turning tables with *Anansi and the Moss-Covered Rock*, *Anansi and the Talking Melon*, and *Anansi Goes Fishing* by Eric A. Kimmel, *Crafty Chameleon* and *Hungry Hyena* by Mwenye Hadithi, and *Tiger Soup: An Anansi Story from Jamaica* by Frances Temple. ALLIGATORS. BEARS. SOUP. TRICKSTER TALES.

92   **Cuyler, Margery.** *That's Good! That's Bad!* **Illus. by David Catrow. Henry Holt, 1991. ISBN 0-8050-1535-3**

A little boy's shiny red balloon lifts him into the sky, starting a wild chain of events that takes him across the river on a hippopotamus, through the air on a vine that's really a snake, across the plain where a lion licks him, and eventually back to the zoo where his parents are waiting. After each encounter, when listeners chant "Oh, that's good!" the story responds, "No, that's bad!" and vice versa. Do have your listeners retell and act out this story in sequence. Like the books *We're Going on a Bear Hunt* by Michael Rosen and *I'm Going on a Bear Hunt* by Sandra Stroner Sivulich, there's plenty of opportunity for sound effects and hand motions. Disasters also work out fortuitously in *I Will Not Go to Market Today* by Harry Allard, *Lucky Me* by Denys Cazet, *Fortunately* by Remy Charlip, *Rosie's Walk* by Pat Hutchins, and *That's Good, That's Bad* by Joan Lexau. ANIMALS. CALL-AND-RESPONSE STORIES. CAUSE AND EFFECT. CHANTABLE REFRAIN. CREATIVE DRAMA. SOUND EFFECTS.

---

93   Dodds, Dayle Ann. *The Color Box.* **Illus. by Giles Laroche. Little, Brown, 1992. ISBN 0-316-18820-4**

Alexander, a monkey, finds a funny-looking box that's all black inside, except for one spot of yellow—an opening that he climbs through to find that everything there is yellow. Each spot he discovers is actually a die-cut hole revealing the color to be found in the collage illustration on the next page, and the winning rhyming story covers eight basic colors. N. N. Charles's *What Am I? Looking Through Shapes at Apples and Grapes*, Lois Ehlert's *Color Farm* and *Color Zoo*, Ann Jonas's *Color Dance*, Arnold Lobel's *The Great Blueness and Other Predicaments*, Bruce McMillan's photo-illustrated *Growing Colors*, Merle Peek's *Mary Wore Her Red Dress and Henry Wore His Green Sneakers*, Mary Serfozo's *Who Said Red?*, Ellen Stoll Walsh's *Mouse Paint*, and Eileen Spinelli's *If You Want to Find Golden* are all variations on the color theme. COLOR. MONKEYS.

---

94   Edwards, Frank B. *Mortimer Mooner Stopped Taking a Bath.* **Illus. by John Bianchi. Bungalo Books, 1990. ISBN 0-921285-21-3**

Each day, pig Mortimer becomes purposely more slovenly, until Sunday, when his visiting grandmother declares that to hug him would surely make her faint, and he cleans up his act. Other odiferous characters encounter water and worse in Brock Cole's *No More Baths*, Iris Hiskey's *Hannah the Hippo's No Mud Day*, Charlotte Pomerantz's *The Piggy in the Puddle*, and Valerie Reddix's *Millie and the Mud Hole*. Reinforce the days of the week with Lorna Balian's *Amelia's Nine Lives*, Tony Blundell's *Joe on Sunday*, and Eric Carle's *Today Is Monday*. BATHS. CLEANLINESS. DAYS OF THE WEEK. GRANDMOTHERS. PIGS.

---

95   Ehlert, Lois. *Circus.* **Illus. by the author. HarperCollins, 1992. ISBN 0-06-020253-X**

Experience a whirlwind performance of the greatest show on earth through Ehlert's signature bold geometric graphics and intense colors. There's the Pretzel brothers' human pyramid, fearless leaping lizards Lena and Lila, Miss Eunice the snake queen, and, of course, the flying Zucchinis. *Ginger Jumps* by Lisa Campbell Ernst shows us competition behind the scenes as dog Ginger is almost upstaged, and *Bearymore* by Don Freeman features a bear without an act. ANIMALS. CIRCUS.

---

96   Ehlert, Lois. *Color Farm.* **Illus. by the author. Lippincott, 1990. ISBN 0-397-32441-3**

A companion book to *Color Zoo*, this shape, color, and animal identification book features die-cut overlaid pages that form a series of animals. More advanced shapes include the hexagon, octagon, diamond, heart, and oval, along with the standard circle, square, rectangle, and triangle. Cathryn Falwell's *Clowning Around* is another fun book of shape compositions, as is Suse MacDonald's ocean-based *Sea Shapes*. Compose your own mix-and-match animals using attribute blocks. Kathleen Sullivan Carroll's *One Red Rooster*, Charles Causley's *"Quack!" Said the Billy-Goat*, Denise Fleming's *Barnyard Banter*, Flora McDonnell's *I Love Animals*, Jill Runcie's *Cock-a-Doodle-Doo!*, and Andrea Zimmerman and David Clemesha's *The Cow Buzzed* all fill in the farm theme. COLOR. DOMESTIC ANIMALS. SHAPES.

97   **Ehlert, Lois. *Fish Eyes: A Book You Can Count On*. Illus. by the author. Harcourt, 1990. ISBN 0-15-228050-2**

The narrator imagines swimming with the fishes, counting varieties of brightly colored fish, such as "4 striped fish plus me makes 5," all the way up to ten. Encourage children to write and read aloud their own "plus me" addition problems, which they can illustrate with bright fish drawings. Mess around with number concepts in *Puzzlers* by Suse MacDonald and Bill Oakes. COUNTING BOOKS. FISHES. MATHEMATICS.

98   **Emberley, Ed. *Go Away, Big Green Monster!* Illus. by the author. Little, Brown, 1993. ISBN 0-316-23653-5**

This monster has two big yellow eyes, a long blue nose, sharp white teeth, two little squiggly ears, scraggly purple hair, and a big scary green face. Are we scared? Only a little, as each die-cut page reveals a bit more of the monster's face. Then we command each feature to go away, and the final pages gradually cover it up, until only the round eyes remain. Like Lois Ehlert's *Color Zoo*, this is a cleverly designed gem that children adore, as it both elicits and calms their fears. Conquer some more monsters in Dick Gackenbach's *Harry and the Terrible Whatzit*, Mercer Mayer's *There's a Nightmare in My Closet*, or Maurice Sendak's *Where the Wild Things Are*. At Halloween time, try it as an appetizer for Bill Martin, Jr.'s *Old Devil Wind*, Dian Curtis Regan's *The Thirteen Hours of Halloween*, Erica Silverman's *Big Pumpkin*, Caroline Stutson's *By the Light of the Halloween Moon*, and Linda Williams's *The Little Old Lady Who Was Not Afraid of Anything*. FEAR. MONSTERS. PICTURE BOOKS FOR ALL AGES.

99   **Ericsson, Jennifer A. *No Milk!* Illus. by Ora Eitan. Tambourine, 1993. ISBN 0-688-11307-9**

A young city boy with silver pail and wooden stool tries valiantly to figure out how to get milk from a genial cow, coaxing her with a kiss, hay, a funny joke, a song and dance, a melange of tricks, and a tantrum before he figures out what he's doing wrong. The short text with its insistent title refrain is perfect to read before a trip to the farm to see how cows work. Use with Chris Babcock's *No Moon, No Milk!*, Paula Brown's *Moon Jump: A Countdown*, David L. Harrison's *When Cows Come Home*, Paul Brett Johnson's *The Cow Who Wouldn't Come Down*, David Kirby and Allen Woodman's *The Cows Are Going to Paris*, and Nancy Van Laan's *The Tiny, Tiny Boy and the Big, Big Cow*. CHANTABLE REFRAIN. COWS. MILK.

100   **Evans, Katie. *Hunky Dory Ate It*. Illus. by Janet Morgan. Dutton, 1992. ISBN 0-525-44847-0**

The young pup eats Clara Lake's cake, Kate Donetti's spaghetti, and other foods that rhyme with the preparers' names. In the also-rhyming sequel, *Hunky Dory Found It* (1994), the dog runs off with the neighbors' toys, clothes, and other treasures. Children will love to chant the title refrain, and to think up new foods for him that rhyme with their own names. Make a class book of their rhymes and accompanying drawings for all to recite. Jim Aylesworth's rhyming *My Son John* is also alluring. Find more food and names in Anne Shelby's alliterative *Potluck,* and more animal-rhyming foods in Cheryl Chapman's *Pass the Fritters, Critters.* Another rhyming story about a naughty dog is Livingston Taylor's *Can I Be Good? One Sun: A Book of Terse Verse,* and its companion *Play Day* by Bruce McMillan, *I Made a Mistake* by Miriam Nerlove, *Down by the Bay* by Raffi, and *Cat Is Back at Bat* by John Stadler are all standout models for putting together rhyming words. CHANTABLE REFRAIN. DOGS. FOOD. NAMES. STORIES IN RHYME.

101　　Everitt, Betsy. *Mean Soup.* Illus. by the author. Harcourt, 1992. ISBN 0-15-253146-7

Horace comes home from school growling until his understanding mother helps him shout and stir away the bad day into a pot of her special broth. The bold, zany watercolors and realistic progression of emotions from furious to genial make this a fine tantrum-stopping story. Children can describe their best strategies for taming a bad mood. Jeanne Modesitt's *Sometimes I Feel Like a Mouse: A Book About Feelings* will help them sort out their emotions. COOKERY. EMOTIONS. MOTHERS AND SONS. SOUP.

102　　Feldman, Judy. *The Alphabet in Nature.* Illus. with photos. Childrens Press, 1991. ISBN 0-516-05101-6

A letter of the alphabet can be discerned in each large color photograph of an animal, plant, or natural wonder. Children can identify and trace each letter, and then search for their own alphabet in their environment. Continue the animal theme with Hope Ryden's *Wild Animals of America ABC.* ALPHABET BOOKS. ANIMALS. NATURE.

103　　Field, Eugene. *The Gingham Dog and the Calico Cat.* Illus. by Janet Street. Philomel, 1990. ISBN 0-399-22151-4

A nursery poem originally published as "The Duel" in the late 1880s, this is the engaging story of two stuffed toys who, left side by side on the table, got into a terrible spat, as witnessed by the old Dutch clock and the Chinese plate, and ate each other up. Far more sanguine is the relationship in Edward Lear's classic 1870 poem *The Owl and the Pussycat* as illustrated by Jan Brett, Paul Galdone, or Louise Voce. ARGUMENTS. CATS–POETRY. STORIES IN RHYME. TOYS–POETRY. STUFFED ANIMALS.

104　　Fleming, Denise. *In the Small, Small Pond.* Illus. by the author. Henry Holt, 1993. ISBN 0-8050-2264-3

Gorgeous huge green handmade paper illustrations transport us to the pond where tadpoles wriggle, geese parade, turtles doze, herons plunge, and other animals go about their business. Like the companion book, *In the Tall, Tall Grass* (1991), only two words per page grace this action-filled rhyming description. Children can act out all the colorful descriptive verbs, along with *2 Is for Dancing: A 1 2 3 of Actions* by Woodleigh Hubbard, *Kitten Can* by Bruce McMillan, and *Jiggle Wiggle Prance* by Sally Noll. In Jim Arnosky's attractive slice of nature story *All Night Near the Water*, a mother mallard leads her 12 ducklings from the nest to the lake. ANIMALS. CREATIVE DRAMA. ENGLISH LANGUAGE–GRAMMAR. POND LIFE. STORIES IN RHYME.

105   Fox, Mem. *Shoes from Grandpa.* Illus. by Patricia Mullins. Orchard, 1990. ISBN 0-531-08448-5

In "This Is the House That Jack Built" cumulative style, Jessie's family buys her a whole new outfit to go with her new shoes. Children can chant the refrain, recall each line, and make up new verses. Bring in clothes to go with the story and have one child dress up as you all recite it. Shirley Nietzel's *The Jacket I Wear in the Snow* uses a similar setup. CHANTABLE REFRAIN. CLOTHING AND DRESS. FAMILY LIFE. SHOES. STORIES IN RHYME.

106   Gackenbach, Dick. *Alice's Special Room.* Illus. by the author. Clarion, 1991. ISBN 0-395-54433-5

Alice's mother tries to guess the special room where Alice can be warm in the winter and sled in the summer, see people, go places, and do things she's already done before. See if your listeners know the place. It's her memory. Children can tell about what's in their special rooms. Those who can't remember a thing will sympathize with the main characters in Tom Birdseye's *Soap! Soap! Don't Forget the Soap!*, Joanna Galdone's *Gertrude the Goose Who Forgot*, Pat Hutchins's *Don't Forget the Bacon!*, Ellen MacGregor's *Theodore Turtle,* and Nancy Patz's *Pumpernickel Tickle and Mean Green Cheese.* Strengthen their memories with Susan Hoguet's *I Unpacked My Grandmother's Trunk.* MEMORY. MOTHERS AND DAUGHTERS.

107   Geraghty, Paul. *Slobcat.* Illus. by the author. Macmillan, 1991. ISBN 0-02-735825-9

While a little girl describes her lazy calico cat, we the readers see from the illustrations how industrious the cat really is. Children can make inferences from the pictures to describe the cat's real adventures. Other irony-laden cat stories include Ruth Brown's *Our Cat Flossie* and Michael Foreman's *Cat and Canary.* CATS.

108   Gershator, Phillis. *Rata-Pata-Scata-Fata: A Caribbean Story.* Illus. by Holly Meade. Little, Brown, 1994. ISBN 0-316-30470-0

Daydreaming Junjun wishes for a dinner fish and a goat to come to him and the tamarind fruit to pick itself, and thanks to coincidence and his lucky magic word, his wishes all come true. Children can repeat the title refrain and make their own wishes. Go to market in Haiti with Sasifi and her mother in Karen Lynn Williams's *Tap-Tap.* Holly Keller's *Island Baby* and Rita Phillips Mitchell's *Hue Boy* are also set on Caribbean islands. CARIBBEAN ISLANDS. ISLANDS. MOTHERS AND SONS. MULTICULTURAL STORIES. WISHES.

109   **Goffin, Josse.** *Oh!* **Illus. by the author. Abrams, 1991. ISBN 0-8109-3660-7**

Open to the first double page where you'll see a hand pointing. Unfold that page, open it out, and now the hand's holding the tail of an alligator balancing a steaming cup of something on his snout. On the next page, there's the cup again, which, when you open it up turns into a large boat with a fish swimming nearby. Your children will be jumping up and down to predict the theme for each page and speculate what it will turn into. *Ah!* (1992) is a companion book that also incorporates famous works of art from major Paris museums. Older children can create new three-paneled transformation drawings. Other attractions for the eye and brain include Linda Bourke's *Eye Spy*, Ruth Brown's *If at First You Do Not See*, Cathryn Falwell's *Clowning Around*, Tana Hoban's *Look Again!* and *Look! Look! Look!*, Ann Jonas's *Reflections*, *Round Trip*, and *The 13th Clue*, and Tomi Ungerer's *One, Two, Where's My Shoe?* PICTURE BOOKS FOR ALL AGES. STORIES WITHOUT WORDS. TRANSFORMATIONS. VISUAL PERCEPTION.

110   **Gordon, Gaelyn.** *Duckat.* **Illus. by Chris Gaskin. Scholastic, 1992. ISBN 0-590-45455-2**

The odd duck that turns up on Mabel's back step seems to think it's a cat, meowing, catching mice, and playing with balls of yarn, so Mabel tries to show it otherwise. Children can have fun extending the odd ending by thinking up ways to convince the quacking cat on Mabel's step that it is not a duck and acting out their dialogues. The animals are all mixed up in Charles Causley's *"Quack!" Said the Billy-Goat*, Victoria Forrester's *The Magnificent Moo*, and Andrea Zimmerman and David Clemesha's *The Cow Buzzed*. Read about a duck that works like a dog in Martin Waddell's *Farmer Duck*. CATS. DUCKS. IDENTITY.

111   **Gordon, Jeffie Ross.** *Six Sleepy Sheep.* **Illus. by John O'Brien. Caroline House/Boyds Mills, 1991. ISBN 1-878093-06-1**

How your tongue will be tangled by this alliterative bedtime subtraction story of snoring sheep who deprive the others of needed sleep! While you're in the mode, try Charles Keller's *Tongue Twisters*, Alvin Schwartz's *Busy Buzzing Bumblebees and Other Tongue Twisters*, and Janice May Udry's *Thump and Plunk*. Another sleepytime subtraction story is Eileen Christelow's riotous *Five Little Monkeys Jumping on the Bed*, while *Ten Pink Piglets: Garth Pig's Wall Song* by Mary Rayner takes place in broad daylight. Sing along with *Sherman the Sheep* by Kevin Kiser, and snore away with *Awful Aardvark* by Mwalimu Kennaway. ALLITERATION. COUNTING BOOKS. SHEEP. SLEEP. SUBTRACTION. TONGUE TWISTERS.

112   **Gordon, Jeffie Ross.** *Two Badd Babies.* **Illus. by Chris L. Demarest. Caroline House/Boyds Mills, 1992. ISBN 1-878093-85-1**

The two Badd twins don't feel like napping, so they rock and bounce and bounce and rock their baby bed out the door and down the street to the center of town where Mrs. Tasty Pastry gives them an éclair, they see a movie, stop for a burger at Greasy Jack's and a nap-time book at their dad's bookstore, and head home again. The exuberant text and watercolors will delight audiences who will chant the bouncy lines with you. Make a detour for the active tots in Pat Hutchins's *Where's the Baby?*, Barbro Lindgren's *The Wild Baby*, and James Stevenson's *Rolling Rose*. BABIES. BEHAVIOR. CHANTABLE REFRAIN.

113 **Gray, Libba Moore.** *Small Green Snake.* **Illus. by Holly Meade. Orchard, 1994. ISBN 0-531-08694-1**

"With a zip and a zag, and a wiggle and a wag," Small Green Snake, a sassy garter snake, lets his curiosity override his mother's admonition not to wander too far, and just as she predicts, he's captured in a glass jelly jar. The onomatopoeia, sound effects, and many chantable lines, along with the quirky colorful torn-paper collage illustrations will make listeners hiss in delight. A snake puts ten mice in a glass jar in Ellen Stoll Walsh's *Mouse Count.* Compare snakes with Nan Bodsworth's fantasy *A Nice Walk in the Jungle* and Faith McNulty's realistic story *A Snake in the House.* CURIOSITY. ENGLISH LANGUAGE–ONOMATOPOEIC WORDS. OBEDIENCE. SNAKES. SOUND EFFECTS.

114 **Greenspan, Adele Aron.** *Daddies.* **Photos by the author. Philomel, 1991. ISBN 0-399-22259-6**

A loving and lovely prose poem about what daddies do, have, give, teach, and need, illustrated by poignant and special large black-and-white photos. The author's essay about her father at the front of the book is not for young children, but will make you cry. There are simply not enough good books for young children about strong and loving fathers, though Robert J. Blake's *The Perfect Spot*, Denys Cazet's *I'm Not Sleepy*, and Laurence Pringle's *Octopus Hug* are all marvelous. FATHERS. LOVE. MULTICULTURAL STORIES.

115 **Haas, Jessie.** *Chipmunk!* **Illus. by Jos. A. Smith. Greenwillow, 1993. ISBN 0-688-11875-5**

When Puss brings a chipmunk into the house, all anyone wants is to get it out again, and in the ensuing ruckus, Dad ends up with the chipmunk on his head. Find out more about this small creature's habits in Joanne Ryder's *Chipmunk Song.* Another chain-reaction story that ends up where it started is Byron Barton's *Buzz Buzz Buzz.* CATS. CHIPMUNKS.

116 **Hale, Sarah Josepha Buell.** *Mary Had a Little Lamb.* **Photos by Bruce McMillan. Scholastic, 1990. ISBN 0-590-43773-9**

Everyone knows this 19th-century poem, but photo-illustrator McMillan has given it new life with his color shots of a bespectacled, yellow-overalled, African American Mary, her male teacher, and of course, that adorable lamb. The illustrations in Tomie dePaola's version are sweet and pretty, while those by Salley Mavor are done with fabrics and stitchery. Humorous picture books *Sherman the Sheep* by Kevin Kiser and *Sheep Out to Eat* by Nancy Shaw give a less sentimental view of the lamb world. NURSERY RHYMES. SCHOOLS. SHEEP. STORIES IN RHYME.

117   Hale, Sarah Josepha Buell. *Mary Had a Little Lamb*. Illus. by Salley Mavor. Orchard, 1995. ISBN 0-531-08725-5

These enchanting textured and three-dimensional illustrations for everyone's favorite lamb song were done in fabric relief. According to the interesting end notes for this picture book version of the famous 1830 nursery rhyme, the first 12 lines may have been written not by Hale but by one John Roulstone. Other versions illustrated by Tomie dePaola and photographed by Bruce McMillan are also lovely. NURSERY RHYMES. SCHOOLS. SHEEP. STORIES IN RHYME.

118   Harrison, David L. *When Cows Come Home*. Illus. by Chris L. Demarest. Boyds Mills, 1994. ISBN 1-56397-143-7

Infectious rhyming verses show what cows do when the farmer looks the other way: play tag, fiddle, square dance, ride bikes, and swim in the pond. There's more frantic farmyard poetry in David McPhail's *Pigs Aplenty, Pigs Galore!*, Reeve Lindburgh's *The Day the Goose Got Loose*, and Nadine Bernard Westcott's *Skip to My Lou*, and prose in Jennifer A. Ericsson's *No Milk!*, David Kirby and Allen Woodman's *The Cows Are Going to Paris*, Kevin Kiser's *Sherman the Sheep*, and Nancy Van Laan's *The Tiny, Tiny Boy and the Big, Big Cow*. COWS. STORIES IN RHYME.

119   Havill, Juanita. *Jamaica and Brianna*. Illus. by Anne Sibley O'Brien. Houghton Mifflin, 1993. ISBN 0-395-64489-5

Jealousy over a new pair of boots leads two best friends to insult each other even though the two girls secretly admire each other's footwear. Dig into fights and how to make up with Paula dePaolo's *Rosie & the Yellow Ribbon*, and jealousy with Ann Martin's *Rachel Parker, Kindergarten Show-Off*. Try on more shoes with Beverly Cleary's *The Growing-Up Feet*, Niki Daly's *Not So Fast, Songololo*, Shirley Hughes's *Alfie's Feet*, Johanna Hurwitz's *New Shoes for Sylvia*, Denise Lewis Patrick's *Red Dancing Shoes*, and Elizabeth Winthrop's *Shoes*. AFRICAN AMERICANS. ASIAN AMERICANS. CONFLICT RESOLUTION. FRIENDSHIP. JEALOUSY. MULTICULTURAL STORIES. SHOES.

120   Hearn, Diane Dawson. *Dad's Dinosaur Day*. Illus. by the author. Macmillan, 1993. ISBN 0-02-743485-0

At breakfast, Mikey's dad isn't himself at all—he's a dinosaur, and he spends the day roaring and playing with his son, much to Mikey's delight. In both *Joe on Sunday* by Tony Blundell and *Matthew Michael's Beastly Day* by Deborah Johnston, it's the child who is transformed. Have a romp with *Dinosaur Roar!* by Paul and Henrietta Stickland, fill in some dino-facts with B. G. Hennessy's *The Dinosaur Who Lived in My Backyard* and Bernard Most's *How Big Were the Dinosaurs?*, and travel back to dino-days with Eric Rohmann's wordless *Time Flies*. Carol Carrick's *Patrick's Dinosaurs* and *What Happened to Patrick's Dinosaurs?*, Robin Pulver's *Mrs. Toggle and the Dinosaur*, and Henry Schwartz's *How I Captured a Dinosaur* are also positively reptilian. DINOSAURS. FATHERS AND SONS. TRANSFORMATIONS.

121   Heller, Nicholas. *Woody.* Illus. by the author. Greenwillow, 1994. ISBN 0-688-12805-X

Sent outside by his mom when he says he's bored, pig Woody idly blows on a dandelion and finds he can make all his wishes come true. Pig Pig undergoes a similar adventure in *Pig Pig and the Magic Photo Album* by David McPhail and a boy's wishes are granted in *Rata-Pata-Scata-Fata: A Caribbean Story* by Phillis Gershator. Make dandelions—or, if the season's right, pick some—blow, and make wishes. Children can draw or act out what the consequences would be. IMAGINATION. PIGS. WISHES.

122   Henkes, Kevin. *Owen.* Illus. by the author. Greenwillow, 1993. ISBN 0-688-11450-4

Though mouse-child Owen thinks his blanket, Fuzzy, is just perfect, next-door neighbor Mrs. Tweezers gives Owen's parents loads of advice on ways to wean him from it, including invoking the Blanket Fairy, the vinegar trick, and just saying no. Just in time for school, his mother comes up with the perfect solution: she turns the blanket into handkerchiefs. Trade a few memories and some secrets with your current or former thumb-sucking, stuffed animal-loving, blanket-toting students. Compare with the solutions offered in other "blanket" books like Nancy Evans Cooney's *The Blanket That Had to Go,* Shirley Hughes's *Alfie Gives a Hand,* Holly Keller's *Geraldine's Blanket,* John Prater's *Tim and the Blanket Thief,* and Deborah Robinson's *Bye-Bye, Old Buddy.* Explore Henkes's other marvelous books about young ones adjusting to change, especially *Chrysanthemum, Sheila Rae, the Brave,* and *Jessica.* BLANKETS. FAMILY LIFE. MICE.

123   Hines, Anna Grossnickle. *What Joe Saw.* Illus. by the author. Greenwillow, 1994. ISBN 0-688-13124-7

While his teacher and the rest of the class set off at a brisk pace on their walk to the park, Joe lags behind and sees what no one else takes the time to notice: a bluebird with a worm in its beak, ants, a chipmunk, a turtle, and a toad. The message is, as the author says in her dedication, to "take time to see." *The Listening Walk* by Paul Showers encourages us to use our ears, while Joe will get your class looking. Take a walk and encourage children to draw and talk about what they observe. Introduce more observation skills with *My Five Senses* by Margaret Miller and Carolyn Otto's *I Can Tell by Touching.* NATURE. SCHOOLS. SENSES AND SENSATION.

124   Hiskey, Iris. *Hannah the Hippo's No Mud Day.* Illus. by Karen Lee Schmidt. Simon & Schuster, 1991. ISBN 0-671-69194-5

With Aunt Lily coming to pay a visit, it's a struggle for Hannah to keep her good pink dress clean, and when the temptation grows too great, she succumbs to a lovely mud puddle. Lucky for Hannah that she helps out an elephant and two birds in distress, for they help her clean up in return. Reluctant bathers and/or mud-lovers abound in Brock Cole's *No More Baths,* Frank B. Edwards's *Mortimer Mooner Stopped Taking a Bath,* Charlotte Pomerantz's *The Piggy in the Puddle,* and Valerie Reddix's *Millie and the Mud Hole,* while those in Bill Martin, Jr.'s rhyming *The Happy Hippopotami* revel in a day at the beach. AUNTS. CLEANLINESS. CLOTHING AND DRESS. COOPERATION. HIPPOPOTAMUS.

125   Hoban, Tana. *Exactly the Opposite*. Photos by the author. Greenwillow, 1990. ISBN 0-688-08862-7

Sets of color photographs depict a variety of opposites, such as open and closed or large and small. Children need to examine the pages and determine what opposites they think each photo represents, as the book is wordless, and there's not always only one correct response. This is a good way to get children thinking about synonyms, and they can make their own opposites pictures. Also see Hoban's *Push, Pull, Empty, Full*, George Mendoza's *The Sesame Street Book of Opposites*, and Niki Yektai's *Bears in Pairs*. ENGLISH LANGUAGE–SYNONYMS AND ANTONYMS. OPPOSITES.

126   Howard, Jane R. *When I'm Hungry*. Illus. by Teri Sloat. Dutton, 1992. ISBN 0-525-44983-3

A little boy puts himself in the place of various animals, such as fish, birds, reptiles, and a smattering of mammals, to show how they eat their food. Celebrate our eating fancies with a chorus or two of Eric Carle's *Today Is Monday*. Joanne Ryder's stunning Just for a Day series, including *Catching the Wind; Lizard in the Sun; Sea Elf; White Bear, Ice Bear;* and *Winter Whale*, delve more deeply into what it might be like if we could turn into another animal. ANIMALS. CREATIVE DRAMA. FOOD.

127   Hubbard, Woodleigh. *2 Is for Dancing: A 1 2 3 of Actions*. Illus. by the author. Chronicle, 1991. ISBN 0-87701-895-2

From "1 is for dreaming" to "12 is for balancing," Hubbard's in-your-face and off-the-wall animal paintings are bright and kooky. As in Denise Fleming's *Count!*, assign each child a number, and as you act out each page, have each child join the growing group. If your class is large, act it out twice so everyone gets a number. Keith Baker's *Big Fat Hen* and Kathleen Sullivan Carroll's *One Red Rooster* are more traditional animal counting books. For acting out, action verbs abound also in *In the Small, Small Pond* by Denise Fleming, *Kitten Can* by Bruce McMillan, and *Jiggle Wiggle Prance* by Sally Noll. COUNTING BOOKS. CREATIVE DRAMA. ENGLISH LANGUAGE–GRAMMAR.

128   Hughes, Shirley. *The Big Alfie Out of Doors Storybook*. Illus. by the author. Lothrop, 1992. ISBN 0-688-11428-8

Alfie and Annie Rose fans will be delighted with this collection of down-to-earth stories and prose poems about sleeping outside in a tent with dad and going to the seashore with a stone named Bonting. Read an Alfie book a day; there's *Alfie Gets in First, Alfie Gives a Hand, Alfie's Feet*, and *An Evening at Alfie's*. BROTHERS AND SISTERS. CAMPING. FAMILY LIFE. SEASHORE. SHEEP.

129   Hurwitz, Johanna. *New Shoes for Sylvia*. Illus. by Jerry Pinkney. Morrow, 1993. ISBN 0-688-05287-8

The beautiful red buckled shoes Tía Rosita sends in the mail to Sylvia in Latin America don't fit yet, so the little girl uses them as doll beds, toys, and pebble holders until one day she is overjoyed to find they are just the right size for her.

Celebrate shoe stories from the United States and other places with Beverly Cleary's *The Growing-Up Feet*, Niki Daly's South African *Not So Fast, Songololo*, Juanita Havill's *Jamaica and Brianna*, Shirley Hughes's English *Alfie's Feet*, Denise Lewis Patrick's *Red Dancing Shoes*, and Elizabeth Winthrop's *Shoes*. Children can bring in their favorite pairs to model for a shoe parade and a shoe mix-and-match game. LATIN AMERICA. SHOES.

130   Hutchins, Pat. *Three-Star Billy*. Illus. by the author. Greenwillow, 1994. ISBN 0-688-13079-8

Monster Billy is just terrible in his new nursery school class, flinging pots of paint, singing dreadful, monstrous songs, and dancing frightful dances—all of which pleases his monster teacher so much she gives him three stars. Use Billy's contrary behavior to kick off a look at opposites with *Dinosaur Roar!* by Paul and Henrietta Stickland. Talk over some of the other monstrous things Billy might do if he were in your class. BEHAVIOR. MONSTERS. NURSERY SCHOOLS. SCHOOLS.

131   Ivimey, John W. *Three Blind Mice: The Classic Nursery Rhyme*. Illus. by Lorinda Bryan Cauley. Putnam, 1991. ISBN 0-399-21775-4

The original song with all its verses is made all the more delightful by Cauley's colorful and genial illustrations of the plump, behatted rodents. The music's on the last page, and surely your listeners will sing the call-and-response parts of the verses. You'll be happy to note that the mice have their excised tails restored by the chemist and his bottle of "Never Too Late to Mend." Two other attractive interpretations are *The Complete Version of Ye Three Blind Mice* illustrated by Walter Corbould and *The Complete Story of the Three Blind Mice* illustrated by Paul Galdone. MICE. NURSERY RHYMES. SONGS. STORIES IN RHYME.

132   Jakob, Donna. *My Bike*. Illus. by Nelle Davis. Hyperion, 1994. ISBN 1-56282-455-4

The narrator describes how he finally learned to ride his two-wheeler today, comparing his heady successes today with yesterday when the pedals got stuck, the front wheel wobbled, and he fell a lot. Riders will have lots of similar stories to relate. Ask the children to tell you about something they couldn't do before but can do just fine now. BICYCLES. PERSEVERANCE.

133   James, Betsy. *Mary Ann*. Illus. by the author. Dutton, 1994. ISBN 0-525-45077-7

Upset when her best friend Mary Ann moves away, Amy finds a praying mantis that she names for her friend and keeps in a terrarium until it lays eggs and dies. When the family returns from a visit to Mary Ann's new house, they find hundreds of baby praying mantises at home. The sensible and sympathetic treatment of a pet's death and the loss a child feels at losing a friend are two themes that are especially well handled here and in Miriam Cohen's *Jim's Dog Muffins*, Connie Heckert's *Dribbles*, Holly Keller's *Goodbye, Max*, Rachel Pank's *Under the Blackberries*, and Judith Viorst's *The Tenth Good Thing About Barney*. Calm fears of moving with *We Are Best Friends* by Aliki, *Good-bye House* by Robin Ballard, *Maggie Doesn't Want to Move* by Elizabeth Lee O'Donnell, *Moving* by Michael

Rosen, and *Anna's Secret Friend* by Yuriko Tsutsui. Barbara Ann Porte's *"Leave That Cricket Be, Alan Lee"* is another good insect-as-pet tale. DEATH. FRIENDSHIP. INSECTS. MOVING, HOUSEHOLD. PRAYING MANTIS.

134   Janovitz, Marilyn. *Look Out, Bird!* Illus. by the author. North-South, 1994. ISBN 1-55858-250-9

Snail slips, hits Bird who frightens Frog who topples Turtle who splashes Salamander, and the alliterative chain reaction proceeds until Moth flutters and startles Snail, when the whole circle starts anew. Act this one out in a circle, with the first child turning to the child on his or her right, and on around until each person has had a turn. There are 15 animals, so you can pantomime the story twice to give everyone at least one action and reaction. Byron Barton's *Buzz Buzz Buzz* and Robert Kalan's *Stop, Thief!* are also circular stories, while in Béatrice Tanaka's *The Chase*, each animal follows after the other when Rabbit starts running. Count all the running animals in David Bennett's *One Cow Moo Moo!* ALLITERATION. ANIMALS. CAUSE AND EFFECT. CREATIVE DRAMA.

135   Johnson, Dolores. *What Will Mommy Do When I'm at School?* Illus. by the author. Macmillan, 1990. ISBN 0-02-747845-9

The narrator, a young African American girl in braids, is worried about starting school and leaving her mom alone and lonely, without her help in singing songs, helping with the grocery shopping, and reading picture books. In a gentle depiction of reverse separation anxiety, Mom reassures her only child that she won't be lonely: she's beginning a brand new job herself. *Chatterbox Jamie* by Nancy Evans Cooney, *Chrysanthemum* by Kevin Henkes, *Waiting for Mom* by Linda Wagner Tyler, and *Timothy Goes to School* by Rosemary Wells all help newcomers adjust to their school environment. Spend a day with a classroom of animal students in *Annie, Bea, and Chi Chi Dolores: A School Day Alphabet* by Donna Maurer. AFRICAN AMERICANS. MOTHERS AND DAUGHTERS. SCHOOLS. SEPARATION ANXIETY.

136   Jonas, Ann. *Color Dance.* Illus. by the author. Greenwillow, 1989. ISBN 0-688-05991-0

Three leotard-clad children dancing with huge scarves demonstrate how each color is formed, using overlaid scarves of red, blue, and yellow to produce the color combinations of the spectrum. Continue the color theme with N. N. Charles's *What Am I? Looking Through Shapes at Apples and Grapes*, Dayle Ann Dodds's *The Color Box*, Lois Ehlert's *Color Farm* and *Color Zoo*, Arnold Lobel's *The Great Blueness and Other Predicaments*, Bruce McMillan's photo-illustrated *Growing Colors*, Merle Peek's *Mary Wore Her Red Dress and Henry Wore His Green Sneakers*, Mary Serfozo's *Who Said Red?*, Ellen Stoll Walsh's *Mouse Paint*, and Eileen Spinelli's *If You Want to Find Golden*. COLOR. DANCING. MULTICULTURAL STORIES.

137   Jones, Carol. *This Old Man.* Illus. by the author. Houghton Mifflin, 1990. ISBN 0-395-54699-0

There's a round windowlike hole in each page to give kids a peek at the next page and guess where the next "knick-knack" will be in this old rhythmic counting song. In the illustrations, we watch a girl and her grandfather spend the day together working in the garden, tending the bees, having a cookout, and gathering eggs. Sing this together and make up some new verses, substituting letters or colors for the numbers. *Knick Knack Paddywack* by Marissa Moss is an updated version, while *Ten Cats Have Hats: A Counting Book* by David McPhail is another rhyming story children can chant. Count back down with *Ten Pink Piglets: Garth Pig's Wall Song* by Mary Rayner. COUNTING BOOKS. FOLK SONGS. SONGS.

138   Kalan, Robert. *Stop, Thief!* Illus. by Yossi Abolafia. Greenwillow, 1993. ISBN 0-688-11877-1

A brown squirrel takes an acorn from the gray squirrel that dug it up, setting off a chain of events with a crow, turtle, otter, fox, dog, and boy, each of whom takes the nut until it winds up back with the first squirrel again. Children can chant the title refrain each time, then retell this and act it out. Other cause-and-effect stories that come full circle include *Buzz Buzz Buzz* by Byron Barton, *Look Out, Bird!* by Marilyn Janovitz and both *If You Give a Moose a Muffin* and *If You Give a Mouse a Cookie* by Laura Joffe Numeroff. CREATIVE DRAMA. ROBBERS AND OUTLAWS. SEQUENCE STORIES. SQUIRRELS.

139   Kandoian, Ellen. *Is Anybody Up?* Illus. by the author. Putnam, 1989. ISBN 0-399-21749-5

While Molly is getting her breakfast on the East Coast of the United States, we see others along the eastern time zone eating theirs as well, from an Inuit woman to an Antarctic seal. Get out your globe to point out each place, and plot the diverse countries in your own time zone. Pair with Molly's nighttime global tour in Kandoian's *Under the Sun,* and follow up with *Milton the Early Riser* by Robert Kraus, *Go to Sleep, Nicholas Joe* by Marjorie Weinman Sharmat, and *'Round and Around* by James Skofield. BREAKFAST. MORNING. MULTICULTURAL STORIES. TIME ZONES.

140   Kasza, Keiko. *A Mother for Choco.* Illus. by the author. Putnam, 1992. ISBN 0-399-21841-6

Little bird Choco sets off to find a mother just like himself, but is taken in by Mrs. Bear, who hugs him, cheers him up, and takes him home to love with her three other adopted animal children. Holly Keller's *Horace* comes at the subject of adoption from another direction, though both make the same point—a parent is someone who loves you. Janell Cannon's *Stellaluna* is about a fruit bat separated from her mother and raised by birds. ADOPTION. BEARS. BIRDS. IDENTITY. LOVE. MOTHERS.

141   Kasza, Keiko. *The Rat and the Tiger.* Illus. by the author. Putnam, 1993. ISBN 0-399-22404-1

Whenever Tiger got the best part in their games, the biggest share of doughnut, or his own way, his best friend would accept his lot without protest: "What could I say? I'm just a tiny little rat." The day Tiger kicks down Rat's castle of blocks, Rat finally gets mad enough to yell back, calling Tiger a bully. Sometimes the meek need to assert themselves, we learn, and teach our more aggressive friends to share. History repeats itself on the last page when the new rhino on the block shows up. Ask children how they'd deal with him. There's more than one way to deal with a bully, as we learn in Barbara Bottner's *Bootsie Barker Bites,* Carol Chapman's *Herbie's Troubles,* Joanna Cole's *Don't Call Me Names,* Phyllis Reynolds Naylor's *King of the Playground,* and Hans Wilhelm's *Tyrone the Horrible.* BULLIES. FRIENDSHIP. RATS. TIGERS.

142   Keller, Holly. *Geraldine's Baby Brother.* **Illus. by the author. Greenwillow, 1994. ISBN 0-688-12006-7**

Pig Geraldine sulks and snarls while the family's attention is focused on placating crying new baby Willie, and it's not until the middle of the night when Geraldine goes in to have a look at him that she relents, makes peace with her jealousy, and begins to like him. Children with babies at home will certainly relate, and will have their own stories to tell, especially when you ask them, "But why is Geraldine acting like that? What's wrong?" Get used to new babies with Alane Ferguson's *That New Pet!,* Kevin Henkes's *Julius, the Baby of the World,* Ezra Jack Keats's *Peter's Chair,* and Frieda Wishinsky's *Oonga Boonga.* BABIES. BROTHERS AND SISTERS. JEALOUSY.

143   Keller, Holly. *Horace.* **Illus. by the author. Greenwillow, 1991. ISBN 0-688-09832-0**

Spotted cat Horace feels out of place when he notices he's the only one in his whole extended family without stripes, and when his attempts at changing his spots don't work, he runs away to a park to find a family where he might belong. His mother's nightly recitation of how he was chosen by them when he lost his first family as a baby is a reassuring and gentle explanation of becoming an adopted or foster child. *Stellaluna* by Janell Cannon and *A Mother for Choco* by Keiko Kasza are picture books about the same sensitive subject. ADOPTION. MOTHERS AND SONS. SELF-ACCEPTANCE. SELF-ESTEEM.

144   Kennaway, Mwalimu. *Awful Aardvark.* **Illus. by Adrienne Kennaway. Little, Brown, 1989. ISBN 0-316-59218-8**

Kept up all night by Aardvark's snoring, Mongoose meets with the Monkeys, Lion, and Rhinoceros, who attempt to waken Aardvark but knock over his tree, leading him to discover the delicacy of nocturnal termites and change his sleeping patterns entirely. Children will love chiming in on the snores—HHHRRR-ZZZZ!—and will also love the sound effects in *Peace at Last* by Jill Murphy. Mwenye Hadithi's *Baby Baboon, Crafty Chameleon, Greedy Zebra, Hungry Hyena, Lazy Lion,* and *Tricky Tortoise,* all illustrated by Adrienne Kennaway, are stories of other engaging animals with less-than-perfect personalities. Beep and kaaaaw with John A. Rowe's noisy story *Baby Crow.* AARDVARKS. ANIMALS. POURQUOI TALES. SLEEP. SOUND EFFECTS.

145   King, Bob. *Sitting on the Farm.* **Illus. by Bill Slavin. Orchard, 1992. ISBN 0-531-08585-6**

An exuberant and funny song recited by a girl who'd love to get rid of all the animals who want to sit on her knee and eat her lunch instead of each other. The music's appended, though you can chant it if you're shy, and everyone will love shouting out the "MUNCH MUNCH MUNCH" parts. Kids can make up their own ending, since it's not conclusive. If you crave more chaos, go to Mona Rabun Reeves's *I Had a Cat*, and Nadine Bernard Westcott's *Skip to My Lou*. ANIMALS–SONGS. CHANTABLE REFRAIN. FOOD. SONGS. STORIES IN RHYME.

146   Kleven, Elisa. *The Paper Princess*. Illus. by the author. Dutton, 1994. IBSN 0-525-45231-1

Before a little girl has a chance to give her hand-drawn paper princess doll any hair, the wind sends the picture flying over a meadow, around a ferris wheel, and into the beak of a blue jay who provides both hair and a trip home. The delicate and detailed collage pictures are wonderful, and children will clamor to cut out and decorate their own paper princes and princesses to send on new journeys. Share a worldwide jaunt with the lost postcard-sending teddy in Dyan Sheldon's *Love, Your Bear Pete*. In both Dick Gackenbach's *Mag the Magnificent* and Susan Jeschke's *Angela and Bear*, children's drawings also come to life as friends. BROTHERS AND SISTERS. DRAWING. LOST. PRINCES AND PRINCESSES.

147   Krensky, Stephen. *Big Time Bears*. Illus. by Maryann Cocca-Leffler. Little, Brown, 1989. ISBN 0-316-50375-4

Time—a second, minute, hour, day, week, month, year, decade, and century—is measured by how long it takes the Bear family to do common tasks. You can time group activities to get an even more concrete idea of what can be done in one second (a sneeze or a blink), ten seconds (a drink from the water fountain), 30 seconds (a verse of a favorite song), five minutes (a short book or story), and so on. If you can get your hands on some inexpensive stopwatches, children would love timing other household or school events such as meals, shopping, and napping. Other time-appropriate stories include Eric Carle's *The Very Grouchy Ladybug* and Pat Hutchins's *Clocks and More Clocks*. BEARS. TIME.

148   Lear, Edward. *The Owl and the Pussycat*. Illus. by Jan Brett. Putnam, 1991. ISBN 0-399-21925-0

Ornate Caribbean scenes and borders add a whole new dimension to Lear's classic poem of the two who set off to sea in a pea-green boat, with an added illustrated subplot of two fish in love who find each other at last. There's so much to see, so read this one several times to let the poem sink in. Compare the illustrations with Paul Galdone's and Louise Voce's versions. For more nonsense, see Janet Stevens's picture-book version of Lear's *The Quangle Wangle's Hat* and *The Walloping Window-Blind* by Charles E. Carryl. There's no love lost in Eugene Field's well-known 18th-century poem *The Gingham Dog and the Calico Cat*. ANIMALS. BOATS AND BOATING. CATS. NONSENSE VERSES. OWLS. PICTURE BOOKS FOR ALL AGES. STORIES IN RHYME.

149   Lear, Edward. *The Owl and the Pussycat*. Illus. by Louise Voce. Lothrop, 1991. ISBN 0-688-09537-2

The two sail off to wed, borrow a piggy's nose ring, and end up on the island where the Bong-tree grows. There's a charming, even goofy, simplicity about the good-natured pen-and-ink and watercolor illustrations, making the classic nonsense poem instantly understandable for the youngest listeners. Compare to the ornate Jan Brett and the amiable Lorinda Bryan Cauley (Putnam, 1986) versions. ANIMALS. BOATS AND BOATING. CATS. NONSENSE VERSES. OWLS. PICTURE BOOKS FOR ALL AGES. STORIES IN RHYME.

150   **Leventhal, Debra.** *What Is Your Language?* **Illus. by Monica Wellington. Dutton, 1994. ISBN 0-525-45133-1**

A young boy travels the world, asking children he meets, "What is your language?" and they tell him the word for "yes" and then "no" in English, German, French, Russian, Inuktitut, Japanese, Chinese, Arabic, and Swahili. Originally a song, the story can be read or sung, with the music, pronunciation, and notes about each language appended. Children should also note the many forms of transportation the boy takes on his jaunt. Hank De Zutter's *Who Says a Dog Goes Bow-Wow?* and Arthur Dorros's *This Is My House* provide more beginning foreign-language experience, while Edith Baer's *This Is the Way We Go to School: A Book About Children Around the World* also introduces other cultures. LANGUAGE. MULTI-CULTURAL STORIES. SONGS. TRANSPORTATION.

151   **Lewison, Wendy Cheyette.** *Shy Vi.* **Illus. by Stephen John Smith. Simon & Schuster, 1993. ISBN 0-671-76968-5**

A shy mouse from a large family takes self-confidence lessons, voice lessons, and acting lessons, all of which pay off when she has a nonspeaking part of a violet in a play. The soft-spoken sheep in Emily Arnold McCully's *Speak Up, Blanche* also goes into the theater. Help your bashful ones with Nancy Evans Cooney's *Chatterbox Jamie*, Joan Lexau's *Benji*, and Rosemary Wells's *Shy Charles*, and then boost their confidence with Mary Hoffman's *Amazing Grace*. ACTING. MICE. PLAYS. SELF-ESTEEM. SHYNESS.

152   **London, Jonathan.** *Froggy Gets Dressed.* **Illus. by Frank Remkiewicz. Viking, 1992. ISBN 0-670-84249-4**

Each time he goes out to play in the snow, Froggy leaves off one important item of clothing, like his pants, his shirt, and even his underwear, and must go back inside to get undressed and then redressed. Your tadpoles will love to act out all the dressing and undressing, with the accompanying noises (flop flop flop). This would make a cute flannelboard story, along with the companion *Let's Go, Froggy*. Try on a few more winter outfits with Louise Borden's *Caps, Hats, Socks, and Mittens*, Jan Brett's *The Mitten* and *Trouble with Trolls*, Shirley Nietzel's *The Jacket I Wear in the Snow*, Eve Rice's *Oh, Lewis!*, and Jean Rogers's *Runaway Mittens*, and spend some time sledding with Cheryl Chapman's *Snow on Snow on Snow*. CLOCKS. CREATIVE DRAMA. FROGS. SNOW. SOUND EFFECTS.

153   **London, Jonathan.** *Let's Go, Froggy.* **Illus. by Frank Remkiewicz. Viking, 1994. ISBN 0-670-85055-1**

Getting ready for a bike trip and a picnic with Dad, Froggy has to figure out where he left his helmet, butterfly net, ball, bag of peaches, and trading cards, for which he scours the house. Children who can never find anything will delight in the search and make all the sound effects along the way. An easy story to act out, it also leads to the questions, "Have you ever lost anything? Where did you look for it? Where did you find it?" How about a classroom treasure hunt to hone their finding skills? Look for other misplaced items in Catherine Bancroft and Hannah Coale Gruenberg's *Felix's Hat* and Shirley Hughes's *Dogger*. CHANTABLE REFRAIN. FATHERS AND SONS. FROGS. LOST. SOUND EFFECTS.

154   Loomis, Christine. *In the Diner.* Illus. by Nancy Poydar. Scholastic, 1994. ISBN 0-590-46716-6

Four word couplets and active watercolors describe a typical day in the diner, where "Waiters hurry. / Busboys scurry. / Bacon sizzles. / Syrup drizzles." Compose new rhyming verses about your school with your children's help, such as "Chalk squeaks. / Faucet leaks. / Balls bounce. / Teacher counts." Other titles using the same structure include Denise Fleming's *In the Small, Small Pond* and *In the Tall, Tall Grass*, and Nancy Shaw's Sheep series. Also fun for simple rhyme-writing are *One Sun: A Book of Terse Verse*, and its companion *Play Day* by Bruce McMillan, *I Made a Mistake* by Miriam Nerlove, *Down by the Bay* by Raffi, and *Cat Is Back at Bat* by John Stadler. CREATIVE WRITING. MULTICULTURAL STORIES. RESTAURANTS. STORIES IN RHYME.

155   Loomis, Christine. *One Cow Coughs: A Counting Book for the Sick and Miserable.* Illus. by Pat Dypold. Ticknor & Fields, 1994. ISBN 0-395-67899-4

One cow coughs, two mules moan, three sheep shake, on up to ten, when we count back to one and find how each group of farm animals cures itself. The rhyming story with amiable and colorful cut-paper collages will get your students fired up to point out every boo-boo and ailment they've had recently. The school nurse might want to read this one aloud. Recover with the aid of Franz Brandenberg's *I Wish I Was Sick, Too,* Marc Brown's *Arthur's Chicken Pox,* Lynne Cherry's rhyming *Who's Sick Today?,* Ursula LeGuin's *A Visit from Dr. Katz,* and Andrea Zimmerman and David Clemesha's *The Cow Buzzed.* Then count up to ten again with the big animal chase scenes of David Bennett's *One Cow Moo Moo!* ALLITERATION. ANIMALS. COUNTING BOOKS. DOMESTIC ANIMALS. SICK. STORIES IN RHYME.

156   MacDonald, Amy. *Little Beaver and the Echo.* Illus. by Sarah Fox-Davies. Putnam, 1990. ISBN 0-399-22203-0

Lonely Little Beaver sets out in his canoe to seek a possible friend whom he hears across the pond crying just like him and who repeats his words. On the way, he meets up with a duck, an otter, and a turtle, all of whom are happy to be friends, and a wise old beaver who fills them all in on the Echo who mirrors your feelings. From the cover with its large endearing portrait of Little Beaver looking searchingly into our eyes, we are entranced with this simple, sweet, and predictable tale and its enchanting watercolors. *Gray Duck Catches a Friend* by Vicki K. Artis, *My Best Friend* by Pat Hutchins, and *The Rainbow Fish* by Marcus Pfister will supplement your exploration of the meaning of friendship. ANIMALS. BEAVERS. ECHOES. FRIENDSHIP.

157   MacDonald, Suse. *Sea Shapes.* Illus. by the author. Harcourt, 1994. ISBN 0-15-200027-5

As she did in *Alphabatics* with letters, MacDonald shows a series of three panels that start with a simple shape that gradually transforms into an ocean animal. A gray square acquires eyes and a tail and in the facing page, we see a colorful cut-paper collage of a seascape with a skate swimming by. The final pages offer a paragraph about the lives and habits of the creatures, which range from starfish and jellyfish to sharks and catfish. View more underwater dwellers in *A House for Hermit Crab* by Eric Carle and *Is This a House for Hermit Crab?* by Megan McDonald, *D Is for Dolphin* by Cami Berg, and *Under the Sea from A to Z* by Anne Doubilet. Also shape-conscious are *Color Farm* and *Color Zoo* by Lois Ehlert and *The Shapes Game* by Paul Rogers. MARINE ANIMALS. SHAPES.

158   McMillan, Bruce. *Beach Ball—Left, Right.* Photos by the author. Holiday House, 1992. ISBN 0-8234-0946-5

A boy on the beach tosses his huge multicolored beach ball into the air, and it travels overhead past an artist at his easel, a dog, a worker up a telephone pole, a farmhouse, cow, fire truck, and a field of flowers before landing in the waves once again. The only text are the words "left" on the left-hand page, and "right" on the right-hand page. Children can narrate their own version of the story and identify on which side of each color photo the ball is traveling. Take a vicarious beach trip with *Reflections* by Ann Jonas, *Not the Piano, Mrs. Medley!* by Evan Levine, *Is This a House for Hermit Crab?* by Megan McDonald, *One Sun: A Book of Terse Verse* by Bruce McMillan, *Beach Days* by Ken Robbins, and *Clams Can't Sing* by James Stevenson. AFRICAN AMERICANS. LEFT AND RIGHT. SEASHORE. VISUAL PERCEPTION.

159   McMillan, Bruce. *Sense Suspense: A Guessing Game for the Five Senses.* Photos by the author. Scholastic, 1994. ISBN 0-590-47904-0

Two children from the Caribbean island of Culebra, part of Puerto Rico, show us the sights, illustrated with McMillan's sharp color photos. For each close-up picture, viewers must first decide what the object is, and then pick which senses they'd use to experience it. We hear a steel drum, see a palm tree, smell a red hibiscus, taste a pineapple, and feel a goat's coat. The five senses are listed on the first page in both English and Spanish, and a list of possible responses, also bilingual, can be found at the back. Continue the guessing game with objects the children bring in, and with *My Five Senses* by Margaret Miller. Delve into individual senses with *What Joe Saw* by Anna Grossnickle Hines, *I Can Tell by Touching* by Carolyn Otto, and *The Listening Walk* by Paul Showers. ISLANDS. MULTICULTURAL STORIES. SENSES AND SENSATION. SPANISH LANGUAGE.

160   Martin, Bill, Jr. *Polar Bear, Polar Bear, What Do You Hear?* Illus. by the author. Henry Holt, 1991. ISBN 0-8050-1759-3

Similar in format to his *Brown Bear, Brown Bear, What Do You See?*, this one uses animal sounds, like a boa constrictor hissing or hippopotamus snorting. Children will need to supply their own interpretations for less typical verbs like fluting, braying, and trumpeting. Add on to the story, with each child drawing an animal and coming up with its voice. Make more noise with Hank De Zutter's international *Who Says a Dog Goes Bow-Wow?* ANIMALS. CALL-AND-RESPONSE STORIES. CHANTABLE REFRAIN. SOUND EFFECTS. ZOOS.

161 Marzollo, Jean. *Pretend You're a Cat.* Illus. by Jerry Pinkney. Dial, 1990. ISBN 0-8037-0774-6

"Can you climb?/ Can you leap?/ Can you stretch?/ Can you sleep?/ Can you hiss?/ Can you scat?/ Can you purr/ Like a cat?/ What else can you do like a cat?" Thirteen animals are described in similar lilting rhyme, with each colored-pencil and watercolor illustration depicting the animal and a winsome group of multiethnic children acting out the rhyme. Read the rhyme before showing the picture so children can guess the animal. Read each one aloud several times—first quickly, then slower, then slow enough for children to pantomime. Continue the poetry with Fay Robinson's *A Frog Inside My Hat.* Other animal guessing books include Marilee Robin Burton's *Tails, Toes, Eyes, Ears, Nose*, Beatrice Schenk de Regniers's *It Does Not Say Meow and Other Animal Riddle Rhymes*, Lois Ehlert's *Color Zoo*, and Deborah Guarino's *Is Your Mama a Llama?* ANIMALS. CREATIVE DRAMA. MULTICULTURAL STORIES. STORIES IN RHYME.

162 Marzollo, Jean. *Ten Cats Have Hats: A Counting Book.* Illus. by David McPhail. Scholastic, 1994. ISBN 0-590-20656-7

"One bear has a chair but I have a hat," declares a child, and on each successive page, we get a new rhyming animal number statement (and a new hat on the contented narrator's head), up to number ten. Heavy stock paper and bright watercolors make this an ideal beginning counting book. Children can come up with new animals and rhymes to count back down again. Ask everyone to bring in hats to show and count. *Big Fat Hen* by Keith Baker and *This Old Man* by Carol Jones are also simple counting stories in rhyme. CHANTABLE REFRAIN. CLOTHING AND DRESS. COUNTING BOOKS. HATS. STORIES IN RHYME.

163 Maurer, Donna. *Annie, Bea, and Chi Chi Dolores: A School Day Alphabet.* Illus. by Denys Cazet. Orchard, 1993. ISBN 0-531-08617-8

From A (all aboard) on the school bus to Z (zip) of the jacket, we sample a typical day with an endearing class of dogs, cats, squirrels, and a cute gray hippo as they count, draw, paint, and run races. Each large illustration contains one letter and word; your scholars will need to examine the action carefully and describe it aloud. Look in on other classes in Nancy Evans Cooney's *Chatterbox Jamie*, James Howe's *The Day the Teacher Went Bananas*, and Elvira Woodruff's *Show and Tell.* ALPHABET BOOKS. SCHOOLS.

164 Meddaugh, Susan. *Tree of Birds.* Illus. by the author. Houghton Mifflin, 1990. ISBN 0-395-53147-0

Harry rescues a wild Green Tufted Tropical he names Sally, but can't bear to let her loose to fly south with her bird compatriots. Compare the surprise ending with *Bird Dogs Can't Fly* by Mary Jane Auch and with a more traditional bird rescue story, *Island Baby* by Holly Keller. BIRDS. MIGRATION.

165   Miller, Margaret. *Guess Who?* Photos by the author. Greenwillow, 1994. ISBN 0-688-12783-5

Using the four-paneled guessing game format of her *Can You Guess?* and *Where Does It Go?*, Miller presents attractive nonstereotyped color photos of men and women demonstrating aspects of their occupations. Children can list other jobs they know, and make up new questions about them. MULTICULTURAL STORIES. OCCUPATIONS. QUESTIONS AND ANSWERS.

166   Miller, Margaret. *Where Does It Go?* Photos by the author. Greenwillow, 1992. ISBN 0-688-10929-2

With the same question-and-choice-of-answers format as her *Can You Guess?* and *Guess Who?*, listeners must identify where to put an assortment of belongings. Along the way, you can reinforce the concepts of connecting words like on, above, between, in, and among. Kathi Appelt's *Elephants Aloft* and Miller's *Where's Jenna?* are also perfect for teaching these concepts. CLOCKS. ENGLISH LANGUAGE–PREPOSITIONS. MULTICULTURAL STORIES. QUESTIONS AND ANSWERS. TOYS.

167   Miller, Margaret. *Where's Jenna?* Photos by the author. Simon & Schuster, 1994. ISBN 0-671-79167-2

The bathtub is full, and Jenna's mother looks for her little girl everywhere, but as we can see from the color photographs, Jenna is hiding. The story shows and tells us where her mother looks—behind the door, under the blanket—but each time Jenna is one step ahead, shedding items of clothing as she goes, and eventually ending up in the tub. Children will need to consider the spatial relationships of each photo and use prepositions to describe where the smiling child is hiding next. *Elephants Aloft* by Kathi Appelt, *Snow on Snow on Snow* by Cheryl Chapman, and Miller's *Where Does It Go?* use prepositions also, while in *Where's the Baby?* by Tom Paxton, we search for a fast-moving toddler. BATHS. CLOTHING AND DRESS. ENGLISH LANGUAGE–PREPOSITIONS.

168   Miller, Margaret. *Whose Shoe?* Photos by the author. Greenwillow, 1991. ISBN 0-688-10009-0

Miller's color photographs show a shoe, and children guess to whom it belongs before turning the page for the answer photos that show both an adult and a child. There's a natural mix of races and sexes, and shoes include baseball cleat, clown shoe, baby shoe, ballet slipper, horseshoe, skate, flipper, running shoe, and hip wader. Miller's *Whose Hat?* follows the same pattern. Try on a few of these for size: Niki Daly's *Not So Fast, Songololo*, Shirley Hughes's *Alfie's Feet*, Johanna Hurwitz's *New Shoes for Sylvia*, Denise Lewis Patrick's *Red Dancing Shoes*, Tomi

Ungerer's *One, Two, Where's My Shoe?*, and Elizabeth Winthrop's *Shoes*. MULTICULTURAL STORIES. OCCUPATIONS. QUESTIONS AND ANSWERS. SHOES.

169   **Modesitt, Jeanne.** *Sometimes I Feel Like a Mouse: A Book About Feelings.* **Illus. by Robin Spowart. Scholastic, 1992. ISBN 0-590-44835-8**

A child describes feeling shy, bold, sad, happy, scared, brave, excited, calm, mad, warm, ashamed, and proud, comparing each to an animal. Have your children try to guess each feeling from the picture and simple description. Delve more deeply into children's emotions with Catherine and Laurence Anholt's *What Makes Me Happy?*, William Cole's *Frances Face Maker*, Marie Hall Ets's *Talking without Words*, Betsy Everitt's *Mean Soup*, and Woodleigh Hubbard's *C Is for Curious: An ABC of Feelings*. Rosemary Wells's Bunny Planet books *First Tomato*, *The Island Light*, and *Moss Pillows* help us transcend a bad day. CREATIVE DRAMA. EMOTIONS.

170   **Modesitt, Jeanne.** *Vegetable Soup.* **Illus. by Robin Spowart. Macmillan, 1988. ISBN 0-02-767630-7**

New to the neighborhood, rabbits Elsie and Theodore visit each nearby house in search of carrots for lunch, and receive instead foods they've never tried before: dandelion leaves, parsley, cherry tomatoes, and cabbage. There's a recipe for the vegetable soup they make and then share with their animal neighbors, which you may want to try, with children each bringing in an ingredient. Since the rabbits are reluctant to taste something new, but find they like it, you may be able to influence a few of your picky eaters into taking more chances. Also take a taste of Doug Cushman's *Possum Stew*, Lois Ehlert's *Eating the Alphabet* and *Growing Vegetable Soup*, Betsy Everitt's *Mean Soup*, and Ann McGovern's or John Warren Stewig's *Stone Soup*. FOOD. NEIGHBORLINESS. RABBITS. SOUP. VEGETABLES.

171   **Mwenye Hadithi.** *Lazy Lion.* **Illus. by Adrienne Kennaway. Little, Brown, 1990. ISBN 0-316-33725-0**

Wanting protection from the impending Big Rain, Lion orders the White Ants, Weaver Birds, Aardvark, Honey Badger, and Crocodile in turn to build him a house, but none of the houses are suitable, so Lion stays on the African plain, houseless to this day. Take a look at real lion behavior in Toshi Yoshida's *Young Lions*. *Baby Baboon*, *Crafty Chameleon*, *Greedy Zebra*, *Hungry Hyena*, and *Tricky Tortoise* are other engaging Mwenye Hadithi animals with less than perfect personalities. AFRICA. ANIMALS. HOUSES. LAZINESS. LIONS.

172   **Nightingale, Sandy.** *A Giraffe on the Moon.* **Illus. by the author. Harcourt, 1992. ISBN 0-15-230950-0**

Beautifully realistic paintings juxtapose the normal and the odd in this two-sentence rhyming poem narrated by a boy who describes the strange things he's seen in his dreams. Children can describe and illustrate some of their more bizarre dreams. Imagine how your pets dream, with the aid of Helen V. Griffith's

Plunk's Dreams and Dav Pilkey's *When Cats Dream*. DREAMS. IMAGINATION. STORIES IN RHYME.

173   Offen, Hilda. *Nice Work, Little Wolf!* Illus. by the author. Dutton, 1992. ISBN 0-525-44880-2

When Brian Porker finds Little Wolf in the cucumber garden, he thinks Little Wolf is a puppy, and takes him in. As the newest and youngest member of a four-pig household, Little Wolf is expected to do all the work. Children will recognize from their own households the humorous chain of command that has Little Wolf first doing dishes, and then building a whole new house before he rebels. Others in the rare collection of stories that have a modicum of sympathy for the poor wolf include Harry Allard's *It's So Nice to Have a Wolf Around the House*, Keiko Kasza's *The Wolf's Chicken Stew*, and Eugene Trivizas's *The Three Little Wolves and the Big Bad Pig*. HELPFULNESS. PIGS. WOLVES.

174   O'Keefe, Susan Heyboer. *One Hungry Monster: A Counting Book in Rhyme*. Illus. by Lynn Munsinger. Joy Street / Little, Brown, 1989. ISBN 0-316-63385-2

From one to ten, the hungry monsters bedevil a little boy until he breaks out the food to appease them, but they scarf down every morsel and clamor for more. Raise more ruckus with *Pigs Aplenty, Pigs Galore!* by David McPhail, and keep counting with *One Cow Moo Moo!* by David Bennett and *Dinner at the Panda Palace* by Stephanie Calmenson. COUNTING BOOKS. FOOD. MONSTERS. STORIES IN RHYME.

175   Patrick, Denise Lewis. *Red Dancing Shoes*. Illus. by James Ransome. Tambourine, 1993. ISBN 0-688-10393-6

A young African American girl is entranced with "the finest, reddest, shiniest shoes that anyone had ever seen," a present from Grandmama, but running to show them off to her aunt, she falls and muddies them. The despair at ruining something new is also palpable in Masako Matsuno's *A Pair of Red Clogs*. Show off some fancy footwear in Niki Daly's *Not So Fast, Songololo*, Shirley Hughes's *Alfie's Feet*, Johanna Hurwitz's *New Shoes for Sylvia*, Tomi Ungerer's *One, Two, Where's My Shoe?*, and Elizabeth Winthrop's *Shoes*. AFRICAN AMERICANS. DANCING. GRANDMOTHERS. SHOES.

176   Polacco, Patricia. *Babushka's Doll*. Illus. by the author. Simon & Schuster, 1990. ISBN 0-671-68343-8

Hating to wait for anything, Natasha demands that her busy grandmother drop what she is doing to play with her and feed her lunch. Babushka retrieves her old doll from a shelf and gives it to the impulsive little girl, and the doll comes to life, insisting that Natasha do her bidding without a rest. Helen Lester's *Cora Copycat*, *Me First*, and *Pookins Gets Her Way*, and Susan Patron's *Burgoo Stew* also teach manners and good behavior. BEHAVIOR. DOLLS. GRANDMOTHERS.

177   Prater, John. *"No!" Said Joe*. Illus. by the author. Candlewick, 1992. ISBN 1-56402-037-1

Trying to lure Joe shopping when he wants to play, his parents delight him with a rhyming account of the giant, witch, or ghosts he might encounter if he stays home alone. Children will echo Joe's cries of "No!" or "Yes!" This good-natured cautionary tale is in the same mode as Maurice Sendak's *Pierre* who always says, "I don't care." CHANTABLE REFRAIN. FEAR. STORIES IN RHYME.

178   Pringle, Laurence. *Octopus Hug*. Illus. by Kate Salley Palmer. Boyds Mills, 1993. ISBN 1-56397-034-1

Mom's out for the evening, and Dad entertains his two young kids with an evening of delicious roughhouse play, giving eight-armed hugs and wild rides on his belly, singing "Rock-a-bye, Sweetie Pies," and playing "tree" and "monster," before he puts them to bed. Soft colored-pencil illustrations show a warm and affectionate African American family. Your children can draw and tell about special games their parents play with them. Denys Cazet's *"I'm Not Sleepy"* and Adele Aron Greenspan's *Daddies* give us more loving dads. AFRICAN AMERICANS. BROTHERS AND SISTERS. FAMILY LIFE. FATHERS. PLAY.

179   Rayner, Mary. *Ten Pink Piglets: Garth Pig's Wall Song*. Illus. by the author. Dutton, 1994. ISBN 0-525-45241-9

One by one, ten piglets fall off the brick wall, and a snoozing wolf awakens and eyes them eagerly. Though the wolf tries to catch them, we find out on the last page that they have all landed safely in the back of their dad's truck. Remember "99 Bottles of Beer on the Wall"? The tune is the same (music is included). Count up in song with *This Old Man* by Carol Jones and *Knick Knack Paddywack* by Marissa Moss; then count down with *Five Little Monkeys Jumping on the Bed* and *Five Little Monkeys Sitting in a Tree* by Eileen Christelow, *Six Sleepy Sheep* by Jeffie Ross Gordon, and *Five Little Ducks* by Raffi. COUNTING BOOKS. PIGS. SONGS. SUBTRACTION. WOLVES.

180   Reddix, Valerie. *Millie and the Mud Hole*. Illus. by Thor Wickstrom. Lothrop, 1992. ISBN 0-688-10213-1

Though one by one the farm animals worry that she's in too deep and implore her to "come out, come out of that mud!," Milly the pig thinks she knows more than they do about mud—until she realizes she's stuck. In a scene reminiscent of the folktale *The Turnip* (as retold by Pierr Morgan or Janina Domanska), everyone stands in a line to pull the silly pig out. Act this one out in narrative pantomime, adding the chantable refrains. Charlotte Pomerantz's *The Piggy in the Puddle* won't come out either. Janice Boland's *Annabel*, Arthur Getz's *Humphrey the Dancing Pig*, David McPhail's *Pigs Aplenty, Pigs Galore!*, and Robert Munsch's *Pigs* will add to the mayhem. CHANTABLE REFRAIN. CREATIVE DRAMA. DOMESTIC ANIMALS. PIGS. STORIES TO TELL.

181   Rogers, Paul. *The Shapes Game*. Illus. by Sian Tucker. Henry Holt, 1990. ISBN 0-8050-1280-X

A rhyming description/finding game in which children must name the shape described and pictured. The circles, triangles, squares, stars, ovals, crescents, rectangles, spirals, and diamonds are portrayed by bold-colored, geometric, batik-like, Matisse-cut-out-ish illustrations. Lois Ehlert's *Color Farm* and *Color Zoo*, Ed Emberley's rhyming *The Wing on a Flea*, and Suse MacDonald's *Sea Shapes* spotlight a plethora of shapes, and Eric Carle's *The Secret Birthday Message* uses them to guide readers through the story. Children can go shape-spotting and draw what they see. GEOMETRY. SHAPES. STORIES IN RHYME.

182   **Rounds, Glen.** *Old MacDonald Had a Farm.* **Illus. by the author. Holiday House, 1989. ISBN 0-8234-0739-X**

Rounds's version of the song, illustrated with large black-lined watercolors of slightly malevolent farm critters, ends with a skunk (with a PEE-YOO here . . .)! Act out each animal and sing with gusto. See also the versions by Lorinda Bryan Cauley, Nancy Hellen, Carol Jones, and Tracey Campbell Pearson, and the surprise ending in Gus Clarke's *EIEIO: The Story of Old MacDonald, Who Had a Farm.* Hank De Zutter's *Who Says a Dog Goes Bow-Wow?* introduces animal sounds in many languages. Spend a day in the country with Dee Dee Duffy's *Barnyard Tracks*, Denise Fleming's *Barnyard Banter*, Kathy Parkinson's and Mary Maki Rae's versions of *The Farmer in the Dell*, Jill Runcie's *Cock-a-Doodle-Doo!*, Martin Waddell's *The Pig in the Pond*, and Nadine Bernard Westcott's *Skip to My Lou.* CHANTABLE REFRAIN. DOMESTIC ANIMALS. FARM LIFE. FOLK SONGS. SOUND EFFECTS.

183   **Rowe, John A.** *Baby Crow.* **Illus. by the author. North-South, 1994. ISBN 1-55858-278-9**

His family just knows Baby Crow will be a great singer when he grows up, but right now, he can only say "beep" instead of "kaaaaaw." A consultation with wise Grandfather Crow reveals the problem—a cherry pit stuck in baby's craw—which, once removed unblocks Baby's very loud and persistent pipes, much to the dismay of the other crows who now can't sleep a wink. This is a purely nonsensical story with strange absurdist acrylic paintings. *Awful Aardvark* by Mwalimu Kennaway keeps everyone up with his snoring, which should add more oomph to an already noisy storytime. Show how noisy kids can be with Quentin Blake's high-spirited poetry book *All Join In.* BIRDS. NOISE. SOUND EFFECTS.

184   **Russo, Marisabina.** *Trade-In Mother.* **Illus. by the author. Greenwillow, 1993. ISBN 0-688-11417-2**

Feeling that nothing's gone right with his day, Max tells his mother that he wishes he could trade her in for a nicer, better mother who would let him wear dirty shirts and eat cookies whenever he wanted. Max finally decides he likes his mother best of all. Meet a few other sympathetic moms in Margaret Wise Brown's *The Runaway Bunny*, Betsy Everitt's *Mean Soup*, and Rosemary Wells's *Hazel's Amazing Mother.* The little girl in *I Am Really a Princess* by Carol Diggory Shields imagines the king and queen would be aghast if they only knew how restrictive her home life is with her everyday family. FAMILY LIFE. MOTHERS AND SONS.

185   **Schindel, John.** *What's for Lunch?* **Illus. by Kevin O'Malley. Lothrop, 1994. ISBN 0-688-13599-4**

It doesn't bother mouse Sidney a bit when the cat threatens to eat him, because a dog runs up planning to chase the cat, a goose plans to bite the dog's tail, and on down the line, as up come a fox, goat, lion, and elephant. "I don't think so," says imperturbable Sidney each time a new threat arises, until he takes charge, scaring the elephant with a giant-sized "BOO!" Act this one out, and share a mouse-sized snack of French bread and cheese afterward. Other chasing stories in the same vein include *One Cow Moo Moo!* by David Bennett, *Lucky Me* by Denys Cazet, *Rosie's Walk* by Pat Hutchins, and *Three Ducks Went Wandering* by Ron Roy, all starring plucky fowl. Rest with *The Napping House* by Audrey Wood, and then get back to the mice with the ravenous rodent in *Lunch!* by Denise Fleming and the mouse family in *Picnic* by Emily Arnold McCully. CHANTABLE REFRAIN. CREATIVE DRAMA. CUMULATIVE STORIES. MICE. PICNICS. SEQUENCE STORIES.

186   **Sharratt, Nick.** *My Mom and Dad Make Me Laugh.* **Illus. by the author. Candlewick, 1994. ISBN 1-56402-250-1**

Mom loves spots, Dad loves stripes, but their son only wears gray. Why? He loves elephants! Have your kids draw pictures depicting their own pattern preferences, from clothes, to food, to animals. *Color Zoo* and *Color Farm* by Lois Ehlert, *Sea Shapes* by Suse MacDonald, and *The Shapes Game* by Paul Rogers will expand their choices. *Little Elephant* by Miela Ford has clear color photographs that will turn you into elephant-lovers too. FAMILY LIFE. PATTERN PERCEPTION. SHAPES.

187   **Showers, Paul.** *The Listening Walk.* **Illus. by Aliki. HarperCollins, 1991. ISBN 0-06-021638-7**

A little girl, her father, and their dachshund Major take a "listening walk" together, contrasting the street noises of a lawn mower, cars, a baby crying, and a jackhammer with the quiet park noises of pigeons, crickets, and bees. On the last page, the child exhorts readers to close the book and count how many sounds they can hear right now. Categorize noises into loud, soft, animal, mechanical, and the like, and ask your listeners to try to imitate each sound. *Rat-a-Tat, Pitter Pat* by Alan Benjamin and the rhyming *Do Bunnies Talk?* by Dayle Ann Dodds are about onomatopoeic words, while in *The Loudest Noise in the World* by Benjamin Elkin, a young prince of the noisy kingdom of Hub-Bub finally hears what silence sounds like. Hank De Zutter's *Who Says a Dog Goes Bow-Wow?* and Marc Robinson's *Cock-a-Doodle-Doo! What Does It Sound Like to You?* offer multilingual animal sounds. Observe closely as Joe does in Anna Grossnickle Hines's *What Joe Saw.* ENGLISH LANGUAGE–ONOMATOPOEIC WORDS. FATHERS AND DAUGHTERS. SENSES AND SENSATION. SOUND. SOUND EFFECTS.

188   **Skofield, James.** *'Round and Around.* **Illus. by James Graham Hale. HarperCollins, 1993. ISBN 0-06-025747-4**

On an after-dinner walk to see the sunset, and while they get ready for bed, Dad explains about circles to young Sam who wants to know why the sun goes down. Find other night and day explanations in *Is Anybody Up?* and *Under the Sun* by

Ellen Kandoian, and *Go to Sleep, Nicholas Joe* by Marjorie Weinman Sharmat. Explore more circles with Donald Crews's *Ten Black Dots*. BEDTIME STORIES. CIRCLES. FATHERS AND SONS. GEOMETRY. SHAPES.

189   **Stickland, Henrietta.** *Dinosaur Roar!* **Illus. by Paul Stickland. Dutton, 1994. ISBN 0-525-45276-1**

"Dinosaur roar, dinosaur squeak, dinosaur fierce, dinosaur meek." The great crashing dinosaur watercolors leap off the page as the rhymes present opposite terms dino-style. Make a class list of other opposites children can illustrate with their own dinosaur pictures, and act out both the book and the children's new additions in narrative pantomime. *Dad's Dinosaur Day* by Diane Dawson Hearn, *The Dinosaur Who Lived in My Backyard* by B. G. Hennessy, *How Big Were the Dinosaurs?* by Bernard Most, *Time Flies* by Eric Rohmann, and *How I Captured a Dinosaur* by Henry Schwartz provide an adventurous mix of fantasy and fact. CREATIVE DRAMA. DINOSAURS. OPPOSITES. STORIES IN RHYME.

190   **Sweet, Melissa.** *Fiddle-I-Fee: A Farmyard Song for the Very Young.* **Illus. by the author. Little, Brown, 1992. ISBN 0-316-82516-6**

"I had a cat and the cat pleased me, I fed my cat under yonder tree; Cat went fiddle-I-fee." We also sing about hen (chipsy-chopsy), duck (quack, quack), goose (swishy-swashy), and other farm critters for children to recall in sequence. Sweet's soft watercolors are pleasing, with much child appeal. Sing also the down-home versions of *Old MacDonald Had a Farm* by Lorinda Bryan Cauley, Nancy Hellen, Carol Jones, Tracey Campbell Pearson, and Glen Rounds, and Gus Clarke's *EIEIO: The Story of Old MacDonald, Who Had a Farm,* plus Kathy Parkinson's and Mary Maki Rae's versions of *The Farmer in the Dell,* and Nadine Bernard Westcott's *Skip to My Lou.* CHANTABLE REFRAIN. CUMULATIVE STORIES. DOMESTIC ANIMALS. FOLK SONGS. NURSERY RHYMES. SONGS.

191   **Tolhurst, Marilyn.** *Somebody and the Three Blairs.* **Illus. by Simone Abel. Orchard, 1991. ISBN 0-531-08478-7**

Mr. and Mrs. and Baby Blair head off for a walk in the park, and Somebody, in the form of a friendly looking large brown bear, stops in to taste the breakfast cereal, try out the chairs, play in the kitchen, investigate the bathroom, and check out the beds. For a very first gentle introduction to parody, this is just right, so pair it with one of the originals, and act out both versions, with all chiming in on the "just right" refrains. There's no shortage of the normal retellings of *The Three Bears,* such as those illustrated by Jan Brett, Lorinda Bryan Cauley, Armand Eisen, Paul Galdone, James Marshall, or Janet Stevens. Goldilocks is the victim of a baby bear in the wordless turnaround *Deep in the Forest* by Brinton Turkle, and in Jane Yolen's *The Three Bears Rhyme Book,* bear and girl have become pals. BEARS. FAIRY TALES–SATIRE. PARODIES.

192   **Tompert, Ann.** *Just a Little Bit.* **Illus. by Lynn Munsinger. Houghton Mifflin, 1993. ISBN 0-395-51527-0**

With Elephant on one end and Mouse on the other, the seesaw won't work, and even though Giraffe, Zebra, Lion, Bear, Crocodile, Mongoose, Monkey, and Ostrich join Mouse to weigh down his side, it's not until a small brown beetle joins the group that they finally balance and can go up and down. Tie this in to a math lesson on balance, using a scale for children to estimate and try out equivalent objects. If there's a playground available, a stint on the seesaw will be in order. Note the differences in the main characters' sizes in *Effie* by Beverly Allinson and *The Ant and the Elephant* by Bill Peet. ANIMALS. FRIENDSHIP. ELEPHANTS. MICE. WEIGHTS AND MEASURES.

193   Trapani, Iza. *The Itsy Bitsy Spider.* Illus. by the author. Whispering Coyote Press, 1993. ISBN 1-879085-77-1

Not only does she climb up the waterspout, but in five beguiling new verses she also climbs the kitchen wall, a yellow pail, a rocking chair, and a maple tree, where she spins a silky web. Music is appended, and it will be challenging for children to devise new hand motions for all the new verses. Eric Carle's *The Very Busy Spider,* Raffi's *Spider on the Floor,* and Nadine Bernard Westcott's *I Know an Old Lady Who Swallowed a Fly* are all either singable or chantable. FOLK SONGS. SPIDERS. STORIES IN RHYME.

194   Turner, Ann. *Hedgehog for Breakfast.* Illus. by Lisa McCue. Macmillan, 1989. ISBN 0-02-789241-7

Sent off to fetch Mrs. Hedgehog for breakfast, fox children Charles and George assume they are supposed to cook her up, but she thinks the pot of water is for a bath and the fireplace spit and oven for drying her spines. Hash over the double meaning of having someone for breakfast. On the same wavelength, see Keiko Kasza's *The Wolf's Chicken Stew* and Betsy and Giulio Maestro's *Lambs for Dinner.* Make music with *The Happy Hedgehog Band* by Martin Waddell. Explain the difference between hedgehogs and porcupines, and read Helen Lester's *A Porcupine Named Fluffy.* FOXES. HEDGEHOGS.

195   Turner, Gwenda. *Over on the Farm.* Illus. by the author. Viking, 1994. ISBN 0-670-85437-9

Prepare for your visit to or study of the farm and countryside with this updated, realistically illustrated version of "Over in the Meadow" using cow and calf, sheep and lambs, and other mother/child animal families as you count to ten. For the original, refer to versions of *Over in the Meadow* by Paul Galdone, John Langstaff, Louise Voce, and Olive A. Wadsworth. Start a collection of names of animal babies. Keith Baker's *Big Fat Hen,* Kathleen Sullivan Carroll's *One Red Rooster,* Denise Fleming's *Count!* are all farm-wise counting books. ANIMALS. CALL-AND-RESPONSE STORIES. COUNTING BOOKS. DOMESTIC ANIMALS. STORIES IN RHYME.

196   Van Laan, Nancy. *People, People, Everywhere!* Illus. by Nadine Bernard Westcott. Knopf, 1992. ISBN 0-679-91063-8

A rhyming text and pulsating watercolors show people all over town, riding the buses, walking dogs in the park, eating hot dogs on the street, constructing tall buildings and subway tunnels, and leading busy lives. All along, we follow a boy, mother, and dog, until they move into the country, which will become the next metropolis. Go realistic with Shelley Rotner and Ken Kreisler's color photos of New York in *Citybook,*while Eileen Spinelli's *If You Want to Find Golden* lets us see the poetry and the colors lurking there. Compare contrasting life-styles using Maxine Bozzo's *Toby in the Country, Toby in the City* and see how a new town grows in Virginia Lee Burton's classic *The Little House*. Your class can construct their own 3-D model neighborhood with clay or milk cartons. CITIES AND TOWNS. COMMUNITIES. STORIES IN RHYME.

197   **Voce, Louise.** *Over in the Meadow: A Traditional Counting Rhyme.* **Illus. by the author. Candlewick, 1994. ISBN 1-56402-428-8**

One turtle digs, two ducklings quack, three little owls who-whoo, and four mice squeak in this version of the beloved nursery rhymelike counting book. The animals romping through Voce's full-page watercolor ink illustrations are friendly and eager. Compare with other versions retold by Paul Galdone, John Langstaff, and Olive A. Wadsworth. *Over on the Farm* by Gwenda Turner is a new farm animal-based version of the old rhyme. ANIMALS–POETRY. COUNTING BOOKS. NURSERY RHYMES. STORIES IN RHYME.

198   **Vollmer, Dennis.** *Joshua Disobeys.* **Illus. by the author. Landmark Editions, 1988. ISBN 0-933849-12-5**

Despite his mother's repeated warnings never to go close to shore, baby whale Joshua wants to get to know B. J., the little boy on shore, and before he knows it he's beached. The final pages offer interesting whale facts. This winning entry in the National Written & Illustrated By . . . Awards Contest for Students will enthrall listeners, especially when they examine the author/illustrator blurb and photo on the back cover and realize the guy was just six years old when the book was published. Identify whales in the ocean with color photo-essay *Going on a Whale Watch* by Bruce McMillan, and pretend you are a humpback whale with *Winter Whale* by Joanne Ryder. Send children to the 599.5s for more whale data. *Small Green Snake* by Libba Moore Gray and *The Grizzly Sisters* by Cathy Bellows give us more naughty young animals who ignore their mothers' warnings and almost pay a steep price. FRIENDSHIP. OBEDIENCE. WHALES.

199   **Waddell, Martin.** *Can't You Sleep, Little Bear?* **Illus. by Barbara Firth. Candlewick, 1992. ISBN 1-56402-007-X**

Big Bear lights up the dark cave with a succession of larger and larger lanterns, but it's not until he carries Little Bear outside to see the moon and the stars that the youngster gets over his fear of the dark. Look for more nighttime insomniacs in Sarah Hayes's *This Is the Bear and the Scary Night*, Russell Hoban's *Bedtime for Frances*, Lenny Hort's *How Many Stars in the Sky?*, Katy Rydell's *Wind Says Good Night*, and Marjorie Weinman Sharmat's *Go to Sleep, Nicholas Joe*. Children will want to discuss their nighttime fears for you to alleviate. BEARS. BEDTIME STORIES. FEAR. NIGHT. MOON.

200   **Waddell, Martin.** *Farmer Duck.* **Illus. by Helen Oxenbury. Candlewick, 1992. ISBN 1-56402-009-6**

"How goes the work?" calls the fat and lazy farmer, and the poor, weary, over-worked duck calls back, "Quack," as he slaves about the fields and farmhouse. Your children will chant this bit of call-and-response all year, and they'll cheer when the duck's animal friends' plan routs the farmer for good. For another reaction to the cooperation theme, read Janina Domanska or Paul Galdone's version of the folktale *The Little Red Hen.* CHANTABLE REFRAIN. COOPERATION. DOMESTIC ANIMALS. DUCKS. FARM LIFE. WORK.

201   **Waddell, Martin.** *Let's Go Home, Little Bear.* **Illus. by Barbara Firth. Candlewick, 1993. ISBN 1-56402-131-9**

Nervous about the sounds of plodding feet, dripping ice, plopping snow, and other noises, Little Bear needs reassurance from Big Bear as they walk home through the snowy woods. A warm and reassuring story, this one goes along with Waddell's *Can't You Sleep, Little Bear?* Celebrate snow with Virginia Lee Burton's *Katy and the Big Snow,* Ezra Jack Keats's *The Snowy Day,* Eve Rice's *Oh, Lewis!,* Millicent Selsam and Joyce Hunt's *Keep Looking,* Keizaburo Tejima's *Fox's Dream,* Harriet Zeifert's *Snow Magic,* and Charlotte Zolotows' *Something Is Going to Happen.* BEARS. FEAR. NOISE. WINTER.

202   **Wadsworth, Olive A.** *Over in the Meadow: An Old Counting Rhyme.* **Illus. by David A. Carter. Scholastic, 1992. ISBN 0-590-44498-0**

Compare the eye-catching cut-paper collages with the illustrations of other versions of this animal counting rhyme retold by Paul Galdone, John Langstaff, and Louise Voce. *Over on the Farm* by Gwenda Turner is a farm-themed variant. Cavort with the animals in Keith Baker's *Big Fat Hen,* Kathleen Sullivan Carroll's *One Red Rooster,* Denise Fleming's *Count!,* and Woodleigh Hubbard's *2 Is for Dancing: A 1 2 3 of Actions.* ANIMALS–POETRY. COUNTING BOOKS. NURSERY RHYMES. STORIES IN RHYME.

203   **Wagner, Karen.** *Silly Fred.* **Illus. by Normand Chartier. Macmillan, 1989. ISBN 0-02-792280-4**

Fred the pig who loves to sing nonsense songs and turn somersaults on his bed meets a humorless beaver who intimidates him into giving up his carefree ways until the irrepressible pig realizes it's more fun to be silly. Make up new nonsense words and tunes and let your listeners know that it's good to act silly sometimes. Janice Boland's *Annabel* and Charlotte Pomerantz's *The Piggy in the Puddle* are also about carefree porkers. BEHAVIOR. PIGS.

204   **Walsh, Ellen Stoll.** *Mouse Paint.* **Illus. by the author. Harcourt, 1989. ISBN 0-15-256025-4**

Three white mice hiding from a cat dip themselves in jars of red, yellow, and blue paint, and discover that mixing paint puddles with their feet results in delightful new colors of orange, green and purple. Dip into the paints and Leo Lionni's *Little Blue and Little Yellow*, Arnold Lobel's *The Great Blueness and Other Predicaments*, and Mary L. O'Neill's poems about color in *Hailstones and Halibut Bones*. For more color, see Dayle Ann Dodds's *The Color Box*, Lois Ehlert's *Color Farm* and *Color Zoo*, Ann Jonas's *Color Dance*, Merle Peek's *Mary Wore Her Red Dress and Henry Wore His Green Sneakers*, and Mary Serfozo's *Who Said Red?* COLOR. MICE.

205   Walsh, Ellen Stoll. *Pip's Magic*. Illus. by the author. Harcourt, 1994. ISBN 0-15-292850-2

Eager to overcome his fear of the dark, red salamander Pip seeks Old Abra the wizard to ask him for magic. His journey through the dark woods, into a black tunnel, and over the hills at nighttime provide the real magic, as the turtle wizard points out, for after the journey Pip has lost his fear. *Go Away, Big Green Monster!* by Ed Emberley allows children power over their fears, while in *Harry and the Terrible Whatzit* by Dick Gackenbach, a young boy vanquishes the monster in his basement by not showing fear. Ask children to describe something they were afraid of once but not anymore, and tell how they stopped being scared. COURAGE. FEAR. SALAMANDERS.

206   Walton, Rick. *How Many, How Many, How Many*. Illus. by Cynthia Jabar. Candlewick, 1993. ISBN 1-56402-062-2

Using the numbers one through 12, each page asks a rhymed question about a well-known set—including how many fingers, seasons, planets, and months—and asks listeners to guess the numbered answer. Make up more number rhymes together about other common facts, such as days of the week, eggs in a carton, or crayons in a box. Suzanne Aker's *What Comes in 2's, 3's & 4's?*, Andrew Clements's *Mother Earth's Counting Book*, Denise Fleming's *Count*, and Marc Harshman's *Only One* cover similar ground. Michael Jay Katz's *Ten Potatoes in a Pot and Other Counting Rhymes* are traditional rhymes using numbers one to 12. COUNTING BOOKS. MULTICULTURAL STORIES. QUESTIONS AND ANSWERS.

207   Weiss, Nicki. *An Egg Is an Egg*. Illus. by the author. Putnam, 1990. ISBN 0-399-22182-4

In simple rhyme with an interspersed refrain, "Nothing stays the same. Everything can change," a boy's mother points out that eggs become chicks, seeds become flowers, and day becomes night, but a mother's baby will always be her baby no matter what. *Changes* by Marjorie N. Allen and Shirley Rotner is a color photo-essay on changes in nature for plants, animals, seasons, and children. Children can name other things that change in their lives, and things that stay the same. CHANGE. CHANTABLE REFRAIN. STORIES IN RHYME.

208   Westcott, Nadine Bernard. *The Pop-Up, Pull-Tab Playtime House That Jack Built*. Illus. by the author. Joy Street / Little, Brown, 1991. ISBN 0-316-93138-1

Bright comic pen-and-ink and watercolors make this enticing pop-up book even more fun as we chant the refrain and marvel at all the complicated goings-on for this old-time favorite cumulative chant. A story-hour delight, it won't stand up to circulation, so keep it in your personal collection. Janet Stevens's *The House That Jack Built* is another good version. Using the same cumulative format are Verna Aardema's *Bringing the Rain to Kapiti Plain*, Mem Fox's *Shoes from Grandpa*, Arnold Lobel's *The Rose in My Garden*, Shirley Nietzel's *The Jacket I Wear in the Snow*, Rose Robart's *The Cake That Mack Ate*, and Colin West's *The King of Kennelwick Castle*. *Old MacDonald Had a Farm* by Nancy Hellen and *The Wheels on the Bus* by Paul O. Zelinsky are also entertaining pop-up-style books. CHANTABLE REFRAIN. CUMULATIVE STORIES. NURSERY RHYMES. TOY AND MOVABLE BOOKS.

209   Wishinsky, Frieda. *Oonga Boonga*. Illus. by Suçie Stevenson. Little, Brown, 1990. ISBN 0-316-94872-1

Baby Louise keeps on crying through all her family's attempts to comfort and amuse her, but it's not until her big brother Daniel says "oonga boonga" to her that her tears dry up. Look into the behavior of more babies in Trish Cooke's *So Much*, Jeffie Ross Gordon's *Two Badd Babies*, Pat Hutchins's monster-ish *Where's the Baby?*, Holly Keller's *Geraldine's Baby Brother*, Tom Paxton's *Where's the Baby?*, James Stevenson's *Rolling Rose*, and Vera B. Williams's *"More More More," Said the Baby*. In *A Teeny Tiny Baby* by Amy Schwartz, the infant narrator describes his life as a baby. Continue the tantrums and tears with *All the Way Home* by Lore Segal. BABIES. BROTHERS AND SISTERS. CRYING.

210   Wolff, Ashley. *Stella & Roy*. Illus. by the author. Dutton, 1993. ISBN 0-525-45081-5

In this updated park-situated version of the tortoise-and-the-hare fable, big sister Stella on her big wheel tells her little brother on his little coasting bike, "Last one to the popcorn stand is a rotten egg." Guess whose perseverance pays off? Read children the original, using Janet Stevens's *The Tortoise and the Hare* or Brian Wildsmith's *The Hare and the Tortoise*, and compare. BICYCLES. BROTHERS AND SISTERS. FABLES. PARODIES. PERSEVERANCE.

211   Wolkstein, Diane. *Step by Step*. Illus. by Jos. A. Smith. Morrow, 1994. ISBN 0-688-10316-2

Shod in four bright red sneakers, a little ant leaves home and walks over a stone, across a leaf, and under a branch, where she meets up with a cricket friend with whom she spends an exciting afternoon. Children will love the repeated "step by step" refrain, and acting it out in narrative pantomime will help them view the world from a small perspective and understand perseverance. *George Shrinks* by William Joyce shows a kid's point of view. For a most personable loud ant, read *Effie* by Beverley Allinson. Find out facts about your subject in *Ant Cities* by Arthur Dorros. ANTS. CHANTABLE REFRAIN. CREATIVE DRAMA. CRICKETS. FRIENDSHIP.

212   Wood, Audrey. *Silly Sally*. Illus. by the author. Harcourt, 1992. ISBN 0-15-274428-2

"Silly Sally went to town, walking backwards, upside down. On the way she met a pig, a silly pig, they danced a jig." Raucous yellow-hued illustrations of her ridiculous encounters with dog, loon, and sheep will keep kids giggling. Now have them write and illustrate new rhymes about "Silly Sally" or alliterative plays on their own names to read aloud and act out. Try some more slapstick rhymes with Cheryl Chapman's *Pass the Fritters, Critters*, Rita Golden Gelman's *I Went to the Zoo*, Bill Morrison's *Squeeze a Sneeze*, Miriam Nerlove's *I Made a Mistake*, Raffi's *Down by the Bay*, and Nancy Shaw's *Sheep in a Jeep* series. CHANTABLE REFRAIN. CREATIVE WRITING. NONSENSE VERSES. STORIES IN RHYME.

213   **Yee, Wong Herbert.** *Big Black Bear.* **Illus. by the author. Houghton Mifflin, 1993. ISBN 0-395-66359-8**

A droll rhyming story about a bear who barges into a girl's house, won't wipe his paws, won't cover his mouth when he coughs and sneezes, and then threatens to eat her as well—which is when the bear's mom shows up and makes him apologize, clean up, and show some manners. Practice your p's and q's with Cheryl Chapman's *Pass the Fritters, Critters*, Marc Brown and Stephen Krensky's *Perfect Pigs*, Helen Lester's *Me First*, and Patricia Polacco's *Babushka's Doll*. BEARS. BEHAVIOR. ETIQUETTE. STORIES IN RHYME.

214   **Zelinsky, Paul O.** *The Wheels on the Bus.* **Illus. by the author. Dutton, 1990. ISBN 0-525-44644-3**

Here's a peerless pop-up book you'll want for your personal collection, as the bus doors really open and shut, the wipers go swish swish swish, and the babies cry waah! waah! waah!, all with moveable parts that bring the old song alive. There's a subplot in the enticing colorful illustrations, as we watch a guitarist and all the moms and babies on the bus on their way to his program at the public library. Both Maryann Kovalski and Raffi have published excellent renditions as well. BUSES. SONGS. STORIES WITH SONGS. TOY AND MOVABLE BOOKS. TRANSPORTATION.

215   **Zimmerman, Andrea, and David Clemesha.** *The Cow Buzzed.* **Illus. by Paul Meisel. HarperCollins, 1993. ISBN 0-06-020809-0**

All the farm animals catch not only the bee's sneezing cold, but each other's voices as well. Children will have a field day with lines like the pig who says, "Moo, moo . . . cough cough, sniffle sniffle, ah-choo!" and perhaps they'll even learn to cover their mouths instead of sneezing on you. Feel better with Lynne Cherry's rhyming *Who's Sick Today?* and Christine Loomis's counting book *One Cow Coughs*. Farm animals trade voices in Charles Causley's *"Quack!" said the Billy Goat*, and Victoria Forrester's *The Magnificent Moo*. If you're looking for another bee story, try Byron Barton's *Buzz Buzz Buzz*. Versions of *Old MacDonald Had a Farm* by Cauley, Hellen, Jones, Pearson, Rounds and Clarke's *EIEIO* can't hurt, not to mention Dee Dee Duffy's *Barnyard Tracks*, Denise Fleming's *Barnyard Banter*, Kathy Parkinson's and Mary Maki Rae's versions of *The Farmer in the Dell*, Martin Waddell's *The Pig in the Pond*, and Nadine Bernard Westcott's *Skip to My Lou*. CHANTABLE REFRAIN. DOMESTIC ANIMALS. FARM LIFE. SICK. SOUND EFFECTS.

Illustration by Peggy Rathmann reprinted by permission of G. P. Putnam's Sons
from BOOTSIE BARKER BITES. Text copyright © 1992 by Barbara Bottner.
Illustrations copyright © 1992 by Peggy Rathmann.

FICTION FOR KINDERGARTEN–GRADE 1

216 **Accorsi, William.** *Friendship's First Thanksgiving.* **Illus. by the author. Holiday House, 1992. ISBN 0-8234-0963-5**

The story of the Pilgrims' first year in the New World is told from Friendship the dog's point of view, culminating in the famous Thanksgiving feast, where Friendship meets Indian dog Caniscoot. Though the story is, of course, fictionalized, it presents the bare facts of the Pilgrim/Indian relationship in a straightforward manner which, coupled with the colorful double-page paintings, will serve your holiday storytime well. According to the final note, the author reveals that by the following Thanksgiving, the two dogs were parents to six puppies. Jean Craighead George's *The First Thanksgiving*, Cheryl Harness's *Three Young Pilgrims*, and Steven Kroll's *Oh, What a Thanksgiving!* supply additional information, while *It's Thanksgiving* by Jack Prelutsky will supply some poetry. DOGS. HISTORICAL FICTION. INDIANS OF NORTH AMERICA. PILGRIMS. THANKSGIVING.

217 **Allinson, Beverly.** *Effie.* **Illus. by Barbara Reid. Scholastic, 1991. ISBN 0-590-44045-4**

Ant Effie's voice is like thunder, and all the other insects shun her, until the day a huge foot almost crushes them all, and the big-mouthed ant speaks up to stop an elephant in her tracks. Two things will enchant the storytime crowd: emulating Effie's shouted dialogue and examining Reid's fabulously detailed plasticine illustrations, after which you can whip out the ingredients for kid-made clay art pictures. Meet up with another mega-volumed small creature in Richard Wilbur's *Loudmouse* (Harcourt, 1991), and see small ones make a difference in Pete Seeger's *Abiyoyo* and Bill Peet's *The Ant and the Elephant*. Try some inviting nonfiction with *Those Amazing Ants* by Patricia Brennan Demuth and *Ant Cities* by Arthur Dorros, do a little math with *One Hundred Hungry Ants* by Elinor J. Pinczes, and go places with the peripatetic ant in *Step by Step* by Diane Wolkstein. ANTS. ELEPHANTS. NOISE. PICTURE BOOKS FOR ALL AGES.

218 **Armour, Peter.** *Stop That Pickle!* **Illus. by Andrew Shachat. Houghton Mifflin, 1993. ISBN 0-395-66375-X**

Unwilling to be eaten, the last fat pickle in the jar runs out of the deli on his little green legs, and darts down the street, chased by a determined peanut-butter-and-jelly sandwich, a braided pretzel, a green pippin apple, and 17 toasted almonds, all crying, "Stop that pickle!" Bring in a jar of kosher dills to crunch, and cucumbers to compare, and restart the chase with folktales P. C. Asbjørnsen's *The Runaway Pancake*, Arnica Esterl's *The Fine Round Cake*, Scott Cook or Paul Galdone's *The Gingerbread Boy*, or Eric A. Kimmel's *The Gingerbread Man*. In Joanne Oppenheim's *You Can't Catch Me!*, it's a fly that leads everyone astray. CHANTABLE REFRAIN. CUMULATIVE STORIES. FOOD.

219   Auch, Mary Jane. *Bird Dogs Can't Fly*. Illus. by the author. Holiday House, 1993. ISBN 0-8234-1050-1

Instead of fetching the injured goose his owner has shot, Blue befriends her and runs away from home so he can attempt to walk south with her, facing surmountable obstacles all along the way. Talk over: How much would you sacrifice for your best friend? Joanne Ryder's *Catching the Wind* transforms us into flying geese, and Jane Yolen's *Honkers* brings us back to earth with a touching, realistic story about a girl and the goose she raises until fall. Another meaty dog tale is *Ginger Jumps* by Lisa Campbell Ernst. CHRISTMAS. DOGS. FRIENDSHIP. GEESE. MIGRATION.

220   Auch, Mary Jane. *The Easter Egg Farm*. Illus. by the author. Holiday House, 1992. ISBN 0-8234-0917-1

Unable to lay regular eggs, hen Pauline insists she's not lazy, just different, and begins producing eggs with shells that look like whatever she sees: the cloudy sky, a ladybug, and a stained-glass light. Delighted with her hen's unusual eggs, Mrs. Pennywort agrees to donate the eggs to an Easter egg hunt, and takes Pauline to the art museum and the ballet for inspiration. Children can draw their own eggs, based on what they see and imagine. Check out more eggs in *Too Many Chickens* by Paulette Bourgeois, *Zinnia and Dot* by Lisa Campbell Ernst, *The Most Wonderful Egg in the World* by Helme Heine, and *Just Plain Fancy* by Patricia Polacco. The title heroes of *Three Cheers for Tacky* by Helen Lester and *The Spooky Tail of Prewitt Peacock* by Bill Peet don't fit the birds-of-a-feather mold either. CHICKENS. EASTER. EGGS. INDIVIDUALITY.

221   Auch, Mary Jane. *Monster Brother*. Illus. by the author. Holiday House, 1994. ISBN 0-8234-1095-1

It's bad enough that a monster sneaks into Rodney's room every night and keeps him awake, but now his mother is planning to bring home a new baby brother, and Rodney's worried, mostly about being alone in his room in the dark with what he imagines to be a monsterlike baby. This whimsical story with its bright paintings of a bug-eyed, skinny-legged family encompasses two real childhood fears, and ably assuages them both. See what a monster brother would be like in *The Very Worst Monster* and *Where's the Baby?* by Pat Hutchins. BABIES. BEDTIME STORIES. BROTHERS. FEAR. MONSTERS.

222   Aylesworth, Jim. *My Son John*. Illus. by David Frampton. Henry Holt, 1994. ISBN 0-8050-1725-9

Keep up the rhythm by chanting the 14 jingle-jangle verses about sons and daughters that takes the "diddle diddle dumpling" nursery rhyme to new heights through one farm day. Children will have tangled tongues as they curl them around delicious twisters like, "Chipper chipper woodpile,/ My son Neil," or "Dilly dilly dingdong,/ My daughter Lynn." Woodcuts of both words and pictures are large, primitive, and eye-catching. Write and illustrate a class book of new verses centered around a typical school day, e.g., "Pointy pointy pencil, my student Jen./ Writes with crayon or with pen./ Now that the sharpener broke again./ Pointy pointy pencil, my student Jen." Students can supply each name, the two words that rhyme with it, and the first lines, while you help them with the rest. Play some more name games with Jane Bayer's *A My Name Is Alice*, and Anita Lobel's books of girls' names *Alison's Zinnia* and boys' names, *Away from Home*. CALL–AND–RESPONSE STORIES. CHANTABLE REFRAIN. CREATIVE WRITING. FARM LIFE. NAMES. NURSERY RHYMES. STORIES IN RHYME.

223   **Aylesworth, Jim. *Old Black Fly*. Illus. by Stephen Gammell. Henry Holt, 1992. ISBN 0-8050-1401-2**

Old Black Fly's been buzzing around, driving everybody crazy in this oozy, sticky, rhyming alphabet book with its chantable, addictive "Shoo fly! Shoo fly! Shoo" refrain. Gammell's splattering colored-pencil-and-watercolor pictures are particularly hideous, which suits viewers just fine. The second time through, have listeners recall the key word for each letter of the alphabet before you show the picture. For more pesky flies, buzz off with Aylesworth's own *Hush Up!*, Lisa Westberg Peters's *When the Fly Flew In . . .*, and Joanne Oppenhem's *You Can't Catch Me*. ALPHABET BOOKS. CHANTABLE REFRAIN. FLIES. INSECTS. STORIES IN RHYME.

224   **Babbitt, Natalie. *Bub: Or, the Very Best Thing*. Illus. by the author. HarperCollins, 1994. ISBN 0-06-205044-3**

Wanting only the best for their son, the Prince, the King and Queen ask their advisors to help them identify what the very best thing for him is, but it's not vegetables and sleep, sunshine, songs, talking and listening; it's bub. Not until the last page do we find out that bub is really love, so ask your listeners what they think is the very best thing for the prince and for themselves. The medieval setting and the family's golden retriever in a blue jester's cap will charm everyone. Explore why love is so important to people of all ages with Susan Jeschke's *Lucky's Choice* and Eileen Spinelli's *Somebody Loves You, Mr. Hatch*. KINGS AND RULERS. LOVE. PRINCES AND PRINCESSES.

225   **Babcock, Chris. *No Moon, No Milk*. Illus. by Mark Teague. Crown, 1993. ISBN 0-517-58780-7**

Rob's cow Martha is sick of her life, and, wanting to do more than cow around in the pasture all day, refuses to give any more milk until Rob helps her go to the moon. Thanks to a moon exhibit at New York's Museum of Natural History, Martha makes a simulated visit. What lunacy! Compare her Neil Armstrong-like pose with the original photograph. Use with Paula Brown's *Moon Jump: A*

Cowntdown, Jennifer A. Ericsson's *No Milk!*, Paul Brett Johnson's *The Cow Who Wouldn't Come Down*, David Kirby and Allen Woodman's *The Cows Are Going to Paris*, and Nancy Van Laan's *The Tiny, Tiny Boy and the Big, Big Cow*. Lisa Campbell Ernst's *When Bluebell Sang* features another cow with big aspirations, and Alice Schertle's poetry picture book *How Now, Brown Cow?* is a treat. Make a return trip to the museum with Hudson Talbott's extraterrestrial dinosaurs in *We're Back!* COWS. MILK. MOON. MUSEUMS. NEW YORK CITY.

226   **Baer, Edith.** *This Is the Way We Go to School: A Book About Children Around the World.* **Illus. by Steve Björkman. Scholastic, 1990. ISBN 0-590-43161-7**

Jaunty rhyming couplets accompany children worldwide as they travel to school on foot, by Staten Island Ferry, cable car in San Francisco, vaporetto in Venice, skiis, train, and bicycle. The last pages tell where each group of children hails from, which is marked on a world map. Show the places on a globe as well. Rose Bursik's *Amelia's Fantastic Flight*, Hank De Zutter's *Who Says a Dog Goes Bow-Wow?*, Arthur Dorros's *This Is My House*, Debra Leventhal's *What Is Your Language?*, Anita Lobel's *Away from Home*, and Marilyn Singer's *Nine O'Clock Lullaby* all have a global outlook. GEOGRAPHY. MULTICULTURAL STORIES. SCHOOLS. STORIES IN RHYME. TRANSPORTATION.

227   **Ball, Duncan.** *Jeremy's Tail.* **Illus. by Donna Rawlins. Orchard, 1991. ISBN 0-531-08551-1**

On his way to pin the tail on the donkey, blindfolded Jeremy boards a bus and a ship, walks past the pyramids, hops a hot air balloon, and is shot out of a cannon before wending his way back to the birthday party. Play a round of the game so children can see how easy it is to become disoriented when blindfolded, and act out Jeremy's long walk in narrative pantomime. Keep traveling with *Magic Carpet* by Pat Brisson, *Amelia's Fantastic Flight* by Rose Bursik, *Away from Home* by Anita Lobel, *How to Make an Apple Pie and See the World* by Marjorie Priceman, *Uncle Lester's Hat* by Howie Schneider, *Love, Your Bear Pete* by Dyan Sheldon, and *Nine O'Clock Lullaby* by Marilyn Singer. CREATIVE DRAMA. GAMES. GEOGRAPHY. VOYAGES AND TRAVELS.

228   **Banks, Kate.** *Peter and the Talking Shoes.* **Illus. by Marc Rosenthal. Knopf, 1994. ISBN 0-394-92723-0**

Sent to the baker's for a loaf of bread, Peter loses his coins and sets out on a cumulative adventure, advised along the way by his sturdy pair of brown shoes, to the locksmith, carpenter, tailor, farmer, and back to the baker. The cheerful, retro 1930s-style illustrations will keep kids laughing, and, if they each bring in a pair of shoes, they can cut loose with some soleful dialogue. Another delightful cumulative tale is *The Old Woman and Her Pig*, as retold by Paul Galdone, Eric A. Kimmel, or Rosanne Litzinger, or Priscilla Lamont's *The Troublesome Pig*, while Nonny Hogrogian's *One Fine Day* is another cumulative tale similar in theme. CUMULATIVE STORIES. SHOES.

229   **Barracca, Debra, and Sal Barracca.** *A Taxi Dog Christmas.* **Illus. by Alan Ayers. Dial, 1994. ISBN 0-8037-1361-4**

After skating at New York City's Rockefeller Center, dog narrator Maxi, his taxi-driving pal Jim, and a new-found kitten spend a night to remember when Santa's sleigh crash-lands nearby. The big guy entreats them to hitch up the reindeer to the taxi, load it with toys, and save Christmas. Keep on trucking with *The Wild Christmas Reindeer* by Jan Brett, *Harvey Slumfenburger's Christmas Present* by John Burningham, *Santa's Book of Names* by David McPhail, and *The Reindeer Christmas* by Moe Price. CHRISTMAS. DOGS. NEW YORK CITY. SANTA CLAUS. STORIES IN RHYME. TAXI-CABS.

230   Bellows, Cathy. *The Grizzly Sisters.* Illus. by the author. Macmillan, 1991. ISBN 0-02-709032-9

"We're big! We're bad! We're the Grizzly sisters!" the two young bears growl delightedly when they scare off seven beavers and even the Wolf brothers, but they can't scare off camera-snapping tourists until their big grizzly Mama steps in to rescue them. Children will take great pleasure in imitating the ferocious faces of the bears. Like *The Tale of Peter Rabbit* by Beatrix Potter, these bears do learn their lesson that "people and bears don't mix," which we could also see in the classic *Blueberries for Sal* by Robert McCloskey. While it's prudent to steer clear of bears, it's safe if you go exploring with Michael Rosen's *We're Going on a Bear Hunt*. Jim Murphy's *Backyard Bear* gives a more realistic taste. Two other creatures who don't listen to their mothers and find themselves in danger are the snake in *Small Green Snake* by Libba Moore Gray and the baby whale in *Joshua Disobeys* by Dennis Vollmer. BEARS. BEHAVIOR. OBEDIENCE.

231   Blake, Robert J. *The Perfect Spot.* Illus. by the author. Philomel, 1992. ISBN 0-399-22132-8

Grumpy Dad, searching the woods for just the right place to paint, and his inquisitive young son, eager to catch frogs and insects, can't agree on a common site to stop. It's not till Dad shares a good splash in the water with his son that he unwinds enough to notice the waterfall, wildlife, and paintable beauty all around. With its radiant watercolor paintings of the New Jersey countryside, this story will motivate children to search for, revel in, and draw or paint their own perfect spots. Tomie dePaola's autobiographical picture book *The Art Lesson* and Cynthia Rylant's story of a painter with a passion for whales *All I See* will also rouse prospective painters to wet their brushes. As an interesting tie-in, Caryn Yacowitz's Chinese folktale *The Jade Stone* tells of a principled sculptor who incurs an emperor's wrath. ARTISTS. FATHERS AND SONS. NATURE. PAINTING.

232   Blundell, Tony. *Beware of Boys.* Illus. by the author. Greenwillow, 1992. ISBN 0-688-10924-1

Captured by a hungry wolf, a small boy offers him very good recipes for Boy Soup, Boy Pie, and Boy Cake, all filled with preposterous ingredients that enable the boy to outwit the wolf and make it home in time for his own supper. Listeners will giggle every time the boy foils the wolf's meal by stating, ". . . silly wolf, you have forgotten the salt!" Compose new recipes just in case the wolf escapes his bricked-up cave and makes it to school in time for lunch. *Yo, Hungry*

Wolf! A Nursery Rap by David Vozar contains three folktale parodies in rhyme. See how one girl gets the best of a hungry fox in Patricia C. McKissack's *Flossie & the Fox*. COOKERY. WOLVES.

233   **Bodsworth, Nan.** *A Nice Walk in the Jungle.* **Illus. by the author. Viking Kestrel, 1989. ISBN 0-670-82476-3**

Intent on not missing the exciting wildlife all around, Miss Jellaby takes her class on a nature walk during which the children are swallowed, one by one, by a grinning boa constrictor (even the child in the wheelchair!). The plucky young teacher rescues them all, but not before your viewers have spotted a slew of creatures, from anteaters to hippos. You'll probably want to break into song with Shel Silverstein's "I'm Being Eaten by a Boa Constrictor" from *Where the Sidewalk Ends*. Boas abound in C. Imbior Kudrna's *To Bathe a Boa*, Robert Leydenfrost's *The Snake That Sneezed*, and Trinka Hakes Noble's *The Day Jimmy's Boa Ate the Wash*, while in Tomi Ungerer's lovable *Crictor*, the snake can even spell! ANIMALS. RAIN FORESTS. SNAKES. TEACHERS.

234   **Bottner, Barbara.** *Bootsie Barker Bites.* **Illus. by Peggy Rathman. Putnam, 1992. ISBN 0-399-22125-5**

Just because their mothers are best friends, the hapless narrator and the diabolical tyrant child Bootsie are expected to play together during visits. Children will laugh and cheer when the overburdened little girl gets even with the "bad seed," and will have their own horror stories to add. Ammunition for coping with bullies abounds in Carol Chapman's *Herbie's Troubles*, Joanna Cole's *Don't Call Me Names*, Phyllis Reynolds Naylor's *King of the Playground*, and Hans Wilhelm's *Tyrone the Horrible*. Rat describes how his best friend used to boss him around until he learned to stand his ground in *The Rat and the Tiger* by Keiko Kasza. BEHAVIOR. BULLIES.

235   **Bourgeois, Paulette.** *Too Many Chickens.* **Illus. by Bill Slavin. Joy Street / Little, Brown, 1991. ISBN 0-316-10358-6**

Farmer Berry gives Mrs. Kerr's class a gift of a dozen chicken eggs, all of which hatch, grow, and lay more eggs; a bunch of angora bunnies, which shed fur for yarn to knit hats; and a nanny goat, which gives milk. The money the class makes from selling all these useful products enables them to buy a farm, and Mrs. Kerr's seed packets on the final page will get listeners thinking about composing a sequel. Amy Ehrlich's *Parents in the Pigpen, Pigs in the Tub* gives a skewed view of farm life when the animals take over, and Lisa Campbell Ernst's *Zinnia and Dot* will give you more empathy for hatching chickens. CHICKENS. DOMESTIC ANIMALS. SCHOOLS. TEACHERS.

236   **Brett, Jan.** *Trouble with Trolls.* **Illus. by the author. Putnam, 1992. ISBN 0-399-22336-3**

On her way to visit her cousin on the other side of Mount Baldy, Treva is waylaid by a succession of furry-tailed trolls who want to take her shepherd dog Tuffi but are satisfied when she gives them pieces of her warm winter clothing instead.

Other troll outwitters include P. C. Asbjørnsen's *The Three Billy Goats Gruff*, George Webbe Dasent's *The Cat on the Dovrefell*, Edward Marshall's *Troll Country*, and Don Arthur Torgersen's *The Girl Who Tricked the Troll*. Stay in the cold climates with Brett's *The Mitten* and *The Wild Christmas Reindeer*. CLOTHING AND DRESS. DOGS. SNOW. TROLLS. WINTER.

237 **Brett, Jan.** *The Wild Christmas Reindeer.* **Illus. by the author. Putnam, 1990. ISBN 0-399-22192-1**

Determined to act strong and firm to train Santa's reindeer in time for Christmas, Teeka instead alienates them with her loud voice and scolding manner until she learns that gentleness and cooperation work best. Brett's ornate paintings and borders are lovely as always, and her winter theme is repeated in *The Mitten*, *Trouble with Trolls*, and *The Twelve Days of Christmas*. Keep the reindeer in harness with *A Taxi Dog Christmas* by Debra and Sal Barracca, *Harvey Slumfenburger's Christmas Present* by John Burningham, *Santa's Book of Names* by David McPhail, and *The Reindeer Christmas* by Moe Price. BEHAVIOR. CHRISTMAS. COOPERATION. REINDEER. SANTA CLAUS.

238 **Brown, Eileen.** *Tick-Tock.* **Illus. by David Parkins. Candlewick, 1994. ISBN 1-56402-300-1**

Mom will be back at four and Skip Squirrel has promised not to jump on the chairs, but when friend Brainy comes over, the temptation is too great. The two of them end up crashing into Mom's precious cuckoo clock, which they then rush first to Weasel, then Hedgehog, and finally Owl who fixes it, more or less. Before reading aloud the final two pages, ask listeners to predict the ending. *Clocks and More Clocks* by Pat Hutchins and *The One and Only Super-Duper Golly-Whopper Jim-Dandy Really-Handy Clock-Tock-Stopper* by Patricia Thomas are also timely. ACCIDENTS. CLOCKS. SQUIRRELS. TIME.

239 **Brown, Marc.** *Arthur's Chicken Pox.* **Illus. by the author. Little, Brown, 1994. ISBN 0-316-11384-0**

Arthur's sister D.W. is jealous of all the attention he receives when he comes down with the chicken pox, and though he's well soon enough to go to the circus, in a surprise ending, it's D.W. who has to stay home. Read this during your next class epidemic, talk over the good and the bad parts of being sick, and make class get-well cards for the kids who are out. Recover with the aid of Franz Brandenberg's *I Wish I Was Sick, Too*, Lynne Cherry's rhyming *Who's Sick Today?*, Ursula LeGuin's *A Visit from Dr. Katz*, and Christine Loomis's *One Cow Coughs: A Counting Book for the Sick and Miserable*. What happens at the circus? Read *Circus* by Lois Ehlert for a quick show. BROTHERS AND SISTERS. CHICKEN POX. SICK.

240 **Brown, Paula.** *Moon Jump: A Countdown.* **Illus. by the author. Viking, 1992. ISBN 0-670-84237-0**

In a charming and original rhyming subtraction story, Angus Le Boeuf is the announcer as each cow attempts—and fails—to jump over the moon with assistance of trapeze, wings, pogo stick, slingshot, and high dive. It's not until the last contestant, Little Miss Heiferton with her pole vault, that we have a winner. Chant the "Oh, no! She missed" refrain for each cow. Compose more cow subtraction problems for your students to figure. The rhyming *Ten Sly Piranhas* by William Wise is a wicked companion, as the fish get eaten one by one. Count back up with *One Cow Moo Moo!* by David Bennett. Keep on mooing with Jennifer A. Ericsson's *No Milk!*, Paul Brett Johnson's *The Cow Who Wouldn't Come Down*, and David Kirby and Allen Woodman's *The Cows Are Going to Paris*. Be sure to review the Mother Goose rhyme "Hey, Diddle Diddle" before you do anything else so your listeners will appreciate the analogy. CHANTABLE REFRAIN. CONTESTS. COUNTING BOOKS. MOON. STORIES IN RHYME. SUBTRACTION.

241   Browne, Anthony. *Changes*. Illus. by the author. Knopf, 1991. ISBN 0-679-91029-8

Joseph's father told him things would change around the house, and indeed, the sink sprouts a face and the chair turns into a gorilla. Read this one twice so children can point out all the transformations and look for clues that show the real change is the arrival of a new baby. Other books to help children adjust to the idea of a newborn include Mary Jane Auch's *Monster Brother*, Jane Cutler's *Darcy and Gran Don't Like Babies*, Alane Ferguson's *That New Pet!*, Kevin Henkes's *Julius, the Baby of the World*, Ezra Jack Keats's *Peter's Chair*, Holly Keller's *Geraldine's Baby Brother*, and James Stevenson's *Worse Than Willy!* BABIES. CHANGE. IMAGINATION. TRANSFORMATIONS.

242   Buehner, Caralyn. *A Job for Wittilda*. Illus. by Mark Buehner. Dial, 1993. ISBN 0-8037-1150-6

Down to her last dried rat, witch Wittilda seeks a job that will feed her 47 cats, and though she's fired from her aunt's hairdressing salon for creating a spiderweb hairstyle, she hits her stride as a delivery person at Dingaling Pizza. Not only will children adore the personable paintings, but sharp-eyed kids will want to spirit the book to a secluded corner to find the dangling spider and inquisitive mouse hidden on each page. Give kids a look at some alternative witchy types with Tomie dePaola's Strega Nona series, Dennis Nolan's *Witch Bazooza*, and Erica Silverman's *Big Pumpkin*. CATS. WITCHES. WORK.

243   Bunting, Eve. *Our Teacher's Having a Baby*. Illus. by Diane de Groat. Clarion, 1992. ISBN 0-395-60470-2

First-grade teacher Mrs. Neal is pregnant, and student Samantha describes how the class prepares for the event, writing letters on the computer for the baby, selecting names, and coping with their teacher's absence when she delivers earlier than expected. When one of our own first-grade teachers got pregnant, we were so thankful for this story, which allayed children's anxieties and prepared them for changes their beloved teacher would soon undergo. Investigate sibling anxiety in Mary Jane Auch's *Monster Brother* and Anthony Browne's *Changes*; jealousy in Kevin Henkes's *Julius, the Baby of the World*, Jane Cutler's *Darcy and Gran Don't Like Babies*, and Alane Ferguson's *That New Pet!*; and embarrassment over a baby brother in Mary Hoffman's *Henry's Baby*. Then find out what the new parents and the new baby will be experiencing with Amy Schwartz's delicious *A Teeny Tiny Baby*. BABIES. MULTICULTURAL STORIES. SCHOOLS. SEPARATION ANXIETY. TEACHERS.

244   Burningham, John. *Harvey Slumfenburger's Christmas Present*. Illus. by the author. Candlewick, 1993. ISBN 1-56402-246-3

Ready for bed after a long night delivering presents, Santa is aghast to discover one he forgot to deliver to Harvey, a boy too poor to get any other gifts and who lives in a hut at the top of the Roly Poly Mountain, which is far, far away. Using every possible means of transportation to get there and back—starting with airplane, jeep, motorbike, skis, and rope—Santa puts the box in Harvey's stocking and heads home. Children can say Santa's speech along with him each time, and act out each step of the journey. Warm up by listing as many means of transportation as possible. Since we never do find out what's in the box, have children pantomime opening it up and tell (or draw) what they would want to be in it. Deliver more holiday fun with Janet and Allan Ahlberg's *The Jolly Christmas Postman*, Debra and Sal Barracca's *A Taxi Dog Christmas*, Jan Brett's *The Wild Christmas Reindeer*, David McPhail's *Santa's Book of Names*, and Moe Price's *The Reindeer Christmas*. CHANTABLE REFRAIN. CHRISTMAS. CREATIVE DRAMA. SANTA CLAUS. TRANSPORTATION.

245   Cannon, Janell. *Stellaluna*. Illus. by the author. Harcourt, 1993. ISBN 0-15-280217-7

Separated from her loving mother by an owl, baby bat Stellaluna lands in a bird's nest where she learns to become one of the the birds until a chance nighttime encounter with other bats leads her back home. Children who express disgust or fear when you mention bats are going to change their minds big time when they meet Stellaluna, a most captivating creature exquisitely rendered in colored pencil and acrylics. Holly Keller's *Horace* and Keiko Kasza's *A Mother for Choco* deal with the adoption-by-a-different-species issue. Fill in more facts with *Shadows of Night: The Hidden World of the Little Brown Bat* by Barbara Bash. Share Paul Goble's Native American folktale *Iktomi and the Boulder*, African folktales in Tololwa M. Mollel's *A Promise to the Sun* and Judy Sierra's *The Elephant's Wrestling Match*, plus Don Freeman's *Hattie the Backstage Bat*, and *Batty Riddles* by Katy Hall and Lisa Eisenberg. ADOPTION. BATS. BIRDS. IDENTITY. PICTURE BOOKS FOR ALL AGES.

246   Carle, Eric. *A House for Hermit Crab*. Illus. by the author. Picture Book Studio, 1987. ISBN 0-88708-056-1

Each month Hermit Crab finds another sea animal to decorate, clean, and protect his new shell, until, at the end of all 12 months, he passes on his lovely ornate house to a smaller hermit crab and eagerly contemplates starting a new one. Continue house hunting with *Is This a House for Hermit Crab?* by Megan McDonald. The color photos in *Under the Sea from A to Z* by Anne Doubilet include some of the sea creatures in Carle's story, as do those in *Sea Shapes* by Suse MacDonald. Reinforce the months with Sara Coleridge's *January Brings the*

Snow and Maurice Sendak's *Chicken Soup with Rice*. CRABS. HERMIT CRABS. HOUSES. MARINE ANIMALS. MONTHS.

247   Carle, Eric. *Pancakes, Pancakes!* Illus. by the author. Scholastic, 1990. ISBN 0-590-44453-0

A yen for a big pancake for breakfast sends Jack cutting and grinding wheat for flour, gathering eggs, milking the cow, churning butter, building a fire, and following his mother's directions for preparing the recipe. Act out the procedure with your hungry crew and consider preparing breakfast with them. Compare with Paul Galdone's *The Little Red Hen* where the chicken does all the work. *How to Make an Apple Pie and See the World* by Marjorie Priceman sends us on a worldwide hunt for ingredients. P. C. Asbjørnsen's *The Runaway Pancake* and Lorinda Bryan Cauley's *The Pancake Boy* are about the pancakes that got away. COOKERY. CREATIVE DRAMA. FOOD.

248   Carle, Eric. *Today Is Monday.* Illus. by the author. Philomel, 1993. ISBN 0-399-21966-8

Sing through the days of the week, along with a menu of corresponding snacks, with Eric Carle's oversized, colorful, tissue-paper-collage animal illustrations accompanying the old song, from Monday's string beans to Sunday's ice cream. Words and music are appended. Children can sing or chant the reverse cumulative verses, and write new ones about the months or colors. Along with Bill Martin, Jr.'s *Brown Bear, Brown Bear, What Do You See?* this should become a staple of primary concept books kids love. Could this be a variant of the 16th-century children's food matching game upon which Audrey Wood based her *Heckedy Peg?* For more eats, Anne Shelby's *Potluck* is an alliterative alphabet of children and the foods they bring with them to a feast. DAYS OF THE WEEK. FOOD. SEQUENCE STORIES. SONGS.

249   Carlson, Nancy L. *A Visit to Grandma's.* Illus. by the author. Viking, 1991. ISBN 0-670-83288-X

Beaver Tina and her parents are shocked at Grandma's new life-style in her Florida condo, but they manage to spend an even more delightful Thanksgiving there than they did on the old farm. Children's stereotyped images will be blown away with this modern aerobic-dancing grandma and other get-up-and-goers like those in Arielle North Olson's *Hurry Home, Grandma!* or James Stevenson's "Grandpa" stories. Lydia Maria Child's *Over the River and Through the Wood: A Song for Thanksgiving* gives a more traditional look. GRANDMOTHERS. THANKS-GIVING.

250   Caseley, Judith. *Dear Annie.* Illus. by the author. Greenwillow, 1991. ISBN 0-688-10011-2

Since Annie was born, her grandpa continued to send her letters and cards until she was old enough to dictate and then write her own replies. The day Annie brings her decorated shoebox filled with Grandpa's 86 letters to school for show-and-tell, all the children decide they want pen pals too, and set up a "Mail from Everybody" bulletin board that is soon covered with correspondence from all over the world. Encourage your class to write to their grandparents and share their responses with the group. Perhaps some of the children's grandparents who live nearby will come to school for a visit. CREATIVE WRITING. FAMILY STORIES. GRANDFATHERS. LETTER WRITING.

251   Child, Lydia Maria. *Over the River and Through the Wood: A Song for Thanksgiving.* **Illus. by Nadine Bernard Westcott. HarperCollins, 1993. ISBN 0-06-021304-3**

In this sprightly illustrated picture book of the old song, we see grandmother and grandfather preparing for their guests as Mom and Dad and their three children drive their car out of the city to the country to join them for the big meal. Prepare for the holiday with Johanna Johnston's *Speak Up, Edie*, Steven Kroll's *Oh, What a Thanksgiving*, the poems in Jack Prelutsky's easy-to-read *It's Thanksgiving*, and Eileen Spinelli's *Thanksgiving at the Tappletons'*. William Accorsi's *Friendship's First Thanksgiving*, Jean Craighead George's *The First Thanksgiving*, and Cheryl Harness's *Three Young Pilgrims* give the history behind the feast. GRANDPARENTS. SONGS. THANKSGIVING.

252   Christelow, Eileen. *Gertrude, the Bulldog Detective.* **Illus. by the author. Clarion, 1992. ISBN 0-395-58701-8**

When Gertrude's friends plant a few fake clues to satisfy the mystery-loving dog, she stumbles upon real crooks who have just pulled off an art heist. Other light-hearted mysteries with animal sleuths include *My Dog and the Birthday Mystery* by David A. Adler and *Chameleon Was a Spy* by Diane Redfield Massie. Explain how mysteries work with Doug Cushman's intrepid, rhyming *The ABC Mystery*. DOGS. MYSTERY AND DETECTIVE STORIES. ROBBERS AND OUTLAWS.

253   Cleary, Beverly. *Petey's Bedtime Story.* **Illus. by David Small. Morrow, 1993. ISBN 0-688-10061-7**

Not yet ready for sleep, young Petey takes over from his exhausted father and tells "the baby story" of his birth, from his parents rushing to the hospital to his father getting a parking ticket. Children can ask their parents to fill them in on their own birth tales, as Marisabina Russo did in *Waiting for Hannah*. Meet another storytelling child in Charlotte Pomerantz's *Posy*. BABIES. BEDTIME STORIES. FAMILY LIFE. FAMILY STORIES. STORYTELLING.

254   Cole, Joanna. *Don't Call Me Names.* **Illus. by Lynn Munsinger. Random House, 1990. ISBN 0-679-90258-9**

Frog Nell is taunted daily by fox Mike and pig Joe until she stands up to them in her monster costume at the costume parade. Barbara Bottner's *Bootsie Barker Bites*, Carol Chapman's *Herbie's Troubles*, Phyllis Reynolds Naylor's *King of the Playground*, and Hans Wilhelm's *Tyrone the Horrible* give additional solutions to the bully problem. Discuss other ways children have discovered to defuse teasing and show how one rat stood up for himself when his best friend wouldn't ever play fair in *The Rat and the Tiger* by Keiko Kasza. BEHAVIOR. BULLIES. FRIENDSHIP. FROGS. TEASING.

255   Cooper, Melrose. *I Got a Family*. Illus. by Dale Gottlieb. Henry Holt, 1993. ISBN 0-8050-1965-0

Meet a young girl's extended loving family as she describes them all in jouncing, metered rhyme, from cuddles with Great-Gran in her wheelchair to expeditions for ice cream, fishing, and night sky-gazing with Grampy, Uncle, and Aunty. The joyful primitive-style black-outlined paintings will make your class want to break out the paints to portray their own favorite family members and make up rhymes about them. *Fathers, Mothers, Sisters, Brothers: A Collection of Family Poems* by Mary Ann Hoberman takes a closer look at the extended family. FAMILY LIFE. STORIES IN RHYME.

256   Cowcher, Helen. *Rain Forest*. Illus. by the author. Farrar, 1988. ISBN 0-374-36167-3

With bright brazen watercolors, we see the animals' panic as toucans, howler monkey, and jaguar spread the warning that machines are cutting down trees and spoiling the land. When the floods come and there are no trees to hold in the soil, the river overflows, washing away man and machine, but the animals are safe on high ground—for now. The conservation message is obvious to even the youngest children. Lynne Cherry's *The Great Kapok Tree*, Judith Heide Gilliland's *River*, and Jane Yolen's *Welcome to the Green House* continue the saga. ANIMALS. ECOLOGY. RAIN FORESTS. TREES.

257   Cowen-Fletcher, Jane. *It Takes a Village*. Illus. by the author. Scholastic, 1994. ISBN 0-590-46573-2

In a small village in Benin, Africa, Yemi is to take care of her little brother Kokou while her mother is selling mangoes at the open-air market. The little boy wanders off, and though Yemi worries that he might be hungry or thirsty or frightened, we see from the pictures that the rest of the villagers are looking out for him. Based on the African proverb "It takes a village to raise a child," the story will make you nostalgic for extended families and close-knit communities that have become less common in these impersonal modern times. See the sights of the African bush where Jamina gets lost in *The Hunter* by Paul Geraghty, and the big city in *Somewhere in Africa* by Ingid Mennem and Niki Daly. In *Masai and I* by Virginia Kroll, an African American girl contrasts her life with how it would be if she lived in East Africa. AFRICA. BENIN, AFRICA. BROTHERS AND SISTERS. MULTICULTURAL STORIES.

258   Crowley, Michael. *New Kid on Spurwink Ave*. Illus. by Abby Carter. Little, Brown, 1992. ISBN 0-316-16230-2

The boys and girls in the Spurwink Gang try to interest new kid Leonard in joining their imaginative play sessions, but Leonard, a realist, isn't interested in make-believe situations, responding with "Naw, man" each time they propose a new one. Instead, Leonard is a genius builder, and his inventions earn him a place in the gang. More inventors tinker in Eileen Christelow's *Mr. Murphy's Marvelous Invention*, John Frank's *Odds 'N' Ends Alvy*, and Dick Gackenbach's *Dog for a Day* and *Tiny for a Day*. Nurture the imagination with Nicholas Heller's *An*

Adventure at Sea, Ezra Jack Keats's *Regards to the Man in the Moon*, and David Wiesner's *Hurricane*. FRIENDSHIP. IMAGINATION. INDIVIDUALITY. INVENTIONS.

259 **Cutler, Jane. *Darcy and Gran Don't Like Babies*. Illus. by Susannah Ryan. Scholastic, 1993. ISBN 0-590-44587-1**

Darcy is relieved when her Gran agrees with her about how annoying babies are, especially since Darcy is trying to cope with her new and unwelcome attention-getting baby brother at home. Warm and honest, the story allows children to allay a few guilt pangs about their true feelings and come to terms with a new sibling. Judith Caseley's *Silly Baby*, Pat Hutchins's monster-filled *Where's the Baby?*, Holly Keller's *Geraldine's Baby Brother*, Alane Ferguson's *That New Pet!*, Kevin Henkes's *Julius, the Baby of the World*, Ezra Jack Keats's *Peter's Chair*, and James Stevenson's *Worse Than Willy!* are all about new-baby jealousy. BABIES. BROTHERS AND SISTERS. GRANDMOTHERS. SIBLING RIVALRY.

260 **Demuth, Patricia Brennan. *The Ornery Morning*. Illus. by Craig McFarland Brown. Dutton, 1991. ISBN 0-525-44688-5**

When Rooster doesn't feel like crowing, Farmer Bill figures he's in a pack of wacky trouble, and sure enough, cow won't give milk, hen won't lay egg, and so on. Daughter comes up with the perfect solution—she tells Pa not to feed the animals, and that gets all them all moving again. The cumulative chantable refrain works like those in Verna Aardema's *Why Mosquitoes Buzz in People's Ears*, Paul Galdone's, Eric A. Kimmel's, or Rosanne Litzinger's *The Old Woman and Her Pig*, Nonny Hogrogian's *One Fine Day*, and Katy Rydell's *Wind Says Good Night*. In Jill Runcie's *Cock-a-Doodle-Doo!*, the rooster is the last one up. Barnyard troubles take over Charles Causley's *"Quack!" Said the Billy-Goat*, Victoria Forrester's *The Magnificent Moo*, and Andrea Zimmerman and David Clemesha's *The Cow Buzzed*. CHANTABLE REFRAIN. CUMULATIVE STORIES. DOMESTIC ANIMALS. FARM LIFE. WORK.

261 **DePaolo, Paula. *Rosie & the Yellow Ribbon*. Illus. by Janet Wolf. Little, Brown, 1992. ISBN 0-316-18100-5**

On Rosie's sixth birthday, her best friend Lucille leaves in a huff after Rosie accuses her of taking a favorite new hair ribbon, one of 20 her grandmother sent. Midway through the story, ask who thinks Lucille took the ribbon and what they would have done about it. When storm winds displace a nest of sparrow eggs nestled in the awning of Mr. Brown's store across the street, the two plucky city kids rush over in mutual concern and discover the real thief. Children who are quick to blame others will have much to ponder, as they too will believe Lucille is guilty. Now, have your children role play how to apologize for hasty accusations. In Gary Soto's *Too Many Tamales*, Maria has to own up to losing her mother's diamond ring. Find out how birds construct their nests with Patricia Brennan Demuth's *Cradles in the Trees: The Story of Bird Nests*. AFRICAN AMERICANS. BIRDS. CONFLICT RESOLUTION. FRIENDSHIP. HONESTY. MULTICULTURAL STORIES.

262 Dodds, Dayle Ann. *Do Bunnies Talk?* Illus. by Arlene Dubanevich. HarperCollins, 1992. ISBN 0-06-020249-1

During all the demonstrations of sounds made by dozens of noisy animals, people, and objects, the rabbits stay mute. In a gleeful, rhyming, day-glo-bright description of onomatopoeic words, bunnies watch as pogo sticks go BOINK BOINK BOINK, trains toot, and birds twitter. Children can listen for and collect other words that define themselves when you say them. *Rat-a-Tat, Pitter Pat* by Alan Benjamin and *The Listening Walk* by Paul Showers present sound words as well, while Hank De Zutter's *Who Says a Dog Goes Bow-Wow?* and Marc Robinson's *Cock-a-Doodle-Doo! What Does It Sound Like to You?* compare animal sounds in many other languages. ENGLISH LANGUAGE–ONOMATOPOEIC WORDS. NOISE. SOUND EFFECTS. STORIES IN RHYME. VOCABULARY.

263 Doherty, Berlie. *Snowy*. Illus. by Keith Bowen. Dial, 1993. ISBN 0-8037-1343-6

Unlike the other children at school, Rachel's only pet is Snowy, the sturdy white horse who pulls Beetle Juice, the barge where Rachel and her parents live, along the canal to take people for rides. So when Rachel can't bring her pet to school, and she is teased by others, her understanding teacher takes the class on a surprise visit to meet the working horse and take a barge ride. Another working horse enters a pet show in *Bonnie's Big Day*, a true account by the late famous writer/veterinarian James Herriot. For other nontraditional living quarters, see *This Is My House* by Arthur Dorros. BARGES. BOATS. HORSES. PETS. SCHOOLS.

264 Donaldson, Julia. *A Squash and a Squeeze*. Illus. by Alex Scheffler. McElderry, 1993. ISBN 0-689-50571-X

A little old lady living all alone who complains to a wise old man that her house does not have enough room, takes his advice and brings in first a hen, then a goat, pig, and cow, who make the place more of a squash and a squeeze than ever. Compare this diverting rhyming retelling, which would be fun to set to music, with the old Jewish folktale on which it is based, as retold in Joanna Cole's *It's Too Noisy*, Marilyn Hirsch's *Could Anything Be Worse?* (Holiday House, 1974), Ann McGovern's *Too Much Noise*, and Margot Zemach's *It Could Always Be Worse*. *Mouse in the House* by Patricia Baehr uses the same more-is-less theme, as does *The One and Only Super-Duper Golly-Whopper Jim-Dandy Really-Handy Clock-Tock-Stopper* by Patricia Thomas with its frantic rhyming narrative. CHANTABLE REFRAIN. DOMESTIC ANIMALS. HOUSES. STORIES IN RHYME.

265 Ehlert, Lois. *Feathers for Lunch*. Illus. by the author. Harcourt, 1990. ISBN 0-15-230550-5

Bold and perky life-sized watercolor collages take us along as a cat prowls unsuccessfully for birds in the garden, passing spring-blooming trees and flowers, and identify 12 bird species along the way. Read this the day you spot your first robin and go out for a walk to search for evidence of spring. Read it first for the rhyme, and again to stop and identify each bird, consulting the final pages for the facts in brief. Lucille Clifton's *The Boy Who Didn't Believe in Spring* and Else Minarik's *It's Spring* will help, too. *Little Robin Redbreast: A Mother Goose Rhyme* illustrated by Shari Halpern shows another futile chase. Read Joanne

Ryder's *Catching the Wind* so your kids can feel like birds, Shirley Climo's folktale *King of the Birds*, Patricia Brennan Demuth's nonfiction picture book *Cradles in the Trees: The Story of Bird Nests*, and Jane Yolen's winter-set *Owl Moon*. BIRDS. CATS. STORIES IN RHYME.

266   **Ehrlich, Amy. *Parents in the Pigpen, Pigs in the Tub*. Illus. by Steven Kellogg. Dial, 1993. ISBN 0-8037-0928-5**

After the cow, chickens, sheep, pigs, horses, and ducks all move into a family's farmhouse and raise a ruckus, Ma, Pa, and the four kids repair to the relative peace of the barn. Stir up some more farmyard madness with David L. Harrison's *When Cows Come Home*, David McPhail's *Pigs Aplenty, Pigs Galore!*, Reeve Lindbergh's *The Day the Goose Got Loose*, Trinka Hakes Noble's *The Day Jimmy's Boa Ate the Wash*, and Nadine Bernard Westcott's *Skip to My Lou*. DOMESTIC ANIMALS. FARM LIFE. HUMOROUS FICTION.

267   **Engel, Diana. *Eleanor, Arthur, and Claire*. Illus. by the author. Macmillan, 1992. ISBN 0-02-733462-7**

Claire, a mouse, stays with her beloved grandparents in the country for an idyllic summer as Grandma Eleanor paints and Grandpa Arthur makes unusual clay sculptures. In the autumn, following a stay in the hospital with heart problems, Grandpa dies, and after a long sad year, Claire finds a way to help her grandmother recover from her grief. Simply and sensitively told, the story will help children with similar losses to comprehend them, as will *The Key into Winter* by Janet S. Andersen, *Abuelita's Paradise* by Carmen Santiago Nodar, and *Saying Good-Bye to Grandma* by Jane Resh Thomas. DEATH. GRANDPARENTS. MICE.

268   **Engel, Diana. *Fishing*. Illus. by the author. Macmillan, 1993. ISBN 0-02-733463-5**

Loretta loves to go fishing with her grandfather, but she and her mother move up north where, lonely for friends and missing him, she pretends they are fishing, throws her line and paper clip hook over the hedge, and catches a new friend. Have children tell what special moments they share with their grandparents. In *Snake Hunt* by Jill Kastner, Granddad and Jessie look for rattlers in the woods but manage not to catch any. Address the second issue in the story—moving and making new friends—by asking children how they "catch" new friends. AFRICAN AMERICANS. FISHING. FRIENDSHIP. GRANDFATHERS. MOVING, HOUSEHOLD. SINGLE-PARENT FAMILIES.

269   **Ernst, Lisa Campbell. *Ginger Jumps*. Illus. by the author. Bradbury, 1990. ISBN 0-02-733565-8**

In the midst of learning a terrifying trick of jumping from atop a staircase onto a small trampoline far below, Ginger, a small brown circus puppy who yearns to find a family with a little girl to love her, loses her nerve and the starring role is given to boastful poodle Prunella. As in all heartstopping shows, at the last possible moment, Ginger prevails. This is one of those special stories that leaves kids cheering for the underdog-makes-good. Mary Jane Auch's *Bird Dogs Can't Fly*,

Susan Meddaugh's *Martha Speaks*, Susan Seligson and Howie Schneider's Amos series, and Marilyn Singer's *Chester the Out-of-Work Dog* all boast spunky mutts as their heroes. Experience the sights and sounds with *Circus* by Lois Ehlert. CIRCUS. DOGS. JEALOUSY. LOVE.

270   **Ernst, Lisa Campbell.** *Walter's Tail.* **Illus. by the author. Bradbury, 1992. ISBN 0-02-733564-X**

As Mrs. Tully's new puppy grows, his wagging tail gets longer too, much to the annoyance of the town merchants, and when his tail knocks over and breaks one too many valuable items, Mrs. Tully and her dog are no longer welcome there. Naturally, the wagging tail saves the day as does Prewitt's in *The Spooky Tail of Prewitt Peacock* by Bill Peet. There's an interesting motif at work here, with the one quality that drives others crazy proving to be a saving grace, as in Susan Meddaugh's *Martha Speaks* and Pete Seeger's *Abiyoyo*. See if listeners can come up with that common thread running through those stories. DOGS.

271   **Ernst, Lisa Campbell.** *Zinnia and Dot.* **Illus. by the author. Viking, 1992. ISBN 0-670-83091-7**

Sharing the egg-sitting is not a pleasant undertaking for either of two fat, vain, competitive chickens left with a single egg between them after a crafty weasel steals the rest. Foul play also plagues the feisty hens in *Peeping Beauty* by Mary Jane Auch and *Wings: A Tale of Two Chickens* by James Marshall. CHICKENS. COOPERATION. EGGS. GENEROSITY. WEASELS.

272   **Falwell, Cathryn.** *Clowning Around.* **Illus. by the author. Orchard, 1991. ISBN 0-531-08552-X**

A red-nosed and suited little clown, juggling with the letters in the title, makes new words to go with a series of transforming pictures. As he changes the letters in the word dog, for instance, straightening out the *g* to form two *l*'s, the picture of a dog changes into a doll, who turns into a ball. It's quite an inventive performance, reminiscent in ways of Josse Goffin's *Oh!* and Suse MacDonald's *Alphabatics*. The author/illustrator was inspired from watching one of her children play with refrigerator magnets, which will also be useful in spelling out these and other new words for children to read. *Eye Spy* by Linda Bourke, *Color Farm* by Lois Ehlert, *Puzzlers* by Suse MacDonald and Bill Oakes, *Sea Shapes* by Suse MacDonald, and *The Shapes Game* by Paul Rogers are also visually stimulating. CLOWNS. SHAPES. VISUAL PERCEPTION. VOCABULARY. WORD GAMES.

273   **Gackenbach, Dick.** *Tiny for a Day.* **Illus. by the author. Clarion, 1993. ISBN 0-395-65616-8**

Sidney, whose changing box let him trade places with his pet in *Dog for a Day*, has just invented a Mini Box, which he uses to shrink the lawn mower, the TV, his baby sister, and then himself. Children can write about their school experiences as three-inch kids, and can design and describe the next invention they think Sidney should try. Stay small with William Joyce's *George Shrinks*, Morris

Lurie's *The Story of Imelda, Who Was Small,* and Elvira Woodruff's *Show and Tell.* Eileen Christelow's *Mr. Murphy's Marvelous Invention,* Michael Crowley's *New Kid on Spurwink Ave.,* and John Frank's *Odds 'N' Ends Alvy* all feature aspiring inventors. INVENTIONS. SCHOOLS. SIZE. TRANSFORMATIONS.

274   Gackenbach, Dick. *Where Are Momma, Poppa, and Sister June?* Illus. by the author. Clarion, 1994. ISBN 0-395-67323-2

Only the dog is in the house when the narrator arrives home from playing baseball, and wondering what could have happened to his family, the little boy fantasizes that perhaps they were eaten by a giant crocodile or zapped into space by aliens. Listeners can puzzle out the message in the note he finds and recall times they were worried too. The hero confronts and vanquishes his fears in Gackenback's *Harry and the Terrible Whatzit.* FAMILY LIFE. IMAGINATION. WORRYING.

275   Gelman, Rita Golden. *I Went to the Zoo.* Illus. by Maryann Kovalski. Scholastic, 1993. ISBN 0-590-45882-5

A little boy cajoles all the bored zoo animals into coming home with him where they make a glorious mess. Children can recall each rhyming animal-themed couplet and make up new ones. Beatrice Schenk de Regniers's *May I Bring a Friend?* and Audrey Wood's *Silly Sally* are also delightful rhyming stories with animals. ANIMALS. CHANTABLE REFRAIN. CUMULATIVE STORIES. STORIES IN RHYME. ZOOS.

276   Gregory, Valiska. *Babysitting for Benjamin.* Illus. by Lynn Munsinger. Little, Brown, 1993. ISBN 0-316-32785-9

Wanting a little company, mouse couple Frances and Ralph baby-sit an exuberant and bouncy rabbit who turns their house upside down until they figure out how to channel his energy into outdoor play and, afterward, a quiet story on the couch. Other stories about sitters, both benign and bumbling, include *Arthur Babysits* by Marc Brown, *Jerome the Babysitter* and *Jerome and the Witchcraft Kids* by Eileen Christelow, *Mr. and Mrs. Pig's Evening Out* by Mary Rayner, *Shy Charles* by Rosemary Wells, and *Bear and Mrs. Duck* by Elizabeth Winthrop. BABY-SITTERS. BEHAVIOR. MICE. RABBITS.

277   Grover, Max. *The Accidental Zucchini: An Unexpected Alphabet.* Illus. by the author. Browndeer Press / Harcourt, 1993. ISBN 0-15-277695-8

For each large, busy acrylic painting, there are two accompanying alliterative words, starting with "Apple autos" and ending with "Zigzag zoos." Cover the words with a piece of cardboard so children can guess each set by examining the illustration. In similar fashion, children can put together two otherwise unrelated alphabet words, make them connect through their illustration, and then let the rest of the class guess what each picture depicts. Jane Bayer's *A My Name Is Alice,* Megan Halsey's *Jump for Joy: A Book of Months,* Anita Lobel's *Alison's Zinnia,* and Anne Shelby's *Potluck* provide more alliteration. ALLITERATION. ALPHABET BOOKS. CREATIVE WRITING.

278   **Guback, Georgia.** *Luka's Quilt.* **Illus. by the author. Greenwillow, 1994. ISBN 0-688-12155-1**

Luka looks forward to the traditional flower-garden quilt her Tutu (Hawaiian for grandmother) is making her, and can't conceal her disappointment when the finished quilt is only green and white with no flower colors. On Lei Day, Tutu and Luka declare a truce and, after making flower leis in the park, Tutu comes up with a compromise for the quilt that brings the two close together again. Use the concepts of declaring a truce and compromising to mediate classroom disputes. Children will recall many instances when they have had such conflicts with family and friends, and evaluate how they resolved them. Valerie Flournoy's *The Patchwork Quilt* is another heartwarming intergenerational story, while Jama Kim Rattigan's *Dumpling Soup* takes us to Hawaii for New Year's Day. ARGUMENTS. CONFLICT RESOLUTION. GRANDMOTHERS. HAWAII. QUILTS.

279   **Halsey, Megan.** *Jump for Joy: A Book of Months.* **Illus. by the author. Bradbury, 1994. ISBN 0-02-742040-X**

For each month there is an accompanying statement, illustrated with a detailed, colorful, double-page paper sculpture collage picture of satisfied children in action. Children will love putting together new alliterative declarative sentences defining the pleasures of each month, starting with an action verb and ending with the month. Try doing these with the seven days of the week. Sara Coleridge's *January Brings the Snow* and Maurice Sendak's *Chicken Soup with Rice* present each month in rhyme. Other alliterative pattern books to consider are Jane Bayer's *A My Name Is Alice*, Max Grover's *The Accidental Zucchini: An Unexpected Alphabet*, Anita Lobel's *Away from Home*, Arnold Lobel's *The Rose in My Garden*, and Anne Shelby's *Potluck*. ALLITERATION. MONTHS.

280   **Harshman, Marc.** *Only One.* **Illus. by Barbara Garrison. Dutton, 1993. ISBN 0-525-65116-0**

At a county fair, we see animals and other sights in terms of the relationships each has to a whole unit, for example, "There may be a million stars, but there is only one sky," or "There may be 11 cows, but there is only one herd." The numbers represented as sets are: one million; 50,000; 500; 100; and then, counting backward, from 12 down to one. Children can think of and illustrate additional sets in like format. Continue counting with Suzanne Aker's *What Comes in 2's, 3's & 4's?*, Andrew Clements's *Mother Earth's Counting Book*, Denise Fleming's *Count*, Michael Jay Katz's *Ten Potatoes in a Pot and Other Counting Rhymes*, and Rick Walton's *How Many, How Many, How Many*. COUNTING BOOKS. FAIRS. MATHEMATICS.

281   **Heller, Nicholas.** *Up the Wall.* **Illus. by the author. Greenwillow, 1992. ISBN 0-688-10634-X**

There's no place to play in his house, so the young narrator fills a big bag with toys and food, calls the dog, and together they walk up the wall to the ceiling, where there's lots of space and everything is upside down. Children can gaze upside down at the school ceilings, then draw and tell what they'd do up there.

The Wrong Side of the Bed by Wallace Keller addresses the same theme. FANTASY. IMAGINATION. PLAY. VISUAL PERCEPTION.

282   **Henkes, Kevin. *Chrysanthemum*. Illus. by the author. Greenwillow, 1991. ISBN 0-688-09700-6**

An endearing young mouse loves her name until she starts school where others tease her mercilessly, until Mrs. Twinkle, an "indescribable wonder" of a music teacher, reveals her own long, flower-based name: Delphinium. Ask your class what wild names they'd choose for themselves if they could. (*The World Almanac* includes a list of the often-surprising original names of many celebrities, if you all want a good laugh.) *Alison's Zinnia* by Anita Lobel is an alphabet of names of both girls and flowers. Don't forget to link *Chrysanthemum* with the longest name of all, from Arlene Mosel's classic Chinese folktale, *Tikki Tikki Tembo*. Helen Lester's *A Porcupine Named Fluffy* also deals with name problems. MICE. NAMES. PICTURE BOOKS FOR ALL AGES. SCHOOLS. TEACHERS.

283   **Henkes, Kevin. *Julius, the Baby of the World*. Illus. by the author. Greenwillow, 1990. ISBN 0-688-08944-5**

Mouse Lily is thrilled about the new baby-to-be—until it arrives. She shows all the typical signs of rage, asking when he's going back, pretending he doesn't exist, spending time in the family's "uncooperative chair," but when Cousin Garland presumes to expresses a dislike for the baby, Lily does an about-face. Here's acknowledgment of an older sibling's true range of emotions. (As one three-year-old daughter of my friend's friend put it, "Can't we just take it back and get a credit?") Explore sibling rivalry and feelings of displacement and love in Judith Caseley's *Silly Baby*, Jane Cutler's *Darcy and Gran Don't Like Babies*, Pat Hutchins's monster-filled *Where's the Baby?*, Ezra Jack Keats's *Peter's Chair*, Holly Keller's *Geraldine's Baby Brother*, Tom Paxton's *Where's the Baby?*, and James Stevenson's *Worse Than Willy*. BABIES. BROTHERS AND SISTERS. JEALOUSY. MICE. SIBLING RIVALRY.

284   **Hennessy, B. G. *The Dinosaur Who Lived in My Backyard*. Illus. by Susan Davis. Viking, 1988. ISBN 0-670-81685-X**

The little boy narrator imagines the size of the dinosaur that might have lived in his backyard long ago, comparing it to sizes he can relate to, such as his car, sandbox, and school bus, and imagining how it might fit into his life now. Bernard Most's *How Big Were the Dinosaurs?* provides interesting facts, while Eric Rohmann's wordless *Time Flies* and Dennis Nolan's *Dinosaur Dreams* take us back to dinosaur times. Henry Schwartz's *How I Captured a Dinosaur* is about a little girl who finds an Albertosaurus while camping. Carol Carrick's *Patrick's Dinosaurs* and *What Happened to Patrick's Dinosaurs?* offers some more imaginative fantasy, and Paul and Henrietta Stickland's *Dinosaur Roar!* will make kids clamor for more. DINOSAURS. IMAGINATION.

285   **Hinton, S. E. *Big David, Little David*. Illus. by Alan Daniel. Doubleday, 1995. ISBN 0-385-31093-5**

Nick comes home from his first day of kindergarten wondering if David, a boy in his class with black hair and glasses just like Dad, could actually be his dad somehow. His jokester father claims he is Little David during the day and Big David after school, and though Nick tries to out-trick his father, it's not until parents' night at school that he succeeds. Midway through, ask your gullible listeners to give reasons to support their opinions as to whether or not Nick's dad is a daytime kid. All three main characters in this wacky story are original and will crack you up with their winning ways. In *Nobody's Mother Is in Second Grade* by Robin Pulver, Cassandra's mom shows up in class disguised as a plant, and in *Bea and Mr. Jones* by Amy Schwartz, a kindergarten girl and her father actually switch roles. FATHERS AND SONS. KINDERGARTEN. NAMES. SCHOOLS.

286   Hoban, Tana. *Look! Look! Look!* **Photos by the author. Greenwillow, 1988. ISBN 0-688-07240-2**

Like Hoban's earlier *Look Again*, but this time in color, here is a collection of photographs covered by all but a two-inch rectangular cut-out, so viewers must try to identify the item by a partial glimpse. The next two pages reveal a close-up photo of the whole object. In *Just Beyond Reach and Other Riddle Poems* by Bonnie Larkin, one must identify each object by the rhyme written about it, and confirm the answer with the photograph of it on the following page. Linda Bourke's *Eye Spy: A Mysterious Alphabet*, Ruth Brown's *If at First You Do Not See*, Beau Gardner's *Guess What?*, Ann Jonas's *Reflections*, *Round Trip*, and *The 13th Clue*, Bruce McMillan's *Mouse Views: What the Class Pet Saw*, and *Puzzlers* by Suse MacDonald and Bill Oakes will keep children looking sharp. PHOTOGRAPHY. VISUAL PERCEPTION.

287   Hoffman, Mary. *Amazing Grace.* **Illus. by Caroline Binch. Dial, 1991. ISBN 0-8037-1040-2**

Upon learning that her class is putting on the play *Peter Pan*, Grace, who loves to act out stories, covets the lead role, and, thanks to her wise grandmother, is undeterred when classmate Natalie tells her, "You can't be Peter Pan. He isn't black." What a self-confidence booster this kid is, with her love of acting out stories and determination to be the best. Discuss how to overcome discouragement, unkind words, and put-downs. If it's acting your students crave, warm them up with Miriam Cohen's *Starring First Grade*, Johanna Johnston's *Speak Up, Edie*, Wendy Cheyette Lewison's *Shy Vi*, Emily Arnold McCully's *Speak Up, Blanche!*, Joan Lowery Nixon's *Gloria Chipmunk, Star!*, and Joanne Oppenheim's *Mrs. Peloki's Class Play*. ACTING. GRANDMOTHERS. MULTICULTURAL STORIES. SCHOOLS. SELF-ESTEEM.

288   Hort, Lenny. *How Many Stars in the Sky?* **Illus. by James Ransome. Tambourine, 1991. ISBN 0-688-10104-6**

A little boy tells about the night his mother was away when he went outside in his pajamas to try to count the stars and his wise father took him on a middle-of-the-night ride to first the city and then the country to look at the sky. For homework, children can go outside and see how many stars they can count. Look in the newspaper for a sky map, and demonstrate how to find the Big Dipper. Check out the sky in the daytime with *It Looked Like Spilt Milk*, a cloud-gazing story by Charles G. Shaw. AFRICAN AMERICANS. COUNTING BOOKS. FATHERS AND SONS. NIGHT. STARS.

289   Hubbard, Woodleigh. *C Is for Curious: An ABC of Feelings*. Illus. by the author. Chronicle, 1990. ISBN 0-87701-679-8

Use an oaktag strip to cover up the word on each page, so viewers can examine the odd and colorful animal illustration, describe what is happening in the picture, and try to guess the emotional adjective it is describing. Delve more deeply into children's emotions with Catherine and Laurence Anholt's *What Makes Me Happy?*, William Cole's *Frances Face Maker*, Marie Hall Ets's *Talking without Words*, Betsy Everitt's *Mean Soup*, and Jean Modesitt's *Sometimes I Feel Like a Mouse: A Book About Feelings*. Children can think of more descriptive adjectives, completing the sentence, "I feel . . . " and acting it out. Continue your alphabetical animal and adjective coverage with Sandra Boynton's *A Is for Angry*, which is done in the same vein. ALPHABET BOOKS. CREATIVE DRAMA. EMOTIONS. ENGLISH LANGUAGE–GRAMMAR

290   Hurwitz, Johanna. *"E" Is for Elisa*. Illus. by Lillian Hoban. Morrow, 1991. ISBN 0-688-10440-1

[6 chapters, 85p.] In trying to catch up with her eight-year-old brother Russell, four-year-old Elisa gets her picture taken, puts another child's tooth under her pillow for the tooth fairy, enjoys a snow day off from nursery school, wears her bathing suit in winter, and breaks her arm. Children will also enjoy stories about other families with real-life foibles such as the Kanes in *Harry and Arney* by Judith Caseley, *Angels on Roller Skates* by Maggie Harrison, and *Junie B. Jones and a Little Monkey Business* by Barbara Park. APARTMENT HOUSES. BROTHERS AND SISTERS. FAMILY LIFE.

291   Jeschke, Susan. *Lucky's Choice*. Illus. by the author. Scholastic, 1987. ISBN 0-590-40520-9

Lucky, a black-and-white housecat who pines for attention and love from his indifferent owner, befriends mouse Ezra and is faced with an ethical dilemma when his owner orders him to kill the mouse or else. Talk over the importance of having someone to love and then read *Bub: Or, the Very Best Thing* by Natalie Babbitt. CATS. LOVE. MICE.

292   Johnson, Paul Brett. *The Cow Who Wouldn't Come Down*. Illus. by the author. Orchard, 1993. ISBN 0-531-08631-3

Though it's a known fact that cows don't fly, Gertrude has a mind of her own, and when the cow takes to the air, farmer Miss Rosemary tries every way she can to lure down the floating beast. Meet some other singular cows in Chris Babcock's *No Moon, No Milk*, Jennifer A. Ericsson's *No Milk!*, Paula Brown's *Moon Jump: A Cowntdown*, Lisa Campbell Ernst's *When Bluebell Sang*, David L.

Harrison's *When Cows Come Home*, David Kirby and Allen Woodman's *The Cows Are Going to Paris*, and Nancy Van Laan's *The Tiny, Tiny Boy and the Big, Big Cow*. Frogs also take to the air in *Tuesday* by David Wiesner. The poems in Alice Schertle's poetry picture book *How Now, Brown Cow?* go a long way toward explaining a cow's motivation. COWS. FLIGHT. JEALOUSY. PICTURE BOOKS FOR ALL AGES.

293   Johnston, Deborah. *Mathew Michael's Beastly Day*. Illus. by Seymour Chwast. Gulliver/ Harcourt, 1992. ISBN 0-15-200521-8

Over the course of one day, a boy wakes up as a sloth, eats as a bear, rides the bus as a timid rabbit, becomes a lion at recess, gets in trouble as a dinosaur, and ends the day as a snoozing chipmunk. Another boy-turned-animal is *Joe on Sunday* by Tony Blundell. Children can describe what animals they resemble at varying parts of the day, and pantomime Mathew's transformations. If they're still in the mood for change, act out Daniel Pinkwater's *Tooth-Gnasher Superflash*. ANIMALS. BEHAVIOR. CREATIVE DRAMA. IMAGINATION. SELF-ESTEEM.

294   Johnston, Tony. *Slither McCreep and His Brother Joe*. Illus. by Victoria Chess. Harcourt, 1992. ISBN 0-15-276100-4

The two squeezing snake brothers bicker when Joe won't share his beach ball, rat robots, or purple sweater, so Slither squeezes his stuff in revenge, an act that only makes him feel better for a bit before guilt sets in. Deal with sibling rivalry through exposure to it in Judy Blume's *The Pain and the Great One*, Crescent Dragonwagon's *I Hate My Brother Harry*, Steven Kellogg's *Much Bigger Than Martin*, P. K. Roche's *Good-Bye, Arnold*, Judith Viorst's *I'll Fix Anthony*, and Dan Yaccarino's *Big Brother Mike*. In the snake department, look for Te Ata's Native American folktale *Baby Rattlesnake*, Nan Bodsworth's *A Nice Walk in the Jungle*, Stefan Czernecki and Timothy Rhodes's Australian folktale *The Singing Snake*, Libba Moore Gray's *Small Green Snake*, Betsy Maestro's nonfiction *Take a Look at Snakes*, Faith McNulty's *A Snake in the House*, and Tomi Ungerer's *Crictor*. BROTHERS. GENEROSITY. SELFISHNESS. SIBLING RIVALRY. SNAKES.

295   Karas, G. Brian. *I Know an Old Lady*. Illus. by the author. Scholastic, 1994. ISBN 0-590-46575-9

Karas's wry illustrations for the song about the gluttonous old gal who swallows a cow to catch the goat, dog, cat, bird, spider, and fly she just scarfed down, are childlike and scratchy, done in gouache, acrylic, and pencil. Other illustrated versions include *I Know an Old Lady Who Swallowed a Fly* by either Glen Rounds or Nadine Bernard Westcott. Also sing Raffi's *Spider on the Floor* and Iza Trapani's *Itsy Bitsy Spider*. ANIMALS. CUMULATIVE STORIES. NONSENSE VERSES. SONGS. STORIES IN RHYME.

296   Keller, Holly. *Island Baby*. Illus. by the author. Greenwillow, 1992. ISBN 0-688-10580-7

On the Caribbean island where Pops runs his bird hospital, young Simon helps feed the birds and clean their cages, but after rescuing a baby flamingo with a broken leg, and, with Pops's help, nursing it back to health, Simon is reluctant to set it free. Introduce another selfless child who rescues a wild creature in Betty Waterton's *A Salmon for Simon*. Even a cricket causes separation anxiety in *"Leave That Cricket Be, Alan Lee"* by Barbara Ann Porte. More Caribbean stories include Phillis Gershator's *Rata-Pata-Scata-Fata*, Rita Phillips Mitchell's *Hue Boy*, and Karen Lynn Williams's *Tap-Tap*. Also sample the poems in John Agard and Grace Nichols's vibrant anthology *A Caribbean Dozen*. BIRDS. CARIBBEAN ISLANDS. ISLANDS. RESPONSIBILITY. WILDLIFE RESCUE.

---

297   **Keller, Wallace. *The Wrong Side of the Bed*. Illus. by the author. Rizzoli, 1992. ISBN 0-8478-1471-8**

Little Matt Turner gets up on the wrong side and, finding himself upside down on the ceiling, spends the day that way, eating breakfast on the wrong side of the plate, sitting on the school bus ceiling, and falling into space. In *Up the Wall* by Nicholas Heller, a little boy happily spends his day on the ceiling. Ruth Brown's clever *If at First You Do Not See* is full of pictures right side up and upside down. Children can draw pictures of common objects, and display them upside down for others to identify. HOUSES. VISUAL PERCEPTION.

---

298   **Kimmel, Eric A. *The Chanukkah Guest*. Illus. by Giora Carmi. Holiday House, 1990. ISBN 0-8234-0788-8**

On the first night of Hanukkah, 97-year-old Bubba Brayna, who doesn't hear or see as well as she once did, mistakes Old Bear for the rabbi, and invites him in for potato latkes. Compare this gentle farce to Phyllis Reynolds Naylor's more sedate *Old Sadie and the Christmas Bear*, where near-sighted Old Sadie shares potato chowder, cinnamon buns, and a box of sweets with her Christmas stranger. Taste a few more potato pancakes with Nina Jaffe's *In the Month of Kislev*. BEARS. ELDERLY. FOOD. HANUKKAH.

---

299   **Kiser, Kevin. *Sherman the Sheep*. Illus. by Rowan Barnes-Murphy. Macmillan, 1994. ISBN 0-02-750825-0**

Obliging the dissatisfied flock who wants him to lead them to the best field in the valley, sheep Sherman misreads all the signs along the way and, singing verses of his "We're sheep" song, guides them back to their own Happy Valley Sheep Ranch. Make up a tune or chant the refrain in this sweet and silly variant of the "there's no place like home" theme. Verna Aardema's Mexican folktale *Borreguita and the Coyote* boasts another sharp sheep, while Nancy Shaw's *Sheep in a Shop* and *Sheep Out to Eat* are a bit more worldly. Rambling cows cause a ruckus in David L. Harrison's *When the Cows Come Home* and David Kirby and Allen Woodman's *The Cows Are Going to Paris*. SHEEP. STORIES WITH SONGS.

---

300   **Knowles, Sheena. *Edward the Emu*. Illus. by Rod Clement. HarperCollins, 1992. ISBN 0-207-17051-7**

Bored with being an emu at the zoo, Edward decides instead to be a seal, a lion, and a snake, but once he tries to go back to his old life-style, he finds another emu taking his place. The theme of admiring and imitating other creatures to be someone you are not is a common one, but Clement's large illustrations of the audacious emu copycatting the expressions of each animal he envies are priceless. Eric Carle's *The Mixed-Up Chameleon*, James Howe's *I Wish I Were a Butterfly*, Keiko Kasza's *The Pigs' Picnic*, Theo LeSieg's *I Wish That I Had Duck Feet*, and Bernard Waber's *"You Look Ridiculous," Said the Rhinoceros to the Hippopotamus* will provide ample comparisons. ANIMALS. BIRDS. EMUS. PICTURE BOOKS FOR ALL AGES. SELF-ACCEPTANCE. STORIES IN RHYME. ZOOS.

301   **Koontz, Robin Michal.** *I See Something You Don't See: A Riddle-Me Picture Book.* **Illus. by the author. Cobblehill, 1992. ISBN 0-525-65077-6**

Each rhyming "riddle-me riddle-me-ree" riddle on the left-hand page describes an object for children to guess that's included in the watercolor illustration on the right. The riddles take us through an idyllic summer day at Grandma's following her two grandchildren plus her cat and dog as they enjoy a round of fishing. Children will be eager to guess each item, and if they get stumped, the answers are on the last page. More easy rhyming riddles abound in Beatrice Schenk de Regniers's *It Does Not Say Meow and Other Animal Riddle Rhymes*, Bonnie Larkin Nims's *Just Beyond Reach and Other Riddle Poems*, and Ruth Young's *Who Says Moo?* Stephanie Calmenson's *What Am I? Very First Riddles* is another interactive book. RIDDLES. STORIES IN RHYME.

302   **Leach, Norman.** *My Wicked Stepmother.* **Illus. by Jane Browne. Macmillan, 1993. ISBN 0-02-754700-0**

Tom thinks his new stepmother is a wicked witch who put a spell on his dad and he can't accept her, no matter how kind she acts, until he starts seeing her as a fairy godmother instead. These days so many children are living with stepparents, and this title is a nifty bit of bibliotherapy that makes a graceful distinction between once-upon-a-time and now. FAMILY PROBLEMS. STEPPARENTS.

303   **Lester, Alison.** *The Journey Home.* **Illus. by the author. Houghton Mifflin, 1991. ISBN 0-395-53355-4**

Brother and sister Wild and Wooley dig a hole in their sandpit and fall through to the North Pole, just the start of a long trip home. On the way they stop for a spell with Santa, the Good Fairy, Prince Charming, the Little Mermaid, the Pirate King, and the Gypsy Queen, each of whom feeds them and gives them a bed for the night. Children can dream up new adventures and draw maps of their journeys. See the real world with *Jeremy's Tail* by Duncan Ball, *Magic Carpet* by Pat Brisson, *Amelia's Fantastic Flight* by Rose Bursik, *Away from Home* by Anita Lobel, *How to Make an Apple Pie and See the World* by Marjorie Priceman, *Uncle Lester's Hat* by Howie Schneider, *Love, Your Bear Pete* by Dyan Sheldon, and *Nine O'Clock Lullaby* by Marilyn Singer. ADVENTURES AND ADVENTURERS. MAPS AND GLOBES. VOYAGES AND TRAVELS.

304   **Lester, Helen.** *Me First.* **Illus. by Lynn Munsinger. Houghton Mifflin, 1992. ISBN 0-395-58706-9**

Pushy Pinkerton, an overly assertive pig, learns that first is not always best on his day trip to the beach with his Pig Scout Troop when a small green creature in a pointy purple hat—a real Sandwitch—hauls him off to her sand castle and allows him to "care" for her. Other pigs who learn about acceptable behavior include Brock Cole's *Nothing But a Pig* and David McPhail's *Pig Pig Grows Up*. Lester delivers more gentle bits of reform for wayward tots in her *Cora Copycat* and *Pookins Gets Her Way*. While discussing the theme of combatting selfishness and self-centeredness, pull in Tony Johnston's *Slither McCreep and His Brother Joe*, Margaret Mahy's *The Great White Man-Eating Shark*, and Ann Martin's *Rachel Parker, Kindergarten Show-Off*. When discussing the difference between sandwich and sandwitch, talk about other potentially confusing homonyms like stake and steak or wait and weight, with more examples from *A Chocolate Moose for Dinner* by Fred Gwynne. BEHAVIOR. ENGLISH LANGUAGE–HOMONYMS. PIGS. SELFISHNESS. WITCHES.

305   **Lester, Helen.** *Three Cheers for Tacky.* **Illus. by Lynn Munsinger. Houghton Mifflin, 1994. ISBN 0-395-66841-7**

Team players may learn to appreciate the iconoclast thanks to this droll little tale of the odd-bird penguin who tries to conform to the cheerleading routines his class is trying to perfect before the Penguin Cheering Contest. Have your students try out the cheers, first the "proper" way, and then work up a wacky one, à la Tacky. Rabbit Pete is another unapologetic individualist in *Pete's Chicken* by Harriet Ziefert. Meet other inadvertant nonconformist birds in *The Easter Egg Farm* by Mary Jane Auch and *The Spooky Tail of Prewitt Peacock* by Bill Peet. Sue Vyner's *The Stolen Egg* shows a more traditional penguin, if you want to show the contrast between types of fiction. INDIVIDUALITY. PENGUINS.

306   **Lindbergh, Reeve.** *The Day the Goose Got Loose.* **Illus. by Steven Kellogg. Dial, 1990. ISBN 0-8037-0409-7**

Mayhem and chaos on the farm when the goose escapes and stirs up all the other animals, and lots of zany illustrations, will make listeners laugh at this bouncy narrative poem. Read this twice so listeners can tune in to the rhyme and chant the title refrain. *There's a Cow in the Road!*, also by Reeve Lindbergh, is similarly silly. *Parents in the Pigpen, Pigs in the Tub* by Amy Ehrlich and Trinka Hakes Noble's *The Day Jimmy's Boa Ate the Wash* are like-minded farm stories also illustrated by Steven Kellogg. CHANTABLE REFRAIN. DOMESTIC ANIMALS. FARM LIFE. STORIES IN RHYME.

307   **Lindbergh, Reeve.** *There's a Cow in the Road!* **Illus. by Tracey Campbell Pearson. Dial, 1993. ISBN 0-8037-1336-3**

A young girl describes, in zesty rhyme, how she notices the cow standing outside in the road at 7:00 A.M. saying, "Moo!" The next thing she knows there's a goat there too, and then, as the minutes tick by, it's joined by a sheep, a horse, a goose, and a pig. All the while, the girl is getting ready for school, until, at a quarter to eight, the school bus arrives. All will enjoy the bounce of the rhyme, the mixture of silly and everyday, and the time-telling motif. Lindbergh's *The Day the Goose*

Got Loose, Amy Ehrlich's *Parents in the Pigpen, Pigs in the Tub*, David L. Harrison's *When Cows Come Home*, and David McPhail's *Pigs Aplenty, Pigs Galore!* will appeal for like reasons. CHANTABLE REFRAIN. COWS. DOMESTIC ANIMALS. STORIES IN RHYME. TIME.

308   **Lionni, Leo.** *Matthew's Dream.* **Illus. by the author. Knopf, 1991. ISBN 0-679-91075-1**

Though his parents have high hopes for their son's future as a doctor, the mouse discovers the world on his first trip to the art museum and decides to become a painter. Bring out the paints and have children paint their dreams. Lionni's other artistic mouse became a poet in the story *Frederick.* Author/illustrator Tomie dePaola decided to became an artist in *The Art Lesson.* See paintings in another light in *When Cats Dream* by Dav Pilkey. ARTISTS. DREAMS. MICE. PAINTING.

309   **Lobel, Anita.** *Alison's Zinnia.* **Illus. by the author. Greenwillow, 1990. ISBN 0-688-08866-X**

"Alison acquired an Amaryllis for Beryl," reads the first page, and each successive page links name with flower, which is displayed in a beautiful watercolor and gouache painting. Children can predict which flower will come next alphabetically and compose their own alliterative flower or vegetable pages. Call a garden supply company like Burpee for their latest catalog. Eve Bunting's *Flower Garden* and Arnold Lobel's *The Rose in My Garden* also honor flowers, with Gail Gibbons's *From Seed to Plant* and Ruth Heller's *The Reason for a Flower* providing factual background for gardeners-to-be. Lobel's *Away from Home* is the male counterpart to this book. Keep alliterating with Jim Aylesworth's rhyming *My Son John*, Jane Bayer's *A My Name Is Alice*, Max Grover's *The Accidental Zucchini: An Unexpected Alphabet*, Megan Halsey's *Jump for Joy: A Book of Months*, Helena Clare Pittman's *Miss Hindy's Cats*, and Anne Shelby's *Potluck.* ALLITERATION. ALPHABET BOOKS. FLOWERS. NAMES.

310   **London, Jonathan.** *The Owl Who Became the Moon.* **Illus. by Ted Rand. Dutton, 1993. ISBN 0-525-45054-8**

A dreamy prose poem takes on a boy's nighttime imaginary train ride through the forest, past the nighttime animals, and to sleep. Rand's breathtaking watercolors are even more astonishing from a distance. Of course you'll want to expand the owl motif with Jane Yolen's *Owl Moon*, and explore the dark with Phyllis Root's *Moon Tiger*, Joanne Ryder's *The Night Flight*, and Cynthia Rylant's *Night in the Country.* ANIMALS. NIGHT. OWLS. TRAINS.

311   **Lurie, Morris.** *The Story of Imelda, Who Was Small.* **Illus. by Terry Denton. Houghton Mifflin, 1988. ISBN 0-395-48663-7**

Tiny Imelda who sleeps in a shoebox is so small her parents take her for a consultation with Dr. Anderson who tells her to eat long foods like spaghetti, runner beans, and licorice sticks and avoid short, dumpy foods like potatoes and pancakes. His advice is erroneous, so before reading aloud the obvious solution, ask listeners what their advice would be. For fun, make a list of long and short foods. Dick

Gackenbach's *Tiny for a Day*, William Joyce's *George Shrinks*, Laura Krauss Melmed's *The Rainbabies*, and Elvira Woodruff's *Show and Tell* will appeal to children who like their heroes pint-sized. SIZE.

312   MacDonald, Amy. *Rachel Fister's Blister*. Illus. by Marjorie Priceman. Houghton Mifflin, 1990. ISBN 0-395-52152-1

In a wild rhyming saga, Rachel's blister on her toe sends everyone into a tizzy wondering how to fix it, but the Queen is the only one who knows what to do. The fuss everyone makes over Rachel's little blister will remind you of the poem about Christopher Robin's "Sneezles" from A. A. Milne's classic *Now We Are Six*. Lynne Cherry's rhyming *Who's Sick Today?*, Ursula LeGuin's *A Visit from Dr. Katz*, and Christine Loomis's *One Cow Coughs: A Counting Book for the Sick and Miserable* will keep kids laughing about their ailments. STORIES IN RHYME. WOUNDS AND INJURIES.

313   McDonald, Megan. *Is This a House for Hermit Crab?* Illus. by S. D. Schindler. Franklin Watts, 1990. ISBN 0-531-08455-8

Grown too big for his old shell, Hermit Crab scritch-scratches along the shore and tries out a rock, a rusty tin can, and other inappropriate containers before a surprise wave and a menacing pricklepine fish send him scurrying into a sea snail shell that fits just right. Children can chant the title refrain, and decide what's inadequate about each house as you read. Keep searching for the perfect place with *A House for Hermit Crab* by Eric Carle. Have a beach party with *Sea Shapes* by Suse MacDonald, Elizabeth Lee O'Donnell's *The Twelve Days of Summer* and James Stevenson's *Clams Can't Sing*. Check your local pet store for hermit crabs, which make interesting classroom pets. CRABS. HERMIT CRABS. HOUSES. SEASHORE. SHELLS.

314   MacDonald, Suse, and Bill Oakes. *Puzzlers*. Illus. by the authors. Dial, 1989. ISBN 0-8037-0690-1

More difficult than it first appears, this one-to-ten counting book features ten animals whose bodies are composed of numbers made of swirly colored-paper collage. For each page, viewers first identify the animal portrayed, and then find the answer to the concept each puzzler poses. Concepts include finding the number in the picture that is widest, tallest, backward, upside down, a pair, back-to-back, facing, a pattern, overlapping, and in sequence. Answers are at the back, along with other finding possibilities for each one. *Fish Eyes: A Book You Can Count On* by Lois Ehlert is also entertaining and original. Take a closer look at the visual games in Linda Bourke's *Eye Spy*, Ruth Brown's *If at First You Do Not See*, Cathryn Falwell's *Clowning Around*, Tana Hoban's *Look Again!* and *Look! Look! Look!*, Ann Jonas's *Reflections*, *Round Trip* and *The 13th Clue*, and Tomi Ungerer's *One, Two, Where's My Shoe?* ALPHABET BOOKS. COUNTING BOOKS. MATHEMATICS. VISUAL PERCEPTION.

315   McMillan, Bruce. *Mouse Views: What the Class Pet Saw*. Photos by the author. Holiday House, 1993. ISBN 0-8234-1008-0

This mouse's-eye view of a classroom, with sharp, full-page, color photographs from alternating perspectives—first the escaped mouse's and then ours—challenges kids to identify common objects the class mouse traverses, such as piano keys, blocks, and books. In addition to enriching children's visual perception skills, there's an aerial diagram map of the school showing all the rooms the mouse visited, which might inspire student cartographers to tour your building and map out what they find. Tana Hoban's *Look! Look! Look!* provides more photographic guessing fun. MAPS AND GLOBES. MICE. SCHOOLS. VISUAL PERCEPTION.

316   McPhail, David. *Lost!* Illus. by the author. Joy Street / Little, Brown, 1990. ISBN 0-316-56329-3

Hearing crying, a city boy discovers a lost bear sitting in the back of a truck, and takes him to the top of a tall building from which the bear spots his home. The park has trees and water, but it is not home after all, so, after spending an enjoyable day there, they try the library for better directions. Play up the library angle with *Once Inside the Library* by Barbara A. Huff. Kids can make maps showing where both boy and bear live. A boy and his squirrel friend design a perfect place to be in *Squirrel Park* by Lisa Campbell Ernst. Based on a true story, *The Bear That Heard Crying* by Natalie Kinsey-Warnock occurred in 1783, when three-year-old Sarah Whitcher got lost in the New Hampshire woods and was rescued by a bear. BEARS. LIBRARIES. LOST. MAPS AND GLOBES. PARKS.

317   McPhail, David. *Pigs Aplenty, Pigs Galore!* Illus. by the author. Dutton, 1993. ISBN 0-525-45079-3

Imagine the author's surprise when he finds his house full of pigs, all manner of pigs, eating pizza and leaving a mess. Told in bouncy rhyme, with bright watercolors depicting dozens of pigs in costumes (even an Elvis impersonator), the tale winds down with the narrator in a pig-jammed bed after he makes them clean up their debris. More greedy creatures chomp their way through Susan Heyboer O'Keefe's *One Hungry Monster: A Counting Book in Rhyme*. Delve deeper into pigs' psyches with Arthur Getz's *Humphrey the Dancing Pig*, Robert Munsch's *Pigs*, Charlotte Pomerantz's *The Piggy in the Puddle*, Mark Teague's *Pigsty*, and Valerie Reddix's *Millie and the Mud Hole*. Another rhyme to get feet tapping is *Skateboard Monsters* by Daniel Kirk. PIGS. STORIES IN RHYME.

318   McPhail, David. *Pig Pig Gets a Job.* Illus. by the author. Dutton, 1990. ISBN 0-525-44619-2

When Pig Pig decides he needs money and his mother suggests he find a job to earn some, he thinks of becoming a cook, builder, auto mechanic, dump worker, and circus trainer. Instead, he settles on working around the house for pay, to which his mother readily agrees. Ask children to list the chores they do around the house for an allowance or for free. For another pig with responsibilities, read Susanna Gretz's *It's Your Turn, Roger!* HELPFULNESS. MONEY. OCCUPATIONS. PIGS.

319   McPhail, David. *Santa's Book of Names.* Illus. by the author. Little, Brown, 1993. ISBN 0-316-56335-8

Although Edward wants more than anything to be able to read, it's not until Christmas Eve, when Santa accidentally drops his Book of Names as he's leaving Edward's house, that he has the motivation to learn. Helping Santa deliver gifts on his sleigh when the old guy loses his specs, Edward has no choice but to decipher the written list of the gift each child is to receive. Would that remedial reading were so simple, but it's a lovely motivational story children will enjoy, along with *The Jolly Christmas Postman* by Janet and Allan Ahlberg, *A Taxi Dog Christmas* by Debra and Sal Barracca, *The Wild Christmas Reindeer* by Jan Brett, *Harvey Slumfenburger's Christmas Present* by John Burningham, *Christmas Eve at Santa's* by Alf Prøysen and Jens Ahlbom, and *The Reindeer Christmas* by Moe Price. BOOKS AND READING. CHRISTMAS. SANTA CLAUS.

320   **Manushkin, Fran.** *My Christmas Safari.* **Illus. by R. W. Alley. Dial, 1993. ISBN 0-8037-1295-2**

In an alternative to "The Twelve Days of Christmas," a little girl's father takes her to Africa on safari where they see 12 elephants trumpeting, 11 lions roaring, ten topis trotting, eight hippos yawning, all the way down to their one green truck. The title page and the final page reveal that the animals they see really come from a box of toys she unwraps for Christmas and an active imagination set in motion when she falls asleep under the tree. George Mendoza's *A Wart Snake in a Fig Tree* is a things-go-bump-in-the-night parody of the original song, as are Carol Greene's *The Thirteen Days of Halloween* and Dian Curtis Regan's *The Thirteen Hours of Halloween*. Kilmeny Niland's *A Bellbird in a Flame Tree* is an Australian version, while Irene Trivas's *Emma's Christmas* turns the song into clever prose. *The Twelve Days of Summer* by Elizabeth Lee O'Donnell is a beach version. ANIMALS–SONGS. CHRISTMAS–SONGS. COUNTING BOOKS. PARODIES. SONGS.

321   **Martin, Ann.** *Rachel Parker, Kindergarten Show-Off.* **Illus. by Nancy Poydar. Holiday House, 1992 ISBN 0-8234-0935-X**

Narrator Olivia is none too pleased with her know-it-all new neighbor and classmate, and competes with her in school and at play until they learn to share the glory. Here's the chance to talk over two pitfalls in a new friendship—competition and jealousy—and how to resolve them. Two friends also compete and squabble in *Jamaica and Brianna* by Juanita Havill. *New Kid on Spurwink Ave.* by Michael Crowley, *Jessica* by Kevin Henkes, *Because of Lozo Brown* by Larry L. King, *Earl's Too Cool for Me* by Leah Komaiko, and *Yo! Yes?* by Chris Raschka all pertain to making new friends. AFRICAN AMERICANS. CONFLICT RESOLUTION. FRIENDSHIP. JEALOUSY. KINDERGARTEN. MULTICULTURAL STORIES. SCHOOLS.

322   **Martin, Bill, Jr.** *The Happy Hippopotami.* **Illus. by Betsy Everitt. Harcourt, 1991. ISBN 0-15-233380-0**

Revel in the wordplay of nonsense verses celebrating a merry May hippopotamus holiday at the beach, as "Happy hippopotapoppas/ Stroll about the candy shoppas/ Giving children dimes and nickels/ To buy their favorite poppasicles." Read along with J. Patrick Lewis's *A Hippopotamustn't*, James Marshall's George and Martha series, and Charlotte Pomerantz's *The Piggy in the Puddle.*

Hippopotamus Hunt by Bernard Most encourages sharp-eyed kids to find hidden words in the word "hippopotamus." HIPPOPOTAMUS. NONSENSE VERSES. STORIES IN RHYME.

323   **Martin, Bill, Jr. *Old Devil Wind*. Illus. by Barry Root. Harcourt, 1993. ISBN 0-15-257768-8**

"One dark and stormy night Ghost floated out of the wall and he began to WAIL." So begins a cumulative tale with thumping stool, swishing broom, flickering candle, smoking fire, rattling window, creaking floor, slamming door, flying witch, and the wind that blows them all away. With your listeners, make up a sound and a motion to go with each new object. Stay in the mood with Eve Bunting's *Scary, Scary Halloween*, Dian Curtis Regan's *The Thirteen Hours of Halloween*, Linda Shute's *Halloween Party*, Erica Silverman's *Big Pumpkin*, Caroline Stutson's *By the Light of the Halloween Moon*, and Linda Williams's *The Little Old Lady Who Was Not Afraid of Anything*. CHANTABLE REFRAIN. CUMULATIVE STORIES. GHOSTS. HALLOWEEN. STORIES TO TELL.

324   **Meltzer, Maxine. *Pups Speak Up*. Illus. by Karen Lee Schmidt. Bradbury, 1994. ISBN 0-02-766710-3**

Perhaps your dog merely barks, but in this colorfully illustrated exposition of dogs around the world, we hear how each says hello and good-bye in its native tongue. From familiar breeds like the Mexican chihuahua and the Irish setter to the lesser known Russian borzoi or an Egyptian pharaoh dog, this amiable book will help children identify countries and languages. Take more round-the-world trips with Edith Baer's *This Is the Way We Go to School*, Rose Bursik's *Amelia's Fantastic Flight*, Anita Lobel's *Away from Home*, and Marilyn Singer's *Nine O'Clock Lullaby*. Talk in tongues globally with Hank De Zutter's *Who Says a Dog Goes Bow-Wow?*, Arthur Dorros's *This Is My House*, Debra Leventhal's *What Is Your Language?*, and Marc Robinson's *Cock-a-Doodle-Doo! What Does It Sound Like to You?* DOGS. GEOGRAPHY. LANGUAGE. MULTICULTURAL STORIES.

325   **Mitchell, Rita Phillips. *Hue Boy*. Illus. by Caroline Binch. Dial, 1993. ISBN 0-8075-1448-3**

The smallest boy on his Caribbean island, Hue Boy seeks the advice of a wise man, a doctor, and Mrs. Frangipani the healer, but it's not until his father arrives home from working on a ship that he is able to stop worrying about growing. Children can discuss the differences between island life and where they live. For an amusing take on the size problem, try Morris Lurie's *The Story of Imelda, Who Was Small*. Linger in the Caribbean with John Agard and Grace Nichols's poetry anthology *A Caribbean Dozen*, Phillis Gershator's *Rata-Pata-Scata-Fata*, Holly Keller's *Island Baby*, and Karen Lynn Williams's *Tap-Tap*. CARIBBEAN ISLANDS. ISLANDS. MULTICULTURAL STORIES. SELF-ESTEEM. SIZE.

326   **Morrison, Bill. *Squeeze a Sneeze*. Illus. by the author. Houghton Mifflin, 1977. ISBN 0-395-25151-6**

Here's one I overlooked until lately, a silly collection of illustrated rhyming phrases ("Make sure it's dark if you bark at a shark.") that readers can roll around their tongues before composing and illustrating new ones. John Stadler's *Cat Is Back at Bat* presents the same idea as Morrison's book, using three rhyming words per sentence. For starters, use the two rhyming word format of books such as *"I Can't," Said the Ant* by Polly Cameron, *Who's Sick Today?* by Lynne Cherry, *One Sun: A Book of Terse Verse*, and its companion *Play Day* by Bruce McMillan, *I Made a Mistake* by Miriam Nerlove, *Down by the Bay* by Raffi, and *Silly Sally* by Audrey Wood. CREATIVE WRITING. NONSENSE VERSES. STORIES IN RHYME.

327   **Moss, Marissa. *Knick Knack Paddywack*. Illus. by the author. Houghton Mifflin, 1992. ISBN 0-395-54701-6**

As the old guy constructs a rocket ship, he first plays not just knick knack, but also "bip bop, tap a shoe" for two, "bim bum bump a knee" for three, and on up till ten, when he counts down and takes off to become the man in the moon. All the inventive nonsense sounds will be fun to sing or chant. Traditionalists will be comforted by the normal version to be found in Carol Jones's *This Old Man*. Count down while singing along with *Ten Pink Piglets: Garth Pig's Wall Song* by Mary Rayner. COUNTING BOOKS. FOLK SONGS. SONGS. SPACE FLIGHT. STORIES IN RHYME.

328   **Moss, Marissa. *Regina's Big Mistake*. Illus. by the author. Houghton Mifflin, 1990. ISBN 0-395-55330-X**

Staring at her big sheet of blank paper on which her teacher has told the class to draw a jungle or rain forest, Regina doesn't know where to start. After she wrecks her first piece, she begins to copy the other kids' pictures until she gains the self-confidence to go with her own ideas. With her picture almost done, she slips and draws a dented sun, but soon fixes her mistake, turning it into a moon. Children need to see that mistakes can be fixed with a little patience and imagination, and this story will prove a good teaching tool for that message the next time you take out the crayons. In *No Good in Art* by Miriam Cohen, Jim learns he can paint, while in *Pete's Chicken* by Harriet Ziefert, a rabbit retains confidence in his drawing ability even when others make fun of his unusual style. Build on the idea of artistic inspiration with Leo Lionni's *Matthew's Dream*. ARTISTS. DRAWING. SCHOOLS. SELF-ESTEEM.

329   **Most, Bernard. *Can You Find It?* Illus. by the author. Harcourt, 1993. ISBN 0-15-292872-3**

"You can look for **it** if you like music. You'll find i̲t in a gu**it**ar." Fifteen clever examples with big, colorful primary-style illustrations show us how to look for the word "it" in bigger words. Children won't throw a f**it** if you ask them to use their w**it**s and compose new "it" sentences to illustrate and read aloud. For more words within words, take a look at Bruce and Brett McMillan's *Puniddles* and Diana Morley's *Marms in the Marmalade*, and Most's *Hippopotamus Hunt* and *Zoodles*. CREATIVE WRITING. ENGLISH LANGUAGE. RIDDLES. WORD GAMES.

330   Munsch, Robert. *Pigs*. Illus. by Michael Martchenko. Annick, 1989. ISBN 1-55037-039-1

Figuring the pigs in the pen are too dumb to get out, Megan opens the gate and is trampled by the rampaging pigs who run riot in her kitchen, at school, and on the school bus before she gets them back in the pen again. This silly tale will make listeners howl, as will Arthur Getz's *Humphrey the Dancing Pig*, David McPhail's *Pigs Aplenty, Pigs Galore!*, and *Pigsty* by Mark Teague. PIGS. STORIES TO TELL.

331   Mwenye Hadithi. *Hungry Hyena*. Illus. by Adrienne Kennaway. Little, Brown, 1994. ISBN 0-316-33715-3

Hyena tricks Fish Eagle out of a shiny, fat fish, but gets his comeuppance when the bird appeals to his greed. This original pourquoi and trickster tale explains why hyenas slink across the great African plains. Mwenye Hadithi's Baby Baboon, Crafty Chameleon, Greedy Zebra, Lazy Lion, and Tricky Tortoise are other flawed but compelling characters who learn their lessons. Greedy tricksters are outwitted in Doug Cushman's *Possum Stew*, and Eric A. Kimmel's *Anansi and the Moss-Covered Rock* and *Anansi Goes Fishing*. EAGLES. GREED. HYENAS. POURQUOI TALES. TRICKSTER TALES.

332   Naylor, Phyllis Reynolds. *King of the Playground*. Illus. by Nola Langner Malone. Atheneum, 1991. ISBN 0-689-31558-9

Kevin is intimidated each time Sammy warns him off the slide or swings or monkey bars by threatening him with dire and outrageous punishments. Each time, Kevin's dad gives him verbal ammunition to stand up to the bully, and when Kevin finally confronts Sammy, the two end up as friends building a shared castle in the sandbox. Barbara Bottner's *Bootsie Barker Bites*, Carol Chapman's *Herbie's Troubles*, Joanna Cole's *Don't Call Me Names*, Keiko Kasza's *The Rat and the Tiger*, and Hans Wilhelm's *Tyrone the Horrible* offer a variety of creative solutions for bully problems. BULLIES. FRIENDSHIP. FATHERS AND SONS.

333   Numeroff, Laura J. *Dogs Don't Wear Sneakers*. Illus. by Joe Mathieu. Simon & Schuster, 1993. ISBN 0-671-79525-2

In a frenetic rhyming story, you witness all the things you'll never see animals doing normally, from bowling moose to ducks riding bikes, with goofy action-filled illustrations that will make kids move. After acting out the verses in narrative pantomime, they can write about, illustrate, and dramatize other ridiculous activities they have never seen undertaken by animals. Spot more unusual behavior in Judi Barrett's *Animals Should Definitely Not Wear Clothing*, Raffi's *Down by the Bay*, and Bernard Most's *Zoodles*. Meet a mess of animals in poetry books like Alan Benjamin's *A Nickel Buys a Rhyme*, William Cole's *A Zooful of Animals*, Richard Edwards's *Moon Frog*, Beverly McLoughland's *A Hippo's a Heap*, and Fay Robinson's *A Frog Inside My Hat*. ANIMALS. CREATIVE DRAMA. HUMOROUS POETRY. IMAGINATION. STORIES IN RHYME.

334   Numeroff, Laura J. *If You Give a Moose a Muffin*. Illus. by Felicia Bond. HarperCollins, 1991. ISBN 0-06-024405-4

A Whole Language teacher's dream, this cyclical story, the companion to *If You Give a Mouse a Cookie*, has a large congenial moose requesting jam, a sweater, sock-puppet accoutrements, a sheet, and finally, more muffins. Felicia Bond's good-natured watercolor and pen-and-ink pictures inspired my first-graders to illustrate their own segments of the story, which they then reassembled and read aloud in sequence, while teacher Pat Frederick's second-grade class wrote another hilarious sequel: "If You Give a Monkey Money." Continue moose calls with James Marshall's *The Guest*, Elise Primavera's *The Three Dots*, Dr. Seuss's *Thidwick the Big-Hearted Moose*, and David Small's *Imogene's Antlers*. CAUSE AND EFFECT. MOOSE. SEQUENCE STORIES.

335   Pank, Rachel. *Under the Blackberries*. Illus. by the author. Scholastic, 1992. ISBN 0-590-45481-1

When her beloved cat Barney dies in a road accident, Sonia finds it hard to believe that he won't be back, though she gets through the sad times by befriending a porcupine in the garden, burying the cat in the yard and planting a rosebush over his grave, and getting a new kitten to love. The grief Sonia feels is not glossed over or rushed, and the addition of the new kitten does not mean she'll ever forget her first cat. A pet's death is handled with dignity also in Miriam Cohen's *Jim's Dog Muffins*, Connie Heckert's *Dribbles*, Ellen Howard's *Murphy and Kate*, Betsy James's *Mary Ann*, Holly Keller's *Goodbye, Max*, and Judith Viorst's *The Tenth Good Thing About Barney*. CATS. DEATH.

336   Peters, Lisa Westberg. *When the Fly Flew In*. Illus. by Brad Sneed. Dial, 1994. ISBN 0-8037-1432-7

A child whispers to his mother, "I can't clean my room . . . All the animals are sleeping." Moments later a fly buzzes in and disrupts the snoozing dog, cat, hamster, and parakeet, all of whom inadvertently dust and straighten the room in their hilarious frenzy to catch the fly. Read this along with Mark Teague's *Pigsty* before you assign everyone tasks to clean up the classroom in one fell swoop. Swat more flies with Jim Aylesworth's *Hush Up!* and *Old Black Fly* and Joanne Oppenheim's *You Can't Catch Me!* It's a flea that interrupts everyone's 40 winks in *The Napping House* by Audrey Wood. CAUSE AND EFFECT. CLEANLINESS. FLIES. INSECTS. PETS.

337   Pfister, Marcus. *The Rainbow Fish*. Trans. by J. Alison James. Illus. by the author. North-South, 1992. ISBN 1-55858-010-7

Beautiful Rainbow Fish, proud of his sparkling silver scales, learns first about loneliness when he is shunned by the other fish for refusing to share his scales with them, and then happiness when he takes a wise octopus's advice and gives away one scale to each fish. Reminiscent of Leo Lionni's bird story *Tico and the*

Golden Wings, it also relates nicely to Lionni's *Fish Is Fish* and *Swimmy*. Children can give examples of how sharing something they valued made them feel special. FISHES. FRIENDSHIP. GENEROSITY. PRIDE AND VANITY.

338   Pittman, Helena Clare. *Miss Hindy's Cats*. Illus. by the author. Carolrhoda, 1990.
       ISBN 0-87614-368-0

The first cat Miss Hindy finds at her front door she names Agnes, followed by Bella found during a snowstorm, Chanticleer at the vegetable store, and on to Winifred at the library, along with newborn kittens Xavier, Yvonne, and Zinnia—all 26 of whom she nurses back to health and happiness. Children will love the surprise open ending where a dog shows up at the door (Anton!) and can consider an alphabetical sequel where each child thinks of a dog's name and draws the circumstances under which Miss Hindy might find it. Fool around with more name alphabets in *A My Name Is Alice* by Jane Bayer, *Alison's Zinnia* and *Away from Home* by Anita Lobel, and *Potluck* by Anne Shelby. ALPHABET BOOKS. CATS. NAMES.

339   Polette, Nancy. *Hole by the Apple Tree: An A–Z Discovery Tale*. Illus. by Nishan
       Akgulian. Greenwillow, 1992. ISBN 0-688-10558-0

Digging a hole by the Apple tree, Harold explains to his friends he is planting Beans to make a beanstalk grow up to the Castle, where he will encounter a giant, monster, and other fairy-tale characters. There's great charm in his imaginative alphabetical wanderings, illustrated as thought bubbles above his head while he recounts his tale. Sit in a circle and compile another adventure with your children, using the same ABC pattern. If you tape record the session and transcribe it, children can illustrate the text for a class book. *Old Black Fly* by Jim Aylesworth and *Alfred's Alphabet Walk* by Victoria Chess also employ the alphabet-within-a-story technique, while *Once Upon a Golden Apple* by Jean Little and Maggie De Vries also plays with the fairy-tale motif. ALPHABET. IMAGINATION. FAIRY TALES–SATIRE.

340   Porte, Barbara Ann. *"Leave That Cricket Be, Alan Lee."* Illus. by Donna Ruff.
       Greenwillow, 1993. ISBN 0-688-11794-5

After his uncle tells him about the cricket cages he used to make as a boy in China, Alan Lee works hard to capture the cricket that's been singing in his house, but once it's in the glass jar, it won't sing or eat. Compare this realistic story of a boy who lets his pet go with the chirping fantasy of Eric Carle's *The Very Quiet Cricket*. In Holly Keller's *Island Baby*, Simon also makes the tough decision to set his wild flamingo free. And in Betsy James's *Mary Ann*, a girl's pet praying mantis dies but leaves behind hundreds of babies. CHINESE AMERICANS. CRICKETS. INSECTS. PETS.

341   Price, Moe. *The Reindeer Christmas*. Illus. by Atsuko Morozumi. Harcourt, 1993.
       ISBN 0-15-266199-9

Santa Claus confides in his chief elf Elwin that this might be his last Christmas because there are too many houses to visit and not enough time to deliver all the presents. The elves build him a magic sleigh and advertise for animals to pull it, but none who apply are quite right for the job until a young reindeer needs help rescuing an injured reindeer friend from a gorge. *A Taxi Dog Christmas* by Debra and Sal Barracca, *The Wild Christmas Reindeer* by Jan Brett, *Harvey Slumfenburger's Christmas Present* by John Burningham, and *Santa's Book of Names* by David McPhail will also delight. CHRISTMAS. ELVES. FLIGHT. REINDEER. SANTA CLAUS.

342 **Primavera, Elise. *The Three Dots*. Illus. by the author. Putnam, 1993. ISBN 0-399-22429-7**

Kindred spirits Henry Frog, Sal Moose, and Margaret Duck, all three of whom have spots on their exteriors, come together by chance in a New York City donut shop, take an apartment together, and form a hit musical trio. A fresh story of fame and fortune in the big time, this one works great with Lisa Campbell Ernst's cow tale *When Bluebell Sang* and Mary Rayner's *Garth Pig Steals the Show*. DUCKS. FRIENDSHIP. FROGS. MOOSE. MUSIC.

343 **Prøysen, Alf. *Christmas Eve at Santa's*. Illus. by Jens Ahlbom. R & S, 1992. ISBN 91-29-62066-X**

On Christmas Eve, Carpenter Anderson, dressed in a Santa suit to surprise his children, bumps into the real Santa who suggests they trade places. Visiting Santa's elf children in their cottage in the woods, the carpenter makes wooden toys for the children, a ladle for Mama, and a walking stick for Grandpa. The Swedish vision of a down-to-earth Santa is a refreshing change from the North Pole toy factory image. Also entertaining are Janet and Allan Ahlberg's *The Jolly Christmas Postman*, Debra and Sal Barracca's *A Taxi Dog Christmas*, *The Wild Christmas Reindeer* by Jan Brett, *Harvey Slumfenburger's Christmas Present* by John Burningham, *Santa's Book of Names* by David McPhail, *The Reindeer Christmas* by Moe Price, and *The Remarkable Christmas of the Cobbler's Sons*, an Austrian folktale by Ruth Sawyer. CARPENTERS. CHRISTMAS. ELVES. SANTA CLAUS.

344 **Pulver, Robin. *Mrs. Toggle and the Dinosaur*. Illus. by R. W. Alley. Four Winds, 1991. ISBN 0-02-775452-9**

Informed by Mr. Stickler, the principal, that her new student is a dinosaur, teacher Mrs. Toggle is aghast, while her helpful class researches dinosaurs in the library and prepares for its arrival. What a relief to find the new child is a little girl—named Dina Sawyer. How could a teacher make such a mistake? Play "Telephone" with your class to see how a message can be misheard and read aloud Janet Stevens's illustrated version of Hans Christian Andersen's *It's Perfectly True* to see the trouble it can cause. DINOSAURS. HUMOROUS FICTION. SCHOOLS. TEACHERS.

345 **Pulver, Robin. *Mrs. Toggle's Beautiful Blue Shoe*. Illus. by R. W. Alley. Four Winds, 1994. ISBN 0-02-775456-1**

In trying to kick the playground ball, teacher Mrs. Toggle sends her shoe sailing into a tree instead, and now everyone—students, principal Mr. Stickler, cook Mrs. Burns, and custodian Mr. Able—has an impractical suggestion for getting it down. Your students will surely think up additional creative ideas. After reading *Mrs. Toggle and the Dinosaur* and *Mrs. Toggle's Zipper*, talk over the differences and similarities between her class and yours. HUMOROUS FICTION. SCHOOLS. SHOES. TEACHERS.

346   **Pulver, Robin.** *Nobody's Mother Is in Second Grade.* **Illus. by G. Brian Karas. Dial, 1992. ISBN 0-8037-1211-1**

Cassandra's curious mother would give anything to visit second grade with her, and comes up with the perfect disguise: a large plant which, once it's settled in the classroom, intrigues the children when it hums, smiles, and even eats lunch in the cafeteria. Comparing all the nice things her mother does for her to the positive attributes of a plant, Cassandra is tickled to have her mother in school. Maybe now is a good time to invite parents to visit your classroom, and they don't need to come incognito—unless they want to. In Amy Schwartz's *Bea and Mr. Jones*, dad and daughter switch places as she goes to the office and he tries kindergarten. Then there's S. E. Hinton's hilarious *Big David, Little David* where Nick's father tries to convince him that by day he is a student in Nick's kindergarten class. MOTHERS AND DAUGHTERS. MULTICULTURAL STORIES. PLANTS. SCHOOLS.

347   **Radcliffe, Theresa.** *Shadow the Deer.* **Illus. by John Butler. Viking, 1993. ISBN 0-670-83852-7**

Luminous realistic paintings grace this slice-of-life story about a deer who protects her three-day-old fawn from Redflank the fox who is hunting for food to feed her two hungry cubs. Irina Korschunow's *The Foundling Fox*, Jonathan London's *The Eyes of Gray Wolf*, Tejima's *Fox's Dream*, and Karen Wallace's *Red Fox* give us the predator's viewpoint. Explore a parallel habitat with William T. George's *Box Turtle at Long Pond*. In Jonathan London's *Gray Fox*, we follow a fox and his family, mourn when the fox is killed by a passing truck, and see how life goes on. DEER. FOXES.

348   **Raffi.** *Spider on the Floor.* **Words and music by Bill Russell. Illus. by True Kelley. Crown, 1993. ISBN 0-517-59464-1**

Part of Raffi's Songs to Read series is this tale of a climbing spider, which children can sing with you, ascending to a higher key with each verse as the spider travels upward. Singers can make up new verses. My kindergartener's sang "There's a spider on my ear, and I'm gonna cry a tear," and "There's a spider on my nose, and he's dancing on his toes." Sing with G. Brian Karas's *I Know an Old Lady*, Glen Rounds's or Nadine Bernard Westcott's *I Know an Old Lady Who Swallowed a Fly*, "I'm Being Eaten by a Boa Constrictor" from Shel Silverstein's *Where the Sidewalk Ends*, and Iza Trapani's *The Itsy Bitsy Spider*. Eric Carle's *The Very Busy Spider* is nicely noisy, too. CHANTABLE REFRAIN. CREATIVE WRITING. SONGS. SPIDERS.

349   Rattigan, Jama Kim. *Dumpling Soup*. Illus. by Lillian Hsu-Flanders. Little, Brown, 1993.
ISBN 0-316-73445-4

At New Year's, Marisa's "chop suey" family—part Korean, Japanese, Chinese,
Hawaiian, and haole (white)—arrives at Grandma's house to make dumplings
for their big family dinner, and this year she is finally old enough to help, though
she worries that her dumplings do not measure up. Your supermarket might sell
wonton wrappers if you want to make easy dumplings in class. Serve up more
ethnic eating pleasure with Norah Dooley's *Everybody Cooks Rice*, Anne Shelby's
Potluck, and Gary Soto's *Too Many Tamales*. *Luka's Quilt* by Georgia Guback gives
us another intergenerational tale from Hawaii. Ring in the American holiday
with Frank Modell's *Goodbye Old Year, Hello New Year* and Chinese New Year
with Ian Wallace's *Chin Chiang and the Dragon Dance*. FAMILY LIFE. FOOD. HAWAII.
MULTICULTURAL STORIES. NEW YEAR.

350   Rohmann, Eric. *Time Flies*. Illus. by the author. Crown, 1994. ISBN 0-517-59599-0

Inspired by the theory that birds and dinosaurs are relatives, Rohmann's heart-
stopping paintings of sweeping brown-toned vistas follow a bird flying through
a dinosaur museum and back to the days of the dinosaurs. What a spectacular
introduction to both fiction and nonfiction dinosaur books. Travel back with
pajama-clad Wilbur as he takes a baby apatosaurus back through each stage of
dinosaur history in Dennis Nolan's *Dinosaur Dreams*. B. G. Hennessy's *The
Dinosaur Who Lived in My Backyard* and Bernard Most's *How Big Were the
Dinosaurs?* are fact filled, while Carol Carrick's *Patrick's Dinosaurs* and *What
Happened to Patrick's Dinosaurs?*, Diane Dawson Hearn's *Dad's Dinosaur Day*,
Robin Pulver's *Mrs. Toggle and the Dinosaur*, and Henry Schwartz's *How I
Captured a Dinosaur* will stir the imagination. BIRDS. DINOSAURS. MUSEUMS. PICTURE
BOOKS FOR ALL AGES. STORIES WITHOUT WORDS.

351   Root, Phyllis. *Coyote and the Magic Words*. Illus. by Sandra Speidel. Lothrop, 1993.
ISBN 0-688-10309-X

When the Maker-of-all-things finished making the world, all words were magic,
and people had but to say "Corn," or "Rain," or "Night" for these things to
appear until the day Coyote got bored and stirred up his usual trouble. Based on
motifs and characters in Southwestern Native American folklore, Root's original
tale gives us a female god and explains how stories are filled with magic words.
Gail E. Haley's African trickster tale *A Story, A Story* about Anansi the Spider also
explains how stories began. Peruse the growing number of Coyote tales with
Verna Aardema's *Borreguita and the Coyote*, Shonto Begay's *Ma'ii and Cousin
Horned Toad*, Jonathan London and Lanny Pinola's *Fire Race*, Gretchen Will
Mayo's *That Tricky Coyote!* and *Meet Tricky Coyote!*, Janet Stevens's *Coyote Steals
the Blanket*, and Harriet Peck Taylor's *Coyote Places the Stars*. COYOTES. CREATION.
INDIANS OF NORTH AMERICA. MAGIC. STORYTELLING.

352   Rosen, Michael. *Moving*. Illus. by Sophy Williams. Viking, 1993. ISBN 0-670-84865-4

What it's like to move to a new house, from an independent house cat's point of view, is "no tickles, no laps, all boxes and boxes and boxes," so the cat hides and won't come to the boy who seeks it until it is tempted with food. Kids aren't mad for moving either, as in Elizabeth Lee O'Donnell's *Maggie Doesn't Want to Move* and Elvira Woodruff's *The Wing Shop*. Joyce McDonald's *Homebody* shows a left-behind cat who is taken in by a new family, while Dav Pilkey's *When Cats Dream* lets us delve into a cat's surreal subconscious. Donald Hall's *I Am the Dog, I Am the Cat* presents both animals' take on the world around them. CATS. MOVING, HOUSEHOLD. PICTURE BOOKS FOR ALL AGES. POINT OF VIEW.

353   Rotner, Shelley, and Ken Kreisler. *Citybook*. Photos by Shelley Rotner. Orchard, 1994. ISBN 0-531-08687-9

A color photo-essay zips us all around Manhattan as Kevin and his mom see a kid's-eye view of the Big Apple. Another rhyming description of city life is Nancy Van Laan's cheery *People, People, Everywhere!* Keep exploring with Arthur Dorros's *Abuela*, Kathy Jakobsen's *My New York*, and E. L. Konigsburg's *Amy Elizabeth Explores Bloomingdale's*. Compare contrasting life-styles using Maxine Bozzo's *Toby in the Country, Toby in the City*. CITIES AND TOWNS. NEW YORK CITY. STORIES IN RHYME.

354   Russo, Marisabina. *Alex Is My Friend*. Illus. by the author. Greenwillow, 1992. ISBN 0-688-10419-3

A young boy explains how he and Alex met and became friends when they were little, a relationship that hasn't changed though Alex will always stay small. Despite Alex's back surgery and recuperation, the boys remain friends, and by the end of the story, we see the narrator is a full head taller than Alex. Other stories that help children to have empathy for people with disabilities include Nancy L. Carlson's *Arnie and the New Kid*, Liz Damrell's *With the Wind*, Jane Cowen-Fletcher's *Mama Zooms*, Audrey Osofsky's *My Buddy*, and Berniece Rabe's *The Balancing Girl*. DWARFS. FRIENDSHIP. HANDICAPS. PHYSICAL DISABILITY. WHEELCHAIRS.

355   Russo, Marisabina. *I Don't Want to Go Back to School*. Illus. by the author. Greenwillow, 1994. ISBN 0-688-04602-9

Apprehensive about meeting his new teacher Mr. Johnson, and intimidated by his older sister's dire warnings, Ben would rather stay home, but once he gets into his classroom, he loves it. Read this on the first day, even if you don't have any hissing cockroaches to show, the way Ben's teacher did. *Chrysanthemum* by Kevin Henkes and *Nobody's Mother Is in Second Grade* by Robin Pulver are also fitting "first day" stories. BROTHERS AND SISTERS. SCHOOLS. TEACHERS.

356   Sadler, Marilyn. *Alistair and the Alien Invasion*. Illus. by Roger Bollen. Simon & Schuster, 1994. ISBN 0-671-75957-4

Searching for an unusual plant for his science project, the boy genius and compulsive neatnik Alistair takes his spaceship for a jaunt around the Milky Way and discovers an alien spaceship heading for Earth. This is another deadpan addition to the series that also includes *Alistair in Outer Space*, *Alistair's Elephant*, and *Alistair's Time Machine*. *Space Case* and *Merry Christmas* by Edward Marshall, and *I'm Coming to Get You* by Tony Ross are also beginning sci-fi titles with a good sense of humor and irony. EXTRATERRESTRIAL LIFE. PLANTS. SCIENCE FICTION. SPACE FLIGHT.

357   Schneider, Howie. *Uncle Lester's Hat*. Illus. by the author. Putnam, 1993. ISBN 0-399-22439-4

While his young nephew wonders why his couch potato Uncle Wilfred is taking so long to come home, the stout bespeckled guy with the bad back is off chasing the hat that once belonged to his own Uncle Lester, the adventurer, all around the world. Tearing through London, Paris, the Alps, the desert, past Japan, Hollywood, and Mount Rushmore, Uncle Wilfred arrives home full of stories, sans backache, ready to give chase once more. Look out for more missing hats in Catherine Bancroft and Hannah Coale Gruenberg's *Felix's Hat*, Eileen Christelow's *Olive and the Magic Hat*, Joan L. Nodset's *Who Took the Farmer's Hat?*, Esphyr Slobodkina's *Caps for Sale*, and Jerry Smath's *A Hat So Simple*. Circumnavigate the globe with *Jeremy's Tail* by Duncan Ball, *Amelia's Fantastic Flight* by Rose Bursik, *Away from Home* by Anita Lobel, *How to Make an Apple Pie and See the World* by Marjorie Priceman, and *Love, Your Bear Pete* by Dyan Sheldon. GEOGRAPHY. HATS. UNCLES. VOYAGES AND TRAVELS.

358   Schwartz, Amy. *A Teeny Tiny Baby*. Illus. by the author. Orchard, 1994. ISBN 0-531-08668-2

"I'm a teeny tiny baby and I know how to get anything I want." So begins a wonderfully endearing and memory-inducing narrative about a newborn's wants, likes, and life experiences so far. Note the doting and exhausted new parents and grandparents cuddling and feeding and catering to the every whim of their benevolent tyrant, and the enchanting and detailed gouache illustrations. Listeners will begin dredging up early memories and can write or record and illustrate them for posterity, before they get too old to remember anymore. Present the personable babies in Pat Hutchins's monster-ish *Where's the Baby?*, Holly Keller's *Geraldine's Baby Brother*, Tom Paxton's *Where's the Baby?*, James Stevenson's *Rolling Rose*, Vera B. Williams's *"More More More," Said the Baby*, and Frieda Wishinsky's *Oonga Boonga*. BABIES. PICTURE BOOKS FOR ALL AGES. POINT OF VIEW.

359   Sharmat, Marjorie Weinman. *A Big Fat Enormous Lie*. Illus. by David McPhail. Dutton, 1978. ISBN 0-525-26510-4

Afraid to admit it when his father asked if he ate the jar of cookies, a little boy is sorry afterward, but the lie follows him and grows like an elephantine green monster until he finally owns up to his deed. As he admits his mistake, the monster shrinks and departs, much like the one fearful Harry faces in *Harry and the Terrible Whatzit* by Dick Gackenbach. Talk over why people lie and how to avoid it. Admitting a mistake is not easy for Maria when she loses her mother's diamond ring in *Too Many Tamales* by Gary Soto. HONESTY.

360   Shaw, Nancy. *Sheep in a Shop.* Illus. by Margot Apple. Houghton Mifflin, 1991. ISBN 0-395-53681-2

"A birthday's coming! Hip Hooray! Five sheep shop for the big big day." So starts another delightful rhyming romp, companion to *Sheep in a Jeep, Sheep on a Ship* (1989), *Sheep Out to Eat,* and *Sheep Take a Hike* (1994). This time, sheep clip their wool, three bags full, to trade for presents. In another rhyming shopping excursion, a young pig gets left behind in *Tommy at the Grocery Store* by Bill Grossman. SHEEP. SHOPPING. STORIES IN RHYME.

361   Shaw, Nancy. *Sheep Out to Eat.* Illus. by Margot Apple. Houghton Mifflin, 1992. ISBN 0-395-61128-8

Sheep manners in the teashop are not the best as they slurp, burp, chomp, sneeze, and knock over the table, before realizing what they really want for lunch is the lawn outside. For more animal havoc in restaurants, see also Stephanie Calmenson's *Dinner at the Panda Palace* and John Stadler's *Animal Cafe.* A similar rhyme scheme shows us how people act when they go out for a bite in *In the Diner* by Christine Loomis. Read all in the Sheep series, and then decide which places the wooly ones might end up next, and what might happen to them there. Speaking of sheep, Kevin Kiser's *Sherman the Sheep* is a charmer, while Sarah Hale's *Mary Had a Little Lamb*, with Bruce McMillan's marvelous color photographs, will also help your listeners remove the wool from their eyes. FOOD. RESTAURANTS. SHEEP. STORIES IN RHYME.

362   Shelby, Anne. *Potluck.* Illus. by Irene Trivas. Orchard, 1991. ISBN 0-531-08519-8

An international alphabet of children with names from A to Z each bring his or her special alliterative dish to a wondrous potluck feast at Alpha and Betty's house. Eric Carle's *Today Is Monday,* Cheryl Chapman's *Pass the Fritters, Critters,* and Norah Dooley's *Everybody Cooks Rice* will get you singing, rhyming, and thinking about lunch. If you're feeling famished, have children write and illustrate their own sentences showing what foods that start with the first letters of their names they'd bring to the table, and then throw a class potluck. Bobbye S. Goldstein's *What's on the Menu?* and Dee Lillegard's *Do Not Feed the Table* provide delectable poetry, while Charles Keller's *Belly Laughs! Food Jokes & Riddles* will keep you chuckling. Jim Aylesworth's rhyming *My Son John,* Jane Bayer's *A My Name Is Alice,* Max Grover's *The Accidental Zucchini,* and Helena Clare Pittman's *Miss Hindy's Cats* are also alphabetical and/or alliterative. ALLITERATION. ALPHABET BOOKS. FOOD. MULTICULTURAL STORIES. NAMES.

363   Sheldon, Dyan. *Love, Your Bear Pete.* Illus. by Tania Hurt-Newton. Candlewick, 1994. ISBN 1-56402-332-X

After leaving her blue bear on the bus, Brenda worries that he'll be lonely without her, until she begins receiving daily postcards from him from London, Paris, Venice, and all over the globe. Chart the peripatetic teddy's trip on a world map, investigating some of the places he visited and some that your students feel he should have visited. Go on a tear with *Jeremy's Tail* by Duncan Ball, *Magic Carpet* by Pat Brisson, *Amelia's Fantastic Flight* by Rose Bursik, *Away from Home* by Anita Lobel, *How to Make an Apple Pie and See the World* by Marjorie Priceman, and *Uncle Lester's Hat* by Howie Schneider. GEOGRAPHY. LETTER WRITING. LOST. TEDDY BEARS. VOYAGES AND TRAVELS.

364   **Silverman, Erica. *Big Pumpkin*. Illus. by S. D. Schindler. Macmillan, 1992. ISBN 0-02-782683-X**

Though the witch tugs and pulls, she cannot pull her pumpkin off the vine, and must accept assistance from the ghost, vampire, mummy, and bat who offer their services in hopes of a taste of pumpkin pie. The setup is reminiscent of Pierr Morgan's or Janina Domanska's retellings of *The Turnip*. Wonderfully ghoulish illustrations and a repeating storyline filled with chantable refrains, this will be a major Halloween hit, especially for acting out using expressive voices. Bring in a pumpkin and carve out a seasonal niche with Tony Johnston's *The Vanishing Pumpkin* and Linda Williams's *The Little Old Lady Who Was Not Afraid of Anything*. Hold the spooky mood with Ed Emberley's *Go Away, Big Green Monster!*, Bill Martin, Jr.'s *Old Devil Wind*, Dian Curtis Regan's *The Thirteen Hours of Halloween*, and Caroline Stutson's *By the Light of the Halloween Moon*. CHANTABLE REFRAIN. COOPERATION. HALLOWEEN. MONSTERS. PUMPKINS. WITCHES.

365   **Silverman, Erica. *Don't Fidget a Feather!* Illus. by S. D. Schindler. Macmillan, 1994. ISBN 0-02-782685-6**

Always competing, Duck and Gander agree on a freeze-in-place contest, with the winner, the one who doesn't move or talk the longest, proclaimed champion of champions. Fox finds the two frozen fowl and carries them home for stew before the stubborn friends come to their senses. Talk over some basic comprehension issues: Why did the two stay frozen when the fox came? Why didn't they move in Fox's cave? Why did Duck finally speak? Relate these questions about stubbornness to their experience: Did you ever act stubborn when you shouldn't have? What happened? In *Bubba and Babba* by Maria Polushkin, two lazy bears agree that whoever is the first to speak will have to wash the dinner dishes. COMPETITION. DUCKS. FOXES. GEESE.

366   **Singer, Marilyn. *Chester the Out-of-Work Dog*. Illus. by Cat Bowman Smith. Henry Holt, 1992. ISBN 0-8050-1828-X**

Sheepdog Chester is thrown out of work and left bored, with nothing to herd, when his family, the Wippenhoopers, sells the farm and moves into an apartment in town. Discuss Chester's dilemma with your students. Why is it so important for him to find something to herd? For a mixture of industrious and not-so driven pets, turn to Steven Kellogg's *Pinkerton, Behave!*, Pija Lindenbaum's *Boodil My Dog*, Susan Meddaugh's *Martha Speaks*, Audrey Osofsky's *My Buddy*, and Frances Ward Weller's *Riptide*. DOGS. SHEEP. WORK.

367   **Smath, Jerry. *A Hat So Simple*. Illus. by the author. BridgeWater, 1993. ISBN 0-8167-3016-4**

All alligator Edna wants is a small and neat little hat to keep her cool while fishing with her husband, but instead she buys a bigger hat that her friends spruce up with a flowerpot, bow, grapes, a balloon, and a candle. Since her now top-heavy hat causes her to fall in the stream, children can discuss the consequences of always taking others' advice instead of depending on ones' own taste. Try on some stunning chapeaus in John Dyke's *Pigwig*, Laura Geringer's *A Three Hat Day*, Ezra Jack Keats's *Jennie's Hat*, and William Jay Smith's *Ho for a Hat!* Uncle Wilfred goes on a world tour chasing after *Uncle Lester's Hat*, as told by Howie Schneider. ALLIGATORS. FISHING. HATS. NARRATIVE POETRY. STORIES IN RHYME.

368   Smith, William Jay. *Ho for a Hat!* Illus. by Lynn Munsinger. Little, Brown, 1989. ISBN 0-316-80120-8

What's the reason for hats, as laid out in this delicious rhyming tribute with jouncing, gleeful illustrations? "They look nice, They feel nice, They *are* nice." Expect everyone to holler the chantable title refrain. Declare Inventive Hat Day, where children create the most outrageous hats with found materials and parade about to show them off. Other hat tales include John Dyke's *Pigwig*, Laura Geringer's *A Three Hat Day*, Ezra Jack Keats's *Jennie's Hat*, and Jerry Smath's *A Hat So Simple*. CHANTABLE REFRAIN. HATS. STORIES IN RHYME.

369   Soto, Gary. *Too Many Tamales*. Illus. by Ed Martinez. Putnam, 1993. ISBN 0-399-22146-8

Helping knead the masa for Christmas tamales, Maria tries on her mother's diamond ring and doesn't remember what she did with it until later when, in a moment of sheer panic, she enlists her cousins to eat all the tamales to find it. Since most children do not have experience with tamales, first discuss Mexican foods they do know—tacos, tortilla chips, nachos, and the like. Swap stories of times kids have had to own up to a big mistake, and how it turned out. In Paula dePaolo's *Rosie & the Yellow Ribbon*, Rosie accuses her best friend of stealing and must eat crow and apologize, and in Marjorie Weinman Sharmat's *A Big Fat Enormous Lie*, a boy eventually owns up to eating a jar of cookies. Norah Dooley's *Everybody Cooks Rice*, Jama Kim Rattigan's *Dumpling Soup*, and Anne Shelby's *Potluck* provide us with more delicious ethnic eats. CHRISTMAS. CONFLICT RESOLUTION. FOOD. HONESTY. MEXICAN AMERICANS.

370   Spinelli, Eileen. *If You Want to Find Golden*. Illus. by Stacey Schuett. Albert Whitman, 1993. ISBN 0-8075-3585-0

There are lots of places in the city to find golden, white, green, orange, blue, yellow, brown, purple, gray, red, copper, black, and silver, and there's one double-page spread devoted to describing each color and where you'll come across it. Children can decide where to go in their neighborhood to find colors, and write and illustrate their descriptions. Kathy Jakobsen's *My New York* is a riot of color and Shelley Rotner and Ken Kreisler give us color-photo shots of pulsing New York in *Citybook*. Dayle Ann Dodds's *The Color Box* takes us on a color tour, Jessica Jenkins's *Thinking About Colors* pulls in our response to color, and Arnold Lobel's *The Great Blueness and Other Predicaments* explains how colors came to be, while Mary L. O'Neill's *Hailstones and Halibut Bones: Adventures in Color* offers one poem for each of 12 colors. CITIES AND TOWNS. COLOR. MULTICULTURAL STORIES.

371   **Spinelli, Eileen.** *Somebody Loves You, Mr. Hatch.* **Illus. by Paul Yalowitz. Bradbury, 1991. ISBN 0-02-786015-9**

A man of lonely habit who keeps to himself, shoelace factory worker Mr. Hatch, one day receives a huge box of candy for Valentine's Day from an unknown admirer. The idea that he has a secret admirer changes his life as he reaches out to his coworkers and neighbors and they return his affection. Imagine his utter devastation when the postman tells him the package was delivered to the wrong address. Valentine's Day is a good time to talk about how, by our actions, we all have the power to improve relations with our friends and classmates. Explore neighborliness in *Smoky Night* by Eve Bunting, about the Los Angeles riots, and love in *Bub: Or, the Very Best Thing* by Natalie Babbitt. FRIENDSHIP. LONELINESS. LOVE. NEIGHBORS. VALENTINE'S DAY.

372   **Stadler, John.** *Cat Is Back at Bat.* **Illus. by the author. Dutton, 1991. ISBN 0-525-44762-8**

In this easy-to-read rhyming word book, each double page contains a simple sentence about an animal, and contains three rhyming words, along with a colorful, cute illustration. Cover the words and see if children can guess each sentence from examining the picture. This is the most basic type of beginning reader, and shows how to present controlled vocabulary in an entertaining and noncondescending way. Children can write, illustrate, and present their own animal sentences, and do more guessing with *"I Can't," Said the Ant* by Polly Cameron, *Who's Sick Today?* by Lynne Cherry, *Hunky Dory Ate It* by Katie Evans, *In the Diner* by Christine Loomis, *One Sun: A Book of Terse Verse* and it's companion *Play Day* by Bruce McMillan, *Squeeze a Sneeze* by Bill Morrison, *I Made a Mistake* by Miriam Nerlove, and *Down by the Bay* by Raffi. ANIMALS. CREATIVE WRITING. STORIES IN RHYME.

373   **Stevenson, James.** *Brrr!* **Illus. by the author. Greenwillow, 1991. ISBN 0-688-09211-X**

Grandpa regales his grandkids Mary Ann and Louie with another "true" story from his adventure-laden boyhood. This one was about the extraordinary winter of 1908, when the snow came down so hard it covered the entire town, and only younger brother Wainey's ear-splitting cry could shatter all the ice that enveloped their house. Stevenson's more than a dozen "Grandpa" books are told in dialogue, with slapdash cartoon panel-style watercolors. All are great fun for children to read aloud in small groups, with each person responsible for delivering one character's lines. Since these stories are usually a child's first exposure to exaggeration and tall tales, teach your tale weavers how to spin a "Grandpa"-style yarn with such story-starters as, "When I was young, it was so cold/hot /dark/light/wet/dry that . . ." BROTHERS. EXAGGERATION. GRANDFATHERS. WEATHER. WINTER.

374   **Stevenson, Robert Louis.** *My Shadow.* **Illus. by Ted Rand. Putnam, 1990. ISBN 0-399-22216-2**

"I have a little shadow that goes in and out with me . . . ." So begins one of Stevenson's most enduring poems, which Ted Rand has turned into a fetching picture book. Go outside at different times of the day to compare your shadows, and using the light from a filmstrip projector, make hand shadows on the wall. SHADOWS–POETRY. STORIES IN RHYME.

375   Taylor, Livingston. *Can I Be Good?* Illus. by Ted Rand. Harcourt, 1993. ISBN 0-15-200436-X

The golden retriever who narrates this adorable picture book in verse spends his day trying to behave, though he howls in the early morning, comes inside all muddy and wet, bounds onto the school bus, and chews Dad's shoe before calming down for a petting by his ever-loving family. Listeners will regale each other with stories of pet misbehavior. *Hunky Dory Ate It* by Katie Evans is another rhyming tribute to a bad dog. BEHAVIOR. DOGS. STORIES IN RHYME.

376   Teague, Mark. *The Field Beyond the Outfield.* Illus. by the author. Scholastic, 1992. ISBN 0-590-45173-1

Ludlow Grebe's parents decide he needs "something real to think about" after he complains about the monsters in his closet and the sharks that swim by his window when it rains, so they sign him up for baseball. A good ballplayer is always ready, but his team puts him far back in the outfield where he finds another ball game going on, and hits a homer for that insect team. *Take Me Out to the Ballgame* by Jack Norworth, Marilyn Sachs's *Matt's Mitt and Fleet-Footed Florence*, and *My Dad's Baseball* by Ron Cohen will please fans. *Simon's Book* by Henrik Drescher and *The Amazing Voyage of Jackie Grace* by Matt Faulkner are imagination stretchers, and *Skateboard Monsters* by Daniel Kirk delivers some sporty new creatures. BASEBALL. IMAGINATION. MONSTERS.

377   Trivas, Irene. *Annie . . . Anya: A Month in Moscow.* Illus. by the author. Orchard, 1992. ISBN 0-531-08602-X

Five-year-old Annie, whose doctor parents bring her with them for a month in Russia, is homesick and miserable for two days at the daycare center until she meets Anya, a little Russian girl just her age. Your listeners will assimilate the over two dozen Russian words introduced in this winning tale of Russian sights, sounds, and foods. Be sure to introduce the Cyrillic alphabet, and, for kids who are already reading, use it as a cipher to send and receive simple messages in class. FRIENDSHIP. LANGUAGE. MULTICULTURAL STORIES. RUSSIA. RUSSIAN LANGUAGE.

378   Trivizas, Eugene. *The Three Little Wolves and the Big Bad Pig.* Illus. by Helen Oxenbury. McElderry, 1993. ISBN 0-689-50569-8

Three cuddly little wolves go out into the world and build a nice house of bricks that the big bad pig can't blow down, so he knocks it down with a sledgehammer. On the next concrete house, the pig uses a pneumatic drill, and on the third house, dynamite, at which point the wolves build their last house . . . of flowers. It's a witty takeoff—though the ending is a bit too sweet to believe—that you can spring on everyone after the traditional *The Three Little Pigs* by Lorinda Bryan Cauley, Paul Galdone, James Marshall, Glen Rounds, or Margot Zemach, and *The Three Little Pigs and the Fox* by William H. Hooks. David Vozar's *Yo, Hungry Wolf! A Nursery Rap* and Tony Blundell's *Beware of Boys* will also amuse. Harry Allard's *It's So Nice to Have a Wolf Around the House,* Keiko Kasza's *The Wolf's Chicken Stew,* and Hilda Offen's *Nice Work, Little Wolf!* all feature nontraditional wolves. FAIRY TALES–SATIRE. HOUSES. PARODIES. PICTURE BOOKS FOR ALL AGES. PIGS. WOLVES.

379   Vyner, Sue. *The Stolen Egg.* Illus. by Tim Vyner. Viking, 1992. ISBN 0-670-84460-8

An albatross picks up an egg, flies far away over the seas, and leaves it in the grass, where a snake takes it, then a crocodile, an ostrich, a tortoise, and finally the albatross again, who flies with it back to the snow. At home, the penguin father nestles it on his feet, and finally, the baby emperor penguin hatches out. Introduce this nature tale with a question: What animals lay eggs? *Chickens Aren't the Only Ones* by Ruth Heller gives more information on the subject, and both should get kids browsing through the nonfiction bird and reptile books in the library. Patricia Brennan Demuth's picture book *Cradles in the Trees: The Story of Bird Nests* will catch everyone's attention. To introduce an egg-laying insect, read about a praying mantis in *Mary Ann* by Betsy James. BIRDS. EGGS. PENGUINS.

380   Wadsworth, Ginger. *Tomorrow Is Daddy's Birthday.* Illus. by Maxie Chambliss. Boyds Mills, 1994. ISBN 1-56397-042-2

One by one, Rachel tells every creature she encounters what she's giving her dad for his birthday, and each time as she whispers her secret to bug, frog, pet rabbit, doll, baby brother, mailman, Grandma, a moth, and a rooster, we overhear a new detail. Ask your children to pay attention to each clue and deduce what her present will be. Give equal time to mom with *Flower Garden* by Eve Bunting, about a girl and her father who plant a flower-filled windowbox for a special birthday present surprise. BIRTHDAYS. FATHERS AND DAUGHTERS. GIFTS.

381   Waters, Fiona (comp.). *The Doubleday Book of Bedtime Stories.* Illus. by Penny Dann. Doubleday, 1992. ISBN 0-385-30790-X

This anthology of 12 cozy just-right stories with large print and sweet watercolor illustrations is not just for bedtime. Feed listeners with the three title foods in "Cheese, Peas, and Chocolate Pudding," Betty Van Witsen's gem about a picky eater. *Stories from Firefly Island* by Benedict Blathwayt will sustain the storytelling mood. BEDTIME STORIES. SHORT STORIES.

382   Watson, Wendy. *Fox Went Out on a Chilly Night.* Illus. by the author. Lothrop, 1994. ISBN 0-688-10766-4

The music is appended, so you can sing this upbeat classic folk song about the fox who abducted the gray goose from old Mother Slipper Slopper's coop to bring home to feed his ten little ones. Listeners can chime in on the repeated refrain, and all will delight in the cheerful, night-lit, branch-bordered pictures. Other stories that generate empathy for the fox include Irina Korshunow's *The*

Foundling Fox, Tejima's *Fox's Dream*, and Karen Wallace's nonfiction *Red Fox*. Another folk ballad to sing or read is John Langstaff's *Frog Went A-Courtin'*. CHANTABLE REFRAIN. FOLK SONGS. FOXES. STORIES IN RHYME. STORIES WITH SONGS.

383   Wells, Rosemary. *Voyage to the Bunny Planet books: First Tomato; The Island Light; Moss Pillows.* Illus. by the author. Dial, 1992. ISBN 0-8037-1175-1; ISBN 0-8037-1178-6; ISBN 0-8037-1177-8

In *First Tomato*, Claire had a bad morning in school; in *The Island Light*, Felix was sent home sick; and in *Moss Pillows*, Robert had to visit his unpleasant relatives. In each of the three cozy books in the set, a dispirited rabbit revels in a comforting trip to the Bunny Planet where Bunny Queen Janet gives them "the day that should have been." Ask your children to compose a double-paneled picture; on the left, they draw their worst day, and on the right, the perfect day Janet would give them. Horace's mother helps him deal with a bad day in Betsy Everitt's *Mean Soup*, and Jeanne Modesitt's *Sometimes I Feel Like a Mouse* helps kids get in touch with their feelings. BEHAVIOR. EMOTIONS. RABBITS. SICK.

384   Wetzel, JoAnne Stewart. *The Christmas Box.* Illus. by Barry Root. Knopf, 1992. ISBN 0-679-91789-6

Author Wetzel recalls the unforgettable Christmas that she spent with her mother and younger brother in 1952, when her father, stationed in Japan with the United States Air Force, mailed them a large wooden box filled with kimonos, clicky clogs called getas, perfumed fans, chopsticks, fans, and a photo album, thus allowing the family to visit vicariously both Japan and their dad. Round up a collection of Japanese artifacts to share with your students, and read this in tandem with Allan Say's *Tree of Cranes*. Gloria Houston's *The Year of the Perfect Christmas Tree* and Harriet Ziefert's *A New Coat for Anna* take us back to the First and Second World Wars. CHRISTMAS. FATHERS. GIFTS. JAPAN.

385   Wiesner, David. *Tuesday.* Illus. by the author. Clarion, 1991. ISBN 0-395-55113-7

In an almost wordless romp, lily-pad-perching frogs rise up into the full moon-lit sky and coast through the neighborhood, startling a late night nosher as they zoom past his kitchen window, watching a little TV, and intimidating a German shepherd before settling back in the swamp at dawn. The last page? "Next Tuesday, 7:58 P.M.," and we see pigs lift off from the barn. Young artists will beg to create a porcine sequel. Keep hopping with Pete Seeger's *The Foolish Frog* and Mark Teague's *Frog Medicine*. For another wordless airborne journey, sweep through Eric Rohmann's dinosaur-filled *Time Flies*. CALDECOTT MEDAL. FROGS. NIGHT. PICTURE BOOKS FOR ALL AGES. STORIES WITHOUT WORDS.

386   Wilcox, Cathy. *Enzo the Wonderfish.* Illus. by the author. Ticknor & Fields, 1994. ISBN 0-395-68382-3

The girl narrator begs her parents for a pet so they give her a goldfish for her birthday, but her attempts to train him with commands like "fetch," "get the ball," and "play dead" are initially unsuccessful. Before reading, ask children to describe tricks their pets have learned, and have them demonstrate how to perform each one. Meet a fish whose owner overfeeds it in Helen Palmer's classic *A Fish Out of Water*, and the talented pets who inadvertently clean up a boy's bedroom in *When the Fly Flew In* by Lisa Westberg Peters. FISHES. PETS.

387 **Wood, Audrey.** *The Tickleoctopus.* **Illus. by Don Wood. Harcourt, 1994. ISBN 0-15-287000-8**

Back about a million years ago, caveboy Bup met up with a pinkish prehistoric creature that crawled out of a pond and tickled him all over, thus causing Bup to feel an unfamiliar warm glow circling his heart. "For the first time in the history of people . . . someone smiled." Bup introduces the creature to his bad-tempered cave parents, and they, in turn, become the first people to laugh and play. Don Wood's design and illustrations for this delightful story are even more fun to view from farther back. The cover is made of heavy board, with scalloped edges, making the effect look charmingly stone-aged, and several pages open out. The best part is the language spoken by Bup, Ughmaw, and Ugpaw. The translation for "OH, MEO, EEH EEH! OM NA GAHS! OOGLIES! OOGLIES!," is "Oh, me, hee hee! That tickles! I like it! I like it!" Students can make up additional words. Take a tour of the Pleistocene era with caveboy Kip in *The First Dog* by Jan Brett. BEHAVIOR. HUMOROUS FICTION. LANGUAGE. MAN, PREHISTORIC.

388 **Woodruff, Elvira.** *Show and Tell.* **Illus. by Denise Brunkus. Holiday House, 1991. ISBN 0-8234-0883-3**

Andy, whose best show-and-tells up till now have been a paper clip and a favorite bent fork, finds a bottle of magic bubbles that shrink his teacher and all the children in his kindergarten and send them airborne for an unusual outdoor field trip. Use props for this one, including the bubbles. As you blow bubbles at classmates, they can describe where they'd go if they could fly. Children can also describe and draw what magical objects they'd like to bring to class and elaborate on their possible consequences. Stay airborne with Woodruff's *The Wing Shop*. Find out what it's like to be small with Dick Gackenbach's *Tiny for a Day*, William Joyce's *George Shrinks*, and Morris Lurie's *The Story of Imelda, Who Was Small*. FLIGHT. SCHOOLS. SIZE. TEACHERS.

389 **Wright, Kit.** *Tigerella.* **Illus. by Peter Bailey. Scholastic, 1994. ISBN 0-590-48171-1**

The grownups would never guess that good little girl Emma changed into a huge tiger at the stroke of midnight and leapt into the air for a bite of the full moon, a tussle with the Bear constellation, and an encounter with the arrow of mighty Orion the Hunter. The rhythm of this enchanting narrative poem lopes and gallops and is a delight to read aloud. Explore with your innocent-looking children: If you had a secret life and could transform yourself into anything at all, what would you do? Take another trip to the sky with Harriet Peck Taylor's Native American trickster tale *Coyote Places the Stars*. *Night of the Gargoyles* by Eve Bunting is about the more sinister nighttime exploits of come-to-life gargoyles, while Joanne Ryder's Just for a Day series, including *White Bear, Ice Bear* and *Winter Whale*, are factual accounts couched in a "you-are-there" fantasy.

BEHAVIOR. CONSTELLATIONS. NIGHT. PICTURE BOOKS FOR ALL AGES. STORIES IN RHYME. TIGERS. TRANSFORMATIONS.

390   Yaccarino, Dan. *Big Brother Mike.* **Illus. by the author. Hyperion, 1993. ISBN 1-56282-330-2**

The unnamed little brother narrator starts out giving reasons why he thinks his big brother doesn't like him, but then he recalls the day his hamster died and Mike was nice to him. The new-wave goofball gouache paintings are fun, and all kids with siblings will relate. Have them list the bad and good things their siblings do for them. Judy Blume's *The Pain and the Great One,* Crescent Dragonwagon's *I Hate My Brother Harry,* Morse Hamilton's *Little Sister for Sale,* Steven Kellogg's *Much Bigger Than Martin,* Jean Little's *Revenge of the Small Small,* P. K. Roche's *Good-Bye, Arnold,* and Judith Viorst's *I'll Fix Anthony* all allow for a bit of venting. BROTHERS. SIBLING RIVALRY.

391   Yolen, Jane. *Honkers.* **Illus. by Leslie Baker. Little, Brown, 1993. ISBN 0-316-96893-5**

With her mother waiting for the birth of a new baby, almost-six-year-old Betsy is sent to stay with Nana and Grandy on their farm where she cares for first a goose egg and then Little Bit, the gosling that hatches from it. Compare this quiet old-fashioned story with its lovely soft watercolors to the brash animal fantasy of *Bird Dogs Can't Fly* by Mary Jane Auch, as both deal with migrating geese. Get a feel for flight with *Catching the Wind* by Joanne Ryder. For an outrageous twist, *Zinnia and Dot* by Lisa Campbell Ernst features two bickering chickens sitting on and claiming the same egg. FARM LIFE. GEESE. GRANDPARENTS. HOMESICKNESS. MIGRATION.

392   Ziefert, Harriet. *Pete's Chicken.* **Illus. by Laura Rader. Tambourine, 1994. ISBN 0-688-13257-X**

Rabbit Pete is secure in the knowledge that there's no one else in the world just like him, and he takes pleasure in doing things his own special way, but when the art teacher asks everyone in class to draw a chicken, and he draws a rainbow-colored one, everyone laughs at him, causing him a moment of self-doubt. Iconoclasts will delight in this story, and conformists might learn to loosen up and be more accepting. In *Regina's Big Mistake* by Marissa Moss a young girl learns how to keep drawing even when she thinks her picture is ruined. *Three Cheers for Tacky* by Helen Lester fits into the same theme of accepting your special talents. Meet a chicken who is capable of hatching a rainbow-colored chick in *The Easter Egg Farm* by Mary Jane Auch. DRAWING. INDIVIDUALITY. RABBITS.

393   Zolotow, Charlotte. *This Quiet Lady.* **Illus. by Anita Lobel. Greenwillow, 1992. ISBN 0-688-09306-X**

From her collection of photographs around the house, a young girl points out sequential pictures of her mother as a baby, child, schoolgirl, graduate, bride, and mother-to-be, culminating in a baby picture of the narrator that she labels

"The Beginning." Your children can bring in photos of their moms' past lives and tell the stories behind them. Use with Charlotte Pomerantz's *The Chalk Doll* and Marisabina Russo's *Waiting for Hannah*. MOTHERS. PHOTOGRAPHY. PICTURE BOOKS FOR ALL AGES.

Illustration from STELLALUNA, copyright © 1993 by Jannell Cannon,
reproduced by permission of Harcourt Brace & Company.

From WHEN CATS DREAM by Dav Pilkey. Copyright © 1992 by Dav Pilkey.
Reprinted by permission from the publisher, Orchard Books, New York.

FICTION FOR GRADES 1–2

394   Abolafia, Yossi. *Fox Tale.* **Illus. by the author. Greenwillow, 1991. ISBN 0-688-09542-9**

Gullible Bear trades his half-empty jar of honey to Fox for the use of Fox's beautiful bushy tail, but Crow, Rabbit, and Donkey, all tired of the tricks Fox has played on them involving cheese, sour grapes, and chestnuts, help Bear get even. For the original tricky fox, see *Three Aesop's Fox Fables*, illustrated by Paul Galdone, and *The Gingerbread Boy* by Scott Cook or Paul Galdone. Have a songfest with Wendy Watson's *The Fox Went Out on a Chilly Night*. In *One Fine Day* by Nonny Hogrogian, the hapless fox makes many trades to get back his tail after an old woman chops it off. Foxes get what they deserve in Mary Jane Auch's *Peeping Beauty*, Patricia C. McKissack's *Flossie and the Fox*, and James Marshall's *Wings: A Tale of Two Chickens*. ANIMALS. BEARS. FOXES. SWINDLERS AND SWINDLING.

395   Ada, Alma Flor. *Dear Peter Rabbit.* **Illus. by Leslie Tryon. Atheneum, 1994. ISBN 0-689-31850-2**

Peter Rabbit, the Three Little Pigs, Goldilocks, Baby Bear, and even the Wolf exchange letters, catching up on all of their local and interconnected fairy-tale gossip and invitations to housewarming parties. The large, soft watercolors cross-hatched with pen and inks are lovely, each one facing a full-paged piece of correspondence. As in *The Jolly Postman* (1986) and *The Jolly Christmas Postman* by Janet and Allan Ahlberg, children will want to compose new letters to and from others in the fairy-tale set. Get to know Goldie and Baby Bear better from the sweet poems in Jane Yolen's *The Three Bears Rhyme Book*. Jon Scieszka's parody *The Frog Prince Continued* shows us the darker underside of the forest. FAIRY TALES–SATIRE. LETTER WRITING. PARODIES. PIGS. RABBITS. WOLVES.

396   Ahlberg, Janet, and Allan Ahlberg. *The Jolly Christmas Postman.* **Illus. by the authors. Little, Brown, 1991. ISBN 0-316-02033-8**

In the equally charming rhyming sequel to *The Jolly Postman* (1986), we follow the postman as he delivers Christmas cards to the fairy-tale and nursery-rhyme characters along his route, ending up with a ride home in Santa's sleigh. For each delivery, there's a miniature postcard, puzzle, game, or letter inserted into its own special envelope that's built into the page. As a library book, this would be wrecked in no time, so I keep a copy of each book for teachers to use. Folklore

215

characters sending letters is also the theme in Alma Flor Ada's delightful *Dear Peter Rabbit*. Children delight in designing and posting their own mail. Writers will also appreciate a rundown of the 5 W's, introduced painlessly in Rosemary Wells' *Max's Christmas*, one of those simple-to-read picture books all ages adore. Celebrate further with *Harvey Slumfenburger's Christmas Present* by John Burningham and *Santa's Book of Names* by David McPhail. CHRISTMAS. CREATIVE WRITING. FAIRY TALES–SATIRE. LETTER WRITING. PARODIES. PICTURE BOOKS FOR ALL AGES.

397   **Albert, Richard E.** *Alejandro's Gift.* **Illus. by Sylvia Long. Chronicle, 1994. ISBN 0-8118-0436-4**

Lonely Alejandro, who lives alone in an adobe house, tends his desert garden, and taking solace from the creatures who visit there, decides to dig a water hole for them. An afterword identifies the many animals that appear in the stately watercolors. Mention to your listeners that the author wrote this book, his first for children, at the age of 83. Brenda Guiberson's *Cactus Hotel*, Pat Mora's bilingual sound poem *Listen to the Desert*, and Diane Siebert's *Mojave* provide more desert background, while *Voices of the Wild* by Jonathan London extends the ecology theme. ANIMALS. DESERTS. ECOLOGY. ELDERLY. WATER.

398   **Andersen, Karen Born.** *An Alphabet in Five Acts.* **Illus. by Flint Born. Dial, 1993. ISBN 0-8037-1441-6**

Sequential alphabetical sentences with one word to a page are illustrated with amusing hand-colored photo-collages. In the five-page spread of Act 1 we see the owner bringing a nice bowl of cat chow to an unconcerned longhaired cat who walks away, and we read "Another bad cat doesn't eat." Five sentences take us all through the alphabet. Children can easily make up and illustrate their own alphabet sentences with three, four, or more words and act out the results, as the author suggests in her note. ALPHABET BOOKS. CREATIVE DRAMA. CREATIVE WRITING.

399   **Armstrong, Jennifer.** *Little Salt Lick and the Sun King.* **Illus. by Jon Goodell. Crown, 1994. ISBN 0-517-59621-0**

Paul's title, down in the kitchen of the palace at Versailles, is the Second Assistant Rotisserie Turner in the Department of Roasted Meats, but since all the dogs follow him to lick the salt from his sweaty arms, he is nicknamed Little Salt Lick. Finding the lost poodle of King Louis XIV earns him new respect and a better job as First Assistant Bearer of the King's Dog. A young page boy saves the day in *King Bidgood's in the Bathtub* by Audrey Wood. Take a closer look at French royalty. Over a century later, in 1826, meet King Charles X as he awaits delivery of France's first giraffe in Nancy Milton's true account, *The Giraffe That Walked to Paris*. And almost a thousand years earlier, in 787 A.D., Emperor Charlemagne of France awaited an elephant as recounted in *Two Travelers* by Christopher Manson. DOGS. FRANCE. KINGS AND RULERS.

400   **Arnold, Tedd.** *The Signmaker's Assistant.* **Illus. by the author. Dial, 1992. ISBN 0-8037-1011-9**

When the old sign maker leaves town for the day, young Norman, in charge of mixing colors and cleaning brushes, takes advantage of his absence and paints ridiculous messages—"Eat Your Hat," "Ants Crossing," and "Knock Heads"—which everyone follows without thinking. Working with magic markers, each pair of children can produce two signs: one that makes sense to obey, and one that does not. As each pair reads aloud its signs, the rest of the group can decide which ones are sensible, and which are foolish. Other apprentices run amok in Joanna Cole's *Doctor Change*, Tomie dePaola's Strega Nona books, and Mercer Mayer's *A Special Trick*. Meet another sign painter who develops a conscience in Roger Roth's *The Sign Painter's Dream* and two sky painters in Pat Cummings's *C.L.O.U.D.S.* and Aaron Shepard's *The Legend of Slappy Hooper*. HONESTY. RESPONSIBILITY. SIGNS AND SIGNBOARDS.

401   **Asch, Frank, and Vladimir Vagin. *Dear Brother*. Illus. by the authors. Scholastic, 1992. ISBN 0-590-43107-2**

While cleaning out the attic, mice brothers Joey and Marvin discover a stack of old letters their great-great-granduncles wrote to each other when one moved to the big city. Children can ask for old pictures and stories of their relatives and write and illustrate similar-styled letters. Model more letter writing with *Dear Peter Rabbit* by Alma Flor Ada, *The Jolly Postman* (1986) and *The Jolly Christmas Postman* by Janet and Allan Ahlberg, *Dear Annie* by Judith Caseley, and *Dear Hildegarde* by Bernard Waber. Also interesting to show is a sampling of titles with mouse protagonists that make a point: *Aunt Isabel Tells a Good One* by Kate Duke defines the elements of a good story; *Ruby* by Michael Emberley is an updated retelling of "Little Red Riding Hood"; and Dav Pilkey's pun-laden, language-enhancing *Dogzilla* and *Kat Kong* present mice as heroes. BROTHERS. CITIES AND TOWNS. COUNTRY LIFE. LETTER WRITING. MICE.

402   **Auch, Mary Jane. *Peeping Beauty*. Illus. by the author. Holiday House, 1993. ISBN 0-8234-1001-3**

Determined to follow her dream of being a famous ballerina, hen Poulette allows herself to be taken in by the sweet talk of a fox who claims to be a talent scout and convinces her to audition for the ballet Peeping Beauty. Fending off the sharp-toothed imposter, Poulette gives him a swift kick, (also known as a *tour jeté*), informing him, "They don't call me 'thunder drumsticks' for nothing!" Lead your troupe in a few grand jetés to celebrate. Chickens and their adversaries mingle in *Zinnia and Dot* by Lisa Campbell Ernst and *Wings: A Tale of Two Chickens* by James Marshall, while foxes are outflanked in *Flossie and the Fox* by Patricia C. McKissack and *Fox Tale* by Yossi Abolafia. CHICKENS. FOXES. BALLET.

403   **Axelrod, Amy. *Pigs Will Be Pigs*. Illus. by Sharon McGinley-Nally. Four Winds, 1994. ISBN 0-02-765415-X**

There's nothing to eat in the refrigerator, and the Pig family's broke, but a money hunt that turns up cash and change all over the house brings in enough for four specials at their favorite restaurant, the Enchanted Enchilada. There's lots of good math to be done here, adding up the money they find, figuring what can be ordered from the menu for $34.67, and calculating the change. The money adds up in *How the Second Grade Got $8,205.50 to Visit the Statue of Liberty* by Nathan Zimelman, and dwindles to nothing in Judith Viorst's *Alexander Who Used to Be Rich Last Sunday*. MATHEMATICS. MONEY. PIGS. RESTAURANTS.

404   Barracca, Debra, and Sal Barracca. *The Adventures of Taxi Dog*. Illus. by Mark Buehner. Dial, 1990. ISBN 0-8037-0672-3

Taxi driver Jim takes in a hungry stray mutt, ties a red scarf around his neck, and names him Maxi. The endearing mutt now rides uptown and down, singing along with an opera-warbling passenger, donning Groucho glasses, moustache, and fake nose to entertain the passengers. Inspired to write this dog-narrated poem after riding in a taxi where the owner kept his dog on the front seat, this husband-and-wife team has come up with a real New York City taxi tribute. Your listeners will love the yellow and black checkerboard borders, and will rush for the sequels, *Maxi, the Hero* (1991), *Maxi the Star* (1993), and *Taxi Dog Christmas*. See some more of the Big Apple in Arthur Dorros's *Abuela*, Kathy Jakobsen's *My New York*, and E. L. Konigsburg's *Amy Elizabeth Explores Bloomingdale's*. CITIES AND TOWNS. DOGS. NEW YORK CITY. STORIES IN RHYME. TRANSPORTATION.

405   Bartone, Elisa. *Peppe the Lamplighter*. Illus. by Ted Lewin. Lothrop, 1993. ISBN 0-688-10269-7

In New York City's Little Italy, back in the days before electricity, Peppe, the only boy among eight sisters, accepts a temporary job as lamplighter, though his father's contempt for the lowly position causes him to shirk his duties one night. The dark but glowing paintings of New York tenement life earned Lewin a Caldecott Honor, and children will be fascinated to compare their lives. To set the mood, also read *The Great Pumpkin Switch* and *The Potato Man*, both by Megan McDonald and illustrated by Ted Lewin, and discuss life in the olden days with ice boxes, peddlers, and working kids. To find out how ice was made back then, read *The Ice Horse* by Candace Christiansen. Compare the streets with the current tour in *My New York* by Kathy Jakobsen. BROTHERS AND SISTERS. FAMILY STORIES. HISTORICAL FICTION. ITALIAN AMERICANS. NEW YORK CITY.

406   Behn, Harry. *Trees*. Illus. by James Endicott. Henry Holt, 1992. ISBN 0-8050-1926-X

"Trees are the kindest things I know,/ They do no harm, they simply grow." Behn's brief, affectionate poem, prettily illustrated with glowing colors, is a tribute to trees and what they give us, such as shade, fruit, wood, and new buds. Janice May Udry's *A Tree Is Nice* tells more advantages, while Dick Gackenbach's *Mighty Tree*, Bruce Hiscock's *The Big Tree*, and George Ella Lyon's *A B Cedar: An Alphabet of Trees* provide some hard facts. A boy and a squirrel save a town's oldest tree in Lisa Campbell Ernst's *Squirrel Park*, but, on the down side, Eve Bunting's *Someday a Tree* is about a tree that's been poisoned by polluters. STORIES IN RHYME. TREES–POETRY.

407   Blathwayt, Benedict. *Stories from Firefly Island*. Illus. by the author. Greenwillow, 1993. ISBN 0-688-12487-9

[10 chapters, 121p.] On warm nights by the beach, Old Tortoise regales the other animal residents of their idyllic island with memories of past inhabitants like former bully Brave Pig, power-monger King Badger, and young Porcupine who climbed the forbidden Snake Tree. With moral leanings on themes of friendship, harmony, solidarity, and kindness, these amiable stories, reminiscent of A. A. Milne's Winnie-the-Pooh tales, allow children to reflect on their own good and not-so-good behavior. ANIMALS. BEHAVIOR. SHORT STORIES. TURTLES.

408   **Booth, Barbara D.** *Mandy.* **Illus. by Jim LaMarche. Lothrop, 1992. ISBN 0-688-10339-1**

When Grandma realizes she's lost her treasured pin, a gift from her late husband, Mandy, who's afraid of the dark, nevertheless slips outside with a flashlight, and with lightning flashing above, trips and miraculously finds it in the grass. A warm tale with large, soft paintings, this has one added wrinkle that children will find fascinating: Mandy is deaf, and communicates with a combination of signing, lip reading, and speech. Check your library for sign-language books to investigate with your class. To demonstrate the difficulties of lip reading, show a taped segment of a television show with the sound turned off, and ask students to describe what was said. Then play the segment again with the sound on and discuss the differences. In Karen Hesse's *Lester's Dog*, Corey is a hearing-impaired boy who rescues an abandoned kitten. DEAF. GRANDMOTHERS. HANDICAPS. LOST.

409   **Bourke, Linda.** *Eye Spy: A Mysterious Alphabet.* **Illus. by the author. Chronicle, 1991. ISBN 0-87701-805-7**

In an ingenious alphabet book of homonyms and homophones, we examine carefully three of four square panels laid across a double-page spread to identify an object, and then name the item in the fourth panel that sounds the same. That last panel also contains a clue as to the word on the following page. For "A," then, we identify an ant. The fourth square shows the head of a white-haired lady wearing a circle pin picturing two bowling pins. She must be an aunt, and the clue for the letter "B" is "bowl." In *A Chocolate Moose for Dinner* by Fred Gwynne, a young boy comically misunderstands standard expressions because of homonyms. Figure out the photographed homonym combos in Bruce and Brett McMillan's *Puniddles*. Other picture games include *Oh!* by Josse Goffin, *The 13th Clue* by Ann Jonas, and *Can You Find It?*, *Hippopotamus Hunt*, and *Zoodles* by Bernard Most. Identify the numbers that form composite animals in *Puzzlers* by Suse MacDonald and Bill Oakes. ALPHABET BOOKS. ENGLISH LANGUAGE–HOMONYMS. VISUAL PERCEPTION. WORD GAMES.

410   **Bradman, Tony.** *It Came from Outer Space.* **Illus. by Carol Wright. Dial, 1992. ISBN 0-8037-1098-4**

The children in a classroom are frightened when an alien spaceship crashes through the roof and they get a good look at the hideous monster who climbs out. It's friendly, however, and it even poses with the class when the teacher snaps a picture. What did the photograph of the monster look like? Children can draw it and share with each other before you reveal the ending: The monster is human, while the children telling the story are green-faced aliens. In *I'm Coming to Get You!* by Tony Ross, we see a space monster from two perspectives as he heads to Earth to eat Tommy Brown. Friendlier aliens include those in Daniel Pinkwater's *Ned Feldman, Space Pirate*, Edward Marshall's *Space Case*, Marilyn Sadler's *Alistair and the Alien Invasion* and *Alistair in Outer Space*, and Arthur Yorinks's *Company's Coming*. EXTRATERRESTRIAL LIFE. MONSTERS. SCIENCE FICTION.

411   Brisson, Pat. *Magic Carpet*. Illus. by Amy Schwartz. Bradbury, 1991. ISBN 0-02-714340-6

Using globe and atlas, Aunt Agatha and her niece Elizabeth invent a round-the-world story, describing how Agatha's Chinese carpet might have traveled from Beijing to Tokyo to Alaska, and then cross-country through U.S. cities starting with the letter "S." Get out your maps and plot out new routes, find alliterative cities, and write up a new adventure. *Away from Home* by Anita Lobel is another alliterative city guide, and you can keep on trucking with *Jeremy's Tail* by Duncan Ball, *Amelia's Fantastic Flight* by Rose Bursik, *How to Make an Apple Pie and See the World* by Marjorie Priceman, *Uncle Lester's Hat* by Howie Schneider, *Love, Your Bear Pete* by Dyan Sheldon, and *Nine O'Clock Lullaby* by Marilyn Singer. AUNTS. GEOGRAPHY. MAPS AND GLOBES. NAMES, GEOGRAPHICAL. VOYAGES AND TRAVELS.

412   Brown, Marc. *Arthur Babysits*. Illus. by the author. Joy Street/ Little, Brown, 1992. ISBN 0-316-11293-3

Nervous about baby-sitting the terrible Tribble twins, Arthur receives advice from his little sister D.W. about showing them who's boss, but it's not until he tells them a nice scary story that they finally calm down. Other valiant sitters who learn how to manage their charges can be found in *Marie Louise's Heyday* by Natalie Savage Carlson, *Jerome and the Witchcraft Kids* and *Jerome the Babysitter* by Eileen Christelow, *Chucky Bellman Was So Bad* by Phyllis Green, and *Babysitting for Benjamin* by Valiska Gregory. BABY-SITTERS. BEHAVIOR. BROTHERS AND SISTERS. STORYTELLING. TWINS.

413   Brown, Marc. *Arthur Meets the President*. Illus. by the author. Little, Brown, 1991. ISBN 0-316-11265-8

The winner of the "How I Can Make America Great" essay contest, aardvark Arthur is invited with his whole class to Washington, D.C., to recite his speech to the president at the White House. After a tour of the Washington Monument, the Capitol, and the White House, a nervous Arthur arrives at the Rose Garden where his mind goes blank and his wisecracking sister D.W. helps him out. Your students can write their own short essays and deliver them as speeches. Look up books on the capital for photographs and additional information. CONTESTS. PRESIDENTS–U.S. PUBLIC SPEAKING. SCHOOLS. WASHINGTON, D.C.

414   Browne, Eileen. *No Problem*. Illus. by David Parkins. Candlewick, 1993. ISBN 1-56402-176-9

Mouse receives a construction kit from Rat, and in her rush to put together the mountain of bits and pieces, she forgets to look at the instructions and fashions a wobbly, wheelie-popping Biker-Riker. Each animal that tries to fix the contraption turns it into another malfunctioning vehicle until Shrew takes over, reads the instructions, and fashions a wonderful airplane. This will dovetail into any lesson you have about following directions, and for a test run there is miniature version of the airplane with full directions for assembly on the dust jacket of the book. Cut out and photocopy a master copy, being careful to label each part and draw in dotted lines for places to cut, and after making the original yourself, have your students color in and assemble their own. *The 13th Clue* by Ann Jonas is another story where children learn about proceeding in sequence. AIRPLANES. ANIMALS. BOOKS AND READING. MICE. TRANSPORTATION.

415   Bunting, Eve. *Fly Away Home*. Illus. by Ronald Himler. Clarion, 1991. ISBN 0-395-55962-6

Living in the airport, the young narrator and his dad do their best to go unnoticed by airport security, washing up in the bathrooms every morning, and staying on the move during the day. Dad works as a janitor on the weekends, and is saving up for the apartment they hope to find someday soon. Heartbreaking in its simplicity, with soft watercolors that match the hopeful matter-of-fact mood, this is one book that explains homelessness in a way younger children can comprehend. Read with DyAnne DiSalvo-Ryan's *Uncle Willie and the Soup Kitchen* and Stephanie S. Tolan's *Sophie and the Sidewalk Man*. AIRPORTS. BIRDS. FATHERS AND SONS. HOMELESSNESS. PICTURE BOOKS FOR ALL AGES.

416   Bunting, Eve. *Someday a Tree*. Illus. by Ronald Himler. Clarion, 1993. ISBN 0-395-61309-4

Across Far Meadow there's a huge and ancient oak tree under which Alice was christened as a baby, and where she and her parents picnic, but today, she notices the grass underneath smells funny and is a weird yellow color. Each day the stain spreads, the tree leaves turn dull and die, and a tree doctor informs them the tree has been poisoned with chemicals someone has dumped there. When the grand old tree dies, we grieve with Alice for such a senseless act of destruction. Lynne Cherry's *A River Ran Wild: An Environmental History*, Gloria Rand's *Prince William*, and Anne Shelby's *What to Do About Pollution* renew our hope. Harry Behn's *Trees*, Lisa Campbell Ernst's *Squirrel Park*, Dick Gackenbach's *Mighty Tree*, Bruce Hiscock's *The Big Tree*, George Ella Lyon's *A B Cedar: An Alphabet of Trees*, and Janice May Udry's *A Tree Is Nice* are all tree-loving books. POLLUTION. TREES.

417   Bursik, Rose. *Amelia's Fantastic Flight*. Illus. by the author. Henry Holt, 1992. ISBN 0-8050-1872-7

Amelia builds an airplane and takes it for a little spin around the world. Each leg of her flight is illustrated, including an inset map tracing each stop. Get out a bigger world map to pinpoint Amelia's travels, as the maps in the book are small. The clever use of both alliteration and global travels is similar in ways to Pat Brisson's *Magic Carpet* and Anita Lobel's *Away from Home*. Keep sightseeing with *Jeremy's Tail* by Duncan Ball, *How to Make an Apple Pie and See the World* by Marjorie Priceman, *Uncle Lester's Hat* by Howie Schneider, *Love, Your Bear Pete* by

Dyan Sheldon, and *Nine O'Clock Lullaby* by Marilyn Singer. AIRPLANES. ALLITERA-TION. FLIGHT. GEOGRAPHY. IMAGINATION. MAPS AND GLOBES. VOYAGES AND TRAVELS.

418   Calhoun, Mary. *Henry the Sailor Cat*. Illus. by Erick Ingraham. Morrow, 1994. ISBN 0-688-10841-5

This time the haughty Siamese stows away aboard The Man's sailboat, discovers he loves sailing, and, when The Man falls overboard, helps The Kid rescue him. Read the series of Henry books and talk over what other feats he might undertake, now that he's mastered skiing (*Cross-Country Cat*), hot-air ballooning (*Hot-Air Henry*), and tightrope walking (*High-Wire Henry*). Children can draw him experiencing his next adventure. CATS. OCEAN. SAILING.

419   Calhoun, Mary. *High-Wire Henry*. Illus. by Erick Ingraham. Morrow, 1991. ISBN 0-688-08984-4

Henry, the self-reliant Siamese cat who skiied his way down a mountain to safety in *Cross-Country Cat*, discovers a new talent of tightrope walking in time to save the family's new dachshund puppy who rambles out on the roof to see a squirrel. Compare Henry's hind-leg-walking feats with those of *Puss in Boots*, as retold by Lorinda Bryan Cauley, Paul Galdone, Gail E. Haley, Lincoln Kirstein, or Fred Marcellino. Find other personable kitties in the poetry of Beatrice Schenk de Regniers's *This Big Cat and Other Cats I've Known*, Lee Bennett Hopkins's *I Am the Cat*, Nancy Larrick's *Cats Are Cats*, Myra Cohn Livingston's *Cat Poems*, and Jane Yolen's *Raining Cats and Dogs*. *When Cats Dream* by Dav Pilkey gives more insight into a cat's psyche, while his *Kat Kong* depicts a cat monster run amok. CATS. DOGS. JEALOUSY.

420   Calmenson, Stephanie. *The Principal's New Clothes*. Illus. by Denise Brunkus. Scholastic, 1989. ISBN 0-590-41822-X

Sharp dresser Mr. Bundy, principal of P.S. 88, is taken in by tricksters who claim to be able to sew him an amazing one-of-a-kind suit that is "invisible to anyone who is no good at his job or just plain stupid." Your principal might get a charge out of reading aloud this droll modern-day parody, which you can analyze alongside Hans Christian Andersen's *The Emperor's New Clothes*. Next compare Andersen's *The Princess and the Pea* with parodies *The Cowboy and the Black-Eyed Pea* by Tony Johnston and *Princess* by Anne Wilsdorf. Ellen Jackson's *Cinder Edna*, Frances Minters' *Cinder-Elly*, and Bernice Myers's *Sidney Rella and the Glass Sneaker* are all Americanized spoofs of "Cinderella." CLOTHING AND DRESS. FAIRY TALES–SATIRE. PARODIES. PICTURE BOOKS FOR ALL AGES. PRINCIPALS. SELF-CONCEPT.

421   Carlson, Nancy L. *Arnie and the New Kid*. Illus. by the author. Viking, 1990. ISBN 0-670-82499-2

No one at Philip's new school knows how to play with a boy in a wheelchair, and Arnie teases the new kid without mercy until he himself breaks his leg and finds out firsthand the difficulties of being disabled. The cast of animal characters (Philip is a dog, Arnie is a cat) deals with and overcomes some of the difficulties of inclusion, which can open up the issue for your learners to confront. Continue the discourse with Liz Damrell's *With the Wind*, Jane Cowen-Fletcher's *Mama Zooms*, Audrey Osofsky's *My Buddy*, Berniece Rabe's *The Balancing Girl*, and Marisabina Russo's *Alec Is My Friend*. FRIENDSHIP. HANDICAPS. PHYSICAL DISABILITY. SCHOOLS. WHEELCHAIRS.

422 Caseley, Judith. *Harry and Arney*. Greenwillow, 1994. ISBN 0-688-12140-3

[7 chapters, 138p.] At the same time Harry is getting stitches in his leg at the emergency room, his mother is being rushed to the same hospital to deliver her fourth child, whom Harry decides should be named Arney after the doctor who took such good care of him. Other titles about the Kane family include *Chloe in the Know* (1993), *Hurricane Harry* (1991), and *Starring Dorothy Kane* (1992). The episodes in each good-natured chapter bring to mind other warm family stories such as the Ramona books by Beverly Cleary, *Russell Sprouts* and *Superduper Teddy* by Johanna Hurwitz, and *Junie B. Jones and a Little Monkey Business* by Barbara Park. BABIES. BROTHERS AND SISTERS. FAMILY LIFE.

423 Cherry, Lynne. *The Armadillo from Amarillo*. Illus. by the author. Harcourt, 1994. ISBN 0-15-200359-2

Texas armadillo Sasparillo wonders what's beyond his woods, and he hikes through the state to find out, even traveling via eagle's back to view the country, continent, and world. What a perfect way to start investigating the 50 states! With a format reminiscent of Joanna Cole's Magic School Bus books and Loreen Leedy's *Postcards from Pluto: A Tour of the Solar System*, Cherry has filled her sweeping watercolor and oil pastel paintings with great detail including the postcards the armadillo sends to his cousin at the Philadelphia Zoo. Told in rhyme, the spectacular story ends with an informative author's note that fills us in on armadillos. Bianca Lavie's nonfiction photo-essay *It's an Armadillo* is a must here as well. For more out-of-this-world experiences, share Andrew Clements's *Mother Earth's Counting Book* and Robert E. Wells's *Is a Blue Whale the Biggest Thing There Is?* ARMADILLOS. EARTH. MAPS AND GLOBES. STORIES IN RHYME. TEXAS.

424 Choi, Sook Nyul. *Halmoni and the Picnic*. Illus. by Karen M. Dugan. Houghton Mifflin, 1993. ISBN 0-395-61626-3

Yunmi's grandmother, Halmoni, newly arrived in New York City from Korea, is having a difficult time acclimating to unfamiliar American ways, and Yunmi's friends pledge to help. When they volunteer Halmoni as chaperone for their annual school picnic in Central Park, Yunmi worries that the other children will make fun of her grandmother's pointed rubber shoes and long Korean dress. Discuss the differences the story points out between American and Korean foods, dress, and manners, and ask children to share knowledge of interesting customs from other cultures. Barbara Cohen's *Molly's Pilgrim*, Sherry Garland's *The Lotus Seed*, and Bud Howlett's *I'm New Here* all expound on the culture shock new immigrants face. GRANDMOTHERS. IMMIGRATION AND EMIGRATION. KOREAN AMERICANS. NEW YORK CITY. PICNICS. SCHOOLS.

425 Christelow, Eileen. *The Five-Dog Night*. Illus. by the author. Clarion, 1993. ISBN 0-395-62399-5

Crusty Ezra, who lives alone with his five dogs for company, considers his concerned neighbor Betty an old busybody, especially when she pesters him to use a blanket each night as the weather gets colder. Ezra claims he doesn't need any blankets, and we see how he keeps warm each night with up to five dogs sprawled across him on the bed, depending on how cold it gets. *Moe the Dog in Tropical Paradise* by Diane Stanley will help you dispel the winter blahs, and *Brrr!* by James Stevenson will warm you right up. DOGS. NEIGHBORLINESS. WINTER.

426 Cole, Brock. *Alpha and the Dirty Baby*. Illus. by the author. Farrar, 1991. ISBN 0-374-30241-3

Alpha's parents' petty argument turns dangerous when a devil's imp and his slovenly wife take over for Mama and Papa, bring in their imp baby for Alpha to mind, and expect her to unclean the house. Alpha breaks the spell by washing the baby and bringing back her real parents and family harmony. Other family quarrels are patched up in *Toby's Toe* by Jane Goodsell, *Spinky Sulks* by William Steig, and *The Quarreling Book* by Charlotte Zolotow. ARGUMENTS. CLEANLINESS. FAMILY LIFE. IMPS. TRANSFORMATIONS.

427 Crowley, Michael. *Shack and Back*. Illus. by Abby Carter. Little, Brown, 1993. ISBN 0-316-16231-0

The Spurwink Gang splits into three boys and four girls after Crater says that cooking is for sissy-girls, but when the four Broad Cove Bullies challenge the boys to a bike race, Crater has to eat his words and apologize, especially to T-Ball, the fastest racer in the gang. For children at an age when boys start to see girls as the enemy, this sequel to *New Kid on Spurwink Ave.* squarely faces the issues of competition and boy-girl dissension, and shows that sticking together works wonders. Boys and girls who get along just fine get to know a storytelling old man in *Mr. Knocky* by Jack Ziegler. ARGUMENTS. BICYCLES. CONFLICT RESOLUTION. FRIENDSHIP.

428 Cushman, Doug. *The ABC Mystery*. Illus. by the author. HarperCollins, 1993. ISBN 0-06-021227-6

A rhyming tale of intrigue and theft of a priceless painting from Dame Agatha, this melodramatic animal alphabet book lays out every facet of a good English-style mystery, from clues to witnesses to solution by Detective Inspector McGroom. Start off your mystery genres unit with this one and have students list the elements of a typical whodunit. Get a handle on the genre with the animal private eyes in *My Dog and the Birthday Mystery* by David A. Adler, *Gertrude, the Bulldog Detective* by Eileen Christelow, and *Chameleon Was a Spy* by Diane Redfield Massie, and the pancake-loving investigator of Marjorie Weinman Sharmat's Nate the Great series. ALPHABET BOOKS. BADGERS. MYSTERY AND DETECTIVE STORIES. PICTURE BOOKS FOR ALL AGES. STORIES IN RHYME.

429   Damrell, Liz. *With the Wind.* Illus. by Stephen Marchesi. Orchard, 1991. ISBN 0-531-08482-5

At first an impassioned account of the freedom and power a boy feels riding a horse, it's not till the last pages that we realize the deeper meaning riding holds for the boy, as we see him lifted from the horse's back and placed in his wheelchair. Be sure to read this brief but effective book twice and ask children to comment on how the story was different for them the second time. Nancy Carlson's *Arnie and the New Kid*, Audrey Osofsky's *My Buddy*, Berniece Rabe's *The Balancing Girl*, and Marisabina Russo's *Alec Is My Friend* all depict children in wheelchairs. HANDICAPS. HORSES. PHYSICAL DISABILITY. WHEELCHAIRS.

430   dePaola, Tomie. *Strega Nona Meets Her Match.* Illus. by the author. Putnam, 1993. ISBN 0-399-22421-1

Strega Nona's old friend Strega Amelia comes for a visit, and seeing how profitable the witch business is, sets up her own competing establishment, advertising the lastest scientific equipment for finding husbands for young ladies, curing headaches, and removing warts. Then Big Anthony goes to work for her, unwittingly sabotaging every cure, and old-fashioned Strega Nona is back in demand once more. Use with the original *Strega Nona* to get a feel for Big Anthony's remarkable level of incompetence. Discuss: What does it mean to "meet your match?" Why didn't Strega Nona get upset over Big Anthony's new job with Strega Amelia? COMPETITION. HUMOROUS FICTION. WITCHES.

431   dePaola, Tomie. *Tom.* Illus. by the author. Putnam, 1993. ISBN 0-399-22417-3

Reading the comics aloud, reciting funny poems, telling stories, and showing him how to open and close a chicken's foot by pulling the tendons, Tommy's Irish grandfather Tom knew how to keep him enthralled. Children will love chanting "Garunge-arunge-a" and hearing about how the famous author/illustrator once spent the day in the principal's office. This delightful autobiographical reminiscence should be read as a companion to the author's *The Art Lesson* and *Nana Upstairs & Nana Downstairs* (Putnam, 1973). Introduce more unforgettable grandparents with Karen Ackerman's *Song and Dance Man*, Lisa Campbell Ernst's *The Luckiest Kid on the Planet*, Eloise Greenfield's *Grandpa's Face*, Dayal Kaur Khalsa's *Tales of a Gambling Grandma*, Patricia Polacco's *Thunder Cake*, Amy Schwartz's *Oma and Bobo*, and David Schwartz's *Supergrandpa*. AUTOBIOGRAPHY. FAMILY STORIES. GRANDFATHERS. PICTURE BOOKS FOR ALL AGES.

432   DiSalvo-Ryan, DyAnne. *Uncle Willie and the Soup Kitchen.* Illus. by the author. Morrow, 1991. ISBN 0-688-09165-2

Frank the Can Man and an old woman sleeping on a park bench are two of the dispossessed folks the young narrator meets the day his uncle takes him to work at the soup kitchen where he prepares lunch every day. It's not easy to explain homelessness and hunger in the United States to children, but Eve Bunting's *Fly Away Home*, Stephanie Tolan's *Sophie and the Sidewalk Man*, and this softly colored picture book will help introduce the subject, and show them how concerned and dedicated people might make a difference. HOMELESSNESS. SOUP. UNCLES.

433   **Dooley, Norah.** *Everybody Cooks Rice.* **Illus. by Peter J. Thornton. Carolrhoda, 1991. ISBN 0-87614-412-1**

Sent to find her younger brother Anthony in time for dinner, narrator Carrie trails him from house to house, sampling each neighbor's delicious rice recipes as she goes, including yellow rice from Puerto Rico, fish sauce over rice from Vietnam, and biryani from India. How can you resist trying one of the nine recipes at the end of the story? Ask your students to describe any other ethnic rice dishes they've tried, and to come up with other types of food common to many cultures, like pasta and bread. Arlene Mosel's *The Funny Little Woman* and Ann Tompert's *Bamboo Hats and a Rice Cake,* both Japanese folktales, shower us with additional forms of rice. For more ethnic treats, sample Jama Kim Rattigan's *Dumpling Soup,* Anne Shelby's *Potluck,* and Gary Soto's *Too Many Tamales.* COOKERY. FOOD. MULTICULTURAL STORIES.

434   **Dorros, Arthur.** *Abuela.* **Illus. by Elisa Kleven. Dutton, 1991. ISBN 0-525-44750-4**

Rosalba and her abuela, or grandmother, visit the park, where the young girl imagines the two of them flying high above New York City, past the Statue of Liberty, and up to the clouds. Adventure-loving Abuela speaks to her in Spanish, pointing out sights she saw when she first came to the United States, while the girl translates her words in the context of the story. For a delightful linguistic bonus, the glossary and pronunciation guide at the back will enable you and your students to absorb several dozen Spanish words and phrases. The vibrant mixed-media collage of watercolors, pastels, and cut paper pulses with colors and tiny details of city life seen from the air. From paper and fabric scraps, put together your own folk-art-style collage bulletin board mural: an aerial view of the school neighborhood. Keep flying throughout New York City with Faith Ringgold's *Tar Beach,* and explore the neighborhoods with Kathy Jakobsen's *My New York.* FLIGHT. GRANDMOTHERS. HISPANIC AMERICANS. LANGUAGE. NEW YORK CITY. SPANISH LANGUAGE.

435   **Dorros, Arthur.** *This Is My House.* **Illus. by the author. Scholastic, 1992. ISBN 0-590-45302-5**

Accompanied by a detailed watercolor-and-pencil painting on each page, children from 20 countries describe their houses, including a yurt in Mongolia, a cave in Turkey, an adobe house in Mexico, and a houseboat in Thailand. The title sentence is repeated in each corresponding language and is spelled phonetically for children to try. Make your own classroom book of houses where everyone draws and describes where he or she lives. Edith Baer's *This Is the Way We Go to School: A Book About Children Around the World* has a similar global concept, while Hank De Zutter's *Who Says a Dog Goes Bow-Wow?* and Debra Leventhal's *What Is Your Language?* teach a few elementary phrases in other languages. HOUSES. LANGUAGE. MULTICULTURAL STORIES.

436   Duke, Kate. *Aunt Isabel Tells a Good One.* **Illus. by the author. Dutton, 1992. ISBN 0-525-44835-7**

Everybody loves a good story, and when young mouse Penelope requests a new tale, her aunt asks for help in making one up about a kidnapped prince who is rescued from Odious Mole by clever Lady Nell. This charming and useful explanation of story structure will assist your class in making up their own adventure yarn using all the plot elements described: a good beginning, interesting main characters, a problem, a villain, a little danger, and a happy ending. *From Pictures to Words: A Book About Making a Book* by Janet Stevens is an author/illustrator's description of how characters, plot, and illustrations become a book. AUNTS. CREATIVE WRITING. MICE. PRINCES AND PRINCESSES. STORYTELLING.

437   Emberley, Michael. *Ruby.* **Illus. by the author. Little, Brown, 1990. ISBN 0-316-23643-8**

On her way to Granny's to drop off a batch of triple-cheese pies, red-cloaked mouse Ruby fails to heed her mother's advice not to talk to strangers, especially cats, when a well-dressed stranger helps her fend off the menacing advances of a grimy reptile. With the help of Granny's neighbor Mrs. Mastiff, Ruby is able to turn the tables on the suave mouse-craving cat, unlike her less street-wise counterpart in the original fairy tale. The story is peppered with tough-guy city dialogue that may give you pause, so don't read this one cold. Make sure your listeners know the earnest Grimm version of *Little Red Riding Hood*, such as the one illustrated by Trina Schart Hyman, before opening up James Marshall's campy *Red Riding Hood*. One third of David Vozar's comical, rap-style *Yo, Hungry Wolf!* is about tough Little Red Rappinghood, while Frances Minters's witty *Cinder-Elly* is another city-set parody. CATS. FAIRY TALES–SATIRE. MICE. PARODIES. PICTURE BOOKS FOR ALL AGES.

438   Emberley, Michael. *Welcome Back Sun.* **Illus. by the author. Little, Brown, 1993. ISBN 0-316-23647-0**

A young Norwegian girl describes how in March, after six months of dark, sunless days they call the *murkitiden* or murky time, her parents and neighbors climb Mount Gausta to see the sun and welcome spring. Jan Brett's *Trouble with Trolls* is a fanciful Norwegian tale that will make an interesting contrast. More thrilling, gripping, realistic winter stories include Jan Andrews's *Very Last First Time*, Lonzo Anderson's *The Ponies of Mykillengi*, and Deborah Hartley's *Up North in Winter*. Prepare for the end of cold weather with Natalie Kinsey-Warnock's *When Spring Comes* and Charles Larry's *Peboan and Seegwun*. NORWAY. SEASONS. SPRING. SUN. WINTER.

439   Ernst, Lisa Campbell. *The Luckiest Kid on the Planet.* **Illus. by the author. Bradbury, 1994. ISBN 0-02-733566-6**

With a great name like Lucky Morgenstern, Lucky grows up thinking he has it made, but when he receives a letter from his Great Aunt Thelma addressed to Herbert, he discovers that Lucky is a nickname his grandfather gave him at birth.

Crushed by this revelation, he won't even listen to the grandfather he adores who tells him, "Someday you'll think of that one thing to prove that you are lucky, after all." Children who blame every misfortune on external forces will see that good luck can be self-directed, especially when we stop to appreciate what we have. Lucky's luck stemmed from his grandfather's love; ask your listeners to identify when and why they've had good luck. Introduce other supportive grandparents in Karen Ackerman's *Song and Dance Man,* Judith Caseley's *Dear Annie,* Tomie dePaola's *Tom,* Eloise Greenfield's *Grandpa's Face,* and Dayal Kaur Khalsa's *Tales of a Gambling Grandma.* BEHAVIOR. GRANDFATHERS. LUCK. SELF-ESTEEM.

440   Ernst, Lisa Campbell. *Squirrel Park.* Illus. by the author. Bradbury, 1993. ISBN 0-02-733562-3

Given the job by his father the builder to design a new town park, Stuart and his best friend Chuck, a squirrel, plan curling paths, playgrounds, and flower garden, with their favorite giant gnarled old oak tree in the center, none of which dovetail with Stuart's father's idea of a treeless park with straight paths. Each of your nature-lovers can design a perfect park for his or her neighborhood. *Lost!* by David McPhail has a nice one. Harry Behn's poem *Trees* and Janice May Udry's *A Tree Is Nice* show arbor appreciation, and Dick Gackenbach's *Mighty Tree,* Bruce Hiscock's *The Big Tree,* George Ella Lyon's *A B Cedar: An Alphabet of Trees,* and Joanne Ryder's *Hello Tree* provide information. Eve Bunting's *Someday a Tree* is about the death of a tree from toxic chemicals. FATHERS AND SONS. PARKS. SQUIRRELS. TREES.

441   Frank, John. *Odds 'N' Ends Alvy.* Illus. by G. Brian Karas. Four Winds, 1993. ISBN 0-02-735675-2

Alvy Flynn keeps a cardboard box beside his desk at school so he can assemble the odds and ends into unexpected inventions, but one day he turns his desk into a high-speed vehicle that zooms him into traffic and a wild city adventure. Listing all the forms of transportation he encounters, children can come up with new ones for him to overcome as they write a class sequel about his next invention, and fill it with onomotopoeic verbs. John Burningham's *Harvey Slumfenburger's Christmas Present* and Daniel Pinkwater's *Tooth-Gnasher Superflash* both cover many bases in the odd transport department. Spot new inventions in picture books like Eileen Christelow's *Mr. Murphy's Marvelous Invention,* Michael Crowley's *New Kid on Spurwink Ave.,* and Dick Gackenbach's *Dog for a Day* and *Tiny for a Day,* while Betsy Duffy's *The Gadget War* is a chapter book for frustrated tinkerers. ENGLISH LANGUAGE–GRAMMAR. INVENTIONS. TRANSPORTATION.

442   Geraghty, Paul. *The Hunter.* Illus. by the author. Crown, 1994. ISBN 0-517-59693-8

Jamina pretends she is a hunter as she walks out into the African bush to collect honey with her grandfather, but when she wanders too far off and becomes separated, she finds a baby elephant by its mother's lifeless body and learns about poachers. The vivid, realistic paintings of the animals and scenery are gorgeous, and the antihunting message hits home. Discuss with your listeners the difference between hunting for food and sport, and describe what illegal hunting has meant to many endangered animals. Find out more about elephants in the 599.6 section of the library, but also examine the up-close color photos in *Little Elephant* by Liela Ford and the component parts in the fable *Seven Blind Mice* by Ed Young. *The Bear That Heard Crying* by Natalie Kinsey-Warnock is another animal story, based on a real occurrence, where a wild animal keeps watch over a lost human child. AFRICA. ELEPHANTS. GRANDFATHERS. HUNTERS AND HUNTING. LOST.

443   Goble, Paul. *Dream Wolf*. Illus. by the author. Bradbury, 1990. ISBN 0-02-736585-9

Countering the wolf's image as an evil predator is this original Plains Indian story of Tiblo and Tanksi, a brother and sister who wander away from berry-picking to climb the hills, and spend the night safe in a wolf's den. When the wolf leads them back safely to their camp, the people reward him with a blanket and beautiful gifts. The final page offers verses of Plains Indian songs about wolves. *To the Top of the World: Adventures with Arctic Wolves* by Jim Brandenberg, *The Eyes of Gray Wolf* by Jonathan London, *The Call of the Wolves* by Jim Murphy, and, for older readers, Jean Craighead George's unforgettable *Julie of the Wolves* also do much to rehabilitate the reputation of the wolf for fearful children. INDIANS OF NORTH AMERICA. LOST. PICTURE BOOKS FOR ALL AGES. PLAINS INDIANS. WOLVES.

444   Green, Phyllis. *Chucky Bellman Was So Bad*. Illus. by Gioia Fiammenghi. Albert Whitman, 1991. ISBN 0-8075-1156-0

Sixteen baby-sitters have refused to take care of obnoxious, obstreperous Chucky, so his mother calls Gaby Bipsey, listed in the yellow pages under "SITTERS," and she agrees to come. Actually, Gaby is a tree-sitter looking forward to spending the day in the the lovely cherry tree in the front yard, but as a sideline she defuses each of Chucky's fits and wins him over with stories about her brother Berke who was a world-class tantrum thrower, thumb sucker, swearer, and messy-room keeper. The humor is in the tall tales Gaby bandies about. See if your students can exaggerate tales of their own about a sibling's bad behavior. In *Bootsie Barker Bites* by Barbara Bottner, a little girl finds a way to overcome Bootsie's rotten treatment. BABY-SITTERS. BEHAVIOR. HUMOROUS FICTION.

445   Greene, Carol. *The Old Ladies Who Liked Cats*. Illus. by Loretta Krupinski. HarperCollins, 1991. ISBN 0-06-022104-6

In this witty ecological tale about interdependence, when an island's cats are prevented by law from chasing mice, a chain reaction ensues, compromising everyone's safety until the law is changed. The story, based on Darwin and other scientists' observations, demonstrates how everything is affected when the balance of nature is upset, just as we see in Lynn Cherry's *The Great Kapok Tree*. Folksinger Pete Seeger's song "The People Are Scratching," about too many rabbits, gives the same message. CATS. CAUSE AND EFFECT. ECOLOGY. INTERDEPENDENCE. PICTURE BOOKS FOR ALL AGES.

446   Griffith, Helen V. *Emily and the Enchanted Frog*. Illus. by Susan Condie Lamb. Greenwillow, 1989. ISBN 0-688-08483-4

Stimulate imaginations with these three amusing stories about Emily's encounters with an enchanted frog, a wish-granting elf, and a crab that thinks it's a mermaid. Use the frog story with Jacob Grimm's original folktale *The Frog Prince*, and with parodies like Fred Gwynne's *Pondlarker*, Jon Scieszka's *The Frog Prince Continued*, and A. Vesey's *The Princess and the Frog*. For more wishes that come true, also read *Barney Bipple's Magic Dandelions* by Carol Chapman and *The Three Wishes*, a folktale by Margot Zemach. CRABS. FROGS. WISHES.

447   Gwynne, Fred. *Pondlarker.* Illus. by the author. Simon & Schuster, 1990. ISBN 0-671-70846-5

Always on the lookout for a princess to kiss him, a frog finds an old one, but before she can pucker up, he reconsiders and decides to stay the way he is. Read Jacob Grimm's folktale *The Frog Prince* for background, and then cut loose with Helen V. Griffith's *Emily and the Enchanted Frog*, Jon Scieszka's *The Frog Prince Continued* and "The Other Frog Prince" from Scieszka's *The Stinky Cheese Man*, and A. Vesey's *The Princess and the Frog*. FAIRY TALES–SATIRE. FROGS. PARODIES. PRINCES AND PRINCESSES. SELF-ACCEPTANCE.

448   Hall, Donald. *I Am the Dog, I Am the Cat.* Illus. by Barry Moser. Dial, 1994. ISBN 0-8037-1505-6

In alternating voices, a complacent rottweiler and his companion, a well-fed bemused tabby, realistically portrayed in handsome watercolors, lay out their contrasting philosophies about food, babies, strangers, rest, and frights. Good readers can reread this aloud in pairs. Before reading, survey your group to gauge their preferences and make a chart of the differences between dogs and cats based on their experiences. Afterward, see if any components of their chart agree with the personalities in the story: the crowd-pleasing dog versus the aloof cat. They can then write profiles of their own pets or pets they have known. *Dribbles* by Connie Heckert and *Moving* by Michael Rosen also show the world from a cat's eyes. CATS. DOGS. PICTURE BOOKS FOR ALL AGES. POINT OF VIEW.

449   Hamanaka, Sheila. *All the Colors of the Earth.* Illus. by the author. Morrow, 1994. ISBN 0-688-11132-7

"Children come in all the colors of the earth . . ." So starts this stunning portrait poem of children worldwide, comparing their skin colors to "roaring browns of bears and soaring eagles," and "whispering golds of late summer grasses." Large exultant double-page oil paintings depict children "in all colors of love" playing together in the sunlight. *The Fire Children: A West African Creation Tale* by Eric Maddern explains how all the races of the earth came to be. "We're all just sailors come ashore off the same deep blue sea," is the lesson new friends learn about being brothers instead of enemies in *Over the Deep Blue Sea* by Daisaku Ikeda. With stories like these, we can start a dialogue on our ties to all humanity and downplay and counter the hatreds and prejudices that help make the adult world so volatile. BROTHERHOOD. MULTICULTURAL STORIES. RACE. STORIES IN RHYME.

450   Hamilton, Morse. *Little Sister for Sale*. **Illus. by Gioia Fiammenghi. Cobblehill, 1992. ISBN 0-525-65078-4**

After Kate discovers her little sister Abby has not only chopped off the pigtail of her favorite doll but used her toothbrush as well, she sets up the lemonade stand and prepares to sell the little pest for just $1.99. Sample some sibling rivalry stories like Judy Blume's *The Pain and the Great One*, Jean Little's *Revenge of the Small Small*, Patricia Polacco's *My Rotten Redheaded Older Brother*, James Stevenson's *Worse Than Willy!*, and Dan Yaccarino's *Big Brother Mike*. Children can make a two-column list of the good and bad things about having siblings or being an only child and compare horror stories. CONFLICT RESOLUTION. GRANDMOTHERS. SIBLING RIVALRY. SISTERS.

451   Harrison, Maggie. *Angels on Roller Skates*. **Illus. by the author. Candlewick, 1992. ISBN 1-56402-003-7**

[5 chapters, 106p.] In five engaging chapters about an affectionate English family with siblings Bigun, Middlun, and the baby Littlun, it's Middlun who rides her brother's new bike without permission, accidentally locks them both in the bathroom, pretends they're all orphans, and wins a prize for her drawing of angels on roller skates. All along the way, your listeners will want to volunteer stories about their own families in similar situations. Joanna Hurwitz's books about Nora, Teddy, Russell, and Elisa are good American counterparts. BROTHERS AND SISTERS. ENGLAND. FAMILY LIFE.

452   Heckert, Connie. *Dribbles*. **Illus. by Elizabeth Sayles. Clarion, 1993. ISBN 0-395-62336-7**

After the old woman dies, the old man and his hissing amber cat Dribbles move into the house where cats Bing, Benny, and Gracie live, and the three try to make overtures to the unhappy new cat, whom they finally befriend. When the old cat takes sick, the three say good-bye and stay by her side until she dies. Told entirely from the cats' point of view, this is a tender story with a calm explanation of death that takes the edge off the hurt listeners will feel for poor Dribbles. Miriam Cohen's *Jim's Dog Muffins*, Ellen Howard's *Murphy and Kate*, Holly Keller's *Goodbye, Max*, Betsy James's *Mary Ann*, Rachel Pank's *Under the Blackberries*, and Judith Viorst's *The Tenth Good Thing About Barney* also concern a pet's death. CATS. DEATH. ELDERLY. POINT OF VIEW.

453   Himmelman, John. *Lights Out!* **Illus. by the author. BridgeWater, 1995. ISBN 0-8167-3450-X**

It's bedtime, but each time Counselor Jim turns out the lights in the cabin, one of the six Camp Badger Scouts imagines another danger awaiting them—a lion, a hypnotizing eyeball on the ceiling, or fluid-drinking mosquitoes. Make light of nighttime fears in *Monster Brother* by Mary Jane Auch, *Ghost's Hour, Spook's Hour* by Eve Bunting, *What's Under My Bed?* by James Stevenson, and *My Mama Says There Aren't Any Zombies, Ghosts, Vampires, Creatures, Demons, Fiends, Goblins, or Things* by Judith Viorst. Take to the woods with a dog and his zooming couch in *Amos Camps Out* by Susan Seligson. BEDTIME STORIES. CAMPING. FEAR. NIGHT. SLEEP.

454 Hoffman, Mary. *Henry's Baby*. Illus. by Susan Winter. Dorling Kindersley, 1993. ISBN 1-56458-196-9

Wanting to belong to the popular gang at his new school, and afraid of not fitting their image of tough, cool, and interesting, Henry doesn't mention he has a baby brother until the afternoon the gang comes over. Look into some bogus baby facts in Jeanne Willis's *Earthlets: As Explained by Professor Xargle*, and ask the real experts—the older brothers and sisters—what it's like to have little ones around. What's different and welcome about this story is that here's a boy who likes his baby brother, and once his friends meet George, they're crazy about him, too. See how two boys become friends in Leah Komaiko's rhyming *Earl's Too Cool for Me*. BABIES. BROTHERS. FRIENDSHIP. POPULARITY.

455 Howard, Elizabeth Fitzgerald. *Mac & Marie & the Train Toss Surprise*. Illus. by Gail Gordon Carter. Four Winds, 1993. ISBN 0-02-744640-9

Based on a true childhood story the author's father shared with her, this soft nighttime tale, illustrated with dark blue-toned watercolors and colored pencil, is about an African American brother and sister who wait by the train tracks behind their house one night. Their Uncle Clem, working aboard a New York-bound train from Florida, plans to throw them a present as he passes at half-past eight. Children can predict what Uncle Clem will be throwing off the train for them. *Freight Train* by Donald Crews and *Train Song* by Diane Siebert will get your listeners in a train mood. *The Potato Man* and *The Great Pumpkin Switch* by Megan McDonald and Alice McClerran's *Roxaben* also look back on childhood memories of the same turn of the century/early 20th century era. AFRICAN AMERICANS. BROTHERS AND SISTERS. FAMILY STORIES. GIFTS. TRAINS. UNCLES.

456 Howe, James. *Creepy-Crawly Birthday*. Illus. by Leslie Morrill. Morrow, 1991. ISBN 0-688-09688-3

During Toby's birthday party, Harold the dog and his cohorts dachshund Howie and paranoid cat Chester come across animal carriers in the bedroom and, suspecting the Monroe family plans to replace them with the seven new pets inside, manage to set free an iguana, boa constrictor, and more. See if listeners can figure out which of animal-handler Mr. Hu's zoo is still missing at the end. Others in Howe's picture book series narrated by the family dog include *The Fright Before Christmas*, *Hot Fudge* (1990), *Rabbit-Cadabra!*, and *Scared Silly*. Go for another birthday scare with *Some Birthday!* by Patricia Polacco. BIRTHDAYS. CATS. DOGS. PETS.

457 Howe, James. *Pinky and Rex and the Spelling Bee*. Illus. by Melissa Sweet. Atheneum, 1991. ISBN 0-689-31618-6

[6 chapters, 40p.] Losing the spelling bee would be the worst thing that ever happened to him, thinks second-grader Pinky, but he wins against the new boy, and then the worst thing ever truly happens: As his class is cheering his victory, he wets his pants, and everybody sees. It happens to many children in school, and talking about the embarrassment and teasing Pinky endures will make it easier for children to overcome their own, especially when they note how best friend

Rex, a girl, is so understanding. Children will want to read all the books in the series, starting with *Pinky and Rex* (1990). CONTESTS. EMBARRASSMENT. FRIENDSHIP. SCHOOLS.

458   Howe, James. *Rabbit-Cadabra!* **Illus. by Alan Daniel. Morrow, 1993. ISBN 0-688-10403-7**

In another delightful entry from the Bunnicula series of picture books about the Monroe family as narrated by the family dog, brothers Toby and Pete are excited about the great magician, The Amazing Karlovsky, who is coming to town. The family pets want to know why a rabbit that looks just like the Monroe's vampire bunny Bunnicula can be seen being lifted out of a top hat on the magician's posters all over town. As always, the solution is a simple one, but dogs Harold and Howie and neurotic cat Chester almost sabotage Karlovsky's show. The final pages of the book give detailed instructions for performing the Bunnicula-out-of-a-hat trick. *The Amazing Felix* by Emily Arnold McCully, *The Amazing Magic Show* by P. J. Petersen, and *The Houdini Box* by Brian Selznick will appeal to magic fanciers, and Roy Broekel's *Now You See It: Easy Magic for Beginners* will give them many useful tips. CATS. DOGS. MAGICIANS. RABBITS. VAMPIRES.

459   Huff, Barbara A. *Once Inside the Library.* **Illus. by Iris Van Rynback. Little, Brown, 1990. ISBN 0-316-37967-0**

One fine day Mrs. Forte's whole fourth-grade class surprised me in the library by reciting a poem they had memorized about the pleasures of books and libraries and made my day. Imagine my delight when I discovered the poem had been turned into a charming picture book, with each pen-and-ink and watercolor illustration showing another place you can go in your imagination with a good book. On the same wavelength are Caroline Feller Bauer's *Too Many Books*, Crosby Bonsall's *Tell Me Some More*, Judith Caseley's *Sophie and Sammy's Library Sleepover*, Ann McGovern's *Drop Everything, It's D.E.A.R. Time!*, Sue Felt's *Rosa-Too-Little*, and Julia L. Sauer's *Mike's House*. Lee Bennett Hopkins has collected a whole book of poems about reading in *Good Books, Good Times!* BOOKS AND READING. LIBRARIES. PICTURE BOOKS FOR ALL AGES. STORIES IN RHYME.

460   Ikeda, Daisaku. English version by Geraldine McCaughrean. *Over the Deep Blue Sea.* **Illus. by Brian Wildsmith. Knopf, 1993. ISBN 0-679-94184-3**

Sister and brother Akiko and Hiroshi, newly moved with their parents to an idyllic island, are lonely until Pablo befriends them, showing them the beguiling sights, including a rusted wrecked ship and wonderful sea turtles. Once Pablo learns that the two are from a country that once attacked the island during a war, he rejects them, but comes through to save Hiroshi when his canoe is pulled out to sea. The children are able to transcend the bitter feelings left by war, reasoning, "How can anyone be enemies . . . if it's only the sea in between that makes us different?" Discuss the concepts of enemies, hatred, and making amends with *Smoky Night* by Eve Bunting and *Baseball Saved Us* by Ken Mochizuki. *All the Colors of the Earth* by Sheila Hamanaka and *The Fire Children: A West African Creation Tale* by Eric Maddern explain how we are all one. ENEMIES. FRIENDSHIP. ISLANDS. OCEAN. PREJUDICE. WAR.

461 **Izen, Marshall, and Jim West.** *Why the Willow Weeps: A Story Told with Hands.* **Photos by the authors. Doubleday, 1992. ISBN 0-385-30683-0**

In an original pourquoi story, illustrated with photographs of colored glove-clad hands acting out each character, we meet a willow who asks a duck, hare, dog, and tortoise not to harm his lovely rose, and then grieves when a heedless young man plucks its petals and destroys it. After a night of weeping, the willow's tears fall on the bush, and another rosebud appears. The final pages of photographs show how to involve children in retelling the story with their own hands. Pick up sets of white gloves at the paint store and paint them with poster paint to act out this and other simple stories such as *Aesop's Fables.* Identify the marvelous hand animals in Mario Mariotti's *Hanimations* and *Hanimals* (Green Tiger/Simon & Schuster, 1982), and experiment making new animal figures with your fingers. CREATIVE DRAMA. FLOWERS. HANDS. PUPPETS. TREES.

462 **Jenkins, Jessica.** *Thinking About Colors.* **Illus. by the author. Dutton, 1992. ISBN 0-525-44908-6**

Simon shows his friends and us his new paint box, describing how each color makes us feel or what it stands for, and naming each different hue. Since he leaves out purple, brown, and white, your students can create new pages for those colors, and contribute additional ideas about all the colors. *If You Want to Find Golden* by Eileen Spinelli is about color in the city, Arnold Lobel's *The Great Blueness and Other Predicaments* is a clever story of how colors came to be, and Mary L. O'Neill's *Hailstones and Halibut Bones: Adventures in Color* includes one poem for each of 12 colors. COLOR. EMOTIONS.

463 **Johnson, Dolores.** *Your Dad Was Just Like You.* **Illus. by the author. Macmillan, 1993. ISBN 0-02-747838-6**

Peter and his father don't get along, but when the boy breaks Dad's treasured purple trophy and his father is too angry to even yell, the boy heads over to seek solace with his adored grandfather. Grandpa regales Peter with stories of Dad's childhood and, revealing the touching story behind the now-broken trophy, helps bring the boy and his father to a new understanding. Children can list how they are like and different from their parents, and interview them to see what they were like as children. AFRICAN AMERICANS. FATHERS AND SONS. GRANDFATHERS. MULTICULTURAL STORIES.

464 **Jonas, Ann.** *The 13th Clue.* **Illus. by the author. Greenwillow, 1992. ISBN 0-688-09743-X**

A girl's diary entry is interrupted when the light goes on in the attic, illuminating a sign tied to the lamp: "Find more clues!" Thirteen clever word and picture clues await her, leading her downstairs, outside, and into the woods, where her friends await her with balloons and a surprise birthday party. Children will love puzzling out the clue on each page, and will want to construct their own treasure hunt replete with clues. Jonas's *Reflections* and *Round Trip* have pictures that change when turned upside down. Kids clamor for what my students call "finding books" like the Waldo books, Linda Bourke's *Eye Spy: A Mysterious Alphabet,* Ruth Brown's *If at First You Do Not See,* Beau Gardner's *Guess What?,* Tana

Hoban's *Look Again!* and *Look! Look! Look!*, and Suse MacDonald and Bill Oakes's *Puzzlers*. Celebrate Patricia's birthday down at the scary Clay Pit Bottoms in *Some Birthday!* by Patricia Polacco. BIRTHDAYS. PARTIES. VISUAL PERCEPTION. WORD GAMES.

465   **Kastner, Jill.** *Snake Hunt.* **Illus. by the author. Four Winds, 1993. ISBN 0-02-749395-4**

Granddad's tall tale about wrestling a rattler sends him and granddaughter Jesse on a snake hunt in the woods where their imaginations scare them but no real snakes surface. James Stevenson's Grandpa tell his grandkids whoppers in *Brrr!*, *That Terrible Halloween Night*, and *What's Under My Bed?*, while Megan McDonald's tells about himself as a boy in *The Great Pumpkin Switch* and *The Potato Man*. Betsy Maestro's nonfiction *Take a Look at Snakes*, Faith McNulty's *A Snake in the House*, Stefan Czernecki and Timothy Rhodes's Australian folktale *The Singing Snake*, and Tomi Ungerer's *Crictor* should satisfy the snake fans. FEAR. GRANDFATHERS. SNAKES.

466   **Keller, Holly.** *Grandfather's Dream.* **Illus. by the author. Greenwillow, 1994. ISBN 0-688-12340-6**

Now that the war in Vietnam is over, Grandfather is hoping that once the land inside the newly built dikes floods, the cranes will return, bringing good luck again. Keller's lovely watercolors show family life in a village by the Mekong delta. When the cranes return and Nam wonders if they will stay, his grandfather tells him, "That is up to you." Ask your students what he means, and what they can do to preserve our own wildlife. Sherry Garland's *The Lotus Seed* is a powerful picture book about one Vietnamese woman's life during and after the war. Lynne Cherry's *The Great Kapok Tree*, Barbara Cooney's *Miss Rumphius*, Susan Jeffers's *Brother Eagle, Sister Sky*, and Jane Yolen's *Welcome to the Green House* are also environmental tales that encourage children to care for the earth and its creatures. BIRDS. CRANES. ENVIRONMENT. GRANDFATHERS. VIETNAM.

467   **King-Smith, Dick.** *The Invisible Dog.* **Illus. by Roger Roth. Crown, 1993. ISBN 0-517-59424-2**

[7 chapters, 73p.] A real black-and-white harlequin Great Dane puppy would cost too much, and though seven-year-old Janie is confident that she'll get one someday, in the meantime she carries a leash with the empty collar dangling and calls her invisible dog Henry. Show Steven Kellogg's Pinkerton books, including the author-with-dog photos at the back of *Pinkerton, Behave!* to see the dog Janie covets. Sam needs to figure out a way to control his enormous dog in *The Big Deal* by Alison Cragin Herzig, while both dog and owner work on training the other in *A Boy in the Doghouse* by Betsy Duffey. Children can research breeds and then draw and describe the dogs they'd want. DOGS. IMAGINATION.

468   **Kinsey-Warnock, Natalie.** *The Bear That Heard Crying.* **Illus. by Ted Rand. Dutton, 1993. ISBN 0-525-65103-9**

One warm day in June 1783, three-year-old Sarah Whitcher got lost in the New Hampshire woods near her home and was looked after by a large black bear until she was found four days later by a man named Mr. Heath who had a dream the night before that revealed to him where she would be found. The child was the author's great-great-great-great-great aunt. *The Bears on Hemlock Mountain* by Alice Dalgliesh and *The Biggest Bear* by Lynd Ward are classic realistic stories about children who meet up with bears, while Jim Murphy's *Backyard Bear* is based on recent bear sightings in more populated areas. BEARS. FAMILY STORIES. HISTORICAL FICTION. LOST. PICTURE BOOKS FOR ALL AGES. SURVIVAL.

469   **Kinsey-Warnock, Natalie.** *When Spring Comes.* **Illus. by Stacey Schuett. Dutton, 1993. ISBN 0-525-45008-4**

As she contemplates the marvels of winter, a young girl eagerly anticipates the coming spring when her family will boil down maple sap from the trees, catch tadpoles, fish, plow the garden, and run barefoot. The old-timey feel of this lush mood piece fits in well with Donald Hall's *Ox-Cart Man*, and Tony Johnston's *Yonder*. Charles Larry's *Peboan and Seegwun*, a Native American legend, explains how winter gives way to spring. Children can tell, write, and illustrate about their preferred season, and what they do each year when spring finally arrives. FAMILY LIFE. FARM LIFE. SEASONS. SPRING. WINTER.

470   **Kinsey-Warnock, Natalie.** *Wilderness Cat.* **Illus. by Mark Graham. Cobblehill, 1992. ISBN 0-525-65068-7**

Moving from Vermont to a small shanty in the Canadian wilderness 50 miles away, Serena must leave behind Moses, her fine black cat. In the winter, when her father has gone off to find food for the family and the cupboard is bare, Moses shows up carrying a large snowshoe hare he has caught that saves the family from starvation. Children are intrigued by stories of spartan life in the late 1700s, when this story is set, and on into the late 19th century. Marion Russell's *Along the Santa Fe Trail*, Scott Russell Sanders's *Here Comes the Mystery Man* and *Warm as Wool*, and David Williams's *Grandma Essie's Covered Wagon* should also suit your vicarious pioneers. CANADA. CATS. FRONTIER AND PIONEER LIFE. HISTORICAL FICTION. INDIANS OF NORTH AMERICA.

471   **Kirby, David, and Allen Woodman.** *The Cows Are Going to Paris.* **Illus. by Chris L. Demarest. Caroline House/Boyds Mills, 1991. ISBN 1-878093-11-8**

Tired of chewing grass in the fields, the cows board the train at Fontainbleu, dress up in the clothes that the frightened passengers left behind, and visit some of the major tourist highlights, such as the Eiffel Tower, Maxim's, and the Louvre. *Zut alors*, this merry bovine inspection of the world's most beautiful city is *très amusant*, and if you can swing a French accent, *c'est parfait*. Write sequels for other major cities and what the cows find there. If you're feeling bullish, then continue with Chris Babcock's *No Moon, No Milk*, Paula Brown's *Moon Jump: A Cowntdown*, Jennifer A. Ericsson's *No Milk!*, Lisa Campbell Ernst's *When Bluebell Sang*, David L. Harrison's *When Cows Come Home*, Paul Brett Johnson's *The Cow Who Wouldn't Come Down*, Alice Schertle's poetry picture book *How Now, Brown Cow?*, and Nancy Van Laan's *The Tiny, Tiny Boy and the Big, Big Cow.* COWS. FRANCE. PARIS. TRAINS.

472   Kirk, Daniel. *Skateboard Monsters*. Illus. by the author. Rizzoli, 1992. ISBN 0-87663-798-5

"All the children jump and run, when the skateboard monsters come!" So starts a zooming, zingy rhyming romp as eight rubber-faced multicolored new-wave creatures carom around the neighborhood. Read it twice for the sheer fun of it. Play in traffic with the high-speed kid inventor of *Odds 'N' Ends Alvy* by John Frank, and pick up the speed with the world's wildest transforming car in *Tooth-Gnasher Superflash*, by Daniel Pinkwater. *Simon's Book* by Henrik Drescher, *No More Monsters for Me* by Peggy Parish, and *The Field Beyond the Outfield* by Mark Teague house an assortment of likeable monsters. Another fast-moving bit of nonsense verse runs through *Pigs Aplenty, Pigs Galore!* by David McPhail. MONSTERS. SKATEBOARDING. STORIES IN RHYME.

473   Kline, Rufus. *Watch Out for Those Weirdos*. Illus. by Nancy Carlson. Viking, 1990. ISBN 0-670-82376-7

Meet Ryan who's always crying, Jenny who won't lend you a penny, Bob who acts like a slob, and eight other not-perfect but real-life kids who all finally arrive at the narrator's birthday party. There's a "Wanted" poster for each of the narrator's quirky friends, covering age, height, weight, hair, eyes, favorite saying, and latest "crime." Compile your own statistics with each classroom "weirdo" making his or her own wanted poster as a lead-in to talking about biographies or a math lesson on simple charts and graphs. Meet a kid who can do anything in Leah Komaiko's *Earl's Too Cool for Me*. FRIENDSHIP. HUMOROUS FICTION.

474   Kline, Suzy. *Horrible Harry and the Christmas Surprise*. Illus. by Frank Remkiewicz. Viking, 1991. ISBN 0-670-83357-6

[4 chapters, 54p.] Krikkity krikk goes Miss Mackle's old rocking chair as she reads "Twas the Night Before Christmas" to her class. When the chair breaks, Miss Mackle ends up in the hospital with a torn ligament and the kids in Room 2B end up with their principal, Mr. Cardini, as a substitute. Children can sing Ida's new "Jingle Bells" song, and perhaps make up one for their own classroom. Not only a good short-chapter book to get into the holiday spirit, this is a good one for introducing the rest of the amiable books in the Horrible Harry series. Of course you'll also want to reprise Clement C. Moore's *The Night Before Christmas*. BEHAVIOR. CHRISTMAS. PRINCIPALS. TEACHERS. SCHOOLS.

475   Kline, Suzy. *Mary Marony and the Snake*. Illus. by Blanche Sims. Putnam, 1992. ISBN 0-399-22044-5

[6 chapters, 64p.] Trouble with the letter "M" means second-grader Mary can't even say her own name without stuttering, and though she's angry at one classmate for teasing her, help from the speech therapist and success at catching an escaped garter snake mark the beginning of a successful year. Readers will want to follow her progress in *Mary Marony Hides Out* (1993). SCHOOLS. SNAKES. SPEECH IMPAIRMENT. STUTTERING.

476   Kline, Suzy. *Song Lee in Room 2B*. Illus. by Frank Remkiewicz. Viking, 1993. ISBN 0-670-84772-0

[4 chapters, 56 pages] Worried about speaking up in class, shy Song Lee brings in a large cardboard cherry-blossom tree to stand behind while she gives an oral report about Korea, where she was born. Three more short and amusing chapters, narrated by classmate Doug about keeping secrets and jealousy, writer's block and class notebooks, and Song Lee's pet salamander and a fire drill round out this addition to the Horrible Harry series about the kids in Miss Mackle's second-grade class. Author Suzy Kline is a teacher, whence comes her ample source of funny incidents, authentic dialogue, and great teaching ideas woven into her narratives. Keep a running list with your students of the memorable moments in your classroom as inspiration for an in-school chapter book of their own. FRIENDSHIP. KOREAN AMERICANS. SCHOOLS.

477   Komaiko, Leah. *Earl's Too Cool for Me*. Illus. by Laura Cornell. Harper & Row, 1988. ISBN 0-06-023282-X

"Earl has a bicycle made of hay. He takes rides on the Milky Way. Earl's too cool for me." He's cool, all right, but, as the narrator finds out after describing all the marvelous things Earl does, he's also perfectly friendly—a regular guy! Listeners will love to tap out the rhythm of this playful rhyme, and chant the title refrain. Before reading, ask your students what it takes to be considered "cool." See how easy it is to cultivate friends in *Henry's Baby* by Mary Hoffman, *Watch Out for Those Weirdos* by Rufus Kline, and *Yo! Yes?* by Chris Raschka. FRIENDSHIP. PICTURE BOOKS FOR ALL AGES. STORIES IN RHYME.

478   Konigsburg, E. L. *Amy Elizabeth Explores Bloomingdale's*. Illus. by the author. Atheneum, 1992. ISBN 0-689-31766-2

The first place Grandma plans to take Amy Elizabeth during her weeklong visit to New York City from Houston is that famous department store New Yorkers call "Bloomies." Instead, they end up watching a protest march, visiting Chinatown by subway, going to the top of the Empire State Building, and eating at the Carnegie Deli. You'll love the bright yellow background and checker cab borders on each page, not to mention getting an insider's view of the Big Apple. Keep touring with Arthur Dorros's *Abuela*, Kathy Jakobsen's *My New York*, Faith Ringgold's *Tar Beach*, and Shelley Rotner and Ken Kreisler's *Citybook*. GRANDMOTHERS. NEW YORK CITY.

479   Kovalski, Maryann. *Pizza for Breakfast*. Illus. by the author. Morrow, 1991. ISBN 0-688-10410-X

In an irresistible update and twist on Grimm's folktale "The Fisherman and His Wife," we meet Frank and Zelda, pizza shop owners who are granted a wish of a thousand customers a day until business becomes too successful for them to bear. Compare the outcomes of the two stories. See how pizza is prepared in Dayal Kaur Khalsa's nostalgic *How Pizza Came to Queens*, and see how it saves a family from flowing lava in Margaret Mahy's *The Rattlebang Picnic*. Then switch from too much pizza to a surfeit of pasta with Tomie dePaola's classic, *Strega*

Nona. Note what happens to people granted wishes in Robert Benton's *Don't Ever Wish for a 7-Foot Bear*, Carol Chapman's *Barney Bipple's Magic Dandelions*, William Steig's *Sylvester and the Magic Pebble*, and Jay Williams's *One Big Wish*. Your crew can write new "wish" tales incorporating what they covet and how it might come to them. HUSBANDS AND WIVES. FAIRY TALES–SATIRE. PARODIES. PICTURE BOOKS FOR ALL AGES. PIZZA. RESTAURANTS. WISHES.

480 **Kroll, Virginia.** *Masai and I.* **Illus. by Nancy Carpenter. Four Winds, 1992. ISBN 0-02-751165-0**

Learning in school about the Masai people of East Africa, an African American girl feels a kinship and compares her life—eating, sleeping, and playing—with what it would be like if she was Masai. On facing pages, the oil-and-color-pencil illustrations contrast the two cultures, depicting both with dignity and affection. *It Takes a Village* by Jane Cowen-Fletcher, *Jambo Means Hello: Swahili Alphabet Book* by Muriel Feelings, *The Hunter* by Paul Geraghty, folktale *The Village of Round and Square Houses* by Ann Grifalconi, and *Somewhere in Africa* by Ingid Mennem and Niki Daly give a first glimpse of Africa to introduce the continent as a whole. Children can read about other countries and write up and illustrate a two-panel picture showing the difference between here and there. AFRICA. AFRICAN AMERICANS. MULTICULTURAL STORIES.

481 **Lebentritt, Julia, and Richard Ploetz.** *The Kooken.* **Illus. by Clément Oubrerie. Henry Holt, 1992. ISBN 0-8050-1749-6**

[1 sitting, unp.] Johanna brings her cello to Granny's Vermont farm for the summer, planning to practice in preparation for a fall concert at Carnegie Hall in New York. Unfortunately, Kooken, Granny's great lummox of a Doberman, eats the instrument, but Johanna discovers Kooken's one remarkable talent—the dog sounds just like a cello when played with a bow. In a perfect example of the willing suspension of disbelief, we are drawn into this bizarre and funny story that ends with a triumphant performance of girl and dog. Keep in tune with *Zin! Zin! Zin! A Violin* by Lloyd Moss and *Mrs. Merriweather's Musical Cat* by Carol Purdy. All manners of dogs cavort through Robert J. Blake's *Dog*, Dick Gackenbach's *Beauty, Brave and Beautiful*, Steven Kellogg's *Pinkerton, Behave!*, Pija Lindenbaum's *Boodil My Dog*, Susan Meddaugh's *Martha Speaks*, Marilyn Singer's poetry book *It's Hard to Read a Map with a Beagle on Your Lap*, and Frances Ward Weller's *Riptide*. CELLO. CONTESTS. DOGS. GRANDMOTHERS. MUSICAL INSTRUMENTS. PICTURE BOOKS FOR ALL AGES.

482 **Leedy, Loreen.** *Fraction Action.* **Illus. by the author. Holiday House, 1994. ISBN 0-8234-1109-5**

Miss Prime, a stylishly dressed hippo teacher, sets up a series of lessons on fractions for her mixed-animal class. Using the overhead projector, marbles, and her students' imagination, she demonstrates the concepts of halves, thirds, fourths, and fifths, which the students carry over into episodes out of school. Your math-conscious learners will enjoy answering the math problems she poses, and will come up with fresh examples as well. Bring in manipulatives, and let your students make up test questions for you to answer. Louise Matthews's *Gator Pie* and Bruce McMillan's *Eating Fractions* also introduce fractions, while Elinor J. Pinczes's *One Hundred Hungry Ants* demonstrates changing sets of numbers. FRACTIONS. MATHEMATICS.

483   Levine, Evan. *Not the Piano, Mrs. Medley!* Illus. by S. D. Schindler. Orchard, 1991. ISBN 0-531-08556-2

Mrs. Medley, her visiting young grandson, Max, and her schnauzer, Word, are heading off to the beach, but first, in successive trips back to the house, they collect towels, raincoats, hats, boots, Monopoly, a table and chairs, a radio, bongo drums, and an accordion, forgetting only one thing—their bathing suits! Children can draw and write about the essential things they take to go swimming, and then can write a sequel where Mrs. M. visits the mountains. To improve your memories, practice with Susan Hoguet's story/game *I Unpacked My Grandmother's Trunk* and Elizabeth Lee O'Donnell's beach-based *The Twelve Days of Summer*. Then explore the ocean in greater depth with Joanna Cole's *The Magic School Bus on the Ocean Floor*, James Stevenson's *Clams Can't Sing*, and Frances Ward Weller's *Riptide*. GRANDMOTHERS. MEMORY. OCEAN. SEASHORE.

484   Lies, Brian. *Hamlet and the Enormous Chinese Dragon Kite*. Illus. by the author. Houghton Mifflin, 1994. ISBN 0-395-68391-2

A risk-taking, adventure-seeking pig refuses to allow his best friend, worrywart porcupine Quince, to talk him out of flying his massive new kite, which pulls him higher than the treetops for a short-lived flight. Discuss with your audience with whom they identify and why: free-thinking Hamlet or his faithful homebody pal. Take to the skies again with *The Wing Shop* by Elvira Woodruff. FLIGHT. KITES. PIGS. PORCUPINES.

485   Lindenbaum, Pija. *Boodil My Dog*. Illus. by the author. Henry Holt, 1992. ISBN 0-8050-2444-1

In an affectionate character sketch, the unseen child narrator describes her white bull terrier as brilliant, fierce, brave, and beautiful, showing us what the dog does on a typical day, from sleeping on Dad's chair to taking reluctant walks in the park, hiding from the vacuum cleaner, and knocking down furniture and little brother during evening play. What we see, to our great amusement, is a preoccupied, almost catatonic dog who is spoiled rotten, and this makes for an incongruous, ironic description. Compare Boodil's behavior to the hyperactive Great Dane in Steven Kellogg's Pinkerton series. Children can write and illustrate a character sketch of a pet they know. Other dogs with personality can be found in Dick Gackenbach's *Beauty, Brave and Beautiful*, Susan Meddaugh's *Martha Speaks*, Julia Lebentritt and Richard Ploetz's *The Kooken*, and Frances Ward Weller's *Riptide*. DOGS.

486   Little, Jean. *Revenge of the Small Small*. Illus. by Janet Wilson. Viking, 1992. ISBN 0-670-84471-3

Teased once too often by her older siblings while recuperating from chicken pox, Patsy Small constructs an entire miniature town from construction paper and plasticine, and includes a cemetery with tombstones for Jim, Jane and Hugo. Discuss everyone's reaction to her revenge, and talk over why her father said, "It did them a world of good," when Patsy confesses to being mean to the three older children. Other protagonists cope with sibling rivalry in Judy Blume's *The Pain and the Great One*, Patricia Polacco's *My Rotten Redheaded Older Brother*, James Stevenson's *Worse Than Willy!*, and Dan Yaccarino's *Big Brother Mike*. BROTHERS AND SISTERS. SIBLING RIVALRY. SICK.

487   Lobel, Anita. *Away from Home*. Illus. by the author. Greenwillow, 1994. ISBN 0-688-10355-3

An around-the-world alphabetical tableau is performed on stage with each of the international cast of 26 boys acting out his arrival in a city that starts with the first letter of his name, in front of a backdrop depicting a famous site or sight (as in "David danced in Detroit"). Large, majestic paintings capture the essence of each city. Act this out in narrative pantomime; have children research each city, finding pictures and additional information; compile your own classroom tour book with each child writing, researching, and illustrating an original, personalized alliterative sentence, and paint backdrops for each so that you can stage your own global theatrical. Girls' names are featured in Lobel's *Alison's Zinnia*. Visit more tourist sites in *Jeremy's Tail* by Duncan Ball, *Magic Carpet* by Pat Brisson, *Amelia's Fantastic Flight* by Rose Bursik, *How to Make an Apple Pie and See the World* by Marjorie Priceman, and *Uncle Lester's Hat* by Howie Schneider. ALLITERATION. ALPHABET BOOKS. CITIES AND TOWNS. GEOGRAPHY. NAMES. VOYAGES AND TRAVELS.

488   London, Jonathan. *The Eyes of Gray Wolf*. Illus. by Jon Van Zyle. Chronicle, 1993. ISBN 0-8118-0285-X

Having lost his mate to a hunter's steel trap, Gray Wolf searches the frozen winter landscape for food and a new companion. A slice-of-life nature study with striking oversized paintings, this can be teamed with other serious and realistic picture books about much maligned animals such as London's *Gray Fox* and *Voices of the Wild*, Jim Murphy's *The Call of the Wolves*, and Tejima's *Fox's Dream*. For older children, Jim Brandenberg's nonfiction photo-essay *To the Top of the World: Adventures with Arctic Wolves* is unforgettable. PICTURE BOOKS FOR ALL AGES. WOLVES.

489   London, Jonathan. *Gray Fox*. Illus. by Robert Sauber. Viking, 1993. ISBN 0-670-84490-X

Magnificent sun-lit paintings take us through the seasons with Gray Fox, and when he is hit and killed by a speeding truck and found, still warm, by a young farm boy, we grieve. The circle of life continues, we see, with Mother Fox raising the cubs who continue through the seasons, growing up and having cubs of their own. Irina Korschunow's *The Foundling Fox*, London's *The Eyes of Gray Wolf*, Theresa Radcliffe's *Shadow the Deer*, and Tejima's *Fox's Dream* are fine companions. DEATH. FOXES. NATURE.

490 Macaulay, David. *Black and White.* Illus. by the author. Houghton Mifflin, 1990. ISBN 0-395-52151-3

Each double-page spread holds a quartet of continuing, interconnected tales involving a boy on a train, a boy and dog playing with a toy train, a train station of newspaper-folding commuters, and an escaping convict camouflaged by Holstein cows. Encourage your kids to find any and all connections among the four seemingly separate stories. (See page 27 for a further description of how this puzzler of a book can be used with children.) David Wiesner's *Tuesday*, with its free-flying frogs, is a nicely strange companion book, and Alice Schertle's poetry picture book *How Now, Brown Cow?* is a treat for cow fanciers. CALDECOTT MEDAL. COWS. PICTURE BOOKS FOR ALL AGES. ROBBERS AND OUTLAWS. TRAINS.

491 McCully, Emily Arnold. *The Amazing Felix.* Illus. by the author. Putnam, 1993. ISBN 0-399-22428-9

Though Papa, a great pianist on a world tour, expects his children to practice the piano on the boat across the Atlantic before meeting up with him in London, Felix does not have the talent of his sister Fanny, and instead practices a coin trick he learned from the ship's magician. Like McCully's heroine in *Mirette on the High Wire*, Felix's determination saves the day when his sister is trapped in a castle tower, earning his father's admiration. The 1920s setting makes a nice change, shown off to great effect by the shimmering watercolors. In *The Houdini Box* by Brian Selznick, we meet up with the greatest magician of all times. Conjure up a few other magicians in James Howe's *Rabbit-Cadabra!* and P. J. Petersen's *The Amazing Magic Show.* For aspiring sleight-of-hand artists, try out a few simple magic tricks with books like Roy Broekel's *Now You See It: Easy Magic for Beginners* from the 793.8 section of the library. CASTLES. MAGICIANS. MUSICIANS. SHIPS. TRICKS.

492 McCully, Emily Arnold. *Mirette on the High Wire.* Illus. by the author. Putnam, 1992. ISBN 0-399-22130-1

In 1890s Paris a sad-faced stranger, retired high-wire walker Bellini, arrives at the well-known boarding house of Mirette's mother, the widow Gâteau. When Mirette finds him in the courtyard crossing the clothesline, she is entranced, but he refuses to instruct her, so she teaches herself until he relents. The astonishing stunts that the story attributes to Bellini were in real life enacted by the French daredevil Blondin who actually crossed Niagara Falls on a wire. McCully's dramatic Toulouse-Lautrec-influenced watercolors are full of mystery and drama. Set a rope on your classroom floor or in the hallway for children to traverse so they can see firsthand the courage required for balancing in the air. CALDECOTT MEDAL. COURAGE. FRANCE. PARIS. PICTURE BOOKS FOR ALL AGES. TIGHTROPE WALKING.

493 McCully, Emily Arnold. *Speak Up, Blanche!* Illus. by the author. HarperCollins, 1991. ISBN 0-06-024228-0

Young sheep Blanche loves the theater but but is too painfully shy to cut it as an actor at the bear family's Farm Theater. Where her real talent lies is in drawing, and when she is permitted to paint the huge sets for the new play, she gains new confidence as an artist. In McCully's *The Evil Spell* (1990), another story about the bear troupe, see how acting bear Edwin gets over his stage fright. Mary Hoffman's *Amazing Grace* and Joanne Oppenheim's *Mrs. Peloki's Class Play* will also appeal to thespians, while Joan Lexau's *Benji* and Rosemary Wells's *Shy Charles* deal with overcoming shyness. ACTING. ARTISTS. BEARS. SHEEP. SHYNESS.

494   McDonald, Joyce. *Homebody.* Illus. by Karl Swanson. Putnam, 1991. ISBN 0-399-21939-0

Left behind when the Peeble family moves away, their nameless thin gray cat stays close to the ramshackle country house, "Because home was home. And that was that." When Joe Budd buys and renovates the house and decides to keep the place for his own family, he takes in and names the loyal cat. Other strays children will want to take in include Nellie Burchardt's *Project Cat*, Wanda Gag's *Millions of Cats*, and Bernard Waber's *Rich Cat, Poor Cat*. See change from a cat's perspective in *Moving* by Michael Rosen. CATS. HOUSES.

495   McDonald, Megan. *The Great Pumpkin Switch.* Illus. by Ted Lewin. Orchard, 1992. ISBN 0-531-08514-7

In this sequel to *The Potato Man*, Grampa relates to his two grandchildren how he accidentally broke his sister's prize pumpkin, and how the Potato Man sold him an even bigger one to replace it. Bring in some apple butter to go along with this one. *Peppe the Lamplighter* by Elisa Bartone brings us back to New York City in the same time frame and *Roxaboxen* is about author Alice McLerran's mother's childhood in the Arizona desert. A girl recalls her late grandmother's stories of her childhood in *Abuelita's Paradise* by Carmen Santiago Nodar. ACCIDENTS. FAMILY STORIES. HISTORICAL FICTION. PUMPKINS.

496   McDonald, Megan. *The Potato Man.* Illus. by Ted Lewin. Orchard, 1991. ISBN 0-531-08600-3

As Grampa sits on the couch with his two attentive grandchildren, he recalls the time he and his boyhood friend Otto first encountered the one-eyed peddler and his horse-drawn wagon one snowy winter way back when. If children endeavor to pump their parents and grandparents for information on what life was like in those ancient times, they'll treasure the resulting tales. Make a class tape recording of the anecdotes they collect about school, play, siblings, and getting in trouble in the olden days before TV. *The Great Pumpkin Switch* continues Grampa's reminiscences. See how ice was harvested before the invention of refrigerators in *The Ice Horse* by Candace Christiansen. Go back another century to 1811 to meet an itinerant peddler in *Here Comes the Mystery Man* by Scott Russell Sanders. FAMILY STORIES. GRANDFATHERS. HISTORICAL FICTION. PEDDLERS AND PEDDLING.

497   McGovern, Ann. *Drop Everything, It's D.E.A.R. Time!* Illus. by Anna DiVito. Scholastic, 1993. ISBN 0-590-45802-7

Is this your school? Everyone's busy in every classroom, when suddenly—it's Drop Everything and Read time, and each student and teacher grabs a book, settles down, and gets lost in the pages. If you've never tried schoolwide D.E.A.R., this paperback explanation is right on the mark. Caroline Feller Bauer's *Too Many Books*, Crosby Bonsall's *Tell Me Some More*, Judith Caseley's *Sophie and Sammy's Library Sleepover*, James Daugherty's *Andy and the Lion*, Henrik Drescher's *Simon's Book*, and Barbara A. Huff's *Once Inside the Library* all promote reading as a contact sport. BOOKS AND READING. SCHOOLS.

498   McGuire, Richard. *Night Becomes Day*. Illus. by the author. Viking, 1994. ISBN 0-670-85547-2

"Night becomes day/ And day becomes bright/ Bright becomes sun/ And sun becomes shine/ Shine becomes sparkle/ And sparkle becomes steam . . ." Almost like a word-association game, the text flows from one image to another related one, and ends up back where it started. The 1940s style of the bright geometric illustrations may help children recall each key word as you read the book again. Try some free associating with the whole group, and then break children into pairs or small groups to see what they come up with. Start with seeds (Seeds become plant and plant becomes flower . . .) or letters (Letters become words and words become books . . .) , or a word the group suggests, and see where it leads. Jim Aylesworth's *Hush Up*, Byron Barton's *Buzz Buzz Buzz*, and Joanne Oppenheimer's *You Can't Catch Me* are farm tales that come full circle, as do *Fortunately* by Remy Charlip and *If You Give a Moose a Muffin* and *If You Give a Mouse a Cookie* by Laura Joffe Numeroff. CAUSE AND EFFECT. TIME.

499   McLerran, Alice. *Roxaboxen*. Illus. by Barbara Cooney. Lothrop, 1991. ISBN 0-688-07593-2

Out of rocks, wooden boxes, bottles, and other scraps, Marian and a group of her playmates build their own play town on a cactus-strewn hill in Yuma, Arizona, designating places for houses, a town hall, a bakery, two ice cream parlors, and even a jail. Based on the childhood memories of the author's mother, this is a beautiful tribute to the range of children's imaginations in making up their own private society. Young builders can create models of their own imagined towns with collected materials, draw maps, and name roads and important landmarks. Ask them to describe the games they make up and play today, not including anything that has to be plugged in! "Deep Dene" is the place all the kids go to play in *Mr. Knocky* by Jack Ziegler, while modern kids invent games in Michael Crowley's *New Kid on Spurwink Ave.*, Nicholas Heller's *An Adventure at Sea*, Ezra Jack Keats's *Regards to the Man in the Moon*, and David Wiesner's *Hurricane*. CITIES AND TOWNS. DESERTS. FAMILY STORIES. IMAGINATION. PLAY.

500   McNulty, Faith. *A Snake in the House*. Illus. by Ted Rand. Scholastic, 1994. ISBN 0-590-44758-0

A boy captures a snake in a glass jar and brings it home for a pet, but the snake escapes and spends days hiding in safe nooks throughout the house before the boy finally finds it and lets it go free. Close-up watercolors from the snake's-eye view give us empathy for the frightened creature who evades Daisy the cat and the terrors of a vacuum cleaner. Compare this realistic story with the slapstick fantasy of Nan Bodsworth's *A Nice Walk in the Jungle*, Libba Moore Gray's *Small*

Green Snake, Imbior C. Kudrna's *To Bathe a Boa*, and Trinka Hakes Noble's *The Day Jimmy's Boa Ate the Wash*, and show the startling photographs in Bianca Lavies's *A Gathering of Garter Snakes* (Dutton, 1993). Jill Kastner's *Snake Hunt* features Jesse and tall-taling Grandad as they search the woods for rattlesnakes and give themselves a scare. SNAKES.

501   **Mahy, Margaret.** *The Great White Man-Eating Shark: A Cautionary Tale.* **Illus. by Jonathan Allen. Dial, 1990. ISBN 0-8037-0749-5**

Talent is easy to abuse, as Norvin finds out to his discredit when he disguises himself as a shark and terrorizes swimmers in Caramel Cove so he can have the water to himself. Unfortunately, he's such a convincing actor that he attracts an amorous female shark who scares the sand out of him. One reviewer called this "a quirky combination of *Jaws* and *The Boy Who Cried Wolf*," and the shark endpapers will start the giggles. Toss out some facts with Betsy Maestro's *A Sea Full of Sharks*. Another greedy-guts learns to cool it in *Me First* by Helen Lester. GREED. PICTURE BOOKS FOR ALL AGES. SELFISHNESS. SHARKS. SWIMMING.

502   **Mahy, Margaret.** *The Rattlebang Picnic.* **Illus. by Steven Kellogg. Dial, 1994. ISBN 0-8037-1319-3**

Granny McTavish's pizza, tough as an old boot, is a perfect stand-in for the tire that falls off the family's jalopy as it plunges down Mount Fogg to outrun the erupting volcano's flowing red-hot lava. Kellogg's large convivial watercolors are just the ticket for the mayhem of this family-style tall tale. For their next picnic, the seven children and their folks plan to drive to Tornado Alley. Children can predict and write about the hair-raising dilemmas that are sure to follow. Since the family's old rattlebang may be on its last legs, they might appreciate a fine new car like Daniel Pinkwater's *Tooth-Gnasher Superflash*. Top your reading menu with Dayal Kaur Khalsa's realistic *How Pizza Came to Queens* and Maryanne Kovalski's folktalelike *Pizza for Breakfast*. AUTOMOBILES. GRANDMOTHERS. HUMOROUS FICTION. PICNICS. PIZZA. TALL TALES. VOLCANOES.

503   **Marshall, James.** *The Cut-Ups Carry On.* **Illus. by the author. Viking, 1990. ISBN 0-670-81645-0**

"I'd rather eat bugs," says Joe when his mother informs him that he and partner-in-crime Spud are signed up for an after-school dance class, but they change their attitude when Captain Kideo announces a TV dance contest with big prizes. Read this when the class is preparing for square dancing in gym and the boys are kicking up a fuss. Keep dancing with Rachel Isadora's *Max*. Angels and troublemakers alike will want to catch up with the other books in the Cut-Ups series. BEHAVIOR. CONTESTS. DANCING. HUMOROUS FICTION.

504   **Martin, Bill, Jr.** *The Maestro Plays.* **Illus. by Vladimir Radunsky. Henry Holt, 1994. ISBN 0-8050-1746-1**

In wonderfully silly nonsense verse studded with adverbs, a bulbous-nosed cartoonlike maestro plays all manner of instruments in a music-mad frenzy. He builds to a crescendo, playing "ringingly, wingingly . . . swingingly flingingly tingingly faster, faster . . ." Musically inclined teachers will want to compose music to go along and conduct the works with their classroom musicians. *Meet the Orchestra* by Ann Hayes and *Zin! Zin! Zin! A Violin* by Lloyd Moss introduce us to the instruments. To teach the joys of adverbs, this can't be beat, along with a bit of formal instruction in Ruth Heller's picture book *Up Up and Away: A Book About Adverbs*. CREATIVE DRAMA. ENGLISH LANGUAGE–GRAMMAR. MUSICIANS. PICTURE BOOKS FOR ALL AGES.

505   Mazer, Anne. *The Yellow Button.* Illus. by Judy Pedersen. Knopf, 1990. ISBN 0-394-92935-7

From a close-up of a girl's round yellow button, the paintings zoom outward to her house, field, mountain, country, and on to the far reaches of the universe, providing a comprehensible description of comparative sizes. To give children a further sense of universal perspective, also read Lynne Cherry's *The Armadillo from Amarillo*, Andrew Clements's *Mother Earth's Counting Book*, and Robert E. Wells's *Is a Blue Whale the Biggest Thing There Is? Something from Nothing* by Phoebe Gilman is a Jewish folktale that takes us on an opposite journey, showing how a boy's coat became a vest, tie, handkerchief, button, and finally a story. BUTTONS. UNIVERSE.

506   Meddaugh, Susan. *Martha Speaks.* Illus. by the author. Houghton Mifflin, 1992. ISBN 0-395-63313-3

When the alphabet soup Martha eats goes up to her brain instead of down to her stomach, lo and behold, the lovable mutt begins to talk. And talk. And talk. Her human family, overwhelmed with her excess verbiage, cries, "Martha, please! SHUT UP!" and the dog, crushed, retreats in silence that lasts until a burglar breaks in. Thanks to her smart mouth, Martha wins a vacation for four at the Come-On-Inn where there are No Dogs Allowed in the merry sequel, *Martha Calling* (1994). Ask your students to really listen to their pets, and transcribe what they think they might be saying. Another burglar buster is the Great Dane in Steven Kellogg's *Pinkerton, Behave!* Dick Gackenbach's *Beauty, Brave and Beautiful*, Julia Lebentritt and Richard Ploetz's *The Kooken*, and Frances Ward Weller's *Riptide* are all about unusual mutts. DOGS. HUMOROUS FICTION. PICTURE BOOKS FOR ALL AGES. ROBBERS AND OUTLAWS. SPEECH.

507   Meddaugh, Susan. *The Witches' Supermarket.* Illus. by the author. Houghton Mifflin, 1991. ISBN 0-395-57034-4

With Helen dressed as a witch for Halloween and her dog Martha (of *Martha Speaks* fame) in a cat costume, at first none of the strangely attired women in the store notice there are intruders in their midst, but when girl and dog realize that this is no ordinary supermarket, they almost don't make it back outside. Children can make itemized shopping lists of staples they might need in such a specialized store. Read the witchy poems in Lilian Moore's *See My Lovely Poison Ivy* to get the juices flowing. In a turnabout, it's the witch who attends in disguise in Linda Shute's *Halloween Party*. COSTUMES. DOGS. HALLOWEEN. WITCHES.

508   Melmed, Laura Krauss. *The Rainbabies.* Illus. by Jim LaMarche. Lothrop, 1992. ISBN 0-688-10755-9

An old woman and man who have always yearned for children have their wish fulfilled after a moonshower when they discover 12 tiny rainbabies in the meadow and care for them, saving them from water, fire, and a covetous weasel. In typical folktale fashion, Mother Moonshower tests their loyalty, and trades them the dozen wee babies for a human one. Stay miniature with Hans Christian Andersen's *Thumbelina*, Barbara Brenner's Japanese folktale *Little One Inch*, Dick Gackenbach's *Tiny for a Day*, William Joyce's *George Shrinks*, Morris Lurie's *The Story of Imelda, Who Was Small*, and Elvira Woodruff's *Show and Tell*. BABIES. LITERARY FAIRY TALES. SIZE.

509   Mennen, Ingrid, and Niki Daly. *Somewhere in Africa.* Illus. by Nicolaas Maritz. Dutton, 1992. ISBN 0-525-44848-9

If you envision only lions and crocs and zebras when you think of Africa, then meet Ashraf, a young South African boy, and have a look at Cape Town, the noisy, busy, modern city where he lives. Maritz's crowded, vivid paintings are full of movement and sound. Contrast Ashraf's urban world with the rural ones in Jane Cowen-Fletcher's *It Takes a Village*, Paul Geraghty's *The Hunter*, Ann Grifalconi's Caldecott Honor folktale *The Village of Round and Square Houses*, and Virginia Kroll's *Masai and I*. Ashraf explores wild Africa in his favorite library book. Children can raid the library shelves to research their own favorite corners of the world and share their findings. Barbara A. Huff's *Once Inside the Library* is a poem that shows all the marvels one can discover with books. AFRICA. BOOKS AND READING. CITIES AND TOWNS. MULTICULTURAL STORIES.

510   Minters, Frances. *Cinder-Elly.* Illus. by G. Brian Karas. Viking, 1993. ISBN 0-670-84417-9

Shod in glass sneakers and a red miniskirt, younger sibling Elly gets to the basketball game where she meets up with star player Prince Charming. This good-natured parody version is told in snappy rhyme, with modern-primitive gouache-and-acrylic illustrations. You'll want to look at other parodies like Ellen Jackson's *Cinder Edna*, and Bernice Myers's *Sidney Rella and the Glass Sneaker*, as well as more tongue-in-cheek retellings like Barbara Karlin's or William Wegman's *Cinderella*. Stephanie Calmenson's *The Principal's New Clothes* is another amusing update. BASKETBALL. CINDERELLA STORIES. FAIRY TALES–SATIRE. PARODIES. SISTERS. STORIES IN RHYME.

511   Modesitt, Jeanne. *The Story of Z.* Illus. by Lonni Sue Johnson. Picture Book Studio, 1990. ISBN 0-88708-105-3

Tired of being last in line, the letter Z walks off the regular alphabet to start up her own, but has trouble recruiting any other letters. When she realizes how much everybody misses and appreciates her, she rejoins the other 25. Children can write sentences with the z's missing, such as one in the story, "Can we go to the oo and see the ebras," and read them aloud for others to figure out. Speculate: What would happen if any other letters bowed out? How about vowels? All can compose sentences without any o's, for instance. ALPHABET. CREATIVE WRITING.

512   **Moss, Lloyd.** *Zin! Zin! Zin! A Violin.* **Illus. by Marjorie Priceman. Simon & Schuster, 1995. ISBN 0-671-88239-2**

"One trombone is playing solo; trumpet joins and makes a duo; french horn enters, makes a trio; quartet's formed with mello cello." Moss's punchy rhymes and Priceman's splashy, zany gouache paintings introduce the whole orchestra, counting up to a chamber group of ten. Review the numbers by having children form into groups of quartets or octets. Each can pantomime playing an orchestra instrument for others to identify. *Meet the Orchestra* by Ann Hayes has a different animal playing each instrument, while *The Maestro Plays* by Bill Martin, Jr. contains an adverb-studded virtuoso performance. *Mrs. Merriweather's Musical Cat* by Carol Purdy, *The Kooken* by Julia Lebentritt and Richard Ploetz, and *Garth Pig Steals the Show* by Mary Rayner are all delightful spoofs of musical life. COUNTING BOOKS. MUSICAL INSTRUMENTS. MUSICIANS. STORIES IN RHYME.

513   **Most, Bernard.** *Hippopotamus Hunt.* **Illus. by the author. Harcourt, 1994. ISBN 0-15-234520-5**

Take a trek through the jungle with five word-hunting children as they search for words that can be formed from the letters in the word "hippopotamus," including map, south, photos, thump, and soap, and incorporate each into a sentence. Children can brainstorm another word search with "elephant" and write and illustrate an all new adventure. The author offers more word searches in *Can You Find It?* and *Zoodles,* while Cathi Hepworth's *Antics!* and Bruce and Brett McMillan's *Puniddles* will also get kids thinking. Fool some more with the sounds of language in Bill Martin, Jr.'s dippy rhyming story *The Happy Hippopotami.* ENGLISH LANGUAGE–SPELLING. HIPPOPOTAMUS. WORD GAMES.

514   **Most, Bernard.** *Zoodles.* **Illus. by the author. Harcourt, 1992. ISBN 0-15-299969-8**

"What do you call a kangaroo that wakes you up every day? A kangarooster!" Children will crow their answers to the 15 riddles about animals with combined names in this jaunty picture book. A stubborn emu is an "emule," and a goat that stands on one leg is a "flamingoat." It's not too hard for children to make up their own zoodles, after brainstorming to come up with a few starter creatures like turtle (turtleopard?), toucan (toucanary?), or gerbil (badgerbil?) to get them thinking. There are four components here: thinking up two animals with linking names, making up a riddle that defines both animals' characteristics, illustrating the answer, and presenting the finished zoodle for others to guess. There are more hidden words in Linda Bourke's *Eye Spy: A Mysterious Alphabet,* Cathi Hepworth's *Antics!,* and Most's *Can You Find It?* and *Hippopotamus Hunt.* ANIMALS. CREATIVE WRITING. RIDDLES. WORD GAMES.

515   **Murphy, Jim.** *Backyard Bear.* **Illus. by Jeffrey Greene. Scholastic, 1993. ISBN 0-590-44375-5**

In a realistic depiction of animal behavior, a young black bear wanders out of the forest one night and into a suburban neighborhood in search of food. A boy and his parents hear noises outside and find the bear by the garage, where the police try but fail to catch it. "The Bear Facts" information at the back of the book describes what to do if a bear visits your yard, a not uncommon situation that happened to my sister Sharron and her family a few years back. Introduce a diverse group of bears with *The Grizzly Sisters* by Cathy Bellows, *Little Tricker the Squirrel Meets Big Double the Bear* by Ken Kesey, *The Bear That Heard Crying* by Natalie Kinsey-Warnock, *The Biggest Bear* by Lynd Ward, and *Swamp Angel* by Paul O. Zelinsky. BEARS. PICTURE BOOKS FOR ALL AGES.

516 **Nabb, Magdalen.** *Josie Smith at School.* **Illus. by Pirkko Vainio. McElderry, 1990. ISBN 0-689-50533-7**

[3 chapters, 106p.] In three entertaining chapters, we get to know English schoolgirl Josie who comes to school filthy and late when she tries to pick roses to bring to her new teacher, takes a new little non-English-speaking girl under her wing, and puts on a brave face when she doesn't get the part she wants in the class play. Students will also enjoy *Josie Smith* (1989), *Josie Smith at the Seashore* (1990), and *Josie Smith and Eileen* (1992). *Ramona the Pest* by Beverly Cleary and the Junie B. Jones books by Barbara Park are also about little girls with irrepressible personalities. FRIENDSHIP. SCHOOLS.

517 **Newman, Nanette.** *There's a Bear in the Bath!* **Illus. by Michael Foreman. Harcourt, 1994. ISBN 0-15-285512-2**

Liza invites Jam, a visiting bear, into her house where he dances the tango, does the newspaper crossword puzzle, drinks shampoo, and puts frilly underwear on his head. What you'll love about the story, along with the glowing watercolors, is the clever and unpredictable dialogue, with memorable lines such as, ". . . boasting is very unattractive in a child, but boasting when you're a bear is quite acceptable." Discuss what makes Jam such a memorable character, and not just a generic stock bear. Students can offer words that describe his personality and describe incidents that bear out their observations. BEARS. PICTURE BOOKS FOR ALL AGES.

518 **Niland, Kilmeny.** *A Bellbird in a Flame Tree.* **Illus. by the author. Tambourine, 1991. ISBN 0-688-10797-4**

Tired of the same old partridge-in-a-pear-tree for your Christmas warbling? How about trading them in for koala, dingoes, numbats, quokkas, lorikeets, and wallabies, all leaping and dancing and knitting and cooking? With such detailed and charming illustrations, you can't go wrong. Compare the words of the original *The Twelve Days of Christmas* with Jan Brett's luscious paintings, and travel to Africa for *My Christmas Safari* by Fran Manushkin. George Mendoza's *A Wart Snake in a Fig Tree* is a coal-in-your-stocking parody, and Irene Trivas's *Emma's Christmas* is a prose version. Warm up with a trip to the beach in *The Twelve Days of Summer* by Elizabeth Lee O'Donnell. *Koala Lou* by Mem Fox and *Wombat Stew* by Marcia K. Vaughn are more stories from Down Under. ANIMALS. AUSTRALIA. CHRISTMAS. SONGS. STORIES IN RHYME.

519   Nodar, Carmen Santiago. *Abuelita's Paradise*. Illus. by Diane Paterson. Albert Whitman, 1992. ISBN 0-8075-0129-8

Adjusting to her grandmother's death becomes easier for young Marita as she sits in Abuelita's rocking chair and relives listening to the idyllic stories her grandmother told her about growing up in Puerto Rico, cutting sugar cane, watching the honeycreeper bird, making pillows, and enjoying the beautiful scenery. *The Key into Winter* by Janet S. Andersen, *Eleanor, Arthur, and Claire* by Diana Engel, and *Saying Good-Bye to Grandma* by Jane Resh Thomas handle the death of a grandparent sensitively. Fly over New York City with Arthur Dorros's *Abuela*. DEATH. FAMILY STORIES. GRANDMOTHERS. HISPANIC AMERICANS. PUERTO RICO.

520   Nolan, Dennis. *Dinosaur Dream*. Illus. by the author. Macmillan, 1990. ISBN 0-02-768145-9

The baby apatosaurus Wilbur discovers outside his bedroom window one night follows the boy through the Ice Age, the Age of Mammals, the Cretaceous period, and all the way back to the Jurassic period, where the dinosaur is reunited with his family. Nolan's paintings of dinosaurs and the changing landscape are luminous and dramatic, and his story is filled with facts and adventure. Eric Rohmann's wordless *Time Flies* is another breathtaking trip back to dinosaur time. Carol Carrick's *Patrick's Dinosaurs* and *What Happened to Patrick's Dinosaurs?*, Henry Schwartz's *How I Captured a Dinosaur*, and Hudson Talbott's extraterrestrial dinosaurs in *We're Back!* will pique listeners's imagination, while B. G. Hennessy's *The Dinosaur Who Lived in My Backyard* and Bernard Most's *How Big Were the Dinosaurs?* will fill in more information. DINOSAURS. DREAMS. PICTURE BOOKS FOR ALL AGES. TIME TRAVEL.

521   Norworth, Jack. *Take Me Out to the Ballgame*. Illus. by Alec Gillman. Four Winds, 1993. ISBN 0-02-735991-3

The original lyrics to the 1908 song that has become baseball's anthem are paired with big, genial illustrations showing Game 5 of the 1947 World Series between the New York Yankees and the Brooklyn Dodgers (with Jackie Robinson at the plate), which is described in the illustrator's notes on the final pages. *Extra Innings: Baseball Poems*, compiled by Lee Bennett Hopkins, *At the Crack of the Bat: Baseball Poems*, compiled by Lillian Morrison, and Ernest Lawrence Thayer's *Casey at the Bat* integrate more poetry with the sport. *Teammates* by Peter Golenbock, a picture book about how Jackie Robinson dealt with prejudice when he became the first black major league player, is a significant title for educating children in the changes that baseball has undergone. *My Dad's Baseball* by Ron Cohen shows us the Yankees in 1955, while *The Field Beyond the Outfield* by Mark Teague is a baseball fantasy for daydreamers. BASEBALL. PICTURE BOOKS FOR ALL AGES. SONGS.

522 Odgers, Sally Farrell. *Drummond: The Search for Sarah*. Illus. by Carol Jones. Holiday House, 1990. ISBN 0-8234-0851-5

[19 chapters, 112p.] The old-fashioned teddy bear that Sarah and her brother Nicholas find at their great-aunt's mansion during the village fair can talk and walk, and he's determined to find his human friend Sarah who left him in a room and never returned. The large format chapter book with its charming pen-and-ink-and-watercolors on nearly every page will beguile children, all of whom will want to go home and see if their teddies will come out of hibernation and talk too. Have children bring in their bears, and work in pairs, with one person engaging in conversation a partner who will assume the personality of his or her bear and become its mouthpiece. Compare Drummond's personality with that of A. A. Milne's Winnie-the-Pooh, and stir up more trouble with Barbara Dillon's *The Teddy Bear Tree*. BROTHERS AND SISTERS. FANTASY. TEDDY BEARS.

523 O'Donnell, Elizabeth Lee. *The Twelve Days of Summer*. Illus. by Karen Lee Schmidt. Morrow, 1991. ISBN 0-088-08203-3

Down by the sea for a day at the beach, a little girl observes 12 gulls a-gliding, 11 waves a-crashing, dolphins, seals, crabs, starfish, squid, flying fish, pipers, jellyfish, pelicans, and a little purple sea anenome. Raffi's *Down by the Bay* is another wonderful beach song to sing. Spend more time at the seashore with *Reflections* by Ann Jonas, *Not the Piano, Mrs. Medley!* by Evan Levine, *Is This a House for Hermit Crab?* by Megan McDonald, *Beach Days* by Ken Robbins, *Clams Can't Sing* by James Stevenson, and *Riptide* by Frances Ward Weller, and then multiply it with Joy N. Hulme's *Sea Squares*. Pick up on the same format with other rewrites including Kilmeny Niland's Australian *A Bellbird in a Flame Tree*, Fran Manushkin's *My Christmas Safari*, George Mendoza's *A Wart Snake in a Fig Tree*, Carol Greene's *The Thirteen Days of Halloween*, Dian Curtis Regan's *The Thirteen Hours of Halloween*, and Irene Trivas's *Emma's Christmas*. COUNTING BOOKS. MARINE ANIMALS. PARODIES. SEASHORE. SONGS.

524 Ogburn, Jacqueline K. *Scarlett Angelina Wolverton-Manning*. Illus. by Brian Ajhar. Dial, 1994. ISBN 0-8037-1377-0

Wealthy young Scarlet Angelina, she of the big toothy smile and the big fine eyes, is kidnapped in the family's lone black car by Ralph, a bogus chauffeur, which doesn't faze her a bit, as long as she's home by dark. What is it about darkness and the full moon that has her family shaken, and just what does the child do to Ralph's parrot, goldfish, and kitty? Some of your listeners will deduce the ending; all will be pleased at the werewolf-filled climax to this veddy Britishlike melodrama. After reading, have children list the many clues to the family's identity. There's a lovely gargoyle on the cover that might lead you into the shivery mood piece *Night of the Gargoyles* by Eve Bunting, and *Wempires* by Daniel Pinkwater is also a nice touch. KIDNAPPING. TRANSFORMATIONS. WEREWOLVES.

525 Okimoto, Jean Davies. *Blumpoe the Grumpoe Meets Arnold the Cat*. Illus. by Howie Schneider. Little, Brown, 1990. ISBN 0-316-63811-0

Even crankier since the death of his dog Raymond, Mr. Blumpoe is on his way to visit his sister when his car breaks down, and he checks in to the Anderson House Hotel, where guests are given the option of selecting a cat for their rooms each night. Shy Arnold follows the bad-tempered man, and by the end of the night, after many hilarious attempts by man to rid himself of cat, the two are great pals. Inspired by an actual hotel in Wabasha, Minnesota, Okimoto's story will make listeners want to check in for a few nights. Meet another bad-tempered fellow in James Stevenson's *Worse Than the Worst* and *The Worst Person's Christmas*. BEHAVIOR. CATS. HOTELS, MOTELS, ETC.

526   Osofsky, Audrey. *My Buddy.* Illus. by Ted Rand. Henry Holt, 1992. ISBN 0-8050-1747-X

The narrator, a young boy with muscular dystrophy, describes in a matter-of-fact manner how his dog Buddy trained to become his service dog, performing all the day-to-day activities a child with muscular dystrophy can't manage alone, like turning out the lights, fetching the phone, and pushing the elevator buttons in the mall. Buoyant watercolors show a child whose love for the personable golden retriever help him with his short-lived jitters at being mainstreamed in a new school. Compare Buddy's role with Stephanie Calmenson's *Rosie: A Visiting Dog's Story*, and the Seeing Eye dog in Sally Hobart Alexander's *Mom's Best Friend*. Stories about children with physical disabilities include Nancy Carlson's *Arnie and the New Kid*, Liz Damrell's *With the Wind*, and Berniece Rabe's *The Balancing Girl*. Children curious about wheelchairs will take to Jane Cowen-Fletcher's *Mama Zooms*. DOGS. HANDICAPS. MUSCULAR DYSTROPHY. PHYSICAL DISABILITY. WHEELCHAIRS.

527   Patron, Susan. *Burgoo Stew.* Illus. by Mike Shenon. Orchard, 1991. ISBN 0-531-08516-3

Stone Soup-style, old Billy Que sends out the hungry crowd of five rowdy bad boys to come up with the extra ingredients he needs to make his special stew, and teaches them a few manners in the meantime. Your ornery crew can act out the story, with each child asking kindly for each ingredient. Compare this to the folktales *Stone Soup*, with versions by Marcia Brown, Ann McGovern, and John Warren Stewig, and *Nail Soup* by Harve Zemach. *Potato Pancakes All Around* by Marilyn Hirsch is a Hanukkah story using the same motif. BEHAVIOR. FOOD. SOUP. STORIES TO TELL.

528   Pearson, Susan. *Lenore's Big Break.* Illus. by Nancy Carlson. Viking, 1992. ISBN 0-670-83474-2

Nerdy Lenore ignores the snickers of her condescending coworkers at the office, for she has big plans. Back home in her apartment every night, she runs her multitude of birds—parrots, flamingos, hummingbirds, cockatoos, and more—through their dancing and other vaudevillelike routines, in preparation for the big night on TV's Amateur Hour, where they are a smash. What's interesting about this treatment is that Lenore never doubts her own talents and abilities, and her hard work and perseverance pay off, as she knew they would. Contrast with stories where the hero must learn to accept him/herself first, such as James Howe's *I Wish I Were a Butterfly* or Bill Peet's *The Spooky Tail of Prewitt Peacock*.

Both *Amazing Grace* by Mary Hoffman and *Cinder Edna* by Ellen Jackson boast spunky heroines who don't allow naysayers or circumstances to stand in their way. BIRDS. PICTURE BOOKS FOR ALL AGES. SECRETARIES. SELF-ESTEEM.

529 Petersen, P. J. *The Amazing Magic Show.* Illus. by Renée Williams-Andriani. Simon & Schuster, 1994. ISBN 0-671-86581-1

[8 chapters, 89p.] In several lighthearted episodes, brothers Chuck and Hal try various means to earn money to see a magic show performed by The Amazing Victor, where the magician makes Chuck disappear, after which Hal takes up magic to put on his own show. Younger siblings will appreciate Hal's ultimate success in one-upping his smug older brother. In your library, visit the magic trick section of nonfiction in 793.8 for easy-to-perform magic tricks, such as those in Roy Broekel's *Now You See It: Easy Magic for Beginners*, that pairs of your students can read, learn, practice, and perform for the rest of the group. Conjure up more tricks with James Howe's *Rabbit-Cadabra!* and *The Amazing Felix* by Emily Arnold McCully. BROTHERS. MAGIC. MAGICIANS.

530 Pilkey, Dav. *Dog Breath: The Horrible Trouble with Hally Tosis.* Illus. by the author. Blue Sky/Scholastic, 1994. ISBN 0-590-47466-9

The Tosis family owns a good dog with one big problem: she has such horrible breath even skunks avoid her. Pun-filled attempts to help her, such as taking her to the top of a breathtaking mountain, have no effect, but when she overpowers two sneaky burglars, all is forgiven, even though the family must hold their noses just to get near her. Like Pilkey's *Dogzilla* and *Kat Kong*, this one will make kids howl. See how other smart but eccentric dogs save the day in *Walter's Tail* by Lisa Campbell Ernst, *Pinkerton, Behave!* by Steven Kellogg, *The Kooken* by Julia Lebentritt and Richard Ploetz, *Martha Speaks* by Susan Meddaugh, and *Amos Camps Out* by Susan Seligson. DOGS. HUMOROUS FICTION. PICTURE BOOKS FOR ALL AGES. SENSES AND SENSATION.

531 Pilkey, Dav. *'Twas the Night Before Thanksgiving.* Illus. by the author. Scholastic, 1990. ISBN 0-590-22901-X

On a school field trip to visit the turkey farm of Farmer Mack Nuggett, once the children realize the eight tiny turkeys will meet their end as Thanksgiving dinners, they smuggle out the gobblers under their coats. Since Pilkey's book is a parody of Clement C. Moore's poem "The Night Before Christmas," you should read that as well so they understand the spoof. The farmer's call, "Now Ollie, now Stanley, now Larry and Moe, on Wally, on Beaver, on Shemp and Groucho," should get you grinning. Another Thanksgiving with no turkey dinner is *Thanksgiving at the Tappletons'* by Eileen Spinelli. Continue the nonsense with the Jack Prelutsky's poem "The Turkey Shot Out of the Oven" from *The New Kid on the Block* and his collection of easy-to-read poems *It's Thanksgiving*. PARODIES. PICTURE BOOKS FOR ALL AGES. STORIES IN RHYME. THANKSGIVING. TURKEYS.

532 Pilkey, Dav. *When Cats Dream.* Illus. by the author. Orchard, 1992. ISBN 0-531-08597-X

Take an impressionistic slow-motion romp through a cat's dream state, where the black-and-white world is transformed into undulating color, the fishtank becomes a welcoming ocean, and a cat can dance on a snoring dog's head and swing from jungle vines. The cat-influenced send-ups of Mona Lisa, Whistler's Mother, and works by Marc Chagall and Henri Rousseau will send readers reeling, though you'll want to keep reproductions of the original paintings nearby so children can first get the visual jokes, and then compare the results. Make a detour to meet other personable cats like those in Mary Calhoun's *Cross-Country Cat*, Jack Gantos's *Rotten Ralph*, Daniel Pinkwater's *The Wuggie Norple Story*, Pilkey's cat run-amok *Kat Kong*, and Bill Slavin's *The Cat Came Back*. Helen V. Griffith's *Plunk's Dreams* speculates on what dogs dream about. Have your students watch a pet as it sleeps and then write down its possible dreams. ART. CATS. DREAMS. PICTURE BOOKS FOR ALL AGES.

533   **Pinczes, Elinor J. *One Hundred Hungry Ants*. Illus. by Bonnie MacKain. Houghton Mifflin, 1993. ISBN 0-395-63116-5**

A hill of hungry ants marches off to their picnic ("a hey and a hi dee ho!") in a long row, when the littlest ant realizes they'll get there quicker if they regroup into two lines of 50, then four lines of 25, then five lines of 20, and finally ten lines of ten. Unfortunately, by the time they get there, all the food is gone, but in the meantime, we've managed to learn a few nifty facts about division. Challenge your students to see how many ways they can regroup themselves to make equal sets. Loreen Leedy's *Fraction Action* and Louise Matthews's *Gator Pie* will help explain fractions. *Effie* by Beverley Allinson introduces an ant with personality and a big voice, *Those Amazing Ants* by Patricia Brennan Demuth and *Ant Cities* by Arthur Dorros give ant facts, *The Ant and the Elephant* by Bill Peet proves little guys can help, and *Two Bad Ants* by Chris Van Allsburg shows how curiosity can be dangerous. ANTS. CALL-AND-RESPONSE STORIES. CHANTABLE REFRAIN. DIVISION. MATHEMATICS. PICNICS. STORIES IN RHYME.

534   **Pinkwater, Daniel. *Doodle Flute*. Illus. by the author. Macmillan, 1991. ISBN 0-02-774635-6**

Already owning everything a kid could possibly want, Kevin Spoon covets the doodle flute that weird Mason Mintz says is the last of its kind, but Mason won't sell it or trade for it. He gives it to Kevin, however, and when Kevin can't figure out how to play it, shares ownership and teaches him. Children who want for nothing will think over the meaning of this one, which would make a good Reader's Theater in three acts. FLUTE. FRIENDSHIP. GENEROSITY. INDIVIDUALITY. MUSICAL INSTRUMENTS.

535   **Pinkwater, Daniel. *Wempires*. Illus. by the author. Macmillan, 1991. ISBN 0-02-774411-6**

Jonathan Harker wears his vampire suit and fake fangs everywhere, and one night, to his great delight, three real vampires—Pinkwater-like triplets—climb through his window and induce him to feed them sardine and onion sandwiches, cold chicken, and corn flakes. Thanks to this ridiculously silly story, in another ten years or so your listeners might be inspired to meet the real Jonathan

Harker when they read Bram Stoker's terrifying classic, *Dracula*. Bunnicula, a vampire bunny, is a silent character in James Howe's *The Fright Before Christmas*, *Rabbit-Cadabra!*, and *Scared Silly*, while the title character of Jacqueline K. Ogburn's deliciously droll *Scarlett Angelina Wolverton-Manning* is a werewolf. HUMOROUS FICTION. PICTURE BOOKS FOR ALL AGES. VAMPIRES.

536   **Polacco, Patricia. *My Rotten Redheaded Older Brother*. Illus. by the author. Simon & Schuster, 1994. ISBN 0-671-72751-6**

As a child, spending the summer in Michigan on her Babushka's farm was bliss for Patricia, spoiled only and incessantly by the presence of brother Richard who always claimed to be able to do everything better: pick more berries, get the dirtiest, or burp the loudest. "And I'm four years older than you . . . Always have been and always will be," he sneers. How the two make peace makes for a realistic and hopeful autobiographical sibling story, bolstered by endpapers covered with snapshots of the two growing up in the 1950s. Revisit the author's grandmother in *Some Birthday!* and *Thunder Cake*. Compare other cases of sibling rivalry in Judy Blume's *The Pain and the Great One*, Jean Little's *Revenge of the Small Small*, James Stevenson's *Worse Than Willy!*, and Dan Yaccarino's *Big Brother Mike*. Ask your children to give examples of love-hate relationships they have experienced and relate how they resolve their conflicts. BROTHERS AND SISTERS. GRANDMOTHERS. PICTURE BOOKS FOR ALL AGES. SIBLING RIVALRY.

537   **Polacco, Patricia. *Some Birthday!* Illus. by the author. Simon & Schuster, 1991. ISBN 0-671-72750-8**

It seems as if Patricia's father has forgotten her birthday, but when he comes home from work he hustles her brother Ritchie, cousin Billy, and her to the haunted Clay Pit to take the first ever picture of the Monster of the Clay Pit Bottoms. All signs indicate that this spooky and funny family story is based on the author's own experience. Solve the birthday mystery in *The 13th Clue* by Ann Jonas, and get another scare with the pets in *Creepy-Crawly Birthday* by James Howe, a hare-raising "Bunnicula" story. Ask your children to relate their most unforgettable birthday experiences. A nice touch in this book is the natural treatment of a divorced father with summertime custody. *Birthday Rhymes, Special Times* selected by Bobbye S. Goldstein and *Happy Birthday*, selected by Lee Bennett Hopkins contain some good companion poems to set up your story. BIRTHDAYS. FATHERS. MONSTERS. SINGLE-PARENT FAMILIES.

538   **Priceman, Marjorie. *How to Make an Apple Pie and See the World*. Illus. by the author. Knopf, 1994. ISBN 0-679-93705-6**

If the market is closed and you need the best ingredients, then follow the dark-haired girl as she gets her semolina wheat in Italy, eggs in France, cinnamon from Sri Lanka, butter from an English cow, sugar from Jamaica, and apples from Vermont. Charming primitive watercolors, with world map route endpapers and an apple pie recipe on the last page make this a most delectable journey. Children can plot out where in the world they'd need to go to make ice cream or fruit salad. *Jeremy's Tail* by Duncan Ball, *Magic Carpet* by Pat Brisson, *Amelia's*

Fantastic Flight by Rose Bursik, *Away from Home* by Anita Lobel, *Uncle Lester's Hat* by Howie Schneider, *Love, Your Bear Pete* by Dyan Sheldon, and *Nine O'Clock Lullaby* by Marilyn Singer will also appeal to map- and globe-trotting tourists. Another step-by-step cooking story is *Pancakes, Pancakes* by Eric Carle. COOKERY. FOOD. FRUIT. GEOGRAPHY. PIES. VOYAGES AND TRAVELS.

539   Purdy, Carol. *Mrs. Merriweather's Musical Cat.* Illus. by Petra Mathers. Putnam, 1994. ISBN 0-399-22543-9

Piano teacher Mrs. Merriwether barely weathers students who mangle the music and a neighbor who complains about the noise until the day a stray cat leaps through the window and onto the piano and starts waving its tail in time to the music. Beethoven, as she call him, helps every student until the sad day he disappears, but in a welcome and not-so-surprise ending, the cat returns, leading her musical triplet kittens. *The Kooken* by Julia Lebentritt and Richard Ploetz features a cello-eating dog who becomes one with the music in a more-than-literal sense. Feature more pets with a purpose in life, such as the Siamese cat Henry in *Cross-Country Cat*, *Henry the Sailor Cat*, and *High Wire Henry* by Mary Calhoun, the verbose dog in *Martha Speaks* by Susan Meddaugh, and the hotel cat in *Blumpoe the Grumpoe Meets Arnold the Cat* by Jean Davies Okimoto. CATS. MUSIC. MUSICAL INSTRUMENTS. PIANO.

540   Rand, Gloria. *Salty Takes Off.* Illus. by Ted Rand. Henry Holt, 1991. ISBN 0-8050-1159-5

Sea dog Salty and his owner Zack plan to lay over in a small Alaskan town for the winter, and while Zack goes to work fixing planes for Jarman Curtis's flying service, the dog goes "flightseeing" with Jarman. On one stormy fight, the dog tumbles out of the plane and into the snow far below—and survives. What an adventure! The dazzling watercolors of mountains, snow, and red plane will make your kids hot to travel. On a more sober subject is Rand's also engrossing *Prince William*, about a baby seal rescued after the 1989 oil slick in Prince William Sound. In *Cross Country Cat*, a realistic fantasy by Mary Calhoun, the resourceful Siamese takes to skiis when he is stranded at the top of a snowy mountain. AIRPLANES. ALASKA. DOGS. PICTURE BOOKS FOR ALL AGES. SNOW. SURVIVAL. WINTER.

541   Raschka, Chris *Yo! Yes?* Illus. by the author. Orchard, 1993. ISBN 0-531-08619-4

A captivating portrait of and dialogue between two boys who encounter each other on opposite pages, and utter a total of just 34 exuberant words, no more than two per page. The boy on the left page is black and confident, the sad sack on the right hand page, white and reticent. The white boy reveals his problem: "No friends." The solution? Friendship. Act this out in pairs. With Aliki's *Communication*, we see how the more we talk, joke, and laugh together, the better. Make more new friends with *Henry's Baby* by Mary Hoffman, *Watch Out for Those Weirdos* by Rufus Kline, and *Earl's Too Cool for Me* by Leah Komaiko. AFRICAN AMERICANS. CREATIVE DRAMA. FRIENDSHIP. MULTICULTURAL STORIES. PICTURE BOOKS FOR ALL AGES.

542   Ray, Mary Lynn. *Pianna.* Illus. by Bobbie Henba. Harcourt, 1994. ISBN 0-15-261357-9

She's 80 now, and still living in the house where she was born, but when Anna was seven, her father bought her a piano and she rode the train into Boston each Saturday for lessons from a professor. For all those lazy students who wonder why they should bother practicing (as in Melinda Green's *Rachel's Recital*), we see how fulfilling Anna's life was as she married, raised a family, and kept on playing. Use with other fond reminiscences such as Barbara Cooney's *Miss Rumphius*, Gloria Houston's *My Great Aunt Arizona* and *The Year of the Perfect Christmas Tree*, and Trinka Hakes Noble's *Apple Tree Christmas*. HISTORICAL FICTION. MUSIC. MUSICAL INSTRUMENTS. PIANO.

543   Rayner, Mary. *Garth Pig Steals the Show*. Illus. by the author. Dutton, 1993. ISBN 0-525-45023-8

Once again, Mrs. Wolf returns, this time disguised as a sousaphone player who volunteers to play at the Pig family's charity concert at the town hall. When Father Pig tells her he can't pay her but that she'd be helping pigs, she replies, "Nothing I like better than a helping of pig, " and indeed, at the concert, she surreptitiously stuffs Garth into her instrument. Find out more about the ten pig siblings in *Garth Pig and the Ice Cream Lady*, *Mr. and Mrs. Pig's Evening Out*, *Mrs. Pig's Bulk Buy*, and *Mrs. Pig Gets Cross and Other Stories* (Dutton, 1987). Performing animals take the stage in Lisa Campbell Ernst's *Ginger Jumps* and *When Bluebell Sang*, Susan Jeschke's *Perfect the Pig*, and Elise Primavera's *The Three Dots*. From solo, duo, and trio up to a chamber group of ten, meet the orchestra in the rhyming *Zin! Zin! Zin! A Violin* by Lloyd Moss. MUSICAL INSTRUMENTS. MUSICIANS. PIGS. WOLVES.

544   Regan, Dian Curtis. *The Thirteen Hours of Halloween*. Illus. by Lieve Baeten. Albert Whitman, 1993. ISBN 0-8075-7876-2

You can read or sing this "Twelve Days of Christmas" parody, told by a little girl who gets 13 ghastly gifts, along with Carol Greene's *The Thirteen Days of Halloween*. Songsters can compose and illustrate new verses for the whole class to try. Bill Martin, Jr.'s *Old Devil Wind*, Linda Shute's *Halloween Party*, Erica Silverman's *Big Pumpkin*, and Caroline Stutson's *By the Light of the Halloween Moon* are all rhythmically spooky. GIFTS. HALLOWEEN. PARODIES. SONGS.

545   Roth, Roger. *The Sign Painter's Dream*. Illus. by the author. Crown, 1993. ISBN 0-517-58921-4

Crabby Clarence complains about everything, especially his boring job painting signs, but after he turns down an old woman who wants him to make a sign saying "FREE APPLES IF YOU NEED 'EM," he has a dream about George Washington that changes his mind and attitude. Poll your children before the story and after as to their views on philanthropy and giving something for nothing, and see if they change their minds any. Don't forget to bring the apples. Norman in Tedd Arnold's *The Signmaker's Assistant* and the sky painters in Pat Cummings's *C.L.O.U.D.S.* and Aaron Shepard's *The Legend of Slappy Hooper: An American Tall Tale* all learn a thing or two about making signs. DREAMS. GENEROSI-

TY. PAINTING. PICTURE BOOKS FOR ALL AGES. SIGNS AND SIGNBOARDS. WASHINGTON, GEORGE.

546   Sanders, Scott Russell. *Warm as Wool*. Illus. by Helen Cogancherry. Bradbury, 1992. ISBN 0-02-778139-9

The Ward family spends a chilling first winter in their rough log cabin in the Ohio woods in 1803, and when spring comes resourceful mother Betsy buys eight shaggy sheep to shear so she can make clothes for her husband and three children. Based on original source material, the story traces the hardships endured by a pioneer family, which should get children thinking about how they acquire clothes and other things they so take for granted. If you have access to it, bring in wool and carders to show how yarn begins. At the least, hand out cotton balls and show how to twist them into a long yarnlike string. Elsa Beskow's *Pelle's New Suit* and Tomie dePaola's *Charlie Needs a Cloak* take us from sheep to shirt. Natalie Kinsey-Warnock's *Wilderness Cat*, Marion Russell's *Along the Santa Fe Trail*, Scott Russell Sanders's *Here Comes the Mystery Man*, and David Williams's *Grandma Essie's Covered Wagon* also embody the pioneer experience. CLOTHING AND DRESS. FAMILY LIFE. FRONTIER AND PIONEER LIFE. HISTORICAL FICTION. OHIO. PICTURE BOOKS FOR ALL AGES. SHEEP.

547   Say, Allen. *Tree of Cranes*. Illus. by the author. Houghton Mifflin, 1991. ISBN 0-395-52024-X

A young Japanese boy is bewildered by his mother's behavior one gray winter day when she digs up a small pine tree from the garden, brings it into the house, and decorates it with hand-folded paper cranes and candles. She describes the customs she recalls from her own childhood in California: "It is a day of love and peace. Enemies stop fighting. Strangers smile at one another. We need more days like it." Allen Say's elegant watercolors, serene and majestic, transport the reader to Japan, where Christmas is not often celebrated. Also read Say's biographical companion, *Grandfather's Journey*. With your students, look into how other countries celebrate the time of the winter solstice. CHRISTMAS. GIFTS. JAPAN. MOTHERS AND SONS.

548   Scieszka, Jon. *The Book That Jack Wrote*. Illus. by Daniel Adel. Viking, 1994. ISBN 0-670-84330-X

Written in the "House That Jack Built" style, this slyly absurd nursery rhyme parody starts off with a book falling on the fez-covered head of a smug, bespeckled Jack (. . . that squashed the Man, that stomped the bug, that tripped the Hatter . . .) and ends up showing the bizarre sequence of Jack's flattening. Each surreal illustration, from Humpty Dumpty to Simple Simon, is painted within a formal frame, and you'll need to examine the illustrations and puzzle out the sequence many times before it makes sense (sort of). Ask your students to note the nursery-rhyme characters they recognize, and to come up with some reasons why the book fell on Jack's head in the first place. Janet Stevens illustrated a pleasing version of the original nursery rhyme *The House that Jack Built*, which you'll need to introduce first. Henrik Drescher's *Simon's Book* is another strange story-within-a-story that will fit in just fine. BOOKS AND READING. CUMULATIVE STORIES. FAIRY TALES–SATIRE. NURSERY RHYMES. PARODIES. PICTURE BOOKS FOR ALL AGES.

549 **Seligson, Susan.** *Amos Camps Out: A Couch Adventure in the Woods.* **Illus. by Howie Schneider. Joy Street/ Little, Brown, 1992. ISBN 0-316-77402-2**

Amos, the floppy red dog we first met in *Amos: The Story of an Old Dog and His Couch*, who travels via zooming sofa, gets lost in the woods on his first camping trip with his owners. Readers will also want to catch up with *The Amazing Amos and the Greatest Couch on Earth* (1989) and *Amos Ahoy! A Couch Adventure on Land and Sea* (1990). Other dogs with extraordinary talents include those in Susan Meddaugh's *Martha Speaks*, Julia Lebentritt and Richard Ploetz's *The Kooken*, and Frances Ward Weller's *Riptide*. CAMPING. DOGS. FURNITURE. PICTURE BOOKS FOR ALL AGES.

550 **Shields, Carol Diggory.** *I Am Really a Princess.* **Illus. by Paul Meisel. Dutton, 1993. ISBN 0-525-45138-2**

A little girl vents that if her "true parents" the king and queen found out how she's expected to clean up around the house, share a room with a little sister, take piano lessons, only have sleep-overs on the weekends, and eat lima beans at dinner, they'd be horrified and allow her to do whatever she wanted. Max isn't satisfied with his lot either in *Trade-In Mother* by Marisabina Russo. For another comic personal rant-and-rave narrative, *Now Everybody Really Hates Me* by Jane Read Martin and Patricia Marx is a pip. FAMILY LIFE. PRINCES AND PRINCESSES.

551 **Shute, Linda.** *Halloween Party.* **Illus. by the author. Lothrop, 1994. ISBN 0-688-11715-5**

Disguised as a witch and Dracula, a woman and a boy attend a big, boisterous Halloween costume party and have a blast, but at midnight, when the masks come off, the two reveal themselves for what they really are: a witch and a vampire kid. Other marvelously spooky and rhythmical stories include Eve Bunting's *Scary, Scary Halloween*, Dian Curtis Regan's *The Thirteen Hours of Halloween*, Erica Silverman's *Big Pumpkin*, and Caroline Stutson's *By the Light of the Halloween Moon*. CHANTABLE REFRAIN. COSTUMES. HALLOWEEN. PARTIES. STORIES IN RHYME.

552 **Siebert, Diane.** *Plane Song.* **Illus. by Vincent Nasta. HarperCollins, 1993. ISBN 0-06-021467-8**

"Through the skyways/ touched by clouds/ over highways/ over crowds/ roaring/ soaring/ at full tilt/ go birds that human hands have built." Even the poetry is laid out in airplane shapes in this throat-catching, high-flying tribute to all types of airplanes. Siebert's *Train Song* and *Truck Song* are just as impressive, especially if you're working up a transportation unit. Meet two daring pilots in Don Brown's *Ruth Law Thrills a Nation*, Robert Burleigh's *Flight: The Journey of Charles Lindbergh*, Chris L. Demarest's *Lindbergh*, and Reeve Lindbergh's *View from the Air: Charles Lindbergh's Earth and Sky*. AIRPLANES–POETRY. FLIGHT. PICTURE BOOKS FOR ALL AGES. STORIES IN RHYME. TRANSPORTATION.

553   Siebert, Diane. *Train Song*. Illus. by Mike Wimmer. Crowell, 1990. ISBN 0-690-04728-2

A train love song that rattles along clickety-clack, this will spice up those transportation units and make a dandy choral reading. Wimmer's huge, close-up paintings are magnificent, as we become spectators watching the train roll through our dusty town. The illustrations in Donald Crews's *Freight Train* also give a great feel for the motion of a fast-moving train. Check out other ways to get around in Siebert's *Plane Song* and *Truck Song*. PICTURE BOOKS FOR ALL AGES. STORIES IN RHYME. TRAINS. TRANSPORTATION.

554   Singer, Marilyn. *Nine O'Clock Lullaby*. Illus. by Frané Lessac. HarperCollins, 1991. ISBN 0-06-025648-6

At the same time you're hearing a bedtime story at 9:00 P.M. in Brooklyn, New York, it's 10:00 P.M. in Puerto Rico, 5:00 A.M. in Moscow, 10:00 A.M. in Guangzhou, China, and 6:00 P.M. on the beach in Los Angeles. Each double-page spread of cheerful, detailed folk-art paintings shows what's going on somewhere else in the world as we travel the time zones. Use the globe as you read this. To develop time sense, also read the poems in Lee Bennett Hopkins's *It's About Time*, and *Is Anybody Up?* and *Under the Sun* by Ellen Kandoian, which explore morning and night around the world. Visit other places worldwide with *This Is the Way We Go to School* by Edith Baer, *Amelia's Fantastic Flight* by Rose Bursik, *Away from Home* by Anita Lobel, *How to Make an Apple Pie and See the World* by Marjorie Priceman, *Uncle Lester's Hat* by Howie Schneider, and *Love, Your Bear Pete* by Dyan Sheldon. GEOGRAPHY. MULTICULTURAL STORIES. TIME. TIME ZONES.

555   Slavin, Bill. *The Cat Came Back*. Illus. by the author. Albert Whitman, 1992. ISBN 0-8075-1097-1

If you never heard the song about old Mr. Johnson's yellow cat who wouldn't stay away, turn to the music on the last page of this picture-book version, and start singing. I learned this song (with many additional verses) at Camp Dark Waters in Medford, N.J., when I was eight and never forgot its wonderfully wicked words. Slavin softens the impact with comical watercolors, and by leaving out the more grisly verses, but dollars to doughnuts your kids will know them by heart. If not, commission them to write new ones. Mary Calhoun's *Cross-Country Cat*, Dav Pilkey's *When Cats Dream* and *Kat Kong*, Jack Gantos's *Rotten Ralph*, and Daniel Pinkwater's *The Wuggie Norple Story* all contain cats who don't quit. CATS. SONGS. STORIES IN RHYME.

556   Stanley, Diane. *Moe the Dog in Tropical Paradise*. Illus. by Elise Primavera. Putnam, 1992. ISBN 0-399-22127-1

It's freezing outside, and Moe the dog, who works in the Brown Cow ice cream factory, and his best friend Arlene are miserable. They can't afford a trip to Tahiti, so he acts on a wonderful idea for a warm and sunny vacation at home. See if your listeners can figure out what he's up to. Read this in the dead of winter and have everyone bring in at least one beach item so you can set up a corner of tropical paradise in school. Watch how other animals cope with the cold in

Cross-Country Cat by Mary Calhoun and *The Five-Dog Night* by Eileen Christelow. DOGS. VACATIONS. WINTER.

557   Stevenson, James. *The Mud Flat Olympics.* Illus. by the author. Greenwillow, 1994. ISBN 0-688-12924-2

Possum Burbank carries the torch to begin the games, which consist of the Deepest Hole Contest, the All-Snail High Hurdle event, the Smelliest Skunk Contest, and the River-Cross Freestyle. Five droll chapters, filled with small but choice watercolors and a priceless assortment of names, will get you started on a class version of the Olympics. (Sharpest Pencil or Neatest Desk contests? Wastebasket Toss? Brainstorm your categories.) Stevenson's dialogue, always so low-key funny, makes a great model for student writing, and these chapters are prime for adapting as Reader's Theater. ANIMALS. COMPETITION. GAMES. OLYMPIC GAMES. READER'S THEATER.

558   Stevenson, James. *That's Exactly the Way It Wasn't.* Illus. by the author. Greenwillow, 1991. ISBN 0-688-09869-X

Louis and Mary Ann's inability to agree on anything reminds Grandpa and his brother Uncle Wainey of the day their parents sent them outside, instructing them not to return until they agreed on something. As in all Grandpa stories, the two had a wild adventure, involving a purple armadillo, a fall from a cliff into an armadillo's mouth, and a giant cherry pie about to explode, but each of them now recalls the events quite differently. Save this one for a day when no one seems able to get along without contradicting each other, and for discussing varying points of view. ARGUMENTS. BROTHERS. GRANDFATHERS. POINT OF VIEW. TALL TALES.

559   Stevenson, James. *The Worst Person's Christmas.* Illus. by the author. Greenwillow, 1991. ISBN 0-688-10211-5

Next-door neighbors young Walker and Jenny decide to give Mr. Worst, a crotchety old man who takes great pleasure in his miserly ways, a fruitcake for Christmas, which sets off a chain of events that mellows him just a bit. He gets his comeuppance in *Worse Than the Worst* when great-nephew Warren comes for a visit. Contrast the Worst's experience with that of the grumpy old woman who celebrates her first real Christmas thanks to the ragged Ugly Child who appears on her doorstep in Louise Moeri's *Star Mother's Youngest Child.* Joan Lowery Nixon's *That's the Spirit, Claude* will get everyone cheering for Sandy Claus as he makes his first visit to Texas way back when. CHRISTMAS. ELDERLY.

560   Stevenson, James. *Worse Than the Worst.* Illus. by the author. Greenwillow, 1994. ISBN 0-688-12250-7

Mr. Worst, a crotchety gentleman who gets his jollies from seeing others miserable, meets his match when his rotten young great-nephew Warren drops by to spend the night, bringing along his huge Great Dane, Arnold. Get into the spirit of Scrooge unreformed in *The Worst Person's Christmas.* Barbara Dugan's *Loop the*

Loop and Jack Ziegler's *Mr. Knocky* both feature seniors with personality. BEHAVIOR. DOGS. ELDERLY. UNCLES.

561   Stutson, Caroline. *By the Light of the Halloween Moon.* Illus. by Kevin Hawkes. Lothrop, 1993. ISBN 0-688-12046-6

A girl "smacks the sprite who bites the ghost who trips the ghoul who swats at the bat . . ." as she taps a tune with her gleaming toe "by the light, by the light, by the silvery light of the Halloween moon!" What a night of shenanigans, all told to an eerie rhythm with a satisfyingly creepy chantable refrain and spooky illustrations. Spread the mystery with Emily Herman's *Hubknuckles*, James Howe's *Scared Silly*, Bill Martin, Jr.'s *Old Devil Wind*, Dian Curtis Regan's *The Thirteen Hours of Halloween*, Linda Shute's *Halloween Party*, Erica Silverman's *Big Pumpkin*, and Linda Williams's *The Little Old Lady Who Was Not Afraid of Anything*. CHANTABLE REFRAIN. CUMULATIVE STORIES. HALLOWEEN.

562   Sun, Chying Feng. *Mama Bear.* Illus. by Lolly Robinson. Houghton Mifflin, 1994. ISBN 0-395-63412-1

To save enough money to buy "the softest warmest bear in the whole world," Mei-Mei helps out at the Chinese restaurant where her mother works, earning almond cookies for her labor, which she then sells to customers, but on Christmas Eve, she must accept that there is not enough money to buy the coveted stuffed animal. In *A Chair for My Mother* by Vera B. Williams, Rosa reaches her goal. Compare the two stories and discuss how children handle their own disappointments. CHINESE AMERICANS. CHRISTMAS. MONEY. RESTAURANTS. SINGLE-PARENT FAMILIES. TEDDY BEARS.

563   Teague, Mark. *Moog-Moog, Space Barber.* Illus. by the author. Scholastic, 1990. ISBN 0-590-43332-6

Luckily for Elmo Freem, who receives an awful haircut the day before school is to start, he finds space monsters drinking milk from the carton in his kitchen and they graciously arrange to take him and his cat Elmo to the planet Moogie for an appointment with the Great Moog. Unfortunately, even that best barber can't undo Elmo's fiasco haircut, but when he returns home, he finds his best friend has the same problem. Elmo has book report problems in *Frog Medicine*. Write new Elmo Freem stories about problems he might encounter that vex your kids too, and the fantastic ways he would solve them. HAIR. HUMOROUS FICTION. SPACE FLIGHT.

564   Teague, Mark. *Pigsty.* Illus. by the author. Scholastic, 1994. ISBN 0-590-45915-5

His mother declares his room a pigsty, and much to Wendell's surprise he finds one pig on his bed on Monday, and more each subsequent day, until the mess gets to him and he organizes the pigs into a cleaning crew. More messes are made in *Pigs* by Robert Munsch, and straightened up in *Pigs Aplenty, Pigs Galore* by David McPhail and *When the Fly Flew In* by Lisa Westberg Peters. Three vampires are frightfully untidy at Jonathan Harker's house one night in Daniel Pinkwater's *Wempires*. CLEANLINESS. PIGS.

565   Tews, Susan. *The Gingerbread Doll*. Illus. by Megan Lloyd. Clarion, 1993. ISBN 0-395-56438-7

In 1930, during the Great Depression, when Great Grandma Rebecca was nine, her large farm family was so poor that instead of the porcelain doll she wanted for Christmas, she received one her mother made from gingerbread, Button Marie, as she named her, became her best-loved doll. *The Chalk Doll* by Charlotte Pomerantz is another family story about a girl whose Jamaican mother loved her homemade rag doll as a child, while in *An Ellis Island Christmas* by Maxine Rhea Leighton, Krysia must leave her doll behind when her family emigrates from Poland. See how people triumph over hard times in *The Rag Coat* by Lauren Mills and *Uncle Jed's Barbershop* by Margaree King Mitchell. Harve Zemach's *Mommy, Buy Me a China Doll*, an Appalachian folk song, is a fitting sing-along. CHRISTMAS. DOLLS. FAMILY STORIES. FARM LIFE. HISTORICAL FICTION. WISCONSIN.

566   Thomas, Patricia. *The One and Only Super-Duper Golly-Whopper Jim-Dandy Really-Handy Clock-Tock-Stopper*. Illus. by John O'Brien. Lothrop, 1990. ISBN 0-688-09341-8

In an entertaining ramble of a narrative poem, a fast-talking rabbit salesman unloads a number of indispensable and outrageous Rube Goldberg-like clock-related gadgets to a grouchy porcupine who can't stand the constant tick-tocking of his clock. Listeners can echo the escalating noises for each new clock addition. With a similar theme, Joanna Cole's *It's Too Noisy*, Julia Donaldson's *A Squash and a Squeeze*, Marilyn Hirsch's *Could Anything Be Worse?* (Holiday House, 1974), Ann McGovern's *Too Much Noise*, and Margot Zemach's *It Could Always Be Worse* are all variants of a traditional folktale about how to make a crowded house seem positively spacious. CLOCKS. NOISE. PORCUPINES. RABBITS. SOUND EFFECTS. STORIES IN RHYME.

567   Tompert, Ann. *Grandfather Tang's Story*. Illus. by Robert Andrew Parker. Crown, 1990. ISBN 0-517-57272-9

Using tangrams to show each character, Grandfather Tang tells his granddaughter Little Soo a story about the fox fairies, best friends Chou and Wu Ling, who transform themselves into many different animals and almost lose their friendship trying to outdo each other. Along with each illustration, there is a black tangram diagram showing how to arrange the seven pieces into each animal. Ideally, you could make up a small poster or flannelboard to display each tangram animal as you read the story, and then hand sets of seven tangrams to pairs of students who could experiment making new shapes from component parts. Your math supplies kits left out the tangrams? Make sets out of squares of construction paper or oak tag according to the diagram on the last page. FOXES. GEOMETRY. GRANDFATHERS. SHAPES. STORYTELLING. TRANSFORMATIONS.

568   Tusa, Tricia. *The Family Reunion*. Illus. by the author. Farrar, 1993. ISBN 0-374-32268-6

Unlike Cynthia Rylant's *The Relatives Came*, this wild reunion of the extended Beneada family incorporates an unfamiliar couple, Esther and Fester, who, the others ascertain, aren't circus performers, Dinky Donut TV commercial actors, belly-button doctors, or even escapees from the state pen. Note how the relatives treat the visiting aliens in Arthur Yorinks's *Company's Coming*. FAMILY LIFE. HUMOROUS FICTION. PARTIES.

569   Tzannes, Robin. *Professor Puffendorf's Secret Potions*. Illus. by Paul Korky. Checkerboard Press, 1992. ISBN 1-56288-267-8

Angry that the professor is rich and famous while he does "all the work," lazy, grumbling assistant Slag delves into the scientist's top-secret cabinet and, before stealing them, tests out the new potions he finds there on hapless guinea pig Chip. In an upbeat ending reminiscent of Chris Van Allsburg's gloomier *The Sweetest Fig*, when Chip tests the "Best Wish" potion, it works, and when the professor returns, she finds her now-giant guinea pig sweeping the lab floor, while a tiny Slag is running around the wheel in the rodent's cage. Children can think up new possible potions and record their consequences. Inventors with promise try out new discoveries in Eileen Christelow's *Mr. Murphy's Marvelous Invention*, Michael Crowley's *New Kid on Spurwink Ave.*, John Frank's *Odds 'N' Ends Alvy*, and Dick Gackenbach's *Dog for a Day*. GUINEA PIGS. INVENTORS. PICTURE BOOKS FOR ALL AGES. SCIENTISTS. TRANSFORMATIONS. WISHES.

570   Vozar, David. *Yo, Hungry Wolf! A Nursery Rap*. Illus. by Betsy Lewin. Doubleday, 1993. ISBN 0-395-30452-8

A send-up of three tales—"The Three Little Pigs," "Little Red Riding Hood," and Aesop's "The Boy Who Cried Wolf"—these wisecracking renditions are told in rap, leaving the wolf unharmed and unrepentant, pondering his next day's meals and moves. From traditional versions of the pig tale by Lorinda Bryan Cauley, Paul Galdone, James Marshall, Glen Rounds, and Margot Zemach, to variants like William H. Hooks's *The Three Little Pigs and the Fox*, other parodies like Jon Scieszka's *The True Story of the 3 Little Pigs*, and turnabouts like Eugene Trivizas's *The Three Little Wolves and the Big Bad Pig*, this is a story that won't quit. Along with Jacob Grimm's traditional folktale and James Marshall's droll *Red Riding Hood*, Vozar's "Little Red Rappinghood" and Michael Emberley's *Ruby* also go well together. FAIRY TALES–SATIRE. PARODIES. PIGS. STORIES IN RHYME. WOLVES.

571   Wegman, William. *ABC*. Illus. by the author. Little, Brown, 1994. ISBN 1-56282-699-9

This is one you either love or hate, and children find partly hilarious and adorable, and partly odd. Wegman, whose color photos of his weimeraners in often humanlike poses have brought him instant recognition, has assembled a dog-filled alphabet. For each letter, there's a color photo of Batty or Chundo or Fay in an arresting pose—as an elephant, dressed as a queen, or balancing a boat—and on the facing page is the alphabet letter itself, comprised of the dogs photographed lying in formation. It's strange but endearing, and is a refreshingly strange change from the run-of-the-mill alphabet book. Given the availability of cameras, each child can take a photo of his or her pet or stuffed animal interacting with an object representing a given alphabet letter. ALPHABET BOOKS. DOGS. PICTURE BOOKS FOR ALL AGES.

572   **Wells, Rosemary.** *Lucy Comes to Stay.* **Illus. by Mark Graham. Dial, 1994. ISBN 0-8037-1214-6**

In a gentle picture book broken into short chapter vignettes, Mary Elizabeth describes bringing home her new white puppy Lucy and, over the next six months, her attempts to train her. Children can recall what they know about the dog's and the girl's personalities, and incorporate what they've deduced about characterization into their own chapters about pets or animals they have known. Robert J. Blake's *Dog*, Pija Lindenbaum's *Boodil My Dog*, and Frances Ward Weller's *Riptide* are also intriguing character studies of real dogs. DOGS.

573   **Wells, Rosemary.** *Max and Ruby's First Greek Myth: Pandora's Box.* **Illus. by the author. Dial, 1993. ISBN 0-8037-1525-0**

Trying to keep dim brother Max out of her room, Ruby nails up a sign, but Max can't read, and catching him lurking around her jewelry box, she reads him a story about sneaking and peeking. The version of "Pandora's Box" she reads is a very funny bunny-based diversion with only the slightest resemblance to the somber tale you've heard, and, of course, as in *Max's Chocolate Chicken* and *Max's Christmas*, rabbit Max doesn't quite learn his lesson. My only concern is that younger children won't understand what's being parodied, so first tell them about the original myth. Older children versed in mythology find Ruby's retelling hilarious. Have them rewrite other famous myths, Ruby-style. Meet another Ruby, the street-smart mouse in *Ruby*, a Red Riding Hood send-up by Michael Emberley, and also try *Princess*, Ann Wilsdorf's skewed version of "The Princess and the Pea." BROTHERS AND SISTERS. CURIOSITY. MYTHOLOGY. OBEDIENCE. PARODIES. PICTURE BOOKS FOR ALL AGES. RABBITS.

574   **Wiesner, David.** *Hurricane.* **Illus. by the author. Clarion, 1990. ISBN 0-395-54382-7**

Brothers David and George are thrilled when, after the big hurricane, they discover one of their yard's two elm trees has toppled over, giving them a perfect place to pretend they're sailing the seven seas, stalking in the jungle, and lost in space. After hearing this read aloud to his first-grade class, one boy said solemnly, "This book really reminds me of another book I like—*Where the Wild Things Are*—where Max's room turns into a jungle." You'll love the last page where you get a window on the boys' black-and-white cat's imagination. Look for other "mind's eye" books like Michael Crowley's *New Kid on Spurwink Ave.*, Matt Faulkner's *The Amazing Voyage of Jackie Grace*, Nicholas Heller's *An Adventure at Sea*, Ezra Jack Keats's *Regards to the Man in the Moon*, and Alice McLerran's *Roxaboxen*, where kids really know how to play. BROTHERS. HURRICANES. IMAGINATION. PLAY. WEATHER.

575   **Williams, Barbara.** *The Author and Squinty Gritt.* **Illus. by Betsy James. Dutton, 1990. ISBN 0-525-44655-9**

[10 chapters, 67p.] Famous children's book author Helena Wright is visiting Squinty's school, and the second-grader decides to enter the school contest for best poster to win the author's special prize, which he figures could be a drive to her mansion in her red sports car. If your school has invited a children's book author or illustrator to speak, read this as preparation for his or her visit, along with Daniel Pinkwater's off-the-wall *Author's Day*. Also see Joan Lowery Nixon's *If You Were a Writer*. AUTHORS. AUTOMOBILES. BOOKS AND READING. SCHOOLS.

576   **Williams, Karen Lynn.** *Tap-Tap.* **Illus. by Catherine Stock. Clarion, 1994. ISBN 0-395-65617-6**

Every market day, Sasifi and her mama carry their baskets of oranges on their heads and walk all the way to the big road, and to the Haitian market where they sell their wares. On one special day, Sasifi decides to spend her few coins on a special treat—a ride home from market in the tap-tap, a brightly colored truck that takes riders back to their village. Phillis Gershator's *Rata-Pata-Scata-Fata: A Caribbean Story*, Holly Keller's *Island Baby* and Rita Phillips Mitchell's *Hue Boy* are also set on Caribbean islands, and all blend so well with the buoyant poems in John Agard and Grace Nichols's poetry collection *A Caribbean Dozen*. HAITI. HATS. MARKETS. MOTHERS AND DAUGHTERS. MULTICULTURAL STORIES. TRUCKS.

577   **Wilsdorf, Anne.** *Princess.* **Illus. by the author. Greenwillow, 1993. ISBN 0-688-11542-X**

Even though he has no trouble vanquishing the evil monsters that guard them, none of the self-absorbed certified genuine princesses Prince Leopold meets are his cup of tea until he meets Princess, a charming shepherd girl whose tumble off the obligatory mattresses produce bruises that convince the queen of her authenticity. Be sure your listeners know the original Hans Christian Andersen "The Princess and the Pea," and continue the parodies with Tony Johnston's *The Cowboy and the Black-Eyed Pea* and "The Princess and the Bowling Ball" from Jon Scieszka's *The Stinky Cheese Man*. Another reworking of a well-loved Andersen tale is *The Principal's New Clothes* by Stephanie Calmenson. FAIRY TALES–SATIRE. LOVE. PARODIES. PRINCES AND PRINCESSES.

578   **Wise, William.** *Ten Sly Piranhas: A Counting Story in Reverse (A Tale of Wickedness and Worse).* **Illus. by Victoria Chess. Dial, 1993. ISBN 0-8037-1201-4**

One by one, the sly, hungry, cannibalistic fish eat each other in a rhyming subtraction story teeming with rain forest creatures. I like to read or sing this one with an English Music Hall kind of flair. Have students make up piranha subtraction word problems. Since most have no idea what this toothsome little fish looks like, have them do a bit of library research to find out a few gruesome details. Another story for counting back is the cow-filled *Moon Jump: A Cowntdown* by Paula Brown. COUNTING BOOKS. FISHES. STORIES IN RHYME. SUBTRACTION.

579   **Wojciechowski, Susan.** *The Best Halloween of All.* **Illus. by Susan Meddaugh. Crown, 1992. ISBN 0-517-57835-2**

A seven-year-old boy describes everything he's ever been for Halloween, from a clown at age one to a bunch of grapes last year, with each costume painstakingly constructed and sewn by his doting parents, but this year he plans on making his costume himself. Ask students to bring in paper bags and other found items and make your own costumes for a pre-Halloween celebration. For an out-of-this-world get-up, read Edward Marshall's *Space Case*. COSTUMES. HALLOWEEN.

580   Woodruff, Elvira. *The Wing Shop*. Illus. by Stephen Gammell. Holiday House, 1991. ISBN 0-8234-0825-6

Not happy with his family's move to a new house, Matthew stumbles upon Featherman's Wing Shop where Lucy, who's watching the store for her grandfather, sends him on a test flight with seagull, bat, and old-timey airplane wings, so he can fly back to his old neighborhood. Once overhead, the boy sees his old house, repainted and with new kids there, and settles for his new house after all. Elizabeth Lee O'Donnell's *Maggie Doesn't Want to Move* is another look at the trauma of relocating. Children find the notion of flying irresistible, as in *Abuela* by Arthur Dorros and in Woodruff's *Show and Tell*, where Andy's magic bubbles shrink his classmates who then zoom above town. Have everyone look at books of birds and other flying creatures, decide what kind of wings they'd want and where they'd go, and draw themselves in flight. FANTASY. FLIGHT. MOVING, HOUSEHOLD. WINGS.

581   Yorinks, Arthur. *Whitefish Will Rides Again!* Illus. by Mort Drucker. HarperCollins, 1994. ISBN 0-06-205037-0

The "best danged sheriff that ever lived" comes back from retirement to rout Bad Bart and his gang of horse thieves, which he does with the help of his trusty harmonica. For older kids, this outrageously silly tale will teach them a thing or two about irony. Add some extra dialogue and sound effects and act out the whole book with improvised dialogue or write up a Reader's Theater version with parts for all. Get a feel for the great outdoors with Alan Axelrod's *Songs of the Wild West* and *Cowboys*, a collection of poems compiled by Charles Sullivan. Roy Gerard's *Rosie and the Rustlers*, Jo Harper's *Jalapeño Hal*, Tony Johnston's *The Cowboy and the Black-Eyed Pea*, Eric A. Kimmel's *Charlie Drives the Stage*, Angela Shelf Medearis's adaption of the folksong *The Zebra-Riding Cowboy*, and Glen Rounds's *Mr. Yowder and the Train Robbers* are all grand choices. BEHAVIOR. HARMONICA. HUMOROUS FICTION. PICTURE BOOKS FOR ALL AGES. ROBBERS AND OUTLAWS. SHERIFFS. WEST.

582   Ziegler, Jack. *Mr. Knocky*. Illus. by the author. Macmillan, 1993. ISBN 0-02-793725-9

When all the kids in town head out to Deep Dene, their favorite place to play, their only drawback is having to put up with the wild, nonsensical tales spun by nearby resident old Mr. Knocky. One child accidentally knocks him out with a snowball, and all are panicked until he comes to, still telling tall tales that the kids now listen to with real pleasure. Your kids can flesh out the stories he tells about moondogs, banana meatballs, talking sailboats, and other delicious nonsense. Meet another irrepressible soul in *Loop the Loop* by Barbara Dugan, and an unrepentant grouch in James Stevenson's *Worse Than the Worst*. ELDERLY. INDIVIDU-ALITY. SNOW. STORYTELLING.

583 **Zimelman, Nathan.** *How the Second Grade Got $8,205.50 to Visit the Statue of Liberty.* **Illus. by Bill Slavin. Albert Whitman, 1992. ISBN 0-8075-3431-5**

In this hilariously understated official "Report on the drive to collect funds . . ." second-grade treasurer and reporter Susan Olson lists their expenses, profits, and experiences undertaking a paper drive, lemonade stand, baby-sitting, dog walk-ing, candy sales, and car wash, all of which net a total of $5.50. However, catch-ing the bank robbers brings them a reward of $8,200. Oh, the marvelous math possibilities here! Kids can try their own fund-raising venture, or write a sequel about the class's NYC adventure and how they spent their dough. Kathy Jakobsen's *My New York* will show the sights. In *Lily and Miss Liberty* by Carla Stevens, Lily finds a way to raise money for the new statue in 1885. Betsy Maestro's *The Story of the Statue of Liberty* will be invaluable, too. Find money around the house in Amy Axelrod's *Pigs Will Be Pigs*, and watch it disappear in Judith Viorst's *Alexander Who Used to Be Rich Last Sunday*. MONEY. MONUMENTS. NEW YORK CITY. ROBBERS AND OUTLAWS. SCHOOLS. STATUE OF LIBERTY. WORK.

FICTION FOR GRADES 2–3

584   Allen, Judy. *Panda*. Illus. by Tudor Humphries. Candlewick, 1993. ISBN 1-56402-142-4

On a botanical expedition in western China, 12-year-old Jake is left behind at the campsite when his father and Professor Beall leave to look for orchids, and a panda visits their tent. Upon returning, neither man believes Jake's remarkable story until the panda comes back. A panda fact sheet at the back of the book explains why they are endangered, and students can locate more information in the library about pandas and other endangered animals. CHINA. ENDANGERED SPECIES. PANDAS.

585   Allen, Judy. *Tiger*. Illus. by Tudor Humphries. Candlewick, 1992. ISBN 1-56402-083-5

Most people believe the rumor about the dangerous tiger out beyond the rice fields, and a great hunter arrives in the village to shoot it. Vivid watercolors of the powerful beast in the wild are thrilling, and it will be interesting to note how many of your listeners guess the hunter is shooting with a camera and not a gun. End notes give information on how to help save endangered tigers. ENDANGERED SPECIES. PHOTOGRAPHY. TIGERS.

586   Andersen, Hans Christian. *The Steadfast Tin Soldier*. Retold by Tor Seidler. Illus. by Fred Marcellino. HarperCollins, 1992. ISBN 0-06-205000-1

If you need a sturdy retelling of Andersen's classic unrequited love story of a one-legged tin toy soldier who suffers stoically for a paper ballerina, this one's tremendously appealing, set at Christmastime with a "Nutcracker" feel to it. First published in 1838, the story is on the maudlin side, with the two destined for each other ending up in the fireplace flames, but it still appeals, especially with Marcellino's sensational illustrations. CHRISTMAS. LITERARY FAIRY TALES. LOVE. PICTURE BOOKS FOR ALL AGES. SOLDIERS. TOYS.

587   Andersen, Janet S. *The Key into Winter*. Illus. by David Soman. Albert Whitman, 1994. ISBN 0-8075-4170-2

Sitting before the hearth where the four keys to the seasons are hung, Clara's mother tells her the story of how, when she was a child, she hid the key into winter to prevent winter from coming and her beloved grandmother from dying. The theme of delaying a grandparent's death will remind you of *Annie and the Old One* by Miska Miles. This is an interesting mythlike story depicting three generations of African American women who control the seasons. As children study the illustration of the four keys, have them identify which one is which and why. *Peboan and Seegwun* by Larry Charles and *Yonder* by Tony Johnston show the seasons as a cycle, while Kris Waldherr's *Persephone and the Pomegranate* and Chris Van Allsburg's *The Stranger* show the consequences of disrupting that cycle. As background, play a recording of Vivaldi's *The Four Seasons* and try to identify the mood of each. AFRICAN AMERICANS. DEATH. GRANDMOTHERS. SEASONS.

588   Armstrong, Jennifer. *Chin Yu Min and the Ginger Cat.* Illus. by Mary Grandpré. Crown, 1993. ISBN 0-517-58657-6

After her prosperous husband dies, proud and haughty Chin Yu Min becomes poor until she encounters a talking cat who becomes her companion, catching fish for her with his tail. The day she gives away an old basket to a beggar, the cat disappears, too. Faced with the loss of the only affection she has known, she gives away all her money in the hopes of getting him back, and learns a valuable lesson about humility and love. Questions to consider: Why did she give away all her money to get her cat back? How did she change at the end of the story? Do you think she'll go back to the way she acted before? Prove that money isn't everything with Jay Williams's *One Big Wish,* about a farmer who wishes for and gets a million dollars. CATS. CHINA. LOVE. MONEY. PICTURE BOOKS FOR ALL AGES. PRIDE AND VANITY. WEALTH.

589   Bahr, Mary. *The Memory Box.* Illus. by David Cunningham. Albert Whitman, 1992. ISBN 0-8075-5052-3

Zach describes how he and Gramps fill an old box with special photos, souvenirs, medals, and written memories to recall their life together after Gramps is diagnosed with Alzheimer's and wants to preserve the memories he still has. *Loop the Loop* by Barbara Dugan is another touching story about a young girl's special friendship with a peppery old woman. ALZHEIMER'S DISEASE. FAMILY STORIES. GRANDFATHERS. GRANDPARENTS. MEMORY.

590   Barber, Antonia. *Catkin.* Illus. by P. J. Lynch. Candlewick, 1994. ISBN 1-56402-485-7

A cat so small he can fit in the palm of a man's hand, Catkin is given the job of looking after Carrie, a human baby, who is carried off by the Little People when Catkin is distracted. Meticulous realistic watercolor paintings transport us to their enchanted land under the green hill where Catkin must answer three riddles before the Lord and Lady there will allow the child to go free. In both *The Changeling* by Selma Langerlöf and *A Ride on the Red Mare's Back* by Ursula K. LeGuin, children are taken from their parents by trolls. Jenny Nimmo's Scottish folktale *The Witches and the Singing Mice* features two cats who must undo the spell cast on two village children, while *Wild Robin* by Susan Jeffers, *The Giant's Apprentice* by Margaret Wetterer, and *The Ghost Fox* by Laurence Yep all involve the undoing of an enchantment. BABIES. CATS. FAIRIES. LITERARY FAIRY TALES. RIDDLES.

591   Blake, Robert J. *Dog.* Illus. by the author. Philomel, 1994. ISBN 0-399-22019-4

Crusty old Peter lives alone in a leaky cottage in the Irish countryside. After he turns away a stray dog during a storm, he can't stop worrying until he finds it safe. Told entirely in Peter's rambling monologue, peppered with a bit of brogue, this is a first-rate character study with an affectionate happy ending as man and dog connect. *Loop the Loop* by Barbara Dugan offers another unsentimental look at old age. Don't miss Frances Ward Weller's dog story *Riptide,* also illustrated with Blake's magnificent sweeping paintings. DOGS. ELDERLY. IRELAND.

592   Bunting, Eve. *A Day's Work.* Illus. by Ronald Himler. Clarion, 1994. ISBN 0-395-67321-6

Waiting with his grandfather in the parking lot hoping to be hired for day work, enterprising young Francisco talks his way into a job pulling weeds, though his Spanish-speaking abuelo, newly arrived from Mexico only days before, tells him he knows nothing about gardening. After they find they have pulled all the plants and left the chickweed, Abuelo insists on working a day for free to undo their mistakes. Francisco learns the hard way about the importance of honesty. Bunting has a brilliant knack of unearthing social issues that matter and making them understandable and compelling to children, as she did in *Fly Away Home,* about a homeless boy and his father who live in an airport, *Smoky Night,* about a boy affected by the Los Angeles riots of 1992, *The Wall,* about the Vietnam Memorial in Washington, D.C., and *The Wednesday Surprise,* about a girl who teaches her grandmother to read. GRANDFATHERS. HONESTY. MEXICAN AMERICANS. RESPONSIBILITY. WORK.

593   Bunting, Eve. *Smoky Night.* Illus. by David Diaz. Harcourt, 1994. ISBN 0-15-269954-6

As Daniel and his mother look out from their apartment at the rioting crowds below, she explains, "It can happen when people get angry. They want to smash and destroy. They don't care anymore what's right and what's wrong." When their building is set afire, there's not enough time to locate David's cat Jasmine, and Daniel and his mother run to a shelter, along with neighbor Mrs. Kim who owns the now-looted market and whose cat is also missing. A firefighter brings in the two bedraggled cats, and we see how it is possible for people to forget their differences and coexist. Dramatic paintings are superimposed over found-item collages, which viewers will want to analyze. Once again, Bunting takes a difficult subject and encourages children to think deeply about it. Interesting follow-ups would be *Chicken Sunday* or *Tikvah Means Hope* by Patricia Polacco. AFRICAN AMERICANS. CALDECOTT MEDAL. KOREAN AMERICANS. MULTICULTURAL STORIES. PICTURE BOOKS FOR ALL AGES. PREJUDICE. RIOTS.

594   Bunting, Eve. *Summer Wheels.* Illus. by Thomas Allen. Harcourt, 1992. ISBN 0-15-207000-1

[6 chapters, unp.] The Bicycle Man fixes old bikes and lends them for the day to neighborhood kids, even to a boy who signs his out under the name "Abrehem Lincoln" and doesn't plan to bring it back. Best friends Lawrence and Brady don't understand why the old man later allows the boy to take out another bike, especially when he trashes it and the rule is, if it breaks while you have it, you must work with the Bicycle Man to fix it. Ask your listeners if they can explain the boy's actions. BICYCLES. FRIENDSHIP. MULTICULTURAL STORIES. RESPONSIBILITY. STEALING.

595   Byars, Betsy. *The Seven Treasure Hunts.* Illus. by Jennifer Barrett. HarperCollins, 1991. ISBN 0-06-020886-4

[7 chapters, 74p.] One Saturday, best friends Jackson and Goat try to outwit each other with a series of treasure maps and clues to decipher, each resulting in the discovery of a bit of hidden treasure, but one prize, a chocolate popsicle, gets them in trouble. Each of your detectives can hide a small object in the classroom and make a map of its whereabouts or create a secret code so another student can figure it out and locate the prize. BROTHERS AND SISTERS. BURIED TREASURE. FRIEND-SHIP.

596   Carryl, Charles E. *The Walloping Window-Blind.* Illus. by Ted Rand. Little, Brown, 1992. ISBN 1-55970-154-4

That "capital ship for an ocean trip," filled with eccentric sailors, sails to the Gulliby Isles where the crew encounters the Tickleteaser, whistling bees, and Binnacle-bats in waterproof hats before appropriating a Chinese junk and putting to sea once more. Music for this adventurous 1885 narrative nonsense poem is on the last page. A choral reading of this would be loads of fun, once children's tongues became untwisted. *The Owl and the Pussycat* by Edward Lear, Janet Stevens's picture-book version of Lear's *The Quangle Wangle's Hat*, and *The Adventures of Isabel* by Ogden Nash are also wonderful fun. NARRATIVE POETRY. NONSENSE VERSES. POETRY–SAILING. STORIES IN RHYME.

597   Christiansen, Candace. *The Ice Horse.* Illus. by Thomas Locker. Dial, 1993. ISBN 0-8037-1401-7

[1 sitting] In the days before refrigerators, 12-year-old Jack relates how men harvested ice from the frozen river with teams of horses and stored the blocks in the icehouse to sell in New York City when the warm weather came. Locker's beautiful paintings make us feel the cold, and an episode where Jack's horse Max falls through the ice provides tension in an otherwise descriptive story. *Waiting for the Evening Star* by Rosemary Wells is a breathtaking picture book that takes place in the Vermont countryside on the eve of World War I. See what city life was like back then with *Peppe the Lamplighter* by Elisa Bartone, and *The Potato Man* and *The Great Pumpkin Switch* by Megan McDonald. HISTORICAL FICTION. HORSES. NEW YORK (STATE). WINTER.

598   Cohen, Barbara. *Make a Wish, Molly.* Illus. by Jan Naimo Jones. Doubleday, 1994. ISBN 0-385-31079-X

[1 sitting, 40p.] Third-grader Molly, a Russian Jewish immigrant to the United States, confronts prejudice and ignorance when she is invited to her friend Emma's birthday party during Passover and declines to eat any cake. A companion story to *Molly's Pilgrim*, in this one her rival, the ever-nasty Elizabeth, repeats her mother's assertion that Jews won't eat in Christian houses, and that if a Christian eats in a Jew's house, the Jew throws the plates and silverware in the garbage. Molly's mother defuses Elizabeth's prejudice, which should churn up some interesting class discussions about the damage misconceptions can do. Another effective story is Eleanor Estes's *The Hundred Dresses*. BIRTHDAYS. HOLIDAYS. JEWS. MOTHERS AND DAUGHTERS. RUSSIAN AMERICANS.

599   Cohen, Ron. *My Dad's Baseball.* Illus. by the author. Lothrop, 1994. ISBN 0-688-12391-0

When Max's dad finds an old baseball in the attic, he tells the story of attending his first professional baseball game in 1955 and catching a ball hit into the stands by New York Yankee Yogi Berra. For those who have never attended a baseball game, William Jaspersohn's *The Ballpark: One Day Behind the Scenes at a Major League Game* should fill in some details. *Extra Innings: Baseball Poems*, compiled by Lee Bennett Hopkins, and *At the Crack of the Bat: Baseball Poems*, compiled by Lillian Morrison, plus the picture book of Ernest Lawrence Thayer's classic narrative poem "Casey at the Bat" will also be welcome, as will Marilyn Sachs's mythic tale of two fictional father-and-daughter superstars in *Matt's Mitt and Fleet-Footed Florence*. Warm up by singing the picture book version of *Take Me Out to the Ball Game* by Jack Norworth, set during game five of 1947 World Series with the Brooklyn Dodgers playing the New York Yankees. BASEBALL. FAMILY STORIES. FATHERS AND SONS. NEW YORK CITY.

600   Conford, Ellen. *Nibble, Nibble, Jenny Archer.* Illus. by Diane Palmisciano. Little, Brown, 1993. ISBN 0-316-15371-0

[9 chapters, 60p.] At the mall, Jenny shows such enthusiasm for the free sample of what looks like trail mix that the people running the taste test make her the star of their commercial for Nibble Nibble, which she discovers afterward is a new gerbil food. Fast and funny, the story can lead into discourse on truth in advertising and how products are pitched. Introduce the magazine *Zillions!* for kid consumers to consult, and write and videotape new commercials for products both good and dreadful. Larry also shoots an embarrassing commercial in *The Secret Life of the Underwear Champ* by Betty Miles. The Jenny Archer books are fast, funny reads with a spunky and appealing heroine who gets in and out of scrapes. Read one aloud, and your kids will devour the rest. ADVERTISING. HUMOROUS FICTION. TELEVISION.

601   Conford, Ellen. *What's Cooking, Jenny Archer?* Illus. by Diane Palmisciano. Little, Brown, 1989. ISBN 0-316-15254-4

[12 chapters, 69p.] Watching her favorite TV show *Kids in the Kitchen* gives entrepreneurial Jenny the idea to start making both her own and, for a fee, her friends' school lunches from now on, but her friends don't appreciate her talents as a chef. Classroom food critics can write a hypothetical revision of the school lunch menu to their satisfaction, taking care not to make the same mistakes as Jenny. See how 19 other young chefs prepare their favorite recipes in Jill Krementz's photo essay *The Fun of Cooking* (Knopf, 1985). In Paul Yee's *Roses Sing on New*

Snow: A Delicious Tale, a young Chinese girl teaches a visiting governor from China a lesson about cooking. COOKERY. FOOD. HUMOROUS FICTION. MONEY. SCHOOLS.

602   **Cutler, Jane.** *No Dogs Allowed.* **Illus. by Tracey Campbell Pearson. Farrar, 1992. ISBN 0-374-35526-6**

[5 chapters, 101p.] Both eight-year-old Jason and his five-year-old brother Edward are allergic to dogs, a situation Edward attempts to remedy by acting like a dog, barking and calling himself Tuffles. Each likable chapter is a just-right depiction of sibling relationships. In the second chapter you'll especially appreciate the story ideas provided by the children at the school assembly when a famous author and illustrator give a presentation. *Angel in Charge* by Judy Delton; Johanna Hurwitz's books about Nora, Teddy, Russell, and Elisa; *Hilary and the Troublemakers* by Kathleen Leverich; *Operation: Dump the Chump* by Barbara Park, *The Amazing Magic Show* by P. J. Petersen, *My Brother Is a Visitor from Another Planet* by Dyan Sheldon, and *Wally* by Judie Wolkoff are all funny and believable family stories of sibling tensions and truces. BROTHERS. FAMILY STORIES. HUMOROUS FICTION. SIBLING RIVALRY.

603   **Danziger, Paula.** *Amber Brown Is Not a Crayon.* **Illus. by Tony Ross. Putnam, 1994. ISBN 0-399-22509-9**

[9 chapters, 80p.] Third-grader Amber's best friend and classmate, Justin Daniels, who is moving to Alabama, won't discuss his feelings about leaving her behind, and when he throws out their treasured chewing gum ball they fight and stop speaking. Ira and Reggie have a similar tough time in Bernard Waber's picture book *Ira Says Goodbye.* For all the new kids in class, or the ones who have lived through a move, Patricia Reilly Giff's Polk Street School spin-off *Matthew Jackson Meets the Wall* is from their point of view, while in *Joshua T. Bates Takes Charge* by Susan Shreve, shrimpy new fifth-grader Sean latches onto Joshua, causing him extra anguish. In Barbara M. Joosse's *Wild Willie and King Kyle Detectives,* Willie spies on the new girl next door after best-friend Kyle moves to "stupid-Cleveland-stupid-Ohio." FRIENDSHIP. MOVING, HOUSEHOLD. SCHOOLS.

604   **DeFelice, Cynthia.** *Mule Eggs.* **Illus. by Mike Shenon. Orchard, 1994. ISBN 0-531-08693-3**

Though a farmer does manage to sell city slicker Patrick a pumpkin for $25.00, telling him he can hatch twin mules from it, Patrick soon wises up and pays the farmer a return trick. Similar to *The Gollywhopper Egg* by Anne Rockwell and Canadian folktale *The Mare's Egg* by Carole Spray, to which you'll want to chart comparisons, the twist ending is a pleasure to read. Bring in a pumpkin for a prop. FARM LIFE. FOOLS. MULES. PRACTICAL JOKES. PUMPKINS.

605   **Duffey, Betsy.** *A Boy in the Doghouse.* **Illus. by Leslie Morrill. Simon & Schuster, 1991. ISBN 0-671-73618-3**

[14 chapters, 84p.] Unless George can teach his new dog Lucky not to bark at night and puddle in the house by the end of the week, it's back to the pound.

Told from alternating points of view, we watch as boy tries to train dog using a book, and dog tries to break in his new boy. Readers will enjoy their further adventures in *Lucky in Left Field* (1992) and *Lucky on the Loose* (1993). Ask your students to observe a pet and write a story about it from both the animal's and their own point of view. In *The Big Deal* by Alison Cragin Herzig, Sam's dog Wally is so huge, the dog walks the boy instead of the other way around. DOGS. POINT OF VIEW.

606   Duffey, Betsy. *The Gadget War.* Illus. by Janet Wilson. Viking, 1991. ISBN 0-670-84152-8

[12 chapters, 74p.] Third-grader Kelly Sparks has already invented 43 gadgets when new student Einstein Anderson Jones, who's even been to Young Inventor's Camp, joins her class, and it's hate at first sight. While you might frown upon your students inventing vengeful gadgets like Kelly's fake pencil, lipstick smear gun, or (heaven forbid!) food-fight catapult, they may come up with some neat and peaceful ideas of their own. John Frank's *Odds 'N' Ends Alvy* is about another kid inventor, while Jim Murphy's *Weird and Wacky Inventions* is full of actual patented inventions for your audience to identify. COMPETITION. CONFLICT RESOLUTION. HUMOROUS FICTION. INVENTIONS. SCHOOLS.

607   Duffey, Betsy. *The Math Whiz.* Illus. by Janet Wilson. Viking, 1991. ISBN 0-670-83422-X

[10 chapters, 68p.] Third-grader Marty Malone, who has always been able to work out any math equation, needs to solve his problem with being the last picked in gym class for every team. Ask your students to write math equations for nonmath problems they need to solve, and decide on the possible solutions. Alvin thinks he can't draw for beans in *Alvin's Famous No-Horse* by William Harry Harding. Other school stories where the protagonist is having problems adjusting include Natalie Honeycutt's *The All-New Jonah Twist*, Johanna Hurwitz's *Class Clown*, Elizabeth Levy's *Keep Ms. Sugarman in the Fourth Grade*, Barbara Park's *Maxie, Rosie, and Earl—Partners in Grime*, and Jerry Spinelli's *Fourth Grade Rats*. FRIENDSHIP. MATHEMATICS. SCHOOLS.

608   Dugan, Barbara. *Loop the Loop.* Illus. by James Stevenson. Greenwillow, 1992. ISBN 0-688-09648-4

Young Anne's unconventional and endearing new friend Mrs. Simpson may be old and in a wheelchair, but she's sharp as a tack. She belts out "Hold that Tiger" at the piano and can still toss a mean yo-yo, until the day she falls and breaks her hip. Pull out your yo-yo for a few spins when you read this aloud, and swap some stories about indomitable grandparents to counter children's stereotypes about the elderly. In *The Wednesday Surprise* by Eve Bunting, Anna teaches her grandmother to read. Make two class lists: one of all the things your children have learned from an older person, and another of what they themselves have taught or given in return. Make the acquaintance of other realistic characters in Robert J. Blake's *Dog*, James Stevenson's *Worse Than the Worst*, and Jack Ziegler's *Mr. Knocky*. CATS. ELDERLY. FRIENDSHIP. HOSPITALS. PICTURE BOOKS FOR ALL AGES. YO-YOS.

609   Garland, Sherry. *The Lotus Seed.* Illus. by Tatsuro Kiuchi. Harcourt, 1993. ISBN 0-15-249465-0

"My grandmother saw the emperor cry the day he lost his golden dragon throne." Wanting something to remember the emperor by, grandmother takes a lotus seed from the Imperial garden and keeps it with her as she begins her odyssey from wartime Vietnam in 1945 to America, at the end of the Vietnam War, where she raises a family. Elegant paintings combined with the spare, dignified story convey the terrors of war and the loneliness of dislocation. Other stories that examine the difficulties of adjusting to a new life in America include Sook Nyul Choi's *Halmoni and the Picnic*, Barbara Cohen's *Molly's Pilgrim*, and Maxine Rhea Leighton's *An Ellis Island Christmas*. Bud Howlett's *I'm New Here* is a nonfiction photo-essay about a girl who has just arrived in the United States from El Salvador. For other perspectives on war, read Eve Bunting's *The Wall*, Florence Parry Heide and Judith Heide Gilliland's *Sami and the Time of the Troubles*, and Holly Keller's *Grandfather's Dream*. FLOWERS. GRANDMOTHERS. IMMIGRATION AND EMIGRATION. PICTURE BOOKS FOR ALL AGES. SEEDS. VIETNAM WAR. WAR.

610   Gerrard, Roy. *Rosie and the Rustlers.* Illus. by the author. Farrar, 1989. ISBN 0-374-36345-5

This galloping ballad about how Rosie Jones, her ranch hands, and their Cherokee friends captured outlaw Greasy Ben and his gang will lasso your listeners. Get into the western mood with *Songs of the Wild West* edited by Alan Axelrod and with *Cowboys*, a collection of poems compiled by Charles Sullivan. Add to the fun with Jo Harper's *Jalapeño Hal*, Tony Johnston's parody *The Cowboy and the Black-Eyed Pea*, Eric A. Kimmel's *Charlie Drives the Stage*, Angela Shelf Medearis's adaptation of the folksong *The Zebra-Riding Cowboy*, and *Whitefish Will Rides Again!* by Arthur Yorinks. COWBOYS. NARRATIVE POETRY. ROBBERS AND OUTLAWS. STORIES IN RHYME. WEST.

611   Giff, Patricia Reilly. *Matthew Jackson Meets the Wall.* Illus. by Blanche Sims. Delacorte, 1990. ISBN 0-385-29972-9

[10 chapters, 91p.] Moving from New York to Ohio, Matthew already misses his friends from Polk Street School, and the weird new kid next door doesn't make his transition any easier when she tells him about the Wall, a big, huge kid who gives everybody a bloody nose. Readers will be eager to see how nonreader Matthew takes to his new teacher in the sequel, *Shark in School* (1994). Paula Danziger's *Amber Brown Is Not a Crayon*, Barbara M. Joosse's *Wild Willie and King Kyle Detectives*, and Susan Shreve's *Joshua T. Bates Takes Charge* are good complementary titles about moving and its consequences. BULLIES. FRIENDSHIP. MOVING, HOUSEHOLD.

612   Haley, Gail E. *Dream Peddler.* Illus. by the author. Dutton, 1993. ISBN 0-525-45153-6

Based on an English folktale, "The Peddler of Swaffham," this alluring story is about John Chapman, an 18th-century chapbook peddler who dreams he will hear news that will bring him great joy if he travels to London Bridge, a six-day journey away. As in Margaret Hodges's *Saint Patrick and the Peddler*, Uri

Shulevitz's *The Treasure*, and Diane Stanley's *Fortune*, he discovers that his treasure—a chest of Roman gold—is back at home, buried in the back yard. John uses his gold to purchase a print shop and bring books and reading to his townsfolk. A lesson on the importance of reading can tie in hieroglyphics, illuminated manuscripts, Johann Gutenberg, hornbooks, and computers, using concrete examples collected on jaunts to bookstores, museums, and libraries. Cathryn Falwell's *Letter Jesters*, Jack Knowlton's factual *Books and Libraries* and Barbara A. Huff's poem *Once Inside the Library* can help get you started. BOOKS AND READING. DREAMS. ENGLAND. LONDON. PICTURE BOOKS FOR ALL AGES.

613   Harding, William Harry. *Alvin's Famous No-Horse.* **Illus. by Michael Chesworth. Henry Holt, 1992. ISBN 0-8050-2227-9**

[10 chapters, 71p.] With the class art exhibit for Parents' Night coming up on Friday, third-grader Alvin would like to be able to paint a decent-looking horse, but he doesn't have the confidence yet, even though his teacher Mrs. Casey brings in her own watercolors for him to use. Ask children how they learn to do something well, and how they keep from psyching themselves out over talents they feel they don't have. In *Mieko and the Fifth Treasure* by Eleanor Coerr, a young girl from Hiroshima is sent to live with her grandparents in the countryside in 1945. A talented artist, she now must regain the use of a hand that was injured in the bombing and gain back her confidence in her abilities. Marty is great at math but lousy at P.E. in *The Math Whiz* by Betsy Duffey. ARTISTS. DRAWING. SCHOOLS. SELF-ESTEEM. TEACHERS.

614   Harness, Cheryl. *Three Young Pilgrims.* **Illus. by the author. Bradbury, 1992. ISBN 0-02-742643-2**

Mary, Remember, and Bartholomew Allerton sailed with their parents to the New World on the Mayflower in 1620. Through richly detailed paintings and a fictionalized but fact-based text, we follow the trials of the next year when their mother and baby sister die, and the Pilgrims plant crops and join with the Indians for a feast of thanksgiving. The final pages picture each of the Saints, Strangers, and Indians, with sidebars providing additional facts. Other excellent selections are William Accorsi's *Friendship's First Thanksgiving*, Jean Craighead George's *The First Thanksgiving*, and Steven Kroll's *Oh, What a Thanksgiving! Merrily Comes Our Harvest In: Poems for Thanksgiving* compiled by Lee Bennett Hopkins and *It's Thanksgiving*, with easy-to-read poems by Jack Prelutsky, will diversify your holiday presentation. HISTORICAL FICTION. MASSACHUSETTS. PILGRIMS. THANKSGIVING.

615   Harper, Jo. *Jalapeño Hal.* **Illus. by Jennifer Beck Harris. Four Winds, 1993. ISBN 0-02-742645-9**

The tough Texas cowboy with scorching-hot breath from the jalapeño peppers he eats ends the drought in Presidio by making all the townsfolk eat so many peppers they breathe steam, causing storm clouds to form. Bring in a jar of jalapeños for all to see, and even taste. Continue spinning Texas tall tales with Roy Gerard's *Rosie and the Rustlers*, Tony Johnston's *The Cowboy and the Black-Eyed Pea*, and Eric A. Kimmel's *Charlie Drives the Stage*. Alan Axelrod's *Songs of the Wild West* and *Cowboys*, a collection of poems compiled by Charles Sullivan will add some realism. Enrich your weather unit with this and other tall tales such as *Cloudy with a Chance of Meatballs* by Judi and Ron Barrett; *The Match Between the Winds*, a folktale from Borneo by Shirley Climo; *C.L.O.U.D.S.* by Pat Cummings; *The Legend of Slappy Hooper* by Aaron Shepard; *Chinook* by Michael O. Tunnell; *Rain Player* by David Wisniewski; and *The Junior Thunder Lord*, a Chinese folktale by Laurence Yep. COWBOYS. DROUGHT. RAIN AND RAINFALL. TALL TALES. TEXAS. WEATHER. WEST.

616   **Heide, Florence Parry, and Judith Heide Gilliland.** *The Day of Ahmed's Secret.* **Illus. by Ted Lewin. Lothrop, 1990. ISBN 0-688-08895-3**

Follow a young Egyptian boy on his rounds through contemporary Cairo, selling cooking gas canisters to earn money for his family. Ahmed's secret is not revealed until the final pages, when he shows his family what he has just learned—to write his name. As Ahmed reminds us, being able to write your name connects you with the ages. Ask your students how their lives would be different if they could neither read nor write. Also read *The Wednesday Surprise* by Eve Bunting where a young girl teaches her grandmother to read; together, they make an eloquent plea for literacy. EGYPT. LITERACY. SECRETS. WRITING.

617   **Herman, Charlotte.** *Max Malone Makes a Million.* **Illus. by Cat Bowman Smith. Henry Holt, 1991. ISBN 0-8050-1374-1**

[9 chapters, 76p.] Max's get-rich-quick schemes with best friend Gordy include baking (and burning) cookies, selling lemonade (and drinking it all themselves), and running a backyard carnival, but he's upstaged each time by six-year-old neighbor Austin Healy, a real entrepreneur who knows his market and understands how to make a profit. Base your math lessons and problems on their exploits. Meet more moneymaking kids in *A Job for Jenny Archer* and *What's Cooking, Jenny Archer?* by Ellen Conford and *Benjy in Business* by Jean Van Leeuwen. Readers will want to follow Max's further exploits in *Max Malone, Superstar* (1992) and *Max Malone the Magnificent* (1993). FRIENDSHIP. HUMOROUS FICTION. MONEY.

618   **Herzig, Alison Cragin.** *The Big Deal.* **Viking, 1992. ISBN 0-670-84251-6**

[10 chapters, 68p.] Unless Sam Bates, the smallest kid in the fourth grade, can figure out a way to train Wally, his enormous, ungainly dog, his parents threaten to take the dog back to the farm. Break the ice with Steven Kellogg's *Pinkerton, Behave!* a picture book about a Great Dane who also flunked obedience school. George tries to teach his new dog Lucky how to behave and vice versa in *A Boy in the Doghouse* by Betsy Duffey, and so far, Janie's Great Dane is just imaginary in *The Invisible Dog* by Dick King-Smith. DOGS. RESPONSIBILITY. SIZE.

619   **Hesse, Karen.** *Lester's Dog.* **Illus. by Nancy Carpenter. Crown, 1993. ISBN 0-517-58358-5**

The narrator relates how he and his fearless best friend Corey, who is deaf, rescue a scrawny kitten Corey has found, save it from the growling dog up the street, and give it to Mr. Frank who's been a "broken man" since his wife died. A slice-of-life tale of friendship, courage, and compassion, told with matter-of-fact directness, this should encourage your children to recount the last brave, selfless deed they did. In Barbara D. Booth's *Mandy*, a deaf girl fights her fear of the dark to find her grandmother's lost pin outside. DEAF. DOGS. FEAR. FRIENDSHIP. HANDICAPS.

620   **Hoffman, Mary. *The Four-Legged Ghosts*. Illus. by Laura L. Seely. Dial, 1993. ISBN 0-8037-1645-1**

[8 chapters, 90p.] Since Alex's younger sister has asthma and furry animals make her wheeze, they have never been able to keep any pets until the doctor says one small pet mouse won't do her any harm. Cedric is not an everyday mouse, however, for, being the 17th son of a 17th son, he has the power of summoning the ghosts of all the past pets of the house, including dogs, cats, a horse, and even a tiger. What will mouse Cedric—who, according to the last line of the book, knows lots of other spells—do next? Children can speculate and then compose new adventures. ASTHMA. GHOSTS. MAGIC. MICE. PETS.

621   **Honeycutt, Natalie. *Juliet Fisher and the Foolproof Plan*. Bradbury, 1992. ISBN 0-02-744845-2**

[9 chapters, 133p.] Considered nosy and bossy for mentioning other students' mistakes, third-grader Juliet just considers herself motivated, so when Mrs. Lacey seats irrepressible chatterbox Lydia Jane next to her, an indignant Juliet takes it upon herself to reform her new seatmate. In this entertaining companion to *The All-New Jonah Twist* and *The Best-Laid Plans of Jonah Twist*, we cheer when Juliet's almost-friends Jonah and Granville hatch a plan to teach the "perfect" child to relax and have fun. Your students will love the extra-long sentence Juliet writes that incorporates all ten spelling words (page 97). See if they can do the same with this week's spelling or vocabulary list. Danny decides to flunk fifth grade on purpose in *My Dog Ate It* by Saragail Katzman Benjamin. BEHAVIOR. FRIENDSHIP. POPULARITY. SCHOOLS. SELF-ESTEEM.

622   **Hopkinson, Deborah. *Sweet Clara and the Freedom Quilt*. Illus. by James Ransome. Knopf, 1993. ISBN 0-679-92311-X**

[1 sitting, unp.] Reassigned from a field hand to a seamstress, 12-year-old Clara, a slave on a plantation near the Ohio River, learns to sew and constructs a quilt with a map that shows the way north on the Underground Railroad. When she and her friend Jack run away to freedom, she leaves the quilt behind to help others who might follow. Additional sensitive stories about slavery are Stacey Chbosky's *Who Owns the Sun?*, Faith Ringgold's *Aunt Harriet's Underground Railroad in the Sky*, Dolores Johnson's *Now Let Me Fly: The Story of a Slave Family*, F. N. Monjo's *The Drinking Gourd*, and Jeannette Winter's *Follow the Drinking Gourd*. AFRICAN AMERICANS. MAPS AND GLOBES. PICTURE BOOKS FOR ALL AGES. QUILTS. SLAVERY. U.S.–HISTORY–1783-1865–FICTION.

623   Howard, Ellen. *Murphy and Kate.* Illus. by Mark Graham. Simon & Schuster, 1995. ISBN 0-671-79775-1

After Kate's 14-year-old dog Murphy dies, she can't imagine feeling happy again, and in a poignantly sentimental remembrance of their life together, illustrated with soft oil paintings, we see how Kate will carry on without him, "one step at a time." Connie Heckert's *Dribbles*, Rachel Pank's *Under the Blackberries*, and Judith Viorst's *The Tenth Good Thing About Barney* help children come to terms with the death of a pet cat. DEATH. DOGS. PICTURE BOOKS FOR ALL AGES.

624   Hulme, Joy N. *Sea Squares.* Illus. by Carol Schwartz. Hyperion, 1991. ISBN 1-56282-080-X

Not only do you count the beautiful sea creatures on each page, but also multiply their parts, squaring each number from one to ten. For eight octopuses with their eight legs, we come up with 64. The final pages provide more information about the sea animals presented, including clown fish, sea stars, and tubfish, along with the better-known sea gulls, seals, and squids. Spend more time at the shore with *D Is for Dolphin* by Cami Berg, *A House for Hermit Crab* by Eric Carle, *Under the Sea from A to Z* by Anne Doubilet, *Sea Shapes* by Suse MacDonald, and *Is This a House for Hermit Crab?* by Megan McDonald, and count up with *The Twelve Days of Summer* by Elizabeth Lee O'Donnell. COUNTING BOOKS. MARINE ANIMALS. MATHEMATICS. MULTIPLICATION. STORIES IN RHYME.

625   Isaacs, Anne. *Swamp Angel.* Illus. by Paul O. Zelinsky. Dutton, 1994. ISBN 0-525-45271-0

Move over Paul Bunyan. Angelica Longrider, Tennessee's greatest woodswoman, born in 1815, is about to share some tall-tale space with all those big boys. This original yarn, with eye-popping oils painted on real wood veneers, is a tribute to the indefatigable giantess, who, the story claims, formed the Great Smoky Mountains during a five-day wrestling match with Thundering Tarnation—a bear to end all bears—laid out Montana's Shortgrass Prairie with his pelt, and, throwing him up into the stars, created a new constellation. Before sending your students off to spin more yarns on paper, in a storytelling circle, or on tape, familiarize them with Steven Kellogg's well-loved tall tale retellings of *Mike Fink* (Morrow, 1992), *Paul Bunyan* (Morrow, 1985), and *Pecos Bill* (Morrow, 1986), and Julius Lester's masterful version of *John Henry.* BEARS. FRONTIER AND PIONEER LIFE. PICTURE BOOKS FOR ALL AGES. TALL TALES. TENNESSEE.

626   Jackson, Ellen. *Cinder Edna.* Illus. by Kevin O'Malley. Lothrop, 1994. ISBN 0-688-12323-6

Cinderella's next-door neighbor, take-charge, resourceful Edna, has too much on the ball to sit around waiting for a fairy godmother to solve her family problems, and finds Prince Charming "borrring." At the ball, she instead hits it off with his socially conscious younger brother Rupert. The side-by-side comparison of the two girls will help kids realize that beauty doesn't matter nearly as much as personality and self-motivation. Team up with other wry parodies such as Frances Minter's *Cinder-Elly*, and Bernice Myers's *Sidney Rella and the Glass Sneaker*, and traditional-based but nicely skewed retellings like Barbara Karlin's or William Wegman's *Cinderella*. *The Principal's New Clothes* by Stephanie Calmenson is a timely update, while *Princess* by Ann Wilsdorf is a funny reworking of *The Princess and the Pea*. CINDERELLA STORIES. FAIRY TALES–SATIRE. PARODIES. PRINCES AND PRINCESSES.

627   Jaffe, Nina. *In the Month of Kislev: A Story for Hanukkah*. Illus. by Louise August. Viking, 1992. ISBN 0-670-82863-7

In traditional folktale fashion, the three hungry daughters of Mendel, a penniless peddler, spend the eight nights of Hanukkah contentedly inhaling the luscious aroma of latkes outside the house of wealthy merchant Feivel, who insists on being compensated one ruble for each night of the children's "thefts." A sagacious rabbi collects a bag of gelt from the assembled townspeople, and shakes it till it jingles, thus helping Mendel pay for the smell of the pancakes with the sound of money. Before reading the ending, allow your children to render their own judgment. Shake a batch of coins in a bag for sound effects, and hand out chocolate-covered coins for a treat. Compare the plot with that of Jane Kurtz's Ethiopian folktale *Fire on the Mountain*. Marilyn Hirsch's *Potato Pancakes All Around*, and Eric A. Kimmel's *Asher and the Capmakers*, *The Chanukkah Guest*, and *Hershel and the Hanukkah Goblins* all give a good flavor of the holiday. FOOD. HANUKKAH. JEWS. MONEY. PICTURE BOOKS FOR ALL AGES.

628   Jeffers, Susan. *Brother Eagle, Sister Sky: A Message from Chief Seattle*. Illus. by the author. Dial, 1991. ISBN 0-8037-0963-3

Leader of one of the Northwest Indian Nations in the mid-1850s, Chief Seattle spoke about preserving land, air, and rivers for future generations. Jeffers's stunning crosshatched illustrations combined with the poetic text are unforgettable. There was controversy over Chief Seattle's words as printed in this book when it was revealed that parts of his speech were actually never said by him at all, but composed by a modern-day speechwriter. Nevertheless, the book still makes a powerful impact, exhorting us to care for the earth, and children will be inspired. Holly Keller's *Grandfather's Dream*, Sheila Hamanaka's *Screen of Frogs*, Jonathan London's *Voices of the Wild*, and Jane Yolen's *Welcome to the Green House* are also message stories to make children ponder their role in preserving their environment. ECOLOGY. ENVIRONMENT. INDIANS OF NORTH AMERICA. PICTURE BOOKS FOR ALL AGES.

629   Johnson, Dolores. *Now Let Me Fly: The Story of a Slave Family*. Illus. by the author. Macmillan, 1993. ISBN 0-02-747699-5

Kidnapped and sold as a slave by fellow villager Dongo, the chief's daughter Minna describes how she was sent from Africa to America in 1815, grew up on Master Clemmons's plantation, and raised three children, all the while facing incomprehensible hardships and sorrows. Additional sensitive stories about slavery are Stacey Chbosky's *Who Owns the Sun?*, Deborah Hopkinson's *Sweet Clara and the Freedom Quilt*, Faith Ringgold's *Aunt Harriet's Underground Railroad in the Sky*, and Jeannette Winter's *Follow the Drinking Gourd*. AFRICAN AMERI-

CANS–HISTORY. FAMILY STORIES. HISTORICAL FICTION. SLAVERY. U.S.–HISTORY–1783-1865–FICTION.

630   **Joosse, Barbara M.** *Wild Willie and King Kyle Detectives.* **Illus. by Sue Truesdale. Clarion, 1993. ISBN 0-395-64338-4**

[10 chapters, 66p.] Next-door neighbors Willie and Kyle are best friends forever until Kyle's dad takes a job in stupid-Cleveland-stupid-Ohio. With the periscope Kyle leaves him, Willie promises to spy on the new girl who moves in and send Kyle his findings. Readers can follow up on their own with the sequel *The Losers Fight Back* (Clarion, 1994). In Paula Danziger's *Amber Brown Is Not a Crayon*, Amber and her best friend Justin have a blow up before he is to move away. Ira and Reggie also mask their separation anxiety with a quarrel in Bernard Waber's picture book *Ira Says Goodbye*. Patricia Reilly Giff's *Matthew Jackson Meets the Wall* is from the new kid's perspective, while in Susan Shreve's *Joshua T. Bates Takes Charge*, Joshua tries not to become friends with uncool new kid Sean. Your children can write about how it feels to move or be the friend of one who does. FRIENDSHIP. MOVING, HOUSEHOLD. MYSTERY AND DETECTIVE STORIES.

631   **Joyce, William.** *Santa Calls.* **Illus. by the author. HarperCollins, 1993. ISBN 0-06-021134-2**

Orphan Art Atchinson Aimsworth from Abilene, Texas, was often mean to his younger sister Esther until the Christmas of 1908, when the two of them, along with best friend Spaulding Littlefeets, went to the North Pole via their Yuletide Flyer flying machine and saved toyland from the Dark Elves and their evil Queen. The stylish oversized book has a campy art-deco look, and the story has a "Babes in Toyland" feel, topped off with an elegant, rotund Santa. *The Polar Express* by Chris Van Allsburg will come to mind, and the final letters that tie up the story will tie in to Janet and Allan Ahlberg's *The Jolly Christmas Postman*. BROTHERS AND SISTERS. CHRISTMAS. PICTURE BOOKS FOR ALL AGES. SANTA CLAUS.

632   **Kalman, Esther.** *Tchaikovsky Discovers America.* **Illus. by Laura Fernandez and Rick Jacobson. Orchard, 1995. ISBN 0-531-06894-3**

On her 11th birthday, Eugenia Petroff attends a concert at the newly opened Carnegie Hall in New York City to hear the famous Russian composer Tchaikovsky conduct a concert. Her fictionalized diary incorporates actual events in the composer's visit to New York and Niagara Falls in 1891, much in the way Christoph chronicles Beethoven's later years through letters to his uncle in *Beethoven Lives Upstairs* by Barbara Nichol. Incorporate Tchaikovsky's music from *Swan Lake* and *The Nutcracker* into your reading of this handsomely illustrated picture book. *Lives of the Musicians: Good Times, Bad Times (And What the Neighbors Thought)* by Kathleen Krull is a spellbinding collection of biographical essays about 19 eccentric and brilliant composers. DIARIES. HISTORICAL FICTION. MUSICIANS. RUSSIAN AMERICANS. TCHAIKOVSKY, PETER ILICH.

633   **Kalman, Maira.** *Max Makes a Million.* **Illus. by the author. Viking, 1990. ISBN 0-670-83545-5**

This zippy stream-of-consciousness narrative by Max, a dog who wants to go to Paris and be a poet is so off-the-wall, so New York adult, avant garde, and new wave that you'll either love it or loathe it. One of my fourth-graders said, "It's like modern art. I love modern art," but the rest of the class was stunned. Iconoclast teacher Carol Shields read it to her third-graders and they simply adored it, chanting the poem, "My life began/ When I was born/ Hold the phone/ I'll eat some corn" as one of their favorite parts. Go figure. Follow Max to Paris with *Ooh La La (Max in Love)* (1991) DOGS. POETS.

634   Kesey, Ken. *Little Tricker the Squirrel Meets Big Double the Bear.* Illus. by Barry Moser. Viking, 1990. ISBN 0-670-81136-X

[1 sitting, 32p.] Ravenous Big Double barrels into Topple's Bottom and swallows up marten Sally Snipster, Longrellers the Rabbit, and Charlie Charles the Woodchuck until he is outdone and overcome by the wily ways of a red squirrel who claims he can fly. A story like this Ozark tall tale, with its rich, rolling language and sly good humor, which most children would never comprehend reading to themselves, makes a powerful justification for the advantages of reading aloud. Key words are emphasized by capitals and italics, just in case someone dares to try and read aloud without a ton of country expression. "Sody Saleratus" in *Grandfather Tales* by Richard Chase is a close cousin, while Paul Galdone's *The Greedy Old Fat Man*, Jack Kent's *The Fat Cat*, Nancy Polette's *The Little Old Woman and the Hungry Cat*, and Jack Prelutsky's narrative poem *The Terrible Tiger* are all variants on the swallowing motif. BEARS. CHANTABLE REFRAIN. SQUIRRELS. TRICKSTER TALES.

635   Kimmel, Eric A. *Asher and the Capmakers: A Hanukkah Story.* Illus. by Will Hillenbrand. Holiday House, 1993. ISBN 0-8234-1031-5

On Hanukkah Eve, Asher sets off in the snow to the neighbor's to borrow an egg so his mother can make the potato pancakes, but ends up at the house of three tiny old women capmakers with whom he is whisked up the chimney to the pasha's palace in Jerusalem. Sentenced to hang by the pasha, Asher's last requests for an egg and the return of his cap are granted, and he magics himself back home where seven years have passed. Make up a tune for the capmakers' wild song and dance, which is actually a Yiddish folk song. For more seasonal trickery, don't forget Eric A. Kimmel's *Hershel and the Hanukkah Goblins.* Sample a few latkes with *In the Month of Kislev* by Nina Jaffe and *Potato Pancakes All Around* by Marilyn Hirsch. Another dancing fellow ends up with all the gold one All Hallows' Eve in *Bill and the Google-Eyed Goblins* by Alice Schertle. EGGS. FAIRIES. HANUKKAH. JERUSALEM. JEWS. LITERARY FAIRY TALES. MAGIC.

636   Langerlöf, Selma. *The Changeling.* Illus. by Jeanette Winter. Trans. from the Swedish by Susanna Stevens. Knopf, 1992. ISBN 0-679-91035-2

A troll crone trades her hideous infant for a human baby, and the farmer's wife, realizing her child has been taken, cares for the troll child as her own, and protects it from harm when her husband tries to kill it. Midway through, ask your listeners what should be done with the troll child and why. Talk about why the mother risked her own safety to take care of the changeling baby, and ask children to relate any extraordinary sacrifices their parents have made for them. In *Catkin* by Antonia Barber, a small cat attempts to rescue Carrie, a toddler who has been taken by the Little People; in *A Ride on the Red Mare's Back* by Ursula K. LeGuin, a sister confronts the trolls to get her brother back; and in *The Ghost Fox* by Laurence Yep, Little Lee saves his mother from great danger. LITERARY FAIRY TALES. LOVE. MOTHERS AND SONS. PICTURE BOOKS FOR ALL AGES. TROLLS.

637 **LeGuin, Ursula K. *A Ride on the Red Mare's Back*. Illus. by Julie Downing. Orchard, 1992. ISBN 0-531-08591-0**

[1–2 sittings, 48p.] With the dark winter coming on, a father takes his young son hunting, but the trolls take the boy. His sister sets off to rescue him, thanks to her toy wooden horse that comes to life and carries her to the High House where the trolls live. Other lyrical and mysterious literary fairy tales include Antonia Barber's *Catkin*, Laurence Houseman's *Rocking-Horse Land*, Susan Jeffers's *Wild Robin*, James Thurber's *The Great Quillow*, Don Arthur Torgersen's *The Girl Who Tricked the Trolls*, and Margaret Wetterer's *The Giant's Apprentice*. In *The Changeling* by Selma Lagerlöf, a mother saves her own son by treating a troll child as her own, and in *The Ghost Fox* by Laurence Yep, a boy's bravery keeps his mother's soul from being stolen by a fox. BROTHERS AND SISTERS. HORSES. LITERARY FAIRY TALES. TROLLS.

638 **Leighton, Maxine Rhea. *An Ellis Island Christmas*. Illus. by Dennis Nolan. Viking, 1992. ISBN 0-670-83182-4**

At the end of the arduous 14-day boat ride, when Krysia and her family disembark at Ellis Island on Christmas Eve to be reunited with Papa, she worries about being sent back to Poland by the doctors who examine all newcomers. Compare the realistic, dark, somber watercolors that capture the voyagers' fears and uncertainty with the bright, primitive-style paintings of *Klara's New World* by Jeanette Winter. Also tie in Carla Stevens' *Lily and Miss Liberty*, and Ellen Levine's factual *If Your Name Was Changed at Ellis Island*. Children can research, write about, and share their own family histories. Sook Nyul Choi's *Halmoni and the Picnic*, Barbara Cohen's *Molly's Pilgrim*, Sherry Garland's *The Lotus Seed*, and Bud Howlett's *I'm New Here* all concern modern-day immigrants and how they adjust to life in America. IMMIGRATION AND EMIGRATION. POLISH AMERICANS. VOYAGES AND TRAVELS.

639 **Leverich, Kathleen. *Best Enemies Again*. Illus. by Walter Lorraine. Greenwillow, 1991. ISBN 0-688-09440-6**

[4 chapters, 96p.] Is there anyone nastier than that snake Felicity Doll? Priscilla's every endeavor is sabotaged by the spiteful blonde in ruffles, from selling lemonade to getting a new bike, but Priscilla prevails anyway in this funny account of kid rivalry. Your students will want to catch up with the first book about the two rivals, *Best Enemies* (1989), and to keep on laughing with *Hilary and the Troublemakers* about a girl with a very real imagination. FRIENDSHIP. HUMOROUS FICTION. SCHOOLS.

640   London, Jonathan. *Voices of the Wild*. Illus. by Wayne McLoughlin. Crown, 1993.
ISBN 0-517-59218-5

In a prose poem graced with extraordinarily beautiful paintings, the wild North-American animals describe their reactions to seeing a solitary man observing them from his kayak. Lynne Cherry's *The Great Kapok Tree* and Marilyn Singer's poetry book *Turtle in July* are also from the animals' points of view, while Sheila Hamanaka's *Screen of Frogs*, Susan Jeffers's *Brother Eagle, Sister Sky*, Holly Keller's *Grandfather's Dream*, and Jane Yolen's *Welcome to the Green House* help as well to develop environmental awareness. Each child can select an animal to research and write about from its perspective. ANIMALS. ECOLOGY. NATURE. PICTURE BOOKS FOR ALL AGES.

641   Manson, Christopher. *The Marvelous Blue Mouse*. Illus. by the author. Henry Holt, 1992.
ISBN 0-8050-1622-8

The Emperor Charlemagne seeks appropriate punishment for the self-important and greedy Lord Mayor's mismanagement of a fine city, and grants clever Isaac permission to humble the man with the aid of a small mouse. Originally written down in A.D. 884 by a monk called Notker the Stammerer, Manson's lively version is illustrated with watercolors in the style of an illuminated manuscript. Manson's *Two Travelers* is also a tale about Charlemagne. Emperors learn pithy lessons about humility in Hans Christian Andersen's *The Nightingale* and Kathryn Hewitt's *King Midas and the Golden Touch*. CHARLEMAGNE, EMPEROR, 742–814. EMPERORS. GREED. HISTORICAL FICTION. MICE. PICTURE BOOKS FOR ALL AGES. PRIDE AND VANITY.

642   Manson, Christopher. *Two Travelers*. Illus. by the author. Henry Holt, 1990. ISBN 0-8050-1214-1

In A.D. 787, the caliph of Baghdad sent the Emperor Charlemagne an elephant named Abulabaz, in the care of Isaac, a servant. Compare Manson's fictionalized story with Nancy Milton's *The Giraffe That Walked to Paris*. Rhoda Blumberg's *Jumbo* describes a famous elephant that made it to the States. Imagine being exposed to an elephant for the first time with Ed Young's fable *Seven Blind Mice*. Another instructive story about the great emperor and his wise friend Isaac is Manson's *The Marvelous Blue Mouse*, which was originally written down in A.D. 884. CHARLEMAGNE, EMPEROR, 742–814. ELEPHANTS. EMPERORS. HISTORICAL FICTION.

643   Marshall, James. *Rats on the Roof and Other Stories*. Illus. by the author. Dial, 1991.
ISBN 0-8037-0835-1

[7 short stories, 79p.] In seven animal-based cautionary tales, Otis and Sophie Dog hire a tomcat to clear off partying rats, a tomcat pops out of a mouse's wedding cake, and wolves and foxes are bettered by illiterate sheep, a vain frog, a talkative swan, and a savvy Christmas goose. Continue with *Rats on the Range* (1993), and ask your children to write some new animal tales. Ingredients: one over-confident predator, and one or more not-so-swift but well-meaning victims who triumph. *Fables* by Arnold Lobel is a bit sophisticated, but in the same vein. ANIMALS. CREATIVE WRITING. HUMOROUS FICTION. SHORT STORIES.

644   **Martin, Jane Read, and Patricia Marx.** *Now Everybody Really Hates Me.* **Illus. by Roz Chast. HarperCollins, 1993. ISBN 0-06-021294-2**

You know all those children's books where the main character is sweet and generous and heroic? This is not one of those. This is about a real kid in a real snit after she's sent to her room for an hour just because she hit her brother Theodore on the head and called him a dumbbell in front of everyone at his birthday party. Patty Jane begs to differ, insisting she just touched him hard and called him a dumb head. In her room she rants and raves about staying there for the rest of her life, and all of your children will understand just how mad and unrepentant she is since they've all had days like that. Ask them about it if you want an earful. Venting can be a lot of fun, and you will laugh a lot at both this character study/monologue and your students' own stories. So there. Find more kids mad at the world in William Cole's *I'm Mad at You*, Jane Goodsell's *Toby's Toe*, Carol Diggory Shields's *I Am Really a Princess*, and William Steig's *Spinky Sulks*. EMOTIONS. FAMILY LIFE. PICTURE BOOKS FOR ALL AGES.

645   **Medearis, Angela Shelf.** *The Zebra-Riding Cowboy: A Folk Song from the Old West.* **Illus. by Maria Cristina Brusca. Henry Holt, 1992. ISBN 0-8050-1712-7**

[1 sitting, unp.] When an educated fellow arrives at the cowboys' campground, they take him for a greenhorn and let him ride the wild outlaw horse Zebra Dun, but the stranger proves himself a "cowboy and not a gent from town." The music for this old cowboy tune is on the inside cover, and the author's note about African American and Mexican cowboys in the Old West will interest your listeners, especially if they're surprised at the portrayal of the stranger as black. Get into the cowboy life-style with *Songs of the Wild West,* edited by Alan Axelrod, and with *Cowboys,* a collection of poems compiled by Charles Sullivan. Follow up with more entertaining sagas including *Rosie and the Rustlers* by Roy Gerard, *Jalapeño Hal* by Jo Harper, *The Cowboy and the Black-Eyed Pea* by Tony Johnston, *Charlie Drives the Stage* by Eric A. Kimmel, and *Whitefish Will Rides Again!* by Arthur Yorinks. AFRICAN AMERICANS. COWBOYS. FOLK SONGS. HORSES. MULTICULTURAL STORIES. STORIES IN RHYME. WEST.

646   **Mills, Lauren.** *The Rag Coat.* **Illus. by the author. Little, Brown, 1991. ISBN 0-316-57407-4**

After Minna's coal-miner father dies, a group of mothers donate rag scraps and piece together a patchwork coat so she can attend the tiny Appalachian schoolhouse for the first time. The butt of her classmates' taunts, Minna demonstrates her spunk and humility and points out how each patch represents a story in her classmates' lives. Based on Dolly Parton's song, "The Coat of Many Colors," this can be compared with Remy Charlip's lyrical *Harlequin and the Coat of Many Colors,* and even the Bible story of Joseph and his coat of many colors. Class discussion point: Would you have made fun of Minna if she came to our school? How do you react when you meet children who look different? Other significant coat stories include Phoebe Gilman's *Something from Nothing,* Amy Hest's *The Purple Coat,* and Harriet Ziefert's *A New Coat for Anna.* Catherine A. Welch's *Danger at the Breaker* is about an eight-year-old boy's first day working in the mines. CLOTHING AND DRESS. CONFLICT RESOLUTION. COUNTRY LIFE. SCHOOLS.

647   Mitchell, Margaree King. *Uncle Jed's Barbershop*. Illus. by James Ransome. Simon & Schuster, 1993. ISBN 0-671-76969-3

Looking back to her childhood in the South, Sarah Jean recalls her favorite uncle who saved all his life to be a barber, through the Great Depression and years of segregation, finally realizing his dream on his 79th birthday. Ask your students: Why didn't Uncle Jed give up on his dream? What dreams are you willing to work all your life to achieve? Faith Ringgold's *Tar Beach* and Ken Mochizuki's *Baseball Saved Us* also deal with the issue of racial prejudice. AFRICAN AMERICANS. FAMILY STORIES. HAIR. PICTURE BOOKS FOR ALL AGES. PREJUDICE. UNCLES. WORK.

648   Moore, Inga. *The Sorcerer's Apprentice*. Illus. by the author. Macmillan, 1989. ISBN 0-02-767645-5

A retelling of an ancient story of magic gone awry, this version is about young Franz who applies for an apprenticeship with Ludvig Hexenmeister, Sorcerer, and at the first opportunity meddles with the broom-bewitching spell, but can't recall the magic words to stop it from fetching pails of water. In both *Strega Nona* by Tomie dePaola and *A Special Trick* by Mercer Mayer, the magic won't stop, while young Tom is more on the ball in *Dr. Change* by Joanna Cole. *The Widow's Broom* by Chris Van Allsburg is about a more cooperative sweeper, though the neighbors are not amused. Children can think which chore or chores they'd like to have performed by a magic object, and write a rhyming spell for it to do so. CREATIVE WRITING. MAGIC. MAGICIANS. PICTURE BOOKS FOR ALL AGES. TRANSFORMATIONS. WIZARDS.

649   Nash, Ogden. *The Adventures of Isabel*. Illus. by James Marshall. Little, Brown, 1991. ISBN 0-316-59874-7

Don't mess with red-headed kid Isabel, as a hungry bear, a wicked old witch, a hideous giant, a troublesome doctor, and a hideous dream all find out the hard way when they threaten her. Most anthologies supply only one or two verses to this deliciously wicked narrative poem; this version is complete and comes with splendid and funny illustrations, peppered with James Marshall's usual trademark chickens. Teachers can break the class into groups to come up with new adventures of our heroine, with verses encountering a fearsome wolf or a screaming ghost. CHANTABLE REFRAIN. HUMOROUS POETRY. NARRATIVE POETRY. PICTURE BOOKS FOR ALL AGES. STORIES IN RHYME.

650   Nixon, Joan Lowery. *That's the Spirit, Claude*. Illus. by Tracey Campbell Pearson. Viking, 1992. ISBN 0-670-83434-3

Not wanting to disappoint their newly adopted young'uns, ten-year-old Tom and eight-year-old Deputy Sheriff Bessie, Shirley talks husband Claude into dressing as Sandy Claus and climbing up on the roof on Christmas Eve, where he crashes into another old coot—the real McCoy. This'un's jist as much fun as the previous four books in Nixon's entertaining Texas-set Claude series, all of which your own young'uns'll pester you to read aloud in sequence. Look in on other Santas in Debra and Sal Barracca's *A Taxi Dog Christmas*, James Flora's *Grandpa's Witched-Up Christmas*, William Joyce's *Santa Calls*, James Stevenson's *The Worst*

Person's Christmas, and Chris Van Allsburg's *The Polar Express*. CHRISTMAS. FRONTIER AND PIONEER LIFE. HUMOROUS FICTION. SANTA CLAUS. TEXAS.

651   Park, Barbara. *Junie B. Jones and a Little Monkey Business*. Illus. by Denise Brunkus.
       Random House, 1993. ISBN 0-679-83886-4

[9 chapters, 68p.] Junie B. is none too thrilled when her parents drop the bombshell about the new B-A-B-Y that her mother's having, especially when they refuse to call it Mrs. Gutzman, a name Junie B. particularly likes, or even Big Teeny. On the day her brother is born, Junie B. misunderstands what her grandmother tells her and announces to her kindergarten class that her new baby brother is "a real, alive, baby MONKEY!!!" In the last chapter, there's a nice scene where Principal explains to the class that some of the things adults say can be confusing to children, and the class volunteers idioms and figures of speech like "couch potato" and "dumb bunny." Amelia Bedelia books will come in handy right about then, as will Fred Gwynne's *A Chocolate Moose for Dinner* and *The King Who Rained*. BABIES. HUMOROUS FICTION. KINDERGARTEN. SCHOOLS.

652   Park, Barbara. *Junie B. Jones and Some Sneaky Peeky Spying*. Illus. by Denise Brunkus.
       Random House, 1994. ISBN 0-679-95101-6

[8 chapters, 66p.] Wanting desperately to discover where her teacher lives so she can visit, Junie B. is shocked and dismayed when she comes upon her teacher at the grocery store and spies her testing some grapes without first paying for them Teachers are supposed to be perfect, and Junie B. decides not to tell what she's seen until she becomes convinced her head will blow up from keeping the secret. The final hilarious confrontation between child, teacher, and principal will start your children talking about right and wrong and how to admit mistakes. Older children will love trying their hands at reading aloud the six-year-old's first-person narration, which is a great starting point for talking about point of view, and composing real-life dialogue in their own writing. HUMOROUS FICTION. KINDERGARTEN. SCHOOLS. SECRETS. SUPERMARKETS. TEACHERS.

653   Park, Barbara. *Junie B. Jones and the Stupid Smelly Bus*. Illus. by Denise Brunkus.
       Random House, 1992. ISBN 0-679-92642-9

[10 chapters, 69p.] Informed by new friend Lucille on the first day of school that kids on the school bus home pour chocolate milk on your head, an indignant Junie B. hides out in the supply closet at the back of the kindergarten classroom until everyone is gone. My students fell over laughing at Junie B.'s frank assessments of the world around her, and volunteered many memories of their early school mishaps. For more first-day recollections, read Amy Schwartz's *Annabelle Swift, Kindergartener*. Though I originally thought younger children would get the most out of the Junie B. Jones series, all of my students from grades one through five have adored the voice and antics of the irrepressible kindergartner and clamor to read all of her books. Buy multiple copies. Other assertive young scholars include Ramona in *Ramona the Pest* by Beverly Cleary and Josie in *Josie Smith at School* by Magdalen Nabb. BUSES. HUMOROUS FICTION. KINDERGARTEN. SCHOOLS.

654   Peters, Julie Anne. *The Stinky Sneakers Contest.* **Illus. by Cat Bowman Smith. Joy Street/Little, Brown, 1992. ISBN 0-316-70214-5**

[9 short chapters, 57p.] Infuriated that his best friend Damien is cheating to win first prize in the Feetfirst factory's contest, Earl righteously prepares his smelly sneakers the old-fashioned way—by wearing them nonstop, day and night—even hanging his sneaker-clad feet over the side of the tub when he takes a bath. One of the Springboard Books series, this pleasant, easy-to-read chapter book about two African American boys will stimulate reflection on what it means to be a winner. A good companion discussion-starter is *Summer Wheels* by Eve Bunting. AFRICAN AMERICANS. CHEATING. CONFLICT RESOLUTION. CONTESTS. FRIENDSHIP. HONESTY.

656   Petersen, P. J. *I Hate Company.* **Illus. by Betsy James. Dutton, 1994. ISBN 0-525-45329-6**

[10 chapters, 87p.] It's bad enough when your own siblings are obnoxious, but Dan is floored when his mother invites her old college chum who has just gotten divorced to bring her three-year-old son Jimmy and stay in their apartment while she looks for a job. Dan does his best to look after the little terror who wrecks books, shoves crayon's up Dan's nose, and listens incessantly to a tape of *The Three Little Pigs,* and eventually even learns to like him. Another funny story about Dan is *I Hate Camping* (1991). Little brothers who drive their big brothers nuts can be found lurking in *Tales of a Fourth Grade Nothing* by Judy Blume and *Operation: Dump the Chump* by Barbara Park. APARTMENT HOUSES. BABY-SITTERS. BEHAVIOR. HUMOROUS FICTION.

655   Petersen, P. J. *The Sub.* **Illus. by Meredith Johnson. Dutton, 1993. ISBN 0-525-45059-9**

[9 chapters, 86p.] Though best friends James and Ray agree to trade seats and identities for the day when their teacher is out sick, their joke causes them much aggravation when they take a shine to Mrs. Walters, a new sub who's no fool. Read this, along with James Marshall's cautionary tales, *Miss Nelson Is Missing,* *Miss Nelson Is Back,* and *Miss Nelson Has a Field Day,* as preparation for discussing your expectations of your children on those days you might be out. FRIENDSHIP. SCHOOLS. SUBSTITUTE TEACHERS. TEACHERS.

657   Pilkey, Dav. *Dogzilla.* **Illus. by the author. Harcourt, 1993 ISBN 0-15-223944-8**

The city of Mousopolis is terrorized by a terrifying Welsh corgi, who chases cars, chews furniture, and digs up old bones, until mouse troops led by the Big Cheese scare him off with a bubble bath. Discuss the original movie the book sends up. While there are loads of folktale parodies out there, this one and Pilkey's *Kat Kong* are a new strain, and when students cry, "We want more like that!" the only comparable parody is Jon Scieszka's *The Stinky Cheese Man and Other Fairly Stupid Tales.* As in *Kat Kong,* children will be entranced by the hilarious photographic collages, and will want to manipulate photos and write stories about their own pets, replete with bad puns. DOGS. MICE. PARODIES. PICTURE BOOKS FOR ALL AGES.

658   Pilkey, Dav. *Kat Kong.* **Illus. by the author. Harcourt, 1993 ISBN 0-15-242036-3**

Catnapping the giant kitty, Kat Kong, from its cat-shaped island, mouse explorers Captain Charles Limburger, Doctor Vincent Varmint, and Rosie Rodent exhibit the beast in Mousopolis where it escapes up the Romano Inn with Rosie in tail. The illustrations to this fabulous pun-filled take-off on the old horror movie *King Kong*—"manipulated photographic collage, heavily touched with acrylic paint"—include photos of Pilkey's own diabolical pets, including three intrepid mice, and the fiercest looking black-and-white alley cat in town. *Dogzilla*, above, is similarly outrageous and captivating. Kids can pick out the puns, and collect new ones to use in their writing, with the help of the the pun-laced riddles in *Riddles to Tell Your Cat* by Caroline Levine and *It's Raining Cats and Dogs* by Charles Keller. CATS. MICE. PARODIES. PICTURE BOOKS FOR ALL AGES.

659   Pinkwater, Daniel. *Author's Day.* **Illus. by the author. Macmillan, 1993. ISBN 0-02-774642-9**

Invited to Melvinville Elementary School to speak to the students, the genial author Bramwell Wink-Porter is taken aback when he finds principal, librarian, teachers, and children prepped to hear him expound on his new book, *The Fuzzy Bunny*, which the entire school has read, even though he has penned an altogether different opus entitled *The Bunny Brothers*. This is an uproariously funny picture book that you'll also want to read aloud at a staff meeting as a reverse handbook on author visits. *The Author and Squinty Gritt* by Barbara Williams is also good, but certainly more conventional. For some excellent advice on sponsoring a disaster-free author and/or illustrator program, consult David Melton's helpful professional book, *How to Capture Live Authors and Bring Them to Your Schools*. AUTHORS. HUMOROUS FICTION. PICTURE BOOKS FOR ALL AGES. SCHOOLS.

660   Pinkwater, Daniel. *Ned Feldman, Space Pirate.* **Illus. by the author. Macmillan, 1994. ISBN 0-02-774633-X**

[11 short chapters, 48p.] Alone in the apartment, Ned hears a noise under the kitchen sink that turns out to be Captain Lumpy Lugo, who has just arrived from the Foon-ping-baba galaxy, and who offers Ned the chance to see what it's like in outer space. Children can write about Ned's next adventures in space. As an introduction to science fiction, this book is fresh and pleasantly foolish, introducing original creatures, the notion of two identical objects (sink and spacecraft) occupying the same space simultaneously, and a romp on another planet where snow and ice are warm. Examine the fantastical elements of *Aliens for Breakfast* by Jonathan Etra and Stephanie Spinner, *The Fallen Spaceman* by Lee Harding, Pinkwater's own *Fat Men from Space*, *Alistair and the Alien Invasion* and *Alistair in Outer Space* by Marilyn Sadler, *My Robot Buddy* by Alfred Slote, *June 29, 1999* by David Wiesner, and *Company's Coming* by Arthur Yorinks. EXTRATERRESTRIAL LIFE. HUMOROUS FICTION. PIRATES. SCIENCE FICTION.

661   Polacco, Patricia. *Chicken Sunday.* **Illus. by the author. Philomel, 1992. ISBN 0-399-22133-6**

Author/illustrator Polacco recalls the summer she and her neighbors, African American brothers Stewart and Winston, went to ask for a job from Mr. Kodinski so they could buy the boys' beloved gramma, "Miss Eula," the Easter bonnet of her dreams, and were falsely accused of throwing eggs at the old man's hat shop. How the three won over the Russian Jewish immigrant shopkeeper with the number tattooed on his forearm by making him decorated Ukrainian "Pysanky" eggs makes for a warmhearted tale of compassion, responsibility, loyalty, and love. Questions to ask include: If the children were not responsible for throwing eggs at Mr. Kodinski's shop, why did they need to prove to him that they were good people? Have you ever been wrongly accused of doing something? What did you do about it and why? Don't forget to show the back-flap photo of Patricia, Stewart, and Winston as they look today, and read her brief color, photo-filled autobiography *Firetalking*. AFRICAN AMERICANS. EASTER. EGGS. ELDERLY. PICTURE BOOKS FOR ALL AGES.

662   Polacco, Patricia. *Just Plain Fancy*. Illus. by the author. Bantam, 1990. ISBN 0-553-05884-3

Naomi, an Amish girl, would like, just once, to have something fancy, and when she finds an odd speckled egg behind the henhouse and hatches a pretty new chick, she names it Fancy. Worried about being shunned by the elders for not wanting to be plain like the rest of the Amish, Naomi hides the bird, who turns out to be a peacock. Try this as a down-to-earth, sympathetic introduction to the ways of the Amish. *The Spooky Tail of Prewitt Peacock* by Bill Peet gives us a peacock who is shunned by his peers for his unusual feather formation. AMISH. EGGS. PEACOCKS. PICTURE BOOKS FOR ALL AGES. PRIDE AND VANITY. SISTERS.

663   Polacco, Patricia. *Mrs. Katz and Tush*. Illus. by the author. Bantam, 1992. ISBN 0-553-08122-5

After the death of Mrs. Katz's husband, a young African American boy named Larnel brings the old Jewish woman a tail-less kitten she names Tush, and the three become fast friends, the old woman telling Larnel about Jewish customs, and Larnel searching for Tush when the cat gets out by accident. You'll cry when you read this, but it's worth it. Follow up with Polacco's autobiographical *Chicken Sunday* and her amiable autobiography *Firetalking*. AFRICAN AMERICANS. CATS. ELDERLY. FRIENDSHIP. JEWS. MULTICULTURAL STORIES. RACE RELATIONS.

664   Polacco, Patricia. *Tikvah Means Hope*. Illus. by the author. Doubleday, 1994. ISBN 0-385-32059-0

Neighbor children Duane and Justine help Mr. Roth build his sukkah, the little hut Jews build for the yearly thanksgiving harvest festival Sukkoth, using cloth for the walls and palm branches for the roof, and camp out in it that night. Over the next several days, a terrible fire sweeps through the Oakland, California, hills, and the Roths lose everything, including their little cat, Tikvah. By a miracle, the sukkah is left standing, unsinged, and at a neighborhood gathering there that night, they find Tikvah hiding inside the barbecue pit. From an author's note, children will be horrified to learn that over 3,400 houses were destroyed and 25 people died in that very real fire. Eve Bunting's Caldecott winner *Smoky Night* chronicles another California disaster—the Los Angeles riots. Compare the two books and see if children can sort out that what they have in common is a sense of hope. CALIFORNIA. CATS. FIRE. HOLIDAYS. JEWS. PICTURE BOOKS FOR ALL AGES. SUKKOTH.

665   Pyle, Howard. *The Swan Maiden*. Illus. by Robert Sauber. Holiday House, 1994. ISBN 0-8234-1088-9

Each night, someone is stealing one of the golden pears from the king's tree, and the youngest of three princes discovers the thief—a swan who can transform herself into a beautiful woman. A literary fairy tale, it contains familiar motifs including the three impossible tasks the prince performs for a witch with three eyes. Ivan catches the firebird stealing golden apples from the king's tree in *Prince Ivan and the Firebird* by Laszlo Gal. In the versions of Hans Christian Andersen's *The Wild Swans* as retold by Amy Ehrlich and Deborah Hautzig, a young girl helps her swan brothers break their enchantment. BIRDS. LITERARY FAIRY TALES. PRINCES AND PRINCESSES. SWANS. TRANSFORMATIONS. WITCHES.

666   Rabin, Staton. *Casey Over There*. Illus. by Greg Shed. Harcourt, 1994. ISBN 0-15-253186-6

Missing his big brother Casey, a sergeant with the Fighting 69th in France during World War I, and worried after three months with no letters, seven-year-old Aubrey writes to Uncle Sam and receives a response from President Wilson instead. Facing pages show us Aubrey's life in sunny Brooklyn contrasted with somber sepia-toned paintings of the French trenches. Set in bucolic Vermont, Rosemary Wells's *Waiting for the Evening Star* takes us to the eve of World War I, while Gloria Houston's *The Year of the Perfect Christmas Tree* unfolds in homefront Appalachia. James Stevenson's autobiographical *Don't You Know There's a War On?* describes life in the United States during World War II. Ask your children to compose their own concerned letters to the current president, which you may decide to send off. Florence Parry Heide and Judith Heide Gilliland's *Sami and the Time of the Troubles* gives us a child living through war today. BROTHERS. FRANCE. PRESIDENTS–U.S. SOLDIERS. WAR. WORLD WAR, 1914-1918–FICTION.

667   Rael, Elsa Okon. *Marushka's Egg*. Illus. by Joanna Wezyk. Four Winds, 1993. ISBN 0-02-775655-6

At the market to buy an egg for her mother's special Easter bread, Marushka pays an old woman a penny for a magic egg and is sucked into it, into the forest where Baba Yaga claims her as a servant and causes her to age one year every time she asks a question. Two of the child's three questions will be interesting to discuss: Why are people selfish? Why are people cruel? The Russian witch stirs up more trouble in Katya Arnold's *Baba Yaga* and *Baba Yaga & the Little Girl*, Becky Hockox Ayres's *Matreshka*, Joanna Cole's *Bony Legs*, Eric A. Kimmel's *Baba Yaga*, Marianna Mayer's *Baba Yaga and Vasilisa the Brave*, Maida Silverman's *Anna and the Seven Swans*, Ernest Small's *Baba Yaga*, and Elizabeth Winthrop's *Vasilissa the Beautiful*. BABA YAGA. EGGS. LITERARY FAIRY TALES. TRANSFORMATIONS. WITCHES.

668   Rand, Gloria. *Prince William*. Illus. by Ted Rand. Henry Holt, 1992. ISBN 0-8050-1841-7

[1 sitting, unp.] In this comely, fact-based, picture book story, three days after a huge tanker hits a reef and releases millions of gallons of oil into Alaska's Prince William Sound in 1989, Denny finds an oil-coated baby seal on the blackened beach and rushes it to the vet at the rescue center. Denny and her mother watch the massive cleanup crews working valiantly to rescue the many birds, otters, and deer caught in the spill. Denny's seal, which she names Prince William, is one of the lucky ones—airlifted to clean waters and released after a ten-week recuperation. Give a global picture with Michele Koch's *World Water Watch*, an easy-to-read nonfiction picture book that introduces endangered sea life. Eve Bunting's *Someday a Tree*, Lynne Cherry's *A River Ran Wild: An Environmental History*, and Anne Shelby's *What to Do About Pollution* all deal with environmental issues. ALASKA. ECOLOGY. POLLUTION. SEALS. WILDLIFE RESCUE.

669   **Regan, Dian Curtis. *The Curse of the Trouble Dolls*. Illus. by Michael Chesworth. Henry Holt, 1992. ISBN 0-8050-1944-8**

[10 short chapters, 58p.] The six pinky-sized dolls Aunt Li sends Angie Wu from Guatemala are supposed to make your troubles go away, but when she brings them to school for Sharing Day, her classmates first beseech her to loan them out and then blame her when their troubles don't go away. If you can get a few tiny bamboo boxes of trouble dolls, often available in crafts stores, hand out a doll to each child and have your worriers write about which troubles they'd love to see disappear. CHINESE AMERICANS. CONFLICT RESOLUTION. DOLLS. SCHOOLS.

670   **Ringgold, Faith. *Aunt Harriet's Underground Railroad in the Sky*. Illus. by the author. Crown, 1992. ISBN 0-517-58768-8**

In this dramatic combination of fact and fantasy, an unforgettable sequel to *Tar Beach*, Cassie and her brother Bebe are flying among the stars where they meet up with the conductor of a phantom train, Harriet Tubman, who shows them how their ancestors survived during slavery times. With Aunt Harriet's guidance, Cassie must retrace the northward escape route, escaping the slave plantation, hiding in safe houses, and evading bounty hunters, before reaching Niagara Falls where she can fly again. An appended Tubman biography, photograph, bibliography, and map provide additional useful information. Also engrossing are the biographies *A Picture Book of Harriet Tubman* by David A. Adler, *Go Free or Die* by Jeri Ferris, and *Runaway Slave* by Ann McGovern, and *Sweet Clara and the Freedom Quilt* by Deborah Hopkinson. AFRICAN AMERICANS–HISTORY. HISTORICAL FICTION. PICTURE BOOKS FOR ALL AGES. TUBMAN, HARRIET. U.S.–HISTORY–1783-1865–FICTION.

671   **Ringgold, Faith. *Tar Beach*. Illus. by the author. Crown, 1991. ISBN 0-517-58031-4**

Lying on a blanket on the roof of her Harlem apartment house one hot summer night, eight-year-old Cassie imagines flying over the George Washington Bridge, which she claims for her very own necklace. Her free-form musings about the prejudice her construction-worker father faces on the job give a sober edge to this exuberant Caldecott Honor picture book, based on one of Ringgold's huge, vibrant story quilts, which is reproduced at the back of the book. Arthur Dorros's *Abuela* provides another aerial view of Manhattan, and E. L. Konigsburg's *Amy*

Elizabeth Explores Bloomingdale's takes us all over town, while Kathy Jakobsen's *My New York* gives the grand tour. *Uncle Jed's Barbershop* by Margaree King Mitchell is an inspiring story about overcoming prejudice. AFRICAN AMERICANS. CITIES AND TOWNS. FLIGHT. NEW YORK CITY. PICTURE BOOKS FOR ALL AGES. PREJUDICE.

672   Sachar, Louis. *Marvin Redpost: Alone in His Teacher's House.* Illus. by Barbara Sullivan. Random House, 1994. ISBN 0-679-91949-X

[12 chapters, 83p.] Imagine Marvin's horror when he returns to his teacher Mrs. North's house where he has been taking care of her elderly dog, Waldo, for the week she's away on vacation, and finds the dog dead. A natural mixture of humor, pathos, and the absurd is a standard component of Sachar's books, and this one will give you plenty to talk over with your students en route. Some possibilities: Why does substitute teacher Miss Hillman take offense at Marvin? Is it Marvin's fault the dog died? What would you have done? What do you think his teacher will say when she comes home and finds out? They'll want to catch up on the earlier titles: *Marvin Redpost: Kidnapped at Birth?* (1992), *Marvin Redpost: Why Pick on Me?* (1993), and *Marvin Redpost: Is He a Girl?* (1993). DEATH. DOGS. RESPONSIBILITY. SUBSTITUTE TEACHERS. TEACHERS.

673   Sanders, Scott Russell. *Here Comes the Mystery Man.* Illus. by Helen Cogancherry. Bradbury, 1993. ISBN 0-02-778145-3

In the fall of 1811, in a remote Indiana village, the four Goodwin children await the yearly arrival of the peddler, who spins thrilling stories of the world outside their farm, and displays such marvels from his pack as an ivory comb, a looking glass, spectacles, a compass, and even a whale's tooth. Along with Sanders's *Warm as Wool*, Donald Hall's *Ox-Cart Man* and Tony Johnston's *Yonder* also portray 18th-century farm life, while Natalie Kinsey-Warnock's *Wilderness Cat*, Marion Russell's *Along the Santa Fe Trail*, and David Williams's *Grandma Essie's Covered Wagon* take us farther west. FAMILY LIFE. FRONTIER AND PIONEER LIFE. HISTORICAL FICTION. PEDDLERS AND PEDDLING.

674   Say, Allen. *Grandfather's Journey.* Illus. by the author. Houghton Mifflin, 1993. ISBN 0-395-57035-2

[1 sitting, unp.] In this companion book to *Tree of Cranes*, breathtakingly illustrated with solemn and still watercolors that look like hand-tinted family photographs, the author expands on his family memories, describing his grandfather's cyclical voyage from Japan to the New World as a young man, and back to Japan with his family, where his daughter married and gave birth to a son. My international mélange of fourth-graders listened to the book in pensive silence and then launched into a spirited, free-ranging discussion about their own family origins, migrations to America, and Ellis Island. Ask your students to bring in their own old family photographs to display and explain. Eleanor Coerr's *Sadako* and *Mieko and the Fifth Treasure*, Ken Mochizuki's *Baseball Saved Us*, Junko Morimoto's *My Hiroshima*, and Ruth Wells's *A to Zen: A Book of Japanese Culture* give a sober picture of Japanese children from wartime through today. CALDECOTT MEDAL. FAMILY STORIES. GRANDFATHERS. JAPAN. PICTURE BOOKS FOR ALL AGES. VOYAGES AND TRAVELS.

675   Schwartz, David. *Supergrandpa*. Illus. by Bert Dodson. Lothrop, 1991. ISBN 0-688-09899-1

At the age of 66, never having raced before, Gustav Hakansson decides to enter the 1,000-mile Tour of Sweden bicycle race, though his family thinks he is too old and one of the judges tells him to go home to his rocking chair. Based on a true story that happened in 1951, Gustav pedaled 600 miles just to get to the starting line, and then unofficially ran and completed the race, becoming a Swedish hero. Stalfarfar, or Steel Grandfather, was one determined guy. Read about other inspirational older folks in Eve Bunting's *The Wednesday Surprise*, Barbara Douglass's *The Great Town and Country Bicycle Balloon Chase*, Barbara Dugan's *Loop the Loop*, and Mary Stolz's *Storm in the Night*. BICYCLES. ELDERLY. GRANDFATHERS. PERSEVERANCE. PICTURE BOOKS FOR ALL AGES. SWEDEN.

676   Scieszka, Jon. *The Frog Prince Continued*. Illus. by Steve Johnson. Viking, 1991. ISBN 0-670-83421-1

In his frantic search for happy-ever-after-ness, and nostalgic for his frog days, this discontented yuppie prince encounters an assortment of sarcastic and/or nasty witches from other folktales before he finally manages to reconcile with his princess. First introduce Jacob Grimm's folktale *The Frog Prince*, and then build a whole scenario with Helen V. Griffith's *Emily and the Enchanted Frog*, Fred Gwynne's *Pondlarker*, Donna Jo Napoli's *The Prince of the Pond* (for older readers), "The Other Frog Prince" from Scieszka's *The Stinky Cheese Man*, and A. Vesey's *The Princess and the Frog*. Raymond Briggs's parody *Jim and the Beanstalk* also takes place after "happy ever after." Children can pick a favorite fairy tale and write the next installment of what might have happened. FAIRY TALES–SATIRE. FROGS. PARODIES. PICTURE BOOKS FOR ALL AGES. PRINCES AND PRINCESSES. WITCHES.

677   Scieszka, Jon. *The Stinky Cheese Man and Other Fairly Stupid Tales*. Illus. by Lane Smith. Viking, 1992. ISBN 0-670-84487-X

This frantic, insanely comic send-up of fairy tales presents nine masterpieces, with a cast that includes "The Princess and the Bowling Ball," "The Other Frog Prince," and "Little Red Running Shorts," and the title character who's too malodorous to eat. Everyone's having a bad day here, from Chicken Licken and company—the table of contents squashes them flat—to the Little Red Hen, who grouses incessantly about her lack of story space. All of this madness is held together by narrator Jack (of beanstalk fame) and the spectacular collage paintings. While reinforcing book terminology in painless and unforgettable ways, this is the ultimate model for constructing a new fairy tale pastiche. After reading this aloud in a variety of appropriate voices, hand it to your students to practice and perform, with each pair or small group of students presenting the tale of their choice. Bring in some stinky cheese to celebrate the production. FAIRY TALES–SATIRE. PARODIES. PICTURE BOOKS FOR ALL AGES.

678   Steig, William. *Zeke Pippin*. Illus. by the author. HarperCollins, 1994. ISBN 0-06-205077-X

Porker Zeke finds a harmonica that he teaches himself to play, but he is so insulted when his family falls asleep after he regales them with a musical number that he runs away from home, taking his raft downriver. Upon realizing that the mouth organ fosters dozing in every listener, a chastened Zeke heads for home, only to be detained by canine villains and a hungry coyote before he can get there. Compare the common elements (magic objects, transformations, outwitting predators) in Steig's classic tales including *The Amazing Bone, Caleb and Kate, Dr. De Soto, Solomon the Rusty Nail, Spinky Sulks,* and *Sylvester and the Magic Pebble.* If you don't own a harmonica, this story will give you a reason to add one to your bag of tricks. HARMONICA. MUSIC. MUSICAL INSTRUMENTS. PIGS. ROBBERS AND OUTLAWS. SLEEP.

679   Stevens, Carla. *Lily and Miss Liberty.* Illus. by Deborah Kogan Ray. Scholastic, 1992. ISBN 0-590-44919-2

[7 chapters, 64p.] In 1885, with the French ship bearing the Statue of Liberty due in New York, Lily thinks of a unique way to raise money to contribute to the Pedestal Fund: She designs and cuts out paper crowns like the one Miss Liberty sports for people to buy and wear. Directions for making Miss Liberty's crown are included. Pair with Betsy Maestro's *The Story of the Statue of Liberty,* and show what life was like for immigrants who greeted Miss Liberty on their way into America with books including Maxine Rhea Leighton's *An Ellis Island Christmas* and Ellen Levine's factual *If Your Name Was Changed at Ellis Island. How the Second Grade Got $8,205.50 to Visit the Statue of Liberty* by Nathan Zimelman is a modern-day fund-raising story. Neil Waldman's sweeping paintings for the song *America the Beautiful* by Katharine Lee Bates are a showcase of America's monuments and natural wonders. HISTORICAL FICTION. MONEY. MONUMENTS. NEW YORK CITY. STATUE OF LIBERTY.

680   Stroud, Virginia A. *Doesn't Fall Off His Horse.* Illus. by the author. Dial, 1994. ISBN 0-8037-1635-4

Saygee, a young Kiowa Indian girl, listens as her great-grandfather recounts the story of how he received his Indian name as a boy when he and several friends made a coup, or raid, on a rival Comanche village to steal ponies, and he was shot during their escape. The issue of stealing as explained by the old man will be interesting to talk about, as this is based on a true story that happened to the author's adoptive grandfather in the Oklahoma Territory in the 1890's. FAMILY STORIES. GRANDFATHERS. HORSES. INDIANS OF NORTH AMERICA. KIOWA INDIANS. STEALING.

681   Teague, Mark. *Frog Medicine.* Illus. by the author. Scholastic, 1991. ISBN 0-590-44177-9

Unwilling to read an assigned book, *Frog Medicine,* Elmo procrastinates, and on the morning his book report is due, is horrified to discover his feet have grown long, slimy, and green. A frog-infested trip to Frogtown leads him to counseling by the book's author Doctor Frank Galoof: "The longer you put a problem off, the worse it becomes." Your readers can surely come up with a list of alternatives to the dreaded book report. Though we are warned not to judge a book by its cover, it's hard not to. Ask your kids to show and talk about books they thought they'd hate but ended up loving. *Wings: A Tale of Two Chickens* by James Marshall tackles the problem of not reading. Check out Elmo's bad haircut in Teague's *Moog-Moog, Space Barber*. BOOKS AND READING. FROGS. PROCRASTINATION.

682   **Thaler, Mike.** *The Teacher from the Black Lagoon.* **Illus. by Jared Lee. Scholastic, 1989. ISBN 0-590-41962-5 (pbk.)**

Move over Miss Viola Swamp from James Marshall's *Miss Nelson Is Missing*. The narrator's new teacher, Mrs. Green, is supposed to be a real monster, and sure enough, she's green with a tail and claws. Teachers and students alike will howl as Mrs. Green breathes fire, gives 200 pages of math homework, and eats several students. Is this for real? Nah. It's just a daydream; the real teacher is swell. For beginning-of-year jitters, this irreverent comedy should loosen everyone up. Children will also appreciate the companion stories *The Gym Teacher from the Black Lagoon* (1994) and *The Principal from the Black Lagoon* (1993). *Mrs. Toggle and the Dinosaur* by Robin Pulver will also guarantee laughs. HUMOROUS FICTION. PICTURE BOOKS FOR ALL AGES. TEACHERS.

683   **Thomas, Jane Resh.** *Saying Good-Bye to Grandma.* **Illus. by Marcia Sewall. Clarion, 1988. ISBN 0-89919-645-4**

[2 sittings, 3 chapters, 48p.] When Susie's grandmother died, the family assembled at Grandpa's and over the course of the next few days went to the church funeral service and cemetery, gathered together with family and friends, and dealt with their grief. Neither overly sad nor maudlin, this story presents all the facets of a funeral, even including the fun Susie has with her cousins playing in a casket room in the funeral home, in a realistic and respectful way. *The Key into Winter* by Janet S. Andersen, *Eleanor, Arthur, and Claire* by Diana Engel, *Abuelita's Paradise* by Carmen Santiago Nodar also concern the death of a grandparent. How one child deals with the impending death of a loved one is handled with tremendous insight in Mavis Jukes's picture book *I'll See You in My Dreams*. DEATH. FUNERALS. GRANDMOTHERS.

684   **Thurber, James.** *The Great Quillow.* **Illus. by Steven Kellogg. Harcourt, 1994. ISBN 0-15-232544-1**

[2 sittings, 56p.] Steven Kellogg's detail-laden illustrations are positively gargantuan in this new edition of Thurber's classic story about Quillow, the village toymaker who comes up with a plan to shake the confidence of Hunder the giant, whose daily demands for sheep, chocolate, clothing, and apple pies could bankrupt the town. Talk over how the affable Quillow, who, due to his short stature, endures daily teasing from the villagers, comes up with so complex and clever a plan to drive Hunder crazy. Take a look at folktale giants with Tomie dePaola's Irish *Fin M'Coul, the Giant of Knockmany Hill* and Italian *The Mysterious Giant of Barletta*, and Teri Sloat's Alaskan *The Hungry Giant of the Tundra*. FANTASY. GIANTS. LITERARY FAIRY TALES. STORYTELLING.

685   Tolan, Stephanie S. *Sophie and the Sidewalk Man*. Illus. by Susan Avishai. Four Winds, 1992. ISBN 0-02-789365-0

[11 chapters, 75p.] While Sophie begins collecting cans and bottles to earn the rest of the money to buy the $42.00 stuffed hedgehog she covets, she can't get the disheveled homeless man sitting with his two garbage bags in front of Rudowski's market out of her thoughts. Her best friend says, "I don't get it . . . That man didn't even say thank you. He's dirty. Maybe he's crazy. Why did you give him half of your money?" And Sophie replies, "Because he's hungry." Eve Bunting's *Fly Away Home* and DyAnne DiSalvo-Ryan's *Uncle Willie and the Soup Kitchen* also address the issues of hunger and homelessness. GENEROSITY. HOMELESSNESS. MONEY.

686   Tomey, Ingrid. *Grandfather's Day*. Illus. by Robert A. McKay. Boyds Mills, 1992. ISBN 1-56397-022-8

[6 chapters, 61p.] What nine-year-old Raydeen sets out to do when her newly widowed grandfather moves in with her family is fix his broken heart, and with the help of her new mouth organ, she succeeds. Other children who help heal broken hearts can be found in Nina Bawden's *Humbug*, John Reynolds Gardiner's *Stone Fox*, Helen V. Griffith's *Grandaddy's Place*, and Robert Kimmell Smith's *The War with Grandpa*. HARMONICA. GRANDFATHERS. MUSICAL INSTRUMENTS.

687   Trivas, Irene. *Emma's Christmas*. Illus. by the author. Orchard, 1988. ISBN 0-531-08380-2

Trivas takes a new look at the sheer volume of true love's largess with her prose version of the 13th-century English carol "The Twelve Days of Christmas." A prince falls for farmer's daughter Emma and implores her to say yes. The cheerful girl does, but not until the farmhouse is filled with leaping lords, swimming swans, and a host of golden rings. If you want the words and music for a bit of a sing-along, don't miss Jan Brett's regal *The Twelve Days of Christmas*. For an alternative, sing Fran Manushkin's *My Christmas Safari*, and for a wicked parody, George Mendoza's *A Wart Snake in a Fig Tree*. CHRISTMAS. GIFTS. PRINCES AND PRINCESSES. SONGS.

688   Tunnell, Michael O. *Chinook!* Illus. by Barry Root. Tambourine, 1993. ISBN 0-688-10870-9

Eccentric old Andy McFadden explains to newcomers Thad and his sister Annie that he's icefishing on the frozen lake in a rowboat so he'll be prepared in case a granddaddy chinook, or hot wind, springs up. He regales the children with tall tales about granddaddies, said to come in the coldest part of winter every 50 years, that melted snow faster than a horse could run and dried out all the streams, lakes, and fish that were in them. In the dead of winter, speculate on what might happen if a chinook hit your town. His storytelling brings to mind Sid Fleischman's *McBroom Tell the Truth* and other books about Josh McBroom's wonderful ten-acre farm. Predict a little more weather with *Cloudy with a Chance of Meatballs* by Judi and Ron Barrett, *The Match Between the Winds* by Shirley Climo, *C.L.O.U.D.S.* by Pat Cummings, *Jalapeño Hal* by Jo Harper, *The Legend of*

Slappy Hooper by Aaron Shepard, and *The Junior Thunder Lord* by Laurence Yep.
STORYTELLING. TALL TALES. WEATHER. WIND. WINTER.

689 **Whelan, Gloria. *Hannah*. Illus. by Leslie Bowman. Knopf, 1991. ISBN 0-679-81397-7**

[7 chapters, 63p.] When Miss Robbin, the new teacher, arrives to board with the family, she insists on nine-year-old Hannah joining her class despite her blindness. This gentle historical novel, narrated by Hannah, takes place in 1887, as Braille was just gaining recognition. Children fascinated with this book and just discovering biographies about Helen Keller will also not want to miss Edith Fisher Hunter's biography, *Child of the Silent Night: The Story of Laura Bridgman*.
BLIND. FARM LIFE. HANDICAPS. HISTORICAL FICTION. TEACHERS.

690 **Wiesner, David. *June 29, 1999*. Illus. by the author. Clarion, 1992. ISBN 0-395-59762-5**

After Holly launches vegetable seedlings in the sky as a science experiment, giant vegetables begin appearing nationwide, and she assumes her experiment is responsible until she hears about vegetable varieties that she never used. The paintings are coolly absurd, with sheep climbing over mega-string beans in Monument Valley and hill-sized turnips in the Rocky Mountains. Read the last two pages carefully, as children tend not to understand the ending until they talk it over and hash out how the octopuslike aliens in their starcruiser connect to the mystery. Speaking of turnips, there's another big one grown in Joanne Oppenheim's *One Gift Deserves Another*, and a spud looms large in Tomie dePaola's *Jamie O'Rourke and the Big Potato*. You may want to work this into a unit on plants. Take a spin through outer space with Daniel Pinkwater's *Ned Feldman, Space Pirate*. EXTRATERRESTRIAL LIFE. PICTURE BOOKS FOR ALL AGES. SCIENCE-EXPERIMENTS. SCIENCE FICTION. SIZE. VEGETABLES.

691 **Williams, David. *Grandma Essie's Covered Wagon*. Illus. by Wiktor Sadowski. Knopf, 1993. ISBN 0-679-90253-8**

Taken from the words of the author's grandmother, this is the remarkable story of her childhood travels from a Missouri log cabin westward to Kansas by covered wagon, and then, when hard times hit, to Oklahoma, and finally back to Missouri, where she married and raised a family. The expressive large-format paintings give a real feel for times past. Natalie Kinsey-Warnock's *Wilderness Cat*, Marion Russell's *Along the Santa Fe Trail*, and Scott Russell Sanders's *Here Comes the Mystery Man* and *Warm as Wool* portray pioneer days, and Donald Hall's *Ox-Cart Man* and Tony Johnston's *Yonder* give a picture of 18th-century farm life.
FAMILY STORIES. FARM LIFE. FRONTIER AND PIONEER LIFE. GRANDMOTHERS. HISTORICAL FICTION. MIDWEST. PICTURE BOOKS FOR ALL AGES.

692 **Willis, Jeanne. *Earthlets: As Explained by Professor Xargle*. Illus. by Tony Ross. Dutton, 1988. ISBN 0-525-44465-3**

Professor Xargle, a green-tentacled alien, lectures his class on Earthlets, also known to us earthlings as babies, describing how they look and act, and why they do what they do. All of his explanations are hilariously skewed, and your listeners should recognize all the incongruities, e.g., "After soaking, they must be dried carefully so they won't shrink. Then they are sprinkled with dust so they won't stick to things." Real Earthkids will want to come up with more brilliant explanations for such Earthlet accoutrements as pacifiers ("Keeps them from exploding," said one of my third-graders), rattles, car seats, and the like, and common events in a baby's life. What if the professor was to visit your school? Children can write about what he'd find there and how he might interpret it. Make a sci-fi tour with *Ned Feldman, Space Pirate* by Daniel Pinkwater and *June 29, 1999* by David Wiesner. BABIES. CREATIVE WRITING. EXTRATERRESTRIAL LIFE.

693   **Winter, Jeanette. *Klara's New World*. Illus. by the author. Knopf, 1992. ISBN 0-679-90626-6**

With life in Sweden too hard to survive, eight-year-old Klara and her family set out for America on a crowded boat for two months, experiencing a raging storm, fever, and the death of a little boy before reaching Castle Garden in New York Harbor, and finally, their new homestead in Minnesota. Maxine Rhea Leighton's *An Ellis Island Christmas* and Betty Waterton's *Petranella* are also stories about immigrants' experiences in the 19th and early 20th centuries. Ellen Levine's factual *If Your Name Was Changed at Ellis Island* will explain further, as will the eloquent photos in Russell Freedman's *Immigrant Kids*. Sook Nyul Choi's *Halmoni and the Picnic*, Barbara Cohen's *Molly's Pilgrim*, and Sherry Garland's *The Lotus Seed* are stories about the experiences of more recent immigrants. FAMILY LIFE. HISTORICAL FICTION. IMMIGRATION AND EMIGRATION. SWEDISH AMERICANS. VOYAGES AND TRAVELS.

694   **Wisniewski, David. *Rain Player*. Illus. by the author. Houghton Mifflin, 1991. ISBN 0-395-55112-9**

With a year of terrible drought foretold, young Pic angers the rain god Chac and tries to earn his forgiveness and bring rain to his people by challenging him to play pok-a-tok, the ancient Mayan soccerlike ball game. As in *Sundiata: Lion King of Mali* and *The Warrior and the Wise Man*, the artist's paper-cut style is powerful and unforgettable. Weather studies become that much more original with books like this and *The Match Between the Winds* by Shirley Climo, *Jalapeño Hal* by Jo Harper, *The Legend of Slappy Hooper* by Aaron Shepard, *Chinook* by Michael O. Tunnell, and *The Junior Thunder Lord* by Laurence Yep. If you're studying early American cultures, also interesting are *The Sad Night: The Story of an Aztec Victory and a Spanish Loss* by Sally Schofer Mathews, *The Tree That Rains: The Flood Myth of the Huichol Indians of Mexico* by Emery Bernhard, and *How Music Came to the World*, an Aztec folktale retold by Hal Ober. DROUGHT. GAMES. INDIANS OF CENTRAL AMERICA. MAYAN INDIANS. PICTURE BOOKS FOR ALL AGES. RAIN AND RAINFALL. WEATHER.

695   **Wojciechowski, Susan. *Don't Call Me Beanhead!* Illus. by Susanna Natti. Candlewick, 1994. ISBN 1-56402-319-2**

[5 chapters, 75p.] Narrator Beany is so involved watching an ant climb into the pencil sharpener she neglects to finish her "Healthy Bodies" test, on which she gets her first "F" and must get the paper signed by a parent. Other entertaining chapters deal with a favorite sweater grown too small, losing a tooth, and the school talent show. For each chapter, children can write their own essays: 1. Watch an ant and write about what it does. 2. Did you ever nag your parents for something you really really wanted? 3. Tell about a favorite item of clothing you loved and outgrew. 4. Write a poem about how you lost one of your teeth. 5. Make a list of all your special talents. FAMILY LIFE.

696   Yee, Paul. *Roses Sing on New Snow: A Delicious Tale.* **Illus. by Harvey Chan. Macmillan, 1992. ISBN 0-02-793622-8**

Maylin's fat, lazy brothers take all the credit and praise for the delicious dishes she cooks in the family's Chinese restaurant in the New World until the visiting governor of South China, delighting in the delectable flavors in the new dish Maylin creates in his honor, demands the recipe. Use this sly turn-of-the-century tale as an appetizer for meaty discussions of gender roles and multicultural contributions to American cuisine. Since there is no description of the tastes and foods comprising "Roses Sing on New Snow," ask your children to write down their list of ingredients and a step-by-step personal recipe for the dish. Next, have them dream up and write down a new world-class recipe of their own creation, or cook up and bring in an existing favorite for all to sample. If your budget allows, bring in some Chinese take-out and chopsticks. CHINESE AMERICANS. COOKERY. FOOD. PICTURE BOOKS FOR ALL AGES.

FICTION FOR GRADES 3–4

697   Alcorn, Johnny. *Rembrandt's Beret*. Illus. by Stephen Alcorn. Tambourine, 1991.
        ISBN 0-688-10207-7

[1 sitting, unp.] Grandfather Tiberius, painting young Marie's portrait, tells her of the day he happened upon the Hall of the Old Masters in Florence's Uffizi Gallery. It seems Rembrandt, Caravaggio, Reubens, and all the other painters climbed out of their picture frames and Rembrandt painted the boy's portrait, and gave him his brushes and his hat to keep forever. Raid the library for books with paintings and self-portraits of the artists including Pascal Bonafoux's *A Weekend with Rembrandt* (Rizzoli, 1992). Art teachers might undertake to have students paint each other's portraits. Ask a few salient questions: Why did the paintings come alive for Tiberius? Why did Rembrandt let the boy keep his painter's crown? If one person could come alive for you and change your life, who would it be and why? Another artist comes back for a longer spell in Elvira Woodruff's *The Disappearing Bike Shop*. Discover how Tomie dePaola decided to became an artist in *The Art Lesson*. ARTISTS. MUSEUMS. PAINTING. PICTURE BOOKS FOR ALL AGES.

698   Alexander, Lloyd. *The Fortune-Tellers*. Illus. by Trina Schart Hyman. Dutton, 1992.
        ISBN 0-525-44849-7

[1 sitting, unp.] A poor carpenter visits a fortune-teller who advises him he will be rich if he earns large sums of money, famous once he becomes well known, happy if he can avoid being miserable, and live a long life unless he has an early demise. The carpenter unwittingly makes his own self-fulfilling prophecy come true by taking over the job of the old fortune-teller, though children will want to debate whether he is deserving of his new status or just another charlatan. Hyman's breathtaking illustrations of life in Cameroon teem with details. Fortunes do not often work so fortuitously. Compare the fates of the three children granted wishes in Bill Brittain's *The Wish Giver*. Question: How responsible are we for our own fate? Explore the concept further with *Dream Peddler* by Gail E. Haley, *Saint Patrick and the Peddler* by Margaret Hodges, *The Treasure* by Uri Shulevitz, and *Fortune* by Diana Stanley. AFRICA. FORTUNE-TELLING. LUCK. PICTURE BOOKS FOR ALL AGES.

699   Andersen, Hans Christian. *The Nightingale.* Illus. by Josef Palecek. Trans. by Naomi Lewis. North-South, 1990. ISBN 1-55858-090-5

[1 sitting, unp.] The Emperor of China treasures the singing of his nightingale until he receives a gift of a mechanical toy bird that can sing the same song perfectly each time. Compare the beautiful Chinese-style paintings with Beni Montressor's version of the same tale. Translator Naomi Lewis includes a brief biography of Andersen as an introduction. For more details, consult *The Amazing Paper Cuttings of Hans Christian Andersen* by Beth Wagner Brust. Barry Moser's mesmerizing rewrite of *The Tinderbox,* Tor Seidler's retelling of *The Steadfast Tin Soldie*r, and Amy Ehrlich's or Deborah Hautzig's retellings of *The Wild Swans* are other fine examples of Andersen's writings. BIRDS. KINGS AND RULERS.

700   Andersen, Hans Christian. *The Wild Swans.* Illus. by Kaarina Kaila. Retold by Deborah Hautzig. Knopf, 1992. ISBN 0-679-93446-4

[1 sitting, unp.] When their father the king marries an evil queen, his 11 sons come under her wicked spell, which turns them into swans, and their devoted sister Elisa almost sacrifices her life to save them. Contrast Kaila's soft watercolors with the brazenly romantic illustrations by Susan Jeffers in Amy Ehrlich's retelling of the same story. In *The Swan Maiden* by Howard Pyle, it's the prince's sweetheart who is a swan. BIRDS. BROTHERS AND SISTERS. KINGS AND RULERS. LITERARY FAIRY TALES. SWANS. TRANSFORMATIONS.

701   Asch, Frank. *Pearl's Promise.* Illus. by the author. Delacorte, 1984. ISBN 0-385-29321-6

[21 chapters, 160p.] Pet-store mouse Pearl must figure out a way to spring her little brother from the cage of a reticulated python before the snake gets hungry again. Satisfy mouse-lovers with the memorable characters in Beverly Cleary's *The Mouse and the Motorcycle,* Roald Dahl's *The Witches,* Dick King-Smith's *Martin's Mice,* and Jean Van Leeuwen's *The Great Christmas Kidnapping Caper* and *The Great Rescue Operation.* Meet up with another evil snake in Rudyard Kipling's classic tale *Rikki-Tikki-Tavi.* FANTASY. MICE. SNAKES.

702   Banks, Lynne Reid. *The Magic Hare.* Illus. by Barry Moser. Morrow, 1993. ISBN 0-688-10896-2

[10 chapters, 49p.] Here are ten rip-roaring stories about the usual assortment of folks—a spoiled queen, an orphan girl, two dim giants, a vampire, a hiccuping prince, a black-and-white witch, a poor king—who meet up with the winsome hare. Like the tricksters from traditional folklore, he solves their problems or gets the better of them, and in the last story even takes a jump to the moon, but decides Earth is the place for his special talents. Children will clamor to compose new "Magic Hare" adventures. Catherine Storr's *Clever Polly and the Stupid Wolf* is also folklore-related, with a wolf who lacks even basic common sense. CREATIVE WRITING. FANTASY. HARES. MAGIC. SHORT STORIES.

703   Bawden, Nina. *Humbug.* Clarion, 1992. ISBN 0-395-62149-6

[15 chapters, 133p.] With her parents off to Japan for six months and Granny laid up with a broken leg, feisty eight-year-old Cora is enraged at being separated from her siblings and sent to stay with a next-door neighbor—too-sweet, phony Aunt Sunday and her horrible, pouting, banshee of a daughter, Angelica—until she strikes up a friendship with Angelica's grandmother, Ma Potter. Raydeen is another strong main character who tries to interest her widowed grandfather in enjoying himself again in *Grandfather's Day* by Ingrid Tomey. ELDERLY. GRANDPARENTS. HONESTY. SELF-RELIANCE.

704   Benjamin, Saragail Katzman. *My Dog Ate It.* **Holiday House, 1994. ISBN 0-8234-1047-1**

[16 chapters, 166p.] Feeling like he's trapped in a science-fiction movie about time warps with no escape forthcoming and no control over his own life, Danny makes a conscious decision to flunk fifth grade so he won't have to go to middle school next year. His teacher, Ms. McCardle, noticing his refusal to do any assignments, implements the Plan, sending her talking dog Homework to help Danny improve his self-esteem. *Juliet Fisher and the Foolproof Plan* by Natalie Honeycutt, *Class Clown* by Johanna Hurwitz, *Maxie, Rosie, and Earl—Partners in Grime* by Barbara Park, and *Fourth Grade Rats* by Jerry Spinelli are also top flight kid-with-school-troubles stories. Another stubborn child meets up with a magic-powered pet on a mission in *Witch-Cat* by Joan Carris. BEHAVIOR. DOGS. FANTASY. HUMOROUS FICTION. MAGIC. SELF-RELIANCE. TEACHERS.

705   Bunting, Eve. *Night of the Gargoyles.* **Illus. by David Wiesner. Clarion, 1994. ISBN 0-395-66553-1**

When night falls, the unblinking stone gargoyles creep down from their perches, on the facade of the museum, peer into the windows at mummies and armor, splash in the fountain, and jeer at the night watchman. The aura of this macabre mood-piece picture book is sardonic, with Van Allsburg-like gray pastel illustrations. Show pictures of real gargoyles before you read. *The Sweetest Fig* and *The Widow's Broom* by Chris Van Allsburg will fit the mood well, while another transformation story, *Tuesday* by David Wiesner, will provide color and a hearty laugh. *Tigerella* by Kit Wright is a daring romp of a poem about a good little girl who becomes a tiger at night, while the title character in Jacqueline K. Ogburn's *Scarlett Angelina Wolverton-Manning* is a werewolf. GARGOYLES. NIGHT. PICTURE BOOKS FOR ALL AGES. TRANSFORMATIONS.

706   Carris, Joan. *Witch-Cat.* **Illus. by Beth Peck. Dell, 1986. ISBN 0-440-49477-X (pbk.)**

[17 chapters, 154p.] For her first job in 200 years, witch-cat Rosetta is sent from Wales to Ohio to become the mistress to practical, magic-scorning Gwen and help the girl discover her own true powers as a witch. Call up some more magic with *Little Witch* by Anna Elizabeth Bennett, *The Chocolate Touch* by Patrick Skene Catling, *Mrs. Tooey & the Terrible Toxic Tar* and *What's Happened to Harry?* by Barbara Dillon, *The Three and Many Wishes of Jason Reid* by Hazel Hutchins, and *Wizard's Hall* by Jane Yolen. A talking dog is assigned to Danny to get him to do his schoolwork in *My Dog Ate It* by Saragail Katzman Benjamin. CATS. DOGS. FANTASY. FRIENDSHIP. MAGIC. WITCHES.

707   Coerr, Eleanor. *Mieko and the Fifth Treasure.* **Calligraphy by Cecil H. Uyehara. Putnam, 1993. ISBN 0-399-22434-3**

[11 chapters, 80p.] Two weeks after The Thunderbolt or atomic bomb is dropped on Nagasaki in 1945, ten-year-old Mieko is sent to live with her grandparents on their farm so her hand can heal from the cut she received from flying glass that day. Formerly a talented calligrapher, she now can't draw, and must overcome her anger and fear at her loss and at being in a new school with children who taunt her. Coerr's picture book *Sadako* and the longer *Sadako & the Thousand Paper Cranes* and Junko Morimoto's autobiographical *My Hiroshima* provide additional background on that terrible time. Ken Mochizuki's *Baseball Saved Us*, Allen Say's *Tree of Cranes* and *Grandfather's Journey*, and Ruth Wells's *A to Zen: A Book of Japanese Culture* are also invaluable. ARTISTS. FRIENDSHIP. HISTORICAL FICTION. JAPAN. SCHOOLS. SELF-ESTEEM. WORLD WAR, 1939-1945–FICTION.

708   Cresswell, Helen. *Time Out.* **Illus. by Peter Elwell. Macmillan, 1990. ISBN 0-02-725425-9**

[5 chapters, 74p.] In a large house in London, on October 8, 1887, Ethel Wilks the parlormaid and her 12-year-old daughter Tweeny the between-maid are hoping to go to the seaside for their first holiday ever. Instead, Ethel's husband, Wilks the butler, convinces them to come with him to 1997, thanks to a book of magic spells he has found. The changes they find 100 years later are mind-boggling: boxes with talking people, conveyances that go without horses, and ladies who show their bare legs! Abigail is brought from 1846 to the present in *Friends in Time* by Grace Chetwin, while the "Time Warp Trio" try prehistoric life in *Your Mother Was a Neanderthal* by Jon Scieszka. Using the "Inventions and Discoveries" section of the *World Almanac*, students can figure out what else had not yet been invented or discovered in 1887 and write a sequel for Tweeny's shocking return to the future. ENGLAND. FANTASY. MAGIC. TIME TRAVEL.

709   Crew, Linda. *Nekomah Creek.* **Illus. by Charles Robinson. Delacorte, 1991. ISBN 0-385-30442-0**

[21 chapters, 191p.] Robby Hummer's fourth-grade teacher sends him to the new school counselor because he reads during recess, and Robby worries that she'll take him away from his role-reversed parents, with mom working and dad cooking and caring for the two-year-old twins in their rustic barn-house in rural Oregon. Book-lovers will especially appreciate page 12, where Robby expounds on the advantages of reading over television. FAMILY LIFE. SCHOOLS. TWINS.

710   Dahl, Roald. *Esio Trot.* **Illus. by Quentin Blake. Viking, 1990. ISBN 0-670-83451-3**

[2 sittings, 62p.] What's tortoise spelled backward? In a whimsical tale of trickery all for the sake of love, Mr. Hoppy lives in the apartment above Mrs. Silver, a widow whom he loves unrequited. In his quest to be noticed by her, he gives her the supposed secret words to make her beloved pet tortoise Alfie grow bigger. Kids will love to read the backward chant and can write new incantations. Once they're hooked on reading words backward, dazzle them with the many palindromes in Jon Agee's *Go Hang a Salami! I'm a Lasagna Hog!* LOVE. SIZE. TURTLES.

711   Greenwald, Sheila. *Rosy Cole Discovers America!* Illus. by the author. Little, Brown, 1992. ISBN 0-316-32721-2

[7 chapters, 96p.] Rosy's assignment for school is to research her own relatives and trace her ancestors, but finding no one famous in her family tree leads her to make up stories about her Great-great-granny Popkin. Readers wanting more about this spunky girl will enjoy the rest of the Rosie Cole series. In *Jenny Archer, Author* by Ellen Conford, Jenny also fabricates her own autobiography to make it more exciting. If you are thinking about starting a genealogy project about family histories for social studies, don't forget Ina R. Friedman's picture book *How My Family Learned to Eat* about how a girl's Japanese mother and American father first got together. FAMILY STORIES. GENEALOGY. SCHOOLS.

712   Havill, Juanita. *Leona and Ike.* Illus. by Emily Arnold McCully. Crown, 1991. ISBN 0-517-57689-2

At first nine-year-old Leona can't stand Ike, the stuck-up new boy on her street who calls her dummy and thinks everything she finds interesting is dumb. Ike's parents are divorced, and Leona worries that her father, who goes on frequent business trips, could leave too. The sequel to *It Always Happens to Leona* (1989), this stands on its own and handles troubling issues with humor and believability. Another story that successfully tackles the issue of divorce is *Don't Make Me Smile* by Barbara Park. Learning to like the new kid is not always problem-free, as we also learn in *The All-New Jonah Twist* by Natalie Honeycutt and *Joshua T. Bates Takes Charge* by Susan Shreve. DIVORCE. FRIENDSHIP. MOVING, HOUSEHOLD.

713   Heide, Florence Parry, and Judith Heide Gilliland. *Sami and the Time of the Troubles.* Illus. by Ted Lewin. Clarion, 1992. ISBN 0-395-55964-2

Sami, the ten-year-old narrator of this somber but hopeful story, waits for the days when he will be able to go outside his uncle's basement in war-torn Beirut and be free of the violence and gunfire that killed his father. It's not easy to explain to children the presence of wars and upheaval, whether in Ireland, the Middle East, former Yugoslavia, or here in America. For more insight, read Eleanor Coerr's *Sadako* and Junko Morimoto's *My Hiroshima* about the atomic bomb, and Sherry Garland's *The Lotus Seed* and Diana Kidd's *Onion Tears* about the aftermath of the Vietnam War. FAMILY LIFE. LEBANON. PICTURE BOOKS FOR ALL AGES. WAR.

714   Hesse, Karen. *Sable.* Illus. by Marcia Sewall. Henry Holt, 1994. ISBN 0-8050-2416-6

[11 short chapters, 81p.] Tate's mother dislikes dogs, but when a near-starved stray wanders down from the mountain, Tate names it Sable and keeps it outside until her parents give it away. In a classic tale of loss, love, and determination, narrator Tate has us rooting for her as she tries to train the gentle but theft-prone dog, builds a fence to keep him in, and deals with his absence. As you read this aloud, have your students keep a running list of words to describe Tate's personality that they can then use to write a character study or a letter to Tate's mother detailing why she should let her daughter keep this dog. Jessie tries to tame a near-wild dog in *Red-Dirt Jessie* by Anna Myers. DOGS.

715   **Hurwitz, Johanna.** *Class President.* **Illus. by Sheila Hamanaka. Morrow, 1990. ISBN 0-688-09114-8**

[8 chapters, 85p.] Though fifth-grader Julio Sanchez would secretly love to be elected class president, he promises to be best friend Lucas Cott's campaign manager instead, a promise that proves impossible to keep. Introduce your class to the other humorous books in Hurwitz's on-target series: *Class Clown, Teacher's Pet* (1988), *School's Out* (1991), and *School Spirit*. Claudia Mills's *Dinah for President* and Barbara Park's *Rosie Swanson, Fourth-Grade Geek for President* put other spins on the campaign process. ELECTIONS. HISPANIC AMERICANS. MULTICULTURAL STORIES. SCHOOLS.

716   **Hurwitz, Johanna.** *School Spirit.* **Illus. by Karen M. Dugan. Morrow, 1994. ISBN 0-688-12825-4**

[12 chapters, 139p.] Julio Sanchez, now fifth-grade class president at Edison-Armstrong School, is incredulous when he hears about the school board's proposal to close the school and, with the support of his teacher, Mr. Flores, and his classmates, including Lucas and Cricket, comes up with practical ideas to rally the students and the community. Not only does this show the difference children can make if they plan together, but in the end we see how Julio deals with another student getting all the public acclaim and credit for his project. Stir up a little school spirit by having students find out about the history of their own school through interviews with senior staff members and older members of the neighborhood. SCHOOLS.

717   **Johnston, Tony.** *The Cowboy and the Black-Eyed Pea.* **Illus. by Warren Ludwig. Putnam, 1992. ISBN 0-399-22330-4**

Texas heiress Farethee Well, looking for a real cowboy who will love her for herself, not just her herd of longhorn cattle, comes up with a test to separate the cowboys from the fortune hunters. How she finds someone sensitive enough to feel a pea hidden under a pile of "fifty saddle blankets, all stacked up like flapjacks" makes for a sly picture-book retelling of Hans Christian Andersen's familiar tale. Don't forget to make sure everyone's heard the original story. Play with the parody "The Princess and the Bowling Ball" from Jon Scieszka's *The Stinky Cheese Man* and Anne Wilsdorf's *Princess*. Stay on horseback with Roy Gerard's *Rosie and the Rustlers*, Jo Harper's *Jalapeño Hal*, Eric A. Kimmel's *Charlie Drives the Stage*, and Arthur Yorinks's *Whitefish Will Rides Again!* Get into the western mood with *Songs of the Wild West* edited by Alan Axelrod and with *Cowboys*, a collection of poems compiled by Charles Sullivan. COWBOYS. FAIRY TALES–SATIRE. PARODIES. PICTURE BOOKS FOR ALL AGES. TEXAS. WEST.

718   **Jukes, Mavis.** *I'll See You in My Dreams.* **Illus. by Stacey Schuett. Knopf, 1993. ISBN 0-679-92690-9**

If she were a skywriter, she would don her leather Amelia Earhart jacket and fly her plane past the hospital where her pilot uncle lies dying, and spell out in clouds the word good-bye. But she's just a kid, flying cross-country with her mother, to see him in the hospital. A poignant and sensitive picture-book, this is not for younger children unless the class is dealing with the death of a friend or relative. Other picture books about death include *The Key into Winter* by Janet S. Andersen, *Eleanor, Arthur, and Claire* by Diana Engel, *Annie and the Old One* by Miska Miles, *Abuelita's Paradise* by Carmen Santiago Nodar, *Saying Good-Bye to Grandma* by Jane Resh Thomas and *The Tenth Good Thing About Barney* by Judith Viorst. When reading aloud fiction books such as *Back to Before* by Jan Slepian and *Dear Napoleon, I Know You're Dead, But . . .* by Elvira Woodruff, pull in this one for its insight. AIRPLANES. DEATH. FLIGHT. PICTURE BOOKS FOR ALL AGES. SICK. TERMINALLY ILL. UNCLES.

719   Kalman, Maira. *Chicken Soup Boots.* Illus. by the author. Viking, 1993. ISBN 0-670-85201-5

[1–2 sittings, unp.] Kalman's books are *très* strange, an acquired taste, and this one, a meandering, musing, and perceptive look at her eccentric family and neighbors in connection with their many jobs, is as odd as picture books come. It's certainly an original way to answer the age-old question, "What do you want to be when you grow up, dear?" Ask your writers to compose and illustrate a portrait of a family member or friend with an unusual job. OCCUPATIONS.

720   Kimmel, Eric A. *Bernal & Florinda: A Spanish Tale.* Illus. by Robert Rayevsky. Holiday House, 1994. ISBN 0-8234-1089-7

Undaunted when his true love's father, the town's mayor, insults him, poor but dashing Bernal vows to marry his Florinda and make his fortune from the grasshoppers that plague his only field. He trades the insects for first a goose, then trades for a sack of charcoal, and finally candles, and tricks the greedy mayor into giving away the hand of his daughter. Illustrated in pen-and-ink and "brilliant" watercolors, the uproarious story is staged like a Spanish play. Bring in a peach pit to hold up as you read the last sentence. Blaming someone for causing the death of an already-dead man is also the plot of "Old Dry Fry" in Richard Chase's *Grandfather Tales*. GRASSHOPPERS. GREED. HUMOROUS FICTION. INSECTS. LOVE. SPAIN.

721   Kimmel, Eric A. *Four Dollars and Fifty Cents.* Illus. by Glen Rounds. Holiday House, 1990. ISBN 0-8234-0817-5

[1 sitting, unp.] Here's a real knee-slapper about how Shorty Long plays dead just so the Widow Macrae can't collect her debt from him. When the widow hauls his casket-clad carcass over to the burial grounds to see if he has truly met his maker, he almost gets his nose sliced off by a trio of train robbers. Roy Gerard's *Rosie and the Rustlers*, Jo Harper's *Jalapeño Hal*, Tony Johnston's parody *The Cowboy and the Black-Eyed Pea*, Kimmel's *Charlie Drives the Stage*, and Angela Shelf Medearis's adaption of the folksong *The Zebra-Riding Cowboy*, Glen Rounds's own *Mr. Yowder and the Train Robbers*, and Arthur Yorinks's *Whitefish*

Will Rides Again! will also keep kids hooting. COWBOYS. MONEY. ROBBERS AND OUT-LAWS. TRICKSTER TALES. WEST.

722   **King-Smith, Dick.** *The Cuckoo Child.* **Illus. by Leslie Bowman. Little, Brown, 1993. ISBN 1-56282-350-7**

[14 chapters, 127p.] Farm boy Jack Daw loves birds best of all, and when his class takes a trip to the wildlife park, he secretly lifts an ostrich egg that the ranger says will not be incubated and places it in the nest of his goose Lydia. Starting with chapter five, we listen in on the birds conversing when Oliver emerges from the strange giant egg and his adopted mother Lydia finds him marvelous. As with all Dick King-Smith stories, his animal dialogue is just right, and you'll learn a great deal about ostriches along the way. The classic tale of raising exotic birds at home is *Mr. Popper's Penguins* by Robert Lawson. BIRDS. FARM LIFE. GEESE. OSTRICHES. STEALING.

723   **King-Smith, Dick.** *Lady Daisy.* **Illus. by Jan Naimo Jones. Delacorte, 1993. ISBN 0-385-30891-4**

[16 chapters, 131p.] Cleaning out a room in his grandmother's attic, Ned comes across a shoebox containing a beautiful old-fashioned doll who speaks to him, telling him her name is Lady Daisy Chain. The doll has been asleep since 1901, and Ned fills her in on modern advancements and takes her home with him, even though he knows boys don't keep dolls. Talk over sex roles and why children feel so bound by them. *William's Doll* by Charlotte Zolotow deals sensitively with this problem. On the historical front, children can do a bit of research to find out what the world was like in 1901, and list the many changes that have come about since then. DOLLS. ENGLAND.

724   **King-Smith, Dick.** *Paddy's Pot of Gold.* **Illus. by David Parkins. Crown, 1992. ISBN 0-517-58136-1**

[10 chapters, 114p.] On the morning of her eighth birthday, Brigid meets P.V.W.R.H. O'Reilly, a 174-year-old leprechaun who promises her his friendship until his dying day. Compare the personalities of leprechauns encountered in Bill Brittain's *All the Money in the World*, Elizabeth Johnson's *Stuck with Luck*, Richard Kennedy's *The Leprechaun's Story*, and Joan Lowery Nixon's *The Gift*. FANTASY. FARM LIFE. FOXES. IRELAND. LEPRECHAUNS.

725   **King-Smith, Dick.** *Pretty Polly.* **Illus. by Marshall Peck. Crown, 1992. ISBN 0-517-58606-1**

[15 chapters, 120p.] With an expensive pet parrot out of the question, Abigail decides instead to train a baby chick to talk, and her hard work pays off. Other interesting fowl can be found in King-Smith's *The Cuckoo Child*, Robert Lawson's *Mr. Popper's Penguins*, Daniel Pinkwater's *The Hoboken Chicken Emergency*, and E. B. White's *The Trumpet of the Swan*. CHICKENS. FARM LIFE. PETS.

726   **King-Smith, Dick.** *The Queen's Nose.* **Illus. by Jill Bennett. HarperCollins, 1994. ISBN 0-06-440450-1**

[11 chapters, 111p.] Harmony's parents won't allow any pets in the house, but when her Uncle Ginger visits for the first time he gives her a riddle to solve leading to the discovery of a magical 50 pence piece that will grant seven wishes. Your listeners will love the way scrappy Harmony categorizes all the people she knows into types of animals (her teacher looks to her like a praying mantis), and might start looking at the folks around them with new eyes. If you can, get hold of an English 50 pence piece so your lot can give proper attention to what they'd wish for and write about the possible consequences. In *The Three and Many Wishes of Jason Reid* by Hazel Hutchins, Jason finds a loophole that allows him unlimited wishes from a magical Elster. ENGLAND. MAGIC. MONEY. WISHES.

727   **King-Smith, Dick.** *The Swoose.* **Illus. by Marie Corner. Hyperion, 1994. ISBN 1-56282-659-X**

[4 chapters, 46p.] Fitzherbert, larger than the rest of the farm's goslings, learns that he is half goose, half swan. As a one-of-a kind swoose, he ventures to Windsor Castle where he becomes a companion to Queen Victoria, making the widow smile for the first time since the death of her husband, Prince Albert, 25 years before. A quick and charming blend of history and animal fantasy, this can foster a research project on Queen Victoria and on whether there are such birds as sweese. ANIMALS, MYTHICAL. BIRDS. ENGLAND. FANTASY. HISTORICAL FICTION. KINGS AND RULERS. VICTORIA, QUEEN OF GREAT BRITAIN, 1819-1901.

728   **Kipling, Rudyard.** *Just So Stories.* **Illus. by David Frampton. HarperCollins, 1991. ISBN 0-06-023296-X**

[12 stories, 122p.] Illustrated with sepia-toned woodcuts that resemble batiks are 12 of Kipling's best-known stories. Another shorter collection includes just five tales illustrated by Victor Ambrus. Vibrant single versions in picture-book format include *The Beginning of the Armadillos* and *The Elephant's Child*, both illustrated by Lorinda Bryan Cauley, *How the Camel Got His Hump* illustrated by Quentin Blake, and *How the Whale Got His Throat* illustrated by Pauline Baynes. ANIMALS. POURQUOI TALES. SHORT STORIES.

729   **Kipling, Rudyard.** *Rikki-Tikki-Tavi.* **Illus. by Lambert Davis. Harcourt, 1992. ISBN 0-15-267015-7**

[2 sittings, 37p.] Written in the 1890s, this classic story, set in India, tells of a brave mongoose who, after being taken in as a pet by an English couple to protect their little son Teddy, defends the child from the deadly cobras Nag and Nagaina. Make the acquaintance of a less fearsome snake in Kipling's *The Elephant's Child*, and a vengeful one in *Pearl's Promise* by Frank Asch. COBRAS. FANTASY. INDIA. MONGOOSE. SNAKES.

730   **Leverich, Kathleen.** *Hilary and the Troublemakers.* **Illus. by Walter Lorraine. Greenwillow, 1992. ISBN 0-688-10857-1**

[5 chapters, 138p.] A giant owl with fierce yellow eyes and a dangerous-looking beak who eats fractions homework, 12 misbehaving sheep, a family of threatening snow people, and a sneaky, selfish piggy bank vex youngest child Hilary Hummer, whose zany imaginary life seems so utterly real to her. Ask your students to write about the joys and aggravations of being the oldest, youngest, middle, or only child. The first chapter is a splendid candidate for Reader's Theater. You'll want to turn it into a script and have your class read and act it out. Ogden Nash's classic, comic, narrative poem *The Adventures of Isabel*, with James Marshall's fiendishly fun illustrations, demonstrates how to take care of any old bugaboo that might bother you, from enormous bear to horrible dream. BEHAVIOR. BROTHERS AND SISTERS. HUMOROUS FICTION. IMAGINATION.

731   Levy, Elizabeth. *Keep Ms. Sugarman in the Fourth Grade.* Illus. by Dave Henderson. HarperCollins, 1991. ISBN 0-06-020427-3

[18 chapters, 83p.] Once every teacher's nightmare, Jackie blooms with the understanding and dynamic Ms. Sugarman until Ms. Sugarman is appointed principal and Jackie vows to stop the promotion by handcuffing herself to her teacher's desk. Ask your students to write about the teacher who made them feel special and explain how that person changed their lives. Saragail Katzman Benjamin's *My Dog Ate It*, Natalie Honeycutt's *Juliet Fisher and the Foolproof Plan*, Johanna Hurwitz's *Class Clown*, Barbara Park's *Maxie, Rosie, and Earl—Partners in Grime*, Barbara Robinson's *The Best School Year Ever*, and Jerry Spinelli's *Fourth Grade Rats* are also middle-grade comedies. BEHAVIOR. SCHOOLS. SELF-ESTEEM. TEACHERS.

732   Mellecker, Judith. *Randolph's Dream.* Illus. by Robert Andrew Parker. Knopf, 1991. ISBN 0-679-81115-X

[1 sitting, unp.] Sent out of London to stay with his aunt and uncle in the safer English countryside during World War II, seven-year-old Randolph dreams of flying every night until the night his mother comes to visit, when his dream of flying to the North African desert and rescuing his own father becomes real. A strangely compelling story, the open-ended conclusion will make you think of Antoine de Saint Exupèry's *The Little Prince*. *War Game*, a heavy-hitting choice for older children by Michael Foreman, and *Don't You Know There's a War On?*, an autobiographical recollection by James Stevenson, are both engrossing picture books about World War II. DREAMS. ENGLAND. FANTASY. FATHERS AND SONS. PICTURE BOOKS FOR ALL AGES. WAR. WORLD WAR, 1939-1945–FICTION.

733   Mochizuki, Ken. *Baseball Saved Us.* Illus. by Dom Lee. Lee & Low Books, 1993. ISBN 1-880000-01-6

[1 sitting, unp.] Somber, sepia-toned paintings, some inspired by Ansel Adams's photographs at Manzanar, accompany a Japanese American child's description of life in the internment camp where he and his family were sent during World War II. Faced with horse-stall barracks, dust storms, and nothing to do, the adults joined together with their children to build a baseball field, sew uniforms, and form teams. With the omnipresent guard in the tower watching, the narrator, normally an "easy out," hits a home run. Back home after the war, when faced once more with prejudice, the boy again proves himself on the baseball field. Get children talking about why people discriminate against those who are different, using a variety of provocative titles such as Peter Golenbock's *Teammates*, Daisaku Ikeda's *Over the Deep Blue Sea*, and Margaree King Mitchell's *Uncle Jed's Barbershop*. BASEBALL. HISTORICAL FICTION. JAPANESE AMERICANS. PREJUDICE. WORLD WAR, 1939-1945–FICTION.

734   **Murphy, Jill.** *Jeffrey Strangeways.* **Illus. by the author. Candlewick, 1992. ISBN 1-56402-018-5**

[11 chapters, 144p.] A poor lad like Jeffrey with a mother depending on him to earn a living should stand little chance of becoming a knight, but the day he meets armor-clad Sir Walter of Winterwood and shares the knight's picnic, he sets out to change his fortune. Rescuing a distressed damsel, clearing out a dragon's lair, and dispensing with a nasty ogre named Grobb are on the knight's list of assignments, and through a series of comical mishaps with an overgrown puppy named Lancelot, Jeffrey comes to the rescue. *Knights of the Kitchen Table* by Jon Scieszka will also prove popular. FANTASY. KNIGHTS AND KNIGHTHOOD. OGRES.

735   **Naylor, Phyllis Reynolds.** *The Boys Start the War.* **Delacorte, 1993. ISBN 0-385-30814-0**

[15 chapters, 133p.] It's the last week of summer vacation, and the four Hatford brothers are outraged to discover that the house where their best friends lived has been rented out to a family with three girls. In alternating rip-roaring chapters, we see how the equally devious and fun-loving Malloy girls and Hatford boys spy on, outmaneuver, and outwit each other in their quest for entertainment and revenge. Readers will want to follow the continued hostilities in *The Girls Get Even* (1993) and *Boys Against Girls* (Delacorte, 1994). BROTHERS. HUMOROUS FICTION. PRACTICAL JOKES. SISTERS.

736   **Park, Barbara.** *Maxie, Rosie, and Earl—Partners in Grime.* **Illus. by Alexander Strogart. Knopf, 1990. ISBN 0-679-90212-0**

[9 chapters, 117p.] Earl Wilbur refuses to read aloud in class, Rosie Swanson tattles once too often, and Maxie Zuckerman cuts a hole in Daniel W.'s shirt after being humiliated by him one time too many. The three oddballs meet in the principal's office for the first time, decide to run out of school together, and end up hiding in a stinky cafeteria dumpster. Once again, Park makes us laugh and identify with the underdog. Your students will enjoy cruising the dictionary for more of Maxie's special words that sound insulting but aren't, such as dipsey, foozle, and niblick. Saragail Katzman Benjamin's *My Dog Ate It*, Natalie Honeycutt's *Juliet Fisher and the Foolproof Plan*, Johanna Hurwitz's *Class Clown*, Elizabeth Levy's *Keep Ms. Sugarman in the Fourth Grade*, Barbara Robinson's *The Best School Year Ever*, and Jerry Spinelli's *Fourth Grade Rats* all concern school kids who don't or won't fit in. BEHAVIOR. FRIENDSHIP. SCHOOLS.

737   **Park, Barbara.** *Rosie Swanson, Fourth-Grade Geek for President.* **Knopf, 1991. ISBN 0-679-92094-3**

[11 chapters, 123p.] Rosie, the self-righteous tattletale of *Maxie, Rosie, and Earl—Partners in Grime*, wonders if an average person has a chance to win as class president, especially when her competition consists of the two most popular kids in the school, one of whom steals both her campaign poem and her idea to campaign for better cafeteria food. Continue campaigning with *Class President* by Johanna Hurwitz and Claudia Mills's *Dinah for President*. ELECTIONS. FRIENDSHIP. HUMOROUS FICTION. POPULARITY. SCHOOLS. TATTLING.

738   Paulsen, Gary. *Dogteam.* Illus. by Ruth Wright Paulsen. Delacorte, 1993. ISBN 0-385-30550-8

[1 sitting, unp.] In a flowing prose poem, two-time Iditarod runner Paulsen rhapsodizes about the beauty and thrill of racing his sled dogs at night. Ruth Paulsen's exquisite night-lit paintings jump off the page. Find out more about the winter wolves they encounter with *The Eyes of Gray Wolf* by Jonathan London and *The Call of the Wolves* by Jim Murphy. *Dream Wolf* by Paul Goble is a compelling Plains Indian story about a brother and sister rescued by a wolf. Bill Littlefield's *Champions: Stories of Ten Remarkable Athletes* devotes a chapter to Susan Butcher, four-time Iditarod winner, and makes us shiver, and Patricia Seibert's *Mush! Across Alaska in the World's Longest Sled-Dog Race* is a picture-book description of the Iditarod. DOGS. PICTURE BOOKS FOR ALL AGES. SLED DOG RACING. WINTER.

739   Rodowsky, Colby. *Dog Days.* Illus. by Kathleen Collins Howell. Farrar, 1990. ISBN 0-374-36342-0

[10 chapters, 131p.] With all the earmarks of a "really *rotten* summer," now that Miss Flossie Scott is coming to baby-sit, along with her grand-niece Destiny, aka Skinny-bones, Rosie is surprised to find excitement next door where famous children's book author Dawn O'Day and Sandy the Super Dog have just moved in. Rosie has a few choice words she has picked up from her thesaurus and enjoys flinging about, including nefarious, abominable, and splendiferous. Each of your wordsmiths can find an outrageous new word to spring on the rest of the group, and incorporate them in stories about that dog star of children's fiction, Sandy. AUTHORS. DOGS. FRIENDSHIP.

740   Roop, Peter, and Connie Roop. *Ahyoka and the Talking Leaves.* Illus. by Yoshi Miyake. Lothrop, 1992. ISBN 0-688-10697-8

[7 chapters, 60p.] A fictionalized biography based on the achievements of Sequoyah, the Cherokee man who in the 19th century became the first person to single-handedly invent a written language from a spoken one, enabling his people to read and write in their own language. Though even her mother can't understand the point in trying to make "talking leaves," as they refer to paper with writing on it, Sequoyah's daughter Ahyoka is determined to support her father in his mission and helps him work out the idea of drawing a picture-letter for every sound in the Tsalagi language. Reproduce the syllabary at the front of the book so children can write each other messages in Cherokee, which, with 86 characters, is tricky but most diverting. *Books and Libraries* by Jack Knowlton gives a brief history of writing that makes Sequoyah's invention seem even more impressive. ALPHABET. CHEROKEE INDIANS. FATHERS AND DAUGHTERS. INDIANS OF NORTH AMERICA–BIOGRAPHY. WRITING.

741   Russell, Ching Yeung. *First Apple.* Illus. by Christopher Zhong-Yuan Zhang. Boyds Mills Press, 1994. ISBN 1-56397-206-9

In a small village in China in the 1940s, nine-year-old Ying decides that she will somehow buy her Ah Pau (grandmother) an apple to share for her 71st birthday, since apples are considered rich man's food and they have never tried one. This gently amusing chapter book, based on the author's childhood, gives us a look at another time and culture. Hand out apple chunks so children can see, smell, and taste the fruit as if for the first time. For contrast, *Yang the Youngest and His Terrible Ear* by Lensey Namioka introduces us to a Chinese family newly arrived in the United States. APPLES. CHINA. GRANDMOTHERS.

742   Schwartz, Amy. *The Lady Who Put Salt in Her Coffee.* Illus. by the author. Harcourt, 1989. ISBN 0-15-243475-5

[1 sitting, unp.] When Mrs. Peterkin puts salt in her coffee instead of sugar, the entire family seeks advice on what to do from the chemist and the herb woman, both of whom try without success to doctor the beverage with dozens of chemical and herbaceous antidotes. It's not until they consult that wise lady from Philadelphia that they hear a reasonable solution: make a fresh cup of coffee! Before you reveal the ending, ask your crew what additions or ideas they'd suggest. A picture-book adaptation from a chapter in Lucretia P. Hale's classic *The Peterkin Papers*, originally published in 1880, the story has the same wry tone and deadpan absurdist humor of Wallace Tripp's *My Uncle Podger*, an English classic tale of a self-important uncle who can't manage to hang a simple painting. FAMILY LIFE. HUMOROUS FICTION.

743   Scieszka, Jon. *Knights of the Kitchen Table.* Illus. by Lane Smith. Viking, 1991. ISBN 0-670-83622-2

[10 short chapters, 55p.] In the first of the Time Warp Trio series, best friends Joe, Fred, and Sam find themselves being threatened by the Black Knight after a magic book Joe receives at his birthday party sends them back to King Arthur's time, with its giants, ogres, and all. The tongue-in-cheek silliness of the series will thrill reluctant readers, with titles like *The Good, the Bad, and the Goofy* (1992), *The Not-So-Jolly Roger* (1991), and *Your Mother Was a Neanderthal.* Gery Greer and Bob Ruddick's *Max and Me and the Time Machine* did it first, with two time-traveling boys who find themselves enmeshed with jousting knights and olde English, but Scieszka's is an easier-to-read book on the same theme. In the same vein are *The Saga of Erik the Viking* by Monty Python's Terry Jones, *Jacob Two-Two Meets the Hooded Fang* by Mordecai Richler, and Pamela Stearns's *Into the Painted Bear Lair.* Kid helps knight held by ogre in Jill Murphy's entertaining *Jeffrey Strangeways.* DRAGONS. FANTASY. GIANTS. HUMOROUS FICTION. KNIGHTS AND KNIGHTHOOD.

744   Scribner, Virginia. *Gopher Takes Heart.* Illus. by Janet Wilson. Viking, 1993. ISBN 0-670-84839-5

[22 chapters, 136p.] Fifth-grader Gopher is trying to figure out a way to get out of handing over his milk money to bully Fletcher every day on the way to school. With its Valentine's Day setting and deft depiction of a problem many kids face, here's a book that will start your class talking about friendship and how to nurture it. BULLIES. SCHOOLS. SELF-ESTEEM. VALENTINE'S DAY.

745   Selznick, Brian. *The Houdini Box.* Illus. by the author. Knopf, 1991. ISBN 0-679-81429-9

[1 sitting, unp.] Ten-year-old Victor, who has tried and failed to duplicate Houdini's famous feats, meets the great magician, who promises to write him a letter telling all, which he does, inviting the boy to his house. Sadly, when Victor arrives on Halloween night, Houdini's wife tells him the magician is dead, and gives him a small locked box engraved with the initials E.W. More of Houdini's marvelous stunts are revealed in Robert Kraske's *Magicians Do Amazing Things* and Florence White's *Escape! The Life of Harry Houdini.* Set in the 1920s, Emily Arnold McCully's *The Amazing Felix* is also about an aspiring child magician. Learn how not to throw your voice with David Macaulay's *Help! Let Me Out!* and climb the tightrope with Emily Arnold McCully's *Mirette on the High Wire,* loosely based on the feats of daredevil Blondin. HOUDINI, HARRY. MAGIC. MAGICIANS.

746   Sheldon, Dyan. *My Brother Is a Visitor from Another Planet.* Illus. by Derek Brazell. Candlewick, 1993. ISBN 1-56402-141-6

[10 chapters, 105p.] Explaining that he is really an alien with special powers, older brother Keith is so convincing, especially when he demonstrates how he can read nine-year-old Adam's mind, that Adam agrees to help him contact his home planet's space ship. Gullible children—and that's most of them—will recall a slew of humiliatingly funny incidents of times their siblings tricked them, too. For an opposite setup, try Barbara Park's equally comic *Operation: Dump the Chump,* where Oscar tries to give his obnoxious younger brother Robert to the nice old couple down the street. Meet a real alien in Daniel Pinkwater's *Ned Feldman, Space Pirate.* BROTHERS. EXTRATERRESTRIAL LIFE. HUMOROUS FICTION. PRACTICAL JOKES. SIBLING RIVALRY.

747   Shreve, Susan. *Joshua T. Bates Takes Charge.* Illus. by Dan Andreasen. Knopf, 1993. ISBN 0-394-84362-2

[10 chapters, 102p.] In the sequel to *The Flunking of Joshua T. Bates* (Knopf, 1984), Joshua is now in fifth grade, and though he seems to be keeping up with his work and dealing with perpetual bully Tommy Wilhelm, his year is shattered when Sean, a new kid, wants to be his friend. Joshua's moral anguish as he balances being nice to the new kid with avoiding trouble from Tommy and his followers, who have labeled Sean a nerd, has a smashing conclusion that children will need to debate. Questions to get kids started: Is it tattling if you tell on someone who is causing real harm? Have you ever had to make a decision like Joshua did? What happened? Patricia Reilly Giff's Polk Street School spin-off *Matthew*

Jackson Meets the Wall is from the point of view of the new kid and will make a fitting contrast. BULLIES. FRIENDSHIP. SCHOOLS.

748   **Singer, Marilyn.** *The Painted Fan.* **Illus. by Wenhai Ma. Morrow, 1994. ISBN 0-688-11743-0**

Told by a soothsayer that the Painted Fan will be his undoing, tyrant Lord Shang falls in love with Bright Willow, a poor goat girl, whom he sends out in pursuit of the Great Pearl that is guarded by a demon. Another lovely literary fairy tale about love and a quest is Diane Stanley's *Fortune*. Search out more pearls in Cheng Hou-Tien's *The Six Chinese Brothers* and Julie Lawson's *The Dragon's Pearl*. In Laurence Yep's *The Ghost Fox*, a boy's bravery saves his mother's soul. CHINA. EMPERORS. LITERARY FAIRY TALES. LOVE. MONSTERS.

749   **Spinelli, Jerry.** *Fourth Grade Rats.* **Illus. by Paul Casale. Scholastic, 1991. ISBN 0-590-44243-0**

[14 chapters, 84p.] Suds Morton, who liked being called an angel last year in third grade, is faced with an ethical dilemma: Should he now live up to the school-yard chant and act like a rat? Spinelli has a fine ear for kids' dialogue. Pair up students to read aloud and act out various chapters. Other stories of students with assorted school problems include Saragail Katzman Benjamin's *My Dog Ate It*, Natalie Honeycutt's *Juliet Fisher and the Foolproof Plan*, Johanna Hurwitz's *Class Clown*, Elizabeth Levy's *Keep Ms. Sugarman in the Fourth Grade*, Barbara Park's *Maxie, Rosie, and Earl—Partners in Grime*, and Barbara Robinson's *The Best School Year Ever*. BEHAVIOR. FRIENDSHIP. SCHOOLS.

750   **Sterman, Betsy, and Samuel Sterman.** *Backyard Dragon.* **Illus. by David Wenzel. HarperCollins, 1993. ISBN 0-06-020784-1**

[17 chapters, 189p.] Lonely Owen has no friends until he discovers Wyrdryn, an enormous Welsh dragon sent forward in time to New Jersey by wizard Gwilym's powerful spell. Great to read at Thanksgiving time so your kids can watch the Macy's Day Parade on TV and see just how Owen, his grandfather, and new friends help the huge creature to get airborne. For another classic seasonal story, see also Daniel Pinkwater's *The Hoboken Chicken Emergency*. Meet up with a few more modern dragons in Stephen Krensky's *The Dragon's Circle*, Seymour Reit's *Benvenuto*, and Barbara Rinkoff's *The Dragon's Handbook*. The poems in Jack Prelutsky's *The Dragons Are Singing Tonight*, and Laura Whipple's compilation, *Eric Carle's Dragons Dragons and Other Creatures That Never Were* will get you prepped. DRAGONS. FANTASY. PARADES. THANKSGIVING. WIZARDS.

751   **Van Allsburg, Chris.** *The Sweetest Fig.* **Illus. by the author. Houghton Mifflin, 1993. ISBN 0-395-67346-1**

[1 sitting, unp.] Fastidious, callous dentist Monsieur Bibot reluctantly accepts as payment from a poor old woman with a toothache two special figs that, as she confides correctly, can make his dreams come true. In the ironic end, in typical, surreal Van Allsburg style, it's Marcel, Bibot's long-suffering dog, who gets the final revenge. Talk over whether Bibot deserved his fate, whether the dog was better or worse than his master, and how the dog-turned-human will react to his new status. Given a bite of dried fig, each child can write about and illustrate his or her dream-come-true. For a more upbeat treatment, read *Professor Puffendorf's Secret Potions* by Robin Tzannes. For similarly provocative ideas, read Van Allsburg's *Jumanji*, *The Widow's Broom*, and *The Wreck of the Zephyr*. Eve Bunting's picture book *Night of the Gargoyles* will give you the willies. DOGS. DREAMS. FRUIT. MAGIC. TRANSFORMATIONS.

752   **Van Allsburg, Chris.** *The Widow's Broom.* **Illus. by the author. Houghton Mifflin, 1992. ISBN 0-395-64051-2**

[1 sitting, unp.] Losing its power, a witch's broom falls to earth one night and lonely widow Minna Shaw, after assisting the wounded witch, is left that most singular broom. Every day it sweeps, does chores, and even picks out a few simple tunes on the piano, but when neighbor Mr. Spivey spies it splitting wood, he declares it a wicked devil. Listeners will find much to talk and argue about after hearing this thought-provoking story about intolerance and Minna Shaw's defiance of it. Some questions to ponder: Was Mr. Spivey justified in his fear of the broom? Was Minna justified in deceiving and scaring off her neighbors? Set up an interview situation, where students take the parts of the different characters, including the broom. For older students, Bill Brittain's *Professor Popkin's Prodigious Polish* and Anne Mazer's *The Oxboy* deal with some of the same themes, and all will enjoy watching brooms run amok in Inga Moore's *The Sorcerer's Apprentice*. BROOMS. MAGIC. PICTURE BOOKS FOR ALL AGES. PREJUDICE. SUPERSTITIONS. WITCHES.

753   **Welch, Catherine A.** *Danger at the Breaker.* **Illus. by Andrea Shine. Carolrhoda, 1992. ISBN 0-87614-693-0**

[1 sitting, 48p.] Andrew is only eight years old when, in lieu of school, he is sent to work in the Pennsylvania coal mines as a "breaker boy" sorting coal to bring in more money for his family, on the day of a serious mine explosion. This is a gritty, day-in-the-life, realistic and easy-to-read story with watercolors aptly depicting the hardships of 19th century mining families that children will find exciting and horrifying. To demonstrate the harrowing conditions that child workers faced, show your class the photographs from Russell Freedman's *Kids at Work: Lewis Hines and the Crusade Against Child Labor* (Clarion, 1994), which includes a chapter on "breaker boys." See how a New York City child helped support his family during the same era in *Peppe the Lamplighter* by Elisa Bartone. Child labor flourishes worldwide, but is restricted in the United States. Debate and discuss issues of whether children should be allowed to work to help their families or be required to attend school. CHILD LABOR. COAL MINES AND MINING.

754   **Wells, Rosemary.** *Waiting for the Evening Star.* **Illus. by Susan Jeffers. Dial, 1993. ISBN 0-8037-1399-1**

Barstow, Vermont, on the eve of World War I is filled with the cycle of the seasons, cutting ice from the river, eating fresh maple syrup over snow, milking cows, and haying, but there's an undercurrent of war, and Berty's older brother Luke is aching to go. This giant picture book has soft, dreamy, cross-hatched watercolors that show the contrast between the idyllic country life and the train that will take him away. The open ending might frustrate listeners needing reassurance of his safe return. Gloria Houston's *The Year of the Perfect Christmas Tree* unfolds in homefront Appalachia, and Staton Rabin's *Casey Over There* takes us to the trenches in France. Contrast the times of the two World Wars with James Stevenson's autobiographical *Don't You Know There's a War On?* Another radiant picture book, which elaborates on how ice was cut in the old days, is *The Ice Horse* by Candace Christiansen. BROTHERS. FARM LIFE. HISTORICAL FICTION. VERMONT. WORLD WAR, 1914–1918–FICTION.

755   Yep, Laurence. *The Ghost Fox*. Illus. by Jean and Mou-Sien Tseng. Scholastic, 1994. ISBN 0-590-47204-6

[11 chapters, 70p.] Once his father Big Lee sails down the Great River to trade his wares, it is up to nine-year-old Little Lee to protect his mother from the fox that tries to steal her soul. Based on a classic Chinese ghost story, this fictionalized retelling, with a mother who overnight turns from loving to cruel and a son who can't rest till he saves her, will generate satisfied sighs from any listeners who have ever felt unappreciated. *Catkin* by Antonia Barber also draws on folklore elements in a story of a baby kidnapped by Little People and the tiny cat who outwits them. In *The Changeling* by Selma Lagerlöf, a mother's undying love saves her son from trolls, and in *A Ride on the Red Mare's Back* by Ursula K. LeGuin, a girl sets out to save her brother who has been captured by trolls. CHINA. FANTASY. FOXES. LITERARY FAIRY TALES. MOTHERS AND SONS. TRANSFORMATIONS.

756   Yolen, Jane. *Encounter*. Illus. by David Shannon. Harcourt, 1992. ISBN 0-15-225962-7

[1 sitting, unp.] Three great-sailed canoes come into the bay, giving birth to many little canoes that land and spit out strange men who hide their bodies like parrots and have voices like barking dogs. The apprehensive young Taino Indian boy narrating the tale tries in vain to warn his people of their impending fate in this chilling picture book that presents the other side to the Columbus story. Christopher Columbus's own *Log of Christopher Columbus*, Michael Dorris's *Morning Girl*, Jean Marzollo's *In 1492*, Peter and Connie Roop's *I, Columbus*, and Peter Sis's *Follow the Dream* offer a variety of viewpoints. *How the Sea Began* is a Taino pourquoi tale retold by George Crespo. COLUMBUS, CHRISTOPHER. HISTORICAL FICTION. INDIANS OF NORTH AMERICA. PICTURE BOOKS FOR ALL AGES.

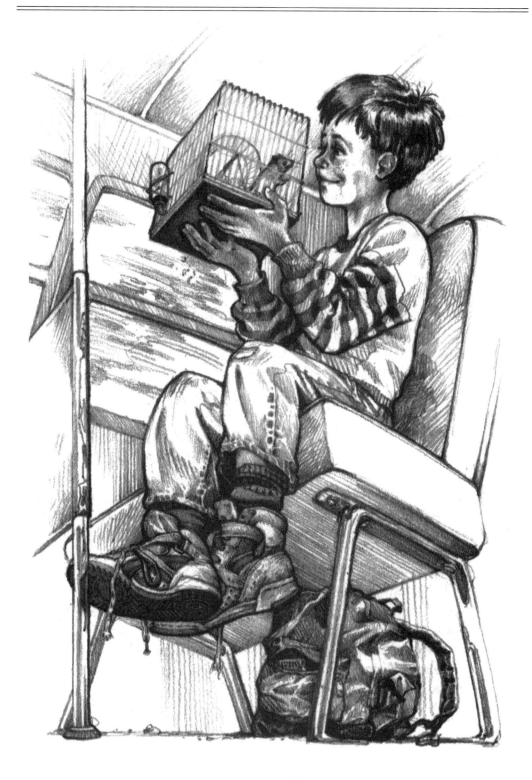

Illustration from WANTED . . . MUD BLOSSOM by Betsy Byars, illustrated by
Jacqueline Rogers. Text copyright © 1991 by Betsy Byars. Illustrations copyright
© 1991 by Jacqueline Rogers. Reprinted by permission of Delacorte Press.

FICTION FOR GRADES 4–5

---

757   Andersen, Hans Christian. *The Tinderbox.* Illus. by Barry Moser. Retold by Barry Moser. Little, Brown, 1990. ISBN 0-316-03938-1

[1 sitting, 29p.] Moser has reset Andersen's tale in the post-Civil War South, where Yoder Ott, a young soldier returning home, meets up with an old curmudgeon who persuades him to brave three huge-eyed dogs to fetch a magic tinderbox. When Yoder strikes the box, the dogs appear, ready to do his bidding, and he uses them to help him get to his true love, the mayor's daughter. Spend time also with the genie in Andrew Lang's *Aladdin and the Wonderful Lamp* or Marianna Mayer's expanded version, *Aladdin and the Enchanted Lamp*, and with Walter McVitty's *Ali Baba and the Forty Thieves* as comparisons to this dark tale. In *Tucker Pfeffercorn*, Moser has also retold Jacob Grimm's "Rumpelstiltskin" and set it in the South. For folklore transported from England to the Appalachians, read aloud Richard Chase's classic *Grandfather Tales*. DOGS. FANTASY. LITERARY FAIRY TALES. U.S.–HISTORY–1865-1898–FICTION.

758   Banks, Lynne Reid. *The Adventures of King Midas.* Illus. by Jos. A Smith. Morrow, 1992. ISBN 0-688-10894-6

[11 chapters, 153p.] In this novel and nicely tongue-in-cheek version of the trouble Midas causes after Nandan the magician grants the King's wish to turn everything he touches into gold, including his daughter Delia, only water from the River Cijam can undo the spell. A wicked witch and a "flandy-bake"-eating young dragon who loves to mispronounce long words round out the cast. Read this fantasy version alongside Midas myths *King Midas and the Golden Touch* by Kathryn Hewitt and *The King Has Horse's Ears* by Peggy Thomson. DRAGONS. FANTASY. GREED. KINGS AND RULERS. MAGIC. MAGICIANS. WITCHES.

759   Birdseye, Tom. *Just Call Me Stupid.* Holiday House, 1993. ISBN 0-8234-1045-5

[25 chapters, 181p.] Fifth-grader Patrick still can't read, though he's a wonderful artist, but when Celina, his new next-door neighbor and classmate, invades his backyard hideout, she reads aloud from T. H. White's *The Sword in the Stone* and inspires him to record his own story on tape. The Tucson setting, especially the scene where Celina can't get a chuckwalla to release its grip on her nose, will send urban kids to look up desert environments in the library. Judie Wolkoff's *Wally* contains more chuckwalla trouble. You might delve a bit into the days of old with books on knights or King Arthur, such as Selina Hastings's *Sir Gawain and the Loathly Lady*, or fictional adventures like Gery Greer and Bob Ruddick's *Max and Me and the Time Machine* or Elizabeth Winthrop's *The Castle in the Attic*. Become part of famous books with the two children in Anne Lindbergh's *Travel Far, Pay No Fare*. BOOKS AND READING. CHESS. FRIENDSHIP. SCHOOLS. SELF-ESTEEM.

760   Brittain, Bill. *Professor Popkin's Prodigious Polish: A Tale of Coven Tree*. Illus. by Andrew Glass. HarperCollins, 1990. ISBN 0-06-020727-2

[9 chapters, 152p.] Farm life is not satisfying to 15-year-old Luther Gilpin, who dreams of getting rich as a traveling salesman until he takes a disastrous job selling bottles of a special new polish guaranteed to "bring new life to household objects." The stuff works all right, as every object that's polished comes to malevolent life. Stuart Meade, known as Stew Meat, narrates this companion tale to *Devil's Donkey*, *Dr. Dredd's Wagon of Wonders*, and *The Wish Giver*, all concerning the New England village where trouble and Satan never give up. In Chris Van Allsburg's *The Widow's Broom*, Minna Shaw's new broom causes quite a stir in her village when the neighbors see it moving by itself. Compare the communities' actions, main characters' reactions, and endings for both books. *The Sorcerer's Apprentice* by Inga Moore is a rich retelling of the story about the boy whose spell to put brooms to work carrying water backfires. DEVIL. FANTASY. SUPERNATURAL.

761   Brittain, Bill. *Shape-Changer*. HarperCollins, 1994. ISBN 0-06-024239-6

[8 chapters, 108p.] Bored with his humdrum life, seventh-grader Frank Dunn gets a jolt when he is recruited by a talking fire hydrant, actually an alien named Zymel who can change into any form, to recapture master criminal Fek before he can take charge of earth. A fast-moving, cleverly predictable bit of sci-fi, this one is fun to use to introduce listeners to the genre. All can predict in what guise Fek is hiding, offering evidence to back up their theories. More space creatures turn up in characters' backyards in Jonathan Etra and Stephanie Spinner's *Aliens for Breakfast*, Lee Harding's *The Fallen Spaceman*, Daniel Pinkwater's *Fat Men from Space*, Pamela Service's *Stinker from Space*, and Louis Slobodkin's *The Spaceship Under the Apple Tree*. EXTRATERRESTRIAL LIFE. SCIENCE FICTION. TRANSFORMATIONS.

762   Byars, Betsy. *McMummy*. Viking, 1993. ISBN 0-670-84995-2

[27 chapters, 150p.] Mozie is looking after the plants in Professor Orloff's greenhouse while the scientist is away and finds what looks like a green life-sized mummy pod growing there, which appears to be humming and growing. The dialogue, descriptions, and scenes with Mozie, his best friend Batty, and Miss Tri-County Tech beauty contestant Valvoline are great fun to read aloud. Read in tandem with John Reynolds Gardiner's *Top Secret*, where Allen's experiments with human photosynthesis turn him into a plant. FANTASY. FRIENDSHIP. MONEY. PLANTS. SINGLE-PARENT FAMILIES.

763   Byars, Betsy. *Wanted . . . Mud Blossom*. Illus. by Jacqueline Rogers. Delacorte, 1991. ISBN 0-385-30428-5

[25 chapters, 148p.] What a variety of connecting problems the Blossom family is juggling! Junior Blossom believes that Pap's dog Mud is responsible for the disappearance of Scooty, the school hamster, and insists that Mud be tried for murder, with sister Maggie as prosecuting attorney; their friend Mad Mary is missing; brother Vern and his pal Michael are in trouble again; and Mom's got a new boyfriend coming to visit. Fifth in the delightful set of books about the never-dull Blossom family, its alternating chapters are a fine way to demonstrate characters' points of view. DOGS. FAMILY LIFE. HAMSTERS. TRIALS.

764   Chetwin, Grace. *Friends in Time.* Bradbury, 1992. ISBN 0-02-718318-1

[12 chapters, 127p.] An impending move, the possible loss of an only best friend, and the chance finding of an old book impel Emma to visit the vacant Bentley mansion next door where she meets up with Abigail Bentley, who has come to the present and wants to return to her family of 1846. The believable and well-plotted fantasy deals with a Brazilian power wand or doll, how to make friends, and what a time-traveling person would encounter in our modern times. In Helen Cresswell's *Time Out,* an English butler and his family leave 1887 to visit 1987. Go further back to the 17th century with Jane Resh Thomas's *The Princess in the Pigpen.* Hollis learns about fitting in and is herself replaced by a powerful doll in *Is There Life on a Plastic Planet?* by Mildred Ames. FANTASY. FRIENDSHIP. MAGIC. MOVING, HOUSEHOLD. TIME TRAVEL.

765   Coville, Bruce. *Jennifer Murdley's Toad.* Illus. by Gary A. Lippincott. Harcourt, 1992. ISBN 0-15-200745-8

[14 chapters, 156p.] Ordinary Jennifer, who thinks of herself as "the kid in the plain brown wrapper," happens upon Elives' Magic Supplies shop where she purchases Bufo as a pet for 75 cents, and the giant toad talks! Like Polly in *The Wish Giver* by Bill Brittain, both Jennifer and her worst enemy, the beautiful Sharra, become toads, and there's plenty of marvelous mayhem from mouthy Bufo before we believe the message about beauty being in the eyes of the beholder. Whether before or after, be sure to read aloud Donna Jo Napoli's *The Prince of the Pond.* Coville's other Magic Shop books are *Jeremy Thatcher, Dragon Hatcher* and *The Monster's Ring.* See if your readers can find first sentences as good as this one: "If Jennifer Murdley hadn't been forced to wear her brother's underpants to school, the whole thing might never have happened." BROTHERS AND SISTERS. FANTASY. FRIENDSHIP. MAGIC. SELF-ESTEEM. TOADS. TRANSFORMATIONS.

766   DeFelice, Cynthia. *Devil's Bridge.* Macmillan, 1992. ISBN 0-380-72117-1

[14 chapters, 95p.] His father, the late Captain Jack Daggett, holds the record on Martha's Vineyard for catching the island's biggest fish, a 66-pound striped bass, and when Ben overhears two men scheming to win this year's contest by less-than-honest methods, he is bound to foil their plans. Still bitter about his fisherman father's death in a hurricane, Ben can't stand his mother's new boyfriend, and his involvement in the fishing derby ultimately allows him to accept change. DEATH. FAMILY PROBLEMS. FISHING.

767 **Dillon, Barbara.** *A Mom by Magic.* **Illus. by Jeffrey Lindberg. HarperCollins, 1990. ISBN 0-397-32449-9**

[9 chapters, 132p.] Shopping with her girlfriend at Milliman's Department Store for Christmas clothes, Jessica Slocum visits the wishing well to choose a holiday present and pulls out a business card good for one wish to be granted by an unusual woman named Philomena Fix. Jessica, whose mother died when she was two, wishes for a mom for Christmas, which is granted in the guise of Amalie Evans, formerly a mannequin at the store, who gives Jessica a holiday to remember. Ask your students to list what makes a good mom, and what skills Amalie might need to learn in her new role. In *Is There Life on a Plastic Planet?* by Mildred Ames, Hollis trades places with a life-sized doll that looks just like her with more sinister results, and in *Konrad* by Christine Nostlinger a factory-made canned kid needs lessons on how not to be perfect. CHRISTMAS. FANTASY. MAGIC. MANNEQUINS. MOTHERS AND DAUGHTERS. WISHES.

768 **Dodds, Bill.** *My Sister Annie.* **Caroline House / Boyds Mills, 1993. ISBN 1-56397-114-3**

[8 chapters, 94p.] Now that he's in sixth grade and wants to appear cool, to ask the alluring Misty to a dance, and to join the Bombers who engage in petty vandalism for fun, Charlie begins to resent and feel embarrassed by his 13-year-old sister Annie who has Down's syndrome. Additional insightful and notable books about retarded children are *A Little Time* by Ann Norris Baldwin, *Crazy Lady!* by Jane Leslie Conly, *Between Friends* by Sheila Garrigue, *Welcome Home, Jellybean* by Marlene Fanta Shyer, and *Risk N' Roses* by Jan Slepian. BASEBALL. DOWN'S SYNDROME. FAMILY STORIES. HANDICAPS. MENTAL RETARDATION.

769 **Duffey, Betsy.** *Coaster.* **Viking, 1994. ISBN 0-670-85480-8**

[17 chapters, 114p.] Since his parents' divorce, 12-year-old Hart sees his father only infrequently, when they go roller coastering in the summer. Now his mom is dating Dub, a celebrity TV weatherman, who takes him to Wonderworld, but an embarrassed and spiteful Hart plays a mean trick on him, rationalizing that he already has a father. With his best friend Frankie, Hart has been building a secret home-made roller coaster along a ravine, and he plans to ride it despite his mother's objections, to demonstrate his bravery. *A Question of Trust* by Marion Dane Bauer and *Strider* by Beverly Cleary are also sensitive and insightful fiction books about boys coming to terms with changes after their parents split up. DIVORCE. FATHERS AND SONS. MOTHERS AND SONS. ROLLER COASTERS.

770 **Greenburg, Dan.** *Young Santa.* **Illus. by Warren Miller. Viking, 1991. ISBN 0-670-83905-1**

[16 short chapters, 72p.] Sophie and Milton Claus tried out many names for their newborn son before deciding to name him for the place they had such a lovely vacation, Santa Fe. When icebox salesman Milton is transferred to a new territory, the North Pole, their son finds he just loves the cold. This prankish version of the Santa Claus legend is stuffed with many cheerful and preposterous twists along the way, including an explanation of just how he found those eight tiny reindeer. Check out some other views of the rotund toybringer in William Joyce's picture book *Santa Calls* and Jean Van Leeuwen's chapter book *The Great Christmas Kidnapping Caper*. CHRISTMAS. HUMOROUS FICTION. PARODIES. REINDEER. SANTA CLAUS.

771   **Hildick, E. W.** *The Case of the Purloined Parrot*. **Macmillan, 1990. ISBN 0-02-743965-8**

[16 chapters, 133p.] Reintroduce children to The McGurk Organization, which now boasts six members including two relative newcomers, the scientifically methodical Brains Bellingham and Mari Yoshimura who can throw her voice and imitate any sound. This time the youthful detective crew are investigating a missing cat and a kidnapped African Gray parrot, and using their various talents, they unmask a ring of cat thieves. When your students see the coat-of-arms shields that narrator Joey designs for each investigator, they'll probably want to design their own emblems, along with Arthurian titles. A loquacious African Gray parrot named Madison is also kidnapped in Dick King-Smith's *Harry's Mad*. MYSTERY AND DETECTIVE STORIES. PARROTS.

772   **Kidd, Diana.** *Onion Tears*. **Illus. by Lucy Montgomery. Orchard, 1991. ISBN 0-531-08470-1**

[2–3 sittings, 62p.] Unable to respond to the teasing of her classmates, Vietnamese refugee Nam-Huong can only confide her feelings through letters she writes to her past pets. Gradually, as she becomes close to her teacher Miss Lily, she is able to reveal her terrible story of fleeing Vietnam by boat with her beloved Grandpa who died en route. Sherry Garland's *The Lotus Seed* is a haunting picture book about the Vietnam War and a woman who survives its many hardships. *The Clay Marble* by Minfong Ho is a novel that takes us to the Cambodian refugee camps. Show a hopeful side of present-day Vietnam with Holly Keller's picture book *Grandfather's Dream*. IMMIGRATION AND EMIGRATION. FOSTER CARE. TEACHERS. VIETNAM WAR. WAR.

773   **LeRoy, Gen.** *Taxi Cat and Huey*. **Illus. by Karen Ritz. HarperCollins, 1992. ISBN 0-06-021769-3**

[18 chapters, 139p.] The langorous life of basset hound Huey is soon under siege when his owners take in an off-the-wall part-Siamese stray cat who fancies himself a Ninja warrior, and repair to a country house for the summer with pets in tow. Chapter four, where the dog and cat are taken to the vet, is a slapstick scene that your students will enjoy reenacting as Reader's Theater. Other funny books told from the animal's viewpoint include James Howe's *Bunnicula*, Dick King-Smith's *Martin's Mice*, and Phyllis Reynolds Naylor's *The Grand Escape*. *High-Wire Henry* by Mary Calhoun is a picture book about another unusual Siamese cat who is jealous when the family adopts a baby dachshund. CATS. DOGS. HUMOROUS FICTION.

774   **Lewis, J. Patrick.** *One Dog Day*. **Illus. by Marcy Dunn Ramsey. Atheneum, 1993. ISBN 0-689-31808-1**

[10 chapters, 52p.] No one would expect a collie to be entered in, much less win, the Third Annual Coon Dog Race and Corn Feed, but Jilly Hawkes's dog Poetry does just that, with a small bit of help from a silent dog whistle. Jilly named her dog for all the Emily Dickinson poems her mother read to her, and you might want to try a few of them out on your students as well. You can read this gem of a novella in two or three sittings, and follow up with more loyal dog tales such as *Stone Fox* by John Reynolds Gardiner, *Old Yeller* by Fred Gibson, *Red-Dirt Jessie* by Anna Myers, *Shiloh* by Phyllis Reynolds Naylor, and the picture books *Dogteam* by Gary Paulsen and *Riptide* by Frances Ward Weller. CONTESTS. DOGS. RACING.

775   **Little, Jean. *From Anna.* Illus. by Joan Sandin. HarperCollins, 1972. ISBN 0-06-023912-3**

[20 chapters, 201p.] After nine-year-old "Awkward" Anna Solden and her family leave fascist Germany for Canada in 1933, she is diagnosed as seriously sight-impaired and placed in a special sight-saving class where a supportive teacher and classmates rescue her from her lifelong loneliness. Encourage your readers to discover Jean Little's triumphant books, many about children who deal with disabilities. The author is herself sight-impaired as you'll discover in her remarkable autobiography, *Little By Little: A Writer's Education*, and many episodes in *From Anna* mirror her own life. CANADA. CHRISTMAS. HANDICAPS. SCHOOLS.

776   **Lowry, Lois. *Attaboy, Sam!* Illus. by Diane de Groat. Houghton Mifflin, 1992. ISBN 0-395-61588-7**

[11 chapters, 116p.] While older sister Anastasia struggles writing a commemorative poem for their mother's 40th birthday, four-year-old Sam collects samples of all his mother's favorite smells—ranging from dad's pipe and chicken soup to yeast and the odor of little babies—and blends them together in a grape-juice jar to invent his own original perfume, which smells terrible and begins to fester in his toybox. Readers who loved *All About Sam* will welcome this droll sequel. Children can bring in one of their favorite smells for the rest of the group to identify. (If you don't mind stinking up the room a bit, this might be a fine time to start a mold-growing science unit.) Bring in some real perfumes for all to sniff, and research the making of it to figure out where Sam went wrong. Collect suggestions for making handmade gifts that will mean more to parents than store-bought. BIRTHDAYS. FAMILY LIFE. GIFTS. HUMOROUS FICTION.

777   **Mahy, Margaret. *Raging Robots and Unruly Uncles.* Illus. by Peter Stevenson. Overlook Press, 1993. ISBN 0-87951-469-8**

[10 chapters, 93p.] Wicked Uncle Jasper, a villain by profession, is ever disappointed in the progress of his seven sons who are not following his evil footsteps, while his twin brother, the virtuous Julian, is equally put out that his only daughter Prudence is not more perfect, leading all the children to run away and open the Television Repair, Fortune-telling and Suburban Transport Service with Associated Gourmet Restaurant. In a slapstick tale of children who never live up to their parents' expectations, add Lilly Rose Blossom, a nauseatingly sweet walkie-talkie doll, and the Nadger, a supervillainous robot who steals from supermarkets, to the cast. Your students can write about what their parents want them to achieve, compared with their own aspirations. FATHERS. HUMOROUS FICTION. ROBOTS. RUNAWAYS.

778   Mills, Claudia. *Dinah for President*. Macmillan, 1992. ISBN 0-02-766999-8

[13 chapters, 103p.] Determined to be more than just an anonymous middle-school student, Dinah prepares to enter the campaign for sixth-grade president, a traditionally male purview, making a school recycling program her campaign platform. The final debate between Dinah and the other candidates may inspire your class to plan a debate on school issues. You'll also want to delve into the importance of recycling as a social issue that effects everybody. A further platform of school election stories would contain Johanna Hurwitz's *Class President* and Barbara Park's *Rosie Swanson, Fourth Grade Geek for President*. ELDERLY. ELECTIONS. RECYCLING. SCHOOLS.

779   Moser, Barry. *Tucker Pfeffercorn: An Old Story Retold*. Illus. by the author. Little, Brown, 1994. ISBN 0-316-58542-4

[1 sitting, unp.] Tall-talester Jefferson Tadlock tells of Bessie Grace Kinzalow, the young widow-woman who he says can spin cotton into gold. Believing him, Hezakiah Sweatt, the mean mine owner, locks her in a room until she does. Like Jacob Grimm's *Rumpelstiltskin*, upon which this Southern-United States retelling is based, a little man comes to the rescue, and he wants her child as payment unless she can guess his name, but this heroine is self-possessed and resourceful. First read aloud Jacob Grimm's *Rumpelstiltskin*, Evaline Ness's English *Tom Tit Tot*, and Harve Zemach's lighthearted *Duffy and the Devil*, and have your students analyze and compare the lot. Moser also retold Hans Christian Andersen's *The Tinderbox*, setting it in the post-Civil War South. FANTASY. LITERARY FAIRY TALES. NAMES–FOLKLORE.

780   Myers, Anna. *Red-Dirt Jessie*. Walker, 1992. ISBN 0-8027-8172-1

[8 chapters, 107p.] After Jessie's little sister Patsy dies of pneumonia, Papa gives up and takes to his bedroom, and while Jessie waits for him to get better, she works on taming Ring, her aunt's near-feral dog. A Depression story set in Oklahoma, this has a gentle tone and a heart-stopping climax. *Sable* by Karen Hesse has a similar feel, and readers could critique and compare the two. DEATH. DOGS. FAMILY LIFE. HISTORICAL FICTION. MENTAL ILLNESS. OKLAHOMA.

781   Namioka, Lensey. *Yang the Youngest and His Terrible Ear*. Illus. by Kees de Kiefte. Joy Street / Little, Brown, 1992. ISBN 0-316-59701-5

[8 chapters, 134p.] Nine-year-old narrator Yingtao, newly immigrated from China to Seattle with his musical family, is tone deaf and plays his newly learned sport of baseball far better than he'll ever play the violin. Luckily, Matthew, Yingtao's new school friend and explainer of American slang and customs, helps him with a plan to escape certain humiliation at the upcoming concert. Discuss cultural differences with your class, asking: How and why do Matthew's and

Yingtao's family, food, behavior, and customs seem unusual to each other? Yingtao's confusion over English vocabulary and idiomatic expressions might remind you of Peggy Parish's Amelia Bedelia books. Make a class list of other words and phrases that would confuse someone just learning English, such as hot dog, rock music, or sweetheart. Using samplings from Marvin Terban's *In a Pickle and Other Funny Idioms* and *Mad as a Wet Hen*, see how well your linguists understand their own language. CHINESE AMERICANS. IDENTITY. MOVING, HOUSEHOLD. MUSICAL INSTRUMENTS. MUSICIANS. VIOLIN.

782   Napoli, Donna Jo. *The Prince of the Pond: Otherwise Known as De Fawg Pin.* Illus. by Judith Byron Schachner. Dutton, 1992. ISBN 0-525-44976-0

[11 chapters, 151p.] "Hep me," the uncoordinated but good-looking frog implores Jade, the female frog narrator, who not only helps him elude the vindictive witch who has just enchanted him, but instructs him in frog behavior and even falls in love with him. This speech-impaired fellow is no ordinary amphibian: he's the original Frog Prince (of Brothers Grimm fairy tale fame). Interview the rest of the characters who come in contact with Pin, such as the witch, the water snake, Pin's tadpoles, and the human woman who finally kisses him, all portrayed by your students. You'll also want to read aloud *Jennifer Murdley's Toad* by Bruce Coville and take a look at Jon Scieszka's astute picture book *The Frog Prince Continued*, which begins after "happy ever after" kicks in. Compare transmutations with another small masterpiece: Mary James' novel *Shoebag*, about a Boston cockroach who awakens one morning to find he's become a human boy. FAIRY TALES–SATIRE. FROGS. PARODIES. PRINCES AND PRINCESSES. TRANSFORMATIONS. WITCHES.

783   Naylor, Phyllis Reynolds. *The Grand Escape.* Illus. by Alan Daniel. Atheneum, 1993. ISBN 0-689-31722-0

[15 chapters, 148p.] Marco and Polo, two English-speaking house cats, run away from their safe and secure lives to look for a ranch like the one Marco read about in the newspaper. When the two cats fall in with a group of other cats, they are expected to prove themselves by solving three of the Important Mysteries of Our Time. Other grand animal fantasies include James Howe's *Bunnicula*, Dick King-Smith's *Martin's Mice*, and Gen LeRoy's *Taxi Cat and Huey*. For a quick pick-me-up, read Dav Pilkey's riotous pun-filled picture book *Kat Kong*. ADVENTURE AND ADVENTURERS. CATS. FANTASY. HUMOROUS FICTION.

784   Nelson, Vaunda Micheaux. *Mayfield Crossing.* Illus. by Leonard Jenkins. Putnam, 1993. ISBN 0-399-22331-2

[13 chapters, 88p.] Meg recalls starting a new school in 1960 with seven neighborhood children, and being the object of racial prejudice until she and her friends challenged the others to a game of baseball. Peter Golenbock's *Teammates* and Ken Mochizuki's *Baseball Saved Us* are two other moving baseball stories about overcoming racial hatred through sports. Discuss other areas of discrimination using Daisaku Ikeda's *Over the Deep Blue Sea*, Lois Lowry's *Number the Stars*, Anne Mazer's *The Oxboy*, Margaree King Mitchell's *Uncle Jed's Barbershop*, and

Chris Van Allburg's *The Widow's Broom*. Chris Raschka's *Yo! Yes?* is a marvelous picture book about friendship that should help put these problems in perspective. AFRICAN AMERICANS. BASEBALL. PREJUDICE. RACE RELATIONS. SCHOOLS.

785   Nichol, Barbara. *Beethoven Lives Upstairs*. Illus. by Scott Cameron. Orchard, 1994. ISBN 0-531-06828-5

[1–2 sittings, unp.] Christoph's uncle reprints his correspondence with his ten-year-old nephew starting in 1822, when the deaf and temperamental Beethoven moved into the boy's house. Woven into the fictional letters are facts about the musician's work and life, including a description of the first performance of his Ninth Symphony. Play samplings of his music as you read, ending, of course, with the Ninth. The letter motif used here would be an interesting format for children to use when researching and reporting on other famous people. Kathleen Krull's *Lives of the Musicians: Good Times, Bad Times (And What the Neighbors Thought)* profiles Beethoven and 18 other idiosyncratic composers. *Tchaikovsky Discovers America* by Esther Kalman borrows the same idea, incorporating diary entries by a young girl who meets that composer during his 1891 visit to New York. BEETHOVEN, LUDWIG VAN. DEAF. HISTORICAL FICTION. LETTER WRITING. MUSICIANS.

786   Polacco, Patricia. *Pink and Say*. Illus. by the author. Philomel, 1994. ISBN 0-399-22671-0

[1 sitting, 48 pages] Polacco drew on her own family history to write an unforgettable and searing Civil War story about Pinkus Aylee, a black soldier who rescues wounded white soldier Sheldon Curtis (Say). Soon after Pink's mother nurses Say back to health she is killed by marauders, and when the two grieving friends set out to rejoin their troops they are captured by Confederates and sent to Andersonville prison, which Say survives but Pink does not. For introducing the causes and effects of the Civil War, this devastating picture book will make more of an impact than any text and will bring listeners to tears. Fill in background on slavery and ongoing prejudice with *Now Let Me Fly: The Story of a Slave Family* by Dolores Johnson, *Uncle Jed's Barbershop* by Margaree King Mitchell, and Vaunda Micheaux Nelson's novel *Mayfield Crossing*. Gwen Everett's provocative *John Brown: One Man Against Slavery* will get students debating. AFRICAN AMERICANS. FAMILY STORIES. FRIENDSHIP. MULTICULTURAL STORIES. SLAVERY. U.S.–HISTORY–CIVIL WAR. WAR.

787   Quattlebaum, Mary. *Jackson Jones and the Puddle of Thorns*. Illus. by Melodye Rosales. Delacorte, 1994. ISBN 0-385-31165-6

[13 chapters, 113p.] Starting the day Jackson hits double digits—"The Big 1-0"— we get to know firsthand an endearing African American kid who is hoping for a birthday basketball from his mother but gets instead his own plot in a nearby community garden. Figuring he can at least grow flowers and sell them to earn the cash for a basketball, he doesn't factor in the bullying he has to endure from Howard "Blood" Green, who gives him the humiliating moniker Bouquet Jones. Bring in some garden catalogs and have your students plan out their own plots of earth, factoring in cost, space, color, height, and design. AFRICAN AMERICANS. FRIENDSHIP. GARDENING. MOTHERS AND SONS. SINGLE-PARENT FAMILIES.

788   Robinson, Barbara. *The Best School Year Ever.* HarperCollins, 1994. ISBN 0-06-023043-6

[9 chapters, 117p.] The horrible Herdmans, all six of them, the worst kids in the history of Woodrow Wilson School, one per grade from first grade on up, are back again in this farcical recounting of their many episodes of malfeasance. As in the first book, *The Best Christmas Pageant Ever*, sixth-grader Beth records her observations about classmate Imogene Herdman and the rest of her siblings. The class assignment for the year is to think of a compliment for each member of the class and then share them on the last day of school. Listeners can predict Beth's compliments for Imogene, plus write some for each other with examples to back them up. Johanna Hurwitz's *Class Clown*, Elizabeth Levy's *Keep Ms. Sugarman in the Fourth Grade*, Barbara Park's *Maxie, Rosie, and Earl—Partners in Grime*, and Jerry Spinelli's *Fourth Grade Rats* are all funny school stories about troublemakers trying hard to adjust. BEHAVIOR. BROTHERS AND SISTERS. HUMOROUS FICTION. SCHOOLS.

789   Rodda, Emily. *Finders Keepers.* Illus. by Noela Young. Greenwillow, 1992. ISBN 0-688-10516-5

[22 chapters, 184p.] Fooling around with a computer at the local computer store, Patrick is startled to receive a personal message on screen inviting him to compete in a million-dollar TV game show on Channel 8, which his mother and sister tell him has never broadcast in their city. Nevertheless, Patrick not only finds the channel, he's pulled into the actual show with quizmaster Lucky Lance Lamont and wheel-spinner Boopie Cupid, and given the challenge to find people's missing treasures lost on the other side of the Barrier that separates their world from ours. After hearing this cleverly plotted and delightfully inventive fantasy from the author of *The Pigs Are Flying*, students will want to go back beyond the Barrier with Patrick in the sequel, *The Timekeeper*. For another explanation of where all our missing items like keys and safety pins get to, *The Borrowers* by Mary Norton is a classic. Chris Van Allsburg's *Jumanji* is another game worth playing. FANTASY. LOST. SPACE AND TIME. TELEVISION.

790   Scieszka, Jon. *Your Mother Was a Neanderthal.* Illus. by Lane Smith. Viking, 1993. ISBN 0-670-84481-0

[12 short chapters, 76p.] This time, Sam, Fred, and narrator Joe use their magic book and end up naked in 40,000 B.C. where they match wits with cave girls Nat-Li, Lin-Say, and Jos-Feen and come up against leader Ma, who's a dead ringer for Joe's own mother, a woolly mammoth, and caveman Duh. As always, the Time Warp Trio series is slapstick funny, though you can meld this one into a science lesson on simple machines and the ideas of Greek mathematician Archimedes. Go back to dinosaur times with *The Bunjee Venture* by Stan McMurty, to ancient Ireland in *The Wizard Children of Finn* by Mary Tannen, and meet Leonardo da Vinci in *The Disappearing Bike Shop* by Elvira Woodruff. FANTASY. HUMOROUS FICTION. MAN, PREHISTORIC. TIME TRAVEL.

791   Spinelli, Jerry. *Report to the Principal's Office.* **Scholastic, 1991. ISBN 0-590-44402-6**

It's the first day at brand new Plumstead Middle School, and principal Mr. Brimlow becomes acquainted with several unique sixth-graders: snarling Sunny, Eddie who refuses to get off the bus, busybody aspiring writer Salem, and master inventor Pickles. The second book in the series, *Who Ran My Underwear Up the Flagpole?* (1992) is equally hilarious. Other true-to-life and comic novels that recount the middle-school experience in all its horror include David Getz's *Almost Famous* and *Thin Air*, Barbara Robinson's *The Best School Year Ever*, Louis Sachar's *Dogs Don't Tell Jokes*, Zilpha Snyder's *Libby on Wednesday*, and Lee Wardlaw's *Seventh-Grade Weirdo*. BEHAVIOR. FRIENDSHIP. HUMOROUS FICTION. PRINCIPALS. SCHOOLS.

792   Springer, Nancy. *Colt.* **Dial, 1991. ISBN 0-8037-1022-4**

[10 chapters, 121p.] Brought to the stables angry and terrified, Colt Vittorio changes his attitude the first time he is placed on the back of homely Appaloosa Liverwurst, as part of the Horses for the Handicapped program. Though falling off or even trotting could be dangerous to a child with spina bifida, Colt becomes determined to learn to ride, which helps him change his negative attitude toward his physical problems and his new stepfamily. *With the Wind* by Liz Damrell is a picture book about the freedom of riding for a disabled boy. *Thin Air* by David Getz is another honest and sometimes scathingly funny portrayal of a boy with severe asthma. HANDICAPS. HORSES. PHYSICAL DISABILITY. SPINA BIFIDA. STEPFAMILIES. STEPPARENTS.

793   Van Leeuwen, Jean. *Bound for Oregon.* **Illus. by James Watling. Dial, 1994. ISBN 0-8037-1527-7**

[16 chapters, 167p.] It took six grueling months for nine-year-old Mary Ellen Todd and her family to travel by covered wagon from their home in Arkansas to their destination in Oregon in 1852. Retold and fleshed out by Van Leeuwen, this is an eye-opening true account, based on a book Todd's daughter wrote detailing her mother's oft-told memories, that will appeal to adventure-seekers. Start with Marion Russell's *Along the Santa Fe Trail*, an eye-catching picture book also based on one traveler's memoirs of her journey from Independence, Missouri, to Albuquerque, New Mexico, in 1852. Get a further feel for the hardships of the times with novels *Weasel* by Cynthia DeFelice, *Dear Levi: Letters from the Overland Trail* by Elvira Woodruff, and picture books *Wilderness Cat* by Natalie Kinsey-Warnock and *Grandma Essie's Covered Wagon* by David Williams. FRONTIER AND PIONEER LIFE. HISTORICAL FICTION. OREGON TRAIL. U.S.–HISTORY–1865-1898–FICTION. WEST.

794   Weiss, Ellen, and Mel Friedman. *The Tiny Parents.* **Knopf, 1989. ISBN 0-394-92418-5**

[10 chapters, 82p.] Marie and Eddie Bicker's eccentric scientist parents work, invent, and argue nonstop in their Brooklyn basement laboratory, but when an experiment goes awry and shrinks them to a mere two-and-a-half inches, the kids take over the household while trying to get them back to normal size in time. There's no great moral message here, but the combination of junk-food-loving kids, a very nosy neighbor, and some very funny dialogue adds up to a most enjoyable diversion. Compare sizes with the characters in Mary Norton's *The Borrowers*, E. Nesbit's *Melisande*, William Sleator's *Among the Dolls*, Kathy Kennedy Tapp's *Moth-Kin Magic*, E. B. White's *Stuart Little*, and Elizabeth Winthrop's *The Castle in the Attic*. Check the point of view in William Joyce's picture book *George Shrinks*. In Elvira Woodruff's *The Summer I Shrank My Grandmother*, Nelly's grandmother gets younger and younger. FAMILY PROBLEMS. FANTASY. HUMOROUS FICTION. INVENTORS. SCIENTISTS. SIZE.

795   **Wolkstein, Diane, reteller.** *The Legend of Sleepy Hollow.* **Illus. by R. W. Alley. Morrow, 1987. ISBN 0-688-06532-5**

[1 sitting, unp.] Wolkstein's retelling of the classic story written in 1819 by Washington Irving about bony schoolmaster Ichabod Crane, his fancy for beautiful and wealthy Katrina Van Tassel, and the scare he receives from practical-joke-playing Brom Bones disguised as the Headless Horseman is made accessible to younger children who couldn't fathom Irving's original ornate prose. Find out the folkloric origin of the carved pumpkin in *Jack-O'-Lantern* by Edna Barth. GHOST STORIES. HISTORICAL FICTION. NEW YORK (STATE). PRACTICAL JOKES. PUMPKINS. TEACHERS.

796   **Woodruff, Elvira.** *Dear Levi: Letters from the Overland Trail.* **Illus. by Beth Peck. Knopf, 1994. ISBN 0-679-94641-1**

[39 short chapters, 119p.] In a collection of letters describing the arduous journey west to Oregon in 1851 to see about his late father's claim, 12-year-old orphan Ausin Ives writes to his younger brother who has stayed behind in Pennsylvania. Rife with adventure and scattered with tragedy, the conversational letters were inspired by the original diaries of Overland Trail travelers in the mid-19th century, and they don't shy away from controversy and tough issues including conflicts with Indians and death. In *Bound for Oregon* by Jean Van Leeuwen, the family of nine-year-old Mary Ellen Todd makes their crossing one year later. Two picture books that will give children a feel for wagon train life are Marion Russell's *Along the Santa Fe Trail* and *Grandma Essie's Covered Wagon* by David Williams. FRONTIER AND PIONEER LIFE. HISTORICAL FICTION. LETTER WRITING. OREGON TRAIL. U.S.–HISTORY–1783-1865–FICTION.

797   **Woodruff, Elvira.** *The Disappearing Bike Shop.* **Holiday House, 1992. ISBN 0-8234-0933-3**

[24 chapters, 169p.] Best friends Tyler and Freckle watch in amazement as an old building up the street rises in the air, vanishes, and then reappears. Could the elderly proprieter of Quigley's Bike Shop be responsible, and is he a wizard, an inventor, or the great Leonardo da Vinci come to modern times via time machine? *A Weekend with Leonardo da Vinci* by Rosabianca Skira-Venturi is a fictionalized autobiography and a good place to find reproductions of his paintings and inventions. Consider other inventions from real to imagined in Webb Garrison's *Why Didn't I Think of That? From Alarm Clocks to Zippers*, Rube Goldberg's *The Best of Rube Goldberg*, Charlotte Foltz Jones's *Mistakes That Worked*, and Jim Murphy's *Weird and Wacky Inventions*. Compare Tyler's confrontations with class bully Mike the Vike with similar themes in Bruce Coville's *The Monster's Ring* and visit prehistoric times in *Your Mother Was a Neanderthal* by Jon Scieszka. BICYCLES. DA VINCI, LEONARDO. INVENTIONS. SCIENCE FICTION. TIME TRAVEL.

798   Woodruff, Elvira. *George Washington's Socks.* **Scholastic, 1991. ISBN 0-590-44035-7**

[23 chapters, 166p.] On an overnight summer campout in the woods, pals Matt, Tony, Hooter, and Matt's pesky little sister Katie find an old rowboat on the lake, and climbing in, are suddenly transported to the Delaware River of Christmas Eve, 1776, as General Washington prepares for a surprise attack on the Hessian soldiers stationed in Trenton, New Jersey. Part adventure, part history lesson, this fine, tightly plotted novel will stir up lively debate as children see the good and bad sides of both the "good guys" and the "enemy." Learn more about George Washington and the Revolutionary War through fiction with *The Fighting Ground* by Avi, *My Brother Sam Is Dead* by James Lincoln Collier and Christopher Collier, *Phoebe and the General* by Judith Berry Griffin, and *Toliver's Secret* by Esther Wood Brady. Then verify the facts with *George Washington: A Picture Book Biography* by James Cross Giblin and *George Washington: Leader of a New Nation* by Mary Pope Osborne. FANTASY. HISTORICAL FICTION. SPACE AND TIME. U.S.–HISTORY–REVOLUTION–FICTION. WASHINGTON, GEORGE.

799   Woodruff, Elvira. *The Magnificent Mummy Maker.* **Scholastic, 1994. ISBN 0-590-45742-X**

[18 chapters, 134p.] Could it be that a 3,000-year-old museum mummy has projected her *ka* or divine nature into Andy's body, helping the ordinarily lackluster student create the most fabulous art project of his life, a mummy that seems to be granting his wishes? Stop reading on page 99 and ask your class to debate whether Andy should wish for his real mother to be alive, thus banishing his rival stepbrother, Jason, whom he refers to as "Mr. Gifted," and what the consequences of that action would be. This amiable chapter book will start your children wondering and writing about what they'd wish for, and send them scurrying to the ancient Egypt and hieroglyphics books in the library to compose inscrutable messages. Travel back in time with Mary Stolz's picture book, *Zekmet, the Stone Carver*, a fictional account of how the Sphinx was created. BROTHERS AND SISTERS. MUMMIES. SCHOOLS. SIBLING RIVALRY. STEPFAMILIES.

800   Woodruff, Elvira. *The Summer I Shrank My Grandmother.* **Illus. Katherine Coville. Holiday House, 1990. ISBN 0-8234-0832-9**

[21 chapters, 153p.] Distressed that her beloved 70-year-old grandmother is getting older, ten-year-old Nelly Brown, scientist-in-training, tries out a formula that reverses the aging process, sending Emma Brown back to her twenties, then teens, and on down to babyhood. Woodruff's lighthearted story encompasses some serious issues, such as how it feels to get older, and accepting inevitable changes in the people we love. Ask your class scientists to write a companion story of what experiment they would request if they found the chemistry set, and what might ensue. For another twist on the age-inversion theme, also read *The Poof Point* by Ellen Weiss and Mel Friedman, and their first book about the Bicker family of scientists, *The Tiny Parents*. ELDERLY. GRANDMOTHERS. MAGIC. SCIENCE-EXPERIMENTS. SIZE.

801   **Yolen, Jane. *Wizard's Hall*. Harcourt, 1991. ISBN 0-15-298132-2**

[22 chapters, 133p.] Shy, quiet, and obedient Henry never wanted to be a wizard, but when he reaches 11, his dear ma packs him off to Wizard's Hall and tells him that talent isn't as important as trying. Sure enough, as a first-year student renamed Thornmallow for acting prickly on the exterior and squishy within, he is welcomed as number 113, and counted upon to help the school rid itself of an impending evil takeover. Explore the imaginative and fantastic realm of high fantasy with more examples, such as *A Hidden Magic* by Vivian Vande Velde, *Into the Painted Bear Lair* by Pamela Stearns, *The Ordinary Princess* by M. M. Kaye, *The Castle in the Attic* by Elizabeth Winthrop, and *Dealing with Dragons* by Patricia Wrede. FANTASY. MAGIC. PERSEVERANCE. WIZARDS.

Illustration from THE DAYDREAMER by Ian McEwan.
Illustrations copyright © 1994 by Anthony Browne.
Reprinted by permission of HarperCollins Publishers and Jonathan Cape Ltd.

FICTION FOR GRADES 5–6

---

802   Alcock, Vivien. *The Trial of Anna Cotman*. Delacorte, 1990. ISBN 0-395-29981-8

[23 chapters, 150p.] Anna, the new girl in town, is snapped up as a best friend by bossy, manipulative Lindy who commands her to join Lindy's brother's new "club," known as the SOM or Society of Masks. At first Anna stays faithful, completing menial cleaning tasks, but when Tom, her one true friend and protector, moves away, the group becomes nasty, tormenting Peter, a victim whom Anna tries to protect, and turns upon Anna, putting her on trial for breaking the rule of loyalty. This chiller works well with *Risk N' Roses* by Jan Slepian, another novel about fitting in and then standing up to repressive group leaders. BEHAVIOR. FRIENDSHIP. PEER PRESSURE. TRIALS.

803   Avi. *The True Confessions of Charlotte Doyle*. Orchard, 1990. ISBN 0-531-08493-0

[22 chapters, 215p.] "Not every 13-year-old girl is accused of murder, brought to trial, and found guilty." So begins Avi's thrilling historical fiction adventure, as recorded in the 1832 journal of Charlotte, an obedient and socially conscious schoolgirl, who relates a chilling tale of cruelty, mutiny, betrayal, and loyalty on the high seas aboard the ship the *Seahawk* during her two-month voyage sailing from England home to America. You should have a field day discussing race/gender roles, values, loyalties, and ethics. The ending is a gold mine for group discussions. Is it possible? Probable? Based on modern mores? And what about Charlotte's future? What will she do next and with the rest of her life? ADVENTURE AND ADVENTURERS. HISTORICAL FICTION. OCEAN. SHIPS. VOYAGES AND TRAVELS.

804   Barre, Shelley A. *Chive*. Simon & Schuster, 1993. ISBN 0-671-75641-9

[23 chapters, 194p.] Interspersed with chapters narrated by Terry, a comfortable suburban boy, are flashback chapters by 12-year-old Chive, Terry's new skateboard companion, who describes how his family lost their farm and moved to a slum apartment where his mother and little sister then died in a fire. Paula Fox's *Monkey Island*, Jerry Spinelli's *Maniac Magee*, and Eve Bunting's moving picture book *Fly Away Home* are all natural companions to *Chive*. Those annual food drives schools sponsor should take on new importance for your students after these up-close looks at homelessness and its consequences. FATHERS AND SONS. FRIENDSHIP. HOMELESSNESS. SKATEBOARDING.

805   **Bauer, Marion Dane.** *A Question of Trust.* **Scholastic, 1994. ISBN 0-590-47915-6**

[13 chapters, 130p.] Exploring themes of parental abandonment, responsibility, and forgiveness, this is a pensive and penetrating novel about 12-year-old Brad and his younger brother Charlie, suffering through their parents' separation after their mother moves out. Secretly caring for a feral cat and her two newborn kittens in the toolshed gives them a sense of purpose, but when they find one kitten dead and half eaten they drive off the mother cat they assume has heartlessly murdered it and struggle to care for the remaining one themselves. Ask your students to write their definition of trust, with examples, and explore the dictionary definitions with their experiences and the events in the novel. Contrast Brad's reaction to his parents' split with that of Leigh Botts in Beverly Cleary's *Strider.* CATS. FAMILY PROBLEMS. FATHERS AND SONS. MOTHERS AND SONS. RESPONSIBILITY.

806   **Cleary, Beverly.** *Strider.* **Illus. by Paul O. Zelinsky. Morrow, 1991. ISBN 0-688-09901-7**

[54 short chapters, 179p.] Leigh Botts of *Dear Mr. Henshaw* is now 14, and in his diary he chronicles how he and friend Barry find an abandoned dog on the beach and decide on joint custody. Skillfully dealing with themes of adjusting to divorce, making friends, and taking responsibility for one's future, Cleary makes us cheer for Leigh as a runner in track and as a winner in life. English teachers will love his two compositions in the story, one about the ancient mariner (page 87), and the other based on a personal experience but using only nouns and verbs. In *A Question of Trust* by Marion Dane Bauer, *Shiloh* by Phyllis Reynolds Naylor, and *The Broccoli Tapes* by Jan Slepian, the main characters deal with problems taking care of secret pets, while *Coaster* by Betsy Duffey explores a boy's adjustment to his divorced mother's new boyfriend. DIVORCE. DOGS. SCHOOLS.

807   **Cole, Sheila.** *The Dragon in the Cliff: A Novel Based on the Life of Mary Anning.* **Illus. by T. C. Farrow. Lothrop, 1991. ISBN 0-688-10196-8**

[23 chapters, 211p.] In 1811, 13-year-old Mary Anning discovered the first complete ichthyosaur skeleton embedded in a cliff near her home in Lyme Regis, England, the first important fossil discovery of the many she would make in her lifetime. Her father dead of consumption when she was 11, Mary worked digging fossils (or curiosities, as they were called then) to support her impoverished family though such manual labor was considered undignified and unsuitable for a female. Cole's novelization of Anning's extraordinary life will find a ready audience among dinosaur fans who will be stunned at her accomplishments and shocked to realize she was never given credit for her work by the all-male scientific establishment. Learn about dinosaurs and other extinct creatures in *And Then There Was One: The Mysteries of Extinction* by Margery Facklam. *Living Dangerously: American Women Who Risked Their Lives for Adventure* by Doreen Rappaport is also inspiring. ENGLAND. FOSSILS. HISTORICAL FICTION. PALEONTOLOGY. WOMEN–BIOGRAPHY.

808   **Conly, Jane Leslie.** *Crazy Lady!* **HarperCollins, 1993. ISBN 0-06-021360-4**

[32 chapters, 180p.] Looking back on seventh grade, the year after his mother died, Vernon tells how he met alcoholic Maxine and befriended her retarded son

Ronald. Omit the infrequent swear words if you need to, but don't miss this powerful inside story of two outcasts told in unsentimental style by the troubled city boy who turns from taunter to supporter. In your discussion, explore how Vernon overcame his mother's death, took the initiative to get academic help from former teacher Miss Annie, and sidestepped his friends' bad influences to take control of his own life. Your class may also want to know more about getting involved in the Special Olympics after reading about it. For a down-to-earth account of Down's syndrome, also read Bill Dodds's *My Sister Annie*. ALCOHOLISM. DEATH. FRIENDSHIP. HANDICAPS. MENTAL RETARDATION.

809   Conrad, Pam. *Pedro's Journal: A Voyage with Christopher Columbus, August 3, 1492–February 14, 1492*. Illus. by Peter Koeppen. Boyds Mills, 1991. ISBN 1-878093-17-7

[35 short chapters, 81p.] Ship's boy Pedro de Salsedo, hired by Columbus because he can read and write, keeps a journal of their voyage, recording the unease of the crew at traveling across the unknown sea, encounters with native peoples, and his own responsibility in the accidental sinking of the Santa María. For a variety of points of view, consult Christopher Columbus's *Log of Christopher Columbus* edited by Steve Lowe, Michael Dorris's *Morning Girl*, Peter and Connie Roop's *I, Columbus*, Peter Sis's *Follow the Dream*, and Jane Yolen's *Encounter*. COLUMBUS, CHRISTOPHER. EXPLORERS. HISTORICAL FICTION. VOYAGES AND TRAVELS.

810   Coville, Bruce. *Jeremy Thatcher, Dragon Hatcher*. Illus. by Gary A. Lippincott. Harcourt, 1991. ISBN 0-15-200748-2

[14 chapters, 148p.] Finding his way to Elives' Magic Supplies shop, Jeremy buys a shimmering ball for a quarter, but when he takes it home and unfolds the paper the old man tucked into the box, he finds directions for hatching a dragon's egg. You'll love Miss Hyacinth Priest, the librarian who tells Jeremy, "No question is silly if you really want to know the answer," and who knows plenty about dragons. Other books in the Magic Shop series are *Jennifer Murdley's Toad* and *The Monster's Ring*. Sarah Sargeant's *Weird Henry Berg*, Brad Strickland's *Dragon's Plunder*, and Patricia Wrede's *Dealing with Dragons* are all essential titles for dragon-lovers. Weave in the poems from Jack Prelutsky's *The Dragons Are Singing Tonight* and Laura Whipple's compilation, *Eric Carle's Dragons Dragons*. DRAGONS. LIBRARIANS.

811   DeFelice, Cynthia. *Lostman's River*. Macmillan, 1994. ISBN 0-02-726466-1

[17 chapters, 157p.] Living in the Florida Everglades in 1906, 13-year-old Tyler, an artistic boy who carves and draws the local wildlife, agrees to go on a scientific expedition with Mr. Strawbridge, who is murdered by local plume hunters, men who shoot birds illegally for their feathers. Complex discussion points include the morality of killing animals for science, Tyler's father's decision to return to New York and give himself up for a murder he thinks he did not commit, and Tyler's betrayal of the location of a secret rookery. As background, also read aloud *Capturing Nature: The Writings and Art of John James Audubon*, taken from his journals, and display pictures of plume birds from his famous reference work *Birds in America*. ADVENTURE AND ADVENTURERS. BIRDS. FLORIDA. HISTORICAL FICTION. RIVERS.

812   DeFelice, Cynthia. *Weasel.* Macmillan, 1990. ISBN 0-02-726457-2

[19 chapters, 119p.] In the Ohio frontier of 1839, 11-year-old Nathan and his nine-year-old sister Molly follow mute Ezra through the woods to a cabin where they find their father seriously wounded after his leg was caught in an animal trap and he was left to die by the murderous Indian hunter called Weasel. Throughout a terrifying, graphic, and riveting tale of classic evil, Nathan wrestles with fear, guilt, rage, and the desire for revenge after Weasel kidnaps him. There is lots to argue about, with the most interesting point being Nathan's dilemma over whether or not to kill Weasel. An unforgettable survival story also dealing with Native American issues is Elizabeth Speare's *The Sign of the Beaver*. For another interesting moral issue, follow up with the 1906 Florida wilderness of deFelice's *Lostman's River*. ADVENTURE AND ADVENTURERS. FRONTIER AND PIONEER LIFE. HISTORICAL FICTION. INDIANS OF NORTH AMERICA.

813   Doherty, Berlie. *Street Child.* Orchard, 1994. ISBN 0-531-08714-X

[27 chapters, 154p.] After his mother dies in the workhouse, Jim Jarvis spends a harrowing year there, passing his days in a dimly lit schoolroom presided over by despotic Mr. Barrack, until he escapes, works for a time with fishmonger Rosie, and is given over to Grimy Nick, who keeps him a virtual slave working on his coal-hauling boat. Victorian London was not a fit place for the poor, and this gripping novel was based on the life of the real Jim Jarvis, who inspired Dr. Thomas Barnardo to found the first Cottage Home for destitute children in 1867. Children will be fascinated by the biography of another workhouse child who overcame his destitution, as related in Diane Stanley and Peter Vennema's *Charles Dickens: The Man Who Had Great Expectations* and Paula Fox's *Monkey Island*, a modern day survival story of a homeless boy in New York City. ENGLAND. HISTORICAL FICTION. HOMELESSNESS. ORPHANS.

814   Dorris, Michael. *Morning Girl.* Houghton Mifflin, 1992. ISBN 1-56282-284-5

[9 chapters, 74p.] This is a lyrical story about a loving island family, told in alternating first-person narratives by Morning Girl and her younger brother, Star Boy, as the two of them cope with the death of their newborn sister, wait out a hurricane, and grow to accept each other's opposite personalities. It's not until the epilogue that we realize who these gentle people are: the Taino Indians who greeted Columbus on his first voyage to the new world (who, Columbus wrote, would make "good and intelligent servants"). You will need to discuss with your students the long-range impact of Columbus's 1492 arrival on that Bahamian island where he "discovered" the ill-fated Taino tribe. Pam Conrad's *Pedro's Journal*, Steve Lowe's editing of Christopher Columbus's own *Log of Christopher Columbus*, Peter and Connie Roop's *I, Columbus*, Peter Sis's *Follow the Dream*, and Jane Yolen's *Encounter* cover the subject from additional angles. *How the Sea Began* is a Taino folktale retold by George Crespo. BROTHERS AND SISTERS. COLUMBUS, CHRISTOPHER. HISTORICAL FICTION. INDIANS OF THE WEST INDIES. ISLANDS.

815   **Fenner, Carol.** *Randall's Wall.* **McElderry, 1991. ISBN 0-689-50518-3**

[85p.] Randall, an outcast boy who is beaten or ignored at home, is rescued from his isolation by Jean, a feisty and loyal girl classmate who helps him uncover his potential. Talk issues with your students. When is it all right to get involved? What should you do if you suspect someone you know is in trouble? Also read *Chive* by Shelley A. Barre, *Cracker Jackson* by Betsy Byars, *Monkey Island* by Paula Fox, and *The Bear's House* by Marilyn Sachs. ARTISTS. FAMILY PROBLEMS. FRIENDSHIP. SCHOOLS. TEACHERS.

816   **Foreman, Michael.** *War Game.* **Illus. by the author. Arcade, 1993. ISBN 1-55970-242-7**

[2 sittings, 72p.] Convinced the war will be over by Christmas, Freddie, Will, Lacey, and Billy enlist and are sent to the trenches in France, overlooking the devastation littering No-Man's Land, with German trenches opposite. On Christmas Eve, the German and British armies serenade each other with Christmas carols, and the following day meet in the middle of No-Man's Land to shake hands, bury the dead, and play an impromptu game of soccer. Based on a true episode, Foreman's sobering story with glowing watercolors and reproductions of posters and period ads give us a window on 1914 Europe. Gloria Houston's *The Year of the Perfect Christmas Tree*, Staton Rabin's *Casey Over There*, and Rosemary Wells's *Waiting for the Evening Star* also take us back to World War I. An interesting World War II picture book is *Randolph's Dream* by Judith Mellecker, while Florence Parry Heide and Judith Heide Gilliland's *Sami and the Time of the Troubles* is a current look at war in Lebanon. ENGLAND. SOCCER. WAR. WORLD WAR–1914-1918–FICTION.

817   **Fox, Paula.** *Monkey Island.* **Orchard, 1991. ISBN 0-531-08562-7**

[10 chapters, 151p.] When 11-year-old Clay Garrity's pregnant mother deserts him at the New York City welfare hotel where they've lived since his father left them, Clay runs away to a park for five harrowing weeks. Horrifyingly realistic in its depiction of homeless people and society's reaction to them, this engrossing novel will generate much discussion, especially if you team it with Eve Bunting's picture book *Fly Away Home*, Shelley A. Barre's *Chive*, and Jerry Spinelli's *Maniac Magee*. HOMELESSNESS. NEW YORK CITY. RUNAWAYS.

818   **Getz, David.** *Almost Famous.* **Henry Holt, 1992. ISBN 0-8050-1940-5**

[19 chapters, 182p.] From the time her now five-year-old brother Wat was born with a heart murmur, Maxine has tried to invent something that will help him get well. Now ten, Maxine yearns to become famous, and begins sending letters to Phil Donohue asking to be a guest on his TV talk show. Maxine and partner Toni actually do invent a useful pillow for Wat, making this quirky and engrossing book a perfect candidate for reading during a unit on inventions when each student must come up with a new product. In pairs, students can act out an interview stint on the "Phil Donohue Show," using questions they have written for each other. Be sure to have a microphone ready. Other tales of school outcasts who attempt to overcome their dilemmas include David Getz's *Thin Air*, Louis

Sachar's *Dogs Don't Tell Jokes*, Zilpha Snyder's *Libby on Wednesday*, Jerry Spinelli's *Report to the Principal's Office*, and Lee Wardlaw's *Seventh-Grade Weirdo*. BROTHERS AND SISTERS. FRIENDSHIP. INVENTORS. LETTER WRITING. SCHOOLS.

819   Getz, David. *Thin Air*. Henry Holt, 1990. ISBN 0-8050-1379-2

[19 chapters, 120p.] Finally being mainstreamed into a sixth-grade class in New York City, Jacob fights to be considered normal, despite his severe asthma and allergies, which he demands no one else acknowledge but which caused him to miss 40 days of school the previous year. It drives Jacob crazy that his older brother is so understanding and sympathetic, and it's not until he meets rebellious classmate Cynthia (who wants him to dance with her Fred Astaire-style) and blind newspaper-vendor Theodore that he begins to get a handle on people's reactions to his chronic illness. Fiercely funny, outrageous, and just plain brilliant, this novel is not to be missed. With all our talk on how to treat others with disabilities, here is a blatantly different point of view that should spur some illuminating discussion on why Jacob has so much trouble in school. Nancy Springer's *Colt*, about a boy with spina bifida, is also outstanding. ASTHMA. BROTHERS. HANDICAPS. NEW YORK CITY. SCHOOLS. SELF-RELIANCE.

820   Hahn, Mary Downing. *Time for Andrew: A Ghost Story*. Clarion, 1994. ISBN 0-395-66556-6

[24 chapters, 165p.] Spending the summer with Aunt Blythe in her old Missouri house while his archaeologist parents are off on a dig, Drew encounters Andrew, a boy who lived there in 1910, is dying of diphtheria, and has time-traveled to the present. Unwillingly, Drew switches places with him. While it's interesting to note the differences in daily life from then to now, the real appeal of this heartfelt story is in the deftly drawn characters, from beautiful tomboy Hannah to whining bully Edward to Drew himself as he becomes more of a "true gent." Incorporate other times with outstanding time-slip stories such as *Tom's Midnight Garden* (late 18th century) by Philippa Pearce, *Fog Magic* (colonial times) by Julia Sauer, *Back to Before* (now and one year ago) by Jan Slepian, *The Princess in the Pigpen* (Elizabethan England) by Jane Resh Thomas, and *Jeremy Visick* (18th century England) by David Wiseman. FAMILY LIFE. FANTASY. GHOST STORIES. SPACE AND TIME.

821   Hesse, Karen. *Phoenix Rising*. Henry Holt, 1994. ISBN 0-8050-3108-1

[29 chapters, 182p.] For the post-Chernobyl generation, this is a startling and affecting story of Nyle, whose grandmother takes in a woman and her 15-year-old son, Ezra, who is dying from the nuclear accident at a nearby power plant that has emptied Boston and contaminated the New England countryside. Initially wary about caring for a stranger, Nyle finds helping Ezra gives her a sense of purpose and connection as she describes his recovery and relapse in her mindful and riveting first-person account. In your class discussion of how the next generation might work to ensure this story won't come true, pull in books on such stark disasters as the Hiroshima bombing, using *Sadako* by Eleanor Coerr and *My Hiroshima* by Junko Morimoto, and modern-day survival stories including Minfong Ho's novel *The Clay Marble* about Cambodian refugees fleeing war. DEATH. DISASTERS. FRIENDSHIP. GRANDMOTHERS.

822   **Hill, Kirkpatrick. *Winter Camp*. McElderry, 1993. ISBN 0-689-50588-4**

[35 short chapters, 185p.] After their parents die, Tough Boy and Sister are taken in by Natasha, the oldest person in their Alaskan village, who takes them to her winter-camp cabin for two months to check her traplines and teach them more of the Indian ways. The sequel to *Toughboy and Sister*, this adventure story of survival at 65 degrees below zero stands on its own. Stay in Alaska with Jean Craighead George's *Julie of the Wolves* and Walt Morey's *Gentle Ben*. Set in the mountains of Wyoming, *The Haymeadow* by Gary Paulsen is another dramatic survival tale. ADVENTURE AND ADVENTURERS. ALASKA. ESKIMOS. INDIANS OF NORTH AMERICA. SURVIVAL.

823   **Ho, Minfong. *The Clay Marble*. Farrar, 1991. ISBN 0-374-31340-7**

[19 chapters, 163p.] Narrated by 12-year-old Dara, this harrowing novel, set in 1980, describes her family's perilous journey to the Thai-Cambodian border refugee camps in hope of obtaining free food, rice seed, and farming tools. "Why must the children suffer, when it's the men who are fighting?" asks one character, a question your listeners will ponder. The picture books *Sadako* by Eleanor Coerr, *The Lotus Seed* by Sherry Garland, *Sami and the Time of the Troubles* by Florence Parry Heide and Judith Heide Gilliland, and *My Hiroshima* by Junko Morimoto also explore the issue of children and war. Diana Kidd's *Onion Tears* is about an orphaned girl who has escaped from Vietnam by boat but lost her family. Bring catastrophe even closer to home with *Phoenix Rising* by Karen Hesse. CAMBODIA. SURVIVAL. WAR.

824   **Holland, Isabelle. *Behind the Lines*. Scholastic, 1994. ISBN 0-590-45113-8**

[14 chapters, 194p.] Working as a kitchen maid for a wealthy family on New York City's Washington Square in 1863, 14-year-old Irish immigrant Katie befriends a skinny puppy she names Paddy, and with the help of Jimmy, a black groom at the stables, tries to keep the puppy from the dog-hating coachman. That's just the first in a series of well-handled subplots, culminating with the New York draft riots that took place when the poor Irish, paid to go to war in place of wealthy young society men, went on a rampage, looting and burning shops, and lynching all blacks they could find. A valuable, stimulating, and shocking addition to any studies of the Civil War, immigration, and slavery, this novel will keep listeners busy debating issues of class, race, and opportunity. Gwen Everett's biographical *John Brown: One Man Against Slavery* will supply some background to those explosive times. AFRICAN AMERICANS. HISTORICAL FICTION. IRISH AMERICANS. RACE RELATIONS. U.S.–HISTORY–CIVIL WAR. WAR.

825   **Jennings, Paul. *Unreal! Eight Surprising Stories*. Viking, 1992. ISBN 0-670-84175-7**

[8 short stories, 107p.] This Australian author's creepy, sometimes scatalogical and crude, but riveting short stories give us Brian Bell, who can't speak without adding the phrase "without a shirt" to the end of each sentence; greedy Giffen, who is undone by his own glue invention; Larry, who finds a ghost outside the outhouse; and Marcus, 16 and never been kissed. It's just the ticket to settle older students who haven't been read to in a while. Also suspenseful and eerily amusing are Ruth Aimsworth's *The Phantom Carousel and Other Ghostly Tales*, Natalie Babbitt's *The Devil's Storybook*, Roald Dahl's *The Wonderful Story of Henry Sugar and Six More*, Dennis Pepper's *The Oxford Book of Scary Stories*, Lance Salway's *A Nasty Piece of Work and Other Ghost Stories*, Alvin Schwartz's *Scary Stories to Tell in the Dark*, and Alfred Slote's *The Devil Rides with Me and Other Fantastic Stories*. GHOST STORIES. SHORT STORIES. SUSPENSE.

826   **Lindbergh, Anne. *Travel Far, Pay No Fare*. HarperCollins, 1992. ISBN 0-06-021775-8**

[18 chapters, 199p.] Owen is shocked to discover that Parsley, using her new bookmark, has somehow entered into the stories of her favorite books to abscond with the Cheshire cat, Snowball from *Stuart Little*, Ramona Quimby's cat Picky-picky, and a dozen others. As Owen's children's-book-writing mother and Parsley's father prepare for their upcoming wedding, the two children venture into Alice's Wonderland and bring home Jody's fawn Flag from Marjorie Kinnen Rawling's *The Yearling*. Your story travelers can write about and reenact going into favorite chapters of memorable books and interacting with the characters. What a natural stimulus for class booktalking and creative dramatics! Patrick in Tom Birdseye's *Just Call Me Stupid* has reading problems until new friend Celina reads him tales of King Arthur. BOOKS AND READING. COUSINS. CREATIVE WRITING. FANTASY. MAGIC. REMARRIAGE. STEPFAMILIES.

827   **Lisle, Janet Taylor. *Forest*. Orchard, 1993. ISBN 0-531-08653-4**

[15 chapters, 150p.] Woodbine and Brown Nut are the first squirrels to witness the young girl alien climbing the large white oak in Upper Forest, while in Lower Forest, eight-year-old Wendell informs his parents that his sister, 12-year-old Amber, disgusted with the fighting and wars she sees on TV and angry with her rigid father, has run away again. With chapters alternating between Upper and Lower Forest, this is a gripping account of the war that develops between humans and squirrels when both groups feel threatened and power-hungry leaders stir up their followers. Children will observe local squirrels in a new light after listening to this engrossing and original fantasy that makes thoughtful points about despots and the rare individuals who are willing to oppose them. Anne Mazer's *The Oxboy*, about a society that hunts down any humans who are part animal, is an interesting choice for a follow-up novel. FANTASY. FORESTS AND FORESTRY. LEADERSHIP. SQUIRRELS. WAR.

828   **Lowry, Lois. *The Giver*. Houghton Mifflin, 1993. ISBN 0-395-64566-2**

[23 chapters, 180p.] In a perfect future society where each family is assigned two children, all needs are provided by the community, and even emotions are regulated, Jonas is content until the year he turns 12 and is assigned his lifetime job: The Receiver of Memory, the only person with access to memories of the world that came before. Starkly original and chillingly plotted, this mesmerizing novel should stimulate invigorating discussions about the concepts of utopia, repression, and conformity. The open-ended ending will drive kids crazy as they debate Jonah's ultimate fate. Madeline L'Engle's *A Wrinkle in Time* and Anne Mazer's *The Oxboy* would make noteworthy follow-ups. FAMILY LIFE. FANTASY. LEADERSHIP. NEWBERY MEDAL. SCIENCE FICTION.

829   **McEwan, Ian. *The Daydreamer.* Illus. by Anthony Browne. HarperCollins, 1994. ISBN 0-06-024427-6**

[8 chapters, 192p.] Peter Fortune may seem silent on the outside, but inside his head his imagination never stops and he becomes a cat, a baby, and even a grown-up, all described with intricate insight. Ask your classroom thinkers to get a handle on their reveries and either write a chapter about themselves, or a further adventure of Peter based on their personal daydreams. Anthony Browne's *Changes* and Matt Faulkner's *The Amazing Voyage of Jackie Grace* are two stimulating picture books that show the imagination at work. In Betsy Byars's *The Two-Thousand-Pound Goldfish*, Warren's escape into movielike fantasies helps him cope with the realities of his daily life. FAMILY LIFE. FANTASY. IMAGINATION.

830   **Maugham, W. Somerset. *Appointment.* Illus. by Roger Essley. Adapted by Alan Benjamin. Green Tiger Press, 1993. ISBN 0-671-75887-X**

[1 sitting, unp.] In the marketplace buying his master's supper, faithful servant Abdullah sees Death, disguised as an old crone, reaching her hand out to him, and he rushes home in terror, begging his master to lend him his horse so he can escape to Samarra. When the merchant seeks out the old woman to ask her why she stared so threateningly at Abdullah, she replies, "It was more a look of surprise. I was taken aback to see him here in Baghdad. You see, I have an appointment with him tonight . . . in Samarra." The dark, gloomy pastels give a further air of exotic mystery to this tantalizing puzzler. You may need to read the story a second time as it will go right over some students' heads. As background, bring up the concept of fate being preordained, using the example of Oedipus as one who fulfilled the Delphic Oracle's predictions in spite of his efforts to circumvent them. DEATH. IRAQ.

831   **Mazer, Anne. *The Oxboy.* Knopf, 1993. ISBN 0-679-84191-1**

[14 chapters, 109p.] A chilling allegory about the son of a human woman and her ox husband, in the days when only Certified Purebred humans are tolerated and hunters track down and kill all animals who dare to intermingle. This spare, strange, and unique story will mesmerize children, with whom you can discuss concepts of prejudice, racial superiority, and oppression. Delve deeper with Daisaku Ikeda's *Over the Deep Blue Sea*, Lois Lowry's *Number the Stars*, Ken Mochizuki's *Baseball Saved Us*, Vaunda Micheaux Nelson's *Mayfield Crossing*, and Chris Van Allburg's *The Widow's Broom*. Lois Lowry's *The Giver* is an unforgettable companion novel for students willing to examine tough issues, while Janet Taylor Lisle's *Forest* is about war between squirrels and humans when both feel threatened. ANIMALS. FANTASY. OXEN. PREJUDICE.

832   Naylor, Phyllis Reynolds. *Shiloh*. Atheneum, 1991. ISBN 0-689-31614-3

[15 chapters, 144p.] In a first-person narrative flavored with West Virginia hill country dialect, 11-year-old Marty Preston is faced with an ethical dilemma when he takes in and hides a maltreated, love-starved beagle that he knows belongs to someone else. In order to keep Shiloh, he finds himself telling an escalating series of lies to his family and best friend, and when the dog is attacked and badly hurt by another dog, Marty must own up to and make amends for his actions. It's a simply told story, and every child will wrestle with the moral dilemma presented: Is it right to steal a dog that is being mistreated? Organize a debate. Betsy Byars's *Wanted . . . Mud Blossom* will make a good counterpart, as will Beverly Cleary's *Strider*. CONFLICT RESOLUTION. DOGS. HONESTY. NEWBERY MEDAL. WEST VIRGINIA.

833   Paulsen, Gary. *A Christmas Sonata*. Illus. by Leslie Bowman. Delacorte, 1992. ISBN 0-385-30441-2

[2–3 sittings, 76p.] Looking back on the Christmas of 1943, the narrator describes the day he stopped believing in Santa Claus and the week he spent with his dying cousin Matthew, when the faith of both boys was restored. This spare, touching short story is well worth brooding over. Paulsen's *The Cookcamp*, written with the same voice and also lovely, is about a young boy who spends a wartime summer with his grandmother. Cynthia Rylant's *Children of Christmas* will also make everyone pensive. CHRISTMAS. DEATH. HISTORICAL FICTION. SANTA CLAUS. SICK. WORLD WAR, 1939-1945–FICTION.

834   Paulsen, Gary. *The Cookcamp*. Orchard, 1991. ISBN 0-531-08527-9

[15 chapters, 115p.] During World War II, the summer the boy was five and his father was away in the army, his mother sent him by train to stay with his grandmother who was working as a cook for a road crew up near the Canadian border. More mood piece than action adventure, the descriptions of life in the Minnesota woods—feeding a chipmunk, riding a caterpillar tractor, missing mother—are told simply, as a young boy would see it. Paulsen's *A Christmas Sonata*, about a boy whose cousin is dying, also takes place in 1943, and packs a wallop. James Stevenson's autobiographical picture book *Don't You Know There's a War On?* shows a typical child's life in the United States at that time. Read aloud the 18 poignant poems in Myra Cohn Livingston's *Poems for Grandmothers*, and ask your students to compile a companion volume of original poems that pay tribute to their own grandparents. FAMILY STORIES. GRANDMOTHERS. HISTORICAL FICTION. WORLD WAR, 1939-1945–FICTION.

835   Paulsen, Gary. *The Haymeadow*. Illus. by Ruth Wright Paulsen. Delacorte, 1992. ISBN 0-385-30621-0

[25 chapters, 195p.] Living on a Wyoming ranch, 14-year-old John Barron yearns for change, granted when his taciturn father assigns him to drive their 6,000 sheep into their summer mountain valley pasture and spend the next three months tending them alone with only two horses and four dogs for companionship and aid. This being a typically introspective yet action-packed Paulsen novel, John copes with a flash flood, coyotes, a bear, and dead and wounded sheep and dogs, all the while learning self-reliance, tolerance, and acceptance of his father and himself. Ask your students to write about a time they overcame fear or took charge of a dangerous or unpleasant situation, first describing the problem, and then detailing their response to it. Move north with the Alaskan survival story *Winter Camp* by Kirkpatrick Hill. ADVENTURE AND ADVENTURERS. RANCH LIFE. SELF-RELIANCE. SHEEP. SURVIVAL. WYOMING.

836   **Pepper, Dennis, ed. *The Oxford Book of Scary Stories*. Oxford University Press, 1992. ISBN 0-19-278131-6**

[35 short stories and poems, 160p.] Starting with the spooky cumulative chant "This Is the Key to the Castle," scare-seekers will find a satisfying assortment of disquieting short stories and poems, some by well-known writers including Vivien Alcock, Adèle Geras, and Susan Price. The large format coupled with the varied styles of dark and brooding illustrations and photos will attract browsers. Unnerve them further with Ruth Ainsworth's *The Phantom Carousel and Other Ghostly Tales*, Natalie Babbitt's *The Devil's Storybook*, Roald Dahl's *The Wonderful Story of Henry Sugar and Six More*, Paul Jennings's *Unreal! Eight Surprising Stories*, Lance Salway's *A Nasty Piece of Work and Other Ghost Stories*, Alvin Schwartz's *Scary Stories to Tell in the Dark*, and Alfred Slote's *The Devil Rides with Me and Other Fantastic Stories*. GHOST STORIES. SHORT STORIES. SUSPENSE.

837   **Price, Leontyne. *Aïda*. Illus. by Leo and Diane Dillon. Gulliver / Harcourt, 1990. ISBN 0-15-200405-X**

[1 sitting, unp.] The story of Giuseppe Verdi's opera is retold by renowned singer Price who has sung the title role in opera houses worldwide. Ethiopian princess Aïda, enslaved by the Egyptians, becomes handmaiden to Princess Amneris and falls in love with Radames, captain of the Egyptian army, whom Amneris fancies for herself. Radames's love for Aïda leads to his downfall, and, entombed, the two die happy in each other's arms. The elaborate drama of the story and the stately, sumptuous acrylic paintings on acetate and marbelized paper will send Egypt fans to the library for books on pharaohs, and get them hooked on the opera. Don't forget to play a recording of the music. For more on Verdi, check out his chapter in Kathleen Krull's *Lives of the Musicians*. Continue the Egypt theme with Shirley Climo's folktale *The Egyptian Cinderella*, and Mary Stolz's *Zekmet the Stone Carver*. EGYPT, ANCIENT. LOVE. OPERA. SLAVERY. WAR.

838   **Radley, Gail. *The Golden Days*. Macmillan, 1992. ISBN 0-02-775652-1**

[14 chapters, 137p.] Corey's third foster home in two years is with Michelle and Dan Kepperman, a caring couple in their early twenties, but fearful of another rejection, the 11-year-old boy vows not to let himself get attached. When he learns Michelle is pregnant, Cory and his new friend, 75-year-old Carlotta, a former circus employee now living in a nursing home, join forces and run away. Shelley A. Barre's *Chive*, Paula Fox's *Monkey Island*, and Jerry Spinelli's *Maniac*

Magee all have in common the themes of abandonment, hiding one's true feelings, and running away, which will make for fascinating comparisons in class discussions. ELDERLY. FOSTER CARE. FRIENDSHIP. RUNAWAYS.

839   Rice, Bebe Faas. *The Year the Wolves Came.* Dutton, 1994. ISBN 0-525-45209-5

[15 chapters, 148p.] In 1910, four years after the Terrible Thing happened, Therese looks back on that Canadian winter, describes the events leading up to her mother's death, and remembers the coming of the white wolf and the mystery that surrounded it. Not wanting to scare your listeners unduly, at the same time read *To the Top of the World: Adventures with Arctic Wolves* by Jim Brandenberg, an inside view of a wolf pack he photographed and studied one summer. CANADA. FANTASY. MOTHERS AND DAUGHTERS. WEREWOLVES. WINTER. WOLVES.

840   Sachar, Louis. *Dogs Don't Tell Jokes.* Knopf, 1991. ISBN 0-679-92017-X

[25 chapters, 215p.] When seventh-grader Gary "Goon" Boone hears about the school talent show, he signs up, planning to write original material for a stand-up comedy routine that he hopes will make him less of an outcast. His parents, worried that he is hiding himself behind a wall of puns and riddles, promise him $100 if he will refrain from telling any jokes for the next three weeks. This sensitive and funny account of a loser who comes out on top will help your students become more accepting and understanding of the "Goons" in their lives. Tune in to the comic possibilities by sponsoring a joke-in where each jokester can search out jokes and riddles to read aloud or tell. Meet other misfits in David Getz's *Almost Famous* and *Thin Air*, Zilpha Snyder's *Libby on Wednesday*, Jerry Spinelli's *Report to the Principal's Office*, and Lee Wardlaw's *Seventh-Grade Weirdo*. COMEDIANS. HUMOROUS FICTION. SCHOOLS.

841   Shreve, Susan. *The Gift of the Girl Who Couldn't Hear.* Tambourine, 1991. ISBN 0-8050-1747-X

[9 chapters, 80p.] Thirteen-year-old talented but angst-filled Eliza Westfield, consumed with insecurity about her weight, grades, and personality, can't decide whether to try out for the lead in "Annie," while her deaf friend, the irrepressible Lucy, decides to learn to sing and try out for the part of an orphan. Though Lucy's parents insist that she use speech and lip-reading to communicate, many deaf people also learn American Sign Language. Start your students signing with Laura Rankin's graceful alphabet book *The Handmade Alphabet*. DEAF. FRIENDSHIP. HANDICAPS. TEACHERS.

842   Shusterman, Neal. *The Eyes of Kid Midas.* Little, Brown, 1992. ISBN 0-316-77542-8

[17 chapters, 185p.] Thirteen-year-old Kevin, on a mountain camping trip with the seventh grade, sets out for the peak of the Divine Watch, where he finds a sleek, dark pair of sunglasses that make everything he says come true. Unfortunately, even though they help him prevail over Bertram, a bully who delights in humiliating his victims, the glasses can't uncreate anything they've created. Other books where a magical power or ability turns sinister include Mildred Ames's *Is There Life on a Plastic Planet?*, Bill Brittain's *Professor Popkin's Prodigious Polish*, Bruce Coville's *Jennifer Murdley's Toad*, and Beatrice Gormley's *Mail-Order Wings*. BULLIES. EYEGLASSES. FANTASY. MAGIC.

843   Slepian, Jan. *Back to Before*. Philomel, 1993. ISBN 0-399-22011-9

[17 chapters, 170p.] Cousins Linny and Hilary can't explain how they find themselves back in Brooklyn one year earlier to the day before his mother died and her father left home, and they try to change time to prevent the inevitable. Discuss with your students: If you could go back and fix something you had said or done one year ago, what would it be? What perspectives on life do you have now that you didn't have last year? Other first-rate time-travel or swap stories include *Time for Andrew: A Ghost Story* by Mary Downing Hahn, *Tom's Midnight Garden* by Philippa Pearce, *Fog Magic* by Julia Sauer, *The Princess in the Pigpen* by Jane Resh Thomas, and *Jeremy Visick* by David Wiseman. If you discuss how one says good-bye to a loved one who is dying, be sure to read the exquisitely touching picture book *I'll See You in My Dreams* by Mavis Jukes. COUSINS. DEATH. FATHERS AND DAUGHTERS. MOTHERS AND SONS. SPACE AND TIME.

844   Slepian, Jan. *The Broccoli Tapes*. Philomel, 1988. ISBN 0-399-21712-6

[6 long chapters, 157p.] Sara and her family are in Hawaii for a five-month sabbatical, during which time she keeps a running cassette-tape log to send back to her teacher Mrs. Hasselbauer in Boston as part of her Oral History social studies project. It's an eventful time: Sara and her older brother Sam secretly befriend a feral cat they name Broccoli, their grandmother takes ill with cancer, and they get to know Eddie, a hostile boy with family problems. Each segment starts with "Click," as Sara turns on the tape recorder, so the book's sound is conversational and immediate. Your students may want to try keeping a talking journal for a while. Leigh Botts keeps a written diary of his days and new dog in *Strider* by Beverly Cleary. BROTHERS AND SISTERS. CATS. DEATH. FRIENDSHIP. GRANDMOTHERS.

845   Slepian, Jan. *Risk N' Roses*. Philomel, 1990. ISBN 0-399-22219-7

[17 chapters, 175p.] Eleven-year-old Skip is expected to look after her beautiful but mildly retarded 15-year-old sister Angela on the stoop of their new Bronx apartment, but Skip, mesmerized by the tough stance of her new friend, Jean Persico, allows Angela to become the butt of Jean's most terrible dare. Neighbor Mr. Kaminski, bitter and alone, befriends Angela and shows her his beautiful roses, each named after a family member killed by the Nazis. Set in 1948, this is a compelling story about peer pressure, cruelty, and being accepted at a great cost, and is almost an American counterpart to Vivian Alcock's *The Trial of Anna Cotman*. Charlie's sister has Down's syndrome and embarrasses him also in *My Sister Annie* by Bill Dodds. If you have never discussed the Holocaust with your students, start with Chana Byers Abels's photo essay *The Children We Remember* and Lois Lowry's *Number the Stars*. BEHAVIOR. FRIENDSHIP. HANDICAPS. HISTORICAL FICTION. JEWS. MENTAL RETARDATION. SISTERS.

846   Snyder, Zilpha Keatley. *Libby on Wednesday*. Delacorte, 1990. ISBN 0-385-29979-6

[20 chapters, 196p.] Precocious 11-year-old Libby, aghast at being enrolled in the local junior high after years of home schooling by her avant-garde literary California family in their marvelous old mansion, wins a writing contest and is assigned to a writer's group with four other talented classmates who slowly evolve into friends. There's sarcastic Gary, punk-hairdoed Tierney, popular, phony Wendy, and awkward Alex, coping with cerebral palsy; their sessions of reading and critiquing each other's work will serve as inspiration for all classroom and closet writers. Meet other kids who have a tough time adjusting to school in David Getz's *Almost Famous* and *Thin Air*, Louis Sachar's *Dogs Don't Tell Jokes*, Jerry Spinelli's *Report to the Principal's Office*, and Lee Wardlaw's *Seventh-Grade Weirdo*. AUTHORS. FRIENDSHIP. SCHOOLS. WRITING.

847   Spinelli, Jerry. *Maniac Magee*. Little, Brown, 1990. ISBN 0-316-80722-2

[46 short chapters, 184p.] Born Jeffrey Lionel Magee, Maniac was orphaned at age three, ran away at 11, and ended up in Two Mills, Pa., where blacks stayed in the East End of town, and whites in the West End. Like the exploits of Paul Bunyan, tales of Maniac's legendary feats spread through both sides of town, and through his example, the rift between two races so suspicious of each other they'd never crossed paths begins to heal. Read aloud, Spinelli's short chapters and direct prose will startle children into rethinking their attitudes toward anyone different. Picking up on the themes of race relations and baseball, pull in Peter Golenbock's *Teammates* and Vaunda Micheaux Nelson's *Mayfield Crossing*. Two more homeless survivors come out on top in Shelley A. Barre's *Chive* and Paula Fox's *Monkey Island*. HOMELESSNESS. MULTICULTURAL STORIES. NEWBERY MEDAL. PREJUDICE. RACE RELATIONS. RUNAWAYS.

848   Strickland, Brad. *Dragon's Plunder*. Illus. by Wayne D. Barlowe Atheneum, 1992. ISBN 0-689-31573-2

[14 chapters, 153p.] Kidnapped by the sailors of the ship *Betty* because of his magic talent of calling up the wind, Jaime Falconer is only too happy to get away from his wearisome duties at the Pirate's Rest Inn and joins the crew voluntarily. The ripsnorting adventure sports a cast that includes a loquacious parrot, a captain who though dead can't rest till he plunders a dragon's hoard, a princess who craves action, and a well-read dragon. Other memorable dragon tales include Bruce Coville's *Jeremy Thatcher, Dragon Hatcher*, Sarah Sargeant's *Weird Henry Berg*, and Patricia Wrede's *Dealing with Dragons*. Also kidnapped, for his supposed ability to see ghosts, is Oliver in Sid Fleischman's pirate tale *The Ghost in the Noonday Sun*. ADVENTURE AND ADVENTURERS. DRAGONS. FANTASY. PIRATES. SHIPS.

849   Wallace, Barbara Brooks. *The Twin in the Tavern*. Atheneum, 1993. ISBN 0-689-31846-4

[21 chapters, 177p.] Orphaned, ten-year-old Taddy is flimflammed by nefarious thieves Lucky and Neezer into working as a slavey in their dismal dockside inn, The Dog's Tail, while he searches for his secret twin. In this fast-moving Victorian melodrama set in 18th-century Alexandria, Virginia, one finds all the satisfying elements of a good mystery yarn, as in the author's earlier companion novel, *Peppermints in the Parlor*. MYSTERY AND DETECTIVE STORIES. ORPHANS. TWINS.

850   **Wardlaw, Lee. *Seventh-Grade Weirdo*. Scholastic, 1992. ISBN 0-590-44805-6**

[18 chapters, 149p.] Christopher "Rob" Robin has a host of problems: his mother runs a children's book business called Heffalump House; his father is a famous former surfing champion who talks in surfing slang; his five-year-old sister Winnie, a certified genius, who taught herself to read at age four, takes on the personality of all her favorite book characters, from Harriet the Spy to King Bidgood; and now Rob's on the wrong side of tough guy Mike "The Shark" Sharkey, and madly in love with Jenner, an eighth-grade girl. Winnie designs "Once Upon a Time," a best-selling board game that's a combination of Trivial Pursuit and Pictionary. Play a book character game where each person secretly chooses a fiction book with a memorable character, and compiles a one-minute speech or skit as that character for rest of the class to guess. Jerry Spinelli's *Report to the Principal's Office* also deals with school traumas. BROTHERS AND SISTERS. BULLIES. FAMILY LIFE. SCHOOLS.

851   **Weiss, Ellen, and Mel Friedman. *The Poof Point*. Knopf, 1992. ISBN 0-679-83257-2**

[16 chapters, 166p.] In the sequel to *The Tiny Parents*, Marie, 12, and Eddie, 9, kidsit their quarrelsome scientist parents whose fifth-dimension-traveling time machine invention has sent them careening back to their own babyhoods in mind but not in body. Hilariously slapstick, the premise of reaching the "poof point," or age zero, and then passing backward into a former life will get your students thinking and writing about who they'd be if they could travel back in hypertime. Elvira Woodruff's *The Summer I Shrank My Grandmother* is a natural companion. FAMILY PROBLEMS. FANTASY. HUMOROUS FICTION. INVENTORS. SCIENTISTS. TIME TRAVEL.

852   **Woodruff, Elvira. *Dear Napoleon, I Know You're Dead, But . . .* Illus. by Noah and Jess Woodruff. Holiday House, 1992. ISBN 0-8234-0962-7**

[26 chapters, 220p.] On a visit to his adored Gramps in the nursing home, Marty shows him the letters he wrote to Napoleon and then to Vincent Van Gogh for a class assignment, and Gramps tells him about a fellow patient, a former mailman who claims he can travel in time to deliver mail to anyone, living or dead. Several weeks later, Marty gets the first response, postmarked Paris, France, from none other than Napoleon Bonaparte, *l'Empereur de la France*, and the ensuing excitement helps Marty come to terms with his grandfather's illness and death. Enliven your biography assignments by asking each student to write a letter to a famous dead person. "Deliver" each letter anonymously to another classmate who will be responsible for researching intriguing biographical tidbits, and responding creditably by mail in the guise of that celebrated figure. DEATH. GRANDFATHERS. LETTER WRITING. SICK.

853   **Wrede, Patricia. *Dealing with Dragons*. Harcourt, 1990. ISBN 0-15-222900-0**

[15 chapters, 212p.] In this crackling first of four books in the Enchanted Forest Chronicles, Cimorene, a youngest princess, rebels against convention and runs off to become cavekeeper for dragon Kazul to escape marriage with a mindless prince. With its challenging, tongue-in-cheek narration, lovers of high fantasy will be reminded of Lloyd Alexander's *The Book of Three* and four other Chronicles of Prydain, and Brian Jacques's mouse epic, *Redwall*. Adventurous readers will continue on their own with *Searching for Dragons* (1992), *Talking to Dragons* (1993) and *Calling on Dragons* (1993). Contrast fairy tale days with modern-set *Jeremy Thatcher, Dragon Hatcher* by Bruce Coville, *Weird Henry Berg* by Sarah Sargeant, and old-time *Dragon's Plunder* by Brad Strickland. Jack Prelutsky's *The Dragons Are Singing Tonight* and Laura Whipple's compilation *Eric Carle's Dragons Dragons* set the stage with poetry. DRAGONS. FANTASY. PRINCES AND PRINCESSES. WIZARDS.

854   **Yep, Laurence.** *The Star Fisher.* **Morrow, 1991. ISBN 0-688-09365-5**

[14 chapters, 150p.] Clarksburg, West Virginia, is the place 15-year-old Joan's parents pick to set up their new laundry in 1927, and, as the only Chinese family in town, they encounter hostility and prejudice from some locals, tempered by many kindnesses from their new landlady, Miss Lucy. This spirited and engrossing book, based on family stories the author collected about his grandparents, will encourage children to ask their parents and grandparents to recall and record their own tales about coming to or growing up in America long ago. *Good Luck Gold and Other Poems* by Janet S. Gold describes growing up in the United States from the point of view of a Chinese American girl. CHINESE AMERICANS. FAMILY LIFE. HISTORICAL FICTION. PREJUDICE. RACE RELATIONS. WEST VIRGINIA.

FOLK & FAIRY TALES, MYTHS & LEGENDS: SINGLE STORIES

855   Aardema, Verna. *Anansi Finds a Fool.* Illus. by Bryna Waldman. Dial, 1992. ISBN 0-8037-1165-4

[Gr. 1–5] Trickster Anansi, in seeking a fool for a fishing partner, teams up with Bonsu who allows Anansi to do all the work making the trap and catching fish while he, Bonsu, gets tired. Set in Ghana, with a human Anansi instead of a spider man, this retelling is more sophisticated than Eric A. Kimmel's slapstick *Anansi Goes Fishing,* and the soft watercolors give us the flavor of life in a small village. Read both and compare text and illustrations. For more stories with Anansi, read Eric Maddern's *The Fire Children,* Gail E. Haley's *A Story, a Story,* Kimmel's *Anansi and the Moss-Covered Rock,* and *Anansi and the Talking Melon,* Gerald McDermott's *Anansi the Spider,* and Frances Temple's Jamaican Anansi story, *Tiger Soup.* Meet some other lazy characters in Arnold Lobel's *A Treeful of Pigs,* Dianne Snyder's *The Boy of the Three Year Nap,* and Diane Wolkstein's *Lazy Stories.* FOLKLORE–AFRICA, WEST. FOOLS–FOLKLORE. LAZINESS–FOLKLORE. TRICKSTER TALES.

856   Aardema, Verna. *Borreguita and the Coyote: A Tale from Ayutla, Mexico.* Illus. by Petra Mathers. Knopf, 1991. ISBN 0-679-90921-X

[Gr. K–3] Three times a demure little lamb outsmarts the fierce coyote who plans to eat her, and your children will root for the weak against the strong. Tony Johnston's *The Story of Rabbit and Coyote,* also from Mexico, incorporates some of the same elements, while we alternately cheer and jeer trickster Coyote in Shonto Begay's *Ma'ii and Cousin Horned Toad,* Valerie Scho Carey's *Quail Song,* Jonathan London and Lanny Pinola's *Fire Race,* Gerald McDermott's *Coyote,* Phyllis Root's *Coyote and the Magic Words,* Janet Stevens's *Coyote Steals the Blanket,* and Harriet Peck Taylor's *Coyote Places the Stars.* Read "The Sky Is Falling!" a variant in Gretchen Will Mayo's collection *That Tricky Coyote!,* along with *Meet Tricky Coyote!* (Walker, 1993). COYOTES–FOLKLORE. FOLKLORE–MEXICO. SHEEP–FOLKLORE. TRICKSTER TALES.

857   Aardema, Verna. *Traveling to Tondo: A Tale of the Nkundo of Zaire.* Illus. by Will Hillenbrand. Knopf, 1991. ISBN 0-679-90081-0

[Gr. Pre–2] Bowane the civet cat invites his friends the pigeon, snake, and tortoise to go with him to meet his intended, but they procrastinate so long that they arrive years too late and find his beautiful bride-to-be already married with children. This is a perfect storyteller's tale, with a chantable refrain, cumulative action, motions and sound effects for the audience to do, plenty of humor, and the added pleasure of acting it out afterward. Check through an animal encyclopedia to display a photo and some info about civet cats, and ask your listeners to explain why the foursome took so absurdly long to get to Tondo. Verna Aardema's *Why Mosquitoes Buzz in People's Ears*, Eric A. Kimmel's *Anansi Goes Fishing*, and Rafe Martin's *Foolish Rabbit's Big Mistake* are folktales that display the same riotously skewed logic. ANIMALS–FOLKLORE. CATS–FOLKLORE. CHANTABLE REFRAIN. CUMULATIVE STORIES. FOLKLORE–AFRICA.

858 Ada, Alma Flor. *The Rooster Who Went to His Uncle's Wedding: A Latin American Folktale.* Illus. by Kathleen Kuchera. Putnam, 1993. ISBN 0-399-22412-2

[Gr. Pre–1] "What to do? Peck or not peck?" a hungry rooster on his way to his uncle's wedding wonders as he weighs getting his beak dirty against passing up eating the single perfect kernel of corn lying in a puddle of mud. Once he gives into temptation, he tries to scare a growing procession of helpers into cleaning his beak, but the grass, lamb, dog, stick, fire, and water all say, "No, I won't. Why should I?" until the sun agrees to cooperate. Act this out in a long line, with several children playing each part. Contrast with Lucie M. Gonzalez's Cuban variant *The Bossy Gallito* and English variant *The Old Woman and Her Pig* as retold by Paul Galdone, Eric A. Kimmel, or Rosanne Litzinger, and *The Troublesome Pig* retold by Priscilla Lamont. CHANTABLE REFRAIN. CREATIVE DRAMA–FOLKLORE. CUMULATIVE STORIES. FOLKLORE–LATIN AMERICA. ROOSTERS–FOLKLORE.

859 Aesop. *The Wind and the Sun.* Retold and illus. by Bernadette Watts. North-South, 1992. ISBN 1-55858-163-4

[Gr. K–2] To settle the argument over who is the strongest, the Wind proposes a test with the Sun: whichever can remove the cloak of the man walking the road below will win. After the Sun shines its warmest and the man removes his cloak, the Sun says ". . . it is easier to influence people with gentleness than with force." In *The Match Between the Winds*, a folktale from Borneo retold by Shirley Climo, it's the gentle wind that wins over the powerful one. Talk over the message of these tales, and ask children if they can think of any examples in their own experience. Keep blowing hot and cold with *Windy Day: Stories and Poems* by Caroline Feller Bauer, *Weather*, the easy-to-read poems collected by Lee Bennett Hopkins, *Old Devil Wind* by Bill Martin, Jr., and *Mirandy and Brother Wind* by Patricia C. McKissack. FABLES. FOLKLORE–GREECE. SUN–FOLKLORE. WIND–FOLKLORE.

860 Arnold, Katya. *Baba Yaga: A Russian Folktale.* Illus. by the author. North-South, 1993. ISBN 1-55858-208-8

[Gr. 1–3] Little Tishka, son of old-age parents who were granted their wish for a child, is captured by Baba Yaga for her supper, but he tricks her back and travels home on the wings of a gosling who takes pity on him. With bright, primitive, hand-colored woodcuts based on Russian folk art "lubok" pictures, this portrait of the witch who lives in a house on chicken legs is positively menacing, with an oven scene reminiscent of Grimm's *Hansel and Gretel*. In Barbara Walker's Turkish variant, *Teeny Tiny and the Witch Woman*, a little boy also outwits an infuriated witch. Baba Yaga fans will also shiver with Arnold's *Baba Yaga & the Little Girl*, Becky Hickox Ayres's *Matreshka*, Joanna Cole's *Bony Legs*, Eric Kimmel's *Baba Yaga*, Elsa Okon Rael's *Marushka's Egg*, Marianna Mayer's *Baba Yaga and Vasilisa the Brave*, Maida Silverman's *Anna and the Seven Swans*, Ernest Small's *Baba Yaga*, and Elizabeth Winthrop's *Vasilissa the Beautiful*. BABA YAGA. FOLKLORE–RUSSIA. GEESE–FOLKLORE. WITCHES–FOLKLORE.

861   **Arnold, Katya.** *Baba Yaga & the Little Girl.* **Illus. by the author. North-South, 1994. ISBN 1-55858-288-6**

[Gr. K–3] Sent by her stepmother to fetch a sewing needle from Baba Yaga, a little girl prevails because she is helpful to the witch's cat, dog, gate, and tree. Compare variants of the same tale, including Maida Silverman's *Anna and the Seven Swans*, Joanna Cole's *Bony Legs*, Eric Kimmel's *Baba Yaga*, and Ernest Small's *Baba Yaga*. Meet up with the Russian witch again in Arnold's *Baba Yaga*, Becky Hickox Ayres's *Matreshka*, Marianna Mayer's *Baba Yaga and Vasilisa the Brave*, Elsa Okon Rael's *Marushka's Egg*, and Elizabeth Winthrop's *Vasilissa the Beautiful*. In Barbara Walker's Turkish variant, *Teeny Tiny and the Witch Woman*, magic objects also aid children in their escape. BABA YAGA. FOLKLORE–RUSSIA. WITCHES–FOLKLORE.

862   **Ata, Te.** *Baby Rattlesnake.* **Adapted by Lynn Moroney. Illus. by Veg Reisberg. Children's Book Press, 1989. ISBN 0-89239-049-2**

[Gr. Pre–1] Though his parents think he is too young and foolish, Baby Rattlesnake wears them down until they give him what he wants—a real rattle on the end of his tail. Children will love chanting his rattle song, "Ch-Ch-Ch!" A good story to tell, this one teaches what happens when one acts irresponsibly, in this case by trying to scare the chief's unflappable daughter. *Snake Hunt* by Jill Kastner takes us out looking for rattlers with a girl and her grandad who claims to have wrestled one bare-handed way back when. Help defuse your children's fear of snakes with Betsy Maestro's nonfiction *Take a Look at Snakes*, Faith McNulty's *A Snake in the House*, Stefan Czernecki and Timothy Rhodes's Australian folktale *The Singing Snake*, and Tomi Ungerer's lovable *Crictor*. CHANTABLE REFRAIN. CHICASAW INDIANS–FOLKLORE. FOLKLORE–INDIANS OF NORTH AMERICA. SNAKES–FOLKLORE. STORIES TO TELL.

863   **Ayres, Becky Hickox.** *Matreshka.* **Illus. by Alexi Natchev. Doubleday, 1992. ISBN 0-385-30657-1**

[Gr. K–3] After sharing her food with an old woman she meets on the way home, Kata receives in return a hand-carved wooden doll that later saves her from becoming Sunday dinner for the evil Baba Yaga. Here is one story that begs for a Russian nesting doll prop. Go on a Baba Yaga binge with Katya Arnold's *Baba Yaga* and *Baba Yaga & the Little Girl*, Joanna Cole's *Bony Legs*, Eric Kimmel's *Baba*

Yaga, Marianna Mayer's *Baba Yaga and Vasilisa the Brave*, Elsa Okon Rael's *Marushka's Egg*, Maida Silverman's *Anna and the Seven Swans*, Ernest Small's *Baba Yaga*, and Elizabeth Winthrop's *Vasilissa the Beautiful*. Compare all these with Jacob Grimm's *Hansel and Gretel* and Barbara Walker's Turkish variant, *Teeny Tiny and the Witch Woman*. BABA YAGA. DOLLS–FOLKLORE. FOLKLORE–RUSSIA. WITCHES–FOLKLORE.

864   Baden, Robert. *And Sunday Makes Seven.* Illus. by Michelle Edwards. Albert Whitman, 1990. ISBN 0-8075-0356-8

[Gr. 2–4] Poor Carlos and his rich cousin Ricardo have something in common: a large brown mole on the ends of their noses—and both get the chance to lose it. When Carlos comes upon a house of 12 witches all singing a song in Spanish about the days of the week, they reward him for finishing their song by removing his mole and giving him 12 bags of gold. Heedless Ricardo ends up with two moles and no money, of course. There's no source given, but you'll be interested to note "The Old Man's Wen" from *The Goblins Giggle and Other Stories* by Molly Bang is a similar version that hails from Japan. To compare motifs, see also Aliki's *The Twelve Months* from Greece, Beatrice Schenk de Regniers's Slavic *Little Sister and the Month Brothers*, Obi Onyefulu's *Chinye* from Nigeria, and Robert San Souci's *The Talking Eggs* from the United States. There's a pronunciation guide in the back so everyone can learn the numbers one to ten and the days of the week in Spanish. DAYS OF THE WEEK–FOLKLORE. FOLKLORE–COSTA RICA. SPANISH LANGUAGE–FOLK-LORE. WITCHES–FOLKLORE.

865   Begay, Shonto. *Ma'ii and Cousin Horned Toad: A Traditional Navajo Story.* Illus. by the author. Scholastic, 1992. ISBN 0-590-45391-2

[Gr. K–4] Horned Toad feeds his coyote trickster cousin with roast corn and squash stew, which the ungrateful Ma'ii rewards by eating Horned Toad and taking over his farm. From inside the scoundrel's belly, Horned Toad is able to make his cousin plenty uncomfortable and teach him a good lesson. Other coyotes get their comeuppance in Verna Aardema's Mexican folktale *Borreguita and the Coyote*, Valerie Scho Carey's Pueblo Indian folktale *Quail Song*, Tony Johnston's *The Story of Rabbit and Coyote*, Gretchen Will Mayo's *That Tricky Coyote!* and *Meet Tricky Coyote!* (Walker, 1993), Gerald McDermott's *Coyote*, Phyllis Root's *Coyote and the Magic Words*, Janet Stevens's *Coyote Steals the Blanket*, and Harriet Peck Taylor's *Coyote Places the Stars*. COYOTES–FOLKLORE. FOLKLORE–INDI-ANS OF NORTH AMERICA. HORNED TOADS–FOLKLORE. NAVAJO INDIANS–FOLKLORE. TOADS–FOLKLORE. TRICKSTER TALES.

866   Bernhard, Emery. *How Snowshoe Hare Rescued the Sun: A Tale from the Arctic.* Illus. by Durga Bernhard. Holiday House, 1993. ISBN 0-8234-1043-9

[Gr. K–3] A long time past, greedy demons who lived under the earth stole the sun for themselves, leaving only the Northern Lights to dispel the gloom, until Snowshoe Hare volunteered to get it back. Thanks to his efforts, we now have as well the moon and all the stars in the Milky Way. Gerald McDermott's *Raven: A Trickster Tale from the Pacific Northwest*, Elphinstone Dayrell's African folktale

Why the Sun and the Moon Live in the Sky, and Mary-Joan Gerson's Brazilian *How Night Came from the Sea* are also interesting to use for astronomy units. Rabbits and hares have the role of trickster in many folktales, among which are Andy Gregg's Algonquian *Great Rabbit and the Long-Tailed Wildcat*, Barbara Knutson's African *Sungura and Leopard*, Gerald McDermott's *Zomo the Rabbit: A Trickster Tale from West Africa*, and Gayle Ross's *How Rabbit Tricked Otter and Other Cherokee Trickster Stories*. ASTRONOMY–FOLKLORE. FOLKLORE, ESKIMO. HARES–FOLKLORE. PICTURE BOOKS FOR ALL AGES. POURQUOI TALES. SUN–FOLKLORE.

867   **Bernhard, Emery. *The Tree That Rains: The Flood Myth of the Huichol Indians of Mexico.* Illus. by Durga Bernhard. Holiday House, 1994. ISBN 0-8234-1108-7**

[Gr. 1–4] With his faithful black dog assisting him, Watakame clears his fields of trees only to find them reappearing each day, thanks to Great-Grandmother Earth who warns him of a devastating flood. Still told by the Huichol Indians of western Mexico, this mystical tale, with primitive gouache paintings influenced by Mexican yarn paintings, will make an interesting counterpart to Ellen Alexander's Peruvian folktale *Llama and the Great Flood*. The black dog who secretly becomes a woman will remind readers of a similar motif in Diane Wolkstein's Chinese folktale *White Wave* and Sumiko Yagawa's Japanese folktale *The Crane Wife*. Pik plays ball with Chak the Mayan rain god to end the drought in David Wisniewski's *Rain Player*. *The Sad Night: The Story of an Aztec Victory and a Spanish Loss* by Sally Schofer Mathews, and *How Music Came to the World*, an Aztec folktale retold by Hal Ober, continue the Mexican theme. FOLKLORE–INDIANS OF MEXICO. HUICHOL INDIANS–FOLKLORE. MULTICULTURAL STORIES–FOLKLORE. RAIN AND RAINFALL–FOLKLORE. TRANSFORMATIONS–FOLKLORE.

868   **Bierhorst, John. *The Woman Who Fell from the Sky: The Iroquois Story of Creation.* Illus. by Robert Andrew Parker. Morrow, 1993. ISBN 0-688-10681-1**

[Gr. 2–6] Pushed by her jealous husband through a hole in the sky, the sky woman lands on a turtle's back and begins to create the earth, sky, sun, and stars. Her sons Sapling and Flint create other good and bad elements, respectively, showing us gentle and hard minds in the universe. Compare this to other Native American creation myths including *Owl Eyes* by Frieda Gates, *Children of the Morning Light: Wampanoag Tales* told by Manitonquat (Medicine Story), *Raven's Light: A Myth from the People of the Northwest Coast* by Susan Hand Shetterly, and *Moon Mother: A Native American Creation Tale* by Ed Young. *The Fire Children: A West African Creation Tale* retold by Eric Maddern makes an interesting contrast. BROTHERS–FOLKLORE. CREATION–FOLKLORE. FOLKLORE–INDIANS OF NORTH AMERICA. IROQUOIS INDIANS–FOLKLORE.

869   **Birdseye, Tom. *Soap! Soap! Don't Forget the Soap! An Appalachian Folktale.* Illus. by Andrew Glass. Holiday House, 1993. ISBN 0-8234-1005-6**

[Gr. 1–3] Up in Sassafras Hollow in North Carolina lives Plug Honeycut, a boy so forgetful he often doesn't recognize his own name, and the day his mama sends him to the store for soap, his absentmindedness gets him in a heap of trouble. Other "forgetful" stories that come full circle include *Ollie Forgot* by Tedd Arnold,

Hans in Luck by Paul Galdone, *Don't Forget the Bacon* by Pat Hutchins, *Farmer Bungle Forgets* by Dick King-Smith, and *Idle Jack* by Anthony Maitland. Prolong that mountain flavor in your storytelling with "Sody Saleratus" from Richard Chase's *Grandfather Tales*. CHANTABLE REFRAIN. FOLKLORE–U.S. FOOLS–FOLKLORE. MEMORY–FOLKLORE. SEQUENCE STORIES.

870   **Bruchac, Joseph.** *The First Strawberries: A Cherokee Story.* **Illus. by Anna Vojtech. Dial, 1993. ISBN 0-8037-1332-0**

[Gr. K–3] When the first man on earth hurts the feelings of his wife, the first woman, she leaves him. In his remorse, he accepts help from the sun which creates the first strawberries as the man's apology for his hard words, and his wife forgives him. Bring in strawberries to share, reminding children to be kind to each other in tribute to the sensible Cherokee belief that "friendship and respect are as sweet as the taste of ripe, red berries." *The Legend of the Cranberry: A Paleo-Indian Tale* by Ellin Greene describes how another fruit came to be, while *How Turtle's Back Was Cracked* by Gayle Ross is another Cherokee pourquoi tale. CHEROKEE INDIANS–FOLKLORE. EMOTIONS–FOLKLORE. FOLKLORE–INDIANS OF NORTH AMERICA. FRUIT–FOLKLORE. POURQUOI TALES.

871   **Bruchac, Joseph.** *The Great Ball Game: A Muskogee Story.* **Illus. by Susan L. Roth. Dial, 1994. ISBN 0-8037-1540-4**

[Gr. K–3] To settle their argument over who is better, the birds and the animals decide to have a ball game and divide themselves into two teams: those with wings and those with teeth. The bat, finally accepted onto the animal team despite his wings, helps win the game and sets the losers' penalty; he deems the birds must leave the land for half of each year. This spare pourquoi tale, illustrated with earth-toned collages made from textured paper, makes an interesting kickoff to a discussion of animal migration. We learn why bats have flattened noses in *Iktomi and the Boulder*, a Plains Indian legend by Paul Goble, and witness more bat/bird conflict in *A Promise to the Sun: An African Story* by Tololwa M. Mollel. *This Way Home* by Lisa Westberg Peters is a description of the annual migration of a flock of sparrows. ANIMALS–FOLKLORE. BATS–FOLKLORE. CREEK INDIANS–FOLKLORE. FOLKLORE–INDIANS OF NORTH AMERICA. MIGRATION–FOLKLORE. POURQUOI TALES.

872   **Bruchac, Joseph, and Jonathan London.** *Thirteen Moons on Turtle's Back: A Native American Year of Moons.* **Illus. by Thomas Locker. Philomel, 1992. ISBN 0-399-22141-7**

[Gr. 2–6] As a young boy's Abenaki grandfather points out, there are always 13 scales on a turtle's back, and 13 moons in each year. In this glowing and gorgeous poetry/folklore book, the legends behind each month are explained from a cross section of Native American tribal nations. *Peboan and Seegwun* by Charles Larry is an Anishinabe or Ojibwa legend about the changes from winter to spring. *Moon Mother: A Native American Creation Tale* by Ed Young and Jane Yolen's poetry in *What Rhymes with Moon?* are also apropos. To find out about turtle's back problems, consult Nigerian pourquoi tale *The Flying Tortoise* by

Tololwa M. Mollel and *How Turtle's Back Was Cracked*, a Cherokee Indian version retold by Gayle Ross. FOLKLORE–INDIANS OF NORTH AMERICA. INDIANS OF NORTH AMERICA–POETRY. MOON–FOLKLORE. MOON–POETRY. SEASONS–POETRY.

873   **Brusca, María Cristina, and Tona Wilson.** *The Blacksmith and the Devils.* **Illus. by María Cristina Brusca. Henry Holt, 1992. ISBN 0-8050-1954-5**

[Gr. 3–6] Out on the pampas, poor Argentinian blacksmith Juan Pobreza refuses to charge for his services when he hammers a new shoe for the mule of an old gaucho, and when the stranger insists he is really San Pedro, guardian of the gates of heaven, Juan accepts the fellow's offer of three wishes. Next, an elegant gent with a pointed tail shows up and offers Pobreza a contract of 20 years of youth and a bag of gold in exchange for his soul. Compare how the devil is outsmarted in variants from the United States including Edna Barth's *Jack-O-Lantern*, Valerie Scho Carey's *The Devil & Mother Crump*, and William H. Hooks's *Mean Jake and the Devils*. DEVIL–FOLKLORE. FOLKLORE–ARGENTINA. WISHES–FOLKLORE.

874   **Brusca, María Cristina, and Tona Wilson.** *The Cook and the King.* **Illus. by María Cristina Brusca. Henry Holt, 1993. ISBN 0-8050-2355-0**

[Gr. 2–4] Independent Florinda goes to work cooking empanadas for the bossy king, but soon finds herself intervening in the foolish judgments he dispenses to his subjects when they come to him with their disputes. *Clever Cooks: A Concoction of Stories, Charms, Recipes and Riddles* by Ellin Greene, *Clever Gretchen and Other Forgotten Folktales* by Alison Lurie, and *Womenfolk and Fairy Tales* by Rosemary Minard all celebrate strong heroines. Another young woman uses her resources to outwit the ruler in the Russian folktale *Vassilisa the Wise* by Josepha Sherman. *In the Month of Kislev: A Story for Hanukkah* by Nina Jaffe, where a rich merchant expects hungry children to pay for smelling his potato pancakes, and Ethiopian folktale *Fire on the Mountain* by Jane Kurtz both incorporate motifs found in Brusca's story. COOKERY–FOLKLORE. FOLKLORE–SOUTH AMERICA. JUDGES–FOLKLORE. KINGS AND RULERS–FOLKLORE. WOMEN–FOLKLORE.

875   **Carey, Valerie Scho.** *Maggie Mab and the Bogey Beast.* **Illus. by Johanna Westerman. Arcade, 1992. ISBN 1-55970-155-2**

[Gr. 2–4] Old Maggie Mab lives in a tiny stone cottage and has little to call her own save for a kind word for everyone she meets, and when she finds an iron pot filled with gold coins that change to a lump of silver, then iron, and then a stone, she utters not a word of disappointment. The bony, donkeylike bogey that takes her on a wild night ride can't get a complaint out of her, and so rewards her with gold for her good nature. Another English tale that starts out similarly is *Beware the Brindlebeast* by Anita Riggio. Compare the endings and ask children to compare the personalities of Maggie Mab and Birdie. Make the acquaintance of other English creatures and characters in Shirley Climo's *Piskies, Spriggans, and Other Magical Beings* and Alan Garner's *A Bag of Moonshine*. FOLKLORE–ENGLAND. MONSTERS–FOLKLORE. SUPERNATURAL–FOLKLORE. TRANSFORMATIONS–FOLKLORE.

876   Carey, Valerie Scho. *Quail Song: A Pueblo Indian Tale.* Illus. by Ivan Barnett. Putnam, 1990. ISBN 0-399-21936-6

[Gr. K–2] Quail cuts herself on sharp grass, but her cry of pain sounds like a beautiful lullaby to forgetful Coyote and he insists that Quail teach him the song over and over again until she thinks of a way to trick him into leaving her be. Coyote makes a further fool of himself in Shonto Begay's *Ma'ii and Cousin Horned Toad*, Gerald McDermott's *Coyote*, and Janet Stevens's *Coyote Steals the Blanket*. In *The Name of the Tree: A Bantu Folktale* by Celia Barker Lottridge, none of the animals can remember the tree's magical name, and in *Lizard's Song* by George Shannon, Bear can't remember the tune he borrows either. BIRDS–FOLKLORE. CHANTABLE REFRAIN. COYOTES–FOLKLORE. CREATIVE DRAMA–FOLKLORE. FOLKLORE–INDIANS OF NORTH AMERICA. PUEBLO INDIANS–FOLKLORE.

877   Chocolate, Deborah M. Newton. *Talk, Talk: An Ashanti Legend.* Illus. by Dave Albers. Troll, 1993. ISBN 0-8167-2817-8

[Gr. 1–5] Farmer Jumaani is digging up his yams when they begin to shout at him to leave them alone, and when the dog, a palm tree branch, a tree, and a stone speak as well, the frightened man sets off running. The original retelling of this farcical folktale comes from Harold Courlander's *The Hat-Shaking Dance and Other Tales from the Gold Coast*. After reading, hand out scripts of the story from Aaron Shepard's *Stories on Stage: Scripts for Reader's Theater*, and act the whole thing out. Trickster tales *Anansi and the Talking Melon* by Eric A. Kimmel and *Tops & Bottoms* by Janet Stevens will also leave you laughing. ENGLISH LANGUAGE–PERSONIFICATION. FOLKLORE–AFRICA, WEST. FOLKLORE, ASHANTI. VEGETABLES–FOLKLORE.

878   Climo, Shirley. *The Korean Cinderella.* Illus. by the author. HarperCollins, 1993. ISBN 0-06-020433-8

[Gr. 1–4] After her mother dies, poor Pear Blossom is miserable ministering to her jealous new stepmother and stepsister who set impossible tasks for her to finish and call her Little Pig for the pigtail style of her hair. Luckily, a tokgabi (goblin), a flock of sparrows, and a black ox help her out, and a lost straw sandal lands her the noble magistrate for a husband. In *The Princess and the Beggar*, a Korean folktale by Anne Sibley O'Brien, the princess marries an outcast peasant. Traverse the globe in search of Cinderella with Climo's *The Egyptian Cinderella*; American variants Joanne Compton's *Ashpet*, William H. Hooks's *Moss Gown*, and Charlotte Huck's *Princess Furball*; Dang Manh Kha's Vietnamese *In the Land of Small Dragon*, Rafe Martin's Algonquian Indian *The Rough-Face Girl*, Robert D. San Souci's African American *Sukey and the Mermaid*, Flora Annie Steele's English *Tattercoats*, and Barbara Ker Wilson's Chinese *Wishbones*. CINDERELLA STORIES. FAIRY TALES. FOLKLORE–KOREA. SHOES–FOLKLORE. STEPMOTHERS–FOLKLORE.

879   Climo, Shirley. *The Match Between the Winds.* Illus. by Roni Shepherd. Macmillan, 1991. ISBN 0-02-719035-8

[Gr. K–3] Wanting to stir up some mischief, the West Wind challenges the East Wind to a contest, but West Wind's great power notwithstanding, it's the gentle

East Wind who is able to coax Kodok the little green tree frog from his palm tree, earning the East Wind the name Rajah Anjin, Lord of the Winds. A variant is Bernadette Watts's retelling of Aesop's *The Wind and the Sun*. *The Stonecutter* by Gerald McDermott and *The Warrior and the Wise Man* by David Wisniewski also demonstrate that force is not always the best solution. *Windy Day: Stories and Poems* by Caroline Feller Bauer, *Weather*, easy-to-read poems collected by Lee Bennett Hopkins, *Old Devil Wind* by Bill Martin, Jr., and *Mirandy and Brother Wind* by Patricia C. McKissack will all help you chart the winds. *The Junior Thunder Lord* by Laurence Yep shows how one man's kindness brings rain to a drought-stricken town. CONTESTS–FOLKLORE. FOLKLORE–BORNEO. FROGS–FOLKLORE. WIND–FOLK-LORE.

880   Climo, Shirley. *Stolen Thunder: A Norse Myth*. Illus. by Alexander Koshkin. Clarion, 1994. ISBN 0-395-64368-6

[Gr. 3–6] Thor has lost Mjolnir, his thunder-making fiery hammer, and trickster Loki finds it in the clutches of giant Thrym the Frost King, who offers to trade it for the hand of Freya, the Goddess of Love. In a comic scene sure to get listeners snickering, Thor, dressed in women's wedding finery, steps in as the bride. Another splendid Norse myth is Marianna Mayer's *Iduna and the Magic Apples*. For another nice bit of deception among giants, read Tomie dePaola's *Fin M'Coul, the Giant of Knockmany Hill*. FOLKLORE–NORWAY. GIANTS–FOLKLORE. MYTHOLOGY. TRICKSTER TALES.

881   Cole, Joanna. *Don't Tell the Whole World!* Illus. by Kate Duke. Crowell, 1990. ISBN 0-690-04811-4

[Gr. K–3] Finding a money box while plowing is a stroke of luck for John, but first he must figure out a way to keep his wife Emma from revealing their good fortune to their rich landlord, Old Mr. Snood. *The Night It Rained Pancakes* by Mirra Ginsburg is a variant featuring two Russian peasant brothers, and the same theme of outwitting authority by feigning stupidity works in Mary Blount Christian's *The April Fool*. BURIED TREASURE–FOLKLORE. FOOLS–FOLKLORE. HUSBANDS AND WIVES–FOLKLORE.

882   Cole, Joanna. *It's Too Noisy!* Illus. by Kate Duke. Crowell, 1989. ISBN 0-690-04737-1

[Gr. Pre–1] Wanting quiet, a poor farmer visits the Wise Man to find out what to do about all the "yelling, singing, snoring, laughing, fighting, and crying" in his overflowing little house. Bringing in all the animals makes things worse, of course. Variants include Julia Donaldson's *A Squash and a Squeeze*, Marilyn Hirsch's *Could Anything Be Worse?* (Holiday House, 1974), Ann McGovern's *Too Much Noise*, and Margot Zemach's *It Could Always Be Worse*. American folktale *Nathaniel Willy, Scared Silly* by Judith Mathews and Fay Robinson and the Puerto Rican variants "The Squeaky Old Bed" from Barbara Baumgartner's folktale collection *Crocodile! Crocodile!* and *The Squeaky Door* by Laura Simms are also loud and fun. *Mouse in the House* by Patricia Baehr and *The One and Only Super-Duper Golly-Whopper Jim-Dandy Really-Handy Clock-Tock-Stopper* by Patricia Thomas use the same theme of not knowing how good you have it until things get worse. DOMESTIC ANIMALS–FOLKLORE. FOLKLORE, JEWISH. NOISE–FOLKLORE.

883   Compton, Joanne. *Ashpet: An Appalachian Tale.* Illus. by Kenn Compton. Holiday House, 1994. ISBN 0-8234-1106-0

[Gr. 1–4] A serving girl hired out to the Widow Hopper and her two ugly and lazy daughters, Myrtle and Ethel, Ashpet is kind to old Granny, who in return fixes the girl up for the big church meeting where she meets the doctor's son. The down-home Cinderella story is illustrated with cartoon-style watercolors, and will make an interesting contrast to the more refined tellings of European American variants William H. Hooks's *Moss Gown* and Charlotte Huck's *Princess Furball*; Native American variants Rafe Martin's Algonquian *The Rough-Face Girl*, Penny Pollock's Zuni *The Turkey Girl*, and Robert D. San Souci's Ojibwa *Sootface* and African American *Sukey and the Mermaid*. Babette Cole's *Prince Cinders*, Ellen Jackson's *Cinder Edna*, Frances Minters's *Cinder-Elly*, and Bernice Myers's *Sidney Rella and the Glass Sneaker* are diverting parodies. CINDERELLA STORIES. FAIRY TALES. FOLKLORE–U.S.

884   Compton, Kenn, and Joanne Compton. *Jack the Giant Chaser: An Appalachian Tale.* Illus. by Kenn Compton. Holiday House, 1993. ISBN 0-8234-0998-8

[Gr. 1–4] When the rock he heaves in the creek kills seven catfish, Jack ambles into town proclaiming, "I just killed me seven with one blow!" which so impresses the mayor that he assigns Jack to chase off the mean old giant living on the mountain. As in *The Valiant Little Tailor* illustrated by Victor Ambrus, Kenn and Joanne Compton's Appalachian *Jack the Giant Chaser*, Christine Price's Turkish *Sixty at a Blow* (Dutton, 1968), Peggy Thomson's *The Brave Little Tailor*, and Dorothy Van Woerkom's Russian *Alexandra the Rock-Eater*, the little guy prevails with his sharp wits. Richard Chase's classic collection *The Jack Tales* (from which this story was adapted), Gail E. Haley's *Jack and the Bean Tree*, and James Still's *Jack and the Bean Tree* are U.S. Jack tales, relatives of all those English versions including those by Lorinda Bryan Cauley, Alan Garner, John Howe, and Susan Pearson, and Paul Galdone's *The History of Mother Twaddle and the Marvelous Achievements of Her Son, Jack.* FOLKLORE–U.S. GIANTS–FOLKLORE.

885   Compton, Patricia A. *The Terrible Eek.* Illus. by Sheila Hamanaka. Simon & Schuster, 1991. ISBN 0-671-73737-6

[Gr. K–3] On a rainy, windy night in the mountains, a boy asks his father what he fears the most, and an eavesdropping wolf and a thief lurking near the small thatched-roof house are baffled by his mis-heard reply: "A terrible leak." A tiger, a monkey, and a deep hole round out this farcical Japanese folktale, leaving the boy and his parents safe in their dry, warm beds. Discuss: How many times have you made up your own imagined definition for a word you didn't know? Next, play a variant of "Dictionary": Supply several nouns they probably won't recognize like blunderbuss, lemming, tirade, or whippet), and ask them to define and draw each one. Share the imaginative results with the whole class. Finally, reveal what each word actually means. Misunderstandings help the heroes in Jacob

Grimm's German folktale *The Bremen Town Musicians* and Laurence Yep's Japanese folktale *The Man Who Tricked a Ghost*. FOLKLORE–JAPAN. PICTURE BOOKS FOR ALL AGES. RAIN AND RAINFALL–FOLKLORE. ROBBERS AND OUTLAWS–FOLKLORE. TIGERS–FOLKLORE. WOLVES–FOLKLORE.

886 **Cook, Joel. *The Rat's Daughter*. Illus. by the author. Boyds Mills, 1993. ISBN 1-56397-140-2**

[Gr. K–2] The parents of a lovely and talented young rat are determined that she only marry the best, which they decide must be the sun. The sun says the cloud is more powerful, the cloud names the wind, the wind points to the wall, and the wall insists the rat is the greatest of all. This story appears in the folk literature of many cultures, including Judith Dupré's Mayan *The Mouse Bride*, Judith Ruth Hurlimann's German *The Proud White Cat*, Eric A. Kimmel's Japanese *The Greatest of All*, Holly H. Kwon's Korean *The Moles and the Mireuk*, and Gerald McDermott's Japanese *The Stonecutter*. MARRIAGE–FOLKLORE. RATS–FOLKLORE. WEDDINGS–FOLKLORE.

887 **Crespo, George. *How the Sea Began: A Taino Myth*. Illus. by the author. Clarion, 1993. ISBN 0-395-63033-9**

[Gr. 1–6] After hunter Yayael disappears in a hurricane, his devoted parents find only his bow and arrows, which they place in a large gourd. The gourd then yields fresh fish and when it is broken by accident, a flowing wave of tear-flavored water—the sea. The author's note states that this West Indian pourquoi tale was collected nearly 500 years ago in what is now the Dominican Republic by a man commissioned by Columbus to record Taino beliefs and customs. Get wet with *Under the Sea from A to Z* by Anne Doubilet and *I Am the Ocean* by Suzanna Marshak, in tandem with the poems in *Splish Splash* by Joan Bransfield Graham and *Until I Saw the Sea* collected by Alison Shaw. Using ocean myths such as Vivian French's *Why the Sea Is Salt* and Jane Langton's *Salt*, contrast with nonfiction books like Seymour Simon's *Oceans* (Morrow, 1990). Also read alongside Michael Dorris's *Morning Girl* and Jane Yolen's *Encounter*, two fiction books about the Taino Indians and the arrival of Christopher Columbus. DEATH–FOLKLORE. FOLKLORE–INDIANS OF THE WEST INDIES. HURRICANES–FOLKLORE. OCEAN–FOLKLORE. POURQUOI TALES. TAINO INDIANS–FOLKLORE.

888 **Croll, Carolyn. *The Three Brothers*. Illus. by the author. Putnam / Whitebird, 1991. ISBN 0-399-22195-6**

[Gr. K–3] Wondering to which of his three worthy sons he should leave his farm, a farmer tells them it will go to whoever can fill up the old barn in one day. Ask your listeners how they would complete this task. As it happens, the eldest fills it with animals, the middle son with hay, but Amos the youngest lights a single candle and fills it with light. Dramatize the ending by lighting a candle in the darkened room. In *Boots and His Brothers: A Norwegian Tale* retold by Eric A. Kimmel, the three fellows set out on a quest and the youngest one also proves himself. BROTHERS–FOLKLORE. FARM LIFE–FOLKLORE. FATHERS AND SONS–FOLKLORE. FOLKLORE–GERMANY.

889 Czernecki, Stefan, and Timothy Rhodes. *The Singing Snake*. Illus. by Stefan Czernecki. Hyperion, 1993. ISBN 1-56282-400-7

[Gr. K–2] To convince the raucous-voiced animals to develop more melodious voices, Old Man promises to make a musical instrument to honor the creature who sings the best. In this pourquoi tale about the first flute, Snake wins by holding Lark at the back of his throat, but when the others discover his deception, he ends up only able to make a hissing sound. *Rainbow Bird* by Eric Maddern is another folktale of the Australian Aborigines. Mix snake fact, folklore, and fiction with Te Ata's *Baby Rattlesnake*, Nan Bodsworth's *A Nice Walk in the Jungle*, Diane L. Burns's *Snakes Alive! Jokes About Snakes*, Katy Hall and Lisa Eisenberg's *Snakey Riddles*, Tony Johnston's *Slither McCreep and His Brother Joe*, Jill Kastner's *Snake Hunt*, Betsy Maestro's nonfiction *Take a Look at Snakes*, Faith McNulty's *A Snake in the House*, and Tomi Ungerer's lovable *Crictor*. FLUTE–FOLKLORE. FOLKLORE–AUSTRALIA. MUSICAL INSTRUMENTS–FOLKLORE. POURQUOI TALES. SINGING–FOLKLORE. SNAKES–FOLKLORE.

890 Dasent, George Webbe, trans. *East o' the Sun and West o' the Moon*. Illus. by P. J. Lynch. Candlewick, 1992. ISBN 1-56402-049-5

[Gr. 3–6] To gain riches, a man gives his youngest daughter to the White Bear who carries her off to his sumptuous castle, where he becomes a man each night. Listening to her mother's advice to look upon the young man as he sleeps proves disastrous for the girl, for the young man is a prince who now must prepare to marry a troll princess far away unless the lassie can get him back in time. Compare the sumptuous and romantic watercolors and retelling with other versions illustrated by Gillian Barlow and by Kathleen and Michael Hague, the American variant "Whitebear Whittington" in Richard Chase's *Grandfather Tales*, and the French *Beauty and the Beast*, retold by Marianna Mayer. Male counterparts to the story include Elizabeth Isele's and J. Patrick Lewis's *The Frog Princess*, Robert D. San Souci's *The Snow Wife*, Diane Wolkstein's *White Wave*, and Sumiko Yagawa's *The Crane Wife*. BEARS–FOLKLORE. FAIRY TALES. FOLKLORE–NORWAY. TRANSFORMATIONS–FOLKLORE. TROLLS–FOLKLORE.

891 Day, David. *The Sleeper*. Illus. by Mark Entwhistle. Ideals, 1990. ISBN 0-8249-8456-0

[Gr. 2–4] After Emperor Chin the Merciless decrees that all the libraries in China be emptied within 100 days, and anyone caught with a book will be put to death, young monk Wu is entrusted with delivering the most valuable ones to the Emperor's officers. Lost in the mountains, Wu finds a cave with two old men playing chess, falls into a deep sleep, and emerges 200 years later with his books intact, just in time to stop an impending battle and bring peace to the land. Here's a feel-good story for underappreciated librarians. Talk over why books are so important, pulling in *Dream Peddler* by Gail E. Haley, the poems in *Good Books, Good Times!* by Lee Bennett Hopkins, the facts in *Books and Libraries* by Jack Knowlton, and the remarkable story of ancient Greek scientist Eratosthenes in *The Librarian Who Measured the Earth* by Kathryn Lasky. BOOKS AND READING–FOLKLORE. CHESS–FOLKLORE. EMPERORS–FOLKLORE. FOLKLORE–CHINA. LIBRARIES–FOLKLORE. SLEEP–FOLKLORE.

892   **Demi. *The Empty Pot*. Illus. by the author. Henry Holt, 1990. ISBN 0-8050-1217-6**

[Gr. K–3] Needing a successor to his throne, the old Emperor gives out special seeds to all the children in the land, proclaiming that whoever can show him the best plant grown from the seed will be chosen. Though Ping nurtures his seed, it never germinates. Ashamed of his failure, he nevertheless brings the empty pot to the palace. As you read, ask your listeners what a seed needs to thrive. At the end, question them on why the Emperor handed out seeds he knew would never grow. *The Jade Stone* by Caryn Yacowitz is a Chinese folktale about a sculptor who sticks to his principles in spite of the Emperor's demands. Both tales validate the old saying that honesty's the best policy. See how healthy seeds grow in *From Seed to Plant* by Gail Gibbons and *The Reason for a Flower* by Ruth Heller. EMPERORS–FOLKLORE. FLOWERS–FOLKLORE. FOLKLORE–CHINA. HONESTY–FOLKLORE. SEEDS–FOLKLORE.

893   **Demi. *The Firebird*. Illus. by the author. Henry Holt, 1994. ISBN 0-8050-3244-4**

[Gr. 2–5] In Demi's version of the Russian fairy tale, archer Dimitri, riding on the Horse of Power, finds a gold feather from the Firebird and brings it to Tsar Ivan, who insists the young man bring the whole bird or lose his head. After his success, he is sent out next to bring back fairy princess Vassilissa for the tsar to marry and falls in love with her. Demi's delicate, gilt-rich, oversized paintings are spectacular. Compare with other variants and versions, including *Prince Ivan and the Firebird* by Laslo Gal, *The Firebird* by Selina Hastings, and *The Firebird* by Robert D. San Souci. ANIMALS, MYTHICAL–FOLKLORE. BIRDS–FOLKLORE. FAIRY TALES. FOLKLORE–RUSSIA. HORSES–FOLKLORE. KINGS AND RULERS–FOLKLORE. PRINCES AND PRINCESSES–FOLKLORE.

894   **Demi. *The Magic Tapestry*. Illus. by the author. Henry Holt, 1994. ISBN 0-8050-2810-2**

[Gr. 1–4] A Chinese widow with three sons weaves the most heavenly tapestry ever made, but as soon as she finishes, it is whisked away on a wind sent by the fairies of Sun Mountain. For a son to retrieve it, he must first knock out his two front teeth and undergo terrible hardships, which, as folktales go, means only the youngest son is brave and loyal enough to try. Compare the delicate gold-toned paintings with the heartier illustrations in variant *The Enchanted Tapestry* by Robert D. San Souci. Jacob Grimm's German *The Water of Life* and Eric A. Kimmel's Norwegian *Boots and His Brothers* are quest tales where the youngest son prevails. BROTHERS–FOLKLORE. FAIRIES–FOLKLORE. FOLKLORE–CHINA.

895   **dePaola, Tomie. *Jamie O'Rourke and the Big Potato: An Irish Folktale*. Illus. by the author. Putnam, 1992. ISBN 0-399-22257-X**

[Gr. K–4] When wife Eileen is laid up in bed with a strained back, lazy husband Jamie is afraid he'll starve, till, on his way to church, he encounters a leprechaun who grants his wish to grow the biggest "pratie," or potato, in the world. Read aloud in your grandest brogue, and bring in spuds for all to sample or sprout. If it's leprechauns you're after, see Lorna Balian's *Leprechauns Never Lie*, Richard Kennedy's *The Leprechaun's Story*, and Linda Shute's *Clever Tom and the*

Leprechaun. Enrich your March 17 storytime further with dePaola's *Fin M'Coul, The Giant of Knockmany Hill*, Margaret Hodges's *Saint Patrick and the Peddler*, and Gerald McDermott's *Daniel O'Rourke* and *Tim O'Toole and the Wee Folk.* Laugh with the lazy ones in Arnold Lobel's *A Treeful of Pigs*, Dianne Snyder's *The Boy of the Three Year Nap*, and Verna Aardema's *Anansi Finds a Fool.* Finally, sample another big veggie in Joanne Oppenheim's folktale *One Gift Deserves Another.* FOLKLORE–IRELAND. LAZINESS–FOLKLORE. LEPRECHAUNS–FOLKLORE. VEGETABLES–FOLK-LORE.

896   **dePaola, Tomie.** *Tony's Bread.* **Illus. by the author. Putnam, 1989. ISBN 0-399-21693-6**

[Gr. 1–4] Tony, a simple bread baker, dreams of fame and owning his own bakery in Milan. When his only daughter Serafina falls in love with Angelo, a Milanese nobleman, those two devise a plan to encourage Tony to create a delicious new bread, pannetone, filled with raisins and candied fruit, and baked in a flowerpot. If you can't rustle up a loaf of pannetone, bring in a raisin bread for all to share. *Bread Bread Bread* by Ann Morris is a photo essay of bread worldwide, and *Make Me a Peanut Butter Sandwich and a Glass of Milk* by Ken Robbins is a behind-the-scenes look at how we get our peanut butter, bread, and milk. If it's Italian food you're craving, read dePaola's *Strega Nona* and Dayal Kaur Khalsa's *How Pizza Came to Queens.* BREAD–FOLKLORE. COOKERY–FOLKLORE. FOLKLORE–ITALY. FOOD–FOLKLORE.

897   **Dixon, Ann.** *How Raven Brought Light to People.* **Illus. by James Watts. McElderry, 1992. ISBN 0-689-50536-1**

[Gr. K–4] Angry because the Great Chief keeps the sun, moon, and stars hidden in wooden boxes, Raven changes himself into a tiny spruce needle. The chief's daughter swallows it unknowingly, and Raven is born again as her son. Based on an Alaskan Tlingit Indian legend, the premise is similar to Gerald McDermott's *Raven* and Susan Hand Shetterly's *Raven's Light*: the "child" cries until he is given each box, and releases its contents for the rest of the people to share. Another explanation lies in Dayrell Elphinstone's African folktale *Why the Sun and Moon Live in the Sky.* ASTRONOMY–FOLKLORE. BIRDS–FOLKLORE. FOLKLORE–ALASKA. FOLKLORE–INDIANS OF NORTH AMERICA. MOON–FOLKLORE. RAVENS–FOLKLORE. SUN–FOLK-LORE.

898   **Dupré, Judith.** *The Mouse Bride: A Mayan Folk Tale.* **Illus. by Fabricio Vanden Broek. Knopf, 1993. ISBN 0-679-83273-4**

[Gr. K–2] Seeking to marry their perfect daughter to the perfect husband, two mice ask the moon to name the most powerful being in the universe. He suggests the sun who recommends the cloud who names the wind, who names the wall, who insists the most powerful of all is a mouse. Before reading, talk over who or what your listeners think is the strongest of all. Afterward, have them review the sequence, assign parts, and act out the story. For second-graders, you could easily write this up into a Reader's Theater script with at least a dozen parts, if you add dialogue for daughter and mouse spouse plus three or four narrators. Far-ranging variants include Joel Cook's *The Rat's Daughter*, Ruth Hurlimann's German *The Proud White Cat*, Eric A. Kimmel's Japanese *The Greatest of All*, Holly H. Kwon's Korean *The Moles and the Mireuk*, and Gerald McDermott's Japanese *The Stonecutter*. CREATIVE DRAMA–FOLKLORE. FOLKLORE–INDIANS OF MEXICO. FOLK-LORE–MEXICO. MARRIAGE–FOLKLORE. MAYAN INDIANS–FOLKLORE. MICE–FOLKLORE. SEQUENCE STORIES.

---

899   **Early, Margaret. *Sleeping Beauty*. Illus. by the author. Abrams, 1993. ISBN 0-8109-3835-9**

[Gr. K–6] Not invited to the christening, the eighth fairy is insulted and presents the princess with her gift of death, which another fairy softens by decreeing a 100-year sleep for the child instead. Readers will swoon over the opulent, gold-filled illuminated-manuscript-style paintings with their gorgeous borders, along with Early's stunning art in both her retelling of *William Tell* and Walter McVitty's *Ali Baba and the Forty Thieves*. Early based her retelling of the fairy tale on the original version first published in 1696 in France by Charles Perrault, to which you can compare the text and illustrations of Trina Schart Hyman's brooding version and Errol Le Cain's illustrated variant *Thorn Rose*, both Jacob Grimm retellings from Germany. FAIRY TALES. FOLKLORE–FRANCE. PRINCES AND PRIN-CESSES–FOLKLORE.

---

900   **Early, Margaret. *William Tell*. Illus. by the author. Abrams, 1991. ISBN 0-8109-3854-5**

[Gr. 2–6] Meticulous gold-leaf-filled paintings illuminate this unforgettable and dramatic retelling about the legendary medieval Swiss hero who drew the wrath of Austrian tyrant Gessler and then set off a revolt that led to the unification of Switzerland. Most children will not have heard the story, even the part where Tell shoots an apple off his son's head, and if you play the *William Tell* overture by Rossini they'll be more likely to connect it with the Lone Ranger. Since the events in the story probably never happened, this is a good story to use to define the term "legend." Read aloud the entry from the *World Book Encyclopedia*, and talk about why the story remains an inspiration for foes of dictators everywhere. Terry Small's *The Legend of William Tell* is a handsome, shortened version of the tale written as a a narrative poem. FOLKLORE–SWITZERLAND. FRUIT–FOLKLORE. TELL, WILLIAM.

---

901   **Edwards, Roberta. *Five Silly Fishermen*. Illus. by Sylvie Wickstrom. Random House, 1989. ISBN 0-679-90092-6**

[Gr. Pre–1] Written as an easy reader, this retelling of an old folktale features five simpletons who, after a successful day fishing, attempt to count each other to make sure no one is missing. Each one counts only four others present, and assuming that one must have drowned, they begin to cry and bemoan their unfortunate friend, until a little girl has them re-count themselves by jumping one at a time into the river. Cast parts and act this out so children can see the humor in it as they count. COUNTING BOOKS–FOLKLORE. CREATIVE DRAMA–FOLKLORE. FOLKLORE. FOOLS–FOLKLORE.

902 Ehlert, Lois. *Moon Rope: Un Lazo a la Luna: A Peruvian Folktale.* Illus. by the author. Harcourt, 1992. ISBN 0-15-255343-6

[Gr. Pre–2] Fox convinces an unwilling Mole to climb to the moon on a woven-grass rope, but Mole bails out and hides underground to avoid the teasing of the other animals, while Fox stays up there. The spare text is in both English and Spanish, and the illustrations, inspired by Peruvian artifacts, with distinct semi-abstract figures in bright colors and luminescent silver, are sensational. Dayrell Elphinstone's African folktale *Why the Sun and Moon Live in the Sky* offers more speculations, while Rabbit ends up on the moon in Tony Johnston's *The Tale of Rabbit and Coyote.* In Harriet Peck Taylor's *Coyote Places the Stars*, the Native American trickster climbs a ladder of arrows to reach the moon and creates constellations. Continue the lunar theme with Frank Asch's *Happy Birthday, Moon* and *Moongame*, Eric Carle's *Papa, Please Get the Moon for Me*, Tim Chadwick's *Cabbage Moon*, and Edna Mitchell Preston's *Squawk to the Moon, Little Goose.* FOLK-LORE–PERU. FOXES–FOLKLORE. MOLES–FOLKLORE. MOON–FOLKLORE. SPANISH LANGUAGE.

903 Esterl, Arnica. *The Fine Round Cake.* Illus. by Andrej Dugin and Olga Dugina. Trans. by Pauline Hejl. Four Winds, 1991. ISBN 0-02-733568-2

[Gr. K–2] The fine round cake jumps out of the oven and rolls away, past the old man and woman, two well diggers, two girls, a bear, a wolf, and, of course, a sly fox. Adapted from Joseph Jacobs's English folktale "Johnny-Cake" and with sly and beautiful medieval-style paintings, you'll want to compare it with the many other variants of this timeless tale, such as P. C. Asbjørnsen's *The Runaway Pancake*, Lorinda Bryan Cauley's *The Pancake Boy*, both Norwegian, Scott Cook or Paul Galdone's *The Gingerbread Boy*, Eric A. Kimmel's *The Gingerbread Man*, and Ruth Sawyer's United States *Journey Cake, Ho!* All are perfect for acting out. Start a modern chase with Peter Armour's *Stop That Pickle!* and Joanne Oppenheim's *You Can't Catch Me!* CHANTABLE REFRAIN. CREATIVE DRAMA–FOLKLORE. CUMULATIVE STORIES. FOLKLORE–ENGLAND. FOOD–FOLKLORE. FOXES–FOLKLORE. SEQUENCE STORIES.

904 Fisher, Leonard Everett. *Cyclops.* Illus. by the author. Holiday House, 1991. ISBN 0-8234-0891-4

[Gr. 4–6] After ten years fighting in Troy, Odysseus and his Greek army set sail for home, but the gods punish them with a storm, and they land instead on an island where the one-eyed giant Polyphemus takes them captive and begins eating them alive, one by one. Children will be alternately fascinated and repelled by the graphic violence in the sensational illustrations, where Odysseus blinds the Cyclops before he escapes. Other impressive picture-book versions of myths include *Theseus and the Minotaur* by Fisher, *Persephone and the Pomegranate* by Kris Waldherr, and *Wings* by Jane Yolen, while Mary Pope Osborne's *Favorite Greek Myths* and Rosemary Sutcliff's *Black Ships Before Troy! The Story of the Iliad* are superior collections. FOLKLORE–GREECE. GIANTS–FOLKLORE. MYTHOLOGY.

905 Freedman, Florence B. *It Happened in Chelm: A Story of the Legendary Town of Fools.* Illus. by Nik Krevitsky. Shapolsky, 1990. ISBN 0-944007-00-7

[Gr. 2–5] High on a hill overlooking Chelm, the Jewish town of fools, the town night watchman, astride a horse tied to a tree, stands guard because of a catastrophe: bandits have robbed every shop in town, and the seven wise men of the Town Council have ruled that a watchman will solve the problem. As in all good Chelm stories, their logic is wonderfully inane, as is that of the protagonist in Amy Schwartz's literary folktale *Yossel Zissel & the Wisdom of Chelm. My Grandmother's Stories: A Collection of Jewish Folk Tales* by Adèle Geras and *When Shlemiel Went to Warsaw & Other Stories* by Isaac Bashevis Singer also contain some entertaining Chelm tales. Compare the dim Chelmites with the trickster in Eric A. Kimmel's *Herschel and the Hanukkah Goblins.* FOOLS–FOLKLORE. FOLKLORE, JEWISH. STORIES TO TELL.

906   French, Vivian. *Why the Sea Is Salt.* Illus. by Patrice Aggs. Candlewick, 1993. ISBN 1-56402-183-1

[Gr. 1–4] On Christmas day, spunky Matilda, oldest of 17 children, sets off to ask her wealthy uncle for food, but all he will give her is a bottle of water and some dried bacon, both of which she gives to an old man who asks her for food and drink. In return, he tells her how to acquire a churn that supplies whatever one requests, and tells her the magic words to stop it from producing. Match the salt motif with Jane Langton's Russian folktale *Salt,* and the unstoppable magic dispenser with Tomie dePaola's *Strega Nona.* The Taino myth *How the Sea Began* by George Crespo has another explanation for the sea's salt flavor. CHRISTMAS–FOLKLORE. FOLKLORE–NORWAY. GREED–FOLKLORE. OCEAN–FOLKLORE. POURQUOI TALES. SALT–FOLKLORE. UNCLES–FOLKLORE.

907   Gabler, Mirko. *Tall, Wide, and Sharp-Eye.* Illus. by the author. Henry Holt, 1994. ISBN 0-8050-2784-X

[Gr. 1–4] The king's only son chooses for his bride a princess who is kept under lock and key in an evil sorcerer's castle, but with the help of the special talents of his three new traveling companions, he gets the girl. The zany cartoon-style watercolors pick up the humor of this Czechoslovakian fairy tale, which shares characteristics with Verna Aardema's Mexican folktale *The Riddle of the Drum* and Arthur Ransome's Russian *The Fool of the World and the Flying Ship.* FOLKLORE–CZECHOSLOVAKIA. PRINCES AND PRINCESSES–FOLKLORE. TRANSFORMATIONS–FOLKLORE. WIZARDS–FOLKLORE.

908   Gal, Laszlo. *Prince Ivan and the Firebird.* Illus. by the author. Firefly, 1992. ISBN 0-920668-98-4

[Gr. 3–6] Pledged to catch the intruder who is stealing gold apples from his father Tsar Vladimir's tree, youngest son Prince Ivan catches a tailfeather from the thief, the beautiful Firebird, and sets out to capture it with the help of a huge gray wolf. Contrast with the equally lovely versions of *The Firebird* by Demi, Selina Hastings, and Robert D. San Souci, and play Igor Stravinsky's music of the ballet to get in the mood for magic. Peaches and rabbits complicate matters in French folktale *Three Sacks of Truth* by Eric A. Kimmel, and missing golden pears trouble the king in Howard Pyle's literary fairy tale *The Swan Maiden.* ANIMALS, MYTHI-

CAL–FOLKLORE. BIRDS–FOLKLORE. FAIRY TALES. FOLKLORE–RUSSIA. KINGS AND RULERS–FOLKLORE. PRINCES AND PRINCESSES–FOLKLORE.

909 **Garland, Sherry.** *Why Ducks Sleep on One Leg.* **Illus. by Jean and Mou-Sien Tseng. Scholastic, 1993. ISBN 0-590-45697-0**

[Gr. 1–4] Long, long ago in Vietnam, when ducks had but one leg instead of two, three of them petitioned the Jade Emperor for three more legs, and each received a golden leg from the village guardian spirit instead. Contrast that pourquoi tale with Katherine Paterson's Japanese folktale *The Tale of the Mandarin Ducks*, where the ducks save a young couple from a cruel lord's wrath. DUCKS–FOLKLORE. FOLK-LORE–VIETNAM. POURQUOI TALES. SLEEP–FOLKLORE.

910 **Garner, Alan.** *Jack and the Beanstalk.* **Illus. by Julek Heller. Doubleday, 1992. ISBN 0-385-30693-8**

[Gr. 1–4] You'll love the language in this most oft-told of tales, and the illustra-tions are nicely scary as well. Lorinda Bryan Cauley, John Howe, and Susan Pearson have all done versions, as did Paul Galdone in *The History of Mother Twaddle and the Marvelous Achievements of Her Son, Jack.* From the United States come Kenn and Joanne Compton's *Jack the Giant Chaser*, Gail E. Haley's *Jack and the Bean Tree*, and James Still's *Jack and the Bean Tree*, while *Jim and the Beanstalk* by Raymond Briggs is a parody that updates the legend. Tomie dePaola's Irish *Fin M'Coul, the Giant of Knockmany Hill* and Italian *The Mysterious Giant of Barletta*, and Teri Sloat's Alaskan *The Hungry Giant of the Tundra* present more giants, both nice and naughty. FAIRY TALES. FOLKLORE–ENGLAND. GIANTS–FOLKLORE.

911 **Gates, Frieda.** *Owl Eyes.* **Illus. by Yoshi Miyake. Lothrop, 1994. ISBN 0-688-12473-9**

[Gr. K–3] In a humorous Mohawk legend, we see how Raweno, Master of All Spirits and Everything-Maker, created first the world and then the animals, allowing the not-completed creatures to choose their own colors and attributes. Nosy, overbearing Owl can't help interfering with Raweno's work, and when he irritates the man one time too many, Raweno gives the annoying bird a short neck, eyes big enough to see in the dark, and a nocturnal life-style as punish-ment. Look into other legends of how the earth and its inhabitants came to be with *The Woman Who Fell from the Sky: The Iroquois Story of Creation* by John Bierhorst, *Children of the Morning Light: Wampanoag Tales* told by Manitonquat (Medicine Story), *Raven's Light: A Myth from the People of the Northwest Coast* by Susan Hand Shetterly, and *Moon Mother: A Native American Creation Tale* by Ed Young. Jane Yolen's *Owl Moon* takes us owling in the snow with a child and her dad. CREATION–FOLKLORE. FOLKLORE–INDIANS OF NORTH AMERICA. MOHAWK INDIANS–FOLKLORE. OWLS–FOLKLORE. POURQUOI TALES.

912 **Gerson, Mary-Joan.** *How Night Came from the Sea: A Story from Brazil.* **Illus. by Carla Golembe. Little, Brown, 1994. ISBN 0-316-30855-2**

[Gr. K–4] The daughter of African goddess Iemanjá leaves her ocean to marry an earth man in the land of daylight, but the constant light and colors are too much for her to bear until her husband orders three servants to beg a bag of night from the girl's sea-dwelling mother. Go from day to night with Pacific Northwest Indian folktales *How Raven Brought Light to People* by Ann Dixon, Gerald McDermott's *Raven* and Susan Hand Shetterley's *Raven's Light*, plus Dayrell Elphinstone's African folktale *Why the Sun and Moon Live in the Sky* and Bernard Emery's Arctic *How Snowshoe Hare Rescued the Sun*. Find out why we have seasons in Kris Waldherr's Greek myth *Persephone and the Pomegranate*. FAIRY TALES. FOLKLORE–BRAZIL. HUSBANDS AND WIVES–FOLKLORE. NIGHT–FOLKLORE. OCEAN–FOLKLORE. POURQUOI TALES.

913   **Gerson, Mary-Joan.** *Why the Sky Is Far Away: A Nigerian Folktale.* **Illus. by Carla Golembe. Joy Street/ Little, Brown, 1992. ISBN 0-316-30852-8**

[Gr. K–4] Though the people were told never to break off more of the delicious-tasting sky than they could finish, one woman, Adese, ignored that warning, and, as punishment, the sky moved upward, forcing people from that day forward to grow and harvest their own crops. In folktales as diverse as Lily Toy Hong's *How the Ox Star Fell from Heaven* and Kristina Rodanas's Native American Zuni *Dragonfly's Tale* we see how other humans were rewarded and punished with food. Ask children to look in the food dumpster at lunchtime and record what they see. Chances are, the amount of food wasted will astonish and dismay them. Have them work in small groups to come up with plans to cut down on or recycle the school's wasted food. On a lighter note, tie in Judi Barrett's *Cloudy with a Chance of Meatballs*, where food falls from the sky three times a day until the weather takes a turn for the worse. FOLKLORE–AFRICA. FOLKLORE–NIGERIA. FOOD–FOLKLORE. POURQUOI TALES. SKY–FOLKLORE.

914   **Gilman, Phoebe.** *Something from Nothing.* **Illus. by the author. Scholastic, 1993. ISBN 0-590-47280-1**

[Gr. Pre–2] Joseph's wonderful blanket is wearing out, and his tailor grandfather fixes it, turning it successively into a jacket, then a vest, a tie, a handkerchief, a button, and finally, a story. A great story to tell and act out, with prop clothing or at least a button, this is adapted from an old Jewish folktale. (I know it as the song "I Had an Old Coat.") Anne Mazer's *The Yellow Button* starts with a small button and then works outward to encompass the entire universe. Leone Castell Anderson's *The Wonderful Shrinking Shirt* keeps shrinking, and Lauren Mills's *The Rag Coat* is made from scraps. BUTTONS–FOLKLORE. CHANTABLE REFRAIN. CLOTHING AND DRESS–FOLKLORE. FOLKLORE, JEWISH. GRANDFATHERS–FOLKLORE.

915   **Goble, Paul.** *Crow Chief: A Plains Indian Story.* **Illus. by the author. Orchard, 1992. ISBN 0-531-08547-3**

[Gr. 2–6] In the days long ago when crows were white, the leader of the Crow Nation would warn the buffalo whenever any hunters were coming, preventing the people from having any meat, until a young man named Falling Star came up with a plan to capture Crow Chief. Ever since that crow's punishment, crows have been black. Add this pourquoi tale to the rest of Goble's retellings of Plains Indian legends, with their dignified language, careful attention to detail, and impressive watercolors. Olaf Baker's *Where the Buffaloes Begin*, Goble's *Buffalo Woman and Her Seven Brothers*, and Nancy Van Laan's *Buffalo Dance: A Blackfoot Legend* are also appropriate, and *Buffalo Hunt* by Russell Freedman tells how the buffalo were hunted and how every part of the buffalo was utilized by the Indians. The crows teach Coyote a lesson in *Coyote: A Trickster Tale from the American Southwest* by Gerald McDermott. BIRDS–FOLKLORE. BUFFALOES–FOLKLORE. CROWS–FOLKLORE. DAKOTA INDIANS–FOLKLORE. FOLKLORE–INDIANS OF NORTH AMERICA. POURQUOI TALES.

916   Goble, Paul. *Love Flute*. Illus. by the author. Bradbury, 1992. ISBN 0-02-736261-2

[Gr. 3–6] So shy that going into battle seems easier than facing the one he loves, a young man follows the path of his arrows into an aspen forest where two Elk Men give him a gift of the first flute, which he uses to woo his beloved. Also describing the first flute is Stefan Czernecki and Timothy Rhodes's *The Singing Snake*, an Australian aboriginal folktale. In *A Boy Becomes a Man at Wounded Knee* by Ted Wood and Wanbli Numpa Afraid of Hawk, follow a nine-year-old boy as he traces the journey of his ancestors who died in the 1890 massacre. FLUTE–FOLKLORE. FOLKLORE–INDIANS OF NORTH AMERICA. LOVE–FOLKLORE. MUSICAL INSTRUMENTS–FOLKLORE. PLAINS INDIANS–FOLKLORE.

917   Gonzalez, Lucie M. *The Bossy Gallito: A Traditional Cuban Folktale*. Illus. by Lulu Delacre. Scholastic, 1994. ISBN 0-590-46843-X

[Gr. K–2] On his way to the wedding of his uncle the parrot, a bossy little rooster dirties his beak and tries to make the grass, a goat, a stick, fire, water, and the sun do his bidding to clean him up. The story is printed in both English and Spanish, and the glossary encourages you to read the English version by substituting the Spanish name for each character. Act this one out, and your children might acquire the pleasant habit of saying "pardon me." Compare with Alma Flor Ada's version from Latin America, *The Rooster Who Went to His Uncle's Wedding*. Paul Galdone, Eric A. Kimmel, and Rosanne Litzinger all put out versions of the well-known English folktale variant, *The Old Woman and Her Pig*, as did Priscilla Lamont in *The Troublesome Pig*. For more fun with Spanish, also read Tony Johnston's Mexican folktale *The Tale of Rabbit and Coyote*, and Arthur Dorros's *Abuela*. CREATIVE DRAMA–FOLKLORE. CUMULATIVE STORIES. FOLKLORE–CUBA. ROOSTERS–FOLKLORE. SPANISH LANGUAGE.

918   Greene, Ellin. *Billy Beg and His Bull*. Illus. by Kimberly Bulcken Root. Holiday House, 1994. ISBN 0-8234-1100-1

[Gr. 2–4] Billy's stepmother claims that only the blood of Billy's beloved bull can heal her, which starts the young prince on a quest in which he fights and cuts off the heads of three many-headed giants, kills a princess-eating dragon, and, like Cinderella, loses a shoe. This time the princess finds the shoe's owner, and the two are married. Contrast to versions of the Cinderella story including Shirley Climo's *The Korean Cinderella*, Joanne Compton's Appalachian *Ashpet*, Rafe Martin's Algonquian *The Rough-Face Girl*, Robert D. San Souci's African American *Sukey and the Mermaid*, and Barbara Ker Wilson's *Wishbones: A Folk Tale from China*. Another fairy-tale hero who loses his beloved pet bovine is Huw in Susan Cooper's *The Silver Cow: A Welsh Tale*. See what makes cows tick in Alice Schertle's poetry picture book *How Now, Brown Cow?* COWS–FOLKLORE. FAIRY TALES. FOLKLORE–IRELAND. GIANTS–FOLKLORE. PRINCES AND PRINCESSES–FOLKLORE.

919 **Greene, Ellin.** *The Legend of the Cranberry: A Paleo-Indian Tale*. **Illus. by Brad Sneed. Simon & Schuster, 1993. ISBN 0-671-75975-2**

[Gr. 1–4] Afraid of the destructive rampages of the once-quiescent mastodons or Yah-qua-whee, the People seek help from the Great Spirit who advises them to undertake a great battle, during which many are killed. In this somber Delaware Indian legend, the Great Spirit rewards the People with a new bitter-tasting berry the color of blood, which the Pilgrims called the crane-berry and we know today as the cranberry. Bring in cranberries to taste, both plain and sugared, and read this at Thanksgiving time, which is tied in to the end of the story. *The First Strawberries: A Cherokee Story* retold by Joseph Bruchac is another fruity pourquoi tale. Some of the stories in *Return of the Sun: Native American Tales from the Northeast Woodlands* by Bruchac come from the same region of the Atlantic coast. ANIMALS, PREHISTORIC–FOLKLORE. DELAWARE INDIANS–FOLKLORE. FOLKLORE–INDIANS OF NORTH AMERICA. FRUIT–FOLKLORE. POURQUOI TALES. THANKSGIVING–FOLKLORE.

920 **Greene, Jacqueline Dembar.** *What His Father Did*. **Illus. by John O'Brien. Houghton Mifflin, 1992. ISBN 0-395-55042-4**

[Gr. 3–6] With the sum of just one lonely kopek in his pocket, prankster Hershel stops at an inn and demands a bed and supper from the innkeeper, threatening her that he'll do what his father used to do if he isn't fed immediately. The frightened woman borrows food from her neighbors and cooks him a fine feast. Ask students to decide what they think Herschel's father used to do in that situation. Other tales where a meal is coaxed from reluctant folks include *Stone Soup* by Marcia Brown and by John Warren Stewig, *Nail Soup* by Margot Zemach, and *Burgoo Stew* by Susan Patron. FOLKLORE, JEWISH. FOOD–FOLKLORE. TRICKSTER TALES.

921 **Gregg, Andy.** *Great Rabbit and the Long-Tailed Wildcat*. **Illus. by Cat Bowman Smith. Albert Whitman, 1993. ISBN 0-8075-3047-6**

[Gr. 2–4] Hungry and on the trail of Great Rabbit, the ruler of all rabbits, Wildcat instead encounters a medicine man with long ears, an old woman with long braids that resemble a rabbit's ears, and a great warrior whose feathers sticking up on each side of his head resemble rabbit's ears. Each time Wildcat is tricked by the wily rabbit he vows revenge, but loses his own tail instead. Gretchen Will Mayo's *Big Trouble for Tricky Rabbit!* and *Here Comes Tricky Rabbit!* (1994) and Gayle Ross's *How Rabbit Tricked Otter and Other Cherokee Trickster Stories* are more humorous Native American trickster tales, to which you can add Tony Johnston's *The Tale of Rabbit and Coyote* from Mexico, Priscilla Jaquith's African American Gullah tales in *Bo Rabbit Smart for True*, Julius Lester's African American *The Tales of Uncle Remus*, and Barbara Knutson's *Sungura and Leopard* and Gerald McDermott's *Zomo the Rabbit*, both from Africa. ALGONQUIN INDIANS–FOLKLORE.

CATS–FOLKLORE. FOLKLORE–INDIANS OF NORTH AMERICA. POURQUOI TALES. RABBITS–FOLK-
LORE. TRICKSTER TALES. WILDCATS–FOLKLORE.

922   **Grimm, Jacob. *The Bear and the Bird King*. Illus. by Robert Byrd. Retold by Robert
       Byrd. Dutton, 1994. ISBN 0-525-45118-8**

[Gr. K–3] Because the bear won't apologize for calling the king of the birds' children nasty, the creatures of the air come to the royal bird couple's defense when
they declare war. Lessons learned by the bear and your listeners? One needs to
apologize for one's mistakes to get along in this world. If you're arbitrating too
many squabbles, this little-known Grimm tale may help spark a bit of sensible
conflict resolution. BEARS–FOLKLORE. BIRDS–FOLKLORE. FOLKLORE–GERMANY. FOXES–
FOLKLORE. WAR–FOLKLORE.

923   **Grimm, Jacob. *The Bremen Town Musicians*. Illus. by Bernadette Watts. Trans. by
       Anthea Bell. North-South, 1992. ISBN 1-55858-140-5**

[Gr. K–2] What a racket the four animals make when they burst in on a houseful
of robbers and scare them away. Compare the styles of illustration with the versions by Anthea Bell and illustrated by Josef Palecek, by Ilse Plume (Doubleday,
1980), and by Hans Wilhelm. In *The Terrible Eek*, a Japanese folktale retold by
Patricia A. Compton, the villains are routed thanks to a similar misunderstanding, while a lone rooster scares off the bad guys in *How the Rooster Saved the Day*
by Arnold Lobel. ANIMALS–FOLKLORE. FOLKLORE–GERMANY. ROBBERS AND OUTLAWS–
FOLKLORE.

924   **Grimm, Jacob. *The Bremen Town Musicians*. Illus. by Hans Wilhelm. Retold by Hans
       Wilhelm. Scholastic, 1992. ISBN 0-590-44795-5**

[Gr. K–2] Four old animals past their prime—a donkey, a dog, a cat, and a
rooster—run away from the masters planning their demises and join forces to
become town musicians, but their first less-than-stellar musical performance
scares away three robbers. Other fine retellings include ones by Anthea Bell,
illustrated by Josef Palecek, by Ilse Plume (Doubleday, 1980), and by Bernadette
Watts. ANIMALS–FOLKLORE. FOLKLORE–GERMANY. ROBBERS AND OUTLAWS–FOLKLORE.

925   **Grimm, Jacob. *The Frog Prince: Or Iron Henry*. Illus. by Binette Schroeder. Trans. by
       Naomi Lewis. North-South, 1989. ISBN 1-55859-015-8**

[Gr. 1–4] Contrast the tale of a frog who rescues a princess's golden ball from the
well and then insists on her keeping her promise of letting him eat from her dish
and sleep in her bed with Donna Jo Napoli's novel *The Prince of the Pond*. What's
interesting in this version with its surreal, oversized paintings is seeing the frog's
transformation from reptile to prince when the princess hurls him against the
wall, and the retention of the original ending, where the bands around the chest
of the prince's faithful servant burst from joy. Paul Galdone's version is lighter in
tone. Take a look at other transformation tales with George Webbe Dasent's
Norwegian *East o' the Sun and West o' the Moon*, Grimm's *The Donkey Prince* and

The Glass Mountain, Elizabeth Isele's or J. Patrick Lewis's Russian *The Frog Princess*, Jane Langton's Latvian *The Hedgehog Boy*, Marianna Mayer's French *Beauty and the Beast*, and Robert D. San Souci's French *The White Cat*. A. Vesey's *The Princess and the Frog* is a funny parody. FAIRY TALES. FOLKLORE–GERMANY. FROGS–FOLKLORE. PRINCES AND PRINCESSES–FOLKLORE. TRANSFORMATIONS–FOLKLORE.

926   **Grimm, Jacob.** *Hansel and Gretel.* **Retold and illus. by James Marshall. Dial, 1990. ISBN 0-8037-0828-9**

[Gr. K–2] Though Hansel is resourceful in the forest, it's Gretel's cleverness that rescues them from the clutches of the nefarious gingerbread house witch. Marshall's wicked witch with her bulging bosom and ribbons in her blonde hair could be a buxom cousin to his character, Miss Viola Swamp. Compare with Paul Galdone's stolid and Paul O. Zelinsky's brooding versions, along with Barbara Walker's Turkish variant, *Teeny Tiny and the Witch Woman*. BROTHERS AND SISTERS–FOLKLORE. FAIRY TALES. FOLKLORE–GERMANY. WITCHES–FOLKLORE.

927   **Grimm, Jacob.** *Iron John.* **Illus. by Trina Schart Hyman. Retold by Eric A. Kimmel. Holiday House, 1994. ISBN 0-8234-1073-0**

[Gr. 2–6] Young Prince Walter frees the wild man Iron John from the king's sturdy cage and accompanies him into the forest where he stays, guarding John's magic spring and growing to manhood. Sent out to a neighboring king to offer himself for work, the prince calls himself Walter-in-the-Mud and becomes a gardener with Elsa the garden girl. With elements of the Cinderella story, this is a satisfyingly romantic tale with a masked ball, a jousting tournament, and a wounded knight saved by the tears of a maid who truly loves him. Follow the fate of another king's child whose loss of a golden ball changes her life in Grimm's better-known *The Frog Prince: Or Iron Henry*. FAIRY TALES. FOLKLORE–GERMANY. LOVE–FOLKLORE. PRINCES AND PRINCESSES–FOLKLORE.

928   **Grimm, Jacob.** *Nanny Goat and the Seven Little Kids.* **Illus. by Janet Stevens. Retold by Eric A. Kimmel. Holiday House, 1990. ISBN 0-8234-0789-6**

[Gr. K–2] The big bad wolf disguises his rough harsh voice with chalk and his horrible hairy feet with flour so he can gain admittance to the house of the seven goat kids, and eats them all up and the nanny goat as well. Mom's sewing scissors and eight heavy stones later, the wolf gets his comeuppance. For another version of this Grimm tale, see *The Wolf and the Seven Little Kids* by Martin Ursell and compare with *Mother Goose and the Sly Fox* by Chris Conover. What happened to *The Three Little Pigs*, as retold by Lorinda Bryan Cauley, Paul Galdone, James Marshall, and Glen Rounds should make us all cautious around unscrupulous bullies. *The Three Billy Goats Gruff*, with versions illustrated by Marcia Brown, Paul Galdone, and Glen Rounds is likewise satisfying. FOLKLORE–GERMANY. GOATS–FOLKLORE. WOLVES–FOLKLORE.

929   **Grimm, Jacob.** *One Gift Deserves Another.* **Illus. by Bo Zaunders. Retold by Joanne Oppenheim. Dutton, 1992. ISBN 0-525-44975-2**

[Gr. 1–4] The poor one of two brothers grows a gigantic turnip and gives it to the king, who rewards him with riches. When the wealthy brother and his wife try to curry the king's favor by giving him all their money, they, in turn, are rewarded too—with the turnip. There's an equally huge spud in *Jamie O'Rourke and the Big Potato: An Irish Folktale* by Tomie dePaola. Janina Domanska's and Pierr Morgan's *The Turnip* and Alexei Tolstoi's *The Great Big Enormous Turnip* are three versions of the same story about pulling up the huge vegetable. *And Sunday Makes Seven* by Robert Baden is a Costa Rican folktale about two cousins, one kind, one not, who also end up with contrasting fortunes. BROTHERS–FOLKLORE. FOLKLORE–GERMANY. GENEROSITY–FOLKLORE. GIFTS–FOLKLORE. KINGS AND RULERS–FOLKLORE. VEGETABLES–FOLKLORE.

930   **Grimm, Jacob.** *Rapunzel.* **Illus. by Kris Waldherr. Retold by Amy Ehrlich. Dial, 1989. ISBN 0-8037-0655-3**

[Gr. 2–4] Given away at birth to the witch woman next door, the lovely lass with the impossibly long tresses is shut up in a tower where the king's son discovers her and climbs her locks for a visit. Waldherr's paintings are softly romantic, and the dignified retelling omits mention of Rapunzel's baby twins. Compare the text and the art with the Barbara Rogasky version, illustrated by Trina Schart Hyman. FAIRY TALES. FOLKLORE–GERMANY. HAIR–FOLKLORE. PRINCES AND PRINCESSES–FOLKLORE. WITCHES–FOLKLORE.

931   **Grimm, Jacob.** *Rumpelstiltskin.* **Illus. by Gennady Spirin. Retold by Alison Sage. Dial, 1990. ISBN 0-8037-0908-0**

[Gr. 1–4] Told by the king to spin straw into gold or lose her head, lovely Rose accepts the assistance of a gray-bearded little man who does the deed three times and makes a bargain to take her firstborn child. In this version, with opulent medieval-style paintings, it's the king who reveals the little man's name. Compare styles of illustrations and retellings of the Grimm versions retold by Barbara Rogasky and Paul O. Zelinsky, and the Russian variant *The Tsar's Promise* by Robert D. San Souci. *Lily and the Wooden Bowl* by Alan Schroeder is a Japanese folktale with similar motifs. FAIRY TALES. FOLKLORE–GERMANY. KINGS AND RULERS–FOLKLORE. NAMES–FOLKLORE.

932   **Grimm, Jacob.** *The Twelve Dancing Princesses.* **Illus. by Ruth Sanderson. Retold by Ruth Sanderson. Little, Brown, 1990. ISBN 0-316-77017-5**

[Gr. 2–4] Where do the princesses go every night that they wear out their dancing shoes? With the aid of a cloak that makes him invisible, commoner Michael, working at the palace as a garden boy, follows them and falls in love with the youngest. Contrast Sanderson's stunningly realistic and romantic oil paintings with the rococo style in Errol Le Cain's version. Another cloak of invisibility turns up in Warwick Hutton's *The Nose Tree*. DANCING–FOLKLORE. FAIRY TALES. FOLKLORE–GERMANY. PRINCES AND PRINCESSES–FOLKLORE.

933   **Haley, Gail E.** *Puss in Boots.* **Illus. by the author. Dutton, 1991. ISBN 0-525-44740-7**

[Gr. 1–4] Haley has personalized Charles Perrault's famous French folktale by giving names to the miller's youngest son (Michael), the fabulous talking cat (Grey), the king's daughter (Theresa), and even the shape-changing ogre (Moustaphus, the Many-Faced). Compare this energetic version with those by Lorinda Bryan Cauley, Paul Galdone, Lincoln Kirstein, and Fred Marcellino. Two courageous tomcats save their town from witches in Jenny Nimmo's Scottish folktale *The Witches and the Singing Mice*. CATS–FOLKLORE. FOLKLORE–FRANCE. KINGS AND RULERS. OGRES.

934   Hamanaka, Sheila. *Screen of Frogs: An Old Tale*. Illus. by the author. Orchard, 1993. ISBN 0-531-05464-0

[Gr. K–3] Wealthy Koji scoffs that working is for fools, and the lazy man sells off almost all his land to pay for his extravagant habits. Dozing by his one remaining lake, he receives a stern lecture from a human-sized frog about the ecological consequences of his unthinking actions, which convinces him to change his ways and lead a productive life. Lynne Cherry's *The Great Kapok Tree*, Susan Jeffers's *Brother Eagle, Sister Sky*, and Holly Keller's *Grandfather's Dream* offer the same basic message. ECOLOGY–FOLKLORE. FOLKLORE–JAPAN. FROGS–FOLKLORE. LAZINESS–FOLKLORE.

935   Han, Oki S., and Stephanie Haboush Plunkett. *Sir Whong and the Golden Pig*. Illus. by Oki S. Han. Dial, 1993. ISBN 0-8037-1345-2

[Gr. 2–5] Known as a kind, gentle, and generous man, Sir Whong is nonetheless taken aback when a complete stranger pays him a visit and requests the loan of 1,000 nyung for one year, offering to leave as collateral a valuable family heirloom. Let your listeners suggest possible ways Sir Whong can get his money back once he discovers the golden pig is a fake. As in *Stories to Solve* and *More Stories to Solve* by George Shannon, you can stop reading at the point where the stranger returns and have them puzzle out just how he is undone. Other insightful Korean folktales include *The Rabbit's Judgment* by Suzanne Crowder Han and *The Princess and the Beggar* by Anne Sibley O'Brien. FOLKLORE–KOREA. MONEY–FOLKLORE. SWINDLERS AND SWINDLING–FOLKLORE.

936   Han, Suzanne Crowder. *The Rabbit's Escape*. Illus. by Yumi Heo. Henry Holt, 1995. ISBN 0-8050-2675-4

[Gr. 1–5] When the Dragon King of the East Sea becomes ill, he is told only the fresh raw liver of a rabbit can cure him, and turtle sets out to bring back a live rabbit. Once the wily rabbit realizes what is needed of him, he tells the king he has left his liver at home and manages to escape his fate. Han's *The Rabbit's Judgment* is another familiar folktale from Korea. Both contain the full text of the stories in both English and Korean. In both Paul Galdone's *The Monkey and the Crocodile* from India and Jose Aruego and Ariane Dewey's *A Crocodile's Tale* from the Philippines, a weaker creature fabricates a story to trick the stronger one as rabbit does. FOLKLORE–KOREA. KOREAN LANGUAGE. RABBITS–FOLKLORE. TIGERS–FOLKLORE. TRICKSTERS–FOLKLORE. TURTLES–FOLKLORE.

937   Han, Suzanne Crowder. *The Rabbit's Judgment.* Illus. by Yumi Heo. Henry Holt, 1994. ISBN 0-8050-2674-6

[Gr. 1–5] A tiger who has fallen into a pit entreats a man to help him out, promising to be forever grateful, but once he is free, he plans to eat the man anyway. Both the pine tree and a passing ox agree the tiger should eat the man, but the rabbit tricks the tiger into reenacting the situation by jumping back into the pit. Children will relish acting this one out and debating whether the man deserves to be eaten, and will be fascinated to see the Korean text of the story on each page. "Rattlesnake's Word" from *Bo Rabbit Smart for True* by Priscilla Jacquith is an African American variation of this "ungrateful beast" story, as is "The Farmer and the Snake" in the *The Knee-High Man and Other Tales* by Julius Lester, while "The Crocodile, the Boy, and the Kind Deed" from Anne Gatti's *Tales from the African Plains* will also seem familiar. CONFLICT RESOLUTION–FOLKLORE. CREATIVE DRAMA–FOLKLORE. FOLKLORE–KOREA. KOREAN LANGUAGE. RABBITS–FOLKLORE. TIGERS–FOLKLORE.

938   Hastings, Selina. *The Firebird.* Illus. by Reg Cartwright. Candlewick, 1993. ISBN 1-56402-096-7

[Gr. 1–4] The king's huntsman, ignoring the sage advice of his faithful horse, picks up from the ground the red-and-gold feather of the firebird and delivers it to the king, who then demands the entire bird. Compare the solid retelling and sensible illustrations with the glamorous gilt-filled version by Demi. In *Prince Ivan and the Firebird* by Laszlo Gal, the prince tries to catch the fabulous bird with the aid of a gray wolf, while *The Firebird* by Robert D. San Souci is based on the story of the classic ballet. ANIMALS, MYTHICAL–FOLKLORE. BIRDS–FOLKLORE. FAIRY TALES. FOLKLORE–RUSSIA. HORSES–FOLKLORE. PRINCES AND PRINCESSES–FOLKLORE.

939   Haviland, Virginia. *The Talking Pot: A Danish Folktale.* Illus. by Melissa Sweet. Little, Brown, 1990. ISBN 0-316-35060-5

[Gr. K–3] A poor man trades his only cow for a talking pot that skips to the rich man's house and brings home pudding, wheat, and even gold coins. The recipe for Baked Danish Apple Pudding on the last page looks mighty tasty and easy enough for the class to assemble. There's a good script for this story in Caroline Feller Bauer's *Presenting Reader's Theater: Plays and Poems to Read Aloud*. A rooster helps a poor couple retrieve their pie-producing oven from a king in Mirra Ginsberg's Russian folktale *The Magic Stove*, while in Lily Toy Hong's Chinese folktale *Two of Everything*, the pot doubles everything put into it, even people. FOLKLORE–DENMARK. MAGIC–FOLKLORE.

940   Hobson, Sally. *Chicken Little.* Illus. by the author. Simon & Schuster, 1994. ISBN 0-671-89548-6

[Gr. Pre–K] Chicken Little and her fowl friends trot off to tell the king the sky is falling until Foxy Loxy lures them into his lair. Full-colored pages with black-lined primitive characters are both bright and sinister, with dark blue shadows lurking underfoot, which add to the drama. *Henny Penny* by Paul Galdone is another well-loved version. Act out the story in sequence with children repeating the "sky is falling" dialogue. *Foolish Rabbit's Big Mistake* by Rafe Martin is a similar story with a happier ending. CHANTABLE REFRAIN. CHICKENS–FOLKLORE. CREATIVE DRAMA–FOLKLORE. FOXES–FOLKLORE. SEQUENCE STORIES.

941   Hodges, Margaret. *Saint Patrick and the Peddler.* Illus. by Paul Brett Johnson. Orchard, 1993. ISBN 0-531-08639-9

[Gr. 1–4] After seeing Saint Patrick in his dreams three times running, a poor peddler finally heeds his advice to travel to Ballymena and hear what he was meant to hear. Once there, a butcher relates his dream of a treasure under an old iron pot, which the peddler finds upon his return home. Adapted from Joseph Jacobs's English folktale "The Pedlar of Swaffam" and Ruth Sawyer's retelling of "The Peddler of Ballagharereen," Hodges's story is set in Ireland. Gail E. Haley's *Dream Peddler* is a retelling of the Jacobs tale, while Uri Shulevitz's *The Treasure* is a Jewish variant, and Diane Stanley's *Fortune* incorporates the same theme. Celebrate Irish folklore with Tomie dePaola's *Fin M'Coul, The Giant of Knockmany Hill* and *Jamie O'Rourke and the Big Potato,* and Gerald McDermott's *Daniel O'Rourke* and *Tim O'Toole and the Wee Folk.* BOOKS AND READING–FOLKLORE. DREAMS–FOLKLORE. FOLKLORE–IRELAND. PEDDLERS AND PEDDLING–FOLKLORE. PATRICK, SAINT.

942   Hong, Lily Toy. *How the Ox Star Fell from Heaven.* Illus. by the author. Albert Whitman, 1991. ISBN 0-8075-3428-5

[Gr. 1–4] In this Chinese picture-book folktale that explains why oxen are now beasts of burden, we learn how the Emperor of All the Heavens, who decreed that hungry peasants would be able to eat once every third day, sent trusted Ox Star to earth with the proclamation which he misread, declaring, ". . . you shall eat three times a day, every day." For an interesting international gastronomic view, compare the food and the art of Hong's dramatic airbrushed acrylic-and-gouache Chinese-style paintings with Xiong Blia's Hmong Laotian folktale variant, *Nine in One, Grr! Grr!,* Mary-Joan Gerson's Nigerian folktale *Why the Sky Is Far Away,* and Kristina Rodanas's Native American *Dragonfly's Tale.* Make a class chart of the different types of food the children eat in one day to track the diversity and quantity they consume. FOLKLORE–CHINA. FOOD–FOLKLORE. OXEN–FOLKLORE. POURQUOI TALES.

943   Hong, Lily Toy. *Two of Everything: A Chinese Folktale.* Illus. by the author. Albert Whitman, 1993. ISBN 0-8075-8157-7

[Gr. K–3] After digging up a large pot in his garden, poor old Mr. Haktak is astonished to find that whatever he throws in the pot automatically doubles, guaranteeing him and his wife instant wealth. Alas, when Mrs. Haktak falls into the pot, he must contend with two identical wives. Mull over the two times table with this one, plus discuss the concept of symmetry. Note how doubling can get out of hand with David Birch's *The King's Chessboard.* In Virginia Haviland's Danish folktale *The Talking Pot,* a three-legged pot skips to the rich man's house to retrieve food and gold for a poor couple. FOLKLORE–CHINA. HUSBANDS AND WIVES–FOLKLORE. MATHEMATICS–FOLKLORE.

944   **Howe, John.** *Jack and the Beanstalk.* **Illus. by the author. Little, Brown, 1989. ISBN 0-316-37579-9**

[Gr. 1–3] A good sturdy version, and clear, bold paintings will make giant-phobic kids shudder. Compare illustrated versions such as Paul Galdone's *The History of Mother Twaddle and the Marvelous Achievements of Her Son, Jack,* and ones by Lorinda Bryan Cauley, Alan Garner, and Susan Pearson. Kenn and Joanne Compton's Appalachian folktale relative *Jack the Giant Chaser,* Gail E. Haley's *Jack and the Bean Tree,* and James Still's *Jack and the Bean Tree* all hail from Appalachia. *Jim and the Beanstalk* by Raymond Briggs fills us in on the giant's later years. Giants abound in folktales Tomie dePaola's Irish *Fin M'Coul, the Giant of Knockmany Hill* and Italian *The Mysterious Giant of Barletta,* and Teri Sloat's Alaskan *The Hungry Giant of the Tundra.* FAIRY TALES. FOLKLORE–ENGLAND. GIANTS–FOLKLORE.

945   **Hughes, Monica.** *Little Fingerling.* **Illus. by Brenda Clark. Ideals, 1992. ISBN 0-8249-8553-2**

[Gr. 1–4] The prayers of a childless couple are answered when a tiny son is born to them, and when the boy is 15 and the height of his father's longest finger, he sets out for Kyoto with his rice bowl and chopsticks to make his way in the world. The unidentified three-eyed giants he defeats to save his beloved Plum Blossom are none other than the wicked Oni who are outsmarted in *The Funny Little Woman* by Arlene Mosel. *Little One Inch* by Barbara Brenner is another retelling of this well-known Japanese folktale about Issun Boshi. Visit with the stalwart tiny folk in Hans Christian Andersen's *Thumbelina,* William Joyce's *George Shrinks,* Morris Lurie's *The Story of Imelda, Who Was Small,* Colin McNaughton's *Anton B. Stanton and the Pirates,* and Laura Krauss Melmed's *The Rainbabies.* FOLKLORE–JAPAN. SIZE–FOLKLORE. TRANSFORMATIONS–FOLKLORE.

946   **Hunter, C. W.** *The Green Gourd: A North Carolina Folktale.* **Illus. by Tony Griego. Whitebird, 1992. ISBN 0-399-22278-2**

[Gr. K–2] Paying no mind to the saying, "Never pull a green gourd afore it's ripe, or it'll witch ye sure," an old woman yanks one off the vine and brings it home to dry, intending to use it to dip water. The gourd commences to chase her, fumping her all over, and fumping the panther and fox that try to stop it. The colloquial language is plenty fun to read, with lots of sound effects and silly goings-on until a little boy squashes that gourd flat. It's a rock that does the chasing in *Iktomi and the Boulder* by Paul Goble and its variant *Coyote Steals the Blanket: A Ute Tale* by Janet Stevens. Inanimate objects come to life in Peter Armour's *Stop That Pickle!,* P. C. Asbjørnsen's *The Runaway Pancake,* Arnica Esterl's *The Fine Round Cake,* Scott Cook or Paul Galdone's *The Gingerbread Boy,* Eric A. Kimmel's *The Gingerbread Man,* and Joanne Oppenheim's *You Can't Catch Me!* For a kinder, gentler gourd, read *Chinye: A West African Folk Tale* by Obi Onyefulu. BEHAVIOR–FOLKLORE. FOLKLORE–U.S. FOXES–FOLKLORE. PANTHERS–FOLKLORE.

947   Johnston, Tony. *The Tale of Rabbit and Coyote*. Illus. by Tomie dePaola. Putnam, 1994.
       ISBN 0-399-22258-8

[Gr. Pre–2] Trapped by the farmer's beeswax doll (shades of Brer Rabbit), Rabbit
thinks fast and talks Coyote into taking his place, then convinces him to hold
back a rock to keep it from crushing the world (as in Verna Aardema's *Borreguita
and the Coyote*), and ends up safe on the moon (as in Lois Ehlert's Peruvian folktale *Moon Rope*). A glossary of Spanish expressions helps listeners translate and
repeat all the funny comments in the illustrations. For more Coyote tales, also
read Shonto Begay's *Ma'ii and Cousin Horned Toad*, Jonathan London and Lanny
Pinola's *Fire Race*, Gerald McDermott's *Coyote*, Phyllis Root's *Coyote and the Magic
Words*, Janet Stevens's *Coyote Steals the Blanket*, and Harriet Peck Taylor's *Coyote
Places the Stars*. Rabbit stars in Andy Gregg's *Great Rabbit and the Long-Tailed
Wildcat*, Barbara Knutson's *Sungura and Leopard*, Gerald McDermott's West
African *Zomo the Rabbit*, and Gayle Ross's *How Rabbit Tricked Otter and Other
Cherokee Trickster Stories*. COYOTES–FOLKLORE. FOLKLORE–INDIANS OF MEXICO.
MOON–FOLKLORE. RABBITS–FOLKLORE. TRICKSTER TALES.

948   Kellogg, Steven. *Mike Fink*. Illus. by the author. Morrow, 1992. ISBN 0-688-07003-5

[Gr. 1–4] "Cock-a-doodle-doo!" crows amiable riverman and champion wrestler
Mike Fink, the King of the Keelboatmen whom even a steamboat couldn't stop.
Kellogg's tall-tale retellings include *Paul Bunyan* (1985), *Pecos Bill* (1986), and
Johnny Appleseed. Meet the rest of the U.S. working heroes in *American Tall Tales*
by Mary Pope Osborne, *Larger Than Life: The Adventures of American Legendary
Heroes* by Robert D. San Souci, and *Big Men, Big Country: A Collection of American
Tall Tales* by Paul Robert Walker. BOATS AND BOATING–FOLKLORE. FOLKLORE–U.S.
RIVERS–FOLKLORE. TALL TALES.

949   Kimmel, Eric A. *Anansi and the Talking Melon*. Illus. by Janet Stevens. Holiday House,
       1994. ISBN 0-8234-1104-4

[Gr. Pre–2] Anansi the Spider eats so much of the inside of a ripe orange can-
taloupe, he's too fat to squeeze back out, so to pass the time, he insults Elephant,
Hippo, Warthog, and even the king, all of whom believe the melon can talk.
Older children will appreciate the contrast between the Ashanti story "Talk" and
Harold Courlander's *The Hat-Shaking Dance*, where a yam does speak, and will
love acting out the play from Aaron Shepard's *Stories on Stage: Scripts for Reader's
Theater*. Deborah M. Newton Chocolate's *Talk, Talk* is another version. For more
stories with Anansi, read Eric Maddern's *The Fire Children*, Gail E. Haley's *A
Story, a Story*, Kimmel's *Anansi and the Moss-Covered Rock* and *Anansi Goes
Fishing*, Gerald McDermott's *Anansi the Spider*, and Frances Temple's *Tiger Soup*.
Verna Aardema's *Rabbit Makes a Monkey Out of Lion*, Gerald McDermott's *Zomo
the Rabbit*, and Janet Stevens's Native American *Coyote Steals the Blanket* introduce
other too-clever tricksters. ANIMALS–FOLKLORE. FOLKLORE–AFRICA. FRUIT–FOLKLORE.
SPIDERS–FOLKLORE. TRICKSTER TALES.

950   Kimmel, Eric A. *Anansi Goes Fishing*. Illus. by Janet Stevens. Holiday House, 1992.
       ISBN 0-8234-0918-X

[Gr. Pre–2] Spider Anansi's plans to let Turtle do all the work backfire when Turtle offers his own irresistible strategy: one will work while the other will get tired. The large watercolors with their trendy modern artifacts—Turtle relaxes in his beach chair with a portable radio—don't attempt to convey the tale's African origins, but they are a delight nonetheless. In Verna Aardema's variant, *Anansi Finds a Fool*, the trickster is in human form. Children also adore Kimmel's *Anansi and the Moss-Covered Rock* and *Anansi and the Talking Melon*. Other tricksters from African folklore include Verna Aardema's *Rabbit Makes a Monkey Out of Lion*, Barbara Knutson's *Sungura and Leopard*, Gerald McDermott's *Zomo the Rabbit*, and Tololwa M. Mollel's *The Flying Tortoise*. From the Americas, try Verna Aardema's *Borreguita and the Coyote*, Gerald McDermott's *Raven*, and Janet Stevens's *Coyote Steals the Blanket* and *Tops & Bottoms*. FISHES–FOLKLORE. FOLKLORE–AFRICA, WEST. LAZINESS–FOLKLORE. SPIDERS–FOLKLORE. TRICKSTER TALES.

951   **Kimmel, Eric A.** *Baba Yaga: A Russian Folktale.* **Illus. by Megan Lloyd. Holiday House, 1991. ISBN 0-8234-0854-X**

[Gr. K–2] Good-hearted Marina would be beautiful if not for the horn growing out of her forehead. When her haughty stepmother sends her to the witch's house to borrow a needle and thread, Marina not only makes it out alive, thanks to her kindness, but is able to shed the horn as well. Baba Yaga fans will also shiver with Katya Arnold's *Baba Yaga* and *Baba Yaga & the Little Girl*, Becky Hickox Ayres's *Matreshka*, Joanna Cole's *Bony Legs*, Marianna Mayer's *Baba Yaga and Vasilisa the Brave*, Elsa Okon Rael's *Marushka's Egg*, Maida Silverman's *Anna and the Seven Swans*, Ernest Small's *Baba Yaga*, and Elizabeth Winthrop's *Vasilissa the Beautiful*. Compare all these with Jacob Grimm's *Hansel and Gretel* and Barbara Walker's Turkish variant, *Teeny Tiny and the Witch Woman*. BABA YAGA. FOLKLORE–RUSSIA. WITCHES–FOLKLORE.

952   **Kimmel, Eric A.** *Boots and His Brothers: A Norwegian Tale.* **Illus. by Kimberly Bulcken Root. Holiday House, 1992. ISBN 0-8234-0886-8**

[Gr. 2–6] Boots's kindness to an old beggar woman nets him useful advice in return: "Whenever you ask a question, do not rest until you find the answer." As the three brothers attempt to chop down the king's oak tree and dig a well in return for their weight in gold, it's Boots's inquisitiveness that leads him to find the three magic objects needed to complete the task. This one's great to act out or turn into a Reader's Theater play. Hand out a variety of folktales where the hero succeeds in his or her quest, such as Demi's *The Magic Tapestry*, Beatrice Schenk de Regniers's *Little Sister and the Month Brothers*, Jacob Grimm's *The Water of Life*, and Claire Martin's *Boots & the Glass Mountain*. List examples of the qualities these heroes have in common, such as loyalty, empathy, kindheartedness, amiability, and generosity. Discuss why these traits are still valued in today's world and what applications modern kids can make from these old stories. BROTHERS–FOLKLORE. FOLKLORE–NORWAY. KINGS AND RULERS–FOLKLORE. TREES–FOLKLORE.

953   **Kimmel, Eric A.** *The Gingerbread Man.* **Illus. by Megan Lloyd. Holiday House, 1993. ISBN 0-8234-0824-8**

[Gr. Pre–1] "I'll run and run as fast as I can. You can't catch me. I'm the ginger-bread man!" The delightful telling, with large, genial illustrations, is perfect for story hour, and a clever ending rhyme reminds us that "gingerbread men return, it's said/ When someone bakes some gingerbread." The timeless story has a fair share of variants to read, retell, and act out: P. C. Asbjørnsen's Norwegian *The Runaway Pancake*, Lorinda Bryan Cauley's Norwegian *The Pancake Boy*, Arnica Esterl's English *The Fine Round Cake*, Scott Cook or Paul Galdone's *The Gingerbread Boy*, and Ruth Sawyer's American *Journey Cake, Ho!* Peter Armour's *Stop That Pickle!* and Joanne Oppenheim's *You Can't Catch Me!* are also merry chase stories. CHANTABLE REFRAIN. CREATIVE DRAMA–FOLKLORE. CUMULATIVE STORIES. FOOD–FOLKLORE. FOXES–FOLKLORE. SEQUENCE STORIES.

954   Kimmel, Eric A. *The Greatest of All: A Japanese Folktale.* Illus. by Giora Carmi. Holiday House, 1991. ISBN 0-8234-0885-X

[Gr. K–2] Chuko Mouse wishes to marry a handsome field mouse, but her proud father seeks someone greater, and asks first the emperor, then the sun, cloud, wind, and wall, finally consenting to a mouse union when he discovers that no one is stronger. Joel Cook's *The Rat's Daughter*, Judith Dupré's Mayan *The Mouse Bride*, Ruth Hurlimann's German *The Proud White Cat*, Holly H. Kwon's Korean *The Moles and the Mireuk*, and Gerald McDermott's Japanese *The Stonecutter* are all variants of that same tale. As with the others, Kimmel's version is ideal for first recalling the sequence and then acting out. CREATIVE DRAMA–FOLKLORE. FOLKLORE–JAPAN. MARRIAGE–FOLKLORE. MICE–FOLKLORE. SEQUENCE STORIES.

955   Kimmel, Eric A. *I-Know-Not-What, I-Know-Not-Where: A Russian Tale.* Illus. by Robert Sauber. Holiday House, 1994. ISBN 0-8234-1020-X

[8 chapters, 64p., Gr. 4–6] After Frol, an archer in the tsar's army, shoots a small white dove, she speaks to him, and after he heals her, becomes his trusted com-panion. In a fortuitous melding of well-loved folktale motifs, we encounter imps, a dangerous Talking Cat, iron-toothed witch Baba Yaga, riddles, the invisible Nobody, an evil czar, and the Water of Life. Familiarize listeners with the charac-ter of Baba Yaga, the Russian witch who lives in a hut on chicken legs, with Katya Arnold's or Ernest Small's *Baba Yaga*, Arnold's *Baba Yaga & the Little Girl*, J. Patrick Lewis's *The Frog Princess*, Marianna Mayer's *Baba Yaga and Vasilisa the Brave*, and Elizabeth Winthrop's *Vasilissa the Beautiful*. Another czar is outwitted in Arthur Ransome's *The Fool of the World and His Flying Ship*, while in Robert D. San Souci's *The Tsar's Promise*, the tsar's son Ivan prevails over a demon. BABA YAGA. BIRDS–FOLKLORE. FAIRY TALES. FOLKLORE–RUSSIA. KINGS AND RULERS.

956   Kimmel, Eric A. *The Old Woman and Her Pig.* Illus. by Giora Carmi. Holiday House, 1992. ISBN 0-8234-0970-8

[Gr. Pre–2] Kimmel lightened the violence in this version of the English folktale, the original of which you can compare in Paul Galdone's book of the same title. When the old woman asks for help getting her piggy over the stile, everyone says no. In the illustrations, every character is posed to spell the word "no," and lis-teners will love finding the letters. Have them retell the story in sequence and act it out. Two other retellings are Priscilla Lamont's *The Troublesome Pig* and Rosanne Litzinger's *The Old Woman and Her Pig*, while Lucie M. Gonzalez's Cuban folktale *Bossy Gallito* is a variant starring a rooster. *One Fine Day* by Nonny Hogrogian is another cumulative tale similar in theme, while *Peter and the Talking Shoes* by Kate Banks is a modern story with a folktale feel. CREATIVE DRAMA–FOLKLORE. CUMULATIVE STORIES. FOLKLORE–ENGLAND. PIGS–FOLKLORE.

957   **Kimmel, Eric A. *The Three Princes: A Tale from the Middle East.* Illus. by Leonard Everett Fisher. Holiday House, 1994. ISBN 0-8234-1115-X**

[Gr. 1–4] Given the task of going out in the world and bringing back the rarest thing they find in their travels, three cousins set out on camelback across the desert to win the princess's hand, and come back a year later with a crystal ball, a flying carpet, and a healing orange. They use their gifts to rush home and save the dying princess, who must then decide which was most responsible for saving her life. Stop reading the story here and let the listeners debate who she chose and why before you continue. Other fairy-tale quests include Cheng Hou-Tien's *The Six Chinese Brothers*, Jacob Grimm's *The Water of Life*, Kimmel's *I-Know-Not-What, I-Know-Not-Where: A Russian Tale*, and Robert D. San Souci's *The White Cat: An Old French Fairy Tale*. FAIRY TALES. FOLKLORE–ARABIA. PRINCES AND PRINCESSES–FOLKLORE.

958   **Kimmel, Eric A. *Three Sacks of Truth: A Story from France.* Illus. by Robert Rayevsky. Holiday House, 1993. ISBN 0-8234-0921-X**

[Gr. 2–5] A dishonest king with a craving for peaches promises his charming daughter in marriage to the man who brings him the perfect peach, though he has no intention of letting anyone near her. The youngest of three brothers is kind and honest to an old woman sitting beside a holy well, and she makes it possible for him to bring his perfect peach to the king and to pass the king's test of herding 10,000 rabbits for four days without losing one. *Two Hundred Rabbits* by Adrienne Adams is a picture book from the 200th rabbit's point of view. Other rousing quest folktales include *Prince Ivan and the Firebird* by Laszlo Gal, *Boots and His Brothers* by Eric A. Kimmel, and *Boots & the Glass Mountain* by Claire Martin. BROTHERS–FOLKLORE. FOLKLORE–FRANCE. FRUIT–FOLKLORE. KINGS AND RULERS–FOLKLORE. PRINCES AND PRINCESSES–FOLKLORE. RABBITS–FOLKLORE.

959   **Kirstein, Lincoln. *Puss in Boots.* Illus. by Alain Vaïs. Little, Brown, 1992. ISBN 0-316-89506-7**

[Gr. 1–4] Robin fits his cat Puss with stout cowhide boots, and the cat, in return, parlays a couple of rabbits into an audience with the king and status for his master. This is the most amusingly ornate version of all, with a king bearing the visage of W. C. Fields, an intelligent-looking personable cat, and a setting amid the chateaux of France. Lorinda Bryan Cauley, Paul Galdone, Gail E. Haley, and Fred Marcellino have all produced admirable retellings as well. Two fearless cats save the day in Jenny Nimmo's Scottish folktale *The Witches and the Singing Mice*. CATS–FOLKLORE. FOLKLORE–FRANCE. OGRES–FOLKLORE. KINGS AND RULERS–FOLKLORE.

960   Knutson, Barbara. *Sungura and Leopard: A Swahili Trickster Tale.* Illus. by the author. Little, Brown, 1993. ISBN 0-316-50010-0

[Gr. K–3] Unbeknownst to each other, both Rabbit Sungura and Leopard begin building the same house on a hill by the river, figuring their ancestors must be helping them finish it so quickly, but when they discover the truth, they are forced to share it. This being a classic trickster tale, Sungura looks for a sneaky way to get Leopard to leave. Rabbits play more tricks in Verna Aardema's *Rabbit Makes a Monkey Out of Lion*, Tony Johnston's *The Story of Rabbit and Coyote*, and Gerald McDermott's *Zomo the Rabbit*. Verna Aardema's *Borreguita and the Coyote*, Eric A. Kimmel's *Anansi and the Moss-Covered Rock* and *Anansi Goes Fishing*, Gerald McDermott's *Raven*, Tololwa M. Mollel's *The Flying Tortoise*, and Janet Stevens's *Coyote Steals the Blanket* are more clever animal tales. FOLKLORE–AFRICA, EAST. HARES–FOLKLORE. LEOPARDS–FOLKLORE. TRICKSTER TALES.

961   Kurtz, Jane. *Fire on the Mountain.* Illus. by E. B. Lewis. Simon & Schuster, 1994. ISBN 0-671-88268-6

[Gr. 2–5] To prove his assertion that he often withstood the mountain cold wearing only a thin cloak to protect him, young Alemayu, watcher of cows, agrees to spend the night outside. The boy survives and says that he kept warm all night by watching the glow from a shepherd's fire across the mountain, but his arrogant master avers that looking at a distant fire is the same as building one and tries to send both the boy and his sister packing. Listeners will be delighted with the trick the servants use to make the rich man admit his faulty reasoning. *In the Month of Kislev: A Story for Hanukkah* by Nina Jaffe, in which a rich merchant expects hungry children to pay for smelling his potato pancakes, has a similar plot structure, which you can compare, as do parts of María Cristina Brusca's Argentinian folktale *The Cook and the King*. FOLKLORE–AFRICA. FOLKLORE–ETHIOPIA.

962   Kwon, Holly H. *The Moles and the Mireuk: A Korean Folktale.* Illus. by Woodleigh Hubbard. Houghton Mifflin, 1993. ISBN 0-395-64347-3

[Gr. K–2] Papa mole rejects the King of the Moles as a suitable husband for his perfect daughter, choosing first the Sky, then the Sun, then the King of the Clouds, the Wind, and finally asking the Mireuk, a wise stone statue who advises him that a mole is the most powerful of all. Review the sequence of events and act this out or write it up as a Reader's Theater script for your students to read aloud. Other versions of the same tale include Joel Cook's *The Rat's Daughter*, Judith Dupré's Mayan *The Mouse Bride*, Ruth Hurlimann's German *The Proud White Cat*, Eric A. Kimmel's Japanese *The Greatest of All*, and Gerald McDermott's Japanese *The Stonecutter*. CREATIVE DRAMA–FOLKLORE. FOLKLORE–KOREA. MARRIAGE–FOLKLORE. MOLES–FOLKLORE.

963   Langton, Jane. *Salt: A Russian Folktale.* Illus. by Ilse Plume. Houghton Mifflin, 1992. ISBN 1-56282-178-4

[Gr. 2–5] Setting out in a ship to learn about the world, Ivan the fool, youngest of three brothers, comes upon an island with a mountain of salt which he then

383

trades to a tsar for gold, silver, precious stones, and the hand of the lovely Tsarevna Marushka. Trouble follows when Ivan comes upon his brothers and they take everything from him, including his devoted bride-to-be. Youngest brothers come out ahead in Norwegian folktales *Boots and His Brothers* by Eric A. Kimmel and *Boots & the Glass Mountain* by Claire Martin, and French folktale *Three Sacks of Truth* by Eric A. Kimmel. Salt plays an important role in *Moss Gown* by William H. Hooks and *Why the Sea Is Salt* by Vivien French. BROTHERS–FOLK-LORE. FOLKLORE–RUSSIA. FOOD–FOLKLORE. GIANTS–FOLKLORE. SALT–FOLKLORE.

964   Larry, Charles. *Peboan and Seegwun*. Illus. by the author. Farrar, 1993. ISBN 0-374-35773-0

[Gr. 1–4] At the end of winter, in the lodge where an old man sits listening to the wind, a young man comes to visit, share a pipe, and swap stories of their power over the seasons. At daybreak, the two are identified: Peboan is Old Man Winter, while Seegwun is the spirit of spring. Dazzling paintings show the transition of the seasons in the daily lives of Anishinabe or Ojibwa in the times before the arrival of Europeans in the northern forests of Michigan, Wisconsin, and Minnesota. *Children of the Morning Light: Wampanoag Tales* told by Manitonquat (Medicine Story) contains "The Great Migration and Old Man Winter," a variant from southeastern Massachusetts. Joseph Bruchac and Jonathan London's *Thirteen Moons on Turtle's Back* is a collection of Native American legends about each of the year's moons. Kris Waldherr's *Persephone and the Pomegranate* is the Greek explanation of the seasons. Janet S. Anderson's *The Key into Winter* is also thought-provoking. FOLKLORE–INDIANS OF NORTH AMERICA. OJIBWAY INDIANS–FOLK-LORE. PICTURE BOOKS FOR ALL AGES. SEASONS–FOLKLORE. WINTER–FOLKLORE.

965   Lawson, Julie. *The Dragon's Pearl*. Illus. by Paul Morin. Clarion, 1993. ISBN 0-395-63623-X

[Gr. 1–4] During a time of terrible drought, hardworking grasscutter Xiao Sheng finds a magic pearl that provides great wealth for him and his mother. When ruffians try to steal it, the boy swallows the pearl and becomes a dragon. Also set in China are *The Six Chinese Brothers* by Cheng Hou-Tien, *Everyone Knows What a Dragon Looks Like* by Jay Williams, and *The Painted Fan* by Marilyn Singer. For dragon folktales of other countries, try Janina Domanska's Polish *King Krakus and the Dragon*, Gail E. Haley's American *Jack and the Fire Dragon*, Margaret Hodges's English *Saint George and the Dragon*, Simon Stern's Russian *Vasily and the Dragon*, and Dorothy Van Woerkum's Russian *Alexandra the Rock-Eater*. DRAGONS–FOLK-LORE. FOLKLORE–CHINA. MOTHERS AND SONS–FOLKLORE.

966   Lemieux, Michèle. *Pied Piper of Hamelin*. Illus. by the author. Morrow, 1993. ISBN 0-688-09849-5

[Gr. 2–5] Thousands of rats converged on the German town of Hamelin at Christmastime in 1283, but a stranger in brightly colored clothes appeared and promised the mayor to rid the town of rats for 1,000 gold pieces. When the piper was not paid what he was owed, he left with the town's 130 children. An author's note explains that the story we think of as merely a legend is in fact a true one. See also Sara and Stephen Corrin's version of the story. FOLKLORE–GERMANY. MIDDLE AGES–FOLKLORE. RATS–FOLKLORE.

967　Lester, Julius. *John Henry.* Illus. by Jerry Pinkney. Dial, 1994. ISBN 0-8037-1607-9

[Gr. 1–4] Based on several versions of the folk song about the larger-than-life African American man who won a contest against a steam hammer and died, this large-sized picture book version has majestic watercolors and a narrative line bursting with humor and wonder combined. Compare the telling with Ezra Jack Keat's version and Steve Sanfield's *A Natural Man: The True Story of John Henry.* *American Tall Tales* by Mary Pope Osborne, *Larger Than Life: The Adventures of American Legendary Heroes* by Robert D. San Souci, and *Big Men, Big Country: A Collection of American Tall Tales* by Paul Robert Walker also contain versions of the tall tale. FOLKLORE, AFRICAN AMERICAN. FOLKLORE–U.S. MACHINES–FOLKLORE. TRAINS–FOLKLORE. TALL TALES.

968　Levine, Arthur A. *The Boy Who Drew Cats: A Japanese Folktale.* Illus. by Frédéric Clément. Dial, 1994. ISBN 0-8037-1173-5

[Gr. 2–6] Kenji strives to please the priests in the village monastery, but unable to restrain himself from drawing cats, he is sent away for his laziness. His one priest friend presents him with a beautiful set of inks and brushes and warns him, "Avoid large places at night—keep to small." Taking shelter in a deserted temple, he paints his cats, which come to life and destroy the menacing Goblin Rat. Photocopy the glossary of Japanese characters on the last page so children can read the one-word message on each page of the story. In Molly Bang's Chinese folktale *Tye May and the Magic Brush,* the girl artist's paintings also come to life. ARTISTS–FOLKLORE. CATS–FOLKLORE. FOLKLORE–JAPAN. GOBLINS–FOLKLORE. PAINTING–FOLKLORE. RATS–FOLKLORE.

969　Lewis, J. Patrick. *The Frog Princess: A Russian Tale.* Illus. by Gennady Spirin. Dial, 1994. ISBN 0-8037-1624-9

[Gr. 2–6] The tsar's youngest son brings home as his wife a little green frog who can weave and bake like a dream, but of course she's actually Princess Vasilisa the Wise under an enchantment. Spirin's paintings are downright gorgeous. Other quest folktales with enchanted royalty include versions of George Webbe Dasent's Norwegian tale *East o' the Sun and West o' the Moon* by Gillian Barlow, Kathleen and Michael Hague, and P. J. Lynch. Then there's Jacob Grimm's *The Frog Prince,* Elizabeth Isele's version of *The Frog Princess,* Eric A. Kimmel's *Three Sacks of Truth,* Jane Langton's *The Hedgehog Boy,* and, of course, the French fairy tale *Beauty and the Beast,* retold by Marianna Mayer. Marianna Mayer's *Baba Yaga and Vasilisa the Brave,* Josepha Sherman's *Vassilisa the Wise,* and Elizabeth Winthrop's *Vasilissa the Beautiful* keep us cheering for the talented Russian heroine. BABA YAGA. FAIRY TALES. FOLKLORE–RUSSIA. FROGS–FOLKLORE. KINGS AND RULERS–FOLKLORE. PRINCES AND PRINCESSES–FOLKLORE. TRANSFORMATIONS–FOLKLORE.

970   Lichtveld, Noni. *I Lost My Arrow in a Kankan Tree*. Illus. by the author. Lothrop, 1994. ISBN 0-688-12749-5

[Gr. K–2] Setting off from the forest to town to find a job, young Jakóno trades useful items with the people he meets, ending up with gold that he gives to the king for a piece of land that his family can farm. This South American folktale has a cumulative refrain that gets longer and longer, and children will try to keep up with you as you speed up your recitation each time. Once children know the story, cast parts and act it out. Paul Galdone's, Eric A. Kimmel's, or Rosanne Litzinger's version of *The Old Woman and Her Pig*, or Priscilla Lamont's *The Troublesome Pig*, and a Cuban variant, Lucie M. Gonzalez's *Bossy Gallito*, all involve listeners recalling a long sequence of events. Both *Peter and the Talking Shoes* by Kate Banks and Nonny Hogrogian's folktale *One Fine Day* incorporate trading as well. CHANTABLE REFRAIN. CREATIVE DRAMA–FOLKLORE. CUMULATIVE STORIES. FOLKLORE–SURINAM. MULTICULTURAL STORIES–FOLKLORE.

971   Litzinger, Rosanne. *The Old Woman and Her Pig: An Old English Tale*. Illus. by the author. Harcourt, 1993 ISBN 0-15-257802-1

[Gr. Pre–1] Not until she gives the cat a saucer of milk does the old woman get any help from the rat, rope, farmer, ox, water, fire, stick, and dog, all of whom she has begged for help in making her pig climb over the stile and go home. Paul Galdone and Eric A. Kimmel also published versions of the same title, as did Priscilla Lamont in *The Troublesome Pig*, and all make wonderful classroom plays to act out. Lucie M. Gonzalez's Cuban folktale *Bossy Gallito* stars a stubborn rooster instead, while Nonny Hogrogian's *One Fine Day* stars a tail-less fox. *Peter and the Talking Shoes* by Kate Banks is another trading story with funky 1930s-style illustrations. CHANTABLE REFRAIN. CREATIVE DRAMA–FOLKORE. CUMULATIVE STORIES. FOLKLORE–ENGLAND. PIGS–FOLKLORE.

972   London, Jonathan, and Lanny Pinola. *Fire Race: A Karuk Coyote Tale About How Fire Came to the People*. Illus. by Sylvia Long. Chronicle, 1993. ISBN 0-8118-0241-8

[Gr. K–3] In the days when the animal people had no fire, Wise Old Coyote devised a plan for Eagle, Mountain Lion, Fox, Bear, Turtle, and Frog to work together with him and steal it from the Yellow Jacket sisters. Eric Maddern's *Rainbow Bird* is an Australian aboriginal folktale about fire, while in Ann Dixon's *How Raven Brought Light to People*, Gerald McDermott's *Raven*, and Susan Hand Shetterley's *Raven's Light*, all Native American legends, we see how Raven brought the sun to all people. Note the preponderance of Indian stories where coyote is a troublemaker: Verna Aardema's *Borreguita and the Coyote*, Shonto Begay's *Ma'ii and Cousin Horned Toad*, Tony Johnston's *The Story of Rabbit and Coyote*, Gretchen Will Mayo's *That Tricky Coyote!* and *Meet Tricky Coyote!* (Walker, 1993), Gerald McDermott's *Coyote*, Phyllis Root's *Coyote and the Magic Words*, Janet Stevens's *Coyote Steals the Blanket*, and Harriet Peck Taylor's *Coyote Places the Stars*. COYOTES–FOLKLORE. FIRE–FOLKLORE. FOLKLORE–INDIANS OF NORTH AMERICA. KARUK INDIANS–FOLKLORE. POURQUOI TALES.

973 Lottridge, Celia Barker. *The Name of the Tree: A Bantu Folktale.* Illus. by Ian Wallace. McElderry, 1989. ISBN 0-689-50490-X

[Gr. Pre–2] In a time of great hunger, the animals band together and find a wondrous tree with delicious-smelling fruit, but until they can find out the tree's name, the fruit will remain out of reach. Each animal that sets out to learn the name from their lion king forgets the name is Ungalli until a young tortoise succeeds, thanks to his concentration on the task at hand. Children can chant the tree's name along with tortoise and describe how the fruit tasted. Take a look at familiar and unusual trees in Barbara Bash's *Tree of Life: The World of the African Baobab,* Harry Behn's poem *Trees,* Dick Gackenbach's *Mighty Tree,* George Ella Lyon's *A B Cedar: An Alphabet of Trees,* and Janice May Udry's *A Tree Is Nice.* Note the different personalities of the tortoises in three other African folktales: *The King and the Tortoise* and *The Flying Tortoise* by Tololwa M. Mollel, and *Tricky Tortoise* by Mwenye Hadithi. ANIMALS–FOLKLORE. FOLKLORE–AFRICA. FRUIT–FOLKLORE. MEMORY–FOLKLORE. TREES–FOLKLORE. TURTLES–FOLKLORE.

974 McCoy, Karen Kawamoto. *A Tale of Two Tengu: A Japanese Folktale.* Illus. by Ken Fossey. Albert Whitman, 1993. ISBN 0-8075-7748-0

[Gr. Pre–2] Kenji and Joji, two sassy tengu or Japanese goblins with long, lovely noses that can stretch out for miles, compete over whose nose can bring back the best prize. Meet two more tengu in *The Badger and the Magic Fan* by Tony Johnston, plus an assortment of well-known creatures from Japanese folklore in *The Funny Little Woman* by Arlene Mosel, and *Momotaro, the Peach Boy* by Linda Shute. See how two more sillies outsmart themselves in *Two Foolish Cats* by Yoshiko Uchida. FOLKLORE–JAPAN. GOBLINS–FOLKLORE.

975 McDermott, Gerald. *Coyote: A Trickster Tale from the American Southwest.* Illus. by the author. Harcourt, 1994. ISBN 0-15-220724-4

[Gr. Pre–2] In a comical Zuni legend, trickster Coyote follows his nose for trouble and attempts to fly with the crows. Annoyed at his attitude, they take back their feathers in midair, leaving him in the dust. *The Flying Tortoise,* an African trickster tale by Tololwa M. Mollel, has similar motifs of feathers, flying, and aggravated birds. Once you introduce tricksters and pourquoi tales, children will clamor for more, so placate them with Verna Aardema's *Borreguita and the Coyote,* Shonto Begay's *Ma'ii and Cousin Horned Toad,* Valerie Scho Carey's *Quail Song,* Paul Goble's *Crow Chief,* Tony Johnston's *The Story of Rabbit and Coyote,* Jonathan London and Lanny Pinola's *Fire Race,* Gretchen Will Mayo's *That Tricky Coyote!* and *Meet Tricky Coyote!* (Walker, 1993), Phyllis Root's *Coyote and the Magic Words,* Janet Stevens's *Coyote Steals the Blanket,* and Harriet Peck Taylor's *Coyote Places the Stars.* BIRDS–FOLKLORE. COYOTES–FOLKLORE. CROWS–FOLKLORE. FOLKLORE–INDIANS OF NORTH AMERICA. TRICKSTER TALES. ZUNI INDIANS–FOLKLORE.

976 McDermott, Gerald. *Raven: A Trickster Tale from the Pacific Northwest.* Illus. by the author. Harcourt, 1993 ISBN 0-15-265661-8

[Gr. K–4] Sorry for the men and women who live in the dark and cold, trickster Raven arranges to be born as a boy child of the Sky Chief's daughter so he can steal the sun that is kept hidden in a box in the lodge and give it to all the people. Compare with the variants *How Raven Brought Light to People* by Ann Dixon and *Raven's Light* by Susan Hand Shetterley. Shonto Begay's *Ma'ii and Cousin Horned Toad* and Paul Goble's *Iktomi and the Boulder* are additional Native American trickster tales. Compare the geometric-styled illustrations in McDermott's many folktales, such as *Anansi the Spider*, *The Stonecutter*, *The Voyage of Osiris*, and *Zomo the Rabbit*. Emery Bernhard's *How Snowshoe Hare Rescued the Sun* and Elphinstone Dayrell's African *Why the Sun and the Moon Live in the Sky* will also supplement your astronomy unit nicely. Both Jonathan London and Lanny Pinola's Native American *Fire Race* and Eric Maddern's Australian tale *Rainbow Bird* explain how we got fire. BIRDS–FOLKLORE. FOLKLORE–INDIANS OF NORTH AMERICA. RAVENS–FOLKLORE. SUN–FOLKLORE. TRICKSTER TALES.

977   McDermott, Gerald. *Zomo the Rabbit: A Trickster Tale from West Africa.* Illus. by the author. Harcourt, 1992. ISBN 0-15-299967-1

[Gr. Pre–1] Not satisfied with cleverness, Zomo asks Sky God for wisdom and is told he can earn it by completing three impossible and dangerous tasks, all of which he pulls off successfully, gaining courage and a bit of sense and learning about caution. Reminiscent in parts of Gail Haley's Anansi tale *A Story, A Story*, the book comes alive with bright gouache paintings in stylized geometric patterns. Verna Aardema's *Rabbit Makes a Monkey Out of Lion*, Tony Johnston's *The Story of Rabbit and Coyote*, Barbara Knutson's *Sungura and Leopard*, Gretchen Will Mayo's *Big Trouble for Tricky Rabbit!* and *Here Comes Tricky Rabbit!* (1994), and Gayle Ross's *How Rabbit Tricked Otter and Other Cherokee Trickster Stories* continue the Rabbit trickster genre. FOLKLORE–AFRICA, WEST. RABBITS–FOLKLORE. TRICKSTER TALES. WISDOM–FOLKLORE.

978   Maddern, Eric. *The Fire Children: A West African Creation Tale.* Illus. by Frané Lessac. Dial, 1993. ISBN 0-8037-1477-7

[Gr. K–3] Two spirit people, Aso Yaa and Kwaku Ananse, propelled to earth when sky god Nyame sneezes, get lonely and shape little clay children, which they bake in the fire and breathe life into. With some baked longer than others, the children's skin comes in varying and equally pleasing hues, which explains why we are all different colors today. This charming pourquoi tale, with primitive-style gouache paintings inspired by West African masks and designs, is perfect for introducing the diverse races of the world and dispelling prejudice against people who look "different," as does Sheila Hamanaka's *All the Colors of the Earth*. Kwaku Ananse is the well-known African spider trickster who also stars in Verna Aardema's *Anansi Finds a Fool*, Gail E. Haley's *A Story, a Story*, Eric A. Kimmel's *Anansi and the Moss-Covered Rock*, *Anansi and the Talking Melon*, and *Anansi Goes Fishing*, Gerald McDermott's *Anansi the Spider*, and Frances Temple's *Tiger Soup*. CHILDREN–FOLKLORE. CREATION–FOLKLORE. FIRE–FOLKLORE. FOLKLORE–AFRICA, WEST. POURQUOI TALES. RACE–FOLKLORE.

979   Maddern, Eric. *Rainbow Bird: An Aboriginal Folktale from Northern Australia*. Illus. by Adrienne Kennaway. Little, Brown, 1993. ISBN 0-316-54314-4

[Gr. K–3] Back in the Time of Dreams, mean and scary Crocodile Man owned fire until Bird Woman snatched it from him and shared it with all people. Jonathan London and Lanny Pinola's *Fire Race* is a Native American coyote trickster tale on the same subject. Another Australian Aboriginal pourquoi tale is Stefan Czernecki and Timothy Rhodes's *The Singing Snake*. Additional folktales about birds include Blia Xiong's Laotian *Nine-in-One, Grr! Grr!*, Shirley Climo's *King of the Birds*, Maggie Duff's Indian *Rum Pum Pum*, Gerald McDermott's Pacific Northwest trickster tale *Raven*, and Joanna Troughton's South American Indian *How the Birds Changed Their Feathers*. AUSTRALIA–FOLKLORE. BIRDS–FOLKLORE. CROCODILES–FOLKLORE. FIRE–FOLKLORE. POURQUOI TALES.

980   Marshall, James. *Old Mother Hubbard and Her Wonderful Dog*. Illus. by the author. Farrar, 1991. ISBN 0-374-35621-1

[Gr. Pre–1] Rats, cats, and chickens run riot in the background while the feisty bulldog plays dead, dances, and reads the news in this Mother Goose rhyme, always perfect for creative dramatics. Compare with other versions by Tomie dePaola, Paul Galdone, Evaline Ness, and a Swedish one by Lennart Helsing (Coward, 1976). CHANTABLE REFRAIN. CREATIVE DRAMA–FOLKLORE. DOGS–FOLKLORE. NURSERY RHYMES. STORIES IN RHYME.

981   Martin, Claire. *Boots & the Glass Mountain*. Illus. by Gennady Spirin. Dial, 1992. ISBN 0-8037-1111-5

[Gr. 2–6] Youngest brother Boots tames three magnificent horses, overpowering their troll magic, and uses them to ride up a sparkling glass mountain built by the Troll Chief and win the hand of a princess perched at the top. A Cinderella story of sorts, Boots tends the kitchen fire and does the chores, but garners the three golden apples from the princess nevertheless. Another tale about our hero is *Boots and His Brothers: A Norwegian Tale* by Eric A. Kimmel. Compare the motifs in Nonny Hogrogian's version of Jacob Grimm's German fairy tale *The Glass Mountain*. BROTHERS–FOLKLORE. FAIRY TALES. FOLKLORE–NORWAY. HORSES–FOLKLORE. KNIGHTS AND KNIGHTHOOD–FOLKLORE. PRINCES AND PRINCESSES–FOLKLORE. TROLLS–FOLKLORE.

982   Martin, Rafe. *The Boy Who Lived with the Seals*. Illus. by David Shannon. Putnam, 1993. ISBN 0-399-22413-0

[Gr. 2–4] Some time after a little boy wanders off and disappears by the river, his grieving parents learn that he has been taken in by seals and arrange to bring him back. The boy grunts and barks, crawls on the ground, and eats only raw fish, but his loving parents reteach him the ways of their Northwest Coast people. *How Raven Brought Light to People* by Ann Dixon and *Raven's Light: A Myth from the People of the Northwest Coast* by Susan Hand Shetterly are creation myths that children will also find interesting. In Mary-Joan Gerson's Brazilian folktale *How*

Night Came from the Sea, a goddess's daughter forsakes her ocean home to marry an earth man. CHINOOK INDIANS–FOLKLORE. FOLKLORE–INDIANS OF NORTH AMERICA. SEALS–FOLKLORE.

983   Martin, Rafe. *The Rough-Face Girl*. Illus. by David Shannon. Putnam, 1992. ISBN 0-399-21859-9

[Gr. 2–6] In this solemn Algonquin Indian Cinderella variant, a young girl, scarred and burned from tending the fire, sets out in tattered moccasins and a dress fashioned from birch bark to meet the Invisible Being only she can see. Robert D. San Souci's *Sootface: An Ojibwa Cinderella Story* is another compelling version, while Penny Pollock's Zuni *The Turkey Girl* does not have the usual happy ending. Compare the details of Martin's solemn retelling and Shannon's majestic paintings with John Steptoe's African Cinderella variant *Mufaro's Beautiful Daughters* and with other American retellings, such as Joanne Compton's *Ashpet*, William Hook's *Moss Gown*, Charlotte Huck's *Princess Furball*, and Robert D. San Souci's *Sukey and the Mermaid*. Martin's *The Boy Who Lived with the Seals* is an interesting companion tale, while *Great Rabbit and the Long-Tailed Wildcat* by Andy Gregg is another Algonquian story. ALGONQUIN INDIANS–FOLKLORE. CINDERELLA STORIES. FAIRY TALES. FOLKLORE–INDIANS OF NORTH AMERICA. INVISIBILITY–FOLKLORE. SISTERS–FOLKLORE.

984   Mathews, Judith, and Fay Robinson. *Nathaniel Willy, Scared Silly*. Illus. by Alexi Natchev. Bradbury, 1994. ISBN 0-02-765285-8

[Gr. Pre–2] Even the cat, dog, pig, and cow his grandmother dumps in his bed one night can't keep Nathaniel from being scared of his squeaky old door until the wise old woman from down the road oils it. Compare this lighthearted, bouncy tale, partly in rhyme, with its Puerto Rican variants "The Squeaky Old Bed" from Barbara Baumgartner's folktale collection *Crocodile! Crocodile!* and *The Squeaky Door* by Laura Simms. Joanna Cole's *It's Too Noisy*, Ann McGovern's *Too Much Noise*, and Margot Zemach's *It Could Always Be Worse* all attempt to adjust the noise level, while *The Little Old Lady Who Was Not Afraid of Anything* by Linda Williams is another sound-effect-filled story. BEDTIME–FOLKLORE. FOLKLORE–U.S. GRANDMOTHERS–FOLKLORE. SEQUENCE STORIES. SOUND EFFECTS–FOLKLORE.

985   Mayer, Marianna. *Baba Yaga and Vasilisa the Brave*. Illus. by K. Y. Craft. Morrow, 1994. ISBN 0-688-08501-6

[Gr. 2–5] Exquisite romantic, bordered, Russian-style paintings with an illustrated initial letter on each page give us a good child, a wicked stepmother who sends her into the clutches of sharp-toothed witch Baba Yaga to ask for a light, and a miracle doll who completes impossible tasks. Elizabeth Winthrop's *Vasilissa the Beautiful* is another variant. Can't get enough Baba Yaga? See Katya Arnold's *Baba Yaga* and *Baba Yaga & the Little Girl*, Becky Hickox Ayres's *Matreshka*, Joanna Cole's *Bony Legs*, Eric Kimmel's *Baba Yaga*, J. Patrick Lewis's *The Frog Princess*, Elsa Okon Rael's *Marushka's Egg*, Maida Silverman's *Anna and the Seven Swans*, and Ernest Small's *Baba Yaga*. BABA YAGA. DOLLS–FOLKLORE. FAIRY TALES. FOLKLORE–RUSSIA. WITCHES–FOLKLORE.

986 Mayer, Marianna. *The Spirit of the Blue Light.* Illus. by Laszlo Gal. Macmillan, 1990. ISBN 0-02-765350-1

[Gr. 3–5] Possessing the innocence and goodness necessary, Michael heeds the advice of old Lawrence to seek the riches inside the White Mountain, and finds the lantern that holds the Spirit of the Blue Light who will give him whatever his heart desires. As in Hans Christian Andersen's story *The Tinderbox,* the young soldier falls for the king's daughter, is condemned to hang for visiting her room, and is saved by the Spirit at the last minute. Compare this German folktale with *The Tinderbox,* Barry Moser's mesmerizing rewrite of Andersen's tale reset in the post-Civil War South, plus Andrew Lang's *Aladdin and the Wonderful Lamp* and Mayer's expanded version, *Aladdin and the Enchanted Lamp.* FAIRY TALES. FOLKLORE–GERMANY. PRINCES AND PRINCESSES–FOLKLORE. WISHES–FOLKLORE.

987 Mollel, Tololwa M. *The Flying Tortoise: An Igbo Tale.* Illus. by Barbara Spurll. Clarion, 1994. ISBN 0-395-68845-0

[Gr. K–2] Hearing of the birds' invitation to a feast with the king of Skyland, Mbeku the tortoise, the always-hungry troublemaker, insists he can show them the way if they will just give him some feathers for wings. His gluttony enrages the birds, and he ends up jumping back down to earth, cracking his prized shell, and hiding inside it, which tortoises still do today. Like *Anansi the Spider,* this Nigerian trickster survives unrepentant. Note the similarity to Gerald McDermott's Native American folktale *Raven,* who convinces crows to help him aloft, while Gayle Ross's *How Turtle's Back Was Cracked* is a Cherokee Indian version. More African tricksters include Verna Aardema's *Rabbit Makes a Monkey Out of Lion,* Eric A. Kimmel's *Anansi and the Moss-Covered Rock* and *Anansi Goes Fishing,* Barbara Knutson's *Sungura and Leopard,* and Gerald McDermott's *Zomo the Rabbit.* The tortoise is the hero of *The Name of the Tree,* an African folktale by Celia Barker Lottridge. BIRDS–FOLKLORE. FOLKLORE–NIGERIA. GREED–FOLKLORE. POURQUOI TALES. TRICKSTER TALES. TURTLES–FOLKLORE.

988 Mollel, Tololwa M. *The King and the Tortoise.* Illus. by Kathy Blankley. Clarion, 1993. ISBN 0-395-64480-1

[Gr. K–3] A king who considers himself the cleverest person in the world challenges his kingdom's creatures to make him a robe of smoke, a task that confounds the hare, fox, leopard, and elephant, but the tortoise proves himself the king's equal. An interesting comparison would be Hans Christian Andersen's *The Emperor's New Clothes.* Other African tales of cunning creatures include Verna Aardema's *Princess Gorilla and a New Kind of Water* and *Rabbit Makes a Monkey Out of Lion,* Ruby Dee's *Two Ways to Count to Ten,* Mwenye Hadithi's *Tricky Tortoise,* and Eric A. Kimmel's *Anansi Goes Fishing.* In *The Name of the Tree,* an African folktale by Celia Barker Lottridge, only the tortoise has the perseverance to help the other animals. FOLKLORE–AFRICA. FOLKLORE–CAMEROON. KINGS AND RULERS–FOLKLORE. TURTLES–FOLKLORE.

989 Mollel, Tololwa M. *The Orphan Boy: A Maasai Story.* Illus. by Paul Morin. Clarion, 1991. ISBN 0-89919-985-2

[Gr. 1–4] A childless old man is overjoyed with the companionship of a boy who calls himself Kileken, though he becomes increasingly driven to discover how the child manages to complete each day's difficult chores without effort. As in Molly Bang's *Dawn*, Diane Wolkstein's *White Wave*, and Sumiko Yagawa's Japanese folktale *The Crane Wife*, once the old man spies on the boy, he loses him forever, for Kileken is the planet Venus come to earth. Morin's brooding moonlit paintings give one much to ponder, especially if you tie in the story to your astronomy unit, with folklore including Barbara Juster Esbensen's *The Star Maiden* and Paul Goble's *Her Seven Brothers*, or fiction like Louise Moeri's *Star Mother's Youngest Child*. ASTRONOMY–FOLKLORE. DROUGHT–FOLKLORE. FOLKLORE–AFRICA. VENUS–FOLK-LORE.

990   Mollel, Tololwa M. *A Promise to the Sun: An African Story*. Illus. by Beatriz Vidal. Joy Street / Little, Brown, 1992. ISBN 0-316-57813-4

[Gr. K–3] At the birds' meeting to discuss the drought, the task of searching for rain falls to Bat, a distant cousin, and after consulting the moon, stars, clouds, and winds, he makes a bargain with the sun to provide it with a nest in exchange for rain. Bat's broken promise is the reason she hides from the sun to this day. Find out more about the bat through folktales like Paul Goble's *Iktomi and the Boulder* and Judy Sierra's *The Elephant's Wrestling Match*, nonfiction including Barbara Bash's *Shadows of Night: The Hidden World of the Little Brown Bat*, and the picture book *Stellaluna* by Janell Cannon, and provide for laughs with *Batty Riddles* by Katy Hall and Lisa Eisenberg. BATS–FOLKLORE. BIRDS–FOLKLORE. FOLK-LORE–AFRICA. SUN–FOLKLORE.

991   Mollel, Tololwa M. *Rhinos for Lunch and Elephants for Supper!* Illus. by Barbara Spurll. Clarion, 1992. ISBN 0-395-60734-5

[Gr. Pre–2] The hare, fox, leopard, rhino, and elephant are all intimidated by the voice booming from the hare's cave, "I am a monster, a monster! I eat rhinos for lunch and elephants for supper! Come in if you dare!" Not until a brazen little frog comes along and threatens the monster with an even scarier retort do they see the creature that tricked them—a tiny caterpillar. Compare this entertaining Masaii tale with the elegant variant *Who's in Rabbit's House?* by Verna Aardema. In Judy Sierra's African folktale *The Elephant's Wrestling Match*, a tiny bat bests the arrogant elephant. ANIMALS–FOLKLORE. CATERPILLARS–FOLKLORE. CHANTABLE REFRAIN. CREATIVE DRAMA–FOLKLORE. FOLKLORE–AFRICA. FROGS–FOLKLORE. TRICKSTER TALES.

992   Nimmo, Jenny. *The Witches and the Singing Mice*. Illus. by Angela Barrett. Dial, 1993. ISBN 0-8037-1509-9

[Gr. 1–4] In the Scottish Highlands, Tam the blacksmith's cat and Rory the carpenter's cat witness three witches' arrival in Glenmagraw. Powerless to prevent the witches from placing enchantments on two village children, the two brave tomcats seek useful advice from wise old Granny Pine. In another sinisterly spooky folktale, Paul Galdone's English *King of the Cats*, the cats also are not what they seem to the people around them. Lorinda Bryan Cauley, Paul Galdone, Gail E. Haley, Lincoln Kirstein, and Fred Marcellino have each retold and/or illustrated the classic English folktale *Puss in Boots* about another stalwart cat. The tiny orange cat in Antonia Barber's *Catkin* saves a child who has been taken by the Little People to their land under the green hill. CATS–FOLKLORE. FOLKLORE–SCOTLAND. MICE–FOLKLORE. WITCHES–FOLKLORE.

993   Ober, Hal. *How Music Came to the World.* Illus. by Carol Ober. Houghton Mifflin, 1994. ISBN 0-395-67523-5

[Gr. 1–4] Sky god Tezcatlipoca convinces wind god Quetzalcoatl to travel to the House of the Sun to bring back the best singers and musicians to earth to wake up the world with music. The bright cutout oil pastel drawings are in the style of pre-Columbian design motifs and Aztec and Mayan codices, as is, on a more somber note, Sally Schofar Mathews's *The Sad Night*, about Cortez's conquest of Mexico in 1519. David Wisniewski's *Rain Player* is an original tale about an ancient Mayan boy who takes on Chac, the god of rain. On the musical theme, Stefan Czernecki and Timothy Rhodes's *The Singing Snake* is an Australian pourquoi tale about the making of the first flute. AZTECS–FOLKLORE. FOLKLORE–INDIANS OF MEXICO. FOLKLORE–MEXICO. MUSIC–FOLKLORE. POURQUOI TALES.

994   O'Brien, Anne Sibley. *The Princess and the Beggar: A Korean Folklore.* Illus. by the author. Scholastic, 1993. ISBN 0-590-46092-7

[Gr. 1–4] Known as the Weeping Princess, the king's youngest daughter is banished when she refuses to marry the nobleman chosen for her, and goes into the forest to be the wife of the beggar Pabo Ondal. *The Korean Cinderella* by Shirley Climo will make an interesting contrast to this riches-to-rags story. BEGGARS–FOLKLORE. FOLKLORE–KOREA. PRINCES AND PRINCESSES–FOLKLORE.

995   Onyefulu, Obi. *Chinye: A West African Folk Tale.* Illus. by Evie Safarewicz. Viking, 1994. ISBN 0-670-85115-9

[Gr. K–3] Sent by her stepmother to fetch water from the stream one night, Chinye is protected by an antelope and a hyena, and aided by an old woman who bids her to take home a magic gourd that gives off great riches. Naturally, her heedless stepsister gets in on the act and takes a big gourd that brings with it bad fortune. What's interesting to note is how many versions of this story there are worldwide, with a few of the more obvious variants including Aliki's *The Twelve Months* from Greece, Robert Baden's *And Sunday Makes Seven* from Spain, Beatrice Schenk de Regniers's Slavic *Little Sister and the Month Brothers*, Jacob Grimm's *Mother Holle* from Germany, and especially Robert D. San Souci's *The Talking Eggs*, an African American tale. Meet up with a gourd that's not so benign in C. W. Hunter's riotous North Carolinan folktale *The Green Gourd*. FOLKLORE–AFRICA, WEST. GREED–FOLKLORE. STEPMOTHERS–FOLKLORE.

996   Paterson, Katherine. *The Tale of the Mandarin Ducks.* Illus. by Leo and Diane Dillon. Lodestar, 1990. ISBN 0-525-67283-4

[Gr. 2–6] A proud and cruel lord cares little for the drake he orders captured and caged so he can show it off, but when sympathetic kitchen maid Yasuko frees the duck, one-eyed former samurai Shozu is falsely accused and the two are condemned to death by drowning. They fall in love and are saved from their sentence by two messengers whom we assume to be the grateful ducks in disguise. The elegant Japanese folktale, done in the style of 18th century *ukiyo-e* or woodblock prints, provides an inspiring message: "Trouble can always be borne when it is shared." Other folktales of birds and humans include Sherry Garland's *Why Ducks Sleep on One Leg*, Momoko Ishii's Japanese *The Tongue-Cut Sparrow*, Eric A. Kimmel's Russian *I-Know-Not-What, I-Know-Not-Where*, Patricia Montgomery Newton's Japanese *The Five Sparrows*, Nami Rhee's Korean *Magic Spring*, and Sumiko Yagawa's Japanese *The Crane Wife*. BIRDS–FOLKLORE. DUCKS–FOLKLORE. FOLKLORE–JAPAN. KINDNESS–FOLKLORE.

997   Perrault, Charles. *Puss in Boots*. Illus. by Fred Marcellino. Trans. by Malcolm Arthur. Farrar, 1990. ISBN 0-374-36160-6

[Gr. 1–4] This Caldecott Honor version is distinguished for its unforgettable cover: the huge, handsome, behatted head of the famous cat, with the titles and illustrator listed on the back cover. Compare this story of the miller's youngest son who, thanks to his quick-thinking cat, becomes the king's son-in-law, with versions illustrated by Lorinda Bryan Cauley, Paul Galdone, Gail E. Haley, and Lincoln Kirstein. CATS–FOLKLORE. FOLKLORE–FRANCE. KINGS AND RULERS. OGRES–FOLKLORE.

998   Pitre, Felix. *Juan Bobo and the Pig: A Puerto Rican Folktale*. Illus. by Christy Hale. Lodestar, 1993. ISBN 0-525-67429-2

[Gr. K–2] Juan Bobo, or "Simple John," the well-loved lazy fool from Puerto Rican folklore, dresses the pig in his mother's finest outfit and sends it off to church. The many Spanish words are translated in context, though you may want to brush up on your pronunciation before reading aloud. Your children can pick up some more Spanish vocabulary with Arthur Dorros's *Abuela*. Other Puerto Rican folktales include Pura Belpré's *Oté* and Laura Simms's *The Squeaky Door*. For another gussied-up pig, see Brock Cole's *Nothing but a Pig*. FOLKLORE–PUERTO RICO. FOOLS–FOLKLORE. MULTICULTURAL STORIES–FOLKLORE. PIGS–FOLKLORE. SPANISH LANGUAGE.

999   Polette, Nancy. *The Little Old Woman and the Hungry Cat*. Illus. by Frank Modell. Greenwillow, 1989. ISBN 0-688-08315-3

[Gr. Pre–2] The old woman's fat gray-and-white cat gobbles down 16 cupcakes and saunters down the road where he meets and slip, slop, slurps down a one-legged man, a squealing pig, a wedding procession, and, to top it off, the old woman herself. Jack Kent's *The Fat Cat* is another version of this Norwegian folktale, while in Virginia Haviland's "The Cat and the Parrot" from *Favorite Fairy Tales Told in India* (Little, Brown, 1973), it's the land crab's sharp claws that save the day. "Sody Saleratus" in both *Crocodile! Crocodile! Stories Told Around the*

World by Barbara Baumgartner and *Grandfather Tales* by Richard Chase, Paul Galdone's *The Greedy Old Fat Man*, Robert Leydenfrost's *The Snake That Sneezed*, and Jack Prelutsky's *The Terrible Tiger* are all "swallowing" stories. Stage this one for acting out. CATS–FOLKLORE. CREATIVE DRAMA–FOLKLORE. CUMULATIVE STORIES. FOLKLORE–DENMARK.

1000   Pollock, Penny. *The Turkey Girl: A Zuni Cinderella Story*. Illus. by Ed Young. Little, Brown, 1996. ISBN 0-316-71314-7

[Gr. 2–5] Wanting to attend the Dance of the Sacred Bird, the Turkey Girl is granted her wish by the turkeys she attends so faithfully, promising to return to them before Father Sun returns to his sacred place. In an ending that will surprise your children, she returns home late to discover the turkeys have abandoned her. Rafe Martin's Algonquian Indian *The Rough-Face Girl* and Robert D. San Souci's *Sootface: An Ojibwa Cinderella Story* are more traditional in their endings, which should provide rich grounds for discussion. Joanne Compton's Appalachian *Ashpet*, William H. Hooks's *Moss Gown* and Charlotte Huck's *Princess Furball* are European-based American variants, while *Sukey and the Mermaid* by Robert D. San Souci is African American. *Dragonfly's Tale* by Kristina Rodanas is another Zuni Indian legend. CINDERELLA STORIES. FAIRY TALES. FOLKLORE–INDIANS OF NORTH AMERICA. TURKEYS–FOLKLORE. ZUNI INDIANS–FOLKLORE.

1001   Renberg, Dalia Hardof. *King Solomon and the Bee*. Illus. by Ruth Heller. HarperCollins, 1994. ISBN 0-06-022902-0

[Gr. K–3] When a bee stings the wise Jewish king on the nose, the enraged ruler becomes amused when the repentant bee begs forgiveness. The bee suggests he may be able to repay the king one day, which he indeed does when the Queen of Sheba presents the king with a difficult puzzle to solve. Before revealing the ending, ask students to predict which of the flower bouquets is real. In Aesop's fable "The Lion and the Rat," the lion also gives the little guy a break and is in turn saved from a hunter's net, while tiny ants prove their worth in Bill Peet's *The Ant and the Elephant*. For another good King Solomon story, read "Bavsi's Feast" from *My Grandmother's Stories* by Adèle Geras. BEES–FOLKLORE. COOPERATION–FOLKLORE. FOLKLORE, JEWISH. HELPFULNESS–FOLKLORE. INSECTS–FOLKLORE. KINGS AND RULERS–FOLKLORE. SIZE–FOLKLORE.

1002   Rhee, Nami. *Magic Spring: A Korean Folktale*. Illus. by the author. Putnam, 1993. ISBN 0-399-22420-3

[Gr. K–3] Following a sweet-singing bluebird over the mountain, an old man discovers a spring that makes him young again, and shares the location with his wife and their greedy neighbor who drinks so much he becomes a baby. Discussion point: What do you think will happen to the baby now that he has the chance to live his life over again? Will he change in any way? In the Japanese folktale *Little Fingerling* by Monica Hughes and Laura Krauss Melmed's *The Rainbabies*, childless couples are rewarded with unusual offspring. BABIES–FOLKLORE. BIRDS–FOLKLORE. FOLKLORE–KOREA. HUSBANDS AND WIVES–FOLKLORE.

1003   Richard, Françoise. *On Cat Mountain*. Illus. by Anne Buguet. Putnam, 1994. ISBN 0-399-22608-7

[Gr. 2–5] In a village in Japan, orphan Sho, servant to a nasty woman who hates both children and cats, cares for a stray black cat she calls Secret until her mistress finds out and frightens it away. Sho journeys to Cat Mountain, from which no one has returned, and is reunited with Secret, now a girl with the face of a cat, who gives her a small bag that buys her freedom. As happens in the Slavic folktale *Little Sister and the Month Brothers* by Beatrice Schenk de Regniers, Russian *Baba Yaga and Vasilisa the Brave* by Marianna Mayer, and African American *The Talking Eggs* by Robert D. San Souci, when the greedy woman seeks riches for herself, she causes her own destruction. The young heroine in San Souci's folktale *The Samurai's Daughter* is also brave in the face of danger. In another unusual Japanese folktale, Alan Schroeder's *Lily and the Wooden Bowl*, the loyal heroine prevails over her spiteful employer. CATS–FOLKLORE. FOLKLORE–JAPAN. KINDNESS–FOLKLORE.

1004   Riggio, Anita. *Beware the Brindlebeast*. Illus. by the author. Boyds Mills, 1994. ISBN 1-56397-133-X

[Gr. K–3] On All Hallows Eve, old Birdie is walking home past the graveyard when she almost trips over a large black kettle that appears to be filled with gold pieces, but on closer inspection seems to be just a barrel of apples. Then it becomes a pumpkin that transforms itself into a hideous beast. Is Birdie scared? Not a bit. Compare her reaction to that of old Maggie in *Maggie Mab and the Bogey Beast*, another English variant by Valerie Scho Carey, and Miss Moody when she unstops the bottle in Brinton Turkle's *Do Not Open*. FEAR. FOLKLORE–ENGLAND. MONSTERS–FOLKLORE. TRANSFORMATIONS–FOLKLORE.

1005   Rodanas, Kristina. *Dragonfly's Tale*. Illus. by the author. Clarion, 1991. ISBN 0-395-57003-4

[Gr. K–3] The head chief's staging of a mock food battle in his Ashiwi pueblo village to celebrate an overabundant harvest alarms two visiting Corn Maidens, disguised as poor old women, and they bring famine to the wasteful tribe until two kind children appease them. Bring in various types of corn and corn products to examine and sample, from popping corn to blue corn chips. Relate old ways to new with Marcia Keegan's *Pueblo Boy: Growing Up in Two Worlds* (Cobblehill, 1991), a lively color photo essay about ten-year-old Timmy Roybal, a member of the San Ildefonso Pueblo near Santa Fe, which still carries on the day-long Green Corn Dance each year. Lily Toy Hong's Chinese *How the Ox Star Fell From Heaven*, Blia Xiong's Hmong Laotian folktale *Nine in One, Grr! Grr!*, and Mary-Joan Gerson's Nigerian *Why the Sky Is Far Away* are also satisfying pourquoi folktales about food and eating. FOLKLORE–INDIANS OF NORTH AMERICA. FOOD–FOLKLORE. INSECTS–FOLKLORE. POURQUOI TALES. PUEBLO INDIANS–FOLKLORE. ZUNI INDIANS–FOLKLORE.

1006   Roddy, Patricia. *Api and the Boy Stranger: A Village Creation Tale*. Illus. by Lynne Russell. Dial, 1994. ISBN 0-8037-1222-7

[Gr. K–2] In a story about their ancestors that parents of the Ivory Coast tell their children when they refuse to share their food, Api's mother is the only one who consents to feed a boy stranger when he wanders into their village on feast days, and he, in turn, advises the villagers to leave home. Though the neighbors scoff, Api and her parents heed his advice, and are the only ones saved when a nearby volcano erupts. As a cautionary tale about kindness and generosity, this legend should lead to a discussion on how we treat strangers, on how we deal with teasing, and the kinds of legacies we wish to leave behind. The many onomatopoeic sounds throughout the tale will involve your listeners, and you will find the story compelling to act out as creative drama. Another somber West African folktale, *The Village of Round and Square Houses* by Ann Grifalconi, is about a volcano. FOLKLORE–AFRICA. FOLKLORE–IVORY COAST. FOOD–FOLKLORE. GENEROSITY–FOLKLORE. MULTICULTURAL STORIES–FOLKLORE. SOUND EFFECTS–FOLKLORE. VOLCANOES–FOLKLORE.

1007   Rosen, Michael. *How the Giraffe Got Such a Long Neck . . . and Why Rhino Is So Grumpy.* Illus. by John Clementson. Dial, 1993. ISBN 0-8037-1621-4

[Gr. Pre–2] In this brightly colored East African pourquoi tale, during the time of drought, it was Man who gave Giraffe the magic herb to help him reach the high tree leaves, but Rhino arrived too late for his portion. *Whistling Thorn* by Helen Cowcher is a nonfiction picture book that explains how long ago on the African grasslands, rhinos and giraffes ate acacia bushes, which led to the acacia developing protective thorns. FOLKLORE–AFRICA, EAST. GIRAFFES–FOLKLORE. POURQOUI TALES. RHINOCEROS–FOLKLORE.

1008   Ross, Gayle. *How Turtle's Back Was Cracked: A Traditional Cherokee Tale.* Illus. by Murv Jacob. Dial, 1995. ISBN 0-8037-1729-6

[Gr. 1–4] Though it was really Possum who killed the persimmon-stealing wolf, Turtle takes the credit, and captures a tribute by cutting off the wolf's ears and fashioning them into wolf-ear spoons. Word gets back to the wolves who threaten to throw him in the fire to boil him up for turtle soup, or throw him in the river. Like Brer Rabbit and other tricksters, Turtle arranges to get tossed in the river, where he cracks his shell on a rock. Nigerian pourquoi tale *The Flying Tortoise* by Tololwa M. Mollel has another explanation for the sorry state of all turtle shells. Ross collected other enjoyable legends in *How Rabbit Tricked Otter and Other Cherokee Trickster Stories*. *The First Strawberries* is a Cherokee legend and pourquoi tale retold by Joseph Bruchac. CHEROKEE INDIANS–FOLKLORE. FOLKLORE–INDIANS OF NORTH AMERICA. POURQUOI TALES. TRICKSTER TALES. TURTLES–FOLKLORE. WOLVES–FOLKLORE.

1009   Rounds, Glen. *The Three Billy Goats Gruff.* Illus. by the author. Holiday House, 1993. ISBN 0-8234-1015-3

[Gr. Pre–2] With its giant typefaces and scraggly black-line-and-crayon illustrations, this version is so satisfying, though it tones down the original wording of the troll and biggest goat's final confrontation a bit. Compare illustration styles with the Marcia Brown and Paul Galdone versions, and bring in George Webbe Dasent's Norwegian Christmas folktale *The Cat on the Dovrefell* and Ingri and

Edgar Parin d'Aulaire's *D'Aulaire's Trolls*. Picture book stories with outwitted trolls include Jan Brett's *Trouble with Trolls*, Edward Marshall's *Troll Country*, and Don Arthur Torgersen's *The Girl Who Tricked the Troll*. Another entertaining and famous Norwegian folktale is P. C. Asbjørnsen's *The Runaway Pancake*, with another version, *The Pancake Boy*, retold by Lorinda Bryan Cauley. The kids also come out ahead in Jacob Grimm's *Nanny Goat and the Seven Little Kids*, as retold by Eric A. Kimmel. FOLKLORE–NORWAY. GOATS–FOLKLORE. TROLLS–FOLKLORE.

1010   Rounds, Glen. *Three Little Pigs and the Big Bad Wolf.* Illus. by the author. Holiday House, 1992. ISBN 0-8234-0923-6

[Gr. Pre–2] While this version is missing the second of the three wolf-planned encounters—the apple tree scene—the rest of the tale is so mischievously told and illustrated that you won't mind. See if children notice the omission when you read one or more of the other wonderful versions of this tale, from those by Lorinda Bryan Cauley, Paul Galdone, James Marshall, and Margot Zemach, to variants like William H. Hooks's *The Three Little Pigs and the Fox* or parodies like Jon Scieszka's *The True Story of the 3 Little Pigs*. CREATIVE DRAMA–FOLKLORE. PIGS–FOLKLORE. WOLVES–FOLKLORE.

1011   San Souci, Robert D. *The Boy and the Ghost.* Illus. by J. Brian Pinkney. Simon & Schuster, 1989. ISBN 0-671-67176-6

[Gr. 1–4] Thomas, a poor African American boy from the South, sets out with his croaker-sack to make some money for his family, and encounters a stranger who tells him of a nearby haunted house whose treasure the boy can keep if he can manage to stay there from sunset to sunrise. As in Spanish folktale *Esteban and the Ghost* by Sibyl Hancock, first the legs, then the arms, body, and head of the ghost drop down from the chimney and try but fail to scare the courageous boy. San Souci's *The Talking Eggs* and *The Man Who Tricked a Ghost* by Laurence Yep both contain related motifs. From the opposite track, meet a timid boy who conquers his fears in the Egyptian folktale *The Monster That Grew Small* by Joan Grant. BURIED TREASURE–FOLKLORE. COURAGE–FOLKLORE. FOLKLORE, AFRICAN AMERICAN. GHOST STORIES. HAUNTED HOUSES–FOLKLORE.

1012   San Souci, Robert D. *The Firebird.* Illus. by Kris Waldherr. Dial, 1992. ISBN 0-8037-0800-9

[Gr. 3–5] In return for her freedom, the captured Firebird grants Prince Ivan a feather and the promise of her help, which he uses to save Princess Elena from the clutches of the wizard Kastchei. In another tale, *Prince Ivan and the Firebird* by Laszlo Gal, the prince sets out to discover who is stealing the golden apples from his father's tree and encounters the fabled bird. In both *The Firebird* by Demi and *The Firebird* by Selina Hastings, a young man risks death to bring back to his king or tsar first the Firebird and then the Princess Vasilissa. ANIMALS, MYTHICAL–FOLKLORE. BIRDS–FOLKLORE. FAIRY TALES. FOLKLORE–RUSSIA. PRINCES AND PRINCESSES–FOLKLORE.

1013   San Souci, Robert D. *The Hobyahs*. Illus. by Alexi Natchev. Doubleday, 1994. ISBN 0-385-30934-1

[Gr. K–2] In this retelling and reworking of a spooky old English tale, the old man chases all five of his dogs into the woods when they disturb his sleep, not realizing that they are protecting the house from the goblins who want to "tear down the hempstalks, eat up the old man and woman, and carry off the little girl!" Less ghoulish than the original Joseph Jacobs tale, which Simon Stern also put out as *The Hobyas: An Old Story*, this one's still plenty titillating, and children will relish chanting the Hobyahs' refrain. For kids old enough to handle the chills, search out the common motifs in Joanna Galdone's American folktale *The Tailypo: A Ghost Story*. CHANTABLE REFRAIN. DOGS–FOLKLORE. FOLKLORE–ENGLAND. GOBLINS–FOLKLORE.

1014   San Souci, Robert D. *The Samurai's Daughter*. Illus. by Stephen T. Johnson. Dial, 1992. ISBN 0-8037-1136-0

[Gr. 3–6] Tokoyo proves herself as brave and loyal as any boy, not only by diving for shellfish with the *amas* or women divers, but by following her samurai father into exile and killing the snakelike sea serpent that is the cause of his banishment. Introduce other strong and assertive females from Japanese folklore in *On Cat Mountain* by Françoise Richard and *Three Strong Women* by Claus Stamm, and from Russian folklore in *Baba Yaga and Vasilisa the Brave* by Marianna Mayer and *Alexandra the Rock-Eater* by Dorothy Van Woerkom. FOLKLORE–JAPAN. LOYALTY–FOLKLORE. MONSTERS–FOLKLORE. OCEAN–FOLKLORE.

1015   San Souci, Robert D. *The Snow Wife*. Illus. by Stephen T. Johnson. Dial, 1993. ISBN 0-8037-1410-6

[Gr. 3–5] Meeting up with the beautiful but chilling Woman of the Snow when she takes the life of an old woodcutter one terrible winter night, apprentice Minokichi promises never to speak a word about her. As in Diane Wolkstein's *White Wave* and Sumiko Yagawa's *The Crane Wife*, he breaks his promise, and loses the wife he loves by forgetting that vow. Then, as in George Webbe Dasent's *East o' the Sun and West o' the Moon*, he faces fearsome odds to ask her forgiveness. FOLKLORE–JAPAN. HUSBANDS AND WIVES–FOLKLORE. SNOW–FOLKLORE. TRANSFORMATIONS–FOLKLORE.

1016   San Souci, Robert D. *Sootface: An Ojibwa Cinderella Story*. Illus. by Daniel San Souci. Doubleday, 1994. ISBN 0-385-31202-4

[Gr. 1–5] Forced to do all the work and tend the fire, poor Sootface must make do with scraps of skins for her dresses and her father's worn-out moccasins for shoes, but though the young men of the village laugh at her, only she passes the test of the invisible warrior. As in Rafe Martin's Algonquian Indian *The Rough-Face Girl*, Sootface sees that his bow is made of the rainbow and is strung with the Milky Way. Penny Pollock's *The Turkey Girl: A Zuni Cinderella Story* is a more poignant Cinderella variant. Other American variants of this universal fairy tale include San Souci's African American *Sukey and the Mermaid*, Joanne Compton's Appalachian *Ashpet*, William H. Hooks's *Moss Gown*, and Charlotte Huck's *Princess Furball*. ALGONQUIN INDIANS–FOLKLORE. CINDERELLA STORIES. FAIRY TALES. FOLKLORE–INDIANS OF NORTH AMERICA. INVISIBILITY–FOLKLORE.

1017   San Souci, Robert D. *Sukey and the Mermaid*. Illus. by Brian Pinkney. Four Winds, 1992. ISBN 0-02-778141-0

[Gr. 2–5] On a little island off the coast of South Carolina, a young hardworking girl who lives with her mother and harsh new stepfather, sings a song and summons up a "beautiful, brown-skinned, black-eyed mermaid" who gives her gold pieces and helps her triumph over the murderous stepfather, Mr. Jones. Illustrated with bold scratchboard and oil pastels, this compelling African American folktale can be linked with other U.S. "Cinderella" variants such as Joanne Compton's *Ashpet*, William Hooks's *Moss Gown*, Charlotte Huck's *Princess Furball*, Rafe Martin's *The Rough-Face Girl*, Penny Pollock's *The Turkey Girl: A Zuni Cinderella Story*, and San Souci's *Sootface: An Ojibwa Cinderella Story*. *Mermaid Tales from Around the World* by Mary Pope Osborne contains 12 more fish-wise stories. FAIRY TALES. FOLKLORE, AFRICAN AMERICAN. MERMAIDS–FOLKLORE. OCEAN–FOLKLORE. SEASHORE–FOLKLORE. STORIES WITH SONGS.

1018   San Souci, Robert D. *The Tsar's Promise*. Illus. by Lauren Mills. Philomel, 1992. ISBN 0-399-21581-6

[Gr. 3–6] In a Russian variant of the "Rumpelstiltskin" story, Ivan outwits the demon to whom he was unwittingly promised as a baby by Ivan's father, Tsar Kojata, and it's all thanks to Maria, a kidnapped princess with whom Ivan escapes. See how the stories intersect by comparing this one with Jacob Grimm's *Rumpelstiltskin* as retold by Alison Sage or Paul O. Zelinsky. Also in the tradition of grandly romantic Russian fairy tales are *The Firebird* by Demi, *Prince Ivan and the Firebird* by Laslo Gal, *I-Know-Not-What, I-Know-Not-Where* by Eric A. Kimmel, *Baba Yaga and Vasilisa the Brave* by Marianna Mayer, *The Fool of the World and His Flying Ship* by Arthur Ransome, and Elizabeth Winthrop's *Vasilissa the Beautiful*. FAIRY TALES. FOLKLORE–RUSSIA. MONSTERS–FOLKLORE. PRINCES AND PRINCESSES–FOLKLORE. TRANSFORMATIONS–FOLKLORE.

1019   San Souci, Robert D. *The White Cat: An Old French Fairy Tale*. Illus. by Gennady Spirin. Orchard, 1990. ISBN 0-531-08409-4

[Gr. 2–5] In search of the prettiest dog to give his father the king, the youngest of three princes finds the ravishing White Cat who helps him win the kingdom. Other quest folktales with enchanted royalty include versions of George Webbe Dasent's Norwegian tale *East o' the Sun and West o' the Moon* by Gillian Barlow, Kathleen and Michael Hague, and P. J. Lynch. Then there's Jacob Grimm's *The Frog Prince*, Elizabeth Isele's and J. Patrick Lewis's *The Frog Princess*, Eric A. Kimmel's *Three Sacks of Truth*, Jane Langton's *The Hedgehog Boy*, and, of course, the French fairy tale *Beauty and the Beast*, retold by Marianna Mayer. CATS–FOLK-LORE. FAIRY TALES. FOLKLORE–FRANCE. PRINCES AND PRINCESSES–FOLKLORE. TRANSFOR-MATIONS–FOLKLORE.

1020   Sawyer, Ruth. *The Remarkable Christmas of the Cobbler's Sons.* Illus. by Barbara Cooney. Viking, 1994. ISBN 0-670-84922-7

[Gr. K–3] In a story about goblin King Laurin that mothers tell their children in the Tirol, a poor cobbler must leave his three hungry sons on Christmas Eve to mend the boots of the soldiers. Against their father's instructions, the boys open the door for a bad-tempered little man who hogs the bed but rewards them with a Christmas feast. Ask listeners to describe how their feelings for the little man changed as the story progressed and why. A carpenter trades places with Santa for the night in *Christmas Eve at Santa's*, a charming Swedish story by Alf Prøysen. BROTHERS–FOLKLORE. CHRISTMAS–FOLKLORE. FOLKLORE–AUSTRIA. GOBLINS–FOLKLORE.

1021   Schroeder, Alan. *Lily and the Wooden Bowl.* Illus. by Yoriko Ito. Doubleday, 1994. ISBN 0-385-30792-5

[Gr. 1–4] On her deathbed, Aya bequeaths to her granddaughter a rice paddle and a folded paper crane, requesting that Lily always wear a large lacquered bowl on her head to hide her beauty from the world and protect her from harm. Working as a servant for a wealthy but jealous woman, Lily falls in love with the woman's son who asks her to marry him, much to his mother's fury. In this compelling and visually lovely Japanese folktale, children will discern elements common to Jacob Grimm's *Rumpelstiltskin*, as retold by Barbara Rogasky, Alison Sage, or Paul O. Zelinsky, and its Russian variant *The Tsar's Promise* by Robert D. San Souci. The wooden spoon Lily uses to turn one grain of rice into a wedding feast is reminiscent of the wicked Oni's magic paddle in *The Funny Little Woman* by Arlene Mosel. *On Cat Mountain*, a Japanese folktale by Françoise Richard, introduces a more assertive heroine who also suffers under an unpleasant employer. FOLKLORE–JAPAN. LOVE–FOLKLORE.

1022   Shannon, Mark. *Gawain and the Green Knight.* Illus. by David Shannon. Putnam, 1994. ISBN 0-399-22446-7

[Gr. 3–6] The youngest and most inexperienced of King Arthur's knights, Gawain accepts the challenge of a strange and fearsome giant knight and cuts off his head with an axe. Undaunted, the red-eyed giant, known as the Knight of the Green Chapel, merely picks up his head and departs. In a year and a day Gawain must undergo a similar test, and his true love Caryn gives him her sash as a good luck keepsake. Wonderfully eerie, this Knights of the Round Table legend is a graphic reminder of the value of loyalty. Compare Selena Hasting's version of the same tale (Lothrop, 1981), and read her *Sir Gawain and the Loathly Lady*, plus *Saint George and the Dragon* by Margaret Hodges. FOLKLORE–ENGLAND. KNIGHTS AND KNIGHTHOOD–FOLKLORE.

1023 Shepard, Aaron. *The Legend of Slappy Hooper: An American Tall Tale*. Illus. by Toni Goffe. Scribner, 1993. ISBN 0-684-19535-6

[Gr. 1–3] Tall-tale hero Slappy Hooper, "the world's biggest, fastest, bestest sign painter," at seven feet tall and 300 pounds, paints pictures so true to life they actually come to life, much to the dismay of local folk who don't appreciate getting sunburned from one of his sunny billboards. Then the Boss from the Heavenly Sign Company commissions him to paint rainbows and even sunrises and sunsets. In Jon Agee's *The Incredible Painting of Felix Clousseau*, the paintings also come to life. Tedd Arnold's *The Signmaker's Assistant* and Roger Roth's *The Sign Painter's Dream* will get you started reading and making signs. Work some tall tales into your weather unit with Judi and Ron Barrett's *Cloudy with a Chance of Meatballs*, Shirley Climo's folktale from Borneo *The Match Between the Winds*, Pat Cummings's *C.L.O.U.D.S.*, Jo Harper's *Jalapeño Hal*, Michael O. Tunnell's *Chinook*, and Laurence Yep's Chinese folktale *The Junior Thunder Lord*. FOLKLORE–U.S. PAINTING–FOLKLORE. RAINBOWS–FOLKLORE. SIGNS AND SIGNBOARDS–FOLK-LORE. SKY–FOLKLORE. TALL TALES.

1024 Shetterly, Susan Hand. *Raven's Light: A Myth from the People of the Northwest Coast*. Illus. by Robert Shetterly. Atheneum, 1991. ISBN 0-689-31629-1

[Gr. 2–5] Raven, the Pacific Northwest Indian trickster and magical being, creates the earth with a stone that slips from his beak, and becomes a child born to the daughter of the Great Chief in order to be able to take day from its round basket and give it to the rest of the people, who have known only darkness. Ann Dixon's *How Raven Brought Light to People* and Gerald McDermott's *Raven* are simpler retellings of the same story. *The Woman Who Fell from the Sky: The Iroquois Story of Creation* by John Bierhorst, *Children of the Morning Light: Wampanoag Tales* told by Manitonquat (Medicine Story), and *Moon Mother: A Native American Creation Tale* by Ed Young also explain how the earth came to be. BIRDS–FOLKLORE. CREATION–FOLKLORE. FOLKLORE–INDIANS OF NORTH AMERICA. RAVENS–FOLKLORE. SUN–FOLKLORE.

1025 Sierra, Judy *The Elephant's Wrestling Match*. Illus. by Brian Pinkney. Dutton, 1992. ISBN 0-525-67366-0

[Gr. Pre–2] Convinced of his great strength, a mighty elephant challenges all the animals to a wrestling match, and monkey beats on his talking drum as leopard, crocodile, and rhinoceros all fall. In this folktale from Cameroon, it's a tiny bat who flies into elephant's ear and brings him to his knees. Demystify the misunderstood bat with folktales Joseph Bruchac's Native American *The Great Ball Game*, Paul Goble's Native American *Iktomi and the Boulder*, Tololwa M. Mollel's *A Promise to the Sun: An African Story*, Katy Hall and Lisa Eisenberg's *Batty Riddles*, Janell Cannon's picture book *Stellaluna*, and Barbara Bash's factual *Shadows of Night: The Hidden World of the Little Brown Bat*. For more mismatched competitions, read Verna Aardema's *Princess Gorilla and a New Kind of Water* and Mwenye Hadithi's *Crafty Chameleon*. ANIMALS–FOLKLORE. BATS–FOLKLORE. ELE-PHANTS–FOLKLORE. FOLKLORE–AFRICA. FOLKLORE–CAMEROON.

1026   Simms, Laura. *The Squeaky Door.* Illus. by Sylvie Wickstrom. Crown, 1991. ISBN 0-517-57583-3

[Gr. Pre–2] Every night at bedtime when his grandmother turns out the light and closes the squeaky door to his room, a little boy gets scared, jumps under the bed and starts to cry, even with the addition of first a cat in his bed, then a dog, a snake, a pig, and finally, a horse. Your listeners will naturally join in on all the chantable refrains and animal wailings in this endearing Puerto Rican folktale, and will be able to retell and act out the entire story in sequence with very little prompting. Keep the volume up with "The Squeaky Old Bed" from Barbara Baumgartner's folktale collection *Crocodile! Crocodile!*, *Nathaniel Willy, Scared Silly*, an American variant by Judith Mathews and Fay Robinson, plus Joanna Cole's *It's Too Noisy*, Ann McGovern's *Too Much Noise*, or Margot Zemach's *It Could Always Be Worse*. If you're still feeling dramatic, don't forget everyone's favorite scary pumpkin story *The Little Old Lady Who Was Not Afraid of Anything* by Linda Williams. ANIMALS–FOLKLORE. BEDTIME–FOLKLORE. FOLKLORE–PUERTO RICO. SEQUENCE STORIES. SOUND EFFECTS–FOLKLORE.

1027   Sloat, Teri. *The Hungry Giant of the Tundra.* Illus. by Robert and Teri Sloat. Dutton, 1993. ISBN 0-525-45126-9

[Gr. K–2] Hungry for his evening meal, the giant A·ka·gua·gan·kak strides across the tundra, scoops up the village children playing there, and drops them into his trouser bag. A strong-beaked chickadee and crane-with-the-long-legs help them to escape in this dramatic Yupik tale from Alaska. Find out more about the lives of the Eskimos in Virginia Kroll's *The Seasons and Someone*. More giants get theirs in Kenn and Joanne Compton's Appalachian folktale *Jack the Giant Chaser*, and versions of *Jack and the Beanstalk* by Lorinda Bryan Cauley, Alan Garner, John Howe, and Susan Pearson. Children defeat other larger-than-life giants in *Harry and the Terrible Whatzit* by Dick Gackenbach and *Abiyoyo* by Pete Seeger. Counter the scary giants with the more benign ones from John F. Green's *Alice and the Birthday Giant*, or Tomie dePaola's folktales *Fin M'Coul, the Giant of Knockmany Hill* and *The Mysterious Giant of Barletta*. FOLKLORE–ALASKA. FOLKLORE, ESKIMO. FOLKLORE–INDIANS OF NORTH AMERICA. GIANTS–FOLKLORE.

1028   Small, Terry. *The Legend of William Tell.* Illus. by the author. Bantam, 1991. ISBN 0-553-07031-2

[Gr. 3–5] By the shores of Lake Lucerne, tyrant Gessler the Black orders all who pass the town square to kneel to his cap, placed upon a pole, and William Tell incurs his fury when he refuses. The dramatic epic poem is accompanied with large, ornate paintings, and makes an interesting contrast to the equally handsome *William Tell* by Margaret Early. Narrative poems about other heroes include *Sir Frances Drake: His Daring Deeds* by Roy Gerrard and *Paul Revere's Ride* by Henry Wadsworth Longfellow. FOLKLORE–SWITZERLAND. FRUIT–FOLKLORE. NARRATIVE POETRY. STORIES IN RHYME. TELL, WILLIAM.

1029   Stevens, Janet. *Coyote Steals the Blanket: A Ute Tale.* Illus. by the author. Holiday House, 1993. ISBN 0-8234-0996-1

[Gr. Pre–3] Though Hummingbird warns him of the danger, Coyote defies her by running off with one of the blankets he finds draped over rocks in the middle of the desert, and now the rock is rumbling after him. Paul Goble's variant, *Iktomi and the Boulder*, also explains why bats have flat noses. Uncover more coyote nonsense in Verna Aardema's *Borreguita and the Coyote*, Shonto Begay's *Ma'ii and Cousin Horned Toad*, Tony Johnston's *The Story of Rabbit and Coyote*, Jonathan London and Lanny Pinola's *Fire Race*, Gretchen Will Mayo's *That Tricky Coyote!*, Gerald McDermott's *Coyote*, Phyllis Root's *Coyote and the Magic Words*, and Harriet Peck Taylor's *Coyote Places the Stars*. Then compare American tricksters with their African counterparts in Verna Aardema's *Rabbit Makes a Monkey Out of Lion*, Eric A. Kimmel's *Anansi and the Moss-Covered Rock* and *Anansi Goes Fishing*, Barbara Knutson's *Sungura and Leopard*, and Gerald McDermott's *Zomo the Rabbit*. COYOTES–FOLKLORE. FOLKLORE–INDIANS OF NORTH AMERICA. HUMMINGBIRDS–FOLKLORE. ROCKS–FOLKLORE. TRICKSTER TALES. UTE INDIANS–FOLKLORE.

1030   **Stevens, Janet. *Tops & Bottoms*. Illus. by the author. Harcourt, 1995. ISBN 0-15-292851-0**

[Gr. Pre–2] A lazy bear who has inherited land and money wishes only to sleep, and when the poor but enterprising hungry hare down the road proposes to plant and harvest crops on Bear's land and split the profit down the middle, it seems too good a deal to pass up. Bear chooses the top half of the crops as his payment, but when Hare harvests the beets and carrots, keeping the succulent roots, Bear demands the bottom half of the next planting. The huge watercolor-and-pencil illustrations are made even more fun by the book's unusual format: it opens up from bottom to top, and the whole story is printed sideways on double-page spreads. In Leslie Conger's *Tops and Bottoms*, it's a farmer who outsmarts a devil in much the same way, while in *Anansi Goes Fishing* by Eric A. Kimmel, Anansi agrees to do all the work while Turtle gets tired. BEARS–FOLKLORE. FARM LIFE–FOLKLORE. FOLKLORE–AFRICAN AMERICAN. GARDENING–FOLKLORE. HARES–FOLKLORE. VEGETABLES–FOLKLORE.

1031   **Stewig, John Warren. *Stone Soup*. Illus. by Margot Tomes. Holiday House, 1991. ISBN 0-8234-0863-9**

[Gr. K–3] On the road to see what she can see, hungry Grethel takes refuge in a village where the stingy villagers claim to have no extra food for her until she contrives to make soup from a stone. Folktale variants include *Stone Soup* by both Marcia Brown and Ann McGovern and *Nail Soup* by Margot Zemach, while Hanukkah story *Potato Pancakes All Around* by Marilyn Hirsch and *Burgoo Stew* by Susan Patron use the same motif of making something from nothing. With its large cast of villagers, each with a different excuse for having no victuals to spare, this is an ideal story to act out as a class. If each person brings in one ingredient, you can cook your own soup and see that too many cooks don't necessarily have to spoil the broth. CREATIVE DRAMA–FOLKLORE. FOLKLORE–FRANCE. FOOD–FOLKLORE. SOUP–FOLKLORE.

1032   **Tanaka, Béatrice. *The Chase: A Kutenai Indian Tale*. Illus. by Michel Gay. Crown, 1991. ISBN 0-517-58624-X**

[Gr. Pre–K] Seeing Rabbit race past, Coyote assumes hunters must be after him, so he runs too, followed by Moose who thinks the river must be flooding, Wolf who figures the forest must be on fire, and Bear, who finally asks why everyone is running. Turns out Rabbit was late for dinner. Children can act this out with invented dialogue, running in place instead of actually chasing each other. In *Foolish Rabbit's Big Mistake* by Rafe Martin and *Why Mosquitoes Buzz in People's Ears* by Verna Aardema, the animals follow each other blindly without knowing why; *One Cow Moo Moo!* by David Bennett, *That's Good! That's Bad!* by Margery Cuyler, and *Look Out, Bird!* by Marilyn Janovitz all demonstrate chain reactions. ANIMALS–FOLKLORE. FOLKLORE–INDIANS OF NORTH AMERICA. RABBITS–FOLKLORE.

1033   Taylor, Harriet Peck. *Coyote Places the Stars.* Illus. by the author. Bradbury, 1993. ISBN 0-02-788845-2

[Gr. 1–3] Eager to climb to the heavens and discover its secrets, Coyote climbs a ladder of arrows to the moon and, shooting his arrows into the sky, finds he can move the stars around to create new sky pictures. Compare this Wasco Indian folktale with colorful batik illustrations to Lois Ehlert's bilingual Peruvian folktale *Moon Rope*, and stay starbound with Paul Goble's Cheyenne folktale *Her Seven Brothers* and Kit Wright's *Tigerella*. If you're working on an astronomy unit, have your children create new constellations, name them, and describe them. Expand on Coyote as a trickster character with Verna Aardema's *Borreguita and the Coyote*, Shonto Begay's *Ma'ii and Cousin Horned Toad*, Tony Johnston's *The Story of Rabbit and Coyote*, Jonathan London and Lanny Pinola's *Fire Race*, Gerald McDermott's *Coyote*, Phyllis Root's *Coyote and the Magic Words*, and Janet Stevens's *Coyote Steals the Blanket*. CONSTELLATIONS–FOLKLORE. COYOTES–FOLKLORE. FOLKLORE–INDIANS OF NORTH AMERICA. STARS–FOLKLORE. WASCO INDIANS–FOLKLORE.

1034   Temple, Frances. *Tiger Soup: An Anansi Story from Jamaica.* Illus. by the author. Orchard, 1994. ISBN 0-531-08709-3

[Gr. Pre–2] Tiger's sweet soup boasts coconut, mango, and even a touch of nutmeg, so when spider Anansi offers to go with Tiger to Blue Hole and teach him how to swim while the hot soup cools, all the while Anansi is scheming to drink the soup himself. On the back of the dust jacket, a Reader's Theater script of the story is printed, so make copies and stage a reading. Anansi the Spider stories originated in Africa, including such delightful retellings as Verna Aardema's *Anansi Finds a Fool*, Gail E. Haley's *a Story, A Story*, Eric A. Kimmel's *Anansi and the Moss-Covered Rock*, *Anansi Goes Fishing*, and *Anansi and the Talking Melon*, Eric Maddern's *The Fire Children*, and Gerald McDermott's *Anansi the Spider*. FOLKLORE–JAMAICA. MONKEYS–FOLKLORE. POURQUOI TALES. READER'S THEATER. SOUP–FOLKLORE. TIGERS–FOLKLORE. TRICKSTER TALES.

1035   Thomson, Peggy. *The Brave Little Tailor.* Illus. by James Warhola. Simon & Schuster, 1992. ISBN 0-671-73736-8

[Gr. 1–4] So pleased at killing seven flies with one swat, the little tailor sews himself a vest with the words "SEVEN AT ONE BLOW" embroidered across the back and sets out to seek his fortune. Encountering a giant, the tailor proves an ample match, using his wits to the giant's brawn. As in Joanne and Kenn Compton's Appalachian *Jack the Giant Chaser*, Jacob Grimm's *The Valiant Little Tailor* illustrated by Victor Ambrus, Christine Price's Turkish *Sixty at a Blow* (Dutton, 1968), and Dorothy Van Woerkom's Russian *Alexandra the Rock-Eater*, the giant loses. For dealing with giants, Richard Chase's classic collection *The Jack Tales*, Gail E. Haley's *Jack and the Bean Tree*, and James Still's *Jack and the Bean Tree* are Jack stories from the United States, relatives of all those English versions including those by Lorinda Bryan Cauley, Alan Garner, John Howe, and Susan Pearson, and Paul Galdone's *The History of Mother Twaddle and the Marvelous Achievements of Her Son, Jack*. FOLKLORE–GERMANY. GIANTS–FOLKLORE. KINGS AND RULERS–FOLKLORE. PRINCES AND PRINCESSES–FOLKLORE. TAILORS–FOLKLORE. UNICORNS–FOLKLORE.

1036   Tompert, Ann. *Bamboo Hats and a Rice Cake: A Tale Adapted from Japanese Folklore.* Illus. by Demi. Crown, 1993. ISBN 0-517-59273-8

[Gr. K–3] A childless old couple decide to sell the wife's treasured wedding kimono to buy rice cakes to celebrate the New Year so fortune will smile on them, but the husband instead trades it for fans, a gold bell, and finally five bamboo hats, which he gives to the six snow-covered statues of Jizo, protector of children. As in Japanese folktale *The Magic Purse* by Yoshiko Uchida, he is rewarded for his goodness. Throughout the text, Japanese calligraphy is used in place of key words, and children will enjoy deciphering the words using the key on the side of each page. After a few pages, you'll be proud to find yourself recognizing the characters for rice cake, kimono, and the rest. FOLKLORE–JAPAN. HATS–FOLKLORE. JAPANESE LANGUAGE. KINDNESS–FOLKLORE. NEW YEAR–FOLKLORE.

1037   Uchida, Yoshiko. *The Magic Purse.* Illus. by Keiko Narahashi. McElderry, 1993. ISBN 0-689-50559-0

[Gr. 1–4] Lost on his way to visit a shrine, a poor young farmer meets a beautiful, sad young girl by the edge of the terrible Black Swamp and agrees to take a letter to her who live by the Red Swamp, from which no one comes out alive. Because of his kind heart and courage, the farmer not only survives but is rewarded for his good deed, as are the main characters in Norwegian folktale *Boots and His Brothers* by Eric A. Kimmel, Ivory Coast folktale *Api and the Boy Stranger* by Patricia Roddy, and Japanese tale *Bamboo Hats and a Rice Cake* by Ann Tompert. COURAGE–FOLKLORE. FOLKLORE–JAPAN. KINDNESS–FOLKLORE. MONEY–FOLKLORE.

1038   Uchida, Yoshiko. *The Wise Old Woman.* Illus. by Martin Springett. McElderry, 1994. ISBN 0-689-50582-5

[Gr. 1–5] "Anyone over 70 is no longer useful," decrees a cruel young lord, and a young farmer defies him, choosing to secret his mother in a cave he digs beneath the kitchen. When a neighboring lord sets out to conquer the village, it is the farmer's mother who solves his three impossible tasks, saves the village, and humbles the young lord into rescinding his ruling. *Three Strong Women* by Claus Stamm is another Japanese folktale that shows respect and admiration for older women. In *Dragonfly's Tale*, a Zuni Indian legend retold by Kristina Rodanas, the two elderly Corn Maidens punish the inhabitants of a wasteful village and help bring them back to their senses. ELDERLY–FOLKLORE. FOLKLORE–JAPAN. MOTHERS AND SONS–FOLKLORE. WISDOM–FOLKLORE.

1039   Van Laan, Nancy. *Buffalo Dance: A Blackfoot Legend.* **Illus. by Beatriz Vidal. Little, Brown, 1993. ISBN 0-316-89728-0**

[Gr. 3–6] Desperate for her village to find food, a young woman rashly promises to marry a buffalo if the rest of the herd will jump over the cliff into the *piscun*, a trap for catching them. Impressed with the woman's powers and kindness when she brings her father back to life, the buffalo chief teaches her the buffalo song and dance to be performed before and after the killing of a buffalo. Aside from the lovely, expressive paintings, the story is also retold in simple pictograph drawings at the bottom of each page of text, which you can photocopy and distribute for children to interpret, arrange in sequence, and use to retell the story. Olaf Baker's *Where the Buffaloes Begin,* and Paul Goble's *Buffalo Woman, Crow Chief,* and *Her Seven Brothers* are additional powerful Plains Indian legends. *Buffalo Hunt* by Russell Freedman describes how the Plains Indians killed and used the buffalo. BLACKFOOT INDIANS–FOLKLORE. BUFFALOES–FOLKLORE. FATHERS AND DAUGHTERS–FOLKLORE. FOLKLORE–INDIANS OF NORTH AMERICA.

1040   Van Laan, Nancy. *The Tiny, Tiny Boy and the Big, Big Cow: A Scottish Folk Tale.* **Illus. by Marjorie Priceman. Knopf, 1993. ISBN 0-679-92078-1**

[Gr. Pre–K] The tiny, tiny boy's mother advises him to shake a fat, fat stick at their recalcitrant cow, to tempt it with a golden gown of silk, and even offer it a cup of tea, but it won't stand still to be milked until they use reverse psychology and order it not to stand still. The cumulative, chantable format is reminiscent of Paul Galdone's *The Old Woman and Her Pig,* and just dandy to group with Chris Babcock's *No Moon, No Milk,* Jennifer A. Ericsson's *No Milk!,* Paul Brett Johnson's *The Cow Who Wouldn't Come Down,* and David Kirby and Allen Woodman's *The Cows Are Going to Paris.* CHANTABLE REFRAIN–FOLKLORE. COWS–FOLKLORE. MILK–FOLKLORE.

1041   Waldherr, Kris. *Persephone and the Pomegranate: A Myth from Greece.* **Illus. by the author. Dial, 1993. ISBN 0-8037-1192-1**

[Gr. 2–6] When Demeter's daughter is kidnapped by Pluto, lord of the underworld, the anguished goddess of the harvests will not rest until she can rescue her child. Penelope Proddow's *Demeter and Persephone* is a classic retelling to compare, along with the versions in Mary Pope Osborne's *Favorite Greek Myths* and *Realms of Gold: Myths & Legends from Around the World* by Ann Pilling. *Cyclops* by Leonard Everett Fisher is another picture book version of a Greek myth, but only if you can stomach the disquieting and violent aspects of the story. Fisher's *Theseus and the Minotaur* and *Wings* by Jane Yolen are companion myths about Ariadne, Theseus, and Daedalus. Aliki's *The Twelve Months,* Beatrice Schenk de Regniers's *Little Sister and the Month Brothers,* Charles Larry's *Peboan and Seegwun,* and Samuel Marshak's *The Month Brothers* are all folktales that explain or describe the seasons. FRUIT–FOLKLORE. MYTHOLOGY. POURQUOI TALES. SEASONS–FOLKLORE.

1042   Wegman, William. *Cinderella*. Photos by the author. Hyperion, 1993. ISBN 1-56282-349-3

[Gr. 1–4] Photographer Wegman has staged an unusual interpretation of the classic fairy tale, told in flowery great detail, using his photogenic weimaraners in all the roles. The juxtaposition of the traditional story with brooding color photographs of costumed, bewigged dogs is jarring but diverting. Read this as a bridge between the traditional tale and more jovial retellings like Joanne Compton's *Ashpet* and Barbara Karlin's *Cinderella* and parodies like Babette Cole's *Prince Cinders*, Ellen Jackson's *Cinder Edna*, Frances Minters's *Cinder-Elly*, and Bernice Myers's *Sidney Rella and the Glass Sneaker*. CINDERELLA STORIES. DOGS–FOLKLORE. FAIRY TALES. PARODIES. PRINCES AND PRINCESSES–FOLKLORE.

1043   Wilson, Barbara Ker. *Wishbones: A Folk Tale from China*. Illus. by Meilo So. Bradbury, 1993. ISBN 0-02-793125-0

[Gr. 2–4] Yeh Hsien's stepmother forces her to draw water from a far-off mountain pool where the young girl catches and befriends a magic fish. In this Cinderella story, the bones of the fish grant the girl's wish to go to the Cave Festival shod in violet silken slippers. Ai-Ling Louie's *Yeh-Shen* is another version. Just look at the multicultural array of Cinderella stories: Shirley Climo's *The Egyptian Cinderella* and *The Korean Cinderella*, American versions including Joanne Compton's Appalachian *Ashpet*, William H. Hooks's *Moss Gown*, Charlotte Huck's *Princess Furball*, and Robert D. San Souci's African American *Sukey and the Mermaid*, Dang Manh Kha's Vietnamese *In the Land of Small Dragon*, Rafe Martin's Algonquian Indian *The Rough-Face Girl*, San Souci's *Sootface: An Ojibwa Cinderella Story*, and Flora Annie Steele's English *Tattercoats*. CINDERELLA STORIES. FAIRY TALES. FISHES–FOLKLORE. FOLKLORE–CHINA. STEPMOTHERS–FOLKLORE.

1044   Winthrop, Elizabeth. *Vasilissa the Beautiful: A Russian Folktale*. Illus. by Alexander Koshkin. HarperCollins, 1991. ISBN 0-06-021663-8

[Gr. 2–5] Sent to Baba Yaga's house for a light by her nasty stepmother and stepsisters, Vasilissa is aided by her little doll in finishing the witch woman's impossible tasks. Another version is Marianna Mayer's *Baba Yaga and Vasilisa the Brave*. Compare the elements of *Cinderella* and *Hansel and Gretel* that run through the story. For a longer read with Baba Yaga as a minor character, see *I-Know-Not-What, I-Know-Not-Where* by Eric A. Kimmel. Go on a Baba Yaga binge with Katya Arnold's *Baba Yaga* and *Baba Yaga & the Little Girl*, Becky Hickox Ayres's *Matreshka*, Joanna Cole's *Bony Legs*, Kimmel's *Baba Yaga*, J. Patrick Lewis's *The Frog Princess*, Elsa Okon Rael's *Marushka's Egg*, Maida Silverman's *Anna and the Seven Swans*, and Ernest Small's *Baba Yaga*. Josepha Sherman's *Vassilisa the Wise* is another resourceful Russian heroine. BABA YAGA. FAIRY TALES. FOLKLORE–RUSSIA. STEPMOTHERS–FOLKLORE. WITCHES–FOLKLORE.

1045   Yacowitz, Caryn. *The Jade Stone: A Chinese Folktale*. Illus. by Ju-Hong Chen. Holiday House, 1992. ISBN 0-8234-0919-8

[Gr. K–4] Though the emperor wants to see a dragon of wind and fire carved out of a perfect piece of jade, stone carver Chan Lo stands by his principles and carves what he hears in the rock: three carp playing in the Celestial Palace pool. Before revealing what Chan Lo carved, ask listeners to sketch what they think the sculpture might be. Another artist who follows his imagination is Gregory, who paints only whales in Cynthia Rylant's *All I See*. Faced with blank pieces of paper and crayons, colored pencil, or watercolors, your young artists can draw and tell about what they see in their mind's eyes. In Robert J. Blake's *The Perfect Spot*, a dad and son search for the best place to paint and explore. *Henry Moore: From Bones and Stones to Sketches and Sculptures* by Jane Mylum Gardner presents the work and life of a famous 20th century sculptor. Break out the clay! ARTISTS–FOLKLORE. EMPERORS–FOLKLORE. FOLKLORE–CHINA. SCULPTORS–FOLKLORE.

1046   Yep, Laurence. *The Junior Thunder Lord*. Illus. by Robert Van Nutt. BridgeWater Books, 1994. ISBN 0-8167-3454-2

[Gr. 1–4] "Those at the top should help those at the bottom" is the lesson Yue lives by, which is why he befriends and feeds Bear Face, a gargantuan man who in return saves Yue from drowning. In this 17th-century Chinese folktale, Bear Face is actually a junior thunder lord who ends the drought in Yue's village. See how other characters control the weather in Jo Harper's Texas tall tale *Jalapeño Hal*, Tololwa M. Mollel's *The Orphan Boy: A Maasai Story*, and David Wisniewski's *Rain Player*, about Chak, the Mayan rain god. DROUGHT–FOLKLORE. FOLKLORE–CHINA. FRIENDSHIP–FOLKLORE. LOYALTY–FOLKLORE. RAIN AND RAINFALL–FOLKLORE. TRANSFORMATIONS–FOLKLORE. WEATHER–FOLKLORE.

1047   Yep, Laurence. *The Man Who Tricked a Ghost*. Illus. by Isadore Seltzer. BridgeWater Books, 1993. ISBN 0-8167-3030-X

[Gr. 1–4] Nothing scares Sung, not even the armor-clad warrior ghost he meets on the way home who tells him he is out to teach a lesson to a fool named Sung who claims he isn't afraid of ghosts. Wily Sung worms out of the ghost that what he fears most is human spit, which is, of course, the ghost's ultimate downfall. An interesting afterword notes that the story was first published in China in the third century A.D. Fear also plays a part in Japanese folktales "The Terrible Black Snake's Revenge" from Yoshiko Uchida's *The Sea of Gold* and Patricia A. Compton's *The Terrible Eek*. Courage saves the day again in *Esteban and the Ghost* by Sibyl Hancock, and *The Boy and the Ghost* and *The Talking Eggs*, both by Robert D. San Souci. COURAGE–FOLKLORE. FEAR–FOLKLORE. FOLKLORE–CHINA. GHOST STORIES. TRICKSTER TALES.

1048   Yolen, Jane. *Tam Lin*. Illus. by Charles Mikolaycak. Harcourt, 1990. ISBN 0-15-284261-6

[Gr. 3–6] Determined to win back her family's castle and land from the Fair Folk (or fairies) and rescue handsome Tam Lin from their power, Jennet pledges to save him on All Hallows Eve. Based on the many versions of the old ballad, both Yolen's retelling and Mikolaycak's paintings are lush and romantic. Contrast both the portrayals of fairies and the way they are outwitted in this and *The Woman Who Flummoxed the Fairies*, a Scottish tale retold by Heather Forest. FAIRIES–FOLKLORE. FOLKLORE–SCOTLAND. HALLOWEEN–FOLKLORE. LOVE–FOLKLORE. MAGIC–FOLKLORE. TRANSFORMATIONS–FOLKLORE.

1049   Yolen, Jane. *Wings.* **Illus. by Dennis Nolan. Harcourt, 1991. ISBN 0-15-297850-X**

[Gr. 4–6] Yolen's retelling of the legend of Daedalus—who built the Minotaur's labyrinth on Crete and fashioned wings so he and his son Icarus could escape the island after Theseus killed the half man-half bull monster—is powerful and stately, as are Nolan's impassioned watercolors. Fill in the rest of the tragic story concluding with Theseus's betrayal of Princess Ariadne and his return to Athens with *Theseus and the Minotaur* by Leonard Everett Fisher. *Demeter and Persephone* by Penelope Proddow and *Persephone and the Pomegranate* by Kris Waldherr are both attractive retellings of another Greek myth, while Fisher's *Cyclops* is not for the faint of heart. FLIGHT–FOLKLORE. FOLKLORE–GREECE. MONSTERS–FOLKLORE. MYTHOLOGY. PRIDE AND VANITY–FOLKLORE.

1050   Young, Ed. *Moon Mother: A Native American Creation Tale.* **Illus. by the author. HarperCollins, 1993. ISBN 0-06-021302-7**

[Gr. 2–6] In this solemn Native American legend, glowing pastel paintings depict the creation of animals and men by the spirit person who came to earth, the arrival of the first spirit woman, the men's discovery of the first baby, and the beginning of the moon. Compare with American Indian creation myths *The Woman Who Fell from the Sky: The Iroquois Story of Creation* by John Bierhorst, *Owl Eyes* by Frieda Gates, *Children of the Morning Light: Wampanoag Tales* told by Manitonquat (Medicine Story), and *Raven's Light: A Myth from the People of the Northwest Coast* by Susan Hand Shetterly, and with *The Fire Children: A West African Creation Tale* retold by Eric Maddern. Learn more about the moon with *The Moon and You* by E. C. Krupp and *One Giant Leap*, a description of the 1969 moon landing by Mary Ann Fraser. Turn to poetry with *Thirteen Moons on Turtle's Back: A Native American Year of Moons* by Joseph Bruchac and Jonathan London, and Jane Yolen's *What Rhymes with Moon?* CREATION–FOLKLORE. FOLKLORE–INDIANS OF NORTH AMERICA. MOON–FOLKLORE.

1051   Young, Ed. *Seven Blind Mice.* **Illus. by the author. Philomel, 1992. ISBN 0-399-22261-8**

[Gr. Pre–3] A recasting of the Indian fable "The Blind Men and the Elephant," using brightly hued collage illustrations and simple language, this visually exciting Caldecott Honor book features seven different-colored blind mice who set out each day of the week to discover an elephant's identity, carefully piecing together information about what manner of creature they have discovered. "Wisdom comes from seeing the whole" is the mouse moral we humans would do well to recall. Compare with Lillian F. Quigley's version of *The Blind Men and the Elephant*. Replicate the experiment by bringing in one or more large objects such as a guitar, a lamp, or a tea kettle for the children to feel and identify without looking. Recall sequence and the seven days with Eric Carle's *Today Is Monday*. COLOR–FOLKLORE. ELEPHANTS–FOLKLORE. FOLKLORE–INDIA. MICE–FOLKLORE. WISDOM–FOLKLORE.

FOLK & FAIRY TALES, MYTHS & LEGENDS: COLLECTIONS

1052   Aardema, Verna. *Misoso: Once Upon a Time Tales from Africa.* Illus. by Reynold Ruffins. Apple Soup / Knopf, 1994. ISBN 0-679-83430-3

[12 tales, 88p., Gr. 2–6] The dozen tellable folktales in this attractive collection introduce us to Anansi the hungry spider trickster who meets up with talking foods that beg him to eat them, the Sloogey Dog who is accused of sniffing a rich man's food, and an ape who returns the favor after a man removes a thorn from its foot. Appealing, brightly colored pencil-and-acrylic paintings accompany each story, and there is also a glossary of African words and an afterword that gives the background of the tale. Other top-notch collections of animal folktales include *Crocodile! Crocodile! Stories Told Around the World* by Barbara Baumgartner, *When Jaguar Ate the Moon: And Other Stories About Animals and Plants of the Americas* by María Cristina Brusca and Tona Wilson, Harold Courlander's classic collections of African folktales *The Hat-Shaking Dance* and *The Cow-Tail Switch,* and *When Lion Could Fly and Other Tales from Africa* by Nick Greaves. ANIMALS–FOLKLORE. FOLKLORE–AFRICA.

1053   Aesop. *Aesop & Company: With Scenes from His Legendary Life.* Illus. by Arthur Geisert. Retold by Barbara Bader. Houghton Mifflin, 1991. ISBN 0-395-50597-6

[19 fables, 64p., Gr. 3–6] What's different about this collection of 19 fables is the introduction, which details the influence Aesop's fables have had on the world of folklore, the scant facts known about the supposed Greek slave from the sixth century B.C., and the last chapter, with stories passed down about him. Detailed pen-and-ink drawings on beige-toned paper accompany the simply told fables, each of which includes a moral. Additional retellings include Stephanie Calmenson's *The Children's Aesop,* Anne Gatti's *Aesop's Fables, Aesop's Fables* as illustrated both by Michael Hague and Heidi Holder, along with Tom Paxton's version in verse, and Barbara McClintock's *Animal Fables from Aesop.* ANIMALS–FOLKLORE. CREATIVE DRAMA–FOLKLORE. FABLES.

1054   Aesop. *Aesop's Fables.* Illus. by Safaya Salter. Retold by Anne Gatti. Gulliver / Harcourt, 1992. ISBN 0-15-200350-9

[60 tales, 79p., Gr. 1–6] The elaborately bordered watercolors will be savored by children as they predict and analyze the morals of these 60 lesser-known tales and act them out in small groups. Find more fables in Barbara Bader's *Aesop & Company*, Stephanie Calmenson's *The Children's Aesop*, Anne Gatti's *Aesop's Fables*, Barbara McClintock's *Animal Fables from Aesop*, and Tom Paxton's *Belling the Cat and Other Aesop's Fables*. ANIMALS–FOLKLORE. CREATIVE DRAMA–FOLKLORE. FABLES.

1055   Aesop. *Animal Fables from Aesop*. Illus. by Barbara McClintock. Retold by Barbara McClintock. Godine, 1991. ISBN 0-87923-913-1

[19 fables, unp., Gr. 2–6] The nine animal tales, all illustrated in 19th-century style of pen-and-ink and watercolors, focus mainly on sly foxes and wolves. The title page introduces us to the animal actors taking a bow onstage, and on the last page, when the players remove their masks, we see they are human actors. Brush up on the fables in Barbara Bader's *Aesop & Company*, Stephanie Calmenson's *The Children's Aesop*, Anne Gatti's *Aesop's Fables*, and Tom Paxton's *Belling the Cat and Other Aesop's Fables*, and act some out with your children. ANIMALS–FOLKLORE. FABLES.

1056   Aesop. *Belling the Cat and Other Aesop's Fables: Retold in Verse*. Illus. by Robert Rayevsky. Retold by Tom Paxton. Morrow, 1990. ISBN 0-688-08159-2

[10 tales, unp., Gr. 3–6] As in Paxton's earlier collections, *Aesop's Fables* and *Androcles and the Lion and Other Aesop's Fables* (1991), a selection of familiar fables have been put into rhyme. Find more fables in Barbara Bader's *Aesop & Company*, Stephanie Calmenson's *The Children's Aesop*, Anne Gatti's *Aesop's Fables*, and Barbara McClintock's *Animal Fables from Aesop*, and see how the prose and poetry versions compare. FABLES. STORIES IN RHYME.

1057   Aesop. *The Children's Aesop: Selected Fables*. Illus. by Robert Byrd. Retold by Stephanie Calmenson. Doubleday, 1988. ISBN 1-56397-041-4

[28 fables, 64p., Gr. 2–5] The conversational narrative story form of these mostly animal fables lends itself to easy rewriting for Reader's Theater plays your children can act out with scripts. Byrd's colorful crosshatched pen-and-ink and watercolors for each one-page tale will also make these sought-after read-alouds. Additional more sophisticated retellings include Barbara Bader's *Aesop & Company*, Anne Gatti's *Aesop's Fables*, *Aesop's Fables* as illustrated both by Michael Hague and Heidi Holder, Barbara McClintock's *Animal Fables from Aesop*, and Tom Paxton's *Aesop's Fables* and *Belling the Cat and Other Aesop's Fables*. ANIMALS–FOLKLORE. FABLES.

1058   Baumgartner, Barbara. *Crocodile! Crocodile! Stories Told Around the World*. Illus. by Judith Moffatt. Dorling Kindersley, 1994. ISBN 1-56458-463-1

[7 tales, 45p., Gr. Pre–2] Six great telling stories with bright cut-paper collages tie so well into other tales. Compare the retelling of "The Squeaky Old Bed" with the American folktale *Nathaniel Willy, Scared Silly* by Judith Mathews and Fay

Robinson and another Puerto Rican variant, *The Squeaky Door* by Laura Simms. Tell the title folktale from India with Paul Galdone's *The Monkey and the Crocodile* and Jose Aruego's Philippine *A Crocodile's Tale*. "Sody Saleratus" is also in Richard Chase's *Grandfather Tales*, and it works wonders with other "swallowing stories" (as my students call them) such as Paul Galdone's *The Greedy Old Fat Man*, Jack Kent's *The Fat Cat*, and Nancy Polette's *The Little Old Woman and the Hungry Cat*, along with another funny Appalachian tale, *Soap! Soap! Don't Forget the Soap!* by Tom Birdseye. All are great fun to act out in person or with stick puppets as the author suggests, along with Mary Medlicott's *Tales for Telling: From Around the World*. ANIMALS–FOLKLORE. CREATIVE DRAMA–FOLKLORE. STORIES TO TELL.

1059   Bruchac, Joseph. *Native American Animal Stories*. Illus. by John Kahionhes Fadden and David Kanietakeron Fadden. Fulcrum, 1992. ISBN 1-55591-127-7 (pbk.)

[24 tales, 135p., Gr. 2–6] The two dozen short and reverential stories in this interesting collection of creation, celebration, and survival legends from many North American tribes are reprinted from Michael J. Caduto and Joseph Bruchac's marvelous teacher resource text, *Keepers of the Animals: Native American Stories and Wildlife Activities for Children*. The afterwords include a detailed glossary and pronunciation key, thorough descriptions of each included tribe, and a resource list of other versions of the stories. Bruchac's *Iroquois Stories: Heroes and Heroines, Monsters and Magic* and *Return of the Sun: Native American Tales from the Northeast Woodlands*, and *Children of the Morning Light: Wampanoag Tales* told by Manitonquat (Medicine Story) are also splendid. Another nice collection of animal folktales is *When Lion Could Fly and Other Tales from Africa* by Nick Greaves. ANIMALS–FOLKLORE. CREATION–FOLKLORE. FOLKLORE–INDIANS OF NORTH AMERICA.

1060   Bruchac, Joseph. *Return of the Sun: Native American Tales from the Northeast Woodlands*. Illus. by Gary Carpenter. Crossing Press, 1989. ISBN 0-89594-344-1

[27 tales, 204p., Gr. 3–6] This splendid collection of 27 creation, pourquoi, and trickster tales is a welcome addition to the many tales available from the western half of the United States. Bruchac's other collections include *Iroquois Stories: Heroes and Heroines, Monsters and Magic* and *Native American Animal Stories*. Ellin Greene's *The Legend of the Cranberry: A Paleo-Indian Tale* is a Delaware Indian tale, and *Children of the Morning Light: Wampanoag Tales* told by Manitonquat (Medicine Story) hails from Massachusetts. ANIMALS–FOLKLORE. CREATION–FOLK-LORE FOLKLORE–INDIANS OF NORTH AMERICA. POURQUOI TALES.

1061   Brusca, María Cristina, and Tona Wilson. *When Jaguar Ate the Moon: And Other Stories About Animals and Plants of the Americas*. Illus. by María Cristina Brusca. Henry Holt, 1995. ISBN 0-8050-2797-1

[31 tales, unp., Gr. 2–6] Here is a welcome and well-chosen collection of folktales native to North and South America, arranged alphabetically by the names of plants and animals, from anteater to zompopo (a type of leaf-cutter ant). Brusca's gorgeous, detailed watercolors of each creature, some of which will be unfamiliar to children (agouti, kinkajou, nutria, olingo), can start off a cocurricular unit combining folklore with nonfiction animal research. *Misoso: Once Upon a Time Tales from Africa* by Verna Aardema, *Crocodile! Crocodile! Stories Told Around the World* by Barbara Baumgartner, *When Lion Could Fly and Other Tales from Africa* by Nick Greaves, and *The Singing Tortoise and Other Animal Folktales* by John Yeoman are all splendid collections of animal stories. ANIMALS–FOLKLORE. FOLKLORE–INDIANS OF NORTH AMERICA. FOLKLORE–INDIANS OF SOUTH AMERICA. PLANTS–FOLKLORE.

1062   **Cecil, Laura, comp. *Boo! Stories to Make You Jump.* Illus. by Emma Chichester Clark. Greenwillow, 1990. ISBN 0-688-09842-8**

[17 tales, 92p., Gr. 1–4] Milder in tone than Maria Leach's *The Thing at the Foot of the Bed* and Alvin Schwartz's Scary Stories series, these 17 selections are slightly scary and attractively laid out with large print and nicely macabre watercolors. Dilys Evans's *Monster Soup and Other Spooky Poems,* Jill Bennett's *Spooky Poems,* Douglas Florian's *Monster Motel,* Diane Goode's *Diane Goode's Book of Scary Stories & Songs,* Jeffie Ross Gordon's *Hide and Shriek: Riddles About Ghosts & Goblins,* Florence Parry Heide's *Grim and Ghastly Goings-On,* Lee Bennett Hopkins's *Ragged Shadows: Poems of Halloween Night,* Myra Cohn Livingston's *Halloween Poems,* Colin McNaughton's *Making Friends with Frankenstein,* and Jane Yolen's *Best Witches* might put a dent in your listeners' insatiable appetite for creepy reads. GHOST STORIES. SUPERNATURAL–FOLKLORE. SUSPENSE–FOLKLORE.

1063   **Cohn, Amy L. *From Sea to Shining Sea: A Treasury of American Folklore and Folk Songs.* Illus. by 11 Caldecott Medal and four Caldecott Honor book artists. Scholastic, 1993. ISBN 0-590-42868-3**

[399p., Gr. 1–6] There are more than 140 songs and stories to suit every taste in Cohn's impeccable and masterful compilation, and an array of colorful and handsome illustrations by 11 Caldecott Medal and four Caldecott Honor book artists. With an assortment of stories ranging from tall tales and ghost stories to historical events and ethnic tales, music and guitar chords provided for the far-ranging collection of songs, as well as an appendix including extensive notes on each selection, this is a book to be savored. You'll also enjoy Kathleen Krull's *Gonna Sing My Head Off! American Folk Songs for Children. Celebrate America in Poetry and Art* edited by Nora Panzer and *Celebrating America: A Collection of Poems and Images of the American Spirit* compiled by Laura Whipple are appealing collections of poetry and paintings. FOLK SONGS. FOLKLORE–ANTHOLOGIES. FOLKLORE–U.S.

1064   **Crouch, Marcus. *Ivan: Stories of Old Russia.* Illus. by Bob Dewar. Oxford University Press, 1989. ISBN 0-19-274135-7**

[16 tales, 80p., Gr. 3–6] Funny exploits of the Russian good-for-nothing fool, sometimes youngest brother, sometimes prince, demonstrate how he usually comes out on top. Other Russian fool stories include Mirra Ginsburg's *The Lazies* and *The Twelve Clever Brothers and Other Fools,* and Arthur Ransome's *The Fool of the World and His Flying Ship,* with Eric A. Kimmel's *I-Know-Not-What, I-Know-Not-Where* providing an interesting contrast. Chart international fools with Uncle Bouki in Harold Courlander's *A Piece of Fire and Other Haitian Tales,* Chelm residents in Isaac Bashevis Singer's *When Shlemiel Went to Warsaw & Other Stories,* and Nasreddin Hoca in Barbara K. Walker's *A Treasury of Turkish Folktales for Children.* FOLKLORE–RUSSIA. FOOLS–FOLKLORE.

1065   Garner, Alan. *Once Upon a Time, Though It Wasn't in Your Time, and It Wasn't in My Time, and It Wasn't in Anybody's Time. . . .* Illus. by Norman Messenger. Dorling Kindersley, 1993. ISBN 1-56458-381-3

[3 tales, 29p., Gr. Pre–2] All three of these lesser-known but delicious tales of nonsense are ripe for telling: "The Fox, the Hare, and the Cock," "The Girl and the Geese," and "Battibeth." CHANTABLE REFRAIN. FOLKLORE.

1066   Gatti, Anne. *Tales from the African Plains.* Illus. by Gregory Alexander. Dutton, 1994. ISBN 0-252-45282-6

[12 tales, 83p., Gr. 3–6] Interesting and unusual tales of animals and people are illustrated with glowing paintings. You'll want to compare "The Crocodile, the Boy, and the Kind Deed" with its African American variant "The Farmer and the Snake" in the *The Knee-High Man and Other Tales* by Julius Lester, and with Suzanne Crowder Han's Korean folktale *The Rabbit's Judgment.* "Why Hyenas Don't Wear Jewelry" is an animal version of Obi Onyefulu's Nigerian folktale *Chinye.* Other outstanding collections of African folklore include Verna Aardema's *Misoso: Once Upon a Time Tales from Africa,* Harold Courlander's classic collections of African folktales *The Hat-Shaking Dance* and *The Cow-Tail Switch,* and *When Lion Could Fly and Other Tales from Africa* by Nick Greaves. FOLKLORE–AFRICA. POURQUOI TALES.

1067   Geras, Adèle. *My Grandmother's Stories: A Collection of Jewish Folk Tales.* Illus. by Jael Jordan. Knopf, 1990. ISBN 0-679-90910-9

[10 tales, 96p., Gr. 3–6] In an extraordinary collection of folktales presenting a range of characters from the fools in Chelm to the wise King Solomon, the author lovingly recalls the time she spent with her grandmother in her apartment listening to her stories. Whether they were making strudel, arranging flowers, or preparing a meal, her grandmother had a story to fit the occasion, and each tale is prefaced by a description of those special times spent together. Spend more time in that mythical village of fools with *It Happened in Chelm: A Story of the Legendary Town of Fools* by Florence B. Freedman and *When Shlemiel Went to Warsaw & Other Stories* by Isaac Bashevis Singer. After reading about wise Solomon in "Bavsi's Feast," present the picture-book version of *King Solomon and the Bee* by Dalia Hardof Renberg. Sample stories in *Elijah's Violin and Other Jewish Fairy Tales,* an impressive collection by Howard Schwartz. FOLKLORE–RUSSIA. FOLKLORE, JEWISH. FOOLS–FOLKLORE. GRANDMOTHERS–FOLKLORE.

1068   Goode, Diane. *Diane Goode's Book of Scary Stories & Songs.* Illus. by Diane Goode. Dutton, 1994. ISBN 0-525-45175-7

[18 stories and poems, 64p., Gr. 2–4] Bordered pages and deliciously macabre watercolors accompany this tidy collection, which includes variants of old favorites such as "My Big Toe," "The Conjure Wives," "Mr. Miacca," and "The Green Ribbon." Don't forget to show the illustrated initial letter for each story. If your scare-mongers decide to write new spooky tales, have them dress up the first letter in the same vein. *Spooky Poems* collected by Jill Bennett, *Boo! Stories to Make You Jump* compiled by Laura Cecil, and *Favorite Scary Stories of American Children* collected by Richard Young and Judy Dockrey Young will keep the chills coming. GHOST STORIES. SUPERNATURAL–FOLKLORE. SUSPENSE–FOLKLORE. SUSPENSE–POETRY.

1069   Goode, Diane. *Diane Goode's Book of Silly Stories and Songs.* Illus. by the author. Dutton, 1992. ISBN 0-525-44967-1

[11 tales, 5 songs, 64p., Gr. 2–5] There are fools and simpletons from all over the world in this amiable collection, including "Sweet Giongio," an Italian variant of Kathryn Hewitt or Paul Galdone's retellings of the English story *The Three Sillies,* and "Bastianello" in Virginia Haviland's *Favorite Fairy Tales Told in Italy.* For more silly songs, you'll treasure Esther L. Nelson's *The Funny Song Book* and Marie Winn's *The Fireside Book of Fun and Game Songs.* FOOLS–FOLKLORE. HUMOROUS SONGS.

1070   Greaves, Nick. *When Lion Could Fly and Other Tales from Africa.* Illus. by Rod Clement. Barrons, 1993. ISBN 0-8120-6344-9

[31 tales, 144p., Gr. 2–6] Not only is this a first-rate collection of animal folktales with handsome realistic color portraits of each creature, but in between each story is a facts page that describes that animal in detail. The lesser-known animals are the most fascinating, including the serval, caracal, eland, pangolin, kudu, bushbuck, duiker, and dung beetle. An interesting follow-up animal project would be for children to research animals and find corresponding folktales to read aloud or tell to the class as part of their presentations. Compare the types of animals and tellings in *Native American Animal Stories* by Joseph Bruchac. *Misoso: Once Upon a Time Tales from Africa* by Verna Aardema, Harold Courlander's state-of-the-art collections of African folktales *The Hat-Shaking Dance* and *The Cow-Tail Switch,* and Anne Gatti's *Tales from the African Plains* include a fair number of animal tales. ANIMALS–FOLKLORE. FOLKLORE–AFRICA.

1071   Hastings, Selina. *Reynard the Fox.* Illus. by Graham Percy. Tambourine, 1991. ISBN 0-688-10156-9

[2–3 sittings, 76p., Gr. 3–6] All of the forest animals demand of Lion that the Fox be brought to justice for his thieving, murderous ways, but the unrepentant Reynard manages to outwit and humiliate each animal that comes to fetch him before the King. Based on William Caxton's version of Reynard stories dating to 1481, this attractively illustrated retelling of episodes about the slick fox has its roots in Aesop's fables, on up through Roman times and the Middle Ages. *Wild Fox* by Cherie Mason and *Reynard: The Story of a Fox Returned to the Wild* by Alice Mills Leighner, both true accounts, along with Betsy Byars's fiction book *The Midnight Fox* will elicit some empathy and encourage readers to do a little research to compare the personality of real foxes with their bad image in folklore. FABLES. FOLKLORE–ENGLAND. FOXES–FOLKLORE. TRICKSTER TALES.

1072   Hodges, Margaret. *Hauntings: Ghosts and Ghouls from Around the World.* Illus. by David Wenzel. Little, Brown, 1991. ISBN 0-316-36796-6

[16 tales, 123p., Gr. 4–6] This international collection of folktale chillers is a satisfying one, with 16 dramatically retold stories. *Scary Stories to Tell in the Dark* and its sequels by Alvin Schwartz and *Favorite Scary Stories of American Children* by Richard and Judith Dockrey Young are also effective compilations to make kids shudder. GHOST STORIES. SUSPENSE–FOLKLORE.

1073   Kherdian, David. *Feathers and Tails: Animal Fables from Around the World.* Illus. by Nonny Hogrogian. Philomel, 1992. ISBN 0-399-21876-9

[21 tales, 95p., Gr. K–4] The 21 appealing, lesser-known stories from African, Asian, European, and Native American folk traditions are accompanied by many soft, colorful, full-page illustrations. Find more animal fables in Stephanie Calmenson's *The Children's Aesop,* Anne Gatti's *Aesop's Fables,* Barbara McClintock's *Animal Fables from Aesop,* Tom Paxton's *Belling the Cat and Other Aesop's Fables,* Jan Thornhill's *Crow & Fox and Other Animal Legends,* and John Yeoman's *The Singing Tortoise and Other Animal Folktales. Crocodile! Crocodile! Stories Told Around the World* by Barbara Baumgartner and *Tales for Telling: From Around the World* by Mary Medlicott are also good sources for animal folktales to share. ANIMALS–FOLKLORE. CREATIVE DRAMA–FOLKLORE. FABLES.

1074   Lang, Andrew. *The Rainbow Fairy Book.* Illus. by Michael Hague. Morrow, 1993. ISBN 0-688-10878-4

[31 tales, 28p., Gr. 3–6] Hague selected his favorite tales from among the 300 in Lang's 12 famous Colored Fairy Books series originally published in the late 19th century and illustrated them in lovely pen-and-ink and watercolors in period style. A mixture of familiar—"Rapunzel," "Jack and the Beanstalk"—and lesser-known stories, this collection should lead readers to the original Lang books, starting with *The Blue Fairy Book.* FAIRY TALES. FOLKLORE–ANTHOLOGIES.

1075   Lester, Julius. *Further Tales of Uncle Remus: The Misadventures of Brer Rabbit, Brer Fox, Brer Wolf, the Doodang, and Other Creatures.* Illus. by Jerry Pinkney. Dial, 1990. ISBN 0-8037-0611-1

[33 tales, 148p., Gr. 2–5] All of the Brers spend their days conniving multiple trickeries, revenges, and mischief-making in this continuation of Lester's informal, shoot-the-breeze style retellings that started with *The Tales of Uncle Remus* and *More Tales of Uncle Remus* (1988), and ends with *The Last Tales of Uncle Remus* (1994). Compare writing styles with Van Dyke Parks and Malcolm Jones's *Jump! The Adventures of Brer Rabbit* and *Jump Again!,* and examine the variants in Priscilla Jaquith's African American Gullah tales in *Bo Rabbit Smart for True.* Contrast these African American rabbit trickster tales with Native American ones in *Big Trouble for Tricky Rabbit!* by Gretchen Will Mayo. ANIMALS–FOLKLORE. FOLK-LORE, AFRICAN AMERICAN. FOLKLORE–U.S. RABBITS–FOLKLORE. TRICKSTER TALES.

1076   MacDonald, Margaret Read. *Peace Tales: World Folktales to Talk About.* **Linnet Books / Shoe String Press, 1992. ISBN 0-208-02329-1**

[36 tales, 116p., Gr. 1–6] An anthology containing dozens of insightful stories and proverbs about war and peace, this will aid children in their discussions about the personal and political choices they will need to make in their lives. The note to storytellers at the back of the book is helpful in planning discussions. With older children, read aloud and discuss MacDonald's "Four Steps to Peace." *War Game* by Michael Foreman, *The Lotus Seed* by Sherry Garland, Florence Parry Heide and Judith Heide Gilliland's *Sami and the Time of the Troubles,* *Randolph's Dream* by Judith Mellecker, *My Hiroshima* by Junko Morimoto, and *Pink and Say* by Patricia Polacco are all picture books that make a profound statement about the meaning of war. Make a further impact with *The Sleeper,* a Chinese folktale retold by David Day, about young monk Wu who stops a battle with the books he brings with him after a 200-year sleep. FOLKLORE–ANTHOLOGIES. PEACE–FOLKLORE. WAR–FOLKLORE.

1077   Manitonquat (Medicine Story). *Children of the Morning Light: Wampanoag Tales.* **Illus. by Mary F. Arquette. Macmillan, 1994. ISBN 0-02-765905-4**

[11 tales, 72p., Gr. 3–6] Retold from Native American stories from southeastern Massachusetts, these are absorbing creation legends about Maushop, or Firstman, who made the world safe for people and his brother Matahdou who created all the bad things in the world. Compare the telling of "The Great Migration and Old Man Winter" with the Ojibway variant *Peboan and Seegwun* retold by Charles Larry. Additional Native American creation legends include *The Woman Who Fell from the Sky: The Iroquois Story of Creation* by John Bierhorst, *Iroquois Stories,* *Native American Animal Stories* and *The Return of the Sun: Native American Tales from the Northeast Woodlands* by Joseph Bruchac, *Owl Eyes* by Frieda Gates, *Raven's Light: A Myth from the People of the Northwest Coast* by Susan Hand Shetterly, and *Moon Mother: A Native American Creation Tale* by Ed Young. CREATION–FOLKLORE. FOLKLORE–INDIANS OF NORTH AMERICA. MASSACHUSETTS–FOLK-LORE. WAMPANOAG INDIANS–FOLKLORE.

1078   Mayo, Gretchen Will. *Big Trouble for Tricky Rabbit!* **Illus. by the author. Walker, 1994. ISBN 0-8027-8276-0**

[6 tales, 37p., Gr. 1–3] All five easy-to-read, cheerful stories about Rabbit's escapades are fine candidates for rewriting as Reader's Theater scripts. Just in case your kids think Bugs Bunny is the only troublemaker around, read from the other choices in the Native American Trickster Tales series, which also includes *Here Comes Tricky Rabbit!* (1994), *Meet Tricky Coyote!* (1993) and *That Tricky Coyote!* Keep going with Andy Gregg's *Great Rabbit and the Long-Tailed Wildcat,* Priscilla Jaquith's African American Gullah tales in *Bo Rabbit Smart for True,* Barbara Knutson's *Sungura and Leopard,* Gerald McDermott's *Zomo the Rabbit: A Trickster Tale from West Africa,* and Gayle Ross's *How Rabbit Tricked Otter and Other*

Cherokee Trickster Stories. FOLKLORE–INDIANS OF NORTH AMERICA. RABBITS–FOLKLORE. TRICKSTER TALES.

1079   Mayo, Gretchen Will. *That Tricky Coyote!* Illus. by the author. Walker, 1993. ISBN 0-8027-8201-9

[5 tales, 35p., Gr. K–2] In five short and simple tales, trickster Coyote meets up with Frog, Lizard, Cicada, Bluebird, and Turtle, all of whom trick him back. Present more Coyote stories in Mayo's companion volume *Meet Tricky Coyote!* (Walker, 1993), plus Verna Aardema's *Borreguita and the Coyote,* Shonto Begay's Navajo folktale *Ma'ii and Cousin Horned Toad,* Valerie Scho Carey's Pueblo Indian *Quail Song,* Jonathan London and Lanny Pinola's *Fire Race,* Gerald McDermott's *Coyote,* Phyllis Root's *Coyote and the Magic Words,* Janet Stevens's *Coyote Steals the Blanket,* and Harriet Peck Taylor's *Coyote Places the Stars.* COYOTES–FOLKLORE. FOLKLORE–INDIANS OF NORTH AMERICA. TRICKSTER TALES.

1080   Medlicott, Mary. *Tales for Telling: From Around the World.* Illus. by Sue Williams. Kingfisher, 1992. ISBN 1-85697-824-9

[15 tales, 93p., Gr. K–4] The stories in this useful and entertaining collection have all been written down by "real, live storytellers," which means the retellings are colloquial, child-directed, and easy to learn to tell your students. Search out more animal stories in *Misoso: Once Upon a Time Tales from Africa* by Verna Aardema, *Crocodile! Crocodile! Stories Told Around the World* by Barbara Baumgartner, *Feathers and Tails: Animal Fables from Around the World* by David Kherdian, *Crow & Fox and Other Animal Legends* by Jan Thornhill, and *The Singing Tortoise and Other Animal Folktales* by John Yeoman. ANIMALS–FOLKLORE. FOLKLORE.

1081   Osborne, Mary Pope. *American Tall Tales.* Illus. by Michael McCurdy. Knopf, 1991. ISBN 0-679-80089-1

[9 stories, 115p., Gr. 3–6] Recounting the exploits of nine uniquely American folklore characters with exuberance and laugh-out-loud gusto, this handsome collection also contains fascinating historical explanations of how these exaggerated characters first became part of our national heritage. Contrast coverage in *Larger Than Life: The Adventures of American Legendary Heroes* by Robert D. San Souci and *Big Men, Big Country: A Collection of American Tall Tales* by Paul Robert Walker. Amy L. Cohn's *From Sea to Shining Sea: A Treasury of American Folklore and Folk Songs* is a more general collection for all U.S. folklore buffs. Practice your exaggerating with Alvin Schwartz's *Whoppers.* FOLKLORE–U.S. TALL TALES.

1082   Osborne, Mary Pope. *Mermaid Tales from Around the World.* Illus. by Troy Howell. Scholastic, 1993. ISBN 0-590-44377-1

[12 tales, 84p., Gr. 3–6] Romantic stories from Japan, Nigeria, Ukraine, Greece, and elsewhere, are each accompanied by breathtaking paintings done in the style of that country. Be sure to have children examine the initial letter of the first word in each story. One more marvelous book is *Sukey and the Mermaid,* an

African American folktale retold by Robert D. San Souci. FOLKLORE–ANTHOLOGIES. MERMAIDS–FOLKLORE. MULTICULTURAL STORIES–FOLKLORE.

1083   **Pilling, Ann.** *Realms of Gold: Myths & Legends from Around the World.* **Illus. by Kady MacDonald Denton. Kingfisher, 1993. ISBN 1-85697-913-X**

[14 tales, 93p, Gr. 4–6] With three sections—Earth, Air, Fire, and Water; Love and Death; and Fools and Heroes—the myths in this visually pleasing collection include African, Asian, North American, and European tales, with familiar tales such as "Persephone," "The Death of Balder," "How Maui Stole Fire from the Gods," and "The Willow Pattern Story," plus other more obscure ones. Continue with Mary Pope Osborne's *Favorite Greek Myths.* FOLKLORE–ANTHOLOGIES. MULTICULTURAL STORIES–FOLKLORE. MYTHOLOGY.

1084   **Ross, Gayle.** *How Rabbit Tricked Otter and Other Cherokee Trickster Stories.* **Illus. by Murv Jacob. HarperCollins, 1994. ISBN 0-06-021286-1**

[15 tales, 79p., Gr. 1–4] Trickster-hero and sassy troublemaker Rabbit gives a hard time to Possum, Wolf, Turtle, Fox, and anyone else naive enough to tangle with him. Gretchen Will Mayo's *Big Trouble for Tricky Rabbit!* is another enjoyable collection of Native American tales. For more rabbit mischief, dig into Andy Gregg's Algonquian Indian folktale *Great Rabbit and the Long-Tailed Wildcat,* Barbara Knutson's African *Sungura and Leopard,* and Gerald McDermott's *Zomo the Rabbit: A Trickster Tale from West Africa.* Priscilla Jaquith's African American Gullah tales in *Bo Rabbit Smart for True,* Julius Lester's four collections of African American Brer Rabbit tales, starting with *The Tales of Uncle Remus: The Adventures of Brer Rabbit,* and Van Dyke Parks and Malcolm Jones's *Jump! The Adventures of Brer Rabbit* are interesting African American counterparts to the Native American stories. ANIMALS–FOLKLORE. CHEROKEE INDIANS–FOLKLORE. FOLKLORE–INDIANS OF NORTH AMERICA. RABBITS–FOLKLORE. TRICKSTER TALES.

1085   **San Souci, Robert D.** *Larger Than Life: The Adventures of American Legendary Heroes.* **Illus. by Andrew Glass. Doubleday, 1991. ISBN 0-385-24907-1**

[5 tales, 59p., Gr. 3–6] Six straight-faced tall-tale characters come to life in this big-hearted, big-format book: John Henry, Old Stormalong, Slue-Foot Sue and her honey Pecos Bill, Texan Strap Buckner, and Paul Bunyan. Look at some of the single-story versions of *John Henry* as told by Ezra Jack Keats and Julius Lester, and Steve Sanfield's *A Natural Man: The True Story of John Henry. Paul Bunyan* by Steven Kellogg (Morrow, 1985) is a rollicking picture-book retelling. *From Sea to Shining Sea: A Treasury of American Folklore and Folk Songs* by Amy L. Cohn, *American Tall Tales* by Mary Pope Osborne, and *Big Men, Big Country: A Collection of American Tall Tales* by Paul Robert Walker are all superb collections. FOLKLORE–U.S. TALL TALES.

1086   **Schwartz, Alvin.** *Scary Stories 3: More Tales to Chill Your Bones.* **Illus. by Stephen Gammell. HarperCollins, 1991. ISBN 0-06-021795-2**

[25 tales, 115p., Gr. 4–6] For all those horror enthusiasts who never got enough *Scary Stories to Tell in the Dark* or *More Scary Stories to Tell in the Dark,* here's a new collection of short, gruesome, fearsome, and disgusting tales, once again collected from American folklore. Want some more screamers? Try *Hauntings: Ghosts and Ghouls from Around the World* by Margaret Hodges, *Favorite Scary Stories of American Children* by Richard and Judith Dockrey Young, and, for the younger set, Laura Cecil's more benign *Boo! Stories to Make You Jump.* GHOST STORIES. FOLKLORE–U.S. SUPERNATURAL–FOLKLORE. SUSPENSE–FOLKLORE.

1087   Shannon, George. *More Stories to Solve: Fifteen Folktales from Around the World.* Illus. by Peter Sis. Greenwillow, 1991. ISBN 0-688-09161-X

[15 tales, 64p., Gr. 3–6] In each brief story-conundrum, which listeners must explain, brains clearly triumph over brawn, whether it is the little deer who becomes a prince, or the clever Chilean bride who outwits her proud young husband. *Stories to Solve* and *Still More Stories to Solve* (1994) provide more puzzlers, as do *Brain Busters* by Louis Philips and, of course, the Encyclopedia Brown mystery series by Donald J. Sobol. FOLKLORE. PROBLEM SOLVING–FOLKLORE. RIDDLES–FOLKLORE.

1088   Sutcliff, Rosemary. *Black Ships Before Troy! The Story of the Iliad.* Illus. by Alan Lee. Delacorte, 1993. ISBN 0-385-31069-2

[19 tales, 128p., Gr. 5–6] When Paris, son of King Priam of Troy, hears about Helen of the Fair Cheeks, the most beautiful of all mortal women, he lures her away from her husband, King Menelaus of Sparta, thus setting in motion ten years of bloody warfare between the armies of Greece and Troy. Included in this huge, stately volume, a prose retelling of Homer's epic poem *The Iliad,* are magnificent sweeping paintings across each page. Ending with the legend of the Trojan horse and the fall of Troy, this is not a story for the faint of heart, as it is remarkably bloody, violent, and cruel. You will most certainly want to read it first yourself, and then decide which sections you want to read aloud to enliven any study of mythology. Mary Pope Osborne's *Favorite Greek Myths* is a stellar collection, and *Cyclops,* Leonard Everett Fisher's thrillingly grotesque picture book, retells one of Odysseus's more unsettling adventures on his way home from Troy. FOLKLORE–GREECE. MYTHOLOGY. TROJAN WAR. WAR–FOLKLORE.

1089   Thornhill, Jan. *Crow & Fox and Other Animal Legends.* Illus. by the author. Simon & Schuster, 1993. ISBN 0-671-87428-4

[8 tales, 32p., Gr. 1–4] Touch down on each continent with these nine beguiling, mostly little-known, two-character animal folktales, attended by color-rich full-page illustrations that are both sensible and captivating. You'll think you know these stories from Aesop, but each one is a surprise. The device of carrying over one animal into the next story will please your listeners, who can search for more animal tales in the 398.2 section of the library. *Crocodile! Crocodile! Stories Told Around the World* by Barbara Baumgartner, *Feathers and Tails: Animal Fables from Around the World* by David Kherdian, and *Tales for Telling: From Around the World* by Mary Medlicott are other agreeable collections. ANIMALS–FOLKLORE.

1090   Walker, Paul Robert. *Big Men, Big Country: A Collection of American Tall Tales.* **Illus. by James Bernardin. Harcourt, 1993. ISBN 0-15-207136-9**

[9 tales, 79p., Gr. 4–6] Boisterous, good-natured yarns about the usual guys—Davy Crockett, Paul Bunyan, John Henry—plus a few lesser-known tall-tale heroes like New York farmer John Darling and New York City fireman Big Mose. Detailed background notes about each story, plus grand full-page paintings make this a collection hard to beat. Pair with *Larger Than Life: The Adventures of American Legendary Heroes* by Robert D. San Souci and *American Tall Tales* by Mary Pope Osborne. Fill in background with Amy L. Cohn's *From Sea to Shining Sea: A Treasury of American Folklore and Folk Songs.* Exaggerate with the help of Alvin Schwartz's *Chin Music* and *Whoppers*, both books of tall talk. FOLKLORE–U.S. TALL TALES.

1091   Yeoman, John. *The Singing Tortoise and Other Animal Folktales.* **Illus. by Quentin Blake. Tambourine, 1993. ISBN 0-688-13366-5**

[11 tales, 95p., Gr. 3–6] The selection of international stories is a thoughtful one, and the retellings range from witty to solemn. Both the Zuni Indian Cinderella variant "The Turkey Girl" (to which you can compare Penny Pollock's picture-book version) and the title story are thoughtful tales without the usual happy ending, but all are balanced with Blake's frazzled, good-natured watercolors. Revisit the animal kingdom with *Misoso: Once Upon a Time Tales from Africa* by Verna Aardema, *When Jaguar Ate the Moon: And Other Stories About Animals and Plants of the Americas* by María Cristina Brusca and Tona Wilson, *Feathers and Tails: Animal Fables from Around the World* by David Kherdian, *Tales for Telling: From Around the World* by Mary Medlicott, and *Crow & Fox and Other Animal Legends* by Jan Thornhill. ANIMALS–FOLKLORE.

1092   Yep, Laurence. *Tongues of Jade.* **Illus. by David Wiesner. HarperCollins, 1991. ISBN 0-06-022471-1**

[17 tales, 194p., Gr. 4–6] The arresting folktales in this collection were collected from Chinese immigrants as part of a WPA project in California in the 1930s. Yep's retellings are elegant and filled with interesting messages about the rewards that accompany behaviors such as morality, honesty, and kindness to others, which children can discuss and relate to themselves. Other inviting collections of Chinese folklore include *Sweet and Sour: Tales from China* by Carol Kendall and Yao-wen Li, *The Magic Boat and Other Folk Stories* by M. A. Jagendorf and Virginia Weng, and *Treasure Mountain* by Catherine Edwards Sadler. FOLK-LORE, CHINESE AMERICAN.

1093   Young, Richard, and Judy Dockrey Young. *Favorite Scary Stories of American Children.* **Illus. by Wendell E. Hall. August House, 1990. ISBN 0-87483-119-9**

[23 tales, 112p., Gr. 3–6] The 23 scary stories in this eclectic, entertaining, and sometimes hair-raising collection are rated for ages 5–6, 7–8, and 9–10, and before telling the scariest ones, you'll want to consider your audience carefully. If your listeners are hooked on *The Thing at the Foot of the Bed* by Maria Leach and *Scary*

Stories to Tell in the Dark and its sequels collected by Alvin Schwartz, they'll eat these up, too. Diane Goode's *Diane Goode's Book of Scary Stories & Songs* and *Hauntings: Ghosts and Ghouls from Around the World* by Margaret Hodges will also please horror fans. FOLKLORE–U.S. GHOST STORIES. SUSPENSE–FOLKLORE.

From AMERICAN TALL TALES by Mary Pope Osborne, illustrated by
Michael McCurdy. Illustrations copyright © 1991 by Michael McCurdy.
Reprinted by permission of Alfred A. Knopf, Inc.

Illustration by Cathi Hepworth reprinted by permission of G. P. Putnam's Sons
from ANTICS! AN ALPHABETICAL ANTHOLOGY,
copyright © 1992 by Cathi Hepworth.

NONFICTION AND BIOGRAPHY

1094 Adams, Barbara Johnston. *The Go-Around Dollar.* Illus. by Joyce Audy Zarins. Four Winds, 1992. ISBN 0-02-700031-1

[1 sitting, unp., Gr. 1–4] After Matt and Eric find a dollar bill on the sidewalk, we track the bill as it changes hands. Sidebars provide extra interesting facts, from how many one-dollar bills make up a pound (490 or so) to how long it takes a bill to wear out (about 18 months). Examine your own dollar bills to locate corresponding information from the text. Students can design new class tender. *The Story of Money* by Betsy Maestro is more complex, and delves into the history of the world's coins and bills. *Pigs Will Be Pigs* by Amy Axelrod, *Max Malone Makes a Million* by Charlotte Herman, and *How the Second Grade Got $8,205.50 to Visit the Statue of Liberty* by Nathan Zimelman are all fiction stories for cash-hungry kids. MONEY.

1095 Adler, David A. *A Picture Book of Harriet Tubman.* Illus. by Samuel Byrd. Holiday House, 1992. ISBN 0-8234-0926-0

[1 sitting, unp., Gr. 1–4] Adler's inspirational retelling of Tubman's difficult life as first a slave and then a major conductor on the Underground Railroad is compelling reading, and the picture-book format makes it a natural for introducing younger children to a complex subject. Also excellent are Jeri Ferris's *Go Free or Die: A Story About Harriet Tubman*, Ann McGovern's *Runaway Slave*, and Faith Ringgold's *Aunt Harriet's Underground Railroad in the Sky*. Extend your children's background with Adler's *A Picture Book of Sojourner Truth*, and picture books Deborah Hopkinson's *Sweet Clara and the Freedom Quilt*, Dolores Johnson's *Now Let Me Fly: The Story of a Slave Family*, F. N. Monjo's *The Drinking Gourd*, and Jeanette Winter's *Follow the Drinking Gourd*. AFRICAN AMERICANS–BIOGRAPHY. BIOGRAPHY. SLAVERY. U.S.–HISTORY–1783-1865.

1096 Adler, David A. *A Picture Book of Sojourner Truth.* Illus. by Gershom Griffith. Holiday House, 1994. ISBN 0-8234-1072-2

[1 sitting, unp., Gr. 2–4] This is an easy-to-read biography with full-page watercolors about the African American woman who was born a slave in New York in

1797 and became a well-known lecturer for the abolitionist cause. Adler's *A Picture Book of Harriet Tubman*, Ann McGovern's *Runaway Slave*, and Faith Ringgold's *Aunt Harriet's Underground Railroad in the Sky* are all essential reads, as are the fiction picture books Deborah Hopkinson's *Sweet Clara and the Freedom Quilt*, Dolores Johnson's *Now Let Me Fly: The Story of a Slave Family*, F. N. Monjo's *The Drinking Gourd*, and Jeanette Winter's *Follow the Drinking Gourd*, all of which deal with the Underground Railroad. ABOLITIONISTS. AFRICAN AMERICANS–BIOGRAPHY. BIOGRAPHY. SLAVERY. U.S.–HISTORY–1783-1865. WOMEN–BIOGRAPHY.

1097   Alexander, Sally Hobart. *Mom Can't See Me*. Photos by George Ancona. Macmillan, 1990. ISBN 0-02-700401-5

[1 sitting, 48p., Gr. 1–4] Describing how her mother went blind at age 26, Leslie describes all the things her mother does: cooking, canoeing, tap dancing, playing piano, and, of course, writing the text of this astonishing black-and-white photo essay on her talking computer. Follow up with *Mom's Best Friend*, below. For a historical look at a blind child's life in 1887, read Gloria Whelan's short novel *Hannah*. BLIND. DOGS. GUIDE DOGS. HANDICAPS. MOTHERS.

1098   Alexander, Sally Hobart. *Mom's Best Friend*. Photos by George Ancona. Macmillan, 1992. ISBN 0-02-700393-0

[1 sitting, 32p., Gr. 2–6] In this appealing follow-up to *Mom Can't See Me*, daughter Leslie continues her affectionate portrayal of her mother in this black-and-white photo essay about the blind author's acquisition of German shepherd Ursula, a new seeing eye dog, after the death of Marit, her first dog. Provide more dog background with James B. Garfield's *Follow My Leader*, a novel about a boy blinded by a firecracker and his new seeing eye dog, Leader, or Audrey Osofsky's picture book *My Buddy*. *Rosie: A Visiting Dog's Story* by Stephanie Calmenson is an uplifting photo essay about a visiting dog. See what life was like for a blind child in 1887 in Gloria Whelan's novel *Hannah*. BLIND. DOGS. GUIDE DOGS. HANDICAPS. MOTHERS.

1099   Aliki. *Communication*. Illus. by the author. Greenwillow, 1993. ISBN 0-688-11248-X

[1 sitting, unp., Gr. 1–3] In a useful and attractive exposition of the ways we communicate to share knowledge, tell news, express feelings, and be heard, Aliki incorporates a raft of realistic dialogues between children, from friendly to angry. The many facets of communicating with people are laid out like color-cartoon-panel storyboards, with short scenes you can photocopy and hand out to students to act out as Reader's Theater. Watch class camaraderie develop as your students act out their own invented dialogues as well, and get to know each other better. Children will also enjoy exploring their emotions in the author's *Feelings* (Greenwillow, 1984). COMMUNICATION. CREATIVE DRAMA. EMOTIONS. READER'S THEATER.

1100   Allen, Marjorie N., and Shelley Rotner. *Changes*. Photos by Shelley Rotner. Macmillan, 1991. ISBN 0-02-700252-7

[1 sitting, unp., Gr. Pre–1] "All things go through changes as they grow," begins this quiet, matter-of-fact color photo essay of how seasonal changes affect plants, animals, and people. *An Egg Is an Egg* by Nicki Weiss is a gentle rhyming explanation by mother to son about how things change. Make a chart of what children observe changing inside and out. Appreciate all the seasons with *Caps, Hats, Socks, and Mittens* by Louise Borden, *January Brings the Snow* by Sara Coleridge, and *When Summer Ends* by Susi Gregg Fowler. CHANGE. NATURE. SEASONS. STORIES IN RHYME.

1101   **Audubon, John James.** *Capturing Nature: The Writings and Art of John James Audubon.* **Edited by Peter Roop and Connie Roop. Illus. by Rick Farley. Walker, 1993. ISBN 0-8027-8205-1**

[2 sittings, 7 short chapters, 39p., Gr. 5–6] Taken from the journals written by the naturalist and painter of birds are interesting anecdotes about Audubon's childhood in nature, a brush with death, and his difficulties in becoming accepted as an artist. Interspersed are reproductions of his magnificent bird paintings. *Urban Roosts: Where Birds Nest in the City* by Barbara Bash is a modern-day naturalist's look at birds. *Bird Watch: A Book of Poetry* by Jane Yolen will help children observe and appreciate the birds around them. ARTISTS. AUDUBON, JOHN JAMES. AUTOBIOGRAPHY. BIRDS. DIARIES. NATURALISTS.

1102   **Ballard, Robert.** *Exploring the Titanic.* **Illus. with photos. Scholastic, 1988. ISBN 0-590-41953-6**

[6 chapters, 64p., Gr. 4–6] In 1986, marine geologist and explorer Robert Ballard and two colleagues discovered the wreck of the *Titanic* and photographed their findings. This extraordinary book recalls his expedition and describes in chilling detail the night of April 14, 1912 when the "unsinkable" ship hit an iceberg. Readers will be riveted both by the text and the illustrations, interweaving large paintings of the ship then and now, photos taken before the voyage and underwater photos of the wreck, and detailed diagrams. Researchers can delve for more information about the *Titanic*, and uncover information and books about other disasters at sea and elsewhere. All will be intrigued with the other titles in the Scholastic Time Quest series, including Ballard's *Exploring the Bismarck* (1991) and *The Lost Wreck of the Isis* (1990), Sara C. Bisel's *Secrets of Vesuvius* (1991), and Shelley Tanaka's *The Disaster of the Hindenburg* (1993). DISASTERS. ICEBERGS. OCEAN. SHIPS. TITANIC.

1103   **Bash, Barbara.** *Shadows of Night: The Hidden World of the Little Brown Bat.* **Illus. by the author. Sierra Club, 1993. ISBN 0-87156-562-5**

[1 sitting, unp., Gr. 1–5] Turn around common fears children harbor about bats with this handsome picture book that lets you observe the life of a newborn little brown bat close up. Pull in fiction with *Stellaluna* by Janell Cannon and *Hattie the Backstage Bat* by Don Freeman, humor with *Batty Riddles* by Katy Hall and Lisa Eisenberg, and folktales with bat characters including Paul Goble's *Iktomi and the Boulder*, Tololwa M. Mollel's *A Promise to the Sun: An African Story*, and Judy Sierra's *The Elephant's Wrestling Match*. BATS.

1104   Bash, Barbara. *Tree of Life: The World of the African Baobab*. Illus. by the author. Sierra Club/ Little, Brown, 1989. ISBN 0-316-08305-4

[1 sitting, unp., Gr. 1–4] A legend told by the bushmen of the African savannahs claims that careless hyena planted the first baobab tree upside down, which is why its branches look more like roots. With a life span of more than one thousand years, the baobab makes a fascinating subject for children to research, and Bash's beautiful watercolors and rich text introduce us to the animals that depend on the tree for survival. Travel the world to view its trees: the U.S. Southwest for Barbara Bash's *Desert Giant: The World of the Saguaro Cactus* and *Cactus Hotel* by Brenda Guiberson, South America for Lynne Cherry's *The Great Kapok Tree*, Africa for Helen Cowcher's *Whistling Thorn*, and the rain forests for Jane Yolen's *Welcome to the Green House*. AFRICA. ECOLOGY. TREES.

1105   Bash, Barbara. *Urban Roosts: Where Birds Nest in the City*. Illus. by the author. Sierra Club/ Little, Brown, 1990. ISBN 0-316-08306-2

[1 sitting, unp., Gr. 3–6] Did you ever wonder where all those pigeons and other city birds live? Look up and you'll spot them on ledges, underpasses, under eaves, and even in traffic-light covers. The intricate pen-and-ink and watercolors will make everyone want to go outside to explore, and the text is sensible, interesting, and unpreachy. Look closer with Patricia Brennan Demuth's *Cradles in the Trees: The Story of Bird Nests*. Get a bird's-eye view of New York City with *Cat and Canary* by Michael Foreman and *Chester Cricket's Pigeon Ride* by George Selden, and wax poetic with *Bird Watch: A Book of Poetry* by Jane Yolen. BIRDS. CITIES AND TOWNS.

1106   Berg, Cami. *D Is for Dolphin*. Illus. by Janet Biondi. Windom, 1991. ISBN 1-879244-01-2

[1 sitting, unp., Gr. Pre–3] "A is for air," starts this lovely dolphin alphabet set against a dark blue ocean background. A glossary further defines each term in simple language that children can read and absorb. Supplement with an assortment of books including Greek legend *Arion and the Dolphins* by Lonzo Anderson, *The Magic School Bus on the Ocean Floor* by Joanna Cole, *How the Sea Began: A Taino Myth* by George Crespo, *Nine True Dolphin Stories* by Margaret Davidson, *Under the Sea from A to Z* by Anne Doubilet, *An Octopus Is Amazing* by Patricia Lauber, *Sea Shapes* by Suse MacDonald, and *I Am the Ocean* by Suzanna Marshak. *If You Ever Meet a Whale*, selected by Myra Cohn Livingston, is a breathtaking book of whale poems. ALPHABET BOOKS. DOLPHINS. MARINE ANIMALS. OCEAN.

1107   Blumberg, Rhoda. *Jumbo*. Illus. by Jonathan Hunt. Bradbury, 1992. ISBN 0-02-711683-2

[1 sitting, unp., Gr. 2–5] The leading attraction at the London Zoo and the world's largest animal in captivity in the mid-nineteenth century was purchased by P. T. Barnum and brought to America with its trainer, Matthew Scott, to appear as the star of Barnum's "Greatest Show on Earth." Jumbo, an invented name, became part of the English language, and is now synonymous with gigantic. The attractive picture book reads like fiction, and children will be enthralled by the story and saddened by the author's note that describes the elephant's untimely death. Give your listeners a laugh with Rudyard Kipling's classic, *The Elephant's Child*, and nurture their perceptions with Lillian F. Quigley's *The Blind Men and the Elephant* and Ed Young's *Seven Blind Mice*. For background on how elephants are still trained in India, read Jeremy Schmidt's color photo essay *In the Village of the Elephants* (Walker, 1994). CIRCUS. ELEPHANTS. ZOOS.

1108   **Brandenberg, Jim.** *To the Top of the World: Adventures with Arctic Wolves.* **Ed. by Joann Bren Guernsey. Photos by the author. Walker, 1993. ISBN 0-8027-8220-5**

[7 chapters, 44p., Gr. 4–6] On assignment for *National Geographic* in Canada's Northwest Territories to photograph the wolves and wildlife of Ellesmere Island, Brandenberg followed a pack of seven adult wolves and six pups for one riveting Arctic summer. Accompanying each page are large, exquisite color photographs that will cause children and adults to rethink their views of wolves as evil predators. Children will also be taken by Alice Mills Leighner's true account, *Reynard: The Story of a Fox Returned to the Wild*. Introduce realistic fiction with picture books *Dream Wolf* by Paul Goble, *The Eyes of Gray Wolf* by Jonathan London, *The Call of the Wolves* by Jim Murphy, and Jean Craighead George's unforgettable *Julie of the Wolves*. ARCTIC REGIONS. PERSONAL NARRATIVES. PHOTOGRAPHY. WOLVES.

1109   **Branley, Franklyn M.** *Shooting Stars.* **Illus. by Holly Keller. Crowell, 1989. ISBN 0-690-04703-7**

[1 sitting, 32p., Gr. 1–3] One of the first-rate Let's-Read-and-Find-Out Science Books series, this introduction explains how shooting stars are not stars at all, but meteors, from the Greek word meaning "something in the air." The facts are easily understood, interesting, and will get kids interested in skygazing on warm nights. Readers will also take a shine to the other astronomy books in the series, such as *The Big Dipper* (1991), *Comets* (1984), and *Eclipse: Darkness in Daytime* (1988). ASTRONOMY. METEORS.

1110   **Brenner, Martha.** *Abe Lincoln's Hat.* **Illus. by Donald Cook. Random House, 1994. ISBN 0-679-94977-1**

[1 sitting, 48p., Gr. 1–4] When Lincoln became a lawyer, he bought a tall black hat, the inside brim of which he used to store his letters and papers. The entertaining series of easy-to-read anecdotes helps put a human face on a fascinating man. Show the photographs in Russell Freedman's more difficult-to-read *Lincoln: A Photobiography*, and also read James Cross Giblin's *George Washington: A Picture Book Biography*, Edith Kunhardt's *Honest Abe*, and Myra Cohn Livingston's narrative poem, *Abraham Lincoln: A Man for All the People*. BIOGRAPHY. HATS. LINCOLN, ABRAHAM. PRESIDENTS–U.S.

1111   **Brown, Don.** *Ruth Law Thrills a Nation.* **Illus. by the author. Ticknor & Fields, 1993. ISBN 0-395-66404-7**

[1 sitting, 32p., Gr. K–4] An inspiring picture-book describes the arduous 1916 flight by the woman pilot who attempted to become the first person to fly from Chicago to New York City in one day, failed, but set a distance record of 590 miles nonstop. Gain additional airborne motivation from Robert Burleigh's *Flight: The Journey of Charles Lindbergh*, Chris L. Demarest's *Lindbergh*, Reeve Lindbergh's *View from the Air: Charles Lindbergh's Earth and Sky*, and Diane Siebert's *Plane Song*. AIRPLANES. BIOGRAPHY. FLIGHT. WOMEN–BIOGRAPHY.

1112   Brown, Laurene Krasny, and Marc Brown. *Dinosaurs to the Rescue! A Guide to Protecting Our Planet*. Illus. by the authors. Joy Street/ Little, Brown, 1992. ISBN 0-316-11087-6

[1 sitting, unp., Gr. Pre–3] "Who cares? It's only one can," rationalizes the Slobosaurus as he litters the grass, but in this amiable and consciousness-raising manual for simple ways we can take care of our earth, we learn otherwise. The dinosaur characters discover ways to conserve or recycle electricity, paper, and plastic, and make clear to us all that each tiny effort helps. A natural for Earth Week and every week, this one melds well with Anne Shelby's *What to Do About Pollution* and poetry books *The Earth Is Painted Green* by Barbara Brenner, *Earth Verses and Water Rhymes* by J. Patrick Lewis, and *Land, Sea, and Sky: Poems to Celebrate the Earth* selected by Catherine Paladino. DINOSAURS. ECOLOGY. ENVIRONMENTAL PROTECTION. RECYCLING.

1113   Brust, Beth Wagner. *Amazing Paper Cuttings of Hans Christian Andersen*. Illus. by Hans Christian Andersen. Ticknor & Fields, 1994. ISBN 0-395-66787-9

[8 chapters, 80p., Gr. 4–6] Not just a biography of the Danish storyteller and author of "The Ugly Duckling," "The Princess and the Pea," and so many other classic tales, this remarkable story tells about and is illustrated by the intricate and original paper cuttings Andersen cut with his scissors to entertain people as he related his stories. Over 250 of these fragile cutouts still exist, and children will want to take to their scissors to see how he did it. Intersperse chapters with readings of his tales. *Lives of the Writers: Comedies, Tragedies (and What the Neighbors Thought)* by Kathleen Krull contains a chapter on Andersen, plus 19 other tortured writers. ANDERSEN, HANS CHRISTIAN. ARTISTS. AUTHORS. BIOGRAPHY.

1114   Burleigh, Robert. *Flight: The Journey of Charles Lindbergh*. Illus. by Mike Wimmer. Philomel, 1991. ISBN 0-399-22272-3

[1 sitting, unp., Gr. 3–6] The terse present-tense narration of this powerful and thrilling picture book, including quotes from Lindbergh's flight diary of May 20, 1927, allows us to accompany him on his miraculous thirty-three-and-a-half-hour ordeal —the first solo nonstop transatlantic flight—and Mike Wimmer's dramatic oil paintings leave us breathless. Use an atlas and globe to plot out his voyage from New York to Paris. Questions to pose: Was his accomplishment worth it? Why? How do you think his life changed afterward? Also read Chris L. Demarest's picture book biography, *Lindbergh*, and Reeve Lindbergh's book of poems along with her father's photos, *View from the Air: Charles Lindbergh's Earth and Sky*. Introduce your frequent flyers to a pilot who broke a flying record more than ten years earlier in Don Brown's *Ruth Law Thrills a Nation*, and see what's so special about flying with Diane Siebert's *Plane Song*. AIRPLANES. BIOGRAPHY. FLIGHT. LINDBERGH, CHARLES A. PICTURE BOOKS FOR ALL AGES.

1115   Byars, Betsy. *The Moon and I*. Messner, 1992. ISBN 0-671-74165-9

[18 chapters, 96p., Gr. 4–6] Betsy Byars uses herself as the main character of her sparkling memoir/writer's advisory and she's every bit as entertaining as her fictional kids like Cracker Jackson, Bingo Brown, or the Blossom family. Her cozy discourse includes close encounters with a handsome wild blacksnake that she names Moon, childhood memories and conversations, and lots of sensible commentary on how she writes her books. Children familiar with Byars' books will be charmed at the way she uses "scraps" from her own life to flesh out her writing. Get acquainted with other authors' autobiographies, such as Roald Dahl's *Boy: Tales of Childhood*, Jean Little's *Little by Little*, and Cynthia Rylant's *Best Wishes*. AUTHORS. AUTOBIOGRAPHY. SNAKES. WRITING.

1116   Calmenson, Stephanie. *Rosie: A Visiting Dog's Story*. Illus. by Justin Sutcliffe. Houghton, 1994. ISBN 0-395-65477-7

[1 sitting, 47p., Gr. 1–4] The author's dog, Rosie, a lovable black-and-white, shaggy-furred Tibetan terrier, is a visiting dog, trained to "cheer up people who are sad, or sick, or lonely," from hospitalized children to elderly residents of nursing homes. An uplifting color photo essay, this will sensitize children to others with problems. Ask them: Why does Miss Calmenson participate in the visiting dog program? Sally Hobart Alexander's *Mom's Best Friend* and Audrey Osofsky's picture book *My Buddy* introduce a seeing eye dog and a helping dog for a child with muscular dystrophy. DOGS. HANDICAPS.

1117   Cherry, Lynne. *A River Ran Wild: An Environmental History*. Illus. by the author. Harcourt, 1992. ISBN 0-15-200542-0

[1 sitting, unp., Gr. 1–4] Over the generations, New Hampshire's Nashua River went from pristine to polluted to clean again as the Nashua Indians were driven off, the Industrial Revolution began the process of pumping waste and chemicals into the water, and, in the 1960s, committed environmentalist Marion Stoddart organized a campaign to rescue the river. As in her *The Great Kapok Tree*, Cherry's lovely and dignified watercolors make this a nonfiction picture book that shows how people can make a difference. *Dinosaurs to the Rescue! A Guide to Protecting Our Planet* by Laurene Krasny Brown and Marc Brown, Eve Bunting's *Someday a Tree*, Gloria Rand's *Prince William*, and Anne Shelby's *What to Do About Pollution* are effective consciousness-raisers as well. Find out more about water in *Follow the Water from Brook to Ocean* by Arthur Dorros and about the ecology of the Amazon River in *River* by Judith Heide Gilliland. ECOLOGY. ENVIRONMENT. POLLUTION. RIVERS. SOCIAL ACTION.

1118   Clements, Andrew. *Mother Earth's Counting Book*. Illus. by Lonni Sue Johnson. Picture Book Studio, 1992. ISBN 0-88708-138-X

[1 sitting, unp., Gr. K–5] Counting to ten and back again takes on global significance in this offbeat and appealing introduction to the planet. Double-page, soft, glowing watercolor washes extend the simplest of texts, showing one earth, two poles, three climate zones, four oceans, plus islands, deserts, continents, birds, mammals, fishes, plants, peoples, insects, seas, mountains, lakes, winds, rivers, and hemispheres. At the back of the book is a brief explanation of each feature. Whether used to introduce Earth to younger students, or to start a geography and globe unit for older ones, this is a thoughtful and gentle way to get children curious about their place in the sun. Explore the universe with Lynne Cherry's *The Armadillo from Amarillo*, Catherine Paladino's *Land, Sea, and Sky: Poems to Celebrate the Earth*, Robert E. Wells's *Is a Blue Whale the Biggest Thing There Is?*, and Jane Yolen's *What Rhymes with Moon?* ASTRONOMY. COUNTING BOOKS. EARTH. GEOGRAPHY. PICTURE BOOKS FOR ALL AGES.

1119   Cleveland, Will, and Mark Alvarez. *Yo, Millard Fillmore! (And All Those Other Presidents You Don't Know)*. Illus. by Tate Nation. Fundamentals, 1992. ISBN 0-9632778-0-4

[112p., Gr. 4–6] This lighthearted review of each president includes dates and facts on the left-hand page, and a cartoon-style illustration with a cumulative mnemonic story to help recall each president's name and sequence on the right. It's comical, it's great fun, and by gum it works! The "Jeopardy"-style quiz at the back will inspire students to undertake additional research about their favorite leaders. Bone up on more fascinating facts with Lila Perl's entertaining and enlightening *It Happened in America: True Stories from the Fifty States*, and then have a few laughs with *Hail to the Chief! Jokes About the Presidents* by Diane and Clint Burns. MNEMONICS. PRESIDENTS–U.S. U.S.–HISTORY.

1120   Coerr, Eleanor. *Sadako*. Illus. by Ed Young. Putnam, 1993. ISBN 0-399-21771-1

[1 sitting, 32 pages, Gr. 2–5] It wasn't until 1954 that a 12-year-old schoolgirl from Hiroshima, Sadako Sasaki, was hospitalized with leukemia or "atom-bomb disease." Recalling the old story that if a sick person folds one thousand paper cranes, the gods will make her well, Sadako folded over 600 cranes before she died, while friends and classmates folded the remaining cranes that were buried with her and kept her memory alive. Originally published as a longer biography, *Sadako and the Thousand Paper Cranes*, Coerr reworked it, first into an award-winning video with art by noted illustrator Ed Young, and now into this touching picture book. Also read Coerr's chapter book *Mieko and the Fifth Treasure*, Junko Morimoto's searing picture-book remembrance, *My Hiroshima*, Allen Say's *Tree of Cranes* and *Grandfather's Journey*, and Ruth Wells's *A to Zen: A Book of Japanese Culture*. BIOGRAPHY. DEATH. JAPAN. SICK. WORLD WAR, 1939-1945.

1121   Cole, Joanna. *The Magic School Bus Lost in the Solar System*. Illus. by Bruce Degen. Scholastic, 1990. ISBN 0-590-41428-3

[1–2 sittings, unp., Gr. 1–4] Though unflappable science teacher Ms. Frizzle plans her latest field trip to see a sky show at the planetarium, it's closed for repairs, and her wisecracking students are not entirely surprised when the bus tilts back and blasts off through the atmosphere for a firsthand look at the moon and the other eight planets. Intrepid Frizzle of the curriculum-coordinated wardrobe assigns her jaded students reports that line the outside margin of each page. The format is perfect to introduce a new astronomy unit or review what you've learned. My third graders crowed, "We knew that" each time I read a new fact aloud. Keep exploring with *Postcards from Pluto: A Tour of the Solar System* by Loreen Leedy and *Is a Blue Whale the Biggest Thing There Is?* by Robert E. Wells. Sally Ride and Susan Okie show us the real thing in *To Space and Back. Blast Off! Poems About Space* selected by Lee Bennett Hopkins and *Spacey Riddles* by Katy Hall and Lisa Eisenberg will also please. ASTRONOMY. BUSES. LOST. PICTURE BOOKS FOR ALL AGES. TEACHERS.

1122   Cole, Joanna. *The Magic School Bus on the Ocean Floor.* Illus. by Bruce Degen. Scholastic, 1992. ISBN 0-590-41430-5

[1 sitting, unp., Gr. 2–4] Taking along Lenny the Lifeguard as a guest passenger, Ms. Frizzle's class investigates a variety of aquatic ecosystems firsthand before returning to dry land. From the acerbic cartoon-bubble comments of the wiseacre class to the many "report" posters on the sides of the pages, this joyride is another informative mélange of facts and fun. Go back for a closer look at marine animals with *D Is for Dolphin* by Cami Berg, *Under the Sea from A to Z* by Anne Doubilet, *An Octopus Is Amazing* by Patricia Lauber, and Elizabeth Tayntor's *Dive to the Coral Reefs. Follow the Water from Brook to Ocean* by Arthur Dorros, *I Am the Ocean* by Suzanna Marshak, and *Until I Saw the Sea: A Collection of Seashore Poems* collected by Alison Shaw offer facts and poetry while *How the Sea Began: A Taino Myth* by George Crespo and *Why the Tides Ebb and Flow* by Joan Chase Bowden will satisfy folklorists. BUSES. MARINE ANIMALS. OCEAN. SEASHORE. TEACHERS.

1123   Cole, Joanna. *My Puppy Is Born.* Photos by Margaret Miller. Morrow, 1991. ISBN 0-688-09771-5

[1 sitting, 48p., Gr. Pre–2] Everyone will fall in love with the subject of this color photo essay, a cuddly newborn Norfolk terrier named Dolly that we follow from birth to eight weeks. Be forewarned that there are two clear photos of the puppy as it emerges from its mother. *Lucy Comes to Stay* by Rosemary Wells is a picture book about a girl and her beloved new white puppy. The poems in *Raining Cats and Dogs* by Jane Yolen will get you talking about new pets. BIRTH. DOGS.

1124   Columbus, Christopher. Ed. by Steve Lowe. *Log of Christopher Columbus.* Illus. by Robert Sabuda. Philomel, 1992. ISBN 0-399-22139-5

[1 sitting, unp., Gr. 4–6] Using selections from the log Columbus made on his first voyage to the west, Sabuda has set out the explorer's observations in a handsome picture book of linoleum-cut illustrations. Peter and Connie Roop's *I, Columbus; My Journal—1492–3* incorporates the same material in longer form. Peter Sis's *Follow the Dream* is an unusual and attractive picture book description of the Columbus story. Get an overview of those early days of exploration with Jean Fritz's *Around the World in a Hundred Years: From Henry the Navigator to Magellan* and Betsy and Giulio Maestro's *The Discovery of the Americas,* and pull in the story of Cortez and his conquest of Mexico with *The Sad Night: The Story of an Aztec Victory and a Spanish Loss* by Sally Schofer Mathews. Flesh out Columbus's story with some fiction, as in Pam Conrad's *Pedro's Journal,* Michael Dorris's

Morning Girl, and Jane Yolen's *Encounter*. AMERICA–DISCOVERY AND EXPLORATION. COLUMBUS, CHRISTOPHER. DIARIES. EXPLORERS.

1125   **Cone, Molly.** *Come Back, Salmon: How a Group of Dedicated Kids Adopted Pigeon Creek and Brought It Back to Life.* **Photos by Sidnee Wheelwright. Sierra Club, 1992. ISBN 0-87156-572-2**

[6 chapters, 48 pages, Gr. 4–6] See how the 450 students of Jackson Elementary School in Everett, Washington, adopted a muddy and polluted creek in 1984, cleaned up and patrolled the creek bed, stopped City Hall from building a storage facility there, and released baby coho salmon into the now-cleaner waters. Wheelwright's vibrant color photos personalize this real-life ecological adventure that should inspire other schools to embark on similar worthwhile missions, such as those described in Phillip Hoose's *It's Our World, Too!* For additional projects that kids can do as a class, consult Patricia Adams and Jean Marzollo's *The Helping Hands Handbook* (Random House, 1992) and *50 Simple Things Kids Can Do to Save the Earth* by The Earth Works Group. Other ecologically important titles include Lynne Cherry's *A River Ran Wild*, Carol Greene's *The Old Ladies Who Liked Cats*, Judith Heide Gilliland's *River*, Gloria Rand's *Prince William*, and Jane Yolen's *Welcome to the Green House*. ECOLOGY. ENVIRONMENT. FISHES. SCHOOLS. SOCIAL ACTION.

1126   **Cowcher, Helen.** *Whistling Thorn.* **Illus. by the author. Scholastic, 1993. ISBN 0-590-47299-2**

[unp., Gr. K–2] In this true ecological tale, we see how the acacia bush developed thorns to protect itself from the rhinos and giraffes when they continued to eat so many of the leaves that the bushes were unable to regenerate. Cowcher's full-page paintings are stunning. *How Giraffe Got Such a Long Neck . . . and Why Rhino Is So Grumpy* is an East African folktale retold by Michael Rosen that ties right in. Look at other plants in Barbara Bash's *Tree of Life: The World of the African Baobab*, Lynne Cherry's *The Great Kapok Tree*, and Brenda Guiberson's *Cactus Hotel*. Give a further picture of African landscapes with *The Hunter* by Paul Geraghty, *Masai and I* by Virginia Kroll, *Learning to Swim in Swaziland: A Child's-Eye View of a Southern African Country* by Nila K. Leigh, *Somewhere in Africa* by Ingid Mennem and Niki Daly, and *Young Lions* by Toshi Yoshida. AFRICA. ECOLOGY. GIRAFFES. PLANTS. RHINOCEROS.

1127   **Cummings, Pat, comp.** *Talking with Artists.* **Bradbury, 1992. ISBN 0-02-724245-5**

[96p., Gr. 2–6] Fourteen personable children's-book illustrators are profiled in this handsome tribute to the creative spirit. Each six-page chapter is illustrated with one childhood and one adult photograph, and color reproductions of two artworks: one recent, and one done when the artist was a child. Through the artists' own remembrances of how they got started, and their answers to a series of questions children might ask (What do you enjoy drawing the most? Where do you get your ideas?), budding artists will be encouraged to keep drawing. Students will easily recognize many of these artists' works, and be delighted to learn more about the artists and read their other books. Also irresistible are

Michael J. Rosen's *Speak! Children's Book Illustrators Brag About Their Dogs* and Zheng Zhensun and Alice Low's *A Young Painter: The Life and Paintings of Wang Yani—China's Extraordinary Young Artist*. ARTISTS. BIOGRAPHY. ILLUSTRATORS.

1128   Demarest, Chris L. *Lindbergh*. Illus. by the author. Crown, 1993. ISBN 0-517-58719-X

[1 sitting, unp., Gr. 2–4] A picture book biography that shows us how a childhood dream can come true with hard work and perseverance, this takes us from Charles Lindbergh's early flying experiences through his famous flight in the Spirit of St. Louis, with an afterword about his later life. Fill in details of his 1927 flight to Paris with Robert Burleigh's spectacular *Flight: The Journey of Charles Lindbergh*, and follow up with his daughter's collection of poems and his photos in Reeve Lindbergh's *View from the Air: Charles Lindbergh's Earth and Sky*. AIRPLANES. FLIGHT. LINDBERGH, CHARLES A.

1129   Demuth, Patricia Brennan. *Cradles in the Trees: The Story of Bird Nests*. Illus. by Suzanne Barnes. Macmillan, 1994. ISBN 0-02-728466-2

[1 sitting, unp., Gr. K–3] Some birds weave their nests using their beaks like sewing machines, and some use mud to hold the twigs and grasses together. The Baltimore oriole's nest hangs from a tree branch like a cradle and rocks with the wind. Facts like these are held together with clear, compelling watercolors that will ensure your listeners will never take birds for granted again. *This Way Home* by Lisa Westberg Peters looks at the annual migration of the savannah sparrow, and *Chickens Aren't the Only Ones* by Ruth Heller identifies a variety of egg-laying animals. See about the birds in *Urban Roosts: Where Birds Nest in the City* by Barbara Bash, *Rosie & the Yellow Ribbon* by Paula DePaolo, and *Feathers for Lunch* by Lois Ehlert. BIRDS.

1130   Demuth, Patricia Brennan. *Those Amazing Ants*. Illus. by S. D. Schindler. Macmillan, 1994. ISBN 0-02-728467-0

[1 sitting, unp., Gr. K–2] Detailed gouache paintings and an engrossing text take us underground where we see the many rooms ants construct, such as sickroom, pantry, and nursery, and get an ant's eye view of daily life. Did you know ants yawn and stretch after awakening from a nap and lick themselves like cats to clean up? Kids won't be so quick to stomp on wandering ants once they read this and *Ant Cities* by Arthur Dorros. Both *Effie* by Beverly Allinson and *The Ant and the Elephant* by Bill Peet show the small coexisting with the mighty, and both the rhyming math story *One Hundred Hungry Ants* by Elinor J. Pinczes and *Step by Step* by Diane Wolkstein show their dogged determination. ANTS. INSECTS.

1131   De Zutter, Hank. *Who Says a Dog Goes Bow-Wow?* Illus. by Suse MacDonald. Doubleday, 1993. ISBN 0-385-30659-8

[1 sitting, unp., Gr. Pre–2] Try out this "international zoo" of animal noises in many languages, with a single- or double-page spread and color collages for each of 16 animals. For instance, dogs say how-how in Russian, huf-huf in Hebrew and Farsi, wan-wan in Japanese, and wah-wah in French, all of which your animal lovers will need to model aloud. Read this one and Marc Robinson's *Cock-a-Doodle-Doo! What Does It Sound Like to You?* when you're introducing the concept of onomatopoeia, plus *Rat-a-Tat, Pitter Pat* by Alan Benjamin, *Do Bunnies Talk?* by Dayle-Ann Dodds, *Who Says That?* by Arnold L. Shapiro, and *The Listening Walk* by Paul Showers. Standards for English animal sounds include Bill Martin, Jr.'s *Polar Bear, Polar Bear, What Do You Hear?* and versions of "Old MacDonald Had a Farm" by Lorinda Bryan Cauley, Carol Jones, Tracey Campbell Pearson, or Glen Rounds. Arthur Dorros's *This Is My House* and Debra Leventhal's *What Is Your Language?* also introduce children to some basic foreign phrases. ANIMALS. ENGLISH LANGUAGE–ONOMATOPOEIC WORDS. LANGUAGE. SOUND EFFECTS.

1132   Dodson, Peter. *An Alphabet of Dinosaurs.* Illus. by Wayne D. Barlowe. Scholastic, 1995. ISBN 0-590-46486-8

[1 sitting. unp., Gr. 1–3] Each of the 26 dinosaurs showcased in this remarkable book is described in a few short sentences and brought to life in an enthralling full-page color painting guaranteed to drive kids wild. Librarians take heed and order several copies! *How Big Were the Dinosaurs?* by Bernard Most and *Dinosaurs! Strange and Wonderful* by Laurence Pringle will take the edge off children's bottomless appetite for facts about the prehistoric reptiles. Carol Carrick's *Patrick's Dinosaurs* and *What Happened to Patrick's Dinosaurs?*, Diane Dawson Hearn's *Dad's Dinosaur Day*, Henry Schwartz's *How I Captured a Dinosaur*, and Paul and Henrietta Stickland's *Dinosaur Roar!* will appeal to fun-lovers, while Dennis Nolan's *Dinosaur Dreams* and Eric Rohmann's wordless *Time Flies* will add a sense of mystery and wonder. ALPHABET BOOKS. DINOSAURS.

1133   Dorros, Arthur. *Follow the Water from Brook to Ocean.* Illus. by the author. HarperCollins, 1991. ISBN 0-06-021599-2

[1 sitting, 32p., Gr. K–3] Ever wonder where water goes as it flows downhill? Dorros explains its journey in understandable language, and on the way touches on erosion, waterfalls, floods, dams, reservoirs, and water pollution. This Let's-Read-and-Find-Out Science Book works well with *Water's Way* by Lisa Westberg Peters, while *Splish Splash* by Joan Bransfield Graham is a book of appealing concrete poems all about water. Go underwater with *How the Sea Began: A Taino Myth* by George Crespo, *Under the Sea from A to Z* by Anne Doubilet, *An Octopus Is Amazing* by Patricia Lauber, *I Am the Ocean* by Suzanna Marshak, and *Until I Saw the Sea: A Collection of Seashore Poems* collected by Alison Shaw. OCEAN. RIVERS. WATER.

1134   Doubilet, Anne. *Under the Sea from A to Z.* Photos by David Doubilet. Crown, 1991. ISBN 0-517-57837-9

[1 sitting, unp., Gr. K–5] Remarkable underwater color photographs capture an alphabet of 26 creatures including the marine iguana, the nudibranch, the poisonous blue-ringed octopus, and the pufferfish. Each is described in a large-print, one-sentence statement and then further defined in a fact-filled paragraph in smaller print. The gorgeous paintings and poems in *If You Ever Meet a Whale,* selected by Myra Cohn Livingston, will make you want to visit the ocean, and *Until I Saw the Sea: A Collection of Seashore Poems* collected by Alison Shaw will have you longing for the beach. Stay close to shore with picture books *A House for Hermit Crab* by Eric Carle and *Is This a House for Hermit Crab?* by Megan McDonald and dive down deep with *D Is for Dolphin* by Cami Berg, *An Octopus Is Amazing* by Patricia Lauber, and *I Am the Ocean* by Suzanna Marshak. Look into a mythic origin of the ocean with *How the Sea Began: A Taino Myth* by George Crespo. ALPHABET BOOKS. MARINE ANIMALS. OCEAN.

1135   Earth Works Group. *50 Simple Things Kids Can Do to Save the Earth.* Illus. by Michele Montez. Andrews & McMeel, 1990. ISBN 0-8362-2301-2 (pbk.)

[156p. Gr. 3–6] While you won't read this straight through like a novel, the 50 suggestions for recycling, protecting animals, using energy wisely, and broadcasting the conservation message are bolstered with projects, fascinating facts, and practical suggestions. Environmentally conscious readers will gleam more ideas from Molly Cone's *Come Back, Salmon*, Patricia Adams and Jean Marzollo's *The Helping Hands Handbook* (Random House, 1992), and Phillip Hoose's *It's Our World, Too!* Picture books that make a point about our role in caring for the earth include Lynne Cherry's *A River Ran Wild*, Carol Greene's *The Old Ladies Who Liked Cats*, Judith Heide Gilliland's *River*, and Gloria Rand's *Prince William*. ECOLOGY. ENVIRONMENTAL PROTECTION. RECYCLING.

1136   Eldin, Peter. *The Trickster's Handbook.* Illus. by Roger Smith. Sterling, 1989. ISBN 0-8069-5740-9

[95p., Gr. 3–6] This clever collection of more than 100 easy-to-pull-off magic tricks and practical jokes will amaze, amuse, and sometimes astonish any gullible audience. Have everyone select a trick to try from this book or Gyles Brandreth's *Brain-Teasers and Mind-Benders*, Richard E. Churchill's *Devilish Bets to Trick Your Friends*, Vicki Cobb and Kathy Darling's *Bet You Can!* and *Bet You Can't!*, Louis Phillips's *263 Brain Busters*, and Laurence B. White, Jr. and Ray Broekel's *The Surprise Book*. JOKES. TRICKS.

1137   Esbensen, Barbara Juster. *Great Northern Diver: The Loon.* Illus. by Mary Barrett Brown. Little, Brown, 1990. ISBN 0-316-24954-6

[1 sitting, unp., Gr. 2–6] A factual but lyrical text and realistic and stately double-page paintings portray the habits and peculiarities of this most primitive of birds whose unflattering name and high-pitched laughing call are all most people know. For older children, contrast the format and the way the information is presented with the facts and color photographs of *Hummingbirds: Jewels in the Sky* by Esther Quesada Tyrrell. *Urban Roosts: Where Birds Nest in the City* by Barbara Bash is also riveting. Take a closer and more lyrical look at birds with *Bird Watch: A Book of Poetry* by Jane Yolen. BIRDS. LOONS.

1138   Everett, Gwen. *John Brown: One Man Against Slavery.* Illus. by Jacob Lawrence. Rizzoli, 1993. ISBN 0-8478-1702-4

[1 sitting, 32 pages, Gr. 5–6] In a fictional but fact-based narration by John Brown's daughter Annie, this is a stark and serious picture book about the motivation behind Brown's abortive raid on Harper's Ferry on October 16, 1859, which he undertook to end slavery. The illustrations, paintings done in 1941 by the renowned African American artist, are harsh and compelling, and the story is bleak. *Go Free or Die: A Story About Harriet Tubman* by Jeri Ferris, and Faith Ringgold's picture book *Aunt Harriet's Underground Railroad in the Sky* give background into the Underground Railroad. *Behind the Lines* by Isabelle Holland examines racial clashes in New York City during the Civil War, while *Pink and Say* by Patricia Polacco is a picture book about two young soldiers, one white, one black, that brings the reasons for the war into sharp focus. ABOLITIONISTS. BIOGRAPHY. BROWN, JOHN. SLAVERY.

1139   Facklam, Margery. *And Then There Was One: The Mysteries of Extinction.* Illus. by Pamela Johnson. Sierra Club/ Little, Brown, 1990. ISBN 0-316-25984-5

[7 chapters, 56p., Gr. 3–6] Starting off with a touching chapter about Lonesome George, the last tortoise of his kind—a saddle-back from Pinta Island—the author makes us care about endangered and extinct animals and see our responsibility to them. She discusses evolution; the death of the dinosaurs; how humans have hastened the death of passenger pigeons, dodos, moas, and auks, and endangered other animals; the *Exxon Valdez* oil disaster; DDT; and acid rain; and ends up with the good news about how we're saving some animals. *Prince William* by Gloria Rand is about a seal rescued from the Alaskan spill. Look for project tie-ins with professional resources Michael J. Caduto and Joseph Bruchac's *Keepers of the Animals: Native American Stories and Wildlife Activities for Children,* and Glenn McGlathery and Norma J. Livo's *Who's Endangered on Noah's Ark? Literary and Scientific Activities for Teachers and Parents.* ANIMALS, EXTINCT. ENDANGERED SPECIES. WILDLIFE CONSERVATION.

1140   Falwell, Cathryn. *The Letter Jesters.* Illus. by the author. Ticknor & Fields, 1994. ISBN 0-395-66898-0

[1 sitting, unp., Gr. 2–4] A cast of two jesters and their little dog Typo introduce the many sizes and styles, or typefaces, of letters as used in typesetting. Bright, sassy graphics present themselves in Roman and italic, light and bold, serif and sans serif, uppercase and lowercase. Children will want to examine the typefaces in books, newspapers, magazines, and product labels to compare styles, and may want to design their own typeface. If you have a computer with a fair amount of fonts, be sure to print out examples. *Dream Peddler* by Gail E. Haley and *Books and Libraries* by Jack Knowlton take listeners from letters and words to books. ALPHABET. BOOKS AND READING. PRINTING.

1141   Ferris, Jeri. *Go Free or Die: A Story About Harriet Tubman.* Illus. by Karen Ritz. Carolrhoda, 1988. ISBN 0-87614-317-6

[5 chapters, 63 pages, Gr. 3–5] In the face of danger and injustice, Harriet Tubman helped lead more than 300 slaves north to freedom from 1850 until the start of the Civil War. Ferris's fictionalized depiction of Tubman's life from childhood until she herself escaped slavery is an effective and exciting introduction to this courageous woman. Also see David A. Adler's *A Picture Book of Harriet Tubman* and *A Picture Book of Sojourner Truth*, Ann McGovern's *Runaway Slave*, and Faith Ringgold's *Aunt Harriet's Underground Railroad in the Sky*. Deborah Hopkinson's *Sweet Clara and the Freedom Quilt*, Dolores Johnson's *Now Let Me Fly: The Story of a Slave Family*, F. N. Monjo's *The Drinking Gourd*, and Jeanette Winter's *Follow the Drinking Gourd* all deal with the Underground Railroad. AFRICAN AMERICANS–BIOGRAPHY. BIOGRAPHY. SLAVERY. U.S.–HISTORY–1783-1865.

1142   **Fraser, Mary Ann.** *One Giant Leap*. **Illus. by the author. Henry Holt, 1993. ISBN 0-8050-2295-3**

[1 sitting, unp., Gr. 4–6] Classes seeking information on the first moon landing by Apollo 11 in 1969 will be transported into the spacecraft and the control room through the quote-filled text and the awesome full-page color paintings in Fraser's absorbing book. Note the updates in technology two decades later with Sally Ride and Susan Okie's *To Space and Back*, a description of the space shuttle. *The Moon and You* by E. C. Krupp provides interesting moon facts. Broaden your scope and imagination with *Why the Sun and Moon Live in the Sky*, an African folktale by Elphinstone Dayrell, *Moon Mother: A Native American Creation Tale* by Ed Young, and the space-based poems in *What Rhymes with Moon?* by Jane Yolen. Robert Burleigh's *Flight: The Journey of Charles Lindbergh* is a close-up account of another memorable journey. ASTRONAUTS. MOON. PROJECT APOLLO. SPACE FLIGHT.

1143   **Fraser, Mary Ann.** *On Top of the World: The Conquest of Mount Everest*. **Illus. by the author. Henry Holt, 1991. ISBN 0-8050-1578-7**

[1 sitting, unp., Gr. 4–6] Climb Everest with Edmund Hillary and Tenzing Norgay, the two adventurers who, in May of 1953, finally conquered the 29,000-foot peak that is still used as a metaphor for achieving the impossible. This thrilling nonfiction picture book description of their ascent, along with the dramatic paintings, will leave children gasping as they contemplate the cold, snow, lack of oxygen, and danger. Pair this with other "firsts," such as Robert Burleigh's *Flight: The Journey of Charles Lindbergh*, and Mary Ann Fraser's Project Apollo description, *One Giant Leap*. Climb more mountains with James Ramsay Ullman's thrilling novel *Banner in the Sky*. EVEREST, MOUNT. MOUNTAINEERING. MOUNTAINS.

1144   **Fritz, Jean.** *Around the World in a Hundred Years: From Henry the Navigator to Magellan*. **Illus. by Anthony Bacon Venti. Putnam, 1994. ISBN 0-399-22527-1**

[12 chapters, 128p., Gr. 5–6] Starting in 1421 with Prince Henry the Navigator who sent out sailors to explore the western coast of Africa, the likes of Diaz, Columbus, da Gama, Cabral, Cabot, Vespucci, Ponce de León, Balboa, and Magellan attempted to find new ocean routes to the Orient. Jean Fritz knows how to make history compelling and entertaining, and each chapter is laced with details that expose both the heroism and rampant greed of those European men who filled in all those empty spaces on their maps. During that time, Cortés invaded Mexico, as described vividly in picture book *The Sad Night: The Story of an Aztec Victory and a Spanish Loss* by Sally Schofer Mathews. *The Log of Christopher Columbus*, edited by Steve Lowe, is another interesting picture-book treatment. EXPLORERS.

1145   Gackenbach, Dick. *Mighty Tree*. Illus. by the author. Harcourt, 1992. ISBN 0-15-200519-6

[1 sitting, unp., Gr. Pre–2] With the simplest of texts, we are introduced to three trees and follow their fates as the first is cut down and turned into paper products for us to use, the second becomes the Christmas tree at Rockefeller Center in New York City, and the third remains standing, providing shelter for the animals and tiny seeds to start the process over again. The bright and friendly watercolors make this a book children will appreciate. Others not to miss include Harry Behn's poem *Trees*, Bruce Hiscock's *The Big Tree*, George Ella Lyon's *A B Cedar: An Alphabet of Trees*, and Janice May Udry's *A Tree Is Nice*. Eve Bunting's *Someday a Tree* is a somber picture book about the death of a tree from toxic chemicals, while in Lisa Campbell Ernst's *Squirrel Park*, a boy and his squirrel save their tree from being cut down. TREES.

1146   Gardner, Jane Mylum. *Henry Moore: From Bones and Stones to Sketches and Sculptures*. Illus. with photos. Four Winds, 1993. ISBN 0-02-735812-7

[1 sitting, 32 p., Gr. 2–5] This black-and-white photo essay about the modern art English sculptor (1898–1986) is just the ticket when discussing how an artist gets an idea and carries it to completion. Children will be intrigued at the photos of Moore in his studio and on his bicycle, of his huge curvy sculptures, and the reproductions of his sketches, all of which will help them appreciate his unusual work. Pull in Tomie dePaola's autobiographical picture book *The Art Lesson*, Cynthia Rylant's story of a whale-obsessed painter in *All I See*, and *The Jade Stone: A Chinese Folktale* by Caryn Yacowitz about a sculptor who paints what he feels and not what the emperor demands. ARTISTS. BIOGRAPHY. SCULPTORS.

1147   George, Jean Craighead. *The First Thanksgiving*. Illus. by Thomas Locker. Philomel, 1993. ISBN 0-399-21991-9

[1 sitting, 32p., Gr. 1–4] Starting with the early 1600s, when armor-clad English sailors kidnapped Squanto and other Pawtuxet men and sold them into slavery, through that first bitter winter in 1620 when the Pilgrims coped with hunger, disease, and death, and were aided by Massasoit and Squanto, the elegant text, coupled with sweeping oil paintings, is a memorable retelling. For a fictionalized take on the Thanksgiving story, also read *Friendship's First Thanksgiving* by William Accorsi, *Three Young Pilgrims* by Cheryl Harness, and *Oh, What a Thanksgiving!* by Steven Kroll. *Thanksgiving: Stories and Poems* compiled by Caroline Feller Bauer is a pleasant collection, as is *Merrily Comes Our Harvest In: Poems for Thanksgiving*, compiled by Lee Bennett Hopkins, and all will enjoy Jack Prelutsky's lighthearted poems in *It's Thanksgiving*. HOLIDAYS. INDIANS OF NORTH AMERICA. PILGRIMS. THANKSGIVING. U.S. HISTORY–COLONIAL PERIOD.

1148   Gibbons, Gail. *From Seed to Plant.* Illus. by the author. Holiday House, 1991. ISBN 0-8234-0872-8

[1 sitting, unp., Gr. K–3] How seeds grow into plants and flowers is detailed with close-up watercolors in this basic introduction, which discusses pollination and the parts of a plant. A final bean seed project is effectively laid out and easy to follow. *Bean and Plant* by Christine Bach and *The Reason for a Flower* by Ruth Heller are also effective nonfiction titles to use, and *Flower Garden* by Eve Bunting, *Alison's Zinnia* by Anita Lobel, and *The Rose in My Garden* by Arnold Lobel pull in the story angle. FLOWERS. PLANTS. SEEDS.

1149   Gibbons, Gail. *Wolves.* Illus. by the author. Holiday House, 1994. ISBN 0-8234-1127-3

[1 sitting, unp., Gr. 1–3] This attractive first primer on the lives and behavior of wolves covers interesting territory, describing organization of a pack, ways wolves communicate, and how they raise their young. Large-scale pen-and-ink and watercolor illustrations are just right for group viewing, though you'll also want to show the astounding color photos in *To the Top of the World: Adventures with Arctic Wolves* by Jim Brandenberg. Picture books *Dream Wolf* by Paul Goble, *The Eyes of Gray Wolf* by Jonathan London, and *The Call of the Wolves* by Jim Murphy buttress the information in Gibbons's factual text. WOLVES.

1150   Giblin, James Cross. *George Washington: A Picture Book Biography.* Illus. by Michael Dooling. Scholastic, 1992. ISBN 0-590-42550-1

[1 sitting, 48p., Gr. 1–4] Literate, engrossing, and intelligent nonfiction for the youngest readers, this hits the highlights of Washington's life, including childhood trouble with spelling, the death of his half brother Lawrence, life at Mount Vernon with Martha and her children, the Revolutionary War, and the first presidency. Majestic paintings, a fascinating afterword consisting of a chronology, a detailed explanation of the fictitious cherry tree incident, a list of Washington's own "Rules of Good Behavior," information about Mount Vernon, and a detailed index help make this a model of biography for younger children. Find out more about the cover painting of Washington crossing the Delaware in Elvira Woodruff's compelling time-travel historical fantasy *George Washington's Socks*. BIOGRAPHY. PRESIDENTS–U.S. U.S.–HISTORY–REVOLUTION. WASHINGTON, GEORGE.

1151   Giff, Patricia Reilly. *Show Time at the Polk Street School: Plays You Can Do Yourself or in the Classroom.* Illus. by Blanche Sims. Delacorte, 1992. ISBN 0-395-30794-2

[101p., Gr. 1–3] In this easy-to-read Reader's Theater book are three plays based on three of Giff's popular Polk Street School books, along with advice on props, costumes, and makeup. Keep kids stagestruck with *Presenting Reader's Theater: Plays and Poems to Read Aloud* by Caroline Feller Bauer, *The Herbie Jones Reader's Theater: Funny Scenes to Read Aloud* by Suzy Kline, *Stories on Stage: Scripts for Reader's Theater* by Aaron Shepard, and *Fantastic Theater: Puppets and Plays for Young Performers and Young Audiences* by Judy Sierra. PLAYS–COLLECTIONS. READER'S THEATER. SCHOOLS.

1152   Gilliland, Judith Heide. *River*. Illus. by Joyce Powzyk. Clarion, 1993. ISBN 0-395-55963-4

[1 sitting, unp., Gr. K–3] Here's a poetic picture book about the world's mightiest river, the Amazon, and the many unusual animals that inhabit the river, forests, trees, and sky, with breathtaking watercolors that will send listeners scurrying to the library for more information. The implied message for conservation makes this a good companion to *The Great Kapok Tree* and *A River Ran Wild: An Environmental History* by Lynne Cherry, *Rain Forest* by Helen Cowcher, *Follow the Water from Brook to Ocean* by Arthur Dorros, and Jane Yolen's *Welcome to the Green House*. AMAZON RIVER. ECOLOGY. PICTURE BOOKS FOR ALL AGES. RAIN FORESTS. RIVERS.

1153   Golenbock, Peter. *Teammates*. Illus. by Paul Bacon. Gulliver/ Harcourt, 1990. ISBN 0-15-200603-6

[1 sitting, unp., Gr. 2–6] In a thought-provoking picture book, we learn how Jackie Robinson was drafted from the Negro Leagues in 1947 by Brooklyn Dodgers general manager Branch Rickey to become the first black major league player. Alec Gillman's illustrations for *Take Me Out to the Ballgame*, a picture book of the song by Jack Norworth, show Robinson up at bat during Game Five of the 1947 World Series. Ken Mochizuki's *Baseball Saved Us* is also about prejudice. Pull in baseball poems collected in *Extra Innings* by Lee Bennett Hopkins and *At the Crack of the Bat* by Lillian Morrison. In Barbara Cohen's fiction book *Thank You, Jackie Robinson*, a ten-year-old white boy shares a passion for Robinson and the Dodgers with his friend, a 60-year-old black man. The narrative poems *Keep on Singing: A Ballad of Marian Anderson* and *Let Freedom Ring: A Ballad of Martin Luther King, Jr.* by Myra Cohn Livingston and *Happy Birthday, Martin Luther King* by Jean Marzollo are tributes to other African American heroes. AFRICAN AMERICANS–BIOGRAPHY. BASEBALL. BIOGRAPHY. PREJUDICE. RACE RELATIONS.

1154   Gryski, Camilla. *Hands On, Thumbs Up: Secret Handshakes, Fingerprints, Sign Languages, and More Handy Ways to Have Fun with Hands*. Illus. by Pat Cupples. Addison Wesley, 1991. ISBN 0-201-56756-3 (pbk.)

[112p., Gr. 3–6] Gryski, the string wizard who wrote the indispensable *Cat's Cradle, Owl's Eyes: A Book of String Games*, has taken a closer look at how we use our hands and has compiled a jim-dandy collection of trivia, tricks, stories, and amazing facts. While you probably won't read this straight through, there's information here to enliven all those times you need some filler to wake the kids up. Students will be astonished to find they can write left to right as described on page 49, and the nine times table described on page 55 will be a hit in math. Also handy are *Why the Willow Weeps: A Story Told with Hands* by Marshall Izen and Jim West, *Hanimations* by Mario Mariotti, and *The Handmade Alphabet* by Laura Rankin, a sign-language alphabet book. HANDS. SENSES AND SENSATION. SIGN LANGUAGE. TOUCH.

1155   Guiberson, Brenda. *Cactus Hotel*. Illus. by Megan Lloyd. Henry Holt, 1991. ISBN 0-8050-1333-4

[1 sitting, unp., Gr. 1–4] This book shows how from the birth of a saguaro (pronounced suh-WAH-ruh or suh-GWA-row, in case you're not from the Southwest) cactus until its death 200 years later, the many desert animals depend on it for food and shelter. Barbara Bash's *Desert Giant: The World of the Saguaro Cactus* is also lovely, and *Alejandro's Gift* by Richard E. Albert, *Listen to the Desert / Oye al Desierto* by Pat Mora, *Mojave* by Diane Siebert, and *Coyote Steals the Blanket: A Ute Tale* by Janet Stevens provide plenty more atmosphere. Investigate other trees with Barbara Bash's *Tree of Life: The World of the African Baobab*, Lynne Cherry's *The Great Kapok Tree*, and Helen Cowcher's *Whistling Thorn*. CACTUS. DESERTS. ECOLOGY.

1156 **Hawes, Judy. *Fireflies in the Night*. Rev. ed. Illus. by Ellen Alexander. HarperCollins, 1991. ISBN 0-06-022485-1**

[1 sitting, 32p., Gr. K–2] One dark night, a young girl relates all the facts her grandfather has told her about fireflies, such as how to get them to glow brighter, how they make light without heat, and how they find their mates. Written as a scientific story, this title from the always excellent Let's-Read-and-Find-Out Science Book series boasts handsome night-lit pastels. Arthur Dorros's *Ant Cities*, part of the same series, is another inviting look at insects. *Water Pennies and Other Poems* by N. M. Bodecker, *Bugs: Poems* by Mary Ann Hoberman, *Flit, Flutter, Fly! Poems About Bugs and Other Crawly Creatures* compiled by Lee Bennett Hopkins, and *Itsy-Bitsy Beasties* by Michael Rosen encourage a celebration of the lowly insect, and *Creepy Crawly Critter Riddles* by Joanne E. Bernstein and Paul Cohen and *Buggy Riddles* by Katy Hall and Lisa Eisenberg pull in a bit of humor. FIRE-FLIES. INSECTS.

1157 **Hayes, Ann. *Meet the Orchestra*. Illus. by Karmen Thompson. Gulliver/Harcourt, 1991. ISBN 0-15-200526-9**

[1 sitting, unp., Gr. K–3] Page by page there's a sparkling, poetic description of each instrument, its characteristics, and special sound, and a stately watercolor of a formally dressed animal demonstrating how to play it, culminating with the lion conductor leading the entire orchestra. Teachers of music will delight in reading a page and either playing a recording of that instrument's music or displaying the real thing for listeners to identify. The rhyming *Zin! Zin! Zin! A Violin* by Lloyd Moss presents instruments and players from one (solo) to ten. Music-based folktales include Stefan Czernecki and Timothy Rhodes's Australian *The Singing Snake*, Hal Ober's Mexican *How Music Came to the World*, and Zuzo Otsuka's Mongolian *Suho and the White Horse*. Stay in concert with *The Cat's Midsummer Jamboree* by David Kherdian, *The Kooken* by Julia Lebentritt and Richard Ploetz, and *Garth Pig Steals the Show* by Mary Rayner. MUSICAL INSTRU-MENTS. ORCHESTRA.

1158 **Heinrich, Bernd. *An Owl in the House: A Naturalist's Diary*. Illus. and photos by the author. Joy Street/ Little, Brown, 1990. ISBN 0-316-35456-2**

[12 chapters, 119p., Gr. 4–6] After finding a baby great horned owl buried in the snow near his Vermont home, the author decided to raise it until it could be released into the wild, and kept a detailed, sketch-filled journal of owl Bubo's progress. Heinrich's descriptions of keeping the possessive owl in his Maine summer cabin are compelling and informative, and show convincingly why raising a wild animal is not an easy or desirable undertaking, though the splendid sketches and black-and-white photos are endearing. Farley Mowat raised two horned owls as a boy, which he chronicles in the very funny *Owls in the Family*. DIARIES. OWLS. WILDLIFE RESCUE.

1159   **Heller, Ruth.** *Animals Born Alive and Well.* **Illus. by the author. Grosset, 1982. ISBN 0-448-01822-5**

[1 sitting, unp., Gr. K–4] A rhyming text and graceful full-color illustrations define the properties of mammals, from elephant to lowly mole, and blue whale to people just like us. Children can each claim a mammal, find out more about its habits, habitats, and various eccentricities, and report back to the class. Heller's *Chickens Aren't the Only Ones* presents animals that lay eggs. ANIMALS. MAMMALS. STORIES IN RHYME.

1160   **Heller, Ruth.** *Chickens Aren't the Only Ones.* **Illus. by the author. Grosset, 1981. ISBN 0-448-01872-1**

[1 sitting, unp., Gr. K–4] Told in rhyme accompanied by glowing color illustrations, the entertaining text introduces animals that lay eggs, including birds, reptiles and amphibians, fish, spiders, insects, and two Australian mammals: the spiny anteater and the platypus. In my school, first-grade teacher Roni Sawin hauls out the incubator each year and the class observes the incubation and hatching of a dozen chicks. *Tracks in the Sand* by Loreen Leedy shows how sea turtles hatch their eggs. Pull in related picture books of hatchings such as *Zinnia and Dot* by Lisa Campbell Ernst (two squabbling chickens, one egg), *Mary Ann* by Betsy James (praying mantis), *Just Plain Fancy* by Patricia Polacco (peacock), and *The Stolen Egg* by Sue Vyner (Emperor penguin). Heller's *Animals Born Alive and Well* covers all types of mammals. See where the birds live in Patricia Brennan Demuth's *Cradles in the Trees: The Story of Bird Nests*. ANIMALS. BIRDS. CHICKENS. EGGS. STORIES IN RHYME.

1161   **Heller, Ruth.** *The Reason for a Flower.* **Illus. by the author. Grosset, 1983. ISBN 0-448-14495-6**

[1 sitting, 42p., Gr. K–4] How flowers are pollinated and how seeds grow are explained in rhyme along with stunning full-page color paintings that will prod listeners to search out the 582 section of the library for more info. Also clear and interesting are *Bean and Plant* by Christine Bach and *From Seed to Plant* by Gail Gibbons. Tie into your plant lessons interesting folktales such as Demi's *The Empty Pot* from China, Tomie dePaola's *The Legend of the Bluebonnet* and *The Legend of the Indian Paintbrush* from the American Southwest, and Barbara Juster Esbensen's Ojibway Indian *The Star Maiden*. Flower-growing picture books include Eve Bunting's *Flower Garden*, Barbara Cooney's *Miss Rumphius*, Anita Lobel's *Alison's Zinnia*, and Arnold Lobel's *The Rose in My Garden*. FLOWERS. PLANTS. SEEDS.

1162   Hiscock, Bruce. *The Big Tree*. Illus. by the author. Atheneum, 1991. ISBN 0-689-31598-8

[1 sitting, unp., Gr. 2–4] Describing a hundred-foot sugar maple standing in northern New York State, the author traces its growth from colonial times till now, tying in a time line description of America's growth along with botanical information. Dick Gackenbach's *Mighty Tree* is a much more elemental rundown, George Ella Lyon's *A B Cedar: An Alphabet of Trees* identifies all types, and Harry Behn's *Trees* is a poem laid out in picture-book format. In Eve Bunting's realistic fiction *Someday a Tree*, we grieve for a tree that has been poisoned, while in Lisa Campbell Ernst's *Squirrel Park*, a boy and squirrel fight to save their favorite tree. Have children choose and examine a favorite tree and draw its bark, leaves, and the tree as a whole, paying attention to details of color, shape, and proportion to the landscape around it. TREES. U.S.–HISTORY.

1163   Hoose, Phillip. *It's Our World, Too! Stories of Young People Who Are Making a Difference*. Illus. with photos. Little, Brown, 1993. ISBN 0-316-37241-2

[166p., Gr. 5–6] Profiled here are 14 groups and individuals who went against convention and took a stand for what they believed. Accounts range from an African American girl from Chicago who spoke out against neighborhood gangs, to a 15-year-old boy who led a successful campaign to convince the big tuna companies to buy only tuna caught in nets that allowed dolphins to escape. The second part of the book lays out the steps for undertaking responsible social change. For another successful example where an entire school got involved, read *Come Back, Salmon: How a Group of Dedicated Kids Adopted Pigeon Creek and Brought It Back to Life* by Molly Cone. Find more pragmatic strategies in Patricia Adams and Jean Marzollo's *The Helping Hands Handbook* (Random House, 1992), *50 Simple Things Kids Can Do to Save the Earth* by The Earth Works Group, and Betty Miles's *Save the Earth: An Action Handbook for Kids* (Knopf, 1991). MULTICULTURAL STORIES. SOCIAL ACTION.

1164   Hoshino, Michio. *The Grizzly Bear Family Book*. Photos by the author. Trans. by Karen Colligan-Taylor. North-South, 1994. ISBN 1-55858-351-3

[1 sitting, unp., Gr. 3–6] The author fills this amiable and informative full-page color-photo-filled essay with his own encounters with and reactions to Alaskan grizzlies. Did you know that a grizzly can eat soapberries for 20 hours a day in late summer, consuming 200,000 berries a day? Hoshino's narrative is filled with facts, but he also imparts a respect for nature and an urgency for experiencing it firsthand. Contrast grizzlies with polar bears using *Polar Bear Cubs* by Downs Matthews and *White Bear, Ice Bear* by Joanne Ryder, and with a bear in captivity in *Andy Bear: A Polar Cub Grows Up at the Zoo* by Ginny Johnston and Judy Cutchins. *The Grizzly Sisters* by Cathy Bellows, *Little Tricker the Squirrel Meets Big Double the Bear* by Ken Kesey, *The Bear That Heard Crying* by Natalie Kinsey-Warnock, and *Backyard Bear* by Jim Murphy will round out the picture with both realism and fantasy. ALASKA. BEARS. PERSONAL NARRATIVES.

1165   Houston, Gloria. *My Great Aunt Arizona*. Illus. by Susan Condie Lamb. HarperCollins, 1992. ISBN 0-06-022607-2

[1 sitting, unp., Gr. 1–6] Though she always intended to visit faraway places, Arizona Houston Hughes, a tall, elegant woman in her long, full dress, white apron, petticoats, and high-button shoes, instead taught school for 57 years and touched the lives of several generations of children, among them her great-niece, author Houston. The combination of Lamb's exquisite double-page paintings and the poetic text of this special picture-book biography and tribute will move our generation of teachers and learners. Especially appreciated is the dedication: "Dedicated for all teachers, members of the most influential profession in the world." Read this to your class, at a faculty meeting, and to all those people who wonder just why you wanted to become a teacher anyway. Continue the pensive mood with Barbara Cooney's *Miss Rumphius* and Mary Lynn Ray's *Pianna*. BIOGRAPHY. FAMILY STORIES. PICTURE BOOKS FOR ALL AGES. TEACHERS. WOMEN–BIOGRAPHY.

1166   Howlett, Bud. *I'm New Here*. Photos by the author. Houghton Mifflin, 1993. ISBN 0-395-64049-0

[1 sitting, 32p., Gr. 2–5] To give children an idea of how it feels to emigrate to America, introduce them to fifth-grader Jazmin Escalante who narrates this perky color photo essay about her first day of school after she moved here from El Salvador speaking Spanish only. Sook Nyul Choi's *Halmoni and the Picnic*, Barbara Cohen's *Molly's Pilgrim*, Sherry Garland's *The Lotus Seed*, and Maxine Rhea Leighton's *An Ellis Island Christmas* also give valuable insight into how it feels to move to a strange new country. BILINGUAL EDUCATION. IMMIGRATION AND EMIGRATION. MULTICULTURAL STORIES. SCHOOLS.

1167   Jakobsen, Kathy. *My New York*. Illus. by the author. Little, Brown, 1993. ISBN 0-316-45653-5

[1 sitting, unp., Gr. K–4] Written in the form of a letter from city girl Becky to Martin, a friend from the Midwest who is planning to visit, this is a dazzling tribute to all the glorious sights to be seen in the Big Apple, taking in the Central Park Zoo, F. A. O. Schwartz, the Plaza Hotel, Chinatown, and far more. Your listeners will want to pore over the detailed oil paintings up close, where they'll find an orange-and-white cat sightseeing on every page, but the best parts are the two pages that open up, taking us to the top of the Empire State Building and detailing the skeleton of both a new skyscraper and a dinosaur at the Museum of Natural History. Endpaper maps of Manhattan show each site visited. Stay in the city with Arthur Dorros's *Abuela*, E. L. Konigsburg's *Amy Elizabeth Explores Bloomingdale's*, Faith Ringgold's *Tar Beach*, and Shelley Rotner and Ken Kreisler's *Citybook*. *Peppe the Lamplighter* by Elisa Bartone takes us back a century to Little Italy. CITIES AND TOWNS. LETTER WRITING. MAPS AND GLOBES. NEW YORK CITY.

1168   Jones, Charlotte Foltz. *Mistakes That Worked*. Illus. by John O'Brien. Doubleday, 1991. ISBN 0-385-26246-9

[40 short chapters, 78 p., Gr. 4–6] Here are the fascinating stories behind the accidental discoveries and inventions of useful and sometimes important items, such as Coca-Cola, potato chips, Silly Putty, and Post-it Notes. One of the most intriguing chapters explains that it is believed that Charles Perraut, in his 1697 print version of the story of Cinderella, somehow confused the slippers of "vair" (fur) of the original French story and substituted the homonym "verre" (glass) instead. Webb Garrison's *Why Didn't I Think of That? From Alarm Clocks to Zippers*, Rube Goldberg's *The Best of Rube Goldberg*, and Jim Murphy's *Weird and Wacky Inventions* will also hold your interest. Meet the great inventor Ben Franklin through biography in Jean Fritz's *What's the Big Idea, Ben Franklin?* and fiction in Robert Lawson's *Ben and Me*. Elvira Woodruff's *The Disappearing Bike Shop* is a fantasy involving that great inventor Leonardo da Vinci. INVENTIONS.

1169   Kamen, Gloria. *Edward Lear, King of Nonsense: A Biography*. Illus. by Edward Lear and Gloria Kamen. Atheneum, 1990. ISBN 0-689-31419-1

[9 chapters, 74p., Gr. 4–6] The 20th of 21 children, Edward Lear hoped to make his mark as a painter, but instead became revered for his many volumes of nonsense poetry and sketches. Kamen's biography will entertain listeners with its many anecdotes and examples of Lear's outrageous wordplay. Also pull in Lear's *Daffy Down Dillies: Silly Limericks* and *How Pleasant to Know Mr. Lear*, compiled by Myra Cohn Livingston, picture book versions of *The Owl and the Pussycat* illustrated by Jan Brett or Paul Galdone, *Of Pelicans and Pussycats: Poems and Limericks*, and *The Quangle Wangle's Hat* illustrated by Janet Stevens. ARTISTS. BIOGRAPHY. ILLUSTRATORS. NONSENSE VERSES. POETS.

1170   Kline, Suzy. *The Herbie Jones Reader's Theater: Funny Scenes to Read Aloud*. Illus. by Richard Williams. Putnam, 1992. ISBN 0-399-22120-4

[21 plays, 177p., Gr. 2–4] Act out school sagas with this collection of 21 of everyone's favorite funny scenes from the first four of the deliciously funny Herbie Jones books. Keep acting with scripts from *Presenting Reader's Theater: Plays and Poems to Read Aloud* by Caroline Feller Bauer, *Show Time at the Polk Street School: Plays You Can Do Yourself or in the Classroom* by Patricia Reilly Giff, *Stories on Stage: Scripts for Reader's Theater* by Aaron Shepard, and *Fantastic Theater: Puppets and Plays for Young Performers and Young Audiences* by Judy Sierra. PLAYS–COLLECTIONS. READER'S THEATER. SCHOOLS.

1171   Knowlton, Jack. *Books and Libraries*. Illus. by Harriet Barton. HarperCollins, 1991. ISBN 0-06-021610-7

[1 sitting, 36p., Gr. 2–5] Starting with cave writing in southern France 30,000 years ago, here is a history of books and writing, as picture writing and hieroglyphics give way to the Greek alphabet, Roman libraries, Gutenberg's movable type, U.S. libraries, and Melville Dewey's Decimal System. The endpapers provide a nifty review of the ten major categories of Dewey. Supplement with artifacts you can make, buy, or find pictures of in books: pages from an illuminated manuscript, a horn book or slate and stylus, a scroll, hieroglyphics, the Rosetta stone, a book galley, or a piece of parchment or papyrus. *Letter Jester* by Cathryn Falwell celebrates typefaces, *Good Books, Good Times!* by Lee Bennett Hopkins is a collection of poems celebrating reading, *Once Inside the Library* by Barbara Huff is a tribute in rhyme, *Dream Peddler* by Gail E. Haley is a legend about an English bookseller, and *The Librarian Who Measured the Earth* by Kathryn Lasky is a biography of Eratosthenes. BOOKS AND READING. LIBRARIES.

1172   **Koch, Michelle. *World Water Watch*. Illus. by the author. Greenwillow, 1993. ISBN 0-688-11465-2**

[1 sitting, unp., Gr. K–2] Give a global picture with this easy-to-understand non-fiction picture book that introduces sea otters, green sea turtles, penguins, fur seals, polar bears, and humpback whales and the reasons they are endangered. Small groups of children can locate other books in the library about each animal and find out more facts to share. *Tracks in the Sand* by Loreen Leedy is a nonfiction picture book that describes the life cycle of the loggerhead sea turtle. ENDANGERED SPECIES. WILDLIFE CONSERVATION.

1173   **Kossman, Nina. *Behind the Border*. Illus. with photos. Lothrop, 1994. ISBN 0-688-13494-7**

[13 chapters, 95p., Gr. 4–6] Until she was ten, the author lived in Moscow under the restrictive Soviet regime, where traveling to another country was called "going behind the border," and where children were expected to love Lenin more than their own parents. In a series of poignant, funny, and sometimes daring episodes, she describes trying to paint Red Square red, anti-Semitism at her school, a young boy considered a Russian hero for turning in his parents to the authorities, and being considered a traitor when her family prepares in secret to emigrate to the West. You'll want your class to do some research on the Soviet government then and now, and discuss the differences of communism versus U.S.-style democracy. AUTOBIOGRAPHY. PERSONAL NARRATIVES. RUSSIA.

1174   **Krull, Kathleen. *Lives of the Musicians: Good Times, Bad Times (and What the Neighbors Thought)*. Illus. by Kathryn Hewitt. Harcourt, 1993 ISBN 0-15-248010-2**

[20 chapters, 96 pages, Gr. 3–6] Did you know that Mozart was scared of ghosts and loud noises? That Beethoven's handwriting was practically unreadable? Or that Brahms ate canned sardines for breakfast? Nineteen eccentric composers are profiled in these four- to six-page biographies, each filled with the most enlightening and amusing trivia, and illustrated with a robust full-page color caricature. Accompany your readings with a sampling of each composer's music. *Beethoven Lives Upstairs* by Barbara Nichol is a fascinating fictionalized account of that composer's last years. Meet the great Russian composer in the fiction story *Tchaikovsky Discovers America* by Esther Kalman, as set down in her diary by 11-year-old Eugenia who encounters him in New York in 1891. BIOGRAPHY. MUSICIANS.

1175   **Krull, Kathleen. *Lives of the Writers: Comedies, Tragedies (and What the Neighbors Thought)*. Illus. by Kathryn Hewitt. Harcourt, 1994. ISBN 0-15-248009-9**

[20 chapters, 96p., Gr. 4–6] This chronological compendium of 20 brief and tantalizing mini-biographies, with winning full-page watercolor caricatures by Kathryn Hewitt, profiles such well-known wordsmiths as Shakespeare, Austen,

Andersen, Poe, Dickens, Dickinson, Alcott, Twain, and Hughes. The book allows us to view their less-public sides, highlighting their many eccentricities, sufferings, and hard roads to success, and inspires us to seek out their poems, plays, and novels. Beth Wagner Brust has written an intriguing biography of the life of the famous storyteller in *The Amazing Paper Cuttings of Hans Christian Andersen*, and Diane Stanley and Peter Vennema fill in a few more blanks in their elegant picture-book biographies *Bard of Avon: The Story of William Shakespeare* (Morrow, 1992) and *Charles Dickens: The Man Who Had Great Expectations* (Morrow, 1993). AUTHORS. BIOGRAPHY.

1176   **Krupp, E. C.** *The Moon and You.* **Illus. by Robin Rector Krupp. Macmillan, 1993. ISBN 0-02-751142-1**

[1 sitting, 48p., Gr. 2–5] This endlessly engrossing nonfiction picture book incorporates descriptions of ancient legends and beliefs with modern scientific knowledge, suggests experiments to try with flashlight and balloons, and boasts huge and stunning pencil illustrations. *The Magic School Bus Lost in the Solar System* by Joanna Cole and *One Giant Leap*, Mary Ann Fraser's description of the 1969 moon landing, will also engross stargazers. Recite some poetry with *What Rhymes with Moon?* by Jane Yolen. *Thirteen Moons on Turtle's Back* by Joseph Bruchac and Jonathan London and *Moon Mother: A Native American Creation Tale* by Ed Young are Native American legends, while both the Peruvian *Moon Rope* by Lois Ehlert and the Mexican *The Tale of Rabbit and Coyote* by Tony Johnston explain the origins of the moon's "face." ASTRONOMY. MOON.

1177   **Krupp, Robin Rector.** *Let's Go Traveling.* **Illus. by the author. Morrow, 1992. ISBN 0-688-08990-9**

[1 sitting, 40p., Gr. 3–5] Rachel Rose, the feisty, bespeckled narrator, takes us on a whirlwind global journey to view ancient ruins and wonders, including the prehistoric caves in western France, Stonehenge, Egyptian and Mayan pyramids, the Great Wall, and the Inca cities of Peru. The vibrant pages are cluttered with notes from her diary, postcards, photographs, maps, and assorted fascinating facts and new words. On the last page, Rachel is planning for a new trip including Easter Island and Colorado's Mesa Verde. Your students can do some advance research on these and other travel spots as Official Worldwide Travel Agents, with each small group presenting its findings to the rest of the agency. CIVILIZATION, ANCIENT. VOYAGES AND TRAVELS.

1178   **Kuklin, Susan** *How My Family Lives in America.* **Bradbury, 1992. ISBN 0-02-751239-8,**

[1 sitting, 32p., Gr. K–3] In three genial, color-photo-filled chapters, we meet three young children firsthand—African American Sanu, Hispanic American Eric, and Chinese American April—as they describe their families, customs, and favorite foods, along with recipes. With their parents' assistance, your students can each compile a new chapter, describing the special foods, recipes, and customs their own families have. An international luncheon could follow. AFRICAN AMERICANS. ASIAN AMERICANS. FOOD. HISPANIC AMERICANS. MULTICULTURAL STORIES.

1179 Kunhardt, Edith. *Honest Abe.* Illus. by Malcah Zeldis. Greenwillow, 1993. ISBN 0-688-11190-4

[1 sitting, unp., Gr. K–3] This simply told biography, with oversized, detailed, colorful gouache, primitive-folk-art-style paintings, is a fitting introduction to the many appealing aspects of Lincoln's persona as renowned storyteller, lover of books, and morally principled leader. An engaging narrative, which is easily understandable for all children, guides us from Lincoln's log-cabin birth through his assassination and funeral train. Appended are the text of the Gettysburg Address and a chronology of his life. Retell the story using Myra Cohn Livingston's powerful narrative poem, *Abraham Lincoln: A Man for All the People.* *Abe Lincoln's Hat* by Barbara Brenner contains interesting true anecdotes about Lincoln and his stovepipe hat. BIOGRAPHY. LINCOLN, ABRAHAM. PRESIDENTS–U.S.

1180 Lasky, Kathryn. *The Librarian Who Measured the Earth.* Illus. by Kevin Hawkes. Little, Brown, 1994. ISBN 0-316-51526-4

[1 sitting, 48p., Gr. 3–6] Despite little written record about the life of Eratosthenes, the ever-curious astronomer and geographer who was chief librarian at the renowned library in Alexandria, Egypt, and lived in the third century B.C., Lasky has pieced together a provocative, unique, and visually striking picture-book biography of the man and his times. What a choice way to encourage children to remain curious about the world, especially when they discover that Eratosthenes figured out a way to measure the circumference of the earth that was only 200 miles off the modern-day figure. *Books and Libraries* by Jack Knowlton catches the library angle, while Sam and Beryl Epstein's *Secret in a Sealed Bottle: Lazzaro Spallanzani's Work with Microbes* portrays another scientist who asked questions. BIOGRAPHY. EARTH. GEOGRAPHY. GREECE, ANCIENT. MEASUREMENT. QUESTIONS AND ANSWERS. SCIENTISTS.

1181 Lauber, Patricia. *An Octopus Is Amazing.* Illus. by Holly Keller. Crowell, 1990. ISBN 0-690-04803-3

[1 sitting, 32p., Gr. 1–3] An angry octopus can turn dark red; a frightened one becomes pale. These and other unusual facts are scattered through the text, along with soft watercolors, in this exemplary addition to the picture-book-like Let's Read-and-Find-Out Science Book series. And how does the octopus really feel? Find out firsthand from Bernard Waber's story *I Was All Thumbs.* Stay wet with *The Magic School Bus on the Ocean Floor* by Joanna Cole, *How the Sea Began: A Taino Myth* by George Crespo, *Under the Sea from A to Z* by Anne Doubilet, and *I Am the Ocean* by Suzanna Marshak. *The Ice Cream Ocean* by Susan Russo is a fittingly gaudy little collection of sea poems. MARINE ANIMALS. OCEAN. OCTOPUS.

1182 Leedy, Loreen. *Postcards from Pluto: A Tour of the Solar System.* Illus. by the author. Holiday House, 1993. ISBN 0-8234-1000-5

[1 sitting, unp., Gr. 1–3] Dr. Quasar, the robot tour guide, takes a multicultural crew of six children to see all the planets via rocket ship from which they send home imaginative and informative postcards to family and friends. A good first introduction to the planets, this is not as detailed as Joanna Cole's *The Magic School Bus Lost in the Solar System*, but it's on the same wavelength. After a bit of research, your future space travelers can design and write up additional postcards. *Blast Off! Poems About Space* selected by Lee Bennett Hopkins contains 20 easy-to-read poems, and *Spacey Riddles* by Katy Hall and Lisa Eisenberg is cheerful and entertaining. ASTRONOMY. LETTER WRITING.

1183 **Leedy, Loreen.** *Tracks in the Sand.* **Illus. by the author. Doubleday, 1993. ISBN 0-385-30658-X**

[1 sitting, unp., Gr. K–2] We are silent witnesses as a loggerhead sea turtle crawls up the beach and lays her eggs in the sand, where dozens of hatchlings emerge two months later and find their way down to the ocean. An afterword fills in more information, including threats to these endangered animals and ways people can help. Leedy's somber color-pencil illustrations make us realize how precarious the turtle's mission is. *World Water Watch* by Michelle Koch presents other endangered sea animals. EGGS. REPTILES. TURTLES.

1184 **Leigh, Nila K.** *Learning to Swim in Swaziland: A Child's-Eye View of a Southern African Country.* **Illus. by the author. Scholastic, 1993. ISBN 0-590-45938-4**

[1 sitting, unp., Gr. 1–4] Fourth-grader Nila Leigh wrote this charming photo essay about the year she spent in Swaziland when she was eight. In her own handwriting and with her own crayon illustrations, she describes life there, showing how the Swazis dress and what the children do, and even includes a Swazi folktale. If you're thinking of having your students compile simple reports on countries, this is an unintimidating and entertaining format to use. Give a broader view of Africa with *Whistling Thorn* by Helen Cowcher, *Jambo Means Hello: Swahili Alphabet Book* by Muriel Feelings, *Masai and I* by Virginia Kroll, *Elephant Have the Right of Way: Life with the Wild Animals of Africa* by Betty Leslie-Melville and *Somewhere in Africa* by Ingrid Mennen and Niki Daly. AFRICA. CHILDREN'S WRITINGS. MULTICULTURAL STORIES. SWAZILAND.

1185 **Leslie-Melville, Betty.** *Elephant Have the Right of Way: Life with the Wild Animals of Africa.* **Photos by the author. Doubleday, 1993. ISBN 0-385-30622-9**

[8 chapters, 48p., Gr. 2–6] Leslie-Melville's *Daisy Rothschild: The Giraffe That Lives with Me* describes how she and her husband raised two giraffes at their home in Nairobi, Kenya. Now she continues the narrative with a discussion of the other animals they adopted or helped to save from poachers, including rhinos, elephants, lions, a cheetah, and a zebra. Helen Cowcher's *Whistling Thorn*, Nila K. Leigh's *Learning to Swim in Swaziland: A Child's-Eye View of a Southern African Country*, and Toshi Yoshida's *Young Lions* provide a window on Africa. Jamina learns about poachers when she gets lost in the African bush and comes upon a baby elephant in the striking picture book *The Hunter* by Paul Geraghty. AFRICA. ANIMALS. ELEPHANTS. GIRAFFES. LIONS. WILDLIFE CONSERVATION.

1186 Levine, Ellen. *If Your Name Was Changed at Ellis Island.* Illus. by Wayne Parmenter Scholastic, 1993. ISBN 0-590-46134-6

[36 short chapters, 80 pages, Gr. 3–6] In a question-and-answer format, this personalizes the common experiences of immigrants who came to America between the 1880s and 1920s, describing the voyage, inspections by doctors for disease, and the conditions at Ellis Island. Russell Freedman's photo essay *Immigrant Kids* discusses conditions for immigrants in the United States from 1890 to the early 20th century. Get more personal with stories such as Maxine Rhea Leighton's *An Ellis Island Christmas*, Carla Stevens's *Lily and Miss Liberty*, and Jeanette Winter's *Clara's New World*. Meet some current immigrants in Sook Nyul Choi's *Halmoni and the Picnic*, Barbara Cohen's *Molly's Pilgrim*, Sherry Garland's *The Lotus Seed*, and Bud Howlett's *I'm New Here*. ELLIS ISLAND. IMMIGRATION AND EMIGRATION. U.S.–HISTORY.

1187 Little, Jean. *Little by Little: A Writer's Education.* Viking Kestrel, 1987. ISBN 0-670-81649-3

[29 chapters, 233p., Gr. 5–6] When Canadian author Jean Little was a little girl growing up in Taiwan, a neighborhood girl informed her she shouldn't climb trees because she had bad eyes, but Jean went ahead and climbed one anyway. This heartfelt autobiography, filled with her love of books and writing, takes us through tauntings by unkind children who called her cross-eyed, her school experiences, and up to her early twenties when her first manuscript, *Mine for Keeps*, won a writing award and was accepted for publication. Students will certainly want to read her many outstanding novels, most about children who must deal with physical disabilities. *From Anna* mirrors Jean's own experiences moving to Canada, entering a Sight Saving class, and weaving a marvelous basket for her parents' Christmas present. Readers can continue with the next volume of her autobiography, *Stars Come Out Within* (1990). Another fine writer's autobiography is *The Moon and I* by Betsy Byars. AUTHORS. AUTOBIOGRAPHY. BLIND. HANDICAPS. WRITING.

1188 Littlefield, Bill. *Champions: Stories of Ten Remarkable Athletes.* Illus. by Bernie Fuchs. Little, Brown, 1993. ISBN 0-316-52805-6

[10 chapters, 132p., Gr. 5–6] Ten rousing, personable biographies about sports heroes, in their various fields, include Satchel Paige the baseball pitcher, jockey Julie Krone, Iditarod winner Susan Butcher, soccer legend Pélé, skier Diana Golden, who lost a leg to cancer, and basketball superstar Nate "Tiny" Archibald. Each engrossing, often gripping profile is accompanied by a full-page painting, though your students may want to search out additional photographs and research additional full-length biographies of these and other sports legends. Read aloud a chapter a day to expose your class to athletes who are in it for more than the money and the glory. ATHLETES–BIOGRAPHY. BIOGRAPHY. MULTICULTURAL STORIES. SPORTS–BIOGRAPHY.

1189 Livingston, Myra Cohn. *Abraham Lincoln: A Man for All the People.* Illus. by Samuel Byrd. Holiday House, 1993. ISBN 0-8234-1049-8

[32p., Gr. K–3] Filled with snippets of Lincoln's own words, this is a simple, brief, fact-filled narrative poem that chronicles Lincoln's life for even the youngest listener. Sources for both the realistic illustrations and quotes are supplied on the last page. Read this in tandem with *Abe Lincoln's Hat* by Barbara Brenner and Edith Kunhardt's also-basic *Honest Abe*, illustrated in folk-art style. James Cross Giblin's *George Washington: A Picture Book Biography*, not as elemental but splendid, will also help you prepare for February birthdays. BIOGRAPHY. LINCOLN, ABRAHAM. NARRATIVE POETRY. POETRY–SINGLE AUTHOR. PRESIDENTS–U.S.–POETRY.

1190   Livingston, Myra Cohn. *Keep on Singing: A Ballad of Marian Anderson.* Illus. by Samuel Byrd. Holiday House, 1994. ISBN 0-8234-1098-6

[1 sitting, unp., Gr. 1–4] A brief biography in verse introduces the great African American singer who dealt with racial prejudice all her life but went on to become an inspiration to all of us. The author's note on the last page will help you elaborate on events referred to briefly in the poem. *Teammates* by Peter Golenbock, a picture book about how Jackie Robinson dealt with prejudice when he joined major league baseball, the narrative poem *Let Freedom Ring: A Ballad of Martin Luther King, Jr.* by Myra Cohn Livingston, and *Happy Birthday, Martin Luther King* by Jean Marzollo also deal with the civil rights struggle. AFRICAN AMERICANS. BIOGRAPHY. NARRATIVE POETRY. PREJUDICE. RACE RELATIONS. WOMEN–BIOGRAPHY.

1191   Livingston, Myra Cohn. *Let Freedom Ring: A Ballad of Martin Luther King, Jr.* Illus. by Samuel Byrd. Holiday House, 1992. ISBN 0-8234-0957-0

[1 sitting, 32p., Gr. 1–6] Incorporating quotes from King's speeches and sermons, Livingston has fashioned a moving narrative poem that takes the civil rights leader from his boyhood in Atlanta through his struggle for equal rights and justice, ending with his death in Memphis. Combined with Byrd's dignified photolike paintings, the poem is moving and will lead listeners to seek out more information. *Happy Birthday, Martin Luther King* by Jean Marzollo is a brief but effective biography, and Livingston's *Keep on Singing: A Ballad of Marian Anderson* and Peter Golenbock's *Teammates*, about Jackie Robinson's experiences as the first African American major league baseball player, are also important titles when discussing heroic Americans who confronted prejudice. AFRICAN AMERICANS–POETRY. KING, MARTIN LUTHER, JR.–POETRY. NARRATIVE POETRY. PREJUDICE. RACE RELATIONS.

1192   Lomas Garza, Carmen. *Family Pictures / Cuadros de Familia.* Illus. by the author. Trans. into Spanish by Rosalma Zubizarreta. Children's Book Press, 1990. ISBN 0-89239-050-6

[1 sitting, 32p., Gr. 1–4] In an affectionate food-filled reminiscence of her childhood in a Texas border town, Mexican American artist Lomas Garza supplies each charming, detailed painting with a paragraph in English and Spanish, describing a family activity. Children can write and illustrate paragraphs about their own family memories, and bind them into their own albums of "Family Pictures." Gary Soto's *Too Many Tamales* is a Mexican American Christmas story.

AUTOBIOGRAPHY. FAMILY STORIES. HISPANIC AMERICANS. MULTICULTURAL STORIES. PERSONAL NARRATIVES. SPANISH LANGUAGE.

1193   McMillan, Bruce. *Eating Fractions*. Photos by the author. Scholastic, 1991. ISBN 0-590-43770-4

[1 sitting, unp., Gr. Pre–1] Two children split a banana and an ear of corn into halves, a roll and a pear jello mold into thirds, and a small pizza and a strawberry tart into fourths, and eat them all with gusto. Full-page color photos of the two kids and a dog, appended recipes, and a detailed author's note all help to make your next fractions lesson a delicious success. Children can work in pairs, trios, and quartets to attempt to divide equally other snacks like pretzel sticks, saltines, and unshelled peanuts. Your fraction instruction will also benefit widely from Loreen Leedy's *Fraction Action*, Louise Matthews's *Gator Pie*, and Elinor J. Pinczes's *One Hundred Hungry Ants*. AFRICAN AMERICANS. FOOD. FRACTIONS. MATHEMATICS. MULTICULTURAL STORIES.

1194   McMillan, Bruce. *Going on a Whale Watch*. Photos by the author. Scholastic, 1992. ISBN 0-590-45768-3

[40p., Gr. K–3] This color photo essay with the simplest of texts takes us as spectators on a whale-watch boat to watch dolphins, fin whales, and humpback whales cavorting off the coast of Maine. Beneath each photograph is a drawing of the whale, showing both what we see above water, and what is hidden to us underwater. At the back are whale statistics and a visual glossary showing and explaining terms such as barnacles, blowholes, and breaching. *If You Ever Meet a Whale* is a stunningly illustrated book of whale poems selected by Myra Cohn Livingston, and *Winter Whale* by Joanne Ryder is a poetic firsthand look at a humpback whale's day. *How the Whale Got His Throat* by Rudyard Kipling will prove a pleasant diversion, while *How the Sea Began: A Taino Myth* by George Crespo, *Under the Sea from A to Z* by Anne Doubilet, *An Octopus Is Amazing* by Patricia Lauber, and *I Am the Ocean* by Suzanna Marshak lead us back to the water. WHALES.

1195   Maestro, Betsy. *The Discovery of the Americas*. Illus. by Giulio Maestro. Lothrop, 1991. ISBN 0-688-06838-3

[1–2 sittings, 48p., Gr. 2–5] This is a first-step overview of American history up to the early 1500s, with thrilling colorful paintings that will draw attention to the various Native American cultures and the explorers up to Columbus, Cabot, Vespucci, Balboa, and Magellan. Focus on Columbus with picture books such as Christopher Columbus's own *Log of Christopher Columbus*, Jean Marzollo's *In 1492*, and Jane Yolen's *Encounter*. AMERICA–DISCOVERY AND EXPLORATION. EXPLORERS.

1196   Maestro, Betsy. *A Sea Full of Sharks*. Illus. by Giulio Maestro. Scholastic, 1990. ISBN 0-590-43100-5

[1 sitting, unp., Gr. 1–3] In picture-book format, with blue-toned watercolors, Maestro presents dozens of compelling shark facts, though she steers clear of blood and gore. When discussing the lure of nonfiction, read this book and make a class list of facts just learned. Encourage students to fulfill their curiosity by investigating other books on this and other fish or animal topics and sharing their new facts with the rest of the group. *The Great White Man-Eating Shark* by Margaret Mahy is a deliciously malevolent story to read alongside. FISHES. SHARKS.

1197   **Maestro, Betsy. *The Story of Money*. Illus. by Giulio Maestro. Clarion, 1993. ISBN 0-395-56242-2**

[2 sittings, 48p., Gr. 3–5] We discover how the ancient Sumerians invented silver money, that the Chinese began using paper money hundreds of years before the Europeans, and that there are about 140 different currencies in the world today. An attractive nonfiction picture book, illustrated with watercolors, this covers money's international history, with emphasis on U.S. currency. *The Go-Around Dollar* by Barbara Johnston Adams provides facts about the U.S. dollar, while Jennifer Armstrong's *Chin Yu Min and the Ginger Cat* and Jay Williams's *One Big Wish* are both fiction picture books that prove money isn't everything, as does Bill Brittain's *All the Money in the World*. MONEY.

1198   **Maestro, Betsy. *Take a Look at Snakes*. Illus. by Giulio Maestro. Scholastic, 1992. ISBN 0-590-44935-4**

[1 sitting, 40p., Gr. 1–4] This well-organized and compelling overview of snake facts, along with realistic and attractive colored-pencil-and-watercolor illustrations, will help listeners overcome their shudders and whet their appetites for investigating snakes more thoroughly. Bring some levity to a scary subject with Diane L. Burns's *Snakes Alive! Jokes About Snakes* and Katy Hall and Lisa Eisenberg's *Snakey Riddles*, and continue with stories such as Stefan Czernecki and Timothy Rhodes's Australian folktale *The Singing Snake*, Jill Kastner's *Snake Hunt*, Faith McNulty's *A Snake in the House*, Trinka Hakes Noble's *The Day Jimmy's Boa Ate the Wash*, and Tomi Ungerer's lovable *Crictor*. SNAKES.

1199   **Mariotti, Mario. *Hanimations*. Photos by the author. Kane/Miller, 1989. ISBN 0-916291-22-7**

[1 sitting, unp., Gr. K–6] In a refinement of hand-shadow puppets, each remarkable page consists of only one or two human hands and forearms, painted and sometimes decorated with eyes, whiskers, or other simple props, and arranged to resemble such animals as a peacock, panda, and flamingo. Children will marvel at each depiction as they guess the animal each page displays, and then try to duplicate the hand positions. *Hanimals* (Green Tiger/Simon & Schuster, 1982) is the artist's first collection of hand pictures. Turn on the filmstrip projector so children can cast shadows on the screen, and read *Why the Willow Weeps: A Story Told with Hands* by Marshall Izen and Jim West. Use that format for creating and acting out new stories. *The Handmade Alphabet* by Laura Rankin, a lovely sign language picture book, would be a natural to use here, while you may want to elaborate on the many functions our hands serve with Camilla Gryski's *Hands On, Thumbs Up*. ANIMALS. PICTURE BOOKS FOR ALL AGES. STORIES WITHOUT WORDS.

1200   Marshak, Suzanna. *I Am the Ocean.* Illus. by James Endicott. Arcade, 1991. ISBN 1-55970-065-3

[1 sitting, unp., Gr. K–4] Told as a prose poem from the ocean's point of view and illustrated with soft but assertive watercolors, this is a lovely stepping point for examining the ocean and the creatures found among the waves. Get into the water with the concrete water poems in *Splish Splash* by Joan Bransfield Graham and *Until I Saw the Sea: A Collection of Seashore Poems* collected by Alison Shaw. *How the Sea Began: A Taino Myth* by George Crespo is a precolumbian creation legend from the Caribbean. *Under the Sea from A to Z* by Anne Doubilet is a photographic look at sea creatures and *An Octopus Is Amazing* by Patricia Lauber gives a closer look. Focus on the world's biggest mammal in *If You Ever Meet a Whale*, a collection of poems selected by Myra Cohn Livingston. MARINE ANIMALS. OCEAN.

1201   Martin, James. *Chameleons: Dragons in the Trees.* Photos by Art Wolfe. Crown, 1991. ISBN 0-517-58389-5

[1 sitting, unp., Gr. 2–5] Eye-popping color photos, along with a clear and compelling text that is loaded with wondrous facts, introduce the many color-changing lizards that live mostly in Africa, Madagascar, and India. You'll experience the same feeling of amazement when reading *Hummingbirds: Jewels in the Sky* by Esther Quesada. The chameleons children keep in terrariums in the United States are really anole lizards that change from green to brown, and in Joanne Ryder's *Lizard in the Sun* we become these lizards for a day. Diane Massie's *Chameleon Was a Spy* is a fun and frantic mystery, and Mwenye Hadithi's picture book *Crafty Chameleon* is a mischievous trickster tale for younger children. CHAMELEONS. REPTILES.

1202   Martin, Rafe. *A Storyteller's Story.* Photos by Jill Krementz. Richard C. Owen, 1992. ISBN 0-913461-03-2

[1 sitting, 32p., Gr. 1–4] Kids always want to know more about their favorite authors as people, and will be delighted to meet children's book author Rafe Martin through color photographs and his own firsthand description of his life as a writer. The bearded and genial Martin takes us through a typical day, and introduces us to some of the kids' books he has written, including *The Rough-Face Girl* and *Will's Mammoth* (Putnam, 1989). Read his other books aloud, including *The Boy Who Lived with the Seals* and *Foolish Rabbit's Big Mistake*. Patricia Polacco's *Firetalking* and Cynthia Rylant's *Best Wishes* are also informative autobiographies in the publisher's Meet the Author series. AUTHORS. AUTOBIOGRAPHY. WRITING.

1203   Marzollo, Jean. *Happy Birthday, Martin Luther King.* Illus. by J. Brian Pinkney. Scholastic, 1993. ISBN 0-590-44065-9

[1 sitting, unp., Gr. Pre–2] Describing how King "helped our country change some of its laws," the pointed narrative of this picture-book biography, with its handsome scratchboard and oil pastel pictures, briefly and clearly explains the contributions of the great civil rights leader. Also read Myra Cohn Livingston's eloquent and moving narrative poem *Let Freedom Ring: A Ballad of Martin Luther King, Jr. Keep on Singing: A Ballad of Marian Anderson* by Myra Cohn Livingston and *Teammates* by Peter Golenbock, a picture book about Jackie Robinson's introduction to major league baseball, are also important books about the civil rights movement in America. AFRICAN AMERICANS–BIOGRAPHY. BIOGRAPHY. KING, MARTIN LUTHER, JR. PREJUDICE. RACE RELATIONS.

1204   **Marzollo, Jean. *In 1492*. Illus. by Steve Björkman. Scholastic, 1991. ISBN 0-590-44413-1**

[1 sitting, unp., Gr. K–3] Marzollo takes that famous old rhyme and expands it into 14 more rhymed couplets describing the mariner's first voyage in ways the youngest child can comprehend, with cheerful full-page watercolor wash illustrations that give us a feel of vast ocean space. An introductory page provides simple background facts. Older students researching Columbus's subsequent voyages could write additional couplets. Other easy-to-understand Columbus books include Peter Sis's *Follow the Dream* and Jane Yolen's *Encounter*. AMERICA–DISCOVERY AND EXPLORATION. COLUMBUS, CHRISTOPHER. EXPLORERS. STORIES IN RHYME.

1205   **Mason, Cherie. *Wild Fox: A True Story*. Illus. by Jo Ellen McAllister Stammen. Down East Books, 1993. ISBN 0-89272-319-X**

[1 sitting, 32p., Gr. 3–6] The author, who lives on Deer Isle off the Maine coast, describes her year of encounters with a wild red fox whose paw was severed in a trap and whom she named Vicky. The soft pastel illustrations are endearing, and the narrative imparts a respect for wild creatures. *Reynard: The Story of a Fox Returned to the Wild* by Alice Mills Leighner is another true account, while Betsy Byars's fiction book *The Midnight Fox* will touch every child. *Reynard the Fox* by Selina Hastings is a collection of folktales about the fox as unconquerable and clever trickster. FOXES. PERSONAL NARRATIVES.

1206   **Mathews, Sally Schofer. *The Sad Night: The Story of an Aztec Victory and a Spanish Loss*. Illus. by the author. Clarion, 1994. ISBN 0-395-63035-5**

[1 sitting, unp., Gr. 5–6] When gold-hungry Spanish explorer Cortés arrived in Tenochtitlán in 1519, he was mistaken for the god Quetzalcoatl by the Aztec leader Moctezuma, which was the beginning of the Aztecs' downfall as related in this unusual nonfiction picture book with remarkable colorful watercolors in the style of the original Aztec codices. If you are delving into Mexican culture, David Wisniewski's *Rain Player* is a literary folktale based on the customs and games of the ancient Mayans. Investigate books on Mexican history to find photos of the pyramids, carvings, and other Aztec artifacts, plus ones that show modern day Mexico City, the former Tenochtitlán. AZTECS. EXPLORERS. INDIANS OF MEXICO. LITERARY FAIRY TALES. MEXICO.

1207   **Miller, Margaret. *My Five Senses*. Photos by the author. Simon & Schuster, 1994. ISBN 0-671-79168-0**

[1 sitting, unp., Gr. Pre–K] In a clear and attractive color photo essay, five children demonstrate what they see, smell, taste, hear, and feel. The basic and pleasant presentation will get your kids started on observing the world around them. If you have access to a camera, it would be logical to put together a senses portfolio starring your own class. Bruce McMillan's *Sense Suspense: A Guessing Game for the Five Senses* is also terrific. Carolyn Otto's *I Can Tell by Touching* is a basic and appealing science book on just that one of the five senses. MULTICULTURAL STORIES. SENSES AND SENSATION.

1208   Milton, Nancy. *The Giraffe That Walked to Paris.* Illus. by Roger Roth. Crown, 1992. ISBN 0-517-58133-7

[1 sitting, 32p., Gr. 2–4] This fascinating true account explains how, in 1826, the pasha of Egypt sent an 11-foot baby giraffe as a present to King Charles X of France 2,100 miles away. From Roger Roth's detailed and endearing watercolors to the final page with the photograph of the actual giraffe, now stuffed and on display in a museum in La Rochelle, here is a book that demonstrates how to make history come alive. Contrast this with Kirby and Woodman's *The Cows Are Going to Paris* as a logical look at the differences between fiction and nonfiction. FRANCE. GIRAFFES. PARIS.

1209   Mora, Pat. *Listen to the Desert / Oye al Desierto.* Illus. by Francisco X. Mora. Clarion, 1994. ISBN 0-395-67292-9

[1 sitting, unp., Gr. Pre–2] In English and Spanish we hear the sounds of the desert animals and their surroundings: owl, toad, snake, dove, coyote, wind, and rain. There are two repeated stanzas for children to join, and the effect is lulling, along with the gentle watercolors. *Mojave* by Diane Siebert is a more dramatic and sweeping poem, while *Alejandro's Gift* by Richard E. Albert, Barbara Bash's *Desert Giant: The World of the Saguaro Cactus* by Barbara Bash, *Cactus Hotel* by Brenda Guiberson, and *Coyote Steals the Blanket: A Ute Tale* by Janet Stevens provide more atmosphere, facts, and folklore. Children can write a similar poem based on the sounds of the forest or seashore. CHANTABLE REFRAIN. DESERTS. ONOMATOPOEIA. SOUND EFFECTS. SPANISH LANGUAGE.

1210   Morimoto, Junko. *My Hiroshima.* Illus. by the author. Viking, 1990. ISBN 0-670-83181-6

[1 sitting, unp., Gr. 3–6] In words and paintings, the author recalls life in her hometown, culminating in her own searing memories of the horrific morning of August 6, 1945, when Hiroshima was devastated by the atomic bomb and of its aftermath. You'll also want to read Eleanor Coerr's biographies, the longer *Sadako and the Thousand Paper Cranes* and both the book and video versions of the remarkable and inspirational picture book *Sadako*, plus her thought-provoking *Meiko and the Fifth Treasure*, where a ten-year-old girl struggles to regain her talent in calligraphy and her self-confidence after her hand is badly hurt in the Nagasaki bombing. Allen Say's *The Bicycle Man*, *Grandfather's Journey* and *Tree of Cranes* also deal eloquently with postwar Japan. Talk about issues of war and peace, using the folktales in Margaret Read MacDonald's *Peace Tales* as an additional catalyst. AUTOBIOGRAPHY. JAPAN. PERSONAL NARRATIVES. WAR. WORLD WAR, 1939-1945.

1211 Morris, Ann. *Bread Bread Bread*. Photos by Ken Heyman. Lothrop, 1989. ISBN 0-688-06335-7

[1 sitting, 32p., Gr. Pre–3] This delightful color photo essay that displays bread and bread-lovers from all over the world. Each child can bring in a different type of bread ranging from bagels to pretzels, rye to white, and many more, and have a taste testing. Find out how it's made in Ken Robbins's *Make Me a Peanut Butter Sandwich and a Glass of Milk*, and then sing or chant Nadine Berard Westcott's manic *Peanut Butter and Jelly: A Play Rhyme*. See how the sweet Italian bread panettone came to be in the folktale *Tony's Bread* by Tomie dePaola. BREAD. FOOD. MULTICULTURAL STORIES.

1212 Most, Bernard. *How Big Were the Dinosaurs?* Illus. by the author. Harcourt, 1994. ISBN 0-15-236800-0

[1 sitting, unp., Gr. K–2] Learn about the size of the dinosaurs by relating each to a concrete modern object children know. T. Rex's teeth were the size of a toothbrush, Supersaurus was longer than a supermarket aisle, and Mamenchisaurus's neck, the longest of any animal, was longer than a school flagpole. Most's casual, lighthearted writing style, along with his colorful, black-lined watercolors, present a wealth of facts to children who will rush for the tape measures to mark off the sizes given for each reptile on the endpapers. *An Alphabet of Dinosaurs* by Peter Dodson is drop-dead gorgeous as is *Dinosaurs! Strange and Wonderful* by Laurence Pringle. Hudson Talbott's hilarious *We're Back: A Dinosaur's Story* continues our fantasies of how the creatures would adapt in today's society. Take a fictional trip back with Dennis Nolan's *Dinosaur Dreams* and Eric Rohmann's wordless *Time Flies*. DINOSAURS. MEASUREMENT. SIZE.

1213 Moutoussamy-Ashe, Jeanne. *Daddy and Me: A Photo Story of Arthur Ashe and His Daughter Camera*. Photos by the author. Knopf, 1993. ISBN 0-679-95096-6

[1 sitting, 40p., Gr. K–6] Arthur Ashe, the world renowned tennis player who contracted AIDS from a blood transfusion in 1985 and died in 1993, is memorialized in this loving black-and-white photo tribute by his wife and young daughter who describes what her daddy's life with AIDS was like on both the good and the bad days, and how they helped each other. AFRICAN AMERICANS–BIOGRAPHY. AIDS. ASHE, ARTHUR. FATHERS AND DAUGHTERS. SICK.

1214 Osborne, Mary Pope. *George Washington: Leader of a New Nation*. Dial, 1991. ISBN 0-8037-0949-8

[10 chapters, 118 pages, Gr. 5–6] Students see the first president as a mythic figure, and this scintillating biography, illustrated with numerous period prints, helps transform him into a person again. Compare the information presented with the briefer but also excellent *George Washington: A Picture Book Biography* by

James Cross Giblin. Read alongside historical fiction titles touching on Washington and his times including Avi's *The Fighting Ground*, Esther Wood Brady's *Toliver's Secret*, James Lincoln Collier's *My Brother Sam Is Dead*, Judith Berry Griffin's *Phoebe and the General*, and Elvira Woodruff's *George Washington's Socks*. BIOGRAPHY. PRESIDENTS–U.S. U.S.–HISTORY–REVOLUTION. WASHINGTON, GEORGE.

1215   Otto, Carolyn. *I Can Tell by Touching*. Illus. by Nadine Bernard Westcott. HarperCollins, 1994. ISBN 0-06-023325-7

[1 sitting, 32p., Gr. Pre–1] A young boy describes how he relates to his world by touch, both indoors and out. The practical examples he gives along with the attractive soft watercolors make this addition to the Let's Read and Find Out Science series another success. Try the simple experiment on the last page of differentiating between the feel of an orange and a baseball, showing the sensitivity of our hands in comparison to the rest of our skin. *Sense Suspense* by Bruce McMillan and *My Five Senses* by Margaret Miller introduce the senses, which you can buttress with individual titles such as *Today Is Monday* by Eric Carle (taste), *What Joe Saw* by Anna Grossnickle Hines (sight), *Dog Breath: The Horrible Trouble with Hally Tosis* by Dav Pilkey (smell), and *The Listening Walk* by Paul Showers (hearing). SENSES AND SENSATION. TOUCH.

1216   Perl, Lila. *It Happened in America: True Stories from the Fifty States*. Illus. by Ib Ohlsson. Henry Holt, 1993. ISBN 0-8050-1719-4

[50 chapters, 302p., Gr. 5–6] For each of the states, Perl gives a description of unusual historical facts and trivia, including the reason behind its nickname, and then retells a riveting true story about its people, some famous, some obscure. Studies of the states come alive with this book, to which you should add *From Sea to Shining Sea: A Treasury of American Folklore and Folk Songs* compiled by Amy L. Cohn, *Celebrate America in Poetry and Art* edited by Nora Panzer, and *Celebrating America: A Collection of Poems and Images of the American Spirit* compiled by Laura Whipple. The text of Katharine Lee Bates's *America the Beautiful*, with ravishing paintings by Neil Waldman, will pull it all together. Try out some presidential trivia with *Yo, Millard Fillmore! (And All Those Other Presidents You Don't Know)* by Will Cleveland and Mark Alvarez. U.S.–HISTORY.

1217   Peters, Lisa Westberg. *This Way Home*. Illus. by Normand Chartier. Henry Holt, 1994. ISBN 0-8050-1368-7

[1 sitting, unp., Gr. K–3] Using the sun, the stars, and earth's invisible magnetic field as compasses to guide them, the savannah sparrows fly from the northern prairie to their winter home on the Atlantic coast more than a thousand miles away. This monthlong journey and its return are described in poetic language accompanied by inviting watercolors. *Wheel on the Chimney* by Margaret Wise Brown is a Caldecott Medal book that describes the migrations of storks each year from Africa to Hungary. *The Great Ball Game: A Muskogee Story* by Joseph Bruchac is a Native American pourquoi tale that tells why birds must migrate each year. Take a closer look at bird homes with Patricia Brennan Demuth's *Cradles in the Trees: The Story of Bird Nests*. BIRDS. MIGRATION.

1218   Peters, Lisa Westberg. *Water's Way*. Illus. by Ted Rand. Arcade, 1991. ISBN 1-55970-062-9

[1 sitting, unp., Gr. K–3] As she did in *The Sun, the Wind, and the Rain*, Peters combines two tales in one, using the analogy of young Tony inside his house heating soup and running a bath to the changes that water undergoes outside as it rises from the sea, falls from clouds, drifts as fog, or turns to ice. It's easy to reproduce Tony's in-house experiments with steam, bubbles, and frost in the classroom. *Follow the Water from Brook to Ocean* by Arthur Dorros, also in an attractive picture-book format, gives additional information. Add some concrete poetry with Joan Bransfield Graham's delightful *Splish Splash*, and more verse with *Weather* by Lee Bennett Hopkins, *Rainy Rainy Saturday* by Jack Prelutsky, and *Rainy Day Rhymes* by Gail Radley. CHANGE. WATER.

1219   Pfeffer, Wendy. *From Tadpole to Frog*. Illus. by Holly Keller. HarperCollins, 1994. ISBN 0-06-023117-3

[1 sitting, 32p., Gr. Pre–1] In a particularly handsome entry from the Let's-Read-and-Find-Out Science series, we follow the frogs from their winter hibernation at the bottom of a pond to their mating in the spring, starting a two-year cycle as tadpoles hatch and grow. Keller's harmonious watercolors fill each double-page spread, taking us below the pond's murky surface. Get your toes wet with *All Night Near the Water* by Jim Arnosky, *In the Small, Small Pond* by Denise Fleming, and *Box Turtle at Long Pond* by William T. George. In a folktale from Borneo, *The Match Between the Winds* by Shirley Climo, the East Wind and West Wind compete to knock a green tree frog from his tree. FROGS. POND LIFE.

1220   Pfeffer, Wendy. *Popcorn Park Zoo: A Haven with a Heart*. Photos by J. Gerard Smith. Messner, 1992. ISBN 0-671-74589-1

[5 chapters, 64p., Gr. 3–5] Saving wildlife is an everyday endeavor for the folks who run the New Jersey Pine Barrens' Popcorn Park Zoo, the only federally licensed zoo in the United States that accepts animals no one else wants and is funded by contributions. There are engrossing anecdotes and colorful photos about blind deer Wonder Boy and Steffie, abandoned circus tiger Tina, overbearing elephant Sonny, and the dozens of other inhabitants. What is horrifying is realizing all the ways humans have been cruel to animals, but all hearts will be warmed at the marvelous work a zoo like this does to accommodate such a wide variety of creatures. Your class might be interested in sponsoring an animal. Call the zoo at (609) 693-1900, or write to Popcorn Park Wildlife Club, Humane Way, P.O. Box 43, Forked River, NJ 08731 for more information. ANIMALS. WILDLIFE RESCUE. ZOOS.

1221   Polacco, Patricia. *Firetalking*. Photos by Lawrence Migdale. Richard C. Owen, 1994. ISBN 0-878450-55-7

[1 sitting, 32p., Gr. 1–4] Master author/artist Polacco describes her childhood, relating incidents in her life that inspired characters and episodes in the many books she has written, and interspersing illustrations from those books with clear, vibrant photographs of family, friends, and herself hard at work. This is an invaluable accompaniment to the author's many outstanding stories, such as *Babushka's Doll, Chicken Sunday, Just Plain Sunday, Mrs. Katz and Tush, Pink and Say,* and *Thunder Cake.* James Howe's *Playing with Words* (1994) and Cynthia Rylant's *Best Wishes* are also autobiographies in the publisher's Meet the Author series. *Talking with Artists,* compiled by Pat Cummings, is another splendid source for getting to know children's book illustrators. Get more firsthand information reading *From Pictures to Words: A Book About Making a Book* by Janet Stevens. ARTISTS. AUTHORS. AUTOBIOGRAPHY. WOMEN–BIOGRAPHY. WRITING.

1222   Pringle, Laurence. *Dinosaurs! Strange and Wonderful.* Illus. by Carol Heyer. Boyds Mills, 1995. ISBN 1-878093-16-9

[1 sitting, unp., Gr. K–4] The bright yellow cover with the slavering mouth and bumpy head of T. Rex will send dinosaur lovers into a swoon before they even open this fact-laden picture-book-style description of a cross section of the great reptiles. Peter Dodson's *An Alphabet of Dinosaurs,* B. G. Hennessy's *The Dinosaur Who Lived in My Backyard* and Bernard Most's *How Big Were the Dinosaurs?* will fill in more facts, while Dennis Nolan's *Dinosaur Dreams* and Eric Rohmann's wordless *Time Flies* are fictional but realistic-seeming trips back to the Age of Reptiles. Stimulate the imagination with Carol Carrick's *Patrick's Dinosaurs* and *What Happened to Patrick's Dinosaurs?,* Diane Dawson Hearn's *Dad's Dinosaur Day,* Henry Schwartz's *How I Captured a Dinosaur,* and Paul and Henrietta Stickland's *Dinosaur Roar!* DINOSAURS.

1223   Rankin, Laura. *The Handmade Alphabet.* Illus. by the author. Dial, 1991. ISBN 0-8037-0975-7

[1 sitting, unp., Gr. K–6] Each page presents one letter, with a single hand shown both signing and interacting with an object that represents the letter: for "A" there is a hand clutching asparagus while forming the sign for that letter; for "B" there are bubbles; a cup dangles from the thumb in "C." Rankin's colored-pencil drawings on charcoal paper illustrate all varieties of hands, from children to adult, and in every human hue. Here's a perfect excuse to start your students signing, though it works equally well as a straight alphabet book with other sophisticated examples like Cathi Hepworth's *Antics.* Use your hands to create the exotic animals in *Why the Willow Weeps: A Story Told with Hands* by Marshall Izen and Jim West and *Hanimations* by Mario Marotti. ALPHABET BOOKS. DEAF. PICTURE BOOKS FOR ALL AGES. SIGN LANGUAGE.

1224   Rappaport, Doreen. *Living Dangerously: American Women Who Risked Their Lives for Adventure.* Illus. with photos. HarperCollins, 1991. ISBN 0-06-025109-3

[6 chapters, 117p., Gr. 4–6] Here are profiles of six courageous and indomitable women including Annie Edson Taylor, who on her 63rd birthday in 1901 went over Niagara Falls in a barrel of her own design and survived, Thecla Mitchell, a triple amputee who completed the 1990 New York Marathon in her wheelchair, and barnstormer Bessie Coleman, the world's first licensed black pilot. There's an appendix listing more than 20 women adventurers so children can research and write new chapters. Continue the excitement with Bill Littlefield's *Champions: Stories of Ten Remarkable Athletes*. ADVENTURE AND ADVENTURERS. BIOGRAPHY. WOMEN–BIOGRAPHY.

1225   Robbins, Ken. *Make Me a Peanut Butter Sandwich and a Glass of Milk*. Photos by the author. Scholastic, 1992. ISBN 0-590-43550-7

[1 sitting, unp., Gr. 1–4] Follow peanuts, wheat, and cows milk as they evolve into that most basic of school lunches in this interesting hand-tinted color photo-essay. Sing or chant Nadine Bernard Westcott's manic *Peanut Butter and Jelly: A Play Rhyme*, and give jelly equal time with John Vernon Lord's *The Giant Jam Sandwich* and Margaret Mahy's *Jam: A True Story*. *Bread Bread Bread* by Ann Morris is a marvelous color photo essay showing people from around the world enjoying bread. And of course you'll want to give the cows their due with Alice Schertle's poems in *How Now, Brown Cow?* BREAD. FOOD. MILK.

1226   Robinson, Marc. *Cock-a-Doodle-Doo! What Does It Sound Like to You?* Illus. by Steve Jenkins. Stewart, Taboori & Chang, 1993. ISBN 1-55670-267-1

[1 sitting, unp., Gr. Pre–2] An English dog barks bow wow, but a Greek one says guv guv, and a Chinese dog wo wo. In a sprightly rhyming story that lays out animal and other sounds first in English and then in other languages, we find that different ears hear different sounds. *Who Says a Dog Goes Bow-Wow?* by Hank De Zutter is another take on the subject, while for onomatopoeic noises in English alone, toot your horn for *Rat-a-Tat, Pitter Pat* by Alan Benjamin, *Polar Bear, Polar Bear, What Do You Hear?* by Bill Martin, Jr., *Do Bunnies Talk?* by Dayle-Ann Dodds, *Who Says That?* by Arnold L. Shapiro, and *The Listening Walk* by Paul Showers. Arthur Dorros's *This Is My House* and Debra Leventhal's *What Is Your Language?* are polyglot stories with phrases children can mimic. ANIMALS. ENGLISH LANGUAGE–ONOMATOPOEIC WORDS. LANGUAGE. SOUND EFFECTS.

1227   Roop, Peter, and Connie Roop. *I, Columbus; My Journal—1492–3*. Illus. by Peter E. Hanson. Walker, 1990. ISBN 0-8027-6978-0

[3 sittings, 57p., Gr. 4–6] Fascinating excerpts from the daily journal Columbus kept on his first voyage humanize the man and provide firsthand insight into his actions for students to talk over and compare with other books on the same topic. Christopher Columbus's own *Log of Christopher Columbus* is a picture book Steve Lowe compiled of the same diary, and Peter Sis's *Follow the Dream* is a brief picture-book biography. Pam Conrad's *Pedro's Journal*, Michael Dorris's *Morning Girl* and Jane Yolen's picture book *Encounter* describe Columbus's arrival from the point of view of native children who greet him. Betsy and Giulio Maestro's *The Discovery of the Americas* gives a look at Columbus and his contemporaries. AMERICA–DISCOVERY AND EXPLORATION. AUTOBIOGRAPHY. COLUMBUS, CHRISTOPHER. DIARIES. EXPLORERS.

1228   Roop, Peter, and Connie Roop. *One Earth, a Multitude of Creatures*. Illus. by Valerie A. Kells. Walker, 1992. ISBN 0-8027-8193-4

[1 sitting, unp., Gr. K–6] Collective nouns are integrated into one-sentence descriptions of animal food-gathering behavior, which is made less callous by the soft yet realistic paintings of the interdependent animals of the Pacific Northwest. The Roops show how unusual collective nouns—an unkindness of ravens, a sleuth of bears—are used in context. Ruth Heller's *A Cache of Jewels and Other Collective Nouns*, Patricia Hooper's poems in *A Bundle of Beasts*, and Patricia MacCarthy's *Herds of Words* also provide exceptionally fine examples. ANIMALS. ENGLISH LANGUAGE–GRAMMAR. PICTURE BOOKS FOR ALL AGES. VOCABULARY.

1229   **Rosen, Michael J., ed.** *Speak! Children's Book Illustrators Brag About Their Dogs.* **Harcourt, 1993 ISBN 0-15-277848-9**

[1–2 sittings, 43p., Gr. 2–6] Editor Rosen contacted 43 known and not-so-known artists, each of whom was granted one page to illustrate and provide written commentary about dogs they have known and loved, and the results range from tender to howlingly funny. Students can research each children's book illustrator to see if any of his or her books include mention of those dogs. Next, each of your students can provide a new dog page of art and text, or branch out to cats and other pets. *Talking with Artists* by Pat Cummings offers additional artistic inspirations. Pick your favorite pooch from Marilyn Singer's poems in *It's Hard to Read a Map with a Beagle on Your Lap.* ARTISTS. CREATIVE WRITING. DOGS. ILLUSTRATORS.

1230   **Russell, Marion. Adapted by Ginger Wadsworth.** *Along the Santa Fe Trail: Marion Russell's Own Story.* **Illus. by James Watling. Albert Whitman, 1993. ISBN 0-8075-0295-2**

[1–2 sittings, unp., Gr. 2–5] Adapted from the memoirs of a woman who traveled the Santa Fe Trail by wagon train with her nine-year-old brother and widowed mother from Independence, Missouri, to Albuquerque, New Mexico, in 1852 at the age of seven, this is a recollection of adversity, awe, and excitement. Gorgeous sweeping watercolors give a feel for the times. *Bound for Oregon* by Jean Van Leeuwen is a novel based on the real life of another nine-year-old girl whose family traveled the Oregon Trail, also in 1852. Natalie Kinsey-Warnock's *Wilderness Cat*, Scott Russell Sanders's *Here Comes the Mystery Man* and *Warm as Wool*, and David Williams's *Grandma Essie's Covered Wagon* are also handsome picture books about the wild frontier, while Opal Whiteley's *Only Opal: The Diary of a Young Girl* is selected from the diary the author kept as a six-year-old orphan in Oregon around 1906. AUTOBIOGRAPHY. FRONTIER AND PIONEER LIFE. PERSONAL NARRATIVES. SANTA FE TRAIL. U.S.–HISTORY–1783-1865.

1231   **Ryder, Joanne.** *Sea Elf.* **Illus. by Michael Rothman. Morrow, 1993. ISBN 0-688-10061-9**

[1 sitting, unp., Gr. K–3] Imagine being a sea otter, wrapped in a blanket of seaweed, cracking open spiny urchins for your breakfast, or napping on your back as you float in the water. As in all the books in the Just for a Day series—including *Catching the Wind, Lizard in the Sun, Winter Whale,* and *White Bear, Ice Bear*—the colorful double-page acrylic paintings are smashing, and play a large part in helping viewers envision themselves as another creature. With your students, look closely at each book to analyze how the author used facts to present his/her stories. As an animal project for older students, either alone or in groups, have them select an animal, research its habitat and habits, and then write a you-are-there story incorporating the facts they've learned. IMAGINATION. OTTERS. PICTURE BOOKS FOR ALL AGES. TRANSFORMATIONS.

1232   **Ryder, Joanne.** *Winter Whale.* **Illus. by Michael Rothman. Morrow, 1991. ISBN 0-688-07177-5**

[1 sitting, unp., Gr. K–3] On a rainy morning, you become a humpback whale, gliding and singing through the warm salty tropical waters where you migrate each winter. Part of the majestic Just for a Day series, which includes *Catching the Wind, Lizard in the Sun, Sea Elf,* and *White Bear, Ice Bear,* this lyrical paean boasts breathtaking acrylic paintings. *If You Ever Meet a Whale,* a gorgeous collection of whale poems selected by Myra Cohn Livingston, is a must, and Bruce Macmillan's *Going on a Whale Watch* has fine color photographs. *Under the Sea from A to Z* by Anne Doubilet and *I Am the Ocean* by Suzanna Marshak will nicely complement your underwater tour. *How the Whale Got His Throat* by Rudyard Kipling and *Burt Dow, Deep-Water Man* by Robert McCloskey are classic fiction reads that fit right in. IMAGINATION. PICTURE BOOKS FOR ALL AGES. TRANSFORMATIONS. WHALES.

1233   **Rylant, Cynthia.** *Best Wishes.* **Photos by Carlo Ontal. Richard C. Owen, 1992. ISBN 1-878450-20-4**

[1 sitting, 32p., Gr. 1–5] When Cynthia Rylant was growing up in West Virginia there was no library or bookstore where she lived, but she learned to love stories from all the comic books she read. From young fans of Rylant's Henry and Mudge series to older readers of *Waiting to Waltz,* students will be curious about her life, augmented by color photographs and a slightly melancholy text. Other fine author autobiographies in the publisher's Meet the Author series include Rafe Martin's *A Storyteller's Story* and Patricia Polacco's *Firetalking.* Betsy Byars's autobiographical *The Moon and I* digs deeper into the way a writer works. *Talking with Artists,* compiled by Pat Cummings, is an outstanding collection of interviews with and illustrations by children's book illustrators. AUTHORS. AUTOBIOGRAPHY. WOMEN–BIOGRAPHY. WRITING.

1234   **Say, Allen.** *El Chino.* **Illus. by the author. Houghton Mifflin, 1990. ISBN 0-395-52023-1**

[1 sitting, unp., Gr. 2–5] Too short to play the professional sports he revered growing up, Chinese American Billy Bong Wong found his true calling while on vacation in Spain when he became enamored of bullfighting and went into training. Told in the first person with warm self-deprecating humor, this brief picture-book biography with its elegant watercolors is winningly inspiring for all of us who dare to deviate from society's norm. Get everyone talking about goals and dreams and what we need to do to achieve them. BIOGRAPHY. BULLFIGHTERS. CHINESE AMERICANS. MULTICULTURAL STORIES.

1235   Seibert, Patricia. *Mush! Across Alaska in the World's Longest Sled-Dog Race.* Illus. by Jan Davey Ellis. Millbrook, 1992. ISBN 1-56294-053-8

[1 sitting, 32p., Gr. 1–4] To honor the team of sled dogs who raced over 1,000 miles from Anchorage to Nome in 1925 bringing urgently needed diptheria medicine, the yearly Iditarod began in 1973. In a colorful and dramatic picture book, we learn how dogs and racers prepare for and undertake the grueling ordeal. Continue with *Dogteam* by Gary Paulsen, a heart-stopping prose poem picture book about racing sled dogs at night. Bill Littlefield's *Champions: Stories of Ten Remarkable Athletes* includes a chapter about four-time Iditerod winner Susan Butcher. For more stories about Alaska, *Prince William* by Gloria Rand describes the cleanup and animal rescue efforts after the 1989 Exxon tanker oil spill into Prince William Sound. ALASKA. DOGS. IDITAROD. RACING. SLED DOG RACING. WINTER.

1236   Shelby, Anne. *What to Do About Pollution.* Illus. by Irene Trivas. Orchard, 1993. ISBN 0-531-08621-6

[1 sitting, unp., Gr. Pre–2] In the simplest possible terms, this picture book demonstrates to children that they can have a say and take some responsibility toward stopping or alleviating pollution, hunger, sickness, and friendlessness. Brainstorm with your children to come up with ways they can help solve big problems with small but caring measures, and adopt one to carry out. Continue with the conservation theme using *Dinosaurs to the Rescue! A Guide to Protecting Our Planet* by Laurene Krasny Brown and Marc Brown, Eve Bunting's *Someday a Tree*, Lynne Cherry's *A River Ran Wild: An Environmental History*, and Gloria Rand's *Prince William.* POLLUTION. SOCIAL ACTION.

1237   Shepard, Aaron. *Stories on Stage: Scripts for Reader's Theater.* H. W. Wilson, 1993. ISBN 0-8242-0851-X

[22 plays, 162p., Gr. 2–6] There are scripts for 22 plays, all taken from children's books, that you can duplicate and use for Reader's Theater. Break your class into groups and work on two or three plays at a time that the players can then stage for the rest of the group. Using these plays as models, older children can select other scenes from kids' books, adapt them for scripts, and perform. *Presenting Reader's Theater: Plays and Poems to Read Aloud* by Caroline Feller Bauer, *Show Time at the Polk Street School: Plays You Can Do Yourself or in the Classroom* by Patricia Reilly Giff, *The Herbie Jones Reader's Theater: Funny Scenes to Read Aloud* by Suzy Kline, and *Fantastic Theater: Puppets and Plays for Young Performers and Young Audiences* by Judy Sierra are all excellent. PLAYS–COLLECTIONS. READER'S THEATER.

1238   Sis, Peter. *Follow the Dream: The Story of Christopher Columbus.* Illus. by the author. Knopf, 1991. ISBN 0-679-90628-2

[1 sitting, unp., Gr. 1–4] Drawing on 15th century maps, these somber oil, ink-and-watercolor, and gouache paintings accompany a pared-down but fact-rich text, exploring Columbus's childhood in Genoa to his first voyage of 1492, when he landed on what he erroneously took to be the shores of Japan. Add details with Christopher Columbus's own *Log of Christopher Columbus*, Pam Conrad's *Pedro's Journal*, Michael Dorris's *Morning Girl*, Jean Marzollo's *In 1492*, Peter and Connie Roop's *I, Columbus*, and Jane Yolen's *Encounter*. Betsy and Giulio Maestro's nonfiction picture book *The Discovery of the Americas* fills in more details. AMERICA–DISCOVERY AND EXPLORATION. BIOGRAPHY. COLUMBUS, CHRISTOPHER. EXPLORERS.

1239   **Skira-Venturi, Rosabianca.** *A Weekend with Leonardo da Vinci.* **Illus. by Leonardo da Vinci. Rizzoli, 1993. ISBN 0-8478-1440-8**

[1–2 sittings, 63p., Gr. 3–8] The left-handed Italian Renaissance genius known as a painter, sculptor, inventor, engineer, and even director of plays reflects back on his life and works in this fictionalized autobiography of the artist at age 60-something, profusely illustrated with paintings, sketches, and pages from his notebooks. Aesthetes will enjoy the artistic license of Dav Pilkey's impressionistic picture book *When Cats Dream* with its send-ups of Mona Lisa, Whistler's Mother, and other famous paintings, and Jon Agee's *The Incredible Painting of Felix Clousseau*, where an artist's masterpieces come to life with often disastrous results. In Elvira Woodruff's *The Disappearing Bike Shop*, two boys befriend an old inventor who just might be da Vinci himself, transported to the present. Other interesting titles in the Weekend with series are about Degas, Rembrandt, Rousseau, Van Gogh, Velazquez, and Winslow Homer. ARTISTS. BIOGRAPHY. PAINTING.

1240   **Skurzynski, Gloria.** *Here Comes the Mail.* **Photos by the author. Bradbury, 1992. ISBN 0-02-782916-2**

[1 sitting, unp., Gr. K–3] In a color photo essay, we trace the route young Kathy's letter takes from Santa Fe to her cousin in Salt Lake City. Children who have composed new letters to go along with stories such as *Dear Peter Rabbit* by Alma Flor Ada or *The Jolly Postman* (Little, Brown, 1986) and *The Jolly Christmas Postman* by Janet and Allan Ahlberg might be curious to know what happens when they mail their letters. LETTER WRITING. POSTAL SERVICE.

1241   **Stanley, Diane, and Peter Vennema.** *Bard of Avon: The Story of William Shakespeare.* **Illus. by Diane Stanley. Morrow, 1992. ISBN 0-688-09109-1**

[1–2 sittings, unp., Gr. 4–6] Though not that much is known about Shakespeare's life, Stanley fills in the gaps with an absorbing profile of 16th century British theater and Elizabethan life, and tidbits about his plays. What makes the picture-book format so attractive are the splendid full-page paintings in period style. *Charles Dickens: The Man Who Had Great Expectations* is another of Stanley and Vennema's author studies. For more fascinating tidbits, see Kathleen Krull's *Lives of the Writers: Comedies, Tragedies (and What the Neighbors Thought)*. AUTHORS. BIOGRAPHY. ENGLAND. PLAYS. POETS. SHAKESPEARE, WILLIAM.

1242   **Stanley, Diane, and Peter Vennema.** *Charles Dickens: The Man Who Had Great Expectations.* **Illus. by Diane Stanley. Morrow, 1993. ISBN 0-688-09111-3**

[2–3 sittings, unp., Gr. 4–6] From his own harsh experiences as a youth, working in a boot-blacking factory at age 12 while his family was in debtor's prison, to his popularity as a writer and performance artist in 19th century England and America, which rivaled that of any modern-day movie star, we see how Dickens's life experiences influenced his novels. Large, exquisitely detailed gouache paintings accompany this picture-book biography, which should begin to lead precocious readers and future writers to Dickens's novels themselves. Stanley and Vennema's *Bard of Avon: The Story of William Shakespeare* is also a treat. Dickens is one of 20 authors profiled in Kathleen Krull's *Lives of the Writers: Comedies, Tragedies (and What the Neighbors Thought)*. AUTHORS. BIOGRAPHY. DICKENS, CHARLES. ENGLAND.

1243   Stanley, Fay. *The Last Princess: The Story of Princess Ka'iulani of Hawai'i*. Illus. by Diane Stanley. Four Winds, 1991. ISBN 0-02-786785-4

[1–2 sittings, 40p., Gr. 4–6] Princess Ka'iulani, heir to the throne of Hawaii's ruling family, died at 23 in 1898, unable to deter the American missionaries, merchants, and politicians from annexing her country and robbing the native Hawaiians of their rights. Large elegant gouache paintings reminiscent of Henri Rousseau accompany this pensive picture-book biography, which you can link to a study of Hawaii. Pull in the poems of the princess's friend, Robert Louis Stevenson. For an interesting account of an African ruler, see David Wisniewski's impressive nonfiction picture book *Sundiata: Lion King of Mali*. BIOGRAPHY. HAWAII. PRINCES AND PRINCESSES.

1244   Stevens, Janet. *From Pictures to Words: A Book About Making a Book*. Illus. by the author. Holiday House, 1995. ISBN 0-8234-1154-0

[1 sitting, unp., Gr. 1–4] With help from a host of imaginary animal characters who share each page with her, illustrator Stevens describes how she came to write her first story and turn it into this very book. Stevens draws herself on each page in pencil and gray watercolor wash, but her Koala Bear, Cat, and Rhino main characters appear in full glowing color. We watch as she decides on her story's setting and plot and lays it out on a storyboard, sends the final story to her editor, and decides what medium to use for the artwork. Patricia Polacco's autobiography *Firetalking* also examines the creative process of writing and illustrating a book, and *Talking with Artists*, compiled by Pat Cummings, offers first-hand advice and anecdotes from many top children's book illustrators. *Aunt Isabel Tells a Good One* by Kate Duke reviews the components of writing an exciting story. Young writers and artists will gain valuable insight into the creative process with these titles. AUTHORS. BOOKS AND READING. CREATIVE WRITING. ILLUSTRATORS.

1245   Stevenson, James. *Don't You Know There's a War On?* Illus. by the author. Greenwillow, 1992. ISBN 0-688-11383-4

[1 sitting, unp., Gr. 2–6] Here's what it was like to live in the United States during World War II, as described by Stevenson in his watercolor-illustrated autobiographical reminiscence that follows *Higher on the Door* (1987), *July* (1990), and

When I Was Nine (1986). Homefront meant a brother in the navy, rationing, tinfoil collecting, enemy plane spotting, Spam, a dad in the army, and war newsreels. Children can interview grandparents to find out more about those times. As autobiography, Stevenson's episodic format is just right for children to emulate when compiling their own memoirs. Gloria Houston's *The Year of the Perfect Christmas Tree*, Staton Rabin's *Casey Over There*, and Rosemary Wells's *Waiting for the Evening Star* take us back to World War I. Judith Mellecker's *Randolph's Dream* is a World War II fantasy, while Florence Parry Heide and Judith Heide Gilliland's *Sami and the Time of the Troubles* is a somber look at a child living through a war right now. AUTOBIOGRAPHY. PERSONAL NARRATIVES. WAR. WORLD WAR, 1939-1945.

1246   Taylor, Clark. *The House That Crack Built*. Illus. by Jan Thompson Dicks. Chronicle, 1992. ISBN 0-8118-0133-0

[1 sitting, unp. Gr. 4–6] Set up like the old "This Is the House That Jack Built" nursery rhyme, this is a powerful picture book that starts with a rich drug lord, and shows the devastating progression the drug makes from grower to dealers to users to a baby with a crack-addicted mother. Far more effective than a lecture or even a book of hard facts, it should break the ice in health classes and get people talking. Appended are addresses of organizations to call for drug abuse problems and information. COCAINE. DRUG ABUSE.

1247   Temple, Lannis, ed. *Dear World: How Children Around the World Feel About Our Environment*. Random House, 1993. ISBN 0-679-84403-1

[45 short chapters, 140p., Gr. 2–6] Concerned about the choking pollution he witnessed in his travels, Lannis Temple visited schools around the globe, interviewing children aged 8 to 13 in over 40 countries as to their hopes and fears for nature's future on earth. A sampling of their touching and inspiring letters—sometimes in their native languages—and energetic drawings are reproduced here, along with color snapshots. Your students, who will want to add their own letters and drawings, will be startled to note how children from far away are so like them. To show what kids can do, read Molly Cone's *Come Back, Salmon: How a Group of Dedicated Kids Adopted Pigeon Creek and Brought It Back to Life* and Phillip Hoose's activist-based *It's Our World, Too! Stories of Young People Who Are Making a Difference*. Confront the issues with Eve Bunting's *Someday a Tree*, Lynne Cherry's *A River Ran Wild*, and Gloria Rand's *Prince William*. CHILDREN'S WRITINGS. ENVIRONMENT. LETTER WRITING. NATURE. POLLUTION.

1248   Tyrrell, Esther Quesada. *Hummingbirds: Jewels in the Sky*. Photos by Robert A. Tyrrell. Crown, 1992. ISBN 0-517-58391-7

[1–2 sittings; 36p., Gr. 3–6] The Tyrrells, a husband-and-wife team, have studied hummingbirds for over 16 years, and will garner huzzahs for their riveting nonfiction writing guaranteed to entrance all readers, and spectacular color photographs to pore over on every page. Were you aware that there are over 300 different kinds of hummingbirds? That they can fly upside down? That their wings can beat up to 200 times a second? That if you burned energy as fast as a hummingbird, you'd need to eat 155,000 calories a day? Of course you'll want to set up a feeder outside your classroom as described, if it's at all feasible. Barbara Juster Esbensen's *Great Northern Diver: The Loon* is another compelling and beautiful book about an unusual bird. In Janet Stevens's Ute Indian folktale, *Coyote Steals the Blanket*, Hummingbird tries to talk sense into trickster Coyote. BIRDS. HUMMINGBIRDS.

1249   Wallace, Karen. *Red Fox.* Illus. by Peter Melnyczuk. Candlewick, 1994. ISBN 1-56402-422-9

[1 sitting, unp., Gr. Pre–2] Large and exquisite colored-pencil illustrations and a sprinkling of hand-lettered facts about foxes help to counter the image of the shifty, untrustworthy fox of folklore in this candid look at a day in the life of a wild red fox as he catches a mouse to eat and checks on his three cubs. Round out the image with Irina Korschunow's *The Foundling Fox*, Jonathan London's *The Eyes of Gray Wolf* and *Gray Fox*, Theresa Radcliffe's *Shadow the Deer*, Tejima's *Fox's Dream*, and Wendy Watson's *Fox Went Out on a Chilly Night*. FOXES.

1250   Waters, Kate. *Samuel Eaton's Day: A Day in the Life of a Pilgrim Boy.* Photos by Russ Kendall. Scholastic, 1993. ISBN 0-590-46311-X

[1 sitting, 40 pages, Gr. 2–4] Similar to the author and photographer's companion book, *Sarah Morton's Day: A Day in the Life of a Pilgrim Girl*, this splendid color photo essay accompanies seven-year-old Samuel as he describes the first time he is allowed to take part in bringing in the rye harvest with his father and neighbor. Now, over 350 years later, your students can compile their own illustrated essays of a typical but significant day in their lives. Jean Fritz's *Who's That Stepping on Plymouth Rock?*, Jean Craighead George's picture book *The First Thanksgiving*, and Marcia Sewall's *The Pilgrims of Plymouth* round out the picture. *Thanksgiving: Stories and Poems* compiled by Caroline Feller Bauer, *Merrily Comes Our Harvest In: Poems for Thanksgiving*, compiled by Lee Bennett Hopkins, and *It's Thanksgiving*, a set of poems by Jack Prelutsky, will help update your celebration. FAMILY LIFE. MASSACHUSETTS. PILGRIMS. U.S. HISTORY–COLONIAL PERIOD.

1251   Wells, Robert E. *Is a Blue Whale the Biggest Thing There Is?* Illus. by the author. Albert Whitman, 1993. ISBN 0-8075-3655-5

[1 sitting, unp., Gr. 2–5] This elongated picture book demonstrates the size of whales relative to Mount Everest, to the Earth, to the Sun, to a supergiant star, to the Milky Way, and to the universe, which is, finally, the biggest thing there is. Pair with *How Big Were the Dinosaurs?* by Bernard Most. David M. Schwartz's *How Much Is a Million?* deals with huge numbers and the space those numbers could occupy. One interesting fact to note: Several recent dinosaur discoveries point to seismosaurus, at a possible 150 feet long, as the biggest animal ever. Use this information to point out that our knowledge changes and grows every time we discover something new. Lynne Cherry's *The Armadillo from Amarillo*, Andrew Clements's *Mother Earth's Counting Book*, Joanna Cole's *The Magic School Bus Lost in the Solar System*, and Anne Mazer's *The Yellow Button* all give pertinent views of Earth and space. ASTRONOMY. SIZE. UNIVERSE.

1252   Wells, Ruth. *A to Zen: A Book of Japanese Culture*. Illus. by Yoshi. Picture Book Studio, 1992. ISBN 0-88708-175-4

[1 sitting, unp., Gr. 3–6] In a Japanese-style format, the text starts at the back of the book and works forward in this informative alphabet book that explains facets of modern Japanese life, covering some familiar and many new terms such as aikido, the martial art eto, the Japanese zodiac, and Tango no Sekku or Children's Day. Each page contains a large, detailed watercolor and a paragraph describing the term, which is written in English and in Japanese characters. Allen Say's *Tree of Cranes* and *Grandfather's Journey*, Taro Yashima's *Crow Boy*, and JoAnne Stewart Wetzel's *The Christmas Box* give a feel for Japan of the past, and Eleanor Coerr's *Mieko and the Fifth Treasure* and *Sadako*, Ken Mochizuki's *Baseball Saved Us*, and Junko Morimoto's *My Hiroshima* expand on the World War II era. ALPHABET BOOKS. JAPAN. JAPANESE LANGUAGE. LANGUAGE.

1253   Whiteley, Opal. *Only Opal: The Diary of a Young Girl*. Illus. by Barbara Cooney. Philomel, 1994. ISBN 0-399-21990-0

[1 sitting, unp., Gr. 2–5] The mama where six-year-old orphan Opal lives keeps the child working and calls her a nuisance, but Opal endures with her pet crow Lars Porsena, her tree, and mouse Felix Mendelsohn for comfort. Whether Opal really wrote this charming and plaintive diary as a child in the early 1900s has caused some discussion and controversy over the years, but the story works regardless. Journal-keepers will take heart at her use of language. Marion Russell's autobiographical picture book *Along the Santa Fe Trail*, Jean Van Leeuwen's fiction book *Bound for Oregon*, David Williams's *Grandma Essie's Covered Wagon*, and Elvira Woodruff's *Dear Levi: Letters from the Overland Trail* take us along on earlier tough journeys west. Picture books Natalie Kinsey-Warnock's *Wilderness Cat* and Scott Russell Sanders's *Here Comes the Mystery Man* and *Warm as Wool* are 19th century slices of hard lives. AUTOBIOGRAPHY. DIARIES. FRONTIER AND PIONEER LIFE. OREGON. ORPHANS. PERSONAL NARRATIVES.

1254   Wisniewski, David. *Sundiata: Lion King of Mali*. Illus. by the author. Clarion, 1992. ISBN 0-395-61302-7

[1 sitting, unp., Gr. 3–5] Passed down orally by the griots of Mali, this sober but stirring account of the rise to power of the great 13th century African king who spent his childhood lame and unable to speak is made memorable with astonishing cut-paper illustrations, a grand spectacle of color, texture, and pattern. The biography of a not-so-successful ruler is presented in *The Last Princess: The Story of Princess Ka'iulani of Hawai'i* by Fay Stanley. Wisniewski's style also works extraordinarily well in his *Rain Player* and *The Warrior and the Wise Man*. AFRICA. AFRICANS–BIOGRAPHY. BIOGRAPHY. KINGS AND RULERS. MALI.

1255   Wood, Ted, and Wanbli Numpa Afraid of Hawk. *A Boy Becomes a Man at Wounded Knee*. Illus. with photos. Walker, 1992. ISBN 0-8027-8175-6

[1–2 sittings, 42p., Gr. 3–6] On the 100th anniversary of the December 1890 massacre at Wounded Knee Creek, South Dakota, a nine-year-old boy recounts how he and his father joined the 150-mile Big Foot Memorial Ride to pray for their Lakota ancestors who were killed there by the U.S. Cavalry. Listeners will empathize with and admire Wanbli Numpa Afraid of Hawk who, in this color photo essay, movingly conveys the importance of their journey despite the cold and hardships. This is an important book that deals with a horrifying aspect of U.S. history, and your students will want to discuss its impact. Take a look at Dakota life long ago with Paul Goble's *Love Flute*. DAKOTA INDIANS. INDIANS OF NORTH AMERICA. PERSONAL NARRATIVES.

1256   **Yolen, Jane. *Welcome to the Green House*. Illus. by Laura Regan. Putnam, 1993. ISBN 0-399-22335-5**

[1 sitting, unp., Gr. K–3] In a prose poem paean to the rain forest, Yolen extolls the many exotic animals that linger there, and Regan's gorgeous full-page paintings allow you to feel the steaminess and to spy on every creature. An author's note relates the sobering statistic that we are destroying 50 acres of the world's rainforests every minute. Lynne Cherry's *The Great Kapok Tree* and Helen Cowcher's *Rain Forest* add environmentally conscious fuel to the controversy. *A River Ran Wild: An Environmental History* by Lynne Cherry, *Follow the Water from Brook to Ocean* by Arthur Dorros, *River* by Judith Heide Gilliland, and *Grandfather's Dream* by Holly Keller tie in to the subject of conservation awareness. ANIMALS. ECOLOGY. RAIN FORESTS.

1257   **Zhensun, Zheng, and Alice Low. *A Young Painter: The Life and Paintings of Wang Yani—China's Extraordinary Young Artist*. Photos by Zheng Zhensun. Illus. by Wang Yani. Scholastic, 1991. ISBN 0-590-44906-0**

[7 chapters, 80p., Gr. 3–6] Wang Yani, a self-taught child artist from China who started painting at age three in her father's art studio, has since become world famous for her remarkable watercolors of monkeys and other animals. A biography as well as a showcase for her paintings, this book will make art teachers smile and children wonder how someone so young could have such a talent and the drive to paint. Pat Cummings's *Talking with Artists* showcases children's book illustrators and their work as both children and adults. ARTISTS. BIOGRAPHY. CHINESE–BIOGRAPHY. PAINTING.

1258   **Zoehfeld, Kathleen Weidner. *What Lives in a Shell?* Illus. by Helen K. Davie. HarperCollins, 1994. ISBN 0-06-022999-3**

[1 sitting, unp., Gr. Pre–2] The clear and simple text of this Let's-Read-and-Find-Out Science Book introduces us to snails, turtles, crabs, clams, and oysters. See if anyone has any good shells to bring in for inspection. *A House for Hermit Crab* by Eric Carle and *Is This a House for Hermit Crab?* by Megan McDonald address the shell problem of this small crab, while *Clams Can't Sing* by James Stevenson is a lighter look at shell-life. There's a cute crab chapter in *Emily and the Enchanted Frog* by Helen V. Griffith, and Elizabeth Lee O'Donnell's *The Twelve Days of Summer* makes us yearn for the seashore. Follow a sea turtle as she lays her eggs in the nonfiction picture book *Tracks in the Sand* by Loreen Leedy. MARINE ANIMALS. SEASHORE. SHELLS.

POETRY, NONSENSE, AND LANGUAGE-ORIENTED NONFICTION

1259   Adoff, Arnold. *Chocolate Dreams.* Illus. by Turi MacCombie. Lothrop, 1989. ISBN 0-688-06823-5

[64 pages, Gr. 5–6] There are over three dozen salivatingly luscious, mostly free-verse poems here, some wistful, others desperate, all tributes to chocolate, and illustrated with large, confectionarily correct watercolors. Read these aloud, and then stop for a well-deserved snack of something sweet—a Hershey's Kiss can't hurt—along with Rosemary Wells's very silly picture book, *Max's Chocolate Chicken.* Candy fanatics can write their own odes to the snacks of their reveries. CANDY–POETRY. FOOD–POETRY. POETRY–SINGLE AUTHOR.

1260   Adoff, Arnold. *In for Winter, Out for Spring.* Illus. by Jerry Pinkney. Harcourt, 1991. ISBN 0-15-238637-8

[unp., Gr. K–4] An around-the-year collection of over two dozen mostly unrhyming open form poems that splash across each page of beautiful watercolors is told from the point of view of Rebecca, a self-assured young African American child who introduces us to her parents and brother, and nudges us from housebound winter to the nature-filled seasons spent outside on their farm. Adoff's distinctive free-verse format needs to be seen as well as heard. Search out more earth-wise poems in Barbara Brenner's *The Earth Is Painted Green,* Barbara Juster Esbensen's *Cold Stars and Fireflies,* Lee Bennett Hopkins's *Moments: Poems About the Seasons, Ring Out, Wild Bells: Poems About Holidays and Seasons,* and *The Sky Is Full of Song,* Shirley Hughes's *Out and About,* Leland B. Jacobs's *Just Around the Corner: Poems About the Seasons,* J. Patrick Lewis's *Earth Verses and Water Rhymes,* and Marilyn Singer's *Turtle in July.* AFRICAN AMERICANS–POETRY. FAMILY LIFE–POETRY. POETRY–SINGLE AUTHOR. SEASONS–POETRY.

1261   Adoff, Arnold. *Street Music: City Poems.* Illus. by Karen Barbour. HarperCollins, 1995. ISBN 0-06-021523-2

[unp., Gr. 2–6] In 15 free-verse poems that pulsate with the bangs and crashes of big-city life, we gaze at tall buildings, play in the park, listen to street musicians, and watch the always-moving profusion of people. Barbour's busy and intensely colorful paintings are filled with people in flux. *The Adventures of Taxi Dog* by Debra and Sal Barracca and *My New York* by Kathy Jakobsen give a further feel for the excitement of New York City. CITIES AND TOWNS–POETRY. POETRY–SINGLE AUTHOR.

1262 **Agard, John, and Grace Nichols, comps.** *A Caribbean Dozen: Poems from Caribbean Poets.* **Illus. by Cathie Felstead. Candlewick Press, 1994. ISBN 1-56402-339-7**

[93p., Gr. 1–6] Each of 13 poets offers up three or more poems detailing island life and reminiscences of growing up in the Caribbean, describing fruits, hurricanes, boats, and school days, all of which are enhanced with bold, beautiful mixed-media paintings. Spend more time in the Caribbean with Phillis Gershator's *Rata-Pata-Scata-Fata*, Holly Keller's *Island Baby*, Rita Phillips Mitchell's *Hue Boy*, and Karen Lynn Williams's *Tap-Tap*. CARIBBEAN ISLANDS–POETRY. ISLANDS–POETRY POETRY–ANTHOLOGIES.

1263 **Agee, Jon.** *Go Hang a Salami! I'm a Lasagna Hog! And Other Palindromes.* **Illus. by the author. Farrar, 1992. ISBN 0-374-33473-0**

[unp., Gr. 2–6] There's "Emil's niece, in slime," and "Mr. Owl ate my metal worm," and even "Oozy rat in a sanitary zoo." The 60-plus palindromes, with amusing pen-and-ink line drawings, will make your students itch to write and illustrate their own. Or hand out some of Agee's palindromes unillustrated, and have your artists try their hands. Send your results to the author c/o the publisher, and see what he thinks. Do note the ISBN number above, and the $12.21 price. Noodle around with more words in the companion book *So Many Dynamos! and Other Palindromes* (1994), *Antics! An Alphabetical Anthology* by Cathi Hepworth, *The Weighty Word Book* by Paul M. Levitt, Douglas A. Burger, and Elissa S. Guralnick, and Marvin Terban's *Funny You Should Ask: How to Make Up Jokes and Riddles with Wordplay.* ENGLISH LANGUAGE. PALINDROMES. WORD GAMES.

1264 **Axelrod, Alan, comp.** *Songs of the Wild West.* **Arrangements by Dan Fox. Simon & Schuster, 1991. ISBN 0-671-74775-4**

[128p., Gr. 1–6] Compiled by the Metropolitan Museum of Art and richly illustrated with reproductions from its collections of paintings, lithographs, sculptures, and assorted western artifacts, this is an elegant song book/history lesson about cowboys, outlaws, railroaders, and westward travelers. Each of the 45 songs is graced by Axelrod's thoughtful commentary explaining the background of both song and artwork, plus piano and guitar arrangements. Charles Sullivan's *Cowboys*, a compilation of poems, is also smashing. Sing some of these when reading aloud Alan Coren's *Arthur the Kid*, Russell Freedman's *Buffalo Hunt* and *Children of the Wild West*, Roy Gerard's *Rosie and the Rustlers*, Gery Greer and Bob Ruddick's *Max and Me and the Wild West*, Jo Harper's *Jalapeño Hal*, Tony Johnston's *The Cowboy and the Black-Eyed Pea*, and Eric A. Kimmel's *Charlie Drives the Stage.* COWBOYS. FOLK SONGS. MUSEUMS. PAINTINGS. WEST.

1265 **Bates, Katharine Lee.** *America the Beautiful.* **Illus. by Neil Waldman. Atheneum, 1983. ISBN 0-689-31861-8** [unp., Gr. Pre–6] Take a further tour of the United States's most thrilling monuments and natural wonders with this picture-book version of the anthemlike song, illustrated in gorgeous pastel acrylics. Children can research the 14 fascinating sites pictured here and prepare a cross-country presentation of these and other marvelous places to familiarize themselves with the Statue of Liberty, the Grand Canyon, Mesa Verde, the coastal redwoods, and more. MONUMENTS. NATURAL MONUMENTS. SONGS. U.S.–POETRY.

1266   Bauer, Caroline Feller, comp. *Thanksgiving: Stories and Poems*. Illus. by Nadine Bernard Westcott. HarperCollins, 1994. ISBN 0-06-023327-3

[26 stories and poems, 86p. Gr. 2–4] A pleasant collection of stories and poems, a recipe for pumpkin pie, directions for making a paper turkey decoration, and an annotated bibliography of additional books to read will get you in the mood for the holiday. *Three Young Pilgrims* by Cheryl Harness, *Oh, What a Thanksgiving!* by Steven Kroll, and *Samuel Eaton's Day: A Day in the Life of a Pilgrim Boy* by Kate Waters give a realistic picture of life in pilgrim times. More poetic choices abound in *Merrily Comes Our Harvest In: Poems for Thanksgiving*, compiled by Lee Bennett Hopkins, and *It's Thanksgiving*, a book of lighthearted poems by Jack Prelutsky. SHORT STORIES. THANKSGIVING. THANKSGIVING–POETRY.

1267   Benjamin, Alan. *A Nickel Buys a Rhyme*. Illus. by Karen Lee Schmidt. Morrow, 1993. ISBN 0-688-06699-2

[unp., Gr. Pre–2] The nursery rhyme set will love to hear and chant these 30 short and bouncy poems and giggle over the animal-laden whimsical watercolors. More verses all will find entertaining include Jill Bennett's *A Cup of Starshine*, William Cole's *A Zooful of Animals*, Richard Edwards's *Moon Frog*, Douglas Florian's *Beast Feast*, J. Patrick Lewis's *A Hippopotamustn't and Other Animal Verses*, Mary Ann Hoberman's *A Fine Fat Pig and Other Animal Poems*, Beverly McLoughland's *A Hippo's a Heap*, Fay Robinson's *A Frog Inside My Hat*, and Jane Yolen's *Alphabestiary*. ANIMALS–POETRY. POETRY–SINGLE AUTHOR.

1268   Bennett, Jill, comp. *A Cup of Starshine: Poems and Pictures for Young Children*. Illus. by Graham Percy. Harcourt, 1991. ISBN 0-15-220982-4

[60p., Gr. Pre–2] This soft, sweet, and thoroughly appealing collection of 69 brief, accessible poems to read and reread is made all the more pleasant by a spacious layout and charming colored-pencil illustrations. Get the youngest listeners hooked on rhymes with *A Nickel Buys a Rhyme* by Alan Benjamin, *Book of Poems* by Tomie dePaola, *Sing a Song of Popcorn* by Beatrice Schenk de Regniers, *Moon Frog* by Richard Edwards, *A Fine Fat Pig and Other Animal Poems* by Mary Ann Hoberman, *April Bubbles Chocolate: An ABC of Poetry* by Lee Bennett Hopkins, *Talking Like the Rain: A First Book of Poems* by Dorothy M. and X. J. Kennedy, *A Hippo's a Heap* by Beverly McLoughland, *Sunflakes* by Lillian Moore, *Read-Aloud Rhymes for the Very Young* by Jack Prelutsky, *A Frog Inside My Hat* by Fay Robinson, and *Poems for the Very Young* selected by Michael Rosen. POETRY–ANTHOLOGIES.

1269   Bennett, Jill, comp. *Spooky Poems*. Illus. by Mary Rees. Little, Brown, 1989. ISBN 0-316-08987-7

[unp., Gr. K–4] Twenty-four faintly macabre poems include mention of a Spangled Pandemonium, a Hairy Toe, an Alphabet Monster, a Marrog, and a Cheeky Little Skeleton, all waiting to get you if you don't watch out. Laura Cecil's *Boo! Stories to Make You Jump*, Dilys Evans's *Monster Soup and Other Spooky Poems*, Douglas Florian's *Monster Motel*, Diane Goode's *Diane Goode's Book of Scary Stories & Songs*, Florence Parry Heide's *Grim and Ghastly Goings-On*, Lee Bennett Hopkins's *Ragged Shadows: Poems of Halloween Night*, Myra Cohn Livingston's *Halloween Poems*, and Colin McNaughton's *Making Friends with Frankenstein* are deliciously creepy, too. HUMOROUS POETRY. SUPERNATURAL–POETRY.

1270   Blake, Quentin. *All Join In*. Illus. by the author. Little, Brown, 1991. ISBN 0-316-09934-1

[unp., Gr. Pre–2] There are seven raucous and free-spirited poems told from the point of view of a gaggle of jolly, active, noisy children who quack with the ducks, slide down the banisters, and ding bong bang the kitchen pans. Read them all at once and expect listeners to help you out with the sound effects and laugh over the frantic watercolors. Together, compose a class noise poem about the sounds you make in school. For more cacophony, in John Rowe's *Baby Crow*, the bird can't caw, but only beeps. CHANTABLE REFRAIN. FAMILY LIFE–POETRY. HUMOROUS POETRY. SOUND EFFECTS.

1271   Bodecker, N. M. *Water Pennies: And Other Poems*. Illus. by Erik Blegvad. McElderry, 1991. ISBN 0-689-50517-5

[52p., Gr. 2–5] A water penny is a tiny, squirming, freshwater insect, and in these 32 wordplay-rich poems, Bodecker takes a microscopic look in verse at other wondrous creatures, mostly from the bug family. *Joyful Noise* by Paul Fleischman, *Bugs: Poems* by Mary Ann Hoberman, *Flit, Flutter, Fly! Poems About Bugs and Other Crawly Creatures* compiled by Lee Bennett Hopkins, and *Itsy-Bitsy Beasties* by Michael Rosen are all poetry books to drive you buggy. *Creepy Crawly Critter Riddles* by Joanne E. Bernstein and Paul Cohen and *Buggy Riddles* by Katy Hall and Lisa Eisenberg pull in broader humor. ANIMALS–POETRY. INSECTS–POETRY. POETRY–SINGLE AUTHOR.

1272   Booth, David, comp. *Doctor Knickerbocker and Other Rhymes*. Illus. by Maryann Kovalski. Ticknor & Fields, 1993. ISBN 0-395-67168-X

[72p., Gr. 2–5] Each page is littered with children's rhymes and nonsense verses, some well-known, some not, and witty, detailed, Victorian-flavored pen-and-inks. Kids can't get enough of these, so make your own classroom volume, and consult James Marshall's *Pocketful of Nonsense*, Lillian Morrison's *Best Wishes, Amen*, Iona and Peter Opie's *I Saw Esau: The Schoolchild's Pocket Book*, Jack Prelutsky's *Poems of A. Nonny Mouse* and *A. Nonny Mouse Writes Again!*, Alvin Schwartz's *And the Green Grass Grew All Around: Folk Poetry from Everyone*, and Carl Withers's *A Rocket in My Pocket: Rhymes and Chants of Young Americans*. HUMOROUS POETRY. NONSENSE VERSES.

1273   **Booth, David, comp. '*Til All the Stars Have Fallen: A Collection of Poems for Children*. Illus. by Kady MacDonald Denton. Viking, 1990. ISBN 0-670-83272-3**

[93p., Gr. 3–5] Here's a fresh, solid, and enormously likeable collection of 73 poems, mostly from Canadian poets, about nature, seasons, and friendship, each illustrated with delicate pen-and-ink and watercolor. Dig in. POETRY–ANTHOLOGIES. POETRY–CANADIAN.

1274   **Brenner, Barbara, comp. *The Earth Is Painted Green: A Garden of Poems About Our Planet*. Illus. by S. D. Schindler. Scholastic, 1994. ISBN 0-590-45134-0**

[96p., Gr. 1–5] A visually beautiful collection of more than 90 poems, arranged in sections about earth, trees, plants, seasons, and environmental well-being, this glorious tribute to nature has instant child appeal. Continue collecting ecologically sound verse with *Snow Toward Evening: A Year in a River Valley: Nature Poems* selected by Josette Frank, *Earth Verses and Water Rhymes* by J. Patrick Lewis and *Land, Sea, and Sky: Poems to Celebrate the Earth* selected by Catherine Paladino. EARTH–POETRY. NATURE–POETRY. POETRY–ANTHOLOGIES.

1275   **Brown, Marc, comp. *Scared Silly: A Book for the Brave*. Illus. by the author. Little, Brown, 1994. ISBN 0-316-11360-3**

[61p., Gr. 1–3] This colorful collection of poems, with a few stories and jokes thrown in for good measure, will raise more laughter than goose bumps. One particularly enjoyable highlight is the double page of tombstones with sly rhyming epitaphs, which, if you all write and design new ones, should make a pleasantly morbid Halloween bulletin board. Poems and tales from Jill Bennett's *Spooky Poems*, Laura Cecil's *Boo! Stories to Make You Jump*, Dilys Evans's *Monster Soup and Other Spooky Poems*, Douglas Florian's *Monster Motel*, Diane Goode's *Diane Goode's Book of Scary Stories & Songs*, Florence Parry Heide's *Grim and Ghastly Goings-On*, Lee Bennett Hopkins's *Ragged Shadows: Poems of Halloween Night*, Myra Cohn Livingston's *Halloween Poems*, and Colin McNaughton's *Making Friends with Frankenstein* should keep kids screaming. Crack a few jokes with Jeffie Ross Gordon's *Hide and Shriek: Riddles About Ghosts & Goblins*. HUMOROUS POETRY. SUPERNATURAL–POETRY. SUSPENSE–POETRY.

1276   **Burns, Diane, and Clint Burns. *Hail to the Chief! Jokes about the Presidents*. Illus. by Joan Hanson. Lerner, 1989. ISBN 0-8225-0971-7**

[unp., Gr. 2–6] Q: Which president made his own clothes? A: Zachary Tailor. While your class is attempting to memorize which president was which, have them sharpen their wits with some presidential humor. A small-sized book with over 50 riddles, many of them plays on the presidents' names, this should spark some new riddle-writing and trivia-sharing. Learn some amusing and amazing facts in *Yo, Millard Fillmore! (And All Those Other Presidents You Don't Know)* by Will Cleveland and Mark Alvarez and *The Last Cow on the White House Lawn & Other Little-Known Facts About the Presidency* by Barbara Seuling. JOKES. PRESIDENTS–U.S. RIDDLES.

1277   Calmenson, Stephanie. *What Am I? Very First Riddles.* **Illus. by Karen Gundersheimer. Harper & Row, 1989. ISBN 0-06-020998-4**

[unp., Gr. Pre–1] Fifteen charming four-line rhymes describe objects for children to identify. Turn the page to see an illustration of the answer. With your help, children can compose new rhyming riddles about things one finds at school. Try out more beginning riddles from Stephanie Calmenson's *It Begins with an A,* Robin Michal Koontz's *I See Something You Don't See,* and Beatrice Schenk de Regniers's *It Does Not Say Meow and Other Animal Riddle Rhymes.* RIDDLES.

1278   Cassedy, Sylvia, and Kunihiro Suetake, trans. *Red Dragonfly on My Shoulder.* **Illus. by Molly Bang. HarperCollins, 1992. ISBN 0-06-0226250-0**

[unp., Gr. 2–6] Thirteen traditional haiku about animals are illustrated with eye-catching fabric and object-laden collages. The imaginative use of everyday items to create animals (such as the fish formed with potato chip fins and a sweet potato body) gives new depth and meaning to the intense images of the poems. Kids will be fascinated by the unique format of this book—the double-paged spreads are printed sideways—and the artist's notes about her choices of found materials will spark ideas for student's own verbal and visual artistic explorations. Demi's *In the Eyes of the Cat* and William J. Higginson's *Wind in the Long Grass* are also fine collections of haiku. ANIMALS–POETRY. CREATIVE WRITING. HAIKU. JAPANESE POETRY.

1279   Cole, Joanna, and Stephanie Calmenson, comps. *The Eentsy, Weentsy Spider: Fingerplays and Action Rhymes.* **Illus. by Alan Tiegreen. Morrow, 1991. ISBN 0-688-09439-2**

[64p., Gr. Pre–2] Liven up your storytimes with these 37 perky fingerplays with black-and-white line drawings depicting the actions for each one. *Hand Rhymes* by Marc Brown, *Ring-a-Round-a-Rosy: Nursery Rhymes, Action Rhymes and Lullabies* by Priscilla Lamont, and *A Day of Rhymes* by Sarah Pooley provide many more examples. Nadine Bernard Westcott's *Peanut Butter and Jelly: A Play Rhyme* and Don and Audrey Wood's *Piggies* are picture books of chantable rhymes. FINGERPLAYS. GAMES. SONGS.

1280   Cole, Joanna, and Stephanie Calmenson, comps. *Six Sick Sheep: 101 Tongue Twisters.* **Illus. by Alan Tiegreen. Morrow, 1993. ISBN 0-688-11140-8**

[64p., Gr. 2–5] Divided into sections, these slippery challengers are laid out on large pages with frantic pen-and-ink illustrations on every page, and include many old favorites, among them "Unique New York." Combine with *Tongue Twisters* by Charles Keller and *Busy Buzzing Bumblebees and Other Tongue Twisters* by Alvin Schwartz for your wordmeisters, and use as a warmup for a lesson on alliteration. ALLITERATION. TONGUE TWISTERS.

1281   Cole, Joanna, and Stephanie Calmenson, comps. *Why Did the Chicken Cross the Road? And Other Riddles Old and New.* **Illus. by Alan Tiegreen. Morrow, 1994. ISBN 0-688-12203-5**

[64p., Gr. 2–5] Illustrated with line drawings, these 200 easy-to-get riddles, long on corn and laughs, are divided into sections on food, animal, spooky, geography, silly-billy, letter, number, Mother Goose, and tricky riddles. Kids will also get a charge out of *And the Green Grass Grew All Around: Folk Poetry from Everyone* by Alvin Schwartz. JOKES. RIDDLES.

1282   Cole, William, comp. *A Zooful of Animals.* Illus. by Lynn Munsinger. Houghton Mifflin, 1992. ISBN 0-395-52278-1

[88 pages, Gr. K–5] A jolly poetry anthology of 45 sparkling poems by the likes of Dennis Lee, Jack Prelutsky, John Ciardi, Dorothy Aldis, and Aileen Fisher is made even more delightful by the large, jaunty illustrations on every page. John Ciardi's "About the Teeth of Sharks" goes wonderfully with Margaret Mahy's *The Great White Man-Eating Shark,* and Wilbur G. Howcroft's "The Personable Porcupine" is perfect for Helen Lester's *A Porcupine Named Fluffy.* Use with other books of animal poetry such as *A Nickel Buys a Rhyme* by Alan Benjamin, *Never Take a Pig to Lunch* by Stephanie Calmenson, *Moon Frog: Animal Poems for Young Children* by Richard Edwards, *Beast Feast* by Douglas Florian, *A Hippopotamustn't and Other Animal Verses* by J. Patrick Lewis, *A Hippo's a Heap: And Other Animal Poems* by Beverly McLoughland, *Zoo Doings* by Jack Prelutsky, *Eric Carle's Animals, Animals,* compiled by Laura Whipple, and *Alphabestiary* by Jane Yolen. ANIMALS–POETRY. NONSENSE VERSES. POETRY–ANTHOLOGIES.

1283   Dakos, Kalli. *If You're Not Here, Please Raise Your Hand: Poems about School.* Illus. by G. Brian Karas. Four Winds, 1990. ISBN 0-02-725581-6

[60p., Gr. 2–6] From an elementary school reading specialist who's seen it all, here are over three dozen entertaining and insightful school poems, both rhyming and free verse, from the vantage of kids and teachers, that take you through the disasters and delights of a typical year. Keep laughing with Kalli Dakos's *Don't Read This Book, Whatever You Do! More Poems About School* (Four Winds, 1993) and *Mrs. Cole on an Onion Roll and Other School Poems* (Simon & Schuster, 1995), plus David L. Harrison's *Somebody Catch My Homework* and Dorothy M. Kennedy's *I Thought I'd Take My Rat to School: Poems for September to June.* HUMOROUS POETRY. POETRY–SINGLE AUTHOR. SCHOOLS–POETRY.

1284   Demi, comp. *In the Eyes of the Cat: Japanese Poetry for All Seasons.* Illus. by the author. Trans. by Tze-si Huang. Henry Holt, 1992. ISBN 0-8050-1955-3

[unp., Gr. 2–6] Divided into seasons, each section features one animal haiku per page along with a delicate and brightly colored painting. The 77 transcendent poems date as far back as the eighth century and both poet and dates are listed when known. Sylvia Cassedy and Kunihiro Suekake's *Red Dragonfly on My Shoulder* and William J. Higginson's *Wind in the Long Grass* are other noteworthy collections. ANIMALS–POETRY. HAIKU. JAPANESE POETRY. NATURE–POETRY. SEASONS–POETRY.

1285   Edwards, Richard. *Moon Frog: Animal Poems for Young Children.* Illus. by Sarah Fox-Davies. Candlewick, 1993. ISBN 1-56402-116-5

[45p., Gr. K–3] The 29 animal poems in this attractive collection are illustrated with gentle watercolors and take an introspective and bemused look at the quirks of creatures including the banana slug, white bear, chameleon, and worm. You'll find a poem to accompany any animal you fancy in Alan Benjamin's *A Nickel Buys a Rhyme*, William Cole's *A Zooful of Animals*, Douglas Florian's *Beast Feast*, Mary Ann Hoberman's *A Fine Fat Pig and Other Animal Poems*, J. Patrick Lewis's *A Hippopotamustn't and Other Animal Verses*, Beverly McLoughland's *A Hippo's a Heap*, Fay Robinson's *A Frog Inside My Hat*, Laura Whipple's *Eric Carle's Animals, Animals*, and Jane Yolen's *Alphabestiary*. ANIMALS–POETRY. POETRY–SINGLE AUTHOR.

1286   Eliot, T. S. *Mr. Mistoffelees with Mungojerrie and Rumpelteazer*. Illus. by Errol Le Cain. Harcourt, 1991. ISBN 0-15-256230-3

[unp., Gr. 3–6] These two exquisitely illustrated poems from Eliot's *Old Possum's Book of Practical Cats*—one about the original magical conjuring cat, the other about two notorious smash-and-grab cat burglars—are a challenge to read aloud, though if you play the record or tape of the Broadway musical *Cats*, you'll pick up the cadence. CATS–POETRY. HUMOROUS POETRY. NARRATIVE POETRY. POETRY–SINGLE AUTHOR.

1287   Esbensen, Barbara Juster. *Who Shrank My Grandmother's House? Poems of Discovery*. Illus. by Eric Beddows. HarperCollins, 1992. ISBN 0-06-021827-4

[47p., Gr. 2–5] Each of these 23 poems is about the discovery of an unexpected side to or close observation of an otherwise ordinary object. Take a better look at a pencil, a door, a prism, a cat, or even homework. Charlotte Huck's *Secret Places* and Valerie Worth's *All the Small Poems and Fourteen More* also encourage readers to pay attention. POETRY–SINGLE AUTHOR.

1288   Evans, Dilys, comp. *Monster Soup and Other Spooky Poems*. Illus. by Jacqueline Rogers. Scholastic, 1992. ISBN 0-590-45208-8

[unp., Gr. 1–5] The entrancing full-page paintings set the stage for the 15 mildly spooky poems about oversized creatures such as dragons, monsters, dinosaurs, and other Halloween types. You'll find more suspenseful rhymes in Marc Brown's *Scared Silly!*, Douglas Florian's *Monster Motel*, Florence Parry Heide's *Grim and Ghastly Goings-On*, Lee Bennett Hopkins's *Ragged Shadows: Poems of Halloween Night*, Myra Cohn Livingston's *Halloween Poems*, Colin McNaughton's *Making Friends with Frankenstein*, and Jane Yolen's *Best Witches*. For a good laugh, try Jeffie Ross *Gordon's Hide and Shriek: Riddles About Ghosts & Goblins*. HAL-LOWEEN–POETRY. MONSTERS–POETRY.

1289   Fatchen, Max. *The Country Mail Is Coming: Poems from Down Under*. Illus. by Catharine O'Neill. Little, Brown, 1990. ISBN 0-316-27493-3

[64p., Gr. 3–6] Australian poet Fatchen has assembled a memorable and witty batch of 41 of his own verses about childhood concerns and observations that will startle you into laughing out loud. Introduce him along with the usual assortment of poetry gurus such as Douglas Florian, Eve Merriam, Jeff Moss, Jack Prelutsky, Shel Silverstein, Judith Viorst, and Jane Yolen. AUSTRALIAN POETRY. COUNTRY LIFE–POETRY. HUMOROUS POETRY. POETRY–SINGLE AUTHOR.

1290   Florian, Douglas. *Beast Feast*. Illus. by the author. Harcourt, 1994. ISBN 0-15-295178-4

[unp., Gr. K–4] Twenty-one animals, from the walrus to the kiwi, cavort and mug across their own double pages, with a large watercolor on one side and a teasing, wordplaying poem on the other. Children can compose animal poems and try their hands at watercolors as well. Encourage the animal theme with Alan Benjamin's *A Nickel Buys a Rhyme*, William Cole's *A Zooful of Animals*, Richard Edwards's *Moon Frog*, Mary Ann Hoberman's *A Fine Fat Pig and Other Animal Poems*, J. Patrick Lewis's *A Hippopotamustn't and Other Animal Verses*, Beverly McLoughland's *A Hippo's a Heap*, Fay Robinson's *A Frog Inside My Hat*, Eric Carle's *Animals, Animals*, compiled by Laura Whipple, and Jane Yolen's *Alphabestiary*. ANIMALS–POETRY. HUMOROUS POETRY. POETRY–SINGLE AUTHOR.

1291   Florian, Douglas. *Bing Bang Boing*. Illus. by the author. Harcourt Brace, 1994. ISBN 0-15-233770-9

[144p., Gr. 1–6] Children who thrive on the nonsense poems of Jack Prelutsky and Shel Silverstein will devour with relish this fat collection of 176 short and punchy poems. Thick-lined pen-and-ink drawings accompany the poems, which are heavy on sharp-witted wordplay and sage observations, including "First": "First things first. / Last things last. / Hours / pass / slowly. / Years pass fast." How true. *The Butterfly Jar* by Jeff Moss and *Sad Underwear and Other Complications* by Judith Viorst will also amuse. HUMOROUS POETRY. NONSENSE VERSES. POETRY–SINGLE AUTHOR.

1292   Florian, Douglas. *Monster Motel*. Illus. by the author. Harcourt, 1993. ISBN 0-15-255320-7

[unp., Gr. K–3] Through a baker's dozen of short, animated rhymes, meet the mostly monstrous monsters that dwell at the horrible horrid Monster Motel: the Gazzygoo, the Fabled Feerz with fifty nifty ears, the crying Crim, polite Purple Po, the tiny Teek, and let's not forget the sneaky Beeky, which might be hiding on your nose. Children can invent and write new poems about prospective tenants. Jack Prelutsky's *The Baby Uggs Are Hatching* and *The Snopp on the Sidewalk* also contain clever and beastly poems. Dilys Evans's *Monster Soup and Other Spooky Poems*, Florence Parry Heide's *Grim and Ghastly Goings-On*, and Colin McNaughton's *Making Friends with Frankenstein* are poetry collections about more typical monsters. ANIMALS, IMAGINARY–POETRY. MONSTERS–POETRY. POETRY–SINGLE AUTHOR.

1293   Foster, John, comp. *Let's Celebrate: Festival Poems*. Oxford University Press, 1989. ISBN 0-19-276083-1

[111p., Gr. 3–6] The 84 poems in this unique collection reflect a year of international holidays such as Ramadan, Idh al-Fitr, Saint Swithin's Day, and Divali, along with more mainstream U.S. holidays. *Ring Out, Wild Bells: Poems About Holidays and Seasons* by Lee Bennett Hopkins and *Callooh! Callay! Holiday Poems for Young Readers* by Myra Cohn Livingston will help fill the need for poems about holidays. HOLIDAYS–POETRY. MULTICULTURAL STORIES. POETRY–ANTHOLOGIES.

1294   Frank, Josette, comp. *Snow Toward Evening: A Year in a River Valley: Nature Poems.* **Illus. by Thomas Locker. Dial, 1990. ISBN 0-8037-0811-4**

[unp., Gr. 3–6] Accompanied by ravishing paintings of Hudson River Valley landscapes, the 13 lyrical nature poems take us through the months from January through New Year's Day. Nature poems are also the theme of *The Earth Is Painted Green* by Barbara Brenner, *Weather* by Lee Bennett Hopkins, *Earth Verses and Water Rhymes* by J. Patrick Lewis, *Land, Sea, and Sky* by Catherine Paladino, and *Turtle in July* by Marilyn Singer, which also presents a poem for each month. Aliki's *The Twelve Months*, Beatrice Schenk de Regniers's *Little Sister and the Month Brothers*, and Samuel Marshak's *The Month Brothers* are folktale variants about the men who rule each season. Charles Larry's *Peboan and Seegwun*, an Ojibway Indian legend about old man winter and young man spring, will fit in perfectly here. MONTHS–POETRY. NATURE–POETRY. SEASONS–POETRY.

1295   Gerberg, Mort. *Geographunny: A Book of Global Riddles.* **Illus. by the author. Clarion, 1991. ISBN 0-395-52449-0**

[64p., Gr. 3–6] Use the full-page comical illustrations to help figure the place-name answers to these funny puns and riddles about North and South America and the rest of the world as well. After puzzling out the answers to these and the ones in *Riddle City, USA! A Book of Geography Riddles* by Marco and Giulio Maestro, students should be raring to make up some geography riddles of their own. For advice in how to go about it, consult Marvin Terban's *Funny You Should Ask: How to Make Up Jokes and Riddles with Wordplay*. GEOGRAPHY–RIDDLES. NAMES, GEOGRAPHICAL–RIDDLES. RIDDLES. U.S.–RIDDLES. WORD GAMES.

1296   Goldstein, Bobbye S., comp. *Bear in Mind: A Book of Bear Poems.* **Illus. by William Pène du Bois. Viking Kestrel, 1989. ISBN 0-670-81907-7**

[32p., Gr. Pre–2] Pair this sweet and colorful collection of 32 bear poems and chants with the many bear picture books out there. *The Three Bears Rhyme Book* by Jane Yolen deals with the friendly relationship between Goldilocks and her new pal, Baby Bear. BEARS–POETRY.

1297   Goldstein, Bobbye S., comp. *Birthday Rhymes, Special Times.* **Illus. by Jose Aruego and Ariane Dewey. Doubleday, 1993. ISBN 0-385-30419-6**

[48p., Gr. Pre–3] In 32 upbeat poems paired with eye-openingly bright and glee-ful pictures, we consider cakes, wishes, presents, and parties. *Happy Birthday*, selected by Lee Bennett Hopkins, shares several poems in common, but is still a pleasant extension. Integrate poetry into birthday stories such as *Benjamin's 365 Birthdays* by Judi Barrett, *Arthur's Birthday* by Marc Brown, *Treasure Hunt* by

Lorinda Bryan Cauley, *The 13th Clue* by Ann Jonas, *Alice and the Birthday Giant* by John F. Green, and *Some Birthday!* by Patricia Polacco. BIRTHDAYS–POETRY.

1298   **Goldstein, Bobbye S., comp.** *Inner Chimes: Poems on Poetry.* **Illus. by Jane Breskin Zalben. Wordsong: Boyds Mills, 1992. ISBN 1-56397-040-6**

[24p., Gr. 2–6] This elegant collection of 20 poems, accompanied by meticulous watercolors, is just what you need to explain the miracles of verse creation. The poems in *Good Books, Good Times!* selected by Lee Bennett Hopkins make a further pitch for reading, and *Letter Jester* by Cathryn Falwell explains the ins and outs of typefaces. *The Sleeper* by David Day and *Dream Peddler* by Gail E. Haley are both folktales about book-lovers. POETRY–ANTHOLOGIES. WRITING.

1299   **Goldstein, Bobbye S., comp.** *What's on the Menu?* **Illus. by Chris L. Demarest. Viking, 1992. ISBN 0-670-83031-3**

[32p., Gr. 1–4] A collection of 25 short and spicy classics, with amusing watercolors by Chris L. Demarest, includes plenty of choices to memorize and recite before lunch. Also sample Arnold Adoff's *Eats*, Rose Agree's *How to Eat a Poem and Other Morsels*, William Cole's *Poem Stew*, Lee Bennett Hopkins's *Munching*, Dee Lillegard's *Do Not Feed the Table*, and Nadine Bernard Westcott's *Never Take a Pig to Lunch*. FOOD–POETRY.

1300   **Gordon, Jeffie Ross.** *Hide and Shriek: Riddles About Ghosts & Goblins.* **Illus. by Susan Slattery Gordon. Lerner, 1991. ISBN 0-8225-2336-1**

[unp., Gr. 2–5] Here are more than five dozen ghost, witch, vampire, and other creepy creature wordplay riddles, in question-and-answer format that children can read aloud in pairs. Stay on the titillating topic with Marc Brown's *Spooky Riddles*, Charles Keller's *Count Draculations! Monster Riddles*, Giulio Maestro's *More Halloween Howls*, and Joseph Rosenbloom's *Monster Madness: Riddles, Jokes, Fun*. Keep the heart rates high with the poems in Dilys Evans's *Monster Soup and Other Spooky Poems*, Florence Parry Heide's *Grim and Ghastly Goings-On*, Lee Bennett Hopkins's *Ragged Shadows: Poems of Halloween Night*, Colin McNaughton's *Making Friends with Frankenstein*, and Jane Yolen's *Best Witches*. GHOSTS–RIDDLES. RIDDLES. WORD GAMES.

1301   **Graham, Joan Bransfield.** *Splish Splash.* **Illus. by Steve Scott. Ticknor & Fields, 1994. ISBN 0-395-70128-7**

[unp., Gr. K–6] Not only are the 21 fast, clever poems in this flamboyant picture book all about water, they're laid out in a graphically colorful and exciting format as concrete poems, which makes them irresistible. With visions of whole-language lessons dancing in their heads, science teachers will smile over the variety of verse on weather, oceans, rivers, steam, ponds, and icicles, and other forms water can take. Each poem is laid out in big print as a shape verse that becomes an integral part of each colorful picture, such as "River," "Sprinkler," and "Ice Cubes." *Weather*, a sprightly assortment of 29 easy-to-read poems compiled by Lee Bennett Hopkins, is a fine companion, as are *Earth Verses and Water Rhymes* by J. Patrick Lewis and *Until I Saw the Sea: A Collection of Seashore Poems* collected by Alison Shaw. For some concrete information, read *Follow the Water from Brook to Ocean* by Arthur Dorros and *Water's Way* by Lisa Westberg Peters. POETRY–SINGLE AUTHOR. WATER–POETRY. WEATHER–POETRY.

1302   **Grimes, Nikki. *Meet Danitra Brown*. Illus. by Floyd Cooper. Lothrop, 1994. ISBN 0-688-12074-1**

[unp., Gr. 3–5] Children will relate to this fresh, upbeat, charming character study in rhyme, with 13 poems narrated by Zuri Jackson about her best friend, Danitra. The two African American city girls crackle with life in Cooper's full-page personable paintings. Children will want to write descriptive poems about their best friends. Tie in Jack Prelutsky's male-oriented portrait poems, *Rolling Harvey Down the Hill*. Lee Bennett Hopkins's *Best Friends* and the spare, small-town memories of Cynthia Rylant's *Waiting to Waltz* will also give them insight. *In for Winter, Out for Spring* by Arnold Adoff, *Pass It On: African-American Poetry for Children* by Wade Hudson, *Brown Angels: An Album of Pictures and Verse* by Walter Dean Myers, and *Families: Poems Celebrating the African American Experience* by Dorothy S. and Michael R. Strickland are also stellar choices. AFRICAN AMERICANS–POETRY. CITIES AND TOWNS–POETRY. FRIENDSHIP–POETRY. POETRY–SINGLE AUTHOR.

1303   **Guthrie, Woody, and Marjorie Mazia Guthrie. *Woody's 20 Grow Big Songs*. Illus. by Woody Guthrie. HarperCollins, 1992. ISBN 0-06-020283-1**

[unp., Gr. Pre–2] A replication of the folksinger's unpublished songbook, which he wrote in the late 1940s with his wife, this charming collection contains words, music, and Guthrie's original watercolors for classics "Cleano," "Put Your Finger in the Air," and "Riding in My Car." *The Mother Goose Songbook* by Tom Glazer, *Gonna Sing My Head Off! American Folk Songs for Children* compiled by Kathleen Krull, *Songs from Mother Goose* by Nancy Larrick, *Shake It to the One That You Love the Best: Play Songs and Lullabies from Black Musical Traditions* by Cheryl Mattox, and *Mother Goose Songbook* by Jane Yolen will keep you humming. SONGS.

1304   **Hall, Katy, and Lisa Eisenberg. *Batty Riddles*. Illus. by Nicole Rubel. Dial, 1993. ISBN 0-8037-1218-9**

[48p., Gr. 1–4] Which bat knows its ABCs? The alpha-bat! Forty-two bat-based riddles rely heavily on the vampire bat's bad reputation, and the clever word-play allows children to laugh at a creature that often frightens them. Help restore the bat's good reputation with the nonfiction *Shadows of Night: The Hidden World of the Little Brown Bat* by Barbara Bash and stories like the charming *Stellaluna* by Janell Cannon and *Hattie the Backstage Bat* by Don Freeman. Folktales featuring bats include Paul Goble's *Iktomi and the Boulder*, Tololwa M. Mollel's *A Promise to the Sun: An African Story*, and Judy Sierra's *The Elephant's Wrestling Match*. Other brightly illustrated titles in this entertaining riddle series include *Buggy Riddles*, *Fishy Riddles* (1983), *Grizzly Riddles* (1989), and *Snaky Riddles*. BATS–RIDDLES. RIDDLES.

1305   Hall, Katy, and Lisa Eisenberg. *Snakey Riddles*. Illus. by Simms Taback. Dial, 1990.
ISBN 0-8037-0670-7

[48p., Gr. 1–4] Why did the snake love to do arithmetic? He was a good little adder! The 42 snake-based riddles in this cheerful collection are truly funny, and, as with *Snakes Alive! Jokes About Snakes* by Diane L. Burns, children will enjoy taking turns reading them aloud. Use riddles as a warm-up for stories such as Native American folktale *Baby Rattlesnake* by Te Ata, *A Nice Walk in the Jungle* by Nan Bodsworth, Australian folktale *The Singing Snake* by Stefan Czernecki and Timothy Rhodes, *Slither McCreep and His Brother Joe* by Tony Johnston, *Snake Hunt* by Jill Kastner, *A Snake in the House* by Faith McNulty, and the lovable *Crictor* by Tomi Ungerer. Betsy Maestro's nonfiction *Take a Look at Snakes* will add facts and take away fears. RIDDLES. SNAKES–RIDDLES.

1306   Hall, Katy, and Lisa Eisenberg. *Spacey Riddles*. Illus. by Simms Taback. Dial, 1992.
ISBN 0-8037-0815-7

[48p., Gr. 2–5] "What is the astronaut's favorite meal? Launch!" The 42 pun-rich riddles are illustrated with watercolors and colored pencils against a black space-set background. Try these out as lead-ins to space stories and nonfiction, ranging from *No Moon, No Milk* by Chris Babcock to *The Magic School Bus Lost in the Solar System* by Joanna Cole. *Blast Off! Poems About Space*, selected by Lee Bennett Hopkins, is also lots of fun. ASTRONOMY–RIDDLES. RIDDLES.

1307   Harrison, David L. *Somebody Catch My Homework*. Illus. by Betsy Lewin. Wordsong:
Boyds Mills, 1993. ISBN 1-878093-87-8

[30p., Gr. 2–5] Twenty genial poems take us through the school day and let us laugh at kids' worries, such as oversleeping, missing homework, naughty students, bad cafeteria food, hard tests, and principal encounters. Equally delightful light verse about school days can be found in Kalli Dakos's *If You're Not Here, Please Raise Your Hand: Poems about School* and the follow-up *Don't Read This Book, Whatever You Do! More Poems about School* (Four Winds, 1993), plus *I Thought I'd Take My Rat to School: Poems for September to June,* selected by Dorothy M. Kennedy. HUMOROUS POETRY. POETRY–SINGLE AUTHOR. SCHOOLS–POETRY.

1308   Hartman, Victoria. *The Silliest Joke Book Ever*. Illus. by R. W. Alley. Lothrop, 1993.
ISBN 0-688-10110-0

[unp., Gr. 3–5] There are food funnies, animal snickers, wacky workers, techie ticklers, journey jests, and gruesome gigglers making up the 100-plus wordplay riddles in this congenial collection with plenty of whimsical pen-and-ink and watercolor illustrations. *Funny You Should Ask: How to Make Up Jokes and Riddles with Wordplay* by Marvin Terban will help punsters think up their own. Charles Keller's *Belly Laughs! Food Jokes & Riddles* and Frederica Young's *Super-Duper Jokes* will also keep kids laughing. JOKES. RIDDLES. WORD GAMES.

1309   Heide, Florence Parry. *Grim and Ghastly Goings-On*. Illus. by Victoria Chess. Lothrop,
1992. ISBN 0-688-08322-6

485

[unp., Gr. 1–4] Curl up with these 21 monster and creature poems, decorated with Chess's usual cheerfully malevolent illustrations. Scream a bit longer with Marc Brown's *Scared Silly!*, Dilys Evans's *Monster Soup and Other Spooky Poems*, Douglas Florian's *Monster Motel*, Lee Bennett Hopkins's *Ragged Shadows: Poems of Halloween Night*, Myra Cohn Livingston's *Halloween Poems*, Colin McNaughton's *Making Friends with Frankenstein*, and Jane Yolen's *Best Witches*. Joke around with Jeffie Ross Gordon's *Hide and Shriek: Riddles About Ghosts & Goblins*. ANIMALS, IMAGINARY–POETRY. MONSTERS–POETRY. POETRY–SINGLE AUTHOR.

1310   **Heller, Ruth. *Merry-Go-Round: A Book About Nouns*. Illus. by the author. Grosset, 1990. ISBN 0-448-40085-5**

[1 sitting, unp., Gr. 1–6] And you thought grammar meant boring? Heller's dazzling illustrations go along with a bouncy rhyming explanation of what a noun is, and describes all types: proper, abstract, concrete, compound, and collective. Much of the text unravels the difficulties and differences between singular and plural nouns, and your students will be able to come up with other examples to add to the list. Heller's *A Cache of Jewels and Other Collective Nouns*, Patricia Hooper's poems in *A Bundle of Beasts*, Patricia MacCarthy's *Herds of Words*, and Peter and Connie Roop's *One Earth, a Multitude of Creatures* deal with collective nouns. Heller's grammar books also hit verbs (*Kites Sail High*), adverbs (*Up, Up and Away*), and adjectives (*Many Luscious Lollipops*, 1989), and all work marvelously as both an introduction to and a review of terms. ENGLISH LANGUAGE–GRAMMAR. STORIES IN RHYME.

1311   **Heller, Ruth. *Up, Up and Away: A Book About Adverbs*. Illus. by the author. Grosset, 1991. ISBN 0-448-40249-1**

[1 sitting, unp., Gr. 2–6] Another rhyming gem with gloriously colorful illustrations, this works marvelously when used with children who are feeling somewhat sick at the thought of learning grammar. Heller's *Many Luscious Lollipops* (1989) covers fascinating adjectives. Ask children to write one rousing adverb and adjective (loudly and loud; angrily and angry) on an index card and place it in a hat or box. Each child or pair then selects a card and acts out the word for others to guess and then use in a sentence. Heller's collection of large rhyming picture books that explain the parts of speech also includes *A Cache of Jewels and Other Collective Nouns*, *Kites Sail High: A Book About Verbs*, and *Merry-Go-Round: A Book About Nouns*. ENGLISH LANGUAGE–GRAMMAR. STORIES IN RHYME.

1312   **Hepworth, Cathi. *Antics! An Alphabetical Anthology*. Illus. by the author. Putnam, 1992. ISBN 0-399-21862-9**

[1 sitting, 32p., Gr. 2–6] Each page of this entertaining and slyly witty alphabet book features one word, like **ant**ique, observ**ant**, and quar**ant**ine, with a large, winning, "ant"-based portrait that shows the meaning of the word in context. Ask them to define each word from its illustration, and compare their answers with the dictionary's. Your kids will love combing their dictionaries to come up with additional "ant" words they can illustrate in similar style. Some of the words (Rembrandt and Kant especially) should lead you to the encyclopedias for more information. Not since *The Weighty Word Book* by Paul M. Levitt, Douglas A. Burger, and Elissa S. Guralnick has there been such a painless way to sop up new words. ALPHABET BOOKS. ANTS. PICTURE BOOKS FOR ALL AGES. VOCABULARY. WORD GAMES.

1313   Higginson, William J., comp. *Wind in the Long Grass: A Collection of Haiku.* Illus. by Sandra Speidel. Simon & Schuster, 1991. ISBN 0-671-67978-3

[unp., Gr. 2–6] Illustrated with lovely smudgy pastels that become clear when you see the book from a distance, this sensitive assemblage of 52 haiku, arranged by season, comes from all over the world. Two other graceful collections are Sylvia Cassedy and Kunihiro Suekake's *Red Dragonfly on My Shoulder* and Demi's *In the Eyes of the Cat: Japanese Poetry for All Seasons.* ANIMALS–POETRY. HAIKU. JAPANESE POETRY. NATURE–POETRY. SEASONS–POETRY.

1314   Hoberman, Mary Ann. *Fathers, Mothers, Sisters, Brothers: A Collection of Family Poems.* Illus. by Marylin Hafner. Little, Brown, 1991. ISBN 0-316-36736-2

[32p., Gr. K–4] The 26 charming poems in this attractive multicultural collection cover the extended family as they spend quality time together. *In for Winter, Out for Spring* by Arnold Adoff and *All Join In* by Quentin Blake engender a cozy family feel, as does the rhyming picture book *I Got a Family* by Melrose Cooper. FAMILY LIFE–POETRY. MULTICULTURAL STORIES. POETRY–SINGLE AUTHOR.

1315   Hoberman, Mary Ann. *A Fine Fat Pig and Other Animal Poems.* Illus. by Malcah Zeldis. HarperCollins, 1991. ISBN 0-06-022426-6

[unp., Gr. K–3] Loud and devilish folk-art paintings face 14 congenial poems, one per double-page spread, about familiar animals from lion to rhino. There are more than enough animal poems to satisfy every young zoologist in collections such as Alan Benjamin's *A Nickel Buys a Rhyme,* William Cole's *A Zooful of Animals,* Richard Edwards's *Moon Frog,* Douglas Florian's *Beast Feast,* J. Patrick Lewis's *A Hippopotamustn't and Other Animal Verses,* Beverly McLoughland's *A Hippo's a Heap,* Fay Robinson's *A Frog Inside My Hat,* and Jane Yolen's *Alphabestiary.* ANIMALS–POETRY. POETRY–SINGLE AUTHOR.

1316   Hopkins, Lee Bennett, comp. *April Bubbles Chocolate: An ABC of Poetry.* Illus. by Barry Root. Simon & Schuster, 1994. ISBN 0-671-75911-6

[40p., Gr. K–3] Master compiler Hopkins has assembled a delightful poetry alphabet representing many of our best children's poets, and illustrated with good-humored paintings. Most of the 26 brief poems are about food or animals, and while all are easy for children to read and understand, they allow us to look at each object in a new way. Children can extend the alphabet, reading, selecting, and copying additional favorite poems from other exemplary anthologies, including *Sunflakes* selected by Lillian Moore, *Poems for the Very Young* selected by Michael Rosen and *Talking Like the Rain: A First Book of Poems* by Dorothy and X. J. Kennedy. ALPHABET–POETRY.

1317   Hopkins, Lee Bennett, comp. *Blast Off! Poems About Space.* Illus. by Melissa Sweet. HarperCollins, 1995. ISBN 0-06-024261-2

[48p., Gr. 1–4] The I Can Read series format of 20 brightly illustrated, easy-to-read poems makes this a perfect companion to a first look at the universe. *Spacey Riddles* by Katy Hall and Lisa Eisenberg add a bit more levity, and *The Magic School Bus Lost in the Solar System* by Joanna Cole and *Postcards from Pluto: A Tour of the Solar System* by Loreen Leedy incorporate facts and a bit of entertaining fantasy. ASTRONOMY–POETRY.

1318   Hopkins, Lee Bennett, comp. *Extra Innings: Baseball Poems.* Illus. by Scott Medlock. Harcourt, 1993. ISBN 0-15-226833-2

[40p., Gr. 4–6] Among the 20 poems here are odes to Joe DiMaggio, Yankee Don Larsen, and Satchel Paige, and tributes to all the boys and girls who play the game. See also *At the Crack of the Bat: Baseball Poems* compiled by Lillian Morrison. Baseball stories range from the realism of *Thank You, Jackie Robinson* by Barbara Cohen and *My Dad's Baseball* by Ron Cohen to the fantasy of Marilyn Sachs's *Matt's Mitt and Fleet-Footed Florence.* Sing along with *Take Me Out to the Ballgame* by Jack Norworth, read the epic *Casey at the Bat* by Ernest Lawrence Thayer, and get an insider's view with *The Ballpark: One Day Behind the Scenes at a Major League Game* by William Jaspersohn. BASEBALL–POETRY. SPORTS–POETRY.

1319   Hopkins, Lee Bennett, comp. *Flit, Flutter, Fly! Poems About Bugs and Other Crawly Creatures.* Illus. by Peter Palagonia. Doubleday, 1992. ISBN 0-385-41468-4

[32p., Gr. K–4] The 20 poems in this dignified and attractively illustrated picture-book collection combine well with the insect verse of *Water Pennies: And Other Poems* by N. M. Bodecker, *Bugs: Poems* by Mary Ann Hoberman, and *Itsy-Bitsy Beasties* by Michael Rosen. *Creepy Crawly Critter Riddles* by Joanne E. Bernstein and Paul Cohen and *Buggy Riddles* by Katy Hall and Lisa Eisenberg also fit in well. *Fireflies in the Night* by Judy Hawes and *Those Amazing Ants* by Patricia Brennan Demuth are both easy-to-read nonfiction titles, while *I Wish I Were a Butterfly* by James Howe, *The Gnats of Knotty Pine* by Bill Peet, and *Two Bad Ants* by Chris Van Allsburg are outstanding picture-book stories. *James and the Giant Peach* by Roald Dahl is an insect chapter book to remember. INSECTS–POETRY.

1320   Hopkins, Lee Bennett, comp. *Good Books, Good Times!* Illus. by Harvey Stevenson. Harper & Row, 1990. ISBN 0-06-022528-9

[32p., Gr. K–4] What better way to celebrate the delights of reading than with these 14 delectable poems? Also try a choral reading of *Once Inside the Library* by Barbara A. Huff, and have the crew chime in on the coolly absurd *The Book That Jack Wrote* by Jon Scieszka. *Inner Chimes: Poems on Poetry* compiled by Bobbye S. Goldstein has a tighter focus, and is also indispensable. *The Sleeper* by David Day, *Letter Jester* by Cathryn Falwell, *Dream Peddler* by Gail E. Haley, *Books and Libraries* by Jack Knowlton, and *Frog Medicine* by Mark Teague also make a definitive case for the necessity of reading. BOOKS AND READING–POETRY.

1321 Hopkins, Lee Bennett, comp. *Happy Birthday: Poems.* Illus. by Hilary Knight. Simon & Schuster, 1991. ISBN 0-671-70973-9

[unp., Gr. K–3] A small collection of 16 short and easy-to-read poems about birthdays takes us through one child's special day as he prepares for and has a fine time at his party, surrounded by friends. The poems in *Birthday Rhymes, Special Times* by Bobbye S. Goldstein provide even more possibilities, all of which you can consider when introducing birthday tales such as *Arthur's Birthday* by Marc Brown, *Treasure Hunt* by Lorinda Bryan Cauley, *The 13th Clue* by Ann Jonas, *Alice and the Birthday Giant* by John F. Green, and *Some Birthday!* by Patricia Polacco. BIRTHDAYS–POETRY.

1322 Hopkins, Lee Bennett, comp. *It's About Time!* Illus. by Matt Novak. Simon & Schuster, 1993. ISBN 0-671-78512-5

[unp., Gr. K–3] Sixteen merry poems take us through a school day from a 7:00 A.M. wake-up call all the way to bedtime with a crew of multiracial kids. Count out the hours with *The Grouchy Ladybug* by Eric Carle, cruise earth's time zones with *Nine O'Clock Lullaby* by Marilyn Singer, and stop the clocks with *Tick-Tock* by Eileen Brown, *Clocks and More Clocks* by Pat Hutchins, and *The One and Only Super-Duper Golly-Whopper Jim-Dandy Really-Handy Clock-Tock-Stopper* by Patricia Thomas. TIME–POETRY.

1323 Hopkins, Lee Bennett, comp. *Merrily Comes Our Harvest In: Poems for Thanksgiving.* Illus. by Ben Shecter. Wordsong: Boyds Mills, 1993. ISBN 1-878093-57-6

[32p., Gr. 2–5] In a slim collection of rhymes, each accompanied by a pleasant line drawing, Hopkins has assembled 20 Thanksgiving poems ranging from the Pilgrims' experiences to current concerns. *Thanksgiving: Stories and Poems* compiled by Caroline Feller Bauer and *It's Thanksgiving*, a set of poems by Jack Prelutsky, are also fine. Interweave the poems between such stories as *The First Thanksgiving* by Jean Craighead George, *Three Young Pilgrims* by Cheryl Harness, *Oh, What a Thanksgiving!* by Steven Kroll, and *Samuel Eaton's Day: A Day in the Life of a Pilgrim Boy* by Kate Waters. THANKSGIVING–POETRY.

1324 Hopkins, Lee Bennett, comp. *Questions.* Illus. by Carolyn Croll. HarperCollins, 1992. ISBN 0-06-022413-4

[64p., Gr. 1–3] Each of the 30 short poems in this I Can Read Books poetry collection incorporates a question asking who, what, when, where, how, and why. Children can compile their own list of questions they have about the world. Meet Max the nervy rabbit who asks the "5 W's" of Santa in *Max's Christmas* by Rosemary Wells. QUESTIONS AND ANSWERS–POETRY.

1325 Hopkins, Lee Bennett, comp. *Ragged Shadows: Poems of Halloween Night.* Illus. by Giles Laroche. Little, Brown, 1993. ISBN 0-316-37276-5

[32 pages, Gr. 1–4] Laroche's cut-out collage illustrations of nighttime trick-or-treat hijinks are an imaginative counterpart to these 14 more-fun-than-frightening poems. Raise a few holiday goose bumps with Marc Brown's *Scared Silly!*, Dilys Evans's *Monster Soup and Other Spooky Poems*, Florence Parry Heide's *Grim and Ghastly Goings-On*, Myra Cohn Livingston's *Halloween Poems*, Colin McNaughton's *Making Friends with Frankenstein*, and Jane Yolen's *Best Witches*. Jeffie Ross Gordon's *Hide and Shriek: Riddles About Ghosts & Goblins* will add a few chortles. HALLOWEEN–POETRY.

1326   Hopkins, Lee Bennett, comp. *Ring Out, Wild Bells: Poems About Holidays and Seasons.* Illus. by Karen Baumann. Harcourt, 1992. ISBN 0-15-267100-5

[80p., Gr. K–5] Go around the year in rhyme with Hopkins's well-chosen collection of 75 poems, one per large page. Check out holiday verse and prose in John Foster's *Let's Celebrate: Festival Poems*, Myra Cohn Livingston's *Callooh! Callay! Holiday Poems for Young Readers*, and Alice Low's *The Family Read-Aloud Holiday Treasury*, and seasonal fare in Arnold Adoff's *In for Winter, Out for Spring*, Barbara Brenner's *The Earth Is Painted Green*, Lee Bennett Hopkins's *The Sky Is Full of Song*, Shirley Hughes's *Out and About*, and Leland B. Jacobs's *Just Around the Corner: Poems About the Seasons*. HOLIDAYS–POETRY. SEASONS–POETRY.

1327   Hopkins, Lee Bennett, comp. *Small Talk: A Book of Short Poems*. Illus. by Susan Graber. Harcourt, 1995. ISBN 0-15-276577-8

[48p., Gr. 2–5] The 33 brief, pleasant, and easy-to-fathom poems in this pleasant collection circle the seasons and peer at robins, rain, caterpillars, and fog. Valerie Worth's *All the Small Poems and Fourteen More* are also brief descriptive poems that pack indelible images into every line. SEASONS–POETRY.

1328   Hopkins, Lee Bennett, comp. *Through Our Eyes: Poems and Pictures About Growing Up.* Photos by Jeffrey Dunn. Little, Brown, 1992. ISBN 0-316-19654-1

[unp., Gr. 2–5] A collection of 16 delicate, often poignant, poems mostly told in the first person relates children's hopes, fears, and desires, and is illustrated with color photographs of real kids. The solitary moods will meld well with those in Charlotte Huck's *Secret Places*. CHILDREN–POETRY. MULTICULTURAL STORIES.

1329   Hopkins, Lee Bennett, comp. *Weather.* Illus. by Melanie Hall. HarperCollins, 1994. ISBN 0-06-021462-7

[63p., Gr. 1–3] Twenty-nine pleasant poems in an easy I Can Read series format are divided into sections on the sun, wind and clouds, rain and fog, and snow and ice, for a class read-aloud session to tie into your science weather unit. Expand your forecasts with *Cloudy with a Chance of Meatballs* by Judi and Ron Barrett, *The Match Between the Winds*, a folktale from Borneo by Shirley Climo, *C.L.O.U.D.S.* by Pat Cummings, *The Legend of Slappy Hooper* by Aaron Shepard, *Brrr!* by James Stevenson, *Chinook* by Michael O. Tunnell, and Chinese folktale *The Junior Thunder Lord* by Laurence Yep. Stay with the same poetic themes in *Windy Day: Stories and Poems* by Caroline Feller Bauer, *The Earth Is Painted Green* by Barbara Brenner, *Out and About* by Shirley Hughes, *Earth Verses and Water*

Rhymes by J. Patrick Lewis, *Rainy Rainy Saturday* by Jack Prelutsky, and *Rainy Day Rhymes* by Gail Radley. WEATHER–POETRY.

1330   **Huck, Charlotte, comp.** *Secret Places.* **Illus. by Lindsay Barrett George. Greenwillow, 1993. ISBN 0-688-11670-1**

[32p., Gr. 1–4] Sometimes it's wonderful to be alone, reveling in a secret hiding space or special place to contemplate the world, as this exquisite and unique collection of 19 poems and huge colorful paintings so eloquently attests. Children can write about the real or imaginary places they've found to get away from it all for a spell. *Through Our Eyes: Poems and Pictures About Growing Up* by Lee Bennett Hopkins is another quiet, introspective, and personal collection of poems about childhood yearnings, and Barbara Esbensen's *Who Shrank My Grandmother's House? Poems of Discovery* offers fresh insights. CHILDREN–POETRY. SOLITUDE–POETRY.

1331   **Hudson, Wade, comp.** *Pass It On: African-American Poetry for Children.* **Illus. by Floyd Cooper. Scholastic, 1993. ISBN 0-590-45770-5**

[32p., Gr. 1–4] Nineteen poems by well-known poets chronicle the range of the African American experience, from personal to political. Dorothy S. and Michael R. Strickland's *Families: Poems Celebrating the African American Experience* is another effective compilation. For more in the personal vein, read *In for Winter, Out for Spring* by Arnold Adoff, *Meet Danitra Brown* by Nikki Grimes, and *Brown Angels: An Album of Pictures and Verse* by Walter Dean Myers, and sing the songs in *Shake It to the One That You Love the Best* collected by Cheryl Warren Mattox. AFRICAN AMERICANS–POETRY.

1332   **Hughes, Langston.** *The Dream Keeper and Other Poems.* **Illus. by Brian Pinkney. Knopf, 1994. ISBN 0-679-94421-4**

[83p., Gr. 4–6] Originally published in 1932, this powerful collection of 66 poems, some in dialect, is still fresh and affecting. Broaden children's knowledge of African American poets with *Pass It On: African-American Poetry for Children* selected by Wade Hudson, *Brown Angels: An Album of Pictures and Verse* by Walter Dean Myers, and Dorothy S. and Michael R. Strickland's *Families: Poems Celebrating the African American Experience.* AFRICAN AMERICANS–POETRY. POETRY–SINGLE AUTHOR.

1333   **Jacobs, Leland B.** *Just Around the Corner: Poems About the Seasons.* **Illus. by Jeff Kaufman. Henry Holt, 1993. ISBN 0-8050-2676-2**

[32p., Gr. Pre–2] Colorful childlike paintings splash across the pages along with 25 easy-to-follow poems, divided into the four seasons. Continue the rhymes with Arnold Adoff's *In for Winter, Out for Spring*, Barbara Brenner's *The Earth Is Painted Green*, Lee Bennett Hopkins's *Ring Out, Wild Bells: Poems About Holidays and Seasons*, and *The Sky Is Full of Song*, and Shirley Hughes's *Out and About*. Circle the seasons with Louise Borden's *Caps, Hats, Socks, and Mittens*, and Susi Gregg Fowler's *When Summer Ends*. POETRY–SINGLE AUTHOR. SEASONS–POETRY.

1334   Janeczko, Paul B., comp. *The Place My Words Are Looking For.* Illus. with photos. Bradbury, 1990. ISBN 0-02-747671-5

[150p., Gr. 5–6] Thirty-nine American poets share their poems and personal thoughts about writing poetry, some of which are exceptionally revealing and useful. The four sections are about people, emotions, nature, and poetry itself. Compare each poem with the poet's musings, and show his or her black-and-white photo to make the experience personal and accessible. Students can search out other examples of that poet's work. The illustrators' counterpart can be found in *Talking with Artists* by Pat Cummings. Janeczko's *Poetry from A to Z: A Guide for Young Writers* is a how-to manual with loads of examples from well-known poets, as is *Poem-Making: Ways to Begin Writing Poetry* by Myra Cohn Livingston. AUTHORS. POETS.

1335   Janeczko, Paul B., comp. *Poetry from A to Z: A Guide for Young Writers.* Illus. by Cathy Bobak. Bradbury, 1994. ISBN 0-02-747672-3

[131p., Gr. 5–6] Incorporating 72 poems arranged alphabetically by subject or theme, this inspirational guide to writing poetry also offers self-help exercises for composing specific types of poems and advice from 23 poets on how to improve one's writing. In Janeczko's companion book, *The Place My Words Are Looking For,* we sample the poems of 39 American poets who talk about their work. *Knock at a Star: A Child's Introduction to Poetry* by X. J. Kennedy, *Let's Do a Poem! Introducing Poetry to Children Through Listening, Singing, Chanting, Impromptu Choral Reading, Body Movement, Dance, and Dramatization* by Nancy Larrick, and *Poem-Making: Ways to Begin Writing Poetry* by Myra Cohn Livingston are gold mines of advice and activities for children and teachers. POETRY–ANTHOLOGIES. WRITING.

1336   Katz, Michael Jay, comp. *Ten Potatoes in a Pot and Other Counting Rhymes.* Illus. by June Otani. Harper & Row, 1990. ISBN 0-06-023107-6

[unp., Gr. Pre–2] When you're fooling around with math, you'll find here at least one nursery or counting rhyme for each number from one to 12 to chant and repeat. *What Comes in 2's, 3's & 4's?* by Suzanne Aker, *Only One* by Marc Harshman, and *How Many, How Many, How Many* by Rick Walton are good math-based books. COUNTING BOOKS. NURSERY RHYMES.

1337   Keller, Charles. *Belly Laughs! Food Jokes & Riddles.* Illus. by Ron Fritz. Simon & Schuster, 1990. ISBN 0-671-70068-5

[32p., Gr. 2–6] What's the best food to eat in the bathroom? Showerkraut. Who writes nursery rhymes and squeezes oranges? Mother Juice. What kind of cheese is made in Scotland? Loch Ness Muenster. Colorful illustrations cap off a cheerful collection, which, along with Victoria Hartman's *The Silliest Joke Book Ever* and Keller's own *Alexander the Grape; Fruit and Vegetable Jokes,* make a delectable before-lunch snack. Sample some droll poems with William Cole's *Poem Stew,* Bobbye S. Goldstein's *What's on the Menu?,* Lee Bennett Hopkins's *Munching: Poems About Eating,* and Dee Lillegard's *Do Not Feed the Table.* FOOD–RIDDLES. JOKES. RIDDLES.

1338   Keller, Charles. *King Henry the Ape: Animal Jokes.* Illus. by Edward Frascino. Pippin Press, 1990. ISBN 0-945912-08-0

[unp., Gr. 2–6] Starting off with the title riddle (What's hairy, ruled England, and eats bananas?), here's a genial collection of animal riddles rife with wordplay. Add to the menagerie with David A. Adler's *The Carsick Zebra and Other Animal Riddles* and Keller's *Llama Beans,* and throw in some funny poems from *Never Take a Pig to Lunch* by Stephanie Calmenson, *Beast Feast* by Douglas Florian, or *A Hippopotamustn't and Other Animal Verses* by J. Patrick Lewis. ANIMALS–RIDDLES. RIDDLES.

1339   Keller, Charles. *Take Me to Your Liter: Science and Math Jokes.* Illus. by Gregory Filling. Pippin Press, 1991. ISBN 0-945912-13-7

[unp., Gr. 3–6] What did Benjamin Franklin say when he discovered electricity? Nothing. He was too shocked. Twelve dozen jokes and riddles will help math and science teachers tweak the brains of their scholars. Keep them stimulated with Vicki Cobb's *Bet You Can* and *Bet You Can't,* Gyles Brandreth's *Brain-Teasers and Mind-Benders,* and Louis Phillips's *263 Brain Busters.* MATHEMATICS–RIDDLES. RIDDLES. SCIENCE–RIDDLES.

1340   Keller, Charles. *Tongue Twisters.* Illus. by Ron Fritz. Simon & Schuster, 1989. ISBN 0-671-67123-5

[unp., Gr. K–3] It's not that these are unfamiliar tongue twisters, as many are old friends, but the colorful watercolors are so appealing they make the twisters fresh all over again. All will also love *Six Sick Sheep: 101 Tongue Twisters* by Joanna Cole and Stephanie Calmenson and *Busy Buzzing Bumblebees and Other Tongue Twisters* by Alvin Schwartz to boot. ALLITERATION. TONGUE TWISTERS.

1341   Kennedy, Dorothy M. *I Thought I'd Take My Rat to School: Poems for September to June.* Illus. by Abby Carter. Little, Brown, 1993. ISBN 0-316-48893-3

[63p., Gr. 3–6] Travel through the school day and year with a sparkling anthology of 57 poems that will have students nodding their heads with recognition. Kalli Dakos's *Don't Read This Book, Whatever You Do! More Poems About School* and *If You're Not Here, Please Raise Your Hand: Poems about School* (Four Winds, 1993), and David L. Harrison's *Somebody Catch My Homework* will also be popular. Have your kids read these aloud to you for a change. HUMOROUS POETRY. POETRY–SINGLE AUTHOR. SCHOOLS–POETRY.

1342   Kennedy, Dorothy M., and X. J. Kennedy, comps. *Talking Like the Rain: A First Book of Poems.* Illus. by Jane Dyer. Little, Brown, 1992. ISBN 0-316-48889-5

[96p., Gr. K–5] A must for libraries, this beguiling anthology, with over 100 poems and soft, evocative watercolors, contains many old favorites and gives a taste of the best children's poets from the past and present. Other worthy anthologies include *A Cup of Starshine* selected by Jill Bennett, *A Zooful of Animals* by William Cole, *April Bubbles Chocolate: An ABC of Poetry* by Lee Bennett

Hopkins, *Sunflakes* by Lillian Moore, *Poems for the Very Young* by Michael Rosen, and *Never Take a Pig to Lunch and Other Poems About the Fun of Eating* by Nadine Bernard Westcott. POETRY–ANTHOLOGIES.

1343   **Kennedy, X. J. *Drat These Brats.* Illus. by James Watts. McElderry, 1993. ISBN 0-689-50589-2**

[44p., Gr. 4–6] Still more nogoodnik kids learn their lessons the hard way in 44 scandalous short wordplay-laced poems in this continuation of the author's *Brats* and *Fresh Brats* (McElderry, 1990). More bad behavior abounds in William Cole's *Beastly Boys and Ghastly Girls,* and James Whitcomb Riley's *The Gobble-Uns'll Git You Ef You Don't Watch Out.* Students can write new brat-style poems using either their own names or those of other children in the class. BEHAVIOR–POETRY. HUMOROUS POETRY. POETRY–SINGLE AUTHOR.

1344   **Krull, Kathleen, comp. *Gonna Sing My Head Off! American Folk Songs for Children.* Illus. by Allen Garns. Knopf, 1992. ISBN 0-394-81991-8**

[146p., Gr. K–5] This friendly collection of 60 stellar tunes spans the United States and includes such all-time greats as "The Cat Came Back," "Take Me Out to the Ball Game," and "Going to the Zoo." The large format, simple piano and guitar arrangements, and colorful pastel illustrations will keep everyone humming. Tie individual songs into your curriculum (e.g. "The Frozen Logger" with a study of tall tales) and your whole-language lessons will be positively tuneful. Amy L. Cohn's *From Sea to Shining Sea: A Treasury of American Folklore and Folk Songs* is another marvelous one. FOLK SONGS. SONGBOOKS.

1345   **Lamont, Priscilla, comp. *Ring-a-Round-a-Rosy: Nursery Rhymes, Action Rhymes and Lullabies.* Illus. by the author. Joy Street / Little, Brown, 1990. ISBN 0-316-51292-3**

[69p., Gr. Pre–1] There are 45 rhymes here, one per page, and a roomy, relaxed format with endearing colored-pencil illustrations showing parents and children acting out the many fingerplays. *Hand Rhymes* by Marc Brown, *The Little Dog Laughed and Other Nursery Rhymes* by Lucy Cousins, *Rain, Rain, Go Away! A Book of Nursery Rhymes* by Jonathan Langley, and *James Marshall's Mother Goose* by James Marshall are just a few of the wonderful companion books in the Mother Goose stable. FINGERPLAYS. NURSERY RHYMES. SONGS.

1346   **Lansky, Bruce, comp. *Kids Pick the Funniest Poems: A Collection of Poems That Will Make You Laugh.* Illus. by Stephen Carpenter. Meadowbrook Press, 1991. ISBN 0-88166-149-X**

[155p., Gr. 2–6] From Lansky's original batch of 500 poems, a panel of 300 elementary school students helped him narrow down the pile to the most hilarious 54 examples. You'll find old favorites from folks including Jack Prelutsky, Jeff Moss, Judith Viorst, Dennis Lee, Lois Simmie, X. J. Kennedy, and, of course, Anonymous. Keep them laughing with *Bing Bang Boing* by Douglas Florian, *The Butterfly Jar* by Jeff Moss, *For Laughing Out Loud: Poems to Tickle Your Funnybone* compiled by Jack Prelutsky, and *Sad Underwear and Other Complications* by Judith Viorst. HUMOROUS POETRY.

1347 **Larrick, Nancy, comp.** *Mice Are Nice.* **Illus. by Ed Young. Philomel, 1988. ISBN 0-399-21495-X**

[45p., Gr. 1–5] The 25 poems gathered together here give an affectionate look at mice, and are illustrated with smudgy brown-toned charcoal drawings. Use these and *Adam Mouse's Book of Poems* by Lillian Moore to lead into mouse-based stories such as *Three Blind Mice: The Classic Nursery Rhyme* by John W. Ivimey, *The Mouse Bride: A Mayan Folk Tale* by Judith Dupré, *The Greatest of All: A Japanese Folktale* by Eric A. Kimmel, and Dav Pilkey's *Dogzilla* and *Kat Kong.* For equal time, also read Larrick's *Cats Are Cats.* MICE–POETRY.

1348 **Lear, Edward.** *Daffy Down Dillies: Silly Limericks.* **Illus. by John O'Brien. Boyds Mills / Caroline House, 1992. ISBN 1-56397-007-4**

[unp., Gr. 3–6] Bright and comical full-page pen-and-ink and watercolors bring out the humor in 37 of Lear's famous limericks. Children will need to keep their dictionaries handy for all the esoteric vocabulary-building adjectives such as imprudent, invidious, and ecstatic. Lear's *Of Pelicans and Pussycats: Poems and Limericks* and *Lots of Limericks* compiled by Myra Cohn Livingston provide even more choices and inspiration for writing new ditties. Find out about the man and his verse in *Edward Lear, King of Nonsense: A Biography* by Gloria Kamen and *How Pleasant to Know Mr. Lear,* compiled by Myra Cohn Livingston. HUMOROUS POETRY. LIMERICKS. NONSENSE VERSES. POETRY–SINGLE AUTHOR.

1349 **Lear, Edward.** *Of Pelicans and Pussycats: Poems and Limericks.* **Illus. by Jill Newton. Dial, 1990. ISBN 0-8037-0728-2**

[26p., Gr. K–5] If you need an illustrated collection of Lear's longer nonsense poems, this will stand you in good stead, including as it does "The Quangle Wangle's Hat," "The Owl and the Pussycat," "The Pelican Chorus" and "The Courtship of the Yonghy-Bonghy Bò," both of which include music, and "The Dong with the Luminous Nose." *Edward Lear, King of Nonsense: A Biography* by Gloria Kamen will help explain his wonderfully odd limericks and longer verse. Also read Lear's *How Pleasant to Know Mr. Lear,* compiled by Myra Cohn Livingston, *Daffy Down Dillies: Silly Limericks* by Lear, picture-book versions of *The Owl and the Pussycat,* illustrated by Jan Brett or Paul Galdone, and *The Quangle Wangle's Hat* illustrated by Janet Stevens. LIMERICKS. NONSENSE VERSES. POETRY–SINGLE AUTHOR.

1350 **Lee, Dennis.** *The Ice Cream Store.* **Illus. by David McPhail. Scholastic, 1992. ISBN 0-590-45861-2**

[unp., Gr. Pre–3] This whimsical and nursery rhyme-ish collection of 69 poems featuring children and animals is made even more charming by McPhail's personable watercolors. *Alligator Pie* and *Jelly Belly* are two more winsome volumes from this beloved Canadian poet. David Booth's *Doctor Knickerbocker and Other*

Rhymes, Douglas Florian's *Bing Bang Boing*, Jack Prelutsky's *Poems of A. Nonny Mouse* and *A. Nonny Mouse Writes Again!*, and Alvin Schwartz's *And the Green Grass Grew All Around* also contain kid-pleasing chantable poems. HUMOROUS POETRY. POETRY–SINGLE AUTHOR.

1351   **Levine, Caroline. *Riddles to Tell Your Cat.* Illus. by Meyer Seltzer. Albert Whitman, 1992. ISBN 0-8075-7006-0**

[unp., Gr. 3–6] What do cats eat for breakfast? Mice Krispies. That's just the first in a small but choice collection of almost 100 very cute cat puns and riddles, hink pinks, poems, jokes, and knock-knocks. Have your kids try these out loud on the rest of the class. Keep chuckling with the cat and dog jokes in *It's Raining Cats and Dogs* by Charles Keller, and sample the many puns, especially after a story like *Kat Kong* by Dav Pilkey. Jean Chapman's *Cat Will Rhyme with Hat*, Lee Bennett Hopkins's *I Am the Cat*, Nancy Larrick's *Cats Are Cats*, Myra Cohn Livingston's *Cat Poems*, and Jane Yolen's *Raining Cats and Dogs* are all outstanding poetry books about cats. CATS–RIDDLES. RIDDLES.

1352   **Lewis, J. Patrick. *Earth Verses and Water Rhymes.* Illus. by Robert Sabuda. Atheneum, 1991. ISBN 0-689-31693-3**

[32p., Gr. 2–4] Follow the roll of the seasons with 17 brief, insightful poems about snowflakes, fog, spring rain, and white wind, red fox, grasshoppers, and blue herons. Sabuda's linoleum prints are lovely and dramatic, especially from a distance. Take a closer look at nature with Arnold Adoff's *In for Winter, Out for Spring*, Barbara Brenner's *The Earth Is Painted Green*, Barbara Juster Esbensen's *Cold Stars and Fireflies*, Josette Frank's *Snow Toward Evening: A Year in a River Valley: Nature Poems*, Leland B. Jacobs's *Just Around the Corner: Poems About the Seasons*, Catherine Paladino's *Land, Sea, and Sky*, and Marilyn Singer's *Turtle in July*. Get wet with the concrete poems about water in *Splish Splash* by Joan Bransfield Graham and Lee Bennett Hopkins's *Weather*. NATURE–POETRY. POETRY–SINGLE AUTHOR. SEASONS–POETRY. WEATHER–POETRY.

1353   **Lewis, J. Patrick. *A Hippopotamustn't and Other Animal Verses.* Illus. by Victoria Chess. Dial, 1990. ISBN 0-8037-0519-0**

[unp., Gr. 1–5] There are 35 very clever, cute, and memorizable animal poems here, including a must-see concrete poem about a flamingo, and one which will forever remind you how to tell the difference between a dromedary and a bactrian camel. Chess's sunny illustrations are perfect foils to the wide variety of both rhyming and unrhyming poems filled with puns and wordplay. Go for the zoo effect with more easy-to-understand poetry books such as Alan Benjamin's *A Nickel Buys a Rhyme*, William Cole's *A Zooful of Animals*, Richard Edwards's *Moon Frog*, Douglas Florian's *Beast Feast*, Mary Ann Hoberman's *A Fine Fat Pig and Other Animal Poems*, Beverly McLoughland's *A Hippo's a Heap*, Fay Robinson's *A Frog Inside My Hat*, Eric Carle's *Animals, Animals*, compiled by Laura Whipple, and Jane Yolen's *Alphabestiary*. ANIMALS–POETRY. HUMOROUS POETRY. POETRY–SINGLE AUTHOR.

1354   Lewis, J. Patrick. *Two-Legged, Four-Legged, No-Legged Rhymes.* Illus. by Pamela Paparone. Knopf, 1991. ISBN 0-679-90771-8

[37p., Gr. K–4] Twenty-eight brief, good-natured animal poems range from non-sensical to pensive, with detailed, charming, and color-intense paintings. Break out Lewis's *A Hippopotamustn't and Other Animal Verses,* as well as other playful books of animal poems such as Alan Benjamin's *A Nickel Buys a Rhyme,* William Cole's *A Zooful of Animals,* Richard Edwards's *Moon Frog,* Douglas Florian's *Beast Feast,* Mary Ann Hoberman's *A Fine Fat Pig and Other Animal Poems,* Beverly McLoughland's *A Hippo's a Heap,* and Fay Robinson's *A Frog Inside My Hat.* ANI-MALS–POETRY. HUMOROUS POETRY. POETRY–SINGLE AUTHOR.

1355   Lillegard, Dee. *Do Not Feed the Table.* Illus. by Keiko Narahashi. Delacorte, 1993. ISBN 0-385-30516-8

[unp., Gr. K–3] There are 30 endearing and clever short poems about the utensils, equipment, and fixtures found in the kitchen: toaster, frying pan, chair, can opener, refrigerator, sponge, rolling pin, and faucet. All will make you hungry for poems about the food prepared there, so follow with Arnold Adoff's *Eats,* Rose Agree's *How to Eat a Poem and Other Morsels,* William Cole's *Poem Stew,* Bobbye S. Goldstein's *What's on the Menu?,* Lee Bennett Hopkins's *Munching,* and Nadine Bernard Westcott's *Never Take a Pig to Lunch.* Young gourmets can bring in additional utensils and compose poems about them. FOOD–POETRY. POETRY–SIN-GLE AUTHOR.

1356   Lindbergh, Reeve. *View from the Air: Charles Lindbergh's Earth and Sky.* Photos by Richard Brown. Viking, 1992. ISBN 0-670-84660-0

[1 sitting, unp., Gr. 3–6] Reeve, daughter of the great aviator, incorporates sweep-ing color photos taken on her father's last flights as a pilot in 1971 and 1972 over New England by a friend and nature photographer, with a poem she wrote in her father's memory. A warning to us on earth to leave nature alone, this tribute to its beauty works well with the picture-book version of the song *America the Beautiful* by Katharine Lee Bates, *The Earth Is Painted Green: A Garden of Poems About Our Planet* by Barbara Brenner, and *Land, Sea, and Sky: Poems to Celebrate the Earth* selected by Catherine Paladino. Also read this with Don Brown's *Ruth Law Thrills a Nation,* Robert Burleigh's *Flight: The Journey of Charles Lindbergh,* Chris L. Demarest's *Lindbergh,* and Diane Siebert's *Plane Song* to become familiar with Lindbergh's life and times. AIRPLANES–POETRY. ENVIRONMENT–POETRY. FLIGHT–POETRY.

1357   Livingston, Myra Cohn, comp. *Halloween Poems.* Illus. by Stephen Gammell. Holiday House, 1989. ISBN 0-8234-0762-4

[32p., Gr. 2–5] A simply splendid assortment of 18 poems that, along with Gammell's creepy gray-and-white illustrations, will set the mood for prospective trick-or-treaters. There's no shortage of companion books, including Marc Brown's *Scared Silly!,* Dilys Evans's *Monster Soup and Other Spooky Poems,* Florence Parry Heide's *Grim and Ghastly Goings-On,* Lee Bennett Hopkins's *Ragged Shadows: Poems of Halloween Night,* Colin McNaughton's *Making Friends with Frankenstein,* and *Best Witches* by Jane Yolen. Joke around with Jeffie Ross Gordon's *Hide and Shriek: Riddles About Ghosts & Goblins.* HALLOWEEN–POETRY.

1358   **Livingston, Myra Cohn, comp.** *If You Ever Meet a Whale.* **Illus. by Leonard Everett Fisher. Holiday House, 1992. ISBN 0-8234-0940-6**

[32p., Gr. 2–5] Seventeen whale poems are made all the more awesome with Fisher's sumptuous full-page paintings. Pull in facts from Gilda Berger's *Whales,* photos from Bruce Macmillan's *Going on a Whale Watch,* vicarious experiences from Joanne Ryder's *Winter Whale,* and stories from Rudyard Kipling's *How the Whale Got His Throat* and Robert McCloskey's *Burt Dow, Deep-Water Man.* On the broader theme of the ocean, there's *How the Sea Began: A Taino Myth* by George Crespo, *Under the Sea from A to Z* by Anne Doubilet, and *I Am the Ocean* by Suzanna Marshak. WHALES–POETRY.

1359   **Livingston, Myra Cohn, comp.** *Lots of Limericks.* **Illus. by Rebecca Perry. McElderry, 1991. ISBN 0-689-50531-0**

[131p., Gr. 4–6] Sorted into 11 chapters including "Peculiar People," "Fabulous Foods," and "Happy Holidays" are more than 200 limericks, ranging from well known to obscure. The index of authors and first lines will help you locate your favorites. *Edward Lear, King of Nonsense: A Biography* by Gloria Kamen, *Daffy Down Dillies: Silly Limericks* by Edward Lear, Lear's *How Pleasant to Know Mr. Lear,* compiled by Myra Cohn Livingston, and Lear's *Of Pelicans and Pussycats: Poems and Limericks* are also most helpful for additional verses and background on the most famous limerick guy of all. HUMOROUS POETRY. LIMERICKS. NONSENSE VERSES. POETRY–ANTHOLOGIES.

1360   **Livingston, Myra Cohn, comp.** *Poems for Grandmothers.* **Illus. by Patricia Cullen-Clark. Holiday House, 1990. ISBN 0-8234-0830-2**

[32p., Gr. 2–6] Some grandmothers are gentle, and some are frail, and others are busy at the office, and in a collection of 18 poems we see that no two grandmothers are alike. Children can see if any of the poems fit the description of their grandmothers. Match poems with grandmother stories like Valerie Flournoy's *The Patchwork Quilt,* Dayal Kaur Khalsa's *Tales of a Gambling Grandma,* Miska Miles's *Annie and the Old One,* Evan Levine's *Not the Piano, Mrs. Medley!,* Amy Schwartz's *Oma and Bobo,* and David Williams's *Grandma Essie's Covered Wagon.* GRANDMOTHERS–POETRY.

1361   **Longfellow, Henry Wadsworth.** *Paul Revere's Ride.* **Illus. by Ted Rand. Dutton, 1990. ISBN 0-525-44610-9**

[1 sitting, unp., Gr. 2–6] That perennial American Revolution poem still dutifully memorized and recited by so many of our students has been given fresh treatment with thrilling moonlit watercolors, which might give your class impetus to stage a dramatic reading and put new life into a grand old chestnut. Find out the whole story with Jean Fritz's entertaining biography, *And Then What Happened, Paul Revere?* Revolutionary War students will be impressed with Drollene P.

Brown's *Sybil Rides for Independence,* about 16-year-old Sybil Luddington who set out on horseback to rouse the patriots to arms after the British set Danbury, Connecticut, ablaze in 1777. NARRATIVE POETRY. POETRY–SINGLE AUTHOR. REVERE, PAUL. STORIES IN RHYME. U.S.–HISTORY–REVOLUTION–POETRY.

1362   **Low, Alice, comp. *The Family Read-Aloud Holiday Treasury.* Illus. by Marc Brown. Little, Brown, 1991. ISBN 0-316-53368-8**

[154p., Gr. 1–4] Read through the year with this marvelous, well-balanced collection of over 60 poems, songs, and excerpts of holiday stories, arranged in month order, and sprinkled throughout with Brown's typical cheery watercolors. *Ring Out, Wild Bells: Poems about Holidays and Seasons* by Lee Bennett Hopkins and *Callooh! Callay! Holiday Poems for Young Readers* by Myra Cohn Livingston are also most useful. HOLIDAYS. HOLIDAYS–POETRY. SHORT STORIES.

1363   **MacCarthy, Patricia. *Herds of Words.* Illus. by the author. Dial, 1991. ISBN 0-8037-0892-0**

[1 sitting, unp., Gr. K–6] Color-infused batik paintings showcase over three dozen collective nouns, for animals mostly, and not the well-known ones either, from a bask of crocodiles to a leap of leopards. Ruth Heller's *A Cache of Jewels and Other Collective Nouns,* Patricia Hooper's poems in *A Bundle of Beasts,* and Peter and Connie Roop's *One Earth, a Multitude of Creatures* provide a wide variety of interesting collective nouns. Children can collect others or make up their own. For straight talk about nouns, see Ruth Heller's *Merry-Go-Round: A Book About Nouns.* ANIMALS. ENGLISH LANGUAGE–GRAMMAR. PICTURE BOOKS FOR ALL AGES. VOCABULARY.

1364   **McLoughland, Beverly. *A Hippo's a Heap: And Other Animal Poems.* Illus. by Laura Rader. Wordsong: Boyds Mills, 1993. ISBN 1-56397-017-1**

[32p., Gr. K–3] Nineteen brief, easy-to-read, and delightfully whimsical poems about animals are guaranteed to get listeners smiling, especially when they see the amiable watercolor and pastel illustrations accompanying each poem. Whip up an animal celebration with Alan Benjamin's *A Nickel Buys a Rhyme,* William Cole's *A Zooful of Animals,* Richard Edwards's *Moon Frog,* Douglas Florian's *Beast Feast,* Mary Ann Hoberman's *A Fine Fat Pig and Other Animal Poems,* J. Patrick Lewis's *A Hippopotamustn't and Other Animal Verses,* Fay Robinson's *A Frog Inside My Hat,* Eric Carle's *Animals, Animals,* compiled by Laura Whipple, and Jane Yolen's *Alphabestiary.* ANIMALS–POETRY. POETRY–SINGLE AUTHOR.

1365   **McMillan, Bruce. *Play Day: A Book of Terse Verse.* Photos by the author. Holiday House, 1991. ISBN 0-8234-0894-9**

[unp., Gr. Pre–1] Like the author's companion *One Sun,* each double page contains two color photographs, this time of young children playing on the lawn, and two rhyming words describing them, like Bear Chair, and Fun Run. As you go, cover up the words on each page so children can guess the rhymes. Kids can make up and illustrate new two-word rhyming couplets around other themes like school, home, or the woods. If your school has cameras for kids, let them loose. Write new rhyming sentences with *"I Can't," Said the Ant* by Polly Cameron, *Who's Sick Today?* by Lynne Cherry, *Hunky Dory Ate It* by Katie Evans, *In the Diner* by Christine Loomis, and *Cat Is Back at Bat* by John Stadler. MULTICUL-TURAL STORIES. PLAY–POETRY. POETRY–SINGLE AUTHOR. STORIES IN RHYME.

1366   McNaughton, Colin. *Making Friends with Frankenstein: A Book of Monstrous Poems and Pictures.* Illus. by the author. Candlewick, 1994. ISBN 1-56402-308-7

[90p., Gr. 2–6] "Cockroach sandwich/ For my lunch,/ Hate the taste/ But love the crunch!" There are 55 other lurid, tasteless, and gross poems to convulse your children in this wicked book, and lots of bright, cheerful, and ghoulish watercol-ors. Keep grinning with poems from Marc Brown's *Scared Silly!*, Dilys Evans's *Monster Soup and Other Spooky Poems*, Douglas Florian's *Monster Motel*, Florence Parry Heide's *Grim and Ghastly Goings-On*, Lee Bennett Hopkins's *Ragged Shadows: Poems of Halloween Night*, Myra Cohn Livingston's *Halloween Poems*, Eve Merriam's *Halloween ABC*, and Jane Yolen's *Best Witches*. Crack a few jokes with Jeffie Ross Gordon's *Hide and Shriek: Riddles About Ghosts & Goblins.* HUMOROUS POETRY. MONSTERS–POETRY. POETRY–SINGLE AUTHOR.

1367   Maestro, Giulio. *More Halloween Howls: Riddles That Come Back to Haunt You.* Illus. by the author. Dutton, 1992. ISBN 0-525-44899-3

[unp., Gr. 2–5] What do goblins mail home while on vacation? Ghostcards. One brightly illustrated riddle per page, with 58 in all, provides a nice bit of spooky wordplay. Marc Brown's *Spooky Riddles*, Charles Keller's *Count Draculations! Monster Riddles*, and Joseph Rosenbloom's *Monster Madness: Riddles, Jokes, Fun* will fill up the empty spaces in any ghastly day. HALLOWEEN–RIDDLES. RIDDLES.

1368   Maestro, Marco, and Giulio Maestro. *Riddle City, USA! A Book of Geography Riddles.* Illus. by Giulio Maestro. HarperCollins, 1994. ISBN 0-06-023369-9

[64p., Gr. 3–6] The answers to each of the five dozen riddles are puns on names of U.S. cities, states, rivers, parks, and well-known places. With each answer at the bottom of the page are a few facts about that site. Some of the riddles are pretty obscure, but many more will provide a chuckle and a challenge to your class, especially if you make them copies of the U.S. map the book provides for consultation. Pair children up with maps to make up new riddles that they can illustrate and present to the rest of the group. *Geographunny: A Book of Global Riddles* by Mort Gerberg and Marvin Terban's *Funny You Should Ask: How to Make Up Jokes and Riddles with Wordplay* will both be appreciated as well. GEOGRAPHY–RIDDLES. NAMES, GEOGRAPHICAL–RIDDLES. RIDDLES. U.S.–RIDDLES.

1369   Marshall, James, comp. *Pocketful of Nonsense.* Illus. by the author. Artists and Writers Guild, 1993. ISBN 0-307-171552-9

[28p., Gr. Pre–3] Along with the 20 large, comic, colorful watercolors sprinkled with droll captions are silly limericks (five of which are by Marshall) and other traditional nonsense rhymes, one to a page. There's no dearth of collections of playful nonsense rhymes, including Jill Bennett's *Tiny Tim: Verses for Children,*

David Booth's *Doctor Knickerbocker and Other Rhymes*, Jack Prelutsky's *Poems of A. Nonny Mouse* and *A. Nonny Mouse Writes Again!*, Alvin Schwartz's *And the Green Grass Grew All Around* and *I Saw You in the Bathtub*, and Wallace Tripp's *A Great Big Ugly Man Came Up and Tied His Horse to Me*. HUMOROUS POETRY. LIMERICKS. NONSENSE VERSES.

1370   Mathews, Judith, and Fay Robinson. *Knock-Knock Knees and Funny Bones: Riddles for Every Body*. Illus. by Jack Desrocher. Albert Whitman, 1994. ISBN 0-8075-4203-2

[unp., Gr. 3–6] How long can you hold your breath? A lung, lung time. One hundred riddles and knock-knocks poke fun at the human body. *Norma Lee I Don't Knock on Doors* by Charles Keller and *Knock Knock! Who's There?* by Joseph Rosenbloom will help satisfy knock-knock fanatics, while health teachers should be pleased to stomach *The Magic School Bus Inside the Human Body* by Joanna Cole. BODY, HUMAN–RIDDLES. KNOCK-KNOCK JOKES. RIDDLES.

1371   Mattox, Cheryl, comp. *Shake It to the One That You Love the Best: Play Songs and Lullabies from Black Musical Traditions*. Illus. by Varnette P. Honeywood and Brenda Joysmith. Warren-Mattox Productions, 1989. ISBN 0-9623381-0-9 (pbk.)

[56p., Gr. Pre–2] The 26 folk songs and chants in this splendid collection include music and chords, descriptions of games that go along, and illustrations including woven cloth borders and exceptional paintings by two major contemporary black artists. *Pass It On: African-American Poetry for Children* selected by Wade Hudson and *Families: Poems Celebrating the African American Experience* selected by Dorothy S. and Michael R. Strickland are more formal collections of modern-day poetry. AFRICAN AMERICANS–SONGS. FOLK SONGS. SONGBOOKS.

1372   Merriam, Eve. *Halloween ABC*. Illus. by Lane Smith. Macmillan, 1987. ISBN 0-02-766870-3

[1 sitting, unp., Gr. 3–6] One macabre poem per letter is accompanied by a shivery painting by Lane Smith (in his first book), about apple, bat, crawler, demon, elf, fiend, and ghost, on up to yeast and zero. Don't read these to the faint-at-heart, though parents get more alarmed at these dark mood poems than kids, who find them just right. Marc Brown's *Scared Silly!*, Dilys Evans's *Monster Soup and Other Spooky Poems*, Florence Parry Heide's *Grim and Ghastly Goings-On*, Lee Bennett Hopkins's *Ragged Shadows: Poems of Halloween Night*, Myra Cohn Livingston's *Halloween Poems*, Colin McNaughton's *Making Friends with Frankenstein*, and Jane Yolen's *Best Witches* are all worth investigating. ALPHABET BOOKS. HALLOWEEN–POETRY. POETRY–SINGLE AUTHOR.

1373   Merriam, Eve. *The Singing Green: New and Selected Poems for All Seasons*. Illus. by Kathleen Collins Howell. Morrow, 1992. ISBN 0-688-11025-8

[102p., Gr. 3–6] The 80 poems in this appealing collection touch on many subjects, ranging from "A Vote for Vanilla" to "A Moose on the Loose," with a sprinkling of just-right selections about reading and writing. Continue with Merriam's *Chortles: New and Selected Wordplay Poems*. Stray from Prelutsky and Silverstein for a breath of new ideas and try out *The Country Mail Is Coming: Poems from Down Under* by Max Fatchen, *Bing Bang Boing* by Douglas Florian, *The Covered Bridge House and Other Poems* by Kaye Starbird, and *Mud, Moon and Me* by Zaro Weil. POETRY–SINGLE AUTHOR. WORD GAMES.

1374   Moore, Lilian. *Adam Mouse's Book of Poems.* Illus. by Kathleen Garry McCord. Atheneum, 1992. ISBN 0-689-31765-4

[51p., Gr. 1–4] The 30 spare and gentle poems in this collection, observations of nature and small creatures, are told from a mouse's point of view, compiled from *I'll Meet You at the Cucumbers* and its sequel, *Don't Be Afraid, Amanda* (1992), plus some new ones. Look at common happenings through another's eyes in *I Am the Dog, I Am the Cat* by Donald Hall and *A Teeny Tiny Baby* by Amy Schwartz before writing poetry from a mouse's point of view. *Mice Are Nice,* compiled by Nancy Larrick, is a collection of poetry about (and not by) mice that will extend your range of opinions. MICE–POETRY. NATURE–POETRY. POETRY–SINGLE AUTHOR. POINT OF VIEW.

1375   Moore, Lillian, comp. *Sunflakes: Poems for Children.* Illus. by Jan Ormerod. Clarion, 1992. ISBN 0-395-58833-2

[96p., Gr. Pre–3] A rewarding collection of 76 poems challenges children to recognize their feelings and become more aware of the world around them. Continue the pleasure with *A Cup of Starshine: Poems and Pictures for Young Children* by Jill Bennett, *Tomie dePaola's Book of Poems* by Tomie dePaola, *Sing a Song of Popcorn* by Beatrice Schenk de Regniers, *April Bubbles Chocolate: An ABC of Poetry* by Lee Bennett Hopkins, *Talking Like the Rain: A First Book of Poems* by Dorothy M. and X. J. Kennedy, *Read-Aloud Rhymes for the Very Young* by Jack Prelutsky, and *Poems for the Very Young* by Michael Rosen. ANIMALS–POETRY. POETRY–ANTHOLOGIES.

1376   Morrison, Lillian, comp. *At the Crack of the Bat: Baseball Poems.* Illus. by Steve Cieslawski. Hyperion, 1992. ISBN 1-56282-177-6

[64p., Gr. 4–6] Sports fans will appreciate the variety of the 44 poems collected here, including ones about legends Nolan Ryan, José Canseco, Hank Aaron, and Roberto Clemente. *Extra Innings: Baseball Poems* compiled by Lee Bennett Hopkins contains a few duplications, but is also a valuable source. Turn to fiction with *Thank You, Jackie Robinson* by Barbara Cohen, *My Dad's Baseball* by Ron Cohen, and *Matt's Mitt and Fleet-Footed Florence* by Marilyn Sachs. William Jaspersohn's *The Ballpark: One Day Behind the Scenes at a Major League Game* is an interesting photo-essay. Finish up by singing the rousing picture book *Take Me Out to the Ball Game* by Jack Norworth and reciting one of the picture-book versions of Ernest Lawrence Thayer's *Casey at the Bat.* BASEBALL–POETRY. SPORTS–POETRY.

1377   Moss, Jeff. *The Butterfly Jar.* Illus. by Chris L. Demarest. Bantam, 1989. ISBN 0-553-05704-9

[115p., Gr. 2–6] More than 80 thoroughly enjoyable, witty, funny, insightful, and original poems that kids will devour, recite, memorize, and love, from a head writer and composer for "Sesame Street." The comparisons to Shel Silverstein's *Where the Sidewalk Ends* and *A Light in the Attic* are obvious. In addition, try Douglas Florian's *Bing Bang Boing*, Jack Prelutsky's *The New Kid on the Block* and *Something Big Has Been Here*, and Judith Viorst's *Sad Underwear and Other Complications*. HUMOROUS POETRY. POETRY–SINGLE AUTHOR.

1378   **Mother Goose.** *Animal Nursery Rhymes.* **Photos by Angela Wilkes. Compiled by Angela Wilkes. Dorling Kindersley, 1992. ISBN 1-56458-122-5**

[29p., Gr. Pre–1] The 55 rhymes are entirely familiar, but the format of color photographs of animals and costumed children superimposed on a huge white background gives the book a clean, nonfiction look. Other typical Mother Goose collections include *Mother Goose Magic* by Kay Chorao, *Mother Goose* by Scott Cook, *The Little Dog Laughed and Other Nursery Rhymes* illustrated by Lucy Cousins, *Michael Foreman's Mother Goose*, *Hickory Dickory Dock and Other Nursery Rhymes* compiled by Carol Jones, *Ring-a-Round-a-Rosy: Nursery Rhymes, Action Rhymes and Lullabies* by Priscilla Lamont, and *Rain, Rain, Go Away! A Book of Nursery Rhymes* by Jonathan Langley. ANIMALS–POETRY. NURSERY RHYMES.

1379   **Mother Goose.** *Hickory Dickory Dock and Other Nursery Rhymes.* **Illus. by Carol Jones. Compiled by Carol Jones. Houghton Mifflin, 1992. ISBN 0-395-60834-1**

[unp., Gr. Pre–1] In the center of each page is a die-cut hole through which children will spy Little Bo Peep's sheep, Miss Muffet's spider, or a snoozing Little Boy Blue. The intricate cross-hatching and colorful watercolors make this a first nursery-rhyme book for children who love to search for details. *Each Peach Pear Plum* by Janet and Allan Ahlberg (Viking, 1979) brings similar satisfaction. More from the overflowing Mother Goose shelf include *Mother Goose Magic* by Kay Chorao, *The Little Dog Laughed and Other Nursery Rhymes* illustrated by Lucy Cousins, and *Animal Nursery Rhymes* with huge color photographs by Angela Wilkes. For a past slew of fine nursery rhyme collections, refer to the Mother Goose listings, Entries 1878–1892, in *Books Kids Will Sit Still For*. NURSERY RHYMES.

1380   **Mother Goose.** *Jane Yolen's Mother Goose Songbook.* **Illus. by Rosekrans Hoffman. Compiled by Jane Yolen. Musical arrangement by Adam Stemple. Caroline House / Boyds Mills, 1992. ISBN 1-878093-52-5**

[95p., Gr. Pre–2] Each of the more than 45 nursery rhymes and old folk songs in this illustrated songbook comes with musical score, guitar chords, and a note about its origin. *Michael Foreman's Mother Goose*, Tom Glazer's *The Mother Goose Songbook*, Nancy Larrick's *Songs from Mother Goose: With the Traditional Melody for Each*, and *The Orchard Book of Nursery Rhymes* selected by Zena Sutherland will further extend your repertoire. *Gonna Sing My Head Off! American Folk Songs for Children* by Kathleen Krull and *Shake It to the One That You Love the Best: Play Songs and Lullabies from Black Musical Traditions* by Cheryl Mattox are other unsurpassed folksong collections. NURSERY RHYMES. SONGS.

1381   Mother Goose. *Rain, Rain, Go Away! A Book of Nursery Rhymes*. Illus. by Jonathan Langley. Compiled by Jonathan Langley. Dial, 1990. ISBN 0-8037-0762-2

[95p., Gr. Pre–2] A pleasant collection of 45 rhymes, some well known, some not, boasts lots of good-natured watercolor and pen-and-ink illustrations that fill the pages. Newer collections include *Mother Goose Magic* by Kay Chorao, *The Little Dog Laughed and Other Nursery Rhymes* by Lucy Cousins, *Michael Foreman's Mother Goose, Ring-a-Round-a-Rosy: Nursery Rhymes, Action Rhymes and Lullabies* by Priscilla Lamont, *Mother Goose's Little Misfortunes* compiled by Leonard S. Marcus and Amy Schwartz, and *The Orchard Book of Nursery Rhymes*, selected by Zena Sutherland. NURSERY RHYMES.

1382   Mother Goose. *Mother Goose Magic*. Illus. by Kay Chorao. Compiled by Kay Chorao. Dutton, 1994. ISBN 0-525-45064-5

[64p., Gr. Pre–K] Eight lesser-known Mother Goose rhymes are spread out, one line to a page, and accompanied by soft, luscious, pastel-colored illustrations of a young, curly-haired boy and his animal companions. Compare with the bright, primitive-art style of Lucy Cousins's *The Little Dog Laughed and Other Nursery Rhymes*, the zany watercolors of *Mother Goose's Little Misfortunes* compiled by Leonard S. Marcus and Amy Schwartz, and the formal watercolors of *The Orchard Book of Nursery Rhymes* selected by Zena Sutherland. Also lovely are *Ring-a-Round-a-Rosy: Nursery Rhymes, Action Rhymes and Lullabies* by Priscilla Lamont and *Rain, Rain, Go Away! A Book of Nursery Rhymes* by Jonathan Langley. Another single rhyme given extended treatment is *Little Robin Redbreast: A Mother Goose Rhyme* cheerily illustrated with cut-paper collages by Shari Halpern. NURSERY RHYMES.

1383   Mother Goose. *Mother Goose's Little Misfortunes*. Illus. by Amy Schwartz. Compiled by Leonard S. Marcus and Amy Schwartz. Bradbury, 1990. ISBN 0-02-781431-9

[unp., Gr. Pre–2] What's purely delightful and different about this collection of 18 Mother Goose rhymes with mischievous pink-faced watercolors is that they're not the same old ones (though we love those same old ones, too), but lesser-known ditties that are sheer fun to spring on kids. Have listeners make up new rhymes about Anna Elise, and see if you can put your heads together to write a sequel to "Little Miss Tuckett," which Miss Muffett fans will surely appreciate. *Mother Goose Magic* by Kay Chorao, *Mother Goose* by Scott Cook, *The Little Dog Laughed and Other Nursery Rhymes* by Lucy Cousins, *Michael Foreman's Mother Goose, Ring-a-Round-a-Rosy: Nursery Rhymes, Action Rhymes and Lullabies* by Priscilla Lamont, and *The Orchard Book of Nursery Rhymes* selected by Zena Sutherland are also wonderful. NURSERY RHYMES.

1384   Mother Goose. *The Little Dog Laughed and Other Nursery Rhymes*. Illus. by Lucy Cousins. Compiled by Lucy Cousins. Dutton, 1990. ISBN 0-525-44573-0

[64p., Gr. Pre–1] For a bit of a change, examine this unique interpretation of 64 nursery rhymes, all illustrated in heavy primary colors with black painted outlines that are childlike and fun. Compare the style of illustration with more clas-

504

sically inclined collections including Kay Chorao's *Mother Goose Magic,* Scott Cook's *Mother Goose, Michael Foreman's Mother Goose, Hickory Dickory Dock and Other Nursery Rhymes* compiled by Carol Jones, Priscilla Lamont's *Ring-a-Round-a-Rosy: Nursery Rhymes, Action Rhymes and Lullabies,* Jonathan Langley's *Rain, Rain, Go Away! A Book of Nursery Rhymes, Mother Goose's Little Misfortunes* compiled by Leonard S. Marcus and Amy Schwartz, and *The Orchard Book of Nursery Rhymes* selected by Zena Sutherland. NURSERY RHYMES.

1385   Mother Goose. *Michael Foreman's Mother Goose.* Illus. by Michael Foreman. Compiled by Michael Foreman. Harcourt, 1991. ISBN 0-15-255820-9

[158p., Gr. Pre–2] A fine specimen with soft, lovely watercolors, and with rhymes grouped by subject and type, this book offers complete verses, instead of just the first, for "Jack and Jill," "Simple Simon," "Cock Robin," and "London Bridge Is Falling Down." Other large, stately collections include *The Mother Goose Treasury* illustrated by Raymond Briggs, *Tomie dePaola's Mother Goose, Ring-a-Round-a-Rosy: Nursery Rhymes, Action Rhymes and Lullabies* by Priscilla Lamont, *Rain, Rain, Go Away! A Book of Nursery Rhymes* by Jonathan Langley, *The Random House Book of Mother Goose* illustrated by Arnold Lobel, *James Marshall's Mother Goose, Tail Feathers from Mother Goose* compiled by Iona and Peter Opie, and *Over the Moon* illustrated by Charlotte Voake. NURSERY RHYMES.

1386   Mother Goose. *Mother Goose.* Illus. by Scott Cook. Compiled by Scott Cook. Apple Soup/ Knopf, 1994. ISBN 0-679-90949-4

[44p., Gr. Pre–1] Here is another nice collection with one or two of the 51 rhymes per page, and soft, smudgy, good-natured watercolors. Just a few of the many Mother Goose collections include *Mother Goose Magic* by Kay Chorao, *The Little Dog Laughed and Other Nursery Rhymes* illustrated by Lucy Cousins, *Hickory Dickory Dock and Other Nursery Rhymes* compiled by Carol Jones, and *Animal Nursery Rhymes* with huge color photographs by Angela Wilkes. NURSERY RHYMES.

1387   Mother Goose. *The Mother Goose Songbook.* Illus. by David McPhail. Compiled by Tom Glazer. Doubleday, 1990. ISBN 0-385-41474-9

[Gr. Pre–2] The 44 familiar rhymes are all set to music, some with tunes composed and new verses added by folksinger Glazer, and each score is illustrated with large and lovely watercolors. Nancy Larrick's *Songs from Mother Goose: With the Traditional Melody for Each* and Jane Yolen's *Mother Goose Songbook* are also most useful. NURSERY RHYMES. SONGS.

1388   Mother Goose. *The Orchard Book of Nursery Rhymes.* Illus. by Faith Jaques. Compiled by Zena Sutherland. Orchard, 1990. ISBN 0-531-05903-0

[88p., Gr. Pre–1] An all-around lovely collection of 77 nursery rhymes, the large, luxurious pages are decorated with delicate late-18th-century-style watercolors. Other standouts in the Mother Goose department include *The Mother Goose Treasury* illustrated by Raymond Briggs, *The Little Dog Laughed and Other Nursery Rhymes* illustrated by Lucy Cousins, *Tomie dePaola's Mother Goose, Michael*

Foreman's Mother Goose, Ring-a-Round-a-Rosy: Nursery Rhymes, Action Rhymes and Lullabies by Priscilla Lamont, *The Random House Book of Mother Goose* illustrated by Arnold Lobel, *Mother Goose's Little Misfortunes* compiled by Leonard S. Marcus and Amy Schwartz, *James Marshall's Mother Goose, Tail Feathers from Mother Goose* compiled by Iona and Peter Opie, and *Over the Moon* illustrated by Charlotte Voake. Use them all as an informal way to gauge your children's personal tastes in styles of illustration. NURSERY RHYMES.

1389   Myers, Walter Dean. *Brown Angels: An Album of Pictures and Verse.* Illus. with photos. HarperCollins, 1993. ISBN 0-06-022918-7

[1 sitting, 40 pages, Gr. 1–6] Spark an interest in children of long ago with the more than three dozen black-and-white and sepia-toned turn-of-the-century photographs of earnest, captivating, African American children, accompanied by 11 of the author's brief, affectionate poems. Your students might have access to their old family photos to examine and write about. Contrast with the modern day children in Arnold Adoff's *In for Winter, Out for Spring* and *Meet Danitra Brown* by Nikki Grimes. *Pass It On: African-American Poetry for Children* compiled by Wade Hudson, and Dorothy S. and Michael R. Strickland's *Families: Poems Celebrating the African American Experience* are both excellent collections. AFRICAN AMERICANS–POETRY. CHILDREN–POETRY. POETRY–SINGLE AUTHOR.

1390   Nims, Bonnie Larkin. *Just Beyond Reach and Other Riddle Poems.* Photos by George Ancona. Scholastic, 1992. ISBN 0-590-44077-2

[unp., Gr. K–3] Each of the 14 short, clever, rhyming riddles describes an object for children to identify; turn the page and there's a color photograph of the answer. Children can select an object to describe—in rhyme, if they can—for the rest of the group to identify. Stephanie Calmenson's *It Begins with an A*, Beatrice Schenk de Regniers's *It Does Not Say Meow and Other Animal Riddle Rhymes*, and Tana Hoban's *Look! Look! Look!* are also for guessers, while for older readers, the poems in Valerie Worth's *All the Small Poems and Fourteen More* describe everyday items with great clarity and zest. POETRY–SINGLE AUTHOR. RIDDLES–POETRY.

1391   Opie, Iona, and Peter Opie, comps. *I Saw Esau: The Schoolchild's Pocket Book.* Illus. by Maurice Sendak. Candlewick, 1992. ISBN 1-56402-046-0

[160p., Gr. 1–5] There are lots of nasty little rhymes in this small-sized book, often the kind children say to each other when they think there are no grown-ups about. Sendak's marvelous watercolors are on nearly every page. While you certainly wouldn't think of reading all of these aloud, the collection, first published in 1946, cannot be ignored, and contains many satisfying chants, rhymes, riddles, tongue twisters, and, of course, insults. David Booth's *Doctor Knickerbocker and Other Rhymes*, James Marshall's *Pocketful of Nonsense*, Jack Prelutsky's *Poems of A. Nonny Mouse* and *A. Nonny Mouse Writes Again!*, Alvin Schwartz's *And the Green Grass Grew All Around: Folk Poetry from Everyone*, and Carl Withers's *A Rocket in My Pocket: Rhymes and Chants of Young Americans* are all terrific collections of nonsense as well. JUMP ROPE RHYMES. NONSENSE VERSES. NURSERY RHYMES.

1392   Paladino, Catherine, comp. *Land, Sea, and Sky: Poems to Celebrate the Earth*. Photos by Catherine Paladino. Joy Street / Little, Brown, 1993. ISBN 0-8075-1720-8

[32p., Gr. 1–5] Nineteen sensible and sensitive poems about animals, trees, weather, and respect for the environment are all coupled with clear and dignified color photographs. Stay with the same poetic themes in *The Earth Is Painted Green* by Barbara Brenner, *Snow Toward Evening: A Year in a River Valley: Nature Poems* by Josette Frank, *Weather* by Lee Bennett Hopkins, and *Earth Verses and Water Rhymes* by J. Patrick Lewis. Note the thoughts children have about their surroundings with Lannis Temple's *Dear World: How Children Around the World Feel About Our Environment*. NATURE–POETRY.

1393   Panzer, Nora, comp. *Celebrate America in Poetry and Art*. Hyperion, 1994. ISBN 1-56282-664-6

[96p., Gr. 4–6] Grandly illustrated with colorful paintings, sculptures, drawings, photographs, and other works of art from the National Museum of Art of the Smithsonian Institution, this is a glorious collection of 52 inspirational poems that reveal our diversity and common ground, and "chronicle the events, rites, and rituals we share as Americans." *Celebrating America: A Collection of Poems and Images of the American Spirit* compiled by Laura Whipple and illustrated with art from the Art Institute of Chicago encompasses the same theme. *Go In and Out the Window: An Illustrated Songbook for Young People* edited by Dan Fox and *Talking to the Sun: An Illustrated Anthology of Poems for Young People* compiled by Kenneth Koch and Kate Farrell are both illustrated with reproductions of art from New York City's Metropolitan Museum of Art. POETRY–ANTHOLOGIES. U.S.–POETRY.

1394   Phillips, Louis. *Invisible Oink: Pig Jokes*. Illus. by Arlene Dubanevich. Viking, 1993. ISBN 0-670-84387-3

[57p., Gr. 3–6] Some of these jokes and riddles are too sophisticated and will go over children's heads, but there is such a vast store of them here you'll have no trouble making everyone squeal with laughter. Try some as an introduction to Jon Scieszka's *The True Story of the Three Little Pigs*. When students do animal reports they can match animals with riddles, using books like *Snakes Alive* by Diane L. Burns, *Batty Riddles* by Katy Hall and Lisa Eisenberg, and *King Henry the Ape: Animal Jokes* by Charles Keller. ANIMALS–RIDDLES. JOKES. PIGS–RIDDLES. RIDDLES.

1395   Prelutsky, Jack, comp. *A. Nonny Mouse Writes Again!* Illus. by Marjorie Priceman. Knopf, 1993. ISBN 0-679-93715-3

[unp., Gr. 1–5] Once again, the prolific A. Nonny Mouse records some of her charming and comical poems, erroneously attributed to "Anonymous" in this companion volume to Prelutsky's *Poems of A. Nonny Mouse*. Four selections are by Prelutsky; see if your sharp-eared children can discern which ones. For more anonymous and nonsense rhymes, read David Booth's *Doctor Knickerbocker and Other Rhymes*, James Marshall's *Pocketful of Nonsense*, Iona and Peter Opie's *I Saw Esau: The Schoolchild's Pocket Book*, Alvin Schwartz's *And the Green Grass Grew All*

Around: Folk Poetry from Everyone, and Carl Withers's *A Rocket in My Pocket: Rhymes and Chants of Young Americans*. HUMOROUS POETRY. NONSENSE VERSES.

1396   Prelutsky, Jack. *The Dragons Are Singing Tonight*. Illus. by Peter Sis. Greenwillow, 1993. ISBN 0-688-12511-5

[40p., Gr. 1–5] Seventeen original poems present dragons in all forms and moods, such as a thunder dragon, an unfriendly one in a boy's computer, a secret one in the tub, and a nasty one just half an inch high. Each generous two-page spread shimmers with Sis's glamorous and mysterious gold-bordered paintings. Laura Whipple's compilation *Eric Carle's Dragons, Dragons* includes additional mythical beasts. Dragon folktales include Janina Domanska's *King Krakus and the Dragon*, Gail E. Haley's *Jack and the Fire Dragon*, Margaret Hodges's *Saint George and the Dragon*, Julie Lawson's *The Dragon's Pearl*, Simon Stern's *Vasily and the Dragon*, and Dorothy Van Woerkum's *Alexandra the Rock-Eater*. Add some fiction with Betsy and Samuel Sterman's *Backyard Dragon*, Bruce Coville's *Jeremy Thatcher, Dragon Hatcher*, and Jay Williams's *Everyone Knows What a Dragon Looks Like*. DRAGONS–POETRY. POETRY–SINGLE AUTHOR.

1397   Prelutsky, Jack, comp. *For Laughing Out Loud: Poems to Tickle Your Funnybone*. Illus. by Marjorie Priceman. Knopf, 1991. ISBN 0-394-82144-0

[84p., Gr. K–5] Browse through and sample the 130 jovial selections from over 50 poets, illustrated with riotous watercolors that dance across each large page. For each favorite poet, see if your researchers can dig up more good poems from the 800s in the library. Many, such as Dennis Lee, Myra Cohn Livingston, Judith Viorst, and of course Prelutsky, have whole volumes of their own poems. Compilations such as Stephanie Calmenson's *Never Take a Pig to Lunch*, Bruce Lansky's *Kids Pick the Funniest Poems*, and James Marshall's *Pocketful of Nonsense* are also entertaining collections. HUMOROUS POETRY. POETRY–ANTHOLOGIES.

1398   Prelutsky, Jack. *Something Big Has Been Here*. Illus. by James Stevenson. Greenwillow, 1990. ISBN 0-688-06434-5

[160p., Gr. K–6] Clear off a bit more space on your desk for the sequel to *The New Kid on the Block*, another masterpiece collection of Prelutsky's comic madness to read aloud at odd moments in the day. There's the usual array of newly hatched beasts like the Wumpaloons, the Addle-pated Paddlepuss, or the morose Twickles who prefer no tickles, and ditties about characters like the unbearably slow Slomona, the disharmonious Disputatious Deeble, and Belinda Blue, bilious to the core when her mother begs her to eat just one green bean. Prolonged reading, memorizing, and reciting of his waggish verse may well trigger a rise in your children's verbal SAT scores. Before lunch, try "The Turkey Shot Out of the Oven" (which also sings nicely to the tune of "My Bonnie"); before science, "My Brother Built a Robot." *Bing Bang Boing* by Douglas Florian, *The Butterfly Jar* by Jeff Moss, and *Sad Underwear and Other Complications* by Judith Viorst will also satisfy. HUMOROUS POETRY. NONSENSE VERSES. POETRY–SINGLE AUTHOR.

1399   Radley, Gail, comp. *Rainy Day Rhymes*. Illus. by Ellen Kandoian. Houghton Mifflin, 1992. ISBN 0-395-59967-9

[48p., Gr. Pre–2] Seventeen short, easy poems, with rainy-day-like watercolor wash paintings, will ease nicely into bad weather days and weather units. Find more rain poems in *Splish Splash* by Joan Bransfield Graham, *Weather* by Lee Bennett Hopkins, and *Rainy Rainy Saturday* by Jack Prelutsky, and find out where all the water goes in *Water's Way* by Lisa Westberg Peters. Read with rain stories such as *The Umbrella Day* by Nancy Evans Cooney, *Mushroom in the Rain* by Mirra Ginsburg, *Listen to the Rain* by Bill Martin, Jr. and John Archambault, *Thunder Cake* by Patricia Polacco, *The Napping House* by Audrey Wood, and Chinese folktale *The Junior Thunder Lord* by Laurence Yep. RAIN AND RAINFALL–POETRY. WEATHER–POETRY.

1400   Raffi, comp. *The Raffi Christmas Treasury*. Illus. by Nadine Bernard Westcott. Crown, 1988. ISBN 0-517-56806-3

[84p., Gr. Pre–2] First come the 14 mostly secular Santa and snow-based songs, illustrated with large, affable watercolors, so each selection looks like an illustrated story poem. The second half contains the music and chords, so they don't intrude on the poetry. Jan Brett's ornate picture book version of the song "The Twelve Days of Christmas," Tomie dePaola's version of Clement C. Moore's *The Night Before Christmas*, and Jack Prelutsky's easy-to-read poetry in *It's Christmas* should get everyone in the spirit. CHRISTMAS–SONGS. SONGS.

1401   Rayner, Shoo. *My First Picture Joke Book*. Illus. by the author. Viking, 1990. ISBN 0-670-82450-X

[unp., Gr. K–2] Fifteen dumb but funny riddles have the question on one side and the answer on the verso, along with cheerful watercolor illustrations. More riddles for younger funnybones include David Adler's *The Carsick Zebra and Other Animal Riddles*, Katy Hall and Lisa Eisenberg's *Batty Riddles, Buggy Riddles*, and *Snakey Riddles*, Joseph Rosenbloom's *The Funniest Riddle Book Ever!*, Alvin Schwartz's *Ten Copycats in a Boat and Other Riddles*, and Andrea Griffing Zimmerman's *The Riddle Zoo*. Children can each select a favorite riddle and illustrate it with the riddle and an illustration on one side of their paper, and the answer and the punch line picture on the other. Have the class keep their riddles secret until they read aloud their finished papers. ANIMALS–RIDDLES. RIDDLES.

1402   Robinson, Fay, comp. *A Frog Inside My Hat: A First Book of Poems*. Illus. by Cyd Moore. Bridgewater Books, 1993. ISBN 0-8167-3129-2

[unp., Gr. Pre–2] The 37 poems here are all very easy to read, and the airy format with bright and colorful watercolors will make it a class favorite for children to share with each other. Many are about animals, with more charmers awaiting you in Alan Benjamin's *A Nickel Buys a Rhyme*, William Cole's *A Zooful of Animals*, Richard Edwards's *Moon Frog*, Douglas Florian's *Beast Feast*, Mary Ann Hoberman's *A Fine Fat Pig and Other Animal Poems*, J. Patrick Lewis's *A Hippopotamustn't and Other Animal Verses*, and Beverly McLoughland's *A Hippo's a Heap*. Lee Bennett Hopkins has compiled many delightful collections of easy-to-read poems, such as *April Bubbles Chocolate: An ABC of Poetry, Questions,* and *More Surprises.* ANIMALS–POETRY.

1403   Rogasky, Barbara, comp. *Winter Poems*. Illus. by Trina Schart Hyman. Scholastic, 1994. ISBN 0-590-42872-1

[40p., Gr. 3–6] Hyman's full-page paintings of wintertime New Hampshire are breathtaking, and if the selection of poetry is more introspective and dark than one usually finds in a children's collection, it will fill those gray and frosty days with warmth. The 25 nonsectarian poems are about the season, and do not include mention of winter holidays. Get a feel for the cold and snow with Janet S. Andersen's *The Key into Winter,* Larry Charles's *Peboan and Seegwun,* Deborah Hartley's *Up North in Winter,* C. S. Lewis's *The Lion, the Witch and the Wardrobe,* Gary Paulsen's *Dogteam,* Robert W. Service's narrative poem *The Cremation of Sam Magee,* Robert Swan's *Destination: Antarctica,* Robert D. San Souci's *The Snow Wife,* and Kris Waldherr's *Persephone and the Pomegranate.* SEASONS–POETRY. WINTER–POETRY.

1404   Rosen, Michael, comp. *Itsy-Bitsy Beasties: Poems from Around the World.* Illus. by Alan Baker. Carolrhoda, 1992. ISBN 0-87614-747-3

[32p., Gr. K–4] Flea, snail, ladybug, lizard, mosquito, caterpillar, and bee take up some of the 31 short poems that feature mostly insects, but other small creatures as well. *Water Pennies: And Other Poems* by N. M. Bodecker, *Bugs: Poems* by Mary Ann Hoberman, and *Flit, Flutter, Fly! Poems About Bugs and Other Crawly Creatures* compiled by Lee Bennett Hopkins, give more selections to hop up those insect studies units, with *Creepy Crawly Critter Riddles* by Joanne E. Bernstein and Paul Cohen and *Buggy Riddles* by Katy Hall and Lisa Eisenberg for more comic relief. Pull in some eye-popping facts with nonfiction such as *Fireflies in the Night* by Judy Hawes and *Those Amazing Ants* by Patricia Brennan Demuth, and then get into anthropomorphic exercises with *James and the Giant Peach* by Roald Dahl, *I Wish I Were a Butterfly* by James Howe, *The Gnats of Knotty Pine* by Bill Peet, and *Two Bad Ants* by Chris Van Allsburg. ANIMALS–POETRY. INSECTS–POETRY.

1405   Rosen, Michael, comp. *Poems for the Very Young.* Illus. by Bob Graham. Kingfisher, 1993. ISBN 1-85697-908-3

[77p., Gr. Pre–2] The busy bright-colored pen-and-ink and watercolors on every page will draw children's attention to this whale-sized collection of more than 100 wonderful poems about animals and relatives, food and friends, and the world around. *A Cup of Starshine: Poems and Pictures for Young Children* selected by Jill Bennett, *A Zooful of Animals* by William Cole, *April Bubbles Chocolate: An ABC of Poetry* by Lee Bennett Hopkins, *Talking Like the Rain: A First Book of Poems* by Dorothy and X. J. Kennedy, *Sunflakes* by Lillian Moore, and *Never Take a Pig to Lunch and Other Poems About the Fun of Eating* by Nadine Bernard Westcott will all get kids grinning and reciting. POETRY–ANTHOLOGIES.

1406   Schertle, Alice. *How Now, Brown Cow?* Illus. by Amanda Schaffer. Browndeer Press, 1994. ISBN 0-15-276648-0 [unp., Gr. 1–6] You'll learn a lot about cows from the 15 refreshing poems, some whimsical, others observant, with each made special by a soulful oversized oil painting on the facing page. Picture books that appreciate a good cow include Chris Babcock's *No Moon, No Milk*, Jennifer A. Ericsson's *No Milk!*, Lisa Campbell Ernst's *When Bluebell Sang*, David L. Harrison's *When Cows Come Home*, and Paul Brett Johnson's *The Cow Who Wouldn't Come Down*. COWS–POETRY. DOMESTIC ANI-MALS–POETRY. POETRY–SINGLE AUTHOR.

1407   **Schwartz, Alvin, comp.** *And the Green Grass Grew All Around: Folk Poetry from Everyone.* **Illus. by Sue Truesdale. HarperCollins, 1992. ISBN 0-06-022758-3**

[195p., Gr. 2–6] Divided into 15 sections, including people, food, school, teases and taunts, and nonsense, the book's roomy layout contains a meaty collection of over 300 poems, songs, riddles, and chants that will keep everyone humming and giggling till June, madcap black-and-white drawings, and meticulously doc-umented source notes. Other kid-friendly Schwartz titles include *Flapdoodle* (Lippincott, 1980), *Tomfoolery, Unriddling* (Lippincott, 1983), and *Witcracks* (Lippincott, 1973). Other similarly scoped titles include David Booth's *Doctor Knickerbocker and Other Rhymes,* Iona and Peter Opie's *I Saw Esau,* Jack Prelutsky's *Poems of A. Nonny Mouse* and *A. Nonny Mouse Writes Again!,* and Carl Withers's *A Rocket in My Pocket.* Students can interview their parents and search their memo-ries to compile both a written and taped classroom collection of additional jump rope rhymes, autograph verse, and other such valuable nonsense. HUMOROUS POETRY. NONSENSE VERSES. SONGS.

1408   **Shaw, Alison, comp.** *Until I Saw the Sea: A Collection of Seashore Poems.* **Photos by Alison Shaw. Henry Holt, 1995. ISBN 0-8050-2755-6**

[32p., Gr. K–4] Illustrated with huge, crisp color photographs of children, this attractive grouping of 19 seaside poems will make you yearn for summer and sand. *Earth Verses and Water Rhymes* by J. Patrick Lewis and the picture book poem *I Am the Ocean* by Suzanna Marshak are also lovely. Take a look under the surface with *The Magic School Bus on the Ocean Floor* by Joanna Cole and *Under the Sea from A to Z* by Anne Doubilet, and pull in the Taino Indian pourquoi tale *How the Sea Began* by George Crespo. OCEAN–POETRY. SEASHORE–POETRY.

1409   **Singer, Marilyn.** *It's Hard to Read a Map with a Beagle on Your Lap.* **Illus. by Clement Oubrerie. Henry Holt, 1993. ISBN 0-8050-2201-5**

[unp., Gr. 3–6] The oddest collection of dog poems, these 27 crawl across the page and take on dachshunds and Saint Bernards, bloodhounds and mongrels, all illustrated with paintings so eccentric you may find it necessary to go and pet a cat. Julia Lebentritt and Richard Ploetz's *The Kooken*, also illustrated by Oubrerie, is a bizarre and oddly endearing picture book about a girl and the dog that eats her priceless cello and then takes over for it. William Cole's *Good Dog Poems*, Lee Bennett Hopkins's *A Dog's Life*, and Jane Yolen's *Raining Cats and Dogs* are also good, if a bit staid by comparison. William Wegman's *Cinderella*, with photographed weimaraners in all the roles, would be a natural here, and *Speak! Children's Book Illustrators Brag About Their Dogs*, edited by Michael J.

Rosen, is a must. Children can research their favorite breeds and write odes. DOGS–POETRY. POETRY–SINGLE AUTHOR.

1410   Singer, Marilyn. *Please Don't Squeeze Your Boa, Noah!* Illus. by Clément Oubrerie. Henry Holt, 1995. ISBN 0-8050-3277-0

[unp., Gr. 3–6] The 22 outrageous and adorable pet poems and illustrations are companions to Singer's dog verse in *It's Hard to Read a Map with a Beagle on Your Lap*. Your poets may want to add to the "Here Are Some of Nature's Laws" verses, including observations about other pets they have known. Keep up the cacophony with the poems in *Never Take a Pig to Lunch* by Stephanie Calmenson, *A Zooful of Animals* by William Cole, *Beast Feast* by Douglas Florian, *A Hippopotamustn't and Other Animal Verses* and *Two-Legged, Four-Legged, No-Legged Rhymes*, both by J. Patrick Lewis, and *Eric Carle's Animals, Animals* compiled by Laura Whipple. ANIMALS–POETRY. PETS–POETRY. POETRY–SINGLE AUTHOR.

1411   Springer, Nancy, comp. *Music of Their Hooves: Poems About Horses.* Illus. by Sandy Rabinowitz. Wordsong: Boyds Mills, 1994. ISBN 1-56397-182-8

[32p., Gr. 3–6] Horse lovers will thrill to the 20 poems, some rhyming, some not, along with majestic watercolors, about horses and the riders who admire them. *The Poetry of Horses* by William Cole and *Cowboys* by Charles Sullivan are books of poetry that will also appeal. HORSES–POETRY. POETRY–SINGLE AUTHOR.

1412   Strickland, Dorothy, and Michael R. Strickland, comps. *Families: Poems Celebrating the African American Experience.* Illus. by John Ward. Wordsong: Boyds Mills, 1994. ISBN 1-56397-288-3

[31p., Gr. K–3] Two dozen poems by well-known writers including Lucille Clifton, Nikki Giovanni, Eloise Greenfield, and Langston Hughes give insight into the lives and thoughts of children. Other first-rate collections are *In for Winter, Out for Spring* by Arnold Adoff, *Meet Danitra Brown* by Nikki Grimes, *Pass It On: African-American Poetry for Children* by Wade Hudson, and *Brown Angels: An Album of Pictures and Verse* by Walter Dean Myers. Add some music with *Shake It to the One That You Love the Best* collected by Cheryl Warren Mattox. AFRICAN AMERICANS–POETRY. FAMILIES–POETRY.

1413   Sullivan, Charles, comp. *Cowboys.* Rizzoli, 1993. ISBN 0-8478-1680-X

[48p., Gr. K–4] Sullivan's 22 poems celebrating the life of cowboys and a few cowgirls are paired with color reproductions of paintings and sculptures by well-known western artists Charles M. Russell, Frederick Remington, and others, plus vintage photographs and even a "Far Side" cartoon by Gary Larson. Get back in the saddle again with *Songs of the Wild West* edited by Alan Axelrod, Roy Gerard's *Rosie and the Rustlers*, Jo Harper's *Jalapeño Hal*, Tony Johnston's *The Cowboy and the Black-Eyed Pea*, and Eric A. Kimmel's *Charlie Drives the Stage*. ART. COWBOYS–POETRY. POETRY–ANTHOLOGIES. WEST.

1414   Terban, Marvin. *Funny You Should Ask: How to Make Up Jokes and Riddles with Wordplay.* Illus. by John O'Brien. Clarion, 1992. ISBN 0-395-60556-3

[4 chapters, 64p., Gr. 3–6] For children who often don't understand the punch line, Terban explains how wordplay works, taking them step by step through jokes with homonyms, almost-sound-alike words, homographs, and idioms, and encouraging them to compose their own. Try out the groaners in collections like *The Silliest Joke Book Ever* by Victoria Hartman and *Super-Duper Jokes* by Frederica Young and see how many your audience gets. Understanding the precepts of wordplay will make all the difference in the world when reading the poems of master punsters, including *Bing Bang Boing* by Douglas Florian, *A Hippopotamustn't and Other Animal Verses* by J. Patrick Lewis, and *Something Big Has Been Here* by Jack Prelutsky. *Go Hang A Salami! I'm a Lasagna Hog! And Other Palindromes* by Jon Agee, *Antics! An Alphabetical Anthology* by Cathi Hepworth, and *The Weighty Word Book* by Paul M. Levitt, Douglas A. Burger, and Elissa S. Guralnick all sharpen a kid's humor supply. ENGLISH LANGUAGE–HOMONYMS. ENGLISH LANGUAGE–IDIOMS. RIDDLES. WORD GAMES.

1415   Thompson, Brian, comp. *Catch It If You Can.* Illus. by Susie Jenkin-Pearce. Viking Kestrel, 1989. ISBN 0-670-82279-5

[unp., Gr. Pre–2] This sprightly collection of 23 nursery rhymelike easy poems with genial watercolors will have children chanting and giggling, especially if you add hand motions to copy. *Hand Rhymes* by Marc Brown, *Mother Goose's Little Misfortunes* compiled by Leonard S. Marcus and Amy Schwartz, *Ring-a-Round-a-Rosy: Nursery Rhymes, Action Rhymes and Lullabies* compiled by Priscilla Lamont, and *Rain, Rain, Go Away! A Book of Nursery Rhymes* by Jonathan Langley will provide more fingerplay fun. HUMOROUS POETRY. NURSERY RHYMES.

1416   Viorst, Judith. *The Alphabet from Z to A: With Much Confusion on the Way.* Illus. by Richard Hull. Atheneum, 1994. ISBN 0-089-31768-9

[1 sitting, unp., Gr. 3–6] Starting at "Z" and working backward, Viorst has created a witty poem pondering the vagaries of the English language and its many spelling exceptions, which make invented spelling seem normal. "U is for UNDERWEAR/ UNCLE, UNWRAP,/ But it can't be for ONION./ Absurd!" You'll need to have children read this one with you so they can see the words and their absurdities. At least, run off a list of all the capitalized words in the poem so listeners can follow along. The intricate acrylic paintings for each letter contain a plethora of objects to identify, but, unfortunately, they're too small for group sharing. This would make a great big book for big kids. For more splendid puns and words, reach for Paul Levitt's The *Weighty Word Book.* ALPHABET. ENGLISH LANGUAGE–POETRY. ENGLISH LANGUAGE–SPELLING. POETRY–SINGLE AUTHOR. STORIES IN RHYME. VOCABULARY.

1417   Viorst, Judith. *Sad Underwear and Other Complications: More Poems for Children and Their Parents.* Illus. by Richard Hull. Atheneum, 1995. ISBN 0-689-31929-0

[78p., Gr. 2–6] In a sequel to the prize poetry collection *If I Were in Charge of the World and Other Worries*, Viorst has come up with 44 more blue-chip verses about children's fears, questions, and special requests. Fairy-tale parody fans will be tickled to note that there are poems musing on the fates of Beauty and the Beast, Rumpelstiltskin, the fisherman and his wife, and Hansel and Gretel. For more cleverness in rhymes, you'll also treasure *Bing Bang Boing* by Douglas Florian, *The Butterfly Jar* by Jeff Moss, and *Something Big Has Been Here* by Jack Prelutsky. FAIRY TALES–POETRY. HUMOROUS POETRY. POETRY–SINGLE AUTHOR.

1418   Walton, Rick, and Ann Walton. *Can You Match This? Jokes About Unlikely Pairs.* Illus. by Joan Hanson. Lerner, 1989. ISBN 0-8225-0973-3

[unp., Gr. 3–6] Q: What do you get when you cross a Chevrolet with a radio? A: Cartunes. There are 60 of these quick-witted riddles in this small-sized book from the Make Me Laugh! series, which will serve to develop children's senses of humor and pun-acuity quotients. As you share the reading of these aloud, discuss how the authors put the jokes together, and see if your pun crew can do the same. Marvin Terban's *Funny You Should Ask: How to Make Up Jokes and Riddles with Wordplay* is a big help, and *Super-Duper Jokes* by Frederica Young is worth laughing over. RIDDLES.

1419   Walton, Rick and Ann Walton. *Kiss a Frog! Jokes About Fairy Tales, Knights, and Dragons.* Illus. by Joan Hanson. Lerner, 1989. ISBN 0-8225-0970-9

[unp., Gr. 1–4] A mini-sized book from the kid-centered Make Me Laugh series, this contains plenty of wordplay puns on "Cinderella," "Sleeping Beauty," and other mainstream fairy tales. You'll find even more in *What Was the Wicked Witch's Real Name? and Other Character Riddles* by Joanne E. Bernstein and Paul Cohen. BOOKS AND READING–RIDDLES. FAIRY TALES–RIDDLES.

1420   Weil, Zaro. *Mud, Moon and Me.* Illus. by Jo Burroughes. Houghton Mifflin, 1992. ISBN 0-395-58038-2

[80p., Gr. 1–4] These 44 brief poems come loaded with child appeal and child-centered insights about the sun, the wind, the sky, and everything in between. Children can read the two-part poems in pairs, and there are many patterned poems just right for modeling in your writer's workshop. CREATIVE WRITING. POETRY–SINGLE AUTHOR.

1421   Westcott, Nadine Bernard, comp. *Never Take a Pig to Lunch and Other Poems About the Fun of Eating.* Illus. by the author. Orchard, 1994. ISBN 0-531-06834-X

[64p., Gr. 1–4] More than 60 funny poems to satisfy the heartiest appetites are illustrated with riotous, detailed, oversized acrylics in hot tropical colors. This is a newly illustrated version of the book originally published in 1972. Satisfy your craving for food poems with Arnold Adoff's *Eats*, Rose Agree's *How to Eat a Poem and Other Morsels*, William Cole's *Poem Stew*, Bobbye S. Goldstein's *What's on the Menu?*, Lee Bennett Hopkins's *Munching*, and Dee Lillegard's *Do Not Feed the Table*. FOOD–POETRY. HUMOROUS POETRY. POETRY–ANTHOLOGIES.

1422   Whipple, Laura, comp. *Celebrating America: A Collection of Poems and Images of the American Spirit.* **Art provided by the Art Institute of Chicago. Philomel, 1994. ISBN 0-399-22036-4**

[79p., Gr. 3–6] There's a resonant match of art and poetry in this large, beautiful, multicultural poetry anthology, and social studies teachers will rejoice in such an intelligent and interesting album. Over five dozen poems are organized into sections on land, stories, heart, people, and spirit, and the layout of one work of art per poem is spacious, well planned, and appealing. *Celebrate America in Poetry and Art* edited by Nora Panzer is another similarly formatted collection that complements this one. ART. PAINTINGS. POETRY–ANTHOLOGIES. U.S.–POETRY.

1423   Whipple, Laura, comp. *Eric Carle's Dragons, Dragons & Other Creatures That Never Were.* **Illus. by Eric Carle. Philomel, 1991. ISBN 0-399-22105-0**

[68p., Gr. 2–6] Introduce your rapt listeners to 34 extraordinary poems, illustrated with audacious tissue-paper collages, about the Hippogriff, Amphisbaena, and Kappa, along with the more well-known beasts such as the Minotaur, Unicorn, Sphinx, or Phoenix. Poets represented include old friends like X. J. Kennedy, Karla Kuskin, and Myra Cohn Livingston, along with traditionalists like William Blake, Elizabeth Barrett Browning, and even Sir Richard Burton, who wrote the first English translation of the *Arabian Nights*. Students can search the library for stories to go with each creature. Jack Prelutsky's poems in *The Dragons Are Singing Tonight* are smart and fun. For a fiction dragon binge, read Bruce Coville's *Jeremy Thatcher, Dragon Hatcher*, Julie Lawson's Chinese folktale *The Dragon's Pearl*, Betsy and Samuel Sterman's *Backyard Dragon*, and Patricia Wrede's *Dealing with Dragons*. ANIMALS, MYTHICAL–POETRY. DRAGONS–POETRY. POETRY–ANTHOLOGIES.

1424   Wong, Janet S. *Good Luck Gold and Other Poems.* **McElderry, 1994. ISBN 0-689-50617-1**

[42p., Gr. 4–6] Drawing on her experiences growing up in California the child of a Chinese father and a Korean mother, Wong's 42 brief insightful poems chronicle love of family, the death of a grandmother, and weave in hurtful brushes with prejudice and discrimination. Your readings of *Yang the Youngest and His Terrible Ear* by Lensey Namioka and *The Star Fisher* by Laurence Yep will be greatly enriched by this combination of rhyming and free verse poems. CHINESE AMERICANS–POETRY. KOREAN AMERICANS–POETRY. MULTICULTURAL STORIES. POETRY–SINGLE AUTHOR.

1425   Worth, Valerie. *All the Small Poems and Fourteen More.* **Illus. by Natalie Babbitt. Farrar, 1994. ISBN 0-374-30211-1**

[194p., Gr. 2–6] Now the four books—*Small Poems, More Small Poems, Still More Small Poems*, and *Small Poems Again*—are packaged together in one satisfying volume, with 14 additional poems added at the end. Each short and perfectly worded poem describes an item or animal in ways that startle and amuse, that make you see it in new ways. Children can select their favorites, bring in an accompanying object, and read the poems to each other, and then compose new ones. Barbara Esbensen's *Who Shrank My Grandmother's House? Poems of Discovery* is also interesting. CREATIVE WRITING. POETRY–SINGLE AUTHOR.

1426   **Yolen, Jane.** *Alphabestiary: Animal Poems from A to Z.* **Illus. by Allan Eitzen. Boyds Mills, 1995. ISBN 1-56397-222-0**

[64p., Gr. 1–4] Except for the usual "difficult" letters, for each alphabet letter there are from two to four thoughtful and friendly poems about ants, bats, cater-pillars, and donkeys, all the way up to the zemmi, zebu, and the zebra, accompa-nied by numerous and pleasantly humorous gouache and watercolor illustrations. Other fine books of animal poetry include Alan Benjamin's *A Nickel Buys a Rhyme*, Stephanie Calmenson's *Never Take a Pig to Lunch*, William Cole's *A Zooful of Animals*, Richard Edwards's *Moon Frog: Animal Poems for Young Children*, Douglas Florian's *Beast Feast*, Mary Ann Hoberman's *A Fine Fat Pig and Other Animal Poems*, J. Patrick Lewis's *A Hippopotamustn't and Other Animal Verses*, Beverly McLoughland's *A Hippo's a Heap*, Fay Robinson's *A Frog Inside My Hat*, Jack Prelutsky's *Zoo Doings*, and *Eric Carle's Animals, Animals*, compiled by Laura Whipple. ANIMALS–POETRY. ALPHABET–POETRY. POETRY–ANTHOLOGIES. POETRY–SINGLE AUTHOR.

1427   **Yolen, Jane.** *Animal Fare.* **Illus. by Janet Street. Harcourt, 1994. ISBN 0-15-203550-8**

[32p., Gr. 1–4] Nonsense animals cavort through this brightly illustrated assem-blage of 16 pleasing poems. There's the Gazealous who "gabounds high over the African plain," the nasty Rhinocerworse, and the Whysel who questions you to death. Catch up with the fanciful creatures in *The Ice Cream Cone Coot And Other Rare Birds* by Arnold Lobel, *No Such Things* by Bill Peet, *The Baby Uggs Are Hatching* by Jack Prelutsky, and assorted Dr. Seuss nonsense titles including *If I Ran the Zoo, McElliot's Pool*, and *On Beyond Zebra.* ANIMALS, IMAGINARY–POETRY HUMOROUS POETRY. NONSENSE VERSES. POETRY–SINGLE AUTHOR.

1428   **Yolen, Jane.** *Best Witches: Poems for Halloween.* **Illus. by Elise Primavera. Putnam, 1989. ISBN 0-399-21539-5**

[48p., Gr. 3–6] Yolen's 21 poems crackle and cackle with wit and cheerful malev-olence, and Primavera's dark and gorgeous full-page paintings are just the ticket to enliven this enchanting collaboration, a Halloween must-read. Scare up a few other tidy titles like Marc Brown's *Scared Silly!*, Dilys Evans's *Monster Soup and Other Spooky Poems*, Florence Parry Heide's *Grim and Ghastly Goings-On*, Lee Bennett Hopkins's *Ragged Shadows: Poems of Halloween Night*, Myra Cohn Livingston's *Halloween Poems*, Colin McNaughton's *Making Friends with Frankenstein*, and Eve Merriam's *Halloween ABC*. Jeffie Ross Gordon's *Hide and Shriek: Riddles About Ghosts & Goblins* provides timely jokes. HALLOWEEN–POETRY. POETRY–SINGLE AUTHOR. WITCHES–POETRY.

1429   **Yolen, Jane.** *Bird Watch: A Book of Poetry.* **Illus. by Ted Lewin. Philomel, 1990. ISBN 0-399-21612-X** [unp., Gr. 3–6] The 17 poems in this glorious book look closely at different types of birds, weaving between woodpecker, great blue heron, swan, robin, cardinal, and turkey. Lewin's watercolors are stunning and the poems introspective. For more animal insights, see Marilyn Singer's *Turtle in July* and the haiku in Sylvia Cassedy and Kunihiro Suekake's *Red Dragonfly on My Shoulder* and Demi's *In the Eyes of the Cat: Japanese Poetry for All Seasons*. *Great Northern Diver: The Loon* by Barbara Juster Esbensen and *Urban Roosts: Where Birds Nest in the City* by Barbara Bash both represent nonfiction at its finest. BIRDS–POETRY. POETRY–SINGLE AUTHOR.

1430   Yolen, Jane. *Raining Cats and Dogs*. Illus. by Janet Street. Harcourt, 1993. ISBN 0-15-265488-7

[unp., Gr. 1–4] It's hard to figure out which side of this genial poetry book goes first. Nine mostly rhyming homey cat poems into the book, you turn the whole thing upside down and, starting over again, find nine more good ones about dogs. Large affectionate illustrations will lead you to a barrage of personal pet stories from your listeners, some of which they may want to record as poems. Open up the pet poetry field with Jean Chapman's *Cat Will Rhyme with Hat*, Beatrice Schenk de Regniers's *This Big Cat and Other Cats I've Known*, Lee Bennett Hopkins's *I Am the Cat* and *A Dog's Life*, Nancy Larrick's *Cats Are Cats*, Myra Cohn Livingston's *Cat Poems*, and Marilyn Singer's *It's Hard to Read a Map with a Beagle on Your Lap*. Provoke laughter with *Riddles to Tell Your Cat* by Caroline Levine. CATS–POETRY. DOGS–POETRY. HUMOROUS POETRY. POETRY–SINGLE AUTHOR.

1431   Yolen, Jane. *What Rhymes with Moon?* Illus. by Ruth Tietjen Councell. Philomel, 1993. ISBN 0-399-22501-3

[40p., Gr. 1–5] Nineteen insightful poems, some rhyming, some free verse, take us on a nighttime moon-gazing spree. Use with Joseph Bruchac's Native American moon poems *Thirteen Moons on a Turtle's Back* and *Moon Mother: A Native American Creation Tale* by Ed Young. Pull in some facts with *The Moon and You* by E. C. Krupp and *One Giant Leap*, a description of the 1969 moon landing, by Mary Ann Fraser. ASTRONOMY–POETRY. MOON–POETRY. POETRY–SINGLE AUTHOR.

1432   Young, Frederica. *Super-Duper Jokes*. Illus. by Chris Murphy. Farrar, 1993. ISBN 0-374-37301-9

[98p., Gr. 3–6] Expand your riddle repertoire with more than 500 funnies in many categories such as kooky definitions, ghostly gimmicks, "What do you get when you cross . . . ?", knock-knocks, wordplay, "Did you hear about . . . ?", and story jokes. Marvin Terban's *Funny You Should Ask: How to Make Up Jokes and Riddles with Wordplay* will direct joke-tellers to create some of their own. Victoria Hartman's *The Silliest Joke Book Ever* is another fun assortment of wordplay riddles, while Rick and Ann Walton's *Can You Match This? Jokes About Unlikely Pairs* contains 60 "crossing" riddles. JOKES. RIDDLES. WORD GAMES.

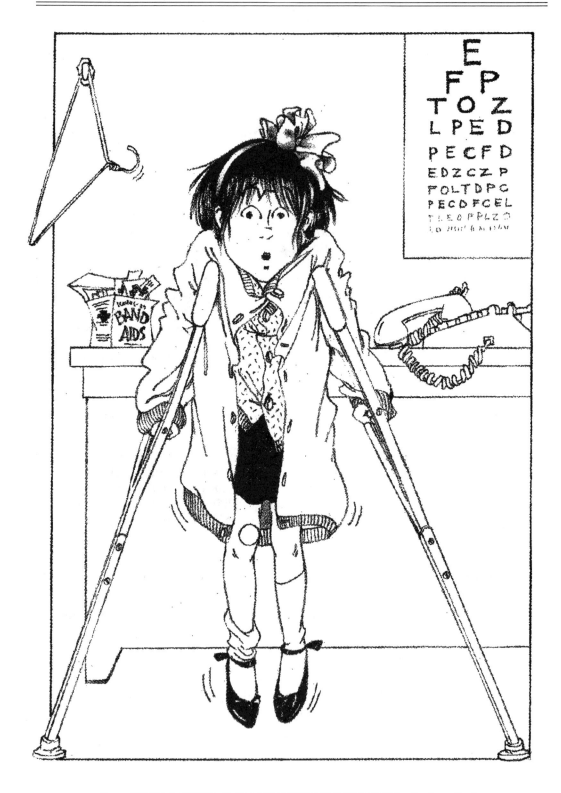

From JUNIE B. JONES AND THE STUPID SMELLY BUS by Barbara Park,
illustrated by Denise Brunkus. Reprinted by permission of Random House, Inc.

Bibliography
and Indexes

TEACHER'S PET

Call a doctor.

Call the vet!

I've just been bitten

By teacher's pet!

"Teacher's Pet" from MAKING FRIENDS WITH FRANKENSTEIN:
A BOOK OF MONSTROUS POEMS AND PICTURES.
Copyright © 1994 by Colin McNaughton. Published in the U.S. by Candlewick
Press, Cambridge, MA, and in the UK by Walker Books Limited, London.

PROFESSIONAL BIBLIOGRAPHY

OVERVIEW OF CHILDREN'S LITERATURE: TEXTS

Cullinan, Bernice E., and Lee Galda. *Literature and the Child.* **3rd ed. Harcourt, 1994. ISBN 0-15-500985-0**

Interspersed with the highly competent text exploring each genre are practical "Teaching Idea" pages that show ways to use books being discussed, and "Profile" pages of well-known authors and illustrators.

Edwards, Margaret A. *The Fair Garden and the Swarm of Beasts: The Library and the Young Adult.* **American Library Association, 1994. ISBN 0-8389-0635-4**

Geared for those who work with older children, this includes excellent practical advice on booktalking.

Huck, Charlotte, Susan Hepler, and Janet Hickman. *Children's Literature in the Elementary School.* **5th ed. Harcourt, 1993. ISBN 0-03-047528-7**

A thorough study of the field, encompassing every aspect of developing a successful literature program. No professional collection is complete without this invaluable text.

Lacy, Lyn Ellen. *Art and Design in Children's Picture Books: An Analysis of Caldecott Award Winning Books.* **American Library Association, 1986. ISBN 0-8389-0446-7**

An in-depth look at thirteen winners.

Lehr, Susan, ed. *Battling Dragons: Issues and Controversies in Children's Literature.* **Heinemann, 1995. ISBN 0-435-08828-9**

A thought-provoking collection of articles about censorship, violence and war, multicultural and gender issues, and political correctness by children's book authors and other professionals in the fray.

Lukens, Rebecca J. *A Critical Handbook of Children's Literature.* **5th ed. HarperCollins, 1994. ISBN 0-06-501108-2**

How to evaluate children's books in terms of genre, characters, plot, setting, theme, point of view, style, and tone.

Norton, Donna E. *Through the Eyes of a Child: An Introduction to Children's Literature.* **4th ed. Merrill, 1994. ISBN 0-675-20725-8**

A competent, attractive, and detailed overview, designed for children's literature classes.

Sloan, Glenna Davis. *The Child as Critic: Teaching Literature in the Elementary School.* **3rd ed. Teachers College Press, 1991. ISBN 0-8077-3156-0**

Includes a fascinating explanation of literary imagery and the four types of literature: comedy, romance, tragedy, and irony-satire.

Sutherland, Zena, and May Hill Arbuthnot. Children and Books. 8th ed. Scott, Foresman, 1990. ISBN 0-673-46357-5

Under each genre, major authors and their works are discussed in detail.

CHILDREN'S LITERATURE: BIBLIOGRAPHIES

Barstow, Barbara, and Judith Riggle. *Beyond Picture Books: A Guide to First Readers.* **R. R. Bowker, 1995. ISBN 0-8352-3519-X**

An annotated bibliography of more than 2,100 books on a first to second grade beginning-to-read level that children can handle independently.

Bodart, Joni. *Booktalk! Booktalking and School Visiting for Young Adult Audiences.* **H. W. Wilson, 1980. ISBN 0-8242-0650-9**

The definitive guide to principals of booktalking, with a plethora of sample booktalks you can give. *Booktalk! 2* (1985), *Booktalk! 3* (1988), *Booktalk! 4* (1992), and *Booktalk! 5* (1993) will help keep your presentations up to date. *Booktalking the Award Winners, 1992–1993* (1994) is the first in a new series of booktalks on prize-winning titles.

Dreyer, Sharon Spredemann. *The Best of Bookfinder: A Guide to Children's Literature About Interests and Concerns of Youth Aged 2–18.* **American Guidance Service, 1992. ISBN 0-88671-440-0**

Over 650 titles selected from volumes 1–3 of the well-respected annotated guide to children's books will help children cope with psychological, behavioral, and developmental problems; titles listed go up to 1987.

Friedberg, Joan Brest, June B. Mullins, and Adelaide Weir Sukiennik. *Portraying Persons with Disabilities: An Annotated Bibliography of Nonfiction for Children and Teenagers.* R. R. Bowker, 1992. ISBN 0-8352-3022-8

The excellent companion volume to *Portraying Persons with Disabilities: An Annotated Bibliography of Fiction for Children and Teenagers* by Debra Robertson.

Gillespie, John T., and Corinne J. Naden. Best Books for Children: Preschool through Grade 6. 5th ed. R. R. Bowker, 1994. ISBN 0-8352-3455-X

Choose from more than 15,000 annotated titles, arranged under general subject categories.

Gillespie, John T., and Corinne J. Naden. *Middleplots 4: A Book Talk Guide for Use with Readers Age 8–12.* R. R. Bowker, 1994. ISBN 0-8352-3446-0

Plots of 80 books, divided by genre, are described in great detail, including thematic and booktalking material and related titles. Earlier books in the series include *Introducing Books* (1970), *Introducing More Books* (1978), and *Introducing Bookplots 3* (1988).

Hearne, Betsy. *Choosing Books for Children: A Commonsense Guide.* Rev. ed. Delacorte, 1990. ISBN 0-385-30084-4

A thoughtful and intelligent analysis of what makes books worthwhile for toddler to teen, with annotated booklists at the end of each chapter.

Kennedy, DayAnn M., Stella S. Spangler, and Mary Ann Vanderwerf. *Science & Technology in Fact and Fiction: A Guide to Children's Books.* R. R. Bowker, 1990. ISBN 0-8352-2708-1

This useful bibliography for use with children ages 3 to 12 is arranged alphabetically by author and contains 350 suggested titles, each with designated age and grade levels, a detailed summary, and an evaluation of illustrations and text.

Kimmel, Mary Margaret, and Elizabeth Segel. *For Reading Out Loud! A Guide to Sharing Books with Children.* Rev. ed. Dell, 1991. ISBN 0-440-50400-7

Full-page detailed write-ups of 300 good books to read aloud, with advice on how to do it.

Kobrin, Beverly. *Eyeopeners! How to Choose and Use Children's Books About Real People, Places, and Things.* Viking, 1988. ISBN 0-14-046830-7

An annotated subject guide to activities and tips for using nonfiction books with children.

Lee, Lauren K., and Linda L. Homa, eds. *The Elementary School Library Collection: A Guide to Books and Other Media.* 19th ed. Bro-Dart, 1994. ISBN 0-87272-096-9

An enormous, annotated catalogue, issued yearly, of suggested new and favorite titles for children. Arranged like a library shelf list, and including copious indexes, reference and AV materials, and subject headings for each entry, this is a tool no librarian should be without.

Leonard, Charlotte. *Tied Together: Topics and Thoughts for Introducing Children's Books.* Scarecrow, 1980. ISBN 0-8108-1293-2

Hundreds of titles, with ways to present them.

Lima, Carolyn W., and John A. Lima. *A to Zoo: Subject Access to Children's Picture Books.* 4th ed. R. R. Bowker, 1993. ISBN 0-8352-3201-8

An enormous bibliography of almost 14,000 titles, with extensive subject indexing that extends the alphabetical author listings.

Lipson, Eden Ross. *The New York Times Parent's Guide to the Best Books for Children.* Times Books, 1991. ISBN 0-8129-1889-4

A competent, well-chosen, annotated booklist of over nine hundred titles, broken into wordless, picture, story, early reading, middle reading, and young adult books.

McElmeel, Sharron L. *Great New Nonfiction Reads.* Libraries Unlimited, 1995. ISBN 1-56308-228-4

Pique children's curiosity about the world with these more than 100 outstanding children's nonfiction titles, arranged alphabetically by subject, and comprehensively annotated with tie-ins to other titles and related activities.

Miller-Lachmann, Lyn. *Our Family, Our Friends, Our World: An Annotated Guide to Significant Multicultural Books for Children and Teenagers.* R. R. Bowker, 1992. ISBN 0-8352-3025-2.

This impressive, comprehensive reference bibliography includes detailed critical annotations of 1,000 fiction and nonfiction books for preschool through high school published since 1970, with each of the 18 chapters covering ethnic groups in the United States and around the globe.

Moir, Hughes, ed., with Melissa Cain and Leslie Prosak-Beres. *Collected Perspectives: Choosing and Using Books for the Classroom.* 2nd ed. Christopher-Gordon, 1992. ISBN 0-926842-19-9

Reviewed are almost 1,000 picture story books, fiction, poetry, and nonfiction titles from 1984 through 1991, each including a summary, classroom-tested ideas for use with children, and related titles for further exploration.

Paulin, Mary Ann. *Creative Uses of Children's Literature.* Library Professional Publications, 1982. ISBN 0-208-01861-1

A vast compendium of ideas, brought up to date in *More Creative Uses of Children's Literature, Volume 1: Introducing Books in All Kinds of Ways* (1992).

Polette, Nancy. *Nancy Polette's E Is for Everybody: A Manual for Bringing Fine Picture Books into the Minds and Hearts of Children.* 2nd ed. Scarecrow, 1982. ISBN 0-8108-1579-6

Annotations and activities for 126 picture books, plus a section on interpreting literature through art and media.

Polette, Nancy. *Picture Books for Gifted Programs.* Scarecrow, 1981. ISBN 0-8108-1461-7

Your students do not need to be geniuses to appreciate the wealth of activities here, which incorporate cognitive development, visual literacy, language development, and productive and critical thinking skills.

Polette, Nancy, and Marjorie Hamlin. *Celebrating with Books.* Scarecrow, 1977. ISBN 0-8108-1032-8

Holiday tie-ins using children's books.

Richey, Virginia H., and Katharyn E. Puckett. *Wordless/Almost Wordless Picture Books: A Guide.* Libraries Unlimited, 1992. ISBN 0-87287-878-3

Arranged alphabetically by author are annotated citations for 685 books, plus separate indexes of book types, series, illustrators, titles, and subjects.

Roberts, Patricia L., Nancy L. Cecil, and Sharon Alexander. *Gender Positive! A Teachers' and Librarians' Guide to Nonstereotyped Children's Literature.* McFarland, 1993. ISBN 0-89950-816-2

A detailed annotated booklist of over 200 books for grades K–8, broken down into contemporary realistic fiction, folk literature, fanciful fiction, historical fiction, and biographies, with excellent target activities for each title.

Robertson, Debra. *Portraying Persons with Disabilities: An Annotated Bibliography of Fiction for Children and Teenagers.* R. R. Bowker, 1992. ISBN 0-8352-3023-6

An essential list of 473 children's books, dealing with physical problems, sensory problems, cognitive and behavior problems, and various other disabilities, each with a detailed, evaluative plot summary and a thoughtful analysis of how the disability is treated within the story.

Rudman, Masha Kabakow, Kathleen Dunne Gagne, and Joanne E. Bernstein. *Books to Help Children Cope with Separation and Loss: An Annotated Bibliography.* 4th ed. R. R. Bowker, 1993. ISBN 0-8352-3412-6

A bibliographic guide to fiction and nonfiction books for young people, ages 3 to 16, that deals with difficult topics such as moving, adoption, illness, death, divorce, and war.

Thomas, James L. *Play, Learn, and Grow: An Annotated Guide to the Best Books and Materials for Very Young Children.* **R. R. Bowker, 1992. ISBN 0-8352-3019-8**

A "highly selective evaluative collection development resource guide" to books, audiocassettes, and videocassettes for infants, toddlers, preschoolers, and kindergartners.

Thomas, Rebecca L. *Primaryplots: A Book Talk Guide for Use with Readers Ages 4–8.* **R. R. Bowker, 1989. ISBN 0-8352-2514-3**

A top-quality reading guidance directory of 150 easy-to-read and picture-book titles, with each entry supplying a plot summary, thematic material, booktalk ideas and activities, and a list of related titles. Whole language teachers will appreciate the detailed descriptions and related activities for these prime 150 easy-to-read and picture books. *Primaryplots 2* (1993) encompasses 150 new titles from 1988-1993.

Totten, Herman L., and Risa W. Brown. *Culturally Diverse Library Collections for Children.* **Neal-Schuman, 1994. ISBN 1-55570-140-X**

An annotated children's literature bibliography of biographies, folklore, picture books, fiction, reference, and nonfiction about Native Americans, Asian Americans, Hispanic Americans, and African Americans.

Trelease, Jim. *The New Read-Aloud Handbook,* **2nd rev. ed. Viking Penguin, 1989. ISBN 0-14-046881-1**

Why and what to read aloud; a treasury of nearly 300 annotated titles.

READING, WRITING, AND LITERATURE: IDEAS AND ANNOTATIONS

Avery, Carol. *. . . And with a Light Touch: Learning About Reading, Writing, and Teaching with First Graders.* **Heinemann, 1993. ISBN 0-435-08787-8**

Completely practical and classroom-based, Avery's fascinating and well-organized text traces her evolution into a whole language teacher, offering anecdotes about her students along with techniques for teaching.

Bauer, Caroline Feller. *Celebrations.* **Illus. by Lynn Gates. H. W. Wilson, 1985. ISBN 0-8242-0708-4**

Innovative children's book-related holiday activities.

Bauer, Caroline Feller. *Read for the Fun of It: Active Programming with Books for Children.* **Illus. by Lynn Gates Bredeson. H.W. Wilson, 1992. ISBN 0-8242-0824-2**

A melange of marvelously do-able ideas for incorporating Reader's Theater, storytelling, poetry, and even magic tricks into your repertoire.

Bauer, Caroline Feller. *This Way to Books.* Illus. by Lynn Gates. H. W. Wilson, 1985. ISBN 0-8242-0678-9

A grand and attractive collection of children's book-related projects.

Benedict, Susan. *Beyond Words: Picture Books for Older Readers and Writers.* Heinemann, 1992. ISBN 0-435-08710-X

Perfect for upper-grade teachers who need sensible and overwhelming evidence that using picture books with their students will be justifiably worthwhile.

Borders, Sarah G., and Alice Phoebe Naylor. *Children Talking About Books.* Oryx, 1993. ISBN 0-89774-737-2

Models the use of 34 (mostly) picture books to "engage children in reflective thinking about stories, themselves, and the world." Each entry includes actual children/teacher dialogues from book discussions. An essential read for all elementary teachers.

Calkins, Lucy McCormick. *The Art of Teaching Writing.* Heinemann, 1994. ISBN 0-7725-2116-6

A personable, insightful, and indispensable guide.

Calkins, Lucy McCormick. *Living Between the Lines.* Heinemann, 1990. ISBN 0-435-08538-7

More than an inspirational text, this is the basis for building an essential link between teacher and student as we teach our children how and why to write.

Canavan, Diane D., and LaVonne H. Sanborn. *Using Children's Books in Reading/Language Arts Programs: A How-to-Do-It Manual for School and Public Librarians.* Neal-Schuman, 1992. ISBN 1-55570-101-9

These annotated lists of children's books fit into literary subcategories that develop reading and language skills, including decoding, vocabulary development, recognizing parts of speech, and identifying components of a story.

Cullinan, Bernice E., ed. *Invitation to Read: More Children's Literature in the Reading Program.* International Reading Association, 1992. ISBN 0-87207-371-8

A collection of practical essays by experts in the field on using children's literature for genre studies, thematic units, and as the basis for a literature-based reading program.

Fisher, Bobbi. *Joyful Learning: A Whole Language Kindergarten.* Heinemann, 1991. ISBN 0-435-08569-7

The author describes the organization of an exciting learning environment in her classroom throughout the year, where an emphasis on reading and writing empowers children to become "authorities of their own learning."

Fraser, Jane, and Donna Skolnick. *On Their Way: Celebrating Second Graders as They Read and Write.* Heinemann, 1994. ISBN 0-435-08830-0

Two teachers chronicle a year of observing their whole language–based second-grade classes flourish through reading, writing, and talking.

Graves, Donald. *Writing: Teachers & Children at Work.* Heinemann, 1983. ISBN 0-435-08203-5

A calm and reassuring assessment, filled with anecdotes and practical information, of how children write and how teachers can help them develop as writers.

Hall, Susan. *Using Picture Storybooks to Teach Literary Devices: Recommended Books for Children and Young Adults.* Vol. 2. Oryx, 1994. ISBN 0-89774-849-2

Volume Two is an all-new, tremendously useful annotated bibliography of over 300 picture books that teachers can use to illustrate 31 common literary elements including alliteration, foreshadowing, irony, paradox, and poetic justice. The first edition, *Using Picture Storybooks to Teach Literary Devices* (1990), is also a must.

Harwayne, Shelley. *Lasting Impressions: Weaving Literature into the Writing Workshop.* Heinemann, 1992. ISBN 0-435-08732-0

Reminding teachers to "beware of the cute idea," Harwayne's anecdote-rich narrative of working with New York City schoolchildren is filled with real examples and small explosions of inspiration, citing two essentials: quality literature and reflective teachers.

Hurst, Carol Otis. *Long Ago and Far Away . . . : An Encyclopedia for Successfully Using Literature with Intermediate Readers.* DLM, 1991. ISBN 1-55924-556-5

This large, handsome, and useful spiral-bound volume includes sections on presenting literature themes, individual novels, and beloved authors, and includes book blurbs, discussion ideas, and author background.

Irving, Jan, and Robin Currie. *Full Speed Ahead! Stories and Activities for Children on Transportation.* Teacher Ideas Press, 1988. ISBN 0-87287-653-5

A compendium of "literature-sharing experiences" for children in preschool through third grade, bursting with themed annotated bibliographies, crafts, games, stories, fingerplays, and songs.

Irving, Jan, and Robin Currie. *Glad Rags: Stories and Activities Featuring Clothes for Children.* Libraries Unlimited, 1987. ISBN 0-87287-562-8

Hundreds of sterling ideas to use with preschoolers through primary grades, all connected with the theme of clothing, including stories, songs, annotated picture-book lists, games, and literature-related activities.

Irving, Jan, and Robin Currie. *Mudluscious: Stories and Activities Featuring Food for Preschool Children.* Libraries Unlimited, 1987. ISBN 0-87287-517-2

Puppet plays, original stories, fingerplay, games, songs, and annotated bibliographies of children's picture books make up this invaluable compendium of ideas for food-related story times.

Irving, Jan, and Robin Currie. *Raising the Roof: Children's Stories and Activities on Houses.* Libraries Unlimited, 1991. ISBN 0-87287-786-8

Another rich source book of folktales, annotated picture-book bibliographies, activities, songs, and fingerplay, all of which are connected to the subject of houses, for preschool and primary grades.

Kruise, Carol Sue. *Learning Through Literature: Activities to Enhance Reading, Writing, and Thinking Skills.* Teacher Ideas Press, 1990. ISBN 0-87287-784-1

After carefully defining her "Think Bank" of cognitive, affective, critical thinking, and creative problem-solving skills, Kruise offers comprehensive units on 17 books for grades 1–3, including activities for predicting, post-reading, thinking, and writing, plus personal information about each author.

Kruise, Carol Sue. *Those Bloomin' Books: A Handbook for Extended Thinking Skills.* Libraries Unlimited, 1986. ISBN 0-87287-548-2

Applies Bloom's Taxonomy to 38 children's books, both fiction and picture books, supplies activities and discussion questions, and serves as a model for developing higher-level thinking skills with other good books.

Lamme, Linda Leonard, Suzanne Lowell Krogh, and Kathy A. Yachmetz. *Literature-Based Moral Education: Children's Books & Activities for Teaching Values, Responsibility, & Good Judgment in the Elementary School.* Oryx, 1992. ISBN 0-89774-773-2

Concrete strategies and discussion points for using children's books to introduce, reinforce, and influence elementary school children in making moral choices, with issues ranging from self-esteem, responsibility, sharing, and truthfulness to conflict resolution.

Lane, Barry. *After the End: Teaching and Learning Creative Revision.* Heinemann, 1993. ISBN 0-435-08714-2

Incisive and sensible methods—with interesting tie-ins to memorable passages from children's literature—to get writers in grades 4 and up to take risks and hone their writing skills.

Larrick, Nancy. *A Parent's Guide to Children's Reading.* 5th rev. ed. Westminster, 1983. ISBN 0-664-32705-2

Hundreds of suggested titles and activities to try at home.

Laughlin, Mildred, and Letty S. Watt. *Developing Learning Skills Through Children's Literature: An Idea Book for K–5 Classrooms and Libraries.* **Oryx, 1986. ISBN 0-89774-258-3**

An interesting and appealing subject approach to introducing books to children, with a lifetime supply of suggestions for literature-based activities.

McElmeel, Sharron L. *My Bag of Book Tricks.* **Illus. by Deborah L. McElmeel. Teacher Ideas Press, 1989. ISBN 0-87287-722-1**

Bibliographies and a plethora of ideas for literature-based activities on a wide variety of themes, plus a useful birthday list of authors and illustrators.

Marantz, Sylvia S. *Picture Books for Looking and Learning: Awakening Visual Perceptions Through the Art of Children's Books.* **Oryx, 1992. ISBN 0-89774-716-X**

This careful page-by-page analysis of the illustrations in 43 picture books for children in preschool through grade four encourages teachers to look at picture books with renewed appreciation.

Montgomery, Paula Kay. *Approaches to Literature Through Literary Form.* **Oryx, 1995. ISBN 0-89774-775-5**

Ties in literary structures (narrative, expository, drama, and persuasive writing) to children's books. One of the Oryx Reading Motivation series, an absorbing, stimulating, well-researched series that allows teachers to plan fifth-through-ninth-grade literature units that work. Also in the series are Montgomery's *Approaches to Literature Through Theme* (1992) and *Approaches to Literature Through Subject* (1992), Lucille W. Van Vliet's *Approaches to Literature Through Genre* (1992), and Mary Elizabeth Wildberger's *Approaches to Literature Through Authors* (1993).

Moss, Joy F. *Focus on Literature: A Context for Literacy Learning.* **Richard C. Owen, 1990. ISBN 0-913461-17-2**

Through 12 themed Focus Units, we see how children can learn about literature and build on their knowledge, using folk and fairy tale picture books as a basis for discussion, writing, and projects.

Polette, Nancy. *Brain Power Through Picture Books: Help Children Develop with Books That Stimulate Specific Parts of Their Minds.* **McFarland, 1992. ISBN 0-89950-708-5**

Provides activities and annotated lists of picture books to stimulate and enhance learning through all four quadrants of the brain: the "intellectual, contextual, affective and creative realms."

Rasinski, Timothy V., and Cindy S. Gillespie. *Sensitive Issues: An Annotated Guide to Children's Literature K–6.* **Oryx, 1992. ISBN 0-89774-777-1**

Within chapters on child abuse, prejudice and cultural differences, substance abuse, death and dying, moving, illness and disability, divorce, and nontraditional home environments, entries include plot summaries and meaningful activity ideas for over 220 titles.

Robb, Laura. *Whole Language, Whole Learners: Creating a Literature-Centered Classroom*. Morrow, 1994. ISBN 0-688-11957-3

Filled with examples of student writing, thoughtful essays by 15 top children's book authors and illustrators, and an intelligent blend of theory and how-to, the book exhorts us to read aloud to our children constantly and with fervor, and incite them to write and read and talk about books.

Routman, Regie. *Invitations: Changing as Teachers and Learners*. Heinemann, 1991. ISBN 0-435-08578-6

Just the intelligent, practical, fun-to-read, and important guide you need about all aspects of running a successful whole language program, from examples of student work and anecdotes to research. Primary-grade teachers also depend on the author's first book, *Transitions: From Literature to Literacy* (1988).

Stewig, John Warren. *Reading to Write: Using Children's Literature as a Springboard for Teaching Writing*. 3rd ed. Richard C. Owens, 1990. ISBN 0-913461-16-4

Ideas for integrating components of good stories, i.e., characterization, plot, language, and poetry, through children's literature, with examples of student writing.

Tuten-Puckett, Katharyn E., and Virginia H. Richey. *Using Wordless Picture Books: Authors and Activities*. Teacher Ideas Press, 1993. ISBN 0-87287-877-5

Ten comprehensive author/illustrator studies cover creative ways to use wordless books across the curriculum, plus an additional analysis of 25 other outstanding titles.

Van Vliet, Lucille W. *Approaches to Literature Through Genre*. Oryx, 1992. ISBN 0-89774-773-9

Annotated recommended reading lists and activities for introducing fiction genres including humor, mystery, fantasy, realistic, historical, animal, and adventure. One of the Oryx Reading Motivation series, an absorbing, stimulating, well-researched series that allows teachers to plan fifth-through-ninth-grade literature units that work. Also in the series are Paula Kay Montgomery's *Approaches to Literature Through Literary Form* (1995), *Approaches to Literature Through Theme* (1992), and *Approaches to Literature Through Subject* (1992), and Mary Elizabeth Wildberger's *Approaches to Literature Through Authors* (1993).

Watt, Letty S., and Terri Parker Street. *Developing Learning Skills Through Children's Literature: An Idea Book for K–5 Classrooms and Libraries*. Vol. 2. Oryx, 1994. ISBN 0-89774-746-1

Within chapters for each overlapping grade (K–1, 1–2, 2–3, 3–4, 4–5, 5–6) are nine first-rate literature units based on an author's work or a specific subject (grandparents, winter, word play, mysteries), which include objectives, recommended readings, and literature-related activities for both groups and individual students.

Weaver, Constance. *Reading Process and Practice: From Socio-Psycholinguistics to Whole Language.* **2nd ed. Heinemann, 1994. ISBN 0-435-08799-1**

A comprehensive hands-on whole language textbook that teachers of reading will find invaluable.

Weaver, Constance. *Understanding Whole Language: From Principles to Practice.* **Heinemann, 1990. ISBN 0-435-08535-2**

The "whole language" philosophy, often misunderstood or misinterpreted by teachers, administrators, and parents, is defined, described, and modeled.

POETRY

Armor, Maureen W. *Poetry, the Magic Language: Children Learn to Read and Write It.* **Teacher Ideas Press, 1994. ISBN 1-56308-033-8**

An intelligent and creative idea-rich source for teaching children to experience poetry.

Baring-Gould, William, and Cecil Baring-Gould, eds. *The Annotated Mother Goose.* **Clarkson N. Potter, 1982. ISBN 0-517-54629-9**

Explanations of the history behind the rhymes.

Bauer, Caroline Feller. *The Poetry Break: An Annotated Anthology with Ideas for Introducing Children to Poetry.* **Illus. by Edith Bingham. H. W. Wilson, 1995. ISBN 0-8242-0852-8**

This collection of poems and corresponding poetry activities is designed to help make poetry enjoyable for children and teachers alike and motivate them to spread poetry schoolwide.

Chatton, Barbara. *Using Poetry Across the Curriculum: A Whole Language Approach.* **Oryx, 1993. ISBN 0-89774-715-1**

Tie poetry into every area of your teaching, using the many specific suggestions of books and individual poems cited in the bibliographies that accompany discussion of each discipline.

Denman, Gregory. *When You've Made It Your Own: Teaching Poetry to Young People.* **Heinemann, 1988. ISBN 0-435-08462-3**

Nudges teachers and students to become comfortable with reading, understanding, and writing poetry.

Hopkins, Lee Bennett. *Pass the Poetry, Please!* **2nd ed. HarperCollins, 1987. ISBN 0-06-446062-2**

Poetry-shy teachers can unwind with biographical sketches and a poem for each of 20 well-loved children's poets, descriptions of types of poetry, and a plethora of activities to try out with students.

Koch, Kenneth. *Rose, Where Did You Get That Red? Teaching Great Poetry to Children.* **Random House, 1973, 1990. ISBN 0-679-72471-0**

This essential groundbreaking book assumes that children are capable of reading, understanding, and enjoying great adult poems, and provides, along with over five dozen selections, "poetry ideas" for teachers to try in conjunction with each poem.

Koch, Kenneth. *Wishes, Lies, and Dreams: Teaching Children to Write Poetry.* **HarperCollins, 1980. ISBN 0-06-080530-7**

Proven techniques for teaching elementary school children to write formula poems, along with scores of examples of children's work.

Larrick, Nancy. *Let's Do a Poem! Introducing Poetry to Children Through Listening, Singing, Chanting, Impromptu Choral Reading, Body Movement, Dance, and Dramatization.* **Delacorte, 1991. ISBN 0-385-30292-4**

This competent hands-on guide uses over five dozen verse examples and demonstrates how to use poetry to stimulate children's imaginations.

Livingston, Myra Cohn. *Poem-Making: Ways to Begin Writing Poetry.* **HarperCollins, 1991. ISBN 0-06-024020-2**

Using scores of outstanding examples from 75 major poets, Livingston introduces and explains the different voices of poetry. Every library needs this book, and every teacher scared off or baffled by poetry should read it.

McElmeel, Sharron. *The Poet Tree.* **Illus. by Deborah L. McElmeel. Teacher Ideas Press, 1993. ISBN 1-56308-102-4**

Poet profiles, including photos, of 20 poets who wrote or write for children, along with ideas and annotated booklists for introducing their work, plus poetry connections across the curriculum.

Steinbergh, Judith W. *Reading and Writing Poetry: A Guide for Teachers.* **Scholastic, 1994. ISBN 0-590-49068-7**

Teachers of children in grades K–4 will appreciate the practical activities and ideas from a Poet-in-Residence who has worked closely with children in several Massachusetts school systems.

STORYTELLING AND CREATIVE DRAMA

Baltuck, Naomi. *Crazy Gibberish and Other Story Hour Stretches (From a Storyteller's Bag of Tricks)*. Illus. by Doug Cushman. Linnett Books, 1993. ISBN 0-208-02336-4

Irresistible chants, audience participation stories, songs and musical games, and jokes that will ensure story-hour success, and if you order the accompanying toe tapping tape, you can learn it all in the car on your way to work.

Bauer, Caroline Feller. *Handbook for Storytellers*. American Library Association, 1977. ISBN 0-8389-0293-6

From planning to delivery, a gold mine of ideas.

Bauer, Caroline Feller. *New Handbook for Storytellers: With Stories, Poems, Magic, and More*. Illus. by Lynn Gates Bredeson. American Library Association, 1993. ISBN 0-8389-0613-3

A compendium of techniques, story sources, activities, and programs that will make you go dizzy with the sheer numbers of do-able and kid-pleasing ideas.

Bauer, Caroline Feller. *Presenting Reader's Theater: Plays and Poems to Read Aloud*. Illus. by Lynn Gates Bredeson. H. W. Wilson, 1987. ISBN 0-8242-0748-3

Over 50 read-aloud scripts based on children's literature.

Bettelheim, Bruno. *The Uses of Enchantment: The Meaning and Importance of Fairy Tales*. Knopf, 1976. ISBN 0-679-72393-5

Fascinating interpretations by the famous child psychologist. Little Red Riding Hood will never be the same.

Bosma, Bette. *Fairy Tales, Fables, Legends, and Myths: Using Folk Literature in Your Classroom*. Teachers College Press, 1987. ISBN 0-8077-2827-6

Comprehension, critical reading, writing, and other creative activities for incorporating the study of folklore into a classroom program.

Brady, Martha and Patsy T. Gleason. *Artstarts: Drama, Music, Movement, Puppetry, and Storytelling Activities*. Teacher Ideas Press, 1994. ISBN 1-56308-148-2

A lesson plan guide to using drama and the arts with children, with scads of do-able ideas and pragmatic instructions.

Breneman, Lucille, and Bren Breneman. *Once Upon a Time: A Storytelling Handbook*. Nelson, 1983. ISBN 0-8304-1007-4

The basics.

Briggs, Nancy E., and Joseph A. Wagner. *Children's Literature Through Storytelling & Drama*. 2nd ed. William C. Brown, 1979. ISBN 0-697-06212-0

A thoroughly professional, pragmatic, and accessible guide, with plenty of useful exercises and examples involving children as tellers and actors.

Caduto, Michael J., and Joseph Bruchac. *Keepers of the Animals: Native American Stories and Wildlife Activities for Children*. Fulcrum Publishing, 1991. ISBN 1-55591-088-2

Enrich wildlife ecology and environmental studies units for grades 1–6 with this rich resource of 27 regional Native American animal folktales and a detailed collection of related activities and background materials to accompany each story. Also valuable are *Keepers of the Earth: Native American Stories and Wildlife Activities for Children* (1988) and *Keepers of the Night: Native American Stories and Nocturnal Activities for Children* (1994).

Chambers, Dewey W. *The Oral Tradition: Storytelling and Creative Drama*. 2nd ed. William C. Brown, 1977. ISBN 0-697-06210-4

Another useful guide, laced with practical suggestions.

Champlin, Connie, and Nancy Renfro. *Storytelling with Puppets*. American Library Association, 1985. ISBN 0-8389-0421-1

A competent overview, including puppet patterns, techniques for storytelling and puppet manipulation, participatory activities, story bibliographies, and plenty of sensible advice.

Clarkson, Atelia, and Gilbert B. Cross. *World Folktales: A Scribner Resource Collection*. Scribner, 1980. ISBN 0-684-16290-3

Over 60 known and not-so-known stories for telling, including notes, principal motifs, and parallel stories for each selection.

Colwell, Eileen. *Storytelling*. Bodley Head, 1983. ISBN 0-370-30228-1

From an old hand.

Dailey, Sheila. *Putting the World in a Nutshell: The Art of the Formula Tale*. H. W. Wilson, 1994. ISBN 0-8242-0860-9

A collection of 38 easy-to-learn stories to tell, with examples of each of nine types of stories: chain, cumulative, circle, endless, catch, compound triad, question, "air castles," and good/bad. Story notes, a story formula outline for telling, and an annotated bibliography of other versions and variants accompanies each tale.

De Vos, Gail. *Storytelling for Young Adults: Techniques and Treasury*. Libraries Unlimited, 1991. ISBN 0-87287-832-5

Describes benefits, basic techniques, and classroom extension activities, and gives plot summaries and sources for 200 fairy tales, myths and legends, ghost stories, urban belief legends, love and romance stories, trickster, tall, and literary tales, plus retellings of 21 stories that will wake up and involve even a jaded teenage audience.

De Wit, Dorothy. *Children's Faces Looking Up: Program Building for the Storyteller.* **American Library Association, 1979. ISBN 0-8389-0272-3**

Develops storytelling programs on a multitude of themes, with suggestions for tales that tie in.

Goforth, Frances S., and Carolyn V. Spillman. *Using Folk Literature in the Classroom: Encouraging Children to Read and Write.* **Oryx, 1994. ISBN 0-89774-747-X**

In setting up instructional units on changes and challenges, overcoming odds, animals, transformations, enchantment, and heroes and heroines, each of the 54 folktale lessons includes a story summary, and activities designed to connect children to prior knowledge of the story, construct personal meaning, and create a verbal, artistic, or written response.

Greene, Ellin. *Storytelling: Art and Technique.* **3rd ed. R. R. Bowker, 1996. ISBN 0-8352-3458-4**

A sensible manual for beginning and experienced storytellers alike.

Hamilton, Martha, and Mitch Weiss. *Children Tell Stories: A Teaching Guide.* **Richard C. Owen, 1990. ISBN 0-913461-20-2**

The authors, a.k.a. Beauty & the Beast Storytellers, describe ways to integrate kids as storytellers into the school curriculum.

Heinig, Ruth Beall. *Improvisation with Favorite Tales: Integrating Drama into the Reading/Writing Classroom.* **Heinemann, 1992. ISBN 0-435-08609-X**

Ways to use creative drama in the classroom to extend 19 mostly well-known folk and fairy tales, including for each an annotated bibliography of related children's book titles, various types of pantomime and verbal exercises, and related writing and art activities.

Heinig, Ruth Beall, and Lydia Stillwell. *Creative Drama for the Classroom Teacher.* **4th ed. Prentice-Hall, 1988. ISBN 0-13-189663-6**

An exhaustive guide that relates children's literature to drama activities.

Irving, Jan, and Robin Currie. *Straw into Gold: Books and Activities About Folktales.* **Libraries Unlimited, 1993. ISBN 1-56308-074-5**

Songs, poems, chants, retellings, and ideas for projects for eight traditional folktales to use with grades K–4.

Kelner, Lenore Blank. *Creative Classroom: A Guide for Using Creative Drama in the Classroom, Pre K–6*. Heinemann, 1993. ISBN 0-435-08628-6

Each of the more than 50 creative drama activities described is written up in a comprehensive lesson plan, encompassing grammar and spelling, classifying and sequencing techniques, comprehension and writing skills, language and thinking skills, and literature enrichment.

Kinghorn, Harriet R., and Mary Helen Pelton. *Every Child a Storyteller: A Handbook of Ideas*. Illus. by Myke Knutson. Teacher Ideas Press, 1991. ISBN 0-87287-868-6

Includes stories, bibliographies, reproducibles, and a slew of ideas for teaching children to tell stories.

Livo, Norma J., and Sandra A. Rietz. *Storytelling: Process and Practice*. Libraries Unlimited, 1986. ISBN 0-87287-443-5

Practical and comprehensive guidance through every aspect of the art.

MacDonald, Margaret Read. *Celebrate the World: Twenty Tellable Folktales for Multicultural Festivals*. Illus. by Roxane Murphy Smith. H. W. Wilson, 1994. ISBN 0-8242-0862-5

A treasure trove of easy-to-learn stories set in ethnopoetic format, to go along with less well known holidays such as Chinese New Years, Girls' Day and Boys' Day in Japan, Mardi Gras, and Diwali in India. Each tale includes notes describing its background and tips for delivery, comparative notes of similar stories, and information about the holiday with suggestions for its celebration with children.

MacDonald, Margaret Read. *Look Back and See: Twenty Lively Tales for Gentle Tellers*. Illus. by Roxane Murphy. H. W. Wilson, 1991. ISBN 0-8242-0810-2

Participation stories from around the globe, many with songs or chantable refrains, with the text laid out in free verse to ensure easy mastery of each tale's natural phrasing, appropriate rhythm, and emphasis.

MacDonald, Margaret Read. *Storyteller's Sourcebook*. Gale, 1982. ISBN 0-8103-0471-6

Comprehensive index of over 700 editions of folktales, by story subject, motif, and title. A necessity for all folklore-minded library collections.

MacDonald, Margaret Read. *Twenty Tellable Tales: Audience Participation Folktales for the Beginning Storyteller*. Illus. by Roxane Murphy. H. W. Wilson, 1986. ISBN 0-8242-0719-X

Step-by-step, for people who are afraid to tell stories.

MacDonald, Margaret Read. *When the Lights Go Out: Twenty Scary Stories to Tell*. Illus. by Roxane Murphy. H. W. Wilson, 1988. ISBN 0-8242-0770-X

Includes extensive notes on how to tell, sources, and variants for each tale.

Pellowski, Anne. *The Family Storytelling Handbook: How to Use Stories, Anecdotes, Rhymes, Handkerchiefs, Paper and Other Objects to Enrich Your Family Traditions.* Illus. by Lynn Sweat. Macmillan, 1987. ISBN 0-02-770610-9

A gem that parents and all other storytellers will treasure.

Pellowski, Anne. *The Storytelling Vine: A Source Book of Unusual and Easy-to-Tell Stories from Around the World.* Illus. by Lynn Sweat. Macmillan, 1984. ISBN 0-02-770590-0

Indispensable "gimmicks," with instructions for string, picture-drawing, sand, doll, fingerplay, and musical instrument stories.

Sawyer, Ruth. *The Way of the Storyteller.* Rev. ed. Viking Penguin, 1977. ISBN 0-14-004436-1

Engrossing commentary on the art by a famous American storyteller, with a sampling of her favorite tales.

Schimmel, Nancy. *Just Enough to Make a Story: A Sourcebook for Telling.* 2nd ed. Sisters Choice Press, 1992. ISBN 0-932164-03-X

Practical, down-to-earth advice, and an assortment of good stories to tell.

Shedlock, Marie L. *The Art of the Story-Teller.* Rev. ed. Dover, n.d. ISBN 0-486-20635-1

Instructions and tales from a renowned American storyteller; originally published in 1915.

Sierra, Judy. *Fantastic Theater: Puppets and Plays for Young Performers and Young Audiences.* H. W. Wilson, 1991. ISBN 0-89774-727-5

Contains 30 short puppet plays taken from folklore, plus production notes, follow-up activities, and instructions and traceable patterns for making puppets, props, and scenery.

Sierra, Judy. *Oryx Multicultural Folktale Series: Cinderella.* Illus. by Joanne Caroselli. Oryx, 1992. ISBN 0-89774-727-5

Examines and compares the texts of 25 versions of the basic Cinderella story from many different cultures. Others in the series include *A Knock at the Door* by George Shannon (1992), *Tom Thumb* by Margaret Read MacDonald (1993), and *Beauties & Beasts* by Betsy Hearne (1993).

Sierra, Judy, and Robert Kaminski. *Multicultural Folktales: Stories to Tell Young Children.* Oryx, 1991. ISBN 0-89774-688-0

Twenty-five easy-to-tell tales from around the globe for children ages 2 to 7, including tips for tellers, suggestions of other story tie-ins, and patterns for making simple flannel board figures or puppets.

Sierra, Judy, and Robert Kaminski. *Twice Upon a Time: Stories to Tell, Retell, Act Out, and Write About.* **H. W. Wilson, 1989. ISBN 0-8242-0775-0**

In addition to the texts of 21 easy-to-learn folktales are tips for telling and suggestions for related creative drama and writing activities.

Yolen, Jane. *Favorite Folktales from Around the World.* **Pantheon, 1986. ISBN 0-394-72960-9**

An intelligent assortment of tellable stories, grouped by types of tales and characters.

Yolen, Jane. *Touch Magic: Fantasy, Faerie and Folklore in the Literature of Childhood.* **Philomel, 1981. ISBN 0-399-20830-5**

Lyrical essays on the art and artistry of storytelling.

Ziskind, Sylvia. *Telling Stories to Children.* **H. W. Wilson, 1976. ISBN 0-8242-0588-X**

The chapter on "Mastering Technique" should be required reading for beginning storytellers.

CHILDREN'S LITERATURE IN THE CONTENT AREAS

Barchers, Suzanne I., and Patricia C. Marden. *Cooking Up U.S. History: Recipes and Research to Share with Children.* **Libraries Unlimited, 1991. ISBN 0-87287-782-5**

Tasteful annotated bibliographies separated into nonfiction and fiction lists accompany a dozen easy-to-follow recipes for each period in U.S. history, starting with American Indians and ending with the West.

Braddon, Kathryn L., Nancy J. Hall, and Dale Taylor. *Math Through Children's Literature: Making the NCTM Standards Come Alive.* **Teacher Ideas Press, 1993. ISBN 0-87287-932-1**

Shows how to enhance math lessons for each NCTM standard using scores of children's books and provides an extensive collection of activities and related titles to accompany each concept.

Burns, Marilyn. *Math and Literature (K–3).* **Heinemann, 1992. ISBN 0-942355-07-1**

Classroom-tested ideas for teaching math lessons using 31 children's books.

Butzow, Carol M., and John W. Butzow. *Science Through Children's Literature: An Integrated Approach.* Libraries Unlimited, 1989. ISBN 0-87287-667-5

In addition to delving into ways to use picture books as a basis for presenting science lessons, there are specific activities for each of 33 children's books, covering life science, earth and space science, and physical science for grades K–3.

Fredericks, Anthony D. *The Integrated Curriculum: Books for Reluctant Readers, Grades 2–5.* Illus. by Robert Michael Seufert and Anthony Allan Stoner. Teacher Ideas Press, 1992. ISBN 0-87287-994-1

For each of the 39 well-chosen books there are critical thinking questions and suggestions for activities in reading/language arts, science/health, art, math, music, social studies, and physical education, all of which will energize and excite reluctant readers.

Fredericks, Anthony D. *Social Studies Through Children's Literature: An Integrated Approach.* Libraries Unlimited, 1991. ISBN 0-87287-970-4

Units on child and self, community and neighborhood, city and country, states and regions, nation and country, and world encompass well-chosen children's books and stimulating activities for social studies teaching.

Griffiths, Rachel, and Margaret Clyne. *Books You Can Count On: Linking Mathematics & Literature.* Heinemann, 1991. ISBN 0-435-08322-8

A range of lessons outlines based on 40 math-related children's books and poems.

Kennemer, Phyllis K. *Using Literature to Teach Middle Grades About War.* Oryx, 1993. ISBN 0-89774-778-X

Each of the six thematic units (from the Revolutionary War to the Gulf War) for grades 6-8 contains chronologies, annotated lists of recommended titles across all genres, sample lesson plans, questions and activities, and glossary.

Latrobe, Kathy Howard, series ed. Exploring the United States Through Literature series. Oryx, 1994.

Each volume in the series is broken down into its states, which are listed in Dewey order, an annotated bibliography of grades K-8 fiction and nonfiction print and nonprint materials, with activities suggestions for each title. The series includes: *Exploring the Northeast States Through Literature* (ISBN 0-89774-779-8), *Southeast States* (ISBN 0-89774-770-4), *Great Lakes States* (ISBN 0-89774-731-3), *Plains States* (ISBN 0-89774-762-3), *Mountain States* (ISBN 0-89774-783-6), *Southwest States* (ISBN 0-89774-765-8), and *Pacific States* (ISBN 0-89774-771-2).

Laughlin, Mildred, and Patricia Payne Kardaleff. *Literature-Based Social Studies: Children's Books and Activities to Enrich the K–5 Curriculum.* Oryx, 1991. ISBN 0-89774-605-8

General units on family, community, and American history include student objectives, annotated "Recommended Reading" lists, and extensive collections of activities.

Laughlin, Mildred, and Claudia Lisman Swisher. *Literature-Based Reading: Children's Books and Activities to Enrich the K–5 Curriculum.* **Oryx, 1990. ISBN 0-89774-562-0**

Introduces literary elements (plot, characterization) and higher-level thinking skills (predicting and sequencing) through activities using children's books for grades K–5.

Laughlin, Mildred, and Terri Parker Street. *Literature-Based Art & Music: Children's Books and Activities to Enrich the K–5 Curriculum.* **Oryx, 1992. ISBN 0-89774-661-9**

Using an exemplary collection of children's books, the authors offer a series of lessons and extending activities that explore a variety of illustrators' use of color, shape, line, texture, and space, and expose young musicians to tempo and rhythm, timbre and dynamics, and form and style.

Levene, Donna B. *Music Through Children's Literature: Theme and Variations.* **Illus. by Susan Kochenberger Stroeher. Teacher Ideas Press, 1993. ISBN 1-56308-021-4**

Sections on rhythm, melody, form and style, instruments, dances, and history are presented using children's books to illustrate each concept.

McElmeel, Sharron L. *McElmeel Booknotes: Literature Across the Curriculum.* **Teacher Ideas Press, 1993. ISBN 0-87287-951-8**

Connects children's books with areas of the curriculum, including annotated booklists with concrete ideas for lessons in writing, math, and the arts.

McGlathery, Glenn, and Norma J. Livo. *Who's Endangered on Noah's Ark? Literacy and Scientific Ideas for Teachers and Parents.* **Illus. by David Stallings. Teacher Ideas Press, 1992. ISBN 0-87287-949-6**

Ten chapters, each focused on one endangered animal, incorporate folktales, a wealth of teaching activities, and a comprehensive bibliography of related books.

Perez-Stable, Maria A., and Mary Hurlbut Cordier. *Understanding American History Through Children's Literature: Instructional Units and Activities for Grades K–8.* **Oryx, 1994. ISBN 0-89774-795-X**

A useful guide to teaching history with nonfiction, biography, folklore, and historical fiction, tied in to a chronological framework of topical units, each including objectives, learning activities, and annotated bibliographies.

Sinclair, Patti K. *E for Environment: An Annotated Bibliography of Children's Books with Environmental Themes.* **R. R. Bowker, 1992. ISBN 0-8352-3028-7**

Thorough annotations of the 517 titles for preschool though age 14 cover such chapter topics as nature, ecology, endangered species, pollution, and activities and experiments.

Walter, Virginia A. *War & Peace: Literature for Children and Young Adults: A Resource Guide to Significant Issues.* **Oryx, 1993. ISBN 0-89774-725-9**

An annotated bibliography of more than 400 books dealing with war and conflict resolution, and how to share such issues in the classroom.

Whitin, David J., and Sandra Wilde. *Read Any Good Math Lately? Children's Books for Mathematical Learning, K–6.* **Heinemann, 1992. ISBN 0-435-08334-1**

Teachers seeking to expand their math lessons from textbook to literature and real life will find lively chapters on classification, counting and addition, fractions, estimation, geometry, and measurement, all incorporating innovative projects and ideas.

AUTHORS AND ILLUSTRATORS

Day, Frances Ann. *Multicultural Voices in Contemporary Literature: A Resource for Teachers.* **Heinemann, 1994. ISBN 0-435-08826-2**

A fascinating study of the lives and works of 39 multicultural authors and illustrators, with each entry containing a biographical sketch, photograph, address, bibliography, and detailed teaching guide for several of the author's works.

Kovacs, Debora K., and Hames Preller. *Meet the Authors and Illustrators: 60 Creators of Favorite Children's Books Talk About Their Work.* **Scholastic, 1991. ISBN 0-590-49097-4**

Each interview fills two pages of quote-filled narrative, a selected bibliography, a black and white photo, and a "Do It Yourself" activity for students to try. *Meet the Authors and Illustrators, Volume Two* (1993) supplies 60 further famous folks.

McElmeel, Sharron L. *An Author a Month (for Nickels).* **Libraries Unlimited, 1990. ISBN 0-87287-527-9**

Chapters celebrating 12 picture-book authors each include an author poster, one brief and one more-detailed biography, and an annotated list of that author's books with a host of activities to try. *An Author a Month (for Pennies)* (1988) features more of the same.

Melton, David. *How to Capture Live Authors and Bring Them to Your Schools.* **Landmark Editions, 1986. ISBN 0-933849-03-6**

Let Melton's breezy step-by-step guide help you organize effective and valuable author programs that will delight teachers, kids, and the chosen authors as well.

Wildberger, Mary Elizabeth. *Approaches to Literature Through Authors.* **Oryx, 1993. ISBN 0-89774-776-3**

Uses works of recognized children's book authors and illustrators to investigate styles, themes, and subjects. One of the Oryx Reading Motivation series, an absorbing, stimulating, well-researched series that allows teachers to plan fifth-through-ninth-grade literature units that work. Also in the series are Paula Kay Montgomery's *Approaches to Literature Through Literary Form* (1995), *Approaches to Literature Through Theme* (1992), *Approaches to Literature Through Subject* (1992), and Lucille W. Van Vliet's *Approaches to Literature Through Genre* (1992).

From THE SUMMER I SHRANK MY GRANDMOTHER by Elvira Woodruff,
illustrated by Katherine Coville. Text copyright © 1990 by Elvira Woodruff;
illustrations copyright © 1990 by Katherine Coville.
Reprinted by permission of Holiday House.

AUTHOR INDEX

Authors are arranged alphabetically by last name. Authors' and joint authors' names are followed by book titles—also arranged alphabetically—and the text entry number. References to entry numbers in this volume appear in boldface type, while references to the companion volume, *Books Kids Will Sit Still For* (R. R. Bowker, 1990), appear in regular type.

Aardema, Verna. *Anansi Finds a Fool*, **855**
  Bimwili and the Zimwi, 1379
  Borreguita and the Coyote, **856**
  Bringing the Rain to Kapiti Plain, 1380
  Misoso, **1052**
  Princess Gorilla and a New Kind of Water, 1381
  Rabbit Makes a Monkey Out of Lion, 1382
  The Riddle of the Drum, 1383
  Traveling to Tondo, **857**
  What's So Funny, Ketu?, 1384
  Who's in Rabbit's House?, 1385
  Why Mosquitoes Buzz in People's Ears, 1386
Abels, Chana Byers. *The Children We Remember*, 1985
Abercrombie, Barbara. *Michael and the Cats*, **1**
Abolafia, Yossi. *Fox Tale*, **394**
Abrashkin, Raymond (jt. author). *Danny Dunn and the Homework Machine*, 1255
  Danny Dunn, Time Traveler, 1256
Accorsi, William. *Friendship's First Thanksgiving*, **216**
Ackerman, Karen. *Song and Dance Man*, 599
Ada, Alma Flor. *Dear Peter Rabbit*, **395**
  The Rooster Who Went to His Uncle's Wedding, **858**
Adams, Adrienne. *A Woggle of Witches*, 1
Adams, Barbara Johnston. *The Go-Around Dollar*, **1094**
Adler, David A. *Eaton Stanley & the Mind Control Experiment*, 1137
  My Dog and the Birthday Mystery, 313
  A Picture Book of Harriet Tubman, **1095**
  A Picture Book of Sojourner Truth, **1096**
  Remember Betsy Floss, 1740
  Wild Pill Hickok and Other Old West Riddles, 1741

Adler, David A. (comp.). *The Carsick Zebra and Other Animal Riddles*, 1739
Adoff, Arnold. *Chocolate Dreams*, **1259**
  Eats, 1742
  In for Winter, Out for Spring, **1260**
  Street Music, **1261**
Aesop. *Aesop & Company*, **1053**
  The Aesop for Children, 1641
  Aesop's Fables, **1054**, 1642, 1643, 1644, 1645, 1646
  Animal Fables from Aesop, **1055**
  Belling the Cat and Other Aesop's Fables, **1056**
  The Children's Aesop, **1057**
  The Fables of Aesop, 1647
  The Miller, His Son and Their Donkey, 1387
  Once in a Wood, 1648
  Seven Fables from Aesop, 1649
  Three Aesop Fox Fables, 1650
  The Tortoise and the Hare, 1388
  Twelve Tales from Aesop, 1651
  The Wind and the Sun, **859**
Afanasev, Alexander (ed.). *Russian Folk Tales*, 1652
Agard, John, and Grace Nichols, comps. *A Caribbean Dozen*, **1262**
Agee, Jon. *Go Hang a Salami! I'm a Lasagna Hog!*, **1263**
  The Incredible Painting of Felix Clousseau, 862
Agree, Rose H. (comp.). *How to Eat a Poem and Other Morsels*, 1743
Ahlberg, Allan (jt. author). *Funnybones*, 314
  The Jolly Christmas Postman, **396**
Ahlberg, Janet, and Allan Ahlberg. *Funnybones*, 314
  The Jolly Christmas Postman, **396**
Aiken, Joan. *The Moon's Revenge*, 1038

Ainsworth, Ruth. *The Phantom Carousel and Other Ghostly Tales*, 1138

Aker, Suzanne. *What Comes in 2's, 3's & 4's?*, **62**

Albert, Richard E. *Alejandro's Gift*, **397**

Alborough, Jez. *It's the Bear!*, **63**
Where's My Teddy?, **2**

Alcock, Vivien. *The Monster Garden*, 1257
The Trial of Anna Cotman, **802**

Alcorn, Johnny. *Rembrandt's Beret*, **697**

Alderson, Brian (comp.). *Cakes and Custard*, 1878

Alderson, Brian (ed.). *Blue Fairy Book*, 1702

Alexander, Ellen. *Llama and the Great Flood*, 1389

Alexander, Lloyd. *The Book of Three*, 1258
The Cat Who Wished to Be a Man, 1259
The First Two Lives of Lucas-Kasha, 1260
The Fortune-Tellers, **698**
The Town Cats and Other Tales, 1261
The Wizard in the Tree, 1262

Alexander, Martha. *Move Over, Twerp*, 315
The Story Grandmother Told, 2

Alexander, Sally Hobart. *Mom Can't See Me*, **1097**
Mom's Best Friend, **1098**

Alexander, Sue. *Dear Phoebe*, 600
There's More . . . Much More, 3

Aliki. *At Mary Bloom's*, 4
Communication, **1099**
Keep Your Mouth Closed, Dear, 5
The Twelve Months, 1390
We Are Best Friends, 6

Allard, Harry. *I Will Not Go to a Market Today*, 316
It's So Nice to Have a Wolf around the House, 317
Miss Nelson Is Missing, 601
The Stupids Die, 318
There's a Party at Mona's Tonight, 319

Allen, Jeffrey. *Mary Alice, Operator Number Nine*, 320

Allen, Judy. *Panda*, **584**
Tiger, **585**

Allen, Marjorie N. *One, Two, Three—Ah-Choo!*, 321

Allen, Marjorie N., and Shelley Rotner. *Changes*, **1100**

Allen, Pamela. *Bertie and the Bear*, 7

Alley, R. W. (reteller). *Seven Fables from Aesop*, 1649

Allinson, Beverly. *Effie*, **217**

Alvarez, Mark (jt. author). *Yo, Millard Fillmore!*, **1119**

Ames, Mildred. *Is There Life on a Plastic Planet?*, 1263

Andersen, Hans Christian. *The Emperor's New Clothes*, 863

It's Perfectly True, 602
The Nightingale, 1039, **699**
The Princess and the Pea, 322
The Steadfast Tin Soldier, **586**
Thumbelina, 864
The Tinderbox, **757**
The Ugly Duckling, 603
The Wild Swans, 1040, **700**

Andersen, Janet S. *The Key into Winter*, **587**

Andersen, Karen Born. *An Alphabet in Five Acts*, **398**

Anderson, Leone Castell. *The Wonderful Shrinking Shirt*, 604

Anderson, Lonzo. *Arion and the Dophins*, 1391
The Halloween Party, 605
The Ponies of Mykillengi, 865
Two Hundred Rabbits, 606

Anderson, Margaret. *The Brain on Quartz Mountain*, 1041

Anderson, Norman D. (jt. author). *Rescue!*, 2004

Andrews, F. Emerson. *Upside-Down Town*, 866

Andrews, Jan. *Very Last First Time*, 867

Anholt, Catherine, and Laurence Anholt. *All About You*, **3**
Kids, **64**
What Makes Me Happy?, **65**

Anholt, Laurence (jt. author). *All About You*, **3**
Kids, **64**
What Makes Me Happy?, **65**

Annett, Cora. *How the Witch Got Alf*, 868

Appelt, Kathi. *Elephants Aloft*, **66**

Appiah, Peggy. *Tales of an Ashanti Father*, 1653

Arbuthnot, Mary Hill (comp.). *Time for Poetry*, 1744

Archambault, John (jt. author). *Barn Dance!*, 505
Chicka Chicka Boom Boom, 205
Listen to the Rain, 746

Archibald, Leon (jt. author). *The Old-Fashioned Storybook*, 1727

Arenstein, Misha (jt. comp.). *Thread One to a Star*, 1829

Arkhurst, Joyce Cooper. *The Adventures of Spider*, 1654

Armitage, David (jt. author). *The Bossing of Josie*, 8

Armitage, Ronda, and David Armitage. *The Bossing of Josie*, 8

Armour, Peter. *Stop That Pickle!*, **218**

Armstrong, Jennifer. *Chin Yu Min and the Ginger Cat*, **588**
Little Salt Lick and the Sun King, **399**

Armstrong, William. *Sounder*, 1264

Arnold, Caroline. *Kangaroo*, 1986
The Terrible Hodag, 1392

Trapped in Tar, 1987

Arnold, Eric H., and Jeffrey Loeb, eds. *I'm Telling!*, 1988

Arnold, Katya. *Baba Yaga*, **860**

Baba Yaga & the Little Girl, **861**

Arnold, Tedd. *Ollie Forgot*, 607

The Signmaker's Assistant, **400**

Arnosky, Jim. *All Night Near the Water*, **67**

Arthur, Malcolm (trans.). *Puss in Boots*, **997**

Arthur, Robert. *The Secret of Terror Castle*, 1265

Artis, Vicki K. *Gray Duck Catches a Friend*, 9

Aruego, Jose, and Ariane Dewey. *A Crocodile's Tale*, 1393

Asbjørnsen, P. C. *The Runaway Pancake*, 1394

The Squire's Bride, 1395

The Three Billy Goats Gruff, 1396

Asch, Frank. *Bear Shadow*, 10

Goodbye House, 11

Happy Birthday, Moon, 12

Just Like Daddy, 13

Moongame, 14

Pearl's Promise, **701**

Popcorn, 15

Turtle Tale, 16

Asch, Frank, and Vladimir Vagin. *Dear Brother*, **401**

Ata, Te. *Baby Rattlesnake*, **862**

Atwater, Florence (jt. author). *Mr. Popper's Penguins*, 1042

Atwater, Richard, and Florence Atwater. *Mr. Popper's Penguins*, 1042

Auch, Mary Jane. *Bird Dogs Can't Fly*, **219**

The Easter Egg Farm, **220**

Monster Brother, **221**

Peeping Beauty, **402**

Audubon, John James. *Capturing Nature*, **1101**

Avi. *Bright Shadow*, 1266

The Fighting Ground, 1267

Night Journeys, 1268

Shadrach's Crossing, 1269

The True Confessions of Charlotte Doyle, **803**

Axelrod, Alan (comp.). *Songs of the Wild West*, **1264**

Axelrod, Amy. *Pigs Will Be Pigs*, **403**

Aylesworth, Jim. *Hush Up!*, 323

My Son John, **222**

Old Black Fly, **223**

One Crow, 17

Two Terrible Frights, 18

Ayres, Becky Hickox. *Matreshka*, **863**

Babbitt, Natalie. *Bub*, **224**

The Devil's Storybook, 1270

The Search for Delicious, 1139

Tuck Everlasting, 1271

Babcock, Chris. *No Moon, No Milk*, **225**

Back, Christine. *Bean and Plant*, 1989

Bacon, Peggy. *The Magic Touch*, 1043

Baden, Robert. *And Sunday Makes Seven*, **864**

Bader, Barbara (reteller). *Aesop & Company*, **1053**

Baehr, Patricia. *Mouse in the House*, **68**

Baer, Edith. *This Is the Way We Go to School*, **226**

Words Are Like Faces, 324

Bahr, Mary. *The Memory Box*, **589**

Baker, Alan. *Benjamin's Book*, 325

Benjamin's Portrait, 326

Baker, Augusta, and Ellin Greene. *Storytelling*, 2160

Baker, Keith. *Big Fat Hen*, **4**

Baker, Olaf. *Where the Buffaloes Begin*, 1397

Baker, Richard (jt. comp.). *The Star-Spangled Banana and Other Revolutionary Riddles*, 1844

Baldwin, Ann Norris. *A Little Time*, 1140

Balian, Lorna. *Amelia's Nine Lives*, 19

The Animal, 327

Bah! Humbug?, 328

Humbug Potion, 608

Humbug Witch, 20

Leprechauns Never Lie, 609

The Sweet Touch, 329

Ball, Duncan. *Jeremy's Tail*, **227**

Ballard, Robert. *Exploring the Titanic*, **1102**

Ballard, Robin. *Good-bye, House*, **69**

Bancroft, Catherine, and Hannah Coale Gruenberg. *Felix's Hat*, **70**

Bang, Molly. *Dawn*, 869

The Goblins Giggle and Other Stories, 1655

The Paper Crane, 610

Tye May and the Magic Brush, 1398

Wiley and the Hairy Man, 1399

Banish, Rosalyn. *Let Me Tell You about My Baby*, 1990

Banks, Kate. *Peter and the Talking Shoes*, **228**

Banks, Lynne Reid. *The Adventures of King Midas*, **758**

The Fairy Rebel, 1141

The Indian in the Cupboard, 1272

The Magic Hare, **702**

Barber, Antonia. *Catkin*, **590**

Bare, Colleen Stanley. *Guinea Pigs Don't Read Books*, 1991

To Love a Dog, 1992

Baring-Gould, Cecil (jt. ed.). *The Annotated Mother Goose*, 2124

Baring-Gould, William, and Cecil Baring-Gould, eds. *The Annotated Mother Goose*, 2124

Barracca, Debra, and Sal Barracca. *The Adventures of Taxi Dog*, **404**

A Taxi Dog Christmas, **229**

Barracca, Sal (jt. author). *The Adventures of Taxi Dog*, **404**

A Taxi Dog Christmas, **229**

Barre, Shelley A. *Chive*, **804**

Barrett, Judi. *Animals Should Definitely Not Wear Clothing*, 870

Benjamin's 365 Birthdays, 330

Cloudy with a Chance of Meatballs, 871

Pickles Have Pimples, 611

Barrol, Grady. *The Little Book of Anagrams*, 1745

Barstow, Barbara, and Judith Riggle. *Beyond Picture Books*, 2125

Barth, Edna. *Jack-O'-Lantern*, 1400

Barton, Byron. *Applebet Story*, 331

Building a House, 1993

Buzz Buzz Buzz, 21

Bartone, Elisa. *Peppe the Lamplighter*, **405**

Bash, Barbara. *Desert Giant*, 1994

Shadows of Night, **1103**

Tree of Life, **1104**

Urban Roosts, **1105**

Basile, Giambattista. *Petrosinella*, 1401

Bate, Lucy. *Little Rabbit's Loose Tooth*, 332

Bates, Katharine Lee. *America the Beautiful*, **1265**

Bauer, Caroline Feller. *Celebrations*, 2126

Handbook for Storytellers, 2161

My Mom Travels a Lot, 612

Presenting Reader's Theater, 2162

This Way to Books, 2127

Too Many Books, 333

Windy Day, 1746

Bauer, Caroline Feller (comp.). *Thanksgiving*, **1266**

Bauer, Marion Dane. *On My Honor*, 1273

A Question of Trust, **805**

Baum, Arline, and Joseph Baum. *Opt*, 1044

Baum, Joseph (jt. author). *Opt*, 1044

Baumgartner, Barbara. *Crocodile! Crocodile!*, **1058**

Bawden, Nina. *Humbug*, **703**

Bayer, Jane. *A My Name Is Alice*, 334

Baylor, Byrd. *Amigo*, 613

The Best Town in the World, 872

Everybody Needs a Rock, 873

Beatty, Jerome. *Matthew Looney's Invasion of the Earth*, 1142

Beatty, Patricia. *That's One Ornery Orphan*, 1274

Begay, Shonto. *Ma'ii and Cousin Horned Toad*, **865**

Behn, Harry. *Trees*, **406**

Bell, Anthea (reteller). *The Bremen Town Musicians*, 1487

The Emperor's New Clothes, 863

Bell, Anthea (trans.). *The Bremen Town Musicians*, **931**

Bellaits, John. *The House with a Clock in Its Walls*, 1143

The Treasure of Alpheus Winterborn, 1275

Bellows, Cathy. *The Grizzly Sisters*, **230**

Belpré, Pura. *Oté*, 1402

Bemelmans, Ludwig. *Madeline's Rescue*, 335

Benet, Sula (jt. comp.). *The American Riddle Book*, 1978

Benjamin, Alan. *A Nickel Buys a Rhyme*, **1267**

Rat-a-Tat, Pitter Pat, 22

Benjamin, Alan (adapt.). *Appointment*, **830**

Benjamin, Saragail Katzman. *My Dog Ate It*, **704**

Bennett, Anna Elizabeth. *Little Witch*, 874

Bennett, David. *One Cow Moo Moo!*, **5**

Bennett, Jill. *Teeny Tiny*, 1403

Bennett, Jill (comp.). *A Cup of Starshine*, **1268**

Spooky Poems, **1269**

Tiny Tim, 1747

Benson, Sally. *Stories of Gods and Heroes*, 1656

Benton, Robert. *Don't Ever Wish for a 7-Foot Bear*, 614

Berg, Cami. *D Is for Dolphin*, **1106**

Berger, Gilda. *Whales*, 1995

Berger, Terry. *The Turtle's Picnic*, 615

Bernhard, Emery. *How Snowshoe Hare Rescued the Sun*, **866**

The Tree That Rains, **867**

Bernstein, Joanne E., and Paul Cohen. *Creepy Crawly Critter Riddles*, 1748

What Was the Wicked Witch's Real Name?, 1749

Beskow, Elsa. *Pelle's New Suit*, 336

Bess, Clayton. *The Truth about the Moon*, 875

Bettleheim, Bruno. *The Uses of Enchantment*, 2163

Bierhorst, John. *The Woman Who Fell from the Sky*, **868**

Birch, David. *The King's Chessboard*, 1045

Birdseye, Tom. *Air Mail to the Moon*, 616

I'm Going to Be Famous, 1144

Just Call Me Stupid, **759**

Soap! Soap! Don't Forget the Soap!, **869**

Biro, Val. *Hungarian Folk-Tales*, 1657

Bishop, Claire. *The Five Chinese Brothers*, 617

Blackburn, George M., III (jt. comp.). *In the Witch's Kitchen*, 1757

My Tang's Tungled and Other Ridiculous Situations, 1759

Blackburn, Lorraine A. (jt. comp.). *In the Witch's Kitchen*, 1757

They've Discovered a Head in the Box for the Bread, 1756

Blake, Quentin. *All Join In*, **1270**

Blake, Robert J. *Dog*, **591**
  The Perfect Spot, **231**
Blathwayt, Benedict. *Stories from Firefly Island*, **407**
Blia, Xiong. *Nine-in-One, Grr! Grr!*, 1404
Blumberg, Rhoda. *The Incredible Journey of Lewis & Clark*, 1996
  Jumbo, **1107**
Blume, Judy. *Freckle Juice*, 618
  The Pain and the Great One, 619
  Superfudge, 1145
  Tales of a Fourth Grade Nothing, 1046
Blundell, Tony. *Beware of Boys*, **232**
  Joe on Sunday, 337
Bodart, Joni. *Booktalk!*, 2128
  Booktalk! 2, 2129
  Booktalk! 3, 2130
Bodecker, N. M. *"It's Raining," Said John Twaining*, 1750
  Let's Marry Said the Cherry and Other Nonsense Poems, 1751
  A Person from Britain Whose Head Was the Shape of a Mitten and Other Limericks, 1752
  Water Pennies, **1271**
Bodsworth, Nan. *A Nice Walk in the Jungle*, **233**
Boland, Janice. *Annabel*, **6**
Bond, Felicia. *Pointsettia and the Firefighters*, 338
Bond, Michael. *A Bear Called Paddington*, 1146
  Paddington's Storybook, 1147
Bonsall, Crosby. *Tell Me Some More*, 23
Booth, Barbara D. *Mandy*, **408**
Booth, David (comp.). *Doctor Knickerbocker and Other Rhymes*, **1272**
  'Til All the Stars Have Fallen, **1273**
Borden, Louise. *Caps, Hats, Socks, and Mittens*, 24
Bosma, Bette. *Fairy Tales, Fables, Legends, and Myths*, 2164
Bottner, Barbara. *Bootsie Barker Bites*, **234**
  Messy, 339
Bourgeois, Paulette. *Too Many Chickens*, **235**
Bourke, Linda. *Eye Spy*, **409**
Bowden, Joan Chase. *The Bean Boy*, 1405
  Why the Tides Ebb and Flow, 1406
Boyd, Pauline (jt. author). *I Met a Polar Bear*, 340
Boyd, Selma, and Pauline Boyd. *I Met a Polar Bear*, 340
Boynton, Sandra. *A Is for Angry*, 341
Bozzo, Maxine. *Toby in the Country, Toby in the City*, 25
Bradman, Tony. *It Came from Outer Space*, **410**
Brady, Esther Wood. *Toliver's Secret*, 1148
Brady, Irene. *Doodlebug*, 620
Brandenberg, Franz. *I Wish I Was Sick, Too*, 26
  No School Today, 342

Brandenberg, Jim. *To the Top of the World*, **1108**
Brandreth, Gyles. *Brain-Teasers and Mind-Benders*, 1997
  The Super Joke Book, 1754
Brandreth, Gyles (comp.). *The Biggest Tongue Twister Book in the World*, 1753
Branley, Franklyn M. *Shooting Stars*, **1109**
  Tornado Alert, 1998
Breneman, Bren (jt. author). *Once Upon a Time*, 2165
Breneman, Lucille, and Bren Breneman. *Once Upon a Time*, 2165
Brenner, Barbara. *A Dog I Know*, 621
  Little One Inch, 1407
  Mr. Tall and Mr. Small, 343
  A Year in the Life of Rosie Bernard, 1149
Brenner, Barbara (comp.). *The Earth Is Painted Green*, **1274**
Brenner, Martha. *Abe Lincoln's Hat*, **1110**
Brett, Jan. *The First Dog*, 622
  Goldilocks and the Three Bears, 1408
  The Mitten, 1409
  Trouble with Trolls, **236**
  The Twelve Days of Christmas, 1755
  The Wild Christmas Reindeer, **237**
Brewton, John E. (jt. comp.). *My Tang's Tungled and Other Ridiculous Situations*, 1759
  Shrieks at Midnight, 1758
Brewton, John E., and Lorraine A. Blackburn, comps. *They've Discovered a Head in the Box for the Bread*, 1756
Brewton, John E., Lorraine A. Blackburn, and George M. Blackburn, III, comps. *In the Witch's Kitchen*, 1757
Brewton, Sara, and John E. Brewton, comps. *Shrieks at Midnight*, 1758
Brewton, Sara, John E. Brewton, and G. Meredith Blackburn, III, comps. *My Tang's Tungled and Other Ridiculous Situations*, 1759
Briggs, Nancy E., and Joseph A. Wagner. *Children's Literature Through Storytelling & Drama*, 2166
Briggs, Raymond. *Jim and the Beanstalk*, 623
Briggs, Raymond (comp.). *The Mother Goose Treasury*, 1885
Brimner, Larry Dane. *Country Bear's Good Neighbor*, 27
Brink, Carol Ryrie. *The Bad Times of Irma Baumline*, 1150
  Caddie Woodlawn, 1151
Brisson, Pat. *Magic Carpet*, **411**
Brittain, Bill. *All the Money in the World*, 1152
  Devil's Donkey, 1276
  Dr. Dredd's Wagon of Wonders, 1277

Professor Popkin's Prodigious Polish, **760**
Shape-Changer, **761**
The Wish Giver, 1278
Broekel, Ray (jt. author). *The Surprise Book*, 2114
Broekel, Ray, and Laurence B. White, Jr. *Now You See It*, 1999
Brooke, L. Leslie. *The Golden Goose Book*, 1658
Brooks, Walter Rollin. *Jimmy Takes Vanishing Lessons*, 876
Brown, Bob. *How to Fool Your Friends*, 2000
Brown, Don. *Ruth Law Thrills a Nation*, **1111**
Brown, Drollene P. *Sybil Rides for Independence*, 2001
Brown, Eileen. *Tick-Tock*, **238**
Brown, Jeff. *Flat Stanley*, 624
Brown, Laurene Krasny, and Marc Brown. *Dinosaurs to the Rescue!*, **1112**
Brown, Marc. *Arthur Babysits*, **412**
Arthur Meets the President, **413**
Arthur's April Fool, 625
Arthur's Baby, 344
Arthur's Birthday, 626
Arthur's Chicken Pox, **239**
Arthur's Eyes, 345
Arthur's Halloween, 627
Arthur's Teacher Trouble, 628
Arthur's Tooth, 629
D.W. Thinks Big, **71**
Hand Rhymes, 1760
Spooky Riddles, 1761
Brown, Marc (jt. author). *Dinosaurs to the Rescue!*, **1112**
Brown, Marc (comp.). *Scared Silly*, **1275**
Brown, Marc, and Stephen Krensky. *Dinosaurs, Beware!*, 2002
Perfect Pigs, 2003
Brown, Marcia. *Cinderella*, 1410
Dick Whittington and His Cat, 1411
How, Hippo!, 28
Peter Piper's Alphabet, 1762
Stone Soup, 1412
Brown, Margaret. *The Important Book*, 630
The Runaway Bunny, 29
The Steamroller, 346
Wheel on the Chimney, 631
Brown, Paula. *Moon Jump*, **240**
Brown, Ruth A. *A Dark, Dark Tale*, 347
If at First You Do Not See, 348
Our Cat Flossie, 632
Brown, Walter R., and Norman D. Anderson. *Rescue!*, 2004
Browne, Anthony. *Bear Hunt*, 30
Changes, **241**
Gorilla, 349

Willy the Wimp, 350
Browne, Eileen. *No Problem*, **414**
Bruchac, Joseph. *The First Strawberries*, **870**
The Great Ball Game, **871**
Iroquois Stories, 1659
Native American Animal Stories, **1059**
Return of the Sun, **1060**
Bruchac, Joseph, and Jonathan London. *Thirteen Moons on Turtle's Back*, **872**
Brusca, María Cristina, and Tona Wilson. *The Blacksmith and the Devils*, **873**
The Cook and the King, **874**
When Jaguars Ate the Moon, **1061**
Brust, Beth Wagner. *Amazing Paper Cuttings of Hans Christian Andersen*, **1113**
Bucknall, Caroline. *One Bear in the Picture*, 31
Buehner, Caralyn. *A Job for Wittilda*, **242**
Bulla, Clyde Robert. *The Sword in the Tree*, 877
Bunting, Eve. *A Day's Work*, **592**
Flower Garden, **72**
Fly Away Home, **415**
Ghost's Hour, Spook's Hour, 351
The Mother's Day Mice, 32
Night of the Gargoyles, **705**
Our Teacher's Having a Baby, **243**
Scary, Scary Halloween, 352
Smoky Night, **593**
Someday a Tree, **416**
Summer Wheels, **594**
The Valentine Bears, 353
The Wall, 354
The Wednesday Surprise, 633
Burch, Robert. *Ida Early Comes Over the Mountain*, 1153
Burchardt, Nellie. *Project Cat*, 878
Burger, Douglas A. (jt. author). *The Weighty Word Book*, 1326
Burleigh, Robert. *Flight*, **1114**
Burnford, Sheila. *The Incredible Journey*, 1279
Burningham, John. *Harvey Slumfenburger's Christmas Present*, **244**
Mr. Gumpy's Outing, 33
Would You Rather . . ., 355
Burns, Clint (jt. author). *Hail to the Chief!*, **1276**
Burns, Diane, and Clint Burns. *Hail to the Chief!*, **1276**
Burns, Diane L. *Snakes Alive!*, 1763
Burroway, Janet (jt. author). *The Giant Jam Sandwich*, 730
Bursik, Rose. *Amelia's Fantastic Flight*, **417**
Burton, Marilee Robin. *Tails, Toes, Eyes, Ears, Nose*, 34
Burton, Virgina Lee. *Katy and the Big Snow*, 35
The Little House, 634

Mike Mulligan and His Steam Shovel, 36
Butterworth, Oliver. *The Enormous Egg*, 1154
Byars, Betsy. *Beans on the Roof*, 879
  Cracker Jackson, 1280
  The 18th Emergency, 1155
  McMummy, **762**
  The Midnight Fox, 1047
  The Moon and I, **1115**
  The Not-Just-Anybody Family, 1156
  The Pinballs, 1281
  The Seven Treasure Hunts, **595**
  The Summer of the Swans, 1282
  The Two-Thousand Pound Goldfish, 1283
  Wanted . . . Mud Blossom, **763**
  The Winged Colt of Casa Mia, 1048
Byrd, Robert (reteller). *The Bear and the Bird
  King*, **929**

Calhoun, Mary. *Cross-Country Cat*, 635
  Henry the Sailor Cat, **418**
  High-Wire Henry, **419**
  The Night the Monster Came, 880
Callen, Larry. *The Deadly Mandrake*, 1284
  Pinch, 1285
  Sorrow's Song, 1286
Calmenson, Stephanie. *Dinner at the Panda
  Palace*, **73**
  It Begins with an A, **74**
  The Principal's New Clothes, **420**
  Rosie, **1116**
  What Am I?, **1277**
Calmenson, Stephanie (comp.). *Never Take a Pig
  to Lunch*, 1764
Calmenson, Stephanie (jt. comp.). *The Eentsy,
  Weentsy Spider*, **1279**
  Laugh Book, 1774
  Six Sick Sheep, **1280**
  Why Did the Chicken Cross the Road?, **1281**
Calmenson, Stephanie (reteller). *The Children's
  Aesop*, **1057**
Cameron, Ann. *The Stories Julian Tells*, 881
Cameron, Polly. *"I Can't," Said the Ant*, 636
Cannon, Janell. *Stellaluna*, **245**
Caple, Kathy. *The Biggest Nose*, 356
Carey, Valerie Scho. *The Devil & Mother Crump*,
  1049
  Maggie Mab and the Bogey Beast, **875**
  Quail Song, **876**
Carle, Eric. *The Grouchy Ladybug*, 37
  A House for Hermit Crab, **246**
  The Mixed-Up Chameleon, 38
  Pancakes, Pancakes!, **247**
  Papa, Please Get the Moon for Me, 39
  The Secret Birthday Message, 40

Today Is Monday, **248**
  The Very Busy Spider, 41
  The Very Hungry Caterpillar, 42
  The Very Quiet Cricket, **75**
Carle, Eric (reteller). *Twelve Tales from Aesop*,
  1651
Carlson, Bernice Wells (comp.). *Listen! And Help
  Tell the Story*, 1765
Carlson, Nancy L. *Arnie and the New Kid*, **421**
  Louanne Pig in the Mysterious Valentine, 637
  A Visit to Grandma's, **249**
Carlson, Natalie Savage. *King of the Cats and
  Other Tales*, 1660
  Marie Louise's Heyday, 638
  The Night the Scarecrow Walked, 639
  Runaway Marie Louise, 43
  Spooky Night, 357
Carlson, Ruth Kearney. *Enrichment Ideas*, 2131
  Writing Aids Through the Grades, 2132
Carlstrom, Nancy White. *How Do You Say It
  Today, Jesse Bear?*, **76**
Carmichael, Carolyn (jt. ed.). *Literature and
  Young Children*, 2133
Carrara, Larry (jt. author). *A Moose for Jessica*,
  2111
Carrick, Carol. *Aladdin and the Wonderful Lamp*,
  1413
  Ben and the Porcupine, 640
  The Foundling, 641
  Patrick's Dinosaurs, 358
  What Happened to Patrick's Dinosaurs?, 642
Carrick, Donald. *Harald and the Giant Knight*, 882
  Harald and the Great Stag, 883
Carris, Joan. *Witch-Cat*, **706**
Carroll, Kathleen Sullivan. *One Red Rooster*, **7**
Carryl, Charles E. *The Walloping Window-Blind*,
  596
Caseley, Judith. *Dear Annie*, **250**
  Harry and Arney, **422**
  Silly Baby, 44
  Sophie and Sammy's Library Sleepover, **77**
Cassedy, Sylvia. *Behind the Attic Wall*, 1287
Cassedy, Sylvia, and Kunihiro Suetake (trans.).
  Red Dragonfly on My Shoulder, **1278**
Catling, Patrick Skene. *The Chocolate Touch*, 884
Caudill, Rebecca. *Did You Carry the Flag Today,
  Charlie?*, 643
Cauley, Lorinda Bryan. *The Cock, the Mouse and
  the Little Red Hen*, 1414
  Goldilocks and the Three Bears, 1415
  The Goose and the Golden Coins, 1416
  Jack and the Beanstalk, 1417
  Old MacDonald Had a Farm, **78**
  The Pancake Boy, 1418

Puss in Boots, 1419
The Three Little Kittens, 45
The Three Little Pigs, 1420
The Town Mouse and the Country Mouse, 1421
Treasure Hunt, **79**
Causley, Charles. *"Quack!" Said the Billy-Goat*, 46
Cazet, Denys. *December 24th*, 359
"I'm Not Sleepy," **80**
Lucky Me, 360
Cecil, Laura (comp.). *Boo!*, **1062**
Cerf, Bennett. *Bennett Cerf's Book of Riddles*, 1766
Chadwick, Tim. *Cabbage Moon*, **81**
Chambers, Dewey W. *The Oral Tradition*, 2167
Champlin, Connie, and Nancy Renfro. *Storytelling with Puppets*, 2168
Chapman, Carol. *Barney Bipple's Magic Dandelions*, 644
Herbie's Troubles, 361
The Tale of Meshka the Kvetch, 885
Chapman, Cheryl. *Pass the Fritters, Critters*, **82**
Snow on Snow on Snow, **83**
Chapman, Jean (comp.). *Cat Will Rhyme with Hat*, 1767
Charles, N. N. *What Am I?*, **84**
Charlip, Remy. *Fortunately*, 645
Harlequin and the Gift of Many Colors, 886
Charlip, Remy, and Burton Supree. *Mother, Mother, I Feel Sick, Send for the Doctor Quick, Quick, Quick*, 646
Chase, Mary. *Loretta Mason Potts*, 1157
Chase, Richard. *Grandfather Tales*, 1661
Jack Tales, 1662
Chbosky, Stacey. *Who Owns the Sun?*, 1158
Cheng, Hou-Tien. *The Six Chinese Brothers*, 1422
Cherry, Lynne. *The Armadillo from Amarillo*, **423**
The Great Kapok Tree, 647
A River Ran Wild, **1117**
Who's Sick Today?, 47
Chess, Victoria. *Alfred's Alphabet Walk*, 648
Chetwin, Grace. *Friends in Time*, **764**
Child, Lydia Maria. *Over the River and Through the Wood*, **251**
Chocolate, Deborah M. Newton. *Talk, Talk*, **877**
Choi, Sook Nyul. *Halmoni and the Picnic*, **424**
Chorao, Kay (comp.). *Mother Goose Magic*, **1382**
Christelow, Eileen. *The Five-Dog Night*, **425**
Five Little Monkeys Jumping on the Bed, 48
Five Little Monkeys Sitting in a Tree, **85**
Gertrude, the Bulldog Detective, **252**
Henry and the Dragon, 49
Henry and the Red Stripes, 362
Jerome and the Babysitter, 364
Jerome and the Witchcraft Kids, 363

Mr. Murphy's Marvelous Invention, 649
Olive and the Magic Hat, 365
Christian, Mary Blount. *April Fool*, 1423
Christiansen, Candace. *The Ice Horse*, **597**
Churchill, E. Richard. *Devilish Bets to Trick Your Friends*, 2005
Churchill, E. Richard (comp.). *The Six-Million Dollar Cucumber*, 1768
Ciardi, John. *Doodle Soup*, 1769
Fast and Slow, 1770
The Hopeful Trout and Other Limericks, 1771
You Read to Me, I'll Read to You, 1772
Clarke, Gus. *EIEIO*, **86**
Clarkson, Atelia, and Gilbert B. Cross. *World Folktales*, 2169
Cleary, Beverly. *Beezus and Ramona*, 887
The Growing-Up Feet, 50
Henry Huggins, 888
The Mouse and the Motorcycle, 1050
Petey's Bedtime Story, **253**
Ralph S. Mouse, 1051
Ramona Quimby, Age 8, 889
Ramona the Pest, 890
Ribsy, 891
Strider, **806**
Clements, Andrew. *Mother Earth's Counting Book*, **1118**
Clemesha, David (jt. author). *The Cow Buzzed*, **215**
Cleveland, David. *The April Rabbits*, 366
Cleveland, Will, and Mark Alvarez. *Yo, Millard Fillmore!*, **1119**
Clifford, Eth. *Harvey's Horrible Snake Disaster*, 1052
Clifford, Sandy. *The Roquefort Gang*, 1053
Clifton, Lucille. *The Boy Who Didn't Believe in Spring*, 650
Climo, Shirley. *The Egyptian Cinderella*, 1424
King of the Birds, 1425
The Korean Cinderella, **878**
The Match Between the Winds, **879**
Piskies, Spriggans, and Other Magical Beings, 1663
Someone Saw a Spider, 1664
Stolen Thunder, **880**
Clymer, Eleanor. *My Brother Stevie*, 1054
Coatsworth, David (jt. comp.). *The Adventures of Nanabush*, 1665
Coatsworth, Emerson, and David Coatsworth, comps. *The Adventures of Nanabush*, 1665
Cobb, Vicki, and Kathy Darling. *Bet You Can!*, 2006
Coerr, Eleanor. *Mieko and the Fifth Treasure*, **707**
Sadako, **1120**

Sadako & the Thousand Paper Cranes, 2007
Cohen, Barbara. *The Carp in the Bathtub*, 892
   Make a Wish, Molly, **598**
   Molly's Pilgrim, 893
   Thank You, Jackie Robinson, 1159
Cohen, Caron Lee. *Renata, Whizbrain and the Ghost*, 894
Cohen, Miriam. *Jim Meets the Thing*, 367
   Jim's Dog Muffins, 368
   Lost in the Museum, 369
   No Good in Art, 370
   Starring First Grade, 371
Cohen, Paul (jt. author). *Creepy Crawly Critter Riddles*, 1748
   What Was the Wicked Witch's Real Name?, 1749
Cohen, Ron. *My Dad's Baseball*, **599**
Cohn, Amy L. *From Sea to Shining Sea*, **1063**
Cohn, Janice. *I Had a Friend Named Peter*, 51
Cole, Brock. *Alpha and the Dirty Baby*, **426**
   The King at the Door, 895
   No More Baths, 52
   Nothing but a Pig, 651
Cole, Joanna. *Best Loved Folktales of the World*, 1666
   Bony-Legs, 1426
   Doctor Change, 896
   Don't Call Me Names, **254**
   Don't Tell the Whole World!, **881**
   Golly Gump Swallowed a Fly, 372
   It's Too Noisy!, **882**
   The Magic School Bus at the Waterworks, 2008
   The Magic School Bus Inside the Earth, 2009
   The Magic School Bus Inside the Human Body, 2010
   The Magic School Bus Lost in the Solar System, **1121**
   The Magic School Bus on the Ocean Floor, **1122**
   My Puppy Is Born, **1123**
Cole, Joanna (comp.). *A New Treasury of Children's Poetry*, 1773
Cole, Joanna, and Stephanie Calmenson, comps. *The Eentsy, Weentsy Spider*, **1279**
   Laugh Book, 1774
   Six Sick Sheep, **1280**
   Why Did the Chicken Cross the Road?, **1281**
Cole, Joanna, and Philip Cole. *Big Goof and Little Goof*, 373
Cole, Philip (jt. author). *Big Goof and Little Goof*, 373
Cole, Sheila. *The Dragon in the Cliff*, **807**
Cole, William. *Frances Face-Maker*, 53
Cole, William (comp.). *Beastly Boys and Ghastly Girls*, 1775
   Dinosaurs and Beasts of Yore, 1776

Good Dog Poems, 1777
   I Went to the Animal Fair, 1778
   I'm Mad at You, 1779
   Oh, Such Foolishness, 1780
   Poem Stew, 1781
   The Poetry of Horses, 1782
   A Zooful of Animals, **1282**
Coleridge, Sara. *January Brings the Snow*, 54
Coletta, Hallie (jt. author). *From A to Z*, 897
Coletta, Irene, and Hallie Coletta. *From A to Z*, 897
Collier, Christopher (jt. author). *My Brother Sam Is Dead*, 1288
Collier, James Lincoln, and Christopher Collier. *My Brother Sam Is Dead*, 1288
Colligan-Taylor, Karen (trans.). *The Grizzly Bear Family Book*, **1164**
Collodi, Carlo. *The Adventures of Pinocchio*, 1160
Columbus, Christopher. *Log of Christopher Columbus*, **1124**
Colwell, Eileen. *Storytelling*, 2170
Compton, Joanne. *Ashpet*, **883**
Compton, Joanne (jt. author). *Jack the Giant Chaser*, **884**
Compton, Kenn, and Joanne Compton. *Jack the Giant Chaser*, **884**
Compton, Patricia A. *The Terrible Eek*, **885**
Cone, Molly. *Come Back, Salmon*, **1125**
Conford, Ellen. *And This Is Laura*, 1289
   Impossible Possum, 652
   Jenny Archer, Author, 898
   A Job for Jenny Archer, 899
   Lenny Kandell, Smart Aleck, 1290
   Me and the Terrible Two, 1161
   Nibble, Nibble, Jenny Archer, **600**
   Revenge of the Incredible Dr. Rancid and His Youthful Assistant, Jeffrey, 1162
   What's Cooking, Jenny Archer?, **601**
Conger, Leslie. *Tops and Bottoms*, 1427
Conly, Jane Leslie. *Crazy Lady!*, **808**
Conover, Chris. *Mother Goose and the Sly Fox*, 1428
Conrad, Pam. *Pedro's Journal*, **809**
Cook, Joel. *The Rat's Daughter*, **886**
Cook, Scott. *The Gingerbread Boy*, 1429
Cook, Scott (comp.). *Mother Goose*, **1386**
Cooke, Trish. *So Much*, 8
Coombs, Patricia. *Dorrie and the Weather Box*, 653
   The Magician and McTree, 900
   Molly Mullett, 901
Cooney, Barbara. *Island Boy*, 1055
   Miss Rumphius, 654

Cooney, Barbara (reteller). *Little Brother and Little Sister*, 1499

Cooney, Nancy Evans. *The Blanket Had to Go*, 55
Chatterbox Jamie, **87**
Donald Says Thumbs Down, 56
Go Away Monsters, Lickety Split, **88**
The Umbrella Day, 57
The Wobbly Tooth, 374

Cooper, Melrose. *I Got a Family*, **255**

Cooper, Susan. *The Silver Cow*, 1430

Corbett, Scott. *The Donkey Planet*, 1163
The Lemonade Trick, 1056
The Limerick Trick, 1057
The Red Room Riddle, 1164

Coren, Alan. *Arthur the Kid*, 902

Corrin, Sara, and Stephen Corrin. *The Faber Book of Favourite Fairy Tales*, 1667
The Pied Piper of Hamelin, 1431

Corrin, Sara, and Stephen Corrin, comps. *Once Upon a Rhyme*, 1783

Corrin, Stephen (jt. author). *The Faber Book of Favourite Fairy Tales*, 1667
The Pied Piper of Hamelin, 1431

Corrin, Stephen (jt. comp.). *Once Upon a Rhyme*, 1783

Courlander, Harold. *The Hat-Shaking Dance*, 1668
The Piece of Fire and Other Haitian Tales, 1669

Courlander, Harold, and George Herzog. *The Cow-Tail Switch and Other West African Stories*, 1670

Cousins, Lucy (comp.). *The Little Dog Laughed and Other Nursery Rhymes*, **1384**

Coville, Bruce. *Jennifer Murdley's Toad*, **765**
Jeremy Thatcher, Dragon Hatcher, **810**
The Monster's Ring, 1165

Cowcher, Helen. *Rain Forest*, **256**
Whistling Thorn, **1126**

Cowen-Fletcher, Jane. *It Takes a Village*, **257**
Mama Zooms, **89**

Cox, David. *Bossyboots*, 655

Cox, James A. *Put Your Foot in Your Mouth and Other Silly Sayings*, 1784

Cox, Miriam. *The Magic and the Sword*, 1671

Craig, M. Jean. *The Dragon in the Clock Box*, 375

Craig, M. Jean (adapt.). *The Donkey Prince*, 1490

Credle, Ellis. *Tall Tales from the High Hills and Other Stories*, 1672

Crespo, George. *How the Sea Began*, **887**

Cresswell, Helen. *Time Out*, **708**

Crew, Linda. *Nekomah Creek*, **709**

Crews, Donald. *Freight Train*, 58
Ten Black Dots, 59

Cricket Magazine, editors of (comp.). *Cricket's Jokes, Riddles & Other Stuff*, 1785

Croll, Carolyn. *The Three Brothers*, **888**

Cross, Gilbert B. (jt. author). *World Folktales*, 2169

Cross, Helen Reader. *The Real Tom Thumb*, 2011

Crouch, Marcus. *Ivan*, **1064**
The Whole World Storybook, 1673

Crowe, Robert L. *Clyde Monster*, 60

Crowley, Michael. *New Kid on Spurwink Ave*, **258**
Shack and Back, **427**

Cullinan, Bernice E. *Literature and the Child*, 2118

Cullinan, Bernice E, and Carolyn Carmichael, eds. *Literature and Young Children*, 2133

Cummings, Pat. *C.L.O.U.D.S.*, 903

Cummings, Pat (comp.). *Talking with Artists*, **1127**

Cummings, Phil. *Goodness Gracious!*, **90**

Curtis, Foley. *The Little Book of Big Tongue Twisters*, 1786

Cushman, Doug. *The ABC Mystery*, **428**
Possum Stew, **91**

Cutchins, Judy (jt. author). *Andy Bear*, 2056

Cutler, Jane. *Darcy and Gran Don't Like Babies*, **259**
No Dogs Allowed, **602**

Cuyler, Margery. *Shadow's Baby*, 61
That's Good! That's Bad!, **92**

Czernecki, Stefan, and Timothy Rhodes. *The Singing Snake*, **889**

Dahl, Roald. *BFG*, 1166
Boy, 2012
Charlie and the Chocolate Factory, 1058
Danny, the Champion of the World, 1291
The Enormous Crocodile, 656
Esio Trot, **710**
The Fantastic Mr. Fox, 904
James and the Giant Peach, 1059
The Magic Finger, 905
Matilda, 1292
Roald Dahl's Revolting Rhymes, 1787
The Witches, 1167
The Wonderful Story of Henry Sugar and Six More, 1293

Dakos, Kalli. *If You're Not Here, Please Raise Your Hand*, **1283**

Dalgliesh, Alice. *The Bears on Hemlock Mountain*, 657

Daly, Niki. *Not So Fast, Songololo*, 62

Daly, Niki (jt. author). *Somewhere in Africa*, **509**

Damrell, Liz. *With the Wind*, **429**

Danziger, Paula. *Amber Brown Is Not a Crayon*, **603**

Darling, Kathy (jt. author). *Bet You Can!*, 2006

Dasent, George Webbe. *The Cat on the Dovrefell*, 1432

East o' the Sun & West o' the Moon, **890**, 1433

Daugherty, James. *Andy and the Lion*, 658

D'Aulaire, Edgar Parin (jt. author). *Benjamin Franklin*, 2013

D'Aulaire's Book of Greek Myths, 1674

D'Aulaire's Trolls, 1434

D'Aulaire, Ingri, and Edgar Parin D'Aulaire. *Benjamin Franklin*, 2013

D'Aulaire's Book of Greek Myths, 1674

D'Aulaire's Trolls, 1434

Davidson, Margaret. *Nine True Dolphin Stories*, 2014

Seven True Dog Stories, 2015

Davis, Gibbs. *Katy's First Haircut*, 63

Davis, Hubert (ed.). *A January Fog Will Freeze a Hog and Other Weather Folklore*, 2016

Day, Alexandra. *Frank and Ernest*, 906

Day, David. *The Sleeper*, **891**

Dayrell, Elphinstone. *Why the Sun and Moon Live in the Sky*, 1435

Dee, Ruby. *Two Ways to Count to Ten*, 1436

DeFelice, Cynthia. *The Dancing Skeleton*, 1437

Devil's Bridge, **766**

Lostman's River, **811**

Mule Eggs, **604**

Weasel, **812**

Degen, Bruce. *Jamberry*, 64

DeJong, Meindert. *Hurry Home, Candy*, 1060

The Wheel on the School, 1168

Delamar, Gloria T. (comp.). *Children's Counting Out Rhymes, Fingerplays, Jump-Rope and Bounce-Ball Chants and Other Rhymes*, 1788

Delton, Judy. *Angel in Charge*, 1061

I'm Telling You Now, 65

Two Good Friends, 66

Demarest, Chris L. *Lindbergh*, **1128**

Morton and Sidney, 67

No Peas for Nellie, 68

Demi. *A Chinese Zoo*, 1675

Demi's Reflective Fables, 1676

Dragon Kites and Dragonflies, 1789

The Empty Pot, **892**

The Firebird, **893**

The Magic Tapestry, **894**

Demi (comp.). *In the Eyes of the Cat*, **1284**

Demuth, Patricia Brennan. *Cradles in the Trees*, **1129**

The Ornery Morning, **260**

Those Amazing Ants, **1130**

dePaola, Tomie. *The Art Lesson*, 907

Big Anthony and the Magic Ring, 908

Charlie Needs a Cloak, 376

The Cloud Book, 2017

The Comic Adventures of Old Mother Hubbard and Her Dog, 1438

Fin M'Coul, the Giant of Knockmary Hill, 1439

Jamie O'Rourke and the Big Potato, **895**

The Legend of the Bluebonnet, 1440

The Legend of the Indian Paintbrush, 1441

Merry Christmas, Strega Nona, 909

The Mysterious Giant of Barletta, 1442

The Popcorn Book, 2018

The Prince of the Dolomites, 1443

The Quicksand Book, 2019

Strega Nona, 1444

Strega Nona Meets Her Match, **430**

Tom, **431**

Tomie dePaola's Book of Poems, 1790

Tony's Bread, **896**

dePaola, Tomie (comp.). *Tomie dePaola's Mother Goose*, 1892

DePaolo, Paula. *Rosie & the Yellow Ribbon*, **261**

De Regniers, Beatrice Schenk. *It Does Not Say Meow and Other Animal Riddle Rhymes*, 1791

Little Sister and the Month Brothers, 1445

May I Bring a Friend?, 69

This Big Cat and Other Cats I've Known, 1793

De Regniers, Beatrice Schenk (ed.). *Sing a Song of Popcorn*, 1792

Desbarats, Peter. *Gabrielle and Selena*, 659

Devlin, Harry, and Wende Devlin. *Cranberry Thanksgiving*, 660

Old Witch Rescues Halloween, 661

Devlin, Wende (jt. author). *Cranberry Thanksgiving*, 660

Old Witch Rescues Halloween, 661

De Vries, Maggie (jt. author). *Once Upon a Golden Apple*, 478

Dewey, Ariane (jt. author). *A Crocodile's Tale*, 1393

De Wit, Dorothy. *Children's Faces Looking Up*, 2171

De Zutter, Hank. *Who Says a Dog Goes Bow-Wow?*, **1131**

Dillon, Barbara. *The Beast in the Bed*, 70

A Mom by Magic, **767**

Mrs. Tooey & the Terrible Toxic Tar, 1062

The Teddy Bear Tree, 662

What's Happened to Harry?, 910

DiSalvo-Ryan, DyAnne. *Uncle Willie and the Soup Kitchen*, **432**

Dixon, Ann. *How Raven Brought Light to People*, **897**

Dodds, Bill. *My Sister Annie*, **768**

Dodds, Dayle Ann. *The Color Box*, **93**

Do Bunnies Talk?, **262**

Wheel Away!, 71

Dodds, Siobhan. *Grandpa Bud*, **9**

Dodson, Peter. *An Alphabet of Dinosaurs*, **1132**

Doherty, Berlie. *Snowy*, **263**

Street Child, **813**

Domanska, Janina. *King Krakus and the Dragon*, 1446

Little Red Hen, 1447

The Turnip, 1448

Donaldson, Julia. *A Squash and a Squeeze*, **264**

Donnelly, Judy. *True-Life Treasure Hunts*, 2020

Dooley, Norah. *Everybody Cooks Rice*, **433**

Dorris, Michael. *Morning Girl*, **814**

Dorros, Arthur. *Abuela*, **434**

Ant Cities, 2021

Follow the Water from Brook to Ocean, **1133**

This Is My House, **435**

Doty, Roy (comp.). *Tinkerbell Is a Ding-a-Ling*, 1794

Doubilet, Anne. *Under the Sea from A to Z*, **1134**

Douglass, Barbara. *Good As New*, **72**

The Great Town and Country Bicycle Balloon Chase, 73

Dragonwagon, Crescent. *I Hate My Brother Harry*, 663

Drescher, Henrik. *Simon's Book*, 664

Dreyer, Sharon Spredemann. *The Bookfinder*, 2134

Drummond, V. H. *Phewtus the Squirrel*, 74

Drury, Roger W. *The Champion of Merrimack County*, 1169

The Finches' Fabulous Furnace, 1170

Du Bois, William Pène. *The Giant*, 1294

Lazy Tommy Pumpkinhead, 911

Lion, 912

The Twenty-One Balloons, 1295

Duff, Maggie. *Rum Pum Pum*, 1449

Duffey, Betsy. *A Boy in the Doghouse*, **605**

Coaster, **769**

The Gadget War, **606**

The Math Whiz, **607**

Duffy, Dee Dee. *Barnyard Tracks*, **10**

Dugan, Barbara. *Loop the Loop*, **608**

Duke, Kate. *Aunt Isabel Tells a Good One*, **436**

Guinea Pigs Far and Near, 75

Seven Froggies Went to School, 377

Dupré, Judith. *The Mouse Bride*, **898**

Duvoisin, Roger. *Petunia*, 378

Dyke, John. *Pigwig*, 379

Early, Margaret. *Sleeping Beauty*, **899**

William Tell, **900**

Earth Works Group. *50 Simple Things Kids Can Do to Save the Earth*, **1135**

Edens, Cooper (comp.). *The Glorious Mother Goose*, 1879

Edwards, Frank B. *Mortimer Mooner Stopped Taking a Bath*, **94**

Edwards, Julie. *The Last of the Really Great Whangdoodles*, 1063

Edwards, Margaret A. *The Fair Garden and the Swarm of Beasts*, 2135

Edwards, Richard. *Moon Frog*, **1285**

Edwards, Roberta. *Five Silly Fishermen*, **901**

Ehlert, Lois. *Circus*, **95**

Color Farm, **96**

Color Zoo, 76

Eating the Alphabet, 77

Feathers for Lunch, **265**

Fish Eyes, **97**

Growing Vegetable Soup, 78

Moon Rope, **902**

Ehrlich, Amy. *Parents in the Pigpen, Pigs in the Tub*, **266**

Ehrlich, Amy (reteller). *Rapunzel*, **923**

Thumbelina, 864

The Wild Swans, 1040

Eichenberg, Fritz. *Ape in a Cape*, 79

Dancing in the Moon, 380

Eisen, Armand. *Goldilocks and the Three Bears*, 1450

Eisenberg, Lisa (jt. author). *Batty Riddles*, **1304**

Buggy Riddles, 1809

Snakey Riddles, **1305**

Spacey Riddles, **1306**

Eldin, Peter. *The Trickster's Handbook*, **1136**

Eliot, T. S. *Mr. Mistoffelees with Mungojerrie and Rumpelteazer*, **1286**

Old Possum's Book of Practical Cats, 1795

Elkin, Benjamin. *The Loudest Noise in the World*, 381

Ellis, Anne. *Dabble Duck*, 382

Emberley, Barbara. *Drummer Hoff*, 80

Emberley, Ed. *Go Away, Big Green Monster!*, **98**

The Wing on a Flea, 81

Emberley, Michael. *Ruby*, **437**

Welcome Back Sun, **438**

Embry, Margaret. *The Blue-Nosed Witch*, 913

Emrich, Duncan (comp.). *The Hodgepodge Book*, 1796

Engel, Diana. *Eleanor, Arthur, and Claire*, **267**

Fishing, **268**

Epstein, Beryl (jt. author). *Secret in a Sealed Bottle*, 2022

Epstein, Sam, and Beryl Epstein. *Secret in a Sealed Bottle*, 2022

Erickson, Paul (jt. author). *Dive to the Coral Reefs*, 2110

Erickson, Russell E. *A Toad for Tuesday*, 665

Ericsson, Jennifer A. *No Milk!*, **99**

Ernst, Lisa Campbell. *Ginger Jumps*, **269**
  The Luckiest Kid on the Planet, **439**
  Squirrel Park, **440**
  Walter's Tail, **270**
  When Bluebell Sang, 383
  Zinnia and Dot, **271**

Esbensen, Barbara Juster. *Cold Stars and Fireflies*, 1797
  Great Northern Diver, **1137**
  The Star Maiden, 1451
  Who Shrank My Grandmother's House?, **1287**

Esterl, Arnica. *The Fine Round Cake*, **903**

Estes, Eleanor. *The Hundred Dresses*, 914

Etra, Jonathan, and Stephanie Spinner. *Aliens for Breakfast*, 915

Ets, Marie Hall. *Talking without Words*, 82

Evans, Dilys (comp.). *Monster Soup and Other Spooky Poems*, **1288**

Evans, Katie. *Hunky Dory Ate It*, **100**

Everett, Gwen. *John Brown*, **1138**

Everitt, Betsy. *Frida the Wondercat*, 384
  Mean Soup, **101**

Facklam, Margery. *And Then There Was One*, **1139**

Falwell, Cathryn. *Clowning Around*, **272**
  Feast for 10, **11**
  The Letter Jesters, **1140**

Farley, Walter. *The Black Stallion*, 1064

Farrell, Kate (jt. comp.). *Talking to the Sun*, 1849

Fatchen, Max. *The Country Mail Is Coming*, **1289**

Fatio, Louise. *The Happy Lion*, 385

Faulkner, Matt. *The Amazing Voyage of Jackie Grace*, 666

Feagles, Anita. *Casey the Utterly Impossible Horse*, 916

Feelings, Muriel. *Jambo Means Hello*, 1798

Feldman, Judy. *The Alphabet in Nature*, **102**

Felt, Sue. *Rosa-Too-Little*, 83

Fenner, Carol. *Randall's Wall*, **815**

Fenton, Edward. *The Big Yellow Balloon*, 667

Ferguson, Alane. *That New Pet!*, 386

Ferris, Jeri. *Go Free or Die*, **1141**

Field, Eugene. *The Gingham Dog and the Calico Cat*, **103**

Fife, Dale. *North of Danger*, 1296
  Who's in Charge of Lincoln?, 917

Finger, Charles. *Tales from Silver Lands*, 1677

Fisher, Leonard Everett. *Cyclops*, **904**
  The Great Wall of China, 2023

Theseus and the Minotaur, 1452

Fisk, Nicholas. *Grinny*, 1297

Fitzgerald, John D. *The Great Brain*, 1171

Fitzhugh, Louise. *Harriet the Spy*, 1298

Flack, Marjorie. *Angus and the Cat*, 84
  Angus and the Ducks, 85
  Angus Lost, 86
  Ask Mr. Bear, 87
  The Story about Ping, 387
  Walter the Lazy Moose, 668

Fleischman, Paul. *Finzel the Farsighted*, 1065
  The Half-a-Moon Inn, 1299
  Joyful Noise, 1799

Fleischman, Sid. *By the Great Horn Spoon*, 1300
  The Ghost in the Noonday Sun, 1301
  The Ghost on Saturday Night, 918
  Jingo Django, 1302
  McBroom Tells the Truth, 1066
  Mr. Mysterious's Secrets of Magic, 2024
  The Whipping Boy, 1172

Fleming, Denise. *Barnyard Banter*, **12**
  Count!, **13**
  In the Small, Small Pond, **104**
  Lunch, **14**

Fleming, Susan. *Trapped on the Golden Flyer*, 1173

Flora, James. *Grandpa's Ghost Stories*, 919
  Grandpa's Witched-Up Christmas, 920
  The Great Green Turkey Creek Monster, 921
  The Joking Man, 922
  Leopold the See-Through Crumbpicker, 669
  Little Hatchy Hen, 923
  My Friend Charlie, 924
  Sherwood Walks Home, 88

Florian, Douglas. *Beast Feast*, **1290**
  Bing Bang Boing, **1291**
  Monster Motel, **1292**

Flournoy, Valerie. *The Patchwork Quilt*, 925

Folsom, Marcia (jt. author). *Easy as Pie*, 670

Folsom, Michael, and Marcia Folsom. *Easy as Pie*, 670

Ford, Miela. *Little Elephant*, **15**

Foreman, Michael. *Cat and Canary*, 388
  War Game, **816**

Foreman, Michael (comp.). *Michael Foreman's Mother Goose*, **1385**

Forest, Heather. *The Woman Who Flummoxed the Fairies*, 1453

Forrester, Victoria. *The Magnificent Moo*, 89

Foster, John (comp.). *Let's Celebrate*, **1293**

Foster, John (ed.). *A First Poetry Book*, 1800

Fowler, Susi Gregg. *When Summer Ends*, 90

Fox, Dan (ed.). *Go In and Out the Window*, 1801

Fox, Mem. *Hattie and the Fox*, 91
  Koala Lou, 389

Shoes from Grandpa, **105**

Fox, Paula. *Monkey Island*, **817**

Frank, John. *Odds 'N' Ends Alvy*, **441**

Frank, Josette (comp.). *Snow Toward Evening*, **1294**

Frascino, Edward. *My Cousin the King*, 390

Fraser, Mary Ann. *On Top of the World*, **1143**
    One Giant Leap, **1142**

Freedman, Florence B. *It Happened in Chelm*, **905**

Freedman, Russell. *Buffalo Hunt*, 2025
    Children of the Wild West, 2026
    Immigrant Kids, 2027
    Lincoln, 2028

Freeman, Don. *Beady Bear*, 92
    Bearymore, 391
    Corduroy, 93
    Dandelion, 392
    Hattie the Backstage Bat, 393
    Mop Top, 94
    Norman the Doorman, 671
    A Pocket for Corduroy, 95
    Quiet! There's a Canary in the Library, 96
    A Rainbow of My Own, 97

French, Vivian. *Why the Sea Is Salt*, **906**

Friedman, Ina R. *How My Parents Learned to Eat*, 672

Friedman, Mel (jt. author). *The Poof Point*, **851**
    The Tiny Parents, **794**

Friedrich, Otto (jt. author). *The Easter Bunny That Overslept*, 394

Friedrich, Priscilla, and Otto Friedrich. *The Easter Bunny That Overslept*, 394

Fritz, Jean. *And Then What Happened, Paul Revere?*, 2029
    Around the World in a Hundred Years, **1144**
    Can't You Make Them Behave, King George?, 2030
    The Double Life of Pocahontas, 2031
    Shh! We're Writing the Constitution, 2032
    What's the Big Idea, Ben Franklin?, 2033
    Where Do You Think You're Going, Christopher Columbus?, 2034
    Who's That Stepping on Plymouth Rock?, 2035

Gabler, Mirko. *Tall, Wide, and Sharp-Eye*, **907**

Gackenbach, Dick. *Alice's Special Room*, **106**
    Arabella and Mr. Crack, 1454
    Beauty, Brave and Beautiful, 395
    Claude Has a Picnic, **16**
    Dog for a Day, 396
    Harry and the Terrible Whatzit, 98
    Harvey the Foolish Pig, 397
    Hurray for Hattie Rabbit, 99
    King Wacky, 673

Mag the Magnificent, 398

Mighty Tree, **1145**

Poppy, the Panda, 100

Tiny for a Day, **273**

What's Claude Doing?, 101

Where Are Momma, Poppa, and Sister June?, **274**

Gaeddert, Lou Ann. *Noisy Nancy Norris*, 102

Gag, Wanda. *The Funny Thing*, 103
    Millions of Cats, 104

Gage, Wilson. *Cully Cully and the Bear*, 399

Gal, Laszlo. *Prince Ivan and the Firebird*, **908**

Galbraith, Kathryn O. *Laura Charlotte*, 105
    Waiting for Jennifer, 400

Galbraith, Richard. *Reuben Runs Away*, 106

Galdone, Joanna. *The Little Girl and the Big Bear*, 1455
    The Tailypo, 1456

Galdone, Joanna, and Paul Galdone. *Gertrude the Goose Who Forgot*, 107

Galdone, Paul. *The Amazing Pig*, 1457
    Cinderella, 1458
    The Gingerbread Boy, 1459
    The Greedy Old Fat Man, 1460
    Henny Penny, 1461
    The History of Mother Twaddle and the Marvelous Achievements of Her Son, Jack, 1462
    King of the Cats, 1463
    The Little Red Hen, 1464
    The Magic Porridge Pot, 1465
    The Monkey and the Crocodile, 1466
    The Monster and the Tailor, 1467
    Old Mother Hubbard and Her Dog, 1468
    The Old Woman and Her Pig, 1469
    Over in the Meadow, 108
    Puss in Boots, 1470
    The Teeny-Tiny Woman, 1471
    The Three Bears, 1472
    The Three Billy Goats Gruff, 1473
    The Three Little Pigs, 1474
    The Three Sillies, 1475
    What's in Fox's Sack?, 1476

Galdone, Paul (jt. author). *Gertrude the Goose Who Forgot*, 107

Galdone, Paul (reteller). *The Elves and the Shoemaker*, 1491
    Three Aesop Fox Fables, 1650

Gammell, Stephen. *Once upon MacDonald's Farm*, 401

Gannett, Ruth Stiles. *My Father's Dragon*, 674

Gantos, Jack. *Greedy Greeny*, 109
    Rotten Ralph, 402

Gardiner, John Reynolds. *Stone Fox*, 1067
    Top Secret, 1303

Gardner, Beau. *Guess What?*, 110

Have You Ever Seen . . .?, 403

The Look Again . . . and Again, and Again, and Again Book, 675

Gardner, Jane Mylum. *Henry Moore*, **1146**

Garfield, James B. *Follow My Leader*, 1174

Garland, Michael. *My Cousin Katie*, **17**

Garland, Sherry. *The Lotus Seed*, **609**

Why Ducks Sleep on One Leg, **909**

Garner, Alan. *A Bag of Moonshine*, 1678

Jack and the Beanstalk, **910**

Once Upon a Time, Though It Wasn't in Your Time, and It Wasn't in My Time, and It Wasn't in Anybody's Time. . . ., **1065**

Garrett, Helen. *Angelo the Naughty One*, 676

Garrigue, Sheila. *Between Friends*, 1175

Garrison, Webb. *Why Didn't I Think of That?*, 2036

Garson, Eugenia (comp.). *The Laura Ingalls Wilder Songbook*, 1802

Gates, Doris. *Lord of the Sky*, 1679

Gates, Frieda. *Owl Eyes*, **911**

Gatti, Anne. *Tales from the African Plains*, **1066**

Gatti, Anne (reteller). *Aesop's Fables*, **1054**

Gauch, Patricia Lee. *This Time, Tempe Wick?*, 926

Gay, Michael. *The Christmas Wolf*, 404

Gelman, Rita Golden. *I Went to the Zoo*, **275**

Gennaro, Joseph (jt. author). *Small Worlds Close Up*, 2043

George, Jean Craighead. *The First Thanksgiving*, **1147**

Julie of the Wolves, 1304

My Side of the Mountain, 1176

George, William T. *Box Turtle at Long Pond*, 2037

Geraghty, Paul. *The Hunter*, **442**

Slobcat, **107**

Geras, Adèle. *My Grandmother's Stories*, **1067**

Gerberg, Mort. *Geographunny*, **1295**

Geringer, Laura. *A Three Hat Day*, 111

Gerler, William R. (comp.). *A Pack of Riddles*, 1803

Gerrard, Roy. *Rosie and the Rustlers*, **610**

Sir Francis Drake, 2038

Gershator, Phillis. *Rata-Pata-Scata-Fata*, **108**

Gerson, Mary-Joan. *How Night Came from the Sea*, **912**

Why the Sky Is Far Away, **913**

Gerstein, Mordicai. *Arnold of the Ducks*, 677

Follow Me!, 112

William, Where Are You?, 113

Getz, Arthur. *Humphrey, the Dancing Pig*, 405

Getz, David. *Almost Famous*, **818**

Thin Air, **819**

Gibbons, Gail. *From Seed to Plant*, **1148**

Wolves, **1149**

Giblin, James Cross. *George Washington*, **1150**

Giff, Patricia Reilly. *Happy Birthday, Ronald Morgan!*, 406

Matthew Jackson Meets the Wall, **611**

Show Time at the Polk Street School, **1151**

Today Was a Terrible Day, 678

The Winter Worm Business, 1177

Gillespie, John T. *More Juniorplots*, 2136

Gillespie, John T., and Diana Lembo. *Introducing Books*, 2137

Juniorplots, 2138

Gillespie, John T., and Corinne J. Naden, eds. *Best Books for Children*, 2139

Gilliland, Judith Heide. *River*, **1152**

Gilliland, Judith Heide (jt. author). *The Day of Ahmed's Secret*, **616**

Sami and the Time of the Troubles, **713**

Gilman, Phoebe. *Something from Nothing*, **914**

Gilson, Jamie. *Dial Leroi Rupert, D.J.*, 1178

Harvey the Beer Can King, 1179

Ginsburg, Mirra. *The Chick and the Duckling*, 114

The Chinese Mirror, 1477

The Fisherman's Son, 1478

The Lazies, 1680

The Magic Stove, 1479

Mushroom in the Rain, 115

The Night It Rained Pancakes, 1480

Three Rolls and One Doughnut, 1681

The Twelve Clever Brothers and Other Fools, 1682

Gipson, Fred. *Old Yeller*, 1180

Gish, Lillian, and Selma Lanes. *An Actor's Life for Me!*, 2039

Glaser, Byron (jt. author). *Action Alphabet*, 758

Glazer, Tom. *On Top of Spaghetti*, 679

Glazer, Tom (comp.). *Eye Winker, Tom Tinker, Chin Chopper*, 1804

The Mother Goose Songbook, **1387**

Tom Glazer's Treasury of Songs for Children, 1805

Goble, Paul. *Buffalo Woman*, 1481

Crow Chief, **915**

Dream Wolf, **443**

Her Seven Brothers, 1482

Iktomi and the Boulder, 1483

Love Flute, **916**

Goffin, Josse. *Oh!*, **109**

Goldberg, Rube. *The Best of Rube Goldberg*, 2040

Goldstein, Bobbye S. (comp.). *Bear in Mind*, **1296**

Birthday Rhymes, Special Times, **1297**

Inner Chimes, **1298**

What's on the Menu?, **1299**

Golenbock, Peter. *Teammates*, **1153**

Gonzalez, Lucie M. *The Bossy Gallito*, **917**

Goodall, Jane. *The Chimpanzee Family Book*, 2041

Goode, Diane. *Diane Goode's Book of Scary Stories & Songs*, **1068**

Diane Goode's Book of Silly Stories and Songs, **1069**

Goodsell, Jane. *Toby's Toe*, 407

Goodspeed, Peter. *A Rhinoceros Wakes Me Up in the Morning*, 116

Gordon, Gaelyn. *Duckat*, **110**

Gordon, Jeffie Ross. *Hide and Shriek*, **1300**

Six Sleepy Sheep, **111**

Two Badd Babies, **112**

Gormley, Beatrice. *Fifth-Grade Magic*, 1181

Mail-Order Wings, 1182

Gould, Deborah. *Aaron's Shirt*, 117

Gounaud, Karen Jo (comp.). *A Very Mice Joke Book*, 1806

Graeber, Charlotte. *Mustard*, 927

Graham, Joan Bransfield. *Splish Splash*, **1301**

Graham, Margaret Bloy. *Benjy and the Barking Bird*, 118

Graham, Thomas. *Mr. Bear's Chair*, 119

Grahame, Kenneth. *The Wind in the Willows*, 1305

Gramatky, Hardie. *Hercules*, 120

Grant, Joan. *The Monster That Grew Small*, 1484

Graves, Robert. *The Big Green Book*, 680

Gray, Libba Moore. *Small Green Snake*, **113**

Gray, Nigel. *A Balloon for Grandad*, 121

Greaves, Nick. *When Lion Could Fly and Other Tales from Africa*, **1070**

Green, John F. *Alice and the Birthday Giant*, 408

Green, Melinda. *Rachel's Recital*, 928

Green, Norma B. *The Hole in the Dike*, 409

Green, Phyllis. *Chucky Bellman Was So Bad*, **444**

Greenburg, Dan. *Young Santa*, **770**

Greene, Bette. *Philip Hall Likes Me. I Reckon, Maybe*, 1183

Greene, Carol. *The Old Ladies Who Liked Cats*, **445**

The Thirteen Days of Halloween, 681

Greene, Ellin. *Billy Beg and His Bull*, **918**

Clever Cooks, 1683

The Legend of the Cranberry, **919**

Greene, Ellin (jt. author). *Storytelling*, 2160

Greene, Jacqueline Dembar. *What His Father Did*, **920**

Greenfield, Eloise. *Grandpa's Face*, 410

Honey, I Love, 1807

Me as Neesie, 411

Under the Sunday Tree, 1808

Greenspan, Adele Aron. *Daddies*, **114**

Greenwald, Sheila. *The Atrocious Two*, 1184

Rosy Cole Discovers America!, **711**

Greer, Gery, and Bob Ruddick. *Max and Me and the Time Machine*, 1306

Max and Me and the Wild West, 1307

Gregg, Andy. *Great Rabbit and the Long-Tailed Wildcat*, **921**

Gregory, Valiska. *Babysitting for Benjamin*, **276**

Gretz, Susanna. *It's Your Turn, Roger!*, 412

Teddy Bears Cure a Cold, 413

Grifalconi, Ann. *The Village of Round and Square Houses*, 1485

Griffin, Judith Berry. *Phoebe and the General*, 2042

Griffith, Helen V. *Emily and the Enchanted Frog*, **446**

Grandaddy's Place, 682

Plunk's Dreams, 122

Grillone, Lisa, and Joseph Gennaro. *Small Worlds Close Up*, 2043

Grimes, Nikki. *Meet Danitra Brown*, **1302**

Grimm, Jacob. *The Bear and the Bird King*, **929**

The Bearskinner, 1486

The Bremen Town Musicians, **925**, **931**, 1487

The Brothers Grimm Popular Folk Tales, 1684

Cinderella, 1488

The Devil with the Three Golden Hairs, 1489

The Donkey Prince, 1490

The Elves and the Shoemaker, 1491

Fairy Tales and the Brothers Grimm, 1685

The Fisherman and His Wife, 1492

The Frog Prince, **932**, 1493

The Glass Mountain, 1494

Grimm's Fairy Tales, 1686

Hans in Luck, 1495

Hansel and Gretel, **926**, 1496, 1497

Iron John, **928**

Jorinda and Joringel, 1498

The Juniper Tree, 1687

Little Brother and Little Sister, 1499

Little Red Cap, 1500

Little Red Riding Hood, 1501

Mother Holly, 1502

Nanny Goat and the Seven Little Kids, **924**

One Gift Deserves Another, **927**

Rapunzel, **923**, 1503

Rumpelstiltskin, 1504, **922**

The Sleeping Beauty, 1505

Snow White, 1506

The Table, the Donkey and the Stick, 1507

Tales from Grimm, 1688

Thorn Rose, 1508

The Twelve Dancing Princesses, **930**, 1509

The Twelve Dancing Princesses and Other Tales from Grimm, 1689

The Valiant Little Tailor, 1510

The Water of Life, 1511
The Wolf and the Seven Little Kids, 1512
Grossman, Bill. *Tommy at the Grocery Store*, 414
Grossman, Joan Adess (jt. author). *Clara's Story*, 2054
Grover, Max. *The Accidental Zucchini*, **277**
Gruenberg, Hannah Coale (jt. author). *Felix's Hat*, **70**
Gryski, Camilla. *Cat's Cradle, Owl's Eyes*, 2044
Hands On, Thumbs Up, **1154**
Guarino, Deborah. *Is Your Mama a Llama?*, 123
Guback, Georgia. *Luka's Quilt*, **278**
Guernsey, Joann Bren (ed.). *To the Top of the World*, **1108**
Guiberson, Brenda. *Cactus Hotel*, **1155**
Guralnick, Elissa S. (jt. author). *The Weighty Word Book*, 1326
Guthrie, Marjorie Mazia (jt. author). *Woody's 20 Grow Big Songs*, **1303**
Guthrie, Woody, and Marjorie Mazia Guthrie. *Woody's 20 Grow Big Songs*, **1303**
Gwynne, Fred. *A Chocolate Moose for Dinner*, 1068
Pondlarker, **447**

Haas, Dorothy F. *Tink in a Tangle*, 929
Haas, Jessie. *Chipmunk!*, **115**
Hadathi, Mwenye. *See* Mwenye Hadathi
Hague, Kathleen, and Michael Hague. *East of the Sun and West of the Moon*, 1513
The Man Who Kept House, 1514
Hague, Michael (jt. author). *East of the Sun and West of the Moon*, 1513
The Man Who Kept House, 1514
Hague, Michael (comp.). *Mother Goose*, 1884
Hague, Michael (sel.). *Aesop's Fables*, 1642
Hahn, Mary Downing. *Time for Andrew*, **820**
Hale, Lucretia. *The Lady Who Put Salt in Her Coffee*, 930
Hale, Sarah Josepha Buell. *Mary Had a Little Lamb*, **116, 117,** 127
Haley, Gail E. *Dream Peddler*, **612**
Jack and the Bean Tree, 1515
Jack and the Fire Dragon, 1516
Puss in Boots, **933**
A Story, a Story, 1517
Hall, Donald. *I Am the Dog, I Am the Cat*, **448**
Ox-Cart Man, 931
Hall, Katy, and Lisa Eisenberg. *Batty Riddles*, **1304**
Buggy Riddles, 1809
Snakey Riddles, **1305**
Spacey Riddles, **1306**

Hall, Lynn. *In Trouble Again, Zelda Hammersmith?*, 1069
Hall, Malcolm. *Headlines*, 932
Hall, Zoe. *It's Pumpkin Time!*, **18**
Halsey, Megan. *Jump for Joy*, **279**
Hamcock, Sibyl. *Esteban and the Ghost*, 1518
Hamanaka, Sheila. *All the Colors of the Earth*, **449**
Screen of Frogs, **934**
Hamilton, Morse. *Little Sister for Sale*, **450**
Hamlin, Marjorie (jt. author). *Celebrating with Books*, 2152
Han, Oki S., and Stephanie Haboush Plunkett. *Sir Whong and the Golden Pig*, **935**
Han, Suzanne Crowder. *The Rabbit's Escape*, **936**
The Rabbit's Judgment, **937**
Harding, Lee. *The Fallen Spaceman*, 1070
Harding, William Harry. *Alvin's Famous No-Horse*, **613**
Harness, Cheryl. *Three Young Pilgrims*, **614**
Harper, Jo. *Jalapeño Hal*, **615**
Harper, Wilhelmina. *Ghosts and Goblins*, 1690
The Gunniwolf, 1519
Harris, Christie. *Mouse Woman and the Mischief-Makers*, 1691
The Trouble with Adventurers, 1692
Harris, Dorothy Joan. *The School Mouse*, 415
Harris, Rosemary. *Beauty and the Beast*, 1520
Harrison, David L. *Somebody Catch My Homework*, **1307**
When Cows Come Home, **118**
Harrison, Maggie. *Angels on Roller Skates*, **451**
Harshman, Marc. *Only One*, **280**
Hart, Jane (comp.). *Singing Bee!*, 1810
Hartley, Deborah. *Up North in Winter*, 683
Hartman, Victoria. *The Silliest Joke Book Ever*, **1308**
Hastings, Selina. *The Firebird*, **938**
Reynard the Fox, **1071**
Sir Gawain and the Loathly Lady, 1521
Hautzig, Deborah (reteller). *The Wild Swans*, **700**
Haviland, Virgina (ed.). *The Fairy Tale Treasury*, 1693
Favorite Fairy Tales Told around the World, 1694
North American Legends, 1695
Haviland, Virginia. *The Talking Pot*, **939**
Havill, Juanita. *Jamaica and Brianna*, **119**
Leona and Ike, **712**
Hawes, Judy. *Fireflies in the Night*, **1156**
Hayes, Ann. *Meet the Orchestra*, **1157**
Hayes, Sarah. *Robin Hood*, 1696
This Is the Bear, 128
This Is the Bear and the Scary Night, **19**
Hayes, William. *Project: Genius*, 1308

Haynes, Betsy. *The Ghost of the Gravestone Hearth*, 1185

Haywood, Carolyn. *A Christmas Fantasy*, 416

Hazen, Barbara Shook. *Fang*, 417
Last, First, Middle and Nick, 2045

Hearn, Diane Dawson. *Dad's Dinosaur Day*, **120**

Heath, W. L. *Max the Great*, 1309

Heckert, Connie. *Dribbles*, **452**

Heide, Florence Parry. *Banana Twist*, 1310
Grim and Ghastly Goings-On, **1309**
The Shrinking of Treehorn, 1071

Heide, Florence Parry, and Judith Heide Gilliland. *The Day of Ahmed's Secret*, **616**
Sami and the Time of the Troubles, **713**

Heide, Florence Parry, and Roxanne Heide. *A Monster Is Coming! A Monster Is Coming!*, 684

Heide, Roxanne (jt. author). *A Monster Is Coming! A Monster Is Coming!*, 684

Heine, Helme. *The Most Wonderful Egg in the World*, 129

Heinig, Ruth Beall, and Lydia Stillwell. *Creative Drama for the Classroom Teacher*, 2172

Heinrich, Bernd. *An Owl in the House*, **1158**

Hejl, Pauline (trans.). *The Fine Round Cake*, 903

Hellen, Nancy. *Old MacDonald Had a Farm*, **20**

Heller, Nicholas. *An Adventure at Sea*, 685
Up the Wall, **281**
Woody, **121**

Heller, Ruth. *Animals Born Alive and Well*, **1159**
A Cache of Jewels and Other Collective Nouns, 1811
Chickens Aren't the Only Ones, **1160**
Kites Sail High, 1812
Merry-Go-Round, **1310**
The Reason for a Flower, **1161**
Up, Up and Away, **1311**

Hellsing, Lennart. *Old Mother Hubbard and Her Dog*, 130

Henkes, Kevin. *Bailey Goes Camping*, 131
Chrysanthemum, **282**
Jessica, 418
Julius, the Baby of the World, **283**
Margaret & Taylor, 419
Owen, **122**
Sheila Rae, the Brave, 132
A Weekend with Wendell, 420

Hennessy, B. G. *The Dinosaur Who Lived in My Backyard*, **284**
The Missing Tarts, 133
Sleep Tight, **21**

Henry, Marguerite. *Misty of Chincoteague*, 1072

Hepworth, Cathi. *Antics!*, **1312**

Herman, Charlotte. *Max Malone Makes a Million*, **617**

Our Snowman Had Olive Eyes, 1186

Herman, Emily. *Hubknuckles*, 686

Herriot, James. *Blossom Comes Home*, 2046
Bonny's Big Day, 2047
The Christmas Day Kitten, 2048

Herzig, Alison Cragin. *The Big Deal*, **618**

Herzig, Alison Cragin, and Jane Lawrence Mali. *Oh, Boy! Babies!*, 2049

Herzog, George (jt. author). *The Cow-Tail Switch and Other West African Stories*, 1670

Hesse, Karen. *Lester's Dog*, **619**
Phoenix Rising, **821**
Sable, **714**

Hest, Amy. *The Mommy Exchange*, 421
The Purple Coat, 422

Hewitt, Kathryn. *King Midas and the Golden Touch*, 1522
The Three Sillies, 1523

Heyward, DuBose. *The Country Bunny and the Little Gold Shoes*, 423

Hicks, Clifford B. *Alvin's Swap Shop*, 1187
Peter Potts, 1188

Higginson, William J. (comp.). *Wind in the Long Grass*, **1313**

Hildick, E. W. *The Case of the Condemned Cat*, 1073
The Case of the Purloined Parrot, **771**
McGurk Gets Good and Mad, 1189

Hill, Elizabeth Starr. *Evan's Corner*, 687

Hill, Kirkpatrick. *Winter Camp*, **822**

Hiller, Catherine. *Abracatabby*, 424

Himmelman, John. *Lights Out!*, **453**
Talester the Lizard, 134

Hines, Anna Grossnickle. *What Joe Saw*, **123**

Hinton, S. E. *Big David, Little David*, **285**

Hirsch, Marilyn. *Potato Pancakes All Around*, 933
The Rabbi and the Twenty-Nine Witches, 1524

Hiscock, Bruce. *The Big Rock*, 2050
The Big Tree, **1162**

Hiskey, Iris. *Hannah the Hippo's No Mud Day*, **124**

Hissey, Jane. *Little Bear's Trousers*, 135

Ho, Minfong. *The Clay Marble*, **823**

Hoban, Lillian. *Arthur's Christmas Cookies*, 425
Arthur's Great Big Valentine, 426
Arthur's Honey Bear, 136
Arthur's Loose Tooth, 427

Hoban, Russell. *A Baby Sister for Frances*, 137
Bedtime for Frances, 428
Bread and Jam for Frances, 429
Egg Thoughts and Other Frances Songs, 1813

Hoban, Tana. *A Children's Zoo*, 430
Exactly the Opposite, **125**
Look Again!, 688

Look! Look! Look!, **286**
Push, Pull, Empty, Full, 138
Hoberman, Mary Ann. *Bugs*, 1814
   Fathers, Mothers, Sisters, Brothers, **1314**
   A Fine Fat Pig and Other Animal Poems, **1315**
   A House Is a House for Me, 431
Hobson, Sally. *Chicken Little*, **940**
Hodges, Margaret. *Hauntings*, **1072**
   The Little Humpbacked Horse, 1525
   Saint Patrick and the Peddler, **941**
   The Wave, 1527
Hodges, Margaret (adapt.). *Saint George and the Dragon*, 1526
Hofer, Angelika. *The Lion Family Book*, 2051
Hoff, Syd. *Lengthy*, 139
   Syd Hoff's Animal Jokes, 1815
   Syd Hoff's Joke Book, 1816
Hoffman, Mary. *Amazing Grace*, **287**
   The Four-Legged Ghosts, **620**
   Henry's Baby, **454**
Hogrogian, Nonny. *One Fine Day*, 1528
Hogrogian, Nonny (reteller). *Cinderella*, 1488
   The Devil with the Three Golden Hairs, 1489
   The Glass Mountain, 1494
Hoguet, Susan. *I Unpacked My Grandmother's Trunk*, 689
Hoke, Helen. *Witches, Witches, Witches*, 1697
Holabird, Katharine. *Alexander and the Dragon*, 140
Holland, Barbara. *Prisoners at the Kitchen Table*, 1190
Holland, Isabelle. *Alan and the Animal Kingdom*, 1311
   Behind the Lines, **824**
Holman, Felice. *The Blackmail Machine*, 1191
Honeycutt, Natalie. *The All New Jonah Twist*, 934
   Juliet Fisher and the Foolproof Plan, **621**
Hong, Lily Toy. *How the Ox Star Fell from Heaven*, **942**
   Two of Everything, **943**
Hooks, William H. *Mean Jake and the Devils*, 1074
   Moss Gown, 1529
   The Three Little Pigs and the Fox, 1530
Hooper, Patricia. *A Bundle of Beasts*, 1817
Hoose, Phillip. *It's Our World, Too!*, **1163**
Hopkins, Lee Bennett. *Pass the Poetry, Please!*, 2140
   Witching Time, 1698
Hopkins, Lee Bennett (comp.). *April Bubbles Chocolate*, **1316**
   Best Friends, 1818
   Blast Off!, **1317**
   Click, Rumble, Roar, 1819
   Creatures, 1820

Dinosaurs, 1821
A Dog's Life, 1822
Extra Innings, **1318**
Flit, Flutter, Fly!, **1319**
Good Books, Good Times!, **1320**
Happy Birthday, **1321**
I Am the Cat, 1823
It's About Time!, **1322**
Merrily Comes Our Harvest In, **1323**
Moments, 1824
More Surprises, 1825
Munching, 1826
Questions, **1324**
Ragged Shadows, **1325**
Ring Out, Wild Bells, **1326**
Side by Side, 1827
The Sky Is Full of Song, 1828
Small Talk, **1327**
Through Our Eyes, **1328**
Weather, **1329**
Hopkins, Lee Bennett (sel.). *Don't You Turn Back*, 1830
Hopkins, Lee Bennett, and Misha Arenstein, comps. *Thread One to a Star*, 1829
Hopkinson, Deborah. *Sweet Clara and the Freedom Quilt*, **622**
Hort, Lenny. *How Many Stars in the Sky?*, **288**
Hoshino, Michio. *The Grizzly Bear Family Book*, **1164**
Houseman, Laurence. *Rocking-Horse Land*, 690
Houston, Gloria. *My Great Aunt Arizona*, **1165**
   The Year of the Perfect Christmas Tree, 691
Howard, Elizabeth Fitzgerald. *Mac & Marie & the Train Toss Surprise*, **455**
Howard, Ellen. *A Circle of Giving*, 1192
   Murphy and Kate, **623**
Howard, Jane R. *When I'm Hungry*, **126**
   When I'm Sleepy, 141
Howe, Deborah, and James Howe. *Bunnicula*, 1193
Howe, James. *Creepy-Crawly Birthday*, **456**
   The Day the Teacher Went Bananas, 142
   The Fright before Christmas, 935
   I Wish I Were a Butterfly, 692
   Nighty-Nightmare, 1194
   Pinky and Rex and the Spelling Bee, **457**
   Rabbit-Cadabra!, **458**
   Scared Silly, 693
Howe, James (jt. author). *Bunnicula*, 1193
Howe, John. *Jack and the Beanstalk*, **944**
Howlett, Bud. *I'm New Here*, **1166**
Huang, Tze-si (trans.). *In the Eyes of the Cat*, **1284**
Hubbard, Woodleigh. *C Is for Curious*, **289**
   2 Is for Dancing, **127**

Huck, Charlotte. *Children's Literature in the Elementary School*, 2119
Princess Furball, **1531**
Huck, Charlotte (comp.). *Secret Places*, **1330**
Hudson, Wade (comp.). *Pass It On*, **1331**
Huff, Barbara A. *Once Inside the Library*, **459**
Hughes, Dean. *Nutty Knows All*, 1312
Hughes, Langston. *Don't You Turn Back*, 1830
The Dream Keeper and Other Poems, **1332**
Hughes, Monica. *Little Fingerling*, **945**
Hughes, Shirley. *Alfie Gets in First*, 143
Alfie Gives a Hand, 144
Alfie's Feet, 145
The Big Alfie Out of Doors Storybook, **128**
Dogger, 146
An Evening at Alfie's, 147
Giving, **22**
Out and About, 1831
Hughes, Ted. *The Iron Giant*, 1075
Hulme, Joy N. *Sea Squares*, **624**
Hunt, Bernice. *The Whatchmacallit Book*, 2052
Hunt, Joyce (jt. author). *Keep Looking!*, 2095
Hunter, C. W. *The Green Gourd*, **946**
Hunter, Edith Fisher. *Child of the Silent Night*, 2053
Hunter, Mollie. *A Furl of Fairy Wind*, 1076
Wicked One, 1313
Hurd, Thacher. *Mama Don't Allow*, 432
Hurlimann, Ruth. *The Proud White Cat*, 1532
Hurmence, Belinda. *A Girl Called Boy*, 1314
Hurwitz, Johanna. *Busybody Nora*, 694
Class Clown, 936
Class President, **715**
"E" Is for Elisa, **290**
Much Ado about Aldo, 937
New Shoes for Sylvia, **129**
Russell Sprouts, 695
School Spirit, **716**
Superduper Teddy, 696
Hutchins, Hazel. *The Three and Many Wishes of Jason Reid*, 1077
Hutchins, Pat. *Clocks and More Clocks*, 433
Don't Forget the Bacon!, 434
Good-Night, Owl, 148
My Best Friend, **23**
Rosie's Walk, 149
Silly Billy!, **24**
The Tale of Thomas Mead, 697
Three-Star Billy, **130**
The Very Worst Monster, 150
Where's the Baby?, 435
Hutton, Warwick. *The Nose Tree*, 1533
Hyman, Trina Schart (reteller). *Little Red Riding Hood*, 1501

The Sleeping Beauty, 1505

Ikeda, Daisaku. *Over the Deep Blue Sea*, **460**
Ipcar, Dahlov. *I Love My Anteater with an A*, 1078
Isaacman, Clara, and Joan Adess Grossman. *Clara's Story*, 2054
Isaacs, Anne. *Swamp Angel*, **625**
Isadora, Rachel. *Max*, 436
Isele, Elizabeth. *The Frog Princess*, 1534
Ishii, Momoko. *The Tongue-Cut Sparrow*, 1535
Ivanov, Anatoly. *Ol' Jake's Lucky Day*, 698
Ivimey, John W. *The Complete Story of the Three Blind Mice*, 151
Complete Version of Ye Three Blind Mice, 152
Three Blind Mice, **131**
Izen, Marshall, and Jim West. *Why the Willow Weeps*, **461**

Jackson, Ellen. *Cinder Edna*, **626**
Jacobs, Joseph (reteller). *The Fables of Aesop*, 1647
Jacobs, Leland B. *Just Around the Corner*, **1333**
Jacques, Brian. *Redwall*, 1315
Jaffe, Nina. *In the Month of Kislev*, **627**
Jagendorf, M. A., and Virginia Weng. *The Magic Boat*, 1699
Jakob, Donna. *My Bike*, **132**
Jakobsen, Kathy. *My New York*, **1167**
James, Betsy. *Mary Ann*, **133**
James, J. Alison (trans.). *The Rainbow Fish*, **337**
James, Mary. *Shoebag*, 1195
Janeczko, Paul B. (comp.). *The Place My Words Are Looking For*, **1334**
Poetry from A to Z, **1335**
Janovitz, Marilyn. *Look Out, Bird!*, **134**
Jaquith, Priscilla. *Bo Rabbit Smart for True*, 1700
Jarrell, Randall (reteller). *The Fisherman and His Wife*, 1492
Jaspersohn, William. *The Ballpark*, 2055
Jeffers, Susan. *Brother Eagle, Sister Sky*, **628**
Wild Robin, 699
Jenkins, Jessica. *Thinking About Colors*, **462**
Jennings, Linda M. (reteller). *The Wolf and the Seven Little Kids*, 1512
Jennings, Paul. *Unreal!*, **825**
Jeschke, Susan. *Angela and Bear*, 437
Lucky's Choice, **291**
Perfect the Pig, 438
John, Timothy (ed.). *The Great Song Book*, 1832
Johnson, Crockett. *Harold and the Purple Crayon*, 153
Will Spring Be Early? or Will Spring Be Late?, 439
Johnson, Dolores. *Now Let Me Fly*, **629**
What Will Mommy Do When I'm at School?, **135**

Your Dad Was Just Like You, **463**

Johnson, Elizabeth. *Stuck with Luck,* 938

Johnson, Jane. *Today I Thought I'd Run Away,* 154

Johnson, Paul Brett. *The Cow Who Wouldn't Come Down,* **292**

Johnston, Deborah. *Mathew Michael's Beastly Day,* **293**

Johnston, Ginny, and Judy Cutchins. *Andy Bear,* 2056

Johnston, Johanna. *Edie Changes Her Mind,* 155
Speak Up, Edie, 440
That's Right, Edie, 441

Johnston, Tony. *The Badger and the Magic Fan,* 1536
The Cowboy and the Black-Eyed Pea, **717**
Mole and Troll Trim the Tree, 442
Slither McCreep and His Brother Joe, **294**
The Tale of Rabbit and Coyote, **947**
The Vanishing Pumpkin, 443
The Witch's Hat, 156
Yonder, 939

Jonas, Ann. *Color Dance,* **136**
Reflections, 700
Round Trip, 701
The 13th Clue, **464**
Where Can It Be?, **25**

Jones, Carol. *Old MacDonald Had a Farm,* 157
This Old Man, **137**

Jones, Carol (comp.). *Hickory Dickory Dock and Other Nursery Rhymes,* **1379**

Jones, Charlotte Foltz. *Mistakes That Worked,* **1168**

Jones, Evelyn (comp.). *World's Wackiest Riddle Book,* 1833

Jones, Malcolm (jt. author). *Jump!,* 1714

Jones, Maurice. *I'm Going on a Dragon Hunt,* 158

Jones, Rebecca C. *Germy Blew It,* 1196

Jones, Terry. *The Saga of Erik the Viking,* 1197

Joosse, Barbara M. *Wild Willie and King Kyle Detectives,* **630**

Jorgensen, Gail. *Crocodile Beat,* 159

Joslin, Sesyle. *What Do You Say, Dear?,* 702

Joyce, William. *George Shrinks,* 444
Santa Calls, **631**

Jukes, Mavis. *I'll See You in My Dreams,* **718**

Julian, Nancy R. *The Peculiar Miss Pickett,* 940

Juster, Norton. *The Phantom Tollbooth,* 1316

Kalan, Robert. *Jump, Frog, Jump,* 160
Stop, Thief!, **138**

Kalman, Esther. *Tchaikovsky Discovers America,* **632**

Kalman, Maira. *Chicken Soup Boots,* **719**
Hey Willy, See the Pyramids, 941

Max Makes a Million, **633**

Kamen, Gloria. *Charlie Chaplin,* 2057
Edward Lear, King of Nonsense, **1169**

Kandoian, Ellen. *Is Anybody Up?,* **139**
Under the Sun, 445

Karas, G. Brian. *I Know an Old Lady,* **295**

Karlin, Barbara. *Cinderella,* 1537

Karlin, Bernie, and Mati Karlin. *Night Ride,* 446

Karlin, Mati (jt. author). *Night Ride,* 446

Karlin, Nurit. *The Tooth Witch,* 447

Kastner, Jill. *Snake Hunt,* **465**

Kasza, Keiko. *A Mother for Choco,* **140**
The Pig's Picnic, 161
The Rat and the Tiger, **141**
The Wolf's Chicken Stew, 162

Katz, Michael Jay (comp.). *Ten Potatoes in a Pot and Other Counting Rhymes,* **1336**

Kaufman, Les (jt. author). *Dive to the Coral Reefs,* 2110

Kaye, M. M. *The Ordinary Princess,* 1079

Keats, Ezra Jack. *Apt. 3,* 942
Dreams, 448
Goggles!, 449
Jennie's Hat, 450
John Henry, 1538
A Letter to Amy, 451
Pet Show!, 163
Peter's Chair, 164
Regards to the Man in the Moon, 703
The Snowy Day, 165
Whistle for Willie, 166

Kehret, Peg. *Deadly Stranger,* 1317

Keller, Beverly. *The Genuine, Ingenious Thrift Shop Genie, Clarissa Mae Bean and Me,* 1198

Keller, Charles. *Belly Laughs!,* **1337**
King Henry the Ape, **1338**
Take Me to Your Liter, **1339**
Tongue Twisters, **1340**

Keller, Charles (comp.). *Alexander the Grape,* 1834
Ballpoint Bananas and Other Jokes for Kids, 1835
Count Draculations!, 1836
It's Raining Cats and Dogs, 1837
Llama Beans, 1838
Norma Lee I Don't Knock on Doors, 1839
The Nutty Joke Book, 1840
Remember the à la Mode!, 1841
School Daze, 1842
Swine Lake, 1843

Keller, Charles, and Richard Baker, comps. *The Star-Spangled Banana and Other Revolutionary Riddles,* 1844

Keller, Holly. *A Bear for Christmas,* 167
Geraldine's Baby Brother, **142**

Geraldine's Blanket, 168
Goodbye, Max, 452
Grandfather's Dream, **466**
Henry's Fourth of July, **26**
Horace, **143**
Island Baby, **296**
Keller, Wallace. *The Wrong Side of the Bed*, **297**
Kellogg, Steven. *Chicken Little*, 704
Johnny Appleseed, 2058
Mike Fink, **948**
Much Bigger than Martin, 453
The Mysterious Tadpole, 705
Pinkerton, Behave, 706
Prehistoric Pinkerton, 707
Kendall, Carol, and Yao-wen Li. *Sweet and Sour*, 1701
Kennaway, Mwalimu. *Awful Aardvark*, **144**
Kennedy, DayAnn M., Stella S. Spangler, and Mary Ann Vanderwerf. *Science & Technology in Fact and Fiction*, 2141
Kennedy, Dorothy M. *I Thought I'd Take My Rat to School*, **1341**
Kennedy, Dorothy M., and X. J. Kennedy, comps. *Talking Like the Rain*, **1342**
Kennedy, Richard. *Come Again in the Spring*, 1080
The Contests at Cowlick, 708
Inside My Feet, 1318
The Leprechaun's Story, 1081
The Lost Kingdom of Karnica, 1082
The Rise and Fall of Ben Gizzard, 1083
Kennedy, X. J. *Brats*, 1845
Drat These Brats, **1343**
Ghastlies, Goops & Pincushions, 1846
Kennedy, X. J. (comp.). *Knock at a Star*, 1847
Kennedy, X. J. (jt. comp.). *Talking Like the Rain*, **1342**
Kent, Jack. *The Fat Cat*, 1539
Jim Jimmy James, 454
Joey Runs Away, 169
Little Peep, 455
Kesey, Ken. *Little Tricker the Squirrel Meets Big Double the Bear*, **634**
Kessler, Leonard. *Old Turtle's Baseball Stories*, 709
Kha, Dang Manh. *In the Land of Small Dragon*, 1540
Khalsa, Dayal Kaur. *How Pizza Came to Queens*, 456
Tales of a Gambling Grandma, 1084
Kherdian, David. *The Cat's Midsummer Jamboree*, 457
Feathers and Tails, **1073**
Kidd, Diana. *Onion Tears*, **772**

Kimmel, Eric A. *Anansi and the Moss-Covered Rock*, 1541
Anansi and the Talking Melon, **949**
Anansi Goes Fishing, **950**
Asher and the Capmakers, **635**
Baba Yaga, **951**
Bernal & Florinda, **720**
Boots and His Brothers, **952**
The Chanukkah Guest, **298**
Charlie Drives the Stage, 943
Four Dollars and Fifty Cents, **721**
The Gingerbread Man, **953**
The Greatest of All, **954**
Hershel and the Hanukkah Goblins, 944
I-Know-Not-What, I-Know-Not-Where, **955**
The Old Woman and Her Pig, **956**
The Three Princes, **957**
Three Sacks of Truth, **958**
Kimmel, Eric A. (reteller). *Iron John*, **928**
Nanny Goat and the Seven Little Kids, **924**
Kimmel, Mary Margaret, and Elizabeth Segel. *For Reading Out Loud!*, 2142
King, Bob. *Sitting on the Farm*, **145**
King, Larry L. *Because of Loza Brown*, 710
King-Smith, Dick. *Babe, the Gallant Pig*, 1319
The Cuckoo Child, **722**
Farmer Bungle Forgets, 458
Harry's Mad, 1199
The Invisible Dog, **467**
Lady Daisy, **723**
Martin's Mice, 1085
Paddy's Pot of Gold, **724**
Pigs Might Fly, 1320
Pretty Polly, **725**
The Queen's Nose, **726**
Sophie's Snail, 711
The Swoose, **727**
Kinsey-Warnock, Natalie. *The Bear That Heard Crying*, **468**
When Spring Comes, **469**
Wilderness Cat, **470**
Kipling, Rudyard. *The Beginning of the Armadillos*, 945
The Elephant's Child, 946
How the Camel Got His Hump, 947
How the Whale Got His Throat, 712
Just So Stories, 948, **728**
Rikki-Tikki-Tavi, **729**
Kirby, David, and Allen Woodman. *The Cows Are Going to Paris*, **471**
Kirby, Susan. *Ike and Porker*, 1200
Kirk, Daniel. *Skateboard Monsters*, **472**
Kirstein, Lincoln. *Puss in Boots*, **959**
Kiser, Kevin. *Sherman the Sheep*, **299**

Kismaric, Carole. *The Rumor of Pavel and Paali*, 1542

Klein, Robin. *Snakes and Ladders*, 1848

Kleven, Elisa. *The Paper Princess*, **146**

Kline, Rufus. *Watch Out for Those Weirdos*, **473**

Kline, Suzy. *Don't Touch!*, 170
The Herbie Jones Reader's Theater, **1170**
Horrible Harry and the Christmas Surprise, **474**
Mary Marony and the Snake, **475**
SHHHH!, 171
Song Lee in Room 2B, **476**
What's the Matter with Herbie Jones?, 949

Knowles, Sheena. *Edward the Emu*, **300**

Knowlton, Jack. *Books and Libraries*, **1171**

Knutson, Barbara. *Sungura and Leopard*, **960**

Kobrin, Beverly. *Eyeopeners!*, 2143

Koch, Kenneth, and Kate Farrell, comps. *Talking to the Sun*, 1849

Koch, Michelle. *World Water Watch*, **1172**

Koide, Tan. *May We Sleep Here Tonight?*, 172

Komaiko, Leah. *Earl's Too Cool for Me*, **477**

Konigsburg, E. L. *Amy Elizabeth Explores Bloomingdale's*, **478**
From the Mixed-Up Files of Mrs. Basil E. Frankweiler, 1201

Koontz, Robin Michal. *I See Something You Don't See*, **301**

Kopper, Lisa. *Daisy Thinks She Is a Baby*, **27**

Korman, Gordon. *This Can't Be Happening at Macdonald Hall*, 1321

Korschunow, Irina. *The Foundling Fox*, 713

Kossman, Nina. *Behind the Border*, **1173**

Kotzwinkle, William. *Trouble in Bugland*, 1322

Kovalski, Maryann. *Pizza for Breakfast*, **479**
The Wheels on the Bus, 173

Kraske, Robert. *Magicians Do Amazing Things*, 2059

Kraus, Robert. *How Spider Saved Christmas*, 459
Leo the Late Bloomer, 460
Milton the Early Riser, 174
Noel the Coward, 175
Owliver, 461
Phil the Ventriloquist, 176
Whose Mouse Are You?, 177

Krauss, Ruth. *The Carrot Seed*, 178
Is This You?, 714

Kreisler, Ken (jt. author). *Citybook*, **353**

Krensky, Stephen. *Big Time Bears*, **147**
The Dragon Circle, 1202

Krensky, Stephen (jt. author). *Dinosaurs, Beware!*, 2002
Perfect Pigs, 2003

Kroll, Steven. *Amanda and Giggling Ghost*, 715
The Candy Witch, 462

Friday the 13th, 716
Happy Mother's Day, 717
Oh, What a Thanksgiving!, 718
The Tyrannosaurus Game, 719

Kroll, Virginia. *Masai and I*, **480**

Krull, Kathleen. *Lives of the Musicians*, **1174**
Lives of the Writers, **1175**

Krull, Kathleen (comp.). *Gonna Sing My Head Off!*, **1344**

Krupp, E. C. *The Comet and You*, 2060
The Moon and You, **1176**

Krupp, Robin Rector. *Let's Go Traveling*, **1177**

Kudrna, C. Imbior. *To Bathe a Boa*, 463

Kuklin, Susa. *How My Family Lives in America*, **1178**

Kunhardt, Edith. *Honest Abe*, **1179**

Kurtz, Jane. *Fire on the Mountain*, **961**

Kwon, Holly H. *The Moles and the Mireuk*, **962**

Lacy, Lyn Ellen. *Art and Design in Children's Picture Books*, 2120

Lamont, Priscilla. *The Troublesome Pig*, 1543

Lamont, Priscilla (comp.). *Ring-a-Round-a-Rosy*, **1345**

Landsman, Sandy. *Castaways on Chimp Island*, 1323

Lanes, Selma (jt. author). *An Actor's Life for Me!*, 2039

Lang, Andrew. *Aladdin and the Wonderful Lamp*, 1544
Blue Fairy Book, 1702
The Rainbow Fairy Book, **1074**

Langerlöf, Selma. *The Changeling*, **636**

Langley, Jonathan (comp.). *Rain, Rain, Go Away!*, **1381**

Langstaff, John. *Frog Went a-Courtin'*, 179
Over in the Meadow, 180

Langstaff, John (jt. comp.). *Jim Along Josie*, 1850

Langstaff, Nancy, and John Langstaff. *Jim Along Josie*, 1850

Langton, Jane. *The Hedgehog Boy*, 1545
Salt, **963**

Lansky, Bruce (comp.). *Kids Pick the Funniest Poems*, **1346**

Laroche, Michel. *The Snow Rose*, 1086

Larrick, Nancy. *A Parent's Guide to Children's Reading*, 2144

Larrick, Nancy (comp.). *Cats Are Cats*, 1851
Mice Are Nice, **1347**
Piping Down the Valleys Wild, 1852
Songs from Mother Goose, 1890

Larry, Charles. *Peboan and Seegwun*, **964**

Lasker, Joe. *The Do-Something Day*, 464

Lasky, Kathryn. *The Librarian Who Measured the Earth*, **1180**

Lauber, Patricia. *Clarence and the Burglar*, 720
Lost Star, 2061
The News about Dinosaurs, 2062
An Octopus Is Amazing, **1181**
Volcano, 2063

Laughlin, Mildred, and Letty S. Watt. *Developing Learning Skills Through Children's Literature*, 2145

Lavies, Bianca. *It's an Armadillo*, 2064

Lawson, Julie. *The Dragon's Pearl*, **965**

Lawson, Robert. *Ben and Me*, 1324

Leach, Maria. *The Rainbow Book of American Folk Tales and Legends*, 1703
The Thing at the Foot of the Bed and Other Scary Tales, 1704

Leach, Norman. *My Wicked Stepmother*, **302**

Leaf, Munro. *The Story of Ferdinand*, 465

Lear, Edward. *Daffy Down Dillies*, **1348**
How Pleasant to Know Mr. Lear!, 1853
Of Pelicans and Pussycats, **1349**
The Owl and the Pussycat, 181, **148**, **149**
The Quangle Wangle's Hat, 466

Lebentritt, Julia, and Richard Ploetz. *The Kooken*, **481**

Lee, Dennis. *Alligator Pie*, 1854
The Ice Cream Store, **1350**
Jelly Belly, 1855

Lee, Jeanne M. *Toad Is the Uncle of Heaven*, 1546

Leedy, Loreen. *Fraction Action*, **482**
A Number of Dragons, 182
Postcards from Pluto, **1182**
Tracks in the Sand, **1183**

Le Guin, Ursula K. *Catwings*, 950
A Ride on the Red Mare's Back, **637**
A Visit from Dr. Katz, 183

Lehane, M. S. *Science Tricks*, 2065

Leigh, Nila K. *Learning to Swim in Swaziland*, **1184**

Leighner, Alice Mills. *Reynard*, 2066

Leighton, Maxine Rhea. *An Ellis Island Christmas*, **638**

Lembo, Diana (jt. author). *Introducing Books*, 2137
Juniorplots, 2138

Lemieux, Michèle. *Pied Piper of Hamelin*, **966**
What's That Noise, 184

L'Engle, Madeleine. *A Wrinkle in Time*, 1325

Leonard, Charlotte. *Tied Together*, 2146

Leonard, Marcia (comp.). *Cricket's Jokes, Riddles & Other Stuff*, 1785

LeRoy, Gen. *Taxi Cat and Huey*, **773**

LeSieg, Theo. *I Wish That I Had Duck Feet*, 467

Leslie-Melville, Betty. *Daisy Rothschild*, 2067
Elephant Have the Right of Way, **1185**

Lesser, Rika (reteller). *Hansel and Gretel*, 1497

Lester, Alison. *The Journey Home*, **303**

Lester, Helen. *Cora Copycat*, 468
It Wasn't My Fault, 469
Me First, **304**
Pookins Gets Her Way, 470
A Porcupine Named Fluffy, 471
Three Cheers for Tacky, **305**
The Wizard, the Fairy and the Magic Chicken, 185

Lester, Julius. *Further Tales of Uncle Remus*, **1075**
How Many Spots Does a Leopard Have?, 1705
John Henry, **967**
The Knee-High Man and Other Tales, 1706
The Tales of Uncle Remus, 1707

Leventhal, Debra. *What Is Your Language?*, **150**

Leverich, Kathleen. *Best Enemies Again*, **639**
Hilary and the Troublemakers, **730**
The Hungry Fox and the Foxy Duck, 186

Levine, Arthur A. *The Boy Who Drew Cats*, **968**

Levine, Caroline. *Riddles to Tell Your Cat*, **1351**

Levine, Ellen. *I Hate English*, 721
If Your Name Was Changed at Ellis Island, **1186**

Levine, Evan. *Not the Piano, Mrs. Medley!*, **483**

Levitin, Sonia. *Jason and the Money Tree*, 1203
Nobody Stole the Pie, 722

Levitt, Paul M., Douglas A. Burger, and Elissa S. Guralnick. *The Weighty Word Book*, 1326

Levy, Elizabeth. *Frankenstein Moved in on the Fourth Floor*, 951
Keep Ms. Sugarman in the Fourth Grade, **731**
Lizzie Lies a Lot, 1087

Lewis, C. S. *The Lion, the Witch and the Wardrobe*, 1088
The Magician's Nephew, 1204

Lewis, J. Patrick. *Earth Verses and Water Rhymes*, **1352**
The Frog Princess, **969**
A Hippopotamustn't and Other Animal Verses, **1353**
One Dog Day, **774**
Two-Legged, Four-Legged, No-Legged Rhymes, **1354**

Lewis, Naomi (ed.). *The Twelve Dancing Princesses and Other Tales from Grimm*, 1689

Lewis, Naomi (trans.). *The Frog Prince*, **932**
The Nightingale, **699**

Lewis, Richard (ed.). *Miracles*, 1856

Lewis, Thomas P. *Hill of Fire*, 723

Lewison, Wendy Cheyette. *Going to Sleep on the Farm*, **28**
The Princess and the Potty, **29**
Shy Vi, **151**

Lexai, Joan. *Benjie*, 472
　I'll Tell on You, 724
　That's Good, That's Bad, 187
Leydenfrost, Robert. *The Snake That Sneezed*, 188
Li, Yao-wen (jt. author). *Sweet and Sour*, 1701
Lichtveld, Noni. *I Lost My Arrow in a Kankan Tree*, **970**
Lies, Brian. *Hamlet and the Enormous Chinese Dragon Kite*, 484
Lillegard, Dee. *Do Not Feed the Table*, **1355**
Lima, Carolyn W., and John A. Lima. *A to Zoo*, 2147
Lima, John A. (jt. author). *A to Zoo*, 2147
Lindbergh, Anne. *Travel Far, Pay No Fare*, **826**
Lindbergh, Reeve. *The Day the Goose Got Loose*, **306**
　There's a Cow in the Road!, **307**
　View from the Air, **1356**
Lindenbaum, Pija. *Boodil My Dog*, **485**
Lindgren, Astrid. *The Ghost of Skinny Jack*, 1089
　I Want a Brother or Sister, 189
　Pippi Longstocking, 1090
　The Tomten, 725
Lindgren, Barbro. *The Wild Baby*, 473
Lionni, Leo. *Alexander and the Wind-Up Mouse*, 726
　Fish Is Fish, 474
　Frederick, 727
　Frederick's Fables, 728
　Inch by Inch, 475
　It's Mine!, 190
　Little Blue and Little Yellow, 191
　Matthew's Dream, **308**
　Swimmy, 476
　Tico and the Golden Wings, 952
　Tillie and the Wall, 477
Lipson, Eden Ross. *The New York Times Parent's Guide to the Best Books for Children*, 2148
Lisle, Janet Taylor. *The Dancing Cats of Applesap*, 1205
　Forest, **827**
Littedale, Freya. *Peter and the North Wind*, 1547
Little, Jean. *From Anna*, **775**
　Home from Far, 1206
　Little by Little, **1187**
　Revenge of the Small Small, **486**
Little, Jean, and Maggie De Vries. *Once Upon a Golden Apple*, 478
Littlefield, Bill. *Champions*, **1188**
Litzinger, Rosanne. *The Old Woman and Her Pig*, **971**
Livingston, Myra Cohn. *Abraham Lincoln*, **1189**
　Higgledy-Piggledy, 953
　Keep on Singing, **1190**

Let Freedom Ring, **1191**
Livingston, Myra Cohn (comp.). *Callooh! Callay!*, 1857
　Cat Poems, 1858
　Christmas Poems, 1859
　Halloween Poems, **1357**
　If You Ever Meet a Whale, **1358**
　Lots of Limericks, **1359**
　Poems for Grandmothers, **1360**
　A Song I Sang to You, 1860
Livingston, Myra Cohn (sel.). *How Pleasant to Know Mr. Lear!*, 1853
Livo, Norma J., and Sandra A. Rietz. *Storytelling*, 2173
Lobel, Anita. *Alison's Zinnia*, **309**
　Away from Home, **487**
Lobel, Arnold. *The Book of Pigericks*, 1861
　Fables, 1207
　Frog and Toad Are Friends, 479
　The Great Blueness and Other Predicaments, 480
　How the Rooster Saved the Day, 192
　The Ice Cream Cone Coot and Other Rare Birds, 954
　Ming Lo Moves the Mountain, 481
　Mouse Tales, 482
　On Market Street, 483
　Owl at Home, 484
　The Rose in My Garden, 485
　A Treeful of Pigs, 729
　Uncle Elephant, 486
　Whiskers & Rhymes, 1862
Lobel, Arnold (comp.). *Gregory Griggs*, 1882
　The Random House Book of Mother Goose, 1887
Loeb, Jeffrey (jt. ed.). *I'm Telling!*, 1988
Lofting, Hugh. *The Story of Doctor Dolittle*, 1091
Lomas Garza, Carmen. *Family Pictures / Cuadros de Familia*, **1192**
London, Jonathan. *The Eyes of Gray Wolf*, **488**
　Froggy Gets Dressed, **152**
　Gray Fox, **489**
　Let's Go, Froggy, **153**
　The Owl Who Became the Moon, **310**
　Voices of the Wild, **640**
London, Jonathan (jt. author). *Thirteen Moons on Turtle's Back*, **872**
London, Jonathan, and Lanny Pinola. *Fire Race*, **972**
Long, Claudia. *Albert's Story*, 487
Longfellow, Henry Wadsworth. *Paul Revere's Ride*, 1863, **1361**
Loomis, Christine. *In the Diner*, **154**
　One Cow Coughs, **155**
Lord, John Vernon, and Janet Burroway. *The Giant Jam Sandwich*, 730

Lottridge, Celia Barker. *The Name of the Tree*, **973**

Louie, Ai-Ling. *Yeh-Shen*, 1548

Low, Alice. *The Witch Who Was Afraid of Witches*, 731

Low, Alice (jt. author). *A Young Painter*, **1257**

Low, Alice (comp.). *The Family Read-Aloud Holiday Treasury*, **1362**

Low, Joseph. *Mice Twice*, 488

Lowe, Steve (ed.). *Log of Christopher Columbus*, **1124**

Lowry, Lois. *All about Sam*, 1327
Attaboy, Sam!, **776**
The Giver, **828**
Number the Stars, 1328

Lukens, Rebecca J. *A Critical Handbook of Children's Literature*, 2121

Lurie, Alison. *Clever Gretchen and Other Forgotten Folktales*, 1708

Lurie, Morris. *The Story of Imelda, Who Was Small*, 311

Luttrell, Ida. *One Day at School*, 732

Lyon, David. *The Biggest Truck*, 193

Lyon, George Ella. *A B Cedar*, 2068

Lystad, Mary. *Jennifer Takes Over P.S. 94*, 733

Macaulay, David. *Black and White*, **490**

MacCarthy, Patricia. *Herds of Words*, **1363**

McCaughrean, Geraldine (trans.). *Over the Deep Blue Sea*, **460**

McCleery, William. *Wolf Story*, 489

McClintock, Barbara (reteller). *Animal Fables from Aesop*, **1055**

McCloskey, Robert. *Blueberries for Sal*, 194
Burt Dow, Deep-Water Man, 955
Homer Price, 1208
Lentil, 956
Make Way for Ducklings, 734
Time of Wonder, 957

McCord, David. *One at a Time*, 1864

McCormick, Dell J. *Paul Bunyan Swings His Axe*, 1709

McCoy, Karen Kawamoto. *A Tale of Two Tengu*, **974**

McCully, Emily Arnold. *The Amazing Felix*, **491**
The Christmas Gift, 195
Mirette on the High Wire, **492**
Picnic, 196
Speak Up, Blanche!, **493**

McCurdy, Michael. *The Devils Who Learned to Be Good*, 1549

McDermott, Gerald. *Anansi the Spider*, 1550
Coyote, **975**
Daniel O'Rourke, 1551
Raven, **976**

The Stonecutter, 1552
Tim O'Toole and the Wee Folk, 1553
The Voyage of Osiris, 1554
Zomo the Rabbit, **977**

MacDonald, Amy. *Little Beaver and the Echo*, **156**
Rachel Fister's Blister, **312**

MacDonald, Betty. *Mrs. Piggle-Wiggle*, 1092

McDonald, Joyce. *Homebody*, **494**

MacDonald, Margaret Read. *Peace Tales*, **1076**
Storyteller's Sourcebook, 2174
Twenty Tellable Tales, 2175
When the Lights Go Out, 2176

McDonald, Megan. *The Great Pumpkin Switch*, **495**
Is This a House for Hermit Crab?, **313**
The Potato Man, **496**

MacDonald, Suse. *Alphabatics*, 490
Sea Shapes, **157**

MacDonald, Suse, and Bill Oakes. *Puzzlers*, **314**

McDonnell, Flora. *I Love Animals*, **30**

McEwan, Ian. *The Daydreamer*, **829**

McGovern, Ann. *Drop Everything, It's D.E.A.R. Time!*, **497**
If You Lived in Colonial Times, 2069
Runaway Slave, 2070
The Secret Soldier, 2071
Stone Soup, 1555
Too Much Noise, 1556

McGovern, Ann (reteller). *Aesop's Fables*, 1644

McGowen, Tom. *The Magician's Apprentice*, 1329

McGraw, Eloise Jarvis. *Joel and the Great Merlini*, 1093

MacGregor, Ellen. *Theodore Turtle*, 491

McGuire, Richard. *Night Becomes Day*, **498**

McKissack, Patricia C. *Flossie & the Fox*, 735
Mirandy and Brother Wind, 958
Nettie Jo's Friends, 492

MacLachlan, Patricia. *Sarah, Plain and Tall*, 1094

McLerran, Alice. *Roxaboxen*, **499**

McLoughland, Beverly. *A Hippo's a Heap*, **1364**

McMillan, Brett (jt. author). *Puniddles*, 959

McMillan, Bruce. *Beach Ball—Left, Right*, **158**
Eating Fractions, **1193**
Going on a Whale Watch, **1194**
Growing Colors, 197
Kitten Can, 198
Mouse Views, **315**
One Sun, 1865
One, Two, One Pair!, **31**
Play Day, **1365**
Sense Suspense, **159**
Super Super Superwords, 199

McMillan, Bruce, and Brett McMillan. *Puniddles*, 959

McMullin, Kate. *The Great Ideas of Lila Fenwick*, 1209

McMurtry, Stan. *The Bunjee Venture*, 1210

McNaughton, Colin. *Anton B. Stanton and the Pirats*, 736
Making Friends with Frankenstein, **1366**

McNulty, Faith. *How to Dig a Hole to the Other Side of the World*, 2072
A Snake in the House, **500**

McPhail, David. *The Bear's Toothache*, 493
Emma's Pet, 200
Emma's Vacation, 201
Fix-It, 494
Great Cat, 495
Lost!, **316**
The Magical Drawings of Mooney B. Finch, 737
Pig Pig and the Magic Photo Album, 496
Pig Pig Gets a Job, **318**
Pig Pig Grows Up, 202
Pigs Aplenty, Pigs Galore!, **317**
Santa's Book of Names, **319**
Something Special, 497

McSwigan, Marie. *Snow Treasure*, 1330

McVitty, Walter. *Ali Baba and the Forty Thieves*, 1557

Madden, Don. *The Wartville Wizard*, 738

Maddern, Eric. *The Fire Children*, **978**
Rainbow Bird, **979**

Maestro, Betsy. *The Discovery of the Americas*, **1195**
A More Perfect Union, 2073
A Sea Full of Sharks, **1196**
The Story of Money, **1197**
The Story of the Statue of Liberty, 2074
Take a Look at Snakes, **1198**

Maestro, Betsy, and Giulio Maestro. *Lambs for Dinner*, 498

Maestro, Giulio. *More Halloween Howls*, **1367**
Razzle-Dazzle Riddles, 1866
A Wise Monkey Tale, 499

Maestro, Giulio (jt. author). *Lambs for Dinner*, 498
Riddle City, USA!, **1368**

Maestro, Marco, and Giulio Maestro. *Riddle City, USA!*, **1368**

Mahy, Margaret. *The Boy Who Was Followed Home*, 739
The Great White Man-Eating Shark, **501**
Jam, 740
Raging Robots and Unruly Uncles, **777**
The Rattlebang Picnic, **502**
The Seven Chinese Brothers, 1558
17 Kings and 42 Elephants, 500

Maitland, Antony. *Idle Jack*, 1559

Major, Beverly. *Playing Sardines*, 741

Mali, Jane Lawrence (jt. author). *Oh, Boy! Babies!*, 2049

Manes, Stephen. *Be a Perfect Person in Just Three Days*, 1095
Chicken Trek, 1211

Manitonquat (Medicine Story). *Children of the Morning Light*, **1077**

Manning-Sanders, Ruth. *A Book of Witches*, 1710

Mansell, Dom. *My Old Teddy*, **32**

Manson, Christopher. *The Marvelous Blue Mouse*, **641**
Two Travelers, **642**

Manushkin, Fran. *My Christmas Safari*, **320**

Marcus, Leonard S. (comp.). *Mother Goose's Little Misfortunes*, **1383**

Margolis, Richard J. *Secrets of a Small Brother*, 1867

Mariotti, Mario. *Hanimations*, **1199**

Marshak, Samuel. *The Month Brothers*, 1560

Marshak, Suzanna. *I Am the Ocean*, **1200**

Marshall, Edward. *Space Case*, 742
Troll Country, 501

Marshall, James. *The Cut-Ups*, 743
The Cut-Ups Carry On, **503**
George and Martha, 502
Goldilocks and the Three Bears, 1561
The Guest, 203
Merry Christmas, Space Case, 744
Old Mother Hubbard and Her Wonderful Dog, **980**
Portly McSwine, 503
Rats on the Roof and Other Stories, **643**
Red Riding Hood, 1562
The Three Little Pigs, 1563
Three Up a Tree, 504
Wings, 745

Marshall, James (comp.). *James Marshall's Mother Goose*, 1883
Pocketful of Nonsense, **1369**

Marshall, James (reteller). *Hansel and Gretel*, **926**

Martin, Ann. *Rachel Parker, Kindergarten Show-Off*, **321**

Martin, Bill, Jr. *Brown Bear, Brown Bear, What Do You See?*, 204
The Happy Hippopotami, **322**
The Maestro Plays, **504**
Old Devil Wind, **323**
Polar Bear, Polar Bear, What Do You Hear?, **160**

Martin, Bill, Jr., and John Archambault. *Barn Dance!*, 505
Chicka Chicka Boom Boom, 205
Listen to the Rain, 746

Martin, Claire. *Boots & the Glass Mountain*, **981**

Martin, Eva. *Tales of the Far North*, 1711
Martin, Jacqueline Briggs. *Bizzy Bones and the Lost Quilt*, 206
Martin, James. *Chameleons*, **1201**
Martin, Jane Read, and Patricia Marx. *Now Everybody Really Hates Me*, **644**
Martin, Rafe. *The Boy Who Lived with the Seals*, **982**
  Foolish Rabbit's Big Mistake, 1564
  The Rough-Face Girl, **983**
  A Storyteller's Story, **1202**
Marx, Patricia (jt. author). *Now Everybody Really Hates Me*, **644**
Marzollo, Jean. *Happy Birthday, Martin Luther King*, **1203**
  In 1492, **1204**
  Pretend You're a Cat, **161**
  Ten Cats Have Hats, **162**
Mason, Cherie. *Wild Fox*, **1205**
Massie, Diane Redfield. *Chameleon Was a Spy*, 960
Masterman-Smith, Virginia. *The Treasure Trap*, 1212
Mathews, Judith, and Fay Robinson. *Knock-Knock Knees and Funny Bones*, **1370**
  Nathaniel Willy, Scared Silly, **984**
Mathews, Sally Schofer. *The Sad Night*, **1206**
Matsuno, Masako. *A Pair of Red Clogs*, 747
Matthews, Downs. *Polar Bear Cubs*, 2075
Matthews, Louise. *Gator Pie*, 506
Mattox, Cheryl (comp.). *Shake It to the One That You Love the Best*, **1371**
Maugham, W. Somerset. *Appointment*, **830**
Maurer, Donna. *Annie, Bea, and Chi Chi Dolores*, **163**
Mayer, Marianna. *Aladdin and the Enchanted Lamp*, 1565
  Baba Yaga and Vasilisa the Brave, **985**
  Beauty and the Beast, 1566
  Iduna and the Magic Apples, 1567
  The Spirit of the Blue Light, **986**
Mayer, Mercer. *Liza Lou and the Yeller Belly Swamp*, 748
  Mrs. Beggs and the Wizard, 749
  A Special Trick, 961
  There's a Nightmare in My Closet, 207
  There's an Alligator under My Bed, 208
  There's Something in My Attic, 209
Mayo, Gretchen Will. *Big Trouble for Tricky Rabbit!*, **1078**
  That Tricky Coyote!, **1079**
Mazer, Anne. *The Oxboy*, **831**
  The Yellow Button, **505**
Meddaugh, Susan. *Beast*, 210

Martha Speaks, **506**
Tree of Birds, **164**
The Witches' Supermarket, **507**
Medearis, Angela Shelf. *The Zebra-Riding Cowboy*, **645**
Medlicott, Mary. *Tales for Telling*, **1080**
Mellecker, Judith. *Randolph's Dream*, **732**
Melmed, Laura Krauss. *The Rainbabies*, **508**
Meltzer, Maxine. *Pups Speak Up*, **324**
Mendoza, George. *Gwot!*, 962
  The Sesame Street Book of Opposites, 211
  A Wart Snake in a Fig Tree, 963
Mennen, Ingrid, and Niki Daly. *Somewhere in Africa*, **509**
Merriam, Eve. *The Birthday Door*, 750
  Blackberry Ink, 1868
  Chortles, 1869
  The Christmas Box, 507
  Halloween ABC, **1372**
  A Poem for a Pickle, 1870
  The Singing Green, **1373**
  Where Is Everybody?, 508
  You Be Good & I'll Be Night, 1871
Merrill, Jean. *The Pushcart War*, 1331
Michel, Anna. *The Story of Nim, the Chimp Who Learned Language*, 2076
Miles, Betty. *The Secret Life of the Underwear Champ*, 1096
Miles, Miska. *Annie and the Old One*, 1213
Miller, Margaret. *Can You Guess?*, **33**
  Guess Who?, **165**
  My Five Senses, **1207**
  Where Does It Go?, **166**
  Where's Jenna?, **167**
  Whose Hat?, 212
  Whose Shoe?, **168**
Miller, Moira. *The Moon Dragon*, 1568
Miller, Virginia. *Eat Your Dinner!*, **34**
Mills, Claudia. *After Fifth Grade, the World!*, 1214
  Dinah for President, **778**
Mills, Lauren. *The Rag Coat*, **646**
Milne, A. A. *Now We Are Six*, 1872
  Winnie-the-Pooh, 964
Milton, Nancy. *The Giraffe That Walked to Paris*, **1208**
Minard, Rosemary. *Womenfolk and Fairy Tales*, 1712
Minarik, Else Holmelund. *It's Spring!*, 213
Minters, Frances. *Cinder-Elly*, **510**
Mitchell, Margaree King. *Uncle Jed's Barbershop*, **647**
Mitchell, Rita Phillips. *Hue Boy*, **325**
Mizamura, Kazue. *Flower Moon Snow*, 1873
Mochizuki, Ken. *Baseball Saved Us*, **733**

Modell, Frank. *Goodbye Old Year, Hello New Year*, 509
One Zillion Valentines, 751
Tooley! Tooley!, 752
Modesitt, Jeanne. *Sometimes I Feel Like a Mouse*, **169**
The Story of Z, **511**
Vegetable Soup, **170**
Moeri, Louise. *Star Mother's Youngest Child*, 1097
Molarsky, Osmond. *Take It or Leave It*, 965
Mollel, Tololwa M. *The Flying Tortoise*, **987**
The King and the Tortoise, **988**
The Orphan Boy, **989**
A Promise to the Sun, **990**
Rhinos for Lunch and Elephants for Supper!, **991**
Monjo, F. N. *The Drinking Gourd*, 966
Moore, Clement C. *The Night before Christmas*, 753
Moore, Inga. *The Sorcerer's Apprentice*, **648**
Moore, Lilian. *Adam Mouse's Book of Poems*, **1374**
I'll Meet You at the Cucumbers, 967
The Snake That Went to School, 968
Moore, Lilian (comp.). *Go with the Poem*, 1874
See My Lovely Poison Ivy, 1875
Sunflakes, **1375**
Mooser, Stephen. *Orphan Jeb at the Massacree*, 1215
Mora, Pat. *Listen to the Desert / Oye al Desierto*, **1209**
Morey, Walt. *Gentle Ben*, 1332
Sandy and the Rock Star, 1333
Morgan, Pierr. *The Turnip*, 1569
Morimoto, Junko. *My Hiroshima*, **1210**
Morley, Diana. *Marms in the Marmalade*, 1876
Moroney, Lynn (adapt.). *Baby Rattlesnake*, 862
Morpurgo, Michael. *War Horse*, 1334
Morris, Ann. *Bread Bread Bread*, **1211**
Morris, Winifred. *The Magic Leaf*, 1570
Morrison, Bill. *Squeeze a Sneeze*, **326**
Morrison, Lillian (comp.). *At the Crack of the Bat*, **1376**
Best Wishes, Amen, 1877
Mosel, Arlene. *The Funny Little Woman*, 1571
Tikki Tikki Tembo, 1572
Moser, Barry. *Tucker Pfeffercorn*, **779**
Moser, Barry (reteller). *The Tinderbox*, **757**
Moskin, Marietta. *The Day of the Blizzard*, 1098
Rosie's Birthday Present, 510
Moss, Jeff. *The Butterfly Jar*, **1377**
Moss, Lloyd. *Zin! Zin! Zin!*, **512**
Moss, Marissa. *Knick Knack Paddywack*, **327**
Regina's Big Mistake, **328**
Most, Bernard. *Can You Find It?*, **329**
Hippopotamus Hunt, **513**

How Big Were the Dinosaurs?, **1212**
Zoodles, **514**
Mother Goose. *Animal Nursery Rhymes*, **1378**
Cakes and Custard, 1878
The Glorious Mother Goose, 1879
Granfa' Grig Had a Pig, 1880
Gray Goose and Gander, 1881
Gregory Griggs, 1882
Hickory Dickory Dock and Other Nursery Rhymes, **1379**
James Marshall's Mother Goose, 1883
Jane Yolen's Mother Goose Songbook, **1380**
The Little Dog Laughed and Other Nursery Rhymes, **1384**
Little Robin Redbreast, **35**
Michael Foreman's Mother Goose, **1385**
Mother Goose, 1884, **1386**
Mother Goose Magic, **1382**
The Mother Goose Songbook, **1387**
The Mother Goose Treasury, 1885
Mother Goose's Little Misfortunes, **1383**
The Orchard Book of Nursery Rhymes, **1388**
Over the Moon, 1886
Rain, Rain, Go Away!, **1381**
The Random House Book of Mother Goose, 1887
The Real Mother Goose, 1888
Richard Scarry's Best Mother Goose Ever, 1889
Songs from Mother Goose, 1890
Tail Feathers from Mother Goose, 1891
Tomie dePaola's Mother Goose, 1892
Moutoussamy-Ashe, Jeanne. *Daddy and Me*, **1213**
Mowat, Farley. *Owls in the Family*, 2077
Mueller, Virginia. *Monster's Birthday Hiccups*, **36**
Munsch, Robert. *Pigs*, **330**
Murphy, Jill. *Jeffrey Strangeways*, **734**
Peace at Last, 214
Murphy, Jim. *Backyard Bear*, **515**
The Call of the Wolves, 969
Weird and Wacky Inventions, 2078
Mwalimu. *See* Kennaway, Mwalimu
Mwenye Hadithi. *Baby Baboon*, **37**
Crafty Chameleon, 124
Greedy Zebra, 125
Hungry Hyena, **331**
Lazy Lion, **171**
Tricky Tortoise, 126
Myers, Anna. *Red-Dirt Jessie*, **780**
Myers, Bernice. *Not This Bear!*, 511
Sidney Rella and the Glass Sneaker, 754
Myers, Walter Dean. *Brown Angels*, **1389**
Myller, Rolf. *How Big Is a Foot?*, 970
A Very Noisy Day, 755

Nabb, Magdalen. *Josie Smith at School*, **516**

Naden, Corinne J. (jt. ed.). *Best Books for Children*, 2139

Namioka, Lensey. *Yang the Youngest and His Terrible Ear*, **781**

Napoli, Donna Jo. *The Prince of the Pond*, **782**

Narahashi, Keiko. *I Have a Friend*, 215

Nash, Ogden. *The Adventures of Isabel*, **649**
Custard and Company, 1893

Naylor, Phyllis Reynolds. *The Bodies in the Besseldorf Hotel*, 1216
The Boys Start the War, **735**
The Grand Escape, **783**
Keeping a Christmas Secret, 216
King of the Playground, **332**
Old Sadie and the Christmas Bear, 512
Shiloh, **832**
Witch's Sister, 1217

Nelson, Esther L. *The Funny Song Book*, 1894

Nelson, Vaunda Micheaux. *Mayfield Crossing*, **784**

Nerlove, Miriam. *I Made a Mistake*, 756

Nesbit, E. *Melisande*, 1218

Ness, Evaline. *Mr. Miacca*, 1573
Sam, Bangs and Moonshine, 757
Tom Tit Tot, 1574

Ness, Evaline (comp.). *Amelia Mixed the Mustard and Other Poems*, 1895

Neumeier, Marty, and Byron Glaser. *Action Alphabet*, 758

Nevins, Ann. *From the Horse's Mouth*, 1896

Newman, Nanette. *There's a Bear in the Bath!*, **517**

Newman, Robert. *The Case of the Baker Street Irregular*, 1335

Newton, Patricia Montgomery. *The Five Sparrows*, 1575

Nichol, Barbara. *Beethoven Lives Upstairs*, **785**

Nichols, Grace (jt. comp.). *A Caribbean Dozen*, **1262**

Nietzel, Shirley. *The Jacket I Wear in the Snow*, 217

Nightingale, Sandy. *A Giraffe on the Moon*, **172**

Nikly, Michelle. *The Emperor's Plum Tree*, 759

Niland, Kilmeny. *A Bellbird in a Flame Tree*, **518**

Nimmo, Jenny. *The Witches and the Singing Mice*, **992**

Nims, Bonnie Larkin. *Just Beyond Reach and Other Riddle Poems*, **1390**

Nixon, Joan Lowery. *The Alligator under the Bed*, 218
Beats Me, Claude, 971
The Gift, 1099
Gloria Chipmunk, Star!, 760

If You Were a Writer, 972
That's the Spirit, Claude, **650**

Noble, Trinka Hakes. *Apple Tree Christmas*, 973
The Day Jimmy's Boa Ate the Wash, 761
Meanwhile Back at the Ranch, 974

Nodar, Carmen Santiago. *Abuelita's Paradise*, **519**

Nodset, Joan L. *Who Took the Farmer's Hat?*, 219

Nolan, Dennis. *Dinosaur Dream*, **520**
Witch Bazooza, 762

Noll, Sally. *Jiggle Wiggle Prance*, 513

North, Sterling. *Rascal*, 2079

Norton, Donna E. *Through the Eyes of a Child*, 2122

Norton, Mary. *The Borrowers*, 1336

Norworth, Jack. *Take Me Out to the Ballgame*, **521**

Nostlinger, Christine. *Konrad*, 1219

Numeroff, Laura J. *Dogs Don't Wear Sneakers*, **333**
If You Give a Moose a Muffin, **334**
If You Give a Mouse a Cookie, 514

Oakes, Bill (jt. author). *Puzzlers*, **314**

Ober, Hal. *How Music Came to the World*, **993**

O'Brien, Anne Sibley. *The Princess and the Beggar*, **994**

O'Brien, Robert C. *Mrs. Frisby and the Rats of NIMH*, 1337

O'Dell, Scott. *The Black Pearl*, 1338
Island of the Blue Dolphins, 1339

Odgers, Sally Farrell. *Drummond*, **522**

O'Donnell, Elizabeth Lee. *Maggie Doesn't Want to Move*, 515
The Twelve Days of Summer, **523**

Offen, Hilda. *Nice Work, Little Wolf!*, **173**

Ogburn, Jacqueline K. *Scarlett Angelina Wolverton-Manning*, **524**

O'Keefe, Susan Heyboer. *One Hungry Monster*, **174**

Okie, Susan (jt. author). *To Space and Back*, 2086

Okimoto, Jean Davies. *Blumpoe the Grumpoe Meets Arnold the Cat*, **525**

Olson, Arielle North. *Hurry Home, Grandma!*, 220

O'Neill, Mary L. *Hailstones and Halibut Bones*, 1897
What Is That Sound!, 1898

Onyefulu, Obi. *Chinye*, **995**

Opie, Iona, and Peter Opie, comps. *I Saw Esau*, **1391**
Tail Feathers from Mother Goose, 1891

Opie, Peter (jt. comp.). *I Saw Esau*, **1391**
Tail Feathers from Mother Goose, 1891

Oppenheim, Joanne. *Mrs. Peloki's Class Play*, 763
You Can't Catch Me!, 516

Oppenheim, Joanne (reteller). *One Gift Deserves Another*, **927**

Ormondroyd, Edward. *David and the Phoenix*, 1100

Osborne, Mary Pope. *American Tall Tales*, **1081**
Favorite Greek Myths, 1713
George Washington, **1214**
Mermaid Tales from Around the World, **1082**

Osofsky, Audrey. *My Buddy*, **526**

Otsuka, Zuzo. *Suho and the White Horse*, 1576

Otto, Carolyn. *I Can Tell by Touching*, **1215**

Padgett, Ron (jt. ed.). *The Whole Word Catalogue 2*, 2159

Paladino, Catherine (comp.). *Land, Sea, and Sky*, **1392**

Palmer, Helen. *A Fish Out of Water*, 221

Panek, Dennis. *Catastrophe Cat*, 222

Pank, Rachel. *Under the Blackberries*, **335**

Panzer, Nora (comp.). *Celebrate America in Poetry and Art*, **1393**

Parish, Peggy. *Amelia Bedelia*, 764
No More Monsters for Me, 517

Park, Barbara. *Don't Make Me Smile*, 1220
Junie B. Jones and a Little Monkey Business, **651**
Junie B. Jones and Some Sneaky Peeky Spying, **652**
Junie B. Jones and the Stupid Smelly Bus, **653**
The Kid in the Red Jacket, 1221
Maxie, Rosie, and Earl—Partners in Grime, **736**
Operation, 1101
Rosie Swanson, Fourth-Grade Geek for President, **737**
Skinnybones, 1222

Parker, Nancy Winslow. *Love from Uncle Clyde*, 518

Parkin, Rex. *The Red Carpet*, 519

Parkinson, Kathy. *The Farmer in the Dell*, 223

Parks, Van Dyke, and Malcolm Jones. *Jump!*, 1714

Paterson, Katherine. *Bridge to Terabithia*, 1340
The Tale of the Mandarin Ducks, **996**

Paton Walsh, Jill. *The Green Book*, 1341

Patrick, Denise Lewis. *Red Dancing Shoes*, **175**

Patron, Susan. *Burgoo Stew*, **527**

Patterson, Francine. *Koko's Kitten*, 2080

Patz, Nancy. *Pumpernickel Tickel and Mean Green Cheese*, 520

Paul, Anthony. *The Tiger Who Lost His Stripes*, 765

Paulin, Mary Ann. *Creative Uses of Children's Literature*, 2149

Paulsen, Gary. *A Christmas Sonata*, 833
The Cookcamp, **834**
Dogteam, **738**

The Haymeadow, **835**

Paxton, Tom. *Jennifer's Rabbit*, 224
Where's the Baby?, 38

Paxton, Tom (reteller). *Aesop's Fables*, 1646
Belling the Cat and Other Aesop's Fables, **1056**

Payne, Emmy. *Katy-No-Pocket*, 225

Pearce, Philippa. *Tom's Midnight Garden*, 1342

Pearson, Susan. *Jack and the Beanstalk*, 1577
Lenore's Big Break, **528**

Pearson, Tracey Campbell. *Old MacDonald Had a Farm*, 226

Peck, Robert Newton. *Bee Tree and Other Stuff*, 1899
Mr. Little, 1343
Soup and Me, 1223

Peek, Merle. *Mary Wore Her Red Dress and Henry Wore His Green Sneakers*, 227

Peet, Bill. *The Ant and the Elephant*, 521
Big Bad Bruce, 766
Capyboppy, 2081
Chester the Worldly Pig, 975
Cowardly Clyde, 976
Cyrus the Unsinkable Sea Serpent, 767
Encore for Eleanor, 768
Gnats of Knotty Pine, 977
How Droofus the Dragon Lost His Head, 769
Hubert's Hair-Raising Adventure, 770
No Such Things, 978
The Spooky Tail of Prewitt Peacock, 771
The Whingdingdilly, 979
The Wump World, 980

Pellowski, Anne. *The Family Storytelling Handbook*, 2177
The Story Vine, 2178

Peppé, Rodney. *The Mice Who Lived in a Shoe*, 772

Pepper, Dennis (ed.). *The Oxford Book of Scary Stories*, 836

Perkins, Al. *Hand, Hand, Fingers, Thumb*, 228

Perl, Lila. *Don't Sing before Breakfast, Don't Sleep in the Moonlight*, 1715
It Happened in America, **1216**

Perrault, Charles. *Puss in Boots*, **997**

Peters, Julie Anne. *The Stinky Sneakers Contest*, **654**

Peters, Lisa Westberg. *The Sun, the Wind and the Rain*, 2082
This Way Home, **1217**
Water's Way, **1218**
When the Fly Flew In, **336**

Petersen, P. J. *The Amazing Magic Show*, **529**
I Hate Company, **655**
The Sub, **656**

Peterson, Esther Allen. *Frederick's Alligator*, 773

Penelope Gets Wheels, 774
Pevear, Richard. *Mr. Cat-and-a-Half*, 1578
Our King Has Horns!, 1579
Pfeffer, Susan Beth. *Kid Power*, 1224
*What Do You Do When Your Mouth Won't
Open?*, 1344
Pfeffer, Wendy. *From Tadpole to Frog*, **1219**
Popcorn Park Zoo, **1220**
Pfister, Marcus. *The Rainbow Fish*, **337**
Phelan, Terry Wolfe. *The Week Mom Unplugged
the TVs*, 1102
Phillips, Louis. *How Do You Get a Horse Out of
the Bathtub?*, 1900
Invisible Oink, **1394**
263 Brain Busters, 2083
The Upside Down Riddle Book, 1901
Pilkey, Dav. *Dog Breath*, **530**
Dogzilla, **657**
Kat Kong, **658**
'Twas the Night Before Thanksgiving, **531**
When Cats Dream, **532**
Pilling, Ann. *Realms of Gold*, **1083**
Pinczes, Elinor J. *One Hundred Hungry Ants*, **533**
Pinkwater, Daniel. *Author's Day*, **659**
Doodle Flute, **534**
Fat Men from Space, 1103
Guys from Space, 522
The Hoboken Chicken Emergency, 1104
Lizard Music, 1225
The Magic Moscow, 1105
Ned Feldman, Space Pirate, **660**
The Slaves of Spiegel, 1226
Three Big Hogs, 229
Tooth-Gnasher Superflash, 523
Wempires, **535**
The Wuggie Norple Story, 524
Yobgorgle, 1227
Pinola, Lanny (jt. author). *Fire Race*, **972**
Pitre, Felix. *Juan Bobo and the Pig*, **998**
Pittman, Helena Clare. *A Grain of Rice*, 1580
Miss Hindy's Cats, **338**
Once When I Was Scared, 775
Ploetz, Richard (jt. author). *The Kooken*, **481**
Plunkett, Stephanie Haboush (jt. author). *Sir
Whong and the Golden Pig*, **935**
Polacco, Patricia. *Babushka's Doll*, **176**
Chicken Sunday, **661**
Firetalking, **1221**
Just Plain Fancy, **662**
Mrs. Katz and Tush, **663**
My Rotten Redheaded Older Brother, **536**
Pink and Say, **786**
Some Birthday!, **537**
Thunder Cake, 525

Tikvah Means Hope, **664**
Polette, Nancy. *Hole by the Apple Tree*, **339**
The Little Old Woman and the Hungry Cat, **999**
Nancy Polette's E Is for Everybody, 2150
Picture Books for Gifted Programs, 2151
Polette, Nancy, and Marjorie Hamlin.
Celebrating with Books, 2152
Pollack, Pamela (ed.). *The Random House Book of
Humor for Children*, 1228
Pollock, Penny. *The Turkey Girl*, **1000**
Polushkin, Maria. *Bubba and Babba*, 526
Mother, Mother, I Want Another, 230
Pomerantz, Charlotte. *The Chalk Doll*, 776
The Downtown Fairy Godmother, 981
If I Had a Paka, 1902
The Piggy in the Puddle, 231
Posy, 232
Pooley, Sarah (comp.). *A Day of Rhymes*, 1903
Porte, Barbara Ann. *Harry in Trouble*, 527
Harry's Dog, 777
"Leave That Cricket Be, Alan Lee," **340**
Porter, David Lord. *Help! Let Me Out*, 982
Potter, Beatrice. *The Tale of Peter Rabbit*, 528
Prater, John. *"No!" Said Joe*, **177**
Prelutsky, Jack. *The Baby Uggs Are Hatching*,
1904
The Dragons Are Singing Tonight, **1396**
It's Christmas, 1905
It's Halloween, 1906
It's Snowing! It's Snowing!, 1907
It's Thanksgiving, 1908
It's Valentine's Day, 1909
The Mean Old Mean Hyena, 983
My Parents Think I'm Sleeping, 1910
The New Kid on the Block, 1911
Nightmares, 1912
The Queen of Eene, 1914
Rainy Rainy Saturday, 1915
The Random House Book of Poetry for Children,
1916
Ride a Purple Pelican, 1918
Rolling Harvey Down the Hill, 1919
The Sheriff of Rottenshot, 1920
The Snopp on the Sidewalk and Other Poems, 1921
Something Big Has Been Here, **1398**
The Terrible Tiger, 778
Tyrannosaurus Was a Beast, 1922
What I Did Last Summer, 1923
Zoo Doings, 1924
Prelutsky, Jack (comp.). *A. Nonny Mouse Writes
Again!*, **1395**
For Laughing Out Loud, **1397**
Poems of A. Nonny Mouse, 1913

Prelutsky, Jack (ed.). *Read-Aloud Rhymes for the Very Young*, 1917

Preston, Edna Mitchell. *Pop Corn & Ma Goodness*, 529
Squawk to the Moon, Little Goose, 233

Price, Leontyne. *Aïda*, **837**

Price, Margaret Evans. *Myths and Enchantment Tales*, 1716

Price, Moe. *The Reindeer Christmas*, **341**

Priceman, Marjorie. *How to Make an Apple Pie and See the World*, **538**

Primavera, Elise. *The Three Dots*, **342**

Pringle, Laurence. *Dinosaurs!*, **1222**
Octopus Hug, **178**

Proddow, Penelope. *Demeter and Persephone*, 1581

Provensen, Alice, and Martin Provensen. *The Glorious Flight*, 2084

Provensen, Martin (jt. author). *The Glorious Flight*, 2084

Prøysen, Alf. *Christmas Eve at Santa's*, **343**

Pulver, Robin. *Mrs. Toggle and the Dinosaur*, **344**
Mrs. Toggle's Beautiful Blue Shoe, **345**
Nobody's Mother Is in Second Grade, **346**

Purdy, Carol. *Mrs. Merriweather's Musical Cat*, **539**

Pyle, Howard. *The Swan Maiden*, **665**

Quackenbush, Robert (comp.). *The Holiday Songbook*, 1925

Quattlebaum, Mary. *Jackson Jones and the Puddle of Thorns*, **787**

Quigley, Lillian F. *The Blind Mice and the Elephant*, 1582

Quinn-Harken, Janet. *Peter Penny's Dance*, 779

Rabe, Berniece. *The Balancing Girl*, 530

Rabin, Staton. *Casey Over There*, **666**

Radcliffe, Theresa. *Shadow the Deer*, **347**

Radley, Gail. *The Golden Days*, **838**

Radley, Gail (comp.). *Rainy Day Rhymes*, **1399**

Rae, Mary Maki. *The Farmer in the Dell*, 234

Rael, Elsa Okon. *Marushka's Egg*, **667**

Raffi. *Down by the Bay*, 780
Five Little Ducks, **39**
The Raffi Singable Songbook, 1926
Spider on the Floor, **348**
Wheels on the Bus, 235

Raffi (comp.). *The Raffi Christmas Treasury*, **1400**

Rand, Gloria. *Prince William*, **668**
Salty Takes Off, **540**

Rankin, Laura. *The Handmade Alphabet*, **1223**

Ransome, Arthur. *The Fool of the World and His Flying Ship*, 1583

Rappaport, Doreen. *Living Dangerously*, **1224**

Raschka, Chris. *Yo! Yes?*, **541**

Rattigan, Jama Kim. *Dumpling Soup*, 349

Ravilious, Robin. *The Runaway Chick*, 236

Ray, Mary Lynn. *Pianna*, **542**

Rayevsky, Inna. *The Talking Tree*, 1584

Rayner, Mary. *Garth Pig and the Ice Cream Lady*, 781
Garth Pig Steals the Show, **543**
Mr. and Mrs. Pig's Evening Out, 782
Mrs. Pig's Bulk Buy, 783
Ten Pink Piglets, **179**

Rayner, Shoo. *My First Picture Joke Book*, **1401**

Reasoner, Charles F. *Releasing Children to Literature*, 2153
Where the Readers Are, 2154

Reddix, Valerie. *Millie and the Mud Hole*, **180**

Reeves, Mona Rabun. *I Had a Cat*, 237

Regan, Dian Curtis. *The Curse of the Trouble Dolls*, **669**
The Thirteen Hours of Halloween, **544**

Reiser, Lynn. *Any Kind of Dog*, **40**

Reit, Seymour. *Behind Rebel Lines*, 2085
Benvenuto, 1106

Renberg, Dalia Hardof. *King Solomon and the Bee*, **1001**

Renfro, Nancy (jt. author). *Storytelling with Puppets*, 2168

Reuter, Bjarne. *The Princess and the Sun, Moon and Stars*, 1585

Rey, H. A. *Curious George*, 238

Rhee, Nami. *Magic Spring*, **1002**

Rhodes, Timothy (jt. author). *The Singing Snake*, **889**

Rice, Bebe Faas. *The Year the Wolves Came*, **839**

Rice, Eve. *Oh, Lewis!*, 239

Rice, Eve (adapt.). *Once in a Wood*, 1648

Richard, Françoise. *On Cat Mountain*, **1003**

Richler, Mordecai. *Jacob Two-Two Meets the Hooded Fang*, 1107

Riddell, Chris. *The Trouble with Elephants*, 240

Ride, Sally, and Susan Okie. *To Space and Back*, 2086

Rietz, Sandra A. (jt. author). *Storytelling*, 2173

Riggio, Anita. *Beware the Brindlebeast*, **1004**

Riggle, Judith (jt. author). *Beyond Picture Books*, 2125

Riley, James Whitcomb. *The Gobble-Uns'll Git You Ef You Don't Watch Out*, 1108

Ringgold, Faith. *Aunt Harriet's Underground Railroad in the Sky*, **670**
Tar Beach, **671**

Rinkoff, Barbara. *The Dragon's Handbooks*, 984
The Remarkable Ramsey, 985

Riordan, James. *The Three Magic Gifts*, 1586
  The Woman in the Moon, 1717
Robart, Rose. *The Cake That Mack Ate*, 241
Robbins, Ken. *Beach Days*, 242
  Make Me a Peanut Butter Sandwich and a Glass of Milk, **1225**
Roberts, Bethany. *Waiting-for-Spring Stories*, 531
Roberts, Willo Davis. *The Girl with the Silver Eyes*, 1345
  The Magic Book, 1229
  The View from the Cherry Tree, 1346
Robertson, Keith. *Henry Reed's Baby-Sitting Service*, 1347
Robinson, Adjai. *Singing Tales of Africa*, 1718
Robinson, Barbara. *The Best Christmas Pageant Ever*, 1230
  The Best School Year Ever, **788**
Robinson, Fay (jt. author). *Knock-Knock Knees and Funny Bones*, **1370**
  Nathaniel Willy, Scared Silly, **984**
Robinson, Fay (comp.). *A Frog Inside My Hat*, **1402**
Robinson, Gail. *Raven the Trickster*, 1719
Robinson, Marc. *Cock-a-Doodle-Doo!*, **1226**
Robinson, Nancy K. *Just Plain Cat*, 986
Robison, Deborah. *Bye-Bye, Old Buddy*, 532
  No Elephants Allowed, 243
Roche, P. K. *Good-Bye, Arnold*, 533
Rockwell, Anne. *The Gollywhopper Egg*, 534
  Puss in Boots & Other Stories, 1720
Rockwell, Anne (comp.). *Gray Goose and Gander*, 1881
Rockwell, Thomas. *How to Eat Fried Worms*, 1109
Rodanas, Kristina. *Dragonfly's Tale*, **1005**
Rodda, Emily. *Finders Keepers*, **789**
  The Pigs Are Flying, 1231
Roddy, Patricia. *Api and the Boy Stranger*, **1006**
Rodowsky, Colby. *Dog Days*, **739**
Rogasky, Barbara (comp.). *Winter Poems*, **1403**
Rogasky, Barbara (reteller). *Rapunzel*, 1503
  The Water of Life, 1511
Rogers, Jean. *Runaway Mittens*, 244
Rogers, Paul. *The Shapes Game*, **181**
Rohmann, Eric. *Time Flies*, 350
Roop, Connie (jt. author). *Ahyoka and the Talking Leaves*, **740**
  I, Columbus; My Journal—1492–3, **1227**
  One Earth, a Multitude of Creatures, **1228**
Roop, Peter, and Connie Roop. *Ahyoka and the Talking Leaves*, **740**
  I, Columbus; My Journal—1492–3, **1227**
  One Earth, a Multitude of Creatures, **1228**
Roop, Peter, and Connie Roop, eds. *Capturing Nature*, **1101**

Connie, Roop (jt. ed.). *Capturing Nature*, **1101**
Root, Phyllis. *Coyote and the Magic Words*, **351**
  Moon Tiger, 535
Rose, Anne. *The Triumphs of Fuzzy Fogtop*, 784
Rosen, Michael. *How the Giraffe Got Such a Long Neck . . . and Why Rhino Is So Grumpy*, **1007**
  Moving, **352**
  We're Going on a Bear Hunt, 245
Rosen, Michael (comp.). *Itsy-Bitsy Beasties*, **1404**
  Poems for the Very Young, **1405**
Rosen, Michael J. (ed.). *Speak!*, **1229**
Rosenbloom, Joseph. *Daffy Definitions*, 1927
  The Funniest Dinosaur Book Ever, 1928
  The Funniest Knock-Knock Book Ever!, 1929
  The Funniest Riddle Book Ever!, 1930
  Giggles, Gags & Groaners, 1932
  Knock Knock! Who's There?, 1933
  The Looniest Limerick Book in the World, 1934
  Spooky Riddles and Jokes, 1937
  The World's Best Sports Riddles and Jokes, 1939
Rosenbloom, Joseph (comp.). *The Gigantic Joke Book*, 1931
  Monster Madness, 1935
  Silly Verse (and Even Worse), 1936
  Twist These on Your Tongue, 1938
Ross, Gayle. *How Rabbit Tricked Otter and Other Cherokee Trickster Stories*, **1084**
  How Turtle's Back Was Cracked, **1008**
Ross, Pat. *Gloria and the Super Soaper*, 987
  M & M and the Santa Secrets, 785
Ross, Tony. *I'm Coming to Get You*, 536
  Super Dooper Jezebel, 786
Roth, Roger. *The Sign Painter's Dream*, **545**
Roth, Susan L. *Kanahena*, 1587
Rotner, Shelley (jt. author). *Changes*, **1100**
Rotner, Shelley, and Ken Kreisler. *Citybook*, **353**
Rounds, Glen. *I Know an Old Lady Who Swallowed a Fly*, 537
  Mr. Yowder and the Train Robbers, 1232
  Ol' Paul, the Mighty Logger, 1721
  Old MacDonald Had a Farm, **182**
  The Three Billy Goats Gruff, **1009**
  Three Little Pigs and the Big Bad Wolf, **1010**
Rowe, John A. *Baby Crow*, **183**
Roy, Ron. *The Chimpanzee Kid*, 1348
  Million Dollar Jeans, 1233
  Nightmare Island, 1234
  Three Ducks Went Wandering, 246
Ruckman, Ivy. *Night of the Twisters*, 1235
Ruddick, Bob (jt. author). *Max and Me and the Time Machine*, 1306
  Max and Me and the Wild West, 1307
Runcie, Jill. *Cock-a-Doodle-Doo!*, **41**
Russell, Ching Yeung. *First Apple*, **741**

Russell, Marion. *Along the Santa Fe Trail*, **1230**
Russo, Marisabina. *Alex Is My Friend*, **354**
  I Don't Want to Go Back to School, **355**
  The Line Up Book, 247
  Only Six More Days, 248
  Trade-In Mother, **184**
  Waiting for Hannah, 538
Russo, Marisabina (comp.). *The Ice Cream Ocean and Other Delectable Poems of the Sea*, 1940
Ryan, Cheli Druan. *Hildilid's Night*, 539
Rydell, Katy. *Wind Says Good Night*, **42**
Ryden, Hope. *Wild Animals of America ABC*, 2087
Ryder, Joanne. *Catching the Wind*, 2088
  Chipmunk Song, 2089
  Lizard in the Sun, 2090
  The Night Flight, 540
  Sea Elf, **1231**
  The Snail's Spell, 249
  White Bear, Ice Bear, 2091
  Winter Whale, **1232**
Rylant, Cynthia. *All I See*, 988
  Best Wishes, **1233**
  Children of Christmas, 1349
  Night in the Country, 541
  The Relatives Came, 542
  Waiting to Waltz, 1941
  When I Was Young in the Mountains, 989

Sachar, Louis. *Dogs Don't Tell Jokes*, **840**
  Marvin Redpost, **672**
  Sideways Stories from Wayside School, 1110
  Wayside School Is Falling Down, 1111
Sachs, Marilyn. *The Bears' House*, 1350
  Matt's Mitt and Fleet-Footed Florence, 990
  Veronica Ganz, 1236
Sadler, Catherine Edwards. *Treasure Mountain*, 1722
Sadler, Marilyn. *Alistair and the Alien Invasion*, **356**
  Alistair in Outer Space, 787
  Alistair's Elephant, 788
  Alistair's Time Machine, 789
Sage, Alison (reteller). *Rumpelstiltskin*, **922**
Salway, Lance. *A Nasty Piece of Work and Other Ghost Stories*, 1351
Samton, Sheila White. *Beside the Bay*, 250
Samuels, Barbara. *Duncan & Dolores*, 251
Sandburg, Carl. *Rainbows Are Made*, 1942
Sanders, Scott Russell. *Here Comes the Mystery Man*, **673**
  Warm as Wool, **546**
Sanderson, Ruth (reteller). *The Twelve Dancing Princesses*, **930**

Sanfield, Steve. *A Natural Man*, 1588
San Souci, Robert D. *The Boy and the Ghost*, **1011**
  The Enchanted Tapestry, 1589
  The Firebird, **1012**
  The Hobyahs, **1013**
  Larger Than Life, **1085**
  The Samurai's Daughter, **1014**
  The Snow Wife, **1015**
  Sootface, **1016**
  Sukey and the Mermaid, **1017**
  The Talking Eggs, 1590
  The Tsar's Promise, **1018**
  The White Cat, **1019**
Sargeant, Sarah. *Weird Henry Berg*, 1352
Sarnoff, Jane. *Take Warning!*, 1723
Sauer, Julie L. *Fog Magic*, 1353
  Mike's House, 252
Saunders, Dennis (comp.). *Magic Lights and Streets of Shining Jet*, 1943
Saunders, Susan. *Fish Fry*, 790
Sawyer, Ruth. *Journey Cake, Ho!*, 1591
  The Remarkable Christmas of the Cobbler's Sons, **1020**
  The Way of the Storyteller, 2179
Say, Allen. *The Bicycle Man*, 791
  El Chino, **1234**
  Grandfather's Journey, **674**
  Once Under the Cherry Blossom Tree, 1592
  Tree of Cranes, **547**
Scarry, Richard (comp.). *Richard Scarry's Best Mother Goose Ever*, 1889
Schatell, Brian. *Farmer Goff and His Turkey Sam*, 543
Schertle, Alice. *The April Fool*, 991
  Bill and Google-Eyed Goblins, 792
  How Now, Brown Cow?, **1406**
  Jeremy Bean's St. Patrick's Day, 544
Schimmel, Nancy. *Just Enough to Make a Story*, 2180
Schindel, John. *What's for Lunch?*, **185**
Schneider, Howie. *Uncle Lester's Hat*, **357**
Schneider, Howie (jt. author). *Amos*, 549
Schotter, Roni. *Captain Snap and the Children of Vinegar Lane*, 793
Schroeder, Alan. *Lily and the Wooden Bowl*, **1021**
Schwartz, Alvin. *Busy Buzzing Bumblebees and Other Tongue Twisters*, 1944
  Gold and Silver, Silver and Gold, 2092
  I Saw You in the Bathtub and Other Folk Rhymes, 1947
  Scary Stories 3, **1086**
  Scary Stories to Tell in the Dark, 1725
  Whoppers, 1726

Schwartz, Alvin (comp.). *And the Green Grass Grew All Around*, **1407**

The Cat's Elbow and Other Secret Languages, 1945

Chin Music, 1946

Cross Your Fingers, Spit in Your Hat, 1724

Kickle Snifters and Other Fearsome Critters Collected from American Folklore, 1593

Ten Copycats in a Boat and Other Riddles, 1948

Tomfoolery, 1949

A Twister of Twists, a Tangler of Tongues, 1950

Schwartz, Amy. *Annabelle Swift, Kindergartner*, 794

Bea and Mr. Jones, 795

Her Majesty, Aunt Essie, 796

The Lady Who Put Salt in Her Coffee, **742**

Oma and Bobo, 545

A Teeny Tiny Baby, **358**

Yossel Zissel & the Wisdom of Chelm, 992

Schwartz, Amy (jt. comp.). *Mother Goose's Little Misfortunes*, **1383**

Schwartz, Betty Ann, and Leon Archibald. *The Old-Fashioned Storybook*, 1727

Schwartz, David. *How Much Is a Million?*, 2093

If You Made a Million, 2094

Supergrandpa, **675**

Schwartz, Henry. *How I Captured a Dinosaur*, 546

Schwartz, Howard. *Elijah's Violin and Other Jewish Fairy Tales*, 1728

Schwartz, Mary Ada. *Spiffen*, 547

Scieszka, Jon. *The Book That Jack Wrote*, **548**

The Frog Prince Continued, **676**

Knights of the Kitchen Table, **743**

The Stinky Cheese Man and Other Fairly Stupid Tales, **677**

The True Story of the 3 Little Pigs, 993

Your Mother Was a Neanderthal, **790**

Scott, Sally. *The Magic Horse*, 1594

The Three Wonderful Beggars, 1595

Scribner, Charles. *The Devil's Bridge*, 1596

Scribner, Virginia. *Gopher Takes Heart*, **744**

Seeger, Charles (jt. author). *The Foolish Frog*, 797

Seeger, Pete. *Abiyoyo*, 548

Seeger, Pete, and Charles Seeger. *The Foolish Frog*, 797

Seeger, Ruth Crawford (comp.). *American Folk Songs for Children*, 1951

Segal, Lore. *All the Way Home*, 253

Tell Me a Mitzi, 798

Segel, Elizabeth (jt. author). *For Reading Out Loud!*, 2142

Seibert, Patricia. *Mush!*, **1235**

Seidler, Tor (reteller). *The Steadfast Tin Soldier*, **586**

Selden, George. *The Cricket in Times Square*, 1237

Sparrow Socks, 799

Seligson, Susan. *Amos Camps Out*, **549**

Seligson, Susan, and Howie Schneider. *Amos*, 549

Selsam, Millicent, and Joyce Hunt. *Keep Looking!*, 2095

Selznick, Brian. *The Houdini Box*, **745**

Sendak, Maurice. *Alligators All Around*, 550

Chicken Soup with Rice, 551

One Was Johnny, 254

Pierre, 552

Where the Wild Things Are, 255

Serfozo, Mary. *Who Said Red?*, 256

Who Wants One?, 257

Service, Pamela F. *Stinker from Space*, 1354

Service, Robert W. *The Cremation of Sam McGee*, 1355

Seuling, Barbara. *The Last Cow on the White House Lawn & Other Little-Known Facts about the Presidency*, 2096

The Triplets, 800

You Can't Eat Peanuts in Church, 2097

Seuss, Dr. *Bartholomew and the Oobleck*, 994

The Cat in the Hat, 258

Dr. Seuss' ABC, 553

The 500 Hats of Bartholomew Cubbins, 995

Green Eggs and Ham, 259

Horton Hatches the Egg, 801

How the Grinch Stole Christmas, 802

If I Ran the Zoo, 803

The King's Stilts, 996

The Lorax, 997

McElligot's Pool, 804

Marvin K. Mooney, Will You Please Go Now, 554

On Beyond Zebra, 805

Thidwick, the Big-Hearted Moose, 806

Sewall, Marcia. *Master of All Masters*, 1597

The Pilgrims of Plimoth, 2098

Shannon, George. *Dance Away*, 260

Lizard's Song, 261

More Stories to Solve, **1087**

Stories to Solve, 1729

The Surprise, 262

Shannon, Mark. *Gawain and the Green Knight*, **1022**

Shapiro, Arnold L. *Who Says That?*, **43**

Sharmat, Marjorie Weinman. *The Best Valentine in the World*, 807

A Big Fat Enormous Lie, **359**

Chasing after Annie, 998

Gila Monsters Meet You at the Airport, 808

Gladys Told Me to Meet Her Here, 809

Go to Sleep, Nicholas Joe, 263

Nate the Great, 810

Sharmat, Mitchell. *Gregory, the Terrible Eater*, 555

Sharratt, Nick. *My Mom and Dad Make Me Laugh*, **186**

Shaw, Alison (comp.). *Until I Saw the Sea*, **1408**

Shaw, Charles G. *It Looked Like Spilt Milk*, 264

Shaw, Nancy. *Sheep in a Jeep*, 556
Sheep in a Shop, **360**
Sheep Out to Eat, **361**

Shedlock, Marie L. *The Art of the Story-Teller*, 2181

Shelby, Anne. *Potluck*, **362**
What to Do About Pollution, **1236**

Sheldon, Dyan. *Love, Your Bear Pete*, **363**
My Brother Is a Visitor from Another Planet, **746**
A Witch Got on at Paddington Station, 265

Shepard, Aaron. *The Legend of Slappy Hooper*, **1023**
Stories on Stage, **1237**

Sheppard, Jeff. *Splash, Splash*, **44**

Sherman, Josepha. *Vassilisa the Wise*, 1598

Sherrow, Victoria. *There Goes the Ghost!*, 557

Shetterly, Susan Hand. *Raven's Light*, **1024**

Shields, Carol Diggory. *I Am Really a Princess*, **550**

Showers, Paul. *The Listening Walk*, **187**

Shreve, Susan. *The Gift of the Girl Who Couldn't Hear*, **841**
Joshua T. Bates Takes Charge, **747**

Shulevitz, Uri. *The Treasure*, 999

Shura, Mary Frances. *Chester*, 1112
Mister Wolf and Me, 1238

Shusterman, Neal. *The Eyes of Kid Midas*, **842**

Shute, Linda. *Clever Tom and the Leprechaun*, 1599
Halloween Party, **551**
Momotaro the Peach Boy, 1600

Shyer, Marlene Fanta. *My Brother, the Thief*, 1356
Welcome Home, Jellybean, 1357

Siebert, Diane. *Mojave*, 1000
Plane Song, **552**
Train Song, **553**
Truck Song, 266

Sierra, Jud. *The Elephant's Wrestling Match*, **1025**

Silverman, Erica. *Big Pumpkin*, **364**
Don't Fidget a Feather!, **365**

Silverman, Maida. *Anna and the Seven Swans*, 1601

Silverstein, Shel. *A Giraffe and a Half*, 811
The Giving Tree, 1001
Where the Sidewalk Ends, 1952
Who Wants a Cheap Rhinoceros?, 812

Simmie, Lois. *Auntie's Knitting a Baby*, 1953

Simms, Laura. *The Squeaky Door*, **1026**

Simon, Seymour. *Animal Fact / Animal Fable*, 2099
The Dinosaur Is the Biggest Animal That Ever Lived and Other Wrong Ideas You Thought Were True, 2100
Einstein Anderson, Science Sleuth, 1239
Galaxies, 2101
Hidden Worlds, 2102
Icebergs and Glaciers, 2103
Stars, 2104
Storms, 2105
Volcanoes, 2106

Singer, Isaac Bashevis. *When Shlemiel Went to Warsaw & Other Stories*, 1730

Singer, Marilyn. *Chester the Out-of-Work Dog*, **366**
It's Hard to Read a Map with a Beagle on Your Lap, **1409**
Nine O'Clock Lullaby, **554**
The Painted Fan, **748**
Please Don't Squeeze Your Boa, Noah!, **1410**
Turtle in July, 1954

Sis, Peter. *Follow the Dream*, **1238**

Sivulich, Sandra Stroner. *I'm Going on a Bear Hunt*, 267

Skira-Venturi, Rosabianca. *A Weekend with Leonardo da Vinci*, **1239**

Skofield, James. *'Round and Around*, **188**

Skurzynski, Gloria. *Here Comes the Mail*, **1240**
Martin by Myself, 813
What Happened to Hamelin, 1358

Slavin, Bill. *The Cat Came Back*, **555**

Sleator, William. *Among the Dolls*, 1240
Into the Dream, 1359

Slepian, Jan. *Back to Before*, **843**
The Broccoli Tapes, **844**
Risk N' Roses, **845**

Sloan, Glenna Davis. *The Child as Critic*, 2155

Sloat, Teri. *The Hungry Giant of the Tundra*, **1027**

Slobodkin, Florence. *Too Many Mittens*, 268

Slobodkin, Louis. *The Spaceship under the Apple Tree*, 1113

Slobodkina, Esphyr. *Caps for Sale*, 269

Slote, Alfred. *The Devil Rides with Me and Other Fantastic Stories*, 1360
Hang Tough, Paul Mather, 1241
My Robot Buddy, 1002
My Trip to Alpha I, 1114

Small, David. *Imogene's Antlers*, 558
Paper John, 814

Small, Ernest. *Baba Yaga*, 1602

Small, Terry. *The Legend of William Tell*, **1028**

Smath, Jerry. *A Hat So Simple*, **367**

Smee, Nicola. *The Tusk Fairy*, **45**

Smith, Alison. *Help! There's a Cat Washing in Here*, 1361

Smith, Janice Lee. *The Monster in the Third Dresser Drawer*, 815
The Show-and-Tell War, 816

Smith, L. J. *The Night of the Solstice*, 1362

Smith, Robert Kimmell. *Chocolate Fever*, 1003
The War with Grandpa, 1115

Smith, William Jay. *Ho for a Hat!*, **368**
Laughing Time, 1955

Snyder, Carol. *Ike and Mama and the Once-a-Year Suit*, 1004

Snyder, Dianne. *The Boy of the Three Year Nap*, 1603

Snyder, Zilpha Keatley. *Libby on Wednesday*, **846**

Sobol, Donald J. *Encyclopedia Brown, Boy Detective*, 1116

Soto, Gary. *Too Many Tamales*, **369**

Spagnoli, Cathy (adapt.). *Nine-in-One, Grr! Grr!*, 1404

Spangler, Stella S. (jt. author). *Science & Technology in Fact and Fiction*, 2141

Speare, Elizabeth George. *The Sign of the Beaver*, 1363

Sperling, Susan Kelz. *Murflies and Wink-a-Peeps*, 1956

Sperry, Armstrong. *Call It Courage*, 1242

Spier, Peter. *Bored, Nothing to Do*, 817
Oh, Were They Ever Happy!, 559

Spinelli, Eileen. *If You Want to Find Golden*, **370**
Somebody Loves You, Mr. Hatch, **371**
Thanksgiving at the Tappletons', 818

Spinelli, Jerry. *Fourth Grade Rats*, **749**
Maniac Magee, **847**
Report to the Principal's Office, **791**

Spinner, Stephanie (jt. author). *Aliens for Breakfast*, 915

Spray, Carole. *The Mare's Egg*, 1604

Springer, Nancy. *Colt*, **792**

Springer, Nancy (comp.). *Music of Their Hooves*, **1411**

Springstubb, Tricia. *The Magic Guinea Pig*, 270

Stadler, John. *Animal Cafe*, 819
Cat Is Back at Bat, **372**

Stamm, Claus. *Three Strong Women*, 1605

Stanley, Diane. *Fortune*, 1117
The Good-Luck Pencil, 1005
Moe the Dog in Tropical Paradise, **556**

Stanley, Diane, and Peter Vennema. *Bard of Avon*, **1241**
Charles Dickens, **1242**

Stanley, Fay. *The Last Princess*, **1243**

Starbird, Kaye. *The Covered Bridge House and Other Poems*, 1957

Stearns, Pamela. *Into the Painted Bear Lair*, 1243

Steckler, Arthur. *101 More Words and How They Began*, 1958

Steel, Flora Annie. *Tattercoats*, 1606

Steig, William. *Abel's Island*, 1364
The Amazing Bone, 1006
Brave Irene, 820
Caleb and Kate, 1118
CDB, 1959
Dr. DeSoto, 1007
Solomon the Rusty Nail, 1008
Spinky Sulks, 1009
Sylvester and the Magic Pebble, 821
Zeke Pippin, **678**

Stein, Sara Bonnett. *Cat*, 2107

Steptoe, John. *Mufaro's Beautiful Daughters*, 1607
Stevie, 1010
The Story of Jumping Mouse, 1608

Sterman, Betsy, and Samuel Sterman. *Backyard Dragon*, **750**
Too Much Magic, 1119

Sterman, Samuel (jt. author). *Backyard Dragon*, **750**
Too Much Magic, 1119

Stern, Simon. *The Hobyas*, 1609
Vasily and the Dragon, 1610

Stevens, Carla. *Lily and Miss Liberty*, **679**

Stevens, Janet. *Coyote Steals the Blanket*, **1029**
From Pictures to Words, **1244**
Goldilocks and the Three Bears, 1611
The House That Jack Built, 271
Tops & Bottoms, **1030**

Stevens, Janet (adapt.). *The Tortoise and the Hare*, 1388

Stevens, Susanna (trans.). *The Changeling*, **636**

Stevenson, James. *Brrr!*, **373**
Clams Can't Sing, 560
Could Be Worse, 822
Don't You Know There's a War On?, **1245**
Happy Valentine's Day, Emma!, 823
Monty, 561
The Mud Flat Olympics, **557**
Rolling Rose, **46**
That Dreadful Day, 1011
That Terrible Halloween Night, 824
That's Exactly the Way It Wasn't, **558**
There's Nothing to Do!, 825
What's Under My Bed?, 826
Worse Than the Worst, **560**
Worse Than Willy!, 827
The Worst Person's Christmas, **559**
Yuck!, 562

Stevenson, Robert Louis. *Block City*, 563
My Shadow, **374**

Stewig, John Warren. *Stone Soup*, **1031**
Stickland, Henrietta. *Dinosaur Roar!*, **189**
Still, James. *Jack and the Wonder Beans*, 1612
Stillwell, Lydia (jt. author). *Creative Drama for the Classroom Teacher*, 2172
Stolz, Mary. *The Bully of Barkham Street*, 1120
  Cat Walk, 1121
  Quentin Corn, 1365
  Storm in the Night, 828
  Zekmet, the Stone Carver, 1244
Stonely, Jack. *Scruffy*, 1245
Storr, Catherine. *Clever Polly and the Stupid Wolf*, 1122
Stott, Dorothy. *Too Much*, **47**
Streatfeild, Noel. *When the Sirens Wailed*, 1366
Strickland, Brad. *Dragon's Plunder*, **848**
Strickland, Dorothy, and Michael R. Strickland, comps. *Families*, **1412**
Strickland, Michael R. (jt. comp.). *Families*, **1412**
Stroud, Virginia A. *Doesn't Fall Off His Horse*, **680**
Stutson, Caroline. *By the Light of the Halloween Moon*, **561**
Suetake, Kunihiro (jt. trans.). *Red Dragonfly on My Shoulder*, **1278**
Sullivan, Charles (comp.). *Cowboys*, **1413**
Sun, Chying Feng. *Mama Bear*, **562**
Sundgaard, Arnold. *Meet Jack Appleknocker*, 272
Supree, Burton (jt. author). *Mother, Mother, I Feel Sick, Send for the Doctor Quick, Quick, Quick*, 646
Sutcliff, Rosemary. *Black Ships Before Troy!*, **1088**
Sutherland, Zena. *Children and Books*, 2123
Sutherland, Zena (comp.). *The Orchard Book of Nursery Rhymes*, **1388**
Sutton, Jane. *Me and the Weirdos*, 1246
Swallow, Pam. *Melvil and Dewey in the Chips*, 1012
Swan, Robert. *Destination*, 2108
Swann, Brian. *A Basket Full of White Eggs*, 1960
Sweet, Melissa. *Fiddle-I-Fee*, **190**
Swinburne, Irene, and Laurence Swinburne. *Behind the Sealed Door*, 2109
Swinburne, Laurence (jt. author). *Behind the Sealed Door*, 2109
Swope, Sam. *The Araboolies of Liberty Street*, 829

Talbott, Hudson. *We're Back!*, 1013
Talon, Robert. *Zoophabets*, 1014
Tanaka, Béatrice. *The Chase*, **1032**
Tannen, Mary. *The Wizard Children of Finn*, 1367
Tapp, Kathy Kennedy. *Moth-Kin Magic*, 1247
Tashjian, Virginia. *Juba This and Juba That*, 1961
  Once There Was and Was Not, 1731

Taylor, Clark. *The House That Crack Built*, **1246**
Taylor, Harriet Peck. *Coyote Places the Stars*, **1033**
Taylor, Livingston. *Can I Be Good?*, **375**
Taylor, Mark. *Henry the Explorer*, 564
Taylor, Mildred D. *The Gold Cadillac*, 1248
Tayntor, Elizabeth, Paul Erickson, and Les Kaufman. *Dive to the Coral Reefs*, 2110
Teague, Mark. *The Field Beyond the Outfield*, **376**
  Frog Medicine, **681**
  Moog-Moog, Space Barber, **563**
  Pigsty, **564**
Tejima, Keizaburo. *Fox's Dream*, **565**
Temple, Frances. *Tiger Soup*, **1034**
Temple, Lannis. (ed.). *Dear World*, **1247**
Terban, Marvin. *The Dove Dove*, 1962
  Funny You Should Ask, **1414**
  I Think I Thought and Other Tricky Verbs, 1963
  In a Pickle and Other Funny Idioms, 1964
  Too Hot to Hoot, 1965
Tews, Susan. *The Gingerbread Doll*, **565**
Thaler, Mike. *The Chocolate Marshmelephant Sundae*, 1966
  The Teacher from the Black Lagoon, **682**
Thayer, Ernest Lawrence. *Casey at the Bat*, 1368
Thayer, Jane. *The Popcorn Dragon*, 273
  The Puppy Who Wanted a Boy, 566
  Quiet on Account of Dinosaur, 567
Thomas, Jane Resh. *The Princess in the Pigpen*, 1369
  Saying Good-Bye to Grandma, **683**
Thomas, Patricia. *The One and Only Super-Duper Golly-Whopper Jim-Dandy Really-Handy Clock-Tock-Stopper*, **566**
  "Stand Back," Said the Elephant, "I'm Going to Sneeze!," 568
Thomas, Rebecca L. *Primaryplots*, 2156
Thompson, Brian (comp.). *Catch It If You Can*, **1415**
Thomson, Peggy. *The Brave Little Tailor*, **1035**
  The King Has Horse's Ears, 1613
Thornhill, Jan. *Crow & Fox and Other Animal Legends*, **1089**
Thurber, James. *The Great Quillow*, **684**
  Many Moons, 1015
Titherington, Jeanne. *A Place for Ben*, 274
Titus, Eve. *Anatole*, 830
  Basil of Baker Street, 1249
Tobias, Tobi. *Chasing the Goblins Away*, 831
Tolan, Stephanie S. *Sophie and the Sidewalk Man*, **685**
Tolhurst, Marilyn. *Somebody and the Three Blairs*, **191**
Tolstoi, Alexie. *The Great Big Enormous Turnip*, 1614

Tomey, Ingrid. *Grandfather's Day*, **686**
Tompert, Ann. *Bamboo Hats and a Rice Cake*, **1036**
  Grandfather Tang's Story, **567**
  Just a Little Bit, **192**
Torgersen, Don Arthur. *The Girl Who Tricked the Troll*, 832
Townson, Hazel. *Terrible Tuesday*, 569
Trapani, Iza. *The Itsy Bitsy Spider*, **193**
Trelease, Jim. *The New Read-Aloud Handbook*, 2157
Tresselt, Alvin. *Hide and Seek Fog*, 833
  The Mitten, 1615
Tripp, Wallace. *My Uncle Podger*, 1123
Tripp, Wallace (comp.). *Granfa' Grig Had a Pig*, 1880
  A Great Big Ugly Man Came Up and Tied His Horse to Me, 1967
Trivas, Irene. *Annie . . . Anya*, **377**
  Emma's Christmas, **687**
Trivizas, Eugene. *The Three Little Wolves and the Big Bad Pig*, **378**
Troughton, Joanna. *How the Birds Changed Their Feathers*, 1616
  Mouse-Deer's Market, 1617
  Tortoise's Dream, 1618
Tsutsui, Yoriko. *Anna's Secret Friend*, 275
Tunnell, Michael O. *Chinook!*, **688**
Turkle, Brinton. *The Adventures of Obadiah*, 834
  Deep in the Forest, 570
  Do Not Open, 1016
Turner, Ann. *Hedgehog for Breakfast*, **194**
Turner, Gwenda. *Over on the Farm*, **195**
Turska, Krystyna. *The Magician of Cracow*, 1619
Tusa, Tricia. *The Family Reunion*, **568**
Tworkov, Jack. *The Camel Who Took a Walk*, 571
Tyler, Linda Wagner. *Waiting for Mom*, 276
Tyrrell, Esther Quesada. *Hummingbirds*, **1248**
Tzannes, Robin. *Professor Puffendorf's Secret Potions*, **569**

Uchida, Yoshiko. *Journey Home*, 1370
  The Magic Purse, **1037**
  The Sea of Gold and Other Tales from Japan, 1732
  The Two Foolish Cats, 1620
  The Wise Old Woman, **1038**
Udry, Janice May. *Alfred*, 572
  Angie, 1017
  Thump and Plunk, 277
  A Tree Is Nice, 278
  What Mary Jo Shared, 279
Ueno, Noriko. *Elephant Buttons*, 280
Ullman, James Ramsay. *Banner in the Sky*, 1371
Ungerer, Tomi. *The Beast of Monsieur Racine*, 1018

Crictor, 573
One, Two, Where's My Shoe?, 281
Untermeyer, Louis (comp.). *The Golden Treasury of Poetry*, 1968
Untermeyer, Louis (sel.). *Aesop's Fables*, 1645

Vagin, Vladimir (jt. author). *Dear Brother*, **401**
Van Allsburg, Chris. *The Garden of Abdul Gasazi*, 1019
  Jumanji, 1020
  The Mysteries of Harris Burdick, 1250
  The Polar Express, 835
  The Stranger, 1124
  The Sweetest Fig, **751**
  Two Bad Ants, 1125
  The Widow's Broom, **752**
  The Wreck of the Zephyr, 1126
Vanderwerf, Mary Ann (jt. author). *Science & Technology in Fact and Fiction*, 2141
Vande Velde, Vivian. *A Hidden Magic*, 1251
Van de Wetering, Janwillem. *Hugh Pine*, 1127
Van Laan, Nancy. *The Big Fat Worm*, 282
  Buffalo Dance, **1039**
  People, People, Everywhere!, **196**
  The Tiny, Tiny Boy and the Big, Big Cow, **1040**
Van Leeuwen, Jean. *Benjy in Business*, 1021
  Bound for Oregon, **793**
  The Great Christmas Kidnapping Caper, 1128
  The Great Rescue Operation, 1252
Van Woerkom, Dorothy. *Alexander the Rock-Eater*, 1621
Vaughn, Marcia K. *Wombat Stew*, 836
Vennema, Peter (jt. author). *Bard of Avon*, **1241**
  Charles Dickens, **1242**
Vernon, Adele. *The Riddle*, 1622
Vesey, A. *The Princess and the Frog*, 837
Viorst, Judith. *Alexander and the Terrible, Horrible, No Good, Very Bad Day*, 838
  Alexander Who Used to Be Rich Last Sunday, 839
  The Alphabet from Z to A, **1416**
  If I Were in Charge of the World and Other Worries, 1969
  I'll Fix Anthony, 574
  My Mama Says There Aren't Any Zombies, Ghosts, Vampires, Creatures, Demons, Monsters, Fiends, Goblins or Things, 840
  Sad Underwear and Other Complications, **1417**
  The Tenth Good Thing about Barney, 575
Vipont, Elfrida. *The Elephant & the Bad Baby*, 283
Voake, Charlotte (comp.). *Over the Moon*, 1886
Voce, Louise. *Over in the Meadow*, **197**
Vollmer, Dennis. *Joshua Disobeys*, **198**
Vozar, David. *Yo, Hungry Wolf!*, **570**

Vreeken, Elizabeth. *The Boy Who Would Not Say His Name*, 576

Vuong, Lynette Dyer. *The Brocaded Slipper and Other Vietnamese Tales*, 1733

Vyner, Sue. *The Stolen Egg*, **379**

Waber, Bernard. *An Anteater Named Arthur*, 577
Dear Hildegarde, 1022
I Was All Thumbs, 1023
Ira Says Goodbye, 841
Ira Sleeps Over, 842
Lyle, Lyle Crocodile, 578
Rich Cat, Poor Cat, 579
"You Look Ridiculous," Said the Rhinoceros to the Hippopotamus, 580

Waddell, Martin. *Can't You Sleep, Little Bear?*, **199**
Farmer Duck, **200**
The Happy Hedgehog Band, **48**
Let's Go Home, Little Bear, **201**
Owl Babies, **49**
The Pig in the Pond, **50**
Sam Vole and His Brothers, **51**
Squeak-a-Lot, **52**

Wade, Barrie. *Little Monster*, 284

Wadsworth, Ginger. *Tomorrow Is Daddy's Birthday*, **380**

Wadsworth, Ginger (adapt.). *Along the Santa Fe Trail*, **1230**

Wadsworth, Olive A. *Over in the Meadow*, **202**

Wagner, Jane. *J. T.*, 1129

Wagner, Jenny. *John Brown, Rose and the Midnight Cat*, 581

Wagner, Joseph A. (jt. author). *Children's Literature Through Storytelling & Drama*, 2166

Wagner, Karen. *Silly Fred*, **203**

Wakefield, Pat A., and Larry Carrara. *A Moose for Jessica*, 2111

Waldherr, Kris. *Persephone and the Pomegranate*, **1041**

Walker, Barbara. *Teeny-Tiny and the Witch Woman*, 1623
A Treasure of Turkish Folktales for Children, 1734

Walker, Paul Robert. *Big Men, Big Country*, **1090**

Wallace, Barbara Brooks. *Peppermints in the Parlor*, 1372
The Twin in the Tavern, **849**

Wallace, Bill. *Beauty*, 1373

Wallace, Daisy (comp.). *Ghost Poems*, 1970

Wallace, Ian. *Chin Chiang and the Dragon Dance*, 843

Wallace, Karen. *Red Fox*, **1249**

Walsh, Ellen Stoll. *Hop Jump*, **53**
Mouse Count, **54**

Mouse Paint, **204**
Pip's Magic, **205**

Walsh, Jill Paton. See Paton Walsh, Jill

Walton, Ann (jt. author). *Can You Match This?*, **1418**
Kiss a Frog!, **1419**
What's Your Name, Again?, 1971

Walton, Rick. *How Many, How Many, How Many*, **206**

Walton, Rick, and Ann Walton. *Can You Match This?*, **1418**
Kiss a Frog!, **1419**
What's Your Name, Again?, 1971

Wanbli Numpa Afraid of Hawk (jt. author). *A Boy Becomes a Man at Wounded Knee*, **1255**

Ward, Lynd. *The Biggest Bear*, 844
The Silver Pony, 1024

Wardlaw, Lee. *Seventh-Grade Weirdo*, **850**

Warner, Gertrude Chandler. *The Boxcar Children*, 1025

Waters, Fiona (comp.). *The Doubleday Book of Bedtime Stories*, **381**

Waters, Kate. *Samuel Eaton's Day*, **1250**
Sarah Morton's Day, 2112

Waterton, Betty. *Petranella*, 845
A Salmon for Simon, 846

Watson, Clyde. *Father Fox's Pennyrhymes*, 1972
How Brown Mouse Kept Christmas, 847

Watson, Pauline. *Wriggles the Little Wishing Pig*, 582

Watson, Wendy. *Fox Went Out on a Chilly Night*, **382**

Watt, Letty S. (jt. author). *Developing Learning Skills Through Children's Literature*, 2145

Watts, Bernadette (reteller). *Mother Holly*, 1502
The Wind and the Sun, **859**

Wegman, William. *ABC*, **571**
Cinderella, **1042**

Weil, Lisl. *Owl and Other Scrambles*, 1026

Weil, Zaro. *Mud, Moon and Me*, **1420**

Weinberg, Larry. *The Forgetful Bears Meet Mr. Memory*, 583

Weisner, William. *Happy-Go-Lucky*, 1625
Turnabout, 1626

Weiss, Ellen, and Mel Friedman. *The Poof Point*, **851**
The Tiny Parents, **794**

Weiss, Nicki. *An Egg Is an Egg*, **207**
Hank and Oogie, 584
If You're Happy and You Know It, 1973

Welch, Catherine A. *Danger at the Breaker*, **753**

Weller, Frances Ward. *Riptide*, 848

Wellington, Monica. *Mr. Cookie Baker*, **55**

Wells, Robert E. *Is a Blue Whale the Biggest Thing There Is?*, **1251**

Wells, Rosemary. *Good Night, Fred*, 285
Hazel's Amazing Mother, 585
Lucy Comes to Stay, **572**
Max and Ruby's First Greek Myth, **573**
Max's Chocolate Chicken, 286
Max's Christmas, 287
Peabody, 288
Shy Charles, 586
Timothy Goes to School, 587
Voyage to the Bunny Planet books, **383**
Waiting for the Evening Star, **754**

Wells, Ruth. *A to Zen*, **1252**

Weng, Virginia (jt. author). *The Magic Boat*, 1699

West, Colin. *The King of Kennelwick Castle*, 289

West, Jim (jt. author). *Why the Willow Weeps*, **461**

Westcott, Nadine Bernard. *I Know an Old Lady Who Swallowed a Fly*, 588
The Lady with the Alligator Purse, 290
Peanut Butter and Jelly, 291
The Pop-Up, Pull-Tab Playtime House That Jack Built, **208**
Skip to My Lou, 292

Westcott, Nadine Bernard (comp.). *Never Take a Pig to Lunch and Other Poems About the Fun of Eating*, **1421**

Westwood, Jennifer. *Going to Squintum's*, 1624

Wetterer, Margaret. *The Giant's Apprentice*, 1130

Wetzel, JoAnne Stewart. *The Christmas Box*, **384**

Whelan, Gloria. *Hannah*, **689**
A Week of Raccoons, 589

Whipple, Laura (comp.). *Celebrating America*, **1422**
Eric Carle's Animals, Animals, 1974
Eric Carle's Dragons, Dragons & Other Creatures That Never Were, **1423**

White, E. B. *Charlotte's Web*, 1027
Stuart Little, 1131
The Trumpet of the Swan, 1253

White, Florence. *Escape!*, 2113

White, Laurence B., Jr. (jt. author). *Now You See It*, 1999

White, Laurence B., Jr., and Ray Broekel. *The Surprise Book*, 2114

Whiteley, Opal. *Only Opal*, **1253**

Whitney, Alma Marshak. *Just Awful*, 293
Leave Herbert Alone, 294

Whybrow, Ian. *Quacky Quack-Quack!*, **56**

Wiesner, David. *Hurricane*, **574**
June 29, 1999, **690**
Tuesday, **385**

Wilcox, Cathy. *Enzo the Wonderfish*, **386**

Wilder, Laura Ingalls. *Farmer Boy*, 1132

Little House in the Big Woods, 1028

Wildsmith, Brian. *The Hare and the Tortoise*, 1627
The Lion and the Rat, 1628

Wilhelm, Hans. *Tyrone the Horrible*, 590

Wilhelm, Hans (reteller). *The Bremen Town Musicians*, **925**

Wilkes, Angela (comp.). *Animal Nursery Rhymes*, **1378**

Willard, Nancy. *Papa's Panda*, 295
Simple Pictures Are Best, 849

Williams, Barbara. *Albert's Toothache*, 296
The Author and Squinty Gritt, **575**
Donna Jean's Disaster, 850

Williams, David. *Grandma Essie's Covered Wagon*, **691**

Williams, Gurney. *True Escape and Survival Stories*, 2115

Williams, Jay. *Everyone Knows What a Dragon Looks Like*, 1029
The Magic Grandfather, 1254
One Big Wish, 1030

Williams, Jay, and Raymond Abrashkin. *Danny Dunn and the Homework Machine*, 1255
Danny Dunn, Time Traveler, 1256

Williams, Karen Lynn. *Tap-Tap*, **576**

Williams, Linda. *The Little Old Lady Who Was Not Afraid of Anything*, 591

Williams, Sue. *I Went Walking*, **57**

Williams, Vera B. *A Chair for My Mother*, 851
Cherries and Cherry Pits, 852
"More More More," Said the Baby, **58**

Willis, Jeanne. *Earthlets*, **692**
The Monster Bed, 592

Willis, Val. *The Secret in the Matchbook*, 593

Willoughby, Elaine. *Boris and the Monsters*, 297

Wilner, Isabel (comp.). *The Poetry Troupe*, 1975

Wilsdorf, Anne. *Princess*, **577**

Wilson, Barbara Ker. *Wishbones*, **1043**

Wilson, Gahan. *Harry the Fat Bear Spy*, 1133

Wilson, Tona (jt. author). *The Blacksmith and the Devils*, **873**
The Cook and the King, **874**
When Jaguars Ate the Moon, **1061**

Winkel, Lois. *The Elementary School Library Collection*, 2158

Winn, Marie (comp.). *The Fireside Book of Fun and Game Songs*, 1976

Winter, Jeanette. *Follow the Drinking Gourd*, 1134
Klara's New World, **693**

Winthrop, Elizabeth. *Bear and Mrs. Duck*, 298
The Castle in the Attic, 1374
Lizzy & Harold, 594
Maggie & the Monster, 299
Shoes, 300

Sloppy Kisses, 595
Vasilissa the Beautiful, **1044**
Wise, William. *Ten Sly Piranhas*, **578**
Wiseman, David. *Jeremy Visick*, 1375
Wishinsky, Frieda. *Oonga Boonga*, **209**
Wisniewski, David. *Rain Player*, **694**
  Sundiata, **1254**
  The Warrior and the Wise Man, 1031
Withers, Carl. *I Saw a Rocket Walk a Mile*, 1735
  Tale of a Black Cat, 853
Withers, Carl (comp.). *A Rocket in My Pocket*, 1977
Withers, Carl, and Sula Benet, comps. *The American Riddle Book*, 1978
Wittman, Sally. *The Wonderful Mrs. Trumbly*, 596
Wojciechowski, Susan. *The Best Halloween of All*, **579**
  Don't Call Me Beanhead!, **695**
Wolff, Ashley. *Stella & Roy*, **210**
Wolitzer, Hilma. *Introducing Shirley Braverman*, 1376
Wolkoff, Judie. *Wally*, 1135
Wolkstein, Diane. *The Banza*, 1629
  Lazy Stories, 1736
  The Legend of Sleepy Hollow, **795**
  The Magic Orange Tree and Other Haitian Folktales, 1737
  The Magic Wings, 1630
  Step by Step, **211**
  White Wave, 1631
Wong, Janet S. *Good Luck Gold and Other Poems*, **1424**
Wood, Audrey. *Heckedy Peg*, 854
  King Bidgood's in the Bathtub, 855
  The Napping House, 301
  Silly Sally, **212**
  The Tickleoctopus, **387**
Wood, Audrey (jt. author). *The Little Mouse, the Red Ripe Strawberry, and the Big Hungry Bear*, **60**
  Piggies, 59
Wood, Don, and Audrey Wood. *The Little Mouse, the Red Ripe Strawberry, and the Big Hungry Bear*, **60**
  Piggies, 59
Wood, Ted, and Wanbli Numpa Afraid of Hawk. *A Boy Becomes a Man at Wounded Knee*, **1255**
Woodman, Allen (jt. author). *The Cows Are Going to Paris*, **471**
Woodruff, Elvira. *Dear Levi*, **796**
  Dear Napoleon, I Know You're Dead, But . . ., **852**
  The Disappearing Bike Shop, **797**
  George Washington's Socks, **798**

The Magnificent Mummy Maker, **799**
Show and Tell, **388**
The Summer I Shrank My Grandmother, **800**
The Wing Shop, **580**
Worth, Valerie. *All the Small Poems and Fourteen More*, **1425**
  Small Poems, 1979
Wrede, Patricia. *Dealing with Dragons*, **853**
Wright, Jill. *The Old Woman and the Jar of Uums*, 856
Wright, Kit. *Tigerella*, **389**
Wuorio, Eva-Lis. *Code: Polonaise*, 1377

Yaccarino, Dan. *Big Brother Mike*, **390**
Yacowitz, Caryn. *The Jade Stone*, **1045**
Yagawa, Sumiko. *The Crane Wife*, 1632
Yashima, Taro. *Crow Boy*, 1032
Yee, Paul. *Roses Sing on New Snow*, **696**
Yee, Wong Herbert. *Big Black Bear*, **213**
Yektai, Niki. *Bears in Pairs*, 302
  What's Missing?, 303
  What's Silly?, 304
Yeoman, John. *The Singing Tortoise and Other Animal Folktales*, **1091**
Yep, Laurence. *The Ghost Fox*, **755**
  The Junior Thunder Lord, **1046**
  The Man Who Tricked a Ghost, **1047**
  The Star Fisher, **854**
  Tongues of Jade, **1092**
Yolen, Jane. *Alphabestiary*, **1426**
  Animal Fare, **1427**
  Best Witches, **1428**
  Bird Watch, **1429**
  Encounter, **756**
  Favorite Folktales from Around the World, 2182
  Honkers, **391**
  Owl Moon, 857
  Raining Cats and Dogs, **1430**
  Sleeping Ugly, 1033
  Tam Lin, **1048**
  The Three Bears Rhyme Book, 1981
  Touch Magic, 2183
  Welcome to the Green House, **1256**
  What Rhymes with Moon?, **1431**
  Wings, **1049**
  Wizard's Hall, **801**
Yolen, Jane (comp.). *The Fireside Song Book of Birds and Beasts*, 1980
  Jane Yolen's Mother Goose Songbook, **1380**
Yorinks, Arthur. *Company's Coming*, 1034
  It Happened in Pinsk, 1035
  Oh, Brother, 1036
  Whitefish Will Rides Again!, **581**

York, Carol Beach. *I Will Make You Disappear*, 1378

Yoshida, Toshi. *Young Lions*, 2116

Young, Ed. *Lon Po Po*, 1633
Moon Mother, **1050**
Seven Blind Mice, **1051**
The Terrible Nung Gwana, 1634

Young, Ed (comp.). *High on a Hill*, 1982

Young, Frederica. *Super-Duper Jokes*, **1432**

Young, Richard and Judy Dockrey Young. *Favorite Scary Stories of American Children*, **1093**

Young, Ruth. *Starring Francine & Dave*, 2117
Who Says Moo?, **61**

Zakhoder, Boris. *How a Piglet Crashed the Christmas Party*, 858

Zaum, Marjorie. *Catlore*, 1738

Zavatsky, Bill, and Ron Padgett, eds. *The Whole Word Catalogue 2*, 2159

Zelinsky, Paul O. *The Lion and the Stoat*, 859
The Maid and the Mouse and the Odd-Shaped House, 860
The Wheels on the Bus, **214**

Zelinsky, Paul O. (reteller). *Rumpelstiltskin*, 1504

Zemach, Harve. *Duffy and the Devil*, 1635
The Judge, 1037
Mommy, Buy Me a China Doll, 305
Nail Soup, 1636
Too Much Noise, 1637

Zemach, Margot. *It Could Always Be Worse*, 1638
The Three Little Pigs, 1639
The Three Wishes, 1640

Zhensun, Zheng, and Alice Low. *A Young Painter*, **1257**

Zhitkov, Boris. *How I Hunted the Little Fellows*, 1136

Ziefert, Harriet. *A New Coat for Anna*, 597
Pete's Chicken, **392**
Snow Magic, 306

Ziegler, Jack. *Mr. Knocky*, **582**

Zimelman, Nathan. *How the Second Grade Got $8,205.50 to Visit the Statue of Liberty*, **583**

Zimmerman, Andrea, and David Clemesha. *The Cow Buzzed*, **215**

Zimmerman, Andrea Griffing (comp.). *The Riddle Zoo*, 1983

Zion, Gene. *Harry by the Sea*, 307
Harry the Dirty Dog, 308
No Roses for Harry, 309
The Plant Sitter, 598

Ziskind, Sylvia. *Telling Stories to Children*, 2184

Zoehfeld, Kathleen Weidner. *What Lives in a Shell?*, **1258**

Zolotow, Charlotte. *Everything Glistens and Everything Sings*, 1984
Mr. Rabbit and the Lovely Present, 310
The Quarreling Book, 861
Something Is Going to Happen, 311
This Quiet Lady, **393**

TITLE INDEX

This index combines titles from this volume and the companion volume, *Books Kids Will Sit Still For* (R. R. Bowker, 1990). References to entry numbers in this volume appear in boldface type, while references to titles in *Books Kids Will Sit Still For* appear in regular type.

A B Cedar: An Alphabet of Trees (Lyon), 2068

A Is for Angry: An Animal and Adjective Alphabet (Boynton), 341

A My Name Is Alice (Bayer), 334

A. Nonny Mouse Writes Again! (Prelutsky), **1395**

A to Zen: A Book of Japanese Culture (Wells), **1252**

A to Zoo: Subject Access to Children's Picture Books (Lima and Lima), 2147

Aaron's Shirt (Gould), 117

ABC (Wegman), **571**

The ABC Mystery (Cushman), **428**

Abe Lincoln's Hat (Brenner), **1110**

Abel's Island (Steig), 1364

Abiyoyo (Seeger), 548

Abracatabby (Hiller), 424

Abraham Lincoln: A Man for All the People (Livingston), **1189**

Abuela (Dorros), **434**

Abuelita's Paradise (Nodar), **519**

The Accidental Zucchini: An Unexpected Alphabet (Grover), **277**

Action Alphabet (Neumeier and Glaser), 758

An Actor's Life for Me! (Gish and Lanes), 2039

Adam Mouse's Book of Poems (Moore), **1374**

An Adventure at Sea (Heller), 685

The Adventures of Isabel (Nash), **649**

The Adventures of King Midas (Banks), **758**

The Adventures of Nanabush: Ojibway Indian Stories (Coatsworth and Coatsworth), 1665

The Adventures of Obadiah (Turkle), 834

The Adventures of Pinocchio (Collodi), 1160

The Adventures of Spider: West African Folktales (Arkhurst), 1654

The Adventures of Taxi Dog (Barracca and Barracca), **404**

Aesop & Company: With Scenes from His Legendary Life (Aesop), **1053**

The Aesop for Children (Aesop), 1641

Aesop's Fables, illus. by Michael Hague (Aesop), 1642

Aesop's Fables, illus. by Heidi Holder (Aesop), 1643

Aesop's Fables, illus. by A. J. McClaskey (Aesop), 1644

Aesop's Fables, illus. by Alice Provensen (Aesop), 1645

Aesop's Fables, illus. by Robert Rayevsky (Aesop), 1646

Aesop's Fables, illus. by Safaya Salter (Aesop), **1054**

After Fifth Grade, the World! (Mills), 1214

Ahyoka and the Talking Leaves (Roop and Roop), **740**

Aïda (Price), **837**

Air Mail to the Moon (Birdseye), 616

Aladdin and the Enchanted Lamp (Mayer), 1565

Aladdin and the Wonderful Lamp (Carrick), 1413

Aladdin and the Wonderful Lamp (Lang), 1544

Alan and the Animal Kingdom (Holland), 1311

Albert's Story (Long), 487

Albert's Toothache (Williams), 296

Alejandro's Gift (Albert), **397**

Alex Is My Friend (Russo), **354**

Alexander and the Dragon (Holabird), 140

Alexander and the Terrible, Horrible, No Good, Very Bad Day (Viorst), 838

Alexander and the Wind-Up Mouse (Lionni), 726

Alexander the Grape: Fruit and Vegetable Jokes (Keller), 1834

Alexander the Rock-Eater (Van Woerkom), 1621

Alexander Who Used to Be Rich Last Sunday (Viorst), 839

Alfie Gets in First (Hughes), 143

Alfie Gives a Hand (Hughes), 144

Alfie's Feet (Hughes), 145

Alfred (Udry), 572

Alfred's Alphabet Walk (Chess), 648

Ali Baba and the Forty Thieves (McVitty), 1557

Alice and the Birthday Giant (Green), 408

Alice's Special Room (Gackenbach), **106**

Aliens for Breakfast (Etra and Spinner), 915

Alison's Zinnia (Lobel), **309**

Alistair and the Alien Invasion (Sadler), **356**

Alistair in Outer Space (Sadler), 787

Alistair's Elephant (Sadler), 788

Alistair's Time Machine (Sadler), 789

All about Sam (Lowry), 1327

All About You (Anholt and Anholt), **3**

All I See (Rylant), 988

All Join In (Blake), **1270**

The All New Jonah Twist (Honeycutt), 934

All Night Near the Water (Arnosky), **67**

All the Colors of the Earth (Hamanaka), **449**

All the Money in the World (Brittain), 1152

All the Small Poems and Fourteen More (Worth), **1425**

All the Way Home (Segal), 253

Alligator Pie (Lee), 1854

The Alligator under the Bed (Nixon), 218

Alligators All Around (Sendak), 550

Almost Famous (Getz), **818**

Along the Santa Fe Trail: Marion Russell's Own Story (Russell), **1230**

Alpha and the Dirty Baby (Cole), **426**

Alphabatics (MacDonald), 490

Alphabestiary: Animal Poems from A to Z (Yolen), **1426**

The Alphabet from Z to A: With Much Confusion on the Way (Viorst), **1416**

An Alphabet in Five Acts (Andersen), **398**

The Alphabet in Nature (Feldman), **102**

An Alphabet of Dinosaurs (Dodson), **1132**

Alvin's Famous No-Horse (Harding), **613**

Alvin's Swap Shop (Hicks), 1187

Amanda and Giggling Ghost (Kroll), 715

The Amazing Bone (Steig), 1006

The Amazing Felix (McCully), **491**

Amazing Grace (Hoffman), **287**

The Amazing Magic Show (Petersen), **529**

Amazing Paper Cuttings of Hans Christian Andersen (Brust), **1113**

The Amazing Pig (Galdone), 1457

The Amazing Voyage of Jackie Grace (Faulkner), 666

Amber Brown Is Not a Crayon (Danziger), **603**

Amelia Bedelia (Parish), 764

Amelia Mixed the Mustard and Other Poems (Ness), 1895

Amelia's Fantastic Flight (Bursik), **417**

Amelia's Nine Lives (Balian), 19

America the Beautiful (Bates), **1265**

American Folk Songs for Children (Seeger), 1951

The American Riddle Book (Withers and Benet), 1978

American Tall Tales (Osborne), **1081**

Amigo (Baylor), 613

Among the Dolls (Sleator), 1240

Amos: The Story of an Old Dog and His Couch (Seligson and Schneider), 549

Amos Camps Out: A Couch Adventure in the Woods (Seligson), **549**

Amy Elizabeth Explores Bloomingdale's (Konigsburg), **478**

Anansi and the Moss-Covered Rock (Kimmel), 1541

Anansi and the Talking Melon (Kimmel), **949**

Anansi Finds a Fool (Aardema), **855**

Anansi Goes Fishing (Kimmel), **950**

Anansi the Spider: A Tale from the Ashanti (McDermott), 1550

Anatole (Titus), 830

And Sunday Makes Seven (Baden), **864**

And the Green Grass Grew All Around: Folk Poetry from Everyone (Schwartz), **1407**

And Then There Was One: The Mysteries of Extinction (Facklam), **1139**

And Then What Happened, Paul Revere? (Fritz), 2029

And This Is Laura (Conford), 1289

Andy and the Lion (Daugherty), 658

Andy Bear: A Polar Bear Cub Grows Up at the Zoo (Johnston and Cutchins), 2056

Angel in Charge (Delton), 1061

Angela and Bear (Jeschke), 437

Angelo the Naughty One (Garrett), 676

Angels on Roller Skates (Harrison), **451**

Angie (Udry), 1017

Angus and the Cat (Flack), 84

Angus and the Ducks (Flack), 85

Angus Lost (Flack), 86

The Animal (Balian), 327

Animal Cafe (Stadler), 819

Animal Fables from Aesop (Aesop), **1055**

Animal Fact / Animal Fable (Simon), 2099

Animal Fare (Yolen), **1427**

Animal Nursery Rhymes (Mother Goose), **1378**

Animals Born Alive and Well (Heller), **1159**

Animals Should Definitely Not Wear Clothing (Barrett), 870

Anna and the Seven Swans (Silverman), 1601

Annabel (Boland), **6**

Annabelle Swift, Kindergartner (Schwartz), 794

Anna's Secret Friend (Tsutsui), 275

Annie and the Old One (Miles), 1213

Annie . . . Anya: A Month in Moscow (Trivas), **377**

Annie, Bea, and Chi Chi Dolores: A School Day Alphabet (Maurer), **163**

The Annotated Mother Goose (Baring-Gould and Baring-Gould), 2124

The Ant and the Elephant (Peet), 521

Ant Cities (Dorros), 2021

An Anteater Named Arthur (Waber), 577

Antics! An Alphabetical Anthology (Hepworth), **1312**

Anton B. Stanton and the Pirats (McNaughton), 736

Any Kind of Dog (Reiser), **40**

Ape in a Cape: An Alphabet of Odd Animals (Eichenberg), 79

Api and the Boy Stranger: A Village Creation Tale (Roddy), **1006**

Apple Tree Christmas (Noble), 973

Applebet Story (Barton), 331

Appointment (Maugham), **830**

April Bubbles Chocolate: An ABC of Poetry (Hopkins), **1316**

The April Fool (Schertle), 991

April Fool (Christian), 1423

The April Rabbits (Cleveland), 366

Apt. 3 (Keats), 942

Arabella and Mr. Crack (Gackenbach), 1454

The Araboolies of Liberty Street (Swope), 829

Arion and the Dophins (Anderson), 1391

The Armadillo from Amarillo (Cherry), **423**

Arnie and the New Kid (Carlson), **421**

Arnold of the Ducks (Gerstein), 677

Around the World in a Hundred Years: From Henry the Navigator to Magellan (Fritz), **1144**

Art and Design in Children's Picture Books: An Analysis of Caldecott Award-Winning Books (Lacy), 2120

The Art Lesson (dePaola), 907

The Art of the Story-Teller (Shedlock), 2181

Arthur Babysits (Brown), **412**

Arthur Meets the President (Brown), **413**

Arthur the Kid (Coren), 902

Arthur's April Fool (Brown), 625

Arthur's Baby (Brown), 344

Arthur's Birthday (Brown), 626

Arthur's Chicken Pox (Brown), **239**

Arthur's Christmas Cookies (Hoban), 425

Arthur's Eyes (Brown), 345

Arthur's Great Big Valentine (Hoban), 426

Arthur's Halloween (Brown), 627

Arthur's Honey Bear (Hoban), 136

Arthur's Loose Tooth (Hoban), 427

Arthur's Teacher Trouble (Brown), 628

Arthur's Tooth (Brown), 629

Asher and the Capmakers: A Hanukkah Story (Kimmel), **635**

Ashpet: An Appalachian Tale (Compton), **883**

Ask Mr. Bear (Flack), 87

At Mary Bloom's (Aliki), 4

At the Crack of the Bat: Baseball Poems (Morrison), **1376**

The Atrocious Two (Greenwald), 1184

Attaboy, Sam! (Lowry), **776**

Aunt Harriet's Underground Railroad in the Sky (Ringgold), **670**

Aunt Isabel Tells a Good One (Duke), **436**

Auntie's Knitting a Baby (Simmie), 1953

The Author and Squinty Gritt (Williams), **575**

Author's Day (Pinkwater), **659**

Away from Home (Lobel), **487**

Awful Aardvark (Kennaway), **144**

Baba Yaga (Small), 1602

Baba Yaga: A Russian Folktale (Arnold), **860**

Baba Yaga: A Russian Folktale (Kimmel), **951**

Baba Yaga & the Little Girl (Arnold), **861**

Baba Yaga and Vasilisa the Brave (Mayer), **985**

Babe, the Gallant Pig (King-Smith), 1319

Babushka's Doll (Polacco), **176**

Baby Baboon (Mwenye Hadithi), **37**

Baby Crow (Rowe), **183**

Baby Rattlesnake (Ata), **862**

A Baby Sister for Frances (Hoban), 137

The Baby Uggs Are Hatching (Prelutsky), 1904

Babysitting for Benjamin (Gregory), **276**

Back to Before (Slepian), **843**

Backyard Bear (Murphy), **515**

Backyard Dragon (Sterman and Sterman), **750**

The Bad Times of Irma Baumline (Brink), 1150

The Badger and the Magic Fan: A Japanese Folktale (Johnston), 1536

A Bag of Moonshine (Garner), 1678

Bah! Humbug? (Balian), 328

Bailey Goes Camping (Henkes), 131

The Balancing Girl (Rabe), 530

A Balloon for Grandad (Gray), 121

The Ballpark: One Day behind the Scenes at a Major League Game (Jaspersohn), 2055

Ballpoint Bananas and Other Jokes for Kids (Keller), 1835

Bamboo Hats and a Rice Cake: A Tale Adapted from Japanese Folklore (Tompert), **1036**

Banana Twist (Heide), 1310

Banner in the Sky (Ullman), 1371

The Banza: A Haitian Story (Wolkstein), 1629

591

Bard of Avon: The Story of William Shakespeare (Stanley and Vennema), **1241**

Barn Dance! (Martin and Archambault), 505

Barney Bipple's Magic Dandelions (Chapman), 644

Barnyard Banter (Fleming), **12**

Barnyard Tracks (Duffy), **10**

Bartholomew and the Oobleck (Seuss), 994

Baseball Saved Us (Mochizuki), **733**

Basil of Baker Street (Titus), 1249

A Basket Full of White Eggs (Swann), 1960

Batty Riddles (Hall and Eisenberg), **1304**

Be a Perfect Person in Just Three Days (Manes), 1095

Bea and Mr. Jones (Schwartz), 795

Beach Ball—Left, Right (McMillan), **158**

Beach Days (Robbins), 242

Beady Bear (Freeman), 92

Bean and Plant (Back), 1989

The Bean Boy (Bowden), 1405

Beans on the Roof (Byars), 879

Bear and Mrs. Duck (Winthrop), 298

The Bear and the Bird King (Grimm), **929**

A Bear Called Paddington (Bond), 1146

A Bear for Christmas (Keller), 167

Bear Hunt (Browne), 30

Bear in Mind: A Book of Bear Poems (Goldstein), **1296**

Bear Shadow (Asch), 10

The Bear That Heard Crying (Kinsey-Warnock), **468**

The Bears' House (Sachs), 1350

Bears in Pairs (Yektai), 302

The Bears on Hemlock Mountain (Dalgliesh), 657

The Bear's Toothache (McPhail), 493

The Bearskinner (Grimm), 1486

Bearymore (Freeman), 391

Beast (Meddaugh), 210

Beast Feast (Florian), **1290**

The Beast in the Bed (Dillon), 70

The Beast of Monsieur Racine (Ungerer), 1018

Beastly Boys and Ghastly Girls (Cole), 1775

Beats Me, Claude (Nixon), 971

Beauty (Wallace), 1373

Beauty and the Beast (Harris), 1520

Beauty and the Beast (Mayer), 1566

Beauty, Brave and Beautiful (Gackenbach), 395

Because of Loza Brown (King), 710

Bedtime for Frances (Hoban), 428

Bee Tree and Other Stuff (Peck), 1899

Beethoven Lives Upstairs (Nichol), **785**

Beezus and Ramona (Cleary), 887

The Beginning of the Armadillos (Kipling), 945

Behind Rebel Lines: The Incredible Story of Emma Edmonds, Civil War Spy (Reit), 2085

Behind the Attic Wall (Cassedy), 1287

Behind the Border (Kossman), **1173**

Behind the Lines (Holland), **824**

Behind the Sealed Door: The Discovery of the Tomb and Treasures of Tutankhamen (Swinburne and Swinburne), 2109

A Bellbird in a Flame Tree (Niland), **518**

Belling the Cat and Other Aesop's Fables: Retold in Verse (Aesop), **1056**

Belly Laughs! Food Jokes & Riddles (Keller), **1337**

Ben and Me (Lawson), 1324

Ben and the Porcupine (Carrick), 640

Benjamin Franklin (D'Aulaire and D'Aulaire), 2013

Benjamin's Book (Baker), 325

Benjamin's Portrait (Baker), 326

Benjamin's 365 Birthdays (Barrett), 330

Benjie (Lexai), 472

Benjy and the Barking Bird (Graham), 118

Benjy in Business (Van Leeuwen), 1021

Bennett Cerf's Book of Riddles (Cerf), 1766

Benvenuto (Reit), 1106

Bernal & Florinda: A Spanish Tale (Kimmel), **720**

Bertie and the Bear (Allen), 7

Beside the Bay (Samton), 250

Best Books for Children: Preschool through Grade 6 (Gillespie and Naden), 2139

The Best Christmas Pageant Ever (Robinson), 1230

Best Enemies Again (Leverich), **639**

Best Friends (Hopkins), 1818

The Best Halloween of All (Wojciechowski), **579**

Best Loved Folktales of the World (Cole), 1666

The Best of Rube Goldberg (Goldberg), 2040

The Best School Year Ever (Robinson), **788**

The Best Town in the World (Baylor), 872

The Best Valentine in the World (Sharmat), 807

Best Wishes (Rylant), **1233**

Best Wishes, Amen (Morrison), 1877

Best Witches: Poems for Halloween (Yolen), **1428**

Bet You Can! Science Possibilities to Fool You (Cobb and Darling), 2006

Between Friends (Garrigue), 1175

Beware of Boys (Blundell), **232**

Beware the Brindlebeast (Riggio), **1004**

Beyond Picture Books: A Gude to First Readers (Barstow and Riggle), 2125

BFG (Dahl), 1166

The Bicycle Man (Say), 791

The Big Alfie Out of Doors Storybook (Hughes), **128**

Big Anthony and the Magic Ring (dePaola), 908

Big Bad Bruce (Peet), 766

Big Black Bear (Yee), **213**

Big Brother Mike (Yaccarino), **390**

Big David, Little David (Hinton), **285**

The Big Deal (Herzig), **618**

A Big Fat Enormous Lie (Sharmat), **359**

Big Fat Hen (Baker), **4**

The Big Fat Worm (Van Laan), 282

Big Goof and Little Goof (Cole and Cole), 373

The Big Green Book (Graves), 680

Big Men, Big Country: A Collection of American Tall Tales (Walker), **1090**

Big Pumpkin (Silverman), **364**

The Big Rock (Hiscock), 2050

Big Time Bears (Krensky), **147**

The Big Tree (Hiscock), **1162**

Big Trouble for Tricky Rabbit! (Mayo), **1078**

The Big Yellow Balloon (Fenton), 667

The Biggest Bear (Ward), 844

The Biggest Nose (Caple), 356

The Biggest Tongue Twister Book in the World (Brandreth), 1753

The Biggest Truck (Lyon), 193

Bill and Google-Eyed Goblins (Schertle), 792

Billy Beg and His Bull (Greene), **918**

Bimwili and the Zimwi (Aardema), 1379

Bing Bang Boing (Florian), **1291**

Bird Dogs Can't Fly (Auch), **219**

Bird Watch: A Book of Poetry (Yolen), **1429**

The Birthday Door (Merriam), 750

Birthday Rhymes, Special Times (Goldstein), **1297**

Bizzy Bones and the Lost Quilt (Martin), 206

Black and White (Macaulay), **490**

The Black Pearl (O'Dell), 1338

Black Ships Before Troy! The Story of the Iliad (Sutcliff), **1088**

The Black Stallion (Farley), 1064

Blackberry Ink (Merriam), 1868

The Blackmail Machine (Holman), 1191

The Blacksmith and the Devils (Brusca and Wilson), **873**

The Blanket Had to Go (Cooney), 55

Blast Off! Poems About Space (Hopkins), **1317**

The Blind Mice and the Elephant (Quigley), 1582

Block City (Stevenson), 563

Blossom Comes Home (Herriot), 2046

Blue Fairy Book (Lang), 1702

The Blue-Nosed Witch (Embry), 913

Blueberries for Sal (McCloskey), 194

Blumpoe the Grumpoe Meets Arnold the Cat (Okimoto), **525**

Bo Rabbit Smart for True: Folktales from the Gullah (Jaquith), 1700

The Bodies in the Besseldorf Hotel (Naylor), 1216

Bonny's Big Day (Herriot), 2047

Bony-Legs (Cole), 1426

Boo! Stories to Make You Jump (Cecil), **1062**

Boodil My Dog (Lindenbaum), **485**

The Book of Pigericks (Lobel), 1861

The Book of Three (Alexander), 1258

A Book of Witches (Manning-Sanders), 1710

The Book That Jack Wrote (Scieszka), **548**

The Bookfinder: A Guide to Children's Literature about the Needs and Problems of Youth Ages 2 to 15 (Dreyer), 2134

Books and Libraries (Knowlton), **1171**

Booktalk! Booktalking and School Visiting for Young Adult Audiences (Bodart), 2128

Booktalk! 2: Booktalking for All Ages and Audiences (Bodart), 2129

Booktalk! 3: More Booktalks for All Ages and Audiences (Bodart), 2130

Boots and His Brothers: A Norwegian Tale (Kimmel), **952**

Boots & the Glass Mountain (Martin), **981**

Bootsie Barker Bites (Bottner), **234**

Bored, Nothing to Do (Spier), 817

Boris and the Monsters (Willoughby), 297

Borreguita and the Coyote: A Tale from Ayutla, Mexico (Aardema), **856**

The Borrowers (Norton), 1336

The Bossing of Josie (Armitage and Armitage), 8

The Bossy Gallito: A Traditional Cuban Folktale (Gonzalez), **917**

Bossyboots (Cox), 655

Bound for Oregon (Van Leeuwen), **793**

Box Turtle at Long Pond (George), 2037

The Boxcar Children (Warner), 1025

Boy (Dahl), 2012

The Boy and the Ghost (San Souci), **1011**

A Boy Becomes a Man at Wounded Knee (Wood and Wanbli Numpa Afraid of Hawk), **1255**

A Boy in the Doghouse (Duffey), **605**

The Boy of the Three Year Nap (Snyder), 1603

The Boy Who Didn't Believe in Spring (Clifton), 650

The Boy Who Drew Cats: A Japanese Folktale (Levine), **968**

The Boy Who Lived with the Seals (Martin), **982**

The Boy Who Was Followed Home (Mahy), 739

The Boy Who Would Not Say His Name (Vreeken), 576

The Boys Start the War (Naylor), **735**

The Brain on Quartz Mountain (Anderson), 1041

Brain-Teasers and Mind-Benders (Brandreth), 1997

Brats (Kennedy), 1845

Brave Irene (Steig), 820

The Brave Little Tailor (Thomson), **1035**

Bread and Jam for Frances (Hoban), 429

Bread Bread Bread (Morris), **1211**

The Bremen Town Musicians, illus by Joseph Palecek (Grimm), 1487

The Bremen Town Musicians, illus. by Bernadette Watts (Grimm), **931**

The Bremen Town Musicians, illus. by Hans Wilhelm (Grimm), **925**

Bridge to Terabithia (Paterson), 1340

Bright Shadow (Avi), 1266

Bringing the Rain to Kapiti Plain (Aardema), 1380

The Brocaded Slipper and Other Vietnamese Tales (Vuong), 1733

The Broccoli Tapes (Slepian), **844**

Brother Eagle, Sister Sky: A Message from Chief Seattle (Jeffers), **628**

The Brothers Grimm Popular Folk Tales (Grimm), 1684

Brown Angels: An Album of Pictures and Verse (Myers), **1389**

Brown Bear, Brown Bear, What Do You See? (Martin), 204

Brrr! (Stevenson), **373**

Bub: Or, the Very Best Thing (Babbitt), **224**

Bubba and Babba (Polushkin), 526

Buffalo Dance: A Blackfoot Legend (Van Laan), **1039**

Buffalo Hunt (Freedman), 2025

Buffalo Woman (Goble), 1481

Buggy Riddles (Hall and Eisenberg), 1809

Bugs: Poems (Hoberman), 1814

Building a House (Barton), 1993

The Bully of Barkham Street (Stolz), 1120

A Bundle of Beasts (Hooper), 1817

The Bunjee Venture (McMurtry), 1210

Bunnicula: A Rabbit-Tale of Mystery (Howe and Howe), 1193

Burgoo Stew (Patron), **527**

Burt Dow, Deep-Water Man (McCloskey), 955

Busy Buzzing Bumblebees and Other Tongue Twisters (Schwartz), 1944

Busybody Nora (Hurwitz), 694

The Butterfly Jar (Moss), **1377**

Buzz Buzz Buzz (Barton), 21

By the Great Horn Spoon (Fleischman), 1300

By the Light of the Halloween Moon (Stutson), **561**

Bye-Bye, Old Buddy (Robison), 532

C Is for Curious: An ABC of Feelings (Hubbard), **289**

Cabbage Moon (Chadwick), **81**

A Cache of Jewels and Other Collective Nouns (Heller), 1811

Cactus Hotel (Guiberson), **1155**

Caddie Woodlawn (Brink), 1151

The Cake That Mack Ate (Robart), 241

Cakes and Custard (Mother Goose), 1878

Caleb and Kate (Steig), 1118

Call It Courage (Sperry), 1242

The Call of the Wolves (Murphy), 969

Callooh! Callay! Holiday Poems for Young Readers (Livingston), 1857

The Camel Who Took a Walk (Tworkov), 571

Can I Be Good? (Taylor), **375**

Can You Find It? (Most), **329**

Can You Guess? (Miller), **33**

Can You Match This? Jokes About Unlikely Pairs (Walton and Walton), **1418**

The Candy Witch (Kroll), 462

Can't You Make Them Behave, King George? (Fritz), 2030

Can't You Sleep, Little Bear? (Waddell), **199**

Caps for Sale (Slobodkina), 269

Caps, Hats, Socks, and Mittens: A Book about the Four Seasons (Borden), 24

Captain Snap and the Children of Vinegar Lane (Schotter), 793

Capturing Nature: The Writings and Art of John James Audubon (Audubon), **1101**

Capyboppy (Peet), 2081

A Caribbean Dozen: Poems from Caribbean Poets (Agard and Nichols), **1262**

The Carp in the Bathtub (Cohen), 892

The Carrot Seed (Krauss), 178

The Carsick Zebra and Other Animal Riddles (Adler), 1739

The Case of the Baker Street Irregular (Newman), 1335

The Case of the Condemned Cat (Hildick), 1073

The Case of the Purloined Parrot (Hildick), **771**

Casey at the Bat: A Ballad of the Republic, Sung in the Year 1888 (Thayer), 1368

Casey Over There (Rabin), **666**

Casey the Utterly Impossible Horse (Feagles), 916

Castaways on Chimp Island (Landsman), 1323

The Castle in the Attic (Winthrop), 1374

Cat (Stein), 2107

Cat and Canary (Foreman), 388

The Cat Came Back (Slavin), **555**

The Cat in the Hat (Seuss), 258

Cat Is Back at Bat (Stadler), **372**

The Cat on the Dovrefell: A Christmas Tale (Dasent), 1432

Cat Poems (Livingston), 1858

Cat Walk (Stolz), 1121

The Cat Who Wished to Be a Man (Alexander), 1259

Cat Will Rhyme with Hat: A Book of Poems (Chapman), 1767

Catastrophe Cat (Panek), 222

Catch It If You Can (Thompson), **1415**

Catching the Wind (Ryder), 2088

Catkin (Barber), **590**

Catlore: Tales from Around the World (Zaum), 1738

Cats Are Cats (Larrick), 1851

Cat's Cradle, Owl's Eyes: A Book of String Games (Gryski), 2044

The Cat's Elbow and Other Secret Languages (Schwartz), 1945

The Cat's Midsummer Jamboree (Kherdian), 457

Catwings (Le Guin), 950

CDB (Steig), 1959

Celebrate America in Poetry and Art (Panzer), **1393**

Celebrating America: A Collection of Poems and Images of the American Spirit (Whipple), **1422**

Celebrating with Books (Polette and Hamlin), 2152

Celebrations: Read-Aloud Holiday & Theme Book Programs (Bauer), 2126

A Chair for My Mother (Williams), 851

The Chalk Doll (Pomerantz), 776

Chameleon Was a Spy (Massie), 960

Chameleons: Dragons in the Trees (Martin), **1201**

The Champion of Merrimack County (Drury), 1169

Champions: Stories of Ten Remarkable Athletes (Littlefield), **1188**

The Changeling (Langerlöf), **636**

Changes (Browne), **241**

Changes (Allen and Rotner), **1100**

The Chanukkah Guest (Kimmel), **298**

Charles Dickens: The Man Who Had Great Expectations (Stanley and Vennema), **1242**

Charlie and the Chocolate Factory (Dahl), 1058

Charlie Chaplin (Kamen), 2057

Charlie Drives the Stage (Kimmel), 943

Charlie Needs a Cloak (dePaola), 376

Charlotte's Web (White), 1027

The Chase: A Kutenai Indian Tale (Tanaka), **1032**

Chasing after Annie (Sharmat), 998

Chasing the Goblins Away (Tobias), 831

Chatterbox Jamie (Cooney), **87**

Cherries and Cherry Pits (Williams), 852

Chester (Shura), 1112

Chester the Out-of-Work Dog (Singer), **366**

Chester the Worldly Pig (Peet), 975

The Chick and the Duckling (Ginsburg), 114

Chicka Chicka Boom Boom (Martin and Archambault), 205

Chicken Little (Kellogg), 704

Chicken Little (Hobson), **940**

Chicken Soup Boots (Kalman), **719**

Chicken Soup with Rice (Sendak), 551

Chicken Sunday (Polacco), **661**

Chicken Trek: The Third Strange Thing That Happened to Oscar J. Noodleman (Manes), 1211

Chickens Aren't the Only Ones (Heller), **1160**

The Child as Critic: Teaching Literature in Elementary and Middle School (Sloan), 2155

Child of the Silent Night: The Story of Laura Bridgman (Hunter), 2053

Children and Books (Sutherland), 2123

Children of Christmas: Stories for the Seasons (Rylant), 1349

Children of the Morning Light: Wampanoag Tales (Manitonquat (Medicine Story)), **1077**

Children of the Wild West (Freedman), 2026

The Children We Remember (Abels), 1985

The Children's Aesop: Selected Fables (Aesop), **1057**

Children's Counting Out Rhymes, Fingerplays, Jump-Rope and Bounce-Ball Chants and Other Rhymes: A Comprehensive English-Language Reference (Delamar), 1788

Children's Faces Looking Up: Program Building for the Storyteller (De Wit), 2171

Children's Literature in the Elementary School (Huck), 2119

Children's Literature Through Storytelling & Drama (Briggs and Wagner), 2166

A Children's Zoo (Hoban), 430

The Chimpanzee Family Book (Goodall), 2041

The Chimpanzee Kid (Roy), 1348

Chin Chiang and the Dragon Dance (Wallace), 843

Chin Music: Tall Talk and Other Talk, Collected from American Folklore (Schwartz), 1946

Chin Yu Min and the Ginger Cat (Armstrong), **588**

The Chinese Mirror (Ginsburg), 1477

A Chinese Zoo: Fables and Proverbs (Demi), 1675

Chinook! (Tunnell), **688**

Chinye: A West African Folk Tale (Onyefulu), **995**

Chipmunk! (Haas), **115**

Chipmunk Song (Ryder), 2089

Chive (Barre), **804**

Chocolate Dreams (Adoff), **1259**

Chocolate Fever (Smith), 1003

The Chocolate Marshmelephant Sundae (Thaler), 1966

A Chocolate Moose for Dinner (Gwynne), 1068

The Chocolate Touch (Catling), 884

Chortles: New and Selected Wordplay Poems (Merriam), 1869

The Christmas Box (Merriam), 507

The Christmas Box (Wetzel), **384**

The Christmas Day Kitten (Herriot), 2048

Christmas Eve at Santa's (Prøysen), **343**

A Christmas Fantasy (Haywood), 416

The Christmas Gift (McCully), 195

Christmas Poems (Livingston), 1859

A Christmas Sonata (Paulsen), **833**

The Christmas Wolf (Gay), 404

Chrysanthemum (Henkes), **282**

Chucky Bellman Was So Bad (Green), **444**

Cinder Edna (Jackson), **626**

Cinder-Elly (Minters), **510**

Cinderella (Galdone), 1458

Cinderella (Grimm), 1488

Cinderella (Karlin), 1537

Cinderella (Wegman), **1042**

Cinderella: Or, The Little Glass Slipper (Brown), 1410

A Circle of Giving (Howard), 1192

Circus (Ehlert), **95**

Citybook (Rotner and Kreisler), **353**

Clams Can't Sing (Stevenson), 560

Clara's Story (Isaacman and Grossman), 2054

Clarence and the Burglar (Lauber), 720

Class Clown (Hurwitz), 936

Class President (Hurwitz), **715**

Claude Has a Picnic (Gackenbach), **16**

The Clay Marble (Ho), **823**

Clever Cooks: A Concoction of Stories, Charms, Recipes and Riddles (Greene), 1683

Clever Gretchen and Other Forgotten Folktales (Lurie), 1708

Clever Polly and the Stupid Wolf (Storr), 1122

Clever Tom and the Leprechaun (Shute), 1599

Click, Rumble, Roar: Poems about Machines (Hopkins), 1819

Clocks and More Clocks (Hutchins), 433

The Cloud Book (dePaola), 2017

C.L.O.U.D.S. (Cummings), 903

Cloudy with a Chance of Meatballs (Barrett), 871

Clowning Around (Falwell), **272**

Clyde Monster (Crowe), 60

Coaster (Duffey), **769**

Cock-a-Doodle-Doo! (Runcie), **41**

Cock-a-Doodle-Doo! What Does It Sound Like to You? (Robinson), **1226**

The Cock, the Mouse and the Little Red Hen (Cauley), 1414

Code: Polonaise (Wuorio), 1377

Cold Stars and Fireflies: Poems of the Four Seasons (Esbensen), 1797

The Color Box (Dodds), **93**

Color Dance (Jonas), **136**

Color Farm (Ehlert), **96**

Color Zoo (Ehlert), 76

Colt (Springer), **792**

Come Again in the Spring (Kennedy), 1080

Come Back, Salmon: How a Group of Dedicated Kids Adopted Pigeon Creek and Brought It Back to Life (Cone), **1125**

The Comet and You (Krupp), 2060

The Comic Adventures of Old Mother Hubbard and Her Dog (dePaola), 1438

Communication (Aliki), **1099**

Company's Coming (Yorinks), 1034

The Complete Story of the Three Blind Mice (Ivimey), 151

Complete Version of Ye Three Blind Mice (Ivimey), 152

The Contests at Cowlick (Kennedy), 708

The Cook and the King (Brusca and Wilson), **874**

The Cookcamp (Paulsen), **834**

Cora Copycat (Lester), 468

Corduroy (Freeman), 93

Could Be Worse (Stevenson), 822

Count! (Fleming), **13**

Count Draculations! Monsters Riddles (Keller), 1836

Country Bear's Good Neighbor (Brimner), 27

The Country Bunny and the Little Gold Shoes (Heyward), 423

The Country Mail Is Coming: Poems from Down Under (Fatchen), **1289**

The Covered Bridge House and Other Poems (Starbird), 1957

The Cow Buzzed (Zimmerman and Clemesha), **215**

The Cow-Tail Switch and Other West African Stories (Courlander and Herzog), 1670

The Cow Who Wouldn't Come Down (Johnson), **292**

Cowardly Clyde (Peet), 976

The Cowboy and the Black-Eyed Pea (Johnston), **717**

Cowboys (Sullivan), **1413**

The Cows Are Going to Paris (Kirby and Woodman), **471**

Coyote: A Trickster Tale from the American Southwest (McDermott), **975**

Coyote and the Magic Words (Root), **351**

Coyote Places the Stars (Taylor), **1033**

Coyote Steals the Blanket: A Ute Tale (Stevens), **1029**

Cracker Jackson (Byars), 1280

Cradles in the Trees: The Story of Bird Nests (Demuth), **1129**

Crafty Chameleon (Mwenye Hadithi), 124

Cranberry Thanksgiving (Devlin and Devlin), 660

The Crane Wife (Yagawa), 1632

Crazy Lady! (Conly), **808**

Creative Drama for the Classroom Teacher (Heinig and Stillwell), 2172

Creative Uses of Children's Literature (Paulin), 2149

Creatures (Hopkins), 1820

Creepy-Crawly Birthday (Howe), **456**

Creepy Crawly Critter Riddles (Bernstein and Cohen), 1748

The Cremation of Sam McGee (Service), 1355

The Cricket in Times Square (Selden), 1237

Cricket's Jokes, Riddles & Other Stuff (Cricket Magazine), 1785

Crictor (Ungerer), 573

A Critical Handbook of Children's Literature (Lukens), 2121

Crocodile Beat (Jorgensen), 159

Crocodile! Crocodile! Stories Told Around the World (Baumgartner), **1058**

A Crocodile's Tale (Aruego and Dewey), 1393

Cross-Country Cat (Calhoun), 635

Cross Your Fingers, Spit in Your Hat: Superstitions and Other Beliefs (Schwartz), 1724

Crow & Fox and Other Animal Legends (Thornhill), **1089**

Crow Boy (Yashima), 1032

Crow Chief: A Plains Indian Story (Goble), **915**

The Cuckoo Child (King-Smith), **722**

Cully Cully and the Bear (Gage), 399

A Cup of Starshine: Poems and Pictures for Young Children (Bennett), **1268**

Curious George (Rey), 238

The Curse of the Trouble Dolls (Regan), **669**

Custard and Company (Nash), 1893

The Cut-Ups (Marshall), 743

The Cut-Ups Carry On (Marshall), **503**

Cyclops (Fisher), **904**

Cyrus the Unsinkable Sea Serpent (Peet), 767

D Is for Dolphin (Berg), **1106**

D.W. Thinks Big (Brown), **71**

Dabble Duck (Ellis), 382

Daddies (Greenspan), **114**

Daddy and Me: A Photo Story of Arthur Ashe and His Daughter Camera (Moutoussamy-Ashe), **1213**

Dad's Dinosaur Day (Hearn), **120**

Daffy Definitions (Rosenbloom), 1927

Daffy Down Dillies: Silly Limericks (Lear), **1348**

Daisy Rothschild: The Giraffe That Lives with Me (Leslie-Melville), 2067

Daisy Thinks She Is a Baby (Kopper), **27**

Dance Away (Shannon), 260

The Dancing Cats of Applesap (Lisle), 1205

Dancing in the Moon (Eichenberg), 380

The Dancing Skeleton (DeFelice), 1437

Dandelion (Freeman), 392

Danger at the Breaker (Welch), **753**

Daniel O'Rourke (McDermott), 1551

Danny Dunn and the Homework Machine (Williams and Abrashkin), 1255

Danny Dunn, Time Traveler (Williams and Abrashkin), 1256

Danny, the Champion of the World (Dahl), 1291

Darcy and Gran Don't Like Babies (Cutler), **259**

A Dark, Dark Tale (Brown), 347

D'Aulaire's Book of Greek Myths (D'Aulaire and D'Aulaire), 1674

D'Aulaire's Trolls (D'Aulaire and D'Aulaire), 1434

David and the Phoenix (Ormondroyd), 1100

Dawn (Bang), 869

The Day Jimmy's Boa Ate the Wash (Noble), 761

The Day of Ahmed's Secret (Heide and Gilliland), **616**

A Day of Rhymes (Pooley), 1903

The Day of the Blizzard (Moskin), 1098

The Day the Goose Got Loose (Lindbergh), **306**

The Day the Teacher Went Bananas (Howe), 142

The Daydreamer (McEwan), **829**

A Day's Work (Bunting), **592**

The Deadly Mandrake (Callen), 1284

Deadly Stranger (Kehret), 1317

Dealing with Dragons (Wrede), **853**

Dear Annie (Caseley), **250**

Dear Brother (Asch and Vagin), **401**

Dear Hildegarde (Waber), 1022

Dear Levi: Letters from the Overland Trail (Woodruff), **796**

Dear Napoleon, I Know You're Dead, But . . . (Woodruff), **852**

Dear Peter Rabbit (Ada), **395**

Dear Phoebe (Alexander), 600

Dear World: How Children Around the World Feel About Our Environment (Temple), **1247**

December 24th (Cazet), 359

Deep in the Forest (Turkle), 570

Demeter and Persephone (Proddow), 1581

Demi's Reflective Fables (Demi), 1676

Desert Giant: The World of the Saguaro Cactus (Bash), 1994

Destination: Antarctica (Swan), 2108

Developing Learning Skills Through Children's Literature: An Idea Book for K–5 Classrooms and Libraries (Laughlin and Watt), 2145

The Devil & Mother Crump (Carey), 1049

The Devil Rides with Me and Other Fantastic Stories (Slote), 1360

The Devil with the Three Golden Hairs (Grimm), 1489

Devilish Bets to Trick Your Friends (Churchill), 2005

The Devil's Bridge (Scribner), 1596

Devil's Bridge (DeFelice), **766**

Devil's Donkey (Brittain), 1276

The Devil's Storybook (Babbitt), 1270

The Devils Who Learned to Be Good (McCurdy), 1549

Dial Leroi Rupert, D.J. (Gilson), 1178

Diane Goode's Book of Scary Stories & Songs (Goode), **1068**

Diane Goode's Book of Silly Stories and Songs (Goode), **1069**

Dick Whittington and His Cat (Brown), 1411

Did You Carry the Flag Today, Charlie? (Caudill), 643

Dinah for President (Mills), **778**

Dinner at the Panda Palace (Calmenson), **73**

Dinosaur Dream (Nolan), **520**

The Dinosaur Is the Biggest Animal That Ever Lived and Other Wrong Ideas You Thought Were True (Simon), 2100

Dinosaur Roar! (Stickland), **189**

The Dinosaur Who Lived in My Backyard (Hennessy), **284**

Dinosaurs (Hopkins), 1821

Dinosaurs! Strange and Wonderful (Pringle), **1222**

Dinosaurs and Beasts of Yore (Cole), 1776

Dinosaurs, Beware! A Safety Guide (Brown and Krensky), 2002

Dinosaurs to the Rescue! A Guide to Protecting Our Planet (Brown and Brown), **1112**

The Disappearing Bike Shop (Woodruff), **797**

The Discovery of the Americas (Maestro), **1195**

Dive to the Coral Reefs: A New England Aquarium Book (Tayntor, Erickson, and Kaufman), 2110

Do Bunnies Talk? (Dodds), **262**

Do Not Feed the Table (Lillegard), **1355**

Do Not Open (Turkle), 1016

The Do-Something Day (Lasker), 464

Doctor Change (Cole), 896

Doctor Knickerbocker and Other Rhymes (Booth), **1272**

Doesn't Fall Off His Horse (Stroud), **680**

Dog (Blake), **591**

Dog Breath: The Horrible Trouble with Hally Tosis (Pilkey), **530**

Dog Days (Rodowsky), **739**

Dog for a Day (Gackenbach), 396

A Dog I Know (Brenner), 621

Dogger (Hughes), 146

Dogs Don't Tell Jokes (Sachar), **840**

Dogs Don't Wear Sneakers (Numeroff), **333**

A Dog's Life (Hopkins), 1822

Dogteam (Paulsen), **738**

Dogzilla (Pilkey), **657**

Donald Says Thumbs Down (Cooney), 56

The Donkey Planet (Corbett), 1163

The Donkey Prince (Grimm), 1490

Donna Jean's Disaster (Williams), 850

Don't Call Me Beanhead! (Wojciechowski), **695**

Don't Call Me Names (Cole), **254**

Don't Ever Wish for a 7-Foot Bear (Benton), 614

Don't Fidget a Feather! (Silverman), **365**

Don't Forget the Bacon! (Hutchins), 434

Don't Make Me Smile (Park), 1220

Don't Sing before Breakfast, Don't Sleep in the Moonlight: Everyday Superstitions and How They Began (Perl), 1715

Don't Tell the Whole World! (Cole), **881**

Don't Touch! (Kline), 170

Don't You Know There's a War On? (Stevenson), **1245**

Don't You Turn Back (Hughes), 1830

Doodle Flute (Pinkwater), **534**

Doodle Soup (Ciardi), 1769

Doodlebug (Brady), 620

Dorrie and the Weather Box (Coombs), 653

The Double Life of Pocahontas (Fritz), 2031

The Doubleday Book of Bedtime Stories (Waters), **381**

The Dove Dove: Funny Homograph Riddles (Terban), 1962

Down by the Bay (Raffi), 780

The Downtown Fairy Godmother (Pomerantz), 981

Dr. DeSoto (Steig), 1007

Dr. Dredd's Wagon of Wonders (Brittain), 1277

Dr. Seuss' ABC (Seuss), 553

The Dragon Circle (Krensky), 1202

The Dragon in the Cliff: A Novel Based on the Life of Mary Anning (Cole), **807**

The Dragon in the Clock Box (Craig), 375

Dragon Kites and Dragonflies: A Collection of Chinese Nursery Rhymes (Demi), 1789

Dragonfly's Tale (Rodanas), **1005**

The Dragons Are Singing Tonight (Prelutsky), **1396**

The Dragon's Handbooks (Rinkoff), 984

The Dragon's Pearl (Lawson), **965**

Dragon's Plunder (Strickland), 848

Drat These Brats (Kennedy), **1343**

The Dream Keeper and Other Poems (Hughes), **1332**

Dream Peddler (Haley), **612**

Dream Wolf (Goble), **443**

Dreams (Keats), 448

Dribbles (Heckert), **452**

The Drinking Gourd (Monjo), 966

Drop Everything, It's D.E.A.R. Time! (McGovern), **497**

Drummer Hoff (Emberley), 80

Drummond: The Search for Sarah (Odgers), **522**

Duckat (Gordon), **110**

Duffy and the Devil (Zemach), 1635

Dumpling Soup (Rattigan), **349**

Duncan & Dolores (Samuels), 251

"E" Is for Elisa (Hurwitz), **290**

Earl's Too Cool for Me (Komaiko), **477**

The Earth Is Painted Green: A Garden of Poems About Our Planet (Brenner), **1274**

Earth Verses and Water Rhymes (Lewis), **1352**

Earthlets: As Explained by Professor Xargle (Willis), **692**

East o' the Sun & West o' the Moon: An Old Norse Tale (Dasent), 1433

East of the Sun and West of the Moon (Hague and Hague), 1513

The Easter Bunny That Overslept (Friedrich and Friedrich), 394

The Easter Egg Farm (Auch), **220**

Easy as Pie: A Guessing Game of Sayings (Folsom and Folsom), 670

Eat Your Dinner! (Miller), **34**

Eating Fractions (McMillan), **1193**

Eating the Alphabet: Fruits and Vegetables from A to Z (Ehlert), 77

Eaton Stanley & the Mind Control Experiment (Adler), 1137

Eats (Adoff), 1742

Edie Changes Her Mind (Johnston), 155

Edward Lear, King of Nonsense: A Biography (Kamen), **1169**

Edward the Emu (Knowles), **300**

The Eentsy, Weentsy Spider: Fingerplays and Action Rhymes (Cole and Calmenson), **1279**

Effie (Allinson), **217**

An Egg Is an Egg (Weiss), **207**

Egg Thoughts and Other Frances Songs (Hoban), 1813

The Egyptian Cinderella (Climo), 1424

EIEIO: The Story of Old MacDonald, Who Had a Farm (Clarke), **86**

The 18th Emergency (Byars), 1155

Einstein Anderson, Science Sleuth (Simon), 1239

El Chino (Say), **1234**

Eleanor, Arthur, and Claire (Engel), **267**

The Elementary School Library Collection: A Guide to Books and Other Media (Winkel), 2158

The Elephant & the Bad Baby (Vipont), 283

Elephant Buttons (Ueno), 280

Elephant Have the Right of Way: Life with the Wild Animals of Africa (Leslie-Melville), **1185**

Elephants Aloft (Appelt), **66**

The Elephant's Child (Kipling), 946

The Elephant's Wrestling Match (Sierra), **1025**

Elijah's Violin and Other Jewish Fairy Tales (Schwartz), 1728

An Ellis Island Christmas (Leighton), **638**

The Elves and the Shoemaker (Grimm), 1491

Emily and the Enchanted Frog (Griffith), **446**

Emma's Christmas (Trivas), **687**

Emma's Pet (McPhail), 200

Emma's Vacation (McPhail), 201

The Emperor's New Clothes: A Fairy Tale (Andersen), 863

The Emperor's Plum Tree (Nikly), 759

The Empty Pot (Demi), **892**

The Enchanted Tapestry: A Chinese Folktale (San Souci), 1589

Encore for Eleanor (Peet), 768

Encounter (Yolen), **756**

Encyclopedia Brown, Boy Detective (Sobol), 1116

The Enormous Crocodile (Dahl), 656

The Enormous Egg (Butterworth), 1154

Enrichment Ideas: Sparking Fireflies (Carlson), 2131

Enzo the Wonderfish (Wilcox), **386**

Eric Carle's Animals, Animals (Whipple), 1974

Eric Carle's Dragons, Dragons & Other Creatures That Never Were (Whipple), **1423**

Escape! The Life of Harry Houdini (White), 2113

Esio Trot (Dahl), **710**

Esteban and the Ghost (Hamcock), 1518

Evan's Corner (Hill), 687

An Evening at Alfie's (Hughes), 147

Everybody Cooks Rice (Dooley), **433**

Everybody Needs a Rock (Baylor), 873

Everyone Knows What a Dragon Looks Like (Williams), 1029

Everything Glistens and Everything Sings (Zolotow), 1984

Exactly the Opposite (Hoban), **125**

Exploring the Titanic (Ballard), **1102**

Extra Innings: Baseball Poems (Hopkins), **1318**

Eye Spy: A Mysterious Alphabet (Bourke), **409**

Eye Winker, Tom Tinker, Chin Chopper: Fifty Musical Fingerplays (Glazer), 1804

Eyeopeners! How to Choose and Use Children's Books about Real People, Places and Things (Kobrin), 2143

The Eyes of Gray Wolf (London), **488**
The Eyes of Kid Midas (Shusterman), **842**

The Faber Book of Favourite Fairy Tales (Corrin and Corrin), 1667
Fables (Lobel), 1207
The Fables of Aesop (Aesop), 1647
The Fair Garden and the Swarm of Beasts: The Library and the Young Adult (Edwards), 2135
The Fairy Rebel (Banks), 1141
The Fairy Tale Treasury (Haviland), 1693
Fairy Tales and the Brothers Grimm (Grimm), 1685
Fairy Tales, Fables, Legends, and Myths: Using Folk Literature in Your Classroom (Bosma), 2164
The Fallen Spaceman (Harding), 1070
Families: Poems Celebrating the African American Experience (Strickland and Strickland), **1412**
Family Pictures / Cuadros de Familia (Lomas Garza), **1192**
The Family Read-Aloud Holiday Treasury (Low), **1362**
The Family Reunion (Tusa), **568**
The Family Storytelling Handbook: How to Use Stories, Anecdotes, Rhymes, Handkerchiefs, Paper and Other Objects to Enrich Your Family Traditions (Pellowski), 2177
Fang (Hazen), 417
The Fantastic Mr. Fox (Dahl), 904
Farmer Boy (Wilder), 1132
Farmer Bungle Forgets (King-Smith), 458
Farmer Duck (Waddell), **200**
Farmer Goff and His Turkey Sam (Schatell), 543
The Farmer in the Dell (Parkinson), 223
The Farmer in the Dell: A Singing Game (Rae), 234
Fast and Slow: Poems for Advanced Children and Beginning Parents (Ciardi), 1770
The Fat Cat (Kent), 1539
Fat Men from Space (Pinkwater), 1103
Father Fox's Pennyrhymes (Watson), 1972
Fathers, Mothers, Sisters, Brothers: A Collection of Family Poems (Hoberman), **1314**
Favorite Fairy Tales Told around the World (Haviland), 1694
Favorite Folktales from Around the World (Yolen), 2182
Favorite Greek Myths (Osborne), 1713
Favorite Scary Stories of American Children (Young), **1093**
Feast for 10 (Falwell), **11**
Feathers and Tails: Animal Fables from Around the World (Kherdian), **1073**
Feathers for Lunch (Ehlert), **265**
Felix's Hat (Bancroft and Gruenberg), **70**

Fiddle-I-Fee: A Farmyard Song for the Very Young (Sweet), **190**
The Field Beyond the Outfield (Teague), **376**
Fifth-Grade Magic (Gormley), 1181
50 Simple Things Kids Can Do to Save the Earth (Earth Works Group), **1135**
The Fighting Ground (Avi), 1267
Fin M'Coul, the Giant of Knockmary Hill (dePaola), **1439**
The Finches' Fabulous Furnace (Drury), 1170
Finders Keepers (Rodda), **789**
A Fine Fat Pig and Other Animal Poems (Hoberman), **1315**
The Fine Round Cake (Esterl), **903**
Finzel the Farsighted (Fleischman), 1065
The Fire Children: A West African Creation Tale (Maddern), **978**
Fire on the Mountain (Kurtz), **961**
Fire Race: A Karuk Coyote Tale About How Fire Came to the People (London and Pinola), **972**
The Firebird (Demi), **893**
The Firebird (Hastings), **938**
The Firebird (San Souci), **1012**
Fireflies in the Night (Hawes), **1156**
The Fireside Book of Fun and Game Songs (Winn), 1976
The Fireside Song Book of Birds and Beasts (Yolen), 1980
Firetalking (Polacco), **1221**
First Apple (Russell), **741**
The First Dog (Brett), 622
A First Poetry Book (Foster), 1800
The First Strawberries: A Cherokee Story (Bruchac), **870**
The First Thanksgiving (George), **1147**
First Tomato (Wells), **383**
The First Two Lives of Lucas-Kasha (Alexander), 1260
Fish Eyes: A Book You Can Count On (Ehlert), **97**
Fish Fry (Saunders), **790**
Fish Is Fish (Lionni), 474
A Fish Out of Water (Palmer), 221
The Fisherman and His Wife (Grimm), 1492
The Fisherman's Son (Ginsburg), 1478
Fishing (Engel), **268**
The Five Chinese Brothers (Bishop), 617
The Five-Dog Night (Christelow), **425**
The 500 Hats of Bartholomew Cubbins (Seuss), 995
Five Little Ducks (Raffi), **39**
Five Little Monkeys Jumping on the Bed (Christelow), 48
Five Little Monkeys Sitting in a Tree (Christelow), **85**
Five Silly Fishermen (Edwards), **901**

The Five Sparrows: A Japanese Folktale (Newton), 1575

Fix-It (McPhail), 494

Flat Stanley (Brown), 624

Flight: The Journey of Charles Lindbergh (Burleigh), **1114**

Flit, Flutter, Fly! Poems About Bugs and Other Crawly Creatures (Hopkins), **1319**

Flossie & the Fox (McKissack), 735

Flower Garden (Bunting), **72**

Flower Moon Snow: A Book of Haiku (Mizamura), 1873

Fly Away Home (Bunting), **415**

The Flying Tortoise: An Igbo Tale (Mollel), **987**

Fog Magic (Sauer), 1353

Follow Me! (Gerstein), 112

Follow My Leader (Garfield), 1174

Follow the Dream: The Story of Christopher Columbus (Sis), **1238**

Follow the Drinking Gourd (Winter), 1134

Follow the Water from Brook to Ocean (Dorros), **1133**

The Fool of the World and His Flying Ship (Ransome), 1583

The Foolish Frog (Seeger and Seeger), 797

Foolish Rabbit's Big Mistake (Martin), 1564

For Laughing Out Loud: Poems to Tickle Your Funnybone (Prelutsky), **1397**

For Reading Out Loud! A Guide to Sharing Books with Children (Kimmel and Segel), 2142

Forest (Lisle), **827**

The Forgetful Bears Meet Mr. Memory (Weinberg), 583

Fortunately (Charlip), 645

Fortune (Stanley), 1117

The Fortune-Tellers (Alexander), **698**

The Foundling (Carrick), 641

The Foundling Fox (Korschunow), 713

Four Dollars and Fifty Cents (Kimmel), **721**

The Four-Legged Ghosts (Hoffman), **620**

Fourth Grade Rats (Spinelli), **749**

Fox Tale (Abolafia), **394**

Fox Went Out on a Chilly Night (Watson), **382**

Fox's Dream (Tejima), 565

Fraction Action (Leedy), **482**

Frances Face-Maker: A Going to Bed Book (Cole), 53

Frank and Ernest (Day), 906

Frankenstein Moved in on the Fourth Floor (Levy), 951

Freckle Juice (Blume), 618

Frederick (Lionni), 727

Frederick's Alligator (Peterson), 773

Frederick's Fables: A Leo Lionni Treasury of Favorite Stories (Lionni), 728

Freight Train (Crews), 58

Frida the Wondercat (Everitt), 384

Friday the 13th (Kroll), 716

Friends in Time (Chetwin), **764**

Friendship's First Thanksgiving (Accorsi), **216**

The Fright before Christmas (Howe), 935

Frog and Toad Are Friends (Lobel), 479

A Frog Inside My Hat: A First Book of Poems (Robinson), **1402**

Frog Medicine (Teague), **681**

The Frog Prince (Grimm), 1493

The Frog Prince: Or Iron Henry, illus. by Binette Schroeder (Grimm), **932**

The Frog Prince Continued (Scieszka), **676**

The Frog Princess (Isele), 1534

The Frog Princess: A Russian Tale (Lewis), **969**

Frog Went a-Courtin' (Langstaff), 179

Froggy Gets Dressed (London), **152**

From A to Z: The Collected Letters of Irene and Hallie Coletta (Coletta and Coletta), 897

From Anna (Little), **775**

From Pictures to Words: A Book About Making a Book (Stevens), **1244**

From Sea to Shining Sea: A Treasury of American Folklore and Folk Songs (Cohn), **1063**

From Seed to Plant (Gibbons), **1148**

From Tadpole to Frog (Pfeffer), **1219**

From the Horse's Mouth (Nevins), **1896**

From the Mixed-Up Files of Mrs. Basil E. Frankweiler (Konigsburg), 1201

The Funniest Dinosaur Book Ever (Rosenbloom), 1928

The Funniest Knock-Knock Book Ever! (Rosenbloom), 1929

The Funniest Riddle Book Ever! (Rosenbloom), 1930

The Funny Little Woman (Mosel), 1571

The Funny Song Book (Nelson), 1894

The Funny Thing (Gag), 103

Funny You Should Ask: How to Make Up Jokes and Riddles with Wordplay (Terban), **1414**

Funnybones (Ahlberg and Ahlberg), 314

A Furl of Fairy Wind (Hunter), 1076

Further Tales of Uncle Remus: The Misadventures of Brer Rabbit, Brer Fox, Brer Wolf, the Doodang, and Other Creatures (Lester), **1075**

Gabrielle and Selena (Desbarats), 659

The Gadget War (Duffey), **606**

Galaxies (Simon), 2101

The Garden of Abdul Gasazi (Van Allsburg), 1019

Garth Pig and the Ice Cream Lady (Rayner), 781

Garth Pig Steals the Show (Rayner), **543**

Gator Pie (Matthews), 506

Gawain and the Green Knight (Shannon), **1022**

Gentle Ben (Morey), 1332

The Genuine, Ingenious Thrift Shop Genie, Clarissa Mae Bean and Me (Keller), 1198

Geographunny: A Book of Global Riddles (Gerberg), **1295**

George and Martha (Marshall), 502

George Shrinks (Joyce), 444

George Washington: A Picture Book Biography (Giblin), **1150**

George Washington: Leader of a New Nation (Osborne), **1214**

George Washington's Socks (Woodruff), **798**

Geraldine's Baby Brother (Keller), **142**

Geraldine's Blanket (Keller), **168**

Germy Blew It (Jones), 1196

Gertrude, the Bulldog Detective (Christelow), **252**

Gertrude the Goose Who Forgot (Galdone and Galdone), 107

Ghastlies, Goops & Pincushions: Nonsense Verse (Kennedy), 1846

The Ghost Fox (Yep), **755**

The Ghost in the Noonday Sun (Fleischman), 1301

The Ghost of Skinny Jack (Lindgren), 1089

The Ghost of the Gravestone Hearth (Haynes), 1185

The Ghost on Saturday Night (Fleischman), 918

Ghost Poems (Wallace), 1970

Ghosts and Goblins: Stories for Halloween (Harper), 1690

Ghost's Hour, Spook's Hour (Bunting), 351

The Giant (Du Bois), 1294

The Giant Jam Sandwich (Lord and Burroway), 730

The Giant's Apprentice (Wetterer), 1130

The Gift (Nixon), 1099

The Gift of the Girl Who Couldn't Hear (Shreve), **841**

The Gigantic Joke Book (Rosenbloom), 1931

Giggles, Gags & Groaners (Rosenbloom), 1932

Gila Monsters Meet You at the Airport (Sharmat), 808

Ginger Jumps (Ernst), **269**

The Gingerbread Boy (Cook), 1429

The Gingerbread Boy (Galdone), 1459

The Gingerbread Doll (Tews), **565**

The Gingerbread Man (Kimmel), **953**

The Gingham Dog and the Calico Cat (Field), **103**

A Giraffe and a Half (Silverstein), 811

A Giraffe on the Moon (Nightingale), **172**

The Giraffe That Walked to Paris (Milton), **1208**

A Girl Called Boy (Hurmence), 1314

The Girl Who Tricked the Troll (Torgersen), 832

The Girl with the Silver Eyes (Roberts), 1345

The Giver (Lowry), **828**

Giving (Hughes), **22**

The Giving Tree (Silverstein), 1001

Gladys Told Me to Meet Her Here (Sharmat), 809

The Glass Mountain (Grimm), 1494

Gloria and the Super Soaper (Ross), 987

Gloria Chipmunk, Star! (Nixon), 760

The Glorious Flight: Across the Channel with Louis Blérot (Provensen and Provensen), 2084

The Glorious Mother Goose (Mother Goose), 1879

Gnats of Knotty Pine (Peet), 977

The Go-Around Dollar (Adams), **1094**

Go Away, Big Green Monster! (Emberley), **98**

Go Away Monsters, Lickety Split (Cooney), **88**

Go Free or Die: A Story About Harriet Tubman (Ferris), **1141**

Go Hang a Salami! I'm a Lasagna Hog! And Other Palindromes (Agee), **1263**

Go In and Out the Window: An Illustrated Songbook for Young People (Fox), 1801

Go to Sleep, Nicholas Joe (Sharmat), 263

Go with the Poem (Moore), 1874

The Gobble-Uns'll Git You Ef You Don't Watch Out (Riley), 1108

The Goblins Giggle and Other Stories (Bang), 1655

Goggles! (Keats), 449

Going on a Whale Watch (McMillan), **1194**

Going to Sleep on the Farm (Lewison), **28**

Going to Squintum's: A Foxy Folktale (Westwood), 1624

Gold and Silver, Silver and Gold: Tales of Hidden Treasure (Schwartz), 2092

The Gold Cadillac (Taylor), 1248

The Golden Days (Radley), **838**

The Golden Goose Book (Brooke), 1658

The Golden Treasury of Poetry (Untermeyer), 1968

Goldilocks and the Three Bears (Brett), 1408

Goldilocks and the Three Bears (Cauley), 1415

Goldilocks and the Three Bears (Eisen), 1450

Goldilocks and the Three Bears (Marshall), 1561

Goldilocks and the Three Bears (Stevens), 1611

Golly Gump Swallowed a Fly (Cole), 372

The Gollywhopper Egg (Rockwell), 534

Gonna Sing My Head Off! American Folk Songs for Children (Krull), **1344**

Good As New (Douglass), 72

Good Books, Good Times! (Hopkins), **1320**

Good-Bye, Arnold (Roche), 533

Goodbye House (Asch), 11

Good-bye, House (Ballard), **69**

Goodbye, Max (Keller), 452

Good Dog Poems (Cole), 1777

Good Luck Gold and Other Poems (Wong), **1424**

The Good-Luck Pencil (Stanley), 1005
Good Night, Fred (Wells), 285
Good-Night, Owl (Hutchins), 148
Goodbye Old Year, Hello New Year (Modell), 509
Goodness Gracious! (Cummings), **90**
The Goose and the Golden Coins (Cauley), 1416
Gopher Takes Heart (Scribner), **744**
Gorilla (Browne), 349
A Grain of Rice (Pittman), 1580
The Grand Escape (Naylor), **783**
Grandaddy's Place (Griffith), 682
Grandfather Tales (Chase), 1661
Grandfather Tang's Story (Tompert), **567**
Grandfather's Day (Tomey), **686**
Grandfather's Dream (Keller), **466**
Grandfather's Journey (Say), **674**
Grandma Essie's Covered Wagon (Williams), **691**
Grandpa Bud (Dodds), **9**
Grandpa's Face (Greenfield), 410
Grandpa's Ghost Stories (Flora), 919
Grandpa's Witched-Up Christmas (Flora), 920
Granfa' Grig Had a Pig: And Other Rhymes without Reason from Mother Goose (Mother Goose), 1880
Gray Duck Catches a Friend (Artis), 9
Gray Fox (London), **489**
Gray Goose and Gander: And Other Mother Goose Rhymes (Mother Goose), 1881
The Great Ball Game: A Muskogee Story (Bruchac), **871**
The Great Big Enormous Turnip (Tolstoi), 1614
A Great Big Ugly Man Came Up and Tied His Horse to Me: A Book of Nonsense Verse (Tripp), 1967
The Great Blueness and Other Predicaments (Lobel), 480
The Great Brain (Fitzgerald), 1171
Great Cat (McPhail), 495
The Great Christmas Kidnapping Caper (Van Leeuwen), 1128
The Great Green Turkey Creek Monster (Flora), 921
The Great Ideas of Lila Fenwick (McMullin), 1209
The Great Kapok Tree: A Tale of the Amazon Rain Forest (Cherry), 647
Great Northern Diver: The Loon (Esbensen), **1137**
The Great Pumpkin Switch (McDonald), **495**
The Great Quillow (Thurber), **684**
Great Rabbit and the Long-Tailed Wildcat (Gregg), **921**
The Great Rescue Operation (Van Leeuwen), 1252
The Great Song Book (John), 1832
The Great Town and Country Bicycle Balloon Chase (Douglass), 73
The Great Wall of China (Fisher), 2023

The Great White Man-Eating Shark: A Cautionary Tale (Mahy), **501**
The Greatest of All: A Japanese Folktale (Kimmel), **954**
Greedy Greeny (Gantos), 109
The Greedy Old Fat Man: An American Folktale (Galdone), 1460
Greedy Zebra (Mwenye Hadithi), 125
The Green Book (Paton Walsh), 1341
Green Eggs and Ham (Seuss), 259
The Green Gourd: A North Carolina Folktale (Hunter), **946**
Gregory Griggs: And Other Nursery Rhyme People (Mother Goose), 1882
Gregory, the Terrible Eater (Sharmat), 555
Grim and Ghastly Goings-On (Heide), **1309**
Grimm's Fairy Tales: 20 Stories (Grimm), 1686
Grinny: A Novel of Science Fiction (Fisk), 1297
The Grizzly Bear Family Book (Hoshino), **1164**
The Grizzly Sisters (Bellows), **230**
The Grouchy Ladybug (Carle), 37
Growing Colors (McMillan), 197
The Growing-Up Feet (Cleary), 50
Growing Vegetable Soup (Ehlert), 78
Guess What? (Gardner), 110
Guess Who? (Miller), **165**
The Guest (Marshall), 203
Guinea Pigs Don't Read Books (Bare), 1991
Guinea Pigs Far and Near (Duke), 75
The Gunniwolf (Harper), 1519
Guys from Space (Pinkwater), 522
Gwot! Horribly Funny Hairticklers (Mendoza), 962

Hail to the Chief! Jokes about the Presidents (Burns and Burns), **1276**
Hailstones and Halibut Bones: Adventures in Color (O'Neill), 1897
The Half-a-Moon Inn (Fleischman), 1299
Halloween ABC (Merriam), **1372**
The Halloween Party (Anderson), 605
Halloween Party (Shute), **551**
Halloween Poems (Livingston), **1357**
Halmoni and the Picnic (Choi), **424**
Hamlet and the Enormous Chinese Dragon Kite (Lies), **484**
Hand, Hand, Fingers, Thumb (Perkins), 228
Hand Rhymes (Brown), 1760
Handbook for Storytellers (Bauer), 2161
The Handmade Alphabet (Rankin), **1223**
Hands On, Thumbs Up: Secret Handshakes, Fingerprints, Sign Languages, and More Handy Ways to Have Fun with Hands (Gryski), **1154**
Hang Tough, Paul Mather (Slote), 1241

Hanimations (Mariotti), **1199**

Hank and Oogie (Weiss), 584

Hannah (Whelan), **689**

Hannah the Hippo's No Mud Day (Hiskey), **124**

Hans in Luck (Grimm), 1495

Hansel and Gretel, illus. by Paul Galdone (Grimm), 1496

Hansel and Gretel, illus. by James Marshall (Grimm), **926**

Hansel and Gretel, illus. by Paul O. Zelinsky (Grimm), 1497

Happy Birthday: Poems (Hopkins), **1321**

Happy Birthday, Martin Luther King (Marzollo), **1203**

Happy Birthday, Moon (Asch), 12

Happy Birthday, Ronald Morgan! (Giff), 406

Happy-Go-Lucky (Weisner), 1625

The Happy Hedgehog Band (Waddell), **48**

The Happy Hippopotami (Martin), **322**

The Happy Lion (Fatio), 385

Happy Mother's Day (Kroll), 717

Happy Valentine's Day, Emma! (Stevenson), 823

Harald and the Giant Knight (Carrick), 882

Harald and the Great Stag (Carrick), 883

The Hare and the Tortoise (Wildsmith), 1627

Harlequin and the Gift of Many Colors (Charlip), 886

Harold and the Purple Crayon (Johnson), 153

Harriet the Spy (Fitzhugh), 1298

Harry and Arney (Caseley), **422**

Harry and the Terrible Whatzit (Gackenbach), 98

Harry by the Sea (Zion), 307

Harry in Trouble (Porte), 527

Harry the Dirty Dog (Zion), 308

Harry the Fat Bear Spy (Wilson), 1133

Harry's Dog (Porte), 777

Harry's Mad (King-Smith), 1199

Harvey Slumfenburger's Christmas Present (Burningham), **244**

Harvey the Beer Can King (Gilson), 1179

Harvey the Foolish Pig (Gackenbach), 397

Harvey's Horrible Snake Disaster (Clifford), 1052

The Hat-Shaking Dance: And Other Tales from the Gold Coast (Courlander), 1668

A Hat So Simple (Smath), **367**

Hattie and the Fox (Fox), 91

Hattie the Backstage Bat (Freeman), 393

Hauntings: Ghosts and Ghouls from Around the World (Hodges), **1072**

Have You Ever Seen . . .? An ABC Book (Gardner), 403

The Haymeadow (Paulsen), **835**

Hazel's Amazing Mother (Wells), 585

Headlines (Hall), 932

Heckedy Peg (Wood), 854

The Hedgehog Boy: A Latvian Folktale (Langton), 1545

Hedgehog for Breakfast (Turner), **194**

Help! Let Me Out (Porter), 982

Help! There's a Cat Washing in Here (Smith), 1361

Henny Penny (Galdone), 1461

Henry and the Dragon (Christelow), 49

Henry and the Red Stripes (Christelow), 362

Henry Huggins (Cleary), 888

Henry Moore: From Bones and Stones to Sketches and Sculptures (Gardner), **1146**

Henry Reed's Baby-Sitting Service (Robertson), 1347

Henry the Explorer (Taylor), 564

Henry the Sailor Cat (Calhoun), **418**

Henry's Baby (Hoffman), **454**

Henry's Fourth of July (Keller), **26**

Her Majesty, Aunt Essie (Schwartz), 796

Her Seven Brothers (Goble), 1482

The Herbie Jones Reader's Theater: Funny Scenes to Read Aloud (Kline), **1170**

Herbie's Troubles (Chapman), 361

Hercules (Gramatky), 120

Herds of Words (MacCarthy), **1363**

Here Comes the Mail (Skurzynski), **1240**

Here Comes the Mystery Man (Sanders), **673**

Hershel and the Hanukkah Goblins (Kimmel), 944

Hey Willy, See the Pyramids (Kalman), 941

Hickory Dickory Dock and Other Nursery Rhymes (Mother Goose), **1379**

A Hidden Magic (Vande Velde), 1251

Hidden Worlds: Pictures of the Invisible (Simon), 2102

Hide and Seek Fog (Tresselt), 833

Hide and Shriek: Riddles About Ghosts & Goblins (Gordon), **1300**

Higgledy-Piggledy: Verses & Pictures (Livingston), 953

High on a Hill: A Book of Chinese Riddles (Young), 1982

High-Wire Henry (Calhoun), **419**

Hilary and the Troublemakers (Leverich), **730**

Hildilid's Night (Ryan), 539

Hill of Fire (Lewis), 723

Hippopotamus Hunt (Most), **513**

A Hippopotamustn't and Other Animal Verses (Lewis), **1353**

A Hippo's a Heap: And Other Animal Poems (McLoughland), **1364**

The History of Mother Twaddle and the Marvelous Achievements of Her Son, Jack (Galdone), 1462

Ho for a Hat! (Smith), **368**

The Hoboken Chicken Emergency (Pinkwater), 1104

The Hobyahs (San Souci), **1013**

The Hobyas: An Old Story (Stern), 1609

The Hodgepodge Book (Emrich), 1796

Hole by the Apple Tree: An A–Z Discovery Tale (Polette), **339**

The Hole in the Dike (Green), 409

The Holiday Songbook (Quackenbush), 1925

Home from Far (Little), 1206

Homebody (McDonald), **494**

Homer Price (McCloskey), 1208

Honest Abe (Kunhardt), **1179**

Honey, I Love (Greenfield), 1807

Honkers (Yolen), **391**

Hop Jump (Walsh), **53**

The Hopeful Trout and Other Limericks (Ciardi), 1771

Horace (Keller), **143**

Horrible Harry and the Christmas Surprise (Kline), **474**

Horton Hatches the Egg (Seuss), 801

The Houdini Box (Selznick), **745**

A House for Hermit Crab (Carle), **246**

A House Is a House for Me (Hoberman), 431

The House That Crack Built (Taylor), **1246**

The House That Jack Built: A Mother Goose Nursery Rhyme (Stevens), 271

The House with a Clock in Its Walls (Bellairs), 1143

How a Piglet Crashed the Christmas Party (Zakhoder), 858

How Big Is a Foot? (Myller), 970

How Big Were the Dinosaurs? (Most), **1212**

How Brown Mouse Kept Christmas (Watson), 847

How Do You Get a Horse Out of the Bathtub? Profound Answers to Preposterous Questions (Phillips), 1900

How Do You Say It Today, Jesse Bear? (Carlstrom), **76**

How Droofus the Dragon Lost His Head (Peet), 769

How, Hippo! (Brown), 28

How I Captured a Dinosaur (Schwartz), 546

How I Hunted the Little Fellows (Zhitkov), 1136

How Many, How Many, How Many (Walton), **206**

How Many Spots Does a Leopard Have? And Other Tales (Lester), 1705

How Many Stars in the Sky? (Hort), **288**

How Much Is a Million? (Schwartz), 2093

How Music Came to the World (Ober), **993**

How My Family Lives in America (Kuklin), **1178**

How My Parents Learned to Eat (Friedman), 672

How Night Came from the Sea: A Story from Brazil (Gerson), **912**

How Now, Brown Cow? (Schertle), **1406**

How Pizza Came to Queens (Khalsa), 456

How Pleasant to Know Mr. Lear! (Lear), 1853

How Rabbit Tricked Otter and Other Cherokee Trickster Stories (Ross), **1084**

How Raven Brought Light to People (Dixon), **897**

How Snowshoe Hare Rescued the Sun: A Tale from the Arctic (Bernhard), **866**

How Spider Saved Christmas (Kraus), 459

How the Birds Changed Their Feathers: A South American Indian Folk Tale (Troughton), 1616

How the Camel Got His Hump (Kipling), 947

How the Giraffe Got Such a Long Neck . . . and Why Rhino Is So Grumpy (Rosen), **1007**

How the Grinch Stole Christmas (Seuss), 802

How the Ox Star Fell from Heaven (Hong), **942**

How the Rooster Saved the Day (Lobel), 192

How the Sea Began: A Taino Myth (Crespo), **887**

How the Second Grade Got $8,205.50 to Visit the Statue of Liberty (Zimelman), **583**

How the Whale Got His Throat (Kipling), 712

How the Witch Got Alf (Annett), 868

How to Dig a Hole to the Other Side of the World (McNulty), 2072

How to Eat a Poem and Other Morsels: Food Poems for Children (Agree), 1743

How to Eat Fried Worms (Rockwell), 1109

How to Fool Your Friends (Brown), 2000

How to Make an Apple Pie and See the World (Priceman), **538**

How Turtle's Back Was Cracked: A Traditional Cherokee Tale (Ross), **1008**

Hubert's Hair-Raising Adventure (Peet), 770

Hubknuckles (Herman), 686

Hue Boy (Mitchell), **325**

Hugh Pine (Van de Wetering), 1127

Humbug (Bawden), **703**

Humbug Potion: An A B Cipher (Balian), 608

Humbug Witch (Balian), 20

Hummingbirds: Jewels in the Sky (Tyrrell), **1248**

Humphrey, the Dancing Pig (Getz), 405

The Hundred Dresses (Estes), 914

Hungarian Folk-Tales (Biro), 1657

The Hungry Fox and the Foxy Duck (Leverich), 186

The Hungry Giant of the Tundra (Sloat), **1027**

Hungry Hyena (Mwenye Hadithi), **331**

Hunky Dory Ate It (Evans), **100**

The Hunter (Geraghty), **442**

Hurray for Hattie Rabbit (Gackenbach), 99

Hurricane (Wiesner), **574**

Hurry Home, Candy (DeJong), 1060

Hurry Home, Grandma! (Olson), 220

Hush Up! (Aylesworth), 323

I Am Really a Princess (Shields), **550**

I Am the Cat (Hopkins), 1823

I Am the Dog, I Am the Cat (Hall), **448**

I Am the Ocean (Marshak), **1200**

I Can Tell by Touching (Otto), **1215**

"I Can't," Said the Ant (Cameron), 636

I, Columbus; My Journal—1492–3 (Roop and Roop), **1227**

I Don't Want to Go Back to School (Russo), **355**

I Got a Family (Cooper), **255**

I Had a Cat (Reeves), 237

I Had a Friend Named Peter: Talking to Children about the Death of a Friend (Cohn), 51

I Hate Company (Petersen), **655**

I Hate English (Levine), 721

I Hate My Brother Harry (Dragonwagon), 663

I Have a Friend (Narahashi), 215

I Know an Old Lady (Karas), **295**

I Know an Old Lady Who Swallowed a Fly (Rounds), 537

I Know an Old Lady Who Swallowed a Fly (Westcott), 588

I-Know-Not-What, I-Know-Not-Where: A Russian Tale (Kimmel), **955**

I Lost My Arrow in a Kankan Tree (Lichtveld), **970**

I Love Animals (McDonnell), **30**

I Love My Anteater with an A (Ipcar), 1078

I Made a Mistake (Nerlove), 756

I Met a Polar Bear (Boyd and Boyd), 340

I Saw a Rocket Walk a Mile: Nonsense Tales, Chants and Songs from Many Lands (Withers), 1735

I Saw Esau: The Schoolchild's Pocket Book (Opie and Opie), **1391**

I Saw You in the Bathtub and Other Folk Rhymes (Schwartz), 1947

I See Something You Don't See: A Riddle-Me Picture Book (Koontz), **301**

I Think I Thought and Other Tricky Verbs (Terban), 1963

I Thought I'd Take My Rat to School: Poems for September to June (Kennedy), **1341**

I Unpacked My Grandmother's Trunk (Hoguet), 689

I Want a Brother or Sister (Lindgren), 189

I Was All Thumbs (Waber), 1023

I Went to the Animal Fair (Cole), 1778

I Went to the Zoo (Gelman), **275**

I Went Walking (Williams), **57**

I Will Make You Disappear (York), 1378

I Will Not Go to a Market Today (Allard), 316

I Wish I Was Sick, Too (Brandenberg), 26

I Wish I Were a Butterfly (Howe), 692

I Wish That I Had Duck Feet (LeSieg), 467

The Ice Cream Cone Coot and Other Rare Birds (Lobel), 954

The Ice Cream Ocean and Other Delectable Poems of the Sea (Russo), 1940

The Ice Cream Store (Lee), **1350**

The Ice Horse (Christiansen), **597**

Icebergs and Glaciers (Simon), 2103

Ida Early Comes Over the Mountain (Burch), 1153

Idle Jack (Maitland), 1559

Iduna and the Magic Apples (Mayer), 1567

If at First You Do Not See (Brown), 348

If I Had a Paka (Pomerantz), 1902

If I Ran the Zoo (Seuss), 803

If I Were in Charge of the World and Other Worries: Poems for Children and Their Parents (Viorst), 1969

If You Ever Meet a Whale (Livingston), **1358**

If You Give a Moose a Muffin (Numeroff), **334**

If You Give a Mouse a Cookie (Numeroff), 514

If You Lived in Colonial Times (McGovern), 2069

If You Made a Million (Schwartz), 2094

If You Want to Find Golden (Spinelli), **370**

If You Were a Writer (Nixon), 972

If Your Name Was Changed at Ellis Island (Levine), **1186**

If You're Happy and You Know It: Eighteen Story Songs Set to Pictures (Weiss), 1973

If You're Not Here, Please Raise Your Hand: Poems about School (Dakos), **1283**

Ike and Mama and the Once-a-Year Suit (Snyder), 1004

Ike and Porker (Kirby), 1200

Iktomi and the Boulder: A Plains Indian Story (Goble), 1483

I'll Fix Anthony (Viorst), 574

I'll Meet You at the Cucumbers (Moore), 967

I'll See You in My Dreams (Jukes), **718**

I'll Tell on You (Lexai), 724

I'm Coming to Get You (Ross), 536

I'm Going on a Bear Hunt (Sivulich), 267

I'm Going on a Dragon Hunt (Jones), 158

I'm Going to Be Famous (Birdseye), 1144

I'm Mad at You (Cole), 1779

I'm New Here (Howlett), **1166**

"I'm Not Sleepy" (Cazet), **80**

I'm Telling! Kids Talk about Brothers and Sisters (Arnold and Loeb), 1988

I'm Telling You Now (Delton), 65

Immigrant Kids (Freedman), 2027

Imogene's Antlers (Small), 558

The Important Book (Brown), 630

Impossible Possum (Conford), 652

In a Pickle and Other Funny Idioms (Terban), 1964

In for Winter, Out for Spring (Adoff), **1260**

In 1492 (Marzollo), **1204**
In the Diner (Loomis), **154**
In the Eyes of the Cat: Japanese Poetry for All Seasons (Demi), **1284**
In the Land of Small Dragon: A Vietnamese Folktale (Kha), 1540
In the Month of Kislev: A Story for Hanukkah (Jaffe), **627**
In the Small, Small Pond (Fleming), **104**
In the Witch's Kitchen: Poems for Halloween (Brewton, Blackburn, and Blackburn), 1757
In Trouble Again, Zelda Hammersmith? (Hall), 1069
Inch by Inch (Lionni), 475
The Incredible Journey (Burnford), 1279
The Incredible Journey of Lewis & Clark (Blumberg), 1996
The Incredible Painting of Felix Clousseau (Agee), 862
The Indian in the Cupboard (Banks), 1272
Inner Chimes: Poems on Poetry (Goldstein), **1298**
Inside My Feet (Kennedy), 1318
Into the Dream (Sleator), 1359
Into the Painted Bear Lair (Stearns), 1243
Introducing Books: A Guide for the Middle Grades (Gillespie and Lembo), 2137
Introducing Shirley Braverman (Wolitzer), 1376
The Invisible Dog (King-Smith), **467**
Invisible Oink: Pig Jokes (Phillips), **1394**
Ira Says Goodbye (Waber), 841
Ira Sleeps Over (Waber), 842
The Iron Giant: A Story in Five Nights (Hughes), 1075
Iron John (Grimm), **928**
Iroquois Stories: Heros and Heroines, Monsters and Magic (Bruchac), 1659
Is a Blue Whale the Biggest Thing There Is? (Wells), **1251**
Is Anybody Up? (Kandoian), **139**
Is There Life on a Plastic Planet? (Ames), 1263
Is This a House for Hermit Crab? (McDonald), **313**
Is This You? (Krauss), 714
Is Your Mama a Llama? (Guarino), 123
Island Baby (Keller), **296**
Island Boy (Cooney), 1055
The Island Light (Wells), **383**
Island of the Blue Dolphins (O'Dell), 1339
It Begins with an A (Calmenson), **74**
It Came from Outer Space (Bradman), **410**
It Could Always Be Worse (Zemach), 1638
It Does Not Say Meow and Other Animal Riddle Rhymes (De Regniers), 1791
It Happened in America: True Stories from the Fifty States (Perl), **1216**

It Happened in Chelm: A Story of the Legendary Town of Fools (Freedman), **905**
It Happened in Pinsk (Yorinks), 1035
It Looked Like Spilt Milk (Shaw), 264
It Takes a Village (Cowen-Fletcher), **257**
It Wasn't My Fault (Lester), 469
It's About Time! (Hopkins), **1322**
It's an Armadillo (Lavies), 2064
It's Christmas (Prelutsky), 1905
It's Halloween (Prelutsky), 1906
It's Hard to Read a Map with a Beagle on Your Lap (Singer), **1409**
It's Mine! (Lionni), 190
It's Our World, Too! Stories of Young People Who Are Making a Difference (Hoose), **1163**
It's Perfectly True (Andersen), 602
It's Pumpkin Time! (Hall), **18**
It's Raining Cats and Dogs: Cat and Dog Jokes (Keller), 1837
"It's Raining," Said John Twaining: Danish Nursery Rhymes (Bodecker), 1750
It's Snowing! It's Snowing! (Prelutsky), 1907
It's So Nice to Have a Wolf around the House (Allard), 317
It's Spring! (Minarik), 213
It's Thanksgiving (Prelutsky), 1908
It's the Bear! (Alborough), **63**
It's Too Noisy! (Cole), **882**
It's Valentine's Day (Prelutsky), 1909
It's Your Turn, Roger! (Gretz), 412
Itsy-Bitsy Beasties: Poems from Around the World (Rosen), **1404**
The Itsy Bitsy Spider (Trapani), **193**
Ivan: Stories of Old Russia (Crouch), **1064**

J. T. (Wagner), 1129
Jack and the Bean Tree (Haley), 1515
Jack and the Beanstalk (Cauley), 1417
Jack and the Beanstalk (Garner), **910**
Jack and the Beanstalk (Howe), **944**
Jack and the Beanstalk (Pearson), 1577
Jack and the Fire Dragon (Haley), 1516
Jack and the Wonder Beans (Still), 1612
Jack-O'-Lantern (Barth), 1400
Jack Tales (Chase), 1662
Jack the Giant Chaser: An Appalachian Tale (Compton and Compton), **884**
The Jacket I Wear in the Snow (Nietzel), 217
Jackson Jones and the Puddle of Thorns (Quattlebaum), **787**
Jacob Two-Two Meets the Hooded Fang (Richler), 1107
The Jade Stone: A Chinese Folktale (Yacowitz), **1045**

Jalapeño Hal (Harper), **615**
Jam: A True Story (Mahy), 740
Jamaica and Brianna (Havill), **119**
Jamberry (Degen), 64
Jambo Means Hello: Swahili Alphabet Book (Feelings), 1798
James and the Giant Peach (Dahl), 1059
James Marshall's Mother Goose (Mother Goose), 1883
Jamie O'Rourke and the Big Potato: An Irish Folktale (dePaola), **895**
Jane Yolen's Mother Goose Songbook (Mother Goose), **1380**
January Brings the Snow: A Book of Months (Coleridge), 54
A January Fog Will Freeze a Hog and Other Weather Folklore (Davis), 2016
Jason and the Money Tree (Levitin), 1203
Jeffrey Strangeways (Murphy), **734**
Jelly Belly: Original Nursery Rhymes (Lee), 1855
Jennie's Hat (Keats), 450
Jennifer Murdley's Toad (Coville), **765**
Jennifer Takes Over P.S. 94 (Lystad), 733
Jennifer's Rabbit (Paxton), 224
Jenny Archer, Author (Conford), 898
Jeremy Bean's St. Patrick's Day (Schertle), 544
Jeremy Thatcher, Dragon Hatcher (Coville), **810**
Jeremy Visick (Wiseman), 1375
Jeremy's Tail (Ball), **227**
Jerome and the Babysitter (Christelow), 364
Jerome and the Witchcraft Kids (Christelow), 363
Jessica (Henkes), 418
Jiggle Wiggle Prance (Noll), 513
Jim Along Josie: A Collection of Folk Songs (Langstaff and Langstaff), 1850
Jim and the Beanstalk (Briggs), 623
Jim Jimmy James (Kent), 454
Jim Meets the Thing (Cohen), 367
Jimmy Takes Vanishing Lessons (Brooks), 876
Jim's Dog Muffins (Cohen), 368
Jingo Django (Fleischman), 1302
A Job for Jenny Archer (Conford), 899
A Job for Wittilda (Buehner), **242**
Joe on Sunday (Blundell), 337
Joel and the Great Merlini (McGraw), 1093
Joey Runs Away (Kent), 169
John Brown: One Man Against Slavery (Everett), **1138**
John Brown, Rose and the Midnight Cat (Wagner), 581
John Henry (Lester), **967**
John Henry: An American Legend (Keats), 1538
Johnny Appleseed (Kellogg), 2058
The Joking Man (Flora), 922

The Jolly Christmas Postman (Ahlberg and Ahlberg), **396**
Jorinda and Joringel (Grimm), 1498
Joshua Disobeys (Vollmer), **198**
Joshua T. Bates Takes Charge (Shreve), **747**
Josie Smith at School (Nabb), **516**
Journey Cake, Ho! (Sawyer), 1591
The Journey Home (Lester), **303**
Journey Home (Uchida), 1370
Joyful Noise: Poems for Two Voices (Fleischman), 1799
Juan Bobo and the Pig: A Puerto Rican Folktale (Pitre), **998**
Juba This and Juba That: Story Hour Stretches for Large or Small Groups (Tashjian), 1961
The Judge: An Untrue Tale (Zemach), 1037
Julie of the Wolves (George), 1304
Juliet Fisher and the Foolproof Plan (Honeycutt), **621**
Julius, the Baby of the World (Henkes), **283**
Jumanji (Van Allsburg), 1020
Jumbo (Blumberg), **1107**
Jump! The Adventures of Brer Rabbit (Parks and Jones), 1714
Jump for Joy: A Book of Months (Halsey), **279**
Jump, Frog, Jump (Kalan), 160
June 29, 1999 (Wiesner), **690**
Junie B. Jones and a Little Monkey Business (Park), **651**
Junie B. Jones and Some Sneaky Peeky Spying (Park), **652**
Junie B. Jones and the Stupid Smelly Bus (Park), **653**
The Junior Thunder Lord (Yep), **1046**
Juniorplots: A Book Talk Manual for Teachers and Librarians (Gillespie and Lembo), 2138
The Juniper Tree: And Other Tales from Grimm (Grimm), 1687
Just a Little Bit (Tompert), **192**
Just Around the Corner: Poems About the Seasons (Jacobs), **1333**
Just Awful (Whitney), 293
Just Beyond Reach and Other Riddle Poems (Nims), **1390**
Just Call Me Stupid (Birdseye), **759**
Just Enough to Make a Story: A Sourcebook for Telling (Schimmel), 2180
Just Like Daddy (Asch), 13
Just Plain Cat (Robinson), 986
Just Plain Fancy (Polacco), **662**
Just So Stories, illus. by Victor Ambrus (Kipling), 948
Just So Stories, illus. by David Frampton (Kipling), **728**

Kanahena: A Cherokee Story (Roth), 1587
Kangaroo (Arnold), 1986
Kat Kong (Pilkey), **658**
Katy and the Big Snow (Burton), 35
Katy-No-Pocket (Payne), 225
Katy's First Haircut (Davis), 63
Keep Looking! (Selsam and Hunt), 2095
Keep Ms. Sugarman in the Fourth Grade (Levy), **731**
Keep on Singing: A Ballad of Marian Anderson (Livingston), **1190**
Keep Your Mouth Closed, Dear (Aliki), 5
Keeping a Christmas Secret (Naylor), 216
The Key into Winter (Andersen), **587**
Kickle Snifters and Other Fearsome Critters Collected from American Folklore (Schwartz), 1593
The Kid in the Red Jacket (Park), 1221
Kid Power (Pfeffer), 1224
Kids (Anholt and Anholt), **64**
Kids Pick the Funniest Poems: A Collection of Poems That Will Make You Laugh (Lansky), **1346**
The King and the Tortoise (Mollel), **988**
The King at the Door (Cole), 895
King Bidgood's in the Bathtub (Wood), 855
The King Has Horse's Ears (Thomson), 1613
King Henry the Ape: Animal Jokes (Keller), **1338**
King Krakus and the Dragon (Domanska), 1446
King Midas and the Golden Touch (Hewitt), 1522
The King of Kennelwick Castle (West), 289
King of the Birds (Climo), 1425
King of the Cats (Galdone), 1463
King of the Cats and Other Tales (Carlson), 1660
King of the Playground (Naylor), **332**
King Solomon and the Bee (Renberg), **1001**
King Wacky (Gackenbach), 673
The King's Chessboard (Birch), 1045
The King's Stilts (Seuss), 996
Kiss a Frog! Jokes About Fairy Tales, Knights, and Dragons (Walton and Walton), **1419**
Kites Sail High: A Book about Verbs (Heller), 1812
Kitten Can (McMillan), 198
Klara's New World (Winter), **693**
The Knee-High Man and Other Tales (Lester), 1706
Knick Knack Paddywack (Moss), **327**
Knights of the Kitchen Table (Scieszka), **743**
Knock at a Star: A Child's Introduction to Poetry (Kennedy), 1847
Knock-Knock Knees and Funny Bones: Riddles for Every Body (Mathews and Robinson), **1370**
Knock Knock! Who's There? (Rosenbloom), 1933
Koala Lou (Fox), 389

Koko's Kitten (Patterson), 2080
Konrad (Nostlinger), 1219
The Kooken (Lebentritt and Ploetz), **481**
The Korean Cinderella (Climo), **878**

Lady Daisy (King-Smith), **723**
The Lady Who Put Salt in Her Coffee (Hale), 930
The Lady Who Put Salt in Her Coffee (Schwartz), **742**
The Lady with the Alligator Purse (Westcott), 290
Lambs for Dinner (Maestro and Maestro), 498
Land, Sea, and Sky: Poems to Celebrate the Earth (Paladino), **1392**
Larger Than Life: The Adventures of American Legendary Heroes (San Souci), **1085**
The Last Cow on the White House Lawn & Other Little-Known Facts about the Presidency (Seuling), 2096
Last, First, Middle and Nick: All about Names (Hazen), 2045
The Last of the Really Great Whangdoodles (Edwards), 1063
The Last Princess: The Story of Princess Ka'iulani of Hawai'i (Stanley), **1243**
Laugh Book: A New Treasury of Humor for Children (Cole and Calmenson), 1774
Laughing Time: Nonsense Poems (Smith), 1955
Laura Charlotte (Galbraith), 105
The Laura Ingalls Wilder Songbook (Garson), 1802
The Lazies (Ginsburg), 1680
Lazy Lion (Mwenye Hadithi), **171**
Lazy Stories (Wolkstein), 1736
Lazy Tommy Pumpkinhead (Du Bois), 911
Learning to Swim in Swaziland: A Child's-Eye View of a Southern African Country (Leigh), **1184**
Leave Herbert Alone (Whitney), 294
"Leave That Cricket Be, Alan Lee" (Porte), **340**
The Legend of Slappy Hooper: An American Tall Tale (Shepard), **1023**
The Legend of Sleepy Hollow (Wolkstein), **795**
The Legend of the Bluebonnet: An Old Tale of Texas (dePaola), 1440
The Legend of the Cranberry: A Paleo-Indian Tale (Greene), **919**
The Legend of the Indian Paintbrush (dePaola), 1441
The Legend of William Tell (Small), **1028**
The Lemonade Trick (Corbett), 1056
Lengthy (Hoff), 139
Lenny Kandell, Smart Aleck (Conford), 1290
Lenore's Big Break (Pearson), **528**
Lentil (McCloskey), 956
Leo the Late Bloomer (Kraus), 460

Leona and Ike (Havill), **712**
Leopold the See-Through Crumbpicker (Flora), 669
Leprechauns Never Lie (Balian), 609
The Leprechaun's Story (Kennedy), 1081
Lester's Dog (Hesse), **619**
Let Freedom Ring: A Ballad of Martin Luther King, Jr. (Livingston), **1191**
Let Me Tell You about My Baby (Banish), 1990
Let's Celebrate: Festival Poems (Foster), **1293**
Let's Go, Froggy (London), **153**
Let's Go Home, Little Bear (Waddell), **201**
Let's Go Traveling (Krupp), **1177**
Let's Marry Said the Cherry and Other Nonsense Poems (Bodecker), 1751
The Letter Jesters (Falwell), **1140**
A Letter to Amy (Keats), 451
Libby on Wednesday (Snyder), **846**
The Librarian Who Measured the Earth (Lasky), **1180**
Lights Out! (Himmelman), **453**
Lily and Miss Liberty (Stevens), **679**
Lily and the Wooden Bowl (Schroeder), **1021**
The Limerick Trick (Corbett), 1057
Lincoln: A Photobiography (Freedman), 2028
Lindbergh (Demarest), **1128**
The Line Up Book (Russo), 247
Lion (Du Bois), 912
The Lion and the Rat (Wildsmith), 1628
The Lion and the Stoat (Zelinsky), 859
The Lion Family Book (Hofer), 2051
The Lion, the Witch and the Wardrobe (Lewis), 1088
Listen! And Help Tell the Story (Carlson), 1765
Listen to the Desert / Oye al Desierto (Mora), **1209**
Listen to the Rain (Martin and Archambault), 746
The Listening Walk (Showers), **187**
Literature and the Child (Cullinan), 2118
Literature and Young Children (Cullinan and Carmichael), 2133
Little Bear's Trousers (Hissey), 135
Little Beaver and the Echo (MacDonald), **156**
Little Blue and Little Yellow (Lionni), 191
The Little Book of Anagrams (Barrol), 1745
The Little Book of Big Tongue Twisters (Curtis), 1786
Little Brother and Little Sister (Grimm), 1499
Little by Little: A Writer's Education (Little), **1187**
The Little Dog Laughed and Other Nursery Rhymes (Mother Goose), **1384**
Little Elephant (Ford), **15**
Little Fingerling (Hughes), **945**
The Little Girl and the Big Bear (Galdone), 1455
Little Hatchy Hen (Flora), 923
The Little House (Burton), 634

Little House in the Big Woods (Wilder), 1028
The Little Humpbacked Horse (Hodges), 1525
Little Monster (Wade), 284
The Little Mouse, the Red Ripe Strawberry, and the Big Hungry Bear (Wood and Wood), **60**
The Little Old Lady Who Was Not Afraid of Anything (Williams), 591
The Little Old Woman and the Hungry Cat (Polette), **999**
Little One Inch (Brenner), **1407**
Little Peep (Kent), 455
Little Rabbit's Loose Tooth (Bate), 332
Little Red Cap (Grimm), 1500
Little Red Hen (Domanska), 1447
The Little Red Hen (Galdone), 1464
Little Red Riding Hood (Grimm), 1501
Little Robin Redbreast: A Mother Goose Rhyme (Mother Goose), **35**
Little Salt Lick and the Sun King (Armstrong), **399**
Little Sister and the Month Brothers (De Regniers), 1445
Little Sister for Sale (Hamilton), **450**
A Little Time (Baldwin), 1140
Little Tricker the Squirrel Meets Big Double the Bear (Kesey), **634**
Little Witch (Bennett), 874
Lives of the Musicians: Good Times, Bad Times (and What the Neighbors Thought) (Krull), **1174**
Lives of the Writers: Comedies, Tragedies (and What the Neighbors Thought) (Krull), **1175**
Living Dangerously: American Women Who Risked Their Lives for Adventure (Rappaport), **1224**
Liza Lou and the Yeller Belly Swamp (Mayer), 748
Lizard in the Sun (Ryder), 2090
Lizard Music (Pinkwater), 1225
Lizard's Song (Shannon), 261
Lizzie Lies a Lot (Levy), 1087
Lizzy & Harold (Winthrop), 594
Llama and the Great Flood: A Folktale from Peru (Alexander), 1389
Llama Beans (Keller), 1838
Log of Christopher Columbus (Columbus), **1124**
Lon Po Po: A Red-Riding Hood Story from China (Young), 1633
Look Again! (Hoban), 688
The Look Again . . . and Again, and Again, and Again Book (Gardner), 675
Look! Look! Look! (Hoban), **286**
Look Out, Bird! (Janovitz), **134**
The Looniest Limerick Book in the World (Rosenbloom), 1934
Loop the Loop (Dugan), **608**
The Lorax (Seuss), 997
Lord of the Sky: Zeus (Gates), 1679

Loretta Mason Potts (Chase), 1157

Lost! (McPhail), **316**

Lost in the Museum (Cohen), 369

The Lost Kingdom of Karnica (Kennedy), 1082

Lost Star: The Story of Amelia Earhart (Lauber), 2061

Lostman's River (DeFelice), **811**

Lots of Limericks (Livingston), **1359**

The Lotus Seed (Garland), **609**

Louanne Pig in the Mysterious Valentine (Carlson), 637

The Loudest Noise in the World (Elkin), 381

Love Flute (Goble), **916**

Love from Uncle Clyde (Parker), 518

Love, Your Bear Pete (Sheldon), **363**

The Luckiest Kid on the Planet (Ernst), **439**

Lucky Me (Cazet), 360

Lucky's Choice (Jeschke), **291**

Lucy Comes to Stay (Wells), **572**

Luka's Quilt (Guback), **278**

Lunch (Fleming), **14**

Lyle, Lyle Crocodile (Waber), 578

M & M and the Santa Secrets (Ross), 785

Mac & Marie & the Train Toss Surprise (Howard), **455**

McBroom Tells the Truth (Fleischman), 1066

McElligot's Pool (Seuss), 804

McGurk Gets Good and Mad (Hildick), 1189

McMummy (Byars), **762**

Madeline's Rescue (Bemelmans), 335

The Maestro Plays (Martin), **504**

Mag the Magnificent (Gackenbach), 398

Maggie & the Monster (Winthrop), 299

Maggie Doesn't Want to Move (O'Donnell), 515

Maggie Mab and the Bogey Beast (Carey), **875**

The Magic and the Sword: The Greek Myths Retold (Cox), 1671

The Magic Boat: And Other Chinese Folk Stories (Jagendorf and Weng), 1699

The Magic Book (Roberts), 1229

Magic Carpet (Brisson), **411**

The Magic Finger (Dahl), 905

The Magic Grandfather (Williams), 1254

The Magic Guinea Pig (Springstubb), 270

The Magic Hare (Banks), **702**

The Magic Horse (Scott), 1594

The Magic Leaf (Morris), 1570

Magic Lights and Streets of Shining Jet (Saunders), 1943

The Magic Moscow (Pinkwater), 1105

The Magic Orange Tree and Other Haitian Folktales (Wolkstein), 1737

The Magic Porridge Pot (Galdone), 1465

The Magic Purse (Uchida), **1037**

The Magic School Bus at the Waterworks (Cole), 2008

The Magic School Bus Inside the Earth (Cole), 2009

The Magic School Bus Inside the Human Body (Cole), 2010

The Magic School Bus Lost in the Solar System (Cole), **1121**

The Magic School Bus on the Ocean Floor (Cole), **1122**

Magic Spring: A Korean Folktale (Rhee), **1002**

The Magic Stove (Ginsburg), 1479

The Magic Tapestry (Demi), **894**

The Magic Touch (Bacon), 1043

The Magic Wings: A Tale from China (Wolkstein), 1630

The Magical Drawings of Mooney B. Finch (McPhail), 737

The Magician and McTree (Coombs), 900

The Magician of Cracow (Turska), 1619

The Magician's Apprentice (McGowen), 1329

Magicians Do Amazing Things (Kraske), 2059

The Magician's Nephew (Lewis), 1204

The Magnificent Moo (Forrester), 89

The Magnificent Mummy Maker (Woodruff), **799**

The Maid and the Mouse and the Odd-Shaped House (Zelinsky), 860

Ma'ii and Cousin Horned Toad: A Traditional Navajo Story (Begay), **865**

Mail-Order Wings (Gormley), 1182

Make a Wish, Molly (Cohen), **598**

Make Me a Peanut Butter Sandwich and a Glass of Milk (Robbins), **1225**

Make Way for Ducklings (McCloskey), 734

Making Friends with Frankenstein: A Book of Monstrous Poems and Pictures (McNaughton), **1366**

Mama Bear (Sun), **562**

Mama Don't Allow (Hurd), 432

Mama Zooms (Cowen-Fletcher), **89**

The Man Who Kept House (Hague and Hague), 1514

The Man Who Tricked a Ghost (Yep), **1047**

Mandy (Booth), **408**

Maniac Magee (Spinelli), **847**

Many Moons (Thurber), 1015

The Mare's Egg: A New World Folk Tale (Spray), 1604

Margaret & Taylor (Henkes), 419

Marie Louise's Heyday (Carlson), 638

Marms in the Marmalade (Morley), 1876

Martha Speaks (Meddaugh), **506**

Martin by Myself (Skurzynski), 813

Martin's Mice (King-Smith), 1085

Marushka's Egg (Rael), **667**

The Marvelous Blue Mouse (Manson), **641**

Marvin K. Mooney, Will You Please Go Now (Seuss), 554

Marvin Redpost: Alone in His Teacher's House (Sachar), **672**

Mary Alice, Operator Number Nine (Allen), 320

Mary Ann (James), 133

Mary Had a Little Lamb, illus. by Tomie dePaola (Hale), 127

Mary Had a Little Lamb, illus. by Bruce McMillan (Hale), **116**

Mary Had a Little Lamb, illus. by Salley Mavor (Hale), **117**

Mary Marony and the Snake (Kline), **475**

Mary Wore Her Red Dress and Henry Wore His Green Sneakers (Peek), 227

Masai and I (Kroll), **480**

Master of All Masters: An English Folktale (Sewall), 1597

The Match Between the Winds (Climo), **879**

The Math Whiz (Duffey), **607**

Mathew Michael's Beastly Day (Johnston), **293**

Matilda (Dahl), 1292

Matreshka (Ayres), **863**

Matthew Jackson Meets the Wall (Giff), **611**

Matthew Looney's Invasion of the Earth (Beatty), 1142

Matthew's Dream (Lionni), **308**

Matt's Mitt and Fleet-Footed Florence (Sachs), 990

Max (Isadora), 436

Max and Me and the Time Machine (Greer and Ruddick), 1306

Max and Me and the Wild West (Greer and Ruddick), 1307

Max and Ruby's First Greek Myth: Pandora's Box (Wells), **573**

Max Makes a Million (Kalman), **633**

Max Malone Makes a Million (Herman), **617**

Max the Great (Heath), 1309

Maxie, Rosie, and Earl—Partners in Grime (Park), **736**

Max's Chocolate Chicken (Wells), 286

Max's Christmas (Wells), 287

May I Bring a Friend? (De Regniers), 69

May We Sleep Here Tonight? (Koide), 172

Mayfield Crossing (Nelson), **784**

Me and the Terrible Two (Conford), 1161

Me and the Weirdos (Sutton), 1246

Me as Neesie (Greenfield), 411

Me First (Lester), **304**

Mean Jake and the Devils (Hooks), 1074

The Mean Old Mean Hyena (Prelutsky), 983

Mean Soup (Everitt), **101**

Meanwhile Back at the Ranch (Noble), 974

Meet Danitra Brown (Grimes), **1302**

Meet Jack Appleknocker (Sundgaard), 272

Meet the Orchestra (Hayes), **1157**

Melisande (Nesbit), 1218

Melvil and Dewey in the Chips (Swallow), 1012

The Memory Box (Bahr), **589**

Mermaid Tales from Around the World (Osborne), **1082**

Merrily Comes Our Harvest In: Poems for Thanksgiving (Hopkins), **1323**

Merry Christmas, Space Case (Marshall), 744

Merry Christmas, Strega Nona (dePaola), 909

Merry-Go-Round: A Book About Nouns (Heller), **1310**

Messy (Bottner), 339

Mice Are Nice (Larrick), **1347**

Mice Twice (Low), 488

The Mice Who Lived in a Shoe (Peppé), 772

Michael and the Cats (Abercrombie), **1**

Michael Foreman's Mother Goose (Mother Goose), **1385**

The Midnight Fox (Byars), 1047

Mieko and the Fifth Treasure (Coerr), **707**

Mighty Tree (Gackenbach), **1145**

Mike Fink (Kellogg), **948**

Mike Mulligan and His Steam Shovel (Burton), 36

Mike's House (Sauer), 252

The Miller, His Son and Their Donkey: A Fable from Aesop (Aesop), 1387

Millie and the Mud Hole (Reddix), **180**

Million Dollar Jeans (Roy), 1233

Millions of Cats (Gag), 104

Milton the Early Riser (Kraus), 174

Ming Lo Moves the Mountain (Lobel), 481

Miracles: Poems by Children of the English-Speaking World (Lewis), 1856

Mirandy and Brother Wind (McKissack), 958

Mirette on the High Wire (McCully), **492**

Misoso: Once Upon a Time Tales from Africa (Aardema), **1052**

Miss Hindy's Cats (Pittman), **338**

Miss Nelson Is Missing (Allard), 601

Miss Rumphius (Cooney), 654

The Missing Tarts (Hennessy), 133

Mistakes That Worked (Jones), **1168**

Mister Wolf and Me (Shura), 1238

Misty of Chincoteague (Henry), 1072

The Mitten (Brett), 1409

The Mitten: An Old Ukranian Folktale (Tresselt), 1615

The Mixed-Up Chameleon (Carle), 38

Moe the Dog in Tropical Paradise (Stanley), **556**

Mojave (Siebert), 1000

Mole and Troll Trim the Tree (Johnston), 442
The Moles and the Mireuk: A Korean Folktale (Kwon), **962**
Molly Mullett (Coombs), 901
Molly's Pilgrim (Cohen), 893
A Mom by Magic (Dillon), **767**
Mom Can't See Me (Alexander), **1097**
Moments: Poems about the Seasons (Hopkins), 1824
Mommy, Buy Me a China Doll (Zemach), 305
The Mommy Exchange (Hest), 421
Momotaro the Peach Boy: A Traditional Japanese Tale (Shute), 1600
Mom's Best Friend (Alexander), **1098**
The Monkey and the Crocodile: A Jataka Tale from India (Galdone), 1466
Monkey Island (Fox), **817**
The Monster and the Tailor (Galdone), 1467
The Monster Bed (Willis), 592
Monster Brother (Auch), **221**
The Monster Garden (Alcock), 1257
The Monster in the Third Dresser Drawer: And Other Stories about Adam Joshua (Smith), 815
A Monster Is Coming! A Monster Is Coming! (Heide and Heide), 684
Monster Madness: Riddles, Jokes, Fun (Rosenbloom), 1935
Monster Motel (Florian), **1292**
Monster Soup and Other Spooky Poems (Evans), **1288**
The Monster That Grew Small: An Egyptian Folktale (Grant), 1484
Monster's Birthday Hiccups (Mueller), **36**
The Monster's Ring (Coville), 1165
The Month Brothers: A Slavic Tale (Marshak), 1560
Monty (Stevenson), 561
Moog-Moog, Space Barber (Teague), **563**
The Moon and I (Byars), **1115**
The Moon and You (Krupp), **1176**
The Moon Dragon (Miller), 1568
Moon Frog: Animal Poems for Young Children (Edwards), **1285**
Moon Jump: A Countdown (Brown), **240**
Moon Mother: A Native American Creation Tale (Young), **1050**
Moon Rope: Un Lazo a la Luna: A Peruvian Folktale (Ehlert), **902**
Moon Tiger (Root), 535
Moongame (Asch), 14
The Moon's Revenge (Aiken), 1038
A Moose for Jessica (Wakefield and Carrara), 2111
Mop Top (Freeman), 94

More Halloween Howls: Riddles That Come Back to Haunt You (Maestro), **1367**
More Juniorplots: A Guide for Teachers and Librarians (Gillespie), 2136
"More More More," Said the Baby: Three Love Stories (Williams), **58**
A More Perfect Union: The Story of Our Constitution (Maestro), 2073
More Stories to Solve: Fifteen Folktales from Around the World (Shannon), **1087**
More Surprises (Hopkins), 1825
Morning Girl (Dorris), **814**
Mortimer Mooner Stopped Taking a Bath (Edwards), **94**
Morton and Sidney (Demarest), 67
Moss Gown (Hooks), 1529
Moss Pillows (Wells), **383**
The Most Wonderful Egg in the World (Heine), 129
Moth-Kin Magic (Tapp), 1247
Mother Earth's Counting Book (Clements), **1118**
A Mother for Choco (Kasza), **140**
Mother Goose (Mother Goose), **1386**
Mother Goose: A Collection of Classic Nursery Rhymes (Mother Goose), 1884
Mother Goose and the Sly Fox (Conover), 1428
Mother Goose Magic (Mother Goose), **1382**
The Mother Goose Songbook (Mother Goose), **1387**
The Mother Goose Treasury (Mother Goose), 1885
Mother Goose's Little Misfortunes (Mother Goose), **1383**
Mother Holly (Grimm), 1502
Mother, Mother, I Feel Sick, Send for the Doctor Quick, Quick, Quick (Charlip and Supree), 646
Mother, Mother, I Want Another (Polushkin), 230
The Mother's Day Mice (Bunting), 32
The Mouse and the Motorcycle (Cleary), 1050
The Mouse Bride: A Mayan Folk Tale (Dupré), **898**
Mouse Count (Walsh), **54**
Mouse-Deer's Market (Troughton), 1617
Mouse in the House (Baehr), **68**
Mouse Paint (Walsh), **204**
Mouse Tales (Lobel), 482
Mouse Views: What the Class Pet Saw (McMillan), **315**
Mouse Woman and the Mischief-Makers (Harris), 1691
Move Over, Twerp (Alexander), 315
Moving (Rosen), **352**
Mr. and Mrs. Pig's Evening Out (Rayner), 782
Mr. Bear's Chair (Graham), 119
Mr. Cat-and-a-Half (Pevear), 1578
Mr. Cookie Baker (Wellington), **55**
Mr. Gumpy's Outing (Burningham), 33
Mr. Knocky (Ziegler), **582**

Mr. Little (Peck), 1343

Mr. Miacca: An English Folktale (Ness), 1573

Mr. Mistoffelees with Mungojerrie and Rumpelteazer (Eliot), **1286**

Mr. Murphy's Marvelous Invention (Christelow), 649

Mr. Mysterious's Secrets of Magic (Fleischman), 2024

Mr. Popper's Penguins (Atwater and Atwater), 1042

Mr. Rabbit and the Lovely Present (Zolotow), 310

Mr. Tall and Mr. Small (Brenner), 343

Mr. Yowder and the Train Robbers (Rounds), 1232

Mrs. Beggs and the Wizard (Mayer), 749

Mrs. Frisby and the Rats of NIMH (O'Brien), 1337

Mrs. Katz and Tush (Polacco), **663**

Mrs. Merriweather's Musical Cat (Purdy), **539**

Mrs. Peloki's Class Play (Oppenheim), 763

Mrs. Piggle-Wiggle (MacDonald), 1092

Mrs. Pig's Bulk Buy (Rayner), 783

Mrs. Toggle and the Dinosaur (Pulver), **344**

Mrs. Toggle's Beautiful Blue Shoe (Pulver), **345**

Mrs. Tooey & the Terrible Toxic Tar (Dillon), 1062

Much Ado about Aldo (Hurwitz), 937

Much Bigger than Martin (Kellogg), 453

The Mud Flat Olympics (Stevenson), **557**

Mud, Moon and Me (Weil), **1420**

Mufaro's Beautiful Daughters: An African Tale (Steptoe), 1607

Mule Eggs (DeFelice), **604**

Munching: Poems about Eating (Hopkins), 1826

Murflies and Wink-a-Peeps: Funny Old Words for Kids (Sperling), 1956

Murphy and Kate (Howard), 623

Mush! Across Alaska in the World's Longest Sled-Dog Race (Seibert), **1235**

Mushroom in the Rain (Ginsburg), 115

Music of Their Hooves: Poems About Horses (Springer), **1411**

Mustard (Graeber), 927

My Best Friend (Hutchins), **23**

My Bike (Jakob), **132**

My Brother Is a Visitor from Another Planet (Sheldon), **746**

My Brother Sam Is Dead (Collier and Collier), 1288

My Brother Stevie (Clymer), 1054

My Brother, the Thief (Shyer), 1356

My Buddy (Osofsky), **526**

My Christmas Safari (Manushkin), **320**

My Cousin Katie (Garland), **17**

My Cousin the King (Frascino), 390

My Dad's Baseball (Cohen), **599**

My Dog and the Birthday Mystery (Adler), 313

My Dog Ate It (Benjamin), **704**

My Father's Dragon (Gannett), 674

My First Picture Joke Book (Rayner), **1401**

My Five Senses (Miller), **1207**

My Friend Charlie (Flora), 924

My Grandmother's Stories: A Collection of Jewish Folk Tales (Geras), **1067**

My Great Aunt Arizona (Houston), **1165**

My Hiroshima (Morimoto), **1210**

My Mama Says There Aren't Any Zombies, Ghosts, Vampires, Creatures, Demons, Monsters, Fiends, Goblins or Things (Viorst), 840

My Mom and Dad Make Me Laugh (Sharratt), **186**

My Mom Travels a Lot (Bauer), 612

My New York (Jakobsen), **1167**

My Old Teddy (Mansell), **32**

My Parents Think I'm Sleeping (Prelutsky), 1910

My Puppy Is Born (Cole), **1123**

My Robot Buddy (Slote), 1002

My Rotten Redheaded Older Brother (Polacco), **536**

My Shadow (Stevenson), **374**

My Side of the Mountain (George), 1176

My Sister Annie (Dodds), **768**

My Son John (Aylesworth), **222**

My Tang's Tungled and Other Ridiculous Situations (Brewton, Brewton, and Blackburn), 1759

My Trip to Alpha I (Slote), 1114

My Uncle Podger (Tripp), 1123

My Wicked Stepmother (Leach), **302**

The Mysteries of Harris Burdick (Van Allsburg), 1250

The Mysterious Giant of Barletta: An Italian Folktale (dePaola), 1442

The Mysterious Tadpole (Kellogg), 705

Myths and Enchantment Tales (Price), 1716

Nail Soup: A Swedish Folk Tale (Zemach), 1636

The Name of the Tree: A Bantu Folktale (Lottridge), **973**

Nancy Polette's E Is for Everybody: A Manual for Bringing Fine Picture Books into the Minds and Hearts of Children (Polette), 2150

Nanny Goat and the Seven Little Kids (Grimm), **924**

The Napping House (Wood), 301

A Nasty Piece of Work and Other Ghost Stories (Salway), 1351

Nate the Great (Sharmat), 810

Nathaniel Willy, Scared Silly (Mathews and Robinson), **984**

Native American Animal Stories (Bruchac), **1059**

A Natural Man: The True Story of John Henry (Sanfield), 1588

Ned Feldman, Space Pirate (Pinkwater), **660**

Nekomah Creek (Crew), **709**

Nettie Jo's Friends (McKissack), 492

Never Take a Pig to Lunch: And Other Funny Poems about Animals (Calmenson), 1764

Never Take a Pig to Lunch and Other Poems About the Fun of Eating (Westcott), **1421**

A New Coat for Anna (Ziefert), 597

New Kid on Spurwink Ave. (Crowley), **258**

The New Kid on the Block (Prelutsky), 1911

The New Read-Aloud Handbook (Trelease), 2157

New Shoes for Sylvia (Hurwitz), **129**

A New Treasury of Children's Poetry: Old Favorites and New Discoveries (Cole), 1773

The New York Times Parent's Guide to the Best Books for Children (Lipson), 2148

The News about Dinosaurs (Lauber), 2062

Nibble, Nibble, Jenny Archer (Conford), **600**

A Nice Walk in the Jungle (Bodsworth), **233**

Nice Work, Little Wolf! (Offen), **173**

A Nickel Buys a Rhyme (Benjamin), **1267**

Night Becomes Day (McGuire), **498**

The Night before Christmas (Moore), 753

The Night Flight (Ryder), 540

Night in the Country (Rylant), 541

The Night It Rained Pancakes (Ginsburg), 1480

Night Journeys (Avi), 1268

Night of the Gargoyles (Bunting), **705**

The Night of the Solstice (Smith), 1362

Night of the Twisters (Ruckman), 1235

Night Ride (Karlin and Karlin), 446

The Night the Monster Came (Calhoun), 880

The Night the Scarecrow Walked (Carlson), 639

The Nightingale, illus. by Beni Montresor (Andersen), 1039

The Nightingale, illus. by Josef Palecek (Andersen), **699**

Nightmare Island (Roy), 1234

Nightmares: Poems to Trouble Your Sleep (Prelutsky), 1912

Nighty-Nightmare (Howe), 1194

Nine-in-One, Grr! Grr! A Folktale from the Hmong People of Laos (Blia), 1404

Nine O'Clock Lullaby (Singer), **554**

Nine True Dolphin Stories (Davidson), 2014

No Dogs Allowed (Cutler), **602**

No Elephants Allowed (Robison), 243

No Good in Art (Cohen), 370

No Milk! (Ericsson), **99**

No Moon, No Milk (Babcock), **225**

No More Baths (Cole), 52

No More Monsters for Me (Parish), 517

No Peas for Nellie (Demarest), 68

No Problem (Browne), **414**

No Roses for Harry (Zion), 309

"No!" Said Joe (Prater), **177**

No School Today (Brandenberg), 342

No Such Things (Peet), 978

Nobody Stole the Pie (Levitin), 722

Nobody's Mother Is in Second Grade (Pulver), **346**

Noel the Coward (Kraus), 175

Noisy Nancy Norris (Gaeddert), 102

Norma Lee I Don't Knock on Doors (Keller), 1839

Norman the Doorman (Freeman), 671

North American Legends (Haviland), 1695

North of Danger (Fife), 1296

The Nose Tree (Hutton), 1533

The Not-Just-Anybody Family (Byars), 1156

Not So Fast, Songololo (Daly), 62

Not the Piano, Mrs. Medley! (Levine), **483**

Not This Bear! (Myers), 511

Nothing but a Pig (Cole), 651

Now Everybody Really Hates Me (Martin and Marx), **644**

Now Let Me Fly: The Story of a Slave Family (Johnson), **629**

Now We Are Six (Milne), 1872

Now You See It: Easy Magic for Beginners (Broekel and White), 1999

A Number of Dragons (Leedy), 182

Number the Stars (Lowry), 1328

The Nutty Joke Book (Keller), 1840

Nutty Knows All (Hughes), 1312

Octopus Hug (Pringle), **178**

An Octopus Is Amazing (Lauber), **1181**

Odds 'N' Ends Alvy (Frank), **441**

Of Pelicans and Pussycats: Poems and Limericks (Lear), **1349**

Oh! (Goffin), **109**

Oh, Boy! Babies! (Herzig and Mali), 2049

Oh, Brother (Yorinks), 1036

Oh, Lewis! (Rice), 239

Oh, Such Foolishness (Cole), 1780

Oh, Were They Ever Happy! (Spier), 559

Oh, What a Thanksgiving! (Kroll), 718

Ol' Jake's Lucky Day (Ivanov), 698

Ol' Paul, the Mighty Logger (Rounds), 1721

Old Black Fly (Aylesworth), **223**

Old Devil Wind (Martin), **323**

The Old-Fashioned Storybook (Schwartz and Archibald), 1727

The Old Ladies Who Liked Cats (Greene), **445**

Old MacDonald Had a Farm (Cauley), **78**

Old MacDonald Had a Farm (Hellen), **20**

Old MacDonald Had a Farm (Jones), 157

Old MacDonald Had a Farm (Pearson), 226

Old MacDonald Had a Farm (Rounds), **182**

Old Mother Hubbard and Her Dog (Galdone), 1468

Old Mother Hubbard and Her Dog (Hellsing), 130

Old Mother Hubbard and Her Wonderful Dog (Marshall), **980**

Old Possum's Book of Practical Cats (Eliot), 1795

Old Sadie and the Christmas Bear (Naylor), 512

Old Turtle's Baseball Stories (Kessler), 709

Old Witch Rescues Halloween (Devlin and Devlin), 661

The Old Woman and Her Pig (Galdone), 1469

The Old Woman and Her Pig (Kimmel), **956**

The Old Woman and Her Pig: An Old English Tale (Litzinger), **971**

The Old Woman and the Jar of Uums (Wright), 856

Old Yeller (Gipson), 1180

Olive and the Magic Hat (Christelow), 365

Ollie Forgot (Arnold), 607

Oma and Bobo (Schwartz), 545

On Beyond Zebra (Seuss), 805

On Cat Mountain (Richard), **1003**

On Market Street (Lobel), 483

On My Honor (Bauer), 1273

On Top of Spaghetti (Glazer), 679

On Top of the World: The Conquest of Mount Everest (Fraser), **1143**

Once in a Wood: Ten Tales from Aesop (Aesop), 1648

Once Inside the Library (Huff), **459**

Once There Was and Was Not: Armenian Tales Retold (Tashjian), 1731

Once Under the Cherry Blossom Tree: An Old Japanese Tale (Say), 1592

Once Upon a Golden Apple (Little and De Vries), 478

Once Upon a Rhyme: 101 Poems for Young Children (Corrin and Corrin), 1783

Once Upon a Time: A Storytelling Handbook (Breneman and Breneman), 2165

Once Upon a Time, Though It Wasn't in Your Time, and It Wasn't in My Time, and It Wasn't in Anybody's Time. . . . (Garner), **1065**

Once upon MacDonald's Farm (Gammell), 401

Once When I Was Scared (Pittman), 775

The One and Only Super-Duper Golly-Whopper Jim-Dandy Really-Handy Clock-Tock-Stopper (Thomas), **566**

One at a Time (McCord), 1864

One Bear in the Picture (Bucknall), 31

One Big Wish (Williams), 1030

One Cow Coughs: A Counting Book for the Sick and Miserable (Loomis), **155**

One Cow Moo Moo! (Bennett), **5**

One Crow: A Counting Rhyme (Aylesworth), 17

One Day at School (Luttrell), 732

One Dog Day (Lewis), **774**

One Earth, a Multitude of Creatures (Roop and Roop), **1228**

One Fine Day (Hogrogian), 1528

One Giant Leap (Fraser), **1142**

One Gift Deserves Another (Grimm), **927**

One Hundred Hungry Ants (Pinczes), **533**

101 More Words and How They Began (Steckler), 1958

One Hungry Monster: A Counting Book in Rhyme (O'Keefe), **174**

One Red Rooster (Carroll), **7**

One Sun (McMillan), 1865

One, Two, One Pair! (McMillan), **31**

One, Two, Three—Ah-Choo! (Allen), 321

One, Two, Where's My Shoe? (Ungerer), 281

One Was Johnny: A Counting Book (Sendak), 254

One Zillion Valentines (Modell), 751

Onion Tears (Kidd), **772**

Only One (Harshman), **280**

Only Opal: The Diary of a Young Girl (Whiteley), **1253**

Only Six More Days (Russo), 248

Oonga Boonga (Wishinsky), **209**

Operation: Dump the Chump (Park), 1101

Opt: An Illusionary Tale (Baum and Baum), 1044

The Oral Tradition: Storytelling and Creative Drama (Chambers), 2167

The Orchard Book of Nursery Rhymes (Mother Goose), **1388**

The Ordinary Princess (Kaye), 1079

The Ornery Morning (Demuth), **260**

The Orphan Boy: A Maasai Story (Mollel), **989**

Orphan Jeb at the Massacree (Mooser), 1215

Oté (Belpré), 1402

Our Cat Flossie (Brown), 632

Our King Has Horns! (Pevear), 1579

Our Snowman Had Olive Eyes (Herman), 1186

Our Teacher's Having a Baby (Bunting), **243**

Out and About (Hughes), 1831

Over in the Meadow (Langstaff), 180

Over in the Meadow: A Traditional Counting Rhyme (Voce), **197**

Over in the Meadow: An Old Counting Rhyme (Wadsworth), **202**

Over in the Meadow: An Old Nursery Counting Rhyme (Galdone), 108

Over on the Farm (Turner), **195**

Over the Deep Blue Sea (Ikeda), **460**

Over the Moon: A Book of Nursery Rhymes (Mother Goose), 1886

Over the River and Through the Wood: A Song for Thanksgiving (Child), **251**

Owen (Henkes), **122**
Owl and Other Scrambles (Weil), 1026
The Owl and the Pussycat, illus. by Jan Brett (Lear), **148**
The Owl and the Pussycat, illus. by Paul Galdone (Lear), **181**
The Owl and the Pussycat, illus. by Loise Voce (Lear), **149**
Owl at Home (Lobel), 484
Owl Babies (Waddell), **49**
Owl Eyes (Gates), **911**
An Owl in the House: A Naturalist's Diary (Heinrich), **1158**
Owl Moon (Yolen), 857
The Owl Who Became the Moon (London), **310**
Owliver (Kraus), 461
Owls in the Family (Mowat), 2077
Ox-Cart Man (Hall), 931
The Oxboy (Mazer), **831**
The Oxford Book of Scary Stories (Pepper), **836**

A Pack of Riddles (Gerler), 1803
Paddington's Storybook (Bond), 1147
Paddy's Pot of Gold (King-Smith), **724**
The Pain and the Great One (Blume), 619
The Painted Fan (Singer), **748**
A Pair of Red Clogs (Matsuno), 747
The Pancake Boy: An Old Norwegian Folk Tale (Cauley), 1418
Pancakes, Pancakes! (Carle), **247**
Panda (Allen), **584**
Papa, Please Get the Moon for Me (Carle), 39
Papa's Panda (Willard), 295
The Paper Crane (Bang), 610
Paper John (Small), 814
The Paper Princess (Kleven), **146**
A Parent's Guide to Children's Reading (Larrick), 2144
Parents in the Pigpen, Pigs in the Tub (Ehrlich), **266**
Pass It On: African-American Poetry for Children (Hudson), **1331**
Pass the Fritters, Critters (Chapman), **82**
Pass the Poetry, Please! (Hopkins), 2140
The Patchwork Quilt (Flournoy), 925
Patrick's Dinosaurs (Carrick), 358
Paul Bunyan Swings His Axe (McCormick), 1709
Paul Revere's Ride, illus. by Paul Galdone (Longfellow), 1863
Paul Revere's Ride, illus. by Ted Rand (Longfellow), **1361**
Peabody (Wells), 288
Peace at Last (Murphy), 214

Peace Tales: World Folktales to Talk About (MacDonald), **1076**
Peanut Butter and Jelly: A Play Rhyme (Westcott), 291
Pearl's Promise (Asch), **701**
Peboan and Seegwun (Larry), **964**
The Peculiar Miss Pickett (Julian), 940
Pedro's Journal: A Voyage with Christopher Columbus, August 3, 1492–February 14, 1492 (Conrad), **809**
Peeping Beauty (Auch), **402**
Pelle's New Suit (Beskow), 336
Penelope Gets Wheels (Peterson), 774
People, People, Everywhere! (Van Laan), **196**
Peppe the Lamplighter (Bartone), **405**
Peppermints in the Parlor (Wallace), 1372
Perfect Pigs: An Introduction to Manners (Brown and Krensky), 2003
The Perfect Spot (Blake), **231**
Perfect the Pig (Jeschke), 438
Persephone and the Pomegranate: A Myth from Greece (Waldherr), **1041**
A Person from Britain Whose Head Was the Shape of a Mitten and Other Limericks (Bodecker), 1752
Pet Show! (Keats), 163
Peter and the North Wind (Littedale), 1547
Peter and the Talking Shoes (Banks), **228**
Peter Penny's Dance (Quinn-Harken), 779
Peter Piper's Alphabet (Brown), 1762
Peter Potts (Hicks), 1188
Peter's Chair (Keats), 164
Pete's Chicken (Ziefert), **392**
Petey's Bedtime Story (Cleary), **253**
Petranella (Waterton), 845
Petrosinella: A Neopolitan Rapunzel (Basile), 1401
Petunia (Duvoisin), 378
The Phantom Carousel and Other Ghostly Tales (Ainsworth), 1138
The Phantom Tollbooth (Juster), 1316
Phewtus the Squirrel (Drummond), 74
Phil the Ventriloquist (Kraus), 176
Philip Hall Likes Me. I Reckon, Maybe (Greene), 1183
Phoebe and the General (Griffin), 2042
Phoenix Rising (Hesse), **821**
Pianna (Ray), **542**
Pickles Have Pimples: And Other Silly Statements (Barrett), 611
Picnic (McCully), 196
A Picture Book of Harriet Tubman (Adler), **1095**
A Picture Book of Sojourner Truth (Adler), **1096**
Picture Books for Gifted Programs (Polette), 2151

The Piece of Fire and Other Haitian Tales (Courlander), 1669

The Pied Piper of Hamelin (Corrin and Corrin), 1431

Pied Piper of Hamelin (Lemieux), **966**

Pierre (Sendak), 552

The Pig in the Pond (Waddell), **50**

Pig Pig and the Magic Photo Album (McPhail), 496

Pig Pig Gets a Job (McPhail), **318**

Pig Pig Grows Up (McPhail), 202

Piggies (Wood and Wood), **59**

The Piggy in the Puddle (Pomerantz), 231

Pigs (Munsch), **330**

Pigs Aplenty, Pigs Galore! (McPhail), **317**

The Pigs Are Flying (Rodda), 1231

Pigs Might Fly (King-Smith), 1320

The Pig's Picnic (Kasza), 161

Pigs Will Be Pigs (Axelrod), **403**

Pigsty (Teague), **564**

Pigwig (Dyke), 379

The Pilgrims of Plimoth (Sewall), 2098

The Pinballs (Byars), 1281

Pinch (Callen), 1285

Pink and Say (Polacco), **786**

Pinkerton, Behave (Kellogg), 706

Pinky and Rex and the Spelling Bee (Howe), **457**

Piping Down the Valleys Wild (Larrick), 1852

Pippi Longstocking (Lindgren), 1090

Pip's Magic (Walsh), **205**

Piskies, Spriggans, and Other Magical Beings (Climo), 1663

Pizza for Breakfast (Kovalski), **479**

A Place for Ben (Titherington), 274

The Place My Words Are Looking For (Janeczko), **1334**

Plane Song (Siebert), **552**

The Plant Sitter (Zion), 598

Play Day: A Book of Terse Verse (McMillan), **1365**

Playing Sardines (Major), 741

Please Don't Squeeze Your Boa, Noah! (Singer), **1410**

Plunk's Dreams (Griffith), 122

A Pocket for Corduroy (Freeman), 95

Pocketful of Nonsense (Marshall), **1369**

A Poem for a Pickle: Funnybone Verses (Merriam), 1870

Poem Stew (Cole), 1781

Poems for Grandmothers (Livingston), **1360**

Poems for the Very Young (Rosen), **1405**

Poems of A. Nonny Mouse (Prelutsky), 1913

Poetry from A to Z: A Guide for Young Writers (Janeczko), **1335**

The Poetry of Horses (Cole), 1782

The Poetry Troupe: An Anthology of Poems to Read Aloud (Wilner), 1975

Pointsettia and the Firefighters (Bond), 338

Polar Bear Cubs (Matthews), 2075

Polar Bear, Polar Bear, What Do You Hear? (Martin), **160**

The Polar Express (Van Allsburg), 835

Pondlarker (Gwynne), **447**

The Ponies of Mykillengi (Anderson), 865

The Poof Point (Weiss and Friedman), **851**

Pookins Gets Her Way (Lester), 470

Pop Corn & Ma Goodness (Preston), 529

The Pop-Up, Pull-Tab Playtime House That Jack Built (Westcott), 208

Popcorn (Asch), 15

The Popcorn Book (dePaola), 2018

The Popcorn Dragon (Thayer), 273

Popcorn Park Zoo: A Haven with a Heart (Pfeffer), **1220**

Poppy, the Panda (Gackenbach), 100

A Porcupine Named Fluffy (Lester), 471

Portly McSwine (Marshall), 503

Possum Stew (Cushman), **91**

Postcards from Pluto: A Tour of the Solar System (Leedy), **1182**

Posy (Pomerantz), 232

The Potato Man (McDonald), **496**

Potato Pancakes All Around: A Hanukkah Tale (Hirsch), 933

Potluck (Shelby), **362**

Prehistoric Pinkerton (Kellogg), 707

Presenting Reader's Theater: Plays and Poems to Read Aloud (Bauer), 2162

Pretend You're a Cat (Marzollo), **161**

Pretty Polly (King-Smith), **725**

Primaryplots: A Book Talk Guide for Use with Readers Ages 4–8 (Thomas), 2156

Prince Ivan and the Firebird (Gal), **908**

The Prince of the Dolomites: An Old Italian Tale (dePaola), 1443

The Prince of the Pond: Otherwise Known as De Fawg Pin (Napoli), **782**

Prince William (Rand), **668**

Princess (Wilsdorf), **577**

The Princess and the Beggar: A Korean Folklore (O'Brien), **994**

The Princess and the Frog (Vesey), 837

The Princess and the Pea (Andersen), 322

The Princess and the Potty (Lewison), **29**

The Princess and the Sun, Moon and Stars (Reuter), 1585

Princess Furball (Huck), 1531

Princess Gorilla and a New Kind of Water (Aardema), 1381

The Princess in the Pigpen (Thomas), 1369
The Principal's New Clothes (Calmenson), **420**
Prisoners at the Kitchen Table (Holland), 1190
Professor Popkin's Prodigious Polish: A Tale of Coven Tree (Brittain), **760**
Professor Puffendorf's Secret Potions (Tzannes), **569**
Project Cat (Burchardt), 878
Project: Genius (Hayes), 1308
A Promise to the Sun: An African Story (Mollel), **990**
The Proud White Cat (Hurlimann), 1532
Pumpernickel Tickel and Mean Green Cheese (Patz), 520
Puniddles (McMillan and McMillan), 959
The Puppy Who Wanted a Boy (Thayer), 566
Pups Speak Up (Meltzer), **324**
The Purple Coat (Hest), 422
Push, Pull, Empty, Full (Hoban), 138
The Pushcart War (Merrill), 1331
Puss in Boots (Cauley), 1419
Puss in Boots (Galdone), 1470
Puss in Boots (Haley), **933**
Puss in Boots (Kirstein), **959**
Puss in Boots (Perrault), **997**
Puss in Boots & Other Stories (Rockwell), 1720
Put Your Foot in Your Mouth and Other Silly Sayings (Cox), 1784
Puzzlers (MacDonald and Oakes), **314**

"Quack!" Said the Billy-Goat (Causley), 46
Quacky Quack-Quack! (Whybrow), **56**
Quail Song: A Pueblo Indian Tale (Carey), **876**
The Quangle Wangle's Hat (Lear), 466
The Quarreling Book (Zolotow), 861
The Queen of Eene (Prelutsky), 1914
The Queen's Nose (King-Smith), **726**
Quentin Corn (Stolz), 1365
A Question of Trust (Bauer), **805**
Questions (Hopkins), **1324**
The Quicksand Book (dePaola), 2019
Quiet on Account of Dinosaur (Thayer), 567
Quiet! There's a Canary in the Library (Freeman), 96

The Rabbi and the Twenty-Nine Witches (Hirsch), 1524
Rabbit-Cadabra! (Howe), **458**
Rabbit Makes a Monkey Out of Lion (Aardema), 1382
The Rabbit's Escape (Han), **936**
The Rabbit's Judgment (Han), **937**
Rachel Fister's Blister (MacDonald), **312**

Rachel Parker, Kindergarten Show-Off (Martin), **321**
Rachel's Recital (Green), 928
The Raffi Christmas Treasury (Raffi), **1400**
The Raffi Singable Songbook: A Collection of 51 Songs from Raffi's First Three Records for Young Children (Raffi), 1926
The Rag Coat (Mills), **646**
Ragged Shadows: Poems of Halloween Night (Hopkins), **1325**
Raging Robots and Unruly Uncles (Mahy), **777**
Rain Forest (Cowcher), **256**
Rain Player (Wisniewski), **694**
Rain, Rain, Go Away! A Book of Nursery Rhymes (Mother Goose), **1381**
The Rainbabies (Melmed), **508**
Rainbow Bird: An Aboriginal Folktale from Northern Australia (Maddern), **979**
The Rainbow Book of American Folk Tales and Legends (Leach), 1703
The Rainbow Fairy Book (Lang), **1074**
The Rainbow Fish (Pfister), **337**
A Rainbow of My Own (Freeman), 97
Rainbows Are Made (Sandburg), 1942
Raining Cats and Dogs (Yolen), **1430**
Rainy Rainy Saturday (Prelutsky), 1915
Ralph S. Mouse (Cleary), 1051
Ramona Quimby, Age 8 (Cleary), 889
Ramona the Pest (Cleary), 890
Randall's Wall (Fenner), **815**
Randolph's Dream (Mellecker), **732**
The Random House Book of Humor for Children (Pollack), 1228
The Random House Book of Mother Goose (Mother Goose), 1887
The Random House Book of Poetry for Children (Prelutsky), 1916
Rapunzel, illus. by Trina Schart Hyman (Grimm), 1503
Rapunzel, illus. by Kris Waldherr (Grimm), **923**
Rascal: A Memoir of a Better Era (North), 2079
Rat-a-Tat, Pitter Pat (Benjamin), 22
The Rat and the Tiger (Kasza), **141**
Rata-Pata-Scata-Fata: A Caribbean Story (Gershator), **108**
The Rat's Daughter (Cook), **886**
Rats on the Roof and Other Stories (Marshall), **643**
The Rattlebang Picnic (Mahy), **502**
Raven: A Trickster Tale from the Pacific Northwest (McDermott), **976**
Raven the Trickster: Legends of the North American Indians (Robinson), 1719
Raven's Light: A Myth from the People of the Northwest Coast (Shetterly), **1024**

Razzle-Dazzle Riddles (Maestro), 1866

Read-Aloud Rhymes for the Very Young (Prelutsky), 1917

The Real Mother Goose (Mother Goose), 1888

The Real Tom Thumb (Cross), 2011

Realms of Gold: Myths & Legends from Around the World (Pilling), **1083**

The Reason for a Flower (Heller), **1161**

The Red Carpet (Parkin), 519

Red Dancing Shoes (Patrick), **175**

Red-Dirt Jessie (Myers), **780**

Red Fox (Wallace), **1249**

Red Riding Hood (Marshall), 1562

The Red Room Riddle (Corbett), 1164

Redwall (Jacques), 1315

Reflections (Jonas), 700

Regards to the Man in the Moon (Keats), 703

Regina's Big Mistake (Moss), **328**

The Reindeer Christmas (Price), **341**

The Relatives Came (Rylant), 542

Releasing Children to Literature (Reasoner), 2153

The Remarkable Christmas of the Cobbler's Sons (Sawyer), **1020**

The Remarkable Ramsey (Rinkoff), 985

Rembrandt's Beret (Alcorn), **697**

Remember Betsy Floss: And Other Colonial American Riddles (Adler), 1740

Remember the à la Mode! Riddles and Puns (Keller), 1841

Renata, Whizbrain and the Ghost (Cohen), 894

Report to the Principal's Office (Spinelli), **791**

Rescue! True Stories of Winners of the Young American Medal for Bravery (Brown and Anderson), 2004

Return of the Sun: Native American Tales from the Northeast Woodlands (Bruchac), **1060**

Reuben Runs Away (Galbraith), 106

Revenge of the Incredible Dr. Rancid and His Youthful Assistant, Jeffrey (Conford), 1162

Revenge of the Small Small (Little), **486**

Reynard: The Story of a Fox Returned to the Wild (Leighner), 2066

Reynard the Fox (Hastings), **1071**

A Rhinoceros Wakes Me Up in the Morning (Goodspeed), 116

Rhinos for Lunch and Elephants for Supper! (Mollel), **991**

Ribsy (Cleary), 891

Rich Cat, Poor Cat (Waber), 579

Richard Scarry's Best Mother Goose Ever (Mother Goose), 1889

The Riddle (Vernon), 1622

Riddle City, USA! A Book of Geography Riddles (Maestro and Maestro), **1368**

The Riddle of the Drum (Aardema), 1383

The Riddle Zoo (Zimmerman), 1983

Riddles to Tell Your Cat (Levine), **1351**

Ride a Purple Pelican (Prelutsky), 1918

A Ride on the Red Mare's Back (LeGuin), **637**

Rikki-Tikki-Tavi (Kipling), **729**

Ring-a-Round-a-Rosy: Nursery Rhymes, Action Rhymes and Lullabies (Lamont), **1345**

Ring Out, Wild Bells: Poems About Holidays and Seasons (Hopkins), **1326**

Riptide (Weller), 848

The Rise and Fall of Ben Gizzard (Kennedy), 1083

Risk N' Roses (Slepian), **845**

River (Gilliland), **1152**

A River Ran Wild: An Environmental History (Cherry), **1117**

Roald Dahl's Revolting Rhymes (Dahl), 1787

Robin Hood (Hayes), 1696

A Rocket in My Pocket: The Rhymes and Chants of Young Americans (Withers), 1977

Rocking-Horse Land (Houseman), 690

Rolling Harvey Down the Hill (Prelutsky), 1919

Rolling Rose (Stevenson), **46**

The Rooster Who Went to His Uncle's Wedding: A Latin American Folktale (Ada), **858**

The Roquefort Gang (Clifford), 1053

Rosa-Too-Little (Felt), 83

The Rose in My Garden (Lobel), 485

Roses Sing on New Snow: A Delicious Tale (Yee), **696**

Rosie: A Visiting Dog's Story (Calmenson), **1116**

Rosie and the Rustlers (Gerrard), **610**

Rosie & the Yellow Ribbon (DePaolo), **261**

Rosie Swanson, Fourth-Grade Geek for President (Park), **737**

Rosie's Birthday Present (Moskin), 510

Rosie's Walk (Hutchins), 149

Rosy Cole Discovers America! (Greenwald), **711**

Rotten Ralph (Gantos), 402

The Rough-Face Girl (Martin), **983**

'Round and Around (Skofield), **188**

Round Trip (Jonas), 701

Roxaboxen (McLerran), **499**

Ruby (Emberley), **437**

Rum Pum Pum (Duff), 1449

The Rumor of Pavel and Paali: A Ukrainian Folktale (Kismaric), 1542

Rumpelstiltskin, illus. by Gennady Spirin (Grimm), **922**

Rumpelstiltskin, illus. by Paul O. Zelinsky (Grimm), 1504

The Runaway Bunny (Brown), 29

The Runaway Chick (Ravilious), 236

Runaway Marie Louise (Carlson), 43

Runaway Mittens (Rogers), 244

The Runaway Pancake (Asbjørnsen), 1394

Runaway Slave: The Story of Harriet Tubman (McGovern), 2070

Russell Sprouts (Hurwitz), 695

Russian Folk Tales (Afanasev), 1652

Ruth Law Thrills a Nation (Brown), **1111**

Sable (Hesse), **714**

The Sad Night: The Story of an Aztec Victory and a Spanish Loss (Mathews), **1206**

Sad Underwear and Other Complications: More Poems for Children and Their Parents (Viorst), **1417**

Sadako (Coerr), **1120**

Sadako & the Thousand Paper Cranes (Coerr), 2007

The Saga of Erik the Viking (Jones), 1197

Saint George and the Dragon: A Golden Legend (Hodges), 1526

Saint Patrick and the Peddler (Hodges), **941**

A Salmon for Simon (Waterton), 846

Salt: A Russian Folktale (Langton), **963**

Salty Takes Off (Rand), **540**

Sam, Bangs and Moonshine (Ness), 757

Sam Vole and His Brothers (Waddell), **51**

Sami and the Time of the Troubles (Heide and Gilliland), **713**

Samuel Eaton's Day: A Day in the Life of a Pilgrim Boy (Waters), **1250**

The Samurai's Daughter (San Souci), **1014**

Sandy and the Rock Star (Morey), 1333

Santa Calls (Joyce), **631**

Santa's Book of Names (McPhail), **319**

Sarah Morton's Day: A Day in the Life of a Pilgrim Girl (Waters), 2112

Sarah, Plain and Tall (MacLachlan), 1094

Saying Good-Bye to Grandma (Thomas), **683**

Scared Silly: A Book for the Brave (Brown), **1275**

Scared Silly: A Halloween Treat (Howe), 693

Scarlett Angelina Wolverton-Manning (Ogburn), **524**

Scary, Scary Halloween (Bunting), 352

Scary Stories 3: More Tales to Chill Your Bones (Schwartz), **1086**

Scary Stories to Tell in the Dark (Schwartz), 1725

School Daze (Keller), 1842

The School Mouse (Harris), 415

School Spirit (Hurwitz), **716**

Science & Technology in Fact and Fiction: A Guide to Children's Books (Kennedy, Spangler, and Vanderwerf), 2141

Science Tricks (Lehane), 2065

Screen of Frogs: An Old Tale (Hamanaka), **934**

Scruffy (Stonely), 1245

Sea Elf (Ryder), **1231**

A Sea Full of Sharks (Maestro), **1196**

The Sea of Gold and Other Tales from Japan (Uchida), 1732

Sea Shapes (MacDonald), **157**

Sea Squares (Hulme), **624**

The Search for Delicious (Babbitt), 1139

The Secret Birthday Message (Carle), 40

Secret in a Sealed Bottle: Lazzaro Spallanzani's Work with Microbes (Epstein and Epstein), 2022

The Secret in the Matchbook (Willis), 593

The Secret Life of the Underwear Champ (Miles), 1096

The Secret of Terror Castle (Arthur), 1265

Secret Places (Huck), **1330**

The Secret Soldier: The Story of Deborah Sampson (McGovern), 2071

Secrets of a Small Brother (Margolis), 1867

See My Lovely Poison Ivy: And Other Verses about Witches, Ghosts and Things (Moore), 1875

Sense Suspense: A Guessing Game for the Five Senses (McMillan), **159**

The Sesame Street Book of Opposites (Mendoza), 211

Seven Blind Mice (Young), **1051**

The Seven Chinese Brothers (Mahy), 1558

Seven Fables from Aesop (Aesop), 1649

Seven Froggies Went to School (Duke), 377

The Seven Treasure Hunts (Byars), **595**

Seven True Dog Stories (Davidson), 2015

17 Kings and 42 Elephants (Mahy), 500

Seventh-Grade Weirdo (Wardlaw), **850**

Shack and Back (Crowley), **427**

Shadow the Deer (Radcliffe), **347**

Shadow's Baby (Cuyler), 61

Shadows of Night: The Hidden World of the Little Brown Bat (Bash), **1103**

Shadrach's Crossing (Avi), 1269

Shake It to the One That You Love the Best: Play Songs and Lullabies from Black Musical Traditions (Mattox), **1371**

Shape-Changer (Brittain), **761**

The Shapes Game (Rogers), **181**

Sheep in a Jeep (Shaw), 556

Sheep in a Shop (Shaw), **360**

Sheep Out to Eat (Shaw), **361**

Sheila Rae, the Brave (Henkes), 132

The Sheriff of Rottenshot (Prelutsky), 1920

Sherman the Sheep (Kiser), **299**

Sherwood Walks Home (Flora), 88

Shh! We're Writing the Constitution (Fritz), 2032

SHHHH! (Kline), 171

Shiloh (Naylor), **832**

Shoebag (James), 1195

Shoes (Winthrop), 300

Shoes from Grandpa (Fox), **105**

Shooting Stars (Branley), **1109**

Show and Tell (Woodruff), **388**

The Show-and-Tell War: And Other Stories about Adam Joshua (Smith), 816

Show Time at the Polk Street School: Plays You Can Do Yourself or in the Classroom (Giff), **1151**

Shrieks at Midnight: Macabre Poems, Eerie and Humorous (Brewton and Brewton), 1758

The Shrinking of Treehorn (Heide), 1071

Shy Charles (Wells), 586

Shy Vi (Lewison), **151**

Side by Side: Poems to Read Together (Hopkins), 1827

Sideways Stories from Wayside School (Sachar), 1110

Sidney Rella and the Glass Sneaker (Myers), 754

The Sign of the Beaver (Speare), 1363

The Sign Painter's Dream (Roth), **545**

The Signmaker's Assistant (Arnold), **400**

The Silliest Joke Book Ever (Hartman), **1308**

Silly Baby (Caseley), 44

Silly Billy! (Hutchins), **24**

Silly Fred (Wagner), **203**

Silly Sally (Wood), **212**

Silly Verse (and Even Worse) (Rosenbloom), 1936

The Silver Cow: A Welsh Tale (Cooper), 1430

The Silver Pony (Ward), 1024

Simon's Book (Drescher), 664

Simple Pictures Are Best (Willard), 849

Sing a Song of Popcorn: Every Child's Book of Poems (De Regniers), 1792

Singing Bee! A Collection of Favorite Children's Songs (Hart), 1810

The Singing Green: New and Selected Poems for All Seasons (Merriam), **1373**

The Singing Snake (Czernecki and Rhodes), **889**

Singing Tales of Africa (Robinson), 1718

The Singing Tortoise and Other Animal Folktales (Yeoman), **1091**

Sir Francis Drake: His Daring Deeds (Gerrard), 2038

Sir Gawain and the Loathly Lady (Hastings), 1521

Sir Whong and the Golden Pig (Han and Plunkett), **935**

Sitting on the Farm (King), **145**

The Six Chinese Brothers: An Ancient Tale (Cheng), 1422

The Six-Million Dollar Cucumber: Riddles and Fun for Children (Churchill), 1768

Six Sick Sheep: 101 Tongue Twisters (Cole and Calmenson), **1280**

Six Sleepy Sheep (Gordon), **111**

Skateboard Monsters (Kirk), **472**

Skinnybones (Park), 1222

Skip to My Lou (Westcott), 292

The Sky Is Full of Song (Hopkins), 1828

The Slaves of Spiegel: A Magic Moscow Story (Pinkwater), 1226

Sleep Tight (Hennessy), **21**

The Sleeper (Day), **891**

Sleeping Beauty (Early), **899**

The Sleeping Beauty (Grimm), 1505

Sleeping Ugly (Yolen), 1033

Slither McCreep and His Brother Joe (Johnston), **294**

Slobcat (Geraghty), **107**

Sloppy Kisses (Winthrop), 595

Small Green Snake (Gray), **113**

Small Poems (Worth), 1979

Small Talk: A Book of Short Poems (Hopkins), **1327**

Small Worlds Close Up (Grillone and Gennaro), 2043

Smoky Night (Bunting), **593**

The Snail's Spell (Ryder), 249

Snake Hunt (Kastner), **465**

A Snake in the House (McNulty), **500**

The Snake That Sneezed (Leydenfrost), 188

The Snake That Went to School (Moore), 968

Snakes Alive! Jokes about Snakes (Burns), 1763

Snakes and Ladders: Poems about the Ups and Downs of Life (Klein), 1848

Snakey Riddles (Hall and Eisenberg), **1305**

The Snopp on the Sidewalk and Other Poems (Prelutsky), 1921

Snow Magic (Ziefert), 306

Snow on Snow on Snow (Chapman), **83**

The Snow Rose (Laroche), 1086

Snow Toward Evening: A Year in a River Valley: Nature Poems (Frank), **1294**

Snow Treasure (McSwigan), 1330

Snow White (Grimm), 1506

The Snow Wife (San Souci), **1015**

Snowy (Doherty), **263**

The Snowy Day (Keats), 165

So Much (Cooke), **8**

Soap! Soap! Don't Forget the Soap! An Appalachian Folktale (Birdseye), **869**

Solomon the Rusty Nail (Steig), 1008

Some Birthday! (Polacco), **537**

Somebody and the Three Blairs (Tolhurst), **191**

Somebody Catch My Homework (Harrison), **1307**

Somebody Loves You, Mr. Hatch (Spinelli), **371**

Someday a Tree (Bunting), **416**

Someone Saw a Spider: Spider Facts and Folktales (Climo), 1664

Something Big Has Been Here (Prelutsky), **1398**

Something from Nothing (Gilman), **914**

Something Is Going to Happen (Zolotow), 311

Something Special (McPhail), 497

Sometimes I Feel Like a Mouse: A Book About Feelings (Modesitt), **169**

Somewhere in Africa (Mennen and Daly), **509**

Song and Dance Man (Ackerman), 599

A Song I Sang to You: A Selection of Poems (Livingston), 1860

Song Lee in Room 2B (Kline), **476**

Songs from Mother Goose: With the Traditional Melody for Each (Mother Goose), 1890

Songs of the Wild West (Axelrod), **1264**

Sootface: An Ojibwa Cinderella Story (San Souci), **1016**

Sophie and Sammy's Library Sleepover (Caseley), **77**

Sophie and the Sidewalk Man (Tolan), **685**

Sophie's Snail (King-Smith), 711

The Sorcerer's Apprentice (Moore), **648**

Sorrow's Song (Callen), 1286

Sounder (Armstrong), 1264

Soup and Me (Peck), 1223

Space Case (Marshall), 742

The Spaceship under the Apple Tree (Slobodkin), 1113

Spacey Riddles (Hall and Eisenberg), **1306**

Sparrow Socks (Selden), 799

Speak! Children's Book Illustrators Brag About Their Dogs (Rosen), **1229**

Speak Up, Blanche! (McCully), **493**

Speak Up, Edie (Johnston), 440

A Special Trick (Mayer), 961

Spider on the Floor (Raffi), **348**

Spiffen: A Tale of a Tidy Pig (Schwartz), 547

Spinky Sulks (Steig), 1009

The Spirit of the Blue Light (Mayer), **986**

Splash, Splash (Sheppard), **44**

Splish Splash (Graham), **1301**

Spooky Night (Carlson), 357

Spooky Poems (Bennett), **1269**

Spooky Riddles (Brown), 1761

Spooky Riddles and Jokes (Rosenbloom), 1937

The Spooky Tail of Prewitt Peacock (Peet), 771

A Squash and a Squeeze (Donaldson), **264**

Squawk to the Moon, Little Goose (Preston), 233

Squeak-a-Lot (Waddell), **52**

The Squeaky Door (Simms), **1026**

Squeeze a Sneeze (Morrison), **326**

The Squire's Bride (Asbjørnsen), 1395

Squirrel Park (Ernst), **440**

"Stand Back," Said the Elephant, "I'm Going to Sneeze!" (Thomas), 568

The Star Fisher (Yep), **854**

The Star Maiden: An Ojibway Tale (Esbensen), 1451

Star Mother's Youngest Child (Moeri), 1097

The Star-Spangled Banana and Other Revolutionary Riddles (Keller and Baker), 1844

Starring First Grade (Cohen), 371

Starring Francine & Dave: Three One-Act Plays (Young), 2117

Stars (Simon), 2104

The Steadfast Tin Soldier (Andersen), **586**

The Steamroller (Brown), 346

Stella & Roy (Wolf), **210**

Stellaluna (Cannon), **245**

Step by Step (Wolkstein), **211**

Stevie (Steptoe), 1010

Stinker from Space (Service), 1354

The Stinky Cheese Man and Other Fairly Stupid Tales (Scieszka), **677**

The Stinky Sneakers Contest (Peters), **654**

The Stolen Egg (Vyner), **379**

Stolen Thunder: A Norse Myth (Climo), **880**

Stone Fox (Gardiner), 1067

Stone Soup (Brown), 1412

Stone Soup (McGovern), 1555

Stone Soup (Stewig), **1031**

The Stonecutter: A Japanese Folk Tale (McDermott), 1552

Stop That Pickle! (Armour), **218**

Stop, Thief! (Kalan), **138**

Stories from Firefly Island (Blathwayt), **407**

The Stories Julian Tells (Cameron), 881

Stories of Gods and Heroes (Benson), 1656

Stories on Stage: Scripts for Reader's Theater (Shepard), **1237**

Stories to Solve: Folktales from Around the World (Shannon), 1729

Storm in the Night (Stolz), 828

Storms (Simon), 2105

A Story, a Story (Haley), 1517

The Story about Ping (Flack), 387

The Story Grandmother Told (Alexander), 2

The Story of Doctor Dolittle (Lofting), 1091

The Story of Ferdinand (Leaf), 465

The Story of Imelda, Who Was Small (Lurie), **311**

The Story of Jumping Mouse: A Native American Legend (Steptoe), 1608

The Story of Money (Maestro), **1197**

The Story of Nim, the Chimp Who Learned Language (Michel), 2076

The Story of the Statue of Liberty (Maestro), 2074

The Story of Z (Modesitt), **511**

The Story Vine: A Source Book of Unusual and Easy-to-Tell Stories from Around the World (Pellowski), 2178

Storyteller's Sourcebook (MacDonald), 2174

A Storyteller's Story (Martin), **1202**

Storytelling (Colwell), 2170

Storytelling: Art and Technique (Baker and Greene), 2160

Storytelling: Process and Practice (Livo and Rietz), 2173

Storytelling with Puppets (Champlin and Renfro), 2168

The Stranger (Van Allsburg), 1124

Street Child (Doherty), **813**

Street Music: City Poems (Adoff), **1261**

Strega Nona (dePaola), 1444

Strega Nona Meets Her Match (dePaola), **430**

Strider (Cleary), **806**

Stuart Little (White), 1131

Stuck with Luck (Johnson), 938

The Stupids Die (Allard), 318

The Sub (Petersen), **656**

Suho and the White Horse: A Legend of Mongolia (Otsuka), 1576

Sukey and the Mermaid (San Souci), **1017**

The Summer I Shrank My Grandmother (Woodruff), **800**

The Summer of the Swans (Byars), 1282

Summer Wheels (Bunting), **594**

The Sun, the Wind and the Rain (Peters), 2082

Sundiata: Lion King of Mali (Wisniewski), **1254**

Sunflakes: Poems for Children (Moore), **1375**

Sungura and Leopard: A Swahili Trickster Tale (Knutson), **960**

Super Dooper Jezebel (Ross), 786

Super-Duper Jokes (Young), **1432**

The Super Joke Book (Brandreth), 1754

Super Super Superwords (McMillan), 199

Superduper Teddy (Hurwitz), 696

Superfudge (Blume), 1145

Supergrandpa (Schwartz), **675**

The Surprise (Shannon), 262

The Surprise Book (White and Broekel), 2114

Swamp Angel (Isaacs), **625**

The Swan Maiden (Pyle), **665**

Sweet and Sour: Tales from China (Kendall and Li), 1701

Sweet Clara and the Freedom Quilt (Hopkinson), **622**

The Sweet Touch (Balian), 329

The Sweetest Fig (Van Allsburg), **751**

Swimmy (Lionni), 476

Swine Lake: Music & Dance Riddles (Keller), 1843

The Swoose (King-Smith), **727**

The Sword in the Tree (Bulla), 877

Sybil Rides for Independence (Brown), 2001

Syd Hoff's Animal Jokes (Hoff), 1815

Syd Hoff's Joke Book (Hoff), 1816

Sylvester and the Magic Pebble (Steig), 821

The Table, the Donkey and the Stick (Grimm), 1507

Tail Feathers from Mother Goose: The Opie Rhyme Book (Mother Goose), 1891

Tails, Toes, Eyes, Ears, Nose (Burton), 34

The Tailypo: A Ghost Story (Galdone), 1456

Take a Look at Snakes (Maestro), **1198**

Take It or Leave It (Molarsky), 965

Take Me Out to the Ballgame (Norworth), **521**

Take Me to Your Liter: Science and Math Jokes (Keller), **1339**

Take Warning! A Book of Superstitions (Sarnoff), 1723

Tale of a Black Cat (Withers), 853

The Tale of Meshka the Kvetch (Chapman), 885

The Tale of Peter Rabbit (Potter), 528

The Tale of Rabbit and Coyote (Johnston), **947**

The Tale of the Mandarin Ducks (Paterson), **996**

The Tale of Thomas Mead (Hutchins), 697

A Tale of Two Tengu: A Japanese Folktale (McCoy), **974**

Tales for Telling: From Around the World (Medlicott), **1080**

Tales from Grimm (Grimm), 1688

Tales from Silver Lands (Finger), 1677

Tales from the African Plains (Gatti), **1066**

Tales of a Fourth Grade Nothing (Blume), 1046

Tales of a Gambling Grandma (Khalsa), 1084

Tales of an Ashanti Father (Appiah), 1653

Tales of the Far North (Martin), 1711

The Tales of Uncle Remus: The Adventures of Brer Rabbit (Lester), 1707

Talester the Lizard (Himmelman), 134

Talk, Talk: An Ashanti Legend (Chocolate), **877**

The Talking Eggs (San Souci), 1590

Talking Like the Rain: A First Book of Poems (Kennedy and Kennedy), **1342**

The Talking Pot: A Danish Folktale (Haviland), **939**

Talking to the Sun (Koch and Farrell), 1849

The Talking Tree (Rayevsky), 1584

Talking with Artists (Cummings), **1127**

Talking without Words (Ets), 82

Tall Tales from the High Hills and Other Stories (Credle), 1672

Tall, Wide, and Sharp-Eye (Gabler), **907**
Tam Lin (Yolen), **1048**
Tap-Tap (Williams), **576**
Tar Beach (Ringgold), **671**
Tattercoats: An Old English Tale (Steel), 1606
Taxi Cat and Huey (LeRoy), **773**
A Taxi Dog Christmas (Barracca and Barracca), **229**
Tchaikovsky Discovers America (Kalman), **632**
The Teacher from the Black Lagoon (Thaler), **682**
Teammates (Golenbock), **1153**
The Teddy Bear Tree (Dillon), 662
Teddy Bears Cure a Cold (Gretz), 413
Teeny Tiny (Bennett), 1403
Teeny-Tiny and the Witch Woman (Walker), 1623
A Teeny Tiny Baby (Schwartz), **358**
The Teeny-Tiny Woman: A Ghost Story (Galdone), 1471
Tell Me a Mitzi (Segal), 798
Tell Me Some More (Bonsall), 23
Telling Stories to Children (Ziskind), 2184
Ten Black Dots (Crews), 59
Ten Cats Have Hats: A Counting Book (Marzollo), **162**
Ten Copycats in a Boat and Other Riddles (Schwartz), 1948
Ten Pink Piglets: Garth Pig's Wall Song (Rayner), **179**
Ten Potatoes in a Pot and Other Counting Rhymes (Katz), **1336**
Ten Sly Piranhas: A Counting Story in Reverse (A Tale of Wickedness and Worse) (Wise), **578**
The Tenth Good Thing about Barney (Viorst), 575
The Terrible Eek (Compton), **885**
The Terrible Hodag (Arnold), 1392
The Terrible Nung Gwana: A Chinese Folktale (Young), 1634
The Terrible Tiger (Prelutsky), 778
Terrible Tuesday (Townson), 569
Thank You, Jackie Robinson (Cohen), 1159
Thanksgiving: Stories and Poems (Bauer), **1266**
Thanksgiving at the Tappletons' (Spinelli), 818
That Dreadful Day (Stevenson), 1011
That New Pet! (Ferguson), 386
That Terrible Halloween Night (Stevenson), 824
That Tricky Coyote! (Mayo), **1079**
That's Exactly the Way It Wasn't (Stevenson), **558**
That's Good! That's Bad! (Cuyler), **92**
That's Good, That's Bad (Lexai), 187
That's One Ornery Orphan (Beatty), 1274
That's Right, Edie (Johnston), 441
That's the Spirit, Claude (Nixon), **650**
Theodore Turtle (MacGregor), 491
There Goes the Ghost! (Sherrow), 557

There's a Bear in the Bath! (Newman), **517**
There's a Cow in the Road! (Lindbergh), **307**
There's a Nightmare in My Closet (Mayer), 207
There's a Party at Mona's Tonight (Allard), 319
There's an Alligator under My Bed (Mayer), 208
There's More . . . Much More (Alexander), 3
There's Nothing to Do! (Stevenson), 825
There's Something in My Attic (Mayer), 209
Theseus and the Minotaur (Fisher), 1452
They've Discovered a Head in the Box for the Bread: And Other Laughable Limericks (Brewton and Blackburn), 1756
Thidwick, the Big-Hearted Moose (Seuss), 806
Thin Air (Getz), **819**
The Thing at the Foot of the Bed and Other Scary Tales (Leach), 1704
Thinking About Colors (Jenkins), **462**
The Thirteen Days of Halloween (Greene), 681
The Thirteen Hours of Halloween (Regan), **544**
Thirteen Moons on Turtle's Back: A Native American Year of Moons (Bruchac and London), **872**
The 13th Clue (Jonas), **464**
This Big Cat and Other Cats I've Known (De Regniers), 1793
This Can't Be Happening at Macdonald Hall (Korman), 1321
This Is My House (Dorros), **435**
This Is the Bear (Hayes), 128
This Is the Bear and the Scary Night (Hayes), **19**
This Is the Way We Go to School: A Book About Children Around the World (Baer), **226**
This Old Man (Jones), **137**
This Quiet Lady (Zolotow), **393**
This Time, Tempe Wick? (Gauch), 926
This Way Home (Peters), **1217**
This Way to Books (Bauer), 2127
Thorn Rose: or, The Sleeping Beauty (Grimm), 1508
Those Amazing Ants (Demuth), **1130**
Thread One to a Star: A Book of Poems (Hopkins and Arenstein), 1829
Three Aesop Fox Fables (Aesop), 1650
The Three and Many Wishes of Jason Reid (Hutchins), 1077
The Three Bears (Galdone), 1472
The Three Bears Rhyme Book (Yolen), 1981
Three Big Hogs (Pinkwater), 229
The Three Billy Goats Gruff (Asbjørnsen), 1396
The Three Billy Goats Gruff (Galdone), 1473
The Three Billy Goats Gruff (Rounds), **1009**
Three Blind Mice: The Classic Nursery Rhyme (Ivimey), **131**
The Three Brothers (Croll), **888**

Three Cheers for Tacky (Lester), **305**
The Three Dots (Primavera), **342**
Three Ducks Went Wandering (Roy), 246
A Three Hat Day (Geringer), 111
The Three Little Kittens (Cauley), 45
The Three Little Pigs (Cauley), 1420
The Three Little Pigs (Galdone), 1474
The Three Little Pigs (Marshall), 1563
The Three Little Pigs: An Old Story (Zemach), 1639
Three Little Pigs and the Big Bad Wolf (Rounds), **1010**
The Three Little Pigs and the Fox (Hooks), 1530
The Three Little Wolves and the Big Bad Pig (Trivizas), **378**
The Three Magic Gifts (Riordan), 1586
The Three Princes: A Tale from the Middle East (Kimmel), **957**
Three Rolls and One Doughnut: Fables from Russia (Ginsburg), 1681
Three Sacks of Truth: A Story from France (Kimmel), **958**
The Three Sillies (Galdone), 1475
The Three Sillies (Hewitt), 1523
Three-Star Billy (Hutchins), **130**
Three Strong Women: A Tall Tale (Stamm), 1605
Three Up a Tree (Marshall), 504
The Three Wishes: An Old Story (Zemach), 1640
The Three Wonderful Beggars (Scott), 1595
Three Young Pilgrims (Harness), **614**
Through Our Eyes: Poems and Pictures About Growing Up (Hopkins), **1328**
Through the Eyes of a Child: An Introduction to Children's Literature (Norton), 2122
Thumbelina (Andersen), 864
Thump and Plunk (Udry), 277
Thunder Cake (Polacco), 525
Tick-Tock (Brown), **238**
The Tickleoctopus (Wood), **387**
Tico and the Golden Wings (Lionni), 952
Tied Together: Topics and Thoughts for Introducing Children's Books (Leonard), 2146
Tiger (Allen), **585**
Tiger Soup: An Anansi Story from Jamaica (Temple), **1034**
The Tiger Who Lost His Stripes (Paul), 765
Tigerella (Wright), **389**
Tikki Tikki Tembo (Mosel), 1572
Tikvah Means Hope (Polacco), **664**
'Til All the Stars Have Fallen: A Collection of Poems for Children (Booth), **1273**
Tillie and the Wall (Lionni), 477
Tim O'Toole and the Wee Folk: An Irish Tale (McDermott), 1553

Time Flies (Rohmann), **350**
Time for Andrew: A Ghost Story (Hahn), **820**
Time for Poetry (Arbuthnot), 1744
Time of Wonder (McCloskey), 957
Time Out (Cresswell), **708**
Timothy Goes to School (Wells), 587
The Tinderbox (Andersen), **757**
Tink in a Tangle (Haas), 929
Tinkerbell Is a Ding-a-Ling (Doty), 1794
Tiny for a Day (Gackenbach), **273**
The Tiny Parents (Weiss and Friedman), **794**
Tiny Tim: Verses for Children (Bennett), 1747
The Tiny, Tiny Boy and the Big, Big Cow: A Scottish Folk Tale (Van Laan), **1040**
To Bathe a Boa (Kudrna), 463
To Love a Dog (Bare), 1992
To Space and Back (Ride and Okie), 2086
To the Top of the World: Adventures with Arctic Wolves (Brandenberg), **1108**
A Toad for Tuesday (Erickson), 665
Toad Is the Uncle of Heaven (Lee), 1546
Toby in the Country, Toby in the City (Bozzo), 25
Toby's Toe (Goodsell), 407
Today I Thought I'd Run Away (Johnson), 154
Today Is Monday (Carle), **248**
Today Was a Terrible Day (Giff), 678
Toliver's Secret (Brady), 1148
Tom (dePaola), **431**
Tom Glazer's Treasury of Songs for Children (Glazer), 1805
Tom Tit Tot (Ness), 1574
Tomfoolery: Trickery and Foolery with Words (Schwartz), 1949
Tomie dePaola's Book of Poems (dePaola), 1790
Tomie dePaola's Mother Goose (Mother Goose), 1892
Tommy at the Grocery Store (Grossman), 414
Tomorrow Is Daddy's Birthday (Wadsworth), **380**
Tom's Midnight Garden (Pearce), 1342
The Tomten (Lindgren), 725
The Tongue-Cut Sparrow (Ishii), 1535
Tongue Twisters (Keller), **1340**
Tongues of Jade (Yep), **1092**
Tony's Bread (dePaola), **896**
Too Hot to Hoot: Funny Palindrome Riddles (Terban), 1965
Too Many Books (Bauer), 333
Too Many Chickens (Bourgeois), **235**
Too Many Mittens (Slobodkin), 268
Too Many Tamales (Soto), **369**
Too Much (Stott), **47**
Too Much Magic (Sterman and Sterman), 1119
Too Much Noise (McGovern), 1556
Too Much Noise: An Italian Tale (Zemach), 1637

Tooley! Tooley! (Modell), 752

Tooth-Gnasher Superflash (Pinkwater), 523

The Tooth Witch (Karlin), 447

Top Secret (Gardiner), 1303

Tops and Bottoms (Conger), 1427

Tops & Bottoms (Stevens), **1030**

Tornado Alert (Branley), 1998

The Tortoise and the Hare (Stevens), 1388

The Tortoise and the Hare: An Aesop Tale (Aesop), 1388

Tortoise's Dream (Troughton), 1618

Touch Magic: Fantasy, Faerie and Folklore in the Literature of Childhood (Yolen), 2183

The Town Cats and Other Tales (Alexander), 1261

The Town Mouse and the Country Mouse (Cauley), 1421

Tracks in the Sand (Leedy), **1183**

Trade-In Mother (Russo), **184**

Train Song (Siebert), **553**

Trapped in Tar: Fossils from the Ice Age (Arnold), 1987

Trapped on the Golden Flyer (Fleming), 1173

Travel Far, Pay No Fare (Lindbergh), **826**

Traveling to Tondo: A Tale of the Nkundo of Zaire (Aardema), **857**

The Treasure (Shulevitz), 999

Treasure Hunt (Cauley), **79**

Treasure Mountain: Folktales from Southern China (Sadler), 1722

The Treasure of Alpheus Winterborn (Bellairs), 1275

A Treasure of Turkish Folktales for Children (Walker), 1734

The Treasure Trap (Masterman-Smith), 1212

A Tree Is Nice (Udry), 278

Tree of Birds (Meddaugh), **164**

Tree of Cranes (Say), **547**

Tree of Life: The World of the African Baobab (Bash), **1104**

The Tree That Rains: The Flood Myth of the Huichol Indians of Mexico (Bernhard), **867**

A Treeful of Pigs (Lobel), 729

Trees (Behn), **406**

The Trial of Anna Cotman (Alcock), **802**

The Trickster's Handbook (Eldin), **1136**

Tricky Tortoise (Mwenye Hadithi), 126

The Triplets (Seuling), 800

The Triumphs of Fuzzy Fogtop (Rose), 784

Troll Country (Marshall), 501

Trouble in Bugland: A Collection of Inspector Mantis Mysteries (Kotzwinkle), 1322

The Trouble with Adventurers (Harris), 1692

The Trouble with Elephants (Riddell), 240

Trouble with Trolls (Brett), **236**

The Troublesome Pig: A Nursery Tale (Lamont), 1543

Truck Song (Siebert), 266

The True Confessions of Charlotte Doyle (Avi), **803**

True Escape and Survival Stories (Williams), 2115

True-Life Treasure Hunts (Donnelly), 2020

The True Story of the 3 Little Pigs (Scieszka), 993

The Trumpet of the Swan (White), 1253

The Truth about the Moon (Bess), 875

The Tsar's Promise (San Souci), **1018**

Tuck Everlasting (Babbitt), 1271

Tucker Pfeffercorn: An Old Story Retold (Moser), **779**

Tuesday (Wiesner), **385**

The Turkey Girl: A Zuni Cinderella Story (Pollock), **1000**

Turnabout (Weisner), 1626

The Turnip (Domanska), 1448

The Turnip: An Old Russian Folktale (Morgan), 1569

Turtle in July (Singer), 1954

Turtle Tale (Asch), 16

The Turtle's Picnic: And Other Nonsense Stories (Berger), 615

The Tusk Fairy (Smee), **45**

'Twas the Night Before Thanksgiving (Pilkey), **531**

The Twelve Clever Brothers and Other Fools (Ginsburg), 1682

The Twelve Dancing Princesses, illus. by Errol Le Cain (Grimm), 1509

The Twelve Dancing Princesses, illus. by Ruth Sanderson (Grimm), **930**

The Twelve Dancing Princesses and Other Tales from Grimm (Grimm), 1689

The Twelve Dancing Princesses and Other Tales from Grimm (Lewis), 1689

The Twelve Days of Christmas (Brett), 1755

The Twelve Days of Summer (O'Donnell), **523**

The Twelve Months (Aliki), 1390

Twelve Tales from Aesop (Aesop), 1651

The Twenty-One Balloons (Du Bois), 1295

Twenty Tellable Tales: Audience Participation for the Beginning Storyteller (MacDonald), 2175

The Twin in the Tavern (Wallace), **849**

Twist These on Your Tongue (Rosenbloom), 1938

A Twister of Twists, a Tangler of Tongues (Schwartz), 1950

Two Bad Ants (Van Allsburg), 1125

Two Badd Babies (Gordon), **112**

The Two Foolish Cats (Uchida), 1620

Two Good Friends (Delton), 66

Two Hundred Rabbits (Anderson), 606

263 Brain Busters: Just How Smart Are You, Anyway? (Phillips), 2083

2 Is for Dancing: A 1 2 3 of Actions (Hubbard), **127**

Two-Legged, Four-Legged, No-Legged Rhymes (Lewis), **1354**

Two of Everything: A Chinese Folktale (Hong), **943**

Two Terrible Frights (Aylesworth), 18

The Two-Thousand Pound Goldfish (Byars), 1283

Two Travelers (Manson), **642**

Two Ways to Count to Ten: A Liberian Folktale (Dee), 1436

Tye May and the Magic Brush (Bang), 1398

The Tyrannosaurus Game (Kroll), 719

Tyrannosaurus Was a Beast (Prelutsky), 1922

Tyrone the Horrible (Wilhelm), 590

The Ugly Duckling (Andersen), 603

The Umbrella Day (Cooney), 57

Uncle Elephant (Lobel), 486

Uncle Jed's Barbershop (Mitchell), **647**

Uncle Lester's Hat (Schneider), **357**

Uncle Willie and the Soup Kitchen (DiSalvo-Ryan), **432**

Under the Blackberries (Pank), **335**

Under the Sea from A to Z (Doubilet), **1134**

Under the Sun (Kandoian), 445

Under the Sunday Tree (Greenfield), 1808

Unreal! Eight Surprising Stories (Jennings), **825**

Until I Saw the Sea: A Collection of Seashore Poems (Shaw), **1408**

Up North in Winter (Hartley), 683

Up the Wall (Heller), **281**

Up, Up and Away: A Book About Adverbs (Heller), **1311**

The Upside Down Riddle Book (Phillips), 1901

Upside-Down Town (Andrews), 866

Urban Roosts: Where Birds Nest in the City (Bash), **1105**

The Uses of Enchantment: The Meaning and Importance of Fairy Tales (Bettleheim), 2163

The Valentine Bears (Bunting), 353

The Valiant Little Tailor (Grimm), 1510

The Vanishing Pumpkin (Johnston), 443

Vasilissa the Beautiful: A Russian Folktale (Winthrop), **1044**

Vasily and the Dragon: An Epic Russian Fairy Tale (Stern), 1610

Vassilisa the Wise: A Tale of Medieval Russia (Sherman), 1598

Vegetable Soup (Modesitt), **170**

Veronica Ganz (Sachs), 1236

The Very Busy Spider (Carle), 41

The Very Hungry Caterpillar (Carle), 42

Very Last First Time (Andrews), 867

A Very Mice Joke Book (Gounaud), 1806

A Very Noisy Day (Myller), 755

The Very Quiet Cricket (Carle), **75**

The Very Worst Monster (Hutchins), 150

View from the Air: Charles Lindbergh's Earth and Sky (Lindbergh), **1356**

The View from the Cherry Tree (Roberts), 1346

The Village of Round and Square Houses (Grifalconi), 1485

A Visit from Dr. Katz (Le Guin), 183

A Visit to Grandma's (Carlson), **249**

Voices of the Wild (London), **640**

Volcano: The Eruption and Healing of Mount St. Helens (Lauber), 2063

Volcanoes (Simon), 2106

The Voyage of Osiris: A Myth of Ancient Egypt (McDermott), 1554

Voyage to the Bunny Planet books (Wells), **383**

Waiting for Hannah (Russo), 538

Waiting for Jennifer (Galbraith), 400

Waiting for Mom (Tyler), 276

Waiting-for-Spring Stories (Roberts), 531

Waiting for the Evening Star (Wells), **754**

Waiting to Waltz: A Childhood (Rylant), 1941

The Wall (Bunting), 354

The Walloping Window-Blind (Carryl), **596**

Wally (Wolkoff), 1135

Walter the Lazy Moose (Flack), 668

Walter's Tail (Ernst), **270**

Wanted . . . Mud Blossom (Byars), **763**

War Game (Foreman), **816**

War Horse (Morpurgo), 1334

The War with Grandpa (Smith), 1115

Warm as Wool (Sanders), **546**

The Warrior and the Wise Man (Wisniewski), 1031

A Wart Snake in a Fig Tree (Mendoza), 963

The Wartville Wizard (Madden), 738

Watch Out for Those Weirdos (Kline), **473**

The Water of Life (Grimm), 1511

Water Pennies: And Other Poems (Bodecker), **1271**

Water's Way (Peters), **1218**

The Wave (Hodges), 1527

The Way of the Storyteller (Sawyer), 2179

Wayside School Is Falling Down (Sachar), 1111

We Are Best Friends (Aliki), 6

Weasel (DeFelice), **812**

Weather (Hopkins), **1329**

The Wednesday Surprise (Bunting), 633

The Week Mom Unplugged the TVs (Phelan), 1102

A Week of Raccoons (Whelan), 589

A Weekend with Leonardo da Vinci (Skira-Venturi), **1239**

A Weekend with Wendell (Henkes), 420

The Weighty Word Book (Levitt, Burger, and Guralnick), 1326

Weird and Wacky Inventions (Murphy), 2078

Weird Henry Berg (Sargeant), 1352

Welcome Back Sun (Emberley), **438**

Welcome Home, Jellybean (Shyer), 1357

Welcome to the Green House (Yolen), **1256**

Wempires (Pinkwater), 535

We're Back! (Talbott), 1013

We're Going on a Bear Hunt (Rosen), 245

Whales (Berger), 1995

What Am I? Looking Through Shapes at Apples and Grapes (Charles), 84

What Am I? Very First Riddles (Calmenson), **1277**

What Comes in 2's, 3's & 4's? (Aker), **62**

What Do You Do When Your Mouth Won't Open? (Pfeffer), 1344

What Do You Say, Dear? (Joslin), 702

What Happened to Hamelin (Skurzynski), 1358

What Happened to Patrick's Dinosaurs? (Carrick), 642

What His Father Did (Greene), **920**

What I Did Last Summer (Prelutsky), 1923

What Is That Sound! (O'Neill), 1898

What Is Your Language? (Leventhal), **150**

What Joe Saw (Hines), **123**

What Lives in a Shell? (Zoehfeld), **1258**

What Makes Me Happy? (Anholt and Anholt), **65**

What Mary Jo Shared (Udry), 279

What Rhymes with Moon? (Yolen), **1431**

What to Do About Pollution (Shelby), **1236**

What Was the Wicked Witch's Real Name? And Other Character Riddles (Bernstein and Cohen), 1749

What Will Mommy Do When I'm at School? (Johnson), **135**

The Whatchmacallit Book (Hunt), 2052

What's Claude Doing? (Gackenbach), 101

What's Cooking, Jenny Archer? (Conford), **601**

What's for Lunch? (Schindel), **185**

What's Happened to Harry? (Dillon), 910

What's in Fox's Sack? (Galdone), 1476

What's Missing? (Yektai), 303

What's on the Menu? (Goldstein), **1299**

What's Silly? (Yektai), 304

What's So Funny, Ketu? (Aardema), 1384

What's That Noise (Lemieux), 184

What's the Big Idea, Ben Franklin? (Fritz), 2033

What's the Matter with Herbie Jones? (Kline), 949

What's Under My Bed? (Stevenson), 826

What's Your Name, Again? More Jokes about Names (Walton and Walton), 1971

Wheel Away! (Dodds), 71

Wheel on the Chimney (Brown), 631

The Wheel on the School (DeJong), 1168

The Wheels on the Bus (Kovalski), 173

Wheels on the Bus (Raffi), 235

The Wheels on the Bus (Zelinsky), **214**

When Bluebell Sang (Ernst), 383

When Cats Dream (Pilkey), **532**

When Cows Come Home (Harrison), **118**

When I Was Young in the Mountains (Rylant), 989

When I'm Hungry (Howard), **126**

When I'm Sleepy (Howard), 141

When Jaguar Ate the Moon: And Other Stories About Animals and Plants of the Americas (Brusca and Wilson), **1061**

When Lion Could Fly and Other Tales from Africa (Greaves), **1070**

When Shlemiel Went to Warsaw & Other Stories (Singer), 1730

When Spring Comes (Kinsey-Warnock), **469**

When Summer Ends (Fowler), 90

When the Fly Flew In (Peters), **336**

When the Lights Go Out: Twenty Scary Tales to Tell (MacDonald), 2176

When the Sirens Wailed (Streatfeild), 1366

Where Are Momma, Poppa, and Sister June? (Gackenbach), **274**

Where Can It Be? (Jonas), **25**

Where Do You Think You're Going, Christopher Columbus? (Fritz), 2034

Where Does It Go? (Miller), **166**

Where Is Everybody? An Animal Alphabet (Merriam), 508

Where the Buffaloes Begin (Baker), 1397

Where the Readers Are (Reasoner), 2154

Where the Sidewalk Ends (Silverstein), 1952

Where the Wild Things Are (Sendak), 255

Where's Jenna? (Miller), **167**

Where's My Teddy? (Alborough), **2**

Where's the Baby? (Hutchins), 435

Where's the Baby? (Paxton), **38**

The Whingdingdilly (Peet), 979

The Whipping Boy (Fleischman), 1172

Whiskers & Rhymes (Lobel), 1862

Whistle for Willie (Keats), 166

Whistling Thorn (Cowcher), **1126**

White Bear, Ice Bear (Ryder), 2091

The White Cat: An Old French Fairy Tale (San Souci), **1019**

White Wave: A Chinese Tale (Wolkstein), 1631

Whitefish Will Rides Again! (Yorinks), **581**

Who Owns the Sun? (Chbosky), 1158

Who Said Red? (Serfozo), 256

Who Says a Dog Goes Bow-Wow? (De Zutter), **1131**

Who Says Moo? (Young), **61**

Who Says That? (Shapiro), **43**

Who Shrank My Grandmother's House? Poems of Discovery (Esbensen), **1287**

Who Took the Farmer's Hat? (Nodset), 219

Who Wants a Cheap Rhinoceros? (Silverstein), 812

Who Wants One? (Serfozo), 257

The Whole Word Catalogue 2 (Zavatsky and Padgett), 2159

The Whole World Storybook (Crouch), 1673

Whoppers: Tall Tales and Other Lies (Schwartz), 1726

Who's in Charge of Lincoln? (Fife), 917

Who's in Rabbit's House? (Aardema), 1385

Who's Sick Today? (Cherry), 47

Who's That Stepping on Plymouth Rock? (Fritz), 2035

Whose Hat? (Miller), 212

Whose Mouse Are You? (Kraus), 177

Whose Shoe? (Miller), **168**

Why Did the Chicken Cross the Road? And Other Riddles Old and New (Cole and Calmenson), **1281**

Why Didn't I Think of That? From Alarm Clock to Zippers (Garrison), 2036

Why Ducks Sleep on One Leg (Garland), **909**

Why Mosquitoes Buzz in People's Ears (Aardema), 1386

Why the Sea Is Salt (French), **906**

Why the Sky Is Far Away: A Nigerian Folktale (Gerson), **913**

Why the Sun and Moon Live in the Sky (Dayrell), 1435

Why the Tides Ebb and Flow (Bowden), 1406

Why the Willow Weeps: A Story Told with Hands (Izen and West), **461**

Wicked One: A Story of Suspense (Hunter), 1313

The Widow's Broom (Van Allsburg), **752**

Wild Animals of America ABC (Ryden), 2087

The Wild Baby (Lindgren), 473

The Wild Christmas Reindeer (Brett), **237**

Wild Fox: A True Story (Mason), **1205**

Wild Pill Hickok and Other Old West Riddles (Adler), 1741

Wild Robin (Jeffers), 699

The Wild Swans, illus. by Susan Jeffers (Andersen), 1040

The Wild Swans, illus. by Kaarina Kaila (Andersen), **700**

Wild Willie and King Kyle Detectives (Joosse), **630**

Wilderness Cat (Kinsey-Warnock), **470**

Wiley and the Hairy Man (Bang), 1399

Will Spring Be Early? or Will Spring Be Late? (Johnson), 439

William Tell (Early), **900**

William, Where Are You? (Gerstein), 113

William's Doll (Zolotow), 312

Willy the Wimp (Browne), 350

The Wind and the Sun (Aesop), **859**

Wind in the Long Grass: A Collection of Haiku (Higginson), **1313**

The Wind in the Willows (Grahame), 1305

Wind Says Good Night (Rydell), **42**

Windy Day: Stories and Poems (Bauer), 1746

The Wing on a Flea (Emberley), 81

The Wing Shop (Woodruff), **580**

The Winged Colt of Casa Mia (Byars), 1048

Wings (Yolen), **1049**

Wings: A Tale of Two Chickens (Marshall), 745

Winnie-the-Pooh (Milne), 964

Winter Camp (Hill), **822**

Winter Poems (Rogasky), **1403**

Winter Whale (Ryder), **1232**

The Winter Worm Business (Giff), 1177

A Wise Monkey Tale (Maestro), 499

The Wise Old Woman (Uchida), **1038**

The Wish Giver: Three Tales of Coven Tree (Brittain), 1278

Wishbones: A Folk Tale from China (Wilson), **1043**

Witch Bazooza (Nolan), 762

Witch-Cat (Carris), **706**

A Witch Got on at Paddington Station (Sheldon), 265

The Witch Who Was Afraid of Witches (Low), 731

The Witches (Dahl), 1167

The Witches and the Singing Mice (Nimmo), **992**

The Witches' Supermarket (Meddaugh), **507**

Witches, Witches, Witches (Hoke), 1697

Witching Time: Mischievous Stories and Poems (Hopkins), 1698

The Witch's Hat (Johnston), 156

Witch's Sister (Naylor), 1217

With the Wind (Damrell), **429**

The Wizard Children of Finn (Tannen), 1367

The Wizard in the Tree (Alexander), 1262

The Wizard, the Fairy and the Magic Chicken (Lester), 185

Wizard's Hall (Yolen), **801**

The Wobbly Tooth (Cooney), 374

A Woggle of Witches (Adams), 1

The Wolf and the Seven Little Kids (Grimm), 1512

Wolf Story (McCleery), 489

The Wolf's Chicken Stew (Kasza), 162

Wolves (Gibbons), **1149**

The Woman in the Moon: And Other Tales of Forgotten Heroines (Riordan), 1717

The Woman Who Fell from the Sky: The Iroquois Story of Creation (Bierhorst), **868**

The Woman Who Flummoxed the Fairies: An Old Tale from Scotland (Forest), 1453

Wombat Stew (Vaughn), 836

Womenfolk and Fairy Tales (Minard), 1712

The Wonderful Mrs. Trumbly (Wittman), 596

The Wonderful Shrinking Shirt (Anderson), 604

The Wonderful Story of Henry Sugar and Six More (Dahl), 1293

Woody (Heller), **121**

Woody's 20 Grow Big Songs (Guthrie and Guthrie), **1303**

Words Are Like Faces (Baer), 324

World Folktales: A Scribner Resource Collection (Clarkson and Cross), 2169

World Water Watch (Koch), **1172**

The World's Best Sports Riddles and Jokes (Rosenbloom), 1939

World's Wackiest Riddle Book (Jones), 1833

Worse Than the Worst (Stevenson), **560**

Worse Than Willy! (Stevenson), 827

The Worst Person's Christmas (Stevenson), **559**

Would You Rather . . . (Burningham), 355

The Wreck of the Zephyr (Van Allsburg), 1126

Wriggles the Little Wishing Pig (Watson), 582

A Wrinkle in Time (L'Engle), 1325

Writing Aids Through the Grades (Carlson), 2132

The Wrong Side of the Bed (Keller), **297**

The Wuggie Norple Story (Pinkwater), 524

The Wump World (Peet), 980

Yang the Youngest and His Terrible Ear (Namioka), **781**

A Year in the Life of Rosie Bernard (Brenner), 1149

The Year of the Perfect Christmas Tree (Houston), 691

The Year the Wolves Came (Rice), **839**

Yeh-Shen: A Cinderella Story from China (Louie), 1548

The Yellow Button (Mazer), **505**

Yo, Hungry Wolf! A Nursery Rap (Vozar), **570**

Yo, Millard Fillmore! (And All Those Other Presidents You Don't Know) (Cleveland and Alvarez), **1119**

Yo! Yes? (Raschka), **541**

Yobgorgle: Mystery Monster of Lake Ontario (Pinkwater), 1227

Yonder (Johnston), 939

Yossel Zissel & the Wisdom of Chelm (Schwartz), 992

You Be Good & I'll Be Night: Jump-on-the-Bed Poems (Merriam), 1871

You Can't Catch Me! (Oppenheim), 516

You Can't Eat Peanuts in Church: And Other Little-Known Laws (Seuling), 2097

"You Look Ridiculous," Said the Rhinoceros to the Hippopotamus (Waber), 580

You Read to Me, I'll Read to You (Ciardi), 1772

Young Lions (Yoshida), 2116

A Young Painter: The Life and Paintings of Wang Yani—China's Extraordinary Young Artist (Zhensun and Low), **1257**

Young Santa (Greenburg), **770**

Your Dad Was Just Like You (Johnson), **463**

Your Mother Was a Neanderthal (Scieszka), **790**

Yuck! (Stevenson), 562

The Zebra-Riding Cowboy: A Folk Song from the Old West (Medearis), **645**

Zeke Pippin (Steig), **678**

Zekmet, the Stone Carver (Stolz), 1244

Zin! Zin! Zin! A Violin (Moss), **512**

Zinnia and Dot (Ernst), **271**

Zomo the Rabbit: A Trickster Tale from West Africa (McDermott), **977**

Zoo Doings (Prelutsky), 1924

Zoodles (Most), **514**

A Zooful of Animals (Cole), **1282**

Zoophabets (Talon), 1014

From THE STINKY SNEAKERS CONTEST by Julie Anne Peters.
Text copyright © 1992 by Julie Anne Peters; illustrations copyright © 1992 by
Cat Bowman Smith. By permission of Little, Brown and Company.

ILLUSTRATOR INDEX

Illustrators and joint illustrators are listed here, as well as photographers. Authors are shown in parentheses following the book title. If no author name is given parenthetically, then the illustrator is also the author of the book. References to entry numbers in this volume appear in boldface type, while references to the companion volume, *Books Kids Will Sit Still For,* appear in regular type.

Abel, Ray. *Why Didn't I Think of That?*
(Garrison), 2036
Abel, Simone. *Somebody and the Three Blairs*
(Tolhurst), **191**
Abolafia, Yossi. *Fox Tale,* **394**
Harry in Trouble (Porte), 527
Harry's Dog (Porte), 777
It's Valentine's Day (Prelutsky), 1909
My Parents Think I'm Sleeping (Prelutsky), 1910
Stop, Thief! (Kalan), **138**
What I Did Last Summer (Prelutsky), 1923
Abrams, Kathie. *Busy Buzzing Bumblebees and
Other Tongue Twisters* (Schwartz), 1944
Accorsi, William. *Friendship's First Thanksgiving,*
216
Adams, Adrienne. *Arion and the Dophins*
(Anderson), 1391
The Easter Bunny That Overslept (Friedrich and
Friedrich), 394
The Halloween Party (Anderson), 605
Jorinda and Joringel (Grimm), 1498
The Ponies of Mykillengi (Anderson), 865
Two Hundred Rabbits (Anderson), 606
A Woggle of Witches, 1
Adel, Daniel. *The Book That Jack Wrote*
(Scieszka), **548**
Agee, Jon. *Go Hang a Salami! I'm a Lasagna Hog!,*
1263
The Incredible Painting of Felix Clousseau, 862
Aggs, Patrice. *Why the Sea Is Salt* (French), **906**
Ahlberg, Allan (jt. illus.). *Funnybones* (Ahlberg
and Ahlberg), 314
The Jolly Christmas Postman (Ahlberg and
Ahlberg), **396**
Ahlberg, Janet, and Allan Ahlberg. *Funnybones,*
314
The Jolly Christmas Postman, **396**

Ahlbom, Jens. *Christmas Eve at Santa's*
(Prøysen), **343**
Ajhar, Brian. *Scarlett Angelina Wolverton-
Manning* (Ogburn), **524**
Akaba, Suekichi. *The Crane Wife* (Yagawa), 1632
Suho and the White Horse (Otsuka), 1576
The Tongue-Cut Sparrow (Ishii), 1535
Akgulian, Nishan. *Hole by the Apple Tree*
(Polette), **339**
Alanen, Erkki. *The Turtle's Picnic* (Berger), 615
Albers, Dave. *Talk, Talk* (Chocolate), **877**
Alborough, Jez. *It's the Bear!,* **63**
Martin's Mice (King-Smith), 1085
Where's My Teddy?, **2**
Alcorn, Stephen. *Rembrandt's Beret* (Alcorn), **697**
Alexander, Ellen. *Fireflies in the Night* (Hawes),
1156
Llama and the Great Flood, 1389
Alexander, Gregory. *Tales from the African Plains*
(Gatti), **1066**
Alexander, Martha. *Move Over, Twerp,* 315
The Story Grandmother Told, 2
Aliki. *At Mary Bloom's,* 4
Communication, **1099**
I Wish I Was Sick, Too (Brandenberg), 26
Keep Your Mouth Closed, Dear, 5
The Listening Walk (Showers), **187**
No School Today (Brandenberg), 342
That's Good, That's Bad (Lexai), 187
The Twelve Months, 1390
We Are Best Friends, 6
Allen, Jonathan. *The Great White Man-Eating
Shark* (Mahy), **501**
Allen, Pamela. *Bertie and the Bear,* 7
Allen, Thomas. *Summer Wheels* (Bunting), **594**
Alley, R. W. *The Legend of Sleepy Hollow*
(Wolkstein), **795**

Mrs. Toggle and the Dinosaur (Pulver), **344**
Mrs. Toggle's Beautiful Blue Shoe (Pulver), **345**
My Christmas Safari (Manushkin), **320**
Seven Fables from Aesop (Aesop), 1649
The Silliest Joke Book Ever (Hartman), **1308**
Ambrus, Glenys. *A Christmas Fantasy* (Haywood), 416
Ambrus, Victor. *Chasing the Goblins Away* (Tobias), 831
Just So Stories (Kipling), 948
The Valiant Little Tailor (Grimm), 1510
Ambrus, Victor (jt. illus.). *A Christmas Fantasy* (Haywood), 416
Ancona, George. *Just Beyond Reach and Other Riddle Poems* (Nims), **1390**
Mom Can't See Me (Alexander), **1097**
Mom's Best Friend (Alexander), **1098**
Andersen, Hans Christian. *Amazing Paper Cuttings of Hans Christian Andersen* (Brust), **1113**
Andreasen, Dan. *Joshua T. Bates Takes Charge* (Shreve), **747**
Anglund, Joan Walsh. *The Golden Treasury of Poetry* (Untermeyer), 1968
Anholt, Catherine. *All About You*, **3**
Anholt, Catherine, and Laurence Anholt. *Kids*, **64**
What Makes Me Happy?, **65**
Anholt, Laurence (jt. illus.). *Kids* (Anholt and Anholt), **64**
What Makes Me Happy? (Anholt and Anholt), **65**
Apple, Margot. *Benjy in Business* (Van Leeuwen), 1021
The Chocolate Touch (Catling), 884
Donna Jean's Disaster (Williams), 850
The Great Rescue Operation (Van Leeuwen), 1252
Sheep in a Jeep (Shaw), 556
Sheep in a Shop (Shaw), **360**
Sheep Out to Eat (Shaw), **361**
Sybil Rides for Independence (Brown), 2001
Tink in a Tangle (Haas), 929
The Wonderful Mrs. Trumbly (Wittman), 596
Armitage, David (jt. illus.). *The Bossing of Josie* (Armitage and Armitage), 8
Armitage, Ronda, and David Armitage. *The Bossing of Josie*, 8
Arno, Enrico. *The Hat-Shaking Dance* (Courlander), 1668
Arnold, Katya. *Baba Yaga*, **860**
Baba Yaga & the Little Girl, **861**
Arnold, Tedd. *Ollie Forgot*, 607
The Signmaker's Assistant, **400**

Arnosky, Jim. *All Night Near the Water*, **67**
The Covered Bridge House and Other Poems (Starbird), 1957
Joel and the Great Merlini (McGraw), 1093
Arquette, Mary F. *Children of the Morning Light* (Manitonquat (Medicine Story)), **1077**
Aruego, Jose. *Leo the Late Bloomer* (Kraus), 460
Whose Mouse Are You? (Kraus), 177
Aruego, Jose, and Ariane Dewey. *Birthday Rhymes, Special Times* (Goldstein), **1297**
The Chick and the Duckling (Ginsburg), 114
A Crocodile's Tale, 1393
Dance Away (Shannon), 260
Five Little Ducks (Raffi), **39**
Gregory, the Terrible Eater (Sharmat), 555
Lizard's Song (Shannon), 261
Marie Louise's Heyday (Carlson), 638
Milton the Early Riser (Kraus), 174
Mushroom in the Rain (Ginsburg), 115
Noel the Coward (Kraus), 175
Owliver (Kraus), 461
Rum Pum Pum (Duff), 1449
Runaway Marie Louise (Carlson), 43
The Surprise (Shannon), 262
Asch, Frank. *Bear Shadow*, 10
Goodbye House, 11
Happy Birthday, Moon, 12
Just Like Daddy, 13
Moongame, 14
Pearl's Promise, **701**
Popcorn, 15
Turtle Tale, 16
Asch, Frank, and Vladimir Vagin. *Dear Brother*, **401**
Astrop, John. *Arthur the Kid* (Coren), 902
Auch, Mary Jane. *Bird Dogs Can't Fly*, **219**
The Easter Egg Farm, **220**
Monster Brother, **221**
Peeping Beauty, **402**
August, Louise. *In the Month of Kislev* (Jaffe), **627**
Avishai, Susan. *Sophie and the Sidewalk Man* (Tolan), **685**
Axworthy, Ann. *Brain-Teasers and Mind-Benders* (Brandreth), 1997
Ayers, Alan. *A Taxi Dog Christmas* (Barracca and Barracca), **229**
Ayers, Donna. *Jennifer's Rabbit* (Paxton), 224
Ayto, Russell. *Quacky Quack-Quack!* (Whybrow), **56**

Babbitt, Natalie. *All the Small Poems and Fourteen More* (Worth), **1425**
Bub, **224**
The Devil's Storybook (Babbit), 1270

The Search for Delicious (Babbit), 1139
Small Poems (Worth), 1979
Tuck Everlasting (Babbit), 1271
Bacon, Paul. *Teammates* (Golenbock), **1153**
Bacon, Peggy. *The Magic Touch*, 1043
Baeten, Lieve. *The Thirteen Hours of Halloween* (Regan), **544**
Bailey, Peter. *Tigerella* (Wright), **389**
Baker, Alan. *Benjamin's Book*, 325
Benjamin's Portrait, 326
Itsy-Bitsy Beasties (Rosen), **1404**
Baker, Keith. *Big Fat Hen*, **4**
Elephants Aloft (Appelt), **66**
Baker, Leslie. *Honkers* (Yolen), **391**
Balian, Lorna. *Amelia's Nine Lives*, 19
The Animal, 327
Bah! Humbug?, 328
Humbug Potion, 608
Humbug Witch, 20
Leprechauns Never Lie, 609
The Sweet Touch, 329
Ballard, Robin. *Good-bye, House*, **69**
Bang, Molly. *Dawn*, 869
The Goblins Giggle and Other Stories, 1655
The Paper Crane, 610
Red Dragonfly on My Shoulder (Cassedy and Suetake), **1278**
Tye May and the Magic Brush, 1398
Wiley and the Hairy Man, 1399
Barbier, Suzette. *One Red Rooster* (Carroll), **7**
Barbour, Karen. *Street Music* (Adoff), **1261**
Barkley, James. *Sounder* (Armstrong), 1264
Barlow, Gillian. *East o' the Sun & West o' the Moon* (Dasent), 1433
Barlowe, Wayne D. *Dragon's Plunder* (Strickland), **848**
An Alphabet of Dinosaurs (Dodson), **1132**
Barnes, Suzanne. *Cradles in the Trees* (Demuth), **1129**
Barnes-Murphy, Rowan. *Sherman the Sheep* (Kiser), **299**
Barnett, Ivan. *Quail Song* (Carey), **876**
Barnett, Moneta. *Me as Neesie* (Greenfield), 411
Barnum, Jay Hyde. *The Popcorn Dragon* (Thayer), 273
Barrett, Angela. *The Witches and the Singing Mice* (Nimmo), **992**
The Woman in the Moon (Riordan), 1717
Barrett, Jennifer. *The Seven Treasure Hunts* (Byars), **595**
Barrett, Ron. *Animals Should Definitely Not Wear Clothing* (Barrett), 870
Benjamin's 365 Birthdays (Barrett), 330
Chicken Trek (Manes), 1211

Cloudy with a Chance of Meatballs (Barrett), 871
Ghastlies, Goops & Pincushions (Kennedy), 1846
Barrios, David. *Ballpoint Bananas and Other Jokes for Kids* (Keller), 1835
Barrow, Ann. *A Visit from Dr. Katz* (Le Guin), 183
Barton, Byron. *Applebet Story*, 331
Building a House, 1993
Buzz Buzz Buzz, 21
Gila Monsters Meet You at the Airport (Sharmat), 808
Jump, Frog, Jump (Kalan), 160
The Snopp on the Sidewalk and Other Poems (Prelutsky), 1921
Truck Song (Siebert), 266
Barton, Harriet. *Books and Libraries* (Knowlton), **1171**
In the Witch's Kitchen (Brewton, Blackburn, and Blackburn), 1757
Barton, Jill. *The Happy Hedgehog Band* (Waddell), **48**
The Pig in the Pond (Waddell), **50**
Bash, Barbara. *Desert Giant*, 1994
Shadows of Night, **1103**
Tree of Life, **1104**
Urban Roosts, **1105**
Bassett, Jeni. *Gator Pie* (Matthews), 506
Baum, Arline, and Joseph Baum. *Opt*, 1044
Baum, Joseph (jt. illus.). *Opt* (Baum and Baum), 1044
Baumann, Karen. *Ring Out, Wild Bells* (Hopkins), **1326**
Baynes, Pauline. *How the Whale Got His Throat* (Kipling), 712
The Lion, the Witch and the Wardrobe (Lewis), 1088
The Magician's Nephew (Lewis), 1204
Beddows, Eric. *Joyful Noise* (Fleischman), 1799
Who Shrank My Grandmother's House? (Esbensen), **1287**
Begay, Shonto. *Ma'ii and Cousin Horned Toad*, **865**
Behr, Joyce. *Daffy Definitions* (Rosenbloom), 1927
The Funny Song Book (Nelson), 1894
The Gigantic Joke Book (Rosenbloom), 1931
Monster Madness (Rosenbloom), 1935
Silly Verse (and Even Worse) (Rosenbloom), 1936
Twist These on Your Tongue (Rosenbloom), 1938
Bellows, Cathy. *The Grizzly Sisters*, **230**
Bemelmans, Ludwig. *Madeline's Rescue*, 335
Bennett, Jill. *Danny, the Champion of the World* (Dahl), 1291

Harry's Mad (King-Smith), 1199

Once Upon a Rhyme (Corrin and Corrin), 1783

The Queen's Nose (King-Smith), **726**

Bennett, Richard. *Magicians Do Amazing Things* (Kraske), 2059

Tall Tales from the High Hills and Other Stories (Credle), 1672

Benson, Patrick. *Owl Babies* (Waddell), **49**

Robin Hood (Hayes), 1696

Benton, Sally. *Don't Ever Wish for a 7-Foot Bear* (Benton), 614

Bernardin, James. *Big Men, Big Country* (Walker), **1090**

Bernhard, Durga. *How Snowshoe Hare Rescued the Sun* (Bernhard), **866**

The Tree That Rains (Bernhard), **867**

Bernstein, Zena. *Mrs. Frisby and the Rats of NIMH* (O'Brien), 1337

Berringer, Nick. *The Super Joke Book* (Brandreth), 1754

Berson, Harold. *Loretta Mason Potts* (Chase), 1157

My Trip to Alpha I (Slote), 1114

Beskow, Elsa. *Pelle's New Suit*, 336

Bianchi, John. *Mortimer Mooner Stopped Taking a Bath* (Edwards), **94**

Bilibin, Ivan I. *Russian Folk Tales* (Afanasev), 1652

Binch, Caroline. *Amazing Grace* (Hoffman), **287**

Hue Boy (Mitchell), **325**

Biondi, Janet. *D Is for Dolphin* (Berg), **1106**

Biro, Val. *Hungarian Folk-Tales*, 1657

Bjorkman, Peter. *I Hate English* (Levine), 721

Björkman, Steve. *Aliens for Breakfast* (Etra and Spinner), 915

In 1492 (Marzollo), **1204**

This Is the Way We Go to School (Baer), **226**

Blades, Ann. *Petranella* (Waterton), 845

A Salmon for Simon (Waterton), 846

Blake, Quentin. *All Join In*, **1270**

BFG (Dahl), 1166

Custard and Company (Nash), 1893

The Enormous Crocodile (Dahl), 656

Esio Trot (Dahl), **710**

How the Camel Got His Hump (Kipling), 947

Matilda (Dahl), 1292

Roald Dahl's Revolting Rhymes (Dahl), 1787

The Singing Tortoise and Other Animal Folktales (Yeoman), **1091**

The Witches (Dahl), 1167

Blake, Robert J. *Dog*, 591

The Perfect Spot, **231**

Riptide (Weller), 848

Blankley, Kathy. *The King and the Tortoise* (Mollel), **988**

Blathwayt, Benedict. *Stories from Firefly Island*, **407**

Blegvad, Erik. *Cat Walk* (Stolz), 1121

The Finches' Fabulous Furnace (Drury), 1170

The Tenth Good Thing about Barney (Viorst), 575

Water Pennies (Bodecker), **1271**

Bloom, Lloyd. *The Green Book* (Paton Walsh), 1341

Yonder (Johnston), 939

Bloom, Tom. *Murflies and Wink-a-Peeps* (Sperling), 1956

Blundell, Tony. *Beware of Boys*, **232**

Joe on Sunday, 337

Bobak, Cathy. *Poetry from A to Z* (Janeczko), **1335**

Bodecker, N. M. *"It's Raining," Said John Twaining*, 1750

Let's Marry Said the Cherry and Other Nonsense Poems, 1751

A Person from Britain Whose Head was the Shape of a Mitten and Other Limericks, 1752

Bodsworth, Nan. *A Nice Walk in the Jungle*, **233**

Bollen, Roger. *Alistair and the Alien Invasion* (Sadler), **356**

Alistair in Outer Space (Sadler), 787

Alistair's Elephant (Sadler), 788

Alistair's Time Machine (Sadler), 789

Bolognese, Don. *Benjie* (Lexai), 472

Jimmy Takes Vanishing Lessons (Brooks), 876

Bond, Felicia. *If You Give a Moose a Muffin* (Numeroff), **334**

If You Give a Mouse a Cookie (Numeroff), 514

Pointsettia and the Firefighters, 338

Bonforte, Lisa. *Whales* (Berger), 1995

Bonners, Susan. *Cold Stars and Fireflies* (Esbensen), 1797

Booth, Graham. *Henry the Explorer* (Taylor), 564

My Tang's Tungled and Other Ridiculous Situations (Brewton, Brewton, and Blackburn), 1759

Born, Flint. *An Alphabet in Five Acts* (Andersen), **398**

Bottner, Barbara. *Messy*, 339

Bourke, Linda. *Eye Spy*, **409**

Bowen, Keith. *Snowy* (Doherty), **263**

Bowman, Leslie. *A Christmas Sonata* (Paulsen), **833**

The Cuckoo Child (King-Smith), **722**

Hannah (Whelan), **689**

Boynton, Sandra. *A Is for Angry*, 341

Brady, Irene. *Doodlebug*, 620

Brandenberg, Jim. *To the Top of the World*, **1108**

Brazell, Derek. *My Brother Is a Visitor from Another Planet* (Sheldon), **746**

Bredeson, Lynn Gates. *Presenting Reader's Theater* (Bauer), 2162

Brenner, Fred. *A Dog I Know* (Brenner), 621
The Drinking Gourd (Monjo), 966
Little One Inch (Brenner), 1407

Brett, Jan. *The First Dog*, 622
Goldilocks and the Three Bears, 1408
The Mitten, 1409
The Mother's Day Mice (Bunting), 32
The Owl and the Pussycat (Lear), **148**
Scary, Scary Halloween (Bunting), 352
Trouble with Trolls, **236**
The Twelve Days of Christmas, 1755
The Valentine Bears (Bunting), 353
The Wild Christmas Reindeer, **237**

Brewster, Patience. *Bear and Mrs. Duck* (Winthrop), 298
Good As New (Douglass), 72
I Met a Polar Bear (Boyd and Boyd), 340
There's More . . . Much More (Alexander), 3

Briggs, Raymond. *The Elephant & the Bad Baby* (Vipont), 283
The Fairy Tale Treasury (Haviland), 1693
Jim and the Beanstalk, 623
The Mother Goose Treasury (Mother Goose), 1885

Broek, Fabricio Vanden. *The Mouse Bride* (Dupré), **898**

Brooke, L. Leslie. *The Golden Goose Book*, 1658

Brooks, Ron. *John Brown, Rose and the Midnight Cat* (Wagner), 581

Brown, Craig McFarland. *The Ornery Morning* (Demuth), **260**

Brown, Don. *Ruth Law Thrills a Nation*, **1111**

Brown, Judith. *Melvil and Dewey in the Chips* (Swallow), 1012

Brown, Judith Gwyn. *The Best Christmas Pageant Ever* (Robinson), 1230
A New Treasury of Children's Poetry (Cole), 1773
The Treasure of Alpheus Winterborn (Bellairs), 1275
When the Sirens Wailed (Streatfeild), 1366

Brown, Laurene Krasny, and Marc Brown. *Dinosaurs to the Rescue!*, **1112**

Brown, M. K. *Big Goof and Little Goof* (Cole and Cole), 373

Brown, Marc. *Arthur Babysits*, **412**
Arthur Meets the President, **413**
Arthur's April Fool, 625
Arthur's Baby, 344
Arthur's Birthday, 626
Arthur's Chicken Pox, **239**
Arthur's Eyes, 345
Arthur's Halloween, 627
Arthur's Teacher Trouble, 628
Arthur's Tooth, 629
The Banza (Wolkstein), 1629
D.W. Thinks Big, **71**
The Family Read-Aloud Holiday Treasury (Low), **1362**
Hand Rhymes, 1760
Read-Aloud Rhymes for the Very Young (Prelutsky), 1917
Scared Silly, **1275**
Spooky Riddles, 1761
What's So Funny, Ketu? (Aardema), 1384
Why the Tides Ebb and Flow (Bowden), 1406

Brown, Marc (jt. illus.). *Dinosaurs to the Rescue!* (Brown and Brown), **1112**

Brown, Marc, and Stephen Krensky. *Dinosaurs, Beware!*, 2002
Perfect Pigs, 2003

Brown, Marcia. *Cinderella*, 1410
Dick Whittington and His Cat, 1411
How, Hippo!, 28
Peter Piper's Alphabet, 1762
Stone Soup, 1412
The Three Billy Goats Gruff (Asbjørnsen), 1396

Brown, Mary Barrett. *Great Northern Diver* (Esbensen), **1137**

Brown, Paula. *Moon Jump*, **240**

Brown, Richard. *View from the Air* (Lindbergh), **1356**

Brown, Rick. *The Princess and the Potty* (Lewison), **29**

Brown, Ruth. *Blossom Comes Home* (Herriot), 2046
Bonny's Big Day (Herriot), 2047
The Christmas Day Kitten (Herriot), 2048
A Dark, Dark Tale (Brown), 347
If at First You Do Not See (Brown), 348
Our Cat Flossie (Brown), 632

Browne, Anthony. *Bear Hunt*, 30
Changes, **241**
The Daydreamer (McEwan), **829**
Gorilla, 349
Willy the Wimp, 350

Browne, Jane. *My Wicked Stepmother* (Leach), **302**

Brunkus, Denise. *Junie B. Jones and a Little Monkey Business* (Park), **651**
Junie B. Jones and Some Sneaky Peeky Spying (Park), **652**
Junie B. Jones and the Stupid Smelly Bus (Park), **653**
The Principal's New Clothes (Calmenson), **420**

Show and Tell (Woodruff), **388**

Brusca, María Cristina. *The Blacksmith and the Devils*, **873**

The Cook and the King, **874**

When Jaguars Ate the Moon, **1061**

The Zebra-Riding Cowboy (Medearis), **645**

Bucknall, Caroline. *One Bear in the Picture*, 31

Buehner, Mark. *The Adventures of Taxi Dog* (Barracca and Baracca), **404**

A Job for Wittilda (Buehner), **242**

Buguet, Anne. *On Cat Mountain* (Richard), **1003**

Burger, Carl. *The Incredible Journey* (Burnford), 1279

Old Yeller (Gipson), 1180

Burgess, Anne. *Sloppy Kisses* (Winthrop), 595

Burgevin, Daniel. *Iroquois Stories* (Bruchac), 1659

Burkert, Nancy Ekholm. *James and the Giant Peach* (Dahl), 1059

Burningham, John. *Harvey Slumfenburger's Christmas Present*, **244**

Mr. Gumpy's Outing, 33

Would You Rather . . ., 355

Burris, Burmah. *Listen! And Help Tell the Story* (Carlson), 1765

Burroughes, Jo. *Mud, Moon and Me* (Weil), **1420**

Bursik, Rose. *Amelia's Fantastic Flight*, **417**

Burton, Marilee Robin. *Tails, Toes, Eyes, Ears, Nose*, 34

Burton, Virgina Lee. *Katy and the Big Snow*, 35

The Little House, 634

Mike Mulligan and His Steam Shovel, 36

Butler, John. *Shadow the Deer* (Radcliffe), **347**

Byrd, Robert. *The Bear and the Bird King* (Grimm and Byrd), **929**

The Children's Aesop (Aesop and Calmenson), **1057**

Byrd, Samuel. *Abraham Lincoln* (Livingston), **1189**

Keep on Singing (Livingston), **1190**

Let Freedom Ring (Livingston), **1191**

A Picture Book of Harriet Tubman (Adler), **1095**

Cain, Errol Le. *Mr. Mistoffelees with Mungojerrie and Rumpelteazer* (Eliot), **1286**

Cameron, Polly. *"I Can't," Said the Ant*, 636

Cameron, Scott. *Beethoven Lives Upstairs* (Nichol), **785**

Cannon, Janell. *Stellaluna*, **245**

Caple, Kathy. *The Biggest Nose*, 356

Carle, Eric. *Brown Bear, Brown Bear, What Do You See?* (Martin), 204

Eric Carle's Animals, Animals (Whipple), 1974

Eric Carle's Dragons, Dragons & Other Creatures That Never Were (Whipple), **1423**

The Grouchy Ladybug, 37

The Hole in the Dike (Green), 409

A House for Hermit Crab, **246**

The Mixed-Up Chameleon, 38

Pancakes, Pancakes!, **247**

Papa, Please Get the Moon for Me, 39

The Secret Birthday Message, 40

Today Is Monday, **248**

Twelve Tales from Aesop (Aesop), 1651

The Very Busy Spider, 41

The Very Hungry Caterpillar, 42

The Very Quiet Cricket, **75**

Carlson, Nancy. *Arnie and the New Kid*, **421**

Lenore's Big Break (Pearson), **528**

Louanne Pig in the Mysterious Valentine, 637

A Visit to Grandma's, **249**

Watch Out for Those Weirdos (Kline), **473**

Carmi, Giora. *The Chanukkah Guest* (Kimmel), **298**

The Greatest of All (Kimmel), **954**

The Old Woman and Her Pig (Kimmel), **956**

Carnabuci, Anthony. *Sleep Tight* (Hennessy), **21**

Carpenter, Gary. *Return of the Sun* (Bruchac), **1060**

Carpenter, Nancy. *Lester's Dog* (Hesse), **619**

Masai and I (Kroll), **480**

Carpenter, Stephen. *Kids Pick the Funniest Poems* (Lansky), **1346**

Carrick, Donald. *Aladdin and the Wonderful Lamp* (Carrick), 1413

Ben and the Porcupine (Carrick), 640

Doctor Change (Cole), 896

The Foundling (Carrick), 641

Ghost's Hour, Spook's Hour (Bunting), 351

Harald and the Giant Knight, 882

Harald and the Great Stag, 883

Moss Gown (Hooks), 1529

Patrick's Dinosaurs (Carrick), 358

Secrets of a Small Brother (Margolis), 1867

The Wednesday Surprise (Bunting), 633

What Happened to Patrick's Dinosaurs? (Carrick), 642

Carrol, Charles. *Me and the Terrible Two* (Conford), 1161

Carter, Abby. *I Thought I'd Take My Rat to School* (Kennedy), **1341**

New Kid on Spurwink Ave. (Crowley), **258**

Shack and Back (Crowley), **427**

Carter, David A. *Over in the Meadow* (Wadsworth), **202**

Carter, Gail Gordon. *Mac & Marie & the Train Toss Surprise* (Howard), **455**

Cartwright, Reg. *The Firebird* (Hastings), **938**

Casale, Paul. *Fourth Grade Rats* (Spinelli), **749**

Caseley, Judith. *Dear Annie*, **250**
  Silly Baby, 44
  Sophie and Sammy's Library Sleepover, **77**
Catalanotto, Peter. *All I See* (Rylant), 988
Catrow, David. *That's Good! That's Bad!*
    (Cuyler), **92**
Cauley, Lorinda Bryan. *The Beginning of the*
    Armadillos (Kipling), 945
  The Cock, the Mouse and the Little Red Hen, 1414
  The Elephant's Child (Kipling), 946
  Goldilocks and the Three Bears, 1415
  The Goose and the Golden Coins, 1416
  Jack and the Beanstalk, 1417
  Old MacDonald Had a Farm, **78**
  The Pancake Boy, 1418
  Puss in Boots, 1419
  Three Blind Mice (Ivimey), **131**
  The Three Little Kittens, 45
  The Three Little Pigs, 1420
  The Town Mouse and the Country Mouse, 1421
  Treasure Hunt, **79**
  The Ugly Duckling (Andersen), 603
Cazet, Denys. *Annie, Bea, and Chi Chi Dolores*
    (Maurer), **163**
  December 24th, 359
  "I'm Not Sleepy," **80**
  Lucky Me, 360
Chaffin, Donald. *The Fantastic Mr. Fox* (Dahl),
    904
Chambliss, Maxie. *Donald Says Thumbs Down*
    (Cooney), 56
  Go Away Monsters, Lickety Split (Cooney), **88**
  Tomorrow Is Daddy's Birthday (Wadsworth),
    380
Chan, Harvey. *Roses Sing on New Snow* (Yee),
    696
Chappell, Warren. *Wolf Story* (McCleery), 489
Charlip, Remy. *Fortunately*, 645
  Harlequin and the Gift of Many Colors, 886
  Mother, Mother, I Feel Sick, Send for the Doctor
    Quick, Quick, Quick, 646
Chartier, Normand. *Keep Looking!* (Selsam and
    Hunt), 2095
  Silly Fred (Wagner), **203**
  This Way Home (Peters), **1217**
Chast, Roz. *Now Everybody Really Hates Me*
    (Martin and Marx), **644**
Chastain, Madye Lee. *The Cow-Tail Switch and*
    Other West African Stories (Courlander and
    Herzog), 1670
Chbosky, Stacey. *Who Owns the Sun?*, 1158
Chen, Ju-Hong. *The Jade Stone* (Yacowitz), **1045**
  The Magic Leaf (Morris), 1570

Chen, Tony. *The Fisherman's Son* (Ginsburg),
    1478
  In the Land of Small Dragon (Kha), 1540
  The Riddle of the Drum (Aardema), 1383
Cheng, Hou-Tien. *The Six Chinese Brothers*, 1422
Cherry, Lynne. *The Armadillo from Amarillo*, **423**
  Chipmunk Song (Ryder), 2089
  The Great Kapok Tree, 647
  If I Were in Charge of the World and Other
    Worries (Viorst), 1969
  A River Ran Wild, **1117**
  The Snail's Spell (Ryder), 249
  When I'm Sleepy (Howard), 141
  Who's Sick Today?, 47
Chess, Victoria. *Alfred's Alphabet Walk*, 648
  Bugs (Hoberman), 1814
  Grim and Ghastly Goings-On (Heide), **1309**
  A Hippopotamustn't and Other Animal Verses
    (Lewis), **1353**
  Princess Gorilla and a New Kind of Water
    (Aardema), 1381
  The Queen of Eene (Prelutsky), 1914
  Rolling Harvey Down the Hill (Prelutsky), 1919
  The Sheriff of Rottenshot (Prelutsky), 1920
  Slither McCreep and His Brother Joe (Johnston),
    294
  Ten Sly Piranhas (Wise), **578**
  Tommy at the Grocery Store (Grossman), 414
Chessare, Michele. *Moth-Kin Magic* (Tapp), 1247
Chesworth, Michael. *Alvin's Famous No-Horse*
    (Harding), **613**
  The Curse of the Trouble Dolls (Regan), **669**
Chin, Alex. *The Biggest Tongue Twister Book in*
    the World (Brandreth), 1753
Chorao, Kay. *Albert's Toothache* (Williams), 296
  Clyde Monster (Crowe), 60
  Mother Goose Magic (Mother Goose and
    Chorao), **1382**
  My Mama Says There Aren't Any Zombies,
    Ghosts, Vampires, Creatures, Demons,
    Monsters, Fiends, Goblins or Things (Viorst),
    840
Christelow, Eileen. *Dear Phoebe* (Alexander), 600
  The Five-Dog Night, **425**
  Five Little Monkeys Jumping on the Bed, 48
  Five Little Monkeys Sitting in a Tree, **85**
  Gertrude, the Bulldog Detective, **252**
  Henry and the Dragon, 49
  Henry and the Red Stripes, 362
  Jerome and the Babysitter, 364
  Jerome and the Witchcraft Kids, 363
  Mr. Murphy's Marvelous Invention, 649
  Olive and the Magic Hat, 365
  Two Terrible Frights (Aylesworth), 18

Christiana, David. *Gold and Silver, Silver and Gold* (Schwartz), 2092

Chwast, Seymour. *Mathew Michael's Beastly Day* (Johnston), **293**

Cieslawski, Steve. *At the Crack of the Bat* (Morrison), **1376**

Clark, Brenda. *Little Fingerling* (Hughes), **945**

Clark, Emma Chichester. *Boo!* (Cecil), **1062**

Clarke, Gus. *EIEIO*, **86**

Clément, Frédéric. *The Boy Who Drew Cats* (Levine), **968**

Clement, Rod. *Edward the Emu* (Knowles), **300**

When Lion Could Fly and Other Tales from Africa (Greaves), **1070**

Clementson, John. *How the Giraffe Got Such a Long Neck . . . and Why Rhino Is So Grumpy* (Rosen), **1007**

Clifford, Sandy. *The Roquefort Gang*, 1053

Climo, Shirley. *The Korean Cinderella*, **878**

Cober, Alan E. *Tale of a Black Cat* (Withers), 853

Cocca-Leffler, Maryann. *Big Time Bears* (Krensky), **147**

Thanksgiving at the Tappletons' (Spinelli), 818

CoConis, Ted. *The Summer of the Swans* (Byars), 1282

Cogancherry, Helen. *Here Comes the Mystery Man* (Sanders), **673**

Warm as Wool (Sanders), **546**

Cohen, Ron. *My Dad's Baseball*, **599**

Cole, Brock. *Alpha and the Dirty Baby*, **426**

The Indian in the Cupboard (Banks), 1272

The King at the Door, 895

No More Baths, 52

Nothing but a Pig, 651

Coletta, Hallie (jt. illus.). *From A to Z* (Coletta and Coletta), 897

Coletta, Irene, and Hallie Coletta. *From A to Z*, 897

Compton, Kenn. *Ashpet* (Compton), **883**

Jack the Giant Chaser, **884**

Conover, Chris. *The Beast in the Bed* (Dillon), 70

The Little Humpbacked Horse (Hodges), 1525

Mother Goose and the Sly Fox, 1428

The School Mouse (Harris), 415

What's Happened to Harry? (Dillon), 910

Cook, Donald. *Abe Lincoln's Hat* (Brenner), **1110**

Cook, Joel. *The Rat's Daughter*, **886**

Cook, Scott. *The Gingerbread Boy*, 1429

Mother Goose (Mother Goose and Cook), **1386**

Nettie Jo's Friends (McKissack), 492

Cooke, Andy. *One Cow Moo Moo!* (Bennett), **5**

Cooke, Donald E. *The Peculiar Miss Pickett* (Julian), 940

Coombs, Patricia. *Bill and Google-Eyed Goblins* (Schertle), 792

Dorrie and the Weather Box, 653

The Magician and McTree, 900

Molly Mullett, 901

Cooney, Barbara. *American Folk Songs for Children* (Seeger), 1951

Demeter and Persephone (Proddow), 1581

The Donkey Prince (Craig), 1490

Island Boy, 1055

Little Brother and Little Sister (Grimm), 1499

Miss Rumphius, 654

Only Opal (Whiteley), **1253**

Ox-Cart Man (Hall), 931

The Remarkable Christmas of the Cobbler's Sons (Sawyer), **1020**

Roxaboxen (McLerran), **499**

Squawk to the Moon, Little Goose (Preston), 233

The Year of the Perfect Christmas Tree (Houston), 691

Cooper, Floyd. *Grandpa's Face* (Greenfield), 410

Laura Charlotte (Galbraith), 105

Meet Danitra Brown (Grimes), **1302**

Pass It On (Hudson), **1331**

Corbould, Walton. *Complete Version of Ye Three Blind Mice* (Ivimey), 152

Cornell, Laura. *Earl's Too Cool for Me* (Komaiko), **477**

Corner, Marie. *The Swoose* (King-Smith), **727**

Councell, Ruth Tietjen. *Country Bear's Good Neighbor* (Brimner), 27

What Rhymes with Moon? (Yolen), **1431**

Cousins, Lucy. *The Little Dog Laughed and Other Nursery Rhymes* (Mother Goose and Cousins), **1384**

Coville, Katherine. *The Monster's Ring* (Coville), 1165

Cowcher, Helen. *Rain Forest*, **256**

Whistling Thorn, **1126**

Cowen-Fletcher, Jane. *It Takes a Village*, **257**

Mama Zooms, **89**

Cox, David. *Bossyboots*, 655

Craft, K. Y. *Baba Yaga and Vasilisa the Brave* (Mayer), **985**

Craig, Helen. *Alexander and the Dragon* (Holabird), **140**

Jam (Mahy), 740

This Is the Bear (Hayes), 128

This Is the Bear and the Scary Night (Hayes), **19**

Crespo, George. *How the Sea Began*, **887**

Crews, Donald. *Freight Train*, 58

Ten Black Dots, 59

Croll, Carolyn. *Questions* (Hopkins), **1324**

The Three Brothers, **888**

Cruz, Ray. *Alexander and the Terrible, Horrible, No Good, Very Bad Day* (Viorst), 838
Alexander Who Used to Be Rich Last Sunday (Viorst), 839
Jennifer Takes Over P.S. 94 (Lystad), 733
Cuffari, Richard. *Thank You, Jackie Robinson* (Cohen), 1159
Toliver's Secret (Brady), 1148
The Winged Colt of Casa Mia (Byars), 1048
Cullen-Clark, Patricia. *Poems for Grandmothers* (Livingston), **1360**
Cummings, Pat. *C.L.O.U.D.S.*, 903
Storm in the Night (Stolz), 828
Cunningham, David. *The Memory Box* (Bahr), **589**
Cupples, Pat. *Hands On, Thumbs Up* (Gryski), **1154**
Cushman, Doug. *The ABC Mystery*, **428**
Possum Stew, **91**
Czernecki, Stefan. *The Singing Snake*, **889**

Dabcovich, Lydia. *Hurry Home, Grandma!* (Olson), 220
Up North in Winter (Hartley), 683
Daly, Niki. *Not So Fast, Songololo*, 62
Daniel, Alan. *Big David, Little David* (Hinton), **285**
Bunnicula (Howe and Howe), 1193
The Grand Escape (Naylor), **783**
Rabbit-Cadabra! (Howe), **458**
This Big Cat and Other Cats I've Known (De Regniers), 1793
Dann, Penny. *The Doubleday Book of Bedtime Stories* (Waters), **381**
Darling, Louis. *Beezus and Ramona* (Cleary), 887
The Enormous Egg (Butterworth), 1154
Henry Huggins (Cleary), 888
The Mouse and the Motorcycle (Cleary), 1050
Ramona the Pest (Cleary), 890
Ribsy (Cleary), 891
Darrow, Whitney, Jr. *The Fireside Book of Fun and Game Songs* (Winn), 1976
Daugherty, James. *Andy and the Lion*, 658
The Loudest Noise in the World (Elkin), 381
D'Aulaire, Edgar Parin (jt. illus.). *Benjamin Franklin* (D'Aulaire and D'Aulaire), 2013
D'Aulaire's Book of Greek Myths (D'Aulaire and D'Aulaire), 1674
D'Aulaire's Trolls (D'Aulaire and D'Aulaire), 1434
D'Aulaire, Ingri, and Edgar Parin D'Aulaire. *Benjamin Franklin*, 2013
D'Aulaire's Book of Greek Myths, 1674
D'Aulaire's Trolls, 1434

Davidson, Raymond. *The Genuine, Ingenious Thrift Shop Genie, Clarissa Mae Bean and Me* (Keller), 1198
Davie, Helen K. *The Star Maiden* (Esbensen), 1451
What Lives in a Shell? (Zoehfeld), **1258**
daVinci, Leonardo. *A Weekend with Leonardo da Vinci* (Skira-Venturi), **1239**
Davis, Lambert. *Rikki-Tikki-Tavi* (Kipling), **729**
The Terrible Hodag (Arnold), 1392
Davis, Nelle. *Munching* (Hopkins), 1826
My Bike (Jakob), **132**
Davis, Susan. *The Dinosaur Who Lived in My Backyard* (Hennessy), **284**
Dawson, Diane. *April Fool* (Christian), 1423
The Blanket Had to Go (Cooney), 55
Gloria Chipmunk, Star! (Nixon), 760
Mother, Mother, I Want Another (Polushkin), 230
See My Lovely Poison Ivy (Moore), 1875
Day, Alexandra. *Frank and Ernest*, 906
Deal, Kate L. *The Boxcar Children* (Warner), 1025
Deas, Michael. *True Escape and Survival Stories* (Williams), 2115
Degen, Bruce. *The Forgetful Bears Meet Mr. Memory* (Weinberg), 583
The Good-Luck Pencil (Stanley), 1005
How Do You Say It Today, Jesse Bear? (Carlstrom), **76**
If You Were a Writer (Nixon), 972
Jamberry, 64
The Magic School Bus at the Waterworks (Cole), 2008
The Magic School Bus Inside the Earth (Cole), 2009
The Magic School Bus Inside the Human Body (Cole), 2010
The Magic School Bus Lost in the Solar System (Cole), **1121**
The Magic School Bus on the Ocean Floor (Cole), **1122**
de Groat, Diane. *All about Sam* (Lowry), 1327
Animal Fact / Animal Fable (Simon), 2099
Attaboy, Sam! (Lowry), **776**
Bears in Pairs (Yektai), 302
Bubba and Babba (Polushkin), 526
The Great Ideas of Lila Fenwick (McMullin), 1209
Little Rabbit's Loose Tooth (Bate), 332
Our Teacher's Having a Baby (Bunting), **243**
Where Is Everybody? (Merriam), 508
Delacre, Lulu. *The Bossy Gallito* (Gonzalez), **917**
Delaney, A. *The Dragon Circle* (Krensky), 1202
de Larrea, Victoria. *Abracatabby* (Hiller), 424
The Blackmail Machine (Holman), 1191

Juba This and Juba That (Tashjian), 1961

Delessert, Etienne. *A Wart Snake in a Fig Tree* (Mendoza), 963

Demarest, Chris L. *The Butterfly Jar* (Moss), **1377**

The Cows Are Going to Paris (Kirby and Woodman), **471**

Lindbergh, **1128**

Morton and Sidney, 67

No Peas for Nellie, 68

Two Badd Babies (Gordon), **112**

What's on the Menu? (Goldstein), **1299**

When Cows Come Home (Harrison), **118**

Demi. *Bamboo Hats and a Rice Cake* (Tompert), **1036**

A Chinese Zoo, 1675

Demi's Reflective Fables, 1676

Dragon Kites and Dragonflies, 1789

The Empty Pot, **892**

The Firebird, **893**

In the Eyes of the Cat, **1284**

The Magic Tapestry, **894**

Dennis, Wesley. *Misty of Chincoteague* (Henry), 1072

Denton, Kady MacDonald. *Realms of Gold* (Pilling), **1083**

'Til All the Stars Have Fallen (Booth), **1273**

Denton, Terry. *The Story of Imelda, Who Was Small* (Lurie), **311**

dePaola, Tomie. *The Art Lesson*, 907

The Badger and the Magic Fan (Johnston), 1536

Big Anthony and the Magic Ring, 908

Can't You Make Them Behave, King George? (Fritz), 2030

The Carsick Zebra and Other Animal Riddles (Adler), 1739

The Cat on the Dovrefell (Dasent), 1432

Charlie Needs a Cloak, 376

The Cloud Book, 2017

The Comic Adventures of Old Mother Hubbard and Her Dog, 1438

Fin M'Coul, the Giant of Knockmary Hill, 1439

Ghost Poems (Wallace), 1970

Jamie O'Rourke and the Big Potato, **895**

The Legend of the Bluebonnet, 1440

The Legend of the Indian Paintbrush, 1441

Maggie & the Monster (Winthrop), 299

Mary Had a Little Lamb (Hale), 127

Merry Christmas, Strega Nona, 909

The Mysterious Giant of Barletta, 1442

The Night before Christmas (Moore), 753

Oh, Such Foolishness (Cole), 1780

The Popcorn Book, 2018

The Prince of the Dolomites, 1443

The Quicksand Book, 2019

Shh! We're Writing the Constitution (Fritz), 2032

Simple Pictures Are Best (Willard), 849

The Star-Spangled Banana and Other Revolutionary Riddles (Keller and Baker), 1844

Strega Nona, 1444

Strega Nona Meets Her Match, **430**

The Tale of Rabbit and Coyote (Johnston), **947**

Teeny Tiny (Bennett), 1403

Tom, **431**

Tomie dePaola's Book of Poems, 1790

Tomie dePaola's Mother Goose (Mother Goose), 1892

Tony's Bread, **896**

The Triumphs of Fuzzy Fogtop (Rose), 784

The Tyrannosaurus Game (Kroll), 719

The Vanishing Pumpkin (Johnston), 443

The Whatchmacallit Book (Hunt), 2052

The Wuggie Norple Story (Pinkwater), 524

Deraney, Michael. *Molly's Pilgrim* (Cohen), 893

Desrocher, Jack. *Knock-Knock Knees and Funny Bones* (Mathews and Robinson), **1370**

Deuchar, Ian. *The Moon Dragon* (Miller), 1568

Devlin, Harry. *Cranberry Thanksgiving*, 660

Devlin, Harry, and Wende Devlin. *Old Witch Rescues Halloween*, 661

Devlin, Wende (jt. illus.). *Old Witch Rescues Halloween* (Devlin and Devlin), 661

Dewar, Bob. *Ivan* (Crouch), **1064**

Dewey, Ariane (jt. illus.). *Birthday Rhymes, Special Times* (Goldstein), **1297**

The Chick and the Duckling (Ginsburg), 114

A Crocodile's Tale (Aruego and Dewey), 1393

Dance Away (Shannon), 260

Five Little Ducks (Raffi), **39**

Gregory, the Terrible Eater (Sharmat), 555

Lizard's Song (Shannon), 261

Marie Louise's Heyday (Carlson), 638

Milton the Early Riser (Kraus), 174

Mushroom in the Rain (Ginsburg), 115

Noel the Coward (Kraus), 175

Owliver (Kraus), 461

Rum Pum Pum (Duff), 1449

Runaway Marie Louise (Carlson), 43

The Surprise (Shannon), 262

Diamond, Donna. *Bridge to Terabithia* (Paterson), 1340

Mustard (Graeber), 927

Diaz, David. *Smoky Night* (Bunting), **593**

Dicks, Jan Thompson. *The House That Crack Built* (Taylor), **1246**

Dickson, Mora. *Tales of an Ashanti Father* (Appiah), 1653

di Fiori, Lawrence. *A Toad for Tuesday* (Erickson), 665

Dillon, Diane (jt. illus.). *Aïda* (Price), **837**
The Tale of the Mandarin Ducks (Paterson), **996**
What Am I? (Charles), **84**
Who's in Rabbit's House? (Aardema), 1385
Why Mosquitoes Buzz in People's Ears (Aardema), 1386
Dillon, Diane, and Leo Dillon. *Honey, I Love* (Greenfield), 1807
Dillon, Leo (jt. illus.). *Honey, I Love* (Greenfield), 1807
Dillon, Leo, and Diane Dillon. *Aïda* (Price), **837**
The Tale of the Mandarin Ducks (Paterson), **996**
What Am I? (Charles), **84**
Who's in Rabbit's House? (Aardema), 1385
Why Mosquitoes Buzz in People's Ears (Aardema), 1386
DiSalvo-Ryan, DyAnne. *The Growing-Up Feet* (Cleary), 50
The Mommy Exchange (Hest), 421
Uncle Willie and the Soup Kitchen, **432**
DiVito, Anna. *Drop Everything, It's D.E.A.R. Time!* (McGovern), **497**
Dodds, Siobhan. *Grandpa Bud*, **9**
Dodson, Bert. *Supergrandpa* (Schwartz), **675**
Domanska, Janina. *King Krakus and the Dragon*, 1446
Little Red Hen, 1447
The Turnip, 1448
Dooling, Michael. *George Washington* (Giblin), **1150**
Dorros, Arthur. *Ant Cities*, 2021
Follow the Water from Brook to Ocean, **1133**
This Is My House, **435**
dos Santos, Joyce Audy. *Million Dollar Jeans* (Roy), 1233
Mrs. Peloki's Class Play (Oppenheim), 763
Orphan Jeb at the Massacree (Mooser), 1215
Piskies, Spriggans, and Other Magical Beings (Climo), 1663
Doty, Roy. *Tales of a Fourth Grade Nothing* (Blume), 1046
Tinkerbell Is a Ding-a-Ling, 1794
Doubilet, David. *Under the Sea from A to Z* (Doubilet), **1134**
Downing, Julie. *I Had a Cat* (Reeves), 237
A Ride on the Red Mare's Back (LeGuin), **637**
Drescher, Henrik. *Poems of A. Nonny Mouse* (Prelutsky), 1913
Simon's Book, 664
Drescher, Joan. *Eaton Stanley & the Mind Control Experiment* (Adler), 1137
Drucker, Mort. *Whitefish Will Rides Again!* (Yorinks), **581**
Drummond, V. H. *Phewtus the Squirrel*, 74

Dubanevich, Arlene. *Do Bunnies Talk?* (Dodds), **262**
Invisible Oink (Phillips), **1394**
Du Bois, William Pène. *Bear in Mind* (Goldstein), **1296**
The Giant, 1294
Lazy Tommy Pumpkinhead, 911
Lion, 912
The Magic Finger (Dahl), 905
The Twenty-One Balloons, 1295
William's Doll (Zolotow), 312
Dugan, Karen M. *Halmoni and the Picnic* (Choi), **424**
School Spirit (Hurwitz), **716**
Dugin, Andrej, and Olga Dugina. *The Fine Round Cake* (Esterl and Hejl), **903**
Dugina, Olga (jt. illus.). *The Fine Round Cake* (Esterl and Hejl), **903**
Duke, Kate. *Aunt Isabel Tells a Good One*, **436**
Don't Tell the Whole World! (Cole), **881**
Guinea Pigs Far and Near, 75
It's Too Noisy! (Cole), **882**
Seven Froggies Went to School, 377
Dunn, Jeffrey. *Through Our Eyes* (Hopkins), **1328**
Dunnington, Tom. *The Girl Who Tricked the Troll* (Torgersen), 832
The Thirteen Days of Halloween (Greene), 681
Duntze, Dorothee. *The Emperor's New Clothes* (Andersen), 863
Duvoisin, Roger. *The Camel Who Took a Walk* (Tworkov), 571
The Happy Lion (Fatio), 385
Hide and Seek Fog (Tresselt), 833
Petunia, 378
Dyer, Jane. *Talking Like the Rain* (Kennedy and Kennedy), **1342**
The Three Bears Rhyme Book (Yolen), 1981
Dyke, John. *Pigwig*, 379
Dypold, Pat. *One Cow Coughs* (Loomis), **155**

Early, Margaret. *Ali Baba and the Forty Thieves* (McVitty), 1557
Sleeping Beauty, **899**
William Tell, **900**
Eastman, P. D. *A Fish Out of Water* (Palmer), 221
Edens, Cooper. *The Glorious Mother Goose* (Mother Goose), 1879
Edwards, Michelle. *And Sunday Makes Seven* (Baden), **864**
Egielski, Richard. *Oh, Brother* (Yorinks), 1036
Ehlert, Lois. *Chicka Chicka Boom Boom* (Martin and Archambault), 205
Circus, **95**
Color Farm, **96**

Color Zoo, 76
Eating the Alphabet, 77
Feathers for Lunch, 265
Fish Eyes, **97**
Growing Vegetable Soup, 78
Moon Rope, **902**
What Is That Sound! (O'Neill), 1898
Eichenberg, Fritz. *Ape in a Cape*, 79
Dancing in the Moon, 380
Rainbows Are Made (Sandburg), 1942
Einzig, Susan. *Tom's Midnight Garden* (Pearce), 1342
Eitan, Ora. *No Milk!* (Ericsson), **99**
Eitzen, Allan. *Alphabestiary* (Yolen), **1426**
Ellis, Jan Davey. *Mush!* (Seibert), **1235**
Elwell, Peter. *Time Out* (Cresswell), **708**
Emberley, Ed. *Drummer Hoff* (Emberley), 80
Go Away, Big Green Monster!, **98**
The Wing on a Flea, 81
Emberley, Michael. *Ruby*, **437**
Welcome Back Sun, **438**
Endicott, James. *I Am the Ocean* (Marshak), **1200**
Listen to the Rain (Martin and Archambault), 746
Trees (Behn), **406**
Engel, Diana. *Eleanor, Arthur, and Claire*, **267**
Fishing, **268**
Entwhistle, Mark. *The Sleeper* (Day), **891**
Eriksson, Eva. *The Wild Baby* (Lindgren), 473
Ernst, Lisa Campbell. *Ginger Jumps*, **269**
The Luckiest Kid on the Planet, **439**
Squirrel Park, **440**
Walter's Tail, **270**
When Bluebell Sang, 383
Who Says Moo? (Young), **61**
Zinnia and Dot, **271**
Essley, Roger. *Appointment* (Maugham and Benjamin), **830**
Ets, Marie Hall. *Talking without Words*, 82
Everitt, Betsy. *Frida the Wondercat*, 384
The Happy Hippopotami (Martin), **322**
Mean Soup, **101**

Fadden, David Kanietakeron (jt. illus.). *Native American Animal Stories* (Bruchac), **1059**
Fadden, John Kahionhes, and David Kanietakeron Fadden. *Native American Animal Stories* (Bruchac), **1059**
Falwell, Cathryn. *Clowning Around*, **272**
Feast for 10, **11**
The Letter Jesters, **1140**
Farley, Rick. *Capturing Nature* (Audubon, Roop, and Roop), **1101**

Farrow, Rachi. *A Monster Is Coming! A Monster Is Coming!* (Heide and Heide), 684
Farrow, T. C. *The Dragon in the Cliff* (Cole), **807**
Faulkner, Matt. *The Amazing Voyage of Jackie Grace*, 666
Feelings, Tom. *Jambo Means Hello* (Feelings), 1798
Fehr, Terrence M. *Science Tricks* (Lehane), 2065
Feiffer, Jules. *The Phantom Tollbooth* (Juster), 1316
Felstead, Cathie. *A Caribbean Dozen* (Agard and Nichols), **1262**
Felt, Sue. *Rosa-Too-Little*, 83
Felts, Shirley. *Sweet and Sour* (Kendall and Li), 1701
Ferguson, Amos. *Under the Sunday Tree* (Greenfield), 1808
Fernandez, Laura, and Rick Jacobson. *Tchaikovsky Discovers America* (Kalman), **632**
Ferris, Lynn Bywaters. *Goldilocks and the Three Bears* (Eisen), 1450
Fiammenghi, Gioia. *Chocolate Fever* (Smith), 1003
Chucky Bellman Was So Bad (Green), **444**
Little Sister for Sale (Hamilton), **450**
Noisy Nancy Norris (Gaeddert), 102
Toby's Toe (Goodsell), 407
Filling, Gregory. *Alexander the Grape* (Keller), 1834
Swine Lake (Keller), 1843
Take Me to Your Liter (Keller), **1339**
Firmin, Charlotte. *I'm Going on a Dragon Hunt* (Jones), 158
Firth, Barbara. *Can't You Sleep, Little Bear?* (Waddell), **199**
Let's Go Home, Little Bear (Waddell), **201**
"Quack!" Said the Billy-Goat (Causley), 46
Sam Vole and His Brothers (Waddell), **51**
Fisher, Leonard Everett. *Cyclops*, **904**
The Great Wall of China, 2023
If You Ever Meet a Whale (Livingston), **1358**
Theseus and the Minotaur, 1452
The Three Princes (Kimmel), **957**
Fitzhugh, Louise. *Harriet the Spy*, 1298
Flack, Marjorie. *Angus and the Cat*, 84
Angus and the Ducks, 85
Angus Lost, 86
Ask Mr. Bear, 87
The Country Bunny and the Little Gold Shoes (Heyward), 423
Fleischman, Seymour. *Quiet on Account of Dinosaur* (Thayer), 567
Fleming, Denise. *Barnyard Banter*, **12**
Count!, **13**

In the Small, Small Pond, **104**
Lunch, **14**
Flora, James. *Grandpa's Ghost Stories*, 919
Grandpa's Witched-Up Christmas, 920
The Great Green Turkey Creek Monster, 921
The Joking Man, 922
Leopold the See-Through Crumbpicker, 669
Little Hatchy Hen, 923
My Friend Charlie, 924
101 More Words and How They Began (Steckler), 1958
Sherwood Walks Home, 88
Florian, Douglas. *Beast Feast*, **1290**
Bing Bang Boing, **1291**
Monster Motel, **1292**
The Night It Rained Pancakes (Ginsburg), 1480
Ford, Jeremy. *A Nasty Piece of Work and Other Ghost Stories* (Salway), 1351
Foreman, Michael. *The Brothers Grimm Popular Folk Tales* (Grimm), 1684
Cat and Canary, 388
Michael Foreman's Mother Goose (Mother Goose and Foreman), **1385**
The Saga of Erik the Viking (Jones), 1197
Teeny-Tiny and the Witch Woman (Walker), 1623
There's a Bear in the Bath! (Newman), **517**
The Tiger Who Lost His Stripes (Paul), 765
War Game, **816**
Forrester, Victoria. *The Magnificent Moo*, 89
Fortnum, Peggy. *A Bear Called Paddington* (Bond), 1146
Paddington's Storybook (Bond), 1147
Fossey, Ken. *A Tale of Two Tengu* (McCoy), **974**
Fox-Davies, Sarah. *Little Beaver and the Echo* (MacDonald), **156**
Moon Frog (Edwards), **1285**
Frampton, David. *Just So Stories* (Kipling), **728**
King of the Cats and Other Tales (Carlson), 1660
My Son John (Aylesworth), **222**
Frankenberg, Robert. *Owls in the Family* (Mowat), 2077
Frascino, Edward. *Count Draculations!* (Keller), 1836
Gladys Told Me to Meet Her Here (Sharmat), 809
King Henry the Ape (Keller), **1338**
My Cousin the King, 390
The Trumpet of the Swan (White), 1253
Fraser, Betty. *A House Is a House for Me* (Hoberman), 431
Fraser, Mary Ann. *On Top of the World*, **1143**
One Giant Leap, **1142**
Freeman, Don. *Beady Bear*, 92
Bearymore, 391

Corduroy, 93
Dandelion, 392
Hattie the Backstage Bat, 393
Mike's House (Sauer), 252
Mop Top, 94
Norman the Doorman, 671
A Pocket for Corduroy, 95
Quiet! There's a Canary in the Library, 96
A Rainbow of My Own, 97
French, Fiona. *Going to Squintum's* (Westwood), 1624
Friedman, Marvin. *Pinch* (Callen), 1285
Sorrow's Song (Callen), 1286
Fritz, Ron. *Belly Laughs!* (Keller), **1337**
Tongue Twisters (Keller), **1340**
Fuchs, Bernie. *Champions* (Littlefield), **1188**

Gaber, Susan. *The Woman Who Flummoxed the Fairies* (Forest), 1453
Gabler, Mirko. *Tall, Wide, and Sharp-Eye*, **907**
Gackenbach, Dick. *Alice's Special Room*, **106**
Amanda and Giggling Ghost (Kroll), 715
Arabella and Mr. Crack, 1454
Beauty, Brave and Beautiful, 395
Claude Has a Picnic, **16**
Dog for a Day, 396
Friday the 13th (Kroll), 716
Harry and the Terrible Whatzit, 98
Harvey the Foolish Pig, 397
Hurray for Hattie Rabbit, 99
I Hate My Brother Harry (Dragonwagon), 663
King Wacky, 673
Mag the Magnificent, 398
Mighty Tree, **1145**
The Monster in the Third Dresser Drawer (Smith), 815
My Dog and the Birthday Mystery (Adler), 313
One, Two, Three—Ah-Choo! (Allen), 321
Poppy, the Panda, 100
The Show-and-Tell War (Smith), 816
Tiny for a Day, **273**
What's Claude Doing?, 101
Where Are Momma, Poppa, and Sister June?, **274**
Gaffney-Kessell, Walter. *Lenny Kandell, Smart Aleck* (Conford), 1290
Gag, Wanda. *The Funny Thing*, 103
Millions of Cats, 104
Tales from Grimm (Grimm), 1688
Gal, Laszlo. *The Enchanted Tapestry* (San Souci), 1589
Iduna and the Magic Apples (Mayer), 1567
Prince Ivan and the Firebird, **908**
The Spirit of the Blue Light (Mayer), **986**
Tales of the Far North (Martin), 1711

Galbraith, Richard. *Reuben Runs Away*, 106
Galdone, Paul. *The Amazing Pig*, 1457
  Anatole (Titus), 830
  Basil of Baker Street (Titus), 1249
  Cinderella, 1458
  Clarence and the Burglar (Lauber), 720
  The Complete Story of the Three Blind Mice
    (Ivimey), 151
  Edie Changes Her Mind (Johnston), 155
  The Elves and the Shoemaker (Grimm), 1491
  The Frog Prince (Grimm), 1493
  Gertrude the Goose Who Forgot (Galdone and
    Galdone), 107
  The Gingerbread Boy, 1459
  The Greedy Old Fat Man, 1460
  Hans in Luck (Grimm), 1495
  Hansel and Gretel (Grimm), 1496
  Henny Penny, 1461
  *The History of Mother Twaddle and the Marvelous
    Achievements of Her Son, Jack*, 1462
  The Hungry Fox and the Foxy Duck (Leverich),
    186
  *It Does Not Say Meow and Other Animal Riddle
    Rhymes* (De Regniers), 1791
  Jack-O'-Lantern (Barth), 1400
  King of the Cats, 1463
  The Lemonade Trick (Corbett), 1056
  The Limerick Trick (Corbett), 1057
  The Little Girl and the Big Bear (Galdone), 1455
  The Little Red Hen, 1464
  The Magic Porridge Pot, 1465
  The Monkey and the Crocodile, 1466
  The Monster and the Tailor, 1467
  Norma Lee I Don't Knock on Doors (Keller), 1839
  Old Mother Hubbard and Her Dog, 1468
  The Old Woman and Her Pig, 1469
  Oté (Belpré), 1402
  Over in the Meadow, 108
  The Owl and the Pussycat (Lear), 181
  Paul Revere's Ride (Longfellow), 1863
  The Princess and the Pea (Andersen), 322
  Puss in Boots, 1470
  Speak Up, Edie (Johnston), 440
  The Sword in the Tree (Bulla), 877
  The Table, the Donkey and the Stick (Grimm),
    1507
  The Tailypo (Galdone), 1456
  The Teeny-Tiny Woman, 1471
  That's Right, Edie (Johnston), 441
  Theodore Turtle (MacGregor), 491
  Three Aesop Fox Fables (Aesop), 1650
  The Three Bears, 1472
  The Three Billy Goats Gruff, 1473
  Three Ducks Went Wandering (Roy), 246

  The Three Little Pigs, 1474
  The Three Sillies, 1475
  What's in Fox's Sack?, 1476
  Who's in Charge of Lincoln? (Fife), 917
  Wriggles the Little Wishing Pig (Watson), 582
Gammell, Stephen. *Air Mail to the Moon*
    (Birdseye), 616
  The Day of the Blizzard (Moskin), 1098
  A Furl of Fairy Wind (Hunter), 1076
  Halloween Poems (Livingston), **1357**
  Old Black Fly (Aylesworth), **223**
  Once upon MacDonald's Farm, 401
  The Real Tom Thumb (Cross), 2011
  The Relatives Came (Rylant), 542
  Scary Stories 3 (Schwartz), **1086**
  Scary Stories to Tell in the Dark (Schwartz), 1725
  Song and Dance Man (Ackerman), 599
  Waiting to Waltz (Rylant), 1941
  Where the Buffaloes Begin (Baker), 1397
  The Wing Shop (Woodruff), **580**
Gannett, Ruth Chrisman. *My Father's Dragon*
    (Gannett), 674
Garcia, Manuel. *Cat* (Stein), 2107
Garcia, Tom. *On Top of Spaghetti* (Glazer), 679
Gardner, Beau. *Guess What?*, 110
  Have You Ever Seen . . . ?, 403
  *The Look Again . . . and Again, and Again, and
    Again Book*, 675
  The Upside Down Riddle Book (Phillips), 1901
Garland, Michael. *My Cousin Katie*, **17**
Garns, Allen. *Gonna Sing My Head Off!* (Krull),
    1344
Garrison, Barbara. *Only One* (Harshman), **280**
Gaskin, Chris. *Duckat* (Gordon), **110**
Gates, Lynn. *Celebrations* (Bauer), 2126
  This Way to Books (Bauer), 2127
Gaver, Becky. *Fast and Slow* (Ciardi), 1770
Gay, Michel. *The Chase* (Tanaka), **1032**
  The Christmas Wolf (Gay), 404
Geisert, Arthur. *Aesop & Company* (Aesop and
    Bader), **1053**
Geldart, William. *The Fairy Rebel* (Banks), 1141
George, Jean Craighead. *My Side of the
    Mountain*, 1176
George, Lindsay Barrett. *Box Turtle at Long Pond*
    (George), 2037
  Secret Places (Huck), **1330**
Geraghty, Paul. *The Hunter*, **442**
  Slobcat, **107**
Gerrard, Roy. *Rosie and the Rustlers*, **610**
Gerberg, Mort. *Geographunny*, **1295**
Gergely, Tibor. *Wheel on the Chimney* (Brown),
    631

Gerlach, Geff. *The Red Room Riddle* (Corbett), 1164

Gerrard, Roy. *Sir Francis Drake*, 2038

Gerstein, Mordicai. *Arnold of the Ducks*, 677
Follow Me!, 112
Frankenstein Moved in on the Fourth Floor (Levy), 951
William, Where Are You?, 113

Getz, Arthur. *Humphrey, the Dancing Pig*, 405

Gibbons, Gail. *From Seed to Plant*, **1148**
Wolves, **1149**

Gillman, Alec. *Take Me Out to the Ballgame* (Norworth), **521**

Gilman, Phoebe. *Once Upon a Golden Apple* (Little and De Vries), 478
Something from Nothing, **914**

Glanzman, Louis S. *Pippi Longstocking* (Lindgren), 1090
Veronica Ganz (Sachs), 1236

Glaser, Byron (jt. illus.). *Action Alphabet* (Neumeier and Glaser), 758

Glass, Andrew. *Devil's Donkey* (Brittain), 1276
Dr. Dredd's Wagon of Wonders (Brittain), 1277
The Gift (Nixon), 1099
Larger Than Life (San Souci), **1085**
Playing Sardines (Major), 741
Professor Popkin's Prodigious Polish (Brittain), **760**
Soap! Soap! Don't Forget the Soap! (Birdseye), **869**
Spooky Night (Carlson), 357
The Wish Giver (Brittain), 1278

Glasser, Judy. *Albert's Story* (Long), 487
Too Much Magic (Sterman and Sterman), 1119

Gobbato, Imero. *Tops and Bottoms* (Conger), 1427

Goble, Paul. *Buffalo Woman*, 1481
Crow Chief, **915**
Dream Wolf, **443**
Her Seven Brothers, 1482
Iktomi and the Boulder, 1483
Love Flute, **916**

Goembel, Ponder. *A Basket Full of White Eggs* (Swann), 1960

Goffe, Toni. *The Legend of Slappy Hooper* (Shepard), **1023**

Goffin, Josse. *Oh!*, **109**

Goldberg, Rube. *The Best of Rube Goldberg*, 2040

Golembe, Carla. *How Night Came from the Sea* (Gerson), **912**
Why the Sky Is Far Away (Gerson), **913**

Goode, Diane. *Diane Goode's Book of Scary Stories & Songs*, **1068**
Diane Goode's Book of Silly Stories and Songs, **1069**
Tattercoats (Steel), 1606
When I Was Young in the Mountains (Rylant), 989

Goodell, Jon. *Little Salt Lick and the Sun King* (Armstrong), **399**

Gordon, Susan Slattery. *Hide and Shriek* (Gordon), **1300**

Gorey, Edward. *The House with a Clock in Its Walls* (Bellairs), 1143
Old Possum's Book of Practical Cats (Eliot), 1795
The Shrinking of Treehorn (Heide), 1071
You Read to Me, I'll Read to You (Ciardi), 1772

Gottlieb, Dale. *I Got a Family* (Cooper), **255**

Graber, Susan. *Small Talk* (Hopkins), **1327**

Graham, Bob. *Poems for the Very Young* (Rosen), **1405**

Graham, Margaret Bloy. *Benjy and the Barking Bird*, 118
Harry by the Sea (Zion), 307
Harry the Dirty Dog (Zion), 308
It's Spring! (Minarik), 213
No Roses for Harry (Zion), 309
The Plant Sitter (Zion), 598

Graham, Mark. *Lucy Comes to Stay* (Wells), **572**
Michael and the Cats (Abercrombie), **1**
Murphy and Kate (Howard), **623**
Where's the Baby? (Paxton), **38**
Wilderness Cat (Kinsey-Warnock), **470**

Graham, Thomas. *Mr. Bear's Chair*, 119

Gramatky, Hardie. *Hercules*, 120

Grandpré, Mary. *Chin Yu Min and the Ginger Cat* (Armstrong), **588**

Grant, Leigh. *Kid Power* (Pfeffer), 1224

Grebu, Devis. *The King's Chessboard* (Birch), 1045

Green, Melinda. *Rachel's Recital*, 928

Greene, Jeffrey. *Backyard Bear* (Murphy), **515**

Greenspan, Adele Aron. *Daddies*, **114**

Greenwald, Sheila. *The Atrocious Two*, 1184
Rosy Cole Discovers America!, **711**

Greiner, Robert. *Follow My Leader* (Garfield), 1174

Gretz, Susanna. *It's Your Turn, Roger!*, 412

Griego, Tony. *The Green Gourd* (Hunter), **946**

Grifalconi, Ann. *Don't You Turn Back* (Hughes), 1830
The Midnight Fox (Byars), 1047
The Secret Soldier (McGovern), 2071
The Village of Round and Square Houses, 1485

Griffith, Gershom. *A Picture Book of Sojourner Truth* (Adler), **1096**

Grossman, Nancy. *Did You Carry the Flag Today, Charlie?* (Caudill), 643

Evan's Corner (Hill), 687

Gabrielle and Selena (Desbarats), 659

Grossman, Robert. *The 18th Emergency* (Byars), 1155

Grover, Max. *The Accidental Zucchini*, **277**

Gruenberg, Hannah Coale. *Felix's Hat* (Bancroft and Gruenberg), **70**

Guback, Georgia. *Luka's Quilt*, **278**

Gundersheimer, Karen. *What Am I? Very First Riddles* (Calmenson), **1277**

The Witch Who Was Afraid of Witches (Low), 731

Words Are Like Faces (Baer), 324

Gurche, John. *The News about Dinosaurs* (Lauber), 2062

Gurney, Eric. *Hand, Hand, Fingers, Thumb* (Perkins), 228

Guthrie, Woody. *Woody's 20 Grow Big Songs*, **1303**

Gwynne, Fred. *A Chocolate Moose for Dinner*, 1068

Pondlarker, **447**

Hack, Konrad. *Mister Wolf and Me* (Shura), 1238

Hafner, Marylin. *The Candy Witch* (Kroll), 462

Chatterbox Jamie (Cooney), **87**

Fathers, Mothers, Sisters, Brothers (Hoberman), **1314**

Happy Mother's Day (Kroll), 717

It's Christmas (Prelutsky), 1905

It's Halloween (Prelutsky), 1906

It's Thanksgiving (Prelutsky), 1908

Laugh Book (Cole and Calmenson), 1774

M & M and the Santa Secrets (Ross), 785

Rainy Rainy Saturday (Prelutsky), 1915

The Wobbly Tooth (Cooney), 374

Hague, Michael. *Aesop's Fables* (Aesop), 1642

East of the Sun and West of the Moon (Hague and Hague), 1513

The Frog Princess (Isele), 1534

The Man Who Kept House (Hague and Hague), 1514

Moments (Hopkins), 1824

Mother Goose (Mother Goose), 1884

The Rainbow Fairy Book (Lang), **1074**

Hale, Christy. *Juan Bobo and the Pig* (Pitre), **998**

Hale, James Graham. *'Round and Around* (Skofield), **188**

Haley, Gail E. *Dream Peddler*, **612**

Jack and the Bean Tree, 1515

Jack and the Fire Dragon, 1516

Puss in Boots, **933**

A Story, a Story, 1517

Hall, Melanie. *Weather* (Hopkins), **1329**

Hall, Wendell E. *Favorite Scary Stories of American Children* (Young), **1093**

Halpern, Joan. *The Carp in the Bathtub* (Cohen), 892

Halpern, Shari. *It's Pumpkin Time!* (Hall), **18**

Little Robin Redbreast (Mother Goose), **35**

Halsey, Megan. *Annabel* (Boland), **6**

Jump for Joy, **279**

Hamanaka, Sheila. *All the Colors of the Earth*, **449**

Chortles (Merriam), 1869

Class Clown (Hurwitz), 936

Class President (Hurwitz), **715**

A Poem for a Pickle (Merriam), 1870

Screen of Frogs, **934**

The Terrible Eek (Compton), **885**

Han, Oki S. *Sir Whong and the Golden Pig* (Han and Plunkett), **935**

Handelsman, J. B. *Who's That Stepping on Plymouth Rock?* (Fritz), 2035

Handville, Robert. *Lord of the Sky* (Gates), 1679

Hanson, Joan. *Can You Match This?* (Walton and Walton), **1418**

Hail to the Chief! (Burns and Burns), **1276**

Kiss a Frog! (Walton and Walton), **1419**

Snakes Alive! (Burns), 1763

What's Your Name, Again? (Walton and Walton), 1971

Hanson, Peter E. *I, Columbus; My Journal—1492–3* (Roop and Roop), **1227**

Harness, Cheryl. *Aaron's Shirt* (Gould), 117

Three Young Pilgrims, **614**

Harper, Piers. *Cabbage Moon* (Chadwick), **81**

Harris, Jennifer Beck. *Jalapeño Hal* (Harper), **615**

Harrison, Maggie. *Angels on Roller Skates*, **451**

Harrison, Ted. *The Cremation of Sam McGee* (Service), 1355

Hawkes, Kevin. *By the Light of the Halloween Moon* (Stutson), **561**

The Librarian Who Measured the Earth (Lasky), **1180**

Hayashi, Akiko. *Anna's Secret Friend* (Tsutsui), 275

Hays, Michael. *Abiyoyo* (Seeger), 548

The Gold Cadillac (Taylor), 1248

Hearn, Diane Dawson. *Dad's Dinosaur Day*, **120**

Heine, Helme. *The Most Wonderful Egg in the World*, 129

Heinrich, Bernd. *An Owl in the House*, **1158**

Hellen, Nancy. *Old MacDonald Had a Farm*, **20**

Heller, Julek. *Jack and the Beanstalk* (Garner), **910**

Heller, Linda. *Elijah's Violin and Other Jewish Fairy Tales* (Schwartz), 1728

The Magic Stove (Ginsburg), 1479

Heller, Nicholas. *An Adventure at Sea*, 685

Up the Wall, **281**

Woody, **121**

Heller, Ruth. *Animals Born Alive and Well,* **1159**

A Cache of Jewels and Other Collective Nouns,
1811

Chickens Aren't the Only Ones, **1160**

The Egyptian Cinderella (Climo), 1424

King of the Birds (Climo), 1425

King Solomon and the Bee (Renberg), **1001**

Kites Sail High, 1812

Merry-Go-Round, **1310**

The Reason for a Flower, **1161**

Up, Up and Away, **1311**

Henba, Bobbie. *Pianna* (Ray), **542**

Henderson, Dave. *Keep Ms. Sugarman in the
Fourth Grade* (Levy), **731**

Henkes, Kevin. *Bailey Goes Camping,* 131

Chrysanthemum, **282**

Jessica, 418

Julius, the Baby of the World, **283**

Margaret & Taylor, 419

Owen, **122**

Sheila Rae, the Brave, 132

A Weekend with Wendell, 420

Henriquez, Elsa. *The Magic Orange Tree and
Other Haitian Folktales* (Wolkstein), 1737

Heo, Yumi. *The Rabbit's Escape* (Han), **936**

The Rabbit's Judgment (Han), **937**

Hepworth, Cathi. *Antics!,* **1312**

Hewitt, Kathryn. *Flower Garden* (Bunting), **72**

King Midas and the Golden Touch, 1522

Lives of the Musicians (Krull), **1174**

Lives of the Writers (Krull), **1175**

The Three Sillies, 1523

Heyer, Carol. *Dinosaurs!* (Pringle), **1222**

Heyman, Ken. *Bread Bread Bread* (Morris), **1211**

Hillenbrand, Will. *Asher and the Capmakers*
(Kimmel), **635**

Traveling to Tondo (Aardema), **857**

Himler, Ronald. *The Best Town in the World*
(Baylor), 872

A Day's Work (Bunting), **592**

Eye Winker, Tom Tinker, Chin Chopper (Glazer),
1804

Fly Away Home (Bunting), **415**

Inside My Feet (Kennedy), 1318

Sadako & the Thousand Paper Cranes (Coerr),
2007

Someday a Tree (Bunting), **416**

The Wall (Bunting), 354

Himmelman, John. *Go to Sleep, Nicholas Joe*
(Sharmat), 263

Lights Out!, **453**

Talester the Lizard, 134

Hines, Anna Grossnickle. *What Joe Saw,* **123**

Hirsch, Marilyn. *Potato Pancakes All Around,* 933

The Rabbi and the Twenty-Nine Witches, 1524

Hiscock, Bruce. *The Big Rock,* 2050

The Big Tree, **1162**

Hissey, Jane. *Little Bear's Trousers,* 135

Hoban, Lillian. *Arthur's Christmas Cookies,* 425

Arthur's Great Big Valentine, 426

Arthur's Honey Bear, 136

Arthur's Loose Tooth, 427

A Baby Sister for Frances (Hoban), 137

The Balancing Girl (Rabe), 530

Bread and Jam for Frances (Hoban), 429

Caps, Hats, Socks, and Mittens (Borden), 24

The Day the Teacher Went Bananas (Howe), 142

"E" Is for Elisa (Hurwitz), **290**

Egg Thoughts and Other Frances Songs (Hoban),
1813

I'm Telling You Now (Delton), 65

Jim Meets the Thing (Cohen), 367

Jim's Dog Muffins (Cohen), 368

Just Awful (Whitney), 293

Lost in the Museum (Cohen), 369

No Good in Art (Cohen), 370

Papa's Panda (Willard), 295

Russell Sprouts (Hurwitz), 695

Starring First Grade (Cohen), 371

Hoban, Tana. *Exactly the Opposite,* **125**

Little Elephant (Ford), **15**

Look! Look! Look!, **286**

Hobson, Sally. *Chicken Little,* **940**

Hockerman, Dennis. *Sideways Stories from
Wayside School* (Sachar), 1110

Hoff, Syd. *I Saw You in the Bathtub and Other
Folk Rhymes* (Schwartz), 1947

Lengthy, 139

Syd Hoff's Animal Jokes, 1815

Syd Hoff's Joke Book, 1816

Hoffman, Felix. *The Bearskinner* (Grimm), 1486

Hoffman, Rosekrans. *Alexander the Rock-Eater*
(Van Woerkom), 1621

Creepy Crawly Critter Riddles (Bernstein and
Cohen), 1748

Jane Yolen's Mother Goose Songbook (Mother
Goose and Yolen), **1380**

The Truth about the Moon (Bess), 875

Hoffman, Sanford. *Devilish Bets to Trick Your
Friends* (Churchill), 2005

Giggles, Gags & Groaners (Rosenbloom), 1932

Knock Knock! Who's There? (Rosenbloom), 1933

The Looniest Limerick Book in the World
(Rosenbloom), 1934

Spooky Riddles and Jokes (Rosenbloom), 1937

The World's Best Sports Riddles and Jokes (Rosenbloom), 1939

Hogrogian, Nonny. *The Cat's Midsummer Jamboree* (Kherdian), 457
Cinderella (Grimm), 1488
The Devil with the Three Golden Hairs (Grimm), 1489
Feathers and Tails (Kherdian), **1073**
The Glass Mountain (Grimm), 1494
Once There Was and Was Not (Tashjian), 1731
One Fine Day, 1528

Hoguet, Susan. *I Unpacked My Grandmother's Trunk*, 689

Holder, Heidi. *Aesop's Fables* (Aesop), 1643

Holland, Janice. *The Blind Mice and the Elephant* (Quigley), 1582

Holmes, Bea. *Child of the Silent Night* (Hunter), 2053

Hom, Nancy. *Nine-in-One, Grr! Grr!* (Blia), 1404

Honeysett, Martin. *Farmer Bungle Forgets* (King-Smith), 458

Honeywood, Varnette P., and Brenda Joysmith. *Shake It to the One That You Love the Best* (Mattox), **1371**

Hong, Lily Toy. *How the Ox Star Fell from Heaven*, **942**
Two of Everything, **943**

Honore, Paul. *Tales from Silver Lands* (Finger), 1677

Hoshino, Michio. *The Grizzly Bear Family Book*, **1164**

Howe, John. *Jack and the Beanstalk*, **944**

Howell, Kathleen Collins. *Dog Days* (Rodowsky), **739**
The Singing Green (Merriam), **1373**

Howell, Troy. *The Donkey Planet* (Corbett), 1163
Favorite Greek Myths (Osborne), 1713
Mermaid Tales from Around the World (Osborne), **1082**
The Old-Fashioned Storybook (Schwartz and Archibald), 1727
Peter and the North Wind (Littedale), 1547

Howlett, Bud. *I'm New Here*, **1166**

Hsu-Flanders, Lillian. *Dumpling Soup* (Rattigan), **349**

Hubbard, Woodleigh. *C Is for Curious*, **289**
The Moles and the Mireuk (Kwon), **962**
2 Is for Dancing, **127**

Huffman, Tom. *Be a Perfect Person in Just Three Days* (Manes), 1095
The Dove Dove (Terban), 1962

Hughes, Jan. *The Alligator under the Bed* (Nixon), 218

Hughes, Shirley. *Alfie Gets in First*, 143

Alfie Gives a Hand, 144
Alfie's Feet, 145
The Big Alfie Out of Doors Storybook, **128**
Dogger, 146
An Evening at Alfie's, 147
Giving, **22**
Out and About, 1831
The Phantom Carousel and Other Ghostly Tales (Ainsworth), 1138

Hull, Richard. *The Alphabet from Z to A* (Viorst), **1416**
Sad Underwear and Other Complications (Viorst), **1417**

Humphries, Tudor. *Panda* (Allen), **584**
Tiger (Allen), **585**

Hunt, Jonathan. *Jumbo* (Blumberg), **1107**

Hurd, Clement. *The Runaway Bunny* (Brown), 29

Hurd, Thacher. *Mama Don't Allow*, 432
Wheel Away! (Dobbs), 71

Hurlimann, Ruth. *The Proud White Cat*, 1532

Hurt-Newton, Tania. *Love, Your Bear Pete* (Sheldon), **363**

Hutchins, Pat. *Clocks and More Clocks*, 433
Don't Forget the Bacon!, 434
Good-Night, Owl, 148
My Best Friend, **23**
Rosie's Walk, 149
Silly Billy!, **24**
The Tale of Thomas Mead, 697
Three-Star Billy, **130**
The Very Worst Monster, 150
Where's the Baby?, 435

Hutton, Warwick. *The Nose Tree*, 1533
The Silver Cow (Cooper), 1430

Hyman, Trina Schart. *Among the Dolls* (Sleator), 1240
The Bad Times of Irma Baumline (Brink), 1150
Cat Poems (Livingston), 1858
Christmas Poems (Livingston), 1859
Clever Cooks (Greene), 1683
The Fortune-Tellers (Alexander), **698**
Hershel and the Hanukkah Goblins (Kimmel), 944
A Hidden Magic (Vande Velde), 1251
Iron John (Grimm and Kimmel), **928**
Little Red Riding Hood (Grimm), 1501
Rapunzel (Grimm), 1503
Saint George and the Dragon (Hodges), 1526
Sing a Song of Popcorn (De Regniers), 1792
The Sleeping Beauty (Grimm), 1505
Snow White (Grimm), 1506
Star Mother's Youngest Child (Moeri), 1097
Stuck with Luck (Johnson), 938
Take It or Leave It (Molarsky), 965
The Water of Life (Grimm), 1511

Winter Poems (Rogasky), **1403**

Ingraham, Erick. *Cross-Country Cat* (Calhoun), 635
  Henry the Sailor Cat (Calhoun), **418**
  High-Wire Henry (Calhoun), **419**
Innocenti, Roberto. *The Adventures of Pinocchio* (Collodi), 1160
Iosa, Ann. *What Was the Wicked Witch's Real Name?* (Bernstein and Cohen), 1749
Ipcar, Dahlov. *I Love My Anteater with an A*, 1078
Isadora, Rachel. *Flossie & the Fox* (McKissack), 735
  Max, 436
Ito, Yoriko. *Lily and the Wooden Bowl* (Schroeder), **1021**
Ivanov, Anatoly. *Ol' Jake's Lucky Day*, 698
Izen, Marshall, and Jim West. *Why the Willow Weeps* (Izen and West), **461**

Jabar, Cynthia. *How Many, How Many, How Many* (Walton), **206**
Jacob, Murv. *How Rabbit Tricked Otter and Other Cherokee Trickster Stories* (Ross), **1084**
  How Turtle's Back Was Cracked (Ross), **1008**
Jacobi, Kathy. *The Half-a-Moon Inn* (Fleischman), 1299
Jacobson, Rick (jt. illus.). *Tchaikovsky Discovers America* (Kalman), 632
Jacques, Robin. *A Book of Witches* (Manning-Sanders), 1710
Jagr, Miroslav. *The Foolish Frog* (Seeger and Seeger), 797
Jakobsen, Kathy. *My New York*, **1167**
James, Ann. *Snakes and Ladders* (Klein), 1848
James, Betsy. *The Author and Squinty Gritt* (Williams), **575**
  I Hate Company (Petersen), **655**
  Mary Ann, **133**
James, Synthia Saint. *Snow on Snow on Snow* (Chapman), **83**
Janovitz, Marilyn. *Look Out, Bird!*, **134**
Jaques, Faith. *The Orchard Book of Nursery Rhymes* (Mother Goose and Sutherland), **1388**
Jeffers, Susan. *Brother Eagle, Sister Sky*, **628**
  Thumbelina (Andersen), 864
  Waiting for the Evening Star (Wells), **754**
  Wild Robin, 699
  The Wild Swans (Andersen), 1040
Jenkin-Pearce, Susie. *Catch It If You Can* (Thompson), **1415**
Jenkins, Jessica. *Thinking About Colors*, **462**

Jenkins, Leonard. *Mayfield Crossing* (Nelson), **784**
Jenkins, Steve. *Cock-a-Doodle-Doo!* (Robinson), **1226**
Jeschke, Susan. *Angela and Bear*, 437
  Busybody Nora (Hurwitz), 694
  Lucky's Choice, **291**
  Perfect the Pig, 438
  Superduper Teddy (Hurwitz), 696
Johnson, Crockett. *The Carrot Seed* (Krauss), 178
  Harold and the Purple Crayon, 153
  Is This You? (Krauss), 714
  Will Spring Be Early? or Will Spring Be Late?, 439
Johnson, Dolores. *Now Let Me Fly*, **629**
  What Will Mommy Do When I'm at School?, **135**
  Your Dad Was Just Like You, **463**
Johnson, Jane. *Today I Thought I'd Run Away*, 154
Johnson, John E. *I Saw a Rocket Walk a Mile* (Withers), 1735
Johnson, Larry. *The Deadly Mandrake* (Callen), 1284
Johnson, Lonni Sue. *Mother Earth's Counting Book* (Clements), **1118**
  Pickles Have Pimples (Barrett), 611
  The Story of Z (Modesitt), **511**
Johnson, Meredith. *The Sub* (Petersen), **656**
Johnson, Milton. *The Black Pearl* (O'Dell), 1338
Johnson, Pamela. *And Then There Was One* (Facklam), **1139**
  Quentin Corn (Stolz), 1365
Johnson, Paul Brett. *The Cow Who Wouldn't Come Down*, **292**
  Saint Patrick and the Peddler (Hodges), **941**
Johnson, Stephen T. *The Samurai's Daughter* (San Souci), **1014**
  The Snow Wife (San Souci), **1015**
Johnson, Steve. *The Frog Prince Continued* (Scieszka), **676**
Jonas, Ann. *Color Dance*, **136**
  Reflections, 700
  Round Trip, 701
  The 13th Clue, **464**
  Where Can It Be?, **25**
Jones, Carol. *Drummond* (Odgers), **522**
  Hickory Dickory Dock and Other Nursery Rhymes (Mother Goose and Jones), **1379**
  Old MacDonald Had a Farm, 157
  This Old Man, **137**
Jones, Dan. *The Secret Life of the Underwear Champ* (Miles), 1096
Jones, Jan Naimo. *Lady Daisy* (King-Smith), **723**
  Make a Wish, Molly (Cohen), **598**

Jordan, Jael. *My Grandmother's Stories* (Geras), **1067**

Jorgensen, David. *Wind Says Good Night* (Rydell), **42**

Joyce, William. *George Shrinks*, 444
Santa Calls, **631**
Shoes (Winthrop), 300
Waiting-for-Spring Stories (Roberts), 531

Joysmith, Brenda (jt. illus.). *Shake It to the One That You Love the Best* (Mattox), **1371**

Kagige, Francis. *The Adventures of Nanabush* (Coatsworth and Coatsworth), 1665

Kaila, Kaarina. *The Wild Swans* (Andersen and Hautzig), **700**

Kalman, Maira. *Chicken Soup Boots*, **719**
Hey Willy, See the Pyramids, 941
Max Makes a Million, **633**

Kamen, Gloria. *Charlie Chaplin*, 2057

Kamen, Gloria (jt. illus.). *Edward Lear, King of Nonsense*, **1169**

Kampen, Owen. *Danny Dunn, Time Traveler* (Williams and Abrashkin), 1256

Kandoian, Ellen. *Is Anybody Up?*, **139**
Rainy Day Rhymes (Radley), **1399**
Under the Sun, 445

Kane, Harry. *The Secret of Terror Castle* (Arthur), 1265

Kane, Henry B. *One at a Time* (McCord), 1864

Karas, G. Brian. *Cinder-Elly* (Minters), **510**
I Know an Old Lady, **295**
If You're Not Here, Please Raise Your Hand (Dakos), **1283**
I'm Telling! (Arnold and Loeb), 1988
Nobody's Mother Is in Second Grade (Pulver), **346**
Odds 'N' Ends Alvy (Frank), **441**

Karlin, Bernie. *Night Ride*, 446
What Comes in 2's, 3's & 4's? (Aker), **62**

Karlin, Nurit. *The April Rabbits* (Cleveland), 366
The Tooth Witch, 447

Kastner, Jill. *Snake Hunt*, **465**

Kasza, Keiko. *A Mother for Choco*, **140**
The Pig's Picnic, 161
The Rat and the Tiger, **141**
The Wolf's Chicken Stew, 162

Kaufman, Jeff. *Just Around the Corner* (Jacobs), **1333**

Keats, Ezra Jack. *Apt. 3*, 942
Danny Dunn and the Homework Machine (Williams and Abrashkin), 1255
Dreams, 448
Goggles!, 449
Jennie's Hat, 450

John Henry, 1538
A Letter to Amy, 451
Pet Show!, 163
Peter's Chair, 164
Regards to the Man in the Moon, 703
The Snowy Day, 165
Whistle for Willie, 166

Keller, Holly. *A Bear for Christmas*, 167
From Tadpole to Frog (Pfeffer), **1219**
Geraldine's Baby Brother, **142**
Geraldine's Blanket, 168
Goodbye, Max, 452
Grandfather's Dream, **466**
Henry's Fourth of July, **26**
Horace, **143**
Island Baby, **296**
An Octopus Is Amazing (Lauber), **1181**
Shooting Stars (Branley), **1109**

Keller, Wallace. *The Wrong Side of the Bed*, **297**

Kelley, True. *Spider on the Floor* (Raffi), **348**

Kellogg, Steven. *A My Name Is Alice* (Bayer), 334
Barney Bipple's Magic Dandelions (Chapman), 644
The Boy Who Was Followed Home (Mahy), 739
Chicken Little, 704
The Day Jimmy's Boa Ate the Wash (Noble), 761
The Day the Goose Got Loose (Lindbergh), **306**
The Great Christmas Kidnapping Caper (Van Leeuwen), 1128
The Great Quillow (Thurber), **684**
Gwot! (Mendoza), 962
How Much Is a Million? (Schwartz), 2093
How the Witch Got Alf (Annett), 868
If You Made a Million (Schwartz), 2094
Is Your Mama a Llama? (Guarino), 123
Johnny Appleseed, 2058
Mike Fink, **948**
Much Bigger than Martin, 453
The Mysterious Tadpole, 705
Parents in the Pigpen, Pigs in the Tub (Ehrlich), **266**
Pinkerton, Behave, 706
Prehistoric Pinkerton, 707
The Rattlebang Picnic (Mahy), **502**

Kells, Valerie A. *One Earth, a Multitude of Creatures* (Roop and Roop), **1228**

Kendall, Russ. *Samuel Eaton's Day* (Waters), **1250**

Kendrick, Dennis. *World's Wackiest Riddle Book* (Jones), 1833

Kennaway, Adrienne. *Awful Aardvark* (Kennaway), **144**
Baby Baboon (Mwenye Hadithi), **37**
Crafty Chameleon (Mwenye Hadithi), 124

Greedy Zebra (Mwenye Hadithi), 125
Hungry Hyena (Mwenye Hadithi), **331**
Lazy Lion (Mwenye Hadithi), **171**
Rainbow Bird (Maddern), **979**
Tricky Tortoise (Mwenye Hadithi), 126
Kent, Jack. *Easy as Pie* (Folsom and Folsom), 670
The Fat Cat, 1539
Jim Jimmy James, 454
Joey Runs Away, 169
Little Peep, 455
Kessler, Leonard. *Old Turtle's Baseball Stories*, 709
Kew, Katinka. *Little Monster* (Wade), 284
Khalsa, Dayal Kaur. *How Pizza Came to Queens*, 456
Tales of a Gambling Grandma, 1084
Kiefte, Kees de. *Yang the Youngest and His Terrible Ear* (Namioka), **781**
Kirk, Daniel. *Skateboard Monsters*, **472**
Kiuchi, Tatsuro. *The Lotus Seed* (Garland), **609**
Klein, Suzanne. *Womenfolk and Fairy Tales* (Minard), 1712
Kleven, Elisa. *Abuela* (Dorros), **434**
The Paper Princess, **146**
Knight, Hilary. *Angie* (Udry), 1017
Happy Birthday (Hopkins), **1321**
Mrs. Piggle-Wiggle (MacDonald), 1092
Never Take a Pig to Lunch (Calmenson), 1764
Side by Side (Hopkins), 1827
Knight, Hilary, and Charles Robinson. *Matt's Mitt and Fleet-Footed Florence* (Sachs), 990
Knutson, Barbara. *Sungura and Leopard*, **960**
Koch, Michelle. *World Water Watch*, **1172**
Koda, Dorothy. *Max the Great* (Heath), 1309
Koeppen, Peter. *Pedro's Journal* (Conrad), **809**
Koide, Yasuko. *May We Sleep Here Tonight?* (Koide), 172
Konigsburg, E. L. *Amy Elizabeth Explores Bloomingdale's*, **478**
From the Mixed-Up Files of Mrs. Basil E. Frankweiler, 1201
Koontz, Robin Michal. *I See Something You Don't See*, **301**
Kopper, Lisa. *Daisy Thinks She Is a Baby*, **27**
Korky, Paul. *Professor Puffendorf's Secret Potions* (Tzannes), **569**
Koshkin, Alexander. *Stolen Thunder* (Climo), **880**
Vasilissa the Beautiful (Winthrop), **1044**
Kossin, Sandy. *Me and the Weirdos* (Sutton), 1246
Kovalski, Maryann. *Alice and the Birthday Giant* (Green), 408
Doctor Knickerbocker and Other Rhymes (Booth), **1272**
I Went to the Zoo (Gelman), **275**

Pizza for Breakfast, **479**
The Wheels on the Bus, 173
Krahn, Fernando. *Laughing Time* (Smith), 1955
Nobody Stole the Pie (Levitin), 722
They've Discovered a Head in the Box for the Bread (Brewton and Blackburn), 1756
Kraus, Robert. *How Spider Saved Christmas*, 459
Phil the Ventriloquist, 176
Krementz, Jill. *A Storyteller's Story* (Martin), **1202**
Krensky, Stephen (jt. illus.). *Dinosaurs, Beware!* (Brown and Krensky), 2002
Perfect Pigs (Brown and Krensky), 2003
Krevitsky, Nik. *It Happened in Chelm* (Freedman), **905**
Krupinski, Loretta. *The Old Ladies Who Liked Cats* (Greene), **445**
Krupp, Robin Rector. *The Comet and You* (Krupp), 2060
Let's Go Traveling, **1177**
The Moon and You (Krupp), **1176**
Krush, Beth, and Joe Krush. *The Borrowers* (Norton), 1336
The Piece of Fire and Other Haitian Tales (Courlander), 1669
Krush, Joe (jt. illus.). *The Borrowers* (Norton), 1336
The Piece of Fire and Other Haitian Tales (Courlander), 1669
Kubinyi, Laslo. *The Town Cats and Other Tales* (Alexander), 1261
The Wizard in the Tree (Alexander), 1262
Kuchera, Kathleen. *The Rooster Who Went to His Uncle's Wedding* (Ada), **858**
Kudrna, C. Imbior. *To Bathe a Boa*, 463
Kuklin, Susan, and Herbert S. Terrace. *The Story of Nim, the Chimp Who Learned Language* (Michel), 2076

LaBlanc, Andre. *Snow Treasure* (McSwigan), 1330
La Fave, Kim. *The Mare's Egg* (Spray), 1604
LaMarche, Jim. *Mandy* (Booth), **408**
The Rainbabies (Melmed), **508**
Lamb, Susan Condie. *Emily and the Enchanted Frog* (Griffith), **446**
My Great Aunt Arizona (Houston), **1165**
Plunk's Dreams (Griffith), 122
Lamont, Priscilla. *Ring-a-Round-a-Rosy*, **1345**
The Troublesome Pig, 1543
Langley, Jonathan. *Rain, Rain, Go Away!* (Mother Goose and Langley), **1381**
Laroche, Giles. *The Color Box* (Dodds), **93**
Ragged Shadows (Hopkins), **1325**

Laroche, Sandra. *The Snow Rose* (Laroche), 1086

Larry, Charles. *Peboan and Seegwun*, **964**

Lasker, Joe. *The Do-Something Day*, **464**

Lattimore, Deborah Nourse. *Zekmet, the Stone Carver* (Stolz), 1244

Lauter, Richard. *The War with Grandpa* (Smith), 1115

Lavies, Bianca. *It's an Armadillo*, 2064

Lawrence, Jacob. *John Brown* (Everett), **1138**

Lawson, Robert. *Ben and Me*, 1324

  Mr. Popper's Penguins (Atwater and Atwater), 1042

  The Story of Ferdinand (Leaf), 465

Lazare, Jerry. *Home from Far* (Little), 1206

Lear, Edward. *How Pleasant to Know Mr. Lear!*, 1853

Lear, Edward, and Gloria Kamen. *Edward Lear, King of Nonsense* (Kamen), **1169**

Le Cain, Errol. *Aladdin and the Wonderful Lamp* (Lang), 1544

  Beauty and the Beast (Harris), 1520

  The Pied Piper of Hamelin (Corrin and Corrin), 1431

  Thorn Rose (Grimm), 1508

  The Three Magic Gifts (Riordan), 1586

  The Twelve Dancing Princesses (Grimm), 1509

Leder, Dora. *Don't Touch!* (Kline), 170

  SHHHH! (Kline), 171

Lee, Alan. *Black Ships Before Troy!* (Sutcliff), **1088**

  The Moon's Revenge (Aiken), 1038

Lee, Dom. *Baseball Saved Us* (Mochizuki), **733**

Lee, Jared. *One Day at School* (Luttrell), 732

  The Teacher from the Black Lagoon (Thaler), **682**

Lee, Jeanne M. *Toad Is the Uncle of Heaven*, 1546

Leedy, Loreen. *Fraction Action*, **482**

  A Number of Dragons, 182

  Postcards from Pluto, **1182**

  Tracks in the Sand, **1183**

Leigh, Nila K. *Learning to Swim in Swaziland*, **1184**

Lemieux, Michèle. *Pied Piper of Hamelin*, **966**

  What's That Noise, 184

Lent, Blair. *Baba Yaga* (Small), 1602

  The Funny Little Woman (Mosel), 1571

  Tikki Tikki Tembo (Mosel), 1572

  The Wave (Hodges), 1527

  Why the Sun and Moon Live in the Sky (Dayrell), 1435

LeSieg, Theo. *I Wish That I Had Duck Feet*, 467

Leslie-Melville, Betty. *Elephant Have the Right of Way*, **1185**

Lessac, Frané. *The Chalk Doll* (Pomerantz), 776

  The Fire Children (Maddern), **978**

  Nine O'Clock Lullaby (Singer), **554**

Lester, Alison. *The Journey Home*, **303**

Lester, Helen. *Cora Copycat*, 468

Levine, David. *The Fables of Aesop* (Aesop), 1647

Lewin, Betsy. *Somebody Catch My Homework* (Harrison), **1307**

  Yo, Hungry Wolf! (Vozar), **570**

Lewin, Ted. *Bird Watch* (Yolen), **1429**

  The Day of Ahmed's Secret (Heide and Gilliland), **616**

  The Great Pumpkin Switch (McDonald), **495**

  Peppe the Lamplighter (Bartone), **405**

  The Potato Man (McDonald), **496**

  Sami and the Time of the Troubles (Heide and Gilliland), **713**

Lewis, E. B. *Fire on the Mountain* (Kurtz), **961**

Leydenfrost, Robert. *The Snake That Sneezed*, 188

Lichtveld, Noni. *I Lost My Arrow in a Kankan Tree*, **970**

Lies, Brian. *Hamlet and the Enormous Chinese Dragon Kite*, **484**

Lilly, Charles. *Philip Hall Likes Me. I Reckon, Maybe* (Greene), 1183

  Soup and Me (Peck), 1223

Lincoln, Patricia Henderson. *An Actor's Life for Me!* (Gish and Lanes), 2039

Lindberg, Jeffrey. *A Mom by Magic* (Dillon), **767**

Lindenbaum, Pija. *Boodil My Dog*, **485**

Lionni, Leo. *Alexander and the Wind-Up Mouse*, 726

  Fish Is Fish, 474

  Frederick, 727

  Frederick's Fables, 728

  Inch by Inch, 475

  It's Mine!, 190

  Little Blue and Little Yellow, 191

  Matthew's Dream, **308**

  Swimmy, 476

  Tico and the Golden Wings, 952

  Tillie and the Wall, 477

Lippincott, Gary A. *Jennifer Murdley's Toad* (Coville), **765**

  Jeremy Thatcher, Dragon Hatcher (Coville), **810**

Lippman, Peter. *Sparrow Socks* (Selden), 799

Lisker, Sonia O. *Freckle Juice* (Blume), 618

Litzinger, Rosanne. *The Old Woman and Her Pig*, **971**

  The Treasure Trap (Masterman-Smith), 1212

Lloyd, Megan. *Baba Yaga* (Kimmel), **951**

  Cactus Hotel (Guiberson), **1155**

  The Gingerbread Doll (Tews), **565**

  The Gingerbread Man (Kimmel), **953**

  The Little Old Lady Who Was Not Afraid of Anything (Williams), 591

  More Surprises (Hopkins), 1825

There Goes the Ghost! (Sherrow), 557
Lobel, Anita. *Alison's Zinnia*, **309**
 Away from Home, **487**
 How the Rooster Saved the Day (Lobel), 192
 A New Coat for Anna (Ziefert), 597
 On Market Street (Lobel), 483
 Peter Penny's Dance (Quinn-Harken), 779
 Princess Furball (Huck), 1531
 The Rose in My Garden (Lobel), 485
 Singing Bee! (Hart), 1810
 This Quiet Lady (Zolotow), **393**
 Three Rolls and One Doughnut (Ginsburg), 1681
 A Treeful of Pigs (Lobel), 729
Lobel, Arnold. *The Book of Pigericks*, 1861
 The Devil & Mother Crump (Carey), 1049
 Fables, 1207
 Frog and Toad Are Friends, 479
 The Great Blueness and Other Predicaments, 480
 Gregory Griggs (Mother Goose), 1882
 Hildilid's Night (Ryan), 539
 The Ice Cream Cone Coot and Other Rare Birds, 954
 I'll Fix Anthony (Viorst), 574
 The Mean Old Mean Hyena (Prelutsky), 983
 Ming Lo Moves the Mountain, 481
 Mouse Tales, 482
 Nightmares (Prelutsky), 1912
 Owl at Home, 484
 The Quarreling Book (Zolotow), 861
 The Random House Book of Mother Goose (Mother Goose), 1887
 The Random House Book of Poetry for Children (Prelutsky), 1916
 The Tale of Meshka the Kvetch (Chapman), 885
 The Terrible Tiger (Prelutsky), 778
 A Three Hat Day (Geringer), 111
 Tyrannosaurus Was a Beast (Prelutsky), 1922
 Uncle Elephant, 486
 Whiskers & Rhymes, 1862
Locker, Thomas. *The First Thanksgiving* (George), **1147**
 The Ice Horse (Christiansen), **597**
 Snow Toward Evening (Frank), **1294**
 Thirteen Moons on Turtle's Back (Bruchac and London), **872**
Lofting, Hugh. *The Story of Doctor Dolittle*, 1091
Lofts, Pamela. *Koala Lou* (Fox), 389
 Wombat Stew (Vaughn), 836
Lohse, W. R. *Witches, Witches, Witches* (Hoke), 1697
Lomas Garza, Carmen. *Family Pictures / Cuadros de Familia*, **1192**
Long, Sylvia. *Alejandro's Gift* (Albert), **397**
 Fire Race (London and Pinola), **972**

Lord, John Vernon. *The Giant Jam Sandwich*, 730
Lorenz, Lee. *Cock-a-Doodle-Doo!* (Runcie), **41**
 Remember the à la Mode! (Keller), 1841
Lorraine, Walter. *Best Enemies Again* (Leverich), **639**
 Hilary and the Troublemakers (Leverich), **730**
 McBroom Tells the Truth (Fleischman), 1066
Low, Joseph. *Mice Twice*, 488
Ludwig, Warren. *The Cowboy and the Black-Eyed Pea* (Johnston), **717**
Lustig, Loretta. *Best Wishes, Amen* (Morrison), 1877
Lydecker, Laura. *Bee Tree and Other Stuff* (Peck), 1899
 Mouse in the House (Baehr), 68
Lynch, P. J. *A Bag of Moonshine* (Garner), 1678
 Catkin (Barber), **590**
 East o' the Sun and West o' the Moon (Dasent), **890**
 Melisande (Nesbit), 1218
Lyon, David. *The Biggest Truck*, 193

Ma, Wenhai. *The Painted Fan* (Singer), **748**
Macaulay, David. *Black and White*, **490**
 Help! Let Me Out (Porter), 982
MacCarthy, Patricia. *Herds of Words*, **1363**
 17 Kings and 42 Elephants (Mahy), 500
MacClain, George. *I'm Mad at You* (Cole), 1779
McClaskey, A. J. *Aesop's Fables* (Aesop), 1644
McClintock, Barbara. *Animal Fables from Aesop* (Aesop and McClintock), **1055**
McCloskey, Robert. *Blueberries for Sal*, 194
 Burt Dow, Deep-Water Man, 955
 Henry Reed's Baby-Sitting Service (Robertson), 1347
 Homer Price, 1208
 Journey Cake, Ho! (Sawyer), 1591
 Lentil, 956
 Make Way for Ducklings, 734
 Time of Wonder, 957
MacCombie, Turi. *Chocolate Dreams* (Adoff), **1259**
McCord, Kathleen Garry. *Adam Mouse's Book of Poems* (Moore), **1374**
McCormick, Dell J. *Paul Bunyan Swings His Axe*, 1709
McCue, Lisa. *Hedgehog for Breakfast* (Turner), **194**
 The Puppy Who Wanted a Boy (Thayer), 566
McCully, Emily Arnold. *The Amazing Felix*, **491**
 The April Fool (Schertle), 991
 The Christmas Gift, 195
 Fifth-Grade Magic (Gormley), 1181
 How to Eat Fried Worms (Rockwell), 1109
 Leona and Ike (Havill), **712**

Mail-Order Wings (Gormley), 1182
Mirette on the High Wire, **492**
Picnic, 196
Speak Up, Blanche!, **493**
McCurdy, Michael. *American Tall Tales* (Osborne), **1081**
    The Devils Who Learned to Be Good, 1549
McDermott, Gerald. *Aladdin and the Enchanted Lamp* (Mayer), 1565
    Anansi the Spider, 1550
    Coyote, **975**
    Daniel O'Rourke, 1551
    Raven, **976**
    The Stonecutter, 1552
    Tim O'Toole and the Wee Folk, 1553
    The Voyage of Osiris, 1554
    Zomo the Rabbit, **977**
MacDonald, Suse. *Alphabatics*, 490
    Sea Shapes, **157**
    Who Says a Dog Goes Bow-Wow? (De Zutter), **1131**
MacDonald, Suse, and Bill Oakes. *Puzzlers*, **314**
McDonnell, Flora. *I Love Animals*, **30**
McGinley-Nally, Sharon. *Pigs Will Be Pigs* (Axelrod), **403**
McGowen, Tom. *The Magician's Apprentice*, 1329
McGuire, Richard. *Night Becomes Day*, **498**
MacKain, Bonnie. *One Hundred Hungry Ants* (Pinczes), **533**
McKay, Robert A. *Grandfather's Day* (Tomey), **686**
McKie, Roy. *Bennett Cerf's Book of Riddles* (Cerf), 1766
MacLean, Robert. *Nightmare Island* (Roy), 1234
McLoughlin, Wayne. *Voices of the Wild* (London), **640**
McMillan, Bruce. *Beach Ball—Left, Right*, **158**
    Eating Fractions, **1193**
    Going on a Whale Watch, **1194**
    Mary Had a Little Lamb (Hale), **116**
    Mouse Views, **315**
    One Sun, 1865
    One, Two, One Pair!, **31**
    Play Day, **1365**
    Sense Suspense, **159**
McMurtry, Stan. *The Bunjee Venture*, 1210
McNaughton, Colin. *Anton B. Stanton and the Pirats*, 736
    Making Friends with Frankenstein, **1366**
McPhail, David. *The Bear's Toothache*, 493
    A Big Fat Enormous Lie (Sharmat), **359**
    Emma's Pet, 200
    Emma's Vacation, 201
    Fix-It, 494

Great Cat, 495
The Ice Cream Store (Lee), **1350**
Leave Herbert Alone (Whitney), 294
Lost!, **316**
The Magical Drawings of Mooney B. Finch, 737
The Mother Goose Songbook (Mother Goose and Glazer), **1387**
Pig Pig and the Magic Photo Album, 496
Pig Pig Gets a Job, **318**
Pig Pig Grows Up, 202
Pigs Aplenty, Pigs Galore!, **317**
Santa's Book of Names, **319**
Something Special, 497
Ten Cats Have Hats (Marzollo), **162**
Madden, Don. *The Wartville Wizard*, 738
Maestro, Giulio. *The Dinosaur Is the Biggest Animal That Ever Lived and Other Wrong Ideas You Thought Were True* (Simon), 2100
    The Discovery of the Americas (Maestro), **1195**
    Gray Duck Catches a Friend (Artis), 9
    I Think I Thought and Other Tricky Verbs (Terban), 1963
    In a Pickle and Other Funny Idioms (Terban), 1964
    Lambs for Dinner (Maestro and Maestro), 498
    More Halloween Howls, **1367**
    A More Perfect Union (Maestro), 2073
    A Pack of Riddles (Gerler), 1803
    Razzle-Dazzle Riddles, 1866
    Riddle City, USA! (Maestro and Maestro), **1368**
    The Riddle Zoo (Zimmerman), 1983
    A Sea Full of Sharks (Maestro), **1196**
    The Story of Money (Maestro), **1197**
    The Story of the Statue of Liberty (Maestro), 2074
    Take a Look at Snakes (Maestro), **1198**
    Too Hot to Hoot (Terban), 1965
    Tornado Alert (Branley), 1998
    Two Good Friends (Delton), 66
    A Wise Monkey Tale, 499
Mai, Vo-Dinh. *The Brocaded Slipper and Other Vietnamese Tales* (Vuong), 1733
Maitland, Antony. *Blue Fairy Book* (Alderson), 1702
    Idle Jack, 1559
Malone, Nola Langner. *King of the Playground* (Naylor), **332**
Mansell, Dom. *My Old Teddy*, **32**
Manson, Christopher. *The Marvelous Blue Mouse*, **641**
    Two Travelers, **642**
Marcellino, Fred. *Puss in Boots* (Perrault and Arthur), **997**
    The Steadfast Tin Soldier (Andersen and Seidler), **586**

Marchesi, Stephen. *With the Wind* (Damrell), **429**

Mariotti, Mario. *Hanimations*, **1199**

Maritz, Nicolaas. *Somewhere in Africa* (Mennen and Daly), **509**

Marshall, James. *The Adventures of Isabel* (Nash), **649**

All the Way Home (Segal), 253

Cinderella (Karlin), 1537

The Cut-Ups, 743

The Cut-Ups Carry On, **503**

George and Martha, 502

Goldilocks and the Three Bears, 1561

The Guest, 203

Hansel and Gretel (Grimm and Marshall), **926**

I Will Not Go to a Market Today (Allard), 316

It's So Nice to Have a Wolf around the House (Allard), 317

James Marshall's Mother Goose (Mother Goose), 1883

Lazy Stories (Wolkstein), 1736

Mary Alice, Operator Number Nine (Allen), 320

Merry Christmas, Space Case, 744

Miss Nelson Is Missing (Allard), 601

Old Mother Hubbard and Her Wonderful Dog, **980**

The Piggy in the Puddle (Pomerantz), 231

Pocketful of Nonsense, **1369**

Portly McSwine, 503

Rats on the Roof and Other Stories, **643**

Red Riding Hood, 1562

Space Case (Marshall), 742

The Stupids Die (Allard), 318

There's a Party at Mona's Tonight (Allard), 319

The Three Little Pigs, 1563

Three Up a Tree, 504

Troll Country (Marshall), 501

Wings, 745

Marshall, Janet. *Barnyard Tracks* (Duffy), **10**

Martchenko, Michael. *Pigs* (Munsch), **330**

Martin, Bill. *Polar Bear, Polar Bear, What Do You Hear?*, **160**

Martin, Jacqueline Briggs. *Bizzy Bones and the Lost Quilt*, 206

Martinez, Ed. *Too Many Tamales* (Soto), **369**

Massie, Diane Redfield. *Chameleon Was a Spy*, 960

Mathers, Petra. *Borreguita and the Coyote* (Aardema), **856**

Mrs. Merriweather's Musical Cat (Purdy), **539**

Mathews, Sally Schofer. *The Sad Night*, **1206**

Mathieu, Joe. *Dogs Don't Wear Sneakers* (Numeroff), **333**

Mathis, Melissa Bay. *The Umbrella Day* (Cooney), 57

Mavor, Salley. *Mary Had a Little Lamb* (Hale), **117**

Mayer, Mercer. *Beauty and the Beast* (Mayer), 1566

Everyone Knows What a Dragon Looks Like (Williams), 1029

The Great Brain (Fitzgerald), 1171

Liza Lou and the Yeller Belly Swamp, 748

Mrs. Beggs and the Wizard, 749

A Special Trick, 961

There's a Nightmare in My Closet, 207

There's an Alligator under My Bed, 208

There's Something in My Attic, 209

Mayo, Gretchen Will. *Big Trouble for Tricky Rabbit!*, **1078**

That Tricky Coyote!, **1079**

Meade, Holly. *Rata-Pata-Scata-Fata* (Gershator), **108**

Small Green Snake (Gray), **113**

Meddaugh, Susan. *Beast*, 210

The Best Halloween of All (Wojciechowski), **579**

Bimwili and the Zimwi (Aardema), 1379

The Hopeful Trout and Other Limericks (Ciardi), 1771

Martha Speaks, **506**

Tree of Birds, **164**

Two Ways to Count to Ten (Dee), 1436

The Witches' Supermarket, **507**

Medlock, Scott. *Extra Innings* (Hopkins), **1318**

Meisel, Paul. *The Cow Buzzed* (Zimmerman and Clemesha), **215**

I Am Really a Princess (Shields), **550**

Melnyczuk, Peter. *Red Fox* (Wallace), **1249**

Messenger, Norman. *Once Upon a Time, Though It Wasn't in Your Time, and It Wasn't in My Time, and It Wasn't in Anybody's Time. . . .* (Garner), **1065**

Michl, Reinard. *The Foundling Fox* (Korschunow), 713

Migdale, Lawrence. *Firetalking* (Polacco), **1221**

Mikolaycak, Charles. *The Rumor of Pavel and Paali* (Kismaric), 1542

Tam Lin (Yolen), **1048**

The Twelve Clever Brothers and Other Fools (Ginsburg), 1682

Mill, Eleanor. *What Mary Jo Shared* (Udry), 279

Miller, Margaret. *Can You Guess?*, **33**

Guess Who?, **165**

My Five Senses, **1207**

My Puppy Is Born (Cole), **1123**

Where Does It Go?, **166**

Where's Jenna?, **167**

Whose Hat?, 212

Whose Shoe?, **168**

Miller, Virginia. *Eat Your Dinner!*, **34**
   Squeak-a-Lot (Waddell), **52**
Miller, Warren. *Young Santa* (Greenburg), **770**
Mills, Lauren. *The Rag Coat*, **646**
   The Tsar's Promise (San Souci), **1018**
Minor, Wendall. *Mojave* (Siebert), 1000
Minter-Kemp, Claire. *Sophie's Snail* (King-Smith), 711
Miyake, Yoshi. *Ahyoka and the Talking Leaves* (Roop and Roop), **740**
   Owl Eyes (Gates), **911**
Mizamura, Kazue. *Flower Moon Snow*, 1873
   A Pair of Red Clogs (Matsuno), 747
Modell, Frank. *Goodbye Old Year, Hello New Year*, 509
   The Little Old Woman and the Hungry Cat (Polette), **999**
   One Zillion Valentines, 751
   Toby in the Country, Toby in the City (Bozzo), 25
   Tooley! Tooley!, 752
Moffatt, Judith. *Crocodile! Crocodile!* (Baumgartner), **1058**
Mohammed, Affie. *This Can't Be Happening at Macdonald Hall* (Korman), 1321
Montez, Michele. *50 Simple Things Kids Can Do to Save the Earth* (Earth Works Group), **1135**
Montgomery, Lucy. *Onion Tears* (Kidd), **772**
Montresor, Beni. *May I Bring a Friend?* (De Regniers), 69
   The Nightingale (Andersen), 1039
Moore, Cyd. *A Frog Inside My Hat* (Robinson), **1402**
Moore, Inga. *The Sorcerer's Apprentice*, **648**
Mora, Francisco X. *Listen to the Desert / Oye al Desierto* (Mora), **1209**
Morgan, Janet. *Hunky Dory Ate It* (Evans), **100**
Morgan, Pierr. *The Turnip*, 1569
Morimoto, Junko. *My Hiroshima*, **1210**
Morin, Paul. *The Dragon's Pearl* (Lawson), **965**
   The Orphan Boy (Mollel), **989**
Morozumi, Atsuko. *The Reindeer Christmas* (Price), **341**
Morrill, Leslie. *Angel in Charge* (Delton), 1061
   A Boy in the Doghouse (Duffey), **605**
   Creepy-Crawly Birthday (Howe), **456**
   Fang (Hazen), 417
   The Fright before Christmas (Howe), 935
   The Night the Monster Came (Calhoun), 880
   Nighty-Nightmare (Howe), 1194
   Scared Silly (Howe), 693
   The Winter Worm Business (Giff), 1177
Morrison, Bill. *Now You See It* (Broekel and White), 1999
   Squeeze a Sneeze, **326**

Moser, Barry. *I Am the Dog, I Am the Cat* (Hall), **448**
   Jump! (Parks and Jones), 1714
   Little Tricker the Squirrel Meets Big Double the Bear (Kesey), **634**
   The Magic Hare (Banks), **702**
   The Tinderbox (Andersen and Moser), **757**
   Tucker Pfeffercorn, **779**
Moss, Marissa. *Knick Knack Paddywack*, **327**
   Regina's Big Mistake, **328**
Most, Bernard. *Can You Find It?*, **329**
   Hippopotamus Hunt, **513**
   How Big Were the Dinosaurs?, **1212**
   Zoodles, **514**
Moutoussamy-Ashe, Jeanne. *Daddy and Me*, **1213**
Mullins, Patricia. *Crocodile Beat* (Jorgensen), 159
   Hattie and the Fox (Fox), 91
   Shoes from Grandpa (Fox), **105**
Munsinger, Lynn. *Babysitting for Benjamin* (Gregory), **276**
   Boris and the Monsters (Willoughby), 297
   Don't Call Me Names (Cole), **254**
   Ho for a Hat! (Smith), **368**
   Hugh Pine (Van de Wetering), 1127
   It Wasn't My Fault (Lester), 469
   Just a Little Bit (Tompert), **192**
   Martin by Myself (Skurzynski), 813
   Me First (Lester), **304**
   Monster's Birthday Hiccups (Mueller), **36**
   One Hungry Monster (O'Keefe), **174**
   Pookins Gets Her Way (Lester), 470
   A Porcupine Named Fluffy (Lester), 471
   Spiffen (Schwartz), 547
   Three Cheers for Tacky (Lester), **305**
   A Very Mice Joke Book (Gounaud), 1806
   A Week of Raccoons (Whelan), 589
   The Wizard, the Fairy and the Magic Chicken (Lester), 185
   A Zooful of Animals (Cole), **1282**
Murdocca, Sal. *The Bean Boy* (Bowden), 1405
Murphy, Chris. *Super-Duper Jokes* (Young), **1432**
Murphy, Jill. *Jeffrey Strangeways*, **734**
   Peace at Last, 214
Murphy, Roxane. *Twenty Tellable Tales* (MacDonald), 2175
   When the Lights Go Out (MacDonald), 2176
Myers, Bernice. *Not This Bear!*, 511
   Sidney Rella and the Glass Sneaker, 754
Myller, Rolf. *How Big Is a Foot?*, 970
   A Very Noisy Day, 755

Nacht, Merle. *Doodle Soup* (Ciardi), 1769
Nadler, Robert. *The Iron Giant* (Hughes), 1075

Narahashi, Keiko. *Do Not Feed the Table* (Lillegard), **1355**
I Have a Friend, 215
The Magic Purse (Uchida), **1037**
Who Said Red? (Serfozo), 256
Who Wants One? (Serfozo), 257
Nasta, Vincent. *Plane Song* (Siebert), **552**
Natchev, Alexi. *The Hobyahs* (San Souci), **1013**
Matreshka (Ayres), **863**
Nathaniel Willy, Scared Silly (Mathews and Robinson), **984**
Nation, Tate. *Yo, Millard Fillmore!* (Cleveland and Alvarez), **1119**
Natti, Susanna. *Dinosaurs and Beasts of Yore* (Cole), 1776
Don't Call Me Beanhead! (Wojciechowski), **695**
The Downtown Fairy Godmother (Pomerantz), 981
Frederick's Alligator (Peterson), 773
Happy Birthday, Ronald Morgan! (Giff), 406
Penelope Gets Wheels (Peterson), 774
Today Was a Terrible Day (Giff), 678
Nerlove, Miriam. *I Made a Mistake*, 756
Ness, Evaline. *Amelia Mixed the Mustard and Other Poems*, 1895
The Devil's Bridge (Scribner), 1596
Mr. Miacca, 1573
Sam, Bangs and Moonshine, 757
The Steamroller (Brown), 346
Tom Tit Tot, 1574
Neumeier, Marty, and Byron Glaser. *Action Alphabet*, 758
Nevins, Dan. *From the Horse's Mouth* (Nevins), 1896
Newfield, Frank. *Alligator Pie* (Lee), 1854
Newsom, Carol. *The Great Town and Country Bicycle Balloon Chase* (Douglass), 73
Newton, Jill. *Of Pelicans and Pussycats* (Lear), **1349**
Newton, Patricia Montgomery. *The Five Sparrows*, 1575
Old Sadie and the Christmas Bear (Naylor), 512
Nicklaus, Carol. *Konrad* (Nostlinger), 1219
The Six-Million Dollar Cucumber (Churchill), 1768
Nielsen, Kay. *Fairy Tales and the Brothers Grimm* (Grimm), 1685
Nightingale, Sandy. *A Giraffe on the Moon*, **172**
Nikly, Michelle. *The Emperor's Plum Tree*, 759
Niland, Kilmeny. *A Bellbird in a Flame Tree*, **518**
Noble, Trinka Hakes. *Apple Tree Christmas*, 973
Nolan, Dennis. *Dinosaur Dream*, **520**
An Ellis Island Christmas (Leighton), **638**
Llama Beans (Keller), 1838

Wings (Yolen), **1049**
Witch Bazooza, 762
Noll, Sally. *Jiggle Wiggle Prance*, 513
Novak, Matt. *It's About Time!* (Hopkins), **1322**
Nutt, Robert Van. *The Junior Thunder Lord* (Yep), **1046**

Oakes, Bill (jt. illus.). *Puzzlers* (MacDonald and Oakes), **314**
Ober, Carol. *How Music Came to the World* (Ober), **993**
Obligado, Lilian. *The Best Valentine in the World* (Sharmat), 807
O'Brien, Anne Sibley. *Jamaica and Brianna* (Havill), 119
The Princess and the Beggar, **994**
O'Brien, John. *Chin Music* (Schwartz), 1946
Daffy Down Dillies (Lear), **1348**
Funny You Should Ask (Terban), **1414**
Mistakes That Worked (Jones), **1168**
The One and Only Super-Duper Golly-Whopper Jim-Dandy Really-Handy Clock-Tock-Stopper (Thomas), **566**
One Big Wish (Williams), 1030
Six Sleepy Sheep (Gordon), **111**
Tom Glazer's Treasury of Songs for Children (Glazer), 1805
What His Father Did (Greene), **920**
Oechsli, Kelly. *The Dragon in the Clock Box* (Craig), 375
The Dragon's Handbooks (Rinkoff), 984
Herbie's Troubles (Chapman), 361
Offen, Hilda. *Nice Work, Little Wolf!*, **173**
Ohlsson, Ib. *The Big Yellow Balloon* (Fenton), 667
The Hodgepodge Book (Emrich), 1796
It Happened in America (Perl), **1216**
Oliver, Jenni. *January Brings the Snow* (Coleridge), 54
Olsen, Ib Spang. *Old Mother Hubbard and Her Dog* (Hellsing), 130
O'Malley, Kevin. *Cinder Edna* (Jackson), **626**
What's for Lunch? (Schindel), **185**
O'Neill, Catharine. *The Country Mail Is Coming* (Fatchen), **1289**
Ontal, Carlo. *Best Wishes* (Rylant), **1233**
Ormai, Stella. *Bet You Can!* (Cobb and Darling), 2006
Creatures (Hopkins), 1820
Ormerod, Jan. *Sunflakes* (Moore), **1375**
Orr, Chris, Martin White, and Joseph Wright. *A First Poetry Book* (Foster), 1800
Otani, June. *Ten Potatoes in a Pot and Other Counting Rhymes* (Katz), **1336**

Otto, Svend. *The Princess and the Sun, Moon and Stars* (Reuter), 1585

The Runaway Pancake (Asbjørnsen), 1394

Oubrerie, Clement. *It's Hard to Read a Map with a Beagle on Your Lap* (Singer), **1409**

The Kooken (Lebentritt and Ploetz), **481**

Please Don't Squeeze Your Boa, Noah! (Singer), **1410**

Owens, Gail. *I Had a Friend Named Peter* (Cohn), 51

I'll Tell on You (Lexai), 724

The Magic Grandfather (Williams), 1254

Witch's Sister (Naylor), 1217

Oxenbury, Helen. *Cakes and Custard* (Mother Goose), 1878

Farmer Duck (Waddell), **200**

The Great Big Enormous Turnip (Tolstoi), 1614

So Much (Cooke), **8**

The Three Little Wolves and the Big Bad Pig (Trivizas), **378**

Tiny Tim (Bennett), 1747

We're Going on a Bear Hunt (Rosen), 245

Paladino, Catherine. *Land, Sea, and Sky*, **1392**

Palagonia, Peter. *Flit, Flutter, Fly!* (Hopkins), **1319**

Palecek, Josef. *The Bremen Town Musicians* (Grimm), 1487

The Nightingale (Andersen and Lewis), **699**

Palmer, Kate Salley. *Octopus Hug* (Pringle), **178**

Palmisciano, Diane. *Jenny Archer, Author* (Conford), 898

A Job for Jenny Archer (Conford), 899

Nibble, Nibble, Jenny Archer (Conford), **600**

What's Cooking, Jenny Archer? (Conford), **601**

Panek, Dennis. *Catastrophe Cat*, 222

A Rhinoceros Wakes Me Up in the Morning (Goodspeed), 116

Splash, Splash (Sheppard), **44**

Pank, Rachel. *Under the Blackberries*, **335**

Paparone, Pamela. *Two-Legged, Four-Legged, No-Legged Rhymes* (Lewis), **1354**

Paradis, Susan. *Gloria and the Super Soaper* (Ross), 987

Parker, Nancy Winslow. *The Jacket I Wear in the Snow* (Nietzel), 217

Love from Uncle Clyde, 518

My Mom Travels a Lot (Bauer), 612

Parker, Robert Andrew. *The Dancing Skeleton* (DeFelice), 1437

Grandfather Tang's Story (Tompert), **567**

The Magic Wings (Wolkstein), 1630

Pop Corn & Ma Goodness (Preston), 529

Randolph's Dream (Mellecker), **732**

The Woman Who Fell from the Sky (Bierhorst), **868**

Parker, Tom. *A B Cedar* (Lyon), 2068

Parkin, Rex. *The Red Carpet*, 519

Parkins, David. *No Problem* (Browne), **414**

Paddy's Pot of Gold (King-Smith), **724**

Tick-Tock (Brown), **238**

Parkinson, Kathy. *The Farmer in the Dell*, 223

Parks, Gordon. *J. T.* (Wagner), 1129

Parmente, Wayne. *If Your Name Was Changed at Ellis Island* (Levine), **1186**

Parnall, Peter. *Annie and the Old One* (Miles), 1213

Cat Will Rhyme with Hat (Chapman), 1767

Everybody Needs a Rock (Baylor), 873

The Fireside Song Book of Birds and Beasts (Yolen), 1980

Parry, Marian. *The Lazies* (Ginsburg), 1680

Paterson, Diane. *Abuelita's Paradise* (Nodar), **519**

Too Many Books (Bauer), 333

Patz, Nancy. *Pumpernickel Tickel and Mean Green Cheese*, 520

Paulsen, Ruth Wright. *Dogteam* (Paulsen), **738**

The Haymeadow (Paulsen), **835**

Pearson, Tracey Campbell. *Beats Me, Claude* (Nixon), 971

The Missing Tarts (Hennessy), 133

No Dogs Allowed (Cutler), **602**

Old MacDonald Had a Farm, 226

That's the Spirit, Claude (Nixon), **650**

There's a Cow in the Road! (Lindbergh), **307**

Peck, Beth. *Dear Levi* (Woodruff), **796**

Witch-Cat (Carris), **706**

Peck, Marshall. *Pretty Polly* (King-Smith), **725**

Pedersen, Judy. *The Yellow Button* (Mazer), **505**

Peek, Merle. *Mary Wore Her Red Dress and Henry Wore His Green Sneakers*, 227

Peet, Bill. *The Ant and the Elephant*, 521

Big Bad Bruce, 766

Capyboppy, 2081

Chester the Worldly Pig, 975

Cowardly Clyde, 976

Cyrus the Unsinkable Sea Serpent, 767

Encore for Eleanor, 768

Gnats of Knotty Pine, 977

How Droofus the Dragon Lost His Head, 769

Hubert's Hair-Raising Adventure, 770

No Such Things, 978

The Spooky Tail of Prewitt Peacock, 771

The Whingdingdilly, 979

The Wump World, 980

Pels, Winslow Pinney. *Stone Soup* (McGovern), 1555

Peppé, Rodney. *The Mice Who Lived in a Shoe*, 772

Percy, Graham. *A Cup of Starshine* (Bennett), **1268**

Reynard the Fox (Hastings), **1071**

Perry, Rebecca. *Lots of Limericks* (Livingston), **1359**

Pfister, Marcus. *The Rainbow Fish*, **337**

Pienkowski, Jan. *Jim Along Josie* (Langstaff and Langstaff), 1850

Pierce, Robert. *How to Fool Your Friends* (Brown), 2000

Pilkey, Dav. *Dog Breath*, **530**

Dogzilla, **657**

Kat Kong, **658**

'Twas the Night Before Thanksgiving, **531**

When Cats Dream, **532**

Pincus, Harriet. *Tell Me a Mitzi* (Segal), 798

Pinkney, J. Brian. *The Boy and the Ghost* (San Souci), **1011**

The Dream Keeper and Other Poems (Hughes), **1332**

The Elephant's Wrestling Match (Sierra), **1025**

Happy Birthday, Martin Luther King (Marzollo), **1203**

Sukey and the Mermaid (San Souci), **1017**

Pinkney, Jerry. *The Adventures of Spider* (Arkhurst), 1654

Further Tales of Uncle Remus (Lester), **1075**

In for Winter, Out for Spring (Adoff), **1260**

John Henry (Lester), **967**

Mirandy and Brother Wind (McKissack), 958

New Shoes for Sylvia (Hurwitz), **129**

The Patchwork Quilt (Flournoy), 925

Pretend You're a Cat (Marzollo), **161**

Rabbit Makes a Monkey Out of Lion (Aardema), 1382

The Tales of Uncle Remus (Lester), 1707

The Talking Eggs (San Souci), 1590

Turtle in July (Singer), 1954

Pinkwater, Daniel. *Author's Day*, **659**

Doodle Flute, **534**

Fat Men from Space, 1103

Guys from Space, 522

The Hoboken Chicken Emergency, 1104

The Magic Moscow, 1105

Ned Feldman, Space Pirate, **660**

Three Big Hogs, 229

Tooth-Gnasher Superflash, 523

Wempires, **535**

Pinto, Ralph. *The Knee-High Man and Other Tales* (Lester), 1706

Pittman, Helena Clare. *A Grain of Rice*, 1580

Miss Hindy's Cats, **338**

Plume, Ilse. *The Hedgehog Boy* (Langston), 1545

Salt (Langton), **963**

Polacco, Patricia. *Babushka's Doll*, **176**

Chicken Sunday, **661**

Just Plain Fancy, **662**

Mrs. Katz and Tush, **663**

My Rotten Redheaded Older Brother, **536**

Pink and Say, **786**

Some Birthday!, **537**

Thunder Cake, 525

Tikvah Means Hope, **664**

Politi, Leo. *Angelo the Naughty One* (Garrett), 676

Pooley, Sarah. *A Day of Rhymes*, 1903

Porter, Pat Grant. *Jason and the Money Tree* (Levitin), 1203

Postma, Lydia. *The Twelve Dancing Princesses and Other Tales from Grimm* (Grimm), 1689

Potter, Beatrix. *The Tale of Peter Rabbit* (Potter), 528

Powers, R. M. *Runaway Slave* (McGovern), 2070

Powzyk, Joyce. *River* (Gilliland), **1152**

Poydar, Nancy. *In the Diner* (Loomis), **154**

Rachel Parker, Kindergarten Show-Off (Martin), **321**

Prater, John. *"No!" Said Joe*, **177**

Price, Christine. *Singing Tales of Africa* (Robinson), 1718

Price, Harold. *The Magic and the Sword* (Cox), 1671

Priceman, Marjorie. *A. Nonny Mouse Writes Again!* (Prelutsky), **1395**

For Laughing Out Loud (Prelutsky), **1397**

How to Make an Apple Pie and See the World, **538**

Rachel Fister's Blister (MacDonald), **312**

The Tiny, Tiny Boy and the Big, Big Cow (Van Laan), **1040**

Zin! Zin! Zin! (Moss), **512**

Primavera, Elise. *Best Witches* (Yolen), **1428**

The Giant's Apprentice (Wetterer), 1130

Moe the Dog in Tropical Paradise (Stanley), **556**

The Three Dots, **342**

Provensen, Alice, and Martin Provensen. *Aesop's Fables* (Aesop), 1645

The Glorious Flight, 2084

Provensen, Martin (jt. illus.). *Aesop's Fables* (Aesop), 1645

The Glorious Flight (Provensen and Provensen), 2084

Quackenbush, Charles. *It's Raining Cats and Dogs* (Keller), 1837

Quackenbush, Robert. *The Holiday Songbook*, 1925

Rabinowitz, Sandy. *Music of Their Hooves* (Springer), **1411**

Rackham, Arthur. *Grimm's Fairy Tales* (Grimm), 1686

Rader, Laura. *A Hippo's a Heap* (McLoughland), **1364**

Pete's Chicken (Ziefert), **392**

Radunsky, Vladimir. *The Maestro Plays* (Martin), **504**

Radunsky, Vladimir (jt. illus.). *The Riddle* (Vernon), 1622

Rae, Mary Maki. *The Farmer in the Dell*, 234

Ramsey, Marcy Dunn. *One Dog Day* (Lewis), **774**

Rand, Ted. *Barn Dance!* (Martin and Archambault), 505

The Bear That Heard Crying (Kinsey-Warnock), **468**

Can I Be Good? (Taylor), **375**

My Buddy (Osofsky), **526**

My Shadow (Stevenson), **374**

Once When I Was Scared (Pittman), 775

The Owl Who Became the Moon (London), **310**

Paul Revere's Ride (Longfellow), **1361**

Prince William (Rand), **668**

Salty Takes Off (Rand), **540**

A Snake in the House (McNulty), **500**

The Sun, the Wind and the Rain (Peters), 2082

The Walloping Window-Blind (Carryl), **596**

Water's Way (Peters), **1218**

Rankin, Laura. *The Handmade Alphabet*, **1223**

Ransome, James. *How Many Stars in the Sky?* (Hort), **288**

Red Dancing Shoes (Patrick), **175**

Sweet Clara and the Freedom Quilt (Hopkinson), **622**

Uncle Jed's Barbershop (Mitchell), **647**

Raschka, Chri. *Yo! Yes?*, **541**

Raskin, Ellen. *Piping Down the Valleys Wild* (Larrick), 1852

Shrieks at Midnight (Brewton and Brewton), 1758

Rathman, Peggy. *Bootsie Barker Bites* (Bottner), **234**

Ravilious, Robin. *The Runaway Chick*, 236

Rawlins, Donna. *Jeremy's Tail* (Ball), **227**

Ray, Deborah Kogan. *Hubknuckles* (Herman), 686

Lily and Miss Liberty (Stevens), **679**

Ray, Jane. *A Balloon for Grandad* (Gray), 121

Rayevsky, Robert. *Aesop's Fables* (Aesop), 1646

Belling the Cat and Other Aesop's Fables (Aesop and Paxton), **1056**

Bernal & Florinda (Kimmel), **720**

Mr. Cat-and-a-Half (Pevear), 1578

Our King Has Horns! (Pevear), 1579

The Talking Tree (Rayevsky), 1584

Three Sacks of Truth (Kimmel), **958**

Rayevsky, Robert, and Vladimir Radunsky. *The Riddle* (Vernon), 1622

Rayner, Mary. *Babe, the Gallant Pig* (King-Smith), 1319

Garth Pig and the Ice Cream Lady, 781

Garth Pig Steals the Show, **543**

Mr. and Mrs. Pig's Evening Out, 782

Mrs. Pig's Bulk Buy, 783

Pigs Might Fly (King-Smith), 1320

Ten Pink Piglets, **179**

Rayner, Shoo. *My First Picture Joke Book*, **1401**

Raysor, Joan. *David and the Phoenix* (Ormondroyd), 1100

Rees, Mary. *Spooky Poems* (Bennett), **1269**

Regan, Laura. *Welcome to the Green House* (Yolen), **1256**

Reid, Barbara. *Effie* (Allinson), **217**

Reisberg, Veg. *Baby Rattlesnake* (Ata and Moroney), **862**

Reiser, Lynn. *Any Kind of Dog*, **40**

Remkiewicz, Frank. *Froggy Gets Dressed* (London), **152**

Horrible Harry and the Christmas Surprise (Kline), **474**

Let's Go, Froggy (London), **153**

Song Lee in Room 2B (Kline), **476**

Rey, H. A. *Curious George*, 238

Katy-No-Pocket (Payne), 225

Rhee, Nami. *Magic Spring*, **1002**

Rice, Eve. *Oh, Lewis!*, 239

Once in a Wood (Aesop), 1648

Richards, Linda Rochester. *A Dog's Life* (Hopkins), 1822

I Am the Cat (Hopkins), 1823

Riddell, Chris. *The Trouble with Elephants*, 240

Riggio, Anita. *Beware the Brindlebeast*, **1004**

Ringgold, Faith. *Aunt Harriet's Underground Railroad in the Sky*, **670**

Tar Beach, **671**

Ritz, Karen. *Go Free or Die* (Ferris), **1141**

Taxi Cat and Huey (LeRoy), **773**

Robart, Rose. *The Cake That Mack Ate*, 241

Robbins, Ken. *Beach Days*, 242

Make Me a Peanut Butter Sandwich and a Glass of Milk, **1225**

Robinson, Charles. *All the Money in the World* (Brittain), 1152

The Brain on Quartz Mountain (Anderson), 1041

Ike and Mama and the Once-a-Year Suit (Snyder), 1004

Journey Home (Uchida), 1370

Nekomah Creek (Crew), **709**

The Night the Scarecrow Walked (Carlson), 639

True-Life Treasure Hunts (Donnelly), 2020

Robinson, Charles (jt. illus.). *Matt's Mitt and Fleet-Footed Florence* (Sachs), 990

Robinson, Lolly. *Mama Bear* (Sun), **562**

Robison, Deborah. *Bye-Bye, Old Buddy*, 532

No Elephants Allowed, 243

Roche, P. K. *Good-Bye, Arnold*, 533

Rocker, Fermin. *Project Cat* (Burchardt), 878

Rockwell, Anne. *The Gollywhopper Egg*, 534

Gray Goose and Gander (Mother Goose), 1881

Puss in Boots & Other Stories, 1720

Rodanas, Kristina. *Dragonfly's Tale*, **1005**

Rocking-Horse Land (Houseman), 690

Rogers, Jacqueline. *Monster Soup and Other Spooky Poems* (Evans), **1288**

The Not-Just-Anybody Family (Byars), 1156

Wanted . . . Mud Blossom (Byars), **763**

Rogers, Jean. *Runaway Mittens*, 244

Rogers, Kathy. *Marms in the Marmalade* (Morley), 1876

Rohmann, Eric. *Time Flies*, **350**

Rojankovsky, Feodor. *Frog Went a-Courtin'* (Langstaff), 179

Over in the Meadow (Langstaff), 180

Root, Barry. *April Bubbles Chocolate* (Hopkins), **1316**

The Araboolies of Liberty Street (Swope), 829

Chinook! (Tunnell), **688**

The Christmas Box (Wetzel), **384**

Old Devil Wind (Martin), **323**

Root, Kimberly Bulcken. *Billy Beg and His Bull* (Greene), **918**

Boots and His Brothers (Kimmel), **952**

Rosales, Melodye. *Beans on the Roof* (Byars), 879

Jackson Jones and the Puddle of Thorns (Quattlebaum), **787**

Rose, Carl. *The Blue-Nosed Witch* (Embry), 913

Rose, David. *Rosie's Birthday Present* (Moskin), 510

The Teddy Bear Tree (Dillon), 662

Rosenberry, Vera. *Witching Time* (Hopkins), 1698

Rosenthal, Marc. *Peter and the Talking Shoes* (Banks), **228**

Ross, David. *The Little Book of Big Tongue Twisters* (Curtis), 1786

Ross, Tony. *Amber Brown Is Not a Crayon* (Danziger), **603**

Earthlets (Willis), **692**

I'm Coming to Get You, 536

Meanwhile Back at the Ranch (Noble), 974

Super Dooper Jezebel, 786

Terrible Tuesday (Townson), 569

Rosselli, Colette. *I Went to the Animal Fair* (Cole), 1778

Roth, Judith Shuman. *Alfred* (Udry), 572

Roth, Roger. *The Giraffe That Walked to Paris* (Milton), **1208**

The Invisible Dog (King-Smith), **467**

The Sign Painter's Dream, **545**

Roth, Susan L. *The Great Ball Game* (Bruchac), **871**

Kanahena, 1587

Pass the Fritters, Critters (Chapman), **82**

Rothman, Michael. *Catching the Wind* (Ryder), 2088

Lizard in the Sun (Ryder), 2090

Sea Elf (Ryder), **1231**

White Bear, Ice Bear (Ryder), 2091

Winter Whale (Ryder), **1232**

Rotner, Shelley. *Changes* (Allen and Rotner), **1100**

Citybook (Rotner and Kreisler), **353**

Rounds, Glen. *Charlie Drives the Stage* (Kimmel), 943

Cross Your Fingers, Spit in Your Hat (Schwartz), 1724

Four Dollars and Fifty Cents (Kimmel), **721**

Hush Up! (Aylesworth), 323

I Know an Old Lady Who Swallowed a Fly, 537

I'm Going on a Bear Hunt (Sivulich), 267

Kickle Snifters and Other Fearsome Critters Collected from American Folklore (Schwartz), 1593

Mr. Yowder and the Train Robbers, 1232

Ol' Paul, the Mighty Logger, 1721

Old MacDonald Had a Farm, **182**

The Old Woman and the Jar of Uums (Wright), 856

The Three Billy Goats Gruff, **1009**

Three Little Pigs and the Big Bad Wolf, **1010**

Tomfoolery (Schwartz), 1949

A Twister of Twists, a Tangler of Tongues (Schwartz), 1950

Whoppers (Schwartz), 1726

Wild Pill Hickok and Other Old West Riddles (Adler), 1741

Rowe, John A. *Baby Crow*, **183**

Rowen, Amy. *Help! There's a Cat Washing in Here* (Smith), 1361

Rubel, Nicole. *Batty Riddles* (Hall and Eisenberg), **1304**

Greedy Greeny (Gantos), 109

Rotten Ralph (Gantos), 402

Ruff, Donna. *"Leave That Cricket Be, Alan Lee"* (Porte), **340**

Ruffins, Reynold. *Misoso* (Aardema), **1052**
Take Warning! (Sarnoff), 1723

Russell, Lynne. *Api and the Boy Stranger* (Roddy), **1006**

Russo, Marisabina. *Alex Is My Friend*, **354**
The Big Fat Worm (Van Laan), 282
I Don't Want to Go Back to School, **355**
It Begins with an A (Calmenson), **74**
The Line Up Book, 247
Only Six More Days, 248
Trade-In Mother, **184**
Waiting for Hannah, 538
When Summer Ends (Fowler), 90

Russo, Susan. *Eats* (Adoff), 1742
The Ice Cream Ocean and Other Delectable Poems of the Sea (Russo), 1940

Ryan, Susannah. *Darcy and Gran Don't Like Babies* (Cutler), **259**
What's Missing? (Yektai), 303
What's Silly? (Yektai), 304

Ryden, Hope. *Wild Animals of America ABC*, 2087

Sabuda, Robert. *Earth Verses and Water Rhymes* (Lewis), **1352**
Log of Christopher Columbus (Columbus and Lowe), **1124**

Sadowski, Wiktor. *Grandma Essie's Covered Wagon* (Williams), **691**

Saether, Haakon. *North of Danger* (Fife), 1296

Safarewicz, Evie. *Chinye* (Onyefulu), **995**

Sage, Alison. *Teddy Bears Cure a Cold* (Gretz), 413

Salter, Safaya. *Aesop's Fables* (Aesop and Gatti), **1054**

Samton, Sheila. *Beside the Bay* (Samton), 250
Meet Jack Appleknocker (Sundgaard), 272

Samuels, Barbara. *Duncan & Dolores*, 251

Sanderson, Ruth. *Good Dog Poems* (Cole), 1777
Into the Dream (Sleator), 1359
The Poetry of Horses (Cole), 1782
The Twelve Dancing Princesses (Grimm and Sanderson), **930**

Sandin, Joan. *From Anna* (Little), **775**
Hill of Fire (Lewis), 723
A Year in the Life of Rosie Bernard (Brenner), 1149

Sankey, Tom. *Cat's Cradle, Owl's Eyes* (Gryski), 2044

San Souci, Daniel. *Sootface* (San Souci), **1016**
Vassilisa the Wise (Sherman), 1598

Sauber, Robert. *Gray Fox* (London), **489**
I-Know-Not-What, I-Know-Not-Where (Kimmel), **955**
The Swan Maiden (Pyle), **665**

Savage, Steele. *Stories of Gods and Heroes* (Benson), 1656

Say, Allen. *The Bicycle Man*, 791
The Boy of the Three Year Nap (Snyder), 1603
El Chino, **1234**
Grandfather's Journey, **674**
How My Parents Learned to Eat (Friedman), 672
Once Under the Cherry Blossom Tree, 1592
Tree of Cranes, **547**

Sayles, Elizabeth. *Dribbles* (Heckert), **452**

Scarry, Richard. *Richard Scarry's Best Mother Goose Ever* (Mother Goose), 1889

Schachner, Judith Byron. *The Prince of the Pond* (Napoli), **782**

Schaffer, Amanda. *How Now, Brown Cow?* (Schertle), **1406**

Schatell, Brian. *Farmer Goff and His Turkey Sam*, 543

Scheffler, Alex. *A Squash and a Squeeze* (Donaldson), **264**

Schick, Joel. *The Gobble-Uns'll Git You Ef You Don't Watch Out* (Riley), 1108
My Robot Buddy (Slote), 1002
Wayside School Is Falling Down (Sachar), 1111
The Week Mom Unplugged the TVs (Phelan), 1102

Schindelman, Joseph. *Charlie and the Chocolate Factory* (Dahl), 1058

Schindler, S. D. *Big Pumpkin* (Silverman), **364**
Catwings (Le Guin), 950
Children of Christmas (Rylant), 1349
Don't Fidget a Feather! (Silverman), **365**
The Earth Is Painted Green (Brenner), **1274**
Favorite Fairy Tales Told around the World (Haviland), 1694
Fish Fry (Saunders), 790
Is This a House for Hermit Crab? (McDonald), 313
Not the Piano, Mrs. Medley! (Levine), **483**
Oh, What a Thanksgiving! (Kroll), 718
Those Amazing Ants (Demuth), **1130**
The Three Little Pigs and the Fox (Hooks), 1530

Schmidt, Karen Lee. *Hannah the Hippo's No Mud Day* (Hiskey), **124**
A Nickel Buys a Rhyme (Benjamin), **1267**
Pups Speak Up (Meltzer), **324**
The Twelve Days of Summer (O'Donnell), **523**
You Be Good & I'll Be Night (Merriam), 1871

Schneider, Howie. *Amos* (Seligson and Schneider), 549

Amos Camps Out (Seligson), **549**
Blumpoe the Grumpoe Meets Arnold the Cat
  (Okimoto), **525**
Uncle Lester's Hat, **357**
Schoenherr, Ian (jt. illus.). *The Fallen Spaceman*
  (Harding), 1070
Schoenherr, John. *Gentle Ben* (Morey), 1332
  Julie of the Wolves (George), 1304
  Owl Moon (Yolen), 857
  Rascal (North), 2079
Schoenherr, John, and Ian Schoenherr. *The*
  Fallen Spaceman (Harding), 1070
Schroeder, Binette. *The Frog Prince* (Grimm and
  Lewis), **932**
Schuett, Stacey. *If You Want to Find Golden*
  (Spinelli), **370**
  I'll See You in My Dreams (Jukes), **718**
  When Spring Comes (Kinsey-Warnock), **469**
Schumacher, Claire. *Snow Magic* (Ziefert), 306
Schwartz, Amy. *Annabelle Swift, Kindergartner*,
  794
  Bea and Mr. Jones, 795
  Because of Loza Brown (King), 710
  Her Majesty, Aunt Essie, 796
  How I Captured a Dinosaur (Schwartz), 546
  The Lady Who Put Salt in Her Coffee, **742**, 930
  Maggie Doesn't Want to Move (O'Donnell), 515
  Magic Carpet (Brisson), **411**
  Mother Goose's Little Misfortunes (Mother
    Goose, Marcus, and Schwartz), **1383**
  The Night Flight (Ryder), 540
  Oma and Bobo, 545
  The Purple Coat (Hest), 422
  A Teeny Tiny Baby, **358**
  Yossel Zissel & the Wisdom of Chelm, 992
Schwartz, Carol. *Sea Squares* (Hulme), **624**
Schwarz, Jill Karla. *Best Loved Folktales of the*
  World (Cole), 1666
  The Monster That Grew Small (Grant), 1484
Schweninger, Ann. *Thump and Plunk* (Udry), 277
Scott, Sally. *The Magic Horse*, 1594
  The Three Wonderful Beggars, 1595
Scott, Steve. *Splish Splash* (Graham), **1301**
Seely, Laura L. *The Four-Legged Ghosts*
  (Hoffman), **620**
Seltzer, Isadore. *The Man Who Tricked a Ghost*
  (Yep), **1047**
Seltzer, Meyer. *Riddles to Tell Your Cat* (Levine),
  1351
Selznick, Brian. *The Houdini Box*, **745**
Sendak, Maurice. *Alligators All Around*, 550
  The Big Green Book (Graves), 680
  Chicken Soup with Rice, 551
  Hurry Home, Candy (DeJong), 1060

I Saw Esau (Opie and Opie), **1391**
  The Juniper Tree (Grimm), 1687
  Mr. Rabbit and the Lovely Present (Zolotow), 310
  One Was Johnny, 254
  Pierre, 552
  What Do You Say, Dear? (Joslin), 702
  The Wheel on the School (DeJong), 1168
  Where the Wild Things Are, 255
Seredy, Kate. *Caddie Woodlawn* (Brink), 1151
Servello, Joe. *Trouble in Bugland* (Kotzwinkle),
  1322
Seuling, Barbara. *The Last Cow on the White*
  House Lawn & Other Little-Known Facts about
  the Presidency, 2096
  The Triplets, 800
  You Can't Eat Peanuts in Church, 2097
Seuss, Dr. *Bartholomew and the Oobleck*, 994
  The Cat in the Hat, 258
  Dr. Seuss' ABC, 553
  The 500 Hats of Bartholomew Cubbins, 995
  Green Eggs and Ham, 259
  Horton Hatches the Egg, 801
  How the Grinch Stole Christmas, 802
  If I Ran the Zoo, 803
  The King's Stilts, 996
  The Lorax, 997
  McElligot's Pool, 804
  Marvin K. Mooney, Will You Please Go Now, 554
  On Beyond Zebra, 805
  Thidwick, the Big-Hearted Moose, 806
Sewall, Marcia. *Captain Snap and the Children of*
  Vinegar Lane (Schotter), 793
  Come Again in the Spring (Kennedy), 1080
  Finzel the Farsighted (Fleischman), 1065
  The Leprechaun's Story (Kennedy), 1081
  Master of All Masters, 1597
  The Pilgrims of Plimoth, 2098
  The Rise and Fall of Ben Gizzard (Kennedy),
    1083
  Sable (Hesse), **714**
  Saying Good-Bye to Grandma (Thomas), **683**
  The Squire's Bride (Asbjørnsen), 1395
  Stone Fox (Gardiner), 1067
Sewell, Helen. *The Bears on Hemlock Mountain*
  (Dalgliesh), 657
Shachat, Andrew. *Stop That Pickle!* (Armour),
  218
  You Can't Catch Me! (Oppenheim), 516
Shannon, David. *The Boy Who Lived with the*
  Seals (Martin), **982**
  Encounter (Yolen), **756**
  Gawain and the Green Knight (Shannon), **1022**
  How Many Spots Does a Leopard Have? (Lester),
    1705

The Rough-Face Girl (Martin), **983**

Sharratt, Nick. *My Mom and Dad Make Me Laugh*, **186**

Shaw, Alison. *Until I Saw the Sea*, **1408**

Shaw, Charles G. *It Looked Like Spilt Milk*, 264

Shecter, Ben. *Merrily Comes Our Harvest In* (Hopkins), **1323**

Shed, Greg. *Casey Over There* (Rabin), **666**

Shefts, Joelle. *The Dancing Cats of Applesap* (Lisle), 1205

Shelley, John. *The Secret in the Matchbook* (Willis), 593

Shenon, Mike. *Burgoo Stew* (Patron), **527**
Mule Eggs (DeFelice), **604**

Shepard, Ernest H. *Now We Are Six* (Milne), 1872
The Wind in the Willows (Grahame), 1305
Winnie-the-Pooh (Milne), 964

Shepherd, Roni. *The Match Between the Winds* (Climo), **879**

Shetterly, Robert. *Raven's Light* (Shetterly), **1024**

Shiffman, Lena. *Keeping a Christmas Secret* (Naylor), 216

Shine, Andrea. *Danger at the Breaker* (Welch), **753**

Shortall, Leonard. *The Boy Who Would Not Say His Name* (Vreeken), 576
The Bully of Barkham Street (Stolz), 1120
Encyclopedia Brown, Boy Detective (Sobol), 1116
The Remarkable Ramsey (Rinkoff), 985

Shulevitz, Uri. *The Fool of the World and His Flying Ship* (Ransome), 1583
The Lost Kingdom of Karnica (Kennedy), 1082
The Treasure, 999

Shute, Linda. *Clever Tom and the Leprechaun*, 1599
Halloween Party, **551**
Jeremy Bean's St. Patrick's Day (Schertle), 544
Katy's First Haircut (Davis), 63
Momotaro the Peach Boy, 1600

Siebel, Fritz. *Amelia Bedelia* (Parish), 764
Tell Me Some More (Bonsall), 23
Who Took the Farmer's Hat? (Nodset), 219

Silverstein, Shel. *A Giraffe and a Half*, 811
The Giving Tree, 1001
Where the Sidewalk Ends, 1952
Who Wants a Cheap Rhinoceros?, 812

Simmie, Anne. *Auntie's Knitting a Baby* (Simmie), 1953

Simont, Marc. *The American Riddle Book* (Withers and Benet), 1978
Chasing after Annie (Sharmat), 998
The Contests at Cowlick (Kennedy), 708

How to Dig a Hole to the Other Side of the World (McNulty), 2072
Nate the Great (Sharmat), 810
No More Monsters for Me (Parish), 517
The Rainbow Book of American Folk Tales and Legends (Leach), 1703
Ten Copycats in a Boat and Other Riddles (Schwartz), 1948
Top Secret (Gardiner), 1303
A Tree Is Nice (Udry), 278

Sims, Blanche. *Mary Marony and the Snake* (Kline), **475**
Matthew Jackson Meets the Wall (Giff), **611**
Renata, Whizbrain and the Ghost (Cohen), 894
Show Time at the Polk Street School (Giff), **1151**

Sis, Peter. *The Dragons Are Singing Tonight* (Prelutsky), **1396**
Follow the Dream, **1238**
The Ghost in the Noonday Sun (Fleischman), 1301
Higgledy-Piggledy (Livingston), 953
More Stories to Solve (Shannon), **1087**
Stories to Solve (Shannon), 1729
The Whipping Boy (Fleischman), 1172

Skurzynski, Gloria. *Here Comes the Mail*, **1240**

Slavin, Bill. *The Cat Came Back*, **555**
How the Second Grade Got $8,205.50 to Visit the Statue of Liberty (Zimelman), **583**
Sitting on the Farm (King), **145**
Too Many Chickens (Bourgeois), **235**

Sloat, Robert, and Teri Sloat. *The Hungry Giant of the Tundra* (Sloat), **1027**

Sloat, Teri. *When I'm Hungry* (Howard), **126**

Sloat, Teri (jt. illus.). *The Hungry Giant of the Tundra*, **1027**

Slobodkin, Florence. *Too Many Mittens*, 268

Slobodkin, Louis. *The Hundred Dresses* (Estes), 914
Many Moons (Thurber), 1015
The Spaceship under the Apple Tree, 1113
Upside-Down Town (Andrews), 866

Slobodkina, Esphyr. *Caps for Sale*, 269

Small, David. *Anna and the Seven Swans* (Silverman), 1601
The Christmas Box (Merriam), 507
Imogene's Antlers, 558
The King Has Horse's Ears (Thomson), 1613
Paper John, 814
Petey's Bedtime Story (Cleary), **253**

Small, Terry. *The Legend of William Tell*, **1028**

Smath, Jerry. *A Hat So Simple*, **367**

Smee, Nicola. *The Tusk Fairy*, **45**

Smith, Cat Bowman. *Chester the Out-of-Work Dog* (Singer), **366**

Great Rabbit and the Long-Tailed Wildcat (Gregg), **921**

Max Malone Makes a Million (Herman), **617**

The Stinky Sneakers Contest (Peters), **654**

Smith, Craig. *Goodness Gracious!* (Cummings), **90**

Smith, J. Gerard. *Popcorn Park Zoo* (Pfeffer), **1220**

Smith, Jos. A. *The Adventures of King Midas* (Banks), **758**

Chipmunk! (Haas), **115**

Step by Step (Wolkstein), **211**

Smith, Lane. *Halloween ABC* (Merriam), **1372**

Knights of the Kitchen Table (Scieszka), **743**

The Stinky Cheese Man and Other Fairly Stupid Tales (Scieszka), **677**

The True Story of the 3 Little Pigs (Scieszka), 993

Your Mother Was a Neanderthal (Scieszka), **790**

Smith, Roger. *The Trickster's Handbook* (Eldin), **1136**

Smith, Stephen John. *Shy Vi* (Lewison), **151**

Smith, Wendy. *A Witch Got on at Paddington Station* (Sheldon), 265

Sneed, Brad. *The Legend of the Cranberry* (Greene), **919**

When the Fly Flew In (Peters), **336**

So, Meilo. *Wishbones* (Wilson), **1043**

Sokol, Bill. *Alvin's Swap Shop* (Hicks), 1187

Solbert, Ronni. *The Pushcart War* (Merrill), 1331

Soman, David. *The Key into Winter* (Andersen), **587**

Sopko, Eugen. *The Miller, His Son and Their Donkey* (Aesop), 1387

Speidel, Sandra. *Coyote and the Magic Words* (Root), **351**

Wind in the Long Grass (Higginson), **1313**

Sperry, Armstrong. *Call It Courage*, 1242

Spier, Peter. *Bored, Nothing to Do*, 817

Oh, Were They Ever Happy!, 559

Spirin, Gennady. *Boots & the Glass Mountain* (Martin), **981**

The Frog Princess (Lewis), **969**

Rumpelstiltskin (Grimm and Sage), **922**

The White Cat (San Souci), **1019**

Spowart, Robin. *Sometimes I Feel Like a Mouse* (Modesitt), **169**

Songs from Mother Goose (Mother Goose), 1890

Vegetable Soup (Modesitt), **170**

Springett, Martin. *The Wise Old Woman* (Uchida), **1038**

Spurll, Barbara. *The Flying Tortoise* (Mollel), **987**

Rhinos for Lunch and Elephants for Supper! (Mollel), **991**

Stadler, John. *Animal Cafe*, 819

Cat Is Back at Bat, **372**

Stammen, Jo Ellen McAllister. *Wild Fox* (Mason), **1205**

Stanley, Diane. *Bard of Avon*, **1241**

Charles Dickens, **1242**

Fortune, 1117

The Last Princess (Stanley), **1243**

The Month Brothers (Marshak), 1560

Petrosinella (Basile), 1401

Sleeping Ugly (Yolen), 1033

Steele, Mark. *A Bundle of Beasts* (Hooper), 1817

Steig, William. *Abel's Island*, 1364

The Amazing Bone, 1006

Brave Irene, 820

Caleb and Kate, 1118

CDB, 1959

Dr. DeSoto, 1007

Solomon the Rusty Nail, 1008

Spinky Sulks, 1009

Sylvester and the Magic Pebble, 821

Zeke Pippin, **678**

Stein, Alex. *Trapped on the Golden Flyer* (Fleming), 1173

Steptoe, John. *Mufaro's Beautiful Daughters*, 1607

Stevie, 1010

The Story of Jumping Mouse, 1608

Stern, Simon. *The Hobyas*, 1609

Vasily and the Dragon, 1610

Sterrett, Jane. *Secret in a Sealed Bottle* (Epstein and Epstein), 2022

Stevens, Janet. *Anansi and the Moss-Covered Rock* (Kimmel), 1541

Anansi and the Talking Melon (Kimmel), **949**

Anansi Goes Fishing (Kimmel), **950**

Callooh! Callay! (Livingston), 1857

Coyote Steals the Blanket, **1029**

From Pictures to Words, **1244**

Goldilocks and the Three Bears, 1611

The House That Jack Built, 271

It's Perfectly True (Andersen), 602

Nanny Goat and the Seven Little Kids (Grimm and Kimmel), **924**

The Quangle Wangle's Hat (Lear), 466

Tops & Bottoms, **1030**

The Tortoise and the Hare (Aesop), 1388

The Weighty Word Book (Levitt, Burger, and Guralnick), 1326

Stevenson, Harvey. *Good Books, Good Times!* (Hopkins), **1320**

Stevenson, James. *The Baby Uggs Are Hatching* (Prelutsky), 1904

Brrr!, **373**

Clams Can't Sing, 560

Could Be Worse, 822

Cully Cully and the Bear (Gage), 399

Don't You Know There's a War On?, **1245**
Grandaddy's Place (Griffith), 682
Happy Valentine's Day, Emma!, 823
How Do You Get a Horse Out of the Bathtub?
 (Phillips), 1900
Loop the Loop (Dugan), **608**
Monty, 561
The Mud Flat Olympics, **557**
The New Kid on the Block (Prelutsky), 1911
Rolling Rose, **46**
Something Big Has Been Here (Prelutsky), **1398**
That Dreadful Day, 1011
That Terrible Halloween Night, 824
That's Exactly the Way It Wasn't, **558**
There's Nothing to Do!, 825
263 Brain Busters (Phillips), 2083
What's Under My Bed?, 826
Worse Than the Worst, **560**
Worse Than Willy!, 827
The Worst Person's Christmas, **559**
Yuck!, 562
Stevenson, Peter. *Raging Robots and Unruly
 Uncles* (Mahy), **777**
Stevenson, Suçie. *Oonga Boonga* (Wishinsky),
 209
Stickland, Paul. *Dinosaur Roar!* (Stickland), **189**
Stobbs, William. *The Whole World Storybook*
 (Crouch), 1673
Stock, Catherine. *Posy* (Pomerantz), 232
 Something Is Going to Happen (Zolotow), 311
 Tap-Tap (Williams), **576**
 That New Pet! (Ferguson), 386
Stone, Helen. *Little Witch* (Bennett), 874
Stott, Dorothy. *Too Much*, **47**
Street, Janet. *Animal Fare* (Yolen), **1427**
 The Gingham Dog and the Calico Cat (Field), **103**
 Raining Cats and Dogs (Yolen), **1430**
Strogart, Alexander. *Maxie, Rosie, and Earl—
 Partners in Grime* (Park), **736**
Stroud, Virginia A. *Doesn't Fall Off His Horse*,
 680
Strugnell, Ann. *Into the Painted Bear Lair*
 (Stearns), 1243
 North American Legends (Haviland), 1695
 The Stories Julian Tells (Cameron), 881
Suares, Jean-Claude. *The Nutty Joke Book*
 (Keller), 1840
Suba, Susanna. *A Rocket in My Pocket* (Withers),
 1977
 Seven True Dog Stories (Davidson), 2015
Sullivan, Barbara. *Marvin Redpost* (Sachar), **672**
Sutcliffe, Justin. *Rosie* (Calmenson), **1116**
Swan, Susan. *Chester* (Shura), 1112
Swanson, Karl. *Homebody* (McDonald), **494**

Sweat, Lynn. *The Family Storytelling Handbook*
 (Pellowski), 2177
 The Story Vine (Pellowski), 2178
Sweet, Melissa. *Blast Off!* (Hopkins), **1317**
 Fiddle-I-Fee, **190**
 Pinky and Rex and the Spelling Bee (Howe), **457**
 The Talking Pot (Haviland), **939**
Szekeres, Cyndy. *Walter the Lazy Moose* (Flack),
 668
Szilagyi, Mary. *Night in the Country* (Rylant),
 541

Taback, Simms. *Buggy Riddles* (Hall and
 Eisenberg), 1809
 Snakey Riddles (Hall and Eisenberg), **1305**
 Spacey Riddles (Hall and Eisenberg), **1306**
 Too Much Noise (McGovern), 1556
Tafuri, Nancy. *If I Had a Paka* (Pomerantz), 1902
Tait, Douglas. *Mouse Woman and the Mischief-
 Makers* (Harris), 1691
 The Trouble with Adventurers (Harris), 1692
Talbott, Hudson. *We're Back!*, 1013
Talon, Robert. *Zoophabets*, 1014
Taylor, Harriet Peck. *Coyote Places the Stars*, **1033**
Teague, Mark. *The Field Beyond the Outfield*, **376**
 Frog Medicine, **681**
 Moog-Moog, Space Barber, **563**
 No Moon, No Milk (Babcock), **225**
 Pigsty, **564**
Tejima, Keizaburo. *Fox's Dream*, 565
Temple, Frances. *Tiger Soup*, **1034**
Tennent, Julie. *The Three and Many Wishes of
 Jason Reid* (Hutchins), 1077
Terrace, Herbert S. (jt. illus.). *The Story of Nim,
 the Chimp Who Learned Language* (Michel),
 2076
Thaler, Mike. *The Chocolate Marshmelephant
 Sundae*, 1966
Thompson, Karmen. *Meet the Orchestra* (Hayes),
 1157
Thornhill, Jan. *Crow & Fox and Other Animal
 Legends*, **1089**
Thornton, Peter J. *The Birthday Door* (Merriam),
 750
 Everybody Cooks Rice (Dooley), **433**
 A Natural Man (Sanfield), 1588
Tiegreen, Alan. *The Eentsy, Weentsy Spider* (Cole
 and Calmenson), **1279**
 Ramona Quimby, Age 8 (Cleary), 889
 Six Sick Sheep (Cole and Calmenson), **1280**
 Why Did the Chicken Cross the Road? (Cole and
 Calmenson), **1281**
Tinkelman, Murray. *Dinosaurs* (Hopkins), 1821

Titherington, Jeanne. *It's Snowing! It's Snowing!* (Prelutsky), 1907
A Place for Ben, 274
Tomei, Lorna. *What Do You Do When Your Mouth Won't Open?* (Pfeffer), 1344
Tomes, Margot. *And Then What Happened, Paul Revere?* (Fritz), 2029
Clever Gretchen and Other Forgotten Folktales (Lurie), 1708
Everything Glistens and Everything Sings (Zolotow), 1984
Jack and the Wonder Beans (Still), 1612
Little Sister and the Month Brothers (De Regniers), 1445
Phoebe and the General (Griffin), 2042
A Song I Sang to You (Livingston), 1860
Stone Soup (Stewig), **1031**
This Time, Tempe Wick? (Gauch), 926
What's the Big Idea, Ben Franklin? (Fritz), 2033
Where Do You Think You're Going, Christopher Columbus? (Fritz), 2034
The Witch's Hat (Johnston), 156
Trapani, Iza. *The Itsy Bitsy Spider*, **193**
Tripp, Wallace. *Casey at the Bat* (Thayer), 1368
Granfa' Grig Had a Pig (Mother Goose), 1880
A Great Big Ugly Man Came Up and Tied His Horse to Me, 1967
Headlines (Hall), 932
Mole and Troll Trim the Tree (Johnston), 442
My Uncle Podger, 1123
"Stand Back," Said the Elephant, "I'm Going to Sneeze!" (Thomas), 568
Trivas, Irene. *Annie . . . Anya*, **377**
Emma's Christmas, **687**
The Pain and the Great One (Blume), 619
Potluck (Shelby), **362**
Waiting for Jennifer (Galbraith), 400
What to Do About Pollution (Shelby), **1236**
The Wonderful Shrinking Shirt (Anderson), 604
Troughton, Joanna. *How the Birds Changed Their Feathers*, 1616
Mouse-Deer's Market, 1617
Raven the Trickster (Robinson), 1719
Tortoise's Dream, 1618
Truesdale, Sue. *And the Green Grass Grew All Around* (Schwartz), **1407**
Dabble Duck (Ellis), 382
Wild Willie and King Kyle Detectives (Joosse), **630**
Tryon, Leslie. *Dear Peter Rabbit* (Ada), **395**
Tseng, Jean, and Mou-Sien Tseng. *The Ghost Fox* (Yep), **755**
The Seven Chinese Brothers (Mahy), 1558
Three Strong Women (Stamm), 1605

Why Ducks Sleep on One Leg (Garland), **909**
Tseng, Mou-Sien (jt. illus.). *The Ghost Fox* (Yep), **755**
The Seven Chinese Brothers (Mahy), 1558
Three Strong Women (Stamm), 1605
Why Ducks Sleep on One Leg (Garland), **909**
Tucker, Sian. *The Shapes Game* (Rogers), **181**
Turkle, Brinton. *The Adventures of Obadiah*, 834
The Boy Who Didn't Believe in Spring (Clifton), 650
Deep in the Forest, 570
Do Not Open, 1016
If You Lived in Colonial Times (McGovern), 2069
Turner, Gwenda. *Over on the Farm*, **195**
Turska, Krystyna. *The Magician of Cracow*, 1619
Tusa, Tricia. *The Family Reunion*, **568**
Tyler, Linda Wagner. *Waiting for Mom*, 276
Tyrrell, Robert A. *Hummingbirds* (Tyrrell), **1248**

Ueno, Noriko. *Elephant Buttons*, 280
Ungerer, Tomi. *The Beast of Monsieur Racine*, 1018
Beastly Boys and Ghastly Girls (Cole), 1775
Crictor, 573
Flat Stanley (Brown), 624
Frances Face-Maker (Cole), 53
The Great Song Book (John), 1832
Mr. Tall and Mr. Small (Brenner), 343
One, Two, Where's My Shoe?, 281
Urbanowich, Evelyn. *Myths and Enchantment Tales* (Price), 1716
Ursell, Martin. *The Wolf and the Seven Little Kids* (Grimm), 1512

Vagin, Vladimir (jt. illus.). *Dear Brother* (Asch and Vagin), **401**
Vainio, Pirkko. *Josie Smith at School* (Nabb), **516**
Vaïs, Alain. *Puss in Boots* (Kirstein), **959**
Van Allsburg, Chris. *The Garden of Abdul Gasazi*, 1019
Jumanji, 1020
The Mysteries of Harris Burdick, 1250
The Polar Express, 835
The Stranger, 1124
The Sweetest Fig, **751**
Two Bad Ants, 1125
The Widow's Broom, **752**
The Wreck of the Zephyr, 1126
Van Rynback, Iris. *Once Inside the Library* (Huff), **459**
Varley, Susan. *The Monster Bed* (Willis), 592
Venti, Anthony Bacon. *Around the World in a Hundred Years* (Fritz), **1144**
Vesey, A. *The Princess and the Frog*, 837

Victor, Liz. *The Little Book of Anagrams* (Barrol), 1745

Vidal, Beatriz. *Bringing the Rain to Kapiti Plain* (Aardema), 1380
Buffalo Dance (Van Laan), **1039**
A Promise to the Sun (Mollel), **990**

Vivas, Julie. *I Went Walking* (Williams), **57**

Voake, Charlotte. *Over the Moon* (Mother Goose), 1886

Voce, Louise. *Over in the Meadow*, **197**
The Owl and the Pussycat (Lear), **149**

Vojtech, Anna. *The First Strawberries* (Bruchac), **870**

Vollmer, Dennis. *Joshua Disobeys*, **198**

Von Schmidt, Eric. *By the Great Horn Spoon* (Fleischman), 1300
The Ghost on Saturday Night (Fleischman), 918
Jingo Django (Fleischman), 1302
Mr. Mysterious's Secrets of Magic (Fleischman), 2024

Vyner, Tim. *The Stolen Egg* (Vyner), **379**

Waber, Bernard. *An Anteater Named Arthur*, 577
Dear Hildegarde, 1022
I Was All Thumbs, 1023
Ira Says Goodbye, 841
Ira Sleeps Over, 842
Lyle, Lyle Crocodile, 578
Rich Cat, Poor Cat, 579
"You Look Ridiculous," Said the Rhinoceros to the Hippopotamus, 580

Waldherr, Kris. *The Firebird* (San Souci), **1012**
Persephone and the Pomegranate, **1041**
Rapunzel (Grimm and Ehrlich), **923**

Waldman, Bryna. *Anansi Finds a Fool* (Aardema), **855**

Waldman, Neil. *America the Beautiful* (Bates), **1265**

Wallace, Ian. *Chin Chiang and the Dragon Dance*, 843
The Name of the Tree (Lottridge), **973**
Very Last First Time (Andrews), 867

Wallner, John. *Dial Leroi Rupert, D.J.* (Gilson), 1178
Hailstones and Halibut Bones (O'Neill), 1897
Harvey the Beer Can King (Gilson), 1179
A January Fog Will Freeze a Hog and Other Weather Folklore (Davis), 2016
Lizzie Lies a Lot (Levy), 1087
Much Ado about Aldo (Hurwitz), 937
Remember Betsy Floss (Adler), 1740

Walsh, Ellen Stoll. *Hop Jump*, 53
Mouse Count, 54
Mouse Paint, **204**

Pip's Magic, **205**

Ward, John. *Families* (Strickland and Strickland), **1412**

Ward, Keith. *The Black Stallion* (Farley), 1064

Ward, Lynd. *The Biggest Bear*, 844
Fog Magic (Sauer), 1353
The Silver Pony, 1024

Warhola, James. *The Brave Little Tailor* (Thomson), **1035**
Jack and the Beanstalk (Pearson), 1577

Watling, James. *Along the Santa Fe Trail* (Russell and Wadsworth), **1230**
Bound for Oregon (Van Leeuwen), **793**

Watson, Wendy. *Father Fox's Pennyrhymes* (Watson), 1972
Fox Went Out on a Chilly Night, **382**
How Brown Mouse Kept Christmas (Watson), 847

Watts, Barrie. *Bean and Plant* (Back), 1989

Watts, Bernadette. *The Bremen Town Musicians* (Grimm and Bell), **931**
Mother Holly (Grimm), 1502
The Wind and the Sun (Aesop and Watts), **859**

Watts, James. *Best Friends* (Hopkins), 1818
Brats (Kennedy), 1845
Drat These Brats (Kennedy), **1343**
How Raven Brought Light to People (Dixon), **897**

Watts, Marjorie-Ann. *Clever Polly and the Stupid Wolf* (Storr), 1122

Weatherby, Mark Alan. *The Call of the Wolves* (Murphy), 969

Wegman, William. *ABC*, **571**
Cinderella, **1042**

Wegner, Fritz. *The Champion of Merrimack County* (Drury), 1169
Jacob Two-Two Meets the Hooded Fang (Richler), 1107

Weihs, Erika. *Don't Sing before Breakfast, Don't Sleep in the Moonlight* (Perl), 1715

Weil, Lisl. *The Case of the Condemned Cat* (Hildick), 1073
McGurk Gets Good and Mad (Hildick), 1189
Owl and Other Scrambles, 1026

Weinhaus, Karen. *Knock at a Star* (Kennedy), 1847
Poem Stew (Cole), 1781

Weisgard, Leonard. *The Important Book* (Brown), 630

Weiss, Ellen. *Shadow's Baby* (Cuyler), 61

Weiss, Nicki. *An Egg Is an Egg*, **207**
Hank and Oogie, 584
If You're Happy and You Know It, 1973

Weissman, Bari. *Golly Gump Swallowed a Fly* (Cole), 372

The Magic Guinea Pig (Springstubb), 270

Weissman, Sam Q. *Last, First, Middle and Nick* (Hazen), 2045

Put Your Foot in Your Mouth and Other Silly Sayings (Cox), 1784

School Daze (Keller), 1842

Wellington, Monica. *Mr. Cookie Baker*, **55**

What Is Your Language? (Leventhal), **150**

Who Says That? (Shapiro), **43**

Wells, Robert E. *Is a Blue Whale the Biggest Thing There Is?*, **1251**

Wells, Rosemary. *Good Night, Fred*, 285

Hazel's Amazing Mother, 585

Impossible Possum (Conford), 652

Max and Ruby's First Greek Myth, **573**

Max's Chocolate Chicken, 286

Max's Christmas, 287

Peabody, 288

Shy Charles, 586

Timothy Goes to School, 587

Voyage to the Bunny Planet books, **383**

Weng, Wan-go. *The Magic Boat* (Jagendorf and Weng), 1699

Wenzel, David. *Backyard Dragon* (Sterman and Sterman), **750**

Hauntings (Hodges), **1072**

Werth, Kurt. *How a Piglet Crashed the Christmas Party* (Zakhoder), 858

The Thing at the Foot of the Bed and Other Scary Tales (Leach), 1704

West, Colin. *The King of Kennelwick Castle*, 289

West, Jim (jt. illus.). *Why the Willow Weeps* (Izen and West), **461**

Westcott, Nadine Bernard. *Dinner at the Panda Palace* (Calmenson), **73**

Down by the Bay (Raffi), 780

I Can Tell by Touching (Otto), **1215**

I Know an Old Lady Who Swallowed a Fly, 588

The Lady with the Alligator Purse, 290

Never Take a Pig to Lunch and Other Poems About the Fun of Eating, **1421**

Over the River and Through the Wood (Child), **251**

Peanut Butter and Jelly, 291

People, People, Everywhere! (Van Laan), **196**

The Pop-Up, Pull-Tab Playtime House That Jack Built, **208**

The Raffi Christmas Treasury (Raffi), **1400**

Skip to My Lou, 292

Thanksgiving (Bauer), **1266**

Westerman, Johanna. *Maggie Mab and the Bogey Beast* (Carey), **875**

Weston, Martha. *Lizzy & Harold* (Winthrop), 594

Wezyk, Joanna. *Marushka's Egg* (Rael), **667**

Wheelwright, Sidnee. *Come Back, Salmon* (Cone), **1125**

White, Martin (jt. illus.). *A First Poetry Book* (Foster), 1800

Wiberg, Harald. *The Tomten* (Lindgren), 725

Wickstrom, Sylvie. *Five Silly Fishermen* (Edwards), **901**

The Squeaky Door (Simms), **1026**

Wheels on the Bus (Raffi), 235

Wickstrom, Thor. *Millie and the Mud Hole* (Reddix), **180**

Wiese, Kurt. *The Five Chinese Brothers* (Bishop), 617

The Story about Ping (Flack), 387

Wiesner, David. *Hurricane*, **574**

June 29, 1999, **690**

Night of the Gargoyles (Bunting), **705**

Tongues of Jade (Yep), **1092**

Tuesday, **385**

Wiesner, William. *Ghosts and Goblins* (Harper), 1690

The Gunniwolf (Harper), 1519

Happy-Go-Lucky (Weisner), 1625

Turnabout (Weisner), 1626

Wijngaard, Juan. *The Faber Book of Favourite Fairy Tales* (Corrin and Corrin), 1667

Going to Sleep on the Farm (Lewison), **28**

Jelly Belly (Lee), 1855

Sir Gawain and the Loathly Lady (Hastings), 1521

Wikland, Ilon. *The Ghost of Skinny Jack* (Lindgren), 1089

I Want a Brother or Sister (Lindgren), 189

Wilcox, Cathy. *Enzo the Wonderfish*, **386**

Wildsmith, Brian. *The Hare and the Tortoise*, 1627

The Lion and the Rat, 1628

Over the Deep Blue Sea (Ikeda and McCaughrean), **460**

Wilhelm, Hans. *Blackberry Ink* (Merriam), 1868

The Bremen Town Musicians (Grimm and Wilhelm), **925**

The Funniest Dinosaur Book Ever (Rosenbloom), 1928

The Funniest Knock-Knock Book Ever! (Rosenbloom), 1929

The Funniest Riddle Book Ever! (Rosenbloom), 1930

Tyrone the Horrible, 590

Wilkes, Angela. *Animal Nursery Rhymes* (Mother Goose and Wilkes), **1378**

Williams, Berkeley, Jr. *Grandfather Tales* (Chase), 1661

Jack Tales (Chase), 1662

Williams, Garth. *Amigo* (Baylor), 613

Bedtime for Frances (Hoban), 428
Charlotte's Web (White), 1027
The Cricket in Times Square (Selden), 1237
Farmer Boy (Wilder), 1132
The Laura Ingalls Wilder Songbook (Garson), 1802
Little House in the Big Woods (Wilder), 1028
Ride a Purple Pelican (Prelutsky), 1918
Stuart Little (White), 1131
Williams, Richard. *The Herbie Jones Reader's Theater* (Kline), **1170**
The Snake That Went to School (Moore), 968
What's the Matter with Herbie Jones? (Kline), 949
Williams, Sophy. *Moving* (Rosen), **352**
Williams, Sue. *Tales for Telling* (Medlicott), **1080**
Williams, Vera B. *A Chair for My Mother*, 851
Cherries and Cherry Pits, 852
"More More More," Said the Baby, **58**
Williams-Andriani, Renée. *The Amazing Magic Show* (Petersen), **529**
Wilner, Isabel. *The Poetry Troupe*, 1975
Wilsdorf, Anne. *Princess*, **577**
Wilson, Dagmar. *Casey the Utterly Impossible Horse* (Feagles), 916
Wilson, Gahan. *Harry the Fat Bear Spy*, 1133
Matthew Looney's Invasion of the Earth (Beatty), 1142
Wilson, Janet. *The Gadget War* (Duffey), **606**
Gopher Takes Heart (Scribner), **744**
The Math Whiz (Duffey), **607**
Revenge of the Small Small (Little), **486**
Wilson, Peggy. *How to Eat a Poem and Other Morsels* (Agree), 1743
Wilson, Roger. *Nine True Dolphin Stories* (Davidson), 2014
Wimmer, Mike. *Flight* (Burleigh), **1114**
Train Song (Siebert), **553**
Winkowski, Fred. *Einstein Anderson, Science Sleuth* (Simon), 1239
Winslow, Will. *Benvenuto* (Reit), 1106
The Surprise Book (White and Broekel), 2114
Winter, Jeanette. *The Changeling* (Langerlöf and Stevens), **636**
Follow the Drinking Gourd, 1134
Klara's New World, **693**
Winter, Milo. *The Aesop for Children* (Aesop), 1641
Winter, Susan. *Henry's Baby* (Hoffman), **454**
Wisniewski, David. *Rain Player*, **694**
Sundiata, **1254**
The Warrior and the Wise Man, 1031
Wolf, Janet. *Rosie & the Yellow Ribbon* (DePaolo), **261**
Wolfe, Art. *Chameleons* (Martin), **1201**

Wolff, Ashley. *Block City* (Stevenson), 563
Stella & Roy, **210**
Wood, Audrey. *Silly Sally*, **212**
Wood, Don. *Heckedy Peg* (Wood), 854
King Bidgood's in the Bathtub (Wood), 855
The Little Mouse, the Red Ripe Strawberry, and the Big Hungry Bear, **60**
The Napping House (Wood), 301
Piggies, **59**
The Tickleoctopus (Wood), **387**
Wooding, Sharon. *I'll Meet You at the Cucumbers* (Moore), 967
Woodruff, Jess (jt. illus.). *Dear Napoleon, I Know You're Dead, But . . .* (Woodruff), **852**
Woodruff, Noah, and Jess Woodruff. *Dear Napoleon, I Know You're Dead, But . . .* (Woodruff), **852**
Wright, Carol. *It Came from Outer Space* (Bradman), **410**
Wright, Joseph (jt. illus.). *A First Poetry Book* (Foster), 1800

Yaccarino, Dan. *Big Brother Mike*, **390**
Yalowitz, Paul. *Somebody Loves You, Mr. Hatch* (Spinelli), **371**
Yamaguchi, Marianne. *The Sea of Gold and Other Tales from Japan* (Uchida), 1732
Yamomoto, Joyce. *The Raffi Singable Songbook* (Raffi), 1926
Yani, Wang, and Zheng Zhensun. *A Young Painter* (Zhensun and Low), **1257**
Yaroslava. *The Mitten* (Tresselt), 1615
Yashima, Taro. *Crow Boy*, 1032
Yee, Wong Herbert. *Big Black Bear*, **213**
Yorinks, Arthur. *Company's Coming*, 1034
It Happened in Pinsk, 1035
Yoshi. *A to Zen* (Wells), **1252**
Yoshida, Toshi. *Young Lions*, 2116
Young, Ed. *Bo Rabbit Smart for True* (Jaquith), 1700
Cats Are Cats (Larrick), 1851
The Double Life of Pocahontas (Fritz), 2031
Foolish Rabbit's Big Mistake (Martin), 1564
High on a Hill, 1982
I Wish I Were a Butterfly (Howe), 692
Lon Po Po, 1633
Mice Are Nice (Larrick), **1347**
Moon Mother, **1050**
Moon Tiger (Root), 535
Sadako (Coerr), **1120**
Seven Blind Mice, **1051**
The Terrible Nung Gwana, 1634
The Turkey Girl (Pollock), **1000**
White Wave (Wolkstein), 1631

Yeh-Shen (Louie), 1548

Young, Noela. *Finders Keepers* (Rodda), **789**
The Pigs Are Flying (Rodda), 1231

Young, Ruth. *One Crow* (Aylesworth), 17
Starring Francine & Dave, 2117

Yun, Cheng Mung. *Treasure Mountain* (Sadler), 1722

Zalben, Jane Breskin. *Inner Chimes* (Goldstein), **1298**

Zarins, Joyce Audy. *The Go-Around Dollar* (Adams), **1094**

Zaum, Marjorie. *Catlore*, 1738

Zaunders, Bo. *One Gift Deserves Another* (Grimm and Oppenheim), **927**

Zeldis, Malcah. *A Fine Fat Pig and Other Animal Poems* (Hoberman), **1315**
Honest Abe (Kunhardt), **1179**

Zelinsky, Paul O. *Hansel and Gretel* (Grimm), 1497
How I Hunted the Little Fellows (Zhitkov), 1136
The Lion and the Stoat, 859
The Maid and the Mouse and the Odd-Shaped House, 860
Ralph S. Mouse (Cleary), 1051
The Random House Book of Humor for Children (Pollack), 1228
Rumpelstiltskin (Grimm), 1504
Strider (Cleary), **806**
Swamp Angel (Isaacs), **625**
The Wheels on the Bus, **214**

Zoo Doings (Prelutsky), 1924

Zemach, Margot. *The Cat's Elbow and Other Secret Languages* (Schwartz), 1945
The Chinese Mirror (Ginsburg), 1477
Duffy and the Devil (Zemach), 1635
The Fisherman and His Wife (Grimm), 1492
It Could Always Be Worse, 1638
The Judge (Zemach), 1037
Mommy, Buy Me a China Doll (Zemach), 305
Nail Soup (Zemach), 1636
The Three Little Pigs, 1639
The Three Wishes, 1640
Too Much Noise (Zemach), 1637
The Two Foolish Cats (Uchida), 1620
When Shlemiel Went to Warsaw & Other Stories (Singer), 1730

Zhang, Christopher Zhong-Yuan. *First Apple* (Russell), **741**

Zhensun, Zheng (jt. illus.). *A Young Painter*, **1257**

Ziegler, Jack. *Mr. Knocky*, **582**

Zimmer, Dirk. *Bony-Legs* (Cole), 1426
Esteban and the Ghost (Hamcock), 1518
Mean Jake and the Devils (Hooks), 1074
The Sky Is Full of Song (Hopkins), 1828
Someone Saw a Spider (Climo), 1664
Windy Day (Bauer), 1746

Zwerger, Lisbeth. *Little Red Cap* (Grimm), 1500

Zyle, Jon Van. *The Eyes of Gray Wolf* (London), **488**

From THE HOUDINI BOX by Brian Selznick. Copyright © 1991 by
Brian Selznick. Reprinted by permission of Alfred A. Knopf, Inc.

SUBJECT INDEX

This index combines titles from this volume and the companion volume, *Books Kids Will Sit Still For* (R. R. Bowker, 1990). References to entry numbers in this volume appear in boldface type, while references to titles in *Books Kids Will Sit Still For* appear in regular type. Recommended reading levels appear in brackets, following the title.

AARDVARKS
Kennaway, Mwalimu. *Awful Aardvark* [Pre-K], **144**

ABOLITIONISTS
Adler, David A. *A Picture Book of Sojourner Truth* [2-4], **1096**
Everett, Gwen. *John Brown: One Man Against Slavery* [5-6], **1138**

ACCIDENTS
Brown, Eileen. *Tick-Tock* [K-1], **238**
McDonald, Megan. *The Great Pumpkin Switch* [1-2], **495**

ACTING
SEE ALSO Creative drama
Cohen, Miriam. *Starring First Grade* [K-1], 371
Ets, Marie Hall. *Talking without Words* [Pre-K], 82
Greenfield, Eloise. *Grandpa's Face* [K-1], 410
Hoffman, Mary. *Amazing Grace* [K-1], **287**
Kraus, Robert. *Owliver* [K-1], 461
Lewison, Wendy Cheyette. *Shy Vi* [Pre-K], **151**
McCully, Emily Arnold. *Speak Up, Blanche!* [1-2], **493**
Nixon, Joan Lowery. *Gloria Chipmunk, Star!* [1-2], 760
Oppenheim, Joanne. *Mrs. Peloki's Class Play* 763

ACTORS AND ACTRESSES
Gish, Lillian, and Selma Lanes. *An Actor's Life for Me!* [4-6], 2039
Kamen, Gloria. *Charlie Chaplin* [4-6], 2057

ADDITION
SEE Counting books; Mathematics

ADJECTIVES
SEE English language–Grammar

ADOPTION
Cannon, Janell. *Stellaluna* [K-1], **245**
Kasza, Keiko. *A Mother for Choco* [Pre-K], **140**
Keller, Holly. *Horace* [Pre-K], **143**

ADVENTURE AND ADVENTURERS
Alexander, Lloyd. *The Book of Three* [5-6], 1258
The First Two Lives of Lucas-Kasha [5-6], 1260
Avi. *The True Confessions of Charlotte Doyle* [5-6], **803**
Babbitt, Natalie. *Tuck Everlasting* [5-6], 1271
Collodi, Carlo. *The Adventures of Pinocchio* [4-5], 1160
DeFelice, Cynthia. *Lostman's River* [5-6], **811**
Weasel [5-6], **812**
Du Bois, William Pène. *The Twenty-One Balloons* [5-6], 1295
Farley, Walter. *The Black Stallion* [3-4], 1064
Fife, Dale. *North of Danger* [5-6], 1296
Fleischman, Sid. *The Ghost in the Noonday Sun* [5-6], 1301
Jingo Django [5-6], 1302
The Whipping Boy [4-5], 1172
George, Jean Craighead. *Julie of the Wolves* [5-6], 1304
Hill, Kirkpatrick. *Winter Camp* [5-6], **822**
Holland, Barbara. *Prisoners at the Kitchen Table* [4-5], 1190
Jones, Terry. *The Saga of Erik the Viking* [4-5], 1197
Kennedy, Richard. *Inside My Feet* [5-6], 1318
Lester, Alison. *The Journey Home* [K-1], **303**
Morey, Walt. *Sandy and the Rock Star* [5-6], 1333
Naylor, Phyllis Reynolds. *The Grand Escape* [4-5], **783**

ADVENTURE AND ADVENTURERS (cont.)

Norton, Mary. *The Borrowers* [5-6], 1336

O'Dell, Scott. *The Black Pearl* [5-6], 1338

Island of the Blue Dolphins [5-6], 1339

Paulsen, Gary. *The Haymeadow* [5-6], **835**

Rappaport, Doreen. *Living Dangerously: American Women Who Risked Their Lives for Adventure* [4-6], **1224**

Sperry, Armstrong. *Call It Courage* [4-5], 1242

Strickland, Brad. *Dragon's Plunder* [5-6], **848**

Ullman, James Ramsay. *Banner in the Sky* [5-6], 1371

Wallace, Barbara Brooks. *Peppermints in the Parlor* [5-6], 1372

Williams, Gurney. *True Escape and Survival Stories* [4-6], 2115

ADVERTISING

Conford, Ellen. *Nibble, Nibble, Jenny Archer* [2-3], **600**

AFRICA

SEE ALSO Folklore–Africa

Alexander, Lloyd. *The Fortune-Tellers* [3-4], **698**

Bash, Barbara. *Tree of Life: The World of the African Baobab* [1-4], **1104**

Bess, Clayton. *The Truth about the Moon* [2-3], 875

Cowcher, Helen. *Whistling Thorn* [K-2], **1126**

Cowen-Fletcher, Jane. *It Takes a Village* [K-1], **257**

Daly, Niki. *Not So Fast, Songololo* [Pre-K], 62

Feelings, Muriel. *Jambo Means Hello: Swahili Alphabet Book* [2-5], 1798

Geraghty, Paul. *The Hunter* [1-2], **442**

Kroll, Virginia. *Masai and I* [1-2], **480**

Leigh, Nila K. *Learning to Swim in Swaziland: A Child's-Eye View of a Southern African Country* [1-4], **1184**

Leslie-Melville, Betty. *Elephant Have the Right of Way: Life with the Wild Animals of Africa* [2-6], **1185**

Lofting, Hugh. *The Story of Doctor Dolittle* [3-4], 1091

Mennen, Ingrid, and Niki Daly. *Somewhere in Africa* [1-2], **509**

Mwenye Hadithi. *Lazy Lion* [Pre-K], **171**

Tricky Tortoise [Pre-K], 126

Wisniewski, David. *Sundiata: Lion King of Mali* [3-5], **1254**

Yoshida, Toshi. *Young Lions* [1-4], 2116

AFRICAN AMERICANS

SEE ALSO Folklore–African American

Andersen, Janet S. *The Key into Winter* [2-3], **587**

Armstrong, William. *Sounder* [5-6], 1264

Brittain, Bill. *All the Money in the World* [4-5], 1152

Bunting, Eve. *Flower Garden* [Pre-K], **72**

Smoky Night [2-3], **593**

Burchardt, Nellie. *Project Cat* [2-3], 878

Cameron, Ann. *The Stories Julian Tells* [2-3], 881

Chapman, Cheryl. *Snow on Snow on Snow* [Pre-K], **83**

Chbosky, Stacey. *Who Owns the Sun?* [4-5], 1158

Clifton, Lucille. *The Boy Who Didn't Believe in Spring* [1-2], 650

Cohen, Barbara. *Thank You, Jackie Robinson* [4-5], 1159

DePaolo, Paula. *Rosie & the Yellow Ribbon* [K-1], **261**

Engel, Diana. *Fishing* [K-1], **268**

Falwell, Cathryn. *Feast for 10* [Pre], **11**

Fife, Dale. *Who's in Charge of Lincoln?* [2-3], 917

Greene, Bette. *Philip Hall Likes Me. I Reckon, Maybe* [4-5], 1183

Greenfield, Eloise. *Grandpa's Face* [K-1], 410

Me as Neesie [K-1], 411

Griffin, Judith Berry. *Phoebe and the General* [2-5], 2042

Havill, Juanita. *Jamaica and Brianna* [Pre-K], 119

Hill, Elizabeth Starr. *Evan's Corner* [1-2], 687

Holland, Isabelle. *Behind the Lines* [5-6], **824**

Hopkinson, Deborah. *Sweet Clara and the Freedom Quilt* [2-3], **622**

Hort, Lenny. *How Many Stars in the Sky?* [K-1], **288**

Howard, Elizabeth Fitzgerald. *Mac & Marie & the Train Toss Surprise* [1-2], **455**

Hurmence, Belinda. *A Girl Called Boy* [5-6], 1314

Hutchins, Pat. *My Best Friend* [Pre], **23**

Johnson, Dolores. *What Will Mommy Do When I'm at School?* [Pre-K], **135**

Your Dad Was Just Like You [1-2], **463**

Keats, Ezra Jack. *Goggles!* [K-1], 449

Pet Show! [Pre-K], 163

Peter's Chair [Pre-K], 164

The Snowy Day [Pre-K], 165

Whistle for Willie [Pre-K], 166

Kroll, Virginia. *Masai and I* [1-2], **480**

Kuklin, Susa. *How My Family Lives in America* [K-3], **1178**

Lexai, Joan. *Benjie* [K-1], 472

Livingston, Myra Cohn. *Keep on Singing: A Ballad of Marian Anderson* [1-4], **1190**

McKissack, Patricia C. *Flossie & the Fox* [1-2], 735

Mirandy and Brother Wind [2-3], 958

Nettie Jo's Friends [K-1], 492

McMillan, Bruce. *Beach Ball—Left, Right* [Pre-K], **158**

Eating Fractions [Pre-1], **1193**

Martin, Ann. *Rachel Parker, Kindergarten Show-Off* [K-1], **321**

Mayer, Mercer. *Liza Lou and the Yeller Belly Swamp* [1-2], 748

Medearis, Angela Shelf. *The Zebra-Riding Cowboy: A Folk Song from the Old West* [2-3], **645**

Mitchell, Margaree King. *Uncle Jed's Barbershop* [2-3], **647**

Monjo, F. N. *The Drinking Gourd* [2-3], 966

Nelson, Vaunda Micheaux. *Mayfield Crossing* [4-5], **784**

Patrick, Denise Lewis. *Red Dancing Shoes* [Pre-K], **175**

Peters, Julie Anne. *The Stinky Sneakers Contest* [2-3], **654**

Polacco, Patricia. *Chicken Sunday* [2-3], **661**
Mrs. Katz and Tush [2-3], **663**
Pink and Say [4-5], **786**

Pringle, Laurence. *Octopus Hug* [Pre-K], **178**

Quattlebaum, Mary. *Jackson Jones and the Puddle of Thorns* [4-5], **787**

Raschka, Chris. *Yo! Yes?* [1-2], **541**

Ringgold, Faith. *Tar Beach* [2-3], **671**

Say, Allen. *The Bicycle Man* [1-2], 791

Springstubb, Tricia. *The Magic Guinea Pig* [Pre-K], 270

Steptoe, John. *Stevie* [2-3], 1010

Stolz, Mary. *Storm in the Night* [1-2], 828

Taylor, Mildred D. *The Gold Cadillac* [4-5], 1248

Udry, Janice May. *What Mary Jo Shared* [Pre-K], 279

Wagner, Jane. *J. T.* [3-4], 1129

Winter, Jeanette. *Follow the Drinking Gourd* [3-4], 1134

AFRICAN AMERICANS–Biography

Adler, David A. *A Picture Book of Harriet Tubman* [1-4], **1095**
A Picture Book of Sojourner Truth [2-4], **1096**

Ferris, Jeri. *Go Free or Die: A Story About Harriet Tubman* [3-5], **1141**

Golenbock, Peter. *Teammates* [2-6], **1153**

McGovern, Ann. *Runaway Slave: The Story of Harriet Tubman* [2-5], 2070

Marzollo, Jean. *Happy Birthday, Martin Luther King* [Pre-2], **1203**

Moutoussamy-Ashe, Jeanne. *Daddy and Me: A Photo Story of Arthur Ashe and His Daughter Camera* [K-6], **1213**

AFRICAN AMERICANS–History

Johnson, Dolores. *Now Let Me Fly: The Story of a Slave Family* [2-3], **629**

Ringgold, Faith. *Aunt Harriet's Underground Railroad in the Sky* [2-3], **670**

AFRICAN AMERICANS–Poetry

Adoff, Arnold. *In for Winter, Out for Spring* [K-4], **1260**

Greenfield, Eloise. *Honey, I Love* [2-5], 1807

Grimes, Nikki. *Meet Danitra Brown* [3-5], **1302**

Hudson, Wade. *Pass It On: African-American Poetry for Children* [1-4], **1331**

Hughes, Langston. *Don't You Turn Back* [3-6], 1830
The Dream Keeper and Other Poems [4-6], **1332**

Livingston, Myra Cohn. *Let Freedom Ring: A Ballad of Martin Luther King, Jr.* [1-6], **1191**

Myers, Walter Dean. *Brown Angels: An Album of Pictures and Verse* [1-6], **1389**

Strickland, Dorothy, and Michael R. Strickland. *Families: Poems Celebrating the African American Experience* [K-3], **1412**

AFRICAN AMERICANS–Songs

Mattox, Cheryl. *Shake It to the One That You Love the Best: Play Songs and Lullabies from Black Musical Traditions* [Pre-2], **1371**

AFRICANS–Biography

Wisniewski, David. *Sundiata: Lion King of Mali* [3-5], **1254**

AIDS

Moutoussamy-Ashe, Jeanne. *Daddy and Me: A Photo Story of Arthur Ashe and His Daughter Camera* [K-6], **1213**

AIR POLLUTION
SEE Pollution

AIRPLANES
SEE ALSO Transportation

Brown, Don. *Ruth Law Thrills a Nation* [K-4], **1111**

Browne, Eileen. *No Problem* [1-2], **414**

Burleigh, Robert. *Flight: The Journey of Charles Lindbergh* [3-6], **1114**

Bursik, Rose. *Amelia's Fantastic Flight* [1-2], **417**

Demarest, Chris L. *Lindbergh* [2-4], **1128**

Jukes, Mavis. *I'll See You in My Dreams* [3-4], **718**

Lauber, Patricia. *Lost Star: The Story of Amelia Earhart* [5-6], 2061

Provensen, Alice, and Martin Provensen. *The Glorious Flight: Across the Channel with Louis Blérot* [K-6], 2084

Rand, Gloria. *Salty Takes Off* [1-2], **540**

AIRPLANES (cont.)

Spier, Peter. *Bored, Nothing to Do* [1-2], 817

AIRPLANES–Poetry

Lindbergh, Reeve. *View from the Air: Charles Lindbergh's Earth and Sky* [3-6], **1356**

Siebert, Diane. *Plane Song* [1-2], **552**

AIRPORTS

Bunting, Eve. *Fly Away Home* [1-2], **415**

ALASKA

SEE ALSO Folklore–Alaska

Hill, Kirkpatrick. *Winter Camp* [5-6], **822**

Hoshino, Michio. *The Grizzly Bear Family Book* [3-6], **1164**

Morey, Walt. *Gentle Ben* [5-6], 1332

Rand, Gloria. *Prince William* [2-3], **668**

Salty Takes Off [1-2], **540**

Rogers, Jean. *Runaway Mittens* [Pre-K], 244

Seibert, Patricia. *Mush! Across Alaska in the World's Longest Sled-Dog Race* [1-4], **1235**

ALCOHOLISM

Conly, Jane Leslie. *Crazy Lady!* [5-6], **808**

ALGONQUIN INDIANS–Folklore

Gregg, Andy. *Great Rabbit and the Long-Tailed Wildcat* [2-4], **921**

Martin, Rafe. *The Rough-Face Girl* [2-6], **983**

San Souci, Robert D. *Sootface: An Ojibwa Cinderella Story* [1-5], **1016**

ALIENS

SEE Extraterrestrial life

ALLERGIES

Allen, Marjorie N. *One, Two, Three—Ah-Choo!* [K-1], 321

Porte, Barbara Ann. *Harry's Dog* [1-2], 777

ALLIGATORS

Aliki. *Keep Your Mouth Closed, Dear* [Pre-K], 5

Christelow, Eileen. *Jerome and the Babysitter* [K-1], 364

Jerome and the Witchcraft Kids [K-1], 363

Cushman, Doug. *Possum Stew* [Pre-K], **91**

Hurd, Thacher. *Mama Don't Allow* [K-1], 432

Matthews, Louise. *Gator Pie* [K-1], 506

Mayer, Mercer. *There's an Alligator under My Bed* [Pre-K], 208

Nixon, Joan Lowery. *The Alligator under the Bed* [Pre-K], 218

Peterson, Esther Allen. *Frederick's Alligator* [1-2], 773

Sendak, Maurice. *Alligators All Around* [K-1], 550

Smath, Jerry. *A Hat So Simple* [K-1], **367**

Stevenson, James. *Monty* [K-1], 561

ALLITERATION

SEE ALSO Tongue twisters; Word games

Bayer, Jane. *A My Name Is Alice* [K-1], 334

Brandreth, Gyles. *The Biggest Tongue Twister Book in the World* [2-6], 1753

Brown, Marcia. *Peter Piper's Alphabet* [1-6], 1762

Bursik, Rose. *Amelia's Fantastic Flight* [1-2], **417**

Chess, Victoria. *Alfred's Alphabet Walk* [1-2], 648

Cole, Joanna, and Stephanie Calmenson. *Six Sick Sheep: 101 Tongue Twisters* [2-5], **1280**

Curtis, Foley. *The Little Book of Big Tongue Twisters* [1-4], 1786

Gordon, Jeffie Ross. *Six Sleepy Sheep* [Pre-K], **111**

Grover, Max. *The Accidental Zucchini: An Unexpected Alphabet* [K-1], **277**

Halsey, Megan. *Jump for Joy: A Book of Months* [K-1], **279**

Janovitz, Marilyn. *Look Out, Bird!* [Pre-K], **134**

Keller, Charles. *Tongue Twisters* [K-3], **1340**

Lobel, Anita. *Alison's Zinnia* [K-1], **309**

Away from Home [1-2], **487**

Loomis, Christine. *One Cow Coughs: A Counting Book for the Sick and Miserable* [Pre-K], **155**

Rosenbloom, Joseph. *Twist These on Your Tongue* [3-6], 1938

Schwartz, Alvin. *Busy Buzzing Bumblebees and Other Tongue Twisters* [Pre-2], 1944

A Twister of Twists, a Tangler of Tongues [2-6], 1950

Seuss, Dr. *Dr. Seuss' ABC* [K-1], 553

Shelby, Anne. *Potluck* [K-1], **362**

ALPHABET

Falwell, Cathryn. *The Letter Jesters* [2-4], **1140**

Modesitt, Jeanne. *The Story of Z* [1-2], **511**

Polette, Nancy. *Hole by the Apple Tree: An A–Z Discovery Tale* [K-1], **339**

Roop, Peter, and Connie Roop. *Ahyoka and the Talking Leaves* [3-4], **740**

Viorst, Judith. *The Alphabet from Z to A: With Much Confusion on the Way* [3-6], **1416**

ALPHABET BOOKS

Andersen, Karen Born. *An Alphabet in Five Acts* [1-2], **398**

Aylesworth, Jim. *Old Black Fly* [K-1], **223**

Balian, Lorna. *Humbug Potion: An A B Cipher* [1-2], 608

Barton, Byron. *Applebet Story* [K-1], 331

Bayer, Jane. *A My Name Is Alice* [K-1], 334

Berg, Cami. *D Is for Dolphin* [Pre-3], **1106**

Bourke, Linda. *Eye Spy: A Mysterious Alphabet* [1-2], **409**

Boynton, Sandra. *A Is for Angry: An Animal and Adjective Alphabet* [K-1], 341

Calmenson, Stephanie. *It Begins with an A* [Pre-K], **74**

Chess, Victoria. *Alfred's Alphabet Walk* [1-2], 648

Coletta, Irene, and Hallie Coletta. *From A to Z: The Collected Letters of Irene and Hallie Coletta* [2-3], 897

Cushman, Doug. *The ABC Mystery* [1-2], **428**

Dodson, Peter. *An Alphabet of Dinosaurs* [1-3], **1132**

Doubilet, Anne. *Under the Sea from A to Z* [K-5], **1134**

Ehlert, Lois. *Eating the Alphabet: Fruits and Vegetables from A to Z* [Pre-K], 77

Eichenberg, Fritz. *Ape in a Cape: An Alphabet of Odd Animals* [Pre-K], 79

Feelings, Muriel. *Jambo Means Hello: Swahili Alphabet Book* [2-5], 1798

Feldman, Judy. *The Alphabet in Nature* [Pre-K], **102**

Folsom, Michael, and Marcia Folsom. *Easy as Pie: A Guessing Game of Sayings* [1-2], 670

Gardner, Beau. *Have You Ever Seen . . .? An ABC Book* [K-1], 403

Grover, Max. *The Accidental Zucchini: An Unexpected Alphabet* [K-1], 277

Hepworth, Cathi. *Antics! An Alphabetical Anthology* [2-6], **1312**

Hoguet, Susan. *I Unpacked My Grandmother's Trunk* [1-2], 689

Hubbard, Woodleigh. *C Is for Curious: An ABC of Feelings* [K-1], **289**

Ipcar, Dahlov. *I Love My Anteater with an A* [3-4], 1078

Lobel, Anita. *Alison's Zinnia* [K-1], **309**
Away from Home [1-2], **487**

Lobel, Arnold. *On Market Street* [K-1], 483

Lyon, George Ella. *A B Cedar: An Alphabet of Trees* [Pre-6], 2068

MacDonald, Suse. *Alphabatics* [K-1], 490

MacDonald, Suse, and Bill Oakes. *Puzzlers* [K-1], **314**

Martin, Bill, Jr., and John Archambault. *Chicka Chicka Boom Boom* [Pre-K], 205

Maurer, Donna. *Annie, Bea, and Chi Chi Dolores: A School Day Alphabet* [Pre-K], **163**

Merriam, Eve. *Halloween ABC* [3-6], **1372**
Where Is Everybody? An Animal Alphabet [K-1], 508

Neumeier, Marty, and Byron Glaser. *Action Alphabet* [1-2], 758

Pittman, Helena Clare. *Miss Hindy's Cats* [K-1], **338**

Rankin, Laura. *The Handmade Alphabet* [K-6], **1223**

Ryden, Hope. *Wild Animals of America ABC* [Pre-2], 2087

Sendak, Maurice. *Alligators All Around* [K-1], 550

Seuss, Dr. *Dr. Seuss' ABC* [K-1], 553
On Beyond Zebra [1-2], 805

Shelby, Anne. *Potluck* [K-1], **362**

Steig, William. *CDB* [2-6], 1959

Talon, Robert. *Zoophabets* [2-3], 1014

Wegman, William. *ABC* [1-2], **571**

Weil, Lisl. *Owl and Other Scrambles* [2-3], 1026

Wells, Ruth. *A to Zen: A Book of Japanese Culture* [3-6], **1252**

ALPHABET–Poetry

Hopkins, Lee Bennett. *April Bubbles Chocolate: An ABC of Poetry* [K-3], **1316**

Yolen, Jane. *Alphabestiary: Animal Poems from A to Z* [1-4], **1426**

ALZHEIMER'S DISEASE

Bahr, Mary. *The Memory Box* [2-3], **589**

AMAZON RIVER

Gilliland, Judith Heide. *River* [K-3], **1152**

AMERICA
SEE United States

AMERICA–Discovery and Exploration

Columbus, Christopher. *Log of Christopher Columbus* [4-6], **1124**

Maestro, Betsy. *The Discovery of the Americas* [2-5], **1195**

Marzollo, Jean. *In 1492* [K-3], **1204**

Roop, Peter, and Connie Roop. *I, Columbus; My Journal—1492–3* [4-6], **1227**

Sis, Peter. *Follow the Dream: The Story of Christopher Columbus* [1-4], **1238**

AMERICAN REVOLUTION
SEE U.S.–History–Revolution

AMISH

Polacco, Patricia. *Just Plain Fancy* [2-3], **662**

ANDERSEN, HANS CHRISTIAN

Brust, Beth Wagner. *Amazing Paper Cuttings of Hans Christian Andersen* [4-6], **1113**

ANGER
SEE Emotions

ANIMAL NOISES
SEE Sound effects

ANIMALS

SEE ALSO individual animals, e.g., Bears; Domestic animals; Pets

Abolafia, Yossi. *Fox Tale* [1-2], **394**

Albert, Richard E. *Alejandro's Gift* [1-2], **397**

Bacon, Peggy. *The Magic Touch* [3-4], 1043

Barrett, Judi. *Animals Should Definitely Not Wear Clothing* [2-3], 870

Bennett, David. *One Cow Moo Moo!* [Pre], **5**

Blathwayt, Benedict. *Stories from Firefly Island* [1-2], **407**

Bodsworth, Nan. *A Nice Walk in the Jungle* [K-1], **233**

Brady, Irene. *Doodlebug* [1-2], 620

Browne, Eileen. *No Problem* [1-2], **414**

Burningham, John. *Mr. Gumpy's Outing* [Pre-K], 33

Burton, Marilee Robin. *Tails, Toes, Eyes, Ears, Nose* [Pre-K], 34

Calmenson, Stephanie. *Dinner at the Panda Palace* [Pre-K], **73**

Carle, Eric. *The Grouchy Ladybug* [Pre-K], 37

Carlson, Natalie Savage. *Marie Louise's Heyday* [1-2], 638

Carroll, Kathleen Sullivan. *One Red Rooster* [Pre], **7**

Chapman, Cheryl. *Pass the Fritters, Critters* [Pre-K], **82**

Cherry, Lynne. *Who's Sick Today?* [Pre-K], 47

Cole, Joanna. *Golly Gump Swallowed a Fly* [K-1], 372

Cowcher, Helen. *Rain Forest* [K-1], **256**

Cuyler, Margery. *That's Good! That's Bad!* [Pre-K], **92**

Dahl, Roald. *The Enormous Crocodile* [1-2], 656

De Regniers, Beatrice Schenk. *May I Bring a Friend?* [Pre-K], 69

De Zutter, Hank. *Who Says a Dog Goes Bow-Wow?* [Pre-2], **1131**

Ehlert, Lois. *Circus* [Pre-K], **95**
Color Zoo [Pre-K], 76

Eichenberg, Fritz. *Ape in a Cape: An Alphabet of Odd Animals* [Pre-K], 79
Dancing in the Moon [K-1], 380

Feldman, Judy. *The Alphabet in Nature* [Pre-K], **102**

Flack, Marjorie. *Ask Mr. Bear* [Pre-K], 87

Fleming, Denise. *Count!* [Pre], **13**
In the Small, Small Pond [Pre-K], **104**

Forrester, Victoria. *The Magnificent Moo* [Pre-K], 89

Fox, Mem. *Koala Lou* [K-1], 389

Freeman, Don. *Quiet! There's a Canary in the Library* [Pre-K], 96

Gammell, Stephen. *Once upon MacDonald's Farm* [K-1], 401

Gardner, Beau. *Guess What?* [Pre-K], 110

Gelman, Rita Golden. *I Went to the Zoo* [K-1], **275**

George, William T. *Box Turtle at Long Pond* [Pre-2], 2037

Ginsburg, Mirra. *Mushroom in the Rain* [Pre-K], 115

Goodspeed, Peter. *A Rhinoceros Wakes Me Up in the Morning* [Pre-K], 116

Grahame, Kenneth. *The Wind in the Willows* [5-6], 1305

Guarino, Deborah. *Is Your Mama a Llama?* [Pre-K], 123

Hall, Malcolm. *Headlines* [2-3], 932

Heller, Ruth. *Animals Born Alive and Well* [K-4], **1159**
Chickens Aren't the Only Ones [K-4], **1160**

Hoban, Tana. *A Children's Zoo* [K-1], 430

Howard, Jane R. *When I'm Hungry* [Pre-K], **126**
When I'm Sleepy [Pre-K], 141

Ipcar, Dahlov. *I Love My Anteater with an A* [3-4], 1078

Jacques, Brian. *Redwall* [5-6], 1315

Janovitz, Marilyn. *Look Out, Bird!* [Pre-K], **134**

Johnston, Deborah. *Mathew Michael's Beastly Day* [K-1], **293**

Jorgensen, Gail. *Crocodile Beat* [Pre-K], 159

Karas, G. Brian. *I Know an Old Lady* [K-1], **295**

Kennaway, Mwalimu. *Awful Aardvark* [Pre-K], **144**

Kessler, Leonard. *Old Turtle's Baseball Stories* [1-2], 709

Kherdian, David. *The Cat's Midsummer Jamboree* [K-1], 457

Kipling, Rudyard. *How the Camel Got His Hump* [2-3], 947
Just So Stories [2-3], 948
Just So Stories [3-4], **728**

Knowles, Sheena. *Edward the Emu* [K-1], **300**

Koide, Tan. *May We Sleep Here Tonight?* [Pre-K], 172

Langstaff, John. *Over in the Meadow* [Pre-K], 180

Lavies, Bianca. *It's an Armadillo* [K-3], 2064

Lear, Edward. *The Owl and the Pussycat* [Pre-K], **148, 149**

Leslie-Melville, Betty. *Elephant Have the Right of Way: Life with the Wild Animals of Africa* [2-6], **1185**

Leydenfrost, Robert. *The Snake That Sneezed* [Pre-K], 188

Lionni, Leo. *Frederick's Fables: A Leo Lionni Treasury of Favorite Stories* [1-2], 728

Lobel, Arnold. *Fables* [4-5], 1207

Lofting, Hugh. *The Story of Doctor Dolittle* [3-4], 1091

London, Jonathan. *The Owl Who Became the Moon* [K-1], **310**
Voices of the Wild [2-3], **640**

Loomis, Christine. *One Cow Coughs: A Counting Book for the Sick and Miserable* [Pre-K], **155**

MacCarthy, Patricia. *Herds of Words* [K-6], **1363**

MacDonald, Amy. *Little Beaver and the Echo* [Pre-K], **156**

McKissack, Patricia C. *Nettie Jo's Friends* [K-1], 492

Maestro, Giulio. *A Wise Monkey Tale* [K-1], 499

Mahy, Margaret. *17 Kings and 42 Elephants* [K-1], 500

Mariotti, Mario. *Hanimations* [K-6], **1199**

Marshall, James. *Rats on the Roof and Other Stories* [2-3], **643**

Martin, Bill, Jr. *Brown Bear, Brown Bear, What Do You See?* [Pre-K], 204
Polar Bear, Polar Bear, What Do You Hear? [Pre-K], **160**

Marzollo, Jean. *Pretend You're a Cat* [Pre-K], **161**

Mazer, Anne. *The Oxboy* [5-6], **831**

Merriam, Eve. *Where Is Everybody? An Animal Alphabet* [K-1], 508

Milne, A. A. *Winnie-the-Pooh* [2-3], 964

Most, Bernard. *Zoodles* [1-2], **514**

Mwenye Hadithi. *Crafty Chameleon* [Pre-K], 124
Greedy Zebra [Pre-K], 125
Lazy Lion [Pre-K], **171**

Niland, Kilmeny. *A Bellbird in a Flame Tree* [1-2], **518**

Nodset, Joan L. *Who Took the Farmer's Hat?* [Pre-K], 219

North, Sterling. *Rascal: A Memoir of a Better Era* [4-6], 2079

Numeroff, Laura J. *Dogs Don't Wear Sneakers* [K-1], **333**

Paul, Anthony. *The Tiger Who Lost His Stripes* [1-2], 765

Paxton, Tom. *Jennifer's Rabbit* [Pre-K], 224

Peek, Merle. *Mary Wore Her Red Dress and Henry Wore His Green Sneakers* [Pre-K], 227

Peet, Bill. *The Ant and the Elephant* [K-1], 521
Capyboppy [2-5], 2081
Gnats of Knotty Pine [2-3], 977
Hubert's Hair-Raising Adventure [1-2], 770

Pfeffer, Wendy. *Popcorn Park Zoo: A Haven with a Heart* [3-5], **1220**

Prelutsky, Jack. *The Mean Old Mean Hyena* [2-3], 983

Raffi. *Down by the Bay* [1-2], 780

Reeves, Mona Rabun. *I Had a Cat* [Pre-K], 237

Robinson, Marc. *Cock-a-Doodle-Doo! What Does It Sound Like to You?* [Pre-2], **1226**

Roop, Peter, and Connie Roop. *One Earth, a Multitude of Creatures* [K-6], **1228**

Rounds, Glen. *I Know an Old Lady Who Swallowed a Fly* [K-1], 537

Ryden, Hope. *Wild Animals of America ABC* [Pre-2], 2087

Selsam, Millicent, and Joyce Hunt. *Keep Looking!* [Pre-2], 2095

Shapiro, Arnold L. *Who Says That?* [Pre], **43**

Sheppard, Jeff. *Splash, Splash* [Pre], **44**

Simon, Seymour. *Animal Fact / Animal Fable* [2-4], 2099

Stadler, John. *Cat Is Back at Bat* [K-1], **372**

Stevenson, James. *Clams Can't Sing* [K-1], 560
Happy Valentine's Day, Emma! [1-2], 823
Monty [K-1], 561
The Mud Flat Olympics [1-2], **557**
Yuck! [K-1], 562

Stolz, Mary. *Cat Walk* [3-4], 1121

Sundgaard, Arnold. *Meet Jack Appleknocker* [Pre-K], 272

Thomas, Patricia. *"Stand Back," Said the Elephant, "I'm Going to Sneeze!"* [K-1], 568

Tompert, Ann. *Just a Little Bit* [Pre-K], **192**

Turner, Gwenda. *Over on the Farm* [Pre-K], **195**

Ueno, Noriko. *Elephant Buttons* [Pre-K], 280

Van Laan, Nancy. *The Big Fat Worm* [Pre-K], 282

Vaughn, Marcia K. *Wombat Stew* [1-2], 836

Waber, Bernard. *An Anteater Named Arthur* [K-1], 577
"You Look Ridiculous," Said the Rhinoceros to the Hippopotamus [K-1], 580

Waddell, Martin. *The Happy Hedgehog Band* [Pre], **48**
Squeak-a-Lot [Pre], **52**

Westcott, Nadine Bernard. *I Know an Old Lady Who Swallowed a Fly* [K-1], 588

Whybrow, Ian. *Quacky Quack-Quack!* [Pre], **56**

Williams, Sue. *I Went Walking* [Pre], **57**

Yolen, Jane. *Welcome to the Green House* [K-3], **1256**

Yoshida, Toshi. *Young Lions* [1-4], 2116

Young, Ruth. *Who Says Moo?* [Pre], **61**

ANIMALS–Creation

Du Bois, William Pène. *Lion* [2-3], 912

Kipling, Rudyard. *The Beginning of the Armadillos* [2-3], 945

ANIMALS–Folklore

Aardema, Verna. *Misoso: Once Upon a Time Tales from Africa* [2-6], **1052**

ANIMALS–Folklore (cont.)

Rabbit Makes a Monkey Out of Lion [Pre-3], 1382

Traveling to Tondo: A Tale of the Nkundo of Zaire [Pre-2], **857**

Who's in Rabbit's House? [2-4], 1385

Why Mosquitoes Buzz in People's Ears [Pre-2], 1386

Aesop. *Aesop & Company: With Scenes from His Legendary Life* [3-6], **1053**

The Aesop for Children [K-3], 1641

Aesop's Fables [2-4], 1642

Aesop's Fables [3-6], 1643, 1646

Aesop's Fables [2-6], 1644

Aesop's Fables [K-3], 1645

Aesop's Fables [1-6], **1054**

Animal Fables from Aesop [2-6], **1055**

The Children's Aesop: Selected Fables [2-5], **1057**

The Fables of Aesop [2-6], 1647

Once in a Wood: Ten Tales from Aesop [Pre-2], 1648

Seven Fables from Aesop [1-4], 1649

Twelve Tales from Aesop [K-3], 1651

Alexander, Ellen. *Llama and the Great Flood: A Folktale from Peru* [2-4], 1389

Appiah, Peggy. *Tales of an Ashanti Father* [3-6], 1653

Arkhurst, Joyce Cooper. *The Adventures of Spider: West African Folktales* [1-4], 1654

Baumgartner, Barbara. *Crocodile! Crocodile! Stories Told Around the World* [Pre-2], **1058**

Brett, Jan. *The Mitten* [Pre-2], 1409

Brooke, L. Leslie. *The Golden Goose Book* [Pre-3], 1658

Bruchac, Joseph. *The Great Ball Game: A Muskogee Story* [K-3], **871**

Native American Animal Stories [2-6], **1059**

Return of the Sun: Native American Tales from the Northeast Woodlands [3-6], **1060**

Brusca, María Cristina, and Tona Wilson. *When Jaguars Ate the Moon: And Other Stories About Animals and Plants of the Americas* [2-6], **1061**

Cauley, Lorinda Bryan. *The Pancake Boy: An Old Norwegian Folk Tale* [1-3], 1418

Courlander, Harold. *The Hat-Shaking Dance: And Other Tales from the Gold Coast* [2-6], 1668

Courlander, Harold, and George Herzog. *The Cow-Tail Switch and Other West African Stories* [2-6], 1670

Dee, Ruby. *Two Ways to Count to Ten: A Liberian Folktale* [K-3], 1436

Ginsburg, Mirra. *The Fisherman's Son* [2-5], 1478

Three Rolls and One Doughnut: Fables from Russia [1-5], 1681

Greaves, Nick. *When Lion Could Fly and Other Tales from Africa* [2-6], **1070**

Grimm, Jacob. *The Bremen Town Musicians* [K-2], **925**, **931**

The Bremen Town Musicians [Pre-3], 1487

Kherdian, David. *Feathers and Tails: Animal Fables from Around the World* [K-4], **1073**

Kimmel, Eric A. *Anansi and the Moss-Covered Rock* [Pre-2], 1541

Anansi and the Talking Melon [Pre-2], **949**

Lamont, Priscilla. *The Troublesome Pig: A Nursery Tale* [Pre-2], 1543

Lester, Julius. *Further Tales of Uncle Remus: The Misadventures of Brer Rabbit, Brer Fox, Brer Wolf, the Doodang, and Other Creatures* [2-5], **1075**

How Many Spots Does a Leopard Have? And Other Tales [1-5], 1705

The Knee-High Man and Other Tales [K-4], 1706

The Tales of Uncle Remus: The Adventures of Brer Rabbit [2-5], 1707

Lottridge, Celia Barker. *The Name of the Tree: A Bantu Folktale* [Pre-2], **973**

McGovern, Ann. *Too Much Noise* [Pre-2], 1556

Martin, Rafe. *Foolish Rabbit's Big Mistake* [Pre-2], 1564

Medlicott, Mary. *Tales for Telling: From Around the World* [K-4], **1080**

Mollel, Tololwa M. *Rhinos for Lunch and Elephants for Supper!* [Pre-2], **991**

Parks, Van Dyke, and Malcolm Jones. *Jump! The Adventures of Brer Rabbit* [2-5], 1714

Robinson, Gail. *Raven the Trickster: Legends of the North American Indians* [4-6], 1719

Rockwell, Anne. *Puss in Boots & Other Stories* [Pre-3], 1720

Ross, Gayle. *How Rabbit Tricked Otter and Other Cherokee Trickster Stories* [1-4], **1084**

Sawyer, Ruth. *Journey Cake, Ho!* [Pre-2], 1591

Sierra, Jud. *The Elephant's Wrestling Match* [Pre-2], **1025**

Simms, Laura. *The Squeaky Door* [Pre-2], **1026**

Tanaka, Béatrice. *The Chase: A Kutenai Indian Tale* [Pre-K], **1032**

Thornhill, Jan. *Crow & Fox and Other Animal Legends* [1-4], **1089**

Tresselt, Alvin. *The Mitten: An Old Ukrainian Folktale* [Pre-2], 1615

Troughton, Joanna. *Mouse-Deer's Market* [Pre-2], 1617

Tortoise's Dream [Pre-2], 1618

Yeoman, John. *The Singing Tortoise and Other Animal Folktales* [3-6], **1091**

ANIMALS–Poetry

Benjamin, Alan. *A Nickel Buys a Rhyme* [Pre-2], **1267**

Bodecker, N. M. *Water Pennies: And Other Poems* [2-5], **1271**

Calmenson, Stephanie. *Never Take a Pig to Lunch: And Other Funny Poems about Animals* [Pre-4], 1764

Cassedy, Sylvia, and Kunihiro Suetake. *Red Dragonfly on My Shoulder* [2-6], **1278**

Cole, William. *I Went to the Animal Fair* [Pre-K], 1778

A Zooful of Animals [K-5], **1282**

Demi. *In the Eyes of the Cat: Japanese Poetry for All Seasons* [2-6], **1284**

Edwards, Richard. *Moon Frog: Animal Poems for Young Children* [K-3], **1285**

Florian, Douglas. *Beast Feast* [K-4], **1290**

Heller, Ruth. *A Cache of Jewels and Other Collective Nouns* [Pre-3], 1811

Higginson, William J. *Wind in the Long Grass: A Collection of Haiku* [2-6], **1313**

Hoberman, Mary Ann. *A Fine Fat Pig and Other Animal Poems* [K-3], **1315**

Hooper, Patricia. *A Bundle of Beasts* [2-5], 1817

Lewis, J. Patrick. *A Hippopotamustn't and Other Animal Verses* [1-5], **1353**

Two-Legged, Four-Legged, No-Legged Rhymes [K-4], 1354

McLoughland, Beverly. *A Hippo's a Heap: And Other Animal Poems* [K-3], **1364**

Moore, Lillian. *Sunflakes: Poems for Children* [Pre-3], **1375**

Mother Goose. *Animal Nursery Rhymes* [Pre-1], **1378**

Prelutsky, Jack. *Zoo Doings* [K-4], 1924

Robinson, Fay. *A Frog Inside My Hat: A First Book of Poems* [Pre-2], **1402**

Rosen, Michael. *Itsy-Bitsy Beasties: Poems from Around the World* [K-4], **1404**

Singer, Marilyn. *Please Don't Squeeze Your Boa, Noah!* [3-6], **1410**

Turtle in July [1-4], 1954

Voce, Louise. *Over in the Meadow: A Traditional Counting Rhyme* [Pre-K], **197**

Wadsworth, Olive A. *Over in the Meadow: An Old Counting Rhyme* [Pre-K], **202**

Whipple, Laura. *Eric Carle's Animals, Animals* [K-4], 1974

Yolen, Jane. *Alphabestiary: Animal Poems from A to Z* [1-4], **1426**

ANIMALS–Riddles

Adler, David A. *The Carsick Zebra and Other Animal Riddles* [K-3], 1739

Churchill, E. Richard. *The Six-Million Dollar Cucumber: Riddles and Fun for Children* [Pre-6], 1768

De Regniers, Beatrice Schenk. *It Does Not Say Meow and Other Animal Riddle Rhymes* [Pre-1], 1791

Hoff, Syd. *Syd Hoff's Animal Jokes* [K-2], 1815

Keller, Charles. *King Henry the Ape: Animal Jokes* [2-6], **1338**

Llama Beans [1-4], 1838

Phillips, Louis. *Invisible Oink: Pig Jokes* [3-6], **1394**

Rayner, Shoo. *My First Picture Joke Book* [K-2], **1401**

Zimmerman, Andrea Griffing. *The Riddle Zoo* [K-2], 1983

ANIMALS–Songs

King, Bob. *Sitting on the Farm* [Pre-K], **145**

Manushkin, Fran. *My Christmas Safari* [K-1], **320**

Seeger, Ruth Crawford. *American Folk Songs for Children* [Pre-4], 1951

Yolen, Jane. *The Fireside Song Book of Birds and Beasts* [Pre-6], 1980

ANIMALS, ENDANGERED

SEE Endangered species

ANIMALS, EXTINCT

Facklam, Margery. *And Then There Was One: The Mysteries of Extinction* [3-6], **1139**

ANIMALS, IMAGINARY

SEE ALSO Animals, mythical

Flora, James. *Leopold the See-Through Crumbpicker* [1-2], 669

Gannett, Ruth Stiles. *My Father's Dragon* [1-2], 674

McMurtry, Stan. *The Bunjee Venture* [4-5], 1210

Peet, Bill. *The Wump World* [2-3], 980

Talon, Robert. *Zoophabets* [2-3], 1014

ANIMALS, IMAGINARY–Poetry

Florian, Douglas. *Monster Motel* [K-3], **1292**

Heide, Florence Parry. *Grim and Ghastly Goings-On* [1-4], **1309**

Lear, Edward. *The Quangle Wangle's Hat* [K-1], 466

Lobel, Arnold. *The Ice Cream Cone Coot and Other Rare Birds* [2-3], 954

Peet, Bill. *No Such Things* [2-3], 978

Prelutsky, Jack. *The Baby Uggs Are Hatching* [K-4], 1904

ANIMALS, IMAGINARY–Poetry (cont.)

The Snopp on the Sidewalk and Other Poems [K-3], 1921

Seuss, Dr. *If I Ran the Zoo* [1-2], 803
McElligot's Pool [1-2], 804
On Beyond Zebra [1-2], 805

Yolen, Jane. *Animal Fare* [1-4], **1427**

ANIMALS, MYTHICAL

SEE ALSO Animals, imaginary

Byars, Betsy. *The Winged Colt of Casa Mia* [3-4], 1048

Edwards, Julie. *The Last of the Really Great Whangdoodles* [3-4], 1063

Kellogg, Steven. *The Mysterious Tadpole* [1-2], 705

King-Smith, Dick. *The Swoose* [3-4], **727**

Lewis, C. S. *The Lion, the Witch and the Wardrobe* [3-4], 1088

Lindgren, Astrid. *The Tomten* [1-2], 725

Ormondroyd, Edward. *David and the Phoenix* 3-4], 1100

ANIMALS, MYTHICAL–Folklore

Arnold, Caroline. *The Terrible Hodag* [1-5], 1392

Carlson, Natalie Savage. *King of the Cats and Other Tales* [3-6], 1660

Demi. *The Firebird* [2-5], **893**

Gal, Laszlo. *Prince Ivan and the Firebird* [3-6], **908**

Hastings, Selina. *The Firebird* [1-4], **938**

San Souci, Robert D. *The Firebird* [3-5], **1012**

Schwartz, Alvin. *Kickle Snifters and Other Fearsome Critters Collected from American Folklore* [2-5], 1593

ANIMALS, MYTHICAL–Poetry

Whipple, Laura. *Eric Carle's Dragons, Dragons & Other Creatures That Never Were* [2-6], **1423**

ANIMALS, PREHISTORIC

SEE ALSO Dinosaurs

Arnold, Caroline. *Trapped in Tar: Fossils from the Ice Age* [4-6], 1987

Brett, Jan. *The First Dog* [1-2], 622

ANIMALS, PREHISTORIC–Folklore

Greene, Ellin. *The Legend of the Cranberry: A Paleo-Indian Tale* [1-4], **919**

ANTS

Allinson, Beverly. *Effie* [K-1], **217**

Cameron, Polly. *"I Can't," Said the Ant* [1-2], 636

Demuth, Patricia Brennan. *Those Amazing Ants* [K-2], **1130**

Dorros, Arthur. *Ant Cities* [K-3], 2021

Hepworth, Cathi. *Antics! An Alphabetical Anthology* [2-6], **1312**

Peet, Bill. *The Ant and the Elephant* [K-1], 521

Pinczes, Elinor J. *One Hundred Hungry Ants* [1-2], **533**

Van Allsburg, Chris. *Two Bad Ants* [3-4], 1125

Wolkstein, Diane. *Step by Step* [Pre-K], **211**

APARTMENT HOUSES

Burchardt, Nellie. *Project Cat* [2-3], 878

Ellis, Anne. *Dabble Duck* [K-1], 382

Gaeddert, Lou Ann. *Noisy Nancy Norris* [Pre-K], 102

Gretz, Susanna. *It's Your Turn, Roger!* [K-1], 412

Hill, Elizabeth Starr. *Evan's Corner* [1-2], 687

Hurwitz, Johanna. *Busybody Nora* [1-2], 694
"E" Is for Elisa [K-1], **290**
Superduper Teddy [1-2], 696

Keats, Ezra Jack. *Apt. 3* [2-3], 942

Levy, Elizabeth. *Frankenstein Moved in on the Fourth Floor* [2-3], 951

Petersen, P. J. *I Hate Company* [2-3], **655**

Williams, Vera B. *A Chair for My Mother* [1-2], 851

APPLES

SEE ALSO Fruit

Russell, Ching Yeung. *First Apple* [3-4], **741**

APRIL FOOL'S DAY

SEE Holidays

ARCHAEOLOGY

Donnelly, Judy. *True-Life Treasure Hunts* [3-5], 2020

Swinburne, Irene, and Laurence Swinburne. *Behind the Sealed Door: The Discovery of the Tomb and Treasures of Tutankhamen* [4-6], 2109

ARCTIC REGIONS

Brandenberg, Jim. *To the Top of the World: Adventures with Arctic Wolves* [4-6], **1108**

ARGUMENTS

Cole, Brock. *Alpha and the Dirty Baby* [1-2], **426**

Crowley, Michael. *Shack and Back* [1-2], **427**

Field, Eugene. *The Gingham Dog and the Calico Cat* [Pre-K], **103**

Guback, Georgia. *Luka's Quilt* [K-1], **278**

Stevenson, James. *That's Exactly the Way It Wasn't* [1-2], **558**

ARITHMETIC

SEE Counting books; Division; Mathematics; Measurement; Multiplication; Subtraction

ARMADILLOS

Cherry, Lynne. *The Armadillo from Amarillo* [1-2], **423**

Kipling, Rudyard. *The Beginning of the Armadillos* [2-3], 945

Lavies, Bianca. *It's an Armadillo* [K-3], 2064

ART

Fox, Dan. *Go In and Out the Window: An Illustrated Songbook for Young People* [Pre-6], 1801

Koch, Kenneth, and Kate Farrell. *Talking to the Sun* [Pre-6], 1849

Pilkey, Dav. *When Cats Dream* [1-2], **532**

Sullivan, Charles. *Cowboys* [K-4], **1413**

Whipple, Laura. *Celebrating America: A Collection of Poems and Images of the American Spirit* [3-6], **1422**

ARTISTS

Agee, Jon. *The Incredible Painting of Felix Clousseau* [2-3], 862

Alcorn, Johnny. *Rembrandt's Beret* [3-4], **697**

Audubon, John James. *Capturing Nature: The Writings and Art of John James Audubon* [5-6], **1101**

Baker, Alan. *Benjamin's Portrait* [K-1], 326

Blake, Robert J. *The Perfect Spot* [K-1], **231**

Brust, Beth Wagner. *Amazing Paper Cuttings of Hans Christian Andersen* [4-6], **1113**

Coerr, Eleanor. *Mieko and the Fifth Treasure* [3-4], **707**

Cummings, Pat. *Talking with Artists* [2-6], **1127**

dePaola, Tomie. *The Art Lesson* [2-3], 907

Du Bois, William Pène. *Lion* [2-3], 912

Fenner, Carol. *Randall's Wall* [5-6], **815**

Freeman, Don. *Norman the Doorman* [1-2], 671

Gardner, Jane Mylum. *Henry Moore: From Bones and Stones to Sketches and Sculptures* [2-5], **1146**

Harding, William Harry. *Alvin's Famous No-Horse* [2-3], **613**

Kamen, Gloria. *Edward Lear, King of Nonsense: A Biography* [4-6], **1169**

Lionni, Leo. *Matthew's Dream* [K-1], **308**

McCully, Emily Arnold. *Speak Up, Blanche!* [1-2], **493**

McPhail, David. *The Magical Drawings of Mooney B. Finch* [1-2], 737
Something Special [K-1], 497

Moss, Marissa. *Regina's Big Mistake* [K-1], **328**

Peet, Bill. *Encore for Eleanor* [1-2], 768

Polacco, Patricia. *Firetalking* [1-4], **1221**

Rosen, Michael J. *Speak! Children's Book Illustrators Brag About Their Dogs* [2-6], **1229**

Rylant, Cynthia. *All I See* [2-3], 988

Skira-Venturi, Rosabianca. *A Weekend with Leonardo da Vinci* [3-8], **1239**

Stolz, Mary. *Zekmet, the Stone Carver* [4-5], 1244

Zelinsky, Paul O. *The Lion and the Stoat* [1-2], 859

Zhensun, Zheng, and Alice Low. *A Young Painter: The Life and Paintings of Wang Yani— China's Extraordinary Young Artist* [3-6], **1257**

ARTISTS–Folklore

Bang, Molly. *Tye May and the Magic Brush* [K-3], 1398

Levine, Arthur A. *The Boy Who Drew Cats: A Japanese Folktale* [2-6], **968**

Yacowitz, Caryn. *The Jade Stone: A Chinese Folktale* [K-4], **1045**

ASHE, ARTHUR

Moutoussamy-Ashe, Jeanne. *Daddy and Me: A Photo Story of Arthur Ashe and His Daughter Camera* [K-6], **1213**

ASIAN AMERICANS

Havill, Juanita. *Jamaica and Brianna* [Pre-K], **119**

Kuklin, Susa. *How My Family Lives in America* [K-3], **1178**

ASTHMA

Getz, David. *Thin Air* [5-6], **819**

Hoffman, Mary. *The Four-Legged Ghosts* [2-3], **620**

ASTRONAUTS

Fraser, Mary Ann. *One Giant Leap* [4-6], **1142**

ASTRONOMY

SEE ALSO Moon; Space flight; Stars; Sun; Universe

Branley, Franklyn M. *Shooting Stars* [1-3], **1109**

Clements, Andrew. *Mother Earth's Counting Book* [K-5], **1118**

Cole, Joanna. *The Magic School Bus Lost in the Solar System* [1-4], **1121**

Krupp, E. C. *The Comet and You* [1-4], 2060
The Moon and You [2-5], **1176**

Leedy, Loreen. *Postcards from Pluto: A Tour of the Solar System* [1-3], **1182**

Ride, Sally, and Susan Okie. *To Space and Back* [3-6], 2086

Simon, Seymour. *Galaxies* [3-6], 2101
Stars [3-6], 2104

Wells, Robert E. *Is a Blue Whale the Biggest Thing There Is?* [2-5], **1251**

ASTRONOMY–Folklore

Bernhard, Emery. *How Snowshoe Hare Rescued the Sun: A Tale from the Arctic* [K-3], **866**

Dixon, Ann. *How Raven Brought Light to People* [K-4], **897**

Mollel, Tololwa M. *The Orphan Boy: A Maasai Story* [1-4], **989**

ASTRONOMY–Poetry

Hopkins, Lee Bennett. *Blast Off! Poems About Space* [1-4], **1317**

Yolen, Jane. *What Rhymes with Moon?* [1-5], **1431**

ASTRONOMY–Riddles

Hall, Katy, and Lisa Eisenberg. *Spacey Riddles* [2-5], **1306**

ATHLETES–Biography

Littlefield, Bill. *Champions: Stories of Ten Remarkable Athletes* [5-6], **1188**

AUDUBON, JOHN JAMES

Audubon, John James. *Capturing Nature: The Writings and Art of John James Audubon* [5-6], **1101**

AUNTS

Brisson, Pat. *Magic Carpet* [1-2], **411**

Brooks, Walter Rollin. *Jimmy Takes Vanishing Lessons* [2-3], 876

Cooney, Barbara. *Miss Rumphius* [1-2], 654

Duke, Kate. *Aunt Isabel Tells a Good One* [1-2], **436**

Fleischman, Sid. *The Ghost on Saturday Night* [2-3], 918

Greenwald, Sheila. *The Atrocious Two* [4-5], 1184

Hiskey, Iris. *Hannah the Hippo's No Mud Day* [Pre-K], **124**

Schwartz, Amy. *Her Majesty, Aunt Essie* [1-2], 796

Wallace, Barbara Brooks. *Peppermints in the Parlor* [5-6], 1372

AUSTRALIA

Cox, David. *Bossyboots* [1-2], 655

Fox, Mem. *Koala Lou* [K-1], 389

Niland, Kilmeny. *A Bellbird in a Flame Tree* [1-2], **518**

Vaughn, Marcia K. *Wombat Stew* [1-2], 836

AUSTRALIA–Folklore

Maddern, Eric. *Rainbow Bird: An Aboriginal Folktale from Northern Australia* [K-3], **979**

AUSTRALIAN POETRY

Fatchen, Max. *The Country Mail Is Coming: Poems from Down Under* [3-6], **1289**

AUTHORS

SEE ALSO Writing

Brust, Beth Wagner. *Amazing Paper Cuttings of Hans Christian Andersen* [4-6], **1113**

Byars, Betsy. *The Moon and I* [4-6], **1115**

Dahl, Roald. *Boy* [5-6], 2012

Janeczko, Paul B. *The Place My Words Are Looking For* [5-6], **1334**

Krauss, Ruth. *Is This You?* [1-2], 714

Krull, Kathleen. *Lives of the Writers: Comedies, Tragedies (and What the Neighbors Thought)* [4-6], **1175**

Little, Jean. *Little by Little: A Writer's Education* [5-6], **1187**

Martin, Rafe. *A Storyteller's Story* [1-4], **1202**

Nixon, Joan Lowery. *If You Were a Writer* [2-3], 972

Pinkwater, Daniel. *Author's Day* [2-3], **659**

Polacco, Patricia. *Firetalking* [1-4], **1221**

Rodowsky, Colby. *Dog Days* [3-4], **739**

Rylant, Cynthia. *Best Wishes* [1-5], **1233**

Snyder, Zilpha Keatley. *Libby on Wednesday* [5-6], **846**

Stanley, Diane, and Peter Vennema. *Bard of Avon: The Story of William Shakespeare* [4-6], **1241**

Charles Dickens: The Man Who Had Great Expectations [4-6], **1242**

Stevens, Janet. *From Pictures to Words: A Book About Making a Book* [1-4], **1244**

Williams, Barbara. *The Author and Squinty Gritt* [1-2], **575**

AUTOBIOGRAPHY

SEE ALSO Biography

Audubon, John James. *Capturing Nature: The Writings and Art of John James Audubon* [5-6], **1101**

Byars, Betsy. *The Moon and I* [4-6], **1115**

Dahl, Roald. *Boy* [5-6], 2012

dePaola, Tomie. *The Art Lesson* [2-3], 907

Tom [1-2], **431**

Fitzgerald, John D. *The Great Brain* [4-5], 1171

Gish, Lillian, and Selma Lanes. *An Actor's Life for Me!* [4-6], 2039

Isaacman, Clara, and Joan Adess Grossman. *Clara's Story* [5-6], 2054

Kossman, Nina. *Behind the Border* [4-6], **1173**

Little, Jean. *Little by Little: A Writer's Education* [5-6], **1187**

Lomas Garza, Carmen. *Family Pictures / Cuadros de Familia* [1-4], **1192**

Martin, Rafe. *A Storyteller's Story* [1-4], **1202**

Morimoto, Junko. *My Hiroshima* [3-6], **1210**

Mowat, Farley. *Owls in the Family* [3-5], 2077

Polacco, Patricia. *Firetalking* [1-4], **1221**

Roop, Peter, and Connie Roop. *I, Columbus; My Journal—1492–3* [4-6], **1227**

Russell, Marion. *Along the Santa Fe Trail: Marion Russell's Own Story* [2-5], **1230**

Rylant, Cynthia. *Best Wishes* [1-5], **1233**

Stevenson, James. *Don't You Know There's a War On?* [2-6], **1245**

Whiteley, Opal. *Only Opal: The Diary of a Young Girl* [2-5], **1253**

Wilder, Laura Ingalls. *Little House in the Big Woods* [2-3], 1028

AUTOMOBILES

SEE ALSO Bicycles; Buses; Transportation; Trucks

Karlin, Bernie, and Mati Karlin. *Night Ride* [K-1], 446

Mahy, Margaret. *The Rattlebang Picnic* [1-2], **502**

Pinkwater, Daniel. *Tooth-Gnasher Superflash* [K-1], 523

Taylor, Mildred D. *The Gold Cadillac* [4-5], 1248

Williams, Barbara. *The Author and Squinty Gritt* [1-2], **575**

AUTUMN

SEE ALSO Seasons

Pittman, Helena Clare. *Once When I Was Scared* [1-2], 775

Van Allsburg, Chris. *The Stranger* [3-4], 1124

AZTECS

Mathews, Sally Schofer. *The Sad Night: The Story of an Aztec Victory and a Spanish Loss* [5-6], **1206**

AZTECS–Folklore

Ober, Hal. *How Music Came to the World* [1-4], **993**

BABA YAGA

Arnold, Katya. *Baba Yaga: A Russian Folktale* [1-3], **860**

Baba Yaga & the Little Girl [K-3], **861**

Ayres, Becky Hickox. *Matreshka* [K-3], **863**

Kimmel, Eric A. *Baba Yaga: A Russian Folktale* [K-2], **951**

I-Know-Not-What, I-Know-Not-Where: A Russian Tale [4-6], **955**

Lewis, J. Patrick. *The Frog Princess: A Russian Tale* [2-6], **969**

Mayer, Marianna. *Baba Yaga and Vasilisa the Brave* [2-5], **985**

Rael, Elsa Okon. *Marushka's Egg* [2-3], **667**

Winthrop, Elizabeth. *Vasilissa the Beautiful: A Russian Folktale* [2-5], **1044**

BABIES

Auch, Mary Jane. *Monster Brother* [K-1], **221**

Banish, Rosalyn. *Let Me Tell You about My Baby* [Pre-1], 1990

Barber, Antonia. *Catkin* [2-3], **590**

Brown, Marc. *Arthur's Baby* [K-1], 344

Browne, Anthony. *Changes* [K-1], **241**

Bunting, Eve. *Our Teacher's Having a Baby* [K-1], **243**

Caseley, Judith. *Harry and Arney* [1-2], **422**

Silly Baby [Pre-K], 44

Cleary, Beverly. *Petey's Bedtime Story* [K-1], **253**

Cooke, Trish. *So Much* [Pre], **8**

Cooney, Nancy Evans. *Chatterbox Jamie* [Pre-K], **87**

Cutler, Jane. *Darcy and Gran Don't Like Babies* [K-1], **259**

Cuyler, Margery. *Shadow's Baby* [Pre-K], 61

Ferguson, Alane. *That New Pet!* [K-1], 386

Galbraith, Kathryn O. *Waiting for Jennifer* [K-1], 400

Gordon, Jeffie Ross. *Two Badd Babies* [Pre-K], **112**

Henkes, Kevin. *Julius, the Baby of the World* [K-1], **283**

Herzig, Alison Cragin, and Jane Lawrence Mali. *Oh, Boy! Babies!* [4-6], 2049

Hoban, Russell. *A Baby Sister for Frances* [Pre-K], 137

Hoffman, Mary. *Henry's Baby* [1-2], **454**

Hutchins, Pat. *Where's the Baby?* [K-1], 435

Keats, Ezra Jack. *Peter's Chair* [Pre-K], 164

Keller, Holly. *Geraldine's Baby Brother* [Pre-K], **142**

Kopper, Lisa. *Daisy Thinks She Is a Baby* [Pre], **27**

Lindgren, Astrid. *I Want a Brother or Sister* [Pre-K], 189

Lindgren, Barbro. *The Wild Baby* [K-1], 473

Lowry, Lois. *All about Sam* [5-6], 1327

Melmed, Laura Krauss. *The Rainbabies* [1-2], **508**

Park, Barbara. *Junie B. Jones and a Little Monkey Business* [2-3], **651**

Paxton, Tom. *Where's the Baby?* [Pre], **38**

Russo, Marisabina. *Waiting for Hannah* [K-1], 538

Schwartz, Amy. *A Teeny Tiny Baby* [K-1], **358**

Smith, Janice Lee. *The Monster in the Third Dresser Drawer: And Other Stories about Adam Joshua* [1-2], 815

Stevenson, James. *Rolling Rose* [Pre], **46**

Worse Than Willy! [1-2], 827

BABIES (cont.)

Titherington, Jeanne. *A Place for Ben* [Pre-K], 274

Vipont, Elfrida. *The Elephant & the Bad Baby* [Pre-K], 283

Whybrow, Ian. *Quacky Quack-Quack!* [Pre], **56**

Williams, Vera B. *"More More More," Said the Baby: Three Love Stories* [Pre], **58**

Willis, Jeanne. *Earthlets: As Explained by Professor Xargle* [2-3], **692**

Wishinsky, Frieda. *Oonga Boonga* [Pre-K], **209**

BABIES–Folklore

Rhee, Nami. *Magic Spring: A Korean Folktale* [K-3], **1002**

BABOONS

Mwenye Hadithi. *Baby Baboon* [Pre], **37**

BABY-SITTERS

Brown, Marc. *Arthur Babysits* [1-2], **412**

Carlson, Natalie Savage. *Marie Louise's Heyday* [1-2], 638

Christelow, Eileen. *Jerome and the Babysitter* [K-1], 364

Jerome and the Witchcraft Kids [K-1], 363

Delton, Judy. *Angel in Charge* [3-4], 1061

Dillon, Barbara. *Mrs. Tooey & the Terrible Toxic Tar* [3-4], 1062

Green, Phyllis. *Chucky Bellman Was So Bad* [1-2], **444**

Gregory, Valiska. *Babysitting for Benjamin* [K-1], **276**

Herzig, Alison Cragin, and Jane Lawrence Mali. *Oh, Boy! Babies!* [4-6], 2049

Hoban, Lillian. *Arthur's Loose Tooth* [K-1], 427

Hughes, Shirley. *An Evening at Alfie's* [Pre-K], 147

Julian, Nancy R. *The Peculiar Miss Pickett* [2-3], 940

Petersen, P. J. *I Hate Company* [2-3], **655**

Rayner, Mary. *Mr. and Mrs. Pig's Evening Out* [1-2], 782

Robertson, Keith. *Henry Reed's Baby-Sitting Service* [5-6], 1347

Smith, Alison. *Help! There's a Cat Washing in Here* [5-6], 1361

Van Leeuwen, Jean. *Benjy in Business* [2-3], 1021

Wells, Rosemary. *Shy Charles* [K-1], 586

Winthrop, Elizabeth. *Bear and Mrs. Duck* [Pre-K], 298

BADGERS

Cushman, Doug. *The ABC Mystery* [1-2], **428**

Hoban, Russell. *A Baby Sister for Frances* [Pre-K], 137

Bedtime for Frances [K-1], 428

Bread and Jam for Frances [K-1], 429

BADGERS–Folklore

Johnston, Tony. *The Badger and the Magic Fan: A Japanese Folktale* [Pre-2], 1536

BADGERS–Poetry

Hoban, Russell. *Egg Thoughts and Other Frances Songs* [K-2], 1813

BAKING

SEE Cookery

BALLET

SEE ALSO Dancing

Auch, Mary Jane. *Peeping Beauty* [1-2], **402**

Isadora, Rachel. *Max* [K-1], 436

Keller, Beverly. *The Genuine, Ingenious Thrift Shop Genie, Clarissa Mae Bean and Me* [4-5], 1198

BALLOONS

Douglass, Barbara. *The Great Town and Country Bicycle Balloon Chase* [Pre-K], 73

Du Bois, William Pène. *The Twenty-One Balloons* [5-6], 1295

Fenton, Edward. *The Big Yellow Balloon* [1-2], 667

Gray, Nigel. *A Balloon for Grandad* [Pre-K], 121

BARGES

Doherty, Berlie. *Snowy* [K-1], **263**

BARTERING

Hicks, Clifford B. *Alvin's Swap Shop* [4-5], 1187

Molarsky, Osmond. *Take It or Leave It* [2-3], 965

BASEBALL

SEE ALSO Sports–Riddles

Anderson, Margaret. *The Brain on Quartz Mountain* [3-4], 1041

Cohen, Barbara. *Thank You, Jackie Robinson* [4-5], 1159

Cohen, Ron. *My Dad's Baseball* [2-3], **599**

Cooney, Nancy Evans. *The Wobbly Tooth* [K-1], 374

Dodds, Bill. *My Sister Annie* [4-5], **768**

Golenbock, Peter. *Teammates* [2-6], **1153**

Hutchins, Hazel. *The Three and Many Wishes of Jason Reid* [3-4], 1077

Isadora, Rachel. *Max* [K-1], 436

Jaspersohn, William. *The Ballpark: One Day behind the Scenes at a Major League Game* [4-6], 2055

Kessler, Leonard. *Old Turtle's Baseball Stories* [1-2], 709

Kroll, Steven. *Friday the 13th* [1-2], 716

Lexai, Joan. *I'll Tell on You* [1-2], 724

Miles, Betty. *The Secret Life of the Underwear Champ* [3-4], 1096

Mochizuki, Ken. *Baseball Saved Us* [3-4], **733**

Nelson, Vaunda Micheaux. *Mayfield Crossing* [4-5], **784**

Norworth, Jack. *Take Me Out to the Ballgame* [1-2], **521**

Park, Barbara. *Skinnybones* [4-5], 1222

Sachs, Marilyn. *Matt's Mitt and Fleet-Footed Florence* [2-3], 990

Slote, Alfred. *Hang Tough, Paul Mather* [4-5], 1241

Teague, Mark. *The Field Beyond the Outfield* [K-1], **376**

BASEBALL–Poetry

Hopkins, Lee Bennett. *Extra Innings: Baseball Poems* [4-6], **1318**

Morrison, Lillian. *At the Crack of the Bat: Baseball Poems* [4-6], **1376**

Thayer, Ernest Lawrence. *Casey at the Bat: A Ballad of the Republic, Sung in the Year 1888* [5-6], 1368

BASKETBALL

Minters, Frances. *Cinder-Elly* [1-2], **510**

BATHS

Cole, Brock. *No More Baths* [Pre-K], 52

Edwards, Frank B. *Mortimer Mooner Stopped Taking a Bath* [Pre-K], **94**

Faulkner, Matt. *The Amazing Voyage of Jackie Grace* [1-2], 666

Garrett, Helen. *Angelo the Naughty One* [1-2], 676

Kudrna, C. Imbior. *To Bathe a Boa* [K-1], 463

Miller, Margaret. *Where's Jenna?* [Pre-K], **167**

Pomerantz, Charlotte. *The Piggy in the Puddle* [Pre-K], 231

Wood, Audrey. *King Bidgood's in the Bathtub* [1-2], 855

Zion, Gene. *Harry the Dirty Dog* [Pre-K], 308

BATS

Bash, Barbara. *Shadows of Night: The Hidden World of the Little Brown Bat* [1-5], **1103**

Cannon, Janell. *Stellaluna* [K-1], **245**

Freeman, Don. *Hattie the Backstage Bat* [K-1], 393

BATS–Folklore

Bruchac, Joseph. *The Great Ball Game: A Muskogee Story* [K-3], **871**

Mollel, Tololwa M. *A Promise to the Sun: An African Story* [K-3], **990**

Sierra, Jud. *The Elephant's Wrestling Match* [Pre-2], **1025**

BATS–Riddles

Hall, Katy, and Lisa Eisenberg. *Batty Riddles* [1-4], **1304**

BAYS

Samton, Sheila White. *Beside the Bay* [Pre-K], 250

BEACHES

SEE Seashore

BEARS

Abolafia, Yossi. *Fox Tale* [1-2], **394**

Alborough, Jez. *It's the Bear!* [Pre-K], **63**

Where's My Teddy? [Pre], **2**

Allen, Pamela. *Bertie and the Bear* [Pre-K], 7

Asch, Frank. *Bear Shadow* [Pre-K], 10

Goodbye House [Pre-K], 11

Happy Birthday, Moon [Pre-K], 12

Just Like Daddy [Pre-K], 13

Moongame [Pre-K], 14

Popcorn [Pre-K], 15

Barrett, Judi. *Benjamin's 365 Birthdays* [K-1], 330

Bellows, Cathy. *The Grizzly Sisters* [K-1], **230**

Benton, Robert. *Don't Ever Wish for a 7-Foot Bear* [1-2], 614

Bond, Michael. *A Bear Called Paddington* [4-5], 1146

Paddington's Storybook [4-5], 1147

Brimner, Larry Dane. *Country Bear's Good Neighbor* [Pre-K], 27

Browne, Anthony. *Bear Hunt* [Pre-K], 30

Bucknall, Caroline. *One Bear in the Picture* [Pre-K], 31

Bunting, Eve. *The Valentine Bears* [K-1], 353

Calhoun, Mary. *The Night the Monster Came* [2-3], 880

Carlstrom, Nancy White. *How Do You Say It Today, Jesse Bear?* [Pre-K], **76**

Cushman, Doug. *Possum Stew* [Pre-K], **91**

Dalgliesh, Alice. *The Bears on Hemlock Mountain* [1-2], 657

Day, Alexandra. *Frank and Ernest* [2-3], 906

Delton, Judy. *Two Good Friends* [Pre-K], 66

Freeman, Don. *Bearymore* [K-1], 391

Gage, Wilson. *Cully Cully and the Bear* [K-1], 399

Graham, Thomas. *Mr. Bear's Chair* [Pre-K], 119

Hissey, Jane. *Little Bear's Trousers* [Pre-K], 135

Hoshino, Michio. *The Grizzly Bear Family Book* [3-6], **1164**

Isaacs, Anne. *Swamp Angel* [2-3], **625**

Jeschke, Susan. *Angela and Bear* [K-1], 437

Johnston, Ginny, and Judy Cutchins. *Andy Bear: A Polar Bear Cub Grows Up at the Zoo* [2-6], 2056

Kasza, Keiko. *A Mother for Choco* [Pre-K], **140**

BEARS (cont.)

Kesey, Ken. *Little Tricker the Squirrel Meets Big Double the Bear* [2-3], **634**

Kimmel, Eric A. *The Chanukkah Guest* [K-1], **298**

Kinsey-Warnock, Natalie. *The Bear That Heard Crying* [1-2], **468**

Krensky, Stephen. *Big Time Bears* [Pre-K], **147**

Lemieux, Michele. *What's That Noise* [Pre-K], 184

McCloskey, Robert. *Blueberries for Sal* [Pre-K], 194

McCully, Emily Arnold. *Speak Up, Blanche!* [1-2], **493**

McPhail, David. *The Bear's Toothache* [K-1], 493
Emma's Pet [Pre-K], 200
Emma's Vacation [Pre-K], 201
Fix-It [K-1], **494**
Lost! [K-1], **316**

Matthews, Downs. *Polar Bear Cubs* [1-4], 2075

Miller, Virginia. *Eat Your Dinner!* [Pre], **34**

Milne, A. A. *Winnie-the-Pooh* [2-3], 964

Morey, Walt. *Gentle Ben* [5-6], 1332

Murphy, Jill. *Peace at Last* [Pre-K], 214

Murphy, Jim. *Backyard Bear* [1-2], **515**

Myers, Bernice. *Not This Bear!* [K-1], 511

Naylor, Phyllis Reynolds. *Old Sadie and the Christmas Bear* [K-1], 512

Newman, Nanette. *There's a Bear in the Bath!* [1-2], **517**

Peet, Bill. *Big Bad Bruce* [1-2], 766

Polushkin, Maria. *Bubba and Babba* [K-1], 526

Rosen, Michael. *We're Going on a Bear Hunt* [Pre-K], 245

Ryder, Joanne. *White Bear, Ice Bear* [Pre-3], 2091

Shannon, George. *Lizard's Song* [Pre-K], 261

Sivulich, Sandra Stroner. *I'm Going on a Bear Hunt* [Pre-K], 267

Stearns, Pamela. *Into the Painted Bear Lair* [4-5], 1243

Tolhurst, Marilyn. *Somebody and the Three Blairs* [Pre-K], **191**

Turkle, Brinton. *Deep in the Forest* [K-1], 570

Waddell, Martin. *Can't You Sleep, Little Bear?* [Pre-K], **199**
Let's Go Home, Little Bear [Pre-K], **201**

Ward, Lynd. *The Biggest Bear* [1-2], 844

Weinberg, Larry. *The Forgetful Bears Meet Mr. Memory* [K-1], 583

Wilson, Gahan. *Harry the Fat Bear Spy* [3-4], 1133

Winthrop, Elizabeth. *Bear and Mrs. Duck* [Pre-K], 298

Yee, Wong Herbert. *Big Black Bear* [Pre-K], **213**

Yektai, Niki. *Bears in Pairs* [Pre-K], 302

BEARS–Folklore

Brett, Jan. *Goldilocks and the Three Bears* [Pre-1], 1408

Cauley, Lorinda Bryan. *Goldilocks and the Three Bears* [Pre-2], 1415

Dasent, George Webbe. *The Cat on the Dovrefell: A Christmas Tale* [Pre-2], 1432
East o' the Sun and West o' the Moon [3-6], **890**

Eisen, Armand. *Goldilocks and the Three Bears* [Pre-1], 1450

Galdone, Joanna. *The Little Girl and the Big Bear* [Pre-2], 1455

Galdone, Paul. *The Three Bears* [Pre-1], 1472

Grimm, Jacob. *The Bear and the Bird King* [K-3], **929**

Hague, Kathleen, and Michael Hague. *East of the Sun and West of the Moon* [3-5], 1513

Marshall, James. *Goldilocks and the Three Bears* [Pre-1], 1561

Stevens, Janet. *Goldilocks and the Three Bears* [Pre-1], 1611
Tops & Bottoms [Pre-2], **1030**

BEARS–Poetry

Goldstein, Bobbye S. *Bear in Mind: A Book of Bear Poems* [Pre-2], **1296**

Yolen, Jane. *The Three Bears Rhyme Book* [Pre-2], 1981

BEAVERS

MacDonald, Amy. *Little Beaver and the Echo* [Pre-K], **156**

BEDTIME–Folklore

Mathews, Judith, and Fay Robinson. *Nathaniel Willy, Scared Silly* [Pre-2], **984**

Simms, Laura. *The Squeaky Door* [Pre-2], **1026**

BEDTIME–Poetry

Merriam, Eve. *You Be Good & I'll Be Night: Jump-on-the-Bed Poems* [Pre-1], 1871

Prelutsky, Jack. *My Parents Think I'm Sleeping* [Pre-3], 1910

BEDTIME STORIES

SEE ALSO Sleep

Auch, Mary Jane. *Monster Brother* [K-1], **221**

Aylesworth, Jim. *Two Terrible Frights* [Pre-K], 18

Bond, Felicia. *Pointsettia and the Firefighters* [K-1], 338

Browne, Anthony. *Gorilla* [K-1], 349

Caseley, Judith. *Sophie and Sammy's Library Sleepover* [Pre-K], **77**

Cazet, Denys. *"I'm Not Sleepy"* [Pre-K], **80**

Chadwick, Tim. *Cabbage Moon* [Pre-K], **81**

Christelow, Eileen. *Five Little Monkeys Jumping on the Bed* [Pre-K], 48
Henry and the Dragon [Pre-K], 49

Cleary, Beverly. *Petey's Bedtime Story* [K-1], **253**

Cole, William. *Frances Face-Maker: A Going to Bed Book* [Pre-K], 53

Cooney, Nancy Evans. *Go Away Monsters, Lickety Split* [Pre-K], **88**

Crowe, Robert L. *Clyde Monster* [Pre-K], 60

Gackenbach, Dick. *Hurray for Hattie Rabbit* [Pre-K], 99

Gerstein, Mordicai. *William, Where Are You?* [Pre-K], 113

Goodspeed, Peter. *A Rhinoceros Wakes Me Up in the Morning* [Pre-K], 116

Hennessy, B. G. *Sleep Tight* [Pre], **21**

Himmelman, John. *Lights Out!* [1-2], **453**

Hoban, Russell. *Bedtime for Frances* [K-1], 428

Holabird, Katharine. *Alexander and the Dragon* [Pre-K], 140

Johnston, Johanna. *Edie Changes Her Mind* [Pre-K], 155

Kalman, Maira. *Hey Willy, See the Pyramids* [2-3], 941

Kandoian, Ellen. *Under the Sun* [K-1], 445

Lewison, Wendy Cheyette. *Going to Sleep on the Farm* [Pre], **28**

Lobel, Arnold. *Mouse Tales* [K-1], 482

Mayer, Mercer. *There's a Nightmare in My Closet* [Pre-K], 207
There's an Alligator under My Bed [Pre-K], 208
There's Something in My Attic [Pre-K], 209

Nixon, Joan Lowery. *The Alligator under the Bed* [Pre-K], 218

Paxton, Tom. *Jennifer's Rabbit* [Pre-K], 224
Where's the Baby? [Pre], **38**

Polushkin, Maria. *Mother, Mother, I Want Another* [Pre-K], 230

Pomerantz, Charlotte. *Posy* [Pre-K], 232

Robison, Deborah. *No Elephants Allowed* [Pre-K], 243

Root, Phyllis. *Moon Tiger* [K-1], 535

Ross, Tony. *I'm Coming to Get You* [K-1], 536

Rydell, Katy. *Wind Says Good Night* [Pre], **42**

Ryder, Joanne. *The Night Flight* [K-1], 540

Rylant, Cynthia. *Night in the Country* [K-1], 541

Sharmat, Marjorie Weinman. *Go to Sleep, Nicholas Joe* [Pre-K], 263

Skofield, James. *'Round and Around* [Pre-K], **188**

Stevenson, James. *What's Under My Bed?* [1-2], 826

Tobias, Tobi. *Chasing the Goblins Away* [1-2], 831

Viorst, Judith. *My Mama Says There Aren't Any Zombies, Ghosts, Vampires, Creatures, Demons, Monsters, Fiends, Goblins or Things* [1-2], 840

Waber, Bernard. *Ira Sleeps Over* [1-2], 842

Waddell, Martin. *Can't You Sleep, Little Bear?* [Pre-K], **199**

Waters, Fiona. *The Doubleday Book of Bedtime Stories* [K-1], **381**

Wells, Rosemary. *Good Night, Fred* [Pre-K], 285

Williams, Vera B. *"More More More," Said the Baby: Three Love Stories* [Pre], **58**

Willis, Jeanne. *The Monster Bed* [K-1], 592

Willoughby, Elaine. *Boris and the Monsters* [Pre-K], 297

Winthrop, Elizabeth. *Maggie & the Monster* [Pre-K], 299

Wood, Don, and Audrey Wood. *Piggies* [Pre], **59**

Zemach, Harve. *Mommy, Buy Me a China Doll* [Pre-K], 305

BEES–Folklore

Renberg, Dalia Hardof. *King Solomon and the Bee* [K-3], **1001**

BEETHOVEN, LUDWIG VAN

Nichol, Barbara. *Beethoven Lives Upstairs* [4-5], **785**

BEGGARS–Folklore

O'Brien, Anne Sibley. *The Princess and the Beggar: A Korean Folklore* [1-4], **994**

BEHAVIOR

Alcock, Vivien. *The Trial of Anna Cotman* [5-6], **802**

Allard, Harry. *Miss Nelson Is Missing* [1-2], 601

Bellows, Cathy. *The Grizzly Sisters* [K-1], **230**

Benjamin, Saragail Katzman. *My Dog Ate It* [3-4], **704**

Blathwayt, Benedict. *Stories from Firefly Island* [1-2], **407**

Blundell, Tony. *Joe on Sunday* [K-1], 337

Bottner, Barbara. *Bootsie Barker Bites* [K-1], **234**

Brett, Jan. *The Wild Christmas Reindeer* [K-1], **237**

Brown, Marc. *Arthur Babysits* [1-2], **412**

Carlson, Natalie Savage. *Runaway Marie Louise* [Pre-K], 43

Cassedy, Sylvia. *Behind the Attic Wall* [5-6], 1287

Caudill, Rebecca. *Did You Carry the Flag Today, Charlie?* [1-2], 643

Chase, Mary. *Loretta Mason Potts* [4-5], 1157

Clymer, Eleanor. *My Brother Stevie* [3-4], 1054

Cole, Brock. *Nothing but a Pig* [1-2], 651

Cole, Joanna. *Don't Call Me Names* [K-1], **254**

Collodi, Carlo. *The Adventures of Pinocchio* [4-5], 1160

BEHAVIOR (cont.)

Corbett, Scott. *The Lemonade Trick* [3-4], 1056

Delton, Judy. *I'm Telling You Now* [Pre-K], 65

Ernst, Lisa Campbell. *The Luckiest Kid on the Planet* [1-2], **439**

Gantos, Jack. *Rotten Ralph* [K-1], 402

Gordon, Jeffie Ross. *Two Badd Babies* [Pre-K], **112**

Green, Phyllis. *Chucky Bellman Was So Bad* [1-2], **444**

Greenwald, Sheila. *The Atrocious Two* [4-5], 1184

Gregory, Valiska. *Babysitting for Benjamin* [K-1], **276**

Honeycutt, Natalie. *Juliet Fisher and the Foolproof Plan* [2-3], **621**

Hurwitz, Johanna. *Class Clown* [2-3], 936

Hutchins, Pat. *Three-Star Billy* [Pre-K], **130**

The Very Worst Monster [Pre-K], 150

Where's the Baby? [K-1], 435

Jeffers, Susan. *Wild Robin* [1-2], 699

Johnston, Deborah. *Mathew Michael's Beastly Day* [K-1], **293**

Kline, Suzy. *Don't Touch!* [Pre-K], 170

Horrible Harry and the Christmas Surprise [1-2], **474**

Lester, Helen. *Cora Copycat* [K-1], 468

Me First [K-1], **304**

Pookins Gets Her Way [K-1], 470

Leverich, Kathleen. *Hilary and the Troublemakers* [3-4], **730**

Levy, Elizabeth. *Keep Ms. Sugarman in the Fourth Grade* [3-4], **731**

Lindgren, Barbro. *The Wild Baby* [K-1], 473

MacDonald, Betty. *Mrs. Piggle-Wiggle* [3-4], 1092

Manes, Stephen. *Be a Perfect Person in Just Three Days* [3-4], 1095

Marshall, James. *The Cut-Ups* [1-2], 743

The Cut-Ups Carry On [1-2], **503**

Nostlinger, Christine. *Konrad* [4-5], 1219

Okimoto, Jean Davies. *Blumpoe the Grumpoe Meets Arnold the Cat* [1-2], **525**

Park, Barbara. *Maxie, Rosie, and Earl—Partners in Grime* [3-4], **736**

Patron, Susan. *Burgoo Stew* [1-2], **527**

Petersen, P. J. *I Hate Company* [2-3], **655**

Polacco, Patricia. *Babushka's Doll* [Pre-K], **176**

Potter, Beatrice. *The Tale of Peter Rabbit* [K-1], 528

Rey, H. A. *Curious George* [Pre-K], 238

Riley, James Whitcomb. *The Gobble-Uns'll Git You Ef You Don't Watch Out* [3-4], 1108

Robinson, Barbara. *The Best Christmas Pageant Ever* [4-5], 1230

The Best School Year Ever [4-5], **788**

Ross, Tony. *Super Dooper Jezebel* [1-2], **786**

Slepian, Jan. *Risk N' Roses* [5-6], **845**

Spinelli, Jerry. *Fourth Grade Rats* [3-4], **749**

Report to the Principal's Office [4-5], **791**

Stevenson, James. *Worse Than the Worst* [1-2], **560**

Taylor, Livingston. *Can I Be Good?* [K-1], **375**

Thayer, Jane. *The Popcorn Dragon* [Pre-K], 273

Viorst, Judith. *Alexander and the Terrible, Horrible, No Good, Very Bad Day* [1-2], 838

Wade, Barrie. *Little Monster* [Pre-K], 284

Wagner, Karen. *Silly Fred* [Pre-K], **203**

Wells, Rosemary. *Voyage to the Bunny Planet books: First Tomato; The Island Light; Moss Pillows* [K-1], **383**

Wood, Audrey. *The Tickleoctopus* [K-1], 387

Wright, Kit. *Tigerella* [K-1], 389

Yee, Wong Herbert. *Big Black Bear* [Pre-K], **213**

Yorinks, Arthur. *Whitefish Will Rides Again!* [1-2], **581**

Zakhoder, Boris. *How a Piglet Crashed the Christmas Party* [1-2], 858

BEHAVIOR–Folklore

Hunter, C. W. *The Green Gourd: A North Carolina Folktale* [K-2], **946**

BEHAVIOR–Poetry

Cole, William. *Beastly Boys and Ghastly Girls* [2-6], 1775

Kennedy, X. J. *Brats* [3-6], 1845

Drat These Brats [4-6], **1343**

Livingston, Myra Cohn. *Higgledy-Piggledy: Verses & Pictures* [2-3], 953

BENIN, AFRICA

Cowen-Fletcher, Jane. *It Takes a Village* [K-1], **257**

BICYCLES

SEE ALSO Transportation

Bunting, Eve. *Summer Wheels* [2-3], **594**

Crowley, Michael. *Shack and Back* [1-2], **427**

Douglass, Barbara. *The Great Town and Country Bicycle Balloon Chase* [Pre-K], 73

Drury, Roger W. *The Champion of Merrimack County* [4-5], 1169

Jakob, Donna. *My Bike* [Pre-K], **132**

Say, Allen. *The Bicycle Man* [1-2], 791

Schwartz, David. *Supergrandpa* [2-3], **675**

Wolf, Ashley. *Stella & Roy* [Pre-K], **210**

Woodruff, Elvira. *The Disappearing Bike Shop* [4-5], **797**

BILINGUAL EDUCATION
Howlett, Bud. *I'm New Here* [2-5], **1166**

BIOGRAPHY
SEE ALSO Autobiography
Adler, David A. *A Picture Book of Harriet Tubman* [1-4], **1095**
A Picture Book of Sojourner Truth [2-4], **1096**
Brenner, Martha. *Abe Lincoln's Hat* [1-4], **1110**
Brown, Don. *Ruth Law Thrills a Nation* [K-4], **1111**
Brown, Drollene P. *Sybil Rides for Independence* [2-4], 2001
Brown, Walter R., and Norman D. Anderson. *Rescue! True Stories of Winners of the Young American Medal for Bravery* [3-6], 2004
Brust, Beth Wagner. *Amazing Paper Cuttings of Hans Christian Andersen* [4-6], **1113**
Burleigh, Robert. *Flight: The Journey of Charles Lindbergh* [3-6], **1114**
Coerr, Eleanor. *Sadako* [2-5], **1120**
Sadako & the Thousand Paper Cranes [3-6], 2007
Cross, Helen Reader. *The Real Tom Thumb* [3-6], 2011
Cummings, Pat. *Talking with Artists* [2-6], **1127**
Dahl, Roald. *Boy* [5-6], 2012
D'Aulaire, Ingri, and Edgar Parin D'Aulaire. *Benjamin Franklin* [2-6], 2013
Epstein, Sam, and Beryl Epstein. *Secret in a Sealed Bottle: Lazzaro Spallanzani's Work with Microbes* [5-6], 2022
Everett, Gwen. *John Brown: One Man Against Slavery* [5-6], **1138**
Ferris, Jeri. *Go Free or Die: A Story About Harriet Tubman* [3-5], **1141**
Freedman, Russell. *Lincoln: A Photobiography* [5-6], 2028
Fritz, Jean. *And Then What Happened, Paul Revere?* [3-6], 2029
Can't You Make Them Behave, King George? [3-6], 2030
The Double Life of Pocahontas [4-6], 2031
What's the Big Idea, Ben Franklin? [3-6], 2033
Where Do You Think You're Going, Christopher Columbus? [4-6], 2034
Gardner, Jane Mylum. *Henry Moore: From Bones and Stones to Sketches and Sculptures* [2-5], **1146**
Giblin, James Cross. *George Washington: A Picture Book Biography* [1-4], **1150**

Gish, Lillian, and Selma Lanes. *An Actor's Life for Me!* [4-6], 2039
Golenbock, Peter. *Teammates* [2-6], **1153**
Griffin, Judith Berry. *Phoebe and the General* [2-5], 2042
Houston, Gloria. *My Great Aunt Arizona* [1-6], **1165**
Hunter, Edith Fisher. *Child of the Silent Night: The Story of Laura Bridgman* [3-5], 2053
Isaacman, Clara, and Joan Adess Grossman. *Clara's Story* [5-6], 2054
Kamen, Gloria. *Charlie Chaplin* [4-6], 2057
Edward Lear, King of Nonsense: A Biography [4-6], **1169**
Kellogg, Steven. *Johnny Appleseed* [1-4], 2058
Krull, Kathleen. *Lives of the Musicians: Good Times, Bad Times (and What the Neighbors Thought)* [3-6], **1174**
Lives of the Writers: Comedies, Tragedies (and What the Neighbors Thought) [4-6], **1175**
Kunhardt, Edith. *Honest Abe* [K-3], **1179**
Lasky, Kathryn. *The Librarian Who Measured the Earth* [3-6], **1180**
Lauber, Patricia. *Lost Star: The Story of Amelia Earhart* [5-6], 2061
Littlefield, Bill. *Champions: Stories of Ten Remarkable Athletes* [5-6], **1188**
Livingston, Myra Cohn. *Abraham Lincoln: A Man for All the People* [K-3], **1189**
Keep on Singing: A Ballad of Marian Anderson [1-4], **1190**
McGovern, Ann. *Runaway Slave: The Story of Harriet Tubman* [2-5], 2070
The Secret Soldier: The Story of Deborah Sampson [3-6], 2071
Marzollo, Jean. *Happy Birthday, Martin Luther King* [Pre-2], **1203**
Osborne, Mary Pope. *George Washington: Leader of a New Nation* [5-6], **1214**
Provensen, Alice, and Martin Provensen. *The Glorious Flight: Across the Channel with Louis Blérot* [K-6], 2084
Rappaport, Doreen. *Living Dangerously: American Women Who Risked Their Lives for Adventure* [4-6], **1224**
Reit, Seymour. *Behind Rebel Lines: The Incredible Story of Emma Edmonds, Civil War Spy* [5-6], 2085
Rylant, Cynthia. *Waiting to Waltz: A Childhood* [5-6], 1941
Say, Allen. *El Chino* [2-5], **1234**

BIOGRAPHY (cont.)

Sis, Peter. *Follow the Dream: The Story of Christopher Columbus* [1-4], **1238**

Skira-Venturi, Rosabianca. *A Weekend with Leonardo da Vinci* [3-8], **1239**

Stanley, Diane, and Peter Vennema. *Bard of Avon: The Story of William Shakespeare* [4-6], **1241**

   Charles Dickens: The Man Who Had Great Expectations [4-6], **1242**

Stanley, Fay. *The Last Princess: The Story of Princess Ka'iulani of Hawai'i* [4-6], **1243**

White, Florence. *Escape! The Life of Harry Houdini* [3-6], 2113

Williams, Gurney. *True Escape and Survival Stories* [4-6], 2115

Wisniewski, David. *Sundiata: Lion King of Mali* [3-5], **1254**

Zhensun, Zheng, and Alice Low. *A Young Painter: The Life and Paintings of Wang Yani— China's Extraordinary Young Artist* [3-6], **1257**

BIRDS

   SEE ALSO Chickens; Ducks; Eagles; Geese; Hummingbirds; Loons; Ostriches; Owls; Parrots; Peacocks; Penguins; Roosters; Swans

Andersen, Hans Christian. *It's Perfectly True* [1-2], 602

   The Nightingale [3-4], 1039, **699**

   The Ugly Duckling [1-2], 603

   The Wild Swans [3-4], **700**, 1040

Atwater, Richard, and Florence Atwater. *Mr. Popper's Penguins* [3-4], 1042

Audubon, John James. *Capturing Nature: The Writings and Art of John James Audubon* [5-6], **1101**

Bang, Molly. *Dawn* [2-3], 869

   The Paper Crane [1-2], 610

Bash, Barbara. *Urban Roosts: Where Birds Nest in the City* [3-6], **1105**

Brown, Margaret. *Wheel on the Chimney* [1-2], 631

Bunting, Eve. *Fly Away Home* [1-2], **415**

Callen, Larry. *Sorrow's Song* [5-6], 1286

Cannon, Janell. *Stellaluna* [K-1], **245**

Dahl, Roald. *Danny, the Champion of the World* [5-6], 1291

DeFelice, Cynthia. *Lostman's River* [5-6], **811**

DeJong, Meindert. *The Wheel on the School* [4-5], 1168

Demuth, Patricia Brennan. *Cradles in the Trees: The Story of Bird Nests* [K-3], **1129**

DePaolo, Paula. *Rosie & the Yellow Ribbon* [K-1], **261**

Duvoisin, Roger. *Petunia* [K-1], 378

Ehlert, Lois. *Feathers for Lunch* [K-1], **265**

Esbensen, Barbara Juster. *Great Northern Diver: The Loon* [2-6], **1137**

Flack, Marjorie. *The Story about Ping* [K-1], 387

Foreman, Michael. *Cat and Canary* [K-1], 388

Gormley, Beatrice. *Mail-Order Wings* [4-5], 1182

Graham, Margaret Bloy. *Benjy and the Barking Bird* [Pre-K], 118

Heller, Ruth. *Chickens Aren't the Only Ones* [K-4], **1160**

Hutchins, Pat. *Good-Night, Owl* [Pre-K], 148

Kasza, Keiko. *A Mother for Choco* [Pre-K], **140**

Keller, Holly. *Grandfather's Dream* [1-2], **466**

   Island Baby [K-1], **296**

Kennedy, Richard. *Come Again in the Spring* [3-4], 1080

   The Rise and Fall of Ben Gizzard [3-4], 1083

King-Smith, Dick. *The Cuckoo Child* [3-4], **722**

   Harry's Mad [4-5], 1199

   The Swoose [3-4], **727**

Knowles, Sheena. *Edward the Emu* [K-1], **300**

Kraus, Robert. *Owliver* [K-1], 461

Lionni, Leo. *Inch by Inch* [K-1], 475

   Tico and the Golden Wings [2-3], 952

Lobel, Arnold. *The Ice Cream Cone Coot and Other Rare Birds* [2-3], 954

   Owl at Home [K-1], 484

McCloskey, Robert. *Burt Dow, Deep-Water Man* [2-3], 955

Meddaugh, Susan. *Tree of Birds* [Pre-K], **164**

Nikly, Michelle. *The Emperor's Plum Tree* [1-2], 759

Ormondroyd, Edward. *David and the Phoenix* [3-4], 1100

Pearson, Susan. *Lenore's Big Break* [1-2], **528**

Peet, Bill. *The Spooky Tail of Prewitt Peacock* [1-2], 771

Peters, Lisa Westberg. *This Way Home* [K-3], **1217**

Pyle, Howard. *The Swan Maiden* [2-3], **665**

Rohmann, Eric. *Time Flies* [K-1], **350**

Rowe, John A. *Baby Crow* [Pre-K], **183**

Ryder, Joanne. *Catching the Wind* [Pre-3], 2088

Selden, George. *Sparrow Socks* [1-2], 799

Seuss, Dr. *The King's Stilts* [2-3], 996

Tyrrell, Esther Quesada. *Hummingbirds: Jewels in the Sky* [3-6], **1248**

Van Laan, Nancy. *The Big Fat Worm* [Pre-K], 282

Vyner, Sue. *The Stolen Egg* [K-1], **379**

Waterton, Betty. *A Salmon for Simon* [1-2], 846

White, E. B. *Stuart Little* [3-4], 1131

   The Trumpet of the Swan [4-5], 1253

Yolen, Jane. *Owl Moon* [1-2], 857

BIRDS–Folklore

Blia, Xiong. *Nine-in-One, Grr! Grr! A Folktale from the Hmong People of Laos* [K-3], 1404

Carey, Valerie Scho. *Quail Song: A Pueblo Indian Tale* [K-2], **876**

Climo, Shirley. *King of the Birds* [K-3], 1425

Demi. *The Firebird* [2-5], **893**

Dixon, Ann. *How Raven Brought Light to People* [K-4], **897**

Duff, Maggie. *Rum Pum Pum* [Pre-2], 1449

Gal, Laszlo. *Prince Ivan and the Firebird* [3-6], **908**

Goble, Paul. *Crow Chief: A Plains Indian Story* [2-6], **915**

Grimm, Jacob. *The Bear and the Bird King* [K-3], **929**

  The Glass Mountain [2-6], 1494

  Jorinda and Joringel [2-4], 1498

Hastings, Selina. *The Firebird* [1-4], **938**

Ishii, Momoko. *The Tongue-Cut Sparrow* [Pre-3], 1535

Kimmel, Eric A. *I-Know-Not-What, I-Know-Not-Where: A Russian Tale* [4-6], **955**

McDermott, Gerald. *Coyote: A Trickster Tale from the American Southwest* [Pre-2], **975**

  Raven: A Trickster Tale from the Pacific Northwest [K-4], **976**

Maddern, Eric. *Rainbow Bird: An Aboriginal Folktale from Northern Australia* [K-3], **979**

Mollel, Tololwa M. *The Flying Tortoise: An Igbo Tale* [K-2], **987**

  A Promise to the Sun: An African Story [K-3], **990**

Newton, Patricia Montgomery. *The Five Sparrows: A Japanese Folktale* [1-4], 1575

Paterson, Katherine. *The Tale of the Mandarin Ducks* [2-6], **996**

Rhee, Nami. *Magic Spring: A Korean Folktale* [K-3], **1002**

Robinson, Gail. *Raven the Trickster: Legends of the North American Indians* [4-6], 1719

San Souci, Robert D. *The Firebird* [3-5], **1012**

Shetterly, Susan Hand. *Raven's Light: A Myth from the People of the Northwest Coast* [2-5], **1024**

Silverman, Maida. *Anna and the Seven Swans* [K-3], 1601

Steptoe, John. *The Story of Jumping Mouse: A Native American Legend* [Pre-4], 1608

Troughton, Joanna. *How the Birds Changed Their Feathers: A South American Indian Folk Tale* [Pre-3], 1616

Yagawa, Sumiko. *The Crane Wife* [2-5], 1632

BIRDS–Poetry

Mother Goose. *Little Robin Redbreast: A Mother Goose Rhyme* [Pre], 35

Yolen, Jane. *Bird Watch: A Book of Poetry* [3-6], **1429**

BIRTH

Cole, Joanna. *My Puppy Is Born* [Pre-2], **1123**

BIRTHDAYS

Adler, David A. *My Dog and the Birthday Mystery* [K-1], 313

Armitage, Ronda, and David Armitage. *The Bossing of Josie* [Pre-K], 8

Asch, Frank. *Happy Birthday, Moon* [Pre-K], 12

Barrett, Judi. *Benjamin's 365 Birthdays* [K-1], 330

Brown, Marc. *Arthur's Birthday* [1-2], 626

Bunting, Eve. *Flower Garden* [Pre-K], **72**

Carle, Eric. *The Secret Birthday Message* [Pre-K], 40

Cazet, Denys. *December 24th* [K-1], 359

Christelow, Eileen. *Olive and the Magic Hat* [K-1], 365

Cohen, Barbara. *Make a Wish, Molly* [2-3], **598**

Flack, Marjorie. *Ask Mr. Bear* [Pre-K], 87

Giff, Patricia Reilly. *Happy Birthday, Ronald Morgan!* [K-1], 406

Green, John F. *Alice and the Birthday Giant* [K-1], 408

Hiller, Catherine. *Abracatabby* [K-1], 424

Houseman, Laurence. *Rocking-Horse Land* [1-2], 690

Howe, James. *Creepy-Crawly Birthday* [1-2], **456**

Hughes, Shirley. *Alfie Gives a Hand* [Pre-K], 144

Johnston, Johanna. *That's Right, Edie* [K-1], 441

Jonas, Ann. *The 13th Clue* [1-2], **464**

Keats, Ezra Jack. *A Letter to Amy* [K-1], 451

Lowry, Lois. *Attaboy, Sam!* [4-5], **776**

Merriam, Eve. *The Birthday Door* [1-2], 750

Moskin, Marietta. *Rosie's Birthday Present* [K-1], 510

Mueller, Virginia. *Monster's Birthday Hiccups* [Pre], **36**

Peterson, Esther Allen. *Penelope Gets Wheels* [1-2], 774

Polacco, Patricia. *Some Birthday!* [1-2], **537**

Russo, Marisabina. *Only Six More Days* [Pre-K], 248

Shannon, George. *The Surprise* [Pre-K], 262

Wadsworth, Ginger. *Tomorrow Is Daddy's Birthday* [K-1], **380**

West, Colin. *The King of Kennelwick Castle* [Pre-K], 289

Willard, Nancy. *Papa's Panda* [Pre-K], 295

BIRTHDAYS–Poetry

Goldstein, Bobbye S. *Birthday Rhymes, Special Times* [Pre-3], **1297**

Hopkins, Lee Bennett. *Happy Birthday: Poems* [K-3], **1321**

BLACKFOOT INDIANS–Folklore

Van Laan, Nancy. *Buffalo Dance: A Blackfoot Legend* [3-6], **1039**

BLACKS

SEE Africa; African Americans

BLANKETS

Cooney, Nancy Evans. *The Blanket Had to Go* [Pre-K], 55

Henkes, Kevin. *Owen* [Pre-K], **122**

Hughes, Shirley. *Alfie Gives a Hand* [Pre-K], 144

Jonas, Ann. *Where Can It Be?* [Pre], **25**

Keller, Holly. *Geraldine's Blanket* [Pre-K], 168

Robison, Deborah. *Bye-Bye, Old Buddy* [K-1], 532

BLIND

SEE ALSO Handicaps

Alexander, Sally Hobart. *Mom Can't See Me* [1-4], **1097**

Mom's Best Friend [2-6], **1098**

Garfield, James B. *Follow My Leader* [4-5], 1174

Hunter, Edith Fisher. *Child of the Silent Night: The Story of Laura Bridgman* [3-5], 2053

Keats, Ezra Jack. *Apt. 3* [2-3], 942

Little, Jean. *Little by Little: A Writer's Education* [5-6], **1187**

Whelan, Gloria. *Hannah* [2-3], **689**

BLIND–Folklore

Quigley, Lillian F. *The Blind Mice and the Elephant* [K-5], 1582

BLIZZARDS

SEE Storms; Weather

BOATS AND BOATING

SEE ALSO Ships

Burningham, John. *Mr. Gumpy's Outing* [Pre-K], 33

Doherty, Berlie. *Snowy* [K-1], **263**

Flack, Marjorie. *The Story about Ping* [K-1], 387

Lear, Edward. *The Owl and the Pussycat* [Pre-K], 181, **148**, **149**

McCloskey, Robert. *Burt Dow, Deep-Water Man* [2-3], 955

Pinkwater, Daniel. *Yobgorgle: Mystery Monster of Lake Ontario* [4-5], 1227

Van Allsburg, Chris. *The Wreck of the Zephyr* [3-4], 1126

BOATS AND BOATING–Folklore

Kellogg, Steven. *Mike Fink* [1-4], **948**

BODY, HUMAN

Cole, Joanna. *The Magic School Bus Inside the Human Body* [2-4], 2010

Cummings, Phil. *Goodness Gracious!* [Pre-K], **90**

BODY, HUMAN–Riddles

Mathews, Judith, and Fay Robinson. *Knock-Knock Knees and Funny Bones: Riddles for Every Body* [3-6], **1370**

BONES

Ahlberg, Janet, and Allan Ahlberg. *Funnybones* [K-1], 314

Steig, William. *The Amazing Bone* [2-3], 1006

BONES–Folklore

Bennett, Jill. *Teeny Tiny* [Pre-2], **1403**

DeFelice, Cynthia C. *The Dancing Skeleton* [2-4], 1437

Galdone, Paul. *The Teeny-Tiny Woman: A Ghost Story* [Pre-2], **1471**

BOOKS AND READING

Baker, Alan. *Benjamin's Book* [K-1], 325

Bauer, Caroline Feller. *Too Many Books* [K-1], 333

Bernstein, Joanne E., and Paul Cohen. *What Was the Wicked Witch's Real Name? And Other Character Riddles* [2-6], 1749

Birdseye, Tom. *Just Call Me Stupid* [4-5], **759**

Bonsall, Crosby. *Tell Me Some More* [Pre-K], 23

Browne, Eileen. *No Problem* [1-2], **414**

Bunting, Eve. *The Wednesday Surprise* [1-2], 633

Caseley, Judith. *Sophie and Sammy's Library Sleepover* [Pre-K], **77**

Daugherty, James. *Andy and the Lion* [1-2], 658

Drescher, Henrik. *Simon's Book* [1-2], 664

Duvoisin, Roger. *Petunia* [K-1], 378

Falwell, Cathryn. *The Letter Jesters* [2-4], **1140**

Felt, Sue. *Rosa-Too-Little* [Pre-K], 83

Haley, Gail E. *Dream Peddler* [2-3], **612**

Huff, Barbara A. *Once Inside the Library* [1-2], **459**

Hutchins, Pat. *The Tale of Thomas Mead* [1-2], 697

Knowlton, Jack. *Books and Libraries* [2-5], **1171**

Krauss, Ruth. *Is This You?* [1-2], 714

Lindbergh, Anne. *Travel Far, Pay No Fare* [5-6], **826**

McGovern, Ann. *Drop Everything, It's D.E.A.R. Time!* [1-2], **497**

McPhail, David. *Fix-It* [K-1], 494
   Santa's Book of Names [K-1], **319**
Marshall, James. *Wings: A Tale of Two Chickens* [1-2], 745
Mennen, Ingrid, and Niki Daly. *Somewhere in Africa* [1-2], **509**
Nixon, Joan Lowery. *If You Were a Writer* [2-3], 972
Paton Walsh, Jill. *The Green Book* [5-6], 1341
Roberts, Willo Davis. *The Magic Book* [4-5], 1229
Sadler, Marilyn. *Alistair in Outer Space* [1-2], 787
Sauer, Julie L. *Mike's House* [Pre-K], 252
Scieszka, Jon. *The Book That Jack Wrote* [1-2], **548**
Stevens, Janet. *From Pictures to Words: A Book About Making a Book* [1-4], **1244**
Teague, Mark. *Frog Medicine* [2-3], **681**
Williams, Barbara. *The Author and Squinty Gritt* [1-2], **575**

BOOKS AND READING–Folklore
Day, David. *The Sleeper* [2-4], **891**
Hodges, Margaret. *Saint Patrick and the Peddler* [1-4], **941**

BOOKS AND READING–Poetry
Hopkins, Lee Bennett. *Good Books, Good Times!* [K-4], **1320**

BOOKS AND READING–Riddles
Walton, Rick, and Ann Walton. *Kiss a Frog! Jokes About Fairy Tales, Knights, and Dragons* [1-4], **1419**

BOOTS
  SEE Shoes

BRAVERY
  SEE Courage

BREAD
  SEE ALSO Cookery; Food
Morris, Ann. *Bread Bread Bread* [Pre-3], **1211**
Robbins, Ken. *Make Me a Peanut Butter Sandwich and a Glass of Milk* [1-4], **1225**

BREAD–Folklore
dePaola, Tomie. *Tony's Bread* [1-4], **896**

BREAKFAST
Kandoian, Ellen. *Is Anybody Up?* [Pre-K], **139**

BROOMS
Van Allsburg, Chris. *The Widow's Broom* [3-4], **752**

BROTHERHOOD
Hamanaka, Sheila. *All the Colors of the Earth* [1-2], **449**

BROTHERS
  SEE ALSO Brothers and Sisters; Sisters
Asch, Frank, and Vladimir Vagin. *Dear Brother* [1-2], **401**
Auch, Mary Jane. *Monster Brother* [K-1], **221**
Avi. *Shadrach's Crossing* [5-6], 1269
Banish, Rosalyn. *Let Me Tell You about My Baby* [Pre-1], 1990
Bishop, Claire. *The Five Chinese Brothers* [1-2], 617
Blume, Judy. *Tales of a Fourth Grade Nothing* [3-4], 1046
Cameron, Ann. *The Stories Julian Tells* [2-3], 881
Carrick, Carol. *Patrick's Dinosaurs* [K-1], 358
Collier, James Lincoln, and Christopher Collier. *My Brother Sam is Dead* [5-6], 1288
Cutler, Jane. *No Dogs Allowed* [2-3], **602**
Fitzgerald, John D. *The Great Brain* [4-5], 1171
Fleischman, Paul. *Finzel the Farsighted* [3-4], 1065
Getz, David. *Thin Air* [5-6], **819**
Hoffman, Mary. *Henry's Baby* [1-2], **454**
Johnston, Tony. *Slither McCreep and His Brother Joe* [K-1], **294**
Kellogg, Steven. *Much Bigger than Martin* [K-1], 453
Levy, Elizabeth. *Frankenstein Moved in on the Fourth Floor* [2-3], 951
Moore, Lilian. *The Snake That Went to School* [2-3], 968
Naylor, Phyllis Reynolds. *The Boys Start the War* [3-4], **735**
Park, Barbara. *Operation: Dump the Chump* [3-4], 1101
Petersen, P. J. *The Amazing Magic Show* [1-2], **529**
Rabin, Staton. *Casey Over There* [2-3], **666**
Roy, Ron. *Nightmare Island* [4-5], 1234
Sheldon, Dyan. *My Brother Is a Visitor from Another Planet* [3-4], **746**
Spier, Peter. *Bored, Nothing to Do* [1-2], 817
Steptoe, John. *Stevie* [2-3], 1010
Sterman, Betsy, and Samuel Sterman. *Too Much Magic* [3-4], 1119
Stevenson, James. *Brrr!* [K-1], **373**
   That's Exactly the Way It Wasn't [1-2], **558**
Titherington, Jeanne. *A Place for Ben* [Pre-K], 274
Waddell, Martin. *Sam Vole and His Brothers* [Pre], **51**
Wells, Rosemary. *Waiting for the Evening Star* [3-4], **754**
Wiesner, David. *Hurricane* [1-2], **574**
Wisniewski, David. *The Warrior and the Wise Man* [2-3], 1031
Yaccarino, Dan. *Big Brother Mike* [K-1], **390**
Yorinks, Arthur. *Oh, Brother* [2-3], 1036

BROTHERS–Folklore

Bierhorst, John. *The Woman Who Fell from the Sky: The Iroquois Story of Creation* [2-6], **868**

Croll, Carolyn. *The Three Brothers* [K-3], **888**

Demi. *The Magic Tapestry* [1-4], **894**

Ginsburg, Mirra. *The Night It Rained Pancakes* [Pre-2], 1480

Grimm, Jacob. *One Gift Deserves Another* [1-4], **927**

The Water of Life [3-6], 1511

Haley, Gail E. *Jack and the Fire Dragon* [2-5], 1516

Kimmel, Eric A. *Boots and His Brothers: A Norwegian Tale* [2-6], **952**

Three Sacks of Truth: A Story from France [2-5], **958**

Kismaric, Carole. *The Rumor of Pavel and Paali: A Ukrainian Folktale* [3-6], 1542

Langton, Jane. *Salt: A Russian Folktale* [2-5], **963**

Mahy, Margaret. *The Seven Chinese Brothers* [K-4], 1558

Martin, Claire. *Boots & the Glass Mountain* [2-6], **981**

Mosel, Arlene. *Tikki Tikki Tembo* [Pre-3], 1572

Riordan, James. *The Three Magic Gifts* [1-4], 1586

San Souci, Robert. *The Enchanted Tapestry: A Chinese Folktale* [1-4], 1589

Sawyer, Ruth. *The Remarkable Christmas of the Cobbler's Sons* [K-3], **1020**

Walker, Barbara. *Teeny-Tiny and the Witch Woman* [2-4], 1623

Zemach, Harve. *Too Much Noise: An Italian Tale* [2-5], 1637

BROTHERS–Poetry

Margolis, Richard J. *Secrets of a Small Brother* [1-4], 1867

BROTHERS AND SISTERS

SEE ALSO Brothers; Sisters

Andersen, Hans Christian. *The Wild Swans* [3-4], 1040, **700**

Anderson, Lonzo. *The Ponies of Mykillengi* [2-3], 865

Andrews, F. Emerson. *Upside-Down Town* [2-3], 866

Arnold, Eric H., and Jeffrey Loeb. *I'm Telling! Kids Talk about Brothers and Sisters* [4-5], 1988

Balian, Lorna. *Bah! Humbug?* [K-1], 328

Bancroft, Catherine, and Hannah Coale Gruenberg. *Felix's Hat* [Pre-K], **70**

Bartone, Elisa. *Peppe the Lamplighter* [1-2], **405**

Blume, Judy. *The Pain and the Great One* [1-2], 619

Superfudge [4-5], 1145

Brandenberg, Franz. *I Wish I Was Sick, Too* [Pre-K], 26

Brown, Marc. *Arthur Babysits* [1-2], **412**

Arthur's April Fool [1-2], 625

Arthur's Baby [K-1], 344

Arthur's Chicken Pox [K-1], **239**

Arthur's Halloween [1-2], 627

D.W. Thinks Big [Pre-K], **71**

Burch, Robert. *Ida Early Comes Over the Mountain* [4-5], 1153

Byars, Betsy. *The Not-Just-Anybody Family* [4-5], 1156

The Seven Treasure Hunts [2-3], **595**

The Summer of the Swans [5-6], 1282

The Two-Thousand Pound Goldfish [5-6], 1283

Carlson, Natalie Savage. *The Night the Scarecrow Walked* [1-2], 639

Caseley, Judith. *Harry and Arney* [1-2], **422**

Sophie and Sammy's Library Sleepover [Pre-K], **77**

Chase, Mary. *Loretta Mason Potts* [4-5], 1157

Cleary, Beverly. *The Growing-Up Feet* [Pre-K], 50

Clymer, Eleanor. *My Brother Stevie* [3-4], 1054

Cohen, Barbara. *The Carp in the Bathtub* [2-3], 892

Conford, Ellen. *Impossible Possum* [1-2], 652

Coville, Bruce. *Jennifer Murdley's Toad* [4-5], **765**

Cowen-Fletcher, Jane. *It Takes a Village* [K-1], **257**

Cutler, Jane. *Darcy and Gran Don't Like Babies* [K-1], **259**

Delton, Judy. *Angel in Charge* [3-4], 1061

Dillon, Barbara. *Mrs. Tooey & the Terrible Toxic Tar* [3-4], 1062

Dorris, Michael. *Morning Girl* [5-6], **814**

Dragonwagon, Crescent. *I Hate My Brother Harry* [1-2], 663

Edwards, Julie. *The Last of the Really Great Whangdoodles* [3-4], 1063

Fisk, Nicholas. *Grinny: A Novel of Science Fiction* [5-6], 1297

Garrigue, Sheila. *Between Friends* [4-5], 1175

Getz, David. *Almost Famous* [5-6], **818**

Green, Melinda. *Rachel's Recital* [2-3], 928

Greenwald, Sheila. *The Atrocious Two* [4-5], 1184

Harrison, Maggie. *Angels on Roller Skates* [1-2], **451**

Haynes, Betsy. *The Ghost of the Gravestone Hearth* [4-5], 1185

Heide, Florence Parry, and Roxanne Heide. *A Monster Is Coming! A Monster Is Coming!* [1-2], 684

Heller, Nicholas. *An Adventure at Sea* [1-2], 685

Henkes, Kevin. *Bailey Goes Camping* [Pre-K], 131

Julius, the Baby of the World [K-1], **283**

Margaret & Taylor [K-1], 419

Henry, Marguerite. *Misty of Chincoteague* [3-4], 1072

Hest, Amy. *The Mommy Exchange* [K-1], 421

Hoban, Lillian. *Arthur's Christmas Cookies* [K-1], 425

Arthur's Great Big Valentine [K-1], 426

Arthur's Loose Tooth [K-1], 427

Howard, Elizabeth Fitzgerald. *Mac & Marie & the Train Toss Surprise* [1-2], **455**

Hughes, Shirley. *Alfie's Feet* [Pre-K], 145

The Big Alfie Out of Doors Storybook [Pre-K], **128**

Hurwitz, Johanna. *Busybody Nora* [1-2], 694

"E" Is for Elisa [K-1], **290**

Superduper Teddy [1-2], 696

Hutchins, Pat. *Silly Billy!* [Pre], **24**

The Very Worst Monster [Pre-K], 150

Jeffers, Susan. *Wild Robin* [1-2], 699

Joyce, William. *Santa Calls* [2-3], **631**

Julian, Nancy R. *The Peculiar Miss Pickett* [2-3], 940

Kalman, Maira. *Hey Willy, See the Pyramids* [2-3], 941

Keller, Holly. *Geraldine's Baby Brother* [Pre-K], **142**

King-Smith, Dick. *Sophie's Snail* [1-2], 711

Kleven, Elisa. *The Paper Princess* [Pre-K], **146**

Krensky, Steven. *The Dragon Circle* [4-6], 1202

LeGuin, Ursula K. *A Ride on the Red Mare's Back* [2-3], **637**

L'Engle, Madeleine. *A Wrinkle in Time* [5-6], 1325

Leverich, Kathleen. *Hilary and the Troublemakers* [3-4], **730**

Lindgren, Astrid. *The Ghost of Skinny Jack* [3-4], 1089

I Want a Brother or Sister [Pre-K], 189

Little, Jean. *Home from Far* [4-5], 1206

Revenge of the Small Small [1-2], **486**

MacLachlan, Patricia. *Sarah, Plain and Tall* [3-4], 1094

McMurtry, Stan. *The Bunjee Venture* [4-5], 1210

Odgers, Sally Farrell. *Drummond: The Search for Sarah* [1-2], **522**

O'Donnell, Elizabeth Lee. *Maggie Doesn't Want to Move* [K-1], 515

Olson, Arielle North. *Hurry Home, Grandma!* [Pre-K], 220

Polacco, Patricia. *My Rotten Redheaded Older Brother* [1-2], **536**

Pringle, Laurence. *Octopus Hug* [Pre-K], **178**

Rayner, Mary. *Garth Pig and the Ice Cream Lady* [1-2], 781

Mr. and Mrs. Pig's Evening Out [1-2], 782

Mrs. Pig's Bulk Buy [1-2], 783

Richler, Mordecai. *Jacob Two-Two Meets the Hooded Fang* [3-4], 1107

Robinson, Barbara. *The Best Christmas Pageant Ever* [4-5], 1230

The Best School Year Ever [4-5], **788**

Roche, P. K. *Good-Bye, Arnold* [K-1], 533

Root, Phyllis. *Moon Tiger* [K-1], 535

Russo, Marisabina. *I Don't Want to Go Back to School* [K-1], **355**

Only Six More Days [Pre-K], 248

Segal, Lore. *Tell Me a Mitzi* [1-2], 798

Shyer, Marlene Fanta. *My Brother, the Thief* [5-6], 1356

Welcome Home, Jellybean [5-6], 1357

Slepian, Jan. *The Broccoli Tapes* [5-6], **844**

Smith, Alison. *Help! There's a Cat Washing in Here* [5-6], 1361

Smith, Janice Lee. *The Monster in the Third Dresser Drawer: And Other Stories about Adam Joshua* [1-2], 815

Smith, L. J. *The Night of the Solstice* [5-6], 1362

Spier, Peter. *Oh, Were They Ever Happy!* [K-1], 559

Stevenson, James. *There's Nothing to Do!* [1-2], 825

Worse Than Willy! [1-2], 827

Streatfeild, Noel. *When the Sirens Wailed* [5-6], 1366

Tannen, Mary. *The Wizard Children of Finn* [5-6], 1367

Udry, Janice May. *Thump and Plunk* [Pre-K], 277

Van Allsburg, Chris. *Jumanji* [2-3], 1020

Van Leeuwen, Jean. *Benjy in Business* [2-3], 1021

Viorst, Judith. *I'll Fix Anthony* [K-1], 574

Wardlaw, Lee. *Seventh-Grade Weirdo* [5-6], **850**

Warner, Gertrude Chandler. *The Boxcar Children* [2-3], 1025

Wells, Rosemary. *Max and Ruby's First Greek Myth: Pandora's Box* [1-2], **573**

Max's Chocolate Chicken [Pre-K], 286

Wishinsky, Frieda. *Oonga Boonga* [Pre-K], **209**

Wolf, Ashley. *Stella & Roy* [Pre-K], **210**

Wolkoff, Judie. *Wally* [3-4], 1135

Woodruff, Elvira. *The Magnificent Mummy Maker* [4-5], **799**

York, Carol Beach. *I Will Make You Disappear* [5-6], 1378

BROTHERS AND SISTERS–Folklore

Goble, Paul. *Her Seven Brothers* [3-6], 1482

Grimm, Jacob. *Hansel and Gretel* [K-2], **926**

Hansel and Gretel [2-4], 1496

BROTHERS AND SISTERS–Folklore (cont.)
Little Brother and Little Sister [2-5], 1499

BROWN, JOHN
Everett, Gwen. *John Brown: One Man Against Slavery* [5-6], **1138**

BUFFALOES
Freedman, Russell. *Buffalo Hunt* [5-6], 2025

BUFFALOES–Folklore
Baker, Olaf. *Where the Buffaloes Begin* [3-6], 1397
Goble, Paul. *Buffalo Woman* [2-6], 1481
  Crow Chief: A Plains Indian Story [2-6], **915**
  Her Seven Brothers [3-6], 1482
Van Laan, Nancy. *Buffalo Dance: A Blackfoot Legend* [3-6], **1039**

BULLFIGHTERS
Say, Allen. *El Chino* [2-5], **1234**

BULLIES
Alexander, Martha. *Move Over, Twerp* [K-1], 315
Bottner, Barbara. *Bootsie Barker Bites* [K-1], **234**
Brown, Marc. *Arthur's April Fool* [1-2], 625
Browne, Anthony. *Willy the Wimp* [K-1], 350
Byars, Betsy. *The 18th Emergency* [4-5], 1155
Chapman, Carol. *Herbie's Troubles* [K-1], 361
Cole, Joanna. *Don't Call Me Names* [K-1], **254**
Conford, Ellen. *Lenny Kandell, Smart Aleck* [5-6], 1290
  Revenge of the Incredible Dr. Rancid and His Youthful Assistant, Jeffrey [4-5], 1162
Coville, Bruce. *The Monster's Ring* [4-5], 1165
Dahl, Roald. *The Enormous Crocodile* [1-2], 656
Giff, Patricia Reilly. *Matthew Jackson Meets the Wall* [2-3], **611**
Kasza, Keiko. *The Rat and the Tiger* [Pre-K], **141**
Keats, Ezra Jack. *Goggles!* [K-1], 449
Kraus, Robert. *Noel the Coward* [Pre-K], 175
Marshall, James. *Merry Christmas, Space Case* [1-2], 744
Mwenye Hadithi. *Crafty Chameleon* [Pre-K], 124
Naylor, Phyllis Reynolds. *King of the Playground* [K-1], **332**
Roberts, Willo Davis. *The Magic Book* [4-5], 1229
Sachs, Marilyn. *Veronica Ganz* [4-5], 1236
Scribner, Virginia. *Gopher Takes Heart* [3-4], **744**
Shreve, Susan. *Joshua T. Bates Takes Charge* [3-4], **747**
Shusterman, Neal. *The Eyes of Kid Midas* [5-6], **842**
Stolz, Mary. *The Bully of Barkham Street* [3-4], 1120
Wardlaw, Lee. *Seventh-Grade Weirdo* [5-6], **850**

Wells, Rosemary. *Hazel's Amazing Mother* [K-1], 585
Wilhelm, Hans. *Tyrone the Horrible* [K-1], 590

BURIED TREASURE
Bellaits, John. *The Treasure of Alpheus Winterborn* [5-6], 1275
Byars, Betsy. *The Seven Treasure Hunts* [2-3], **595**
Cohen, Caron Lee. *Renata, Whizbrain and the Ghost* [2-3], 894
Donnelly, Judy. *True-Life Treasure Hunts* [3-5], 2020
Fleischman, Sid. *The Ghost in the Noonday Sun* [5-6], 1301
Haynes, Betsy. *The Ghost of the Gravestone Hearth* [4-5], 1185
Masterman-Smith, Virginia. *The Treasure Trap* [4-5], 1212
Mooser, Stephen. *Orphan Jeb at the Massacree* [4-5], 1215
Schwartz, Alvin. *Gold and Silver, Silver and Gold: Tales of Hidden Treasure* [4-6], 2092
Swinburne, Irene, and Laurence Swinburne. *Behind the Sealed Door: The Discovery of the Tomb and Treasures of Tutankhamen* [4-6], 2109

BURIED TREASURE–Folklore
Cole, Joanna. *Don't Tell the Whole World!* [K-3], **881**
San Souci, Robert D. *The Boy and the Ghost* [1-4], **1011**

BUSES
SEE ALSO Automobiles; Transportation; Trucks
Alexander, Martha. *Move Over, Twerp* [K-1], 315
Cole, Joanna. *The Magic School Bus Lost in the Solar System* [1-4], **1121**
  The Magic School Bus on the Ocean Floor [2-4], **1122**
Kovalski, Maryann. *The Wheels on the Bus* [Pre-K], 173
Park, Barbara. *Junie B. Jones and the Stupid Smelly Bus* [2-3], **653**
Raffi. *Wheels on the Bus* [Pre-K], 235
Sheldon, Dyan. *A Witch Got on at Paddington Station* [Pre-K], 265
Zelinsky, Paul O. *The Wheels on the Bus* [Pre-K], **214**

BUTTERFLIES
SEE ALSO Insects
Brown, Ruth A. *If at First You Do Not See* [K-1], 348
Carle, Eric. *The Very Hungry Caterpillar* [Pre-K], 42

BUTTONS

Mazer, Anne. *The Yellow Button* [1-2], **505**

BUTTONS–Folklore

Gilman, Phoebe. *Something from Nothing* [Pre-2], **914**

CACTUS

Guiberson, Brenda. *Cactus Hotel* [1-4], **1155**

CAKE

SEE Cookery; Food

CALDECOTT MEDAL

Aardema, Verna. *Why Mosquitoes Buzz in People's Ears* [Pre-2], 1386

Ackerman, Karen. *Song and Dance Man* [1-2], 599

Bemelmans, Ludwig. *Madeline's Rescue* [K-1], 335

Brown, Marcia. *Cinderella: Or, The Little Glass Slipper* [1-4], 1410

Brown, Margaret. *Wheel on the Chimney* [1-2], 631

Bunting, Eve. *Smoky Night* [2-3], **593**

Burton, Virginia Lee. *The Little House* [1-2], 634

De Regniers, Beatrice Schenk. *May I Bring a Friend?* [Pre-K], 69

Emberley, Barbara. *Drummer Hoff* [Pre-K], 80

Haley, Gail E. *A Story, a Story* [K-3], 1517

Hall, Donald. *Ox-Cart Man* [2-3], 931

Hodges, Margaret. *Saint George and the Dragon: A Golden Legend* [3-6], 1526

Hogrogian, Nonny. *One Fine Day* [Pre-2], 1528

Keats, Ezra Jack. *The Snowy Day* [Pre-K], 165

Lobel, Arnold. *Fables* [4-5], 1207

Macaulay, David. *Black and White* [1-2], **490**

McCloskey, Robert. *Make Way for Ducklings* [1-2], 734

Time of Wonder [2-3], 957

McCully, Emily Arnold. *Mirette on the High Wire* [1-2], **492**

Mosel, Arlene. *The Funny Little Woman* [Pre-3], 1571

Ness, Evaline. *Sam, Bangs and Moonshine* [1-2], 757

Provensen, Alice, and Martin Provensen. *The Glorious Flight: Across the Channel with Louis Blérot* [K-6], 2084

Ransome, Arthur. *The Fool of the World and His Flying Ship* [2-4], 1583

Say, Allen. *Grandfather's Journey* [2-3], **674**

Sendak, Maurice. *Where the Wild Things Are* [Pre-K], 255

Steig, William. *Sylvester and the Magic Pebble* [1-2], 821

Thurber, James. *Many Moons* [2-3], 1015

Udry, Janice May. *A Tree Is Nice* [Pre-K], 278

Van Allsburg, Chris. *Jumanji* [2-3], 1020

The Polar Express [1-2], 835

Ward, Lynd. *The Biggest Bear* [1-2], 844

Wiesner, David. *Tuesday* [K-1], **385**

Yolen, Jane. *Owl Moon* [1-2], 857

Young, Ed. *Lon Po Po: A Red-Riding Hood Story from China* [K-2], 1633

Zemach, Harve. *Duffy and the Devil* [2-5], 1635

CALIFORNIA

Fleischman, Sid. *By the Great Horn Spoon* [5-6], 1300

Polacco, Patricia. *Tikvah Means Hope* [2-3], **664**

CALL-AND-RESPONSE STORIES

Aylesworth, Jim. *My Son John* [K-1], **222**

Carlson, Bernice Wells. *Listen! And Help Tell the Story* [Pre-2], 1765

Crews, Donald. *Freight Train* [Pre-K], 58

Cuyler, Margery. *That's Good! That's Bad!* [Pre-K], **92**

Duke, Kate. *Seven Froggies Went to School* [K-1], 377

Galdone, Paul. *Over in the Meadow: An Old Nursery Counting Rhyme* [Pre-K], 108

Jones, Maurice. *I'm Going on a Dragon Hunt* [Pre-K], 158

Leedy, Loreen. *A Number of Dragons* [Pre-K], 182

Martin, Bill, Jr. *Brown Bear, Brown Bear, What Do You See?* [Pre-K], 204

Polar Bear, Polar Bear, What Do You Hear? [Pre-K], **160**

Paxton, Tom. *Where's the Baby?* [Pre], **38**

Pinczes, Elinor J. *One Hundred Hungry Ants* [1-2], **533**

Rosen, Michael. *We're Going on a Bear Hunt* [Pre-K], 245

Sivulich, Sandra Stroner. *I'm Going on a Bear Hunt* [Pre-K], 267

Turner, Gwenda. *Over on the Farm* [Pre-K], **195**

Williams, Sue. *I Went Walking* [Pre], **57**

CAMBODIA

Ho, Minfong. *The Clay Marble* [5-6], **823**

CAMELS

Kipling, Rudyard. *How the Camel Got His Hump* [2-3], 947

Tworkov, Jack. *The Camel Who Took a Walk* [K-1], 571

CAMPING

Henkes, Kevin. *Bailey Goes Camping* [Pre-K], 131

CAMPING (cont.)

Himmelman, John. *Lights Out!* [1-2], **453**

Howe, James. *Nighty-Nightmare* [4-5], 1194

Hughes, Shirley. *The Big Alfie Out of Doors Storybook* [Pre-K], **128**

Roy, Ron. *Nightmare Island* [4-5], 1234

Seligson, Susan. *Amos Camps Out: A Couch Adventure in the Woods* [1-2], **549**

CANADA

SEE ALSO Folklore–Canada

Andrews, Jan. *Very Last First Time* [2-3], 867

Burnford, Sheila. *The Incredible Journey* [5-6], 1279

Kinsey-Warnock, Natalie. *Wilderness Cat* [1-2], **470**

Little, Jean. *From Anna* [4-5], **775**

Mowat, Farley. *Owls in the Family* [3-5], 2077

Rice, Bebe Faas. *The Year the Wolves Came* [5-6], **839**

Waterton, Betty. *A Salmon for Simon* [1-2], 846

CANADA–Poetry

Service, Robert W. *The Cremation of Sam McGee* [5-6], 1355

CANDY

Balian, Lorna. *The Sweet Touch* [K-1], 329

Catling, Patrick Skene. *The Chocolate Touch* [2-3], 884

Dahl, Roald. *Charlie and the Chocolate Factory* [3-4], 1058

Kroll, Steven. *The Candy Witch* [K-1], 462

Smith, Robert Kimmell. *Chocolate Fever* [2-3], 1003

Wells, Rosemary. *Max's Chocolate Chicken* [Pre-K], 286

CANDY–Poetry

Adoff, Arnold. *Chocolate Dreams* [5-6], **1259**

CAREERS

SEE Occupations

CARIBBEAN ISLANDS

Gershator, Phillis. *Rata-Pata-Scata-Fata: A Caribbean Story* [Pre-K], **108**

Keller, Holly. *Island Baby* [K-1], **296**

Mitchell, Rita Phillips. *Hue Boy* [K-1], **325**

CARIBBEAN ISLANDS–Poetry

Agard, John, and Grace Nichols. *A Caribbean Dozen: Poems from Caribbean Poets* [1-6], **1262**

CARPENTERS

Prøysen, Alf. *Christmas Eve at Santa's* [K-1], 343

CASTLES

McCully, Emily Arnold. *The Amazing Felix* [1-2], **491**

CATERPILLARS

SEE ALSO Insects

Brown, Ruth A. *If at First You Do Not See* [K-1], 348

Carle, Eric. *The Very Hungry Caterpillar* [Pre-K], 42

CATERPILLARS–Folklore

Mollel, Tololwa M. *Rhinos for Lunch and Elephants for Supper!* [Pre-2], **991**

CATS

Abercrombie, Barbara. *Michael and the Cats* [Pre], **1**

Alexander, Lloyd. *The Cat Who Wished to Be a Man* [5-6], 1259

The Town Cats and Other Tales [5-6], 1261

Alexander, Martha. *The Story Grandmother Told* [Pre-K], **2**

Armstrong, Jennifer. *Chin Yu Min and the Ginger Cat* [2-3], **588**

Balian, Lorna. *Amelia's Nine Lives* [Pre-K], 19

Barber, Antonia. *Catkin* [2-3], **590**

Bauer, Marion Dane. *A Question of Trust* [5-6], **805**

Brandenberg, Franz. *I Wish I Was Sick, Too* [Pre-K], 26

No School Today [K-1], 342

Brown, Ruth A. *A Dark, Dark Tale* [K-1], 347

Our Cat Flossie [1-2], 632

Buehner, Caralyn. *A Job for Wittilda* [K-1], **242**

Bunting, Eve. *Scary, Scary Halloween* [K-1], 352

Burchardt, Nellie. *Project Cat* [2-3], 878

Burnford, Sheila. *The Incredible Journey* [5-6], 1279

Calhoun, Mary. *Cross-Country Cat* [1-2], 635

Henry the Sailor Cat [1-2], **418**

High-Wire Henry [1-2], **419**

Carlson, Natalie Savage. *Spooky Night* [K-1], 357

Carris, Joan. *Witch-Cat* [3-4], **706**

Cauley, Lorinda Bryan. *The Three Little Kittens* [Pre-K], 45

Clifford, Sandy. *The Roquefort Gang* [3-4], 1053

Coombs, Patricia. *Dorrie and the Weather Box* [1-2], 653

The Magician and McTree [2-3], 900

Cooney, Nancy Evans. *Go Away Monsters, Lickety Split* [Pre-K], 88

Dugan, Barbara. *Loop the Loop* [2-3], **608**

Ehlert, Lois. *Feathers for Lunch* [K-1], **265**

Emberley, Michael. *Ruby* [1-2], **437**

Everitt, Betsy. *Frida the Wondercat* [K-1], 384

Fenton, Edward. *The Big Yellow Balloon* [1-2], 667

Ferguson, Alane. *That New Pet!* [K-1], 386

Flack, Marjorie. *Angus and the Cat* [Pre-K], 84

Foreman, Michael. *Cat and Canary* [K-1], 388

Frascino, Edward. *My Cousin the King* [K-1], 390

Gag, Wanda. *Millions of Cats* [Pre-K], 104

Gantos, Jack. *Rotten Ralph* [K-1], 402

Geraghty, Paul. *Slobcat* [Pre-K], **107**

Gordon, Gaelyn. *Duckat* [Pre-K], **110**

Graeber, Charlotte. *Mustard* [2-3], 927

Greene, Carol. *The Old Ladies Who Liked Cats* [1-2], **445**

Haas, Jessie. *Chipmunk!* [Pre-K], **115**

Hall, Donald. *I Am the Dog, I Am the Cat* [1-2], **448**

Heckert, Connie. *Dribbles* [1-2], **452**

Herriot, James. *The Christmas Day Kitten* [2-4], 2048

Hildick, E. W. *The Case of the Condemned Cat* [3-4], 1073

Hiller, Catherine. *Abracatabby* [K-1], 424

Howe, Deborah, and James Howe. *Bunnicula: A Rabbit-Tale of Mystery* [4-5], 1193

Howe, James. *Creepy-Crawly Birthday* [1-2], **456**
The Fright before Christmas [2-3], 935
Nighty-Nightmare [4-5], 1194
Rabbit-Cadabra! [1-2], **458**

Jeschke, Susan. *Lucky's Choice* [K-1], **291**

Keats, Ezra Jack. *Pet Show!* [Pre-K], 163

Kherdian, David. *The Cat's Midsummer Jamboree* [K-1], 457

King-Smith, Dick. *Martin's Mice* [3-4], 1085

Kinsey-Warnock, Natalie. *Wilderness Cat* [1-2], **470**

Lear, Edward. *The Owl and the Pussycat* [Pre-K], 181, **148**, **149**

Le Guin, Ursula K. *Catwings* [2-3], 950
A Visit from Dr. Katz [Pre-K], 183

LeRoy, Gen. *Taxi Cat and Huey* [4-5], **773**

Lisle, Janet Taylor. *The Dancing Cats of Applesap* [4-5], 1205

Low, Joseph. *Mice Twice* [K-1], 488

McDonald, Joyce. *Homebody* [1-2], **494**

McMillan, Bruce. *Kitten Can* [Pre-K], 198

McPhail, David. *Great Cat* [K-1], 495

Minarik, Else Holmelund. *It's Spring!* [Pre-K], 213

Morey, Walt. *Sandy and the Rock Star* [5-6], 1333

Naylor, Phyllis Reynolds. *The Grand Escape* [4-5], **783**

Ness, Evaline. *Sam, Bangs and Moonshine* [1-2], 757

Nolan, Dennis. *Witch Bazooza* [1-2], 762

Okimoto, Jean Davies. *Blumpoe the Grumpoe Meets Arnold the Cat* [1-2], **525**

Panek, Dennis. *Catastrophe Cat* [Pre-K], 222

Pank, Rachel. *Under the Blackberries* [K-1], **335**

Park, Barbara. *Skinnybones* [4-5], 1222

Peppé, Rodney. *The Mice Who Lived in a Shoe* [1-2], 772

Pilkey, Dav. *Kat Kong* [2-3], **658**
When Cats Dream [1-2], **532**

Pinkwater, Daniel. *The Wuggie Norple Story* [K-1], 524

Pittman, Helena Clare. *Miss Hindy's Cats* [K-1], **338**

Polacco, Patricia. *Mrs. Katz and Tush* [2-3], **663**
Tikvah Means Hope [2-3], **664**

Purdy, Carol. *Mrs. Merriweather's Musical Cat* [1-2], **539**

Ravilious, Robin. *The Runaway Chick* [Pre-K], 236

Reeves, Mona Rabun. *I Had a Cat* [Pre-K], 237

Robinson, Nancy K. *Just Plain Cat* [2-3], 986

Rosen, Michael. *Moving* [K-1], **352**

Samuels, Barbara. *Duncan & Dolores* [Pre-K], 251

Selden, George. *The Cricket in Times Square* [4-5], 1237

Seuss, Dr. *The Cat in the Hat* [Pre-K], 258

Slavin, Bill. *The Cat Came Back* [1-2], **555**

Slepian, Jan. *The Broccoli Tapes* [5-6], **844**

Stadler, John. *Animal Cafe* [1-2], 819

Steig, William. *Solomon the Rusty Nail* [2-3], 1008

Stein, Sara Bonnett. *Cat* [Pre-1], 2107

Stolz, Mary. *Cat Walk* [3-4], 1121

Turkle, Brinton. *Do Not Open* [2-3], 1016

Viorst, Judith. *The Tenth Good Thing about Barney* [K-1], 575

Waber, Bernard. *Rich Cat, Poor Cat* [K-1], 579

Wagner, Jane. *J. T.* [3-4], 1129

Wagner, Jenny. *John Brown, Rose and the Midnight Cat* [K-1], 581

Whitney, Alma Marshak. *Leave Herbert Alone* [Pre-K], 294

Withers, Carl. *Tale of a Black Cat* [1-2], 853

Zelinsky, Paul O. *The Maid and the Mouse and the Odd-Shaped House* [1-2], 860

CATS–Folklore

Aardema, Verna. *Traveling to Tondo: A Tale of the Nkundo of Zaire* [Pre-2], **857**

Brown, Marcia. *Dick Whittington and His Cat* [1-4], 1411

Cauley, Lorinda Bryan. *Puss in Boots* [K-4], 1419

Galdone, Paul. *King of the Cats* [2-4], 1463
Puss in Boots [K-4], 1470

CATS–Folklore (cont.)

Gregg, Andy. *Great Rabbit and the Long-Tailed Wildcat* [2-4], **921**

Haley, Gail E. *Puss in Boots* [1-4], **933**

Hurlimann, Ruth. *The Proud White Cat* [Pre-2], 1532

Kent, Jack. *The Fat Cat* [Pre-2], 1539

Kirstein, Lincoln. *Puss in Boots* [1-4], **959**

Levine, Arthur A. *The Boy Who Drew Cats: A Japanese Folktale* [2-6], **968**

Nimmo, Jenny. *The Witches and the Singing Mice* [1-4], **992**

Perrault, Charles. *Puss in Boots* [1-4], **997**

Pevear, Richard. *Mr. Cat-and-a-Half* [1-3], 1578

Polette, Nancy. *The Little Old Woman and the Hungry Cat* [Pre-2], **999**

Richard, Françoise. *On Cat Mountain* [2-5], **1003**

San Souci, Robert D. *The White Cat: An Old French Fairy Tale* [2-5], **1019**

Uchida, Yoshiko. *The Two Foolish Cats* [Pre-2], 1620

Zaum, Marjorie. *Catlore: Tales from Around the World* [2-6], 1738

CATS–Poetry

Chapman, Jean. *Cat Will Rhyme with Hat: A Book of Poems* [3-6], 1767

De Regniers, Beatrice Schenk. *This Big Cat and Other Cats I've Known* [Pre-2], 1793

Eliot, T. S. *Mr. Mistoffelees with Mungojerrie and Rumpelteazer* [3-6], **1286**

Old Possum's Book of Practical Cats [4-6], 1795

Field, Eugene. *The Gingham Dog and the Calico Cat* [Pre-K], **103**

Hopkins, Lee Bennett. *I Am the Cat* [K-6], 1823

Larrick, Nancy. *Cats Are Cats* [3-6], 1851

Livingston, Myra Cohn. *Cat Poems* [2-5], 1858

Mother Goose. *Little Robin Redbreast: A Mother Goose Rhyme* [Pre], **35**

Yolen, Jane. *Raining Cats and Dogs* [1-4], **1430**

CATS–Riddles

Keller, Charles. *It's Raining Cats and Dogs: Cat and Dog Jokes* [2-5], 1837

Levine, Caroline. *Riddles to Tell Your Cat* [3-6], **1351**

CAUSE AND EFFECT

Aylesworth, Jim. *Hush Up!* [K-1], 323

Barton, Byron. *Buzz Buzz Buzz* [Pre-K], 21

Bennett, David. *One Cow Moo Moo!* [Pre], **5**

Charlip, Remy. *Fortunately* [1-2], 645

Cuyler, Margery. *That's Good! That's Bad!* [Pre-K], **92**

Gackenbach, Dick. *Claude Has a Picnic* [Pre], 16

Goldberg, Rube. *The Best of Rube Goldberg* [3-6], 2040

Goodsell, Jane. *Toby's Toe* [K-1], 407

Greene, Carol. *The Old Ladies Who Liked Cats* [1-2], **445**

Janovitz, Marilyn. *Look Out, Bird!* [Pre-K], **134**

Lester, Helen. *It Wasn't My Fault* [K-1], 469

Lexai, Joan. *That's Good, That's Bad* [Pre-K], 187

McGuire, Richard. *Night Becomes Day* [1-2], **498**

Noble, Trinka Hakes. *The Day Jimmy's Boa Ate the Wash* [1-2], 761

Numeroff, Laura J. *If You Give a Moose a Muffin* [K-1], **334**

If You Give a Mouse a Cookie [K-1], 514

Peters, Lisa Westberg. *When the Fly Flew In* [K-1], **336**

Runcie, Jill. *Cock-a-Doodle-Doo!* [Pre], **41**

Zolotow, Charlotte. *The Quarreling Book* [1-2], 861

CAVES

Taylor, Mark. *Henry the Explorer* [K-1], 564

CELLO

Lebentritt, Julia, and Richard Ploetz. *The Kooken* [1-2], **481**

CHAIRS

Graham, Thomas. *Mr. Bear's Chair* [Pre-K], 119

Williams, Vera B. *A Chair for My Mother* [1-2], 851

CHAMELEONS

SEE ALSO Reptiles

Carle, Eric. *The Mixed-Up Chameleon* [Pre-K], 38

Martin, James. *Chameleons: Dragons in the Trees* [2-5], **1201**

Massie, Diane Redfield. *Chameleon Was a Spy* [2-3], 960

Mwenye Hadithi. *Crafty Chameleon* [Pre-K], 124

CHANGE

Allen, Marjorie N., and Shelley Rotner. *Changes* [Pre-1], **1100**

Browne, Anthony. *Changes* [K-1], **241**

Peters, Lisa Westberg. *Water's Way* [K-3], **1218**

Weiss, Nicki. *An Egg Is an Egg* [Pre-K], **207**

CHANTABLE REFRAIN

Aardema, Verna. *The Riddle of the Drum* [1-4], 1383

Traveling to Tondo: A Tale of the Nkundo of Zaire [Pre-2], **857**

Ada, Alma Flor. *The Rooster Who Went to His Uncle's Wedding: A Latin American Folktale* [Pre-1], **858**

Anderson, Leone Castell. *The Wonderful Shrinking Shirt* [1-2], 604

Armour, Peter. *Stop That Pickle!* [K-1], **218**

Arnold, Tedd. *Ollie Forgot* [1-2], 607

Asch, Frank. *Just Like Daddy* [Pre-K], 13

Ata, Te. *Baby Rattlesnake* [Pre-1], **862**

Aylesworth, Jim. *My Son John* [K-1], **222**
Old Black Fly [K-1], **223**

Bennett, David. *One Cow Moo Moo!* [Pre], **5**

Birdseye, Tom. *Soap! Soap! Don't Forget the Soap! An Appalachian Folktale* [1-3], **869**

Blake, Quentin. *All Join In* [Pre-2], **1270**

Blia, Xiong. *Nine-in-One, Grr! Grr! A Folktale from the Hmong People of Laos* [K-3], 1404

Bowden, Joan Chase. *The Bean Boy* [Pre-1], 1405

Brown, Paula. *Moon Jump: A Cowntdown* [K-1], **240**

Brown, Ruth A. *A Dark, Dark Tale* [K-1], 347

Burningham, John. *Harvey Slumfenburger's Christmas Present* [K-1], **244**

Carey, Valerie Scho. *Quail Song: A Pueblo Indian Tale* [K-2], **876**

Carle, Eric. *The Grouchy Ladybug* [Pre-K], 37
The Very Quiet Cricket [Pre-K], **75**

Carlson, Bernice Wells. *Listen! And Help Tell the Story* [Pre-2], 1765

Cauley, Lorinda Bryan. *Old MacDonald Had a Farm* [Pre-K], **78**
The Pancake Boy: An Old Norwegian Folk Tale [1-3], 1418

Christelow, Eileen. *Five Little Monkeys Jumping on the Bed* [Pre-K], 48
Five Little Monkeys Sitting in a Tree [Pre-K], **85**

Clarke, Gus. *EIEIO: The Story of Old MacDonald, Who Had a Farm* [Pre-K], **86**

Cook, Scott. *The Gingerbread Boy* [Pre-1], 1429

Cuyler, Margery. *That's Good! That's Bad!* [Pre-K], **92**

Demuth, Patricia Brennan. *The Ornery Morning* [K-1], **260**

Dodds, Dayle Ann. *Wheel Away!* [Pre-K], 71

Dodds, Siobhan. *Grandpa Bud* [Pre], **9**

Domanska, Janina. *Little Red Hen* [Pre-1], 1447

Donaldson, Julia. *A Squash and a Squeeze* [K-1], **264**

Duff, Maggie. *Rum Pum Pum* [Pre-2], 1449

Ericsson, Jennifer A. *No Milk!* [Pre-K], 99

Esterl, Arnica. *The Fine Round Cake* [K-2], **903**

Evans, Katie. *Hunky Dory Ate It* [Pre-K], **100**

Fox, Mem. *Shoes from Grandpa* [Pre-K], **105**

Gag, Wanda. *Millions of Cats* [Pre-K], 104

Galdone, Joanna, and Paul Galdone. *Gertrude the Goose Who Forgot* [Pre-K], 107

Galdone, Paul. *The Gingerbread Boy* [Pre-K], 1459
The Greedy Old Fat Man: An American Folktale [Pre-2], 1460
Henny Penny [Pre-1], 1461
The Little Red Hen [Pre-1], 1464
Old Mother Hubbard and Her Dog [Pre-1], 1468
The Old Woman and Her Pig [Pre-1], 1469

Garner, Alan. *Once Upon a Time, Though It Wasn't in Your Time, and It Wasn't in My Time, and It Wasn't in Anybody's Time. . . .* [Pre-2], **1065**

Gelman, Rita Golden. *I Went to the Zoo* [K-1], **275**

Gilman, Phoebe. *Something from Nothing* [Pre-2], **914**

Gordon, Jeffie Ross. *Two Badd Babies* [Pre-K], **112**

Harper, Wilhelmina. *The Gunniwolf* [Pre-1], 1519

Hellen, Nancy. *Old MacDonald Had a Farm* [Pre], **20**

Hobson, Sally. *Chicken Little* [Pre-K], **940**

Hutchins, Pat. *Don't Forget the Bacon!* [K-1], 434

Ishii, Momoko. *The Tongue-Cut Sparrow* [Pre-3], 1535

Johnston, Tony. *The Vanishing Pumpkin* [K-1], 443
Yonder [2-3], 939

Kalan, Robert. *Jump, Frog, Jump* [Pre-K], 160

Kesey, Ken. *Little Tricker the Squirrel Meets Big Double the Bear* [2-3], **634**

Kimmel, Eric A. *The Gingerbread Man* [Pre-1], **953**

King, Bob. *Sitting on the Farm* [Pre-K], **145**

Koide, Tan. *May We Sleep Here Tonight?* [Pre-K], 172

Lamont, Priscilla. *The Troublesome Pig: A Nursery Tale* [Pre-2], 1543

Levitin, Sonia. *Nobody Stole the Pie* [1-2], 722

Lichtveld, Noni. *I Lost My Arrow in a Kankan Tree* [K-2], **970**

Lindbergh, Reeve. *The Day the Goose Got Loose* [K-1], **306**
There's a Cow in the Road! [K-1], **307**

Little, Jean, and Maggie De Vries. *Once Upon a Golden Apple* [K-1], **478**

Litzinger, Rosanne. *The Old Woman and Her Pig: An Old English Tale* [Pre-1], **971**

Lobel, Arnold. *The Rose in My Garden* [K-1], 485

CHANTABLE REFRAIN (cont.)

London, Jonathan. *Let's Go, Froggy* [Pre-K], **153**

Mansell, Dom. *My Old Teddy* [Pre], **32**

Marshall, James. *Old Mother Hubbard and Her Wonderful Dog* [Pre-1], **980**

Martin, Bill, Jr. *Brown Bear, Brown Bear, What Do You See?* [Pre-K], 204

   Old Devil Wind [K-1], **323**

   Polar Bear, Polar Bear, What Do You Hear? [Pre-K], **160**

Marzollo, Jean. *Ten Cats Have Hats: A Counting Book* [Pre-K], **162**

Mollel, Tololwa M. *Rhinos for Lunch and Elephants for Supper!* [Pre-2], **991**

Mora, Pat. *Listen to the Desert / Oye al Desierto* [Pre-2], **1209**

Mosel, Arlene. *Tikki Tikki Tembo* [Pre-3], 1572

Nash, Ogden. *The Adventures of Isabel* [2-3], **649**

Oppenheim, Joanne. *You Can't Catch Me!* [K-1], 516

Patz, Nancy. *Pumpernickel Tickel and Mean Green Cheese* [K-1], 520

Paxton, Tom. *Where's the Baby?* [Pre], **38**

Perkins, Al. *Hand, Hand, Fingers, Thumb* [Pre-K], 228

Pinczes, Elinor J. *One Hundred Hungry Ants* [1-2], **533**

Polushkin, Maria. *Mother, Mother, I Want Another* [Pre-K], 230

Prater, John. *"No!" Said Joe* [Pre-K], **177**

Prelutsky, Jack. *The Mean Old Mean Hyena* [2-3], 983

   The Terrible Tiger [1-2], 778

Preston, Edna Mitchell. *Pop Corn & Ma Goodness* [K-1], 529

Raffi. *Spider on the Floor* [K-1], 348

Reddix, Valerie. *Millie and the Mud Hole* [Pre-K], **180**

Reiser, Lynn. *Any Kind of Dog* [Pre], **40**

Rounds, Glen. *Old MacDonald Had a Farm* [Pre-K], **182**

San Souci, Robert D. *The Hobyahs* [K-2], **1013**

Sawyer, Ruth. *Journey Cake, Ho!* [Pre-2], 1591

Schindel, John. *What's for Lunch?* [Pre-K], **185**

Shapiro, Arnold L. *Who Says That?* [Pre], **43**

Shute, Linda. *Halloween Party* [1-2], **551**

Silverman, Erica. *Big Pumpkin* [K-1], **364**

Smith, William Jay. *Ho for a Hat!* [K-1], **368**

Stern, Simon. *The Hobyas: An Old Story* [Pre-1], 1609

Stevens, Janet. *The House That Jack Built: A Mother Goose Nursery Rhyme* [Pre-K], 271

Stutson, Caroline. *By the Light of the Halloween Moon* [1-2], **561**

Sweet, Melissa. *Fiddle-I-Fee: A Farmyard Song for the Very Young* [Pre-K], **190**

Thomas, Patricia. *"Stand Back," Said the Elephant, "I'm Going to Sneeze!"* [K-1], 568

Van Laan, Nancy. *The Tiny, Tiny Boy and the Big, Big Cow: A Scottish Folk Tale* [Pre-K], **1040**

Waddell, Martin. *Farmer Duck* [Pre-K], **200**

   The Happy Hedgehog Band [Pre], **48**

Watson, Wendy. *Fox Went Out on a Chilly Night* [K-1], **382**

Weiss, Nicki. *An Egg Is an Egg* [Pre-K], **207**

West, Colin. *The King of Kennelwick Castle* [Pre-K], 289

Westcott, Nadine Bernard. *The Lady with the Alligator Purse* [Pre-K], 290

   Peanut Butter and Jelly: A Play Rhyme [Pre-K], 291

   The Pop-Up, Pull-Tab Playtime House That Jack Built [Pre-K], 208

Willard, Nancy. *Simple Pictures Are Best* [1-2], 849

Williams, Sue. *I Went Walking* [Pre], **57**

Wolkstein, Diane. *Step by Step* [Pre-K], **211**

Wood, Audrey. *King Bidgood's in the Bathtub* [1-2], 855

   Silly Sally [Pre-K], **212**

Zimmerman, Andrea, and David Clemesha. *The Cow Buzzed* [Pre-K], **215**

CHARLEMAGNE, EMPEROR, 742–814

Manson, Christopher. *The Marvelous Blue Mouse* [2-3], **641**

   Two Travelers [2-3], **642**

CHEATING

Peters, Julie Anne. *The Stinky Sneakers Contest* [2-3], **654**

CHEMISTRY

SEE Science–Experiments

CHEROKEE INDIANS

Roop, Peter, and Connie Roop. *Ahyoka and the Talking Leaves* [3-4], **740**

CHEROKEE INDIANS–Folklore

Bruchac, Joseph. *The First Strawberries: A Cherokee Story* [K-3], **870**

Ross, Gayle. *How Rabbit Tricked Otter and Other Cherokee Trickster Stories* [1-4], **1084**

   How Turtle's Back Was Cracked: A Traditional Cherokee Tale [1-4], **1008**

CHESS

Birdseye, Tom. *Just Call Me Stupid* [4-5], **759**

CHESS–Folklore
Day, David. *The Sleeper* [2-4], **891**

CHICASAW INDIANS–Folklore
Ata, Te. *Baby Rattlesnake* [Pre-1], **862**

CHICKEN POX
Brown, Marc. *Arthur's Chicken Pox* [K-1], **239**

CHICKENS
SEE ALSO Birds; Ducks; Geese; Owls; Parrots;
Roosters
Allard, Harry. *I Will Not Go to a Market Today*
[K-1], 316
Andersen, Hans Christian. *It's Perfectly True*
[1-2], 602
Anderson, Margaret. *The Brain on Quartz
Mountain* [3-4], 1041
Auch, Mary Jane. *The Easter Egg Farm* [K-1], **220**
Peeping Beauty [1-2], **402**
Baker, Keith. *Big Fat Hen* [Pre], **4**
Bourgeois, Paulette. *Too Many Chickens* [K-1],
235
Cazet, Denys. *Lucky Me* [K-1], 360
Ernst, Lisa Campbell. *Zinnia and Dot* [K-1], **271**
Flora, James. *Little Hatchy Hen* [2-3], 923
Fox, Mem. *Hattie and the Fox* [Pre-K], 91
Ginsburg, Mirra. *The Chick and the Duckling*
[Pre-K], 114
Heine, Helme. *The Most Wonderful Egg in the
World* [Pre-K], 129
Heller, Ruth. *Chickens Aren't the Only Ones*
[K-4], **1160**
Hutchins, Pat. *Rosie's Walk* [Pre-K], 149
Kasza, Keiko. *The Wolf's Chicken Stew* [Pre-K],
162
Kellogg, Steven. *Chicken Little* [1-2], 704
Kent, Jack. *Little Peep* [K-1], 455
King-Smith, Dick. *Pretty Polly* [3-4], **725**
Lester, Helen. *The Wizard, the Fairy and the Magic
Chicken* [Pre-K], 185
McCleery, William. *Wolf Story* [K-1], 489
Manes, Stephen. *Chicken Trek: The Third Strange
Thing That Happened to Oscar J. Noodleman*
[4-5], 1211
Marshall, James. *Wings: A Tale of Two Chickens*
[1-2], 745
Pinkwater, Daniel. *The Hoboken Chicken
Emergency* [3-4], 1104
Ravilious, Robin. *The Runaway Chick* [Pre-K],
236

CHICKENS–Folklore
Cauley, Lorinda Bryan. *The Cock, the Mouse and
the Little Red Hen* [Pre-2], 1414
Domanska, Janina. *Little Red Hen* [Pre-1], 1447

Galdone, Paul. *Henny Penny* [Pre-1], 1461
The Little Red Hen [Pre-1], 1464
Hobson, Sally. *Chicken Little* [Pre-K], **940**

CHILD LABOR
Welch, Catherine A. *Danger at the Breaker* [3-4],
753

CHILDREN
Anholt, Catherine, and Laurence Anholt. *All
About You* [Pre], **3**
Kids [Pre-K], **64**

CHILDREN–Folklore
Maddern, Eric. *The Fire Children: A West African
Creation Tale* [K-3], **978**

CHILDREN–Poetry
Hopkins, Lee Bennett. *Through Our Eyes: Poems
and Pictures About Growing Up* [2-5], **1328**
Huck, Charlotte. *Secret Places* [1-4], **1330**
Myers, Walter Dean. *Brown Angels: An Album of
Pictures and Verse* [1-6], **1389**

CHILDREN'S WRITINGS
Leigh, Nila K. *Learning to Swim in Swaziland: A
Child's-Eye View of a Southern African Country*
[1-4], **1184**
Temple, Lannis. *Dear World: How Children
Around the World Feel About Our Environment*
[2-6], **1247**

CHIMPANZEES
SEE ALSO Gorillas; Monkeys
Browne, Anthony. *Willy the Wimp* [K-1], 350
Goodall, Jane. *The Chimpanzee Family Book* [3-6],
2041
Hoban, Lillian. *Arthur's Christmas Cookies* [K-1],
425
Arthur's Great Big Valentine [K-1], 426
Arthur's Honey Bear [Pre-K], 136
Arthur's Loose Tooth [K-1], 427
Landsman, Sandy. *Castaways on Chimp Island*
[5-6], 1323
Michel, Anna. *The Story of Nim, the Chimp Who
Learned Language* [3-6], 2076
Roy, Ron. *The Chimpanzee Kid* [5-6], 1348

CHINA
SEE ALSO Folklore–China
Allen, Judy. *Panda* [2-3], **584**
Armstrong, Jennifer. *Chin Yu Min and the Ginger
Cat* [2-3], **588**
Fisher, Leonard Everett. *The Great Wall of China*
[2-6], 2023
Flack, Marjorie. *The Story about Ping* [K-1], 387
Russell, Ching Yeung. *First Apple* [3-4], **741**

CHINA (cont.)

Singer, Marilyn. *The Painted Fan* [3-4], **748**

Williams, Jay. *Everyone Knows What a Dragon Looks Like* [2-3], 1029

Yep, Laurence. *The Ghost Fox* [3-4], **755**

CHINESE–Biography

Zhensun, Zheng, and Alice Low. *A Young Painter: The Life and Paintings of Wang Yani—China's Extraordinary Young Artist* [3-6], **1257**

CHINESE AMERICANS

Levine, Ellen. *I Hate English* [1-2], 721

Namioka, Lensey. *Yang the Youngest and His Terrible Ear* [4-5], **781**

Porte, Barbara Ann. *"Leave That Cricket Be, Alan Lee"* [K-1], **340**

Regan, Dian Curtis. *The Curse of the Trouble Dolls* [2-3], **669**

Say, Allen. *El Chino* [2-5], **1234**

Sun, Chying Feng. *Mama Bear* [1-2], **562**

Yee, Paul. *Roses Sing on New Snow: A Delicious Tale* [2-3], **696**

Yep, Laurence. *The Star Fisher* [5-6], **854**

CHINESE AMERICANS–Poetry

Wong, Janet S. *Good Luck Gold and Other Poems* [4-6], **1424**

CHINESE NEW YEAR

SEE Holidays

CHINESE POETRY

Demi. *Dragon Kites and Dragonflies: A Collection of Chinese Nursery Rhymes* [Pre-3], 1789

CHINOOK INDIANS–Folklore

Martin, Rafe. *The Boy Who Lived with the Seals* [2-4], **982**

CHIPMUNKS

Haas, Jessie. *Chipmunk!* [Pre-K], **115**

Nixon, Joan Lowery. *Gloria Chipmunk, Star!* [1-2], 760

Ryder, Joanne. *Chipmunk Song* [Pre-2], 2089

CHOCOLATE

SEE Candy

CHRISTMAS

Ahlberg, Janet, and Allan Ahlberg. *The Jolly Christmas Postman* [1-2], 396

Andersen, Hans Christian. *The Steadfast Tin Soldier* [2-3], **586**

Auch, Mary Jane. *Bird Dogs Can't Fly* [K-1], **219**

Balian, Lorna. *Bah! Humbug?* [K-1], 328

Barracca, Debra, and Sal Barracca. *A Taxi Dog Christmas* [K-1], **229**

Brett, Jan. *The Wild Christmas Reindeer* [K-1], **237**

Brown, Margaret. *The Steamroller* [K-1], 346

Burningham, John. *Harvey Slumfenburger's Christmas Present* [K-1], **244**

Cazet, Denys. *December 24th* [K-1], 359

dePaola, Tomie. *Merry Christmas, Strega Nona* [2-3], 909

Dillon, Barbara. *A Mom by Magic* [4-5], **767**

Flora, James. *Grandpa's Witched-Up Christmas* [2-3], 920

Gay, Michael. *The Christmas Wolf* [K-1], 404

Greenburg, Dan. *Young Santa* [4-5], **770**

Haywood, Carolyn. *A Christmas Fantasy* [K-1], 416

Herriot, James. *The Christmas Day Kitten* [2-4], 2048

Hoban, Lillian. *Arthur's Christmas Cookies* [K-1], 425

Houston, Gloria. *The Year of the Perfect Christmas Tree* [1-2], 691

Howe, James. *The Fright before Christmas* [2-3], 935

Johnston, Tony. *Mole and Troll Trim the Tree* [K-1], 442

Joyce, William. *Santa Calls* [2-3], **631**

Keller, Holly. *A Bear for Christmas* [Pre-K], 167

Kline, Suzy. *Horrible Harry and the Christmas Surprise* [1-2], **474**

Kraus, Robert. *How Spider Saved Christmas* [K-1], 459

Little, Jean. *From Anna* [4-5], **775**

McCully, Emily Arnold. *The Christmas Gift* [Pre-K], 195

McPhail, David. *Santa's Book of Names* [K-1], **319**

Marshall, James. *Merry Christmas, Space Case* [1-2], 744

Mendoza, George. *A Wart Snake in a Fig Tree* [2-3], 963

Merriam, Eve. *The Christmas Box* [K-1], 507

Moeri, Louise. *Star Mother's Youngest Child* [3-4], 1097

Naylor, Phyllis Reynolds. *Keeping a Christmas Secret* [Pre-K], 216

Old Sadie and the Christmas Bear [K-1], 512

Niland, Kilmeny. *A Bellbird in a Flame Tree* [1-2], **518**

Nixon, Joan Lowery. *That's the Spirit, Claude* [2-3], **650**

Noble, Trinka Hakes. *Apple Tree Christmas* [2-3], 973

Olson, Arielle North. *Hurry Home, Grandma!* [Pre-K], 220

Paulsen, Gary. *A Christmas Sonata* [5-6], **833**

Price, Moe. *The Reindeer Christmas* [K-1], **341**

Prøysen, Alf. *Christmas Eve at Santa's* [K-1], **343**

Robinson, Barbara. *The Best Christmas Pageant Ever* [4-5], 1230

Ross, Pat. *M & M and the Santa Secrets* [1-2], 785

Rylant, Cynthia. *Children of Christmas: Stories for the Seasons* [5-6], 1349

Say, Allen. *Tree of Cranes* [1-2], **547**

Seuss, Dr. *How the Grinch Stole Christmas* [1-2], 802

Soto, Gary. *Too Many Tamales* [K-1], **369**

Stevenson, James. *The Worst Person's Christmas* [1-2], **559**

Sun, Chying Feng. *Mama Bear* [1-2], **562**

Tews, Susan. *The Gingerbread Doll* [1-2], **565**

Thayer, Jane. *The Puppy Who Wanted a Boy* [K-1], 566

Trivas, Irene. *Emma's Christmas* [2-3], **687**

Van Allsburg, Chris. *The Polar Express* [1-2], 835

Watson, Clyde. *How Brown Mouse Kept Christmas* [1-2], 847

Wells, Rosemary. *Max's Christmas* [Pre-K], 287

Wetzel, JoAnne Stewart. *The Christmas Box* [K-1], **384**

Zakhoder, Boris. *How a Piglet Crashed the Christmas Party* [1-2], 858

Ziefert, Harriet. *A New Coat for Anna* [K-1], 597

CHRISTMAS–Folklore

Dasent, George Webbe. *The Cat on the Dovrefell: A Christmas Tale* [Pre-2], 1432

French, Vivian. *Why the Sea Is Salt* [1-4], **906**

Sawyer, Ruth. *The Remarkable Christmas of the Cobbler's Sons* [K-3], **1020**

CHRISTMAS–Poetry

Livingston, Myra Cohn. *Christmas Poems* [3-6], 1859

Moore, Clement C. *The Night before Christmas* [1-2], 753

Prelutsky, Jack. *It's Christmas* [Pre-3], 1905

CHRISTMAS–Songs

Brett, Jan. *The Twelve Days of Christmas* [Pre-6], 1755

Manushkin, Fran. *My Christmas Safari* [K-1], **320**

Raffi. *The Raffi Christmas Treasury* [Pre-2], **1400**

CINDERELLA STORIES

Climo, Shirley. *The Korean Cinderella* [1-4], **878**

Compton, Joanne. *Ashpet: An Appalachian Tale* [1-4], **883**

Jackson, Ellen. *Cinder Edna* [2-3], **626**

Martin, Rafe. *The Rough-Face Girl* [2-6], **983**

Minters, Frances. *Cinder-Elly* [1-2], **510**

Pollock, Penny. *The Turkey Girl: A Zuni Cinderella Story* [2-5], **1000**

San Souci, Robert D. *Sootface: An Ojibwa Cinderella Story* [1-5], **1016**

Wegman, William. *Cinderella* [1-4], **1042**

Wilson, Barbara Ker. *Wishbones: A Folk Tale from China* [2-4], **1043**

CIPHERS

SEE Codes and Ciphers

CIRCLES

Skofield, James. *'Round and Around* [Pre-K], **188**

CIRCUS

Blumberg, Rhoda. *Jumbo* [2-5], **1107**

Ehlert, Lois. *Circus* [Pre-K], **95**

Ernst, Lisa Campbell. *Ginger Jumps* [K-1], **269**

Freeman, Don. *Bearymore* [K-1], 391

Peet, Bill. *Chester the Worldly Pig* [2-3], 975

CITIES AND TOWNS

Asch, Frank, and Vladimir Vagin. *Dear Brother* [1-2], **401**

Barracca, Debra, and Sal Barracca. *The Adventures of Taxi Dog* [1-2], **404**

Bash, Barbara. *Urban Roosts: Where Birds Nest in the City* [3-6], **1105**

Baylor, Byrd. *The Best Town in the World* [2-3], 872

Bozzo, Maxine. *Toby in the Country, Toby in the City* [Pre-K], 25

Bunting, Eve. *Flower Garden* [Pre-K], **72**

Burton, Virgina Lee. *The Little House* [1-2], 634

Calhoun, Mary. *Cross-Country Cat* [Pre-K], 635

Clifton, Lucille. *The Boy Who Didn't Believe in Spring* [1-2], 650

Clymer, Eleanor. *My Brother Stevie* [3-4], 1054

Ellis, Anne. *Dabble Duck* [K-1], 382

Jakobsen, Kathy. *My New York* [K-4], **1167**

Keats, Ezra Jack. *Apt. 3* [2-3], 942

Lobel, Anita. *Away from Home* [1-2], **487**

McCloskey, Robert. *Make Way for Ducklings* [1-2], 734

McLerran, Alice. *Roxaboxen* [1-2], **499**

Mennen, Ingrid, and Niki Daly. *Somewhere in Africa* [1-2], **509**

Ringgold, Faith. *Tar Beach* [2-3], **671**

Rotner, Shelley, and Ken Kreisler. *Citybook* [K-1], **353**

Snyder, Carol. *Ike and Mama and the Once-a-Year Suit* [2-3], 1004

Spinelli, Eileen. *If You Want to Find Golden* [K-1], **370**

Van Laan, Nancy. *People, People, Everywhere!* [Pre-K], **196**

Wagner, Jane. *J. T.* [3-4], 1129

CITIES AND TOWNS–Poetry

Adoff, Arnold. *Street Music: City Poems* [2-6], **1261**

Grimes, Nikki. *Meet Danitra Brown* [3-5], **1302**

CIVIL WAR

SEE U.S.–History–1783-1865;
U.S.–History–Civil War

CIVILIZATION, ANCIENT

Krupp, Robin Rector. *Let's Go Traveling* [3-5], **1177**

CLAIRVOYANCE

SEE Extrasensory perception

CLEANLINESS

Bucknall, Caroline. *One Bear in the Picture* [Pre-K], 31

Cole, Brock. *Alpha and the Dirty Baby* [1-2], **426**

Edwards, Frank B. *Mortimer Mooner Stopped Taking a Bath* [Pre-K], **94**

Hiskey, Iris. *Hannah the Hippo's No Mud Day* [Pre-K], **124**

Peters, Lisa Westberg. *When the Fly Flew In* [K-1], **336**

Teague, Mark. *Pigsty* [1-2], **564**

CLOCKS

Bellairs, John. *The House with a Clock in Its Walls* [4-5], 1143

Brown, Eileen. *Tick-Tock* [K-1], **238**

Hutchins, Pat. *Clocks and More Clocks* [K-1], 433

London, Jonathan. *Froggy Gets Dressed* [Pre-K], **152**

Miller, Margaret. *Where Does It Go?* [Pre-K], **166**

Thomas, Patricia. *The One and Only Super-Duper Golly-Whopper Jim-Dandy Really-Handy Clock-Tock-Stopper* [1-2], **566**

Turkle, Brinton. *Do Not Open* [2-3], 1016

CLOTHING AND DRESS

SEE ALSO Costumes; Shoes

Allard, Harry. *There's a Party at Mona's Tonight* [K-1], 319

Andersen, Hans Christian. *The Emperor's New Clothes: A Fairy Tale* [2-3], 863

Anderson, Leone Castell. *The Wonderful Shrinking Shirt* [1-2], 604

Balian, Lorna. *Humbug Witch* [Pre-K], 20

Barrett, Judi. *Animals Should Definitely Not Wear Clothing* [2-3], 870

Beskow, Elsa. *Pelle's New Suit* [K-1], 336

Borden, Louise. *Caps, Hats, Socks, and Mittens: A Book about the Four Seasons* [Pre-K], 24

Brett, Jan. *Trouble with Trolls* [K-1], **236**

Calmenson, Stephanie. *The Principal's New Clothes* [1-2], **420**

Cauley, Lorinda Bryan. *The Three Little Kittens* [Pre-K], 45

Charlip, Remy. *Harlequin and the Gift of Many Colors* [2-3], 886

Christelow, Eileen. *Olive and the Magic Hat* [K-1], 365

dePaola, Tomie. *Charlie Needs a Cloak* [K-1], 376

Estes, Eleanor. *The Hundred Dresses* [2-3], 914

Fox, Mem. *Shoes from Grandpa* [Pre-K], **105**

Freeman, Don. *A Pocket for Corduroy* [Pre-K], 95

Gackenbach, Dick. *Poppy, the Panda* [Pre-K], 100

Gould, Deborah. *Aaron's Shirt* [Pre-K], 117

Hest, Amy. *The Purple Coat* [K-1], 422

Hiskey, Iris. *Hannah the Hippo's No Mud Day* [Pre-K], **124**

Hissey, Jane. *Little Bear's Trousers* [Pre-K], 135

Marzollo, Jean. *Ten Cats Have Hats: A Counting Book* [Pre-K], **162**

Miles, Betty. *The Secret Life of the Underwear Champ* [3-4], 1096

Miller, Margaret. *Where's Jenna?* [Pre-K], **167**

Mills, Lauren. *The Rag Coat* [2-3], **646**

Nietzel, Shirley. *The Jacket I Wear in the Snow* [Pre-K], 217

Rice, Eve. *Oh, Lewis!* [Pre-K], 239

Rogers, Jean. *Runaway Mittens* [Pre-K], 244

Roy, Ron. *Million Dollar Jeans* [4-5], 1233

Sanders, Scott Russell. *Warm as Wool* [1-2], **546**

Selden, George. *Sparrow Socks* [1-2], 799

Slobodkin, Florence. *Too Many Mittens* [Pre-K], 268

Snyder, Carol. *Ike and Mama and the Once-a-Year Suit* [2-3], 1004

Steig, William. *Brave Irene* [1-2], 820

Ziefert, Harriet. *A New Coat for Anna* [K-1], 597

Zion, Gene. *No Roses for Harry* [Pre-K], 309

CLOTHING AND DRESS–Folklore

Galdone, Paul. *The Monster and the Tailor* [2-4], 1467

Gilman, Phoebe. *Something from Nothing* [Pre-2], **914**

CLOUDS

Cummings, Pat. *C.L.O.U.D.S.* [2-3], 903

Shaw, Charles G. *It Looked Like Spilt Milk* [Pre-K], 264

CLOWNS

Falwell, Cathryn. *Clowning Around* [K-1], **272**

COAL MINES AND MINING

Welch, Catherine A. *Danger at the Breaker* [3-4], **753**

COBRAS
Kipling, Rudyard. *Rikki-Tikki-Tavi* [3-4], **729**

COCAINE
Taylor, Clark. *The House That Crack Built* [4-6], **1246**

CODES AND CIPHERS
Balian, Lorna. *Humbug Potion: An A B Cipher* [1-2], 608
Carle, Eric. *The Secret Birthday Message* [Pre-K], 40
Schwartz, Alvin. *The Cat's Elbow and Other Secret Languages* [2-6], 1945

COLLECTIVE NOUNS
SEE English language–Grammar

COLONIAL LIFE
SEE U.S.–History–Colonial Period

COLOR
Carle, Eric. *The Mixed-Up Chameleon* [Pre-K], 38
Charles, N. N. *What Am I? Looking Through Shapes at Apples and Grapes* [Pre-K], **84**
Crews, Donald. *Freight Train* [Pre-K], 58
Dodds, Dayle Ann. *The Color Box* [Pre-K], **93**
Ehlert, Lois. *Color Farm* [Pre-K], **96**
Color Zoo [Pre-K], 76
Fleming, Denise. *Lunch* [Pre], **14**
Gerstein, Mordicai. *Follow Me!* [Pre-K], 112
Hest, Amy. *The Purple Coat* [K-1], 422
Jenkins, Jessica. *Thinking About Colors* [1-2], **462**
Jonas, Ann. *Color Dance* [Pre-K], **136**
Lionni, Leo. *Little Blue and Little Yellow* [Pre-K], 191
Lobel, Arnold. *The Great Blueness and Other Predicaments* [K-1], 480
McMillan, Bruce. *Growing Colors* [Pre-K], 197
Martin, Bill, Jr. *Brown Bear, Brown Bear, What Do You See?* [Pre-K], 204
Peek, Merle. *Mary Wore Her Red Dress and Henry Wore His Green Sneakers* [Pre-K], 227
Samton, Sheila White. *Beside the Bay* [Pre-K], 250
Serfozo, Mary. *Who Said Red?* [Pre-K], 256
Spinelli, Eileen. *If You Want to Find Golden* [K-1], **370**
Walsh, Ellen Stoll. *Mouse Paint* [Pre-K], **204**
Williams, Sue. *I Went Walking* [Pre], **57**
Yektai, Niki. *Bears in Pairs* [Pre-K], 302
Zolotow, Charlotte. *Mr. Rabbit and the Lovely Present* [Pre-K], 310

COLOR–Folklore
Young, Ed. *Seven Blind Mice* [Pre-3], **1051**

COLOR–Poetry
O'Neill, Mary L. *Hailstones and Halibut Bones: Adventures in Color* [Pre-3], 1897

COLUMBUS, CHRISTOPHER
Columbus, Christopher. *Log of Christopher Columbus* [4-6], **1124**
Conrad, Pam. *Pedro's Journal: A Voyage with Christopher Columbus, August 3, 1492–February 14, 1492* [5-6], **809**
Dorris, Michael. *Morning Girl* [5-6], **814**
Marzollo, Jean. *In 1492* [K-3], **1204**
Roop, Peter, and Connie Roop. *I, Columbus; My Journal—1492–3* [4-6], **1227**
Sis, Peter. *Follow the Dream: The Story of Christopher Columbus* [1-4], **1238**
Yolen, Jane. *Encounter* [3-4], **756**

COMEDIANS
Sachar, Louis. *Dogs Don't Tell Jokes* [5-6], **840**

COMETS
SEE Astronomy

COMMUNICATION
Aliki. *Communication* [1-3], **1099**
Ets, Marie Hall. *Talking without Words* [Pre-K], 82
Michel, Anna. *The Story of Nim, the Chimp Who Learned Language* [3-6], 2076
Patterson, Francine. *Koko's Kitten* [2-6], 2080

COMMUNITIES
Van Laan, Nancy. *People, People, Everywhere!* [Pre-K], **196**

COMPETITION
dePaola, Tomie. *Strega Nona Meets Her Match* [1-2], **430**
Duffey, Betsy. *The Gadget War* [2-3], **606**
Silverman, Erica. *Don't Fidget a Feather!* [K-1], **365**
Stevenson, James. *The Mud Flat Olympics* [1-2], **557**

CONDUCT
SEE Behavior

CONFECTIONARY
SEE Candy

CONFLICT RESOLUTION
SEE ALSO Problem solving
Crowley, Michael. *Shack and Back* [1-2], **427**
DePaolo, Paula. *Rosie & the Yellow Ribbon* [K-1], **261**
Duffey, Betsy. *The Gadget War* [2-3], **606**
Guback, Georgia. *Luka's Quilt* [K-1], **278**
Hamilton, Morse. *Little Sister for Sale* [1-2], **450**

CONFLICT RESOLUTION (cont.)

Havill, Juanita. *Jamaica and Brianna* [Pre-K], **119**

Martin, Ann. *Rachel Parker, Kindergarten Show-Off* [K-1], **321**

Mills, Lauren. *The Rag Coat* [2-3], **646**

Naylor, Phyllis Reynolds. *Shiloh* [5-6], **832**

Peters, Julie Anne. *The Stinky Sneakers Contest* [2-3], **654**

Regan, Dian Curtis. *The Curse of the Trouble Dolls* [2-3], **669**

Soto, Gary. *Too Many Tamales* [K-1], **369**

CONFLICT RESOLUTION–Folklore

Han, Suzanne Crowder. *The Rabbit's Judgment* [1-5], **937**

CONSERVATION

SEE Environment; Pollution; Recycling; Wildlife conservation

CONSTELLATIONS

Wright, Kit. *Tigerella* [K-1], **389**

CONSTELLATIONS–Folklore

Taylor, Harriet Peck. *Coyote Places the Stars* [1-3], **1033**

CONSTITUTION

SEE U.S.–Constitutional history

CONTESTS

Brown, Marc. *Arthur Meets the President* [1-2], **413**

Brown, Paula. *Moon Jump: A Countdown* [K-1], **240**

Gilson, Jamie. *Harvey the Beer Can King* [4-5], 1179

Howe, James. *Pinky and Rex and the Spelling Bee* [1-2], **457**

Jones, Rebecca C. *Germy Blew It* [4-5], 1196

Kennedy, Richard. *The Contests at Cowlick* [1-2], 708

Lebentritt, Julia, and Richard Ploetz. *The Kooken* [1-2], **481**

Lewis, J. Patrick. *One Dog Day* [4-5], **774**

Marshall, James. *The Cut-Ups Carry On* [1-2], **503**

Peters, Julie Anne. *The Stinky Sneakers Contest* [2-3], **654**

CONTESTS–Folklore

Climo, Shirley. *The Match Between the Winds* [K-3], **879**

COOKERY

SEE ALSO Food; Fruit; Pies; Soup; Vegetables

Bacon, Peggy. *The Magic Touch* [3-4], 1043

Blundell, Tony. *Beware of Boys* [K-1], **232**

Brimner, Larry Dane. *Country Bear's Good Neighbor* [Pre-K], 27

Carle, Eric. *Pancakes, Pancakes!* [K-1], **247**

Conford, Ellen. *What's Cooking, Jenny Archer?* [2-3], **601**

Delton, Judy. *Two Good Friends* [Pre-K], 66

Devlin, Harry, and Wende Devlin. *Cranberry Thanksgiving* [1-2], 660

Dooley, Norah. *Everybody Cooks Rice* [1-2], **433**

Ehlert, Lois. *Growing Vegetable Soup* [Pre-K], 78

Everitt, Betsy. *Mean Soup* [Pre-K], **101**

Hirsch, Marilyn. *Potato Pancakes All Around: A Hanukkah Tale* [2-3], 933

Hoban, Lillian. *Arthur's Christmas Cookies* [K-1], 425

Hoban, Russell. *Bread and Jam for Frances* [K-1], 429

Khalsa, Dayal Kaur. *How Pizza Came to Queens* [K-1], 456

Mahy, Margaret. *Jam: A True Story* [1-2], 740

Priceman, Marjorie. *How to Make an Apple Pie and See the World* [1-2], **538**

Robart, Rose. *The Cake That Mack Ate* [Pre-K], 241

Wellington, Monica. *Mr. Cookie Baker* [Pre], **55**

Yee, Paul. *Roses Sing on New Snow: A Delicious Tale* [2-3], **696**

COOKERY–Folklore

Brusca, María Cristina, and Tona Wilson. *The Cook and the King* [2-4], **874**

dePaola, Tomie. *Tony's Bread* [1-4], **896**

Domanska, Janina. *Little Red Hen* [Pre-1], 1447

Galdone, Paul. *The Little Red Hen* [Pre-1], 1464
The Magic Porridge Pot [Pre-2], 1465

McGovern, Ann. *Stone Soup* [Pre-2], 1555

Zemach, Harve. *Nail Soup: A Swedish Folk Tale* [1-4], 1636

COOKIES

SEE Cookery

COOPERATION

Brett, Jan. *The Wild Christmas Reindeer* [K-1], **237**

Ernst, Lisa Campbell. *Zinnia and Dot* [K-1], **271**

Hiskey, Iris. *Hannah the Hippo's No Mud Day* [Pre-K], **124**

Lionni, Leo. *Swimmy* [K-1], 476

Peet, Bill. *The Ant and the Elephant* [K-1], 521

Silverman, Erica. *Big Pumpkin* [K-1], **364**

Waddell, Martin. *Farmer Duck* [Pre-K], **200**

COOPERATION–Folklore

Domanska, Janina. *Little Red Hen* [Pre-1], 1447

Renberg, Dalia Hardof. *King Solomon and the Bee* [K-3], **1001**

COSTUMES

Allard, Harry. *There's a Party at Mona's Tonight* [K-1], 319

Armitage, Ronda, and David Armitage. *The Bossing of Josie* [Pre-K], 8

Balian, Lorna. *Humbug Witch* [Pre-K], 20

Charlip, Remy. *Harlequin and the Gift of Many Colors* [2-3], 886

Meddaugh, Susan. *The Witches' Supermarket* [1-2], **507**

Shute, Linda. *Halloween Party* [1-2], 551

Wojciechowski, Susan. *The Best Halloween of All* [1-2], **579**

COUNTING BOOKS

SEE ALSO Mathematics; Measurement

Aker, Suzanne. *What Comes in 2's, 3's & 4's?* [Pre-K], **62**

Aylesworth, Jim. *One Crow: A Counting Rhyme* [Pre-K], 17

Baker, Keith. *Big Fat Hen* [Pre], **4**

Bennett, David. *One Cow Moo Moo!* [Pre], **5**

Brown, Paula. *Moon Jump: A Cowntdown* [K-1], **240**

Calmenson, Stephanie. *Dinner at the Panda Palace* [Pre-K], **73**

Carroll, Kathleen Sullivan. *One Red Rooster* [Pre], **7**

Christelow, Eileen. *Five Little Monkeys Jumping on the Bed* [Pre-K], 48

Five Little Monkeys Sitting in a Tree [Pre-K], **85**

Clements, Andrew. *Mother Earth's Counting Book* [K-5], **1118**

Cleveland, David. *The April Rabbits* [K-1], 366

Crews, Donald. *Ten Black Dots* [Pre-K], 59

Ehlert, Lois. *Fish Eyes: A Book You Can Count On* [Pre-K], **97**

Eichenberg, Fritz. *Dancing in the Moon* [K-1], 380

Falwell, Cathryn. *Feast for 10* [Pre], **11**

Fleming, Denise. *Count!* [Pre], **13**

Galdone, Paul. *Over in the Meadow: An Old Nursery Counting Rhyme* [Pre-K], 108

Gordon, Jeffie Ross. *Six Sleepy Sheep* [Pre-K], **111**

Harshman, Marc. *Only One* [K-1], **280**

Hort, Lenny. *How Many Stars in the Sky?* [K-1], **288**

Hubbard, Woodleigh. *2 Is for Dancing: A 1 2 3 of Actions* [Pre-K], **127**

Hulme, Joy N. *Sea Squares* [2-3], **624**

Jones, Carol. *This Old Man* [Pre-K], **137**

Katz, Michael Jay. *Ten Potatoes in a Pot and Other Counting Rhymes* [Pre-2], **1336**

Langstaff, John. *Over in the Meadow* [Pre-K], 180

Leedy, Loreen. *A Number of Dragons* [Pre-K], 182

Loomis, Christine. *One Cow Coughs: A Counting Book for the Sick and Miserable* [Pre-K], **155**

MacDonald, Suse, and Bill Oakes. *Puzzlers* [K-1], **314**

McMillan, Bruce. *One, Two, One Pair!* [Pre], **31**

Manushkin, Fran. *My Christmas Safari* [K-1], **320**

Marzollo, Jean. *Ten Cats Have Hats: A Counting Book* [Pre-K], **162**

Moss, Lloyd. *Zin! Zin! Zin! A Violin* [1-2], **512**

Moss, Marissa. *Knick Knack Paddywack* [K-1], **327**

O'Donnell, Elizabeth Lee. *The Twelve Days of Summer* [1-2], **523**

O'Keefe, Susan Heyboer. *One Hungry Monster: A Counting Book in Rhyme* [Pre-K], **174**

Raffi. *Five Little Ducks* [Pre], **39**

Rayner, Mary. *Ten Pink Piglets: Garth Pig's Wall Song* [Pre-K], **179**

Sendak, Maurice. *One Was Johnny: A Counting Book* [Pre-K], 254

Serfozo, Mary. *Who Wants One?* [Pre-K], **257**

Turner, Gwenda. *Over on the Farm* [Pre-K], **195**

Voce, Louise. *Over in the Meadow: A Traditional Counting Rhyme* [Pre-K], **197**

Wadsworth, Olive A. *Over in the Meadow: An Old Counting Rhyme* [Pre-K], **202**

Walsh, Ellen Stoll. *Mouse Count* [Pre], **54**

Walton, Rick. *How Many, How Many, How Many* [Pre-K], **206**

Wise, William. *Ten Sly Piranhas: A Counting Story in Reverse (A Tale of Wickedness and Worse)* [1-2], **578**

COUNTING BOOKS–Folklore

Edwards, Roberta. *Five Silly Fishermen* [Pre-1], **901**

COUNTRY FAIRS

SEE Fairs

COUNTRY LIFE

SEE ALSO Cities and towns; Farm life

Asch, Frank, and Vladimir Vagin. *Dear Brother* [1-2], **401**

Bozzo, Maxine. *Toby in the Country, Toby in the City* [Pre-K], 25

Burch, Robert. *Ida Early Comes Over the Mountain* [4-5], 1153

Burton, Virgina Lee. *The Little House* [1-2], 634

Callen, Larry. *The Deadly Mandrake* [5-6], 1284

Pinch [5-6], 1285

COUNTRY LIFE (cont.)

Sorrow's Song [5-6], 1286

Caudill, Rebecca. *Did You Carry the Flag Today, Charlie?* [1-2], 643

Dalgliesh, Alice. *The Bears on Hemlock Mountain* [1-2], 657

Hall, Donald. *Ox-Cart Man* [2-3], 931

Johnston, Tony. *Yonder* [2-3], 939

McPhail, David. *Emma's Vacation* [Pre-K], 201

Mills, Lauren. *The Rag Coat* [2-3], **646**

Rylant, Cynthia. *Night in the Country* [K-1], 541
    When I Was Young in the Mountains [2-3], 989

Saunders, Susan. *Fish Fry* [1-2], 790

Sundgaard, Arnold. *Meet Jack Appleknocker* [Pre-K], 272

Wakefield, Pat A., and Larry Carrara. *A Moose for Jessica* [3-6], 2111

Whelan, Gloria. *A Week of Raccoons* [K-1], 589

COUNTRY LIFE–Poetry

Fatchen, Max. *The Country Mail Is Coming: Poems from Down Under* [3-6], **1289**

COURAGE

Avi. *Shadrach's Crossing* [5-6], 1269

Brady, Esther Wood. *Toliver's Secret* [4-5], 1148

Brown, Walter R., and Norman D. Anderson. *Rescue! True Stories of Winners of the Young American Medal for Bravery* [3-6], 2004

Calhoun, Mary. *The Night the Monster Came* [2-3], 880

Coombs, Patricia. *Molly Mullett* [2-3], 901

Gackenbach, Dick. *Harry and the Terrible Whatzit* [Pre-K], 98

Green, Norma B. *The Hole in the Dike* [K-1], 409

Henkes, Kevin. *Sheila Rae, the Brave* [Pre-K], 132

Hoban, Lillian. *Arthur's Loose Tooth* [K-1], 427

Kraus, Robert. *Noel the Coward* [Pre-K], 175

McCully, Emily Arnold. *Mirette on the High Wire* [1-2], **492**

McSwigan, Marie. *Snow Treasure* [5-6], 1330

Monjo, F. N. *The Drinking Gourd* [2-3], 966

Peet, Bill. *Cowardly Clyde* [2-3], 976

Sperry, Armstrong. *Call It Courage* [4-5], 1242

Steig, William. *Brave Irene* [1-2], 820

Ullman, James Ramsay. *Banner in the Sky* [5-6], 1371

Walsh, Ellen Stoll. *Pip's Magic* [Pre-K], **205**

Williams, Gurney. *True Escape and Survival Stories* [4-6], 2115

Wuorio, Eva-Lis. *Code: Polonaise* [5-6], 1377

COURAGE–Folklore

Grant, Joan. *The Monster That Grew Small: An Egyptian Folktale* [1-4], 1484

San Souci, Robert D. *The Boy and the Ghost* [1-4], **1011**

Uchida, Yoshiko. *The Magic Purse* [1-4], **1037**

Yep, Laurence. *The Man Who Tricked a Ghost* [1-4], **1047**

COUSINS

Clifford, Eth. *Harvey's Horrible Snake Disaster* [3-4], 1052

Garland, Michael. *My Cousin Katie* [Pre], **17**

Giff, Patricia Reilly. *The Winter Worm Business* [4-5], 1177

Lindbergh, Anne. *Travel Far, Pay No Fare* [5-6], **826**

Slepian, Jan. *Back to Before* [5-6], **843**

COWBOYS

Axelrod, Alan. *Songs of the Wild West* [1-6], **1264**

Gerrard, Roy. *Rosie and the Rustlers* [2-3], **610**

Harper, Jo. *Jalapeño Hal* [2-3], **615**

Johnston, Tony. *The Cowboy and the Black-Eyed Pea* [3-4], **717**

Kimmel, Eric A. *Four Dollars and Fifty Cents* [3-4], **721**

Medearis, Angela Shelf. *The Zebra-Riding Cowboy: A Folk Song from the Old West* [2-3], **645**

COWBOYS–Poetry

Sullivan, Charles. *Cowboys* [K-4], **1413**

COWS

Babcock, Chris. *No Moon, No Milk* [K-1], **225**

Ericsson, Jennifer A. *No Milk!* [Pre-K], **99**

Ernst, Lisa Campbell. *When Bluebell Sang* [K-1], 383

Forrester, Victoria. *The Magnificent Moo* [Pre-K], 89

Harrison, David L. *When Cows Come Home* [Pre-K], **118**

Herriot, James. *Blossom Comes Home* [2-5], 2046

Johnson, Paul Brett. *The Cow Who Wouldn't Come Down* [K-1], **292**

Kirby, David, and Allen Woodman. *The Cows Are Going to Paris* [1-2], **471**

Lindbergh, Reeve. *There's a Cow in the Road!* [K-1], **307**

Macaulay, David. *Black and White* [1-2], **490**

Wakefield, Pat A., and Larry Carrara. *A Moose for Jessica* [3-6], 2111

COWS–Folklore

Cooper, Susan. *The Silver Cow: A Welsh Tale* [2-5], 1430

Greene, Ellin. *Billy Beg and His Bull* [2-4], **918**

Van Laan, Nancy. *The Tiny, Tiny Boy and the Big, Big Cow: A Scottish Folk Tale* [Pre-K], **1040**

COWS–Poetry

Schertle, Alice. *How Now, Brown Cow?* [1-6], **1406**

COYOTES

Root, Phyllis. *Coyote and the Magic Words* [K-1], **351**

COYOTES–Folklore

Aardema, Verna. *Borreguita and the Coyote: A Tale from Ayutla, Mexico* [K-3], **856**

Begay, Shonto. *Ma'ii and Cousin Horned Toad: A Traditional Navajo Story* [K-4], **865**

Carey, Valerie Scho. *Quail Song: A Pueblo Indian Tale* [K-2], **876**

Johnston, Tony. *The Tale of Rabbit and Coyote* [Pre-2], **947**

London, Jonathan, and Lanny Pinola. *Fire Race: A Karuk Coyote Tale About How Fire Came to the People* [K-3], **972**

McDermott, Gerald. *Coyote: A Trickster Tale from the American Southwest* [Pre-2], **975**

Mayo, Gretchen Will. *That Tricky Coyote!* [K-2], **1079**

Stevens, Janet. *Coyote Steals the Blanket: A Ute Tale* [Pre-3], **1029**

Taylor, Harriet Peck. *Coyote Places the Stars* [1-3], **1033**

CRABS

Carle, Eric. *A House for Hermit Crab* [K-1], **246**

Griffith, Helen V. *Emily and the Enchanted Frog* [1-2], **446**

McDonald, Megan. *Is This a House for Hermit Crab?* [K-1], **313**

CRANES

Keller, Holly. *Grandfather's Dream* [1-2], **466**

CREATION

Root, Phyllis. *Coyote and the Magic Words* [K-1], **351**

CREATION–Folklore

Bierhorst, John. *The Woman Who Fell from the Sky: The Iroquois Story of Creation* [2-6], **868**

Bruchac, Joseph. *Native American Animal Stories* [2-6], **1059**

Return of the Sun: Native American Tales from the Northeast Woodlands [3-6], **1060**

Gates, Frieda. *Owl Eyes* [K-3], **911**

Maddern, Eric. *The Fire Children: A West African Creation Tale* [K-3], **978**

Manitonquat (Medicine Story). *Children of the Morning Light: Wampanoag Tales* [3-6], **1077**

Shetterly, Susan Hand. *Raven's Light: A Myth from the People of the Northwest Coast* [2-5], **1024**

Young, Ed. *Moon Mother: A Native American Creation Tale* [2-6], **1050**

CREATIVE DRAMA

SEE ALSO Acting

Adams, Adrienne. *A Woggle of Witches* [Pre-K], 1

Agee, Jon. *The Incredible Painting of Felix Clousseau* [2-3], 862

Aliki. *At Mary Bloom's* [Pre-K], 4

Communication [1-3], **1099**

Allard, Harry. *I Will Not Go to a Market Today* [K-1], 316

Allen, Pamela. *Bertie and the Bear* [Pre-K], 7

Andersen, Karen Born. *An Alphabet in Five Acts* [1-2], **398**

Appelt, Kathi. *Elephants Aloft* [Pre-K], **66**

Arnold, Tedd. *Ollie Forgot* [1-2], 607

Artis, Vicki K. *Gray Duck Catches a Friend* [Pre-K], 9

Asch, Frank. *Happy Birthday, Moon* [Pre-K], 12

Just Like Daddy [Pre-K], 13

Ball, Duncan. *Jeremy's Tail* [K-1], **227**

Bond, Michael. *A Bear Called Paddington* [4-5], 1146

Boynton, Sandra. *A Is for Angry: An Animal and Adjective Alphabet* [K-1], 341

Brown, Margaret. *The Steamroller* [K-1], 346

Burningham, John. *Harvey Slumfenburger's Christmas Present* [K-1], **244**

Mr. Gumpy's Outing [Pre-K], 33

Carle, Eric. *Pancakes, Pancakes!* [K-1], **247**

Charlip, Remy, and Burton Supree. *Mother, Mother, I Feel Sick, Send for the Doctor Quick, Quick, Quick* [1-2], 646

Cole, Brock. *No More Baths* [Pre-K], 52

Cole, William. *Frances Face-Maker: A Going to Bed Book* [Pre-K], 53

Cooney, Nancy Evans. *The Umbrella Day* [Pre-K], 57

Cuyler, Margery. *That's Good! That's Bad!* [Pre-K], **92**

dePaola, Tomie. *Charlie Needs a Cloak* [K-1], 376

Duke, Kate. *Guinea Pigs Far and Near* [Pre-K], 75

CREATIVE DRAMA (cont.)

Eichenberg, Fritz. *Dancing in the Moon* [K-1], 380

Emberley, Barbara. *Drummer Hoff* [Pre-K], 80

Fenton, Edward. *The Big Yellow Balloon* [1-2], 667

Flack, Marjorie. *Ask Mr. Bear* [Pre-K], 87

Fleming, Denise. *Count!* [Pre], **13**

In the Small, Small Pond [Pre-K], **104**

Freeman, Don. *Quiet! There's a Canary in the Library* [Pre-K], 96

A Rainbow of My Own [Pre-K], 97

Gage, Wilson. *Cully Cully and the Bear* [K-1], 399

Gannett, Ruth Stiles. *My Father's Dragon* [1-2], 674

Gantos, Jack. *Greedy Greeny* [Pre-K], 109

Gerstein, Mordicai. *Arnold of the Ducks* [1-2], 677

Follow Me! [Pre-K], 112

Ginsburg, Mirra. *The Chick and the Duckling* [Pre-K], 114

Mushroom in the Rain [Pre-K], 115

Glazer, Tom. *Eye Winker, Tom Tinker, Chin Chopper: Fifty Musical Fingerplays* [Pre-2], 1804

Goodsell, Jane. *Toby's Toe* [K-1], 407

Hellsing, Lennart. *Old Mother Hubbard and Her Dog* [Pre-K], 130

Himmelman, John. *Talester the Lizard* [Pre-K], 134

Howard, Jane R. *When I'm Hungry* [Pre-K], **126**

Hubbard, Woodleigh. *C Is for Curious: An ABC of Feelings* [K-1], **289**

2 Is for Dancing: A 1 2 3 of Actions [Pre-K], **127**

Hutchins, Pat. *Rosie's Walk* [Pre-K], 149

Izen, Marshall, and Jim West. *Why the Willow Weeps: A Story Told with Hands* [1-2], **461**

Janovitz, Marilyn. *Look Out, Bird!* [Pre-K], **134**

Johnson, Jane. *Today I Thought I'd Run Away* [Pre-K], 154

Johnston, Deborah. *Mathew Michael's Beastly Day* [K-1], **293**

Johnston, Tony. *The Witch's Hat* [Pre-K], 156

Jones, Maurice. *I'm Going on a Dragon Hunt* [Pre-K], 158

Joslin, Sesyle. *What Do You Say, Dear?* [1-2], 702

Joyce, William. *George Shrinks* [K-1], 444

Kalan, Robert. *Stop, Thief!* [Pre-K], **138**

Keller, Charles. *School Daze* [2-5], 1842

Kent, Jack. *Jim Jimmy James* [K-1], 454

Koide, Tan. *May We Sleep Here Tonight?* [Pre-K], 172

Kraus, Robert. *Milton the Early Riser* [Pre-K], 174

Owliver [K-1], 461

Leedy, Loreen. *A Number of Dragons* [Pre-K], 182

Leydenfrost, Robert. *The Snake That Sneezed* [Pre-K], 188

Lobel, Arnold. *Fables* [4-5], 1207

Mouse Tales [K-1], 482

London, Jonathan. *Froggy Gets Dressed* [Pre-K], **152**

McCloskey, Robert. *Homer Price* [4-5], 1208

McMillan, Bruce. *Kitten Can* [Pre-K], 198

McPhail, David. *The Bear's Toothache* [K-1], 493

Pig Pig and the Magic Photo Album [K-1], 496

Marshall, James. *George and Martha* [K-1], 502

Martin, Bill, Jr. *The Maestro Plays* [1-2], **504**

Marzollo, Jean. *Pretend You're a Cat* [Pre-K], **161**

Modell, Frank. *Goodbye Old Year, Hello New Year* [K-1], 509

Modesitt, Jeanne. *Sometimes I Feel Like a Mouse: A Book About Feelings* [Pre-K], **169**

Murphy, Jill. *Peace at Last* [Pre-K], 214

Myers, Bernice. *Not This Bear!* [K-1], 511

Nerlove, Miriam. *I Made a Mistake* [1-2], 756

Noll, Sally. *Jiggle Wiggle Prance* [K-1], 513

Numeroff, Laura J. *Dogs Don't Wear Sneakers* [K-1], **333**

Panek, Dennis. *Catastrophe Cat* [Pre-K], 222

Perkins, Al. *Hand, Hand, Fingers, Thumb* [Pre-K], 228

Pinkwater, Daniel. *Tooth-Gnasher Superflash* [K-1], 523

Raschka, Chris. *Yo! Yes?* [1-2], **541**

Reddix, Valerie. *Millie and the Mud Hole* [Pre-K], **180**

Rosen, Michael. *We're Going on a Bear Hunt* [Pre-K], 245

Runcie, Jill. *Cock-a-Doodle-Doo!* [Pre], **41**

Ryan, Cheli Druan. *Hildilid's Night* [K-1], 539

Rydell, Katy. *Wind Says Good Night* [Pre], **42**

Ryder, Joanne. *Lizard in the Sun* [Pre-3], 2090

The Snail's Spell [Pre-K], 249

Schindel, John. *What's for Lunch?* [Pre-K], **185**

Seeger, Pete. *Abiyoyo* [K-1], 548

Sendak, Maurice. *Alligators All Around* [K-1], 550

One Was Johnny: A Counting Book [Pre-K], 254

Shannon, George. *Lizard's Song* [Pre-K], 261

Shaw, Charles G. *It Looked Like Spilt Milk* [Pre-K], 264

Shaw, Nancy. *Sheep in a Jeep* [K-1], 556

Sivulich, Sandra Stroner. *I'm Going on a Bear Hunt* [Pre-K], 267

Slobodkina, Esphyr. *Caps for Sale* [Pre-K], 269

Stevenson, James. *Could Be Worse* [1-2], 822

There's Nothing to Do! [1-2], 825

Yuck! [K-1], 562

Stickland, Henrietta. *Dinosaur Roar!* [Pre-K], **189**

Tripp, Wallace. *My Uncle Podger* [3-4], 1123

Ueno, Noriko. *Elephant Buttons* [Pre-K], 280

Ungerer, Tomi. *Crictor* [K-1], 573

Van Laan, Nancy. *The Big Fat Worm* [Pre-K], 282

Vipont, Elfrida. *The Elephant & the Bad Baby* [Pre-K], 283

Walsh, Ellen Stoll. *Hop Jump* [Pre], **53**

Wellington, Monica. *Mr. Cookie Baker* [Pre], **55**

Westcott, Nadine Bernard. *Skip to My Lou* [Pre-K], 292

Whitney, Alma Marshak. *Leave Herbert Alone* [Pre-K], 294

Williams, Linda. *The Little Old Lady Who Was Not Afraid of Anything* [K-1], 591

Wolkstein, Diane. *Step by Step* [Pre-K], **211**

Yektai, Niki. *What's Missing?* [Pre-K], 303

Young, Ruth. *Starring Francine & Dave: Three One-Act Plays* [Pre-2], 2117

Zemach, Harve. *The Judge: An Untrue Tale* [2-3], 1037

Zolotow, Charlotte. *The Quarreling Book* [1-2], 861

CREATIVE DRAMA–Folklore

Aardema, Verna. *Princess Gorilla and a New Kind of Water* [Pre-2], 1381

Who's in Rabbit's House? [2-4], 1385

Ada, Alma Flor. *The Rooster Who Went to His Uncle's Wedding: A Latin American Folktale* [Pre-1], **858**

Aesop. *Aesop & Company: With Scenes from His Legendary Life* [3-6], **1053**

Aesop's Fables [1-6], **1054**

Aesop's Fables [2-4], 1642

Aesop's Fables [3-6], 1643

Aesop's Fables [2-6], 1644

Aesop's Fables [K-3], 1645

The Fables of Aesop [2-6], 1647

Once in a Wood: Ten Tales from Aesop [Pre-2], 1648

Seven Fables from Aesop [1-4], 1649

Three Aesop Fox Fables [K-2], 1650

Twelve Tales from Aesop [K-3], 1651

Aruego, Jose, and Ariane Dewey. *A Crocodile's Tale* [Pre-1], 1393

Asbjørnsen, P. C. *The Runaway Pancake* [Pre-1], 1394

The Three Billy Goats Gruff [Pre-2], 1396

Basile, Giambattista. *Petrosinella: A Neopolitan Rapunzel* [4-6], 1401

Baumgartner, Barbara. *Crocodile! Crocodile! Stories Told Around the World* [Pre-2], **1058**

Belpré, Pura. *Oté* [1-4], 1402

Bowden, Joan Chase. *The Bean Boy* [Pre-1], 1405

Carey, Valerie Scho. *Quail Song: A Pueblo Indian Tale* [K-2], **876**

Cauley, Lorinda Bryan. *The Cock, the Mouse and the Little Red Hen* [Pre-2], 1414

The Three Little Pigs [Pre-2], 1420

Cook, Scott. *The Gingerbread Boy* [Pre-1], 1429

dePaola, Tomie. *The Comic Adventures of Old Mother Hubbard and Her Dog* [Pre-1], 1438

Domanska, Janina. *The Turnip* [Pre-1], 1448

Dupré, Judith. *The Mouse Bride: A Mayan Folk Tale* [K-2], **898**

Edwards, Roberta. *Five Silly Fishermen* [Pre-1], **901**

Esterl, Arnica. *The Fine Round Cake* [K-2], **903**

Galdone, Paul. *The Gingerbread Boy* [Pre-1], 1459

The Greedy Old Fat Man: An American Folktale [Pre-2], 1460

Old Mother Hubbard and Her Dog [Pre-1], 1468

The Old Woman and Her Pig [Pre-1], 1469

The Three Little Pigs [Pre-1], 1474

What's in Fox's Sack? [Pre-2], 1476

Gonzalez, Lucie M. *The Bossy Gallito: A Traditional Cuban Folktale* [K-2], **917**

Han, Suzanne Crowder. *The Rabbit's Judgment* [1-5], **937**

Harper, Wilhelmina. *The Gunniwolf* [Pre-1], 1519

Hobson, Sally. *Chicken Little* [Pre-K], **940**

Hogrogian, Nonny. *One Fine Day* [Pre-2], 1528

Kent, Jack. *The Fat Cat* [Pre-2], 1539

Kherdian, David. *Feathers and Tails: Animal Fables from Around the World* [K-4], **1073**

Kimmel, Eric A. *The Gingerbread Man* [Pre-1], **953**

The Greatest of All: A Japanese Folktale [K-2], **954**

The Old Woman and Her Pig [Pre-2], **956**

Kwon, Holly H. *The Moles and the Mireuk: A Korean Folktale* [K-2], **962**

Lichtveld, Noni. *I Lost My Arrow in a Kankan Tree* [K-2], **970**

Litzinger, Rosanne. *The Old Woman and Her Pig: An Old English Tale* [Pre-1], **971**

McGovern, Ann. *Too Much Noise* [Pre-2], 1556

Marshak, Samuel. *The Month Brothers: A Slavic Tale* [K-3], 1560

Marshall, James. *Old Mother Hubbard and Her Wonderful Dog* [Pre-1], **980**

The Three Little Pigs [Pre-1], 1563

Mollel, Tololwa M. *Rhinos for Lunch and Elephants for Supper!* [Pre-2], **991**

Morgan, Pierr. *The Turnip: An Old Russian Folktale* [Pre-1], 1569

Polette, Nancy. *The Little Old Woman and the Hungry Cat* [Pre-2], **999**

CREATIVE DRAMA–Folklore (cont.)

Rounds, Glen. *Three Little Pigs and the Big Bad Wolf* [Pre-2], **1010**

Silverman, Maida. *Anna and the Seven Swans* [K-3], 1601

Stern, Simon. *The Hobyas: An Old Story* [Pre-1], 1609

Stewig, John Warren. *Stone Soup* [K-3], **1031**

Tolstoi, Alexie. *The Great Big Enormous Turnip* [Pre-1], 1614

Westwood, Jennifer. *Going to Squintum's: A Foxy Folktale* [Pre-2], 1624

Wildsmith, Brian. *The Lion and the Rat* [Pre-3], 1628

Zemach, Margot. *It Could Always Be Worse* [1-4], 1638

The Three Little Pigs: An Old Story [Pre-2], 1639

CREATIVE WRITING

SEE ALSO Authors; Writing

Ahlberg, Janet, and Allan Ahlberg. *The Jolly Christmas Postman* [1-2], **396**

Andersen, Hans Christian. *Thumbelina* [2-3], 864

Andersen, Karen Born. *An Alphabet in Five Acts* [1-2], **398**

Andrews, F. Emerson. *Upside-Down Town* [2-3], 866

Aylesworth, Jim. *My Son John* [K-1], **222**

Bacon, Peggy. *The Magic Touch* [3-4], 1043

Banks, Lynne Reid. *The Magic Hare* [3-4], **702**

Barrett, Judi. *Animals Should Definitely Not Wear Clothing* [2-3], 870

Cloudy with a Chance of Meatballs [2-3], 871

Pickles Have Pimples: And Other Silly Statements [1-2], 611

Bauer, Caroline Feller. *My Mom Travels a Lot* [1-2], 612

Baylor, Byrd. *Everybody Needs a Rock* [2-3], 873

Brandreth, Gyles. *The Biggest Tongue Twister Book in the World* [2-6], 1753

Brenner, Barbara. *A Dog I Know* [1-2], 621

Brett, Jan. *The Twelve Days of Christmas* [Pre-6], 1755

Brewton, John E., and Lorraine A. Blackburn. *They've Discovered a Head in the Box for the Bread: And Other Laughable Limericks* [3-6], 1756

Brittain, Bill. *The Wish Giver: Three Tales of Coven Tree* [5-6], 1278

Brown, Jeff. *Flat Stanley* [1-2], 624

Brown, Marcia. *Peter Piper's Alphabet* [1-6], 1762

Brown, Margaret. *The Important Book* [1-2], 630

Byars, Betsy. *Beans on the Roof* [2-3], 879

Caseley, Judith. *Dear Annie* [K-1], **250**

Cassedy, Sylvia, and Kunihiro Suetake. *Red Dragonfly on My Shoulder* [2-6], **1278**

Cherry, Lynne. *Who's Sick Today?* [Pre-K], 47

Chess, Victoria. *Alfred's Alphabet Walk* [1-2], 648

Clifford, Sandy. *The Roquefort Gang* [3-4], 1053

Cole, Joanna. *Doctor Change* [2-3], 896

Coletta, Irene, and Hallie Coletta. *From A to Z: The Collected Letters of Irene and Hallie Coletta* [2-3], 897

Coombs, Patricia. *The Magician and McTree* [2-3], 900

Dahl, Roald. *Roald Dahl's Revolting Rhymes* [3-6], 1787

Duke, Kate. *Aunt Isabel Tells a Good One* [1-2], **436**

Eichenberg, Fritz. *Ape in a Cape: An Alphabet of Odd Animals* [Pre-K], 79

Dancing in the Moon [K-1], 380

Fleischman, Sid. *McBroom Tells the Truth* [3-4], 1066

Flora, James. *Grandpa's Ghost Stories* [2-3], 919

My Friend Charlie [2-3], 924

Gerrard, Roy. *Sir Francis Drake: His Daring Deeds* [4-6], 2038

Grover, Max. *The Accidental Zucchini: An Unexpected Alphabet* [K-1], **277**

Gwynne, Fred. *A Chocolate Moose for Dinner* [3-4], 1068

Hall, Malcolm. *Headlines* [2-3], 932

Hoban, Tana. *A Children's Zoo* [K-1], 430

Hughes, Dean. *Nutty Knows All* [5-6], 1312

Ipcar, Dahlov. *I Love My Anteater with an A* [3-4], 1078

Joslin, Sesyle. *What Do You Say, Dear?* [1-2], 702

Kalman, Maira. *Hey Willy, See the Pyramids* [2-3], 941

Kennedy, Richard. *Come Again in the Spring* [3-4], 1080

Khalsa, Dayal Kaur. *Tales of a Gambling Grandma* [3-4], 1084

Krauss, Ruth. *Is This You?* [1-2], 714

Levitt, Paul M., Douglas A. Burger, and Elissa S. Guralnick. *The Weighty Word Book* [5-6], 1326

Lindbergh, Anne. *Travel Far, Pay No Fare* [5-6], **826**

Lobel, Arnold. *Fables* [4-5], 1207

The Ice Cream Cone Coot and Other Rare Birds [2-3], 954

Loomis, Christine. *In the Diner* [Pre-K], **154**

Marshall, James. *Rats on the Roof and Other Stories* [2-3], **643**

Modesitt, Jeanne. *The Story of Z* [1-2], **511**

Moore, Inga. *The Sorcerer's Apprentice* [2-3], **648**

Morley, Diana. *Marms in the Marmalade* [1-4], 1876

Morrison, Bill. *Squeeze a Sneeze* [K-1], **326**

Most, Bernard. *Can You Find It?* [K-1], **329**
Zoodles [1-2], **514**

Nerlove, Miriam. *I Made a Mistake* [1-2], 756

Nixon, Joan Lowery. *If You Were a Writer* [2-3], 972

Paton Walsh, Jill. *The Green Book* [5-6], 1341

Peet, Bill. *No Such Things* [2-3], 978

Phillips, Louis. *How Do You Get a Horse Out of the Bathtub? Profound Answers to Preposterous Questions* [5-6], 1900

Raffi. *Down by the Bay* [1-2], 780
Spider on the Floor [K-1], **348**

Rosen, Michael J. *Speak! Children's Book Illustrators Brag About Their Dogs* [2-6], **1229**

Rosenbloom, Joseph. *Daffy Definitions* [4-6], 1927

Rylant, Cynthia. *Waiting to Waltz: A Childhood* [5-6], 1941
When I Was Young in the Mountains [2-3], 989

Sachar, Louis. *Sideways Stories from Wayside School* [3-4], 1110
Wayside School Is Falling Down [3-4], 1111

Schwartz, Alvin. *Whoppers: Tall Tales and Other Lies* [3-6], 1726

Schwartz, Amy. *Bea and Mr. Jones* [1-2], 795

Seuss, Dr. *If I Ran the Zoo* [1-2], 803
McElligot's Pool [1-2], 804
On Beyond Zebra [1-2], 805

Sharmat, Marjorie Weinman. *Chasing after Annie* [2-3], 998

Silverstein, Shel. *Who Wants a Cheap Rhinoceros?* [1-2], 812

Stadler, John. *Cat Is Back at Bat* [K-1], **372**

Stanley, Diane. *The Good-Luck Pencil* [2-3], 1005

Steig, William. *CDB* [2-6], 1959

Stevens, Janet. *From Pictures to Words: A Book About Making a Book* [1-4], **1244**

Storr, Catherine. *Clever Polly and the Stupid Wolf* [3-4], 1122

Talon, Robert. *Zoophabets* [2-3], 1014

Tripp, Wallace. *My Uncle Podger* [3-4], 1123

Van Allsburg, Chris. *The Mysteries of Harris Burdick* [4-5], 1250
Two Bad Ants [3-4], 1125

Waber, Bernard. *Dear Hildegarde* [2-3], 1022

Walton, Rick, and Ann Walton. *What's Your Name, Again? More Jokes about Names* [1-6], 1971

Ward, Lynd. *The Silver Pony* [2-3], 1024

Weil, Zaro. *Mud, Moon and Me* [1-4], **1420**

Williams, Vera B. *Cherries and Cherry Pits* [1-2], 852

Willis, Jeanne. *Earthlets: As Explained by Professor Xargle* [2-3], **692**

Wood, Audrey. *Silly Sally* [Pre-K], **212**

Worth, Valerie. *All the Small Poems and Fourteen More* [2-6], **1425**
Small Poems [2-6], 1979

CREEK INDIANS–Folklore

Bruchac, Joseph. *The Great Ball Game: A Muskogee Story* [K-3], **871**

CRICKETS

SEE ALSO Insects

Carle, Eric. *The Very Quiet Cricket* [Pre-K], **75**

Porte, Barbara Ann. *"Leave That Cricket Be, Alan Lee"* [K-1], **340**

Wolkstein, Diane. *Step by Step* [Pre-K], **211**

CROCODILES

Brown, Marcia. *How, Hippo!* [Pre-K], 28

Christelow, Eileen. *Five Little Monkeys Sitting in a Tree* [Pre-K], **85**

Dahl, Roald. *The Enormous Crocodile* [1-2], 656

Jorgensen, Gail. *Crocodile Beat* [Pre-K], 159

Kipling, Rudyard. *The Elephant's Child* [2-3], 946

Waber, Bernard. *Lyle, Lyle Crocodile* [K-1], 578

CROCODILES–Folklore

Aruego, Jose, and Ariane Dewey. *A Crocodile's Tale* [Pre-1], 1393

Galdone, Paul. *The Monkey and the Crocodile: A Jataka Tale from India* [Pre-2], 1466

Maddern, Eric. *Rainbow Bird: An Aboriginal Folktale from Northern Australia* [K-3], **979**

CROWS–Folklore

Goble, Paul. *Crow Chief: A Plains Indian Story* [2-6], **915**

McDermott, Gerald. *Coyote: A Trickster Tale from the American Southwest* [Pre-2], **975**

CRYING

Wishinsky, Frieda. *Oonga Boonga* [Pre-K], **209**

CUMULATIVE STORIES

Aardema, Verna. *Bringing the Rain to Kapiti Plain* [Pre-2], 1380
The Riddle of the Drum [1-4], 1383
Traveling to Tondo: A Tale of the Nkundo of Zaire [Pre-2], **857**
Why Mosquitoes Buzz in People's Ears [Pre-2], 1386

Ada, Alma Flor. *The Rooster Who Went to His Uncle's Wedding: A Latin American Folktale* [Pre-1], **858**

Armour, Peter. *Stop That Pickle!* [K-1], **218**

CUMULATIVE STORIES (cont.)

Asbjørnsen, P. C. *The Runaway Pancake* [Pre-1], 1394

Banks, Kate. *Peter and the Talking Shoes* [K-1], **228**

Bennett, David. *One Cow Moo Moo!* [Pre], **5**

Cole, Joanna. *Golly Gump Swallowed a Fly* [K-1], 372

Demuth, Patricia Brennan. *The Ornery Morning* [K-1], **260**

Duff, Maggie. *Rum Pum Pum* [Pre-2], 1449

Emberley, Barbara. *Drummer Hoff* [Pre-K], 80

Esterl, Arnica. *The Fine Round Cake* [K-2], **903**

Galdone, Paul. *The Greedy Old Fat Man: An American Folktale* [Pre-2], 1460
The Old Woman and Her Pig [Pre-1], 1469

Gelman, Rita Golden. *I Went to the Zoo* [K-1], **275**

Gonzalez, Lucie M. *The Bossy Gallito: A Traditional Cuban Folktale* [K-2], **917**

Kalan, Robert. *Jump, Frog, Jump* [Pre-K], 160

Karas, G. Brian. *I Know an Old Lady* [K-1], **295**

Kent, Jack. *The Fat Cat* [Pre-2], 1539

Kimmel, Eric A. *The Gingerbread Man* [Pre-1], **953**
The Old Woman and Her Pig [Pre-2], **956**

Lamont, Priscilla. *The Troublesome Pig: A Nursery Tale* [Pre-2], 1543

Lichtveld, Noni. *I Lost My Arrow in a Kankan Tree* [K-2], **970**

Litzinger, Rosanne. *The Old Woman and Her Pig: An Old English Tale* [Pre-1], **971**

Lobel, Arnold. *The Rose in My Garden* [K-1], 485

McGovern, Ann. *Too Much Noise* [Pre-2], 1556

Martin, Bill, Jr. *Old Devil Wind* [K-1], **323**

Nietzel, Shirley. *The Jacket I Wear in the Snow* [Pre-K], 217

Polette, Nancy. *The Little Old Woman and the Hungry Cat* [Pre-2], **999**

Robart, Rose. *The Cake That Mack Ate* [Pre-K], 241

Rounds, Glen. *I Know an Old Lady Who Swallowed a Fly* [K-1], 537

Rydell, Katy. *Wind Says Good Night* [Pre], **42**

Schindel, John. *What's for Lunch?* [Pre-K], **185**

Scieszka, Jon. *The Book That Jack Wrote* [1-2], **548**

Silverstein, Shel. *A Giraffe and a Half* [1-2], 811

Stevens, Janet. *The House That Jack Built: A Mother Goose Nursery Rhyme* [Pre-K], 271

Stutson, Caroline. *By the Light of the Halloween Moon* [1-2], **561**

Sweet, Melissa. *Fiddle-I-Fee: A Farmyard Song for the Very Young* [Pre-K], **190**

West, Colin. *The King of Kennelwick Castle* [Pre-K], 289

Westcott, Nadine Bernard. *I Know an Old Lady Who Swallowed a Fly* [K-1], 588
The Pop-Up, Pull-Tab Playtime House That Jack Built [Pre-K], **208**

Wood, Audrey. *The Napping House* [Pre-K], 301

Zemach, Harve. *Mommy, Buy Me a China Doll* [Pre-K], 305

CURIOSITY

Gray, Libba Moore. *Small Green Snake* [Pre-K], **113**

Kipling, Rudyard. *The Elephant's Child* [2-3], 946

Rey, H. A. *Curious George* [Pre-K], 238

Wells, Rosemary. *Max and Ruby's First Greek Myth: Pandora's Box* [1-2], **573**

DAKOTA INDIANS

Wood, Ted, and Wanbli Numpa Afraid of Hawk. *A Boy Becomes a Man at Wounded Knee* [3-6], **1255**

DAKOTA INDIANS–Folklore

Goble, Paul. *Crow Chief: A Plains Indian Story* [2-6], **915**

DANCING

Ackerman, Karen. *Song and Dance Man* [1-2], 599

Bang, Molly. *The Paper Crane* [1-2], 610

Getz, Arthur. *Humphrey, the Dancing Pig* [K-1], 405

Isadora, Rachel. *Max* [K-1], 436

Jonas, Ann. *Color Dance* [Pre-K], **136**

Keller, Beverly. *The Genuine, Ingenious Thrift Shop Genie, Clarissa Mae Bean and Me* [4-5], 1198

Lobel, Arnold. *Ming Lo Moves the Mountain* [K-1], 481

McKissack, Patricia C. *Mirandy and Brother Wind* [2-3], 958

Marshall, James. *The Cut-Ups Carry On* [1-2], **503**

Martin, Bill, Jr., and John Archambault. *Barn Dance!* [K-1], 505

Patrick, Denise Lewis. *Red Dancing Shoes* [Pre-K], **175**

Quinn-Harken, Janet. *Peter Penny's Dance* [1-2], 779

Schertle, Alice. *Bill and Google-Eyed Goblins* [1-2], 792

Shannon, George. *Dance Away* [Pre-K], 260

Wallace, Ian. *Chin Chiang and the Dragon Dance* [1-2], 843

Walsh, Ellen Stoll. *Hop Jump* [Pre], **53**

DANCING–Folklore

Grimm, Jacob. *The Twelve Dancing Princesses* [1-4], 1509

The Twelve Dancing Princesses [2-4], **930**

DA VINCI, LEONARDO

Woodruff, Elvira. *The Disappearing Bike Shop* [4-5], **797**

DAYS OF THE WEEK

Balian, Lorna. *Amelia's Nine Lives* [Pre-K], 19

Blundell, Tony. *Joe on Sunday* [K-1], 337

Carle, Eric. *Today Is Monday* [K-1], **248**

Edwards, Frank B. *Mortimer Mooner Stopped Taking a Bath* [Pre-K], **94**

Sundgaard, Arnold. *Meet Jack Appleknocker* [Pre-K], 272

Wood, Audrey. *Heckedy Peg* [1-2], 854

DAYS OF THE WEEK–Folklore

Baden, Robert. *And Sunday Makes Seven* [2-4], **864**

Maitland, Antony. *Idle Jack* [K-3], 1559

DEAF

Booth, Barbara D. *Mandy* [1-2], **408**

Hesse, Karen. *Lester's Dog* [2-3], **619**

Nichol, Barbara. *Beethoven Lives Upstairs* [4-5], **785**

Rankin, Laura. *The Handmade Alphabet* [K-6], **1223**

Shreve, Susan. *The Gift of the Girl Who Couldn't Hear* [5-6], **841**

DEATH

Andersen, Janet S. *The Key into Winter* [2-3], **587**

Bauer, Marion Dane. *On My Honor* [5-6], 1273

Coerr, Eleanor. *Sadako* [2-5], **1120**

Cohen, Miriam. *Jim's Dog Muffins* [K-1], 368

Cohn, Janice. *I Had a Friend Named Peter: Talking to Children about the Death of a Friend* [Pre-K], 51

Conly, Jane Leslie. *Crazy Lady!* [5-6], **808**

DeFelice, Cynthia. *Devil's Bridge* [4-5], **766**

Engel, Diana. *Eleanor, Arthur, and Claire* [K-1], **267**

Graeber, Charlotte. *Mustard* [2-3], 927

Heckert, Connie. *Dribbles* [1-2], **452**

Hesse, Karen. *Phoenix Rising* [5-6], **821**

Howard, Ellen. *Murphy and Kate* [2-3], **623**

James, Betsy. *Mary Ann* [Pre-K], **133**

Jukes, Mavis. *I'll See You in My Dreams* [3-4], **718**

Keller, Holly. *Goodbye, Max* [K-1], 452

Kennedy, Richard. *Come Again in the Spring* [3-4], 1080

Little, Jean. *Home from Far* [4-5], 1206

London, Jonathan. *Gray Fox* [1-2], 489

Maugham, W. Somerset. *Appointment* [5-6], **830**

Miles, Miska. *Annie and the Old One* [4-5], 1213

Myers, Anna. *Red-Dirt Jessie* [4-5], **780**

Nodar, Carmen Santiago. *Abuelita's Paradise* [1-2], **519**

Pank, Rachel. *Under the Blackberries* [K-1], **335**

Paterson, Katherine. *Bridge to Terabithia* [5-6], 1340

Paulsen, Gary. *A Christmas Sonata* [5-6], **833**

Sachar, Louis. *Marvin Redpost: Alone in His Teacher's House* [2-3], **672**

Slepian, Jan. *Back to Before* [5-6], **843**

The Broccoli Tapes [5-6], **844**

Thomas, Jane Resh. *Saying Good-Bye to Grandma* [2-3], **683**

Viorst, Judith. *The Tenth Good Thing about Barney* [K-1], 575

Woodruff, Elvira. *Dear Napoleon, I Know You're Dead, But . . .* [5-6], **852**

DEATH–Folklore

Crespo, George. *How the Sea Began: A Taino Myth* [1-6], **887**

DEER

Carrick, Donald. *Harald and the Great Stag* [2-3], 883

Radcliffe, Theresa. *Shadow the Deer* [K-1], **347**

DELAWARE INDIANS–Folklore

Greene, Ellin. *The Legend of the Cranberry: A Paleo-Indian Tale* [1-4], **919**

DEMONS

SEE Monsters

DENMARK–Folklore

SEE Folklore–Denmark

DESERTS

Albert, Richard E. *Alejandro's Gift* [1-2], **397**

Bash, Barbara. *Desert Giant: The World of the Saguaro Cactus* [2-5], 1994

Guiberson, Brenda. *Cactus Hotel* [1-4], **1155**

McLerran, Alice. *Roxaboxen* [1-2], **499**

Mora, Pat. *Listen to the Desert / Oye al Desierto* [Pre-2], **1209**

DESERTS–Poetry

Baylor, Byrd. *Amigo* [1-2], 613

Siebert, Diane. *Mojave* [2-3], 1000

DEVIL

Babbitt, Natalie. *The Devil's Storybook* [5-6], 1270

Brittain, Bill. *Devil's Donkey* [5-6], 1276

Professor Popkin's Prodigious Polish: A Tale of Coven Tree [4-5], **760**

DEVIL (cont.)

Carey, Valerie Soho. *The Devil & Mother Crump* [3-4], 1049

Hooks, William H. *Mean Jake and the Devils* [3-4], 1074

Small, David. *Paper John* [1-2], 814

DEVIL–Folklore

Barth, Edna. *Jack-O'-Lantern* [3-6], 1400

Basile, Giambattista. *Petrosinella: A Neopolitan Rapunzel* [4-6], 1401

Belpré, Pura. *Oté* [1-4], 1402

Brusca, María Cristina, and Tona Wilson. *The Blacksmith and the Devils* [3-6], **873**

Conger, Leslie. *Tops and Bottoms* [Pre-3], 1427

Grimm, Jacob. *The Bearskinner* [2-4], 1486
    The Devil with the Three Golden Hairs [2-4], 1489

McCurdy, Michael. *The Devils Who Learned to Be Good* [K-3], 1549

Scribner, Charles. *The Devil's Bridge* [2-4], 1596

Turska, Krystyna. *The Magician of Cracow* [2-5], 1619

Zemach, Harve. *Duffy and the Devil* [2-5], 1635

DIARIES

Audubon, John James. *Capturing Nature: The Writings and Art of John James Audubon* [5-6], **1101**

Columbus, Christopher. *Log of Christopher Columbus* [4-6], **1124**

Heinrich, Bernd. *An Owl in the House: A Naturalist's Diary* [4-6], **1158**

Kalman, Esther. *Tchaikovsky Discovers America* [2-3], **632**

Roop, Peter, and Connie Roop. *I, Columbus; My Journal—1492–3* [4-6], **1227**

Whiteley, Opal. *Only Opal: The Diary of a Young Girl* [2-5], **1253**

DICKENS, CHARLES

Stanley, Diane, and Peter Vennema. *Charles Dickens: The Man Who Had Great Expectations* [4-6], **1242**

DICTIONARIES

Babbitt, Natalie. *The Search for Delicious* [4-5], 1139

Rosenbloom, Joseph. *Daffy Definitions* [4-6], 1927

DINOSAURS

SEE ALSO Animals, prehistoric

Brown, Laurene Krasny, and Marc Brown. *Dinosaurs to the Rescue! A Guide to Protecting Our Planet* [Pre-3], **1112**

Brown, Marc, and Stephen Krensky. *Dinosaurs, Beware! A Safety Guide* [Pre-3], 2002

Butterworth, Oliver. *The Enormous Egg* [4-5], 1154

Carrick, Carol. *Patrick's Dinosaurs* [K-1], 358
    What Happened to Patrick's Dinosaurs? [1-2], 642

Dodson, Peter. *An Alphabet of Dinosaurs* [1-3], **1132**

Hearn, Diane Dawson. *Dad's Dinosaur Day* [Pre-K], **120**

Hennessy, B. G. *The Dinosaur Who Lived in My Backyard* [K-1], **284**

Kellogg, Steven. *Prehistoric Pinkerton* [1-2], 707

Kroll, Steven. *The Tyrannosaurus Game* [1-2], 719

Lauber, Patricia. *The News about Dinosaurs* [2-6], 2062

Most, Bernard. *How Big Were the Dinosaurs?* [K-2], **1212**

Nolan, Dennis. *Dinosaur Dream* [1-2], **520**

Pringle, Laurence. *Dinosaurs! Strange and Wonderful* [K-4], **1222**

Pulver, Robin. *Mrs. Toggle and the Dinosaur* [K-1], **344**

Rohmann, Eric. *Time Flies* [K-1], **350**

Schwartz, Henry. *How I Captured a Dinosaur* [Pre-K], 546

Stickland, Henrietta. *Dinosaur Roar!* [Pre-K], **189**

Talbott, Hudson. *We're Back!* [2-3], 1013

Thayer, Jane. *Quiet on Account of Dinosaur* [K-1], 567

Wilhelm, Hans. *Tyrone the Horrible* [K-1], 590

DINOSAURS–Poetry

Cole, William. *Dinosaurs and Beasts of Yore* [1-4], 1776

Hopkins, Lee Bennett. *Dinosaurs* [K-6], 1821

Prelutsky, Jack. *Tyrannosaurus Was a Beast* [1-6], 1922

DINOSAURS–Riddles

Rosenbloom, Joseph. *The Funniest Dinosaur Book Ever* [Pre-3], 1928

DISASTERS

Ballard, Robert. *Exploring the Titanic* [4-6], **1102**

Hesse, Karen. *Phoenix Rising* [5-6], **821**

DISOBEDIENCE

SEE Obedience

DIVISION

Pinczes, Elinor J. *One Hundred Hungry Ants* [1-2], **533**

DIVORCE

Cleary, Beverly. *Strider* [5-6], **806**

Duffey, Betsy. *Coaster* [4-5], **769**

Havill, Juanita. *Leona and Ike* [3-4], **712**

Park, Barbara. *Don't Make Me Smile* [4-5], 1220

Roy, Ron. *The Chimpanzee Kid* [5-6], 1348

DOGS

Accorsi, William. *Friendship's First Thanksgiving* [K-1], **216**

Adler, David A. *My Dog and the Birthday Mystery* [K-1], 313

Alexander, Sally Hobart. *Mom Can't See Me* [1-4], **1097**

Mom's Best Friend [2-6], **1098**

Andersen, Hans Christian. *The Tinderbox* [4-5], **757**

Armstrong, Jennifer. *Little Salt Lick and the Sun King* [1-2], **399**

Armstrong, William. *Sounder* [5-6], 1264

Auch, Mary Jane. *Bird Dogs Can't Fly* [K-1], **219**

Bare, Colleen Stanley. *To Love a Dog* [Pre-2], 1992

Barracca, Debra, and Sal Barracca. *The Adventures of Taxi Dog* [1-2], **404**

A Taxi Dog Christmas [K-1], **229**

Bemelmans, Ludwig. *Madeline's Rescue* [K-1], 335

Benjamin, Saragail Katzman. *My Dog Ate It* [3-4], **704**

Berger, Terry. *The Turtle's Picnic: And Other Nonsense Stories* [1-2], 615

Blake, Robert J. *Dog* [2-3], **591**

Brenner, Barbara. *A Dog I Know* [1-2], 621

Brett, Jan. *The First Dog* [1-2], 622

Trouble with Trolls [K-1], **236**

Bunting, Eve. *Ghost's Hour, Spook's Hour* [K-1], 351

Burnford, Sheila. *The Incredible Journey* [5-6], 1279

Byars, Betsy. *The Not-Just-Anybody Family* [4-5], 1156

Wanted . . . Mud Blossom [4-5], **763**

Calhoun, Mary. *High-Wire Henry* [1-2], **419**

Calmenson, Stephanie. *Rosie: A Visiting Dog's Story* [1-4], **1116**

Carrick, Carol. *Ben and the Porcupine* [1-2], 640

The Foundling [1-2], 641

Carris, Joan. *Witch-Cat* [3-4], **706**

Chapman, Carol. *Barney Bipple's Magic Dandelions* [1-2], 644

Chapman, Cheryl. *Snow on Snow on Snow* [Pre-K], **83**

Christelow, Eileen. *The Five-Dog Night* [1-2], **425**

Gertrude, the Bulldog Detective [K-1], **252**

Cleary, Beverly. *Henry Huggins* [2-3], 888

Ribsy [2-3], 891

Strider [5-6], **806**

Cohen, Miriam. *Jim's Dog Muffins* [K-1], 368

Cole, Joanna. *My Puppy Is Born* [Pre-2], **1123**

Cuyler, Margery. *Shadow's Baby* [Pre-K], 61

Davidson, Margaret. *Seven True Dog Stories* [2-4], 2015

DeJong, Meindert. *Hurry Home, Candy* [3-4], 1060

Dillon, Barbara. *What's Happened to Harry?* [2-3], 910

Duffey, Betsy. *A Boy in the Doghouse* [2-3], **605**

Ellis, Anne. *Dabble Duck* [K-1], 382

Ernst, Lisa Campbell. *Ginger Jumps* [K-1], **269**

Walter's Tail [K-1], **270**

Evans, Katie. *Hunky Dory Ate It* [Pre-K], **100**

Flack, Marjorie. *Angus and the Cat* [Pre-K], 84

Angus and the Ducks [Pre-K], 85

Angus Lost [Pre-K], 86

Gackenbach, Dick. *Beauty, Brave and Beautiful* [K-1], 395

Claude Has a Picnic [Pre], **16**

Dog for a Day [K-1], 396

What's Claude Doing? [Pre-K], 101

Gardiner, John Reynolds. *Stone Fox* [3-4], 1067

Garfield, James B. *Follow My Leader* [4-5], 1174

Gipson, Fred. *Old Yeller* [4-5], 1180

Graham, Margaret Bloy. *Benjy and the Barking Bird* [Pre-K], 118

Griffith, Helen V. *Plunk's Dreams* [Pre-K], 122

Hall, Donald. *I Am the Dog, I Am the Cat* [1-2], **448**

Hayes, Sarah. *This Is the Bear* [Pre-K], 128

Hazen, Barbara Shook. *Fang* [K-1], 417

Heath, W. L. *Max the Great* [5-6], 1309

Herzig, Alison Cragin. *The Big Deal* [2-3], **618**

Hesse, Karen. *Lester's Dog* [2-3], **619**

Sable [3-4], **714**

Hoff, Syd. *Lengthy* [Pre-K], 139

Howard, Ellen. *Murphy and Kate* [2-3], **623**

Howe, Deborah, and James Howe. *Bunnicula: A Rabbit-Tale of Mystery* [4-5], 1193

Howe, James. *Creepy-Crawly Birthday* [1-2], **456**

The Fright before Christmas [2-3], 935

Nighty-Nightmare [4-5], 1194

Rabbit-Cadabra! [1-2], **458**

Juster, Norton. *The Phantom Tollbooth* [5-6], 1316

Kalman, Maira. *Max Makes a Million* [2-3], **633**

Keats, Ezra Jack. *Goggles!* [K-1], 449

Whistle for Willie [Pre-K], 166

Keller, Holly. *Goodbye, Max* [K-1], 452

Kellogg, Steven. *Pinkerton, Behave* [1-2], 706

Prehistoric Pinkerton [1-2], 707

King-Smith, Dick. *The Invisible Dog* [1-2], **467**

Kopper, Lisa. *Daisy Thinks She Is a Baby* [Pre], **27**

Lauber, Patricia. *Clarence and the Burglar* [1-2], 720

DOGS (cont.)

Lebentritt, Julia, and Richard Ploetz. *The Kooken* [1-2], **481**

LeRoy, Gen. *Taxi Cat and Huey* [4-5], **773**

Lewis, J. Patrick. *One Dog Day* [4-5], **774**

Lexai, Joan. *I'll Tell on You* [1-2], 724

Lindenbaum, Pija. *Boodil My Dog* [1-2], **485**

Low, Joseph. *Mice Twice* [K-1], 488

Meddaugh, Susan. *Martha Speaks* [1-2], **506**
The Witches' Supermarket [1-2], **507**

Meltzer, Maxine. *Pups Speak Up* [K-1], **324**

Modell, Frank. *Tooley! Tooley!* [1-2], 752

Molarsky, Osmond. *Take It or Leave It* [2-3], 965

Mowat, Farley. *Owls in the Family* [3-5], 2077

Myers, Anna. *Red-Dirt Jessie* [4-5], **780**

Myller, Rolf. *A Very Noisy Day* [1-2], 755

Naylor, Phyllis Reynolds. *Shiloh* [5-6], **832**

Osofsky, Audrey. *My Buddy* [1-2], **526**

Paulsen, Gary. *Dogteam* [3-4], **738**

Peet, Bill. *The Whingdingdilly* [2-3], 979

Pilkey, Dav. *Dog Breath: The Horrible Trouble with Hally Tosis* [1-2], **530**
Dogzilla [2-3], **657**

Pinkwater, Daniel. *The Magic Moscow* [3-4], 1105

Porte, Barbara Ann. *Harry's Dog* [1-2], 777

Rand, Gloria. *Salty Takes Off* [1-2], **540**

Reiser, Lynn. *Any Kind of Dog* [Pre], **40**

Rinkoff, Barbara. *The Remarkable Ramsey* [2-3], 985

Robart, Rose. *The Cake That Mack Ate* [Pre-K], 241

Rodowsky, Colby. *Dog Days* [3-4], **739**

Rosen, Michael J. *Speak! Children's Book Illustrators Brag About Their Dogs* [2-6], **1229**

Sachar, Louis. *Marvin Redpost: Alone in His Teacher's House* [2-3], **672**

Schwartz, Amy. *Her Majesty, Aunt Essie* [1-2], 796
Oma and Bobo [K-1], 545

Seibert, Patricia. *Mush! Across Alaska in the World's Longest Sled-Dog Race* [1-4], **1235**

Selden, George. *The Cricket in Times Square* [4-5], 1237

Seligson, Susan. *Amos Camps Out: A Couch Adventure in the Woods* [1-2], **549**

Seligson, Susan, and Howie Schneider. *Amos: The Story of an Old Dog and His Couch* [K-1], 549

Sharmat, Marjorie Weinman. *Chasing after Annie* [2-3], 998
Nate the Great [1-2], 810

Shura, Mary Frances. *Mister Wolf and Me* [4-5], 1238

Singer, Marilyn. *Chester the Out-of-Work Dog* [K-1], **366**

Skurzynski, Gloria. *Martin by Myself* [1-2], 813

Stadler, John. *Animal Cafe* [1-2], 819

Stanley, Diane. *Moe the Dog in Tropical Paradise* [1-2], **556**

Steig, William. *Caleb and Kate* [3-4], 1118

Stevenson, James. *Worse Than the Worst* [1-2], **560**

Stolz, Mary. *The Bully of Barkham Street* [3-4], 1120

Stonely, Jack. *Scruffy* [4-5], **1245**

Swallow, Pam. *Melvil and Dewey in the Chips* [2-3], 1012

Taylor, Livingston. *Can I Be Good?* [K-1], **375**

Taylor, Mark. *Henry the Explorer* [K-1], 564

Thayer, Jane. *The Puppy Who Wanted a Boy* [K-1], 566

Udry, Janice May. *Alfred* [K-1], 572

Van Allsburg, Chris. *The Garden of Abdul Gasazi* [2-3], 1019
The Sweetest Fig [3-4], **751**

Wagner, Jenny. *John Brown, Rose and the Midnight Cat* [K-1], 581

Wegman, William. *ABC* [1-2], **571**

Weller, Frances Ward. *Riptide* [1-2], 848

Wells, Rosemary. *Lucy Comes to Stay* [1-2], **572**

Willoughby, Elaine. *Boris and the Monsters* [Pre-K], 297

Zion, Gene. *Harry by the Sea* [Pre-K], 307
Harry the Dirty Dog [Pre-K], 308
No Roses for Harry [Pre-K], 309

DOGS–Folklore

dePaola, Tomie. *The Comic Adventures of Old Mother Hubbard and Her Dog* [Pre-1], 1438

Galdone, Paul. *Old Mother Hubbard and Her Dog* [Pre-1], 1468

Marshall, James. *Old Mother Hubbard and Her Wonderful Dog* [Pre-1], **980**

San Souci, Robert D. *The Hobyahs* [K-2], **1013**

Stern, Simon. *The Hobyas: An Old Story* [Pre-1], 1609

Wegman, William. *Cinderella* [1-4], **1042**

DOGS–Poetry

Cole, William. *Good Dog Poems* [4-6], 1777

Hellsing, Lennart. *Old Mother Hubbard and Her Dog* [Pre-K], 130

Hopkins, Lee Bennett. *A Dog's Life* [K-6], 1822

Singer, Marilyn. *It's Hard to Read a Map with a Beagle on Your Lap* [3-6], **1409**

Yolen, Jane. *Raining Cats and Dogs* [1-4], **1430**

DOGS–Riddles

Keller, Charles. *It's Raining Cats and Dogs: Cat and Dog Jokes* [2-5], 1837

DOLLS

Ames, Mildred. *Is There Life on a Plastic Planet?* [5-6], 1263

Brink, Carol Ryrie. *The Bad Times of Irma Baumline* [4-5], 1150

Cassedy, Sylvia. *Behind the Attic Wall* [5-6], 1287

Cohen, Barbara. *Molly's Pilgrim* [2-3], 893

King-Smith, Dick. *Lady Daisy* [3-4], **723**

McKissack, Patricia C. *Nettie Jo's Friends* [K-1], 492

Polacco, Patricia. *Babushka's Doll* [Pre-K], **176**

Pomerantz, Charlotte. *The Chalk Doll* [1-2], 776

Regan, Dian Curtis. *The Curse of the Trouble Dolls* [2-3], **669**

Sachs, Marilyn. *The Bears' House* [5-6], 1350

Sleator, William. *Among the Dolls* [4-5], 1240

Tews, Susan. *The Gingerbread Doll* [1-2], **565**

Wells, Rosemary. *Hazel's Amazing Mother* [K-1], 585

Peabody [Pre-K], 288

Zemach, Harve. *Mommy, Buy Me a China Doll* [Pre-K], 305

Zolotow, Charlotte. *William's Doll* [Pre-K], 312

DOLLS–Folklore

Ayres, Becky Hickox. *Matreshka* [K-3], **863**

Mayer, Marianna. *Baba Yaga and Vasilisa the Brave* [2-5], **985**

DOLPHINS

Berg, Cami. *D Is for Dolphin* [Pre-3], **1106**

Davidson, Margaret. *Nine True Dolphin Stories* [2-4], 2014

DOLPHINS–Folklore

Anderson, Lonzo. *Arion and the Dophins* [K-3], 1391

DOMESTIC ANIMALS

SEE ALSO individual animals, e.g., Dogs; ALSO Animals; Pets

Aylesworth, Jim. *Hush Up!* [K-1], 323

One Crow: A Counting Rhyme [Pre-K], 17

Boland, Janice. *Annabel* [Pre], 6

Bourgeois, Paulette. *Too Many Chickens* [K-1], **235**

Carle, Eric. *The Very Busy Spider* [Pre-K], 41

Carroll, Kathleen Sullivan. *One Red Rooster* [Pre], **7**

Cauley, Lorinda Bryan. *Old MacDonald Had a Farm* [Pre-K], **78**

Causley, Charles. *"Quack!" Said the Billy-Goat* [Pre-K], 46

Clarke, Gus. *EIEIO: The Story of Old MacDonald, Who Had a Farm* [Pre-K], **86**

Cole, Brock. *No More Baths* [Pre-K], 52

Demuth, Patricia Brennan. *The Ornery Morning* [K-1], **260**

Donaldson, Julia. *A Squash and a Squeeze* [K-1], **264**

Duffy, Dee Dee. *Barnyard Tracks* [Pre], **10**

Ehlert, Lois. *Color Farm* [Pre-K], **96**

Ehrlich, Amy. *Parents in the Pigpen, Pigs in the Tub* [K-1], **266**

Fleming, Denise. *Barnyard Banter* [Pre], **12**

Fox, Mem. *Hattie and the Fox* [Pre-K], 91

Frascino, Edward. *My Cousin the King* [K-1], 390

Hellen, Nancy. *Old MacDonald Had a Farm* [Pre], **20**

King-Smith, Dick. *Babe, the Gallant Pig* [5-6], 1319

Leaf, Munro. *The Story of Ferdinand* [K-1], 465

Lewison, Wendy Cheyette. *Going to Sleep on the Farm* [Pre], **28**

Lindbergh, Reeve. *The Day the Goose Got Loose* [K-1], **306**

There's a Cow in the Road! [K-1], **307**

Loomis, Christine. *One Cow Coughs: A Counting Book for the Sick and Miserable* [Pre-K], **155**

McDonnell, Flora. *I Love Animals* [Pre], **30**

Martin, Bill, Jr., and John Archambault. *Barn Dance!* [K-1], **505**

Parkinson, Kathy. *The Farmer in the Dell* [Pre-K], 223

Rae, Mary Maki. *The Farmer in the Dell: A Singing Game* [Pre-K], 234

Reddix, Valerie. *Millie and the Mud Hole* [Pre-K], **180**

Rounds, Glen. *Old MacDonald Had a Farm* [Pre-K], **182**

Runcie, Jill. *Cock-a-Doodle-Doo!* [Pre], **41**

Sweet, Melissa. *Fiddle-I-Fee: A Farmyard Song for the Very Young* [Pre-K], **190**

Turner, Gwenda. *Over on the Farm* [Pre-K], **195**

Waddell, Martin. *Farmer Duck* [Pre-K], **200**

The Pig in the Pond [Pre], **50**

Westcott, Nadine Bernard. *Skip to My Lou* [Pre-K], 292

Zakhoder, Boris. *How a Piglet Crashed the Christmas Party* [1-2], 858

Zimmerman, Andrea, and David Clemesha. *The Cow Buzzed* [Pre-K], **215**

DOMESTIC ANIMALS–Folklore

Cole, Joanna. *It's Too Noisy!* [Pre-1], **882**

DOMESTIC ANIMALS–Poetry

Schertle, Alice. *How Now, Brown Cow?* [1-6], **1406**

DONKEYS

Annett, Cora. *How the Witch Got Alf* [2-3], 868

Corbett, Scott. *The Donkey Planet* [4-5], 1163

Steig, William. *Sylvester and the Magic Pebble* [1-2], 821

DONKEYS–Folklore

Aesop. *The Miller, His Son and Their Donkey: A Fable from Aesop* [K-2], 1387

Grimm, Jacob. *The Donkey Prince* [2-4], 1490
The Table, the Donkey and the Stick [1-4], 1507

DOWN'S SYNDROME

Dodds, Bill. *My Sister Annie* [4-5], **768**

DRAGONS

Banks, Lynne Reid. *The Adventures of King Midas* [4-5], **758**

Coville, Bruce. *Jeremy Thatcher, Dragon Hatcher* [5-6], **810**

Craig, M. Jean. *The Dragon in the Clock Box* [K-1], 375

Gag, Wanda. *The Funny Thing* [Pre-K], 103

Gannett, Ruth Stiles. *My Father's Dragon* [1-2], 674

Holabird, Katharine. *Alexander and the Dragon* [Pre-K], 140

Jones, Maurice. *I'm Going on a Dragon Hunt* [Pre-K], 158

Krensky, Steven. *The Dragon Circle* [4-5], 1202

Leedy, Loreen. *A Number of Dragons* [Pre-K], 182

Long, Claudia. *Albert's Story* [K-1], 487

McPhail, David. *The Magical Drawings of Mooney B. Finch* [1-2], 737

Peet, Bill. *How Droofus the Dragon Lost His Head* [1-2], 769

Reit, Seymour. *Benvenuto* [3-4], 1106

Rinkoff, Barbara. *The Dragon's Handbooks* [2-3], 984

Sargeant, Sarah. *Weird Henry Berg* [5-6], 1352

Schwartz, Mary Ada. *Spiffen: A Tale of a Tidy Pig* [K-1], 547

Scieszka, Jon. *Knights of the Kitchen Table* [3-4], **743**

Sterman, Betsy, and Samuel Sterman. *Backyard Dragon* [3-4], **750**

Strickland, Brad. *Dragon's Plunder* [5-6], **848**

Thayer, Jane. *The Popcorn Dragon* [Pre-K], 273

Wallace, Ian. *Chin Chiang and the Dragon Dance* [1-2], 843

Williams, Jay. *Everyone Knows What a Dragon Looks Like* [2-3], 1029

Willis, Val. *The Secret in the Matchbook* [K-1], 593

Wrede, Patricia. *Dealing with Dragons* [5-6], **853**

DRAGONS–Folklore

Domanska, Janina. *King Krakus and the Dragon* [K-2], 1446

Haley, Gail E. *Jack and the Fire Dragon* [2-5], 1516

Hodges, Margaret. *Saint George and the Dragon: A Golden Legend* [3-6], 1526

Lawson, Julie. *The Dragon's Pearl* [1-4], **965**

Scott, Sally. *The Three Wonderful Beggars* [1-4], 1595

Stern, Simon. *Vasily and the Dragon: An Epic Russian Fairy Tale* [3-6], 1610

Van Woerkom, Dorothy. *Alexander the Rock-Eater* [1-4], 1621

DRAGONS–Poetry

Prelutsky, Jack. *The Dragons Are Singing Tonight* [1-5], **1396**

Whipple, Laura. *Eric Carle's Dragons, Dragons & Other Creatures That Never Were* [2-6], **1423**

DRAWING

Browne, Anthony. *Bear Hunt* [Pre-K], 30

Cohen, Miriam. *No Good in Art* [K-1], 370

dePaola, Tomie. *The Art Lesson* [2-3], 907

Drescher, Henrik. *Simon's Book* [1-2], 664

Gackenbach, Dick. *Mag the Magnificent* [K-1], 398

Harding, William Harry. *Alvin's Famous No-Horse* [2-3], **613**

Jeschke, Susan. *Angela and Bear* [K-1], 437

Johnson, Crockett. *Harold and the Purple Crayon* [Pre-K], 153

Kleven, Elisa. *The Paper Princess* [Pre-K], **146**

McPhail, David. *The Magical Drawings of Mooney B. Finch* [1-2], 737

Moss, Marissa. *Regina's Big Mistake* [K-1], **328**

Noble, Trinka Hakes. *Apple Tree Christmas* [2-3], 973

Peet, Bill. *Encore for Eleanor* [1-2], 768

Withers, Carl. *Tale of a Black Cat* [1-2], 853

Zelinsky, Paul O. *The Maid and the Mouse and the Odd-Shaped House* [1-2], 860

Ziefert, Harriet. *Pete's Chicken* [K-1], **392**

DREAMS

Griffith, Helen V. *Plunk's Dreams* [Pre-K], 122

Haley, Gail E. *Dream Peddler* [2-3], **612**

Lionni, Leo. *Matthew's Dream* [K-1], **308**

Mellecker, Judith. *Randolph's Dream* [3-4], **732**

Nightingale, Sandy. *A Giraffe on the Moon* [Pre-K], **172**

Nolan, Dennis. *Dinosaur Dream* [1-2], **520**

Pilkey, Dav. *When Cats Dream* [1-2], **532**

Roth, Roger. *The Sign Painter's Dream* [1-2], **545**

Ryder, Joanne. *The Night Flight* [K-1], 540

Sleator, William. *Into the Dream* [5-6], 1359

Van Allsburg, Chris. *The Sweetest Fig* [3-4], **751**

DREAMS–Folklore

Hodges, Margaret. *Saint Patrick and the Peddler* [1-4], **941**

Troughton, Joanna. *Tortoise's Dream* [Pre-2], 1618

DROUGHT

Harper, Jo. *Jalapeño Hal* [2-3], **615**

Wisniewski, David. *Rain Player* [2-3], **694**

DROUGHT–Folklore

Mollel, Tololwa M. *The Orphan Boy: A Maasai Story* [1-4], **989**

Yep, Laurence. *The Junior Thunder Lord* [1-4], **1046**

DRUG ABUSE

Taylor, Clark. *The House That Crack Built* [4-6], **1246**

DUCKS

SEE ALSO Birds; Chickens; Geese; Owls; Parrots; Roosters

Allen, Jeffrey. *Mary Alice, Operator Number Nine* [K-1], 320

Andersen, Hans Christian. *The Ugly Duckling* [1-2], 603

Arnosky, Jim. *All Night Near the Water* [Pre-K], **67**

Artis, Vicki K. *Gray Duck Catches a Friend* [Pre-K], 9

Dahl, Roald. *The Magic Finger* [2-3], 905

Delton, Judy. *Two Good Friends* [Pre-K], 66

Ellis, Anne. *Dabble Duck* [K-1], 382

Flack, Marjorie. *Angus and the Ducks* [Pre-K], 85
The Story about Ping [K-1], 387

Gerstein, Mordicai. *Arnold of the Ducks* [1-2], 677
Follow Me! [Pre-K], 112

Ginsburg, Mirra. *The Chick and the Duckling* [Pre-K], 114

Gordon, Gaelyn. *Duckat* [Pre-K], **110**

Leverich, Kathleen. *The Hungry Fox and the Foxy Duck* [Pre-K], 186

McCloskey, Robert. *Make Way for Ducklings* [1-2], 734

Primavera, Elise. *The Three Dots* [K-1], **342**

Raffi. *Five Little Ducks* [Pre], **39**

Roy, Ron. *Three Ducks Went Wandering* [Pre-K], 246

Silverman, Erica. *Don't Fidget a Feather!* [K-1], **365**

Stott, Dorothy. *Too Much* [Pre], **47**

Van Allsburg, Chris. *The Garden of Abdul Gasazi* [2-3], 1019

Waddell, Martin. *Farmer Duck* [Pre-K], **200**

Whybrow, Ian. *Quacky Quack-Quack!* [Pre], **56**

Winthrop, Elizabeth. *Bear and Mrs. Duck* [Pre-K], 298

DUCKS–Folklore

Garland, Sherry. *Why Ducks Sleep on One Leg* [1-4], **909**

Paterson, Katherine. *The Tale of the Mandarin Ducks* [2-6], **996**

DWARFS

Cross, Helen Reader. *The Real Tom Thumb* [3-6], 2011

Russo, Marisabina. *Alex Is My Friend* [K-1], **354**

EAGLES

SEE ALSO Birds

Mwenye Hadithi. *Hungry Hyena* [K-1], **331**

EARTH

SEE ALSO Geology

Beatty, Jerome. *Matthew Looney's Invasion of the Earth* [4-5], 1142

Cherry, Lynne. *The Armadillo from Amarillo* [1-2], **423**

Clements, Andrew. *Mother Earth's Counting Book* [K-5], **1118**

Cole, Joanna. *The Magic School Bus Inside the Earth* [2-4], 2009

Lasky, Kathryn. *The Librarian Who Measured the Earth* [3-6], **1180**

McNulty, Faith. *How to Dig a Hole to the Other Side of the World* [1-4], 2072

EARTH–Poetry

Brenner, Barbara. *The Earth Is Painted Green: A Garden of Poems About Our Planet* [1-5], **1274**

EASTER

Auch, Mary Jane. *The Easter Egg Farm* [K-1], **220**

Friedrich, Priscilla, and Otto Friedrich. *The Easter Bunny That Overslept* [K-1], 394

Heyward, DuBose. *The Country Bunny and the Little Gold Shoes* [K-1], 423

Polacco, Patricia. *Chicken Sunday* [2-3], **661**

Wells, Rosemary. *Max's Chocolate Chicken* [Pre-K], 286

EATING

SEE Cookery; Food

ECHOES

MacDonald, Amy. *Little Beaver and the Echo* [Pre-K], **156**

ECOLOGY

Albert, Richard E. *Alejandro's Gift* [1-2], **397**

Bash, Barbara. *Desert Giant: The World of the Saguaro Cactus* [2-5], 1994

Tree of Life: The World of the African Baobab [1-4], **1104**

Brown, Laurene Krasny, and Marc Brown. *Dinosaurs to the Rescue! A Guide to Protecting Our Planet* [Pre-3], **1112**

Cherry, Lynne. *The Great Kapok Tree: A Tale of the Amazon Rain Forest* [1-2], 647

A River Ran Wild: An Environmental History [1-4], **1117**

Cone, Molly. *Come Back, Salmon: How a Group of Dedicated Kids Adopted Pigeon Creek and Brought It Back to Life* [4-6], **1125**

Cowcher, Helen. *Rain Forest* [K-1], **256**

Whistling Thorn [K-2], **1126**

Earth Works Group. *50 Simple Things Kids Can Do to Save the Earth* [3-6], **1135**

Gilliland, Judith Heide. *River* [K-3], **1152**

Greene, Carol. *The Old Ladies Who Liked Cats* [1-2], **445**

Guiberson, Brenda. *Cactus Hotel* [1-4], **1155**

Jeffers, Susan. *Brother Eagle, Sister Sky: A Message from Chief Seattle* [2-3], **628**

London, Jonathan. *Voices of the Wild* [2-3], **640**

Peet, Bill. *The Wump World* [2-3], 980

Rand, Gloria. *Prince William* [2-3], **668**

Seuss, Dr. *The Lorax* [2-3], 997

Yolen, Jane. *Welcome to the Green House* [K-3], **1256**

ECOLOGY–Folklore

Hamanaka, Sheila. *Screen of Frogs: An Old Tale* [K-3], **934**

EGGS

Auch, Mary Jane. *The Easter Egg Farm* [K-1], **220**

Baker, Keith. *Big Fat Hen* [Pre], **4**

Butterworth, Oliver. *The Enormous Egg* [4-5], 1154

Craig, M. Jean. *The Dragon in the Clock Box* [K-1], 375

Ernst, Lisa Campbell. *Zinnia and Dot* [K-1], **271**

Heine, Helme. *The Most Wonderful Egg in the World* [Pre-K], 129

Heller, Ruth. *Chickens Aren't the Only Ones* [K-4], **1160**

Kimmel, Eric A. *Asher and the Capmakers: A Hanukkah Story* [2-3], **635**

Leedy, Loreen. *Tracks in the Sand* [K-2], **1183**

Lester, Helen. *It Wasn't My Fault* [K-1], 469

McKissack, Patricia C. *Flossie & the Fox* [1-2], 735

Polacco, Patricia. *Chicken Sunday* [2-3], **661**

Just Plain Fancy [2-3], **662**

Rael, Elsa Okon. *Marushka's Egg* [2-3], **667**

Rockwell, Anne. *The Gollywhopper Egg* [K-1], 534

Sargeant, Sarah. *Weird Henry Berg* [5-6], 1352

Seuss, Dr. *Green Eggs and Ham* [Pre-K], 259

Horton Hatches the Egg [1-2], 801

Vyner, Sue. *The Stolen Egg* [K-1], **379**

EGGS–Folklore

San Souci, Robert. *The Talking Eggs* [1-4], 1590

EGYPT

Heide, Florence Parry, and Judith Heide Gilliland. *The Day of Ahmed's Secret* [2-3], **616**

EGYPT, ANCIENT

SEE ALSO Folklore–Egypt

Price, Leontyne. *Aïda* [5-6], **837**

Stolz, Mary. *Zekmet, the Stone Carver* [4-5], 1244

Swinburne, Irene, and Laurence Swinburne. *Behind the Sealed Door: The Discovery of the Tomb and Treasures of Tutankhamen* [4-6], 2109

ELDERLY

SEE ALSO Grandfathers; Grandmothers; Grandparents

Albert, Richard E. *Alejandro's Gift* [1-2], **397**

Bawden, Nina. *Humbug* [3-4], **703**

Blake, Robert J. *Dog* [2-3], **591**

Dugan, Barbara. *Loop the Loop* [2-3], **608**

Heckert, Connie. *Dribbles* [1-2], **452**

Kimmel, Eric A. *The Chanukkah Guest* [K-1], **298**

Mills, Claudia. *Dinah for President* [4-5], **778**

Polacco, Patricia. *Chicken Sunday* [2-3], **661**

Mrs. Katz and Tush [2-3], **663**

Radley, Gail. *The Golden Days* [5-6], **838**

Schwartz, David. *Supergrandpa* [2-3], **675**

Stevenson, James. *Worse Than the Worst* [1-2], **560**

The Worst Person's Christmas [1-2], **559**

Woodruff, Elvira. *The Summer I Shrank My Grandmother* [4-5], **800**

Ziegler, Jack. *Mr. Knocky* [1-2], **582**

ELDERLY–Folklore

Uchida, Yoshiko. *The Wise Old Woman* [1-5], **1038**

ELECTIONS

Hurwitz, Johanna. *Class President* [3-4], **715**

Mills, Claudia. *Dinah for President* [4-5], **778**

Park, Barbara. *Rosie Swanson, Fourth-Grade Geek for President* [3-4], **737**

ELECTIVE MUTISM

SEE Mutism, Elective

ELEPHANTS

Allinson, Beverly. *Effie* [K-1], **217**

Appelt, Kathi. *Elephants Aloft* [Pre-K], **66**

Blumberg, Rhoda. *Jumbo* [2-5], **1107**

Caple, Kathy. *The Biggest Nose* [K-1], 356

Day, Alexandra. *Frank and Ernest* [2-3], 906

Ford, Miela. *Little Elephant* [Pre], **15**

Geraghty, Paul. *The Hunter* [1-2], **442**

Kipling, Rudyard. *The Elephant's Child* [2-3], 946

Leslie-Melville, Betty. *Elephant Have the Right of Way: Life with the Wild Animals of Africa* [2-6], **1185**

Lobel, Arnold. *Uncle Elephant* [K-1], 486

Mahy, Margaret. *17 Kings and 42 Elephants* [K-1], 500

Manson, Christopher. *Two Travelers* [2-3], **642**

Mwenye Hadithi. *Tricky Tortoise* [Pre-K], 126

Patz, Nancy. *Pumpernickel Tickel and Mean Green Cheese* [K-1], 520

Peet, Bill. *The Ant and the Elephant* [K-1], 521
Encore for Eleanor [1-2], 768

Riddell, Chris. *The Trouble with Elephants* [Pre-K], 240

Robison, Deborah. *No Elephants Allowed* [Pre-K], 243

Sadler, Marilyn. *Alistair's Elephant* [1-2], 788

Seuss, Dr. *Horton Hatches the Egg* [1-2], 801

Smee, Nicola. *The Tusk Fairy* [Pre], **45**

Thomas, Patricia. *"Stand Back," Said the Elephant, "I'm Going to Sneeze!"* [K-1], 568

Tompert, Ann. *Just a Little Bit* [Pre-K], **192**

Vipont, Elfrida. *The Elephant & the Bad Baby* [Pre-K], 283

Weinberg, Larry. *The Forgetful Bears Meet Mr. Memory* [K-1], 583

Westcott, Nadine Bernard. *Peanut Butter and Jelly: A Play Rhyme* [Pre-K], 291

ELEPHANTS–Folklore

Quigley, Lillian F. *The Blind Mice and the Elephant* [K-5], 1582

Sierra, Jud. *The Elephant's Wrestling Match* [Pre-2], **1025**

Young, Ed. *Seven Blind Mice* [Pre-3], 1051

ELLIS ISLAND

Levine, Ellen. *If Your Name Was Changed at Ellis Island* [3-6], **1186**

ELVES

Lindgren, Astrid. *The Tomten* [1-2], 725

Price, Moe. *The Reindeer Christmas* [K-1], **341**

Prøysen, Alf. *Christmas Eve at Santa's* [K-1], **343**

ELVES–Folklore

Grimm, Jacob. *The Elves and the Shoemaker* [Pre-2], 1491

EMBARRASSMENT

Howe, James. *Pinky and Rex and the Spelling Bee* [1-2], **457**

EMOTIONS

Aliki. *Communication* [1-3], **1099**

Anholt, Catherine, and Laurence Anholt. *What Makes Me Happy?* [Pre-K], **65**

Cole, William. *Frances Face-Maker: A Going to Bed Book* [Pre-K], 53

Ets, Marie Hall. *Talking without Words* [Pre-K], 82

Everitt, Betsy. *Mean Soup* [Pre-K], **101**

Greenfield, Eloise. *Grandpa's Face* [K-1], 410

Hubbard, Woodleigh. *C Is for Curious: An ABC of Feelings* [K-1], **289**

Jenkins, Jessica. *Thinking About Colors* [1-2], **462**

Martin, Jane Read, and Patricia Marx. *Now Everybody Really Hates Me* [2-3], **644**

Modesitt, Jeanne. *Sometimes I Feel Like a Mouse: A Book About Feelings* [Pre-K], **169**

Steig, William. *Spinky Sulks* [2-3], 1009

Viorst, Judith. *Alexander and the Terrible, Horrible, No Good, Very Bad Day* [1-2], 838

Wells, Rosemary. *Voyage to the Bunny Planet* books: *First Tomato; The Island Light; Moss Pillows* [K-1], **383**

Zolotow, Charlotte. *The Quarreling Book* [1-2], 861

EMOTIONS–Folklore

Bruchac, Joseph. *The First Strawberries: A Cherokee Story* [K-3], **870**

EMOTIONS–Poetry

Cole, William. *I'm Mad at You* [1-4], 1779

EMPERORS

SEE ALSO Kings and rulers

Manson, Christopher. *The Marvelous Blue Mouse* [2-3], **641**
Two Travelers [2-3], **642**

Singer, Marilyn. *The Painted Fan* [3-4], **748**

EMPERORS–Folklore

Day, David. *The Sleeper* [2-4], **891**

Demi. *The Empty Pot* [K-3], **892**

Yacowitz, Caryn. *The Jade Stone: A Chinese Folktale* [K-4], **1045**

EMUS

Knowles, Sheena. *Edward the Emu* [K-1], **300**

ENDANGERED SPECIES

Allen, Judy. *Panda* [2-3], **584**

Tiger [2-3], **585**

Facklam, Margery. *And Then There Was One: The Mysteries of Extinction* [3-6], **1139**

Koch, Michelle. *World Water Watch* [K-2], **1172**

ENEMIES

Ikeda, Daisaku. *Over the Deep Blue Sea* [1-2], **460**

ENGLAND

SEE ALSO Folklore–England

Banks, Lynne Reid. *The Indian in the Cupboard* [5-6], 1272

Bond, Michael. *A Bear Called Paddington* [4-5], 1146

Paddington's Storybook [4-5], 1147

Bulla, Clyde Robert. *The Sword in the Tree* [2-3], 877

Carrick, Donald. *Harald and the Giant Knight* [2-3], 882

Harald and the Great Stag [2-3], 883

Cole, Sheila. *The Dragon in the Cliff: A Novel Based on the Life of Mary Anning* [5-6], **807**

Cresswell, Helen. *Time Out* [3-4], **708**

Doherty, Berlie. *Street Child* [5-6], **813**

Foreman, Michael. *War Game* [5-6], **816**

Greer, Gery, and Bob Ruddick. *Max and Me and the Time Machine* [5-6], 1306

Haley, Gail E. *Dream Peddler* [2-3], **612**

Harrison, Maggie. *Angels on Roller Skates* [1-2], **451**

Herriot, James. *Blossom Comes Home* [2-5], 2046

Bonny's Big Day [2-5], 2047

The Christmas Day Kitten [2-4], 2048

Hughes, Shirley. *Alfie Gets in First* [Pre-K], 143

Alfie Gives a Hand [Pre-K], 144

Alfie's Feet [Pre-K], 145

Dogger [Pre-K], 146

An Evening at Alfie's [Pre-K], 147

King-Smith, Dick. *Farmer Bungle Forgets* [K-1], 458

Lady Daisy [3-4], **723**

Pigs Might Fly [5-6], 1320

The Queen's Nose [3-4], **726**

Sophie's Snail [1-2], 711

The Swoose [3-4], **727**

Mellecker, Judith. *Randolph's Dream* [3-4], **732**

Newman, Robert. *The Case of the Baker Street Irregular* [5-6], 1335

Pearce, Philippa. *Tom's Midnight Garden* [5-6], 1342

Sheldon, Dyan. *A Witch Got on at Paddington Station* [Pre-K], 265

Stanley, Diane, and Peter Vennema. *Bard of Avon: The Story of William Shakespeare* [4-6], **1241**

Charles Dickens: The Man Who Had Great Expectations [4-6], **1242**

Streatfeild, Noel. *When the Sirens Wailed* [5-6], 1366

Thomas, Jane Resh. *The Princess in the Pigpen* [5-6], 1369

Wiseman, David. *Jeremy Visick* [5-6], 1375

ENGLISH LANGUAGE

SEE ALSO Alliteration; Language; Vocabulary; Word games

Agee, Jon. *Go Hang a Salami! I'm a Lasagna Hog! And Other Palindromes* [2-6], **1263**

Dahl, Roald. *BFG* [4-5], 1166

Day, Alexandra. *Frank and Ernest* [2-3], 906

Juster, Norton. *The Phantom Tollbooth* [5-6], 1316

Levine, Ellen. *I Hate English* [1-2], 721

Merriam, Eve. *Chortles: New and Selected Wordplay Poems* [3-6], 1869

Morley, Diana. *Marms in the Marmalade* [1-4], 1876

Most, Bernard. *Can You Find It?* [K-1], **329**

Schwartz, Alvin. *Chin Music: Tall Talk and Other Talk, Collected from American Folklore* [3-6], 1946

Sperling, Susan Kelz. *Murflies and Wink-a-Peeps: Funny Old Words for Kids* [2-6], 1956

Steckler, Arthur. *101 More Words and How They Began* [3-6], 1958

Boynton, Sandra. *A Is for Angry: An Animal and Adjective Alphabet* [K-1], 341

Fleming, Denise. *In the Small, Small Pond* [Pre-K], **104**

Frank, John. *Odds 'N' Ends Alvy* [1-2], **441**

Heller, Ruth. *A Cache of Jewels and Other Collective Nouns* [Pre-3], 1811

Kites Sail High: A Book about Verbs [3-5], 1812

Merry-Go-Round: A Book About Nouns [1-6], **1310**

Up, Up and Away: A Book About Adverbs [2-6], **1311**

Hooper, Patricia. *A Bundle of Beasts* [2-5], 1817

ENGLISH LANGUAGE–Grammar

Hubbard, Woodleigh. *C Is for Curious: An ABC of Feelings* [K-1], **289**

 2 Is for Dancing: A 1 2 3 of Actions [Pre-K], **127**

MacCarthy, Patricia. *Herds of Words* [K-6], **1363**

McMillan, Bruce. *Kitten Can* [Pre-K], **198**

Martin, Bill, Jr. *The Maestro Plays* [1-2], **504**

Noll, Sally. *Jiggle Wiggle Prance* [K-1], **513**

Roop, Peter, and Connie Roop. *One Earth, a Multitude of Creatures* [K-6], **1228**

Stott, Dorothy. *Too Much* [Pre], **47**

Terban, Marvin. *I Think I Thought and Other Tricky Verbs* [2-4], 1963

ENGLISH LANGUAGE–Homonyms

Bourke, Linda. *Eye Spy: A Mysterious Alphabet* [1-2], **409**

Lester, Helen. *Me First* [K-1], **304**

Terban, Marvin. *The Dove Dove: Funny Homograph Riddles* [3-6], 1962

 Funny You Should Ask: How to Make Up Jokes and Riddles with Wordplay [3-6], **1414**

ENGLISH LANGUAGE–Idioms

Cox, James A. *Put Your Foot in Your Mouth and Other Silly Sayings* [2-6], 1784

Folsom, Michael, and Marcia Folsom. *Easy as Pie: A Guessing Game of Sayings* [1-2], 670

Gwynne, Fred. *A Chocolate Moose for Dinner* [3-4], 1068

Nevins, Ann. *From the Horse's Mouth* [3-6], 1896

Parish, Peggy. *Amelia Bedelia* [1-2], 764

Terban, Marvin. *Funny You Should Ask: How to Make Up Jokes and Riddles with Wordplay* [3-6], **1414**

 In a Pickle and Other Funny Idioms [3-6], 1964

ENGLISH LANGUAGE–Onomatopoeic Words

De Zutter, Hank. *Who Says a Dog Goes Bow-Wow?* [Pre-2], **1131**

Dodds, Dayle Ann. *Do Bunnies Talk?* [K-1], **262**

Gray, Libba Moore. *Small Green Snake* [Pre-K], **113**

Robinson, Marc. *Cock-a-Doodle-Doo! What Does It Sound Like to You?* [Pre-2], **1226**

Showers, Paul. *The Listening Walk* [Pre-K], **187**

ENGLISH LANGUAGE–Personification

Chocolate, Deborah M. Newton. *Talk, Talk: An Ashanti Legend* [1-5], **877**

ENGLISH LANGUAGE–Poetry

Viorst, Judith. *The Alphabet from Z to A: With Much Confusion on the Way* [3-6], **1416**

ENGLISH LANGUAGE–Prepositions

Appelt, Kathi. *Elephants Aloft* [Pre-K], **66**

Chapman, Cheryl. *Snow on Snow on Snow* [Pre-K], **83**

Miller, Margaret. *Where Does It Go?* [Pre-K], **166**

 Where's Jenna? [Pre-K], **167**

ENGLISH LANGUAGE–Spelling

Most, Bernard. *Hippopotamus Hunt* [1-2], **513**

Viorst, Judith. *The Alphabet from Z to A: With Much Confusion on the Way* [3-6], **1416**

ENGLISH LANGUAGE–Synonyms and Antonyms

Hoban, Tana. *Exactly the Opposite* [Pre-K], **125**

ENVIRONMENT

Cherry, Lynne. *A River Ran Wild: An Environmental History* [1-4], **1117**

Cone, Molly. *Come Back, Salmon: How a Group of Dedicated Kids Adopted Pigeon Creek and Brought It Back to Life* [4-6], **1125**

Jeffers, Susan. *Brother Eagle, Sister Sky: A Message from Chief Seattle* [2-3], **628**

Keller, Holly. *Grandfather's Dream* [1-2], **466**

Temple, Lannis. *Dear World: How Children Around the World Feel About Our Environment* [2-6], **1247**

ENVIRONMENT–Poetry

Lindbergh, Reeve. *View from the Air: Charles Lindbergh's Earth and Sky* [3-6], **1356**

ENVIRONMENTAL PROTECTION

Brown, Laurene Krasny, and Marc Brown. *Dinosaurs to the Rescue! A Guide to Protecting Our Planet* [Pre-3], **1112**

Earth Works Group. *50 Simple Things Kids Can Do to Save the Earth* [3-6], **1135**

ENVY

SEE Jealousy

ESKIMOS

Andrews, Jan. *Very Last First Time* [2-3], 867

George, Jean Craighead. *Julie of the Wolves* [5-6], 1304

Hill, Kirkpatrick. *Winter Camp* [5-6], **822**

ETIQUETTE

Brown, Marc, and Stephen Krensky. *Perfect Pigs: An Introduction to Manners* [Pre-3], 2003

Chapman, Cheryl. *Pass the Fritters, Critters* [Pre-K], **82**

Joslin, Sesyle. *What Do You Say, Dear?* [1-2], 702

MacDonald, Betty. *Mrs. Piggle-Wiggle* [3-4], 1092

Yee, Wong Herbert. *Big Black Bear* [Pre-K], **213**

ETIQUETTE (cont.)

Zakhoder, Boris. *How a Piglet Crashed the Christmas Party* [1-2], 858

EVEREST, MOUNT

Fraser, Mary Ann. *On Top of the World: The Conquest of Mount Everest* [4-6], **1143**

EXAGGERATION

Boyd, Selma, and Pauline Boyd. *I Met a Polar Bear* [K-1], 340

Fleischman, Sid. *McBroom Tells the Truth* [3-4], 1066

Galdone, Paul. *The Amazing Pig* [2-4], 1457

Peterson, Esther Allen. *Frederick's Alligator* [1-2], 773

Rounds, Glen. *Ol' Paul, the Mighty Logger* [4-6], 1721

Schwartz, Alvin. *Whoppers: Tall Tales and Other Lies* [3-6], 1726

Stevenson, James. *Brrr!* [K-1], **373**

EXPERIMENTS

SEE Science–Experiments

EXPLORERS

Blumberg, Rhoda. *The Incredible Journey of Lewis & Clark* [5-6], 1996

Columbus, Christopher. *Log of Christopher Columbus* [4-6], **1124**

Conrad, Pam. *Pedro's Journal: A Voyage with Christopher Columbus, August 3, 1492–February 14, 1492* [5-6], **809**

Fritz, Jean. *Around the World in a Hundred Years: From Henry the Navigator to Magellan* [5-6], **1144**

Where Do You Think You're Going, Christopher Columbus? [4-6], 2034

Gerrard, Roy. *Sir Francis Drake: His Daring Deeds* [4-6], 2038

Maestro, Betsy. *The Discovery of the Americas* [2-5], **1195**

Marzollo, Jean. *In 1492* [K-3], **1204**

Mathews, Sally Schofer. *The Sad Night: The Story of an Aztec Victory and a Spanish Loss* [5-6], **1206**

Roop, Peter, and Connie Roop. *I, Columbus; My Journal—1492–3* [4-6], **1227**

Sis, Peter. *Follow the Dream: The Story of Christopher Columbus* [1-4], **1238**

Swan, Robert. *Destination: Antarctica* [4-6], 2108

EXTRASENSORY PERCEPTION

Conford, Ellen. *And This Is Laura* [5-6], 1289

Dahl, Roald. *Matilda* [5-6], 1292

Roberts, Willo Davis. *The Girl with the Silver Eyes* [5-6], 1345

Sleator, William. *Into the Dream* [5-6], 1359

EXTRATERRESTRIAL LIFE

Bradman, Tony. *It Came from Outer Space* [1-2], **410**

Brittain, Bill. *Shape-Changer* [4-5], **761**

Etra, Jonathan, and Stephanie Spinner. *Aliens for Breakfast* [2-3], 915

Fisk, Nicholas. *Grinny: A Novel of Science Fiction* [5-6], 1297

Harding, Lee. *The Fallen Spaceman* [3-4], 1070

Marshall, Edward. *Space Case* [1-2], 742

Marshall, James. *Merry Christmas, Space Case* [1-2], 744

Pinkwater, Daniel. *Fat Men from Space* [3-4], 1103

Guys from Space [K-1], 522

Ned Feldman, Space Pirate [2-3], **660**

The Slaves of Spiegel: A Magic Moscow Story [4-5], 1226

Sadler, Marilyn. *Alistair and the Alien Invasion* [K-1], **356**

Service, Pamela F. *Stinker from Space* [5-6], 1354

Sheldon, Dyan. *My Brother Is a Visitor from Another Planet* [3-4], **746**

Slobodkin, Louis. *The Spaceship under the Apple Tree* [3-4], 1113

Wiesner, David. *June 29, 1999* [2-3], **690**

Willis, Jeanne. *Earthlets: As Explained by Professor Xargle* [2-3], **692**

Yorinks, Arthur. *Company's Coming* [2-3], 1034

EYEGLASSES

Brown, Marc. *Arthur's Eyes* [K-1], 345

Keats, Ezra Jack. *Goggles!* [K-1], 449

Shusterman, Neal. *The Eyes of Kid Midas* [5-6], **842**

FABLES

Aesop. *Aesop & Company: With Scenes from His Legendary Life* [3-6], **1053**

The Aesop for Children [K-3], 1641

Aesop's Fables [1-6], **1054**

Aesop's Fables [2-4], 1642

Aesop's Fables [3-6], 1643, 1646

Aesop's Fables [2-6], 1644

Aesop's Fables [K-3], 1645

Animal Fables from Aesop [2-6], **1055**

Belling the Cat and Other Aesop's Fables: Retold in Verse [3-6], **1056**

The Children's Aesop: Selected Fables [2-5], **1057**

The Fables of Aesop [2-6], 1647

The Miller, His Son and Their Donkey: A Fable from Aesop [K-2], 1387

Once in a Wood: Ten Tales from Aesop [Pre-2], 1648

Seven Fables from Aesop [1-4], 1649

Three Aesop Fox Fables [K-2], 1650

The Tortoise and the Hare: An Aesop Tale [Pre-2], 1388

Twelve Tales from Aesop [K-3], 1651

The Wind and the Sun [K-2], **859**

Cauley, Lorinda Bryan. *The Town Mouse and the Country Mouse* [Pre-2], 1421

Demi. *A Chinese Zoo: Fables and Proverbs* [2-6], 1675

Demi's Reflective Fables [2-6], 1676

Ginsburg, Mirra. *Three Rolls and One Doughnut: Fables from Russia* [1-5], 1681

Hastings, Selina. *Reynard the Fox* [3-6], **1071**

Kherdian, David. *Feathers and Tails: Animal Fables from Around the World* [K-4], **1073**

Lionni, Leo. *Frederick's Fables: A Leo Lionni Treasury of Favorite Stories* [1-2], 728

Tillie and the Wall [K-1], 477

Lobel, Arnold. *Fables* [4-5], 1207

Quigley, Lillian F. *The Blind Mice and the Elephant* [K-5], 1582

Wildsmith, Brian. *The Hare and the Tortoise* [Pre-3], 1627

The Lion and the Rat [Pre-3], 1628

Wolf, Ashley. *Stella & Roy* [Pre-K], **210**

FACTS

Seuling, Barbara. *The Last Cow on the White House Lawn & Other Little-Known Facts about the Presidency* [3-5], 2096

You Can't Eat Peanuts in Church: And Other Little-Known Laws [3-5], 2097

FAIRIES

SEE ALSO Elves; Giants; Imps; Leprechauns; Monsters; Ogres; Trolls

Banks, Lynne Reid. *The Fairy Rebel* [4-5], 1141

Barber, Antonia. *Catkin* [2-3], **590**

Gormley, Beatrice. *Fifth-Grade Magic* [4-5], 1181

Hunter, Mollie. *A Furl of Fairy Wind* [3-4], 1076

Jeffers, Susan. *Wild Robin* [1-2], 699

Karlin, Nurit. *The Tooth Witch* [K-1], 447

Kimmel, Eric A. *Asher and the Capmakers: A Hanukkah Story* [2-3], **635**

Hershel and the Hanukkah Goblins [2-3], 944

Lester, Helen. *Pookins Gets Her Way* [K-1], 470

The Wizard, the Fairy and the Magic Chicken [Pre-K], 185

Myers, Bernice. *Sidney Rella and the Glass Sneaker* [1-2], 754

Pomerantz, Charlotte. *The Downtown Fairy Godmother* [2-3], 981

Schertle, Alice. *Bill and Google-Eyed Goblins* [1-2], 792

Yolen, Jane. *Sleeping Ugly* [2-3], 1033

FAIRIES–Folklore

Climo, Shirley. *Piskies, Spriggans, and Other Magical Beings* [3-6], 1663

Cooper, Susan. *The Silver Cow: A Welsh Tale* [2-5], 1430

Demi. *The Magic Tapestry* [1-4], **894**

Forest, Heather. *The Woman Who Flummoxed the Fairies: An Old Tale from Scotland* [1-4], 1453

McDermott, Gerald. *Tim O'Toole and the Wee Folk: An Irish Tale* [1-4], 1553

San Souci, Robert. *The Enchanted Tapestry: A Chinese Folktale* [1-4], 1589

Yolen, Jane. *Tam Lin* [3-6], **1048**

FAIRS

Harshman, Marc. *Only One* [K-1], **280**

FAIRY GODPARENTS

SEE Fairies

FAIRY TALES

Climo, Shirley. *The Korean Cinderella* [1-4], **878**

Compton, Joanne. *Ashpet: An Appalachian Tale* [1-4], **883**

Dasent, George Webbe. *East o' the Sun and West o' the Moon* [3-6], **890**

Demi. *The Firebird* [2-5], **893**

Early, Margaret. *Sleeping Beauty* [K-6], **899**

Gal, Laszlo. *Prince Ivan and the Firebird* [3-6], **908**

Garner, Alan. *Jack and the Beanstalk* [1-4], **910**

Gerson, Mary-Joan. *How Night Came from the Sea: A Story from Brazil* [K-4], **912**

Greene, Ellin. *Billy Beg and His Bull* [2-4], **918**

Grimm, Jacob. *The Frog Prince: Or Iron Henry* [1-4], **932**

Hansel and Gretel [K-2], **926**

Iron John [2-6], **928**

Rapunzel [2-4], **923**

Rumpelstiltskin [1-4], **922**

The Twelve Dancing Princesses [2-4], **930**

Hastings, Selina. *The Firebird* [1-4], **938**

Howe, John. *Jack and the Beanstalk* [1-3], **944**

Kimmel, Eric A. *I-Know-Not-What, I-Know-Not-Where: A Russian Tale* [4-6], **955**

The Three Princes: A Tale from the Middle East [1-4], **957**

FAIRY TALES (cont.)

Lang, Andrew. *The Rainbow Fairy Book* [3-6], **1074**

Lewis, J. Patrick. *The Frog Princess: A Russian Tale* [2-6], **969**

Martin, Claire. *Boots & the Glass Mountain* [2-6], **981**

Martin, Rafe. *The Rough-Face Girl* [2-6], **983**

Mayer, Marianna. *Baba Yaga and Vasilisa the Brave* [2-5], **985**

The Spirit of the Blue Light [3-5], **986**

Pollock, Penny. *The Turkey Girl: A Zuni Cinderella Story* [2-5], **1000**

San Souci, Robert D. *The Firebird* [3-5], **1012**

Sootface: An Ojibwa Cinderella Story [1-5], **1016**

Sukey and the Mermaid [2-5], **1017**

The Tsar's Promise [3-6], **1018**

The White Cat: An Old French Fairy Tale [2-5], **1019**

Wegman, William. *Cinderella* [1-4], **1042**

Wilson, Barbara Ker. *Wishbones: A Folk Tale from China* [2-4], **1043**

Winthrop, Elizabeth. *Vasilissa the Beautiful: A Russian Folktale* [2-5], **1044**

FAIRY TALES–Poetry

Dahl, Roald. *Roald Dahl's Revolting Rhymes* [3-6], 1787

Viorst, Judith. *If I Were in Charge of the World and Other Worries: Poems for Children and Their Parents* [2-5], 1969

Sad Underwear and Other Complications: More Poems for Children and Their Parents [2-6], **1417**

Yolen, Jane. *The Three Bears Rhyme Book* [Pre-2], 1981

FAIRY TALES–Riddles

Walton, Rick, and Ann Walton. *Kiss a Frog! Jokes About Fairy Tales, Knights, and Dragons* [1-4], **1419**

FAIRY TALES–Satire

Ada, Alma Flor. *Dear Peter Rabbit* [1-2], **395**

Ahlberg, Janet, and Allan Ahlberg. *The Jolly Christmas Postman* [1-2], **396**

Briggs, Raymond. *Jim and the Beanstalk* [1-2], 623

Calmenson, Stephanie. *The Principal's New Clothes* [1-2], **420**

Emberley, Michael. *Ruby* [1-2], **437**

Gwynne, Fred. *Pondlarker* [1-2], **447**

Jackson, Ellen. *Cinder Edna* [2-3], **626**

Johnston, Tony. *The Cowboy and the Black-Eyed Pea* [3-4], **717**

Kovalski, Maryanne. *Pizza for Breakfast* [1-2], **479**

Little, Jean, and Maggie De Vries. *Once Upon a Golden Apple* [K-1], 478

Minters, Frances. *Cinder-Elly* [1-2], **510**

Myers, Bernice. *Sidney Rella and the Glass Sneaker* [1-2], 754

Napoli, Donna Jo. *The Prince of the Pond: Otherwise Known as De Fawg Pin* [4-5], **782**

Polette, Nancy. *Hole by the Apple Tree: An A–Z Discovery Tale* [K-1], **339**

Scieszka, Jon. *The Book That Jack Wrote* [1-2], **548**

The Frog Prince Continued [2-3], **676**

The Stinky Cheese Man and Other Fairly Stupid Tales [2-3], **677**

The True Story of the 3 Little Pigs [2-3], 993

Stearns, Pamela. *Into the Painted Bear Lair* [4-5], 1243

Storr, Catherine. *Clever Polly and the Stupid Wolf* [3-4], 1122

Tolhurst, Marilyn. *Somebody and the Three Blairs* [Pre-K], 191

Trivizas, Eugene. *The Three Little Wolves and the Big Bad Pig* [K-1], 378

Vande Velde, Vivian. *A Hidden Magic* [4-5], 1251

Vesey, A. *The Princess and the Frog* [1-2], 837

Vozar, David. *Yo, Hungry Wolf! A Nursery Rap* [1-2], 570

Wilsdorf, Anne. *Princess* [1-2], **577**

Yolen, Jane. *Sleeping Ugly* [2-3], 1033

FALL

SEE Autumn

FAMILY LIFE

SEE ALSO Aunts; Brothers; Brothers and sisters; Grandfathers; Grandmothers; Mothers; Sisters; Uncles

Allard, Harry. *The Stupids Die* [K-1], 318

Anderson, Leone Castell. *The Wonderful Shrinking Shirt* [1-2], 604

Armitage, Ronda, and David Armitage. *The Bossing of Josie* [Pre-K], 8

Birdseye, Tom. *Air Mail to the Moon* [1-2], 616

Blume, Judy. *Superfudge* [4-5], 1145

Tales of a Fourth Grade Nothing [3-4], 1046

Brenner, Barbara. *A Year in the Life of Rosie Bernard* [4-5], 1149

Burch, Robert. *Ida Early Comes Over the Mountain* [4-5], 1153

Byars, Betsy. *Beans on the Roof* [2-3], 879

The Two-Thousand Pound Goldfish [5-6], 1283

Wanted . . . Mud Blossom [4-5], **763**

Cameron, Ann. *The Stories Julian Tells* [2-3], 881

Caseley, Judith. *Harry and Arney* [1-2], **422**

Silly Baby [Pre-K], 44

Cleary, Beverly. *Beezus and Ramona* [2-3], 887

Petey's Bedtime Story [K-1], **253**

Ramona Quimby, Age 8 [2-3], 889

Cole, Brock. *Alpha and the Dirty Baby* [1-2], **426**

Conford, Ellen. *And This Is Laura* [5-6], 1289

Cooney, Barbara. *Island Boy* [3-4], 1055

Cooper, Melrose. *I Got a Family* [K-1], **255**

Crew, Linda. *Nekomah Creek* [3-4], **709**

Delton, Judy. *Angel in Charge* [3-4], 1061

Desbarats, Peter. *Gabrielle and Selena* [1-2], 659

Dillon, Barbara. *The Teddy Bear Tree* [1-2], 662

Falwell, Cathryn. *Feast for 10* [Pre], **11**

Ferguson, Alane. *That New Pet!* [K-1], 386

Fitzgerald, John D. *The Great Brain* [4-5], 1171

Flournoy, Valerie. *The Patchwork Quilt* [2-3], 925

Fox, Mem. *Shoes from Grandpa* [Pre-K], **105**

Gackenbach, Dick. *Where Are Momma, Poppa, and Sister June?* [K-1], **274**

Greenfield, Eloise. *Me as Neesie* [K-1], 411

Hahn, Mary Downing. *Time for Andrew: A Ghost Story* [5-6], **820**

Hall, Donald. *Ox-Cart Man* [2-3], 931

Harrison, Maggie. *Angels on Roller Skates* [1-2], **451**

Heide, Florence Parry, and Judith Heide Gilliland. *Sami and the Time of the Troubles* [3-4], **713**

Henkes, Kevin. *Owen* [Pre-K], **122**

Hest, Amy. *The Mommy Exchange* [K-1], 421

Hill, Elizabeth Starr. *Evan's Corner* [1-2], 687

Hoban, Russell. *A Baby Sister for Frances* [Pre-K], 137

Bread and Jam for Frances [K-1], 429

Hughes, Shirley. *The Big Alfie Out of Doors Storybook* [Pre-K], **128**

An Evening at Alfie's [Pre-K], 147

Hurwitz, Johanna. *Busybody Nora* [1-2], 694

"E" Is for Elisa [K-1], **290**

Russell Sprouts [1-2], 695

Superduper Teddy [1-2], 696

Johnston, Tony. *Yonder* [2-3], 939

King-Smith, Dick. *Sophie's Snail* [1-2], 711

Kinsey-Warnock, Natalie. *When Spring Comes* [1-2], **469**

Kraus, Robert. *Whose Mouse Are You?* [Pre-K], 177

Kroll, Steven. *Happy Mother's Day* [1-2], 717

Oh, What a Thanksgiving! [1-2], 718

Lasker, Joe. *The Do-Something Day* [K-1], 464

Lowry, Lois. *All about Sam* [5-6], 1327

Attaboy, Sam! [4-5], **776**

The Giver [5-6], **828**

McCully, Emily Arnold. *Picnic* [Pre-K], 196

McEwan, Ian. *The Daydreamer* [5-6], **829**

MacLachlan, Patricia. *Sarah, Plain and Tall* [3-4], 1094

McPhail, David. *Emma's Vacation* [Pre-K], 201

Something Special [K-1], 497

Mahy, Margaret. *Jam: A True Story* [1-2], 740

Martin, Jane Read, and Patricia Marx. *Now Everybody Really Hates Me* [2-3], **644**

Merriam, Eve. *The Christmas Box* [K-1], 507

Myers, Anna. *Red-Dirt Jessie* [4-5], **780**

Naylor, Phyllis Reynolds. *Keeping a Christmas Secret* [Pre-K], 216

O'Donnell, Elizabeth Lee. *Maggie Doesn't Want to Move* [K-1], 515

Park, Barbara. *The Kid in the Red Jacket* [4-5], 1221

Paton Walsh, Jill. *The Green Book* [5-6], 1341

Pfeffer, Susan Beth. *Kid Power* [4-5], 1224

Phelan, Terry Wolfe. *The Week Mom Unplugged the TVs* [3-4], 1102

Pringle, Laurence. *Octopus Hug* [Pre-K], **178**

Rattigan, Jama Kim. *Dumpling Soup* [K-1], **349**

Russo, Marisabina. *Trade-In Mother* [Pre-K], **184**

Rylant, Cynthia. *The Relatives Came* [K-1], 542

Sanders, Scott Russell. *Here Comes the Mystery Man* [2-3], **673**

Warm as Wool [1-2], **546**

Schwartz, Amy. *The Lady Who Put Salt in Her Coffee* [3-4], **742**

Segal, Lore. *Tell Me a Mitzi* [1-2], 798

Sharratt, Nick. *My Mom and Dad Make Me Laugh* [Pre-K], **186**

Shields, Carol Diggory. *I Am Really a Princess* [1-2], **550**

Shyer, Marlene Fanta. *Welcome Home, Jellybean* [5-6], 1357

Smith, Alison. *Help! There's a Cat Washing in Here* [5-6], 1361

Smith, Janice Lee. *The Monster in the Third Dresser Drawer: And Other Stories about Adam Joshua* [1-2], 815

Smith, Robert Kimmell. *The War with Grandpa* [3-4], 1115

Spinelli, Eileen. *Thanksgiving at the Tappletons'* [1-2], 818

Steig, William. *Spinky Sulks* [2-3], 1009

Sutton, Jane. *Me and the Weirdos* [4-5], 1246

Titherington, Jeanne. *A Place for Ben* [Pre-K], 274

Townson, Hazel. *Terrible Tuesday* [K-1], 569

Turkle, Brinton. *The Adventures of Obadiah* [1-2], 834

Tusa, Tricia. *The Family Reunion* [1-2], **568**

Uchida, Yoshiko. *Journey Home* [5-6], 1370

Van Leeuwen, Jean. *Benjy in Business* [2-3], 1021

FAMILY LIFE (cont.)

Viorst, Judith. *Alexander and the Terrible, Horrible, No Good, Very Bad Day* [1-2], 838

Alexander Who Used to Be Rich Last Sunday [1-2], 839

Wardlaw, Lee. *Seventh-Grade Weirdo* [5-6], **850**

Waters, Kate. *Samuel Eaton's Day: A Day in the Life of a Pilgrim Boy* [2-4], **1250**

Wilder, Laura Ingalls. *Little House in the Big Woods* [2-3], 1028

Williams, Barbara. *Albert's Toothache* [Pre-K], 296

Williams, Vera B. *A Chair for My Mother* [1-2], 851

"More More More," Said the Baby: Three Love Stories [Pre], **58**

Winter, Jeanette. *Klara's New World* [2-3], **693**

Winthrop, Elizabeth. *Sloppy Kisses* [K-1], 595

Wojciechowski, Susan. *Don't Call Me Beanhead!* [2-3], **695**

Wolitzer, Hilma. *Introducing Shirley Braverman* [5-6], 1376

Yep, Laurence. *The Star Fisher* [5-6], **854**

Zemach, Harve. *Mommy, Buy Me a China Doll* [Pre-K], 305

Zolotow, Charlotte. *The Quarreling Book* [1-2], 861

Something Is Going to Happen [Pre-K], 311

FAMILY LIFE–Poetry

Adoff, Arnold. *In for Winter, Out for Spring* [K-4], **1260**

Blake, Quentin. *All Join In* [Pre-2], **1270**

Hoberman, Mary Ann. *Fathers, Mothers, Sisters, Brothers: A Collection of Family Poems* [K-4], **1314**

Rylant, Cynthia. *Waiting to Waltz: A Childhood* [5-6], 1941

Strickland, Dorothy, and Michael R. Strickland. *Families: Poems Celebrating the African American Experience* [K-3], **1412**

FAMILY PROBLEMS

Baldwin, Ann Norris. *A Little Time* [4-5], 1140

Bauer, Marion Dane. *A Question of Trust* [5-6], **805**

Byars, Betsy. *Cracker Jackson* [5-6], 1280

The Not-Just-Anybody Family [4-5], 1156

The Pinballs [5-6], 1281

DeFelice, Cynthia. *Devil's Bridge* [4-5], **766**

Fenner, Carol. *Randall's Wall* [5-6], **815**

Leach, Norman. *My Wicked Stepmother* [K-1], **302**

Levy, Elizabeth. *Lizzie Lies a Lot* [3-4], 1087

Little, Jean. *Home from Far* [4-5], 1206

Park, Barbara. *Don't Make Me Smile* [4-5], 1220

Roy, Ron. *The Chimpanzee Kid* [5-6], 1348

Sachs, Marilyn. *The Bears' House* [5-6], 1350

Shyer, Marlene Fanta. *My Brother, the Thief* [5-6], 1356

Wallace, Bill. *Beauty* [5-6], 1373

Weiss, Ellen, and Mel Friedman. *The Poof Point* [5-6], **851**

The Tiny Parents [4-5], **794**

FAMILY STORIES

Ackerman, Karen. *Song and Dance Man* [1-2], 599

Bahr, Mary. *The Memory Box* [2-3], **589**

Bartone, Elisa. *Peppe the Lamplighter* [1-2], **405**

Caseley, Judith. *Dear Annie* [K-1], **250**

Cleary, Beverly. *Petey's Bedtime Story* [K-1], **253**

Cohen, Ron. *My Dad's Baseball* [2-3], **599**

Cooney, Barbara. *Miss Rumphius* [1-2], **654**

Cutler, Jane. *No Dogs Allowed* [2-3], **602**

dePaola, Tomie. *Tom* [1-2], **431**

Dodds, Bill. *My Sister Annie* [4-5], **768**

Flournoy, Valerie. *The Patchwork Quilt* [2-3], 925

Friedman, Ina R. *How My Parents Learned to Eat* [1-2], 672

Galbraith, Kathryn O. *Laura Charlotte* [Pre-K], 105

Gray, Nigel. *A Balloon for Grandad* [Pre-K], 121

Greenwald, Sheila. *Rosy Cole Discovers America!* [3-4], **711**

Hartley, Deborah. *Up North in Winter* [1-2], 683

Houston, Gloria. *My Great Aunt Arizona* [1-6], **1165**

The Year of the Perfect Christmas Tree [1-2], 691

Howard, Elizabeth Fitzgerald. *Mac & Marie & the Train Toss Surprise* [1-2], **455**

Johnson, Dolores. *Now Let Me Fly: The Story of a Slave Family* [2-3], **629**

Kinsey-Warnock, Natalie. *The Bear That Heard Crying* [1-2], **468**

Lomas Garza, Carmen. *Family Pictures / Cuadros de Familia* [1-4], **1192**

McDonald, Megan. *The Great Pumpkin Switch* [1-2], **495**

The Potato Man [1-2], **496**

McLerran, Alice. *Roxaboxen* [1-2], **499**

Mitchell, Margaree King. *Uncle Jed's Barbershop* [2-3], **647**

Nodar, Carmen Santiago. *Abuelita's Paradise* [1-2], **519**

Paulsen, Gary. *The Cookcamp* [5-6], **834**

Polacco, Patricia. *Pink and Say* [4-5], **786**

Pomerantz, Charlotte. *The Chalk Doll* [1-2], 776

Russo, Marisabina. *Waiting for Hannah* [K-1], 538

Say, Allen. *Grandfather's Journey* [2-3], **674**

Stroud, Virginia A. *Doesn't Fall Off His Horse* [2-3], **680**

Tews, Susan. *The Gingerbread Doll* [1-2], **565**

Williams, David. *Grandma Essie's Covered Wagon* [2-3], **691**

FANTASY

Aiken, Joan. *The Moon's Revenge* [3-4], 1038

Alcock, Vivien. *The Monster Garden* [5-6], 1257

Alexander, Lloyd. *The Book of Three* [5-6], 1258

The Cat Who Wished to Be a Man [5-6], 1259

The First Two Lives of Lucas-Kasha [5-6], 1260

The Wizard in the Tree [5-6], 1262

Ames, Mildred. *Is There Life on a Plastic Planet?* [5-6], 1263

Andersen, Hans Christian. *The Tinderbox* [4-5], **757**

Asch, Frank. *Pearl's Promise* [3-4], **701**

Avi. *Bright Shadow* [5-6], 1266

Babbitt, Natalie. *The Search for Delicious* [4-5], 1139

Banks, Lynne Reid. *The Adventures of King Midas* [4-5], **758**

The Fairy Rebel [4-5], 1141

The Indian in the Cupboard [5-6], 1272

The Magic Hare [3-4], **702**

Bellaits, John. *The House with a Clock in Its Walls* [4-5], 1143

Benjamin, Saragail Katzman. *My Dog Ate It* [3-4], **704**

Bond, Michael. *Paddington's Storybook* [4-5], 1147

Brittain, Bill. *Devil's Donkey* [5-6], 1276

Dr. Dredd's Wagon of Wonders [5-6], 1277

Professor Popkin's Prodigious Polish: A Tale of Coven Tree [4-5], **760**

The Wish Giver: Three Tales of Coven Tree [5-6], 1278

Byars, Betsy. *McMummy* [4-5], **762**

Carris, Joan. *Witch-Cat* [3-4], **706**

Cassedy, Sylvia. *Behind the Attic Wall* [5-6], 1287

Chase, Mary. *Loretta Mason Potts* [4-5], 1157

Chetwin, Grace. *Friends in Time* [4-5], **764**

Cleary, Beverly. *The Mouse and the Motorcycle* [3-4], 1050

Ralph S. Mouse [3-4], 1051

Collodi, Carlo. *The Adventures of Pinocchio* [4-5], 1160

Coville, Bruce. *Jennifer Murdley's Toad* [4-5], **765**

Cresswell, Helen. *Time Out* [3-4], **708**

Dahl, Roald. *BFG* [4-5], 1166

Charlie and the Chocolate Factory [3-4], 1058

James and the Giant Peach [3-4], 1059

The Witches [4-5], 1167

Dillon, Barbara. *A Mom by Magic* [4-5], **767**

Du Bois, William Pène. *The Giant* [5-6], 1294

The Twenty-One Balloons [5-6], 1295

Edwards, Julie. *The Last of the Really Great Whangdoodles* [3-4], 1063

Gormley, Beatrice. *Fifth-Grade Magic* [4-5], 1181

Mail-Order Wings [4-5], 1182

Grahame, Kenneth. *The Wind in the Willows* [5-6], 1305

Hahn, Mary Downing. *Time for Andrew: A Ghost Story* [5-6], **820**

Heller, Nicholas. *Up the Wall* [K-1], **281**

Hughes, Ted. *The Iron Giant: A Story in Five Nights* [3-4], 1075

Hunter, Mollie. *A Furl of Fairy Wind* [3-4], 1076

Hutchins, Hazel. *The Three and Many Wishes of Jason Reid* [3-4], 1077

Jacques, Brian. *Redwall* [5-6], 1315

James, Mary. *Shoebag* [4-5], 1195

Jones, Terry. *The Saga of Erik the Viking* [4-5], 1197

Juster, Norton. *The Phantom Tollbooth* [5-6], 1316

Kaye, M. M. *The Ordinary Princess* [3-4], 1079

Kennedy, Richard. *Inside My Feet* [5-6], 1318

King-Smith, Dick. *Martin's Mice* [3-4], 1085

Paddy's Pot of Gold [3-4], **724**

Pigs Might Fly [5-6], 1320

The Swoose [3-4], **727**

Kipling, Rudyard. *Rikki-Tikki-Tavi* [3-4], **729**

Krensky, Steven. *The Dragon Circle* [4-5], 1202

Levitin, Sonia. *Jason and the Money Tree* [4-5], 1203

Lewis, C. S. *The Lion, the Witch and the Wardrobe* [3-4], 1088

The Magician's Nephew [4-5], 1204

Lindbergh, Anne. *Travel Far, Pay No Fare* [5-6], **826**

Lisle, Janet Taylor. *Forest* [5-6], **827**

Lofting, Hugh. *The Story of Doctor Dolittle* [3-4], 1091

Lowry, Lois. *The Giver* [5-6], **828**

McEwan, Ian. *The Daydreamer* [5-6], **829**

McGowen, Tom. *The Magician's Apprentice* [5-6], 1329

McGraw, Eloise Jarvis. *Joel and the Great Merlini* [3-5], 1093

McMurtry, Stan. *The Bunjee Venture* [4-5], 1210

Manes, Stephen. *Chicken Trek: The Third Strange Thing That Happened to Oscar J. Noodleman* [4-5], 1211

Mazer, Anne. *The Oxboy* [5-6], **831**

Mellecker, Judith. *Randolph's Dream* [3-4], **732**

FANTASY (cont.)

Milne, A. A. *Winnie-the-Pooh* [2-3], 964

Moeri, Louise. *Star Mother's Youngest Child* [3-4], 1097

Moser, Barry. *Tucker Pfeffercorn: An Old Story Retold* [4-5], **779**

Murphy, Jill. *Jeffrey Strangeways* [3-4], **734**

Naylor, Phyllis Reynolds. *The Grand Escape* [4-5], **783**

Norton, Mary. *The Borrowers* [5-6], 1336

Nostlinger, Christine. *Konrad* [4-5], 1219

O'Brien, Robert C. *Mrs. Frisby and the Rats of NIMH* [5-6], 1337

Odgers, Sally Farrell. *Drummond: The Search for Sarah* [1-2], **522**

Ormondroyd, Edward. *David and the Phoenix* [3-4], 1100

Pinkwater, Daniel. *The Hoboken Chicken Emergency* [3-4], 1104
Lizard Music [4-5], 1225

Reit, Seymour. *Benvenuto* [3-4], 1106

Rice, Bebe Faas. *The Year the Wolves Came* [5-6], **839**

Richler, Mordecai. *Jacob Two-Two Meets the Hooded Fang* [3-4], 1107

Roberts, Willo Davis. *The Girl with the Silver Eyes* [5-6], 1345

Rodda, Emily. *Finders Keepers* [4-5], **789**
The Pigs Are Flying [4-5], 1231

Sargeant, Sarah. *Weird Henry Berg* [5-6], 1352

Sauer, Julie L. *Fog Magic* [5-6], 1353

Scieszka, Jon. *Knights of the Kitchen Table* [3-4], **743**
Your Mother Was a Neanderthal [4-5], **790**

Shusterman, Neal. *The Eyes of Kid Midas* [5-6], **842**

Sleator, William. *Among the Dolls* [4-5], 1240

Slote, Alfred. *The Devil Rides with Me and Other Fantastic Stories* [5-6], 1360

Smith, L. J. *The Night of the Solstice* [5-6], 1362

Stearns, Pamela. *Into the Painted Bear Lair* [4-5], 1243

Sterman, Betsy, and Samuel Sterman. *Backyard Dragon* [3-4], **750**

Stolz, Mary. *Cat Walk* [3-4], 1121
Quentin Corn [5-6], 1365

Storr, Catherine. *Clever Polly and the Stupid Wolf* [3-4], 1122

Strickland, Brad. *Dragon's Plunder* [5-6], **848**

Swallow, Pam. *Melvil and Dewey in the Chips* [2-3], 1012

Tannen, Mary. *The Wizard Children of Finn* [5-6], 1367

Tapp, Kathy Kennedy. *Moth-Kin Magic* [4-5], 1247

Thurber, James. *The Great Quillow* [2-3], **684**

Van de Wetering, Janwillem. *Hugh Pine* [3-4], 1127

Van Leeuwen, Jean. *The Great Christmas Kidnapping Caper* [3-4], 1128

Weiss, Ellen, and Mel Friedman. *The Poof Point* [5-6], **851**
The Tiny Parents [4-5], **794**

Wetterer, Margaret. *The Giant's Apprentice* [3-4], 1130

White, E. B. *Stuart Little* [3-4], 1131
The Trumpet of the Swan [4-5], 1253

Williams, Jay. *The Magic Grandfather* [4-5], 1254

Winthrop, Elizabeth. *The Castle in the Attic* [5-6], 1374

Woodruff, Elvira. *George Washington's Socks* [4-5], **798**
The Wing Shop [1-2], **580**

Wrede, Patricia. *Dealing with Dragons* [5-6], **853**

Yep, Laurence. *The Ghost Fox* [3-4], **755**

Yolen, Jane. *Wizard's Hall* [4-5], **801**

FARM ANIMALS
SEE Domestic animals

FARM LIFE
SEE ALSO Cities and towns; Country life

Aylesworth, Jim. *My Son John* [K-1], **222**
One Crow: A Counting Rhyme [Pre-K], 17

Barton, Byron. *Buzz Buzz Buzz* [Pre-K], 21

Butterworth, Oliver. *The Enormous Egg* [4-5], 1154

Byars, Betsy. *The Midnight Fox* [3-4], 1047

Cauley, Lorinda Bryan. *Old MacDonald Had a Farm* [Pre-K], 78

Clarke, Gus. *EIEIO: The Story of Old MacDonald, Who Had a Farm* [Pre-K], 86

Dalgliesh, Alice. *The Bears on Hemlock Mountain* [1-2], 657

DeFelice, Cynthia. *Mule Eggs* [2-3], **604**

Demuth, Patricia Brennan. *The Ornery Morning* [K-1], **260**

Dyke, John. *Pigwig* [K-1], 379

Ehrlich, Amy. *Parents in the Pigpen, Pigs in the Tub* [K-1], **266**

Fleischman, Sid. *McBroom Tells the Truth* [3-4], 1066

Gammell, Stephen. *Once upon MacDonald's Farm* [K-1], 401

Gardiner, John Reynolds. *Stone Fox* [3-4], 1067

Garland, Michael. *My Cousin Katie* [Pre], **17**

Getz, Arthur. *Humphrey, the Dancing Pig* [K-1], 405

Greene, Bette. *Philip Hall Likes Me. I Reckon, Maybe* [4-5], 1183

Griffith, Helen V. *Grandaddy's Place* [1-2], 682

Hall, Donald. *Ox-Cart Man* [2-3], 931

Hellen, Nancy. *Old MacDonald Had a Farm* [Pre], **20**

Herriot, James. *Blossom Comes Home* [2-5], 2046
Bonny's Big Day [2-5], 2047

Hutchins, Pat. *Rosie's Walk* [Pre-K], 149

Johnston, Tony. *Yonder* [2-3], 939

Jones, Carol. *Old MacDonald Had a Farm* [Pre-K], 157

Kent, Jack. *Little Peep* [K-1], 455

King-Smith, Dick. *Babe, the Gallant Pig* [5-6], 1319
The Cuckoo Child [3-4], **722**
Farmer Bungle Forgets [K-1], 458
Martin's Mice [3-4], 1085
Paddy's Pot of Gold [3-4], **724**
Pigs Might Fly [5-6], 1320
Pretty Polly [3-4], **725**

Kinsey-Warnock, Natalie. *When Spring Comes* [1-2], **469**

Lindbergh, Reeve. *The Day the Goose Got Loose* [K-1], **306**

Lindgren, Astrid. *The Tomten* [1-2], 725

Lobel, Arnold. *How the Rooster Saved the Day* [Pre-K], 192
A Treeful of Pigs [1-2], 729

Martin, Bill, Jr., and John Archambault. *Barn Dance!* [K-1], 505

Noble, Trinka Hakes. *Apple Tree Christmas* [2-3], 973
The Day Jimmy's Boa Ate the Wash [1-2], 761
Meanwhile Back at the Ranch [2-3], 974

Nodset, Joan L. *Who Took the Farmer's Hat?* [Pre-K], 219

Parkinson, Kathy. *The Farmer in the Dell* [Pre-K], 223

Pearson, Tracey Campbell. *Old MacDonald Had a Farm* [Pre-K], 226

Preston, Edna Mitchell. *Pop Corn & Ma Goodness* [K-1], 529
Squawk to the Moon, Little Goose [Pre-K], 233

Rae, Mary Maki. *The Farmer in the Dell: A Singing Game* [Pre-K], 234

Rockwell, Anne. *The Gollywhopper Egg* [K-1], 534

Rounds, Glen. *Old MacDonald Had a Farm* [Pre-K], **182**

Runcie, Jill. *Cock-a-Doodle-Doo!* [Pre], **41**

Serfozo, Mary. *Who Said Red?* [Pre-K], 256

Sherrow, Victoria. *There Goes the Ghost!* [K-1], 557

Tews, Susan. *The Gingerbread Doll* [1-2], **565**

Thomas, Jane Resh. *The Princess in the Pigpen* [5-6], 1369

Torgersen, Don Arthur. *The Girl Who Tricked the Troll* [1-2], 832

Van Allsburg, Chris. *The Stranger* [3-4], 1124

Waddell, Martin. *Farmer Duck* [Pre-K], **200**
The Pig in the Pond [Pre], **50**

Wallace, Bill. *Beauty* [5-6], 1373

Ward, Lynd. *The Biggest Bear* [1-2], 844

Wells, Rosemary. *Waiting for the Evening Star* [3-4], **754**

Westcott, Nadine Bernard. *Skip to My Lou* [Pre-K], 292

Whelan, Gloria. *Hannah* [2-3], **689**

White, E. B. *Charlotte's Web* [2-3], 1027

Wilder, Laura Ingalls. *Farmer Boy* [3-4], 1132

Williams, David. *Grandma Essie's Covered Wagon* [2-3], **691**

Williams, Jay. *One Big Wish* [2-3], 1030

Yolen, Jane. *Honkers* [K-1], **391**

Zimmerman, Andrea, and David Clemesha. *The Cow Buzzed* [Pre-K], **215**

FARM LIFE–Folklore

Conger, Leslie. *Tops and Bottoms* [Pre-3], 1427

Croll, Carolyn. *The Three Brothers* [K-3], **888**

Stevens, Janet. *Tops & Bottoms* [Pre-2], **1030**

Weisner, William. *Happy-Go-Lucky* [1-4], 1625
Turnabout [K-4], 1626

Wolkstein, Diane. *White Wave: A Chinese Tale* [2-6], 1631

FARM LIFE–Poetry

Peck, Robert Newton. *Bee Tree and Other Stuff* [4-6], 1899

FATHERS

Greenspan, Adele Aron. *Daddies* [Pre-K], **114**

Mahy, Margaret. *Raging Robots and Unruly Uncles* [4-5], **777**

Polacco, Patricia. *Some Birthday!* [1-2], **537**

Pringle, Laurence. *Octopus Hug* [Pre-K], **178**

Wetzel, JoAnne Stewart. *The Christmas Box* [K-1], **384**

FATHERS AND DAUGHTERS

Asch, Frank. *Just Like Daddy* [Pre-K], 13

Browne, Anthony. *Gorilla* [K-1], 349

Carle, Eric. *Papa, Please Get the Moon for Me* [Pre-K], 39

Carlson, Nancy L. *Louanne Pig in the Mysterious Valentine* [1-2], 637

Houston, Gloria. *The Year of the Perfect Christmas Tree* [1-2], 691

McPhail, David. *Emma's Pet* [Pre-K], 200

FATHERS AND DAUGHTERS (cont.)

Moutoussamy-Ashe, Jeanne. *Daddy and Me: A Photo Story of Arthur Ashe and His Daughter Camera* [K-6], **1213**

Pomerantz, Charlotte. *Posy* [Pre-K], 232

Roop, Peter, and Connie Roop. *Ahyoka and the Talking Leaves* [3-4], **740**

Schwartz, Amy. *Bea and Mr. Jones* [1-2], 795

Showers, Paul. *The Listening Walk* [Pre-K], **187**

Slepian, Jan. *Back to Before* [5-6], **843**

Udry, Janice May. *What Mary Jo Shared* [Pre-K], 279

Wadsworth, Ginger. *Tomorrow Is Daddy's Birthday* [K-1], **380**

Yolen, Jane. *Owl Moon* [1-2], 857

FATHERS AND DAUGHTERS–Folklore

Hooks, William H. *Moss Gown* [2-6], 1529

Van Laan, Nancy. *Buffalo Dance: A Blackfoot Legend* [3-6], **1039**

FATHERS AND SONS

Barre, Shelley A. *Chive* [5-6], **804**

Bauer, Marion Dane. *A Question of Trust* [5-6], **805**

Blake, Robert J. *The Perfect Spot* [K-1], **231**

Bunting, Eve. *Fly Away Home* [1-2], **415**
The Wall [K-1], 354

Cazet, Denys. *"I'm Not Sleepy"* [Pre-K], **80**

Chbosky, Stacey. *Who Owns the Sun?* [4-5], 1158

Cohen, Ron. *My Dad's Baseball* [2-3], **599**

Collodi, Carlo. *The Adventures of Pinocchio* [4-5], 1160

Dahl, Roald. *Danny, the Champion of the World* [5-6], 1291

Duffey, Betsy. *Coaster* [4-5], **769**

Ernst, Lisa Campbell. *Squirrel Park* [1-2], **440**

Hearn, Diane Dawson. *Dad's Dinosaur Day* [Pre-K], **120**

Hinton, S. E. *Big David, Little David* [K-1], **285**

Hort, Lenny. *How Many Stars in the Sky?* [K-1], **288**

Johnson, Dolores. *Your Dad Was Just Like You* [1-2], **463**

Lewison, Wendy Cheyette. *Going to Sleep on the Farm* [Pre], **28**

London, Jonathan. *Let's Go, Froggy* [Pre-K], **153**

McCleery, William. *Wolf Story* [K-1], 489

Mellecker, Judith. *Randolph's Dream* [3-4], **732**

Naylor, Phyllis Reynolds. *King of the Playground* [K-1], **332**

Porte, Barbara Ann. *Harry's Dog* [1-2], 777

Skofield, James. *'Round and Around* [Pre-K], **188**

Willard, Nancy. *Papa's Panda* [Pre-K], 295

Zolotow, Charlotte. *William's Doll* [Pre-K], 312

FATHERS AND SONS–Folklore

Croll, Carolyn. *The Three Brothers* [K-3], **888**

FEAR

Alborough, Jez. *It's the Bear!* [Pre-K], **63**

Auch, Mary Jane. *Monster Brother* [K-1], **221**

Aylesworth, Jim. *Two Terrible Frights* [Pre-K], 18

Bond, Felicia. *Pointsettia and the Firefighters* [K-1], 338

Bunting, Eve. *Ghost's Hour, Spook's Hour* [K-1], 351

Carlson, Natalie Savage. *The Night the Scarecrow Walked* [1-2], 639

Christelow, Eileen. *Henry and the Dragon* [Pre-K], 49

Cohen, Miriam. *Jim Meets the Thing* [K-1], 367

Cooney, Nancy Evans. *Go Away Monsters, Lickety Split* [Pre-K], **88**

Crowe, Robert L. *Clyde Monster* [Pre-K], 60

Dalgliesh, Alice. *The Bears on Hemlock Mountain* [1-2], 657

Emberley, Ed. *Go Away, Big Green Monster!* [Pre-K], **98**

Hazen, Barbara Shook. *Fang* [K-1], 417

Hesse, Karen. *Lester's Dog* [2-3], **619**

Himmelman, John. *Lights Out!* [1-2], **453**

Hoban, Russell. *Bedtime for Frances* [K-1], 428

Holabird, Katharine. *Alexander and the Dragon* [Pre-K], 140

Howe, James. *The Fright before Christmas* [2-3], 935

Johnston, Johanna. *Speak Up, Edie* [K-1], 440

Kastner, Jill. *Snake Hunt* [1-2], **465**

King, Larry L. *Because of Loza Brown* [1-2], 710

Mayer, Mercer. *There's a Nightmare in My Closet* [Pre-K], 207
There's an Alligator under My Bed [Pre-K], 208
There's Something in My Attic [Pre-K], 209

Nixon, Joan Lowery. *The Alligator under the Bed* [Pre-K], 218

Pfeffer, Susan Beth. *What Do You Do When Your Mouth Won't Open?* [5-6], 1344

Pittman, Helena Clare. *Once When I Was Scared* [1-2], 775

Polacco, Patricia. *Thunder Cake* [K-1], 525

Prater, John. *"No!" Said Joe* [Pre-K], **177**

Robison, Deborah. *No Elephants Allowed* [Pre-K], 243

Ross, Tony. *I'm Coming to Get You* [K-1], 536

Stevenson, James. *That Terrible Halloween Night* [1-2], 824
What's Under My Bed? [1-2], 826

Stolz, Mary. *Storm in the Night* [1-2], 828

Tobias, Tobi. *Chasing the Goblins Away* [1-2], 831

Udry, Janice May. *Alfred* [K-1], 572

Viorst, Judith. *My Mama Says There Aren't Any Zombies, Ghosts, Vampires, Creatures, Demons, Monsters, Fiends, Goblins or Things* [1-2], 840

Waddell, Martin. *Can't You Sleep, Little Bear?* [Pre-K], **199**

Let's Go Home, Little Bear [Pre-K], **201**

Walsh, Ellen Stoll. *Pip's Magic* [Pre-K], **205**

Whitney, Alma Marshak. *Just Awful* [Pre-K], 293

Williams, Barbara. *Donna Jean's Disaster* [1-2], 850

Williams, Linda. *The Little Old Lady Who Was Not Afraid of Anything* [K-1], 591

Willis, Jeanne. *The Monster Bed* [K-1], 592

Willoughby, Elaine. *Boris and the Monsters* [Pre-K], 297

Winthrop, Elizabeth. *Maggie & the Monster* [Pre-K], 299

FEAR–Folklore

Bennett, Jill. *Teeny Tiny* [Pre-2], 1403

Dasent, George Webbe. *East o' the Sun & West o' the Moon: An Old Norse Tale* [2-6], 1433

Galdone, Paul. *The Teeny-Tiny Woman: A Ghost Story* [Pre-2], 1471

Grant, Joan. *The Monster That Grew Small: An Egyptian Folktale* [1-4], 1484

Riggio, Anita. *Beware the Brindlebeast* [K-3], **1004**

Yep, Laurence. *The Man Who Tricked a Ghost* [1-4], **1047**

FEELINGS
SEE Emotions

FEET
SEE Foot

FIGHTING

Kraus, Robert. *Noel the Coward* [Pre-K], 175

Udry, Janice May. *Thump and Plunk* [Pre-K], 277

FIGURES OF SPEECH
SEE English language–Idioms

FINGERPLAYS

Brown, Marc. *Hand Rhymes* [Pre-2], 1760

Carlson, Bernice Wells. *Listen! And Help Tell the Story* [Pre-2], 1765

Cole, Joanna, and Stephanie Calmenson. *The Eentsy, Weentsy Spider: Fingerplays and Action Rhymes* [Pre-2], **1279**

Delamar, Gloria T. *Children's Counting Out Rhymes, Fingerplays, Jump-Rope and Bounce-Ball Chants and Other Rhymes: A Comprehensive English-Language Reference* [Pre-3], 1788

Glazer, Tom. *Eye Winker, Tom Tinker, Chin Chopper: Fifty Musical Fingerplays* [Pre-2], 1804

Lamont, Priscilla. *Ring-a-Round-a-Rosy: Nursery Rhymes, Action Rhymes and Lullabies* [Pre-1], **1345**

Langstaff, Nancy, and John Langstaff. *Jim Along Josie: A Collection of Folk Songs* [Pre-2], 1850

Pooley, Sarah. *A Day of Rhymes* [Pre-1], 1903

Tashjian, Virginia. *Juba This and Juba That: Story Hour Stretches for Large or Small Groups* [Pre-4], 1961

Westcott, Nadine Bernard. *Peanut Butter and Jelly: A Play Rhyme* [Pre-K], 291

Wood, Don, and Audrey Wood. *Piggies* [Pre], **59**

FIRE

Allen, Jeffrey. *Mary Alice, Operator Number Nine* [Pre-K], 320

Bond, Felicia. *Pointsettia and the Firefighters* [K-1], 338

Brenner, Barbara. *Mr. Tall and Mr. Small* [K-1], 343

Polacco, Patricia. *Tikvah Means Hope* [2-3], **664**

Roy, Ron. *Nightmare Island* [4-5], 1234

Williams, Vera B. *A Chair for My Mother* [1-2], 851

FIRE–Folklore

London, Jonathan, and Lanny Pinola. *Fire Race: A Karuk Coyote Tale About How Fire Came to the People* [K-3], **972**

Maddern, Eric. *The Fire Children: A West African Creation Tale* [K-3], **978**

Rainbow Bird: An Aboriginal Folktale from Northern Australia [K-3], **979**

FIREFLIES

Hawes, Judy. *Fireflies in the Night* [K-2], **1156**

FISHES

Cohen, Barbara. *The Carp in the Bathtub* [2-3], 892

Cone, Molly. *Come Back, Salmon: How a Group of Dedicated Kids Adopted Pigeon Creek and Brought It Back to Life* [4-6], **1125**

Ehlert, Lois. *Fish Eyes: A Book You Can Count On* [Pre-K], **97**

Griffith, Helen V. *Grandaddy's Place* [1-2], 682

Lionni, Leo. *Fish Is Fish* [K-1], 474

Swimmy [K-1], 476

McCloskey, Robert. *Burt Dow, Deep-Water Man* [2-3], 955

Maestro, Betsy. *A Sea Full of Sharks* [1-3], **1196**

O'Dell, Scott. *The Black Pearl* [5-6], 1338

Palmer, Helen. *A Fish Out of Water* [Pre-K], 221

FISHES (cont.)

Pfister, Marcus. *The Rainbow Fish* [K-1], **337**

Seuss, Dr. *McElligot's Pool* [1-2], 804

Tayntor, Elizabeth, Paul Erickson, and Les Kaufman. *Dive to the Coral Reefs: A New England Aquarium Book* [3-6], 2110

Waber, Bernard. *I Was All Thumbs* [2-3], 1023

Waterton, Betty. *A Salmon for Simon* [1-2], 846

Wilcox, Cathy. *Enzo the Wonderfish* [K-1], **386**

Wise, William. *Ten Sly Piranhas: A Counting Story in Reverse (A Tale of Wickedness and Worse)* [1-2], **578**

FISHES–Folklore

Grimm, Jacob. *The Fisherman and His Wife* [2-4], 1492

Kimmel, Eric A. *Anansi Goes Fishing* [Pre-2], **950**

Louie, Ai-Ling. *Yeh-Shen: A Cinderella Story from China* [3-5], 1548

Wilson, Barbara Ker. *Wishbones: A Folk Tale from China* [2-4], **1043**

FISHING

DeFelice, Cynthia. *Devil's Bridge* [4-5], **766**

Engel, Diana. *Fishing* [K-1], **268**

Smath, Jerry. *A Hat So Simple* [K-1], **367**

FLIES

SEE ALSO Insects

Aylesworth, Jim. *Old Black Fly* [K-1], **223**

Peters, Lisa Westberg. *When the Fly Flew In* [K-1], **336**

FLIGHT

Adams, Adrienne. *A Woggle of Witches* [Pre-K], 1

Brown, Don. *Ruth Law Thrills a Nation* [K-4], **1111**

Burleigh, Robert. *Flight: The Journey of Charles Lindbergh* [3-6], **1114**

Bursik, Rose. *Amelia's Fantastic Flight* [1-2], **417**

Byars, Betsy. *The Winged Colt of Casa Mia* [3-4], 1048

Demarest, Chris L. *Lindbergh* [2-4], **1128**

Dorros, Arthur. *Abuela* [1-2], **434**

Foreman, Michael. *Cat and Canary* [K-1], 388

Gerstein, Mordicai. *Arnold of the Ducks* [1-2], 677

Gormley, Beatrice. *Mail-Order Wings* [4-5], 1182

Holman, Felice. *The Blackmail Machine* [4-5], 1191

Jeschke, Susan. *Perfect the Pig* [K-1], 438

Johnson, Paul Brett. *The Cow Who Wouldn't Come Down* [K-1], **292**

Jukes, Mavis. *I'll See You in My Dreams* [3-4], **718**

Lauber, Patricia. *Lost Star: The Story of Amelia Earhart* [5-6], 2061

Le Guin, Ursula K. *Catwings* [2-3], 950

Lies, Brian. *Hamlet and the Enormous Chinese Dragon Kite* [1-2], **484**

Price, Moe. *The Reindeer Christmas* [K-1], **341**

Provensen, Alice, and Martin Provensen. *The Glorious Flight: Across the Channel with Louis Blérot* [K-6], 2084

Ringgold, Faith. *Tar Beach* [2-3], **671**

Siebert, Diane. *Plane Song* [1-2], **552**

Woodruff, Elvira. *Show and Tell* [K-1], **388**

The Wing Shop [1-2], **580**

FLIGHT–Folklore

Miller, Moira. *The Moon Dragon* [1-4], 1568

Wolkstein, Diane. *The Magic Wings: A Tale from China* [Pre-4], 1630

Yolen, Jane. *Wings* [4-6], **1049**

FLIGHT–Poetry

Lindbergh, Reeve. *View from the Air: Charles Lindbergh's Earth and Sky* [3-6], **1356**

FLORIDA

DeFelice, Cynthia. *Lostman's River* [5-6], **811**

FLOWERS

SEE ALSO Gardens; Plants; Vegetables

Cooney, Barbara. *Miss Rumphius* [1-2], 654

Garland, Sherry. *The Lotus Seed* [2-3], **609**

Gibbons, Gail. *From Seed to Plant* [K-3], **1148**

Heller, Ruth. *The Reason for a Flower* [K-4], **1161**

Izen, Marshall, and Jim West. *Why the Willow Weeps: A Story Told with Hands* [1-2], **461**

Lobel, Anita. *Alison's Zinnia* [K-1], **309**

Lobel, Arnold. *The Rose in My Garden* [K-1], 485

Waterton, Betty. *Petranella* [1-2], 845

FLOWERS–Folklore

Demi. *The Empty Pot* [K-3], **892**

dePaola, Tomie. *The Legend of the Bluebonnet: An Old Tale of Texas* [1-4], 1440

The Legend of the Indian Paintbrush [1-3], 1441

Esbensen, Barbara Juster. *The Star Maiden: An Ojibway Tale* [2-5], 1451

FLUTE

Pinkwater, Daniel. *Doodle Flute* [1-2], **534**

FLUTE–Folklore

Czernecki, Stefan, and Timothy Rhodes. *The Singing Snake* [K-2], **889**

Goble, Paul. *Love Flute* [3-6], **916**

FOLK SONGS

Axelrod, Alan. *Songs of the Wild West* [1-6], **1264**

Brett, Jan. *The Twelve Days of Christmas* [Pre-6], 1755

Cauley, Lorinda Bryan. *Old MacDonald Had a Farm* [Pre-K], **78**

Clarke, Gus. *EIEIO: The Story of Old MacDonald, Who Had a Farm* [Pre-K], **86**

Cohn, Amy L. *From Sea to Shining Sea: A Treasury of American Folklore and Folk Songs* [1-6], **1063**

Fox, Dan. *Go In and Out the Window: An Illustrated Songbook for Young People* [Pre-6], 1801

Garson, Eugenia. *The Laura Ingalls Wilder Songbook* [2-5], 1802

Glazer, Tom. *Eye Winker, Tom Tinker, Chin Chopper: Fifty Musical Fingerplays* [Pre-2], 1804

Tom Glazer's Treasury of Songs for Children [Pre-6], 1805

Hart, Jane. *Singing Bee! A Collection of Favorite Children's Songs* [K-2], 1810

Hellen, Nancy. *Old MacDonald Had a Farm* [Pre], **20**

John, Timothy. *The Great Song Book* [Pre-5], 1832

Jones, Carol. *This Old Man* [Pre-K], **137**

Krull, Kathleen. *Gonna Sing My Head Off! American Folk Songs for Children* [K-5], **1344**

Langstaff, Nancy, and John Langstaff. *Jim Along Josie: A Collection of Folk Songs* [Pre-2], 1850

Mattox, Cheryl. *Shake It to the One That You Love the Best: Play Songs and Lullabies from Black Musical Traditions* [Pre-2], **1371**

Medearis, Angela Shelf. *The Zebra-Riding Cowboy: A Folk Song from the Old West* [2-3], **645**

Moss, Marissa. *Knick Knack Paddywack* [K-1], **327**

Nelson, Esther L. *The Funny Song Book* [Pre-6], 1894

Raffi. *The Raffi Singable Songbook: A Collection of 51 Songs from Raffi's First Three Records for Young Children* [Pre-2], 1926

Rounds, Glen. *Old MacDonald Had a Farm* [Pre-K], **182**

Seeger, Pete, and Charles Seeger. *The Foolish Frog* [1-2], 797

Seeger, Ruth Crawford. *American Folk Songs for Children* [Pre-4], 1951

Sweet, Melissa. *Fiddle-I-Fee: A Farmyard Song for the Very Young* [Pre-K], **190**

Watson, Wendy. *Fox Went Out on a Chilly Night* [K-1], **382**

Weiss, Nicki. *If You're Happy and You Know It: Eighteen Story Songs Set to Pictures* [Pre-2], 1973

Winn, Marie. *The Fireside Book of Fun and Game Songs* [Pre-6], 1976

Yolen, Jane. *The Fireside Song Book of Birds and Beasts* [Pre-6], 1980

FOLKLORE

Edwards, Roberta. *Five Silly Fishermen* [Pre-1], **901**

Garner, Alan. *Once Upon a Time, Though It Wasn't in Your Time, and It Wasn't in My Time, and It Wasn't in Anybody's Time. . . .* [Pre-2], **1065**

Medlicott, Mary. *Tales for Telling: From Around the World* [K-4], **1080**

Shannon, George. *More Stories to Solve: Fifteen Folktales from Around the World* [3-6], **1087**

FOLKLORE–Africa

Aardema, Verna. *Bimwili and the Zimwi* [K-2], 1379

Misoso: Once Upon a Time Tales from Africa [2-6], **1052**

Princess Gorilla and a New Kind of Water [Pre-2], 1381

Rabbit Makes a Monkey Out of Lion [Pre-3], 1382

Traveling to Tondo: A Tale of the Nkundo of Zaire [Pre-2], **857**

What's So Funny, Ketu? [1-4], 1384

Who's in Rabbit's House? [2-4], 1385

Why Mosquitoes Buzz in People's Ears [Pre-2], 1386

Appiah, Peggy. *Tales of an Ashanti Father* [3-6], 1653

Arkhurst, Joyce Cooper. *The Adventures of Spider: West African Folktales* [1-4], 1654

Courlander, Harold. *The Hat-Shaking Dance: And Other Tales from the Gold Coast* [2-6], 1668

Courlander, Harold, and George Herzog. *The Cow-Tail Switch and Other West African Stories* [2-6], 1670

Dayrell, Elphinstone. *Why the Sun and Moon Live in the Sky* [Pre-2], 1435

Dee, Ruby. *Two Ways to Count to Ten: A Liberian Folktale* [K-3], 1436

Gatti, Anne. *Tales from the African Plains* [3-6], **1066**

Gerson, Mary-Joan. *Why the Sky Is Far Away: A Nigerian Folktale* [K-4], **913**

Greaves, Nick. *When Lion Could Fly and Other Tales from Africa* [2-6], **1070**

Grifalconi, Ann. *The Village of Round and Square Houses* [K-4], 1485

Haley, Gail E. *A Story, a Story* [K-3], 1517

Kimmel, Eric A. *Anansi and the Moss-Covered Rock* [Pre-2], 1541

Anansi and the Talking Melon [Pre-2], **949**

Kurtz, Jane. *Fire on the Mountain* [2-5], **961**

Lester, Julius. *How Many Spots Does a Leopard Have? And Other Tales* [1-5], 1705

FOLKLORE–Africa (cont.)

Lottridge, Celia Barker. *The Name of the Tree: A Bantu Folktale* [Pre-2], **973**

McDermott, Gerald. *Anansi the Spider: A Tale from the Ashanti* [Pre-3], 1550

Mollel, Tololwa M. *The King and the Tortoise* [K-3], **988**

The Orphan Boy: A Maasai Story [1-4], **989**

A Promise to the Sun: An African Story [K-3], **990**

Rhinos for Lunch and Elephants for Supper! [Pre-2], **991**

Robinson, Adjai. *Singing Tales of Africa* [1-4], 1718

Roddy, Patricia. *Api and the Boy Stranger: A Village Creation Tale* [K-2], **1006**

Sierra, Jud. *The Elephant's Wrestling Match* [Pre-2], **1025**

Steptoe, John. *Mufaro's Beautiful Daughters: An African Tale* [1-4], 1607

Troughton, Joanna. *Tortoise's Dream* [Pre-2], 1618

FOLKLORE–Africa, East

Knutson, Barbara. *Sungura and Leopard: A Swahili Trickster Tale* [K-3], **960**

Rosen, Michael. *How the Giraffe Got Such a Long Neck . . . and Why Rhino Is So Grumpy* [Pre-2], **1007**

FOLKLORE–Africa, West

Aardema, Verna. *Anansi Finds a Fool* [1-5], **855**

Chocolate, Deborah M. Newton. *Talk, Talk: An Ashanti Legend* [1-5], **877**

Kimmel, Eric A. *Anansi Goes Fishing* [Pre-2], **950**

McDermott, Gerald. *Zomo the Rabbit: A Trickster Tale from West Africa* [Pre-1], **977**

Maddern, Eric. *The Fire Children: A West African Creation Tale* [K-3], **978**

Onyefulu, Obi. *Chinye: A West African Folk Tale* [K-3], **995**

FOLKLORE–Alaska

Dixon, Ann. *How Raven Brought Light to People* [K-4], **897**

Sloat, Teri. *The Hungry Giant of the Tundra* [K-2], **1027**

FOLKLORE–Anthologies

Cohn, Amy L. *From Sea to Shining Sea: A Treasury of American Folklore and Folk Songs* [1-6], **1063**

Cole, Joanna. *Best Loved Folktales of the World* [2-6], 1666

Corrin, Sara, and Stephen Corrin. *The Faber Book of Favourite Fairy Tales* [1-5], 1667

Crouch, Marcus. *The Whole World Storybook* [3-6], 1673

Haviland, Virgina. *The Fairy Tale Treasury* [Pre-3], 1693

Favorite Fairy Tales Told around the World [1-4], 1694

Lang, Andrew. *Blue Fairy Book* [2-6], 1702

The Rainbow Fairy Book [3-6], **1074**

Leach, Maria. *The Rainbow Book of American Folk Tales and Legends* [3-6], 1703

MacDonald, Margaret Read. *Peace Tales: World Folktales to Talk About* [1-6], **1076**

Osborne, Mary Pope. *Mermaid Tales from Around the World* [3-6], **1082**

Pilling, Ann. *Realms of Gold: Myths & Legends from Around the World* [4-6], **1083**

Schwartz, Betty Ann, and Leon Archibald. *The Old-Fashioned Storybook* [1-4], 1727

Terban, Marvin. *Too Hot to Hoot: Funny Palindrome Riddles* [4-6], 1965

Withers, Carl. *I Saw a Rocket Walk a Mile: Nonsense Tales, Chants and Songs from Many Lands* [K-6], 1735

FOLKLORE–Arabia

Carrick, Carol. *Aladdin and the Wonderful Lamp* [2-4], 1413

Kimmel, Eric A. *The Three Princes: A Tale from the Middle East* [1-4], **957**

Lang, Andrew. *Aladdin and the Wonderful Lamp* [2-5], 1544

McVitty, Walter. *Ali Baba and the Forty Thieves* [3-6], 1557

Mayer, Marianna. *Aladdin and the Enchanted Lamp* [4-6], 1565

FOLKLORE–Argentina

Brusca, María Cristina, and Tona Wilson. *The Blacksmith and the Devils* [3-6], **873**

FOLKLORE–Armenia

Tashjian, Virginia. *Once There Was and Was Not: Armenian Tales Retold* [2-6], 1731

FOLKLORE–Australia

Czernecki, Stefan, and Timothy Rhodes. *The Singing Snake* [K-2], **889**

FOLKLORE–Austria

Sawyer, Ruth. *The Remarkable Christmas of the Cobbler's Sons* [K-3], **1020**

FOLKLORE–Borneo

Climo, Shirley. *The Match Between the Winds* [K-3], **879**

Troughton, Joanna. *Mouse-Deer's Market* [Pre-2], 1617

FOLKLORE–Brazil

Gerson, Mary-Joan. *How Night Came from the Sea: A Story from Brazil* [K-4], **912**

FOLKLORE–Cameroon

Mollel, Tololwa M. *The King and the Tortoise* [K-3], **988**

Sierra, Jud. *The Elephant's Wrestling Match* [Pre-2], **1025**

FOLKLORE–Canada

Coatsworth, Emerson, and David Coatsworth. *The Adventures of Nanabush: Ojibway Indian Stories* [2-5], 1665

Martin, Eva. *Tales of the Far North* [4-6], 1711

Spray, Carole. *The Mare's Egg: A New World Folk Tale* [2-5], 1604

FOLKLORE–China

Bang, Molly. *Tye May and the Magic Brush* [K-3], 1398

Bishop, Claire. *The Five Chinese Brothers* [1-2], 617

Cheng, Hou-Tien. *The Six Chinese Brothers: An Ancient Tale* [Pre-2], 1422

Day, David. *The Sleeper* [2-4], **891**

Demi. *A Chinese Zoo: Fables and Proverbs* [2-6], 1675

Demi's Reflective Fables [2-6], 1676

Dragon Kites and Dragonflies: A Collection of Chinese Nursery Rhymes [Pre-3], 1789

The Empty Pot [K-3], **892**

The Magic Tapestry [1-4], **894**

Hong, Lily Toy. *How the Ox Star Fell from Heaven* [1-4], **942**

Two of Everything: A Chinese Folktale [K-3], **943**

Jagendorf, M. A., and Virginia Weng. *The Magic Boat: And Other Chinese Folk Stories* [2-6], 1699

Kendall, Carol, and Yao-wen Li. *Sweet and Sour: Tales from China* [3-6], 1701

Lawson, Julie. *The Dragon's Pearl* [1-4], **965**

Louie, Ai-Ling. *Yeh-Shen: A Cinderella Story from China* [3-5], 1548

Mahy, Margaret. *The Seven Chinese Brothers* [K-4], 1558

Miller, Moira. *The Moon Dragon* [1-4], 1568

Morris, Winifred. *The Magic Leaf* [2-4], 1570

Mosel, Arlene. *Tikki Tikki Tembo* [Pre-3], 1572

Pittman, Helena Clare. *A Grain of Rice* [2-4], 1580

Reuter, Bjarne. *The Princess and the Sun, Moon and Stars* [1-4], 1585

Sadler, Catherine Edwards. *Treasure Mountain: Folktales from Southern China* [4-6], 1722

San Souci, Robert. *The Enchanted Tapestry: A Chinese Folktale* [1-4], 1589

Wilson, Barbara Ker. *Wishbones: A Folk Tale from China* [2-4], **1043**

Wolkstein, Diane. *The Magic Wings: A Tale from China* [Pre-4], 1630

White Wave: A Chinese Tale [2-6], 1631

Yacowitz, Caryn. *The Jade Stone: A Chinese Folktale* [K-4], **1045**

Yep, Laurence. *The Junior Thunder Lord* [1-4], **1046**

The Man Who Tricked a Ghost [1-4], **1047**

Young, Ed. *High on a Hill: A Book of Chinese Riddles* [2-4], 1982

Lon Po Po: A Red-Riding Hood Story from China [K-2], 1633

The Terrible Nung Gwana: A Chinese Folktale [1-4], 1634

FOLKLORE–Costa Rica

Baden, Robert. *And Sunday Makes Seven* [2-4], **864**

FOLKLORE–Cuba

Gonzalez, Lucie M. *The Bossy Gallito: A Traditional Cuban Folktale* [K-2], **917**

FOLKLORE–Czechoslovakia

Gabler, Mirko. *Tall, Wide, and Sharp-Eye* [1-4], **907**

Marshak, Samuel. *The Month Brothers: A Slavic Tale* [K-3], 1560

FOLKLORE–Denmark

Haviland, Virginia. *The Talking Pot: A Danish Folktale* [K-3], **939**

Polette, Nancy. *The Little Old Woman and the Hungry Cat* [Pre-2], **999**

FOLKLORE–Egypt

Climo, Shirley. *The Egyptian Cinderella* [2-6], 1424

Grant, Joan. *The Monster That Grew Small: An Egyptian Folktale* [1-4], 1484

McDermott, Gerald. *The Voyage of Osiris: A Myth of Ancient Egypt* [2-6], 1554

FOLKLORE–England

Bennett, Jill. *Teeny Tiny* [Pre-2], 1403

Brown, Marcia. *Dick Whittington and His Cat* [1-4], 1411

Carey, Valerie Scho. *Maggie Mab and the Bogey Beast* [2-4], **875**

Cauley, Lorinda Bryan. *Jack and the Beanstalk* [1-3], 1417

Christian, Mary Blount. *April Fool* [1-3], 1423

FOLKLORE–England (cont.)

Climo, Shirley. *Piskies, Spriggans, and Other Magical Beings* [3-6], 1663

Esterl, Arnica. *The Fine Round Cake* [K-2], **903**

Gackenbach, Dick. *Arabella and Mr. Crack* [K-3], 1454

Galdone, Paul. *The History of Mother Twaddle and the Marvelous Achievements of Her Son, Jack* [K-3], 1462

King of the Cats [2-4], 1463

The Old Woman and Her Pig [Pre-1], 1469

The Teeny-Tiny Woman: A Ghost Story [Pre-2], 1471

The Three Sillies [1-4], 1475

What's in Fox's Sack? [Pre-2], 1476

Garner, Alan. *A Bag of Moonshine* [2-5], 1678

Jack and the Beanstalk [1-4], **910**

Hastings, Selina. *Reynard the Fox* [3-6], **1071**

Sir Gawain and the Loathly Lady [3-6], 1521

Hayes, Sarah. *Robin Hood* [4-6], 1696

Hewitt, Kathryn. *The Three Sillies* [1-4], 1523

Hodges, Margaret. *Saint George and the Dragon: A Golden Legend* [3-6], 1526

Howe, John. *Jack and the Beanstalk* [1-3], **944**

Huck, Charlotte. *Princess Furball* [1-4], 1531

Kimmel, Eric A. *The Old Woman and Her Pig* [Pre-2], **956**

Lamont, Priscilla. *The Troublesome Pig: A Nursery Tale* [Pre-2], 1543

Litzinger, Rosanne. *The Old Woman and Her Pig: An Old English Tale* [Pre-1], **971**

Maitland, Antony. *Idle Jack* [K-3], 1559

Ness, Evaline. *Mr. Miacca: An English Folktale* [Pre-2], 1573

Tom Tit Tot [2-4], 1574

Pearson, Susan. *Jack and the Beanstalk* [K-4], 1577

Riggio, Anita. *Beware the Brindlebeast* [K-3], **1004**

San Souci, Robert D. *The Hobyahs* [K-2], **1013**

Sewall, Marcia. *Master of All Masters: An English Folktale* [K-3], 1597

Shannon, Mark. *Gawain and the Green Knight* [3-6], **1022**

Steel, Flora Annie. *Tattercoats: An Old English Tale* [2-5], 1606

Stern, Simon. *The Hobyas: An Old Story* [Pre-1], 1609

Westwood, Jennifer. *Going to Squintum's: A Foxy Folktale* [Pre-2], 1624

Zemach, Harve. *Duffy and the Devil* [2-5], 1635

FOLKLORE–Ethiopia

Kurtz, Jane. *Fire on the Mountain* [2-5], **961**

FOLKLORE–France

Brown, Marcia. *Cinderella: Or, The Little Glass Slipper* [1-4], 1410

Stone Soup [1-4], 1412

Carlson, Natalie Savage. *King of the Cats and Other Tales* [3-6], 1660

Cauley, Lorinda Bryan. *Puss in Boots* [K-4], 1419

Early, Margaret. *Sleeping Beauty* [K-6], **899**

Galdone, Paul. *Cinderella* [1-4], 1458

Puss in Boots [K-4], 1470

Haley, Gail E. *Puss in Boots* [1-4], **933**

Harris, Rosemary. *Beauty and the Beast* [2-5], 1520

Karlin, Barbara. *Cinderella* [Pre-2], 1537

Kimmel, Eric A. *Three Sacks of Truth: A Story from France* [2-5], **958**

Kirstein, Lincoln. *Puss in Boots* [1-4], **959**

Mayer, Marianna. *Beauty and the Beast* [2-5], 1566

Perrault, Charles. *Puss in Boots* [1-4], **997**

San Souci, Robert D. *The White Cat: An Old French Fairy Tale* [2-5], **1019**

Scribner, Charles. *The Devil's Bridge* [2-4], 1596

Stewig, John Warren. *Stone Soup* [K-3], **1031**

FOLKLORE–Germany

Corrin, Sara, and Stephen Corrin. *The Pied Piper of Hamelin* [2-6], 1431

Croll, Carolyn. *The Three Brothers* [K-3], **888**

Grimm, Jacob. *The Bear and the Bird King* [K-3], **922**

The Bearskinner [2-4], 1486

The Bremen Town Musicians [Pre-3], 1487

The Bremen Town Musicians [K-2], **923, 924**

The Brothers Grimm Popular Folk Tales [2-5], 1684

Cinderella [1-4], 1488

The Devil with the Three Golden Hairs [2-4], 1489

The Donkey Prince [2-4], 1490

The Elves and the Shoemaker [Pre-2], 1491

Fairy Tales and the Brothers Grimm [2-5], 1685

The Fisherman and His Wife [2-4], 1492

The Frog Prince [K-3], 1493

The Frog Prince: Or Iron Henry [1-4], **925**

The Glass Mountain [2-6], 1494

Grimm's Fairy Tales: 20 Stories [3-6], 1686

Hans in Luck [K-3], 1495

Hansel and Gretel [K-2], **926**

Hansel and Gretel [2-4], 1496, 1497

Iron John [2-6], **927**

Jorinda and Joringel [2-4], 1498

The Juniper Tree: And Other Tales from Grimm [3-6], 1687

Little Brother and Little Sister [2-5], 1499

Little Red Cap [Pre-2], 1500
Little Red Riding Hood [Pre-2], 1501
Mother Holly [Pre-2], 1502
Nanny Goat and the Seven Little Kids [K-2], **928**
One Gift Deserves Another [1-4], **929**
Rapunzel [2-4], 1503, **930**
Rumpelstiltskin [1-4], 1504, **931**
The Sleeping Beauty [2-5], 1505
Snow White [2-5], 1506
The Table, the Donkey and the Stick [1-4], 1507
Tales from Grimm [1-4], 1688
Thorn Rose: or, The Sleeping Beauty [1-4], 1508
The Twelve Dancing Princesses [1-4], 1509
The Twelve Dancing Princesses [2-4], **930**
The Twelve Dancing Princesses and Other Tales from Grimm [3-6], 1689
The Valiant Little Tailor [1-4], 1510
The Water of Life [3-6], 1511
The Wolf and the Seven Little Kids [Pre-1], 1512
Hurlimann, Ruth. *The Proud White Cat* [Pre-2], 1532
Hutton, Warwick. *The Nose Tree* [2-5], 1533
Lemieux, Michèle. *Pied Piper of Hamelin* [2-5], **966**
Marshall, James. *Red Riding Hood* [Pre-2], 1562
Mayer, Marianna. *The Spirit of the Blue Light* [3-5], **986**
Thomson, Peggy. *The Brave Little Tailor* [1-4], **1035**

FOLKLORE–Greece
Aesop. *The Wind and the Sun* [K-2], **859**
Aliki. *The Twelve Months* [1-3], 1390
Anderson, Lonzo. *Arion and the Dophins* [K-3], 1391
Cox, Miriam. *The Magic and the Sword: The Greek Myths Retold* [4-6], 1671
D'Aulaire, Ingri, and Edgar Parin D'Aulaire. *D'Aulaire's Book of Greek Myths* [4-6], 1674
Fisher, Leonard Everett. *Cyclops* [4-6], **904**
Theseus and the Minotaur [4-6], 1452
Gates, Doris. *Lord of the Sky: Zeus* [5-6], 1679
Hewitt, Kathryn. *King Midas and the Golden Touch* [1-4], 1522
Osborne, Mary Pope. *Favorite Greek Myths* [5-6], 1713
Proddow, Penelope. *Demeter and Persephone* [5-6], 1581
Sutcliff, Rosemary. *Black Ships Before Troy! The Story of the Iliad* [5-6], **1088**
Yolen, Jane. *Wings* [4-6], **1049**

FOLKLORE–Haiti
Courlander, Harold. *The Piece of Fire and Other Haitian Tales* [3-6], 1669

Wolkstein, Diane. *The Banza: A Haitian Story* [Pre-2], 1629
The Magic Orange Tree and Other Haitian Folktales [2-6], 1737

FOLKLORE–Hungary
Biro, Val. *Hungarian Folk-Tales* [3-6], 1657
Galdone, Paul. *The Amazing Pig* [2-4], 1457

FOLKLORE–India
Duff, Maggie. *Rum Pum Pum* [Pre-2], 1449
Galdone, Paul. *The Monkey and the Crocodile: A Jataka Tale from India* [Pre-2], 1466
Quigley, Lillian F. *The Blind Mice and the Elephant* [K-5], 1582
Young, Ed. *Seven Blind Mice* [Pre-3], **1051**

FOLKLORE–Indians of Mexico
Bernhard, Emery. *The Tree That Rains: The Flood Myth of the Huichol Indians of Mexico* [1-4], **867**
Dupré, Judith. *The Mouse Bride: A Mayan Folk Tale* [K-2], **898**
Johnston, Tony. *The Tale of Rabbit and Coyote* [Pre-2], **947**
Ober, Hal. *How Music Came to the World* [1-4], **993**

FOLKLORE–Indians of North America
Ata, Te. *Baby Rattlesnake* [Pre-1], **862**
Baker, Olaf. *Where the Buffaloes Begin* [3-6], 1397
Begay, Shonto. *Ma'ii and Cousin Horned Toad: A Traditional Navajo Story* [K-4], **865**
Bierhorst, John. *The Woman Who Fell from the Sky: The Iroquois Story of Creation* [2-6], **868**
Bruchac, Joseph. *The First Strawberries: A Cherokee Story* [K-3], **870**
The Great Ball Game: A Muskogee Story [K-3], **871**
Iroquois Stories: Heros and Heroines, Monsters and Magic [3-6], 1659
Native American Animal Stories [2-6], **1059**
Return of the Sun: Native American Tales from the Northeast Woodlands [3-6], **1060**
Bruchac, Joseph, and Jonathan London. *Thirteen Moons on Turtle's Back: A Native American Year of Moons* [2-6], **872**
Brusca, María Cristina, and Tona Wilson. *When Jaguars Ate the Moon: And Other Stories About Animals and Plants of the Americas* [2-6], **1061**
Carey, Valerie Scho. *Quail Song: A Pueblo Indian Tale* [K-2], **876**
Coatsworth, Emerson, and David Coatsworth. *The Adventures of Nanabush: Ojibway Indian Stories* [2-5], 1665
dePaola, Tomie. *The Legend of the Bluebonnet: An Old Tale of Texas* [1-4], 1440

FOLKLORE–Indians of North America (cont.)

The Legend of the Indian Paintbrush [1-3], 1441

Dixon, Ann. *How Raven Brought Light to People* [K-4], **897**

Esbensen, Barbara Juster. *The Star Maiden: An Ojibway Tale* [2-5], 1451

Gates, Frieda. *Owl Eyes* [K-3], **911**

Goble, Paul. *Buffalo Woman* [2-6], 1481
Crow Chief: A Plains Indian Story [2-6], **915**
Her Seven Brothers [3-6], 1482
Iktomi and the Boulder: A Plains Indian Story [K-3], 1483
Love Flute [3-6], **916**

Greene, Ellin. *The Legend of the Cranberry: A Paleo-Indian Tale* [1-4], **919**

Gregg, Andy. *Great Rabbit and the Long-Tailed Wildcat* [2-4], **921**

Harris, Christie. *Mouse Woman and the Mischief-Makers* [4-6], 1691
The Trouble with Adventurers [4-6], 1692

Haviland, Virginia. *North American Legends* [4-6], 1695

Larry, Charles. *Peboan and Seegwun* [1-4], **964**

London, Jonathan, and Lanny Pinola. *Fire Race: A Karuk Coyote Tale About How Fire Came to the People* [K-3], **972**

McDermott, Gerald. *Coyote: A Trickster Tale from the American Southwest* [Pre-2], **975**
Raven: A Trickster Tale from the Pacific Northwest [K-4], **976**

Manitonquat (Medicine Story). *Children of the Morning Light: Wampanoag Tales* [3-6], **1077**

Martin, Rafe. *The Boy Who Lived with the Seals* [2-4], **982**
The Rough-Face Girl [2-6], **983**

Mayo, Gretchen Will. *Big Trouble for Tricky Rabbit!* [1-3], **1078**
That Tricky Coyote! [K-2], **1079**

Pollock, Penny. *The Turkey Girl: A Zuni Cinderella Story* [2-5], **1000**

Robinson, Gail. *Raven the Trickster: Legends of the North American Indians* [4-6], 1719

Rodanas, Kristina. *Dragonfly's Tale* [K-3], **1005**

Ross, Gayle. *How Rabbit Tricked Otter and Other Cherokee Trickster Stories* [1-4], **1084**
How Turtle's Back Was Cracked: A Traditional Cherokee Tale [1-4], **1008**

Roth, Susan L. *Kanahena: A Cherokee Story* [Pre-2], 1587

San Souci, Robert D. *Sootface: An Ojibwa Cinderella Story* [1-5], **1016**

Shetterly, Susan Hand. *Raven's Light: A Myth from the People of the Northwest Coast* [2-5], **1024**

Sloat, Teri. *The Hungry Giant of the Tundra* [K-2], **1027**

Steptoe, John. *The Story of Jumping Mouse: A Native American Legend* [Pre-4], 1608

Stevens, Janet. *Coyote Steals the Blanket: A Ute Tale* [Pre-3], **1029**

Tanaka, Béatrice. *The Chase: A Kutenai Indian Tale* [Pre-K], **1032**

Taylor, Harriet Peck. *Coyote Places the Stars* [1-3], **1033**

Van Laan, Nancy. *Buffalo Dance: A Blackfoot Legend* [3-6], **1039**

Young, Ed. *Moon Mother: A Native American Creation Tale* [2-6], **1050**

FOLKLORE–Indians of South America

Brusca, María Cristina, and Tona Wilson. *When Jaguars Ate the Moon: And Other Stories About Animals and Plants of the Americas* [2-6], **1061**

Troughton, Joanna. *How the Birds Changed Their Feathers: A South American Indian Folk Tale* [Pre-3], 1616

FOLKLORE–Indians of the West Indies

Crespo, George. *How the Sea Began: A Taino Myth* [1-6], **887**

FOLKLORE–Ireland

dePaola, Tomie. *Fin M'Coul, the Giant of Knockmary Hill* [1-4], 1439
Jamie O'Rourke and the Big Potato: An Irish Folktale [K-4], **895**

Greene, Ellin. *Billy Beg and His Bull* [2-4], **918**

Hodges, Margaret. *Saint Patrick and the Peddler* [1-4], **941**

McDermott, Gerald. *Daniel O'Rourke* [1-4], 1551
Tim O'Toole and the Wee Folk: An Irish Tale [1-4], 1553

Shute, Linda. *Clever Tom and the Leprechaun* [Pre-3], 1599

FOLKLORE–Italy

Basile, Giambattista. *Petrosinella: A Neopolitan Rapunzel* [4-6], 1401

dePaola, Tomie. *The Mysterious Giant of Barletta: An Italian Folktale* [1-4], 1442
The Prince of the Dolomites: An Old Italian Tale [2-4], 1443
Strega Nona [K-4], 1444
Tony's Bread [1-4], **896**

Rayevsky, Inna. *The Talking Tree* [2-5], 1584

Zemach, Harve. *Too Much Noise: An Italian Tale* [2-5], 1637

FOLKLORE–Ivory Coast

Roddy, Patricia. *Api and the Boy Stranger: A Village Creation Tale* [K-2], **1006**

FOLKLORE–Jamaica

Temple, Frances. *Tiger Soup: An Anansi Story from Jamaica* [Pre-2], **1034**

FOLKLORE–Japan

Brenner, Barbara. *Little One Inch* [K-4], 1407

Compton, Patricia A. *The Terrible Eek* [K-3], **885**

Hamanaka, Sheila. *Screen of Frogs: An Old Tale* [K-3], **934**

Hodges, Margaret. *The Wave* [K-4], 1527

Hughes, Monica. *Little Fingerling* [1-4], **945**

Ishii, Momoko. *The Tongue-Cut Sparrow* [Pre-3], 1535

Johnston, Tony. *The Badger and the Magic Fan: A Japanese Folktale* [Pre-2], 1536

Kimmel, Eric A. *The Greatest of All: A Japanese Folktale* [K-2], **954**

Levine, Arthur A. *The Boy Who Drew Cats: A Japanese Folktale* [2-6], **968**

McCoy, Karen Kawamoto. *A Tale of Two Tengu: A Japanese Folktale* [Pre-2], **974**

McDermott, Gerald. *The Stonecutter: A Japanese Folk Tale* [K-4], 1552

Mosel, Arlene. *The Funny Little Woman* [Pre-3], 1571

Newton, Patricia Montgomery. *The Five Sparrows: A Japanese Folktale* [1-4], 1575

Paterson, Katherine. *The Tale of the Mandarin Ducks* [2-6], **996**

Richard, Françoise. *On Cat Mountain* [2-5], **1003**

San Souci, Robert D. *The Samurai's Daughter* [3-6], **1014**

The Snow Wife [3-5], **1015**

Say, Allen. *Once Under the Cherry Blossom Tree: An Old Japanese Tale* [1-4], 1592

Schroeder, Alan. *Lily and the Wooden Bowl* [1-4], **1021**

Shute, Linda. *Momotaro the Peach Boy: A Traditional Japanese Tale* [1-4], 1600

Snyder, Dianne. *The Boy of the Three Year Nap* [2-5], 1603

Stamm, Claus. *Three Strong Women: A Tall Tale* [2-4], 1605

Tompert, Ann. *Bamboo Hats and a Rice Cake: A Tale Adapted from Japanese Folklore* [K-3], **1036**

Uchida, Yoshiko. *The Magic Purse* [1-4], **1037**

The Sea of Gold and Other Tales from Japan [2-6], 1732

The Two Foolish Cats [Pre-2], 1620

The Wise Old Woman [1-5], **1038**

Wolkstein, Diane. *Lazy Stories* [1-4], 1736

Yagawa, Sumiko. *The Crane Wife* [2-5], 1632

FOLKLORE–Korea

Climo, Shirley. *The Korean Cinderella* [1-4], **878**

Ginsburg, Mirra. *The Chinese Mirror* [1-4], 1477

Han, Oki S., and Stephanie Haboush Plunkett. *Sir Whong and the Golden Pig* [2-5], **935**

Han, Suzanne Crowder. *The Rabbit's Escape* [1-5], **936**

The Rabbit's Judgment [1-5], **937**

Kwon, Holly H. *The Moles and the Mireuk: A Korean Folktale* [K-2], **962**

O'Brien, Anne Sibley. *The Princess and the Beggar: A Korean Folklore* [1-4], **994**

Rhee, Nami. *Magic Spring: A Korean Folktale* [K-3], **1002**

FOLKLORE–Laos

Blia, Xiong. *Nine-in-One, Grr! Grr! A Folktale from the Hmong People of Laos* [K-3], 1404

Wolkstein, Diane. *Lazy Stories* [1-4], 1736

FOLKLORE–Latin America

Ada, Alma Flor. *The Rooster Who Went to His Uncle's Wedding: A Latin American Folktale* [Pre-1], **858**

FOLKLORE–Latvia

Langton, Jane. *The Hedgehog Boy: A Latvian Folktale* [K-3], 1545

FOLKLORE–Mexico

Aardema, Verna. *Borreguita and the Coyote: A Tale from Ayutla, Mexico* [K-3], **856**

The Riddle of the Drum [1-4], 1383

Dupré, Judith. *The Mouse Bride: A Mayan Folk Tale* [K-2], **898**

Ober, Hal. *How Music Came to the World* [1-4], **993**

Wolkstein, Diane. *Lazy Stories* [1-4], 1736

FOLKLORE–Mongolia

Otsuka, Zuzo. *Suho and the White Horse: A Legend of Mongolia* [2-4], 1576

FOLKLORE–Nigeria

Gerson, Mary-Joan. *Why the Sky Is Far Away: A Nigerian Folktale* [K-4], **913**

Mollel, Tololwa M. *The Flying Tortoise: An Igbo Tale* [K-2], **987**

FOLKLORE–Norway

Asbjørnsen, P. C. *The Runaway Pancake* [Pre-1], 1394

The Squire's Bride [1-4], 1395

The Three Billy Goats Gruff [Pre-2], 1396

Cauley, Lorinda Bryan. *The Pancake Boy: An Old Norwegian Folk Tale* [1-3], 1418

FOLKLORE–Norway (cont.)

Climo, Shirley. *Stolen Thunder: A Norse Myth* [3-6], **880**

Dasent, George Webbe. *The Cat on the Dovrefell: A Christmas Tale* [Pre-2], 1432

East o' the Sun and West o' the Moon [3-6], **890**

East o' the Sun & West o' the Moon: An Old Norse Tale [2-6], 1433

D'Aulaire, Ingri, and Edgar Parin D'Aulaire. *D'Aulaire's Trolls* [K-3], 1434

French, Vivian. *Why the Sea Is Salt* [1-4], **906**

Galdone, Paul. *The Three Billy Goats Gruff* [Pre-1], 1473

Hague, Kathleen, and Michael Hague. *East of the Sun and West of the Moon* [3-5], 1513

The Man Who Kept House [K-4], 1514

Kimmel, Eric A. *Boots and His Brothers: A Norwegian Tale* [2-6], **952**

Littedale, Freya. *Peter and the North Wind* [Pre-3], 1547

Martin, Claire. *Boots & the Glass Mountain* [2-6], **981**

Mayer, Marianna. *Iduna and the Magic Apples* [4-6], 1567

Rounds, Glen. *The Three Billy Goats Gruff* [Pre-2], **1009**

Weisner, William. *Happy-Go-Lucky* [1-4], 1625

Turnabout [K-4], 1626

FOLKLORE–Persia

Scott, Sally. *The Magic Horse* [1-4], 1594

FOLKLORE–Peru

Alexander, Ellen. *Llama and the Great Flood: A Folktale from Peru* [2-4], 1389

Ehlert, Lois. *Moon Rope: Un Lazo a la Luna: A Peruvian Folktale* [Pre-2], **902**

FOLKLORE–Philippines

Aruego, Jose, and Ariane Dewey. *A Crocodile's Tale* [Pre-1], 1393

FOLKLORE–Poland

Domanska, Janina. *King Krakus and the Dragon* [K-2], 1446

Turska, Krystyna. *The Magician of Cracow* [2-5], 1619

FOLKLORE–Puerto Rico

Belpré, Pura. *Oté* [1-4], 1402

Pitre, Felix. *Juan Bobo and the Pig: A Puerto Rican Folktale* [K-2], **998**

Simms, Laura. *The Squeaky Door* [Pre-2], **1026**

FOLKLORE–Russia

Afanasev, Alexander. *Russian Folk Tales* [3-6], 1652

Arnold, Katya. *Baba Yaga: A Russian Folktale* [1-3], **860**

Baba Yaga & the Little Girl [K-3], **861**

Ayres, Becky Hickox. *Matreshka* [K-3], **863**

Cole, Joanna. *Bony-Legs* [K-2], **1426**

Crouch, Marcus. *Ivan: Stories of Old Russia* [3-6], **1064**

Demi. *The Firebird* [2-5], **893**

Gal, Laszlo. *Prince Ivan and the Firebird* [3-6], **908**

Geras, Adèle. *My Grandmother's Stories: A Collection of Jewish Folk Tales* [3-6], **1067**

Ginsburg, Mirra. *The Fisherman's Son* [2-5], 1478

The Lazies [2-4], 1680

The Magic Stove [K-3], 1479

The Night It Rained Pancakes [Pre-2], 1480

Three Rolls and One Doughnut: Fables from Russia [1-5], 1681

The Twelve Clever Brothers and Other Fools [2-5], 1682

Hastings, Selina. *The Firebird* [1-4], **938**

Hodges, Margaret. *The Little Humpbacked Horse* [3-5], 1525

Isele, Elizabeth. *The Frog Princess* [2-5], 1534

Kimmel, Eric A. *Baba Yaga: A Russian Folktale* [K-2], **951**

I-Know-Not-What, I-Know-Not-Where: A Russian Tale [4-6], **955**

Langton, Jane. *Salt: A Russian Folktale* [2-5], **963**

Lewis, J. Patrick. *The Frog Princess: A Russian Tale* [2-6], **969**

McCurdy, Michael. *The Devils Who Learned to Be Good* [K-3], 1549

Mayer, Marianna. *Baba Yaga and Vasilisa the Brave* [2-5], **985**

Morgan, Pierr. *The Turnip: An Old Russian Folktale* [Pre-1], 1569

Pevear, Richard. *Mr. Cat-and-a-Half* [1-3], 1578

Our King Has Horns! [2-5], 1579

Ransome, Arthur. *The Fool of the World and His Flying Ship* [2-4], 1583

Riordan, James. *The Three Magic Gifts* [1-4], 1586

San Souci, Robert D. *The Firebird* [3-5], **1012**

The Tsar's Promise [3-6], **1018**

Scott, Sally. *The Three Wonderful Beggars* [1-4], 1595

Sherman, Josepha. *Vassilisa the Wise: A Tale of Medieval Russia* [2-5], 1598

Silverman, Maida. *Anna and the Seven Swans* [K-3], 1601

Small, Ernest. *Baba Yaga* [1-4], 1602

Stern, Simon. *Vasily and the Dragon: An Epic Russian Fairy Tale* [3-6], 1610

Tolstoi, Alexie. *The Great Big Enormous Turnip* [Pre-1], 1614

Van Woerkom, Dorothy. *Alexander the Rock-Eater* [1-4], 1621

Winthrop, Elizabeth. *Vasilissa the Beautiful: A Russian Folktale* [2-5], **1044**

FOLKLORE–Scotland

Forest, Heather. *The Woman Who Flummoxed the Fairies: An Old Tale from Scotland* [1-4], 1453

Nimmo, Jenny. *The Witches and the Singing Mice* [1-4], **992**

Yolen, Jane. *Tam Lin* [3-6], **1048**

FOLKLORE–South America

Brusca, María Cristina, and Tona Wilson. *The Cook and the King* [2-4], **874**

Finger, Charles. *Tales from Silver Lands* [3-6], 1677

FOLKLORE–Spain

Hamcock, Sibyl. *Esteban and the Ghost* [2-4], 1518

Vernon, Adele. *The Riddle* [3-6], 1622

FOLKLORE–Surinam

Lichtveld, Noni. *I Lost My Arrow in a Kankan Tree* [K-2], **970**

FOLKLORE–Sweden

Zemach, Harve. *Nail Soup: A Swedish Folk Tale* [1-4], 1636

FOLKLORE–Switzerland

Early, Margaret. *William Tell* [2-6], **900**

Small, Terry. *The Legend of William Tell* [3-5], **1028**

FOLKLORE–Turkey

Walker, Barbara. *Teeny-Tiny and the Witch Woman* [2-4], 1623

Walker, Barbara K. *A Treasure of Turkish Folktales for Children* [2-6], 1734

FOLKLORE–Ukraine

Brett, Jan. *The Mitten* [Pre-2], 1409

Kismaric, Carole. *The Rumor of Pavel and Paali: A Ukrainian Folktale* [3-6], 1542

Tresselt, Alvin. *The Mitten: An Old Ukrainian Folktale* [Pre-2], 1615

FOLKLORE–U.S.

Arnold, Caroline. *The Terrible Hodag* [1-5], 1392

Birdseye, Tom. *Soap! Soap! Don't Forget the Soap! An Appalachian Folktale* [1-3], **869**

Chase, Richard. *Grandfather Tales* [K-6], 1661
Jack Tales [4-6], 1662

Cohn, Amy L. *From Sea to Shining Sea: A Treasury of American Folklore and Folk Songs* [1-6], **1063**

Compton, Joanne. *Ashpet: An Appalachian Tale* [1-4], **883**

Compton, Kenn, and Joanne Compton. *Jack the Giant Chaser: An Appalachian Tale* [1-4], **884**

Credle, Ellis. *Tall Tales from the High Hills and Other Stories* [4-6], 1672

DeFelice, Cynthia C. *The Dancing Skeleton* [2-4], 1437

Emrich, Duncan. *The Hodgepodge Book* [2-6], 1796

Galdone, Joanna. *The Tailypo: A Ghost Story* [2-4], 1456

Galdone, Paul. *The Greedy Old Fat Man: An American Folktale* [Pre-2], 1460

Haley, Gail E. *Jack and the Bean Tree* [1-4], 1515
Jack and the Fire Dragon [2-5], 1516

Haviland, Virginia. *North American Legends* [4-6], 1695

Hooks, William H. *Moss Gown* [2-6], 1529
The Three Little Pigs and the Fox [Pre-2], 1530

Hunter, C. W. *The Green Gourd: A North Carolina Folktale* [K-2], **946**

Jaquith, Priscilla. *Bo Rabbit Smart for True: Folktales from the Gullah* [K-4], 1700

Keats, Ezra Jack. *John Henry: An American Legend* [1-4], 1538

Kellogg, Steven. *Mike Fink* [1-4], **948**

Leach, Maria. *The Rainbow Book of American Folk Tales and Legends* [3-6], 1703

Lester, Julius. *Further Tales of Uncle Remus: The Misadventures of Brer Rabbit, Brer Fox, Brer Wolf, the Doodang, and Other Creatures* [2-5], **1075**
John Henry [1-4], **967**
The Tales of Uncle Remus: The Adventures of Brer Rabbit [2-5], 1707

McCormick, Dell J. *Paul Bunyan Swings His Axe* [3-6], 1709

Mathews, Judith, and Fay Robinson. *Nathaniel Willy, Scared Silly* [Pre-2], **984**

Osborne, Mary Pope. *American Tall Tales* [3-6], **1081**

Parks, Van Dyke, and Malcolm Jones. *Jump! The Adventures of Brer Rabbit* [2-5], 1714

Rounds, Glen. *Ol' Paul, the Mighty Logger* [4-6], 1721

Sanfield, Steve. *A Natural Man: The True Story of John Henry* [4-6], 1588

San Souci, Robert D. *Larger Than Life: The Adventures of American Legendary Heroes* [3-6], **1085**
The Talking Eggs [1-4], 1590

Sawyer, Ruth. *Journey Cake, Ho!* [Pre-2], 1591

Schwartz, Alvin. *Chin Music: Tall Talk and Other Talk, Collected from American Folklore* [3-6], 1946

FOLKLORE–U.S. (cont.)

Cross Your Fingers, Spit in Your Hat: Superstitions and Other Beliefs [3-6], 1724

Kickle Snifters and Other Fearsome Critters Collected from American Folklore [2-5], 1593

Scary Stories 3: More Tales to Chill Your Bones [4-6], **1086**

Scary Stories to Tell in the Dark [4-6], 1725

Tomfoolery: Trickery and Foolery with Words [1-6], 1949

Whoppers: Tall Tales and Other Lies [3-6], 1726

Shepard, Aaron. *The Legend of Slappy Hooper: An American Tall Tale* [1-3], **1023**

Still, James. *Jack and the Wonder Beans* [2-4], 1612

Walker, Paul Robert. *Big Men, Big Country: A Collection of American Tall Tales* [4-6], **1090**

Withers, Carl. *A Rocket in My Pocket: The Rhymes and Chants of Young Americans* [K-4], 1977

Young, Richard, and Judy Dockrey Young. *Favorite Scary Stories of American Children* [3-6], **1093**

FOLKLORE–Vietnam

Garland, Sherry. *Why Ducks Sleep on One Leg* [1-4], **909**

Kha, Dang Manh. *In the Land of Small Dragon: A Vietnamese Folktale* [3-5], 1540

Lee, Jeanne M. *Toad Is the Uncle of Heaven* [Pre-2], 1546

Vuong, Lynette Dyer. *The Brocaded Slipper and Other Vietnamese Tales* [3-6], 1733

FOLKLORE–Wales

Cooper, Susan. *The Silver Cow: A Welsh Tale* [2-5], 1430

Garner, Alan. *A Bag of Moonshine* [2-5], 1678

FOLKLORE, AFRICAN AMERICAN

Bang, Molly. *Wiley and the Hairy Man* [K-3], 1399

Haviland, Virginia. *North American Legends* [4-6], 1695

Jaquith, Priscilla. *Bo Rabbit Smart for True: Folktales from the Gullah* [K-4], 1700

Keats, Ezra Jack. *John Henry: An American Legend* [1-4], 1538

Lester, Julius. *Further Tales of Uncle Remus: The Misadventures of Brer Rabbit, Brer Fox, Brer Wolf, the Doodang, and Other Creatures* [2-5], **1075**

John Henry [1-4], **967**

The Knee-High Man and Other Tales [K-4], 1706

The Tales of Uncle Remus: The Adventures of Brer Rabbit [2-5], 1707

Parks, Van Dyke, and Malcolm Jones. *Jump! The Adventures of Brer Rabbit* [2-5], 1714

Sanfield, Steve. *A Natural Man: The True Story of John Henry* [4-6], 1588

San Souci, Robert D. *The Boy and the Ghost* [1-4], **1011**

Sukey and the Mermaid [2-5], **1017**

The Talking Eggs [1-4], 1590

Stevens, Janet. *Tops & Bottoms* [Pre-2], **1030**

FOLKLORE, ASHANTI

Chocolate, Deborah M. Newton. *Talk, Talk: An Ashanti Legend* [1-5], **877**

FOLKLORE, CHINESE AMERICAN

Yep, Laurence. *Tongues of Jade* [4-6], **1092**

FOLKLORE, ESKIMO

Bernhard, Emery. *How Snowshoe Hare Rescued the Sun: A Tale from the Arctic* [K-3], 866

Sloat, Teri. *The Hungry Giant of the Tundra* [K-2], **1027**

FOLKLORE, JEWISH

Cole, Joanna. *It's Too Noisy!* [Pre-1], **882**

Freedman, Florence B. *It Happened in Chelm: A Story of the Legendary Town of Fools* [2-5], **905**

Geras, Adèle. *My Grandmother's Stories: A Collection of Jewish Folk Tales* [3-6], **1067**

Gilman, Phoebe. *Something from Nothing* [Pre-2], **914**

Greene, Jacqueline Dembar. *What His Father Did* [3-6], **920**

Hirsch, Marilyn. *The Rabbi and the Twenty-Nine Witches* [K-2], 1524

Renberg, Dalia Hardof. *King Solomon and the Bee* [K-3], **1001**

Schwartz, Howard. *Elijah's Violin and Other Jewish Fairy Tales* [4-6], 1728

Singer, Isaac Bashevis. *When Shlemiel Went to Warsaw & Other Stories* [4-6], 1730

Zemach, Margot. *It Could Always Be Worse* [1-4], 1638

FOLKLORE, SLAVIC

De Regniers, Beatrice Schenk. *Little Sister and the Month Brothers* [K-3], 1445

Galdone, Joanna. *The Little Girl and the Big Bear* [Pre-2], 1455

FOOD

SEE ALSO Cookery; Fruit; Pies; Soup; Vegetables

Armour, Peter. *Stop That Pickle!* [K-1], **218**

Asch, Frank. *Popcorn* [Pre-K], 15

Babbitt, Natalie. *The Search for Delicious* [4-5], 1139

Barrett, Judi. *Cloudy with a Chance of Meatballs* [2-3], 871

Brimner, Larry Dane. *Country Bear's Good Neighbor* [Pre-K], 27

Brown, Ruth A. *If at First You Do Not See* [K-1], 348

Carle, Eric. *Pancakes, Pancakes!* [K-1], **247**
Today Is Monday [K-1], **248**
The Very Hungry Caterpillar [Pre-K], 42

Cazet, Denys. *Lucky Me* [K-1], 360

Chadwick, Tim. *Cabbage Moon* [Pre-K], **81**

Chapman, Cheryl. *Pass the Fritters, Critters* [Pre-K], **82**

Charlip, Remy, and Burton Supree. *Mother, Mother, I Feel Sick, Send for the Doctor Quick, Quick, Quick* [1-2], 646

Conford, Ellen. *What's Cooking, Jenny Archer?* [2-3], **601**

Day, Alexandra. *Frank and Ernest* [2-3], 906

Degen, Bruce. *Jamberry* [Pre-1], 64

Demarest, Chris L. *No Peas for Nellie* [Pre-K], 68

Devlin, Harry, and Wende Devlin. *Cranberry Thanksgiving* [1-2], 660

Dodds, Siobhan. *Grandpa Bud* [Pre], **9**

Dooley, Norah. *Everybody Cooks Rice* [1-2], **433**

Ehlert, Lois. *Growing Vegetable Soup* [Pre-K], 78

Evans, Katie. *Hunky Dory Ate It* [Pre-K], **100**

Fleming, Denise. *Lunch* [Pre], **14**

Flora, James. *Leopold the See-Through Crumbpicker* [1-2], 669

Friedman, Ina R. *How My Parents Learned to Eat* [1-2], 672

Glazer, Tom. *On Top of Spaghetti* [1-2], 679

Hirsch, Marilyn. *Potato Pancakes All Around: A Hanukkah Tale* [2-3], 933

Hoban, Lillian. *Arthur's Christmas Cookies* [K-1], 425

Hoban, Russell. *Bread and Jam for Frances* [K-1], 429

Howard, Jane R. *When I'm Hungry* [Pre-K], **126**

Hurwitz, Johanna. *Much Ado about Aldo* [2-3], 937

Jaffe, Nina. *In the Month of Kislev: A Story for Hanukkah* [2-3], 627

Kasza, Keiko. *The Wolf's Chicken Stew* [Pre-K], 162

Khalsa, Dayal Kaur. *How Pizza Came to Queens* [K-1], 456

Kimmel, Eric A. *The Chanukkah Guest* [K-1], **298**

King, Bob. *Sitting on the Farm* [Pre-K], **145**

Kuklin, Susa. *How My Family Lives in America* [K-3], **1178**

Levitin, Sonia. *Nobody Stole the Pie* [1-2], 722

Lord, John Vernon, and Janet Burroway. *The Giant Jam Sandwich* [1-2], 730

McCloskey, Robert. *Blueberries for Sal* [Pre-K], 194

McMillan, Bruce. *Eating Fractions* [Pre-1], **1193**

Maestro, Betsy, and Giulio Maestro. *Lambs for Dinner* [K-1], 498

Mahy, Margaret. *Jam: A True Story* [1-2], 740

Massie, Diane Redfield. *Chameleon Was a Spy* [2-3], 960

Miller, Virginia. *Eat Your Dinner!* [Pre], **34**

Modesitt, Jeanne. *Vegetable Soup* [Pre-K], **170**

Morris, Ann. *Bread Bread Bread* [Pre-3], **1211**

Nixon, Joan Lowery. *Beats Me, Claude* [2-3], 971

O'Keefe, Susan Heyboer. *One Hungry Monster: A Counting Book in Rhyme* [Pre-K], **174**

Patron, Susan. *Burgoo Stew* [1-2], **527**

Patz, Nancy. *Pumpernickel Tickel and Mean Green Cheese* [K-1], 520

Pinkwater, Daniel. *The Slaves of Spiegel: A Magic Moscow Story* [4-5], 1226
Yobgorgle: Mystery Monster of Lake Ontario [4-5], 1227

Priceman, Marjorie. *How to Make an Apple Pie and See the World* [1-2], **538**

Rattigan, Jama Kim. *Dumpling Soup* [K-1], **349**

Rayner, Mary. *Garth Pig and the Ice Cream Lady* [1-2], 781
Mrs. Pig's Bulk Buy [1-2], 783

Robart, Rose. *The Cake That Mack Ate* [Pre-K], 241

Robbins, Ken. *Make Me a Peanut Butter Sandwich and a Glass of Milk* [1-4], **1225**

Rockwell, Thomas. *How to Eat Fried Worms* [3-4], 1109

Sendak, Maurice. *Chicken Soup with Rice* [K-1], 551

Seuss, Dr. *Green Eggs and Ham* [Pre-K], 259

Sharmat, Mitchell. *Gregory, the Terrible Eater* [K-1], 555

Shaw, Nancy. *Sheep Out to Eat* [K-1], **361**

Shelby, Anne. *Potluck* [K-1], **362**

Soto, Gary. *Too Many Tamales* [K-1], **369**

Stadler, John. *Animal Cafe* [1-2], 819

Stevenson, James. *Yuck!* [K-1], 562

Thayer, Jane. *The Popcorn Dragon* [Pre-K], 273

Titus, Eve. *Anatole* [1-2], 830

Wellington, Monica. *Mr. Cookie Baker* [Pre], **55**

Westcott, Nadine Bernard. *Peanut Butter and Jelly: A Play Rhyme* [Pre-K], 291

Williams, Vera B. *Cherries and Cherry Pits* [1-2], 852

Wilson, Gahan. *Harry the Fat Bear Spy* [3-4], 1133

Wood, Audrey. *Heckedy Peg* [1-2], 854

Yee, Paul. *Roses Sing on New Snow: A Delicious Tale* [2-3], **696**

FOOD (cont.)

Young, Ruth. *Starring Francine & Dave: Three One-Act Plays* [Pre-2], 2117

FOOD–Folklore

Brown, Marcia. *Stone Soup* [1-4], 1412

Cauley, Lorinda Bryan. *The Pancake Boy: An Old Norwegian Folk Tale* [1-3], 1418

dePaola, Tomie. *Strega Nona* [K-4], 1444
Tony's Bread [1-4], **896**

Esterl, Arnica. *The Fine Round Cake* [K-2], **903**

Forest, Heather. *The Woman Who Flummoxed the Fairies: An Old Tale from Scotland* [1-4], 1453

Galdone, Paul. *The Little Red Hen* [Pre-1], 1464
The Magic Porridge Pot [Pre-2], 1465

Gerson, Mary-Joan. *Why the Sky Is Far Away: A Nigerian Folktale* [K-4], **913**

Greene, Ellin. *Clever Cooks: A Concoction of Stories, Charms, Recipes and Riddles* [2-5], 1683

Greene, Jacqueline Dembar. *What His Father Did* [3-6], **920**

Hong, Lily Toy. *How the Ox Star Fell from Heaven* [1-4], **942**

Kimmel, Eric A. *The Gingerbread Man* [Pre-1], **953**

Langton, Jane. *Salt: A Russian Folktale* [2-5], **963**

McGovern, Ann. *Stone Soup* [Pre-2], 1555

Martin, Rafe. *Foolish Rabbit's Big Mistake* [Pre-2], 1564

Mayer, Marianna. *Iduna and the Magic Apples* [4-6], 1567

Rodanas, Kristina. *Dragonfly's Tale* [K-3], **1005**

Roddy, Patricia. *Api and the Boy Stranger: A Village Creation Tale* [K-2], **1006**

Stewig, John Warren. *Stone Soup* [K-3], **1031**

Zemach, Harve. *Nail Soup: A Swedish Folk Tale* [1-4], 1636

FOOD–Poetry

Adoff, Arnold. *Chocolate Dreams* [5-6], **1259**
Eats [2-6], 1742

Agree, Rose H. *How to Eat a Poem and Other Morsels: Food Poems for Children* [2-6], 1743

Cole, William. *Poem Stew* [2-5], 1781

Goldstein, Bobbye S. *What's on the Menu?* [1-4], **1299**

Hopkins, Lee Bennett. *Munching: Poems about Eating* [K-3], 1826

Lillegard, Dee. *Do Not Feed the Table* [K-3], **1355**

Westcott, Nadine Bernard. *Never Take a Pig to Lunch and Other Poems About the Fun of Eating* [1-4], **1421**

FOOD–Riddles

Keller, Charles. *Alexander the Grape: Fruit and Vegetable Jokes* [2-6], 1834
Belly Laughs! Food Jokes & Riddles [2-6], **1337**
The Nutty Joke Book [2-5], 1840

FOOLS

Arnold, Tedd. *Ollie Forgot* [1-2], 607

Cole, Joanna, and Philip Cole. *Big Goof and Little Goof* [K-1], 373

DeFelice, Cynthia. *Mule Eggs* [2-3], **604**

Hale, Lucretia. *The Lady Who Put Salt in Her Coffee* [2-3], 930

Rose, Anne. *The Triumphs of Fuzzy Fogtop* [1-2], 784

Schertle, Alice. *The April Fool* [2-3], 991

Schwartz, Amy. *Yossel Zissel & the Wisdom of Chelm* [2-3], 992

FOOLS–Folklore

Aardema, Verna. *Anansi Finds a Fool* [1-5], **855**

Birdseye, Tom. *Soap! Soap! Don't Forget the Soap! An Appalachian Folktale* [1-3], **869**

Christian, Mary Blount. *April Fool* [1-3], 1423

Cole, Joanna. *Don't Tell the Whole World!* [K-3], **881**

Courlander, Harold. *The Piece of Fire and Other Haitian Tales* [3-6], 1669

Crouch, Marcus. *Ivan: Stories of Old Russia* [3-6], **1064**

Edwards, Roberta. *Five Silly Fishermen* [Pre-1], **901**

Freedman, Florence B. *It Happened in Chelm: A Story of the Legendary Town of Fools* [2-5], **905**

Galdone, Paul. *The Three Sillies* [1-4], 1475

Geras, Adèle. *My Grandmother's Stories: A Collection of Jewish Folk Tales* [3-6], **1067**

Ginsburg, Mirra. *The Lazies* [2-4], 1680
The Night It Rained Pancakes [Pre-2], 1480
The Twelve Clever Brothers and Other Fools [2-5], 1682

Goode, Diane. *Diane Goode's Book of Silly Stories and Songs* [2-5], **1069**

Grimm, Jacob. *Hans in Luck* [K-3], 1495

Hewitt, Kathryn. *The Three Sillies* [1-4], 1523

Hodges, Margaret. *The Little Humpbacked Horse* [3-5], 1525

Maitland, Antony. *Idle Jack* [K-3], 1559

Morris, Winifred. *The Magic Leaf* [2-4], 1570

Pitre, Felix. *Juan Bobo and the Pig: A Puerto Rican Folktale* [K-2], **998**

Ransome, Arthur. *The Fool of the World and His Flying Ship* [2-4], 1583

Singer, Isaac Bashevis. *When Shlemiel Went to Warsaw & Other Stories* [4-6], 1730

Spray, Carole. *The Mare's Egg: A New World Folk Tale* [2-5], 1604

Walker, Barbara K. *A Treasure of Turkish Folktales for Children* [2-6], 1734

FOOT

SEE ALSO Shoes

Cleary, Beverly. *The Growing-Up Feet* [Pre-K], 50

Hughes, Shirley. *Alfie's Feet* [Pre-K], 145

Winthrop, Elizabeth. *Shoes* [Pre-K], 300

FOOTBALL

SEE ALSO Baseball; Sports–Riddles

Myers, Bernice. *Sidney Rella and the Glass Sneaker* [1-2], 754

FORESTS AND FORESTRY

Carrick, Donald. *Harald and the Great Stag* [2-3], 883

Lisle, Janet Taylor. *Forest* [5-6], **827**

Pittman, Helena Clare. *Once When I Was Scared* [1-2], 775

Turkle, Brinton. *Deep in the Forest* [K-1], 570

FORTUNE-TELLING

Alexander, Lloyd. *The Fortune-Tellers* [3-4], **698**

FOSSILS

SEE ALSO Animals, Prehistoric; Dinosaurs

Cole, Sheila. *The Dragon in the Cliff: A Novel Based on the Life of Mary Anning* [5-6], **807**

FOSTER CARE

Kidd, Diana. *Onion Tears* [4-5], **772**

Radley, Gail. *The Golden Days* [5-6], **838**

FOURTH OF JULY

Keller, Holly. *Henry's Fourth of July* [Pre], **26**

FOXES

Abolafia, Yossi. *Fox Tale* [1-2], **394**

Auch, Mary Jane. *Peeping Beauty* [1-2], **402**

Byars, Betsy. *The Midnight Fox* [3-4], 1047

Christelow, Eileen. *Henry and the Red Stripes* [K-1], 362

  Olive and the Magic Hat [K-1], 365

Dahl, Roald. *The Fantastic Mr. Fox* [2-3], 904

Fox, Mem. *Hattie and the Fox* [Pre-K], 91

Hartley, Deborah. *Up North in Winter* [1-2], 683

Hutchins, Pat. *Rosie's Walk* [Pre-K], 149

Kellogg, Steven. *Chicken Little* [1-2], 704

King-Smith, Dick. *Paddy's Pot of Gold* [3-4], **724**

Korschunow, Irina. *The Foundling Fox* [1-2], 713

Leighner, Alice Mills. *Reynard: The Story of a Fox Returned to the Wild* [1-5], 2066

Leverich, Kathleen. *The Hungry Fox and the Foxy Duck* [Pre-K], 186

London, Jonathan. *Gray Fox* [1-2], **489**

McKissack, Patricia C. *Flossie & the Fox* [1-2], 735

Marshall, James. *Wings: A Tale of Two Chickens* [1-2], 745

Mason, Cherie. *Wild Fox: A True Story* [3-6], **1205**

Preston, Edna Mitchell. *Squawk to the Moon, Little Goose* [Pre-K], 233

Radcliffe, Theresa. *Shadow the Deer* [K-1], **347**

Shannon, George. *Dance Away* [Pre-K], 260

Sharmat, Marjorie Weinman. *The Best Valentine in the World* [1-2], 807

Silverman, Erica. *Don't Fidget a Feather!* [K-1], **365**

Steig, William. *The Amazing Bone* [2-3], 1006

  Dr. DeSoto [2-3], 1007

Tejima, Keizaburo. *Fox's Dream* [K-1], 565

Tompert, Ann. *Grandfather Tang's Story* [1-2], **567**

Turner, Ann. *Hedgehog for Breakfast* [Pre-K], **194**

Wallace, Karen. *Red Fox* [Pre-2], **1249**

Watson, Wendy. *Fox Went Out on a Chilly Night* [K-1], **382**

Yep, Laurence. *The Ghost Fox* [3-4], **755**

FOXES–Folklore

Aesop. *Three Aesop Fox Fables* [K-2], 1650

Cauley, Lorinda Bryan. *The Cock, the Mouse and the Little Red Hen* [Pre-2], 1414

Conover, Chris. *Mother Goose and the Sly Fox* [Pre-1], 1428

Cook, Scott. *The Gingerbread Boy* [Pre-1], 1429

Ehlert, Lois. *Moon Rope: Un Lazo a la Luna: A Peruvian Folktale* [Pre-2], **902**

Esterl, Arnica. *The Fine Round Cake* [K-2], **903**

Galdone, Paul. *The Gingerbread Boy* [Pre-1], 1459

  Henny Penny [Pre-1], 1461

  What's in Fox's Sack? [Pre-2], 1476

Grimm, Jacob. *The Bear and the Bird King* [K-3], **929**

Hastings, Selina. *Reynard the Fox* [3-6], **1071**

Hobson, Sally. *Chicken Little* [Pre-K], **940**

Hogrogian, Nonny. *One Fine Day* [Pre-2], 1528

Hooks, William H. *The Three Little Pigs and the Fox* [Pre-2], 1530

Hunter, C. W. *The Green Gourd: A North Carolina Folktale* [K-2], **946**

Kimmel, Eric A. *The Gingerbread Man* [Pre-1], **953**

Pevear, Richard. *Mr. Cat-and-a-Half* [1-3], 1578

Westwood, Jennifer. *Going to Squintum's: A Foxy Folktale* [Pre-2], 1624

FRACTIONS

SEE ALSO Mathematics

Leedy, Loreen. *Fraction Action* [1-2], **482**

McMillan, Bruce. *Eating Fractions* [Pre-1], **1193**

FRANCE

Armstrong, Jennifer. *Little Salt Lick and the Sun King* [1-2], **399**

Fatio, Louise. *The Happy Lion* [K-1], 385

Kirby, David, and Allen Woodman. *The Cows Are Going to Paris* [1-2], **471**

Lawson, Robert. *Ben and Me* [5-6], 1324

McCully, Emily Arnold. *Mirette on the High Wire* [1-2], **492**

Milton, Nancy. *The Giraffe That Walked to Paris* [2-4], **1208**

Rabin, Staton. *Casey Over There* [2-3], **666**

Titus, Eve. *Anatole* [1-2], 830

Ungerer, Tomi. *The Beast of Monsieur Racine* [2-3], 1018

FRIENDSHIP

Alcock, Vivien. *The Trial of Anna Cotman* [5-6], **802**

Aliki. *We Are Best Friends* [Pre-K], 6

Artis, Vicki K. *Gray Duck Catches a Friend* [Pre-K], 9

Auch, Mary Jane. *Bird Dogs Can't Fly* [K-1], **219**

Barre, Shelley A. *Chive* [5-6], **804**

Bauer, Marion Dane. *On My Honor* [5-6], 1273

Birdseye, Tom. *Just Call Me Stupid* [4-5], **759**

Brown, Marc. *Arthur's Birthday* [1-2], 626

Bunting, Eve. *Summer Wheels* [2-3], **594**

Byars, Betsy. *Cracker Jackson* [5-6], 1280
McMummy [4-5], **762**
The Pinballs [5-6], 1281
The Seven Treasure Hunts [2-3], **595**

Carlson, Nancy L. *Arnie and the New Kid* [1-2], **421**

Carris, Joan. *Witch-Cat* [3-4], **706**

Charlip, Remy. *Harlequin and the Gift of Many Colors* [2-3], 886

Chetwin, Grace. *Friends in Time* [4-5], **764**

Coerr, Eleanor. *Mieko and the Fifth Treasure* [3-4], **707**

Cohen, Barbara. *Thank You, Jackie Robinson* [4-5], 1159

Cole, Joanna. *Don't Call Me Names* [K-1], **254**

Cole, Joanna, and Philip Cole. *Big Goof and Little Goof* [K-1], 373

Conford, Ellen. *Me and the Terrible Two* [4-5], 1161

Conly, Jane Leslie. *Crazy Lady!* [5-6], **808**

Coville, Bruce. *Jennifer Murdley's Toad* [4-5], **765**

Crowley, Michael. *New Kid on Spurwink Ave* [K-1], **258**
Shack and Back [1-2], **427**

Danziger, Paula. *Amber Brown Is Not a Crayon* [2-3], **603**

Delton, Judy. *Two Good Friends* [Pre-K], 66

DePaolo, Paula. *Rosie & the Yellow Ribbon* [K-1], **261**

Desbarats, Peter. *Gabrielle and Selena* [1-2], 659

Duffey, Betsy. *The Math Whiz* [2-3], **607**

Dugan, Barbara. *Loop the Loop* [2-3], **608**

Ellis, Anne. *Dabble Duck* [K-1], 382

Engel, Diana. *Fishing* [K-1], **268**

Erickson, Russell E. *A Toad for Tuesday* [1-2], 665

Fenner, Carol. *Randall's Wall* [5-6], **815**

Fitzhugh, Louise. *Harriet the Spy* [5-6], 1298

Flora, James. *My Friend Charlie* [2-3], 924

Gackenbach, Dick. *What's Claude Doing?* [Pre-K], 101

Garrigue, Sheila. *Between Friends* [4-5], 1175

Getz, David. *Almost Famous* [5-6], **818**

Giff, Patricia Reilly. *Matthew Jackson Meets the Wall* [2-3], **611**
The Winter Worm Business [4-5], 1177

Greene, Bette. *Philip Hall Likes Me. I Reckon, Maybe* [4-5], 1183

Greenfield, Eloise. *Me as Neesie* [K-1], 411

Havill, Juanita. *Jamaica and Brianna* [Pre-K], **119**
Leona and Ike [3-4], **712**

Heide, Florence Parry. *Banana Twist* [5-6], 1310

Henkes, Kevin. *Jessica* [K-1], 418
A Weekend with Wendell [K-1], 420

Herman, Charlotte. *Max Malone Makes a Million* [2-3], **617**

Hesse, Karen. *Lester's Dog* [2-3], **619**
Phoenix Rising [5-6], **821**

Hest, Amy. *The Mommy Exchange* [K-1], 421

Hiller, Catherine. *Abracatabby* [K-1], 424

Hoban, Lillian. *Arthur's Great Big Valentine* [K-1], 426

Hoffman, Mary. *Henry's Baby* [1-2], **454**

Honeycutt, Natalie. *The All New Jonah Twist* [2-3], 934
Juliet Fisher and the Foolproof Plan [2-3], **621**

Howard, Ellen. *A Circle of Giving* [4-5], 1192

Howe, James. *Pinky and Rex and the Spelling Bee* [1-2], **457**

Hurwitz, Johanna. *Russell Sprouts* [1-2], 695

Hutchins, Pat. *My Best Friend* [Pre], **23**

Ikeda, Daisaku. *Over the Deep Blue Sea* [1-2], **460**

James, Betsy. *Mary Ann* [Pre-K], **133**

Johnston, Tony. *Mole and Troll Trim the Tree* [K-1], 442

Joosse, Barbara M. *Wild Willie and King Kyle Detectives* [2-3], **630**

Kasza, Keiko. *The Rat and the Tiger* [Pre-K], **141**

Keats, Ezra Jack. *A Letter to Amy* [K-1], 451

Keller, Beverly. *The Genuine, Ingenious Thrift Shop Genie, Clarissa Mae Bean and Me* [4-5], 1198

King, Larry L. *Because of Loza Brown* [1-2], 710

Kline, Rufus. *Watch Out for Those Weirdos* [1-2], **473**

Kline, Suzy. *Song Lee in Room 2B* [1-2], **476**
What's the Matter with Herbie Jones? [2-3], 949

Komaiko, Leah. *Earl's Too Cool for Me* [1-2], **477**

Korman, Gordon. *This Can't Be Happening at Macdonald Hall* [5-6], 1321

Lester, Helen. *The Wizard, the Fairy and the Magic Chicken* [Pre-K], 185

Leverich, Kathleen. *Best Enemies Again* [2-3], **639**

Lionni, Leo. *Little Blue and Little Yellow* [Pre-K], 191

Lobel, Arnold. *Frog and Toad Are Friends* [K-1], 479

Lowry, Lois. *Number the Stars* [5-6], 1328

MacDonald, Amy. *Little Beaver and the Echo* [Pre-K], **156**

Marshall, James. *The Cut-Ups* [1-2], 743
George and Martha [K-1], 502
The Guest [Pre-K], 203
Three Up a Tree [K-1], 504

Martin, Ann. *Rachel Parker, Kindergarten Show-Off* [K-1], **321**

Masterman-Smith, Virginia. *The Treasure Trap* [4-5], 1212

Mills, Claudia. *After Fifth Grade, the World!* [4-5], 1214

Moore, Lilian. *I'll Meet You at the Cucumbers* [2-3], 967

Nabb, Magdalen. *Josie Smith at School* [1-2], **516**

Naylor, Phyllis Reynolds. *King of the Playground* [K-1], **332**

Park, Barbara. *Maxie, Rosie, and Earl—Partners in Grime* [3-4], **736**
Rosie Swanson, Fourth-Grade Geek for President [3-4], **737**

Paterson, Katherine. *Bridge to Terabithia* [5-6], 1340

Peck, Robert Newton. *Soup and Me* [4-5], 1223

Peet, Bill. *How Droofus the Dragon Lost His Head* [1-2], 769

Peters, Julie Anne. *The Stinky Sneakers Contest* [2-3], **654**

Petersen, P. J. *The Sub* [2-3], **656**

Pfister, Marcus. *The Rainbow Fish* [K-1], **337**

Pinkwater, Daniel. *Doodle Flute* [1-2], **534**

Polacco, Patricia. *Mrs. Katz and Tush* [2-3], **663**
Pink and Say [4-5], **786**

Primavera, Elise. *The Three Dots* [K-1], **342**

Quattlebaum, Mary. *Jackson Jones and the Puddle of Thorns* [4-5], **787**

Radley, Gail. *The Golden Days* [5-6], **838**

Raschka, Chris. *Yo! Yes?* [1-2], **541**

Rodowsky, Colby. *Dog Days* [3-4], **739**

Ross, Pat. *M & M and the Santa Secrets* [1-2], 785

Roy, Ron. *The Chimpanzee Kid* [5-6], 1348

Russo, Marisabina. *Alex Is My Friend* [K-1], **354**

Sachs, Marilyn. *Veronica Ganz* [4-5], 1236

Schotter, Roni. *Captain Snap and the Children of Vinegar Lane* [1-2], 793

Sharmat, Marjorie Weinman. *The Best Valentine in the World* [1-2], 807
Gladys Told Me to Meet Her Here [1-2], 809

Shreve, Susan. *The Gift of the Girl Who Couldn't Hear* [5-6], 841
Joshua T. Bates Takes Charge [3-4], **747**

Shura, Mary Frances. *Chester* [3-4], 1112

Slepian, Jan. *The Broccoli Tapes* [5-6], **844**
Risk N' Roses [5-6], **845**

Slote, Alfred. *My Robot Buddy* [2-3], 1002

Snyder, Zilpha Keatley. *Libby on Wednesday* [5-6], **846**

Speare, Elizabeth George. *The Sign of the Beaver* [5-6], 1363

Spinelli, Eileen. *Somebody Loves You, Mr. Hatch* [K-1], **371**

Spinelli, Jerry. *Fourth Grade Rats* [3-4], **749**
Report to the Principal's Office [4-5], **791**

Stevenson, James. *Happy Valentine's Day, Emma!* [1-2], 823

Thayer, Jane. *The Popcorn Dragon* [Pre-K], 273

Tompert, Ann. *Just a Little Bit* [Pre-K], **192**

Trivas, Irene. *Annie . . . Anya: A Month in Moscow* [K-1], **377**

Tsutsui, Yoriko. *Anna's Secret Friend* [Pre-K], 275

Ungerer, Tomi. *The Beast of Monsieur Racine* [2-3], 1018

Vollmer, Dennis. *Joshua Disobeys* [Pre-K], **198**

Waber, Bernard. *I Was All Thumbs* [2-3], 1023
Ira Says Goodbye [1-2], 841
Ira Sleeps Over [1-2], 842

Wells, Rosemary. *Timothy Goes to School* [K-1], 587

Winthrop, Elizabeth. *Lizzy & Harold* [K-1], 594

Wolkstein, Diane. *Step by Step* [Pre-K], **211**

FRIENDSHIP–Folklore

Yep, Laurence. *The Banza: A Haitian Story* [Pre-2], 1629
The Junior Thunder Lord [1-4], **1046**

FRIENDSHIP–Poetry

Grimes, Nikki. *Meet Danitra Brown* [3-5], **1302**

Hopkins, Lee Bennett. *Best Friends* [1-4], 1818

Prelutsky, Jack. *Rolling Harvey Down the Hill* [2-4], 1919

FROGS

SEE ALSO Reptiles; Toads

Bancroft, Catherine, and Hannah Coale Gruenberg. *Felix's Hat* [Pre-K], **70**

Cole, Joanna. *Don't Call Me Names* [K-1], **254**

Devlin, Harry, and Wende Devlin. *Old Witch Rescues Halloween* [1-2], 661

Duke, Kate. *Seven Froggies Went to School* [K-1], 377

Griffith, Helen V. *Emily and the Enchanted Frog* [1-2], **446**

Gwynne, Fred. *Pondlarker* [1-2], **447**

Kalan, Robert. *Jump, Frog, Jump* [Pre-K], 160

Langstaff, John. *Frog Went a-Courtin'* [Pre-K], 179

Lionni, Leo. *Fish Is Fish* [K-1], 474

It's Mine! [Pre-K], 190

Lobel, Arnold. *Frog and Toad Are Friends* [K-1], 479

London, Jonathan. *Froggy Gets Dressed* [Pre-K], **152**

Let's Go, Froggy [Pre-K], **153**

Napoli, Donna Jo. *The Prince of the Pond: Otherwise Known as De Fawg Pin* [4-5], **782**

Pfeffer, Wendy. *From Tadpole to Frog* [Pre-1], **1219**

Primavera, Elise. *The Three Dots* [K-1], **342**

Scieszka, Jon. *The Frog Prince Continued* [2-3], **676**

Seeger, Pete, and Charles Seeger. *The Foolish Frog* [1-2], 797

Teague, Mark. *Frog Medicine* [2-3], **681**

Vesey, A. *The Princess and the Frog* [1-2], 837

Walsh, Ellen Stoll. *Hop Jump* [Pre], **53**

Wiesner, David. *Tuesday* [K-1], **385**

FROGS–Folklore

Climo, Shirley. *The Match Between the Winds* [K-3], **879**

Grimm, Jacob. *The Frog Prince* [K-3], 1493

The Frog Prince: Or Iron Henry [1-4], **932**

Hamanaka, Sheila. *Screen of Frogs: An Old Tale* [K-3], **934**

Isele, Elizabeth. *The Frog Princess* [2-5], 1534

Lewis, J. Patrick. *The Frog Princess: A Russian Tale* [2-6], **969**

Mollel, Tololwa M. *Rhinos for Lunch and Elephants for Supper!* [Pre-2], **991**

FRONTIER AND PIONEER LIFE

Adler, David A. *Wild Pill Hickok and Other Old West Riddles* [2-5], 1741

Brink, Carol Ryrie. *Caddie Woodlawn* [4-5], 1151

Cox, David. *Bossyboots* [1-2], 655

DeFelice, Cynthia. *Weasel* [5-6], **812**

Gipson, Fred. *Old Yeller* [4-5], 1180

Isaacs, Anne. *Swamp Angel* [2-3], **625**

Kellogg, Steven. *Johnny Appleseed* [1-4], 2058

Kinsey-Warnock, Natalie. *Wilderness Cat* [1-2], **470**

Kirby, Susan. *Ike and Porker* [4-5], 1200

MacLachlan, Patricia. *Sarah, Plain and Tall* [3-4], 1094

Nixon, Joan Lowery. *Beats Me, Claude* [2-3], 971

That's the Spirit, Claude [2-3], **650**

Russell, Marion. *Along the Santa Fe Trail: Marion Russell's Own Story* [2-5], **1230**

Sanders, Scott Russell. *Here Comes the Mystery Man* [2-3], **673**

Warm as Wool [1-2], **546**

Speare, Elizabeth George. *The Sign of the Beaver* [5-6], 1363

Spray, Carole. *The Mare's Egg: A New World Folk Tale* [2-5], 1604

Van Leeuwen, Jean. *Bound for Oregon* [4-5], **793**

Waterton, Betty. *Petranella* [1-2], 845

Whiteley, Opal. *Only Opal: The Diary of a Young Girl* [2-5], **1253**

Wilder, Laura Ingalls. *Little House in the Big Woods* [2-3], 1028

Williams, David. *Grandma Essie's Covered Wagon* [2-3], **691**

Woodruff, Elvira. *Dear Levi: Letters from the Overland Trail* [4-5], **796**

FRUIT

SEE ALSO Cookery; Food; Pies; Vegetables

Barton, Byron. *Applebet Story* [K-1], 331

Brimner, Larry Dane. *Country Bear's Good Neighbor* [Pre-K], 27

Charles, N. N. *What Am I? Looking Through Shapes at Apples and Grapes* [Pre-K], **84**

Dahl, Roald. *James and the Giant Peach* [3-4], 1059

Degen, Bruce. *Jamberry* [Pre-K], 64

Ehlert, Lois. *Eating the Alphabet: Fruits and Vegetables from A to Z* [Pre-K], 77

Gantos, Jack. *Greedy Greeny* [Pre-K], 109

McCloskey, Robert. *Blueberries for Sal* [Pre-K], 194

Lentil [2-3], 956

McMillan, Bruce. *Growing Colors* [Pre-K], 197

Priceman, Marjorie. *How to Make an Apple Pie and See the World* [1-2], **538**

Van Allsburg, Chris. *The Sweetest Fig* [3-4], **751**

Williams, Vera B. *Cherries and Cherry Pits* [1-2], 852

Wood, Don, and Audrey Wood. *The Little Mouse, the Red Ripe Strawberry, and the Big Hungry Bear* [Pre], **60**

Zolotow, Charlotte. *Mr. Rabbit and the Lovely Present* [Pre-K], 310

FRUIT–Folklore

Bruchac, Joseph. *The First Strawberries: A Cherokee Story* [K-3], **870**

Early, Margaret. *William Tell* [2-6], **900**

Greene, Ellin. *The Legend of the Cranberry: A Paleo-Indian Tale* [1-4], **919**

Kellogg, Steven. *Johnny Appleseed* [1-4], 2058

Kimmel, Eric A. *Anansi and the Talking Melon* [Pre-2], **949**

 Three Sacks of Truth: A Story from France [2-5], **958**

Lottridge, Celia Barker. *The Name of the Tree: A Bantu Folktale* [Pre-2], **973**

Martin, Rafe. *Foolish Rabbit's Big Mistake* [Pre-2], 1564

Mayer, Marianna. *Iduna and the Magic Apples* [4-6], 1567

Say, Allen. *Once Under the Cherry Blossom Tree: An Old Japanese Tale* [1-4], 1592

Small, Terry. *The Legend of William Tell* [3-5], **1028**

Waldherr, Kris. *Persephone and the Pomegranate: A Myth from Greece* [2-6], **1041**

FRUIT–Riddles

Keller, Charles. *Alexander the Grape: Fruit and Vegetable Jokes* [2-6], 1834

FUNERALS

Thomas, Jane Resh. *Saying Good-Bye to Grandma* [2-3], **683**

FURNITURE

Seligson, Susan. *Amos Camps Out: A Couch Adventure in the Woods* [1-2], **549**

GAMES

 SEE ALSO Play; Word games

Asch, Frank. *Moongame* [Pre-K], 14

Ball, Duncan. *Jeremy's Tail* [K-1], **227**

Brandreth, Gyles. *Brain-Teasers and Mind-Benders* [3-6], 1997

Brown, Marc. *Hand Rhymes* [Pre-2], 1760

Churchill, E. Richard. *Devilish Bets to Trick Your Friends* [3-6], 2005

Cole, Joanna, and Stephanie Calmenson. *The Eentsy, Weentsy Spider: Fingerplays and Action Rhymes* [Pre-2], **1279**

Delamar, Gloria T. *Children's Counting Out Rhymes, Fingerplays, Jump-Rope and Bounce-Ball Chants and Other Rhymes: A Comprehensive English-Language Reference* [Pre-3], 1788

Gryski, Camilla. *Cat's Cradle, Owl's Eyes: A Book of String Games* [2-6], 2044

Heide, Florence Parry. *The Shrinking of Treehorn* [3-4], 1071

Major, Beverly. *Playing Sardines* [1-2], 741

Parkinson, Kathy. *The Farmer in the Dell* [Pre-K], 223

Rae, Mary Maki. *The Farmer in the Dell: A Singing Game* [Pre-K], 234

Stevenson, James. *The Mud Flat Olympics* [1-2], **557**

Van Allsburg, Chris. *Jumanji* [2-3], 1020

White, Laurence B., Jr., and Ray Broekel. *The Surprise Book* [2-6], 2114

Wisniewski, David. *Rain Player* [2-3], **694**

Wood, Don, and Audrey Wood. *Piggies* [Pre], **59**

GARDENING

Bunting, Eve. *Flower Garden* [Pre-K], **72**

Ehlert, Lois. *Growing Vegetable Soup* [Pre-K], 78

Krauss, Ruth. *The Carrot Seed* [Pre-K], 178

Quattlebaum, Mary. *Jackson Jones and the Puddle of Thorns* [4-5], **787**

GARDENING–Folklore

Stevens, Janet. *Tops & Bottoms* [Pre-2], **1030**

GARDENS

 SEE ALSO Flowers; Plants; Trees; Vegetables

Lobel, Arnold. *The Rose in My Garden* [K-1], 485

Potter, Beatrice. *The Tale of Peter Rabbit* [K-1], 528

GARGOYLES

Bunting, Eve. *Night of the Gargoyles* [3-4], **705**

GEESE

 SEE ALSO Birds; Chickens; Ducks; Owls; Parrots; Roosters

Auch, Mary Jane. *Bird Dogs Can't Fly* [K-1], **219**

Bang, Molly. *Dawn* [2-3], 869

Duvoisin, Roger. *Petunia* [K-1], 378

Fleming, Denise. *Barnyard Banter* [Pre], **12**

Galdone, Joanna, and Paul Galdone. *Gertrude the Goose Who Forgot* [Pre-K], 107

Gerstein, Mordicai. *Follow Me!* [Pre-K], 112

King-Smith, Dick. *The Cuckoo Child* [3-4], **722**

GEESE (cont.)

Preston, Edna Mitchell. *Squawk to the Moon, Little Goose* [Pre-K], 233

Ryder, Joanne. *Catching the Wind* [Pre-3], 2088

Silverman, Erica. *Don't Fidget a Feather!* [K-1], **365**

Yolen, Jane. *Honkers* [K-1], **391**

GEESE–Folklore

Arnold, Katya. *Baba Yaga: A Russian Folktale* [1-3], **860**

Cauley, Lorinda Bryan. *The Goose and the Golden Coins* [K-1], 1416

Conover, Chris. *Mother Goose and the Sly Fox* [Pre-1], 1428

GENEALOGY

Greenwald, Sheila. *Rosy Cole Discovers America!* [3-4], **711**

GENEROSITY

Ernst, Lisa Campbell. *Zinnia and Dot* [K-1], **271**

Hughes, Shirley. *Giving* [Pre], **22**

Johnston, Tony. *Slither McCreep and His Brother Joe* [K-1], **294**

Lionni, Leo. *Tico and the Golden Wings* [2-3], 952

Pfister, Marcus. *The Rainbow Fish* [K-1], **337**

Pinkwater, Daniel. *Doodle Flute* [1-2], **534**

Roth, Roger. *The Sign Painter's Dream* [1-2], **545**

Seuss, Dr. *Thidwick, the Big-Hearted Moose* [1-2], 806

Tolan, Stephanie S. *Sophie and the Sidewalk Man* [2-3], **685**

GENEROSITY–Folklore

Grimm, Jacob. *One Gift Deserves Another* [1-4], **927**

Roddy, Patricia. *Api and the Boy Stranger: A Village Creation Tale* [K-2], **1006**

GENIES

Balian, Lorna. *The Sweet Touch* [K-1], 329

GENIES–Folklore

Carrick, Carol. *Aladdin and the Wonderful Lamp* [2-4], 1413

Lang, Andrew. *Aladdin and the Wonderful Lamp* [2-5], 1544

Mayer, Marianna. *Aladdin and the Enchanted Lamp* [4-6], 1565

GEOGRAPHY

Baer, Edith. *This Is the Way We Go to School: A Book About Children Around the World* [K-1], **226**

Ball, Duncan. *Jeremy's Tail* [K-1], **227**

Brisson, Pat. *Magic Carpet* [1-2], **411**

Bursik, Rose. *Amelia's Fantastic Flight* [1-2], **417**

Clements, Andrew. *Mother Earth's Counting Book* [K-5], **1118**

Lasky, Kathryn. *The Librarian Who Measured the Earth* [3-6], **1180**

Lobel, Anita. *Away from Home* [1-2], **487**

Meltzer, Maxine. *Pups Speak Up* [K-1], **324**

Peet, Bill. *Chester the Worldly Pig* [2-3], 975

Priceman, Marjorie. *How to Make an Apple Pie and See the World* [1-2], **538**

Schneider, Howie. *Uncle Lester's Hat* [K-1], **357**

Sheldon, Dyan. *Love, Your Bear Pete* [K-1], **363**

Singer, Marilyn. *Nine O'Clock Lullaby* [1-2], **554**

GEOGRAPHY–Riddles

Gerberg, Mort. *Geographunny: A Book of Global Riddles* [3-6], **1295**

Maestro, Marco, and Giulio Maestro. *Riddle City, USA! A Book of Geography Riddles* [3-6], **1368**

GEOLOGY

SEE ALSO Mountains

Cole, Joanna. *The Magic School Bus Inside the Earth* [2-4], 2009

dePaola, Tomie. *The Quicksand Book* [1-4], 2019

Hiscock, Bruce. *The Big Rock* [1-4], 2050

McNulty, Faith. *How to Dig a Hole to the Other Side of the World* [1-4], 2072

Peters, Lisa Westberg. *The Sun, the Wind and the Rain* [Pre-2], 2082

Simon, Seymour. *Volcanoes* [2-6], 2106

GEOMETRY

Rogers, Paul. *The Shapes Game* [Pre-K], **181**

Skofield, James. *'Round and Around* [Pre-K], **188**

Tompert, Ann. *Grandfather Tang's Story* [1-2], **567**

GERBILS

Swallow, Pam. *Melvil and Dewey in the Chips* [2-3], 1012

GERMANY

Skurzynski, Gloria. *What Happened to Hamelin* [5-6], 1358

GHOST STORIES

Ainsworth, Ruth. *The Phantom Carousel and Other Ghostly Tales* [4-5], 1138

Cecil, Laura. *Boo! Stories to Make You Jump* [1-4], **1062**

Corbett, Scott. *The Red Room Riddle* [4-5], 1164

DeFelice, Cynthia C. *The Dancing Skeleton* [2-4], 1437

Flora, James. *Grandpa's Ghost Stories* [2-3], 919

Galdone, Joanna. *The Tailypo: A Ghost Story* [2-4], 1456

Goode, Diane. *Diane Goode's Book of Scary Stories & Songs* [2-4], **1068**

Hahn, Mary Downing. *Time for Andrew: A Ghost Story* [5-6], **820**

Hamcock, Sibyl. *Esteban and the Ghost* [2-4], 1518

Harper, Wilhelmina. *Ghosts and Goblins: Stories for Halloween* [2-5], 1690

Hodges, Margaret. *Hauntings: Ghosts and Ghouls from Around the World* [4-6], **1072**

Jennings, Paul. *Unreal! Eight Surprising Stories* [5-6], **825**

Leach, Maria. *The Thing at the Foot of the Bed and Other Scary Tales* [2-6], 1704

Lindgren, Astrid. *The Ghost of Skinny Jack* [3-4], 1089

Pepper, Dennis. *The Oxford Book of Scary Stories* [5-6], **836**

Salway, Lance. *A Nasty Piece of Work and Other Ghost Stories* [5-6], 1351

San Souci, Robert D. *The Boy and the Ghost* [1-4], **1011**

Schwartz, Alvin. *Scary Stories 3: More Tales to Chill Your Bones* [4-6], **1086**

Scary Stories to Tell in the Dark [4-6], 1725

Wolkstein, Diane. *The Legend of Sleepy Hollow* [4-5], **795**

Yep, Laurence. *The Man Who Tricked a Ghost* [1-4], **1047**

Young, Richard and Judy Dockrey Young. *Favorite Scary Stories of American Children* [3-6], **1093**

GHOSTS

SEE ALSO Halloween; Supernatural; Witches; Wizards

Brooks, Walter Rollin. *Jimmy Takes Vanishing Lessons* [2-3], 876

Cassedy, Sylvia. *Behind the Attic Wall* [5-6], 1287

Cohen, Caron Lee. *Renata, Whizbrain and the Ghost* [2-3], 894

Fleischman, Sid. *The Ghost on Saturday Night* [2-3], 918

Haynes, Betsy. *The Ghost of the Gravestone Hearth* [4-5], 1185

Herman, Emily. *Hubknuckles* [1-2], 686

Hoffman, Mary. *The Four-Legged Ghosts* [2-3], **620**

Kroll, Steven. *Amanda and Giggling Ghost* [1-2], 715

Martin, Bill, Jr. *Old Devil Wind* [K-1], **323**

Sherrow, Victoria. *There Goes the Ghost!* [K-1], 557

GHOSTS–Poetry

Wallace, Daisy. *Ghost Poems* [K-4], 1970

GHOSTS–Riddles

Gordon, Jeffie Ross. *Hide and Shriek: Riddles About Ghosts & Goblins* [2-5], **1300**

GIANTS

SEE ALSO Fairies; Leprechauns; Monsters; Ogres; Trolls

Briggs, Raymond. *Jim and the Beanstalk* [1-2], 623

Dahl, Roald. *BFG* [4-5], 1166

Du Bois, William Pène. *The Giant* [5-6], 1294

Green, John F. *Alice and the Birthday Giant* [K-1], 408

Hughes, Ted. *The Iron Giant: A Story in Five Nights* [3-4], 1075

Kennedy, Richard. *Inside My Feet* [5-6], 1318

Scieszka, Jon. *Knights of the Kitchen Table* [3-4], **743**

Thurber, James. *The Great Quillow* [2-3], **684**

Wetterer, Margaret. *The Giant's Apprentice* [3-4], 1130

GIANTS–Folklore

Cauley, Lorinda Bryan. *Jack and the Beanstalk* [1-3], 1417

Climo, Shirley. *Stolen Thunder: A Norse Myth* [3-6], **880**

Compton, Kenn, and Joanne Compton. *Jack the Giant Chaser: An Appalachian Tale* [1-4], **884**

dePaola, Tomie. *Fin M'Coul, the Giant of Knockmary Hill* [1-4], 1439

The Mysterious Giant of Barletta: An Italian Folktale [1-4], 1442

Fisher, Leonard Everett. *Cyclops* [4-6], **904**

Galdone, Paul. *The History of Mother Twaddle and the Marvelous Achievements of Her Son, Jack* [K-3], 1462

Garner, Alan. *Jack and the Beanstalk* [1-4], **910**

Greene, Ellin. *Billy Beg and His Bull* [2-4], **918**

Grimm, Jacob. *The Valiant Little Tailor* [1-4], 1510

Haley, Gail E. *Jack and the Bean Tree* [1-4], 1515

Howe, John. *Jack and the Beanstalk* [1-3], **944**

Langton, Jane. *Salt: A Russian Folktale* [2-5], **963**

Mayer, Marianna. *Iduna and the Magic Apples* [4-6], 1567

Pearson, Susan. *Jack and the Beanstalk* [K-4], 1577

Sloat, Teri. *The Hungry Giant of the Tundra* [K-2], **1027**

Still, James. *Jack and the Wonder Beans* [2-4], 1612

Thomson, Peggy. *The Brave Little Tailor* [1-4], **1035**

GIFTS

Asch, Frank. *Happy Birthday, Moon* [Pre-K], 12

GIFTS (cont.)

Barrett, Judi. *Benjamin's 365 Birthdays* [K-1], 330

Bunting, Eve. *The Mother's Day Mice* [Pre-K], 32

Carle, Eric. *The Secret Birthday Message* [Pre-K], 40

Flack, Marjorie. *Ask Mr. Bear* [Pre-K], 87

Gay, Michael. *The Christmas Wolf* [K-1], 404

Haywood, Carolyn. *A Christmas Fantasy* [K-1], 416

Houston, Gloria. *The Year of the Perfect Christmas Tree* [1-2], 691

Howard, Elizabeth Fitzgerald. *Mac & Marie & the Train Toss Surprise* [1-2], **455**

Hughes, Shirley. *Giving* [Pre], **22**

Keller, Holly. *A Bear for Christmas* [Pre-K], 167

Kraus, Robert. *How Spider Saved Christmas* [K-1], 459

Kroll, Steven. *Happy Mother's Day* [1-2], 717

Lowry, Lois. *Attaboy, Sam!* [4-5], **776**

McCully, Emily Arnold. *The Christmas Gift* [Pre-K], 195

Merriam, Eve. *The Christmas Box* [K-1], 507

Moskin, Marietta. *Rosie's Birthday Present* [K-1], 510

Naylor, Phyllis Reynolds. *Keeping a Christmas Secret* [Pre-K], 216

Regan, Dian Curtis. *The Thirteen Hours of Halloween* [1-2], **544**

Ross, Pat. *M & M and the Santa Secrets* [1-2], 785

Say, Allen. *Tree of Cranes* [1-2], **547**

Seuss, Dr. *How the Grinch Stole Christmas* [1-2], 802

Shannon, George. *The Surprise* [Pre-K], 262

Trivas, Irene. *Emma's Christmas* [2-3], **687**

Van Allsburg, Chris. *The Polar Express* [1-2], 835

Wadsworth, Ginger. *Tomorrow Is Daddy's Birthday* [K-1], **380**

Wetzel, JoAnne Stewart. *The Christmas Box* [K-1], **384**

Zolotow, Charlotte. *Mr. Rabbit and the Lovely Present* [Pre-K], 310

GIFTS–Folklore

Grimm, Jacob. *One Gift Deserves Another* [1-4], **927**

GIRAFFES

Brenner, Barbara. *Mr. Tall and Mr. Small* [K-1], 343

Cowcher, Helen. *Whistling Thorn* [K-2], **1126**

Leslie-Melville, Betty. *Daisy Rothschild: The Giraffe That Lives with Me* [2-6], 2067

Elephant Have the Right of Way: Life with the Wild Animals of Africa [2-6], **1185**

Milton, Nancy. *The Giraffe That Walked to Paris* [2-4], **1208**

Silverstein, Shel. *A Giraffe and a Half* [1-2], 811

GIRAFFES–Folklore

Rosen, Michael. *How the Giraffe Got Such a Long Neck . . . and Why Rhino Is So Grumpy* [Pre-2], **1007**

GLASSES

SEE Eyeglasses

GNOMES

SEE Fairies

GOATS

Sharmat, Mitchell. *Gregory, the Terrible Eater* [K-1], 555

GOATS–Folklore

Galdone, Paul. *The Three Billy Goats Gruff* [Pre-1], 1473

Grimm, Jacob. *Nanny Goat and the Seven Little Kids* [K-2], **924**

The Table, the Donkey and the Stick [1-4], 1507

The Wolf and the Seven Little Kids [Pre-1], 1512

Rounds, Glen. *The Three Billy Goats Gruff* [Pre-2], **1009**

Wolkstein, Diane. *The Banza: A Haitian Story* [Pre-2], 1629

GOBLINS

SEE Fairies

GOBLINS–Folklore

SEE ALSO Fairies; Imps

Levine, Arthur A. *The Boy Who Drew Cats: A Japanese Folktale* [2-6], **968**

McCoy, Karen Kawamoto. *A Tale of Two Tengu: A Japanese Folktale* [Pre-2], **974**

San Souci, Robert D. *The Hobyahs* [K-2], **1013**

Sawyer, Ruth. *The Remarkable Christmas of the Cobbler's Sons* [K-3], **1020**

GORILLAS

SEE ALSO Chimpanzees; Monkeys

Browne, Anthony. *Gorilla* [K-1], 349

Howe, James. *The Day the Teacher Went Bananas* [Pre-K], 142

Patterson, Francine. *Koko's Kitten* [2-6], 2080

GORILLAS–Folklore

Aardema, Verna. *Princess Gorilla and a New Kind of Water* [Pre-2], 1381

GOSSIP

Andersen, Hans Christian. *It's Perfectly True* [1-2], 602

GRAMMAR
SEE English language–Grammar

GRANDFATHERS

Ackerman, Karen. *Song and Dance Man* [1-2], 599

Bahr, Mary. *The Memory Box* [2-3], **589**

Bunting, Eve. *A Day's Work* [2-3], **592**

Byars, Betsy. *The Not-Just-Anybody Family* [4-5], 1156

Caseley, Judith. *Dear Annie* [K-1], **250**

Cazet, Denys. *December 24th* [K-1], 359

dePaola, Tomie. *Tom* [1-2], **431**

Dodds, Siobhan. *Grandpa Bud* [Pre], **9**

Douglass, Barbara. *Good As New* [Pre-K], 72
The Great Town and Country Bicycle Balloon Chase [Pre-K], 73

Engel, Diana. *Fishing* [K-1], **268**

Ernst, Lisa Campbell. *The Luckiest Kid on the Planet* [1-2], **439**

Flora, James. *Grandpa's Ghost Stories* [2-3], 919
Grandpa's Witched-Up Christmas [2-3], 920

Gardiner, John Reynolds. *Stone Fox* [3-4], 1067
Top Secret [5-6], 1303

Geraghty, Paul. *The Hunter* [1-2], **442**

Gray, Nigel. *A Balloon for Grandad* [Pre-K], 121

Greenfield, Eloise. *Grandpa's Face* [K-1], 410

Griffith, Helen V. *Grandaddy's Place* [1-2], 682

Henkes, Kevin. *Margaret & Taylor* [K-1], 419

Hest, Amy. *The Purple Coat* [K-1], 422

Johnson, Dolores. *Your Dad Was Just Like You* [1-2], **463**

Kastner, Jill. *Snake Hunt* [1-2], **465**

Keller, Holly. *Grandfather's Dream* [1-2], **466**

McCully, Emily Arnold. *The Christmas Gift* [Pre-K], 195

McDonald, Megan. *The Potato Man* [1-2], **496**

Nixon, Joan Lowery. *The Gift* [3-4], 1099

Pittman, Helena Clare. *Once When I Was Scared* [1-2], 775

Say, Allen. *Grandfather's Journey* [2-3], **674**

Schwartz, David. *Supergrandpa* [2-3], **675**

Smith, Robert Kimmell. *The War with Grandpa* [3-4], 1115

Stevenson, James. *Brrr!* [K-1], **373**
Could Be Worse [1-2], 822
That Dreadful Day [2-3], 1011
That Terrible Halloween Night [1-2], 824
That's Exactly the Way It Wasn't [1-2], **558**
There's Nothing to Do! [1-2], 825
What's Under My Bed? [1-2], 826

Stolz, Mary. *Storm in the Night* [1-2], 828

Stroud, Virginia A. *Doesn't Fall Off His Horse* [2-3], **680**

Tomey, Ingrid. *Grandfather's Day* [2-3], **686**

Tompert, Ann. *Grandfather Tang's Story* [1-2], **567**

Wallace, Bill. *Beauty* [5-6], 1373

Wallace, Ian. *Chin Chiang and the Dragon Dance* [1-2], 843

Warner, Gertrude Chandler. *The Boxcar Children* [2-3], 1025

Williams, Jay. *The Magic Grandfather* [4-5], 1254

Woodruff, Elvira. *Dear Napoleon, I Know You're Dead, But . . .* [5-6], **852**

GRANDFATHERS–Folklore

Gilman, Phoebe. *Something from Nothing* [Pre-2], **914**

GRANDMOTHERS

Alexander, Martha. *The Story Grandmother Told* [Pre-K], 2

Andersen, Janet S. *The Key into Winter* [2-3], **587**

Balian, Lorna. *Leprechauns Never Lie* [1-2], 609

Booth, Barbara D. *Mandy* [1-2], **408**

Bunting, Eve. *The Wednesday Surprise* [1-2], 633

Byars, Betsy. *The Two-Thousand Pound Goldfish* [5-6], 1283

Carlson, Nancy L. *A Visit to Grandma's* [K-1], **249**

Choi, Sook Nyul. *Halmoni and the Picnic* [1-2], **424**

Cutler, Jane. *Darcy and Gran Don't Like Babies* [K-1], **259**

Dahl, Roald. *The Witches* [4-5], 1167

Daly, Niki. *Not So Fast, Songololo* [Pre-K], 62

Devlin, Harry, and Wende Devlin. *Cranberry Thanksgiving* [1-2], 660

Dorros, Arthur. *Abuela* [1-2], **434**

Edwards, Frank B. *Mortimer Mooner Stopped Taking a Bath* [Pre-K], **94**

Flournoy, Valerie. *The Patchwork Quilt* [2-3], 925

Garland, Sherry. *The Lotus Seed* [2-3], **609**

Guback, Georgia. *Luka's Quilt* [K-1], **278**

Hamilton, Morse. *Little Sister for Sale* [1-2], **450**

Herman, Charlotte. *Our Snowman Had Olive Eyes* [4-5], 1186

Hesse, Karen. *Phoenix Rising* [5-6], **821**

Hirsch, Marilyn. *Potato Pancakes All Around: A Hanukkah Tale* [2-3], 933

Hoffman, Mary. *Amazing Grace* [K-1], **287**

Hutchins, Pat. *Where's the Baby?* [K-1], 435

Khalsa, Dayal Kaur. *Tales of a Gambling Grandma* [3-4], 1084

Konigsburg, E. L. *Amy Elizabeth Explores Bloomingdale's* [1-2], **478**

Lebentritt, Julia, and Richard Ploetz. *The Kooken* [1-2], **481**

GRANDMOTHERS (cont.)

Levine, Evan. *Not the Piano, Mrs. Medley!* [1-2], **483**

Levy, Elizabeth. *Lizzie Lies a Lot* [3-4], 1087

Lexai, Joan. *Benjie* [K-1], 472

Lindgren, Astrid. *The Ghost of Skinny Jack* [3-4], 1089

Mahy, Margaret. *The Rattlebang Picnic* [1-2], **502**

Miles, Miska. *Annie and the Old One* [4-5], 1213

Nodar, Carmen Santiago. *Abuelita's Paradise* [1-2], **519**

Olson, Arielle North. *Hurry Home, Grandma!* [Pre-K], 220

Patrick, Denise Lewis. *Red Dancing Shoes* [Pre-K], **175**

Paulsen, Gary. *The Cookcamp* [5-6], **834**

Polacco, Patricia. *Babushka's Doll* [Pre-K], **176**
My Rotten Redheaded Older Brother [1-2], **536**
Thunder Cake [K-1], 525

Russell, Ching Yeung. *First Apple* [3-4], **741**

Schwartz, Amy. *Oma and Bobo* [K-1], 545

Segal, Lore. *Tell Me a Mitzi* [1-2], 798

Slepian, Jan. *The Broccoli Tapes* [5-6], **844**

Smee, Nicola. *The Tusk Fairy* [Pre], **45**

Thomas, Jane Resh. *Saying Good-Bye to Grandma* [2-3], **683**

Wells, Rosemary. *Good Night, Fred* [Pre-K], 285

Williams, Barbara. *Albert's Toothache* [Pre-K], 296

Williams, David. *Grandma Essie's Covered Wagon* [2-3], **691**

Woodruff, Elvira. *The Summer I Shrank My Grandmother* [4-5], **800**

Zhitkov, Boris. *How I Hunted the Little Fellows* [3-4], 1136

GRANDMOTHERS–Folklore

Baylor, Byrd. *The Best Town in the World* [2-3], 872

Geras, Adèle. *My Grandmother's Stories: A Collection of Jewish Folk Tales* [3-6], **1067**

Grifalconi, Ann. *The Village of Round and Square Houses* [K-4], 1485

Grimm, Jacob. *Little Red Cap* [Pre-2], 1500
Little Red Riding Hood [Pre-2], 1501

Henry, Marguerite. *Misty of Chincoteague* [3-4], 1072

Marshall, James. *Red Riding Hood* [Pre-2], 1562

Mathews, Judith, and Fay Robinson. *Nathaniel Willy, Scared Silly* [Pre-2], **984**

GRANDMOTHERS–Poetry

Livingston, Myra Cohn. *Poems for Grandmothers* [2-6], **1360**

GRANDPARENTS

Bahr, Mary. *The Memory Box* [2-3], **589**

Bawden, Nina. *Humbug* [3-4], **703**

Child, Lydia Maria. *Over the River and Through the Wood: A Song for Thanksgiving* [K-1], **251**

Engel, Diana. *Eleanor, Arthur, and Claire* [K-1], **267**

Hurwitz, Johanna. *Busybody Nora* [1-2], 694
Superduper Teddy [1-2], 696

Rylant, Cynthia. *When I Was Young in the Mountains* [2-3], 989

Yolen, Jane. *Honkers* [K-1], **391**

GRASSHOPPERS

SEE ALSO Insects

Kimmel, Eric A. *Bernal & Florinda: A Spanish Tale* [3-4], **720**

GREECE, ANCIENT

Lasky, Kathryn. *The Librarian Who Measured the Earth* [3-6], **1180**

GREED

Banks, Lynne Reid. *The Adventures of King Midas* [4-5], **758**

Gantos, Jack. *Greedy Greeny* [Pre-K], 109

Kennedy, Richard. *The Lost Kingdom of Karnica* [3-4], 1082

Kimmel, Eric A. *Bernal & Florinda: A Spanish Tale* [3-4], **720**

Mahy, Margaret. *The Great White Man-Eating Shark: A Cautionary Tale* [1-2], **501**

Manson, Christopher. *The Marvelous Blue Mouse* [2-3], **641**

Mwenye Hadithi. *Hungry Hyena* [K-1], **331**

GREED–Folklore

French, Vivian. *Why the Sea Is Salt* [1-4], **906**

Hewitt, Kathryn. *King Midas and the Golden Touch* [1-4], 1522

Mollel, Tololwa M. *The Flying Tortoise: An Igbo Tale* [K-2], **987**

Onyefulu, Obi. *Chinye: A West African Folk Tale* [K-3], **995**

Uchida, Yoshiko. *The Two Foolish Cats* [Pre-2], 1620

GREEK MYTHOLOGY

SEE Mythology

GROCERY STORES

SEE Shopping; Supermarkets

GUIDE DOGS

Alexander, Sally Hobart. *Mom Can't See Me* [1-4], **1097**
Mom's Best Friend [2-6], **1098**

GUINEA PIGS

Bare, Colleen Stanley. *Guinea Pigs Don't Read Books* [Pre-1], 1991

Duke, Kate. *Guinea Pigs Far and Near* [Pre-K], 75

Springstubb, Tricia. *The Magic Guinea Pig* [Pre-K], 270

Tzannes, Robin. *Professor Puffendorf's Secret Potions* [1-2], **569**

HABITS

Cooney, Nancy Evans. *The Blanket Had to Go* [Pre-K], 55

Donald Says Thumbs Down [Pre-K], 56

Hughes, Shirley. *Alfie Gives a Hand* [Pre-K], 144

Keller, Holly. *Geraldine's Blanket* [Pre-K], 168

Robison, Deborah. *Bye-Bye, Old Buddy* [K-1], 532

HAIKU

Cassedy, Sylvia, and Kunihiro Suetake. *Red Dragonfly on My Shoulder* [2-6], **1278**

Demi. *In the Eyes of the Cat: Japanese Poetry for All Seasons* [2-6], **1284**

Higginson, William J. *Wind in the Long Grass: A Collection of Haiku* [2-6], **1313**

HAIR

Davis, Gibbs. *Katy's First Haircut* [Pre-K], 63

Freeman, Don. *Mop Top* [Pre-K], 94

Haas, Dorothy F. *Tink in a Tangle* [2-3], 929

Mitchell, Margaree King. *Uncle Jed's Barbershop* [2-3], **647**

Nesbit, E. *Melisande* [4-5], 1218

Teague, Mark. *Moog-Moog, Space Barber* [1-2], **563**

HAIR–Folklore

Grimm, Jacob. *Rapunzel* [2-4], **923**

HAITI

Williams, Karen Lynn. *Tap-Tap* [1-2], **576**

HALLOWEEN

SEE ALSO Ghosts; Haunted houses; Supernatural; Witches; Wizards

Adams, Adrienne. *A Woggle of Witches* [Pre-K], 1

Ahlberg, Janet, and Allan Ahlberg. *Funnybones* [K-1], 314

Anderson, Lonzo. *The Halloween Party* [1-2], 605

Asch, Frank. *Popcorn* [Pre-K], 15

Brown, Marc. *Arthur's Halloween* [1-2], 627

Bunting, Eve. *Scary, Scary Halloween* [K-1], 352

Carlson, Natalie Savage. *The Night the Scarecrow Walked* [1-2], 639

Spooky Night [K-1], 357

Christelow, Eileen. *Jerome and the Witchcraft Kids* [K-1], 363

Corbett, Scott. *The Red Room Riddle* [4-5], 1164

Coville, Bruce. *The Monster's Ring* [4-5], 1165

Devlin, Harry, and Wende Devlin. *Old Witch Rescues Halloween* [1-2], 661

Dillon, Barbara. *What's Happened to Harry?* [2-3], 910

Embry, Margaret. *The Blue-Nosed Witch* [2-3], 913

Greene, Carol. *The Thirteen Days of Halloween* [1-2], 681

Hall, Zoe. *It's Pumpkin Time!* [Pre], **18**

Herman, Emily. *Hubknuckles* [1-2], 686

Hooks, William H. *Mean Jake and the Devils* [3-4], 1074

Howe, James. *Scared Silly: A Halloween Treat* [1-2], 693

Johnston, Tony. *The Vanishing Pumpkin* [K-1], 443

Kroll, Steven. *The Candy Witch* [K-1], 462

Low, Alice. *The Witch Who Was Afraid of Witches* [1-2], 731

Marshall, Edward. *Space Case* [1-2], 742

Martin, Bill, Jr. *Old Devil Wind* [K-1], **323**

Meddaugh, Susan. *The Witches' Supermarket* [1-2], **507**

Nolan, Dennis. *Witch Bazooza* [1-2], 762

Regan, Dian Curtis. *The Thirteen Hours of Halloween* [1-2], **544**

Schertle, Alice. *Bill and Google-Eyed Goblins* [1-2], 792

Shute, Linda. *Halloween Party* [1-2], **551**

Silverman, Erica. *Big Pumpkin* [K-1], **364**

Stevenson, James. *That Terrible Halloween Night* [1-2], 824

Stutson, Caroline. *By the Light of the Halloween Moon* [1-2], **561**

Wetterer, Margaret. *The Giant's Apprentice* [3-4], 1130

Williams, Linda. *The Little Old Lady Who Was Not Afraid of Anything* [K-1], 591

Wojciechowski, Susan. *The Best Halloween of All* [1-2], **579**

HALLOWEEN–Folklore

Barth, Edna. *Jack-O'-Lantern* [3-6], 1400

Hamcock, Sibyl. *Esteban and the Ghost* [2-4], 1518

Harper, Wilhelmina. *Ghosts and Goblins: Stories for Halloween* [2-5], 1690

Yolen, Jane. *Tam Lin* [3-6], **1048**

HALLOWEEN–Poetry

Brewton, John E., Lorraine A. Blackburn, and George M. Blackburn, III. *In the Witch's Kitchen: Poems for Halloween* [K-3], 1757

HALLOWEEN–Poetry (cont.)

Brewton, Sara, and John E. Brewton. *Shrieks at Midnight: Macabre Poems, Eerie and Humorous* [4-6], 1758

Evans, Dilys. *Monster Soup and Other Spooky Poems* [1-5], **1288**

Hopkins, Lee Bennett. *Ragged Shadows: Poems of Halloween Night* [1-4], **1325**

Livingston, Myra Cohn. *Halloween Poems* [2-5], **1357**

Merriam, Eve. *Halloween ABC* [3-6], **1372**

Moore, Lillian. *See My Lovely Poison Ivy: And Other Verses about Witches, Ghosts and Things* [K-3], 1875

Prelutsky, Jack. *It's Halloween* [Pre-3], 1906
Nightmares: Poems to Trouble Your Sleep [3-6], 1912

Wallace, Daisy. *Ghost Poems* [K-4], 1970

Yolen, Jane. *Best Witches: Poems for Halloween* [3-6], **1428**

HALLOWEEN–Riddles

Brown, Marc. *Spooky Riddles* [K-3], 1761

Keller, Charles. *Count Draculations! Monsters Riddles* [2-6], 1836

Maestro, Giulio. *More Halloween Howls: Riddles That Come Back to Haunt You* [2-5], **1367**

Rosenbloom, Joseph. *Spooky Riddles and Jokes* [2-6], 1937

HAMSTERS

Baker, Alan. *Benjamin's Book* [K-1], 325
Benjamin's Portrait [K-1], 326

Byars, Betsy. *Wanted . . . Mud Blossom* [4-5], **763**

HANDICAPS

SEE ALSO Asthma; Blind; Deaf; Down's syndrome; Mental retardation; Spina bifida

Alexander, Sally Hobart. *Mom Can't See Me* [1-4], **1097**
Mom's Best Friend [2-6], **1098**

Baldwin, Ann Norris. *A Little Time* [4-5], 1140

Booth, Barbara D. *Mandy* [1-2], **408**

Byars, Betsy. *The Summer of the Swans* [5-6], 1282

Callen, Larry. *Sorrow's Song* [5-6], 1286

Calmenson, Stephanie. *Rosie: A Visiting Dog's Story* [1-4], **1116**

Carlson, Nancy L. *Arnie and the New Kid* [1-2], **421**

Conly, Jane Leslie. *Crazy Lady!* [5-6], 808

Cowen-Fletcher, Jane. *Mama Zooms* [Pre-K], **89**

Cross, Helen Reader. *The Real Tom Thumb* [3-6], 2011

Damrell, Liz. *With the Wind* [1-2], **429**

Dodds, Bill. *My Sister Annie* [4-5], **768**

Fleischman, Paul. *The Half-a-Moon Inn* [5-6], 1299

Garfield, James B. *Follow My Leader* [4-5], 1174

Garrigue, Sheila. *Between Friends* [4-5], 1175

Getz, David. *Thin Air* [5-6], **819**

Hesse, Karen. *Lester's Dog* [2-3], **619**

Howard, Ellen. *A Circle of Giving* [4-5], 1192

Hunter, Edith Fisher. *Child of the Silent Night: The Story of Laura Bridgman* [3-5], 2053

Little, Jean. *From Anna* [4-5], 775
Little by Little: A Writer's Education [5-6], **1187**

Osofsky, Audrey. *My Buddy* [1-2], **526**

Rabe, Berniece. *The Balancing Girl* [K-1], 530

Russo, Marisabina. *Alex Is My Friend* [K-1], **354**

Shreve, Susan. *The Gift of the Girl Who Couldn't Hear* [5-6], **841**

Shyer, Marlene Fanta. *Welcome Home, Jellybean* [5-6], 1357

Slepian, Jan. *Risk N' Roses* [5-6], **845**

Springer, Nancy. *Colt* [4-5], **792**

Whelan, Gloria. *Hannah* [2-3], **689**

White, E. B. *The Trumpet of the Swan* [4-5], 1253

HANDS

Gryski, Camilla. *Hands On, Thumbs Up: Secret Handshakes, Fingerprints, Sign Languages, and More Handy Ways to Have Fun with Hands* [3-6], **1154**

Izen, Marshall, and Jim West. *Why the Willow Weeps: A Story Told with Hands* [1-2], **461**

HANUKKAH

Hirsch, Marilyn. *Potato Pancakes All Around: A Hanukkah Tale* [2-3], 933

Jaffe, Nina. *In the Month of Kislev: A Story for Hanukkah* [2-3], **627**

Kimmel, Eric A. *Asher and the Capmakers: A Hanukkah Story* [2-3], **635**
The Chanukkah Guest [K-1], **298**
Hershel and the Hanukkah Goblins [2-3], 944

HARES

SEE ALSO Rabbits

Banks, Lynne Reid. *The Magic Hare* [3-4], **702**

Mwenye Hadithi. *Baby Baboon* [Pre], **37**

HARES–Folklore

SEE ALSO Rabbits–Folklore

Bernhard, Emery. *How Snowshoe Hare Rescued the Sun: A Tale from the Arctic* [K-3], **866**

Knutson, Barbara. *Sungura and Leopard: A Swahili Trickster Tale* [K-3], **960**

Stevens, Janet. *Tops & Bottoms* [Pre-2], **1030**

HARMONICAS

SEE ALSO Musical instruments

Steig, William. *Zeke Pippin* [2-3], **678**

Tomey, Ingrid. *Grandfather's Day* [2-3], **686**

Yorinks, Arthur. *Whitefish Will Rides Again!* [1-2], **581**

HATS

Bancroft, Catherine, and Hannah Coale Gruenberg. *Felix's Hat* [Pre-K], **70**

Brenner, Martha. *Abe Lincoln's Hat* [1-4], **1110**

Christelow, Eileen. *Olive and the Magic Hat* [K-1], 365

Dyke, John. *Pigwig* [K-1], 379

Geringer, Laura. *A Three Hat Day* [Pre-K], 111

Keats, Ezra Jack. *Jennie's Hat* [K-1], 450

Marzollo, Jean. *Ten Cats Have Hats: A Counting Book* [Pre-K], **162**

Miller, Margaret. *Whose Hat?* [Pre-K], 212

Nodset, Joan L. *Who Took the Farmer's Hat?* [Pre-K], 219

Schneider, Howie. *Uncle Lester's Hat* [K-1], **357**

Seuss, Dr. *The 500 Hats of Bartholomew Cubbins* [2-3], **995**

Slobodkina, Esphyr. *Caps for Sale* [Pre-K], 269

Smath, Jerry. *A Hat So Simple* [K-1], **367**

Smith, William Jay. *Ho for a Hat!* [K-1], **368**

Williams, Karen Lynn. *Tap-Tap* [1-2], **576**

HATS–Folklore

Tompert, Ann. *Bamboo Hats and a Rice Cake: A Tale Adapted from Japanese Folklore* [K-3], **1036**

HAUNTED HOUSES

Brooks, Walter Rollin. *Jimmy Takes Vanishing Lessons* [2-3], 876

Brown, Marc. *Arthur's Halloween* [1-2], 627

Stevenson, James. *That Terrible Halloween Night* [1-2], 824

HAUNTED HOUSES–Folklore

San Souci, Robert D. *The Boy and the Ghost* [1-4], **1011**

HAWAII

Guback, Georgia. *Luka's Quilt* [K-1], **278**

Rattigan, Jama Kim. *Dumpling Soup* [K-1], **349**

Stanley, Fay. *The Last Princess: The Story of Princess Ka'iulani of Hawai'i* [4-6], **1243**

HEDGEHOGS

Turner, Ann. *Hedgehog for Breakfast* [Pre-K], **194**

Waddell, Martin. *The Happy Hedgehog Band* [Pre], **48**

HELPFULNESS

Gackenbach, Dick. *Claude Has a Picnic* [Pre], **16**

Gretz, Susanna. *It's Your Turn, Roger!* [K-1], 412

Lasker, Joe. *The Do-Something Day* [K-1], 464

McPhail, David. *Pig Pig Gets a Job* [K-1], **318**

Offen, Hilda. *Nice Work, Little Wolf!* [Pre-K], **173**

Peet, Bill. *The Ant and the Elephant* [K-1], 521

HELPFULNESS–Folklore

Renberg, Dalia Hardof. *King Solomon and the Bee* [K-3], **1001**

HERMIT CRABS

Carle, Eric. *A House for Hermit Crab* [K-1], **246**

McDonald, Megan. *Is This a House for Hermit Crab?* [K-1], **313**

HEROES

Brown, Walter R., and Norman D. Anderson. *Rescue! True Stories of Winners of the Young American Medal for Bravery* [3-6], 2004

Williams, Gurney. *True Escape and Survival Stories* [4-6], 2115

HIBERNATION

Bunting, Eve. *The Valentine Bears* [K-1], 353

Freeman, Don. *Bearymore* [K-1], 391

Lemieux, Michele. *What's That Noise* [Pre-K], 184

Ryder, Joanne. *Chipmunk Song* [Pre-2], 2089

HICCUPS

Mueller, Virginia. *Monster's Birthday Hiccups* [Pre], **36**

HIPPOPOTAMUS

Brown, Marcia. *How, Hippo!* [Pre-K], 28

Hiskey, Iris. *Hannah the Hippo's No Mud Day* [Pre-K], **124**

Mahy, Margaret. *The Boy Who Was Followed Home* [1-2], 739

Marshall, James. *George and Martha* [K-1], 502

Martin, Bill, Jr. *The Happy Hippopotami* [K-1], **322**

Most, Bernard. *Hippopotamus Hunt* [1-2], **513**

Parker, Nancy Winslow. *Love from Uncle Clyde* [K-1], 518

Tyler, Linda Wagner. *Waiting for Mom* [Pre-K], 276

Waber, Bernard. *"You Look Ridiculous," Said the Rhinoceros to the Hippopotamus* [K-1], 580

HISPANIC AMERICANS

Dorros, Arthur. *Abuela* [1-2], **434**

Hurwitz, Johanna. *Class President* [3-4], **715**

Kuklin, Susa. *How My Family Lives in America* [K-3], **1178**

Lomas Garza, Carmen. *Family Pictures / Cuadros de Familia* [1-4], **1192**

Nodar, Carmen Santiago. *Abuelita's Paradise* [1-2], **519**

HISTORICAL FICTION

Accorsi, William. *Friendship's First Thanksgiving* [K-1], **216**

Avi. *The Fighting Ground* [5-6], 1267
Night Journeys [5-6], 1268
The True Confessions of Charlotte Doyle [5-6], **803**

Bartone, Elisa. *Peppe the Lamplighter* [1-2], **405**

Beatty, Patricia. *That's One Ornery Orphan* [5-6], 1274

Brady, Esther Wood. *Toliver's Secret* [4-5], 1148

Brenner, Barbara. *A Year in the Life of Rosie Bernard* [4-5], 1149

Brink, Carol Ryrie. *Caddie Woodlawn* [4-5], 1151

Bulla, Clyde Robert. *The Sword in the Tree* [2-3], 877

Burch, Robert. *Ida Early Comes Over the Mountain* [4-5], 1153

Christiansen, Candace. *The Ice Horse* [2-3], **597**

Coerr, Eleanor. *Mieko and the Fifth Treasure* [3-4], **707**

Cole, Sheila. *The Dragon in the Cliff: A Novel Based on the Life of Mary Anning* [5-6], **807**

Collier, James Lincoln, and Christopher Collier. *My Brother Sam Is Dead* [5-6], 1288

Conrad, Pam. *Pedro's Journal: A Voyage with Christopher Columbus, August 3, 1492–February 14, 1492* [5-6], **809**

Cooney, Barbara. *Island Boy* [3-4], 1055

DeFelice, Cynthia. *Lostman's River* [5-6], **811**
Weasel [5-6], **812**

Doherty, Berlie. *Street Child* [5-6], **813**

Dorris, Michael. *Morning Girl* [5-6], **814**

Fife, Dale. *North of Danger* [5-6], 1296

Fitzgerald, John D. *The Great Brain* [4-5], 1171

Fleischman, Sid. *By the Great Horn Spoon* [5-6], 1300

Gauch, Patricia Lee. *This Time, Tempe Wick?* [2-3], 926

Greer, Gery, and Bob Ruddick. *Max and Me and the Time Machine* [5-6], 1306
Max and Me and the Wild West [5-6], 1307

Harness, Cheryl. *Three Young Pilgrims* [2-3], **614**

Holland, Isabelle. *Behind the Lines* [5-6], **824**

Hurmence, Belinda. *A Girl Called Boy* [5-6], 1314

Johnson, Dolores. *Now Let Me Fly: The Story of a Slave Family* [2-3], **629**

Kalman, Esther. *Tchaikovsky Discovers America* [2-3], **632**

King-Smith, Dick. *The Swoose* [3-4], **727**

Kinsey-Warnock, Natalie. *The Bear That Heard Crying* [1-2], **468**
Wilderness Cat [1-2], **470**

Kirby, Susan. *Ike and Porker* [4-5], 1200

Lawson, Robert. *Ben and Me* [5-6], 1324

Lowry, Lois. *Number the Stars* [5-6], 1328

McDonald, Megan. *The Great Pumpkin Switch* [1-2], **495**
The Potato Man [1-2], **496**

MacLachlan, Patricia. *Sarah, Plain and Tall* [3-4], 1094

McSwigan, Marie. *Snow Treasure* [5-6], 1330

Manson, Christopher. *The Marvelous Blue Mouse* [2-3], **641**
Two Travelers [2-3], **642**

Mochizuki, Ken. *Baseball Saved Us* [3-4], **733**

Monjo, F. N. *The Drinking Gourd* [2-3], 966

Mooser, Stephen. *Orphan Jeb at the Massacree* [4-5], 1215

Morpurgo, Michael. *War Horse* [5-6], 1334

Moskin, Marietta. *The Day of the Blizzard* [3-4], 1098

Myers, Anna. *Red-Dirt Jessie* [4-5], **780**

Nichol, Barbara. *Beethoven Lives Upstairs* [4-5], **785**

O'Dell, Scott. *Island of the Blue Dolphins* [5-6], 1339

Paulsen, Gary. *A Christmas Sonata* [5-6], **833**
The Cookcamp [5-6], **834**

Ray, Mary Lynn. *Pianna* [1-2], **542**

Ringgold, Faith. *Aunt Harriet's Underground Railroad in the Sky* [2-3], **670**

Sanders, Scott Russell. *Here Comes the Mystery Man* [2-3], **673**
Warm as Wool [1-2], **546**

Sauer, Julie L. *Fog Magic* [5-6], 1353

Skurzynski, Gloria. *What Happened to Hamelin* [5-6], 1358

Slepian, Jan. *Risk N' Roses* [5-6], **845**

Snyder, Carol. *Ike and Mama and the Once-a-Year Suit* [2-3], 1004

Speare, Elizabeth George. *The Sign of the Beaver* [5-6], 1363

Stevens, Carla. *Lily and Miss Liberty* [2-3], **679**

Stolz, Mary. *Zekmet, the Stone Carver* [4-5], 1244

Streatfeild, Noel. *When the Sirens Wailed* [5-6], 1366

Tews, Susan. *The Gingerbread Doll* [1-2], **565**

Thomas, Jane Resh. *The Princess in the Pigpen* [5-6], 1369

Turkle, Brinton. *The Adventures of Obadiah* [1-2], 834

Uchida, Yoshiko. *Journey Home* [5-6], 1370

Ullman, James Ramsay. *Banner in the Sky* [5-6], 1371

Van Leeuwen, Jean. *Bound for Oregon* [4-5], **793**

Wells, Rosemary. *Waiting for the Evening Star* [3-4], **754**

Whelan, Gloria. *Hannah* [2-3], **689**

Wilder, Laura Ingalls. *Farmer Boy* [3-4], 1132
  Little House in the Big Woods [2-3], 1028
Williams, David. *Grandma Essie's Covered Wagon*
  [2-3], **691**
Williams, Jay, and Raymond Abrashkin. *Danny*
  Dunn, Time Traveler [4-5], 1256
Winter, Jeanette. *Follow the Drinking Gourd* [3-4],
  1134
  Klara's New World [2-3], **693**
Wiseman, David. *Jeremy Visick* [5-6], 1375
Wolitzer, Hilma. *Introducing Shirley Braverman*
  [5-6], 1376
Wolkstein, Diane. *The Legend of Sleepy Hollow*
  [4-5], **795**
Woodruff, Elvira. *Dear Levi: Letters from the*
  Overland Trail [4-5], **796**
  George Washington's Socks [4-5], **798**
Wuorio, Eva-Lis. *Code: Polonaise* [5-6], 1377
Yep, Laurence. *The Star Fisher* [5-6], **854**
Yolen, Jane. *Encounter* [3-4], **756**
Zhitkov, Boris. *How I Hunted the Little Fellows*
  [3-4], 1136

HISTORY–U.S.

SEE U.S.–History

HOLIDAYS

SEE ALSO Christmas; Easter; Halloween;
  Hanukkah; Thanksgiving; Valentine's Day
Brown, Marc. *Arthur's April Fool* [1-2], 625
Carlstrom, Nancy White. *How Do You Say It*
  Today, Jesse Bear? [Pre-K], **76**
Cazet, Denys. *December 24th* [K-1], 359
Cohen, Barbara. *The Carp in the Bathtub* [2-3],
  892
  Make a Wish, Molly [2-3], **598**
George, Jean Craighead. *The First Thanksgiving*
  [1-4], **1147**
Johnson, Crockett. *Will Spring Be Early? or Will*
  Spring Be Late? [K-1], 439
Keller, Holly. *Henry's Fourth of July* [Pre], **26**
Low, Alice. *The Family Read-Aloud Holiday*
  Treasury [1-4], **1362**
Modell, Frank. *Goodbye Old Year, Hello New Year*
  [K-1], 509
Polacco, Patricia. *Tikvah Means Hope* [2-3], **664**
Schertle, Alice. *Jeremy Bean's St. Patrick's Day*
  [K-1], 544
Wallace, Ian. *Chin Chiang and the Dragon Dance*
  [1-2], 843

HOLIDAYS–Poetry

Foster, John. *Let's Celebrate: Festival Poems* [3-6],
  1293

Hopkins, Lee Bennett. *Ring Out, Wild Bells:*
  Poems About Holidays and Seasons [K-5], **1326**
Livingston, Myra Cohn. *Callooh! Callay! Holiday*
  Poems for Young Readers [2-5], 1857
Low, Alice. *The Family Read-Aloud Holiday*
  Treasury [1-4], **1362**

HOLIDAYS–Songs

Quackenbush, Robert. *The Holiday Songbook*
  [Pre-5], 1925

HOMELESSNESS

Barre, Shelley A. *Chive* [5-6], **804**
Bunting, Eve. *Fly Away Home* [1-2], **415**
DiSalvo-Ryan, DyAnne. *Uncle Willie and the*
  Soup Kitchen [1-2], **432**
Doherty, Berlie. *Street Child* [5-6], **813**
Fox, Paula. *Monkey Island* [5-6], **817**
Spinelli, Jerry. *Maniac Magee* [5-6], **847**
Tolan, Stephanie S. *Sophie and the Sidewalk Man*
  [2-3], **685**

HOMESICKNESS

Yolen, Jane. *Honkers* [K-1], **391**

HOMONYMS

SEE English language–Homonyms

HONESTY

SEE ALSO Stealing
Andersen, Hans Christian. *The Emperor's New*
  Clothes: A Fairy Tale [2-3], 863
Arnold, Tedd. *The Signmaker's Assistant* [1-2],
  400
Bawden, Nina. *Humbug* [3-4], **703**
Brink, Carol Ryrie. *The Bad Times of Irma*
  Baumline [4-5], 1150
Bunting, Eve. *A Day's Work* [2-3], **592**
DePaola, Paula. *Rosie & the Yellow Ribbon* [K-1],
  261
Kroll, Steven. *Amanda and Giggling Ghost* [1-2],
  715
Levy, Elizabeth. *Lizzie Lies a Lot* [3-4], 1087
Lexai, Joan. *I'll Tell on You* [1-2], 724
Matsuno, Masako. *A Pair of Red Clogs* [1-2], 747
Naylor, Phyllis Reynolds. *Shiloh* [5-6], **832**
Ness, Evaline. *Sam, Bangs and Moonshine* [1-2],
  757
Peters, Julie Anne. *The Stinky Sneakers Contest*
  [2-3], **654**
Peterson, Esther Allen. *Frederick's Alligator* [1-2],
  773
Sharmat, Marjorie Weinman. *A Big Fat*
  Enormous Lie [K-1], **359**
Soto, Gary. *Too Many Tamales* [K-1], **369**

HONESTY (cont.)

Turkle, Brinton. *The Adventures of Obadiah* [1-2], 834

HONESTY–Folklore

Demi. *The Empty Pot* [K-3], **892**

HORNED TOADS–Folklore

Begay, Shonto. *Ma'ii and Cousin Horned Toad: A Traditional Navajo Story* [K-4], **865**

HORSES

Anderson, Lonzo. *The Ponies of Mykillengi* [2-3], 865

Brady, Irene. *Doodlebug* [1-2], 620

Byars, Betsy. *The Winged Colt of Casa Mia* [3-4], 1048

Christiansen, Candace. *The Ice Horse* [2-3], **597**

Damrell, Liz. *With the Wind* [1-2], **429**

Doherty, Berlie. *Snowy* [K-1], **263**

Farley, Walter. *The Black Stallion* [3-4], 1064

Feagles, Anita. *Casey the Utterly Impossible Horse* [2-3], 916

Gauch, Patricia Lee. *This Time, Tempe Wick?* [2-3], 926

Henry, Marguerite. *Misty of Chincoteague* [3-4], 1072

Herriot, James. *Bonny's Big Day* [2-5], 2047

Houseman, Laurence. *Rocking-Horse Land* [1-2], 690

LeGuin, Ursula K. *A Ride on the Red Mare's Back* [2-3], **637**

Medearis, Angela Shelf. *The Zebra-Riding Cowboy: A Folk Song from the Old West* [2-3], **645**

Morpurgo, Michael. *War Horse* [5-6], 1334

Peet, Bill. *Cowardly Clyde* [2-3], 976

Springer, Nancy. *Colt* [4-5], **792**

Stroud, Virginia A. *Doesn't Fall Off His Horse* [2-3], **680**

Wallace, Bill. *Beauty* [5-6], 1373

Ward, Lynd. *The Silver Pony* [2-3], 1024

HORSES–Folklore

Asbjørnsen, P. C. *The Squire's Bride* [1-4], 1395

Demi. *The Firebird* [2-5], **893**

Hastings, Selina. *The Firebird* [1-4], **938**

Hodges, Margaret. *The Little Humpbacked Horse* [3-5], 1525

Martin, Claire. *Boots & the Glass Mountain* [2-6], **981**

Otsuka, Zuzo. *Suho and the White Horse: A Legend of Mongolia* [2-4], 1576

Spray, Carole. *The Mare's Egg: A New World Folk Tale* [2-5], 1604

HORSES–Poetry

Cole, William. *The Poetry of Horses* [4-6], 1782

Springer, Nancy. *Music of Their Hooves: Poems About Horses* [3-6], **1411**

HOSPITALS

Dugan, Barbara. *Loop the Loop* [2-3], **608**

HOTELS, MOTELS, ETC

Okimoto, Jean Davies. *Blumpoe the Grumpoe Meets Arnold the Cat* [1-2], **525**

HOUDINI, HARRY

Selznick, Brian. *The Houdini Box* [3-4], **745**

HOUSES

Asch, Frank. *Goodbye House* [Pre-K], 11

Ballard, Robin. *Good-bye, House* [Pre-K], **69**

Barton, Byron. *Building a House* [Pre-1], 1993

Burton, Virgina Lee. *The Little House* [1-2], 634

Carle, Eric. *A House for Hermit Crab* [K-1], **246**

Donaldson, Julia. *A Squash and a Squeeze* [K-1], **264**

Dorros, Arthur. *This Is My House* [1-2], **435**

Hoberman, Mary Ann. *A House Is a House for Me* [K-1], 431

Keller, Wallace. *The Wrong Side of the Bed* [K-1], **297**

Lobel, Arnold. *Ming Lo Moves the Mountain* [K-1], 481

McDonald, Joyce. *Homebody* [1-2], **494**

McDonald, Megan. *Is This a House for Hermit Crab?* [K-1], **313**

Mwenye Hadithi. *Lazy Lion* [Pre-K], **171**

Peppé, Rodney. *The Mice Who Lived in a Shoe* [1-2], 772

Shannon, George. *Lizard's Song* [Pre-K], 261

Spier, Peter. *Oh, Were They Ever Happy!* [K-1], 559

Stevens, Janet. *The House That Jack Built: A Mother Goose Nursery Rhyme* [Pre-K], 271

Trivizas, Eugene. *The Three Little Wolves and the Big Bad Pig* [K-1], **378**

Zelinsky, Paul O. *The Maid and the Mouse and the Odd-Shaped House* [1-2], 860

HUICHOL INDIANS–Folklore

Bernhard, Emery. *The Tree That Rains: The Flood Myth of the Huichol Indians of Mexico* [1-4], **867**

HUMMINGBIRDS

Tyrrell, Esther Quesada. *Hummingbirds: Jewels in the Sky* [3-6], **1248**

HUMMINGBIRDS–Folklore

Stevens, Janet. *Coyote Steals the Blanket: A Ute Tale* [Pre-3], **1029**

HUMOROUS FICTION

Andrews, F. Emerson. *Upside-Down Town* [2-3], 866

Atwater, Richard, and Florence Atwater. *Mr. Popper's Penguins* [3-4], 1042

Benjamin, Saragail Katzman. *My Dog Ate It* [3-4], **704**

Birdseye, Tom. *I'm Going to Be Famous* [4-5], 1144

Blume, Judy. *Superfudge* [4-5], 1145
Tales of a Fourth Grade Nothing [3-4], 1046

Bond, Michael. *A Bear Called Paddington* [4-5], 1146
Paddington's Storybook [4-5], 1147

Butterworth, Oliver. *The Enormous Egg* [4-5], 1154

Byars, Betsy. *The 18th Emergency* [4-5], 1155

Callen, Larry. *Pinch* [5-6], 1285

Cleary, Beverly. *Beezus and Ramona* [2-3], 887
Henry Huggins [2-3], 888
Ramona the Pest [2-3], 890

Clifford, Eth. *Harvey's Horrible Snake Disaster* [3-4], 1052

Cole, Joanna, and Stephanie Calmenson. *Laugh Book: A New Treasury of Humor for Children* [2-5], 1774

Conford, Ellen. *Lenny Kandell, Smart Aleck* [5-6], 1290
Nibble, Nibble, Jenny Archer [2-3], **600**
What's Cooking, Jenny Archer? [2-3], **601**

Cutler, Jane. *No Dogs Allowed* [2-3], **602**

Dahl, Roald. *Matilda* [5-6], 1292

dePaola, Tomie. *Strega Nona Meets Her Match* [1-2], **430**

Drury, Roger W. *The Champion of Merrimack County* [4-5], 1169

Duffey, Betsy. *The Gadget War* [2-3], **606**

Ehrlich, Amy. *Parents in the Pigpen, Pigs in the Tub* [K-1], **266**

Gilson, Jamie. *Dial Leroi Rupert, D.J.* [4-5], 1178
Harvey the Beer Can King [4-5], 1179

Green, Phyllis. *Chucky Bellman Was So Bad* [1-2], **444**

Greenburg, Dan. *Young Santa* [4-5], **770**

Greer, Gery, and Bob Ruddick. *Max and Me and the Time Machine* [5-6], 1306
Max and Me and the Wild West [5-6], 1307

Hall, Lynn. *In Trouble Again, Zelda Hammersmith?* [3-4], 1069

Heide, Florence Parry. *Banana Twist* [5-6], 1310

Herman, Charlotte. *Max Malone Makes a Million* [2-3], **617**

Hicks, Clifford B. *Peter Potts* [4-5], 1188

Howe, James. *Nighty-Nightmare* [4-5], 1194

Keller, Beverly. *The Genuine, Ingenious Thrift Shop Genie, Clarissa Mae Bean and Me* [4-5], 1198

Kimmel, Eric A. *Bernal & Florinda: A Spanish Tale* [3-4], **720**

King-Smith, Dick. *Harry's Mad* [4-5], 1199
Sophie's Snail [1-2], 711

Kline, Rufus. *Watch Out for Those Weirdos* [1-2], **473**

Kline, Suzy. *What's the Matter with Herbie Jones?* [2-3], 949

Korman, Gordon. *This Can't Be Happening at Macdonald Hall* [5-6], 1321

LeRoy, Gen. *Taxi Cat and Huey* [4-5], **773**

Leverich, Kathleen. *Best Enemies Again* [2-3], **639**
Hilary and the Troublemakers [3-4], **730**

Lindgren, Astrid. *Pippi Longstocking* [3-4], 1090

Lowry, Lois. *All about Sam* [5-6], 1327
Attaboy, Sam! [4-5], **776**

McCloskey, Robert. *Homer Price* [4-5], 1208

McMurtry, Stan. *The Bunjee Venture* [4-5], 1210

Mahy, Margaret. *Raging Robots and Unruly Uncles* [4-5], **777**
The Rattlebang Picnic [1-2], **502**

Manes, Stephen. *Be a Perfect Person in Just Three Days* [3-4], 1095
Chicken Trek: The Third Strange Thing That Happened to Oscar J. Noodleman [4-5], 1211

Marshall, James. *The Cut-Ups Carry On* [1-2], **503**
Rats on the Roof and Other Stories [2-3], **643**

Meddaugh, Susan. *Martha Speaks* [1-2], **506**

Miles, Betty. *The Secret Life of the Underwear Champ* [3-4], 1096

Naylor, Phyllis Reynolds. *The Bodies in the Besseldorf Hotel* [4-5], 1216
The Boys Start the War [3-4], **735**
The Grand Escape [4-5], **783**

Nixon, Joan Lowery. *That's the Spirit, Claude* [2-3], **650**

Nostlinger, Christine. *Konrad* [4-5], 1219

Park, Barbara. *Junie B. Jones and a Little Monkey Business* [2-3], **651**
Junie B. Jones and Some Sneaky Peeky Spying [2-3], **652**
Junie B. Jones and the Stupid Smelly Bus [2-3], **653**
The Kid in the Red Jacket [4-5], 1221
Operation: Dump the Chump [3-4], 1101
Rosie Swanson, Fourth-Grade Geek for President [3-4], **737**
Skinnybones [4-5], 1222

Peck, Robert Newton. *Mr. Little* [5-6], 1343
Soup and Me [4-5], 1223

Petersen, P. J. *I Hate Company* [2-3], **655**

HUMOROUS FICTION (cont.)

Pilkey, Dav. *Dog Breath: The Horrible Trouble with Hally Tosis* [1-2], **530**

Pinkwater, Daniel. *Author's Day* [2-3], **659**

Fat Men from Space [3-4], 1103

The Hoboken Chicken Emergency [3-4], 1104

The Magic Moscow [3-4], 1105

Ned Feldman, Space Pirate [2-3], **660**

The Slaves of Spiegel: A Magic Moscow Story [4-5], 1226

Wempires [1-2], **535**

Yobgorgle: Mystery Monster of Lake Ontario [4-5], 1227

Pollack, Pamela. *The Random House Book of Humor for Children* [4-5], 1228

Pulver, Robin. *Mrs. Toggle and the Dinosaur* [K-1], **344**

Mrs. Toggle's Beautiful Blue Shoe [K-1], **345**

Robinson, Barbara. *The Best Christmas Pageant Ever* [4-5], 1230

The Best School Year Ever [4-5], **788**

Rockwell, Thomas. *How to Eat Fried Worms* [3-4], 1109

Rounds, Glen. *Mr. Yowder and the Train Robbers* [4-5], 1232

Sachar, Louis. *Dogs Don't Tell Jokes* [5-6], **840**

Sideways Stories from Wayside School [3-4], 1110

Wayside School Is Falling Down [3-4], 1111

Schwartz, Amy. *The Lady Who Put Salt in Her Coffee* [3-4], **742**

Scieszka, Jon. *Knights of the Kitchen Table* [3-4], **743**

Your Mother Was a Neanderthal [4-5], **790**

Sheldon, Dyan. *My Brother Is a Visitor from Another Planet* [3-4], **746**

Smith, Alison. *Help! There's a Cat Washing in Here* [5-6], 1361

Smith, Janice Lee. *The Show-and-Tell War: And Other Stories about Adam Joshua* [1-2], 816

Spinelli, Jerry. *Report to the Principal's Office* [4-5], **791**

Sutton, Jane. *Me and the Weirdos* [4-5], 1246

Swallow, Pam. *Melvil and Dewey in the Chips* [2-3], 1012

Teague, Mark. *Moog-Moog, Space Barber* [1-2], **563**

Thaler, Mike. *The Teacher from the Black Lagoon* [2-3], **682**

Tripp, Wallace. *My Uncle Podger* [3-4], 1123

Tusa, Tricia. *The Family Reunion* [1-2], **568**

Van Leeuwen, Jean. *The Great Rescue Operation* [4-5], 1252

Weiss, Ellen, and Mel Friedman. *The Poof Point* [5-6], **851**

The Tiny Parents [4-5], **794**

Wilson, Gahan. *Harry the Fat Bear Spy* [3-4], 1133

Wolkoff, Judie. *Wally* [3-4], 1135

Wood, Audrey. *The Tickleoctopus* [K-1], **387**

Yorinks, Arthur. *Whitefish Will Rides Again!* [1-2], **581**

HUMOROUS POETRY

Bennett, Jill. *Spooky Poems* [K-4], **1269**

Tiny Tim: Verses for Children [Pre-2], **1747**

Blake, Quentin. *All Join In* [Pre-2], **1270**

Bodecker, N. M. *Let's Marry Said the Cherry and Other Nonsense Poems* [K-5], **1751**

Booth, David. *Doctor Knickerbocker and Other Rhymes* [2-5], **1272**

Brewton, John E., and Lorraine A. Blackburn. *They've Discovered a Head in the Box for the Bread: And Other Laughable Limericks* [3-6], 1756

Brewton, Sara, John E. Brewton, and G. Meredith Blackburn, III. *My Tang's Tungled and Other Ridiculous Situations* [2-6], 1759

Brown, Marc. *Scared Silly: A Book for the Brave* [1-3], **1275**

Calmenson, Stephanie. *Never Take a Pig to Lunch: And Other Funny Poems about Animals* [Pre-4], 1764

Ciardi, John. *Doodle Soup* [1-4], 1769

Fast and Slow: Poems for Advanced Children and Beginning Parents [2-5], 1770

The Hopeful Trout and Other Limericks [3-6], 1771

You Read to Me, I'll Read to You [1-3], 1772

Cole, Joanna, and Stephanie Calmenson. *Laugh Book: A New Treasury of Humor for Children* [2-5], 1774

Cole, William. *Beastly Boys and Ghastly Girls* [2-6], 1775

Dahl, Roald. *Roald Dahl's Revolting Rhymes* [3-6], 1787

Dakos, Kalli. *If You're Not Here, Please Raise Your Hand: Poems about School* [2-6], **1283**

Eliot, T. S. *Mr. Mistoffelees with Mungojerrie and Rumpelteazer* [3-6], **1286**

Fatchen, Max. *The Country Mail Is Coming: Poems from Down Under* [3-6], **1289**

Florian, Douglas. *Beast Feast* [K-4], **1290**

Bing Bang Boing [1-6], **1291**

Ginsburg, Mirra. *The Night It Rained Pancakes* [2-6], 1480

Harrison, David L. *Somebody Catch My Homework* [2-5], **1307**

Hoban, Russell. *Egg Thoughts and Other Frances Songs* [K-2], 1813

Keller, Charles. *Ballpoint Bananas and Other Jokes for Kids* [2-6], 1835

Kennedy, Dorothy M. *I Thought I'd Take My Rat to School: Poems for September to June* [3-6], **1341**

Kennedy, X. J. *Brats* [3-6], 1845
Drat These Brats [4-6], **1343**
Ghastlies, Goops & Pincushions: Nonsense Verse [3-6], 1846

Klein, Robin. *Snakes and Ladders: Poems about the Ups and Downs of Life* [3-6], 1848

Lansky, Bruce. *Kids Pick the Funniest Poems: A Collection of Poems That Will Make You Laugh* [2-6], **1346**

Lear, Edward. *Daffy Down Dillies: Silly Limericks* [3-6], **1348**
How Pleasant to Know Mr. Lear! [4-6], 1853

Lee, Dennis. *Alligator Pie* [Pre-4], 1854
The Ice Cream Store [Pre-3], **1350**
Jelly Belly: Original Nursery Rhymes [Pre-3], 1855

Lewis, J. Patrick. *A Hippopotamustn't and Other Animal Verses* [1-5], **1353**
Two-Legged, Four-Legged, No-Legged Rhymes [K-4], **1354**

Livingston, Myra Cohn. *Lots of Limericks* [4-6], **1359**

Lobel, Arnold. *The Book of Pigericks* [2-6], 1861
Whiskers & Rhymes [Pre-3], 1862

McNaughton, Colin. *Making Friends with Frankenstein: A Book of Monstrous Poems and Pictures* [2-6], **1366**

Marshall, James. *Pocketful of Nonsense* [Pre-3], **1369**

Merriam, Eve. *Blackberry Ink* [Pre-2], 1868
A Poem for a Pickle: Funnybone Verses [K-4], 1870

Milne, A. A. *Now We Are Six* [Pre-3], 1872

Morrison, Lillian. *Best Wishes, Amen* [2-6], 1877

Moss, Jeff. *The Butterfly Jar* [2-6], **1377**

Nash, Ogden. *The Adventures of Isabel* [2-3], **649**
Custard and Company [3-6], 1893

Numeroff, Laura J. *Dogs Don't Wear Sneakers* [K-1], **333**

Prelutsky, Jack. *A. Nonny Mouse Writes Again!* [1-5], **1395**
The Baby Uggs Are Hatching [K-4], 1904
For Laughing Out Loud: Poems to Tickle Your Funnybone [K-5], **1397**
The New Kid on the Block [K-5], 1911
Poems of A. Nonny Mouse [K-4], 1913
The Queen of Eene [2-4], 1914
Rolling Harvey Down the Hill [2-4], 1919
The Sheriff of Rottenshot [2-4], 1920

Something Big Has Been Here [K-6], **1398**

Riley, James Whitcomb. *The Gobble-Uns'll Git You Ef You Don't Watch Out* [3-4], 1108

Rosenbloom, Joseph. *The Looniest Limerick Book in the World* [4-6], 1934
Silly Verse (and Even Worse) [3-6], 1936

Schwartz, Alvin. *And the Green Grass Grew All Around: Folk Poetry from Everyone* [2-6], **1407**
I Saw You in the Bathtub and Other Folk Rhymes [K-3], 1947
Tomfoolery: Trickery and Foolery with Words [1-6], 1949

Silverstein, Shel. *Where the Sidewalk Ends* [Pre-6], 1952

Simmie, Lois. *Auntie's Knitting a Baby* [2-5], 1953

Smith, William Jay. *Laughing Time: Nonsense Poems* [K-3], 1955

Thompson, Brian. *Catch It If You Can* [Pre-2], **1415**

Tripp, Wallace. *A Great Big Ugly Man Came Up and Tied His Horse to Me: A Book of Nonsense Verse* [K-3], 1967

Viorst, Judith. *If I Were in Charge of the World and Other Worries: Poems for Children and Their Parents* [2-5], 1969
Sad Underwear and Other Complications: More Poems for Children and Their Parents [2-6], **1417**

Westcott, Nadine Bernard. *Never Take a Pig to Lunch and Other Poems About the Fun of Eating* [1-4], **1421**

Yolen, Jane. *Animal Fare* [1-4], **1427**
Raining Cats and Dogs [1-4], **1430**

HUMOROUS SONGS

Goode, Diane. *Diane Goode's Book of Silly Stories and Songs* [2-5], **1069**

Nelson, Esther L. *The Funny Song Book* [Pre-6], 1894

Winn, Marie. *The Fireside Book of Fun and Game Songs* [Pre-6], 1976

HUMOROUS STORIES
SEE Humorous fiction

HUNTERS AND HUNTING

Browne, Anthony. *Bear Hunt* [Pre-K], 30

Carrick, Donald. *Harald and the Great Stag* [2-3], 883

Dahl, Roald. *The Fantastic Mr. Fox* [2-3], 904
The Magic Finger [2-3], 905

Geraghty, Paul. *The Hunter* [1-2], **442**

Ivanov, Anatoly. *Ol' Jake's Lucky Day* [1-2], 698

Morey, Walt. *Sandy and the Rock Star* [5-6], 1333

Murphy, Jim. *The Call of the Wolves* [2-3], 969

HUNTERS AND HUNTING (cont.)
Peet, Bill. *Gnats of Knotty Pine* [2-3], 977

Seuss, Dr. *Thidwick, the Big-Hearted Moose* [1-2], 806

HURRICANES
Wiesner, David. *Hurricane* [1-2], **574**

HURRICANES–Folklore
Crespo, George. *How the Sea Began: A Taino Myth* [1-6], **887**

HUSBANDS AND WIVES
Kovalski, Maryann. *Pizza for Breakfast* [1-2], **479**

HUSBANDS AND WIVES–Folklore
Cole, Joanna. *Don't Tell the Whole World!* [K-3], **881**

Gerson, Mary-Joan. *How Night Came from the Sea: A Story from Brazil* [K-4], **912**

Grimm, Jacob. *The Fisherman and His Wife* [2-4], 1492

Hague, Kathleen, and Michael Hague. *The Man Who Kept House* [K-4], 1514

Hong, Lily Toy. *Two of Everything: A Chinese Folktale* [K-3], **943**

Rhee, Nami. *Magic Spring: A Korean Folktale* [K-3], **1002**

San Souci, Robert D. *The Snow Wife* [3-5], **1015**

Weisner, William. *Happy-Go-Lucky* [1-4], 1625
Turnabout [K-4], 1626

HYENAS
Mwenye Hadithi. *Hungry Hyena* [K-1], **331**

HYGIENE
Bottner, Barbara. *Messy* [K-1], 339

Schwartz, Mary Ada. *Spiffen: A Tale of a Tidy Pig* [K-1], 547

ICEBERGS
Ballard, Robert. *Exploring the Titanic* [4-6], **1102**

IDENTITY
Cannon, Janell. *Stellaluna* [K-1], **245**

Gordon, Gaelyn. *Duckat* [Pre-K], **110**

Kasza, Keiko. *A Mother for Choco* [Pre-K], **140**

Namioka, Lensey. *Yang the Youngest and His Terrible Ear* [4-5], **781**

IDIOMS
SEE English language–Idioms

IDITAROD
Seibert, Patricia. *Mush! Across Alaska in the World's Longest Sled-Dog Race* [1-4], **1235**

ILLNESS
SEE Sick

ILLUSTRATION OF BOOKS
Brown, Ruth A. *If at First You Do Not See* [K-1], 348

Drescher, Henrik. *Simon's Book* [1-2], 664

Jonas, Ann. *Reflections* [1-2], 700
Round Trip [1-2], 701

Krauss, Ruth. *Is This You?* [1-2], 714

Withers, Carl. *Tale of a Black Cat* [1-2], 853

ILLUSTRATORS
Cummings, Pat. *Talking with Artists* [2-6], **1127**

Kamen, Gloria. *Edward Lear, King of Nonsense: A Biography* [4-6], **1169**

Rosen, Michael J. *Speak! Children's Book Illustrators Brag About Their Dogs* [2-6], **1229**

Stevens, Janet. *From Pictures to Words: A Book About Making a Book* [1-4], **1244**

IMAGINATION
Balian, Lorna. *The Animal* [K-1], 327

Boyd, Selma, and Pauline Boyd. *I Met a Polar Bear* [K-1], 340

Browne, Anthony. *Changes* [K-1], **241**

Burningham, John. *Would You Rather . . .* [K-1], 355

Bursik, Rose. *Amelia's Fantastic Flight* [1-2], **417**

Byars, Betsy. *The Two-Thousand Pound Goldfish* [5-6], **1283**

Carrick, Carol. *Patrick's Dinosaurs* [K-1], 358
What Happened to Patrick's Dinosaurs? [1-2], 642

Chadwick, Tim. *Cabbage Moon* [Pre-K], **81**

Conford, Ellen. *Jenny Archer, Author* [2-3], 898

Cooney, Nancy Evans. *The Umbrella Day* [Pre-K], 57

Craig, M. Jean. *The Dragon in the Clock Box* [K-1], 375

Crowley, Michael. *New Kid on Spurwink Ave.* [K-1], **258**

Faulkner, Matt. *The Amazing Voyage of Jackie Grace* [1-2], 666

Fife, Dale. *Who's in Charge of Lincoln?* [2-3], 917

Freeman, Don. *A Rainbow of My Own* [Pre-K], 97

Gackenbach, Dick. *Where Are Momma, Poppa, and Sister June?* [K-1], **274**

Gardner, Beau. *The Look Again . . . and Again, and Again, and Again Book* [1-2], 675

Greenfield, Eloise. *Me as Neesie* [K-1], 411

Griffith, Helen V. *Plunk's Dreams* [Pre-K], 122

Haas, Dorothy F. *Tink in a Tangle* [2-3], 929

Heller, Nicholas. *An Adventure at Sea* [1-2], 685
Up the Wall [K-1], **281**
Woody [Pre-K], **121**

Henkes, Kevin. *Jessica* [K-1], 418

Hennessy, B. G. *The Dinosaur Who Lived in My Backyard* [K-1], **284**

Johnston, Deborah. *Mathew Michael's Beastly Day* [K-1], **293**

Keats, Ezra Jack. *Regards to the Man in the Moon* [1-2], 703

King-Smith, Dick. *The Invisible Dog* [1-2], **467**

Leverich, Kathleen. *Hilary and the Troublemakers* [3-4], **730**

Lionni, Leo. *Fish Is Fish* [K-1], 474

Long, Claudia. *Albert's Story* [K-1], 487

Lystad, Mary. *Jennifer Takes Over P.S. 94* [1-2], 733

McEwan, Ian. *The Daydreamer* [5-6], **829**

McLerran, Alice. *Roxaboxen* [1-2], **499**

Nightingale, Sandy. *A Giraffe on the Moon* [Pre-K], **172**

Numeroff, Laura J. *Dogs Don't Wear Sneakers* [K-1], **333**

Pittman, Helena Clare. *Once When I Was Scared* [1-2], 775

Polette, Nancy. *Hole by the Apple Tree: An A–Z Discovery Tale* [K-1], **339**

Ryder, Joanne. *Sea Elf* [K-3], **1231**
    Winter Whale [K-3], **1232**

Rylant, Cynthia. *All I See* [2-3], 988

Shaw, Charles G. *It Looked Like Spilt Milk* [Pre-K], 264

Small, David. *Imogene's Antlers* [K-1], 558

Stevenson, Robert Louis. *Block City* [K-1], 563

Teague, Mark. *The Field Beyond the Outfield* [K-1], **376**

Townson, Hazel. *Terrible Tuesday* [K-1], 569

Van Allsburg, Chris. *The Mysteries of Harris Burdick* [4-5], 1250

Vreeken, Elizabeth. *The Boy Who Would Not Say His Name* [K-1], 576

Ward, Lynd. *The Silver Pony* [2-3], 1024

Wiesner, David. *Hurricane* [1-2], **574**

Zhitkov, Boris. *How I Hunted the Little Fellows* [3-4], 1136

IMMIGRATION AND EMIGRATION

Choi, Sook Nyul. *Halmoni and the Picnic* [1-2], **424**

Cohen, Barbara. *Molly's Pilgrim* [2-3], 893

Freedman, Russell. *Immigrant Kids* [4-6], 2027

Garland, Sherry. *The Lotus Seed* [2-3], **609**

Howlett, Bud. *I'm New Here* [2-5], **1166**

Kidd, Diana. *Onion Tears* [4-5], **772**

Leighton, Maxine Rhea. *An Ellis Island Christmas* [2-3], **638**

Levine, Ellen. *If Your Name Was Changed at Ellis Island* [3-6], **1186**

Waterton, Betty. *Petranella* [1-2], 845

Winter, Jeanette. *Klara's New World* [2-3], **693**

IMPS

SEE ALSO Fairies

Cole, Brock. *Alpha and the Dirty Baby* [1-2], **426**

INDIA

Kipling, Rudyard. *Rikki-Tikki-Tavi* [3-4], **729**

INDIANS OF CENTRAL AMERICA

Wisniewski, David. *Rain Player* [2-3], **694**

INDIANS OF MEXICO

Mathews, Sally Schofer. *The Sad Night: The Story of an Aztec Victory and a Spanish Loss* [5-6], **1206**

INDIANS OF NORTH AMERICA

SEE ALSO Folklore–Indians of North America

Accorsi, William. *Friendship's First Thanksgiving* [K-1], **216**

Banks, Lynne Reid. *The Indian in the Cupboard* [5-6], 1272

Brink, Carol Ryrie. *Caddie Woodlawn* [4-5], 1151

DeFelice, Cynthia. *Weasel* [5-6], **812**

Freedman, Russell. *Buffalo Hunt* [5-6], 2025

Gardiner, John Reynolds. *Stone Fox* [3-4], 1067

George, Jean Craighead. *The First Thanksgiving* [1-4], **1147**

Goble, Paul. *Dream Wolf* [1-2], **443**

Hill, Kirkpatrick. *Winter Camp* [5-6], **822**

Jeffers, Susan. *Brother Eagle, Sister Sky: A Message from Chief Seattle* [2-3], **628**

Kinsey-Warnock, Natalie. *Wilderness Cat* [1-2], **470**

Miles, Miska. *Annie and the Old One* [4-5], 1213

O'Dell, Scott. *Island of the Blue Dolphins* [5-6], 1339

Root, Phyllis. *Coyote and the Magic Words* [K-1], **351**

Speare, Elizabeth George. *The Sign of the Beaver* [5-6], 1363

Stroud, Virginia A. *Doesn't Fall Off His Horse* [2-3], **680**

Wood, Ted, and Wanbli Numpa Afraid of Hawk. *A Boy Becomes a Man at Wounded Knee* [3-6], **1255**

Yolen, Jane. *Encounter* [3-4], **756**

INDIANS OF NORTH AMERICA–Biography

Fritz, Jean. *The Double Life of Pocahontas* [4-6], 2031

Roop, Peter, and Connie Roop. *Ahyoka and the Talking Leaves* [3-4], **740**

INDIANS OF NORTH AMERICA–Poetry

Bruchac, Joseph, and Jonathan London. *Thirteen Moons on Turtle's Back: A Native American Year of Moons* [2-6], **872**

INDIANS OF THE WEST INDIES
SEE ALSO Folklore–Indians of the West Indies
Dorris, Michael. *Morning Girl* [5-6], **814**

INDIVIDUALITY
Anholt, Catherine, and Laurence Anholt. *All About You* [Pre], **3**
Kids [Pre-K], **64**
Auch, Mary Jane. *The Easter Egg Farm* [K-1], **220**
Boland, Janice. *Annabel* [Pre], **6**
Conford, Ellen. *And This Is Laura* [5-6], 1289
Crowley, Michael. *New Kid on Spurwink Ave* [K-1], **258**
dePaola, Tomie. *The Art Lesson* [2-3], 907
Lester, Helen. *Three Cheers for Tacky* [K-1], **305**
Pinkwater, Daniel. *Doodle Flute* [1-2], **534**
Seuling, Barbara. *The Triplets* [1-2], 800
Swope, Sam. *The Araboolies of Liberty Street* [1-2], 829
Walsh, Ellen Stoll. *Hop Jump* [Pre], **53**
Willard, Nancy. *Simple Pictures Are Best* [1-2], 849
Yashima, Taro. *Crow Boy* [2-3], 1032
Ziefert, Harriet. *Pete's Chicken* [K-1], **392**
Ziegler, Jack. *Mr. Knocky* [1-2], **582**

INSECTS
Aylesworth, Jim. *Hush Up!* [K-1], 323
Old Black Fly [K-1], **223**
Cameron, Polly. *"I Can't," Said the Ant* [1-2], 636
Carle, Eric. *The Grouchy Ladybug* [Pre-K], 37
The Very Hungry Caterpillar [Pre-K], 42
The Very Quiet Cricket [Pre-K], **75**
Dahl, Roald. *James and the Giant Peach* [3-4], 1059
Demuth, Patricia Brennan. *Those Amazing Ants* [K-2], **1130**
Dorros, Arthur. *Ant Cities* [K-3], 2021
Hawes, Judy. *Fireflies in the Night* [K-2], **1156**
Howe, James. *I Wish I Were a Butterfly* [1-2], 692
Hurwitz, Johanna. *Much Ado about Aldo* [2-3], 937
James, Betsy. *Mary Ann* [Pre-K], **133**
James, Mary. *Shoebag* [4-5], 1195
Kimmel, Eric A. *Bernal & Florinda: A Spanish Tale* [3-4], **720**
Kotzwinkle, William. *Trouble in Bugland: A Collection of Inspector Mantis Mysteries* [5-6], 1322
Kraus, Robert. *How Spider Saved Christmas* [K-1], 459
Lord, John Vernon, and Janet Burroway. *The Giant Jam Sandwich* [1-2], 730
Oppenheim, Joanne. *You Can't Catch Me!* [K-1], 516
Peet, Bill. *Gnats of Knotty Pine* [2-3], 977

Peters, Lisa Westberg. *When the Fly Flew In* [K-1], **336**
Porte, Barbara Ann. *"Leave That Cricket Be, Alan Lee"* [K-1], **340**
Selden, George. *The Cricket in Times Square* [4-5], 1237
Van Allsburg, Chris. *Two Bad Ants* [3-4], 1125

INSECTS–Folklore
Renberg, Dalia Hardof. *King Solomon and the Bee* [K-3], **1001**
Rodanas, Kristina. *Dragonfly's Tale* [K-3], **1005**

INSECTS–Poetry
Bodecker, N. M. *Water Pennies: And Other Poems* [2-5], **1271**
Fleischman, Paul. *Joyful Noise: Poems for Two Voices* [5-6], 1799
Hoberman, Mary Ann. *Bugs: Poems* [1-4], 1814
Hopkins, Lee Bennett. *Flit, Flutter, Fly! Poems About Bugs and Other Crawly Creatures* [K-4], **1319**
Rosen, Michael. *Itsy-Bitsy Beasties: Poems from Around the World* [K-4], **1404**

INSECTS–Riddles
Bernstein, Joanne E., and Paul Cohen. *Creepy Crawly Critter Riddles* [2-5], 1748
Hall, Katy, and Lisa Eisenberg. *Buggy Riddles* [Pre-2], 1809

INTERDEPENDENCE
Greene, Carol. *The Old Ladies Who Liked Cats* [1-2], **445**

INVENTIONS
Christelow, Eileen. *Mr. Murphy's Marvelous Invention* [1-2], 649
Crowley, Michael. *New Kid on Spurwink Ave* [K-1], **258**
D'Aulaire, Ingri, and Edgar Parin D'Aulaire. *Benjamin Franklin* [2-6], 2013
Duffey, Betsy. *The Gadget War* [2-3], **606**
Frank, John. *Odds 'N' Ends Alvy* [1-2], **441**
Fritz, Jean. *What's the Big Idea, Ben Franklin?* [3-6], 2033
Gackenbach, Dick. *Dog for a Day* [K-1], 396
Tiny for a Day [K-1], **273**
Garrison, Webb. *Why Didn't I Think of That? From Alarm Clock to Zippers* [4-6], 2036
Goldberg, Rube. *The Best of Rube Goldberg* [3-6], 2040
Jones, Charlotte Foltz. *Mistakes That Worked* [4-6], **1168**
Lawson, Robert. *Ben and Me* [5-6], 1324

Murphy, Jim. *Weird and Wacky Inventions* [3-6], 2078

Woodruff, Elvira. *The Disappearing Bike Shop* [4-5], **797**

INVENTORS

Getz, David. *Almost Famous* [5-6], **818**

Tzannes, Robin. *Professor Puffendorf's Secret Potions* [1-2], **569**

Weiss, Ellen, and Mel Friedman. *The Poof Point* [5-6], **851**

The Tiny Parents [4-5], **794**

INVISIBILITY–Folklore

Martin, Rafe. *The Rough-Face Girl* [2-6], **983**

San Souci, Robert D. *Sootface: An Ojibwa Cinderella Story* [1-5], **1016**

IRAQ

Maugham, W. Somerset. *Appointment* [5-6], **830**

IRELAND

Blake, Robert J. *Dog* [2-3], **591**

Kennedy, Richard. *The Leprechaun's Story* [3-4], 1081

King-Smith, Dick. *Paddy's Pot of Gold* [3-4], **724**

Nixon, Joan Lowery. *The Gift* [3-4], 1099

Tannen, Mary. *The Wizard Children of Finn* [5-6], 1367

Wetterer, Margaret. *The Giant's Apprentice* [3-4], 1130

IRISH AMERICANS

Holland, Isabelle. *Behind the Lines* [5-6], **824**

IROQUOIS INDIANS–Folklore

Bierhorst, John. *The Woman Who Fell from the Sky: The Iroquois Story of Creation* [2-6], **868**

ISLANDS

Avi. *Shadrach's Crossing* [5-6], 1269

Cooney, Barbara. *Island Boy* [3-4], 1055

Dorris, Michael. *Morning Girl* [5-6], **814**

Farley, Walter. *The Black Stallion* [3-4], 1064

Gannett, Ruth Stiles. *My Father's Dragon* [1-2], 674

Gershator, Phillis. *Rata-Pata-Scata-Fata: A Caribbean Story* [Pre-K], **108**

Greenfield, Eloise. *Under the Sunday Tree* [2-5], 1808

Ikeda, Daisaku. *Over the Deep Blue Sea* [1-2], **460**

Keller, Holly. *Island Baby* [K-1], **296**

McCloskey, Robert. *Time of Wonder* [2-3], 957

McMillan, Bruce. *Sense Suspense: A Guessing Game for the Five Senses* [Pre-K], **159**

Mitchell, Rita Phillips. *Hue Boy* [K-1], **325**

Morey, Walt. *Sandy and the Rock Star* [5-6], 1333

Roy, Ron. *Nightmare Island* [4-5], 1234

Steig, William. *Abel's Island* [5-6], 1364

Tayntor, Elizabeth, Paul Erickson, and Les Kaufman. *Dive to the Coral Reefs: A New England Aquarium Book* [3-6], 2110

ISLANDS–Poetry

Agard, John, and Grace Nichols. *A Caribbean Dozen: Poems from Caribbean Poets* [1-6], **1262**

ITALIAN AMERICANS

Bartone, Elisa. *Peppe the Lamplighter* [1-2], **405**

ITALY

Charlip, Remy. *Harlequin and the Gift of Many Colors* [2-3], 886

dePaola, Tomie. *Merry Christmas, Strega Nona* [2-3], 909

JACK-O-LANTERNS

SEE Pumpkins

JAMAICA–Folklore

SEE Folklore–Jamaica

JAPAN

SEE ALSO Folklore–Japan

Coerr, Eleanor. *Mieko and the Fifth Treasure* [3-4], **707**

Sadako [2-5], **1120**

Sadako & the Thousand Paper Cranes [3-6], 2007

Friedman, Ina R. *How My Parents Learned to Eat* [1-2], 672

Matsuno, Masako. *A Pair of Red Clogs* [1-2], 747

Morimoto, Junko. *My Hiroshima* [3-6], **1210**

Nikly, Michelle. *The Emperor's Plum Tree* [1-2], 759

Say, Allen. *The Bicycle Man* [1-2], 791

Grandfather's Journey [2-3], **674**

Tree of Cranes [1-2], **547**

Wells, Ruth. *A to Zen: A Book of Japanese Culture* [3-6], **1252**

Wetzel, JoAnne Stewart. *The Christmas Box* [K-1], **384**

Wisniewski, David. *The Warrior and the Wise Man* [2-3], 1031

Yashima, Taro. *Crow Boy* [2-3], 1032

JAPANESE AMERICANS

Mochizuki, Ken. *Baseball Saved Us* [3-4], **733**

JAPANESE LANGUAGE

Tompert, Ann. *Bamboo Hats and a Rice Cake: A Tale Adapted from Japanese Folklore* [K-3], **1036**

Wells, Ruth. *A to Zen: A Book of Japanese Culture* [3-6], **1252**

JAPANESE POETRY

Cassedy, Sylvia, and Kunihiro Suetake. *Red Dragonfly on My Shoulder* [2-6], **1278**

Demi. *In the Eyes of the Cat: Japanese Poetry for All Seasons* [2-6], **1284**

Higginson, William J. *Wind in the Long Grass: A Collection of Haiku* [2-6], **1313**

JEALOUSY

Alexander, Martha. *The Story Grandmother Told* [Pre-K], 2

Annett, Cora. *How the Witch Got Alf* [2-3], 868

Brandenberg, Franz. *I Wish I Was Sick, Too* [Pre-K], 26

Calhoun, Mary. *High-Wire Henry* [1-2], **419**

Ernst, Lisa Campbell. *Ginger Jumps* [K-1], **269**

Ferguson, Alane. *That New Pet!* [K-1], 386

Graham, Margaret Bloy. *Benjy and the Barking Bird* [Pre-K], 118

Havill, Juanita. *Jamaica and Brianna* [Pre-K], **119**

Henkes, Kevin. *Bailey Goes Camping* [Pre-K], 131

Julius, the Baby of the World [K-1], **283**

Hoban, Russell. *A Baby Sister for Frances* [Pre-K], 137

Johnson, Paul Brett. *The Cow Who Wouldn't Come Down* [K-1], **292**

Keats, Ezra Jack. *Peter's Chair* [Pre-K], 164

Keller, Holly. *Geraldine's Baby Brother* [Pre-K], **142**

Kellogg, Steven. *Much Bigger than Martin* [K-1], 453

Kopper, Lisa. *Daisy Thinks She Is a Baby* [Pre], **27**

Lindgren, Astrid. *I Want a Brother or Sister* [Pre-K], 189

Martin, Ann. *Rachel Parker, Kindergarten Show-Off* [K-1], **321**

Wagner, Jenny. *John Brown, Rose and the Midnight Cat* [K-1], 581

JEALOUSY–Folklore

McDermott, Gerald. *The Stonecutter: A Japanese Folk Tale* [K-4], 1552

JERUSALEM

Kimmel, Eric A. *Asher and the Capmakers: A Hanukkah Story* [2-3], **635**

JEWS

SEE ALSO Folklore, Jewish

Abels, Chana Byers. *The Children We Remember* [4-6], 1985

Cohen, Barbara. *The Carp in the Bathtub* [2-3], 892

Make a Wish, Molly [2-3], **598**

Isaacman, Clara, and Joan Adess Grossman. *Clara's Story* [5-6], 2054

Jaffe, Nina. *In the Month of Kislev: A Story for Hanukkah* [2-3], **627**

Kimmel, Eric A. *Asher and the Capmakers: A Hanukkah Story* [2-3], **635**

Hershel and the Hanukkah Goblins [2-3], 944

Lowry, Lois. *Number the Stars* [5-6], 1328

Polacco, Patricia. *Mrs. Katz and Tush* [2-3], **663**

Tikvah Means Hope [2-3], **664**

Slepian, Jan. *Risk N' Roses* [5-6], **845**

JOKES

SEE ALSO Knock-knock jokes; Riddles

Bernstein, Joanne E., and Paul Cohen. *Creepy Crawly Critter Riddles* [2-5], 1748

Brandreth, Gyles. *The Super Joke Book* [3-6], 1754

Burns, Diane, and Clint Burns. *Hail to the Chief! Jokes about the Presidents* [2-6], **1276**

Cole, Joanna, and Stephanie Calmenson. *Why Did the Chicken Cross the Road? And Other Riddles Old and New* [2-5], **1281**

Eldin, Peter. *The Trickster's Handbook* [3-6], **1136**

Hartman, Victoria. *The Silliest Joke Book Ever* [3-5], **1308**

Hoff, Syd. *Syd Hoff's Animal Jokes* [K-2], 1815

Syd Hoff's Joke Book [2-4], 1816

Keller, Charles. *Belly Laughs! Food Jokes & Riddles* [2-6], **1337**

Norma Lee I Don't Knock on Doors [K-3], 1839

School Daze [2-5], 1842

Phillips, Louis. *How Do You Get a Horse Out of the Bathtub? Profound Answers to Preposterous Questions* [5-6], 1900

Invisible Oink: Pig Jokes [3-6], **1394**

Rosenbloom, Joseph. *Daffy Definitions* [4-6], 1927

The Funniest Knock-Knock Book Ever! [Pre-3], 1929

The Gigantic Joke Book [3-6], 1931

Giggles, Gags & Groaners [3-6], **1932**

Knock Knock! Who's There? [3-6], 1933

Spooky Riddles and Jokes [2-6], 1937

Thaler, Mike. *The Chocolate Marshmelephant Sundae* [3-6], 1966

Young, Frederica. *Super-Duper Jokes* [3-6], **1432**

JOURNALS

SEE Diaries

JUDGES–Folklore

Brusca, María Cristina, and Tona Wilson. *The Cook and the King* [2-4], **874**

JUMP ROPE RHYMES

Delamar, Gloria T. *Children's Counting Out Rhymes, Fingerplays, Jump-Rope and Bounce-Ball Chants and Other Rhymes: A*

Comprehensive English-Language Reference [Pre-3], 1788

Nerlove, Miriam. *I Made a Mistake* [1-2], 756

Opie, Iona, and Peter Opie. *I Saw Esau: The Schoolchild's Pocket Book* [1-5], **1391**

JUNGLES

SEE ALSO Rain forests

Cherry, Lynne. *The Great Kapok Tree: A Tale of the Amazon Rain Forest* [1-2], 647

Maestro, Giulio. *A Wise Monkey Tale* [K-1], 499

Mahy, Margaret. *17 Kings and 42 Elephants* [K-1], 500

Tworkov, Jack. *The Camel Who Took a Walk* [K-1], 571

KANGAROOS

Arnold, Caroline. *Kangaroo* [2-6], 1986

Kent, Jack. *Joey Runs Away* [Pre-K], 169

Kraus, Robert. *Noel the Coward* [Pre-K], 175

Payne, Emmy. *Katy-No-Pocket* [Pre-K], 225

KARUK INDIANS–Folklore

London, Jonathan, and Lanny Pinola. *Fire Race: A Karuk Coyote Tale About How Fire Came to the People* [K-3], **972**

KIDNAPPING

Fleischman, Paul. *The Half-a-Moon Inn* [5-6], 1299

Fleischman, Sid. *The Ghost in the Noonday Sun* [5-6], 1301

Holland, Barbara. *Prisoners at the Kitchen Table* [4-5], 1190

Kehret, Peg. *Deadly Stranger* [5-6], 1317

Ogburn, Jacqueline K. *Scarlett Angelina Wolverton-Manning* [1-2], **524**

KINDERGARTEN

SEE ALSO Nursery schools; Schools

Hinton, S. E. *Big David, Little David* [K-1], **285**

Martin, Ann. *Rachel Parker, Kindergarten Show-Off* [K-1], **321**

Park, Barbara. *Junie B. Jones and a Little Monkey Business* [2-3], **651**

Junie B. Jones and Some Sneaky Peeky Spying [2-3], **652**

Junie B. Jones and the Stupid Smelly Bus [2-3], **653**

KINDNESS–Folklore

Paterson, Katherine. *The Tale of the Mandarin Ducks* [2-6], **996**

Richard, Françoise. *On Cat Mountain* [2-5], **1003**

Tompert, Ann. *Bamboo Hats and a Rice Cake: A Tale Adapted from Japanese Folklore* [K-3], **1036**

Uchida, Yoshiko. *The Magic Purse* [1-4], **1037**

KING, MARTIN LUTHER, JR.

Marzollo, Jean. *Happy Birthday, Martin Luther King* [Pre-2], **1203**

KING, MARTIN LUTHER, JR.–Poetry

Livingston, Myra Cohn. *Let Freedom Ring: A Ballad of Martin Luther King, Jr.* [1-6], **1191**

KINGS AND RULERS

Andersen, Hans Christian. *The Emperor's New Clothes: A Fairy Tale* [2-3], 863

The Nightingale [3-4], **699**, 1039

The Wild Swans [3-4], **700**, 1040

Anderson, Lonzo. *Two Hundred Rabbits* [1-2], 606

Armstrong, Jennifer. *Little Salt Lick and the Sun King* [1-2], **399**

Babbitt, Natalie. *Bub: Or, the Very Best Thing* [K-1], **224**

The Search for Delicious [4-5], 1139

Banks, Lynne Reid. *The Adventures of King Midas* [4-5], **758**

Birch, David. *The King's Chessboard* [3-4], 1045

Cole, Brock. *The King at the Door* [2-3], 895

Coombs, Patricia. *The Magician and McTree* [2-3], 900

Molly Mullett [2-3], 901

De Regniers, Beatrice Schenk. *May I Bring a Friend?* [Pre-K], 69

Fritz, Jean. *Can't You Make Them Behave, King George?* [3-6], 2030

Gackenbach, Dick. *King Wacky* [1-2], 673

Heine, Helme. *The Most Wonderful Egg in the World* [Pre-K], 129

Hennessy, B. G. *The Missing Tarts* [Pre-K], 133

Kennedy, Richard. *The Lost Kingdom of Karnica* [3-4], 1082

Kimmel, Eric A. *I-Know-Not-What, I-Know-Not-Where: A Russian Tale* [4-6], **955**

King-Smith, Dick. *The Swoose* [3-4], **727**

Mahy, Margaret. *17 Kings and 42 Elephants* [K-1], 500

Myller, Rolf. *How Big Is a Foot?* [2-3], 970

Nikly, Michelle. *The Emperor's Plum Tree* [1-2], 759

Perrault, Charles. *Puss in Boots* [1-4], **997**

Schertle, Alice. *The April Fool* [2-3], 991

Schwartz, Amy. *Her Majesty, Aunt Essie* [1-2], 796

Seuss, Dr. *Bartholomew and the Oobleck* [2-3], 994

The 500 Hats of Bartholomew Cubbins [2-3], 995

The King's Stilts [2-3], 996

Thurber, James. *Many Moons* [2-3], 1015

Vesey, A. *The Princess and the Frog* [1-2], 837

KINGS AND RULERS (cont.)

West, Colin. *The King of Kennelwick Castle* [Pre-K], 289

Wisniewski, David. *Sundiata: Lion King of Mali* [3-5], **1254**

Wood, Audrey. *King Bidgood's in the Bathtub* [1-2], 855

KINGS AND RULERS–Folklore

Brusca, María Cristina, and Tona Wilson. *The Cook and the King* [2-4], **874**

Christian, Mary Blount. *April Fool* [1-3], 1423

Climo, Shirley. *The Egyptian Cinderella* [2-6], 1424

Demi. *The Firebird* [2-5], **893**

Domanska, Janina. *King Krakus and the Dragon* [K-2], 1446

Duff, Maggie. *Rum Pum Pum* [Pre-2], 1449

Gal, Laszlo. *Prince Ivan and the Firebird* [3-6], **908**

Galdone, Paul. *The Amazing Pig* [2-4], 1457

Ginsburg, Mirra. *The Magic Stove* [K-3], 1479

Grimm, Jacob. *Little Brother and Little Sister* [2-5], 1499

One Gift Deserves Another [1-4], **927**

Rumpelstiltskin [1-4], 1504, **922**

The Water of Life [3-6], 1511

Haley, Gail E. *Puss in Boots* [1-4], **933**

Hastings, Selina. *Sir Gawain and the Loathly Lady* [3-6], 1521

Hewitt, Kathryn. *King Midas and the Golden Touch* [1-4], 1522

Kimmel, Eric A. *Boots and His Brothers: A Norwegian Tale* [2-6], **952**

Three Sacks of Truth: A Story from France [2-5], **958**

Kirstein, Lincoln. *Puss in Boots* [1-4], **959**

Lewis, J. Patrick. *The Frog Princess: A Russian Tale* [2-6], **969**

Mollel, Tololwa M. *The King and the Tortoise* [K-3], **988**

Pevear, Richard. *Our King Has Horns!* [2-5], 1579

Pittman, Helena Clare. *A Grain of Rice* [2-4], 1580

Rayevsky, Inna. *The Talking Tree* [2-5], 1584

Renberg, Dalia Hardof. *King Solomon and the Bee* [K-3], **1001**

Steptoe, John. *Mufaro's Beautiful Daughters: An African Tale* [1-4], 1607

Thomson, Peggy. *The Brave Little Tailor* [1-4], **1035**

The King Has Horse's Ears [2-5], 1613

Vernon, Adele. *The Riddle* [3-6], 1622

KIOWA INDIANS

Stroud, Virginia A. *Doesn't Fall Off His Horse* [2-3], **680**

KITES

Lies, Brian. *Hamlet and the Enormous Chinese Dragon Kite* [1-2], **484**

KNIGHTS AND KNIGHTHOOD

Bulla, Clyde Robert. *The Sword in the Tree* [2-3], 877

Carrick, Donald. *Harald and the Giant Knight* [2-3], 882

Murphy, Jill. *Jeffrey Strangeways* [3-4], **734**

Peet, Bill. *Cowardly Clyde* [2-3], 976

How Droofus the Dragon Lost His Head [1-2], 769

Scieszka, Jon. *Knights of the Kitchen Table* [3-4], **743**

Stearns, Pamela. *Into the Painted Bear Lair* [4-5], 1243

Winthrop, Elizabeth. *The Castle in the Attic* [5-6], 1374

KNIGHTS AND KNIGHTHOOD–Folklore

Hastings, Selina. *Sir Gawain and the Loathly Lady* [3-6], 1521

Hodges, Margaret. *Saint George and the Dragon: A Golden Legend* [3-6], 1526

Martin, Claire. *Boots & the Glass Mountain* [2-6], **981**

Shannon, Mark. *Gawain and the Green Knight* [3-6], **1022**

KNOCK-KNOCK JOKES

SEE ALSO Jokes; Riddles

Keller, Charles. *Norma Lee I Don't Knock on Doors* [K-3], 1839 [3-6], **1022**

Mathews, Judith, and Fay Robinson. *Knock-Knock Knees and Funny Bones: Riddles for Every Body* [3-6], **1370**

Rosenbloom, Joseph. *The Funniest Knock-Knock Book Ever!* [Pre-3], 1929

Knock Knock! Who's There? [3-6], 1933

KOALAS

Fox, Mem. *Koala Lou* [K-1], 389

KOREA–Folklore

SEE Folklore–Korea

KOREAN AMERICANS

Bunting, Eve. *Smoky Night* [2-3], **593**

Choi, Sook Nyul. *Halmoni and the Picnic* [1-2], **424**

Kline, Suzy. *Song Lee in Room 2B* [1-2], **476**

KOREAN AMERICANS–Poetry

Wong, Janet S. *Good Luck Gold and Other Poems* [4-6], **1424**

KOREAN LANGUAGE

Han, Suzanne Crowder. *The Rabbit's Escape* [1-5], **936**
The Rabbit's Judgment [1-5], **937**

LAKES

SEE Pond life

LAMBS

SEE Sheep

LANGUAGE

SEE ALSO English language; Sign language; Vocabulary; Word games
De Zutter, Hank. *Who Says a Dog Goes Bow-Wow?* [Pre-2], **1131**
Dorros, Arthur. *Abuela* [1-2], **434**
This Is My House [1-2], **435**
Feelings, Muriel. *Jambo Means Hello: Swahili Alphabet Book* [2-5], 1798
Leventhal, Debra. *What Is Your Language?* [Pre-K], **150**
Meltzer, Maxine. *Pups Speak Up* [K-1], **324**
Robinson, Marc. *Cock-a-Doodle-Doo! What Does It Sound Like to You?* [Pre-2], **1226**
Schwartz, Alvin. *The Cat's Elbow and Other Secret Languages* [2-6], 1945
Trivas, Irene. *Annie . . . Anya: A Month in Moscow* [K-1], **377**
Wells, Ruth. *A to Zen: A Book of Japanese Culture* [3-6], **1252**
Wood, Audrey. *The Tickleoctopus* [K-1], **387**

LANGUAGE–Poetry

Pomerantz, Charlotte. *If I Had a Paka* [K-4], 1902

LATIN AMERICA

Hurwitz, Johanna. *New Shoes for Sylvia* [Pre-K], **129**

LAZINESS

Balian, Lorna. *Leprechauns Never Lie* [1-2], 609
Du Bois, William Pène. *Lazy Tommy Pumpkinhead* [2-3], 911
Lobel, Arnold. *A Treeful of Pigs* [1-2], 729
Mwenye Hadithi. *Lazy Lion* [Pre-K], **171**
Polushkin, Maria. *Bubba and Babba* [K-1], 526

LAZINESS–Folklore

Aardema, Verna. *Anansi Finds a Fool* [1-5], **855**
dePaola, Tomie. *Jamie O'Rourke and the Big Potato: An Irish Folktale* [K-4], **895**

Hamanaka, Sheila. *Screen of Frogs: An Old Tale* [K-3], **934**
Kimmel, Eric A. *Anansi Goes Fishing* [Pre-2], **950**
Snyder, Dianne. *The Boy of the Three Year Nap* [2-5], 1603
Wolkstein, Diane. *Lazy Stories* [1-4], 1736

LEADERSHIP

Lisle, Janet Taylor. *Forest* [5-6], **827**
Lowry, Lois. *The Giver* [5-6], **828**

LEBANON

Heide, Florence Parry, and Judith Heide Gilliland. *Sami and the Time of the Troubles* [3-4], **713**

LEFT AND RIGHT

McMillan, Bruce. *Beach Ball—Left, Right* [Pre-K], **158**

LEOPARDS

Mwenye Hadithi. *Baby Baboon* [Pre], **37**

LEOPARDS–Folklore

Knutson, Barbara. *Sungura and Leopard: A Swahili Trickster Tale* [K-3], **960**

LEPRECHAUNS

SEE ALSO Fairies; Giants; Monsters; Ogres; Trolls
Balian, Lorna. *Leprechauns Never Lie* [1-2], 609
Brittain, Bill. *All the Money in the World* [4-5], 1152
Johnson, Elizabeth. *Stuck with Luck* [2-3], 938
Kennedy, Richard. *The Leprechaun's Story* [3-4], 1081
King-Smith, Dick. *Paddy's Pot of Gold* [3-4], **724**
Nixon, Joan Lowery. *The Gift* [3-4], 1099

LEPRECHAUNS–Folklore

dePaola, Tomie. *Jamie O'Rourke and the Big Potato: An Irish Folktale* [K-4], **895**
Nixon, Joan Lowery. *The Gift* [Pre-3], 1099

LETTER WRITING

Ada, Alma Flor. *Dear Peter Rabbit* [1-2], **395**
Ahlberg, Janet, and Allan Ahlberg. *The Jolly Christmas Postman* [1-2], **396**
Alexander, Sue. *Dear Phoebe* [1-2], 600
Asch, Frank, and Vladimir Vagin. *Dear Brother* [1-2], **401**
Caseley, Judith. *Dear Annie* [K-1], **250**
Getz, David. *Almost Famous* [5-6], 818
Jakobsen, Kathy. *My New York* [K-4], **1167**
Keats, Ezra Jack. *A Letter to Amy* [K-1], 451

LETTER WRITING (cont.)

Leedy, Loreen. *Postcards from Pluto: A Tour of the Solar System* [1-3], **1182**

Nichol, Barbara. *Beethoven Lives Upstairs* [4-5], **785**

Parker, Nancy Winslow. *Love from Uncle Clyde* [K-1], 518

Payne, Emmy. *Katy-No-Pocket* [Pre-K], 225

Sheldon, Dyan. *Love, Your Bear Pete* [K-1], **363**

Skurzynski, Gloria. *Here Comes the Mail* [K-3], **1240**

Temple, Lannis. *Dear World: How Children Around the World Feel About Our Environment* [2-6], **1247**

Tsutsui, Yoriko. *Anna's Secret Friend* [Pre-K], 275

Waber, Bernard. *Dear Hildegarde* [2-3], 1022

Woodruff, Elvira. *Dear Levi: Letters from the Overland Trail* [4-5], **796**

Dear Napoleon, I Know You're Dead, But . . . [5-6], **852**

LIBRARIANS

Coville, Bruce. *Jeremy Thatcher, Dragon Hatcher* [5-6], **810**

LIBRARIES

Bellaits, John. *The Treasure of Alpheus Winterborn* [5-6], 1275

Bonsall, Crosby. *Tell Me Some More* [Pre-K], 23

Caseley, Judith. *Sophie and Sammy's Library Sleepover* [Pre-K], **77**

Daugherty, James. *Andy and the Lion* [1-2], 658

Felt, Sue. *Rosa-Too-Little* [Pre-K], 83

Freeman, Don. *Quiet! There's a Canary in the Library* [Pre-K], 96

Green, John F. *Alice and the Birthday Giant* [K-1], 408

Huff, Barbara A. *Once Inside the Library* [1-2], **459**

Knowlton, Jack. *Books and Libraries* [2-5], **1171**

McPhail, David. *Lost!* [K-1], **316**

Porte, Barbara Ann. *Harry in Trouble* [K-1], 527

Sauer, Julie L. *Mike's House* [Pre-K], 252

Swallow, Pam. *Melvil and Dewey in the Chips* [2-3], 1012

LIBRARIES–Folklore

Day, David. *The Sleeper* [2-4], **891**

LIMERICKS

SEE ALSO Humorous poetry

Bodecker, N. M. *A Person from Britain Whose Head Was the Shape of a Mitten and Other Limericks* [3-6], 1752

Brewton, John E., and Lorraine A. Blackburn. *They've Discovered a Head in the Box for the Bread: And Other Laughable Limericks* [3-6], 1756

Brewton, Sara, John E. Brewton, and G. Meredith Blackburn, III. *My Tang's Tungled and Other Ridiculous Situations* [2-6], 1759

Ciardi, John. *The Hopeful Trout and Other Limericks* [3-6], 1771

Cricket Magazine, editors of. *Cricket's Jokes, Riddles & Other Stuff* [K-5], 1785

Lear, Edward. *Daffy Down Dillies: Silly Limericks* [3-6], **1348**

How Pleasant to Know Mr. Lear! [4-6], 1853

Of Pelicans and Pussycats: Poems and Limericks [K-5], **1349**

Livingston, Myra Cohn. *Lots of Limericks* [4-6], **1359**

Lobel, Arnold. *The Book of Pigericks* [2-6], 1861

Marshall, James. *Pocketful of Nonsense* [Pre-3], **1369**

Rosenbloom, Joseph. *The Looniest Limerick Book in the World* [4-6], 1934

Silly Verse (and Even Worse) [3-6], 1936

LINCOLN, ABRAHAM

Brenner, Martha. *Abe Lincoln's Hat* [1-4], **1110**

Kunhardt, Edith. *Honest Abe* [K-3], **1179**

Livingston, Myra Cohn. *Abraham Lincoln: A Man for All the People* [K-3], **1189**

LINDBERGH, CHARLES A.

Burleigh, Robert. *Flight: The Journey of Charles Lindbergh* [3-6], **1114**

Demarest, Chris L. *Lindbergh* [2-4], **1128**

LIONS

Berger, Terry. *The Turtle's Picnic: And Other Nonsense Stories* [1-2], 615

Daugherty, James. *Andy and the Lion* [1-2], 658

Du Bois, William Pène. *Lion* [2-3], 912

Fatio, Louise. *The Happy Lion* [K-1], 385

Frascino, Edward. *My Cousin the King* [K-1], 390

Freeman, Don. *Dandelion* [K-1], 392

Hofer, Angelika. *The Lion Family Book* [1-6], 2051

Leslie-Melville, Betty. *Elephant Have the Right of Way: Life with the Wild Animals of Africa* [2-6], **1185**

Lewis, C. S. *The Lion, the Witch and the Wardrobe* [3-4], 1088

Mwenye Hadithi. *Lazy Lion* [Pre-K], **171**

Peet, Bill. *Hubert's Hair-Raising Adventure* [1-2], 770

Sendak, Maurice. *Pierre* [K-1], 552

Yoshida, Toshi. *Young Lions* [1-4], 2116

LIONS–Folklore

Aardema, Verna. *Rabbit Makes a Monkey Out of Lion* [Pre-3], 1382

Martin, Rafe. *Foolish Rabbit's Big Mistake* [Pre-2], 1564

Wildsmith, Brian. *The Lion and the Rat* [Pre-3], 1628

LITERACY

Heide, Florence Parry, and Judith Heide Gilliland. *The Day of Ahmed's Secret* [2-3], **616**

LITERARY FAIRY TALES

Andersen, Hans Christian. *The Steadfast Tin Soldier* [2-3], **586**

The Tinderbox [4-5], **757**

The Wild Swans [3-4], **700**

Barber, Antonia. *Catkin* [2-3], **590**

Houseman, Laurence. *Rocking-Horse Land* [1-2], 690

Kimmel, Eric A. *Asher and the Capmakers: A Hanukkah Story* [2-3], **635**

Langerlöf, Selma. *The Changeling* [2-3], **636**

LeGuin, Ursula K. *A Ride on the Red Mare's Back* [2-3], **637**

Mathews, Sally Schofer. *The Sad Night: The Story of an Aztec Victory and a Spanish Loss* [5-6], **1206**

Melmed, Laura Krauss. *The Rainbabies* [1-2], **508**

Moser, Barry. *Tucker Pfeffercorn: An Old Story Retold* [4-5], **779**

Nesbit, E. *Melisande* [4-5], 1218

Pyle, Howard. *The Swan Maiden* [2-3], **665**

Rael, Elsa Okon. *Marushka's Egg* [2-3], **667**

Singer, Marilyn. *The Painted Fan* [3-4], **748**

Stanley, Diane. *Fortune* [3-4], 1117

Thurber, James. *The Great Quillow* [2-3], **684**

Yep, Laurence. *The Ghost Fox* [3-4], **755**

LIZARDS

SEE ALSO Reptiles; Salamanders

Himmelman, John. *Talester the Lizard* [Pre-K], 134

Pinkwater, Daniel. *Lizard Music* [4-5], 1225

Ryder, Joanne. *Lizard in the Sun* [Pre-3], 2090

Sargeant, Sarah. *Weird Henry Berg* [5-6], 1352

LONDON

SEE ALSO England

Haley, Gail E. *Dream Peddler* [2-3], **612**

LONELINESS

Spinelli, Eileen. *Somebody Loves You, Mr. Hatch* [K-1], **371**

Waddell, Martin. *Sam Vole and His Brothers* [Pre], **51**

LOONS

Esbensen, Barbara Juster. *Great Northern Diver: The Loon* [2-6], **1137**

LOST

Alborough, Jez. *Where's My Teddy?* [Pre], **2**

Bancroft, Catherine, and Hannah Coale Gruenberg. *Felix's Hat* [Pre-K], **70**

Booth, Barbara D. *Mandy* [1-2], **408**

Byars, Betsy. *The Summer of the Swans* [5-6], 1282

Cleary, Beverly. *Ribsy* [2-3], 891

Clifford, Sandy. *The Roquefort Gang* [3-4], 1053

Cohen, Miriam. *Lost in the Museum* [K-1], 369

Cole, Joanna. *The Magic School Bus Lost in the Solar System* [1-4], **1121**

DeJong, Meindert. *Hurry Home, Candy* [3-4], 1060

Drummond, V. H. *Phewtus the Squirrel* [Pre-K], 74

Flack, Marjorie. *Angus Lost* [Pre-K], 86

Walter the Lazy Moose [1-2], 668

Flora, James. *Sherwood Walks Home* [Pre-K], 88

Geraghty, Paul. *The Hunter* [1-2], **442**

Gerstein, Mordicai. *Follow Me!* [Pre-K], 112

Goble, Paul. *Dream Wolf* [1-2], **443**

Hayes, Sarah. *This Is the Bear* [Pre-K], 128

This Is the Bear and the Scary Night [Pre], **19**

Henkes, Kevin. *Sheila Rae, the Brave* [Pre-K], 132

Hughes, Shirley. *Dogger* [Pre-K], 146

Jonas, Ann. *Where Can It Be?* [Pre], **25**

Kinsey-Warnock, Natalie. *The Bear That Heard Crying* [1-2], **468**

Kleven, Elisa. *The Paper Princess* [Pre-K], **146**

London, Jonathan. *Let's Go, Froggy* [Pre-K], **153**

McCully, Emily Arnold. *Picnic* [Pre-K], 196

McPhail, David. *Lost!* [K-1], **316**

Modell, Frank. *Tooley! Tooley!* [1-2], 752

Pinkwater, Daniel. *The Hoboken Chicken Emergency* [3-4], 1104

Porte, Barbara Ann. *Harry in Trouble* [K-1], 527

Rodda, Emily. *Finders Keepers* [4-5], **789**

Sauer, Julie L. *Mike's House* [Pre-K], 252

Sharmat, Marjorie Weinman. *Chasing after Annie* [2-3], **998**

Sheldon, Dyan. *Love, Your Bear Pete* [K-1], **363**

Stonely, Jack. *Scruffy* [4-5], 1245

Taylor, Mark. *Henry the Explorer* [K-1], 564

Vreeken, Elizabeth. *The Boy Who Would Not Say His Name* [K-1], 576

Wells, Rosemary. *Hazel's Amazing Mother* [K-1], 585

Zion, Gene. *Harry by the Sea* [Pre-K], 307

LOVE

Andersen, Hans Christian. *The Steadfast Tin Soldier* [2-3], **586**

Armstrong, Jennifer. *Chin Yu Min and the Ginger Cat* [2-3], **588**

Babbitt, Natalie. *Bub: Or, the Very Best Thing* [K-1], **224**

Carlstrom, Nancy White. *How Do You Say It Today, Jesse Bear?* [Pre-K], **76**

Cooke, Trish. *So Much* [Pre], **8**

Dahl, Roald. *Esio Trot* [3-4], **710**

dePaola, Tomie. *Big Anthony and the Magic Ring* [2-3], 908

Ernst, Lisa Campbell. *Ginger Jumps* [K-1], **269**

Fox, Mem. *Koala Lou* [K-1], **389**

Friedman, Ina R. *How My Parents Learned to Eat* [1-2], 672

Geringer, Laura. *A Three Hat Day* [Pre-K], 111

Greenspan, Adele Aron. *Daddies* [Pre-K], **114**

Jeschke, Susan. *Lucky's Choice* [K-1], **291**

Kasza, Keiko. *A Mother for Choco* [Pre-K], **140**

Kimmel, Eric A. *Bernal & Florinda: A Spanish Tale* [3-4], **720**

Langerlöf, Selma. *The Changeling* [2-3], **636**

Laroche, Michel. *The Snow Rose* [3-4], 1086

Price, Leontyne. *Aïda* [5-6], **837**

Silverstein, Shel. *The Giving Tree* [2-3], 1001

Singer, Marilyn. *The Painted Fan* [3-4], **748**

Spinelli, Eileen. *Somebody Loves You, Mr. Hatch* [K-1], **371**

Wade, Barrie. *Little Monster* [Pre-K], 284

Williams, Vera B. *"More More More," Said the Baby: Three Love Stories* [Pre], **58**

Wilsdorf, Anne. *Princess* [1-2], **577**

LOVE–Folklore

Goble, Paul. *Buffalo Woman* [2-6], 1481
Love Flute [3-6], **916**

Grimm, Jacob. *Iron John* [2-6], **928**

Schroeder, Alan. *Lily and the Wooden Bowl* [1-4], **1021**

Yolen, Jane. *Tam Lin* [3-6], **1048**

LOYALTY–Folklore

San Souci, Robert D. *The Samurai's Daughter* [3-6], **1014**

Yep, Laurence. *The Junior Thunder Lord* [1-4], **1046**

LUCK

Alexander, Lloyd. *The Fortune-Tellers* [3-4], **698**

Allard, Harry. *I Will Not Go to a Market Today* [K-1], 316

Charlip, Remy. *Fortunately* [1-2], 645

Ernst, Lisa Campbell. *The Luckiest Kid on the Planet* [1-2], **439**

Gackenbach, Dick. *Harvey the Foolish Pig* [K-1], 397

Kroll, Steven. *Friday the 13th* [1-2], 716

LYING

SEE Honesty

MACHINES

Brown, Margaret. *The Steamroller* [K-1], 346

Burton, Virgina Lee. *Katy and the Big Snow* [Pre-K], 35
Mike Mulligan and His Steam Shovel [Pre-K], 36

Du Bois, William Pène. *Lazy Tommy Pumpkinhead* [2-3], **911**

Goldberg, Rube. *The Best of Rube Goldberg* [3-6], 2040

Gramatky, Hardie. *Hercules* [Pre-K], 120

Selden, George. *Sparrow Socks* [1-2], 799

MACHINES–Folklore

Lester, Julius. *John Henry* [1-4], **967**

Sanfield, Steve. *A Natural Man: The True Story of John Henry* [4-6], 1588

MACHINES–Poetry

Hopkins, Lee Bennett. *Click, Rumble, Roar: Poems about Machines* [2-5], 1819

MAGIC

SEE ALSO Tricks

Ainsworth, Ruth. *The Phantom Carousel and Other Ghostly Tales* [4-5], 1138

Alexander, Lloyd. *The Cat Who Wished to Be a Man* [5-6], 1259

Bacon, Peggy. *The Magic Touch* [3-4], 1043

Balian, Lorna. *The Sweet Touch* [K-1], 329

Banks, Lynne Reid. *The Adventures of King Midas* [4-5], **758**
The Magic Hare [3-4], **702**

Benjamin, Saragail Katzman. *My Dog Ate It* [3-4], **704**

Bennett, Anna Elizabeth. *Little Witch* [2-3], 874

Brittain, Bill. *All the Money in the World* [4-5], 1152
Devil's Donkey [5-6], 1276
Dr. Dredd's Wagon of Wonders [5-6], 1277
The Wish Giver: Three Tales of Coven Tree [5-6], 1278

Broekel, Ray, and Laurence B. White, Jr. *Now You See It: Easy Magic for Beginners* [2-5], 1999

Brown, Bob. *How to Fool Your Friends* [3-5], 2000

Carris, Joan. *Witch-Cat* [3-4], **706**

Catling, Patrick Skene. *The Chocolate Touch* [2-3], 884

Chapman, Carol. *Barney Bipple's Magic Dandelions* [1-2], 644

Chetwin, Grace. *Friends in Time* [4-5], **764**

Coombs, Patricia. *Dorrie and the Weather Box* [1-2], 653

Corbett, Scott. *The Lemonade Trick* [3-4], 1056
The Limerick Trick [3-4], 1057

Coville, Bruce. *Jennifer Murdley's Toad* [4-5], **765**

Cresswell, Helen. *Time Out* [3-4], **708**

dePaola, Tomie. *Big Anthony and the Magic Ring* [2-3], 908

Dillon, Barbara. *A Mom by Magic* [4-5], **767**
Mrs. Tooey & the Terrible Toxic Tar [3-4], 1062

Everitt, Betsy. *Frida the Wondercat* [K-1], 384

Fleischman, Sid. *Mr. Mysterious's Secrets of Magic* [3-6], 2024

Gackenbach, Dick. *Mag the Magnificent* [K-1], 398

Graves, Robert. *The Big Green Book* [1-2], 680

Green, John F. *Alice and the Birthday Giant* [K-1], 408

Hiller, Catherine. *Abracatabby* [K-1], 424

Hoffman, Mary. *The Four-Legged Ghosts* [2-3], **620**

Hunter, Mollie. *Wicked One: A Story of Suspense* [5-6], 1313

Hutchins, Hazel. *The Three and Many Wishes of Jason Reid* [3-4], 1077

Julian, Nancy R. *The Peculiar Miss Pickett* [2-4], 940

Kimmel, Eric A. *Asher and the Capmakers: A Hanukkah Story* [2-3], **635**

King-Smith, Dick. *The Queen's Nose* [3-4], **726**

Kipling, Rudyard. *How the Camel Got His Hump* [2-3], 947

Kraske, Robert. *Magicians Do Amazing Things* [3-6], 2059

Krensky, Steven. *The Dragon Circle* [4-5], 1202

Lester, Helen. *The Wizard, the Fairy and the Magic Chicken* [Pre-K], 185

Lindbergh, Anne. *Travel Far, Pay No Fare* [5-6], **826**

McGowen, Tom. *The Magician's Apprentice* [5-6], 1329

McGraw, Eloise Jarvis. *Joel and the Great Merlini* [3-4], 1093

McPhail, David. *The Magical Drawings of Mooney B. Finch* [1-2], 737

Mayer, Mercer. *Mrs. Beggs and the Wizard* [1-2], 749
A Special Trick [2-3], 961

Moore, Inga. *The Sorcerer's Apprentice* [2-3], **648**

Petersen, P. J. *The Amazing Magic Show* [1-2], **529**

Pomerantz, Charlotte. *The Downtown Fairy Godmother* [2-3], 981

Rinkoff, Barbara. *The Dragon's Handbooks* [2-3], 984

Roberts, Willo Davis. *The Magic Book* [4-5], 1229

Root, Phyllis. *Coyote and the Magic Words* [K-1], **351**

Seeger, Pete. *Abiyoyo* [K-1], 548

Selznick, Brian. *The Houdini Box* [3-4], **745**

Seuss, Dr. *Bartholomew and the Oobleck* [2-3], 994

Shusterman, Neal. *The Eyes of Kid Midas* [5-6], **842**

Smith, L. J. *The Night of the Solstice* [5-6], 1362

Stanley, Diane. *The Good-Luck Pencil* [2-3], 1005

Steig, William. *Solomon the Rusty Nail* [2-3], 1008

Sterman, Betsy, and Samuel Sterman. *Too Much Magic* [3-4], 1119

Turkle, Brinton. *Do Not Open* [2-3], 1016

Van Allsburg, Chris. *The Sweetest Fig* [3-4], **751**
The Widow's Broom [3-4], **752**

Vande Velde, Vivian. *A Hidden Magic* [4-5], 1251

Williams, Jay. *The Magic Grandfather* [4-5], 1254

Woodruff, Elvira. *The Summer I Shrank My Grandmother* [4-5], **800**

Wright, Jill. *The Old Woman and the Jar of Uums* [1-2], 856

Yolen, Jane. *Wizard's Hall* [4-5], **801**

MAGIC–Folklore

dePaola, Tomie. *Strega Nona* [K-4], 1444

Galdone, Paul. *The Magic Porridge Pot* [Pre-2], 1465

Haviland, Virginia. *The Talking Pot: A Danish Folktale* [K-3], **939**

Johnston, Tony. *The Badger and the Magic Fan: A Japanese Folktale* [Pre-2], 1536

Yolen, Jane. *Tam Lin* [3-6], **1048**

MAGICIANS

Banks, Lynne Reid. *The Adventures of King Midas* [4-5], **758**

Cole, Joanna. *Doctor Change* [2-3], 896

Coombs, Patricia. *The Magician and McTree* [2-3], 900

Howe, James. *Rabbit-Cadabra!* [1-2], **458**

Kraske, Robert. *Magicians Do Amazing Things* [3-6], 2059

Lewis, C. S. *The Magician's Nephew* [4-5], 1204

McCully, Emily Arnold. *The Amazing Felix* [1-2], **491**

McGowen, Tom. *The Magician's Apprentice* [5-6], 1329

Mayer, Mercer. *A Special Trick* [2-3], 961

Moore, Inga. *The Sorcerer's Apprentice* [2-3], **648**

MAGICIANS (cont.)

Petersen, P. J. *The Amazing Magic Show* [1-2], **529**

Selznick, Brian. *The Houdini Box* [3-4], **745**

Seuss, Dr. *Bartholomew and the Oobleck* [2-3], **994**

Van Allsburg, Chris. *The Garden of Abdul Gasazi* [2-3], 1019

White, Florence. *Escape! The Life of Harry Houdini* [3-6], 2113

MAGICIANS–Folklore

Turska, Krystyna. *The Magician of Cracow* [2-5], 1619

MAINE

McCloskey, Robert. *Burt Dow, Deep-Water Man* [2-3], 955

Time of Wonder [2-3], 957

Van de Wetering, Janwillem. *Hugh Pine* [3-4], 1127

MALI

Wisniewski, David. *Sundiata: Lion King of Mali* [3-5], **1254**

MAMMALS

Heller, Ruth. *Animals Born Alive and Well* [K-4], **1159**

MANNEQUINS

Dillon, Barbara. *A Mom by Magic* [4-5], **767**

MANNERS

SEE Etiquette

MAN, PREHISTORIC

Scieszka, Jon. *Your Mother Was a Neanderthal* [4-5], **790**

Wood, Audrey. *The Tickleoctopus* [K-1], **387**

MAPS AND GLOBES

Brisson, Pat. *Magic Carpet* [1-2], **411**

Bursik, Rose. *Amelia's Fantastic Flight* [1-2], **417**

Cherry, Lynne. *The Armadillo from Amarillo* [1-2], **423**

Hopkinson, Deborah. *Sweet Clara and the Freedom Quilt* [2-3], **622**

Jakobsen, Kathy. *My New York* [K-4], **1167**

Lester, Alison. *The Journey Home* [K-1], **303**

McMillan, Bruce. *Mouse Views: What the Class Pet Saw* [K-1], **315**

McPhail, David. *Lost!* [K-1], **316**

MARINE ANIMALS

Berg, Cami. *D Is for Dolphin* [Pre-3], **1106**

Carle, Eric. *A House for Hermit Crab* [K-1], **246**

Cole, Joanna. *The Magic School Bus on the Ocean Floor* [2-4], **1122**

Doubilet, Anne. *Under the Sea from A to Z* [K-5], **1134**

Hulme, Joy N. *Sea Squares* [2-3], **624**

Lauber, Patricia. *An Octopus Is Amazing* [1-3], **1181**

MacDonald, Suse. *Sea Shapes* [Pre-K], **157**

Marshak, Suzanna. *I Am the Ocean* [K-4], **1200**

O'Donnell, Elizabeth Lee. *The Twelve Days of Summer* [1-2], **523**

Zoehfeld, Kathleen Weidner. *What Lives in a Shell?* [Pre-2], **1258**

MARKETS

Williams, Karen Lynn. *Tap-Tap* [1-2], **576**

MARRIAGE–Folklore

Cook, Joel. *The Rat's Daughter* [K-2], **886**

Dupré, Judith. *The Mouse Bride: A Mayan Folk Tale* [K-2], **898**

Kimmel, Eric A. *The Greatest of All: A Japanese Folktale* [K-2], **954**

Kwon, Holly H. *The Moles and the Mireuk: A Korean Folktale* [K-2], **962**

MASSACHUSETTS

Harness, Cheryl. *Three Young Pilgrims* [2-3], **614**

Waters, Kate. *Samuel Eaton's Day: A Day in the Life of a Pilgrim Boy* [2-4], **1250**

MASSACHUSETTS–Folklore

Manitonquat (Medicine Story). *Children of the Morning Light: Wampanoag Tales* [3-6], **1077**

MATHEMATICS

SEE ALSO Counting books; Division; Measurement; Multiplication; Subtraction

Axelrod, Amy. *Pigs Will Be Pigs* [1-2], **403**

Birch, David. *The King's Chessboard* [3-4], 1045[4-5], **790**

Brandreth, Gyles. *Brain-Teasers and Mind-Benders* [3-6], 1997

Churchill, E. Richard. *Devilish Bets to Trick Your Friends* [3-6], 2005

Duffey, Betsy. *The Math Whiz* [2-3], **607**

Ehlert, Lois. *Fish Eyes: A Book You Can Count On* [Pre-K], **97**

Harshman, Marc. *Only One* [K-1], **280**

Hulme, Joy N. *Sea Squares* [2-3], **624**

Leedy, Loreen. *Fraction Action* [1-2], **482**

MacDonald, Suse, and Bill Oakes. *Puzzlers* [K-1], **314**

McMillan, Bruce. *Eating Fractions* [Pre-1], **1193**

Matthews, Louise. *Gator Pie* [K-1], 506

Phillips, Louis. *263 Brain Busters: Just How Smart Are You, Anyway?* [3-6], 2083

Pinczes, Elinor J. *One Hundred Hungry Ants* [1-2], **533**
Schwartz, David M. *How Much Is a Million?* [1-4], 2093
  If You Made a Million [2-4], 2094

MATHEMATICS–Folklore
Dee, Ruby. *Two Ways to Count to Ten: A Liberian Folktale* [K-3], 1436
Hong, Lily Toy. *Two of Everything: A Chinese Folktale* [K-3], **943**

MATHEMATICS–Riddles
Keller, Charles. *Take Me to Your Liter: Science and Math Jokes* [3-6], **1339**

MATURITY
Kraus, Robert. *Leo the Late Bloomer* [K-1], 460
McPhail, David. *Pig Pig Grows Up* [Pre-K], 202

MAYAN INDIANS
Wisniewski, David. *Rain Player* [2-3], **694**

MAYAN INDIANS–Folklore
Dupré, Judith. *The Mouse Bride: A Mayan Folk Tale* [K-2], **898**

MEASUREMENT
SEE ALSO Counting books; Mathematics
Lasky, Kathryn. *The Librarian Who Measured the Earth* [3-6], **1180**
Lionni, Leo. *Inch by Inch* [K-1], 475
Most, Bernard. *How Big Were the Dinosaurs?* [K-2], **1212**
Myller, Rolf. *How Big Is a Foot?* [2-3], 970
Russo, Marisabina. *The Line Up Book* [Pre-K], 247

MEMORY
Arnold, Tedd. *Ollie Forgot* [1-2], 607
Bahr, Mary. *The Memory Box* [2-3], **589**
Gackenbach, Dick. *Alice's Special Room* [Pre-K], **106**
Galdone, Joanna, and Paul Galdone. *Gertrude the Goose Who Forgot* [Pre-K], 107
Hoguet, Susan. *I Unpacked My Grandmother's Trunk* [1-2], 689
Hutchins, Pat. *Don't Forget the Bacon!* [K-1], 434
King-Smith, Dick. *Farmer Bungle Forgets* [K-1], 458
Levine, Evan. *Not the Piano, Mrs. Medley!* [1-2], **483**
MacGregor, Ellen. *Theodore Turtle* [K-1], 491
Patz, Nancy. *Pumpernickel Tickel and Mean Green Cheese* [K-1], 520
Weinberg, Larry. *The Forgetful Bears Meet Mr. Memory* [K-1], 583

MEMORY–Folklore
Birdseye, Tom. *Soap! Soap! Don't Forget the Soap! An Appalachian Folktale* [1-3], **869**
Lottridge, Celia Barker. *The Name of the Tree: A Bantu Folktale* [Pre-2], **973**

MENTAL ILLNESS
Myers, Anna. *Red-Dirt Jessie* [4-5], **780**

MENTAL RETARDATION
Conly, Jane Leslie. *Crazy Lady!* [5-6], **808**
Dodds, Bill. *My Sister Annie* [4-5], **768**
Slepian, Jan. *Risk N' Roses* [5-6], **845**

MENTALLY HANDICAPPED
SEE Handicaps; Mental retardation

MERMAIDS–Folklore
Osborne, Mary Pope. *Mermaid Tales from Around the World* [3-6], **1082**
San Souci, Robert D. *Sukey and the Mermaid* [2-5], **1017**

METEORS
Branley, Franklyn M. *Shooting Stars* [1-3], **1109**

MEXICAN AMERICANS
Bunting, Eve. *A Day's Work* [2-3], **592**
Soto, Gary. *Too Many Tamales* [K-1], **369**

MEXICO
Garrett, Helen. *Angelo the Naughty One* [1-2], 676
Lewis, Thomas P. *Hill of Fire* [1-2], 723
Mathews, Sally Schofer. *The Sad Night: The Story of an Aztec Victory and a Spanish Loss* [5-6], **1206**

MICE
Alexander, Sue. *Dear Phoebe* [1-2], 600
Asch, Frank. *Pearl's Promise* [3-4], **701**
Asch, Frank, and Vladimir Vagin. *Dear Brother* [1-2], **401**
Aylesworth, Jim. *Two Terrible Frights* [Pre-K], 18
Baehr, Patricia. *Mouse in the House* [Pre-K], **68**
Brenner, Barbara. *Mr. Tall and Mr. Small* [K-1], 343
Browne, Eileen. *No Problem* [1-2], **414**
Bunting, Eve. *The Mother's Day Mice* [Pre-K], 32
Cleary, Beverly. *The Mouse and the Motorcycle* [3-4], 1050
  Ralph S. Mouse [3-4], 1051
Clifford, Sandy. *The Roquefort Gang* [3-4], 1053
Dahl, Roald. *The Witches* [4-5], 1167
Drury, Roger W. *The Champion of Merrimack County* [4-5], 1169
Duke, Kate. *Aunt Isabel Tells a Good One* [1-2], **436**
Emberley, Michael. *Ruby* [1-2], **437**

MICE (cont.)

Engel, Diana. *Eleanor, Arthur, and Claire* [K-1], **267**

Flack, Marjorie. *Walter the Lazy Moose* [1-2], 668

Fleming, Denise. *Lunch* [Pre], **14**

Freeman, Don. *Norman the Doorman* [1-2], 671

Gregory, Valiska. *Babysitting for Benjamin* [K-1], **276**

Harris, Dorothy Joan. *The School Mouse* [K-1], 415

Henkes, Kevin. *Chrysanthemum* [K-1], **282**

Julius, the Baby of the World [K-1], **283**

Owen [Pre-K], **122**

Sheila Rae, the Brave [Pre-K], 132

A Weekend with Wendell [K-1], 420

Hoffman, Mary. *The Four-Legged Ghosts* [2-3], **620**

Ivimey, John W. *The Complete Story of the Three Blind Mice* [Pre-K], 151

Complete Version of Ye Three Blind Mice [Pre-K], 152

Three Blind Mice: The Classic Nursery Rhyme [Pre-K], **131**

Jacques, Brian. *Redwall* [5-6], 1315

Jeschke, Susan. *Lucky's Choice* [K-1], **291**

King-Smith, Dick. *Martin's Mice* [3-4], 1085

Kraus, Robert. *Whose Mouse Are You?* [Pre-K], 177

Langstaff, John. *Frog Went a-Courtin'* [Pre-K], 179

Lawson, Robert. *Ben and Me* [5-6], 1324

Lewison, Wendy Cheyette. *Shy Vi* [Pre-K], **151**

Lionni, Leo. *Alexander and the Wind-Up Mouse* [1-2], 726

Frederick [1-2], 727

Frederick's Fables: A Leo Lionni Treasury of Favorite Stories [1-2], 728

Matthew's Dream [K-1], **308**

Tillie and the Wall [K-1], 477

Lobel, Arnold. *Mouse Tales* [K-1], 482

Low, Joseph. *Mice Twice* [K-1], 488

McCully, Emily Arnold. *The Christmas Gift* [Pre-K], 195

Picnic [Pre-K], 196

McMillan, Bruce. *Mouse Views: What the Class Pet Saw* [K-1], **315**

Manson, Christopher. *The Marvelous Blue Mouse* [2-3], **641**

Martin, Jacqueline Briggs. *Bizzy Bones and the Lost Quilt* [Pre-K], 206

Moore, Lilian. *I'll Meet You at the Cucumbers* [2-3], 967

Numeroff, Laura. *If You Give a Mouse a Cookie* [K-1], 514

O'Brien, Robert C. *Mrs. Frisby and the Rats of NIMH* [5-6], 1337

Peppé, Rodney. *The Mice Who Lived in a Shoe* [1-2], 772

Pilkey, Dav. *Dogzilla* [2-3], **657**

Kat Kong [2-3], **658**

Polushkin, Maria. *Mother, Mother, I Want Another* [Pre-K], 230

Roche, P. K. *Good-Bye, Arnold* [K-1], 533

Schindel, John. *What's for Lunch?* [Pre-K], **185**

Selden, George. *The Cricket in Times Square* [4-5], 1237

Steig, William. *Abel's Island* [5-6], 1364

Dr. DeSoto [2-3], 1007

Titus, Eve. *Anatole* [1-2], 830

Basil of Baker Street [4-5], 1249

Tompert, Ann. *Just a Little Bit* [Pre-K], **192**

Udry, Janice May. *Thump and Plunk* [Pre-K], 277

Van Leeuwen, Jean. *The Great Christmas Kidnapping Caper* [3-4], 1128

The Great Rescue Operation [4-5], 1252

Waddell, Martin. *Squeak-a-Lot* [Pre], **52**

Walsh, Ellen Stoll. *Mouse Count* [Pre], **54**

Mouse Paint [Pre-K], **204**

Watson, Clyde. *How Brown Mouse Kept Christmas* [1-2], 847

Wells, Rosemary. *Shy Charles* [K-1], 586

White, E. B. *Stuart Little* [3-4], 1131

Wood, Don, and Audrey Wood. *The Little Mouse, the Red Ripe Strawberry, and the Big Hungry Bear* [Pre], **60**

Zelinsky, Paul O. *The Maid and the Mouse and the Odd-Shaped House* [1-2], 860

MICE–Folklore

Cauley, Lorinda Bryan. *The Town Mouse and the Country Mouse* [Pre-2], 1421

Dupré, Judith. *The Mouse Bride: A Mayan Folk Tale* [K-2], **898**

Kimmel, Eric A. *The Greatest of All: A Japanese Folktale* [K-2], **954**

Nimmo, Jenny. *The Witches and the Singing Mice* [1-4], **992**

Steptoe, John. *The Story of Jumping Mouse: A Native American Legend* [Pre-4], 1608

Young, Ed. *Seven Blind Mice* [Pre-3], **1051**

MICE–Poetry

Larrick, Nancy. *Mice Are Nice* [1-5], **1347**

Moore, Lilian. *Adam Mouse's Book of Poems* [1-4], **1374**

MICE–Riddles
Gounaud, Karen Jo. *A Very Mice Joke Book* [1-5], 1806

MICROSCOPES AND MICROSCOPY
Grillone, Lisa, and Joseph Gennaro. *Small Worlds Close Up* [4-6], 2043
Simon, Seymour. *Hidden Worlds: Pictures of the Invisible* [4-6], 2102

MIDDLE AGES
Bulla, Clyde Robert. *The Sword in the Tree* [2-3], 877
Carrick, Donald. *Harald and the Giant Knight* [2-3], 882
 Harald and the Great Stag [2-3], 883
Greer, Gery, and Bob Ruddick. *Max and Me and the Time Machine* [5-6], 1306
Skurzynski, Gloria. *What Happened to Hamelin* [5-6], 1358

MIDDLE AGES–Folklore
Corrin, Sara, and Stephen Corrin. *The Pied Piper of Hamelin* [2-6], 1431
Lemieux, Michèle. *Pied Piper of Hamelin* [2-5], **966**

MIDDLE WEST
 SEE Midwest

MIDWEST
Williams, David. *Grandma Essie's Covered Wagon* [2-3], **691**

MIGRATION
Auch, Mary Jane. *Bird Dogs Can't Fly* [K-1], **219**
Meddaugh, Susan. *Tree of Birds* [Pre-K], **164**
Peters, Lisa Westberg. *This Way Home* [K-3], **1217**
Yolen, Jane. *Honkers* [K-1], **391**

MIGRATION–Folklore
Bruchac, Joseph. *The Great Ball Game: A Muskogee Story* [K-3], **871**

MILK
Babcock, Chris. *No Moon, No Milk* [K-1], **225**
Ericsson, Jennifer A. *No Milk!* [Pre-K], **99**
Robbins, Ken. *Make Me a Peanut Butter Sandwich and a Glass of Milk* [1-4], **1225**

MILK–Folklore
Van Laan, Nancy. *The Tiny, Tiny Boy and the Big, Big Cow: A Scottish Folk Tale* [Pre-K], **1040**

MITTENS
 SEE ALSO Clothing and dress
Rogers, Jean. *Runaway Mittens* [Pre-K], 244

Slobodkin, Florence. *Too Many Mittens* [Pre-K], 268

MITTENS–Folklore
Brett, Jan. *The Mitten* [Pre-2], 1409
Tresselt, Alvin. *The Mitten: An Old Ukrainian Folktale* [Pre-2], 1615

MNEMONICS
Cleveland, Will, and Mark Alvarez. *Yo, Millard Fillmore! (And All Those Other Presidents You Don't Know)* [4-6], **1119**

MOHAWK INDIANS–Folklore
Gates, Frieda. *Owl Eyes* [K-3], **911**

MOLES–Folklore
Ehlert, Lois. *Moon Rope: Un Lazo a la Luna: A Peruvian Folktale* [Pre-2], **902**
Kwon, Holly H. *The M*oles and the Mireuk: A Korean Folktale* [K-2], **962**

MONEY
Adams, Barbara Johnston. *The Go-Around Dollar* [1-4], **1094**
Armstrong, Jennifer. *Chin Yu Min and the Ginger Cat* [2-3], **588**
Axelrod, Amy. *Pigs Will Be Pigs* [1-2], **403**
Brittain, Bill. *All the Money in the World* [4-5], 1152
Byars, Betsy. *McMummy* [4-5], **762**
Cauley, Lorinda Bryan. *The Goose and the Golden Coins* [K-1], 1416
Conford, Ellen. *A Job for Jenny Archer* [2-3], 899
 What's Cooking, Jenny Archer? [2-3], **601**
Gackenbach, Dick. *Harvey the Foolish Pig* [K-1], 397
Gilson, Jamie. *Dial Leroi Rupert, D.J.* [4-5], 1178
Herman, Charlotte. *Max Malone Makes a Million* [2-3], **617**
Jaffe, Nina. *In the Month of Kislev: A Story for Hanukkah* [2-3], **627**
Kimmel, Eric A. *Four Dollars and Fifty Cents* [3-4], **721**
King-Smith, Dick. *The Queen's Nose* [3-4], **726**
Levitin, Sonia. *Jason and the Money Tree* [4-5], 1203
McPhail, David. *Pig Pig Gets a Job* [K-1], **318**
Maestro, Betsy. *The Story of Money* [3-5], **1197**
Peterson, Esther Allen. *Penelope Gets Wheels* [1-2], 774
Pfeffer, Susan Beth. *Kid Power* [4-5], 1224
Robertson, Keith. *Henry Reed's Baby-Sitting Service* [5-6], 1347
Roy, Ron. *Million Dollar Jeans* [4-5], 1233

MONEY (cont.)

Schertle, Alice. *Bill and Google-Eyed Goblins* [1-2], 792

Schwartz, Alvin. *Gold and Silver, Silver and Gold: Tales of Hidden Treasure* [4-6], 2092

Schwartz, David M. *If You Made a Million* [2-4], 2094

Stevens, Carla. *Lily and Miss Liberty* [2-3], **679**

Sun, Chying Feng. *Mama Bear* [1-2], **562**

Tolan, Stephanie S. *Sophie and the Sidewalk Man* [2-3], **685**

Van Leeuwen, Jean. *Benjy in Business* [2-3], 1021

Viorst, Judith. *Alexander Who Used to Be Rich Last Sunday* [1-2], 839

Williams, Jay. *One Big Wish* [2-3], 1030

Williams, Vera B. *A Chair for My Mother* [1-2], 851

Zimelman, Nathan. *How the Second Grade Got $8,205.50 to Visit the Statue of Liberty* [1-2], **583**

MONEY–Folklore

Han, Oki S., and Stephanie Haboush Plunkett. *Sir Whong and the Golden Pig* [2-5], **935**

Uchida, Yoshiko. *The Magic Purse* [1-4], **1037**

MONGOOSE

Kipling, Rudyard. *Rikki-Tikki-Tavi* [3-4], **729**

MONKEYS

SEE ALSO Chimpanzees; Gorillas

Christelow, Eileen. *Five Little Monkeys Jumping on the Bed* [Pre-K], 48

Five Little Monkeys Sitting in a Tree [Pre-K], **85**

Dodds, Dayle Ann. *The Color Box* [Pre-K], **93**

Heath, W. L. *Max the Great* [5-6], 1309

Lindgren, Astrid. *Pippi Longstocking* [3-4], 1090

Maestro, Giulio. *A Wise Monkey Tale* [K-1], 499

Perkins, Al. *Hand, Hand, Fingers, Thumb* [Pre-K], 228

Rey, H. A. *Curious George* [Pre-K], 238

Slobodkina, Esphyr. *Caps for Sale* [Pre-K], 269

MONKEYS–Folklore

Galdone, Paul. *The Monkey and the Crocodile: A Jataka Tale from India* [Pre-2], 1466

Temple, Frances. *Tiger Soup: An Anansi Story from Jamaica* [Pre-2], **1034**

MONSTERS

SEE ALSO Fairies; Giants; Leprechauns; Ogres; Trolls

Alcock, Vivien. *The Monster Garden* [5-6], 1257

Auch, Mary Jane. *Monster Brother* [K-1], **221**

Bennett, David. *One Cow Moo Moo!* [Pre], **5**

Bradman, Tony. *It Came from Outer Space* [1-2], **410**

Calhoun, Mary. *The Night the Monster Came* [2-3], 880

Coville, Bruce. *The Monster's Ring* [4-5], 1165

Crowe, Robert L. *Clyde Monster* [Pre-K], 60

Demarest, Chris L. *Morton and Sidney* [Pre-K], 67

Dillon, Barbara. *The Beast in the Bed* [Pre-K], 70

Drescher, Henrik. *Simon's Book* [1-2], 664

Emberley, Ed. *Go Away, Big Green Monster!* [Pre-K], **98**

Flora, James. *The Great Green Turkey Creek Monster* [2-3], 921

Gackenbach, Dick. *Harry and the Terrible Whatzit* [Pre-K], 98

Mag the Magnificent [K-1], 398

Gantos, Jack. *Greedy Greeny* [Pre-K], 109

Heide, Florence Parry, and Roxanne Heide. *A Monster Is Coming! A Monster Is Coming!* [1-2], 684

Hughes, Ted. *The Iron Giant: A Story in Five Nights* [3-4], 1075

Hutchins, Pat. *Silly Billy!* [Pre], **24**

Three-Star Billy [Pre-K], **130**

The Very Worst Monster [Pre-K], 150

Where's the Baby? [K-1], 435

Johnson, Jane. *Today I Thought I'd Run Away* [Pre-K], 154

Kirk, Daniel. *Skateboard Monsters* [1-2], **472**

Lester, Helen. *Cora Copycat* [K-1], 468

The Wizard, the Fairy and the Magic Chicken [Pre-K], 185

Mayer, Mercer. *Liza Lou and the Yeller Belly Swamp* [1-2], 748

A Special Trick [2-3], 961

There's a Nightmare in My Closet [Pre-K], 207

There's Something in My Attic [Pre-K], 209

Meddaugh, Susan. *Beast* [Pre-K], 210

Mueller, Virginia. *Monster's Birthday Hiccups* [Pre], **36**

O'Keefe, Susan Heyboer. *One Hungry Monster: A Counting Book in Rhyme* [Pre-K], **174**

Parish, Peggy. *No More Monsters for Me* [K-1], 517

Peet, Bill. *Cowardly Clyde* [2-3], 976

Cyrus the Unsinkable Sea Serpent [1-2], 767

Polacco, Patricia. *Some Birthday!* [1-2], **537**

Ross, Tony. *I'm Coming to Get You* [K-1], 536

Seeger, Pete. *Abiyoyo* [K-1], 548

Sendak, Maurice. *Where the Wild Things Are* [Pre-K], 255

Silverman, Erica. *Big Pumpkin* [K-1], **364**

Singer, Marilyn. *The Painted Fan* [3-4], **748**

Teague, Mark. *The Field Beyond the Outfield* [K-1], **376**

Tobias, Tobi. *Chasing the Goblins Away* [1-2], 831

Turkle, Brinton. *Do Not Open* [2-3], 1016

Ungerer, Tomi. *The Beast of Monsieur Racine* [2-3], 1018

Viorst, Judith. *My Mama Says There Aren't Any Zombies, Ghosts, Vampires, Creatures, Demons, Monsters, Fiends, Goblins or Things* [1-2], 840

Willis, Jeanne. *The Monster Bed* [K-1], 592

Willoughby, Elaine. *Boris and the Monsters* [Pre-K], 297

Winthrop, Elizabeth. *Maggie & the Monster* [Pre-K], 299

Zemach, Harve. *The Judge: An Untrue Tale* [2-3], 1037

MONSTERS–Folklore

Carey, Valerie Scho. *Maggie Mab and the Bogey Beast* [2-4], **875**

Fisher, Leonard Everett. *Theseus and the Minotaur* [4-6], 1452

Galdone, Paul. *The Monster and the Tailor* [2-4], 1467

Grant, Joan. *The Monster That Grew Small: An Egyptian Folktale* [1-4], 1484

Harris, Rosemary. *Beauty and the Beast* [2-5], 1520

Mayer, Marianna. *Beauty and the Beast* [2-5], 1566

Riggio, Anita. *Beware the Brindlebeast* [K-3], **1004**

San Souci, Robert D. *The Samurai's Daughter* [3-6], **1014**

   The Tsar's Promise [3-6], **1018**

Shute, Linda. *Momotaro the Peach Boy: A Traditional Japanese Tale* [1-4], 1600

Yolen, Jane. *Wings* [4-6], **1049**

Young, Ed. *The Terrible Nung Gwana: A Chinese Folktale* [1-4], 1634

MONSTERS–Poetry

Evans, Dilys. *Monster Soup and Other Spooky Poems* [1-5], **1288**

Florian, Douglas. *Monster Motel* [K-3], **1292**

Heide, Florence Parry. *Grim and Ghastly Goings-On* [1-4], **1309**

Hopkins, Lee Bennett. *Creatures* [2-5], 1820

McNaughton, Colin. *Making Friends with Frankenstein: A Book of Monstrous Poems and Pictures* [2-6], **1366**

MONSTERS–Riddles

Brown, Marc. *Spooky Riddles* [K-3], 1761

Keller, Charles. *Count Draculations! Monsters Riddles* [2-6], 1836

Rosenbloom, Joseph. *Monster Madness: Riddles, Jokes, Fun* [3-6], 1935

MONTHS

SEE ALSO Seasons

Carle, Eric. *A House for Hermit Crab* [K-1], **246**

Carlstrom, Nancy White. *How Do You Say It Today, Jesse Bear?* [Pre-K], **76**

Coleridge, Sara. *January Brings the Snow: A Book of Months* [Pre-K], 54

Halsey, Megan. *Jump for Joy: A Book of Months* [K-1], **279**

Sendak, Maurice. *Chicken Soup with Rice* [K-1], 551

MONTHS–Folklore

Aliki. *The Twelve Months* [1-3], 1390

De Regniers, Beatrice Schenk. *Little Sister and the Month Brothers* [K-3], 1445

Marshak, Samuel. *The Month Brothers: A Slavic Tale* [K-3], 1560

MONTHS–Poetry

Frank, Josette. *Snow Toward Evening: A Year in a River Valley: Nature Poems* [3-6], **1294**

Singer, Marilyn. *Turtle in July* [1-4], 1954

MONUMENTS

Bates, Katharine Lee. *America the Beautiful* [Pre-6], **1265**

Bunting, Eve. *The Wall* [K-1], 354

Fisher, Leonard Everett. *The Great Wall of China* [2-6], 2023

Maestro, Betsy. *The Story of the Statue of Liberty* [2-5], 2074

Stevens, Carla. *Lily and Miss Liberty* [2-3], **679**

Zimelman, Nathan. *How the Second Grade Got $8,205.50 to Visit the Statue of Liberty* [1-2], **583**

MOON

SEE ALSO Astronomy; Space flight; Sun

Aiken, Joan. *The Moon's Revenge* [3-4], 1038

Asch, Frank. *Happy Birthday, Moon* [Pre-K], 12

   Moongame [Pre-K], 14

Babcock, Chris. *No Moon, No Milk* [K-1], **225**

Beatty, Jerome. *Matthew Looney's Invasion of the Earth* [4-5], 1142

Bess, Clayton. *The Truth about the Moon* [2-3], 875

Brown, Paula. *Moon Jump: A Cowntdown* [K-1], **240**

Carle, Eric. *Papa, Please Get the Moon for Me* [Pre-K], 39

Carlson, Natalie Savage. *Spooky Night* [K-1], 357

Chadwick, Tim. *Cabbage Moon* [Pre-K], **81**

Fraser, Mary Ann. *One Giant Leap* [4-6], **1142**

Krupp, E. C. *The Moon and You* [2-5], **1176**

Preston, Edna Mitchell. *Squawk to the Moon, Little Goose* [Pre-K], 233

MOON (cont.)

Thurber, James. *Many Moons* [2-3], 1015

Waddell, Martin. *Can't You Sleep, Little Bear?* [Pre-K], **199**

MOON–Folklore

Bruchac, Joseph, and Jonathan London. *Thirteen Moons on Turtle's Back: A Native American Year of Moons* [2-6], **872**

Dayrell, Elphinstone. *Why the Sun and Moon Live in the Sky* [Pre-2], 1435

dePaola, Tomie. *The Prince of the Dolomites: An Old Italian Tale* [2-4], 1443

Dixon, Ann. *How Raven Brought Light to People* [K-4], **897**

Ehlert, Lois. *Moon Rope: Un Lazo a la Luna: A Peruvian Folktale* [Pre-2], **902**

Johnston, Tony. *The Tale of Rabbit and Coyote* [Pre-2], **947**

McDermott, Gerald. *Anansi the Spider: A Tale from the Ashanti* [Pre-3], 1550

Daniel O'Rourke [1-4], 1551

Young, Ed. *Moon Mother: A Native American Creation Tale* [2-6], **1050**

MOON–Poetry

Bruchac, Joseph, and Jonathan London. *Thirteen Moons on Turtle's Back: A Native American Year of Moons* [2-6], **872**

Yolen, Jane. *What Rhymes with Moon?* [1-5], **1431**

MOOSE

Marshall, James. *The Guest* [Pre-K], 203

Numeroff, Laura J. *If You Give a Moose a Muffin* [K-1], **334**

Primavera, Elise. *The Three Dots* [K-1], **342**

Seuss, Dr. *Thidwick, the Big-Hearted Moose* [1-2], 806

Wakefield, Pat A., and Larry Carrara. *A Moose for Jessica* [3-6], 2111

MORNING

Kandoian, Ellen. *Is Anybody Up?* [Pre-K], **139**

MOTHER GOOSE

SEE Nursery rhymes

MOTHERS

Alexander, Sally Hobart. *Mom Can't See Me* [1-4], **1097**

Mom's Best Friend [2-6], **1098**

Bunting, Eve. *The Mother's Day Mice* [Pre-K], 32

Byars, Betsy. *The Two-Thousand Pound Goldfish* [5-6], 1283

Hest, Amy. *The Mommy Exchange* [K-1], 421

Kasza, Keiko. *A Mother for Choco* [Pre-K], **140**

Korschunow, Irina. *The Foundling Fox* [1-2], 713

Smith, Alison. *Help! There's a Cat Washing in Here* [5-6], 1361

Waddell, Martin. *Owl Babies* [Pre], **49**

Zolotow, Charlotte. *This Quiet Lady* [K-1], **393**

MOTHERS AND DAUGHTERS

Alexander, Sue. *Dear Phoebe* [1-2], 600

Bauer, Caroline Feller. *My Mom Travels a Lot* [1-2], 612

Carlson, Natalie Savage. *Runaway Marie Louise* [Pre-K], 43

Cohen, Barbara. *Make a Wish, Molly* [2-3], **598**

Coombs, Patricia. *Molly Mullett* [2-3], 901

Dillon, Barbara. *A Mom by Magic* [4-5], **767**

Fox, Mem. *Koala Lou* [K-1], 389

Gackenbach, Dick. *Alice's Special Room* [Pre-K], **106**

Hurray for Hattie Rabbit [Pre-K], 99

Galbraith, Kathryn O. *Laura Charlotte* [Pre-K], 105

Hall, Lynn. *In Trouble Again, Zelda Hammersmith?* [3-4], 1069

Hest, Amy. *The Purple Coat* [K-1], 422

Houston, Gloria. *The Year of the Perfect Christmas Tree* [1-2], 691

Johnson, Dolores. *What Will Mommy Do When I'm at School?* [Pre-K], **135**

Moskin, Marietta. *Rosie's Birthday Present* [K-1], 510

Nixon, Joan Lowery. *If You Were a Writer* [2-3], 972

Parish, Peggy. *No More Monsters for Me* [K-1], 517

Pomerantz, Charlotte. *The Chalk Doll* [1-2], 776

Pulver, Robin. *Nobody's Mother Is in Second Grade* [K-1], **346**

Rice, Bebe Faas. *The Year the Wolves Came* [5-6], **839**

Russo, Marisabina. *Waiting for Hannah* [K-1], 538

Tyler, Linda Wagner. *Waiting for Mom* [Pre-K], 276

Wells, Rosemary. *Hazel's Amazing Mother* [K-1], 585

Williams, Karen Lynn. *Tap-Tap* [1-2], **576**

Zolotow, Charlotte. *Mr. Rabbit and the Lovely Present* [Pre-K], 310

MOTHERS AND SONS

Bauer, Marion Dane. *A Question of Trust* [5-6], **805**

Brown, Margaret. *The Runaway Bunny* [Pre-K], 29

Cowen-Fletcher, Jane. *Mama Zooms* [Pre-K], **89**

Delton, Judy. *I'm Telling You Now* [Pre-K], 65

Duffey, Betsy. *Coaster* [4-5], **769**

Everitt, Betsy. *Mean Soup* [Pre-K], **101**

Gackenbach, Dick. *Harry and the Terrible Whatzit* [Pre-K], 98

Gershator, Phillis. *Rata-Pata-Scata-Fata: A Caribbean Story* [Pre-K], **108**

Hughes, Shirley. *Alfie Gets in First* [Pre-K], 143

Keller, Holly. *Horace* [Pre-K], **143**

Kent, Jack. *Joey Runs Away* [Pre-K], 169

Langerlöf, Selma. *The Changeling* [2-3], **636**

Lindgren, Barbro. *The Wild Baby* [K-1], 473

Nostlinger, Christine. *Konrad* [4-5], 1219

Polushkin, Maria. *Mother, Mother, I Want Another* [Pre-K], 230

Quattlebaum, Mary. *Jackson Jones and the Puddle of Thorns* [4-5], **787**

Russo, Marisabina. *The Line Up Book* [Pre-K], 247
  Trade-In Mother [Pre-K], **184**

Say, Allen. *Tree of Cranes* [1-2], **547**

Shannon, George. *The Surprise* [Pre-K], 262

Skurzynski, Gloria. *Martin by Myself* [1-2], 813

Slepian, Jan. *Back to Before* [5-6], **843**

Snyder, Carol. *Ike and Mama and the Once-a-Year Suit* [2-3], 1004

Viorst, Judith. *My Mama Says There Aren't Any Zombies, Ghosts, Vampires, Creatures, Demons, Monsters, Fiends, Goblins or Things* [1-2], 840

Waber, Bernard. *An Anteater Named Arthur* [K-1], 577

Yep, Laurence. *The Ghost Fox* [3-4], **755**

MOTHERS AND SONS–Folklore

Lawson, Julie. *The Dragon's Pearl* [1-4], **965**

Uchida, Yoshiko. *The Wise Old Woman* [1-5], **1038**

MOTHER'S DAY

Bunting, Eve. *The Mother's Day Mice* [Pre-K], 32

Kroll, Steven. *Happy Mother's Day* [1-2], 717

MOUNTAINEERING

Fraser, Mary Ann. *On Top of the World: The Conquest of Mount Everest* [4-6], **1143**

MOUNTAINS

SEE ALSO Geology

Dalgliesh, Alice. *The Bears on Hemlock Mountain* [1-2], 657

Fraser, Mary Ann. *On Top of the World: The Conquest of Mount Everest* [4-6], **1143**

George, Jean Craighead. *My Side of the Mountain* [4-5], 1176

Lobel, Arnold. *Ming Lo Moves the Mountain* [K-1], 481

Peters, Lisa Westberg. *The Sun, the Wind and the Rain* [Pre-2], 2082

Rylant, Cynthia. *When I Was Young in the Mountains* [2-3], 989

Ullman, James Ramsay. *Banner in the Sky* [5-6], 1371

MOUNTAINS–Folklore

dePaola, Tomie. *The Prince of the Dolomites: An Old Italian Tale* [2-4], 1443

McDermott, Gerald. *The Stonecutter: A Japanese Folk Tale* [K-4], 1552

MOVING, HOUSEHOLD

Aliki. *We Are Best Friends* [Pre-K], 6

Asch, Frank. *Goodbye House* [Pre-K], 11

Ballard, Robin. *Good-bye, House* [Pre-K], **69**

Chetwin, Grace. *Friends in Time* [4-5], **764**

Danziger, Paula. *Amber Brown Is Not a Crayon* [2-3], **603**

Engel, Diana. *Fishing* [K-1], **268**

Garrigue, Sheila. *Between Friends* [4-5], 1175

Giff, Patricia Reilly. *Matthew Jackson Meets the Wall* [2-3], **611**

Havill, Juanita. *Leona and Ike* [3-4], **712**

Howard, Ellen. *A Circle of Giving* [4-5], 1192

James, Betsy. *Mary Ann* [Pre-K], **133**

Joosse, Barbara M. *Wild Willie and King Kyle Detectives* [2-3], **630**

King, Larry L. *Because of Loza Brown* [1-2], 710

Namioka, Lensey. *Yang the Youngest and His Terrible Ear* [4-5], **781**

O'Donnell, Elizabeth Lee. *Maggie Doesn't Want to Move* [K-1], 515

Park, Barbara. *The Kid in the Red Jacket* [4-5], 1221

Rosen, Michael. *Moving* [K-1], **352**

Sharmat, Marjorie Weinman. *Gila Monsters Meet You at the Airport* [1-2], 808

Smith, Janice Lee. *The Monster in the Third Dresser Drawer: And Other Stories about Adam Joshua* [1-2], 815

Tsutsui, Yoriko. *Anna's Secret Friend* [Pre-K], 275

Waber, Bernard. *I Was All Thumbs* [2-3], 1023
  Ira Says Goodbye [1-2], 841

Wolkoff, Judie. *Wally* [3-4], 1135

Woodruff, Elvira. *The Wing Shop* [1-2], **580**

MULES

DeFelice, Cynthia. *Mule Eggs* [2-3], **604**

MULTICULTURAL STORIES

SEE ALSO African Americans; Asian Americans; Chinese Americans; Hispanic Americans; Indians of North America; Irish Americans; Italian Americans; Japanese Americans; Jews;

MULTICULTURAL STORIES (cont.)

Korean Americans; Russian Americans; Swedish Americans

Anholt, Catherine, and Laurence Anholt. *Kids* [Pre-K], **64**

What Makes Me Happy? [Pre-K], **65**

Baer, Edith. *This Is the Way We Go to School: A Book About Children Around the World* [K-1], **226**

Bunting, Eve. *Our Teacher's Having a Baby* [K-1], **243**

Smoky Night [2-3], **593**

Summer Wheels [2-3], **594**

Chapman, Cheryl. *Snow on Snow on Snow* [Pre-K], **83**

Cooke, Trish. *So Much* [Pre], **8**

Cowen-Fletcher, Jane. *It Takes a Village* [K-1], **257**

DePaolo, Paula. *Rosie & the Yellow Ribbon* [K-1], **261**

Dooley, Norah. *Everybody Cooks Rice* [1-2], **433**

Dorros, Arthur. *This Is My House* [1-2], **435**

Foster, John. *Let's Celebrate: Festival Poems* [3-6], **1293**

Gershator, Phillis. *Rata-Pata-Scata-Fata: A Caribbean Story* [Pre-K], **108**

Greenspan, Adele Aron. *Daddies* [Pre-K], **114**

Hamanaka, Sheila. *All the Colors of the Earth* [1-2], **449**

Havill, Juanita. *Jamaica and Brianna* [Pre-K], **119**

Hoberman, Mary Ann. *Fathers, Mothers, Sisters, Brothers: A Collection of Family Poems* [K-4], **1314**

Hoffman, Mary. *Amazing Grace* [K-1], **287**

Hoose, Phillip. *It's Our World, Too! Stories of Young People Who Are Making a Difference* [5-6], **1163**

Hopkins, Lee Bennett. *Through Our Eyes: Poems and Pictures About Growing Up* [2-5], **1328**

Howlett, Bud. *I'm New Here* [2-5], **1166**

Hurwitz, Johanna. *Class President* [3-4], **715**

Hutchins, Pat. *My Best Friend* [Pre], **23**

Johnson, Dolores. *Your Dad Was Just Like You* [1-2], **463**

Jonas, Ann. *Color Dance* [Pre-K], **136**

Kandoian, Ellen. *Is Anybody Up?* [Pre-K], **139**

Kroll, Virginia. *Masai and I* [1-2], **480**

Kuklin, Susa. *How My Family Lives in America* [K-3], **1178**

Leigh, Nila K. *Learning to Swim in Swaziland: A Child's-Eye View of a Southern African Country* [1-4], **1184**

Leventhal, Debra. *What Is Your Language?* [Pre-K], **150**

Littlefield, Bill. *Champions: Stories of Ten Remarkable Athletes* [5-6], **1188**

Lomas Garza, Carmen. *Family Pictures / Cuadros de Familia* [1-4], **1192**

Loomis, Christine. *In the Diner* [Pre-K], **154**

McMillan, Bruce. *Eating Fractions* [Pre-1], **1193**

Play Day: A Book of Terse Verse [Pre-1], **1365**

Sense Suspense: A Guessing Game for the Five Senses [Pre-K], **159**

Martin, Ann. *Rachel Parker, Kindergarten Show-Off* [K-1], **321**

Marzollo, Jean. *Pretend You're a Cat* [Pre-K], **161**

Medearis, Angela Shelf. *The Zebra-Riding Cowboy: A Folk Song from the Old West* [2-3], **645**

Meltzer, Maxine. *Pups Speak Up* [K-1], **324**

Mennen, Ingrid, and Niki Daly. *Somewhere in Africa* [1-2], **509**

Miller, Margaret. *Can You Guess?* [Pre], **33**

Guess Who? [Pre-K], **165**

My Five Senses [Pre-K], **1207**

Where Does It Go? [Pre-K], **166**

Whose Shoe? [Pre-K], **168**

Mitchell, Rita Phillips. *Hue Boy* [K-1], **325**

Morris, Ann. *Bread Bread Bread* [Pre-3], **1211**

Polacco, Patricia. *Mrs. Katz and Tush* [2-3], **663**

Pink and Say [4-5], **786**

Pulver, Robin. *Nobody's Mother Is in Second Grade* [K-1], **346**

Raschka, Chris. *Yo! Yes?* [1-2], **541**

Rattigan, Jama Kim. *Dumpling Soup* [K-1], **349**

Say, Allen. *El Chino* [2-5], **1234**

Shelby, Anne. *Potluck* [K-1], **362**

Singer, Marilyn. *Nine O'Clock Lullaby* [1-2], **554**

Spinelli, Eileen. *If You Want to Find Golden* [K-1], **370**

Spinelli, Jerry. *Maniac Magee* [5-6], **847**

Trivas, Irene. *Annie . . . Anya: A Month in Moscow* [K-1], **377**

Walton, Rick. *How Many, How Many, How Many* [Pre-K], **206**

Williams, Karen Lynn. *Tap-Tap* [1-2], **576**

Williams, Vera B. *"More More More," Said the Baby: Three Love Stories* [Pre], **58**

Wong, Janet S. *Good Luck Gold and Other Poems* [4-6], **1424**

MULTICULTURAL STORIES–Folklore

SEE ALSO entries under Folklore; e.g., Folklore, African American; Folklore–Jamaica

Bernhard, Emery. *The Tree That Rains: The Flood Myth of the Huichol Indians of Mexico* [1-4], **867**

Lichtveld, Noni. *I Lost My Arrow in a Kankan Tree* [K-2], **970**

Osborne, Mary Pope. *Mermaid Tales from Around the World* [3-6], **1082**

Pilling, Ann. *Realms of Gold: Myths & Legends from Around the World* [4-6], **1083**

Pitre, Felix. *Juan Bobo and the Pig: A Puerto Rican Folktale* [K-2], **998**

Roddy, Patricia. *Api and the Boy Stranger: A Village Creation Tale* [K-2], **1006**

MULTIPLICATION
SEE ALSO Mathematics

Hulme, Joy N. *Sea Squares* [2-3], **624**

MUMMIES
Woodruff, Elvira. *The Magnificent Mummy Maker* [4-5], **799**

MURDER
Babbitt, Natalie. *Tuck Everlasting* [5-6], 1271

Roberts, Willo Davis. *The View from the Cherry Tree* [5-6], 1346

MUSCULAR DYSTROPHY
Osofsky, Audrey. *My Buddy* [1-2], **526**

MUSEUMS
Alcorn, Johnny. *Rembrandt's Beret* [3-4], **697**

Axelrod, Alan. *Songs of the Wild West* [1-6], **1264**

Babcock, Chris. *No Moon, No Milk* [K-1], **225**

Cohen, Miriam. *Lost in the Museum* [K-1], 369

Freeman, Don. *Norman the Doorman* [1-2], 671

Kellogg, Steven. *Prehistoric Pinkerton* [1-2], 707

Konigsburg, E. L. *From the Mixed-Up Files of Mrs. Basil E. Frankweiler* [4-5], 1201

Rohmann, Eric. *Time Flies* [K-1], **350**

Talbott, Hudson. *We're Back!* [2-3], 1013

MUSIC
SEE ALSO Songbooks; Songs; Stories with songs

Aiken, Joan. *The Moon's Revenge* [3-4], 1038

Ernst, Lisa Campbell. *When Bluebell Sang* [K-1], 383

Green, Melinda. *Rachel's Recital* [2-3], 928

Hurd, Thacher. *Mama Don't Allow* [K-1], 432

Kherdian, David. *The Cat's Midsummer Jamboree* [K-1], 457

McCloskey, Robert. *Lentil* [2-3], 956

Perkins, Al. *Hand, Hand, Fingers, Thumb* [Pre-K], 228

Primavera, Elise. *The Three Dots* [K-1], **342**

Purdy, Carol. *Mrs. Merriweather's Musical Cat* [1-2], **539**

Ray, Mary Lynn. *Pianna* [1-2], **542**

Steig, William. *Zeke Pippin* [2-3], **678**

Waddell, Martin. *The Happy Hedgehog Band* [Pre], **48**

MUSIC–Folklore
Aardema, Verna. *Bimwili and the Zimwi* [K-2], 1379

Anderson, Lonzo. *Arion and the Dophins* [K-3], 1391

Ober, Hal. *How Music Came to the World* [1-4], **993**

Otsuka, Zuzo. *Suho and the White Horse: A Legend of Mongolia* [2-4], 1576

MUSIC–Riddles
Keller, Charles. *Swine Lake: Music & Dance Riddles* [3-6], 1843

MUSICAL INSTRUMENTS
SEE ALSO Cello; Flute; Harmonicas; Piano; Violin

Hayes, Ann. *Meet the Orchestra* [K-3], **1157**

Lebentritt, Julia, and Richard Ploetz. *The Kooken* [1-2], **481**

Moss, Lloyd. *Zin! Zin! Zin! A Violin* [1-2], **512**

Namioka, Lensey. *Yang the Youngest and His Terrible Ear* [4-5], **781**

Pinkwater, Daniel. *Doodle Flute* [1-2], **534**

Purdy, Carol. *Mrs. Merriweather's Musical Cat* [1-2], **539**

Ray, Mary Lynn. *Pianna* [1-2], **542**

Rayner, Mary. *Garth Pig Steals the Show* [1-2], **543**

Steig, William. *Zeke Pippin* [2-3], **678**

Tomey, Ingrid. *Grandfather's Day* [2-3], **686**

MUSICAL INSTRUMENTS–Folklore
Czernecki, Stefan, and Timothy Rhodes. *The Singing Snake* [K-2], **889**

Goble, Paul. *Love Flute* [3-6], **916**

MUSICIANS
Kalman, Esther. *Tchaikovsky Discovers America* [2-3], **632**

Krull, Kathleen. *Lives of the Musicians: Good Times, Bad Times (and What the Neighbors Thought)* [3-6], **1174**

McCully, Emily Arnold. *The Amazing Felix* [1-2], **491**

Martin, Bill, Jr. *The Maestro Plays* [1-2], **504**

Moss, Lloyd. *Zin! Zin! Zin! A Violin* [1-2], **512**

Namioka, Lensey. *Yang the Youngest and His Terrible Ear* [4-5], **781**

Nichol, Barbara. *Beethoven Lives Upstairs* [4-5], **785**

MUSICIANS (cont.)

Rayner, Mary. *Garth Pig Steals the Show* [1-2], **543**

MUTISM, ELECTIVE

Cooney, Nancy Evans. *Chatterbox Jamie* [Pre-K], **87**

MYSTERY AND DETECTIVE STORIES

Adler, David A. *My Dog and the Birthday Mystery* [K-1], 313

Arthur, Robert. *The Secret of Terror Castle* [5-6], 1265

Bellaits, John. *The Treasure of Alpheus Winterborn* [5-6], 1275

Christelow, Eileen. *Gertrude, the Bulldog Detective* [K-1], **252**

Cushman, Doug. *The ABC Mystery* [1-2], **428**

Greene, Bette. *Philip Hall Likes Me. I Reckon, Maybe* [4-5], 1183

Greenwald, Sheila. *The Atrocious Two* [4-5], 1184

Hicks, Clifford B. *Alvin's Swap Shop* [4-5], 1187

Hildick, E. W. *The Case of the Condemned Cat* [3-4], 1073

The Case of the Purloined Parrot [4-5], **771**

McGurk Gets Good and Mad [4-5], 1189

Howe, Deborah, and James Howe. *Bunnicula: A Rabbit-Tale of Mystery* [4-5], 1193

Howe, James. *Nighty-Nightmare* [4-5], 1194

Joosse, Barbara M. *Wild Willie and King Kyle Detectives* [2-3], **630**

Konigsburg, E. L. *From the Mixed-Up Files of Mrs. Basil E. Frankweiler* [4-5], 1201

Kotzwinkle, William. *Trouble in Bugland: A Collection of Inspector Mantis Mysteries* [5-6], 1322

Massie, Diane Redfield. *Chameleon Was a Spy* [2-3], **960**

Masterman-Smith, Virginia. *The Treasure Trap* [4-5], 1212

Naylor, Phyllis Reynolds. *The Bodies in the Besseldorf Hotel* [4-5], 1216

Newman, Robert. *The Case of the Baker Street Irregular* [5-6], 1335

Roberts, Willo Davis. *The View from the Cherry Tree* [5-6], 1346

Sharmat, Marjorie Weinman. *Nate the Great* [1-2], 810

Simon, Seymour. *Einstein Anderson, Science Sleuth* [4-5], 1239

Sobol, Donald J. *Encyclopedia Brown, Boy Detective* [3-4], 1116

Titus, Eve. *Basil of Baker Street* [4-5], 1249

Van Leeuwen, Jean. *The Great Christmas Kidnapping Caper* [3-4], 1128

Wallace, Barbara Brooks. *The Twin in the Tavern* [5-6], **849**

Wilson, Gahan. *Harry the Fat Bear Spy* [3-4], 1133

MYTHOLOGY

Benson, Sally. *Stories of Gods and Heroes* [4-6], 1656

Climo, Shirley. *Stolen Thunder: A Norse Myth* [3-6], **880**

Cox, Miriam. *The Magic and the Sword: The Greek Myths Retold* [4-6], 1671

D'Aulaire, Ingri, and Edgar Parin D'Aulaire. *D'Aulaire's Book of Greek Myths* [4-6], 1674

Fisher, Leonard Everett. *Cyclops* [4-6], **904**

Theseus and the Minotaur [4-6], 1452

Gates, Doris. *Lord of the Sky: Zeus* [5-6], 1679

Hewitt, Kathryn. *King Midas and the Golden Touch* [1-4], 1522

McDermott, Gerald. *The Voyage of Osiris: A Myth of Ancient Egypt* [2-6], 1554

Mayer, Marianna. *Iduna and the Magic Apples* [4-6], 1567

Osborne, Mary Pope. *Favorite Greek Myths* [5-6], 1713

Pilling, Ann. *Realms of Gold: Myths & Legends from Around the World* [4-6], **1083**

Price, Margaret Evans. *Myths and Enchantment Tales* [4-6], 1716

Proddow, Penelope. *Demeter and Persephone* [5-6], 1581

Sutcliff, Rosemary. *Black Ships Before Troy! The Story of the Iliad* [5-6], **1088**

Waldherr, Kris. *Persephone and the Pomegranate: A Myth from Greece* [2-6], **1041**

Wells, Rosemary. *Max and Ruby's First Greek Myth: Pandora's Box* [1-2], **573**

Yolen, Jane. *Wings* [4-6], **1049**

NAMES

Aylesworth, Jim. *My Son John* [K-1], **222**

Evans, Katie. *Hunky Dory Ate It* [Pre-K], **100**

Hazen, Barbara Shook. *Last, First, Middle and Nick: All about Names* [4-6], 2045

Henkes, Kevin. *Chrysanthemum* [K-1], **282**

Hinton, S. E. *Big David, Little David* [K-1], **285**

Lester, Helen. *A Porcupine Named Fluffy* [K-1], 471

Lobel, Anita. *Alison's Zinnia* [K-1], **309**

Away from Home [1-2], **487**

Pinkwater, Daniel. *The Wuggie Norple Story* [K-1], 524

Pittman, Helena Clare. *Miss Hindy's Cats* [K-1], **338**

Shelby, Anne. *Potluck* [K-1], **362**

Walton, Rick, and Ann Walton. *What's Your Name, Again? More Jokes about Names* [1-6], 1971

NAMES–Folklore

Grimm, Jacob. *Rumpelstiltskin* [1-4], 1504, **922**

Mosel, Arlene. *Tikki Tikki Tembo* [Pre-3], 1572

Moser, Barry. *Tucker Pfeffercorn: An Old Story Retold* [4-5], **779**

Ness, Evaline. *Tom Tit Tot* [2-4], 1574

Zemach, Harve. *Duffy and the Devil* [2-5], 1635

NAMES, GEOGRAPHICAL

Brisson, Pat. *Magic Carpet* [1-2], **411**

NAMES, GEOGRAPHICAL–Riddles

Gerberg, Mort. *Geographunny: A Book of Global Riddles* [3-6], **1295**

Maestro, Marco, and Giulio Maestro. *Riddle City, USA! A Book of Geography Riddles* [3-6], **1368**

NARRATIVE POETRY

SEE ALSO Poetry–Single author; Stories in rhyme

Baylor, Byrd. *Amigo* [1-2], 613

Carryl, Charles E. *The Walloping Window-Blind* [2-3], **596**

Dahl, Roald. *Roald Dahl's Revolting Rhymes* [3-6], 1787

Eliot, T. S. *Mr. Mistoffelees with Mungojerrie and Rumpelteazer* [3-6], **1286**

Gerrard, Roy. *Rosie and the Rustlers* [2-3], **610**
Sir Francis Drake: His Daring Deeds [4-6], 2038

Livingston, Myra Cohn. *Abraham Lincoln: A Man for All the People* [K-3], **1189**
Keep on Singing: A Ballad of Marian Anderson [1-4], **1190**
Let Freedom Ring: A Ballad of Martin Luther King, Jr. [1-6], **1191**

Longfellow, Henry Wadsworth. *Paul Revere's Ride* [2-6], **1361**
Paul Revere's Ride [4-6], 1863

Moore, Clement C. *The Night before Christmas* [1-2], 753

Nash, Ogden. *The Adventures of Isabel* [2-3], **649**

Peet, Bill. *Hubert's Hair-Raising Adventure* [1-2], 770

Prelutsky, Jack. *The Mean Old Mean Hyena* [2-3], 983

Service, Robert W. *The Cremation of Sam McGee* [5-6], 1355

Seuss, Dr. *Horton Hatches the Egg* [1-2], 801
How the Grinch Stole Christmas [1-2], 802
The Lorax [2-3], 997
Thidwick, the Big-Hearted Moose [1-2], 806

Small, Terry. *The Legend of William Tell* [3-5], **1028**

Smath, Jerry. *A Hat So Simple* [K-1], **367**

Thayer, Ernest Lawrence. *Casey at the Bat: A Ballad of the Republic, Sung in the Year 1888* [5-6], 1368

NATIVE AMERICANS

SEE Indians of North America

NATURAL MONUMENTS

Bates, Katharine Lee. *America the Beautiful* [Pre-6], **1265**

NATURALISTS

Audubon, John James. *Capturing Nature: The Writings and Art of John James Audubon* [5-6], **1101**

NATURE

Allen, Marjorie N., and Shelley Rotner. *Changes* [Pre-1], **1100**

Blake, Robert J. *The Perfect Spot* [K-1], **231**

Feldman, Judy. *The Alphabet in Nature* [Pre-K], **102**

Hines, Anna Grossnickle. *What Joe Saw* [Pre-K], **123**

London, Jonathan. *Gray Fox* [1-2], **489**
Voices of the Wild [2-3], **640**

Peters, Lisa Westberg. *The Sun, the Wind and the Rain* [Pre-2], 2082

Selsam, Millicent, and Joyce Hunt. *Keep Looking!* [Pre-2], 2095

Temple, Lannis. *Dear World: How Children Around the World Feel About Our Environment* [2-6], **1247**

Udry, Janice May. *A Tree Is Nice* [Pre-K], 278

NATURE–Poetry

Brenner, Barbara. *The Earth Is Painted Green: A Garden of Poems About Our Planet* [1-5], **1274**

Demi. *In the Eyes of the Cat: Japanese Poetry for All Seasons* [2-6], **1284**

Frank, Josette. *Snow Toward Evening: A Year in a River Valley: Nature Poems* [3-6], **1294**

Higginson, William J. *Wind in the Long Grass: A Collection of Haiku* [2-6], **1313**

Lewis, J. Patrick. *Earth Verses and Water Rhymes* [2-4], **1352**

Mizamura, Kazue. *Flower Moon Snow: A Book of Haiku* [2-6], 1873

NATURE–Poetry (cont.)

Moore, Lilian. *Adam Mouse's Book of Poems* [1-4], **1374**

Paladino, Catherine. *Land, Sea, and Sky: Poems to Celebrate the Earth* [1-5], **1392**

NAVAJO INDIANS–Folklore

Begay, Shonto. *Ma'ii and Cousin Horned Toad: A Traditional Navajo Story* [K-4], **865**

NEIGHBORLINESS

Christelow, Eileen. *The Five-Dog Night* [1-2], **425**

Modesitt, Jeanne. *Vegetable Soup* [Pre-K], **170**

NEIGHBORS

Brimner, Larry Dane. *Country Bear's Good Neighbor* [Pre-K], 27

Gackenbach, Dick. *Claude Has a Picnic* [Pre], **16**

Levy, Elizabeth. *Frankenstein Moved in on the Fourth Floor* [2-3], 951

Spinelli, Eileen. *Somebody Loves You, Mr. Hatch* [K-1], **371**

NETHERLANDS

DeJong, Meindert. *The Wheel on the School* [4-5], 1168

NEW YEAR

Rattigan, Jama Kim. *Dumpling Soup* [K-1], **349**

NEW YEAR–Folklore

Tompert, Ann. *Bamboo Hats and a Rice Cake: A Tale Adapted from Japanese Folklore* [K-3], **1036**

NEW YORK CITY

Babcock, Chris. *No Moon, No Milk* [K-1], **225**

Barracca, Debra, and Sal Barracca. *The Adventures of Taxi Dog* [1-2], **404**

A Taxi Dog Christmas [K-1], **229**

Bartone, Elisa. *Peppe the Lamplighter* [1-2], **405**

Choi, Sook Nyul. *Halmoni and the Picnic* [1-2], **424**

Cohen, Barbara. *The Carp in the Bathtub* [2-3], 892

Cohen, Ron. *My Dad's Baseball* [2-3], **599**

Cummings, Pat. *C.L.O.U.D.S.* [2-3], 903

Dorros, Arthur. *Abuela* [1-2], **434**

Foreman, Michael. *Cat and Canary* [K-1], 388

Fox, Paula. *Monkey Island* [5-6], **817**

Getz, David. *Thin Air* [5-6], **819**

Holland, Isabella. *Alan and the Animal Kingdom* [5-6], 1311

Jakobsen, Kathy. *My New York* [K-4], **1167**

Konigsburg, E. L. *Amy Elizabeth Explores Bloomingdale's* [1-2], **478**

From the Mixed-Up Files of Mrs. Basil E. Frankweiler [4-5], 1201

Merrill, Jean. *The Pushcart War* [5-6], 1331

Moskin, Marietta. *The Day of the Blizzard* [3-4], 1098

Pomerantz, Charlotte. *The Downtown Fairy Godmother* [2-3], 981

Reit, Seymour. *Benvenuto* [3-4], 1106

Ringgold, Faith. *Tar Beach* [2-3], **671**

Rotner, Shelley, and Ken Kreisler. *Citybook* [K-1], **353**

Selden, George. *The Cricket in Times Square* [4-5], 1237

Snyder, Carol. *Ike and Mama and the Once-a-Year Suit* [2-3], 1004

Stevens, Carla. *Lily and Miss Liberty* [2-3], **679**

Talbott, Hudson. *We're Back!* [2-3], 1013

Van Leeuwen, Jean. *The Great Rescue Operation* [4-5], 1252

Waber, Bernard. *Lyle, Lyle Crocodile* [K-1], 578

White, E. B. *Stuart Little* [3-4], 1131

Wolitzer, Hilma. *Introducing Shirley Braverman* [5-6], 1376

Zimelman, Nathan. *How the Second Grade Got $8,205.50 to Visit the Statue of Liberty* [1-2], **583**

NEW YORK (STATE)

Christiansen, Candace. *The Ice Horse* [2-3], **597**

Wolkstein, Diane. *The Legend of Sleepy Hollow* [4-5], **795**

NEWBERY MEDAL

Armstrong, William. *Sounder* [5-6], 1264

Brink, Carol Ryrie. *Caddie Woodlawn* [4-5], 1151

Byars, Betsy. *The Summer of the Swans* [5-6], 1282

DeJong, Meindert. *The Wheel on the School* [4-5], 1168

Du Bois, William Pène. *The Twenty-One Balloons* [5-6], 1295

Finger, Charles. *Tales from Silver Lands* [3-6], 1677

Fleischman, Paul. *Joyful Noise: Poems for Two Voices* [5-6], 1799

Freedman, Russell. *Lincoln: A Photobiography* [5-6], 2028

George, Jean Craighead. *Julie of the Wolves* [5-6], 1304

Konigsburg, E. L. *From the Mixed-Up Files of Mrs. Basil E. Frankweiler* [4-5], 1201

L'Engle, Madeleine. *A Wrinkle in Time* [5-6], 1325

Lowry, Lois. *The Giver* [5-6], **828**

Number the Stars [5-6], 1328

MacLachlan, Patricia. *Sarah, Plain and Tall* [3-4], 1094

Naylor, Phyllis Reynolds. *Shiloh* [5-6], **832**

O'Brien, Robert C. *Mrs. Frisby and the Rats of NIMH* [5-6], 1337

O'Dell, Scott. *Island of the Blue Dolphins* [5-6], 1339

Paterson, Katherine. *Bridge to Terabithia* [5-6], 1340

Sperry, Armstrong. *Call It Courage* [4-5], 1242

Spinelli, Jerry. *Maniac Magee* [5-6], **847**

NIGHT

Bond, Felicia. *Pointsettia and the Firefighters* [K-1], 338

Bunting, Eve. *Ghost's Hour, Spook's Hour* [K-1], 351

Night of the Gargoyles [3-4], **705**

Carle, Eric. *Papa, Please Get the Moon for Me* [Pre-K], 39

Christelow, Eileen. *Henry and the Dragon* [Pre-K], 49

Cooney, Nancy Evans. *Go Away Monsters, Lickety Split* [Pre-K], **88**

Crowe, Robert L. *Clyde Monster* [Pre-K], 60

Himmelman, John. *Lights Out!* [1-2], **453**

Hort, Lenny. *How Many Stars in the Sky?* [K-1], **288**

Johnston, Johanna. *Edie Changes Her Mind* [Pre-K], 155

Kandoian, Ellen. *Under the Sun* [K-1], 445

Karlin, Bernie, and Mati Karlin. *Night Ride* [K-1], 446

Keats, Ezra Jack. *Dreams* [K-1], 448

London, Jonathan. *The Owl Who Became the Moon* [K-1], **310**

Mayer, Mercer. *There's a Nightmare in My Closet* [Pre-K], 207

Murphy, Jill. *Peace at Last* [Pre-K], 214

Robison, Deborah. *No Elephants Allowed* [Pre-K], 243

Root, Phyllis. *Moon Tiger* [K-1], 535

Ryan, Cheli Druan. *Hildilid's Night* [K-1], 539

Rydell, Katy. *Wind Says Good Night* [Pre], **42**

Ryder, Joanne. *The Night Flight* [K-1], 540

Rylant, Cynthia. *Night in the Country* [K-1], 541

Sharmat, Marjorie Weinman. *Go to Sleep, Nicholas Joe* [Pre-K], 263

Tejima, Keizaburo. *Fox's Dream* [K-1], 565

Waber, Bernard. *Ira Sleeps Over* [1-2], 842

Waddell, Martin. *Can't You Sleep, Little Bear?* [Pre-K], **199**

Owl Babies [Pre], **49**

Wiesner, David. *Tuesday* [K-1], **385**

Winthrop, Elizabeth. *Maggie & the Monster* [Pre-K], 299

Wright, Kit. *Tigerella* [K-1], **389**

NIGHT–Folklore

Gerson, Mary-Joan. *How Night Came from the Sea: A Story from Brazil* [K-4], **912**

NOISE

SEE ALSO Sound

Allinson, Beverly. *Effie* [K-1], **217**

Benjamin, Alan. *Rat-a-Tat, Pitter Pat* [Pre-K], 22

Dodds, Dayle Ann. *Do Bunnies Talk?* [K-1], **262**

Elkin, Benjamin. *The Loudest Noise in the World* [K-1], 381

Gaeddert, Lou Ann. *Noisy Nancy Norris* [Pre-K], 102

Kline, Suzy. *SHHHH! We're Writing the Constitution* [Pre-K], 171

Rowe, John A. *Baby Crow* [Pre-K], **183**

Segal, Lore. *All the Way Home* [Pre-K], 253

Shapiro, Arnold L. *Who Says That?* [Pre], **43**

Stevenson, James. *What's Under My Bed?* [1-2], 826

Thomas, Patricia. *The One and Only Super-Duper Golly-Whopper Jim-Dandy Really-Handy Clock-Tock-Stopper* [1-2], **566**

Waddell, Martin. *Let's Go Home, Little Bear* [Pre-K], **201**

NOISE–Folklore

Cole, Joanna. *It's Too Noisy!* [Pre-1], **882**

McGovern, Ann. *Too Much Noise* [Pre-2], 1556

NONSENSE

Emrich, Duncan. *The Hodgepodge Book* [2-6], 1796

Schwartz, Alvin. *Tomfoolery: Trickery and Foolery with Words* [1-6], 1949

Tashjian, Virginia. *Juba This and Juba That: Story Hour Stretches for Large or Small Groups* [Pre-4], 1961

Withers, Carl. *I Saw a Rocket Walk a Mile: Nonsense Tales, Chants and Songs from Many Lands* [K-6], 1735

NONSENSE VERSES

SEE ALSO Humorous Poetry; Limericks; Nursery rhymes; Stories in rhyme

Bennett, Jill. *Tiny Tim: Verses for Children* [Pre-2], 1747

Booth, David. *Doctor Knickerbocker and Other Rhymes* [2-5], **1272**

Brewton, Sara, John E. Brewton, and G. Meredith Blackburn, III. *My Tang's Tungled and Other Ridiculous Situations* [2-6], 1759

Carryl, Charles E. *The Walloping Window-Blind* [2-3], **596**

Cole, William. *Oh, Such Foolishness* [2-6], 1780

NONSENSE VERSES (cont.)

A Zooful of Animals [K-5], **1282**

Florian, Douglas. *Bing Bang Boing* [1-6], **1291**

Kamen, Gloria. *Edward Lear, King of Nonsense: A Biography* [4-6], **1169**

Karas, G. Brian. *I Know an Old Lady* [K-1], **295**

Keller, Charles. *Ballpoint Bananas and Other Jokes for Kids* [2-6], 1835

Kennedy, X. J. *Ghastlies, Goops & Pincushions: Nonsense Verse* [3-6], 1846

Lear, Edward. *Daffy Down Dillies: Silly Limericks* [3-6], **1348**

How Pleasant to Know Mr. Lear! [4-6], 1853

Of Pelicans and Pussycats: Poems and Limericks [K-5], **1349**

The Owl and the Pussycat [Pre-K], **148, 149**, 181

The Quangle Wangle's Hat [K-1], 466

Lee, Dennis. *Alligator Pie* [Pre-4], 1854

Jelly Belly: Original Nursery Rhymes [Pre-3], 1855

Livingston, Myra Cohn. *Lots of Limericks* [4-6], **1359**

Marshall, James. *Pocketful of Nonsense* [Pre-3], **1369**

Martin, Bill, Jr. *The Happy Hippopotami* [K-1], **322**

Morrison, Bill. *Squeeze a Sneeze* [K-1], **326**

Mother Goose. *Granfa' Grig Had a Pig: And Other Rhymes without Reason from Mother Goose* [Pre-4], 1880

Nash, Ogden. *Custard and Company* [3-6], 1893

Opie, Iona, and Peter Opie. *I Saw Esau: The Schoolchild's Pocket Book* [1-5], **1391**

Prelutsky, Jack. *A. Nonny Mouse Writes Again!* [1-5], **1395**

The Baby Uggs Are Hatching [K-4], 1904

The New Kid on the Block [K-5], 1911

Poems of A. Nonny Mouse [K-4], 1913

Ride a Purple Pelican [Pre-2], 1918

Something Big Has Been Here [K-6], **1398**

Raffi. *Down by the Bay* [1-2], 780

Rosenbloom, Joseph. *Silly Verse (and Even Worse)* [3-6], 1936

Rounds, Glen. *I Know an Old Lady Who Swallowed a Fly* [K-1], 537

Schwartz, Alvin. *And the Green Grass Grew All Around: Folk Poetry from Everyone* [2-6], **1407**

I Saw You in the Bathtub and Other Folk Rhymes [K-3], 1947

Silverstein, Shel. *Where the Sidewalk Ends* [Pre-6], 1952

Smith, William Jay. *Laughing Time: Nonsense Poems* [K-3], 1955

Tripp, Wallace. *A Great Big Ugly Man Came Up and Tied His Horse to Me: A Book of Nonsense Verse* [K-3], 1967

Westcott, Nadine Bernard. *I Know an Old Lady Who Swallowed a Fly* [K-1], 588

The Lady with the Alligator Purse [Pre-K], 290

Withers, Carl. *A Rocket in My Pocket: The Rhymes and Chants of Young Americans* [K-4], 1977

Wood, Audrey. *Silly Sally* [Pre-K], **212**

Yolen, Jane. *Animal Fare* [1-4], **1427**

NORSE MYTHOLOGY

SEE Mythology

NORWAY

Emberley, Michael. *Welcome Back Sun* [1-2], **438**

McSwigan, Marie. *Snow Treasure* [5-6], 1330

NOSES

Caple, Kathy. *The Biggest Nose* [K-1], 356

Embry, Margaret. *The Blue-Nosed Witch* [2-3], 913

NOSES–Folklore

Hutton, Warwick. *The Nose Tree* [2-5], 1533

Zemach, Harve. *Too Much Noise: An Italian Tale* [2-5], 1637

NOUNS

SEE English language–Grammar

NUMBERS

SEE Counting books; Mathematics; Measurement

NURSERY RHYMES

SEE ALSO Humorous poetry; Nonsense verses

Aylesworth, Jim. *My Son John* [K-1], **222**

Baker, Keith. *Big Fat Hen* [Pre], **4**

Bodecker, N. M. *"It's Raining," Said John Twaining: Danish Nursery Rhymes* [Pre-2], 1750

Brown, Marc. *Hand Rhymes* [Pre-2], 1760

Cauley, Lorinda Bryan. *The Three Little Kittens* [Pre-K], 45

Coleridge, Sara. *January Brings the Snow: A Book of Months* [Pre-K], 54

Demi. *Dragon Kites and Dragonflies: A Collection of Chinese Nursery Rhymes* [Pre-3], 1789

dePaola, Tomie. *The Comic Adventures of Old Mother Hubbard and Her Dog* [Pre-1], 1438

Galdone, Paul. *Old Mother Hubbard and Her Dog* [Pre-1], 1468

Over in the Meadow: An Old Nursery Counting Rhyme [Pre-K], 108

Hale, Sarah Josepha Buell. *Mary Had a Little Lamb* [Pre-K], **116, 117**, 127

Hellsing, Lennart. *Old Mother Hubbard and Her Dog* [Pre-K], 130

Hennessy, B. G. *The Missing Tarts* [Pre-K], 133

Ivimey, John W. *The Complete Story of the Three Blind Mice* [Pre-K], 151

 Complete Version of Ye Three Blind Mice [Pre-K], 152

 Three Blind Mice: The Classic Nursery Rhyme [Pre-K], **131**

Katz, Michael Jay. *Ten Potatoes in a Pot and Other Counting Rhymes* [Pre-2], **1336**

Lamont, Priscilla. *Ring-a-Round-a-Rosy: Nursery Rhymes, Action Rhymes and Lullabies* [Pre-1], **1345**

Lee, Dennis. *Alligator Pie* [Pre-4], 1854

 Jelly Belly: Original Nursery Rhymes [Pre-3], 1855

Lobel, Arnold. *Whiskers & Rhymes* [Pre-3], 1862

Marshall, James. *Old Mother Hubbard and Her Wonderful Dog* [Pre-1], **980**

Mother Goose. *Animal Nursery Rhymes* [Pre-1], **1378**

 Cakes and Custard [Pre-1], 1878

 The Glorious Mother Goose [Pre-2], 1879

 Granfa' Grig Had a Pig: And Other Rhymes without Reason from Mother Goose [Pre-4], 1880

 Gray Goose and Gander: And Other Mother Goose Rhymes [Pre-1], 1881

 Gregory Griggs: And Other Nursery Rhyme People [Pre-2], 1882

 Hickory Dickory Dock and Other Nursery Rhymes [Pre-1], **1379**

 James Marshall's Mother Goose [Pre-2], 1883

 Jane Yolen's Mother Goose Songbook [Pre-2], **1380**

 The Little Dog Laughed and Other Nursery Rhymes [Pre-1], **1384**

 Little Robin Redbreast: A Mother Goose Rhyme [Pre], **35**

 Michael Foreman's Mother Goose [Pre-2], **1385**

 Mother Goose [Pre-1] **1386**

 Mother Goose: A Collection of Classic Nursery Rhymes [Pre-1], 1884

 Mother Goose Magic [Pre-K], **1382**

 The Mother Goose Songbook [Pre-2], **1387**

 The Mother Goose Treasury [Pre-2], 1885

 Mother Goose's Little Misfortunes [Pre-2], **1383**

 The Orchard Book of Nursery Rhymes [Pre-1], **1388**

 Over the Moon: A Book of Nursery Rhymes [Pre-2], 1886

 Rain, Rain, Go Away! A Book of Nursery Rhymes [Pre-2], **1381**

 The Random House Book of Mother Goose [Pre-2], 1887

 The Real Mother Goose [Pre-1], 1888

 Richard Scarry's Best Mother Goose Ever [Pre-1], 1889

 Songs from Mother Goose: With the Traditional Melody for Each [Pre-2], 1890

 Tail Feathers from Mother Goose: The Opie Rhyme Book [Pre-3], 1891

 Tomie dePaola's Mother Goose [Pre-2], 1892

Opie, Iona, and Peter Opie. *I Saw Esau: The Schoolchild's Pocket Book* [1-5], **1391**

Pooley, Sarah. *A Day of Rhymes* [Pre-1], 1903

Prelutsky, Jack. *Ride a Purple Pelican* [Pre-2], 1918

Scieszka, Jon. *The Book That Jack Wrote* [1-2], **548**

Stevens, Janet. *The House That Jack Built: A Mother Goose Nursery Rhyme* [Pre-K], 271

Sweet, Melissa. *Fiddle-I-Fee: A Farmyard Song for the Very Young* [Pre-K], **190**

Thompson, Brian. *Catch It If You Can* [Pre-2], **1415**

Voce, Louise. *Over in the Meadow: A Traditional Counting Rhyme* [Pre-K], **197**

Wadsworth, Olive A. *Over in the Meadow: An Old Counting Rhyme* [Pre-K], **202**

Watson, Clyde. *Father Fox's Pennyrhymes* [Pre-1], 1972

Westcott, Nadine Bernard. *The Pop-Up, Pull-Tab Playtime House That Jack Built* [Pre-K], **208**

NURSERY SCHOOLS

SEE ALSO Kindergarten; Schools

Hutchins, Pat. *Three-Star Billy* [Pre-K], **130**

OBEDIENCE

Bauer, Marion Dane. *On My Honor* [5-6], 1273

Bellows, Cathy. *The Grizzly Sisters* [K-1], **230**

Gray, Libba Moore. *Small Green Snake* [Pre-K], **113**

Vollmer, Dennis. *Joshua Disobeys* [Pre-K], **198**

Wells, Rosemary. *Max and Ruby's First Greek Myth: Pandora's Box* [1-2], **573**

OBEDIENCE–Folklore

Cauley, Lorinda Bryan. *Goldilocks and the Three Bears* [Pre-2], 1415

Eisen, Armand. *Goldilocks and the Three Bears* [Pre-1], 1450

Galdone, Paul. *The Three Bears* [Pre-1], 1472

Green, John F. *Alice and the Birthday Giant* [Pre-1], 408

Grimm, Jacob. *Little Red Cap* [Pre-2], 1500

 Little Red Riding Hood [Pre-2], 1501

Harper, Wilhelmina. *The Gunniwolf* [Pre-1], 1519

OBEDIENCE–Folklore (cont.)

Marshall, James. *Goldilocks and the Three Bears* [Pre-1], 1561

Mosel, Arlene. *Tikki Tikki Tembo* [Pre-3], 1572

Ness, Evaline. *Mr. Miacca: An English Folktale* [Pre-2], 1573

Stevens, Janet. *Goldilocks and the Three Bears* [Pre-1], 1611

OCCUPATIONS

Kalman, Maira. *Chicken Soup Boots* [3-4], **719**

Kraus, Robert. *Owliver* [K-1], 461

McPhail, David. *Pig Pig Gets a Job* [K-1], **318**

Miller, Margaret. *Guess Who?* [Pre-K], **165**
  Whose Hat? [Pre-K], 212
  Whose Shoe? [Pre-K], **168**

OCEAN

SEE ALSO Seashore

Avi. *The True Confessions of Charlotte Doyle* [5-6], **803**

Ballard, Robert. *Exploring the Titanic* [4-6], **1102**

Berg, Cami. *D Is for Dolphin* [Pre-3], **1106**

Bowden, Joan Chase. *Why the Tides Ebb and Flow* [1-6], 1406

Calhoun, Mary. *Henry the Sailor Cat* [1-2], **418**

Cole, Joanna. *The Magic School Bus on the Ocean Floor* [2-4], **1122**

Dorros, Arthur. *Follow the Water from Brook to Ocean* [K-3], **1133**

Doubilet, Anne. *Under the Sea from A to Z* [K-5], **1134**

Faulkner, Matt. *The Amazing Voyage of Jackie Grace* [1-2], 666

Ikeda, Daisaku. *Over the Deep Blue Sea* [1-2], **460**

Lauber, Patricia. *An Octopus Is Amazing* [1-3], **1181**

Levine, Evan. *Not the Piano, Mrs. Medley!* [1-2], **483**

Marshak, Suzanna. *I Am the Ocean* [K-4], **1200**

O'Dell, Scott. *The Black Pearl* [5-6], 1338

Paxton, Tom. *Jennifer's Rabbit* [Pre-K], 224

Peet, Bill. *Cyrus the Unsinkable Sea Serpent* [1-2], 767

Seuss, Dr. *The King's Stilts* [2-3], 996

Simon, Seymour. *Icebergs and Glaciers* [3-5], 2103

Sperry, Armstrong. *Call It Courage* [4-5], 1242

Tayntor, Elizabeth, Paul Erickson, and Les Kaufman. *Dive to the Coral Reefs: A New England Aquarium Book* [3-6], 2110

Waber, Bernard. *I Was All Thumbs* [2-3], 1023

OCEAN–Folklore

Crespo, George. *How the Sea Began: A Taino Myth* [1-6], **887**

French, Vivian. *Why the Sea Is Salt* [1-4], **906**

Gerson, Mary-Joan. *How Night Came from the Sea: A Story from Brazil* [K-4], **912**

San Souci, Robert D. *The Samurai's Daughter* [3-6], **1014**
  Sukey and the Mermaid [2-5], **1017**

OCEAN–Poetry

Russo, Marisabina. *The Ice Cream Ocean and Other Delectable Poems of the Sea* [Pre-3], 1940

Shaw, Alison. *Until I Saw the Sea: A Collection of Seashore Poems* [K-4], **1408**

OCTOPUS

Lauber, Patricia. *An Octopus Is Amazing* [1-3], **1181**

OGRES

SEE ALSO Fairies; Giants; Leprechauns; Monsters; Trolls

Basile, Giambattista. *Petrosinella: A Neopolitan Rapunzel* [4-6], 1401

Coombs, Patricia. *Molly Mullett* [2-3], 901

Murphy, Jill. *Jeffrey Strangeways* [3-4], **734**

Peet, Bill. *Cowardly Clyde* [2-3], 976

OGRES–Folklore

Haley, Gail E. *Puss in Boots* [1-4], **933**

Kirstein, Lincoln. *Puss in Boots* [1-4], **959**

Perrault, Charles. *Puss in Boots* [1-4], **997**

OHIO

Sanders, Scott Russell. *Warm as Wool* [1-2], **546**

OJIBWAY INDIANS–Folklore

Larry, Charles. *Peboan and Seegwun* [1-4], **964**

OKLAHOMA

Myers, Anna. *Red-Dirt Jessie* [4-5], **780**

OLD AGE

SEE Elderly

OLYMPIC GAMES

Stevenson, James. *The Mud Flat Olympics* [1-2], **557**

ONOMATOPOEIA

SEE ALSO English language–Onomatopoeic words

Mora, Pat. *Listen to the Desert / Oye al Desierto* [Pre-2], **1209**

OPERA

Price, Leontyne. *Aïda* [5-6], **837**

OPOSSUMS

Carlson, Natalie Savage. *Marie Louise's Heyday* [1-2], 638

Christelow, Eileen. *Olive and the Magic Hat* [K-1], 365

Conford, Ellen. *Impossible Possum* [1-2], 652

Hurd, Thacher. *Mama Don't Allow* [K-1], 432

Keller, Holly. *Henry's Fourth of July* [Pre], **26**

OPPOSITES

Andrews, F. Emerson. *Upside-Down Town* [2-3], 866

Gackenbach, Dick. *King Wacky* [1-2], 673

Hoban, Tana. *Exactly the Opposite* [Pre-K], **125**
Push, Pull, Empty, Full [Pre-K], 138

Mendoza, George. *The Sesame Street Book of Opposites* [Pre-K], 211

Stickland, Henrietta. *Dinosaur Roar!* [Pre-K], **189**

Yektai, Niki. *Bears in Pairs* [Pre-K], 302

OPTICAL ILLUSIONS

Baum, Arline, and Joseph Baum. *Opt: An Illusionary Tale* [3-4], 1044

ORCHESTRA

Hayes, Ann. *Meet the Orchestra* [K-3], **1157**

OREGON

Whiteley, Opal. *Only Opal: The Diary of a Young Girl* [2-5], **1253**

OREGON TRAIL

SEE ALSO Frontier and pioneer life; Santa Fe Trail

Van Leeuwen, Jean. *Bound for Oregon* [4-5], **793**

Woodruff, Elvira. *Dear Levi: Letters from the Overland Trail* [4-5], **796**

ORIGAMI

Coerr, Eleanor. *Sadako & the Thousand Paper Cranes* [3-6], 2007

Small, David. *Paper John* [1-2], 814

ORPHANS

Beatty, Patricia. *That's One Ornery Orphan* [5-6], 1274

Cassedy, Sylvia. *Behind the Attic Wall* [5-6], 1287

Dahl, Roald. *BFG* [4-5], 1166
James and the Giant Peach [3-4], 1059

Doherty, Berlie. *Street Child* [5-6], **813**

Holland, Isabella. *Alan and the Animal Kingdom* [5-6], 1311

Skurzynski, Gloria. *What Happened to Hamelin* [5-6], 1358

Wallace, Barbara Brooks. *Peppermints in the Parlor* [5-6], 1372
The Twin in the Tavern [5-6], **849**

Whiteley, Opal. *Only Opal: The Diary of a Young Girl* [2-5], **1253**

OSTRICHES

King-Smith, Dick. *The Cuckoo Child* [3-4], **722**

OTTERS

Ryder, Joanne. *Sea Elf* [K-3], **1231**

OUTER SPACE

SEE Astronomy; Planets; Space flight

OUTLAWS

SEE Robbers and outlaws

OWLS

SEE ALSO Birds; Chickens; Ducks; Geese; Parrots; Roosters

Erickson, Russell E. *A Toad for Tuesday* [1-2], 665

Heinrich, Bernd. *An Owl in the House: A Naturalist's Diary* [4-6], **1158**

Hutchins, Pat. *Good-Night, Owl* [Pre-K], 148

Kraus, Robert. *Owliver* [K-1], 461

Lear, Edward. *The Owl and the Pussycat* [Pre-K], **148, 149**, 181

Lobel, Arnold. *Owl at Home* [K-1], 484

London, Jonathan. *The Owl Who Became the Moon* [K-1], **310**

Mowat, Farley. *Owls in the Family* [3-5], 2077

Waber, Bernard. *Dear Hildegarde* [2-3], 1022

Waddell, Martin. *Owl Babies* [Pre], **49**

Yolen, Jane. *Owl Moon* [1-2], 857

OWLS–Folklore

Gates, Frieda. *Owl Eyes* [K-3], **911**

OXEN

Mazer, Anne. *The Oxboy* [5-6], **831**

OXEN–Folklore

Hong, Lily Toy. *How the Ox Star Fell from Heaven* [1-4], **942**

PAINTING

Agee, Jon. *The Incredible Painting of Felix Clousseau* [2-3], 862

Alcorn, Johnny. *Rembrandt's Beret* [3-4], **697**

Baker, Alan. *Benjamin's Portrait* [K-1], 326

Blake, Robert J. *The Perfect Spot* [K-1], **231**

Lionni, Leo. *Matthew's Dream* [K-1], **308**

McPhail, David. *Something Special* [K-1], 497

Roth, Roger. *The Sign Painter's Dream* [1-2], **545**

Rylant, Cynthia. *All I See* [2-3], 988

Skira-Venturi, Rosabianca. *A Weekend with Leonardo da Vinci* [3-8], **1239**

Spier, Peter. *Oh, Were They Ever Happy!* [K-1], 559

Zelinsky, Paul O. *The Lion and the Stoat* [1-2], 859

Zhensun, Zheng, and Alice Low. *A Young Painter: The Life and Paintings of Wang Yani—China's Extraordinary Young Artist* [3-6], **1257**

PAINTING–Folklore

Bang, Molly. *Tye May and the Magic Brush* [K-3], 1398

dePaola, Tomie. *The Legend of the Indian Paintbrush* [1-3], 1441

PAINTING–Folklore (cont.)

Levine, Arthur A. *The Boy Who Drew Cats: A Japanese Folktale* [2-6], **968**

Shepard, Aaron. *The Legend of Slappy Hooper: An American Tall Tale* [1-3], **1023**

PAINTINGS

Axelrod, Alan. *Songs of the Wild West* [1-6], **1264**

Fox, Dan. *Go In and Out the Window: An Illustrated Songbook for Young People* [Pre-6], 1801

Koch, Kenneth, and Kate Farrell. *Talking to the Sun* [Pre-6], 1849

Whipple, Laura. *Celebrating America: A Collection of Poems and Images of the American Spirit* [3-6], **1422**

PALEONTOLOGY

Cole, Sheila. *The Dragon in the Cliff: A Novel Based on the Life of Mary Anning* [5-6], **807**

PALINDROMES

Agee, Jon. *Go Hang a Salami! I'm a Lasagna Hog! And Other Palindromes* [2-6], **1263**

PANDAS

Allen, Judy. *Panda* [2-3], **584**

Calmenson, Stephanie. *Dinner at the Panda Palace* [Pre-K], **73**

Gackenbach, Dick. *Poppy, the Panda* [Pre-K], 100

Kraus, Robert. *Milton the Early Riser* [Pre-K], 174

Willard, Nancy. *Papa's Panda* [Pre-K], 295

PANTHERS–Folklore

Hunter, C. W. *The Green Gourd: A North Carolina Folktale* [K-2], **946**

PARADES

Sterman, Betsy, and Samuel Sterman. *Backyard Dragon* [3-4], **750**

PARENT AND CHILD

SEE Family life; Family problems; Fathers and daughters; Fathers and sons; Mothers and daughters; Mothers and sons

PARIS

Kirby, David, and Allen Woodman. *The Cows Are Going to Paris* [1-2], **471**

McCully, Emily Arnold. *Mirette on the High Wire* [1-2], **492**

Milton, Nancy. *The Giraffe That Walked to Paris* [2-4], **1208**

PARKS

Ernst, Lisa Campbell. *Squirrel Park* [1-2], **440**

McPhail, David. *Lost!* [K-1], **316**

PARODIES

Ada, Alma Flor. *Dear Peter Rabbit* [1-2], **395**

Ahlberg, Janet, and Allan Ahlberg. *The Jolly Christmas Postman* [1-2], **396**

Briggs, Raymond. *Jim and the Beanstalk* [1-2], 623

Calmenson, Stephanie. *The Principal's New Clothes* [1-2], **420**

Dahl, Roald. *Roald Dahl's Revolting Rhymes* [3-6], 1787

Emberley, Michael. *Ruby* [1-2], **437**

Greenburg, Dan. *Young Santa* [4-5], **770**

Greene, Carol. *The Thirteen Days of Halloween* [1-2], **681**

Gwynne, Fred. *Pondlarker* [1-2], **447**

Jackson, Ellen. *Cinder Edna* [2-3], **626**

Johnston, Tony. *The Cowboy and the Black-Eyed Pea* [3-4], **717**

Kovalski, Maryanne. *Pizza for Breakfast* [1-2], **479**

Manushkin, Fran. *My Christmas Safari* [K-1], **320**

Mendoza, George. *A Wart Snake in a Fig Tree* 2-3], 963

Minters, Frances. *Cinder-Elly* [1-2], **510**

Myers, Bernice. *Sidney Rella and the Glass Sneaker* [1-2], 754

Napoli, Donna Jo. *The Prince of the Pond: Otherwise Known as De Fawg Pin* [4-5], **782**

O'Donnell, Elizabeth Lee. *The Twelve Days of Summer* [1-2], **523**

Pilkey, Dav. *Dogzilla* [2-3], **657**
Kat Kong [2-3], **658**
'Twas the Night Before Thanksgiving [1-2], **531**

Regan, Dian Curtis. *The Thirteen Hours of Halloween* [1-2], **544**

Scieszka, Jon. *The Book That Jack Wrote* [1-2], **548**
The Frog Prince Continued [2-3], **676**
The Stinky Cheese Man and Other Fairly Stupid Tales [2-3], **677**

Tolhurst, Marilyn. *Somebody and the Three Blairs* [Pre-K], **191**

Trivizas, Eugene. *The Three Little Wolves and the Big Bad Pig* [K-1], **378**

Vesey, A. *The Princess and the Frog* [1-2], 837

Vozar, David. *Yo, Hungry Wolf! A Nursery Rap* [1-2], **570**

Wegman, William. *Cinderella* [1-4], **1042**

Wells, Rosemary. *Max and Ruby's First Greek Myth: Pandora's Box* [1-2], **573**

Wilsdorf, Anne. *Princess* [1-2], **577**

Wolf, Ashley. *Stella & Roy* [Pre-K], **210**

Yolen, Jane. *Sleeping Ugly* [2-3], 1033

PARROTS

SEE ALSO Birds; Chickens; Ducks; Geese; Owls; Roosters

Douglass, Barbara. *The Great Town and Country Bicycle Balloon Chase* [Pre-K], 73

Graham, Margaret Bloy. *Benjy and the Barking Bird* [Pre-K], 118

Hildick, E. W. *The Case of the Purloined Parrot* [4-5], **771**

King-Smith, Dick. *Harry's Mad* [4-5], 1199

PARTIES

Allard, Harry. *The Stupids Die* [K-1], 318

There's a Party at Mona's Tonight [K-1], 319

Anderson, Lonzo. *The Halloween Party* [1-2], 605

Asch, Frank. *Popcorn* [Pre-K], 15

Brown, Marc. *Arthur's Birthday* [1-2], 626

Freeman, Don. *Dandelion* [K-1], 392

Giff, Patricia Reilly. *Happy Birthday, Ronald Morgan!* [K-1], 406

Jonas, Ann. *The 13th Clue* [1-2], **464**

Keats, Ezra Jack. *A Letter to Amy* [K-1], 451

Marshall, James. *Portly McSwine* [K-1], 503

Mueller, Virginia. *Monster's Birthday Hiccups* [Pre], 36

Peek, Merle. *Mary Wore Her Red Dress and Henry Wore His Green Sneakers* [Pre-K], 227

Shute, Linda. *Halloween Party* [1-2], **551**

Tusa, Tricia. *The Family Reunion* [1-2], **568**

Yektai, Niki. *Bears in Pairs* [Pre-K], 302

PARTS OF SPEECH

SEE English language–Grammar

PASSOVER

SEE Holidays; Jews

PATRICK, SAINT

Hodges, Margaret. *Saint Patrick and the Peddler* [1-4], **941**

PATTERN PERCEPTION

Sharratt, Nick. *My Mom and Dad Make Me Laugh* [Pre-K], **186**

PEACE–Folklore

MacDonald, Margaret Read. *Peace Tales: World Folktales to Talk About* [1-6], **1076**

PEACOCKS

Polacco, Patricia. *Just Plain Fancy* [2-3], **662**

PEDDLERS AND PEDDLING

Hirsch, Marilyn. *Potato Pancakes All Around: A Hanukkah Tale* [2-3], 933

McDonald, Megan. *The Potato Man* [1-2], **496**

Rockwell, Anne. *The Gollywhopper Egg* [K-1], 534

Sanders, Scott Russell. *Here Comes the Mystery Man* [2-3], **673**

Slobodkina, Esphyr. *Caps for Sale* [Pre-K], 269

PEDDLERS AND PEDDLING–Folklore

Hodges, Margaret. *Saint Patrick and the Peddler* [1-4], **941**

PEER PRESSURE

Alcock, Vivien. *The Trial of Anna Cotman* [5-6], **802**

PENGUINS

SEE ALSO Birds

Lester, Helen. *Three Cheers for Tacky* [K-1], **305**

Vyner, Sue. *The Stolen Egg* [K-1], **379**

PERSEVERANCE

Conford, Ellen. *Impossible Possum* [1-2], 652

Jakob, Donna. *My Bike* [Pre-K], **132**

Lionni, Leo. *Tillie and the Wall* [K-1], 477

Schwartz, David. *Supergrandpa* [2-3], **675**

Wolf, Ashley. *Stella & Roy* [Pre-K], **210**

Yolen, Jane. *Wizard's Hall* [4-5], **801**

PERSONAL NARRATIVES

Brandenberg, Jim. *To the Top of the World: Adventures with Arctic Wolves* [4-6], **1108**

Hoshino, Michio. *The Grizzly Bear Family Book* [3-6], **1164**

Kossman, Nina. *Behind the Border* [4-6], **1173**

Lomas Garza, Carmen. *Family Pictures / Cuadros de Familia* [1-4], **1192**

Mason, Cherie. *Wild Fox: A True Story* [3-6], **1205**

Morimoto, Junko. *My Hiroshima* [3-6], **1210**

Russell, Marion. *Along the Santa Fe Trail: Marion Russell's Own Story* [2-5], **1230**

Stevenson, James. *Don't You Know There's a War On?* [2-6], **1245**

Whiteley, Opal. *Only Opal: The Diary of a Young Girl* [2-5], **1253**

Wood, Ted, and Wanbli Numpa Afraid of Hawk. *A Boy Becomes a Man at Wounded Knee* [3-6], **1255**

PETS

SEE ALSO Cats; Dogs; Domestic animals; Gerbils; Hamsters; Horses; Mice; Parrots; Snakes

Abercrombie, Barbara. *Michael and the Cats* [Pre], 1

Aliki. *At Mary Bloom's* [Pre-K], 4

Allen, Marjorie N. *One, Two, Three—Ah-Choo!* [K-1], 321

Baehr, Patricia. *Mouse in the House* [Pre-K], **68**

PETS (cont.)

Bare, Colleen Stanley. *Guinea Pigs Don't Read Books* [Pre-1], 1991

Baylor, Byrd. *Amigo* [1-2], 613

Doherty, Berlie. *Snowy* [K-1], **263**

Ferguson, Alane. *That New Pet!* [K-1], 386

Flora, James. *Leopold the See-Through Crumbpicker* [1-2], 669

Gerstein, Mordicai. *William, Where Are You?* [Pre-K], 113

Herriot, James. *Bonny's Big Day* [2-5], 2047

Hoffman, Mary. *The Four-Legged Ghosts* [2-3], **620**

Holland, Isabella. *Alan and the Animal Kingdom* [5-6], 1311

Howe, James. *Creepy-Crawly Birthday* [1-2], **456**
Scared Silly: A Halloween Treat [1-2], 693

Keats, Ezra Jack. *Pet Show!* [Pre-K], 163

Kellogg, Steven. *The Mysterious Tadpole* [1-2], 705

King-Smith, Dick. *Harry's Mad* [4-5], 1199
Pretty Polly [3-4], **725**

Kudrna, C. Imbior. *To Bathe a Boa* [K-1], 463

McPhail, David. *Emma's Pet* [Pre-K], 200

Mowat, Farley. *Owls in the Family* [3-5], 2077

Noble, Trinka Hakes. *The Day Jimmy's Boa Ate the Wash* [1-2], 761

North, Sterling. *Rascal: A Memoir of a Better Era* [4-6], 2079

Peet, Bill. *Capyboppy* [2-5], 2081

Peters, Lisa Westberg. *When the Fly Flew In* [K-1], **336**

Porte, Barbara Ann. *"Leave That Cricket Be, Alan Lee"* [K-1], **340**

Reiser, Lynn. *Any Kind of Dog* [Pre], **40**

Shura, Mary Frances. *Chester* [3-4], 1112

Springstubb, Tricia. *The Magic Guinea Pig* [Pre-K], 270

Wilcox, Cathy. *Enzo the Wonderfish* [K-1], 386

Wolkoff, Judie. *Wally* [3-4], 1135

PETS–Poetry

Singer, Marilyn. *Please Don't Squeeze Your Boa, Noah!* [3-6], **1410**

PHOTOGRAPHY

Allen, Judy. *Tiger* [2-3], **585**

Brandenberg, Jim. *To the Top of the World: Adventures with Arctic Wolves* [4-6], **1108**

Bucknall, Caroline. *One Bear in the Picture* [Pre-K], 31

Hoban, Tana. *Look Again!* [1-2], 688
Look! Look! Look! [K-1], **286**

McPhail, David. *Pig Pig and the Magic Photo Album* [K-1], 496

Willard, Nancy. *Simple Pictures Are Best* [1-2], 849

Zolotow, Charlotte. *This Quiet Lady* [K-1], **393**

PHYSICAL DISABILITY

Carlson, Nancy L. *Arnie and the New Kid* [1-2], **421**

Cowen-Fletcher, Jane. *Mama Zooms* [Pre-K], **89**

Damrell, Liz. *With the Wind* [1-2], **429**

Osofsky, Audrey. *My Buddy* [1-2], **526**

Russo, Marisabina. *Alex Is My Friend* [K-1], **354**

Springer, Nancy. *Colt* [4-5], **792**

PHYSICALLY HANDICAPPED
SEE Handicaps

PIANO

Purdy, Carol. *Mrs. Merriweather's Musical Cat* [1-2], **539**

Ray, Mary Lynn. *Pianna* [1-2], **542**

PICNICS

Alborough, Jez. *It's the Bear!* [Pre-K], **63**

Cauley, Lorinda Bryan. *Treasure Hunt* [Pre-K], **79**

Choi, Sook Nyul. *Halmoni and the Picnic* [1-2], **424**

Gackenbach, Dick. *Claude Has a Picnic* [Pre], **16**

Kasza, Keiko. *The Pig's Picnic* [Pre-K], 161

Keller, Holly. *Henry's Fourth of July* [Pre], **26**

McCully, Emily Arnold. *Picnic* [Pre-K], 196

Mahy, Margaret. *The Rattlebang Picnic* [1-2], **502**

Pinczes, Elinor J. *One Hundred Hungry Ants* [1-2], **533**

Saunders, Susan. *Fish Fry* [1-2], 790

Schindel, John. *What's for Lunch?* [Pre-K], **185**

PICTURE BOOKS FOR ALL AGES

Ahlberg, Janet, and Allan Ahlberg. *The Jolly Christmas Postman* [1-2], **396**

Alcorn, Johnny. *Rembrandt's Beret* [3-4], **697**

Alexander, Lloyd. *The Fortune-Tellers* [3-4], **698**

Allinson, Beverly. *Effie* [K-1], **217**

Andersen, Hans Christian. *The Emperor's New Clothes: A Fairy Tale* [2-3], 863
It's Perfectly True [1-2], 602
The Steadfast Tin Soldier [2-3], **586**

Armstrong, Jennifer. *Chin Yu Min and the Ginger Cat* [2-3], **588**

Bernhard, Emery. *How Snowshoe Hare Rescued the Sun: A Tale from the Arctic* [K-3], **866**

Bunting, Eve. *Fly Away Home* [1-2], **415**
Night of the Gargoyles [3-4], **705**

Smoky Night [2-3], **593**
The Wall [K-1], 354
Burleigh, Robert. *Flight: The Journey of Charles Lindbergh* [3-6], **1114**
Calmenson, Stephanie. *The Principal's New Clothes* [1-2], **420**
Cannon, Janell. *Stellaluna* [K-1], **245**
Cherry, Lynne. *The Great Kapok Tree: A Tale of the Amazon Rain Forest* [1-2], 647
Clements, Andrew. *Mother Earth's Counting Book* [K-5], **1118**
Cole, Joanna. *The Magic School Bus Lost in the Solar System* [1-4], **1121**
Compton, Patricia A. *The Terrible Eek* [K-3], **885**
Cooney, Barbara. *Miss Rumphius* [1-2], 654
Cushman, Doug. *The ABC Mystery* [1-2], **428**
dePaola, Tomie. *The Art Lesson* [2-3], 907
Tom [1-2], **431**
Dugan, Barbara. *Loop the Loop* [2-3], **608**
Ehlert, Lois. *Color Zoo* [Pre-K], 76
Emberley, Ed. *Go Away, Big Green Monster!* [Pre-K], **98**
Emberley, Michael. *Ruby* [1-2], **437**
Gammell, Stephen. *Once upon MacDonald's Farm* [K-1], 401
Gardner, Beau. *The Look Again . . . and Again, and Again, and Again Book* [1-2], 675
Garland, Sherry. *The Lotus Seed* [2-3], **609**
Gilliland, Judith Heide. *River* [K-3], **1152**
Goble, Paul. *Dream Wolf* [1-2], **443**
Goffin, Josse. *Oh!* [Pre-K], **109**
Greene, Carol. *The Old Ladies Who Liked Cats* [1-2], **445**
Haley, Gail E. *Dream Peddler* [2-3], **612**
Hall, Donald. *I Am the Dog, I Am the Cat* [1-2], **448**
Heide, Florence Parry, and Judith Heide Gilliland. *Sami and the Time of the Troubles* [3-4], **713**
Henkes, Kevin. *Chrysanthemum* [K-1], **282**
Hepworth, Cathi. *Antics! An Alphabetical Anthology* [2-6], **1312**
Hopkinson, Deborah. *Sweet Clara and the Freedom Quilt* [2-3], **622**
Houston, Gloria. *My Great Aunt Arizona* [1-6], **1165**
Howard, Ellen. *Murphy and Kate* [2-3], **623**
Howe, James. *Scared Silly: A Halloween Treat* [1-2], 693
Huff, Barbara A. *Once Inside the Library* [1-2], **459**
Ipcar, Dahlov. *I Love My Anteater with an A* [3-4], 1078
Isaacs, Anne. *Swamp Angel* [2-3], **625**

Jaffe, Nina. *In the Month of Kislev: A Story for Hanukkah* [2-3], **627**
Jeffers, Susan. *Brother Eagle, Sister Sky: A Message from Chief Seattle* [2-3], **628**
Johnson, Paul Brett. *The Cow Who Wouldn't Come Down* [K-1], **292**
Johnston, Tony. *The Cowboy and the Black-Eyed Pea* [3-4], **717**
Jonas, Ann. *Reflections* [1-2], 700
Round Trip [1-2], 701
Joyce, William. *Santa Calls* [2-3], **631**
Jukes, Mavis. *I'll See You in My Dreams* [3-4], **718**
Kalman, Maira. *Hey Willy, See the Pyramids* [2-3], 941
Kennedy, Richard. *The Leprechaun's Story* [3-4], 1081
Kimmel, Eric A. *Hershel and the Hanukkah Goblins* [2-3], 944
Kinsey-Warnock, Natalie. *The Bear That Heard Crying* [1-2], **468**
Knowles, Sheena. *Edward the Emu* [K-1], **300**
Komaiko, Leah. *Earl's Too Cool for Me* [1-2], **477**
Kovalski, Maryanne. *Pizza for Breakfast* [1-2], **479**
Kraus, Robert. *Leo the Late Bloomer* [K-1], 460
Langerlöf, Selma. *The Changeling* [2-3], **636**
Larry, Charles. *Peboan and Seegwun* [1-4], **964**
Leaf, Munro. *The Story of Ferdinand* [K-1], 465
Lear, Edward. *The Owl and the Pussycat* [Pre-K], **148, 149**
Lebentritt, Julia, and Richard Ploetz. *The Kooken* [1-2], **481**
Lionni, Leo. *Tillie and the Wall* [K-1], 477
Lobel, Arnold. *On Market Street* [K-1], 483
London, Jonathan. *The Eyes of Gray Wolf* [1-2], **488**
Voices of the Wild [2-3], **640**
Macaulay, David. *Black and White* [1-2], **490**
MacCarthy, Patricia. *Herds of Words* [K-6], **1363**
McCully, Emily Arnold. *Mirette on the High Wire* [1-2], **492**
McPhail, David. *Fix-It* [K-1], 494
Mahy, Margaret. *The Great White Man-Eating Shark: A Cautionary Tale* [1-2], **501**
Manson, Christopher. *The Marvelous Blue Mouse* [2-3], **641**
Mariotti, Mario. *Hanimations* [K-6], **1199**
Marshall, James. *The Cut-Ups* [1-2], 743
George and Martha [K-1], 502
Wings: A Tale of Two Chickens [1-2], 745
Martin, Bill, Jr. *The Maestro Plays* [1-2], **504**
Martin, Jane Read, and Patricia Marx. *Now Everybody Really Hates Me* [2-3], **644**
Meddaugh, Susan. *Martha Speaks* [1-2], **506**
Mellecker, Judith. *Randolph's Dream* [3-4], **732**

PICTURE BOOKS FOR ALL AGES (cont.)

Mitchell, Margaree King. *Uncle Jed's Barbershop* [2-3], **647**

Moore, Clement C. *The Night before Christmas* [1-2], 753

Moore, Inga. *The Sorcerer's Apprentice* [2-3], **648**

Murphy, Jim. *Backyard Bear* [1-2], **515**

Nash, Ogden. *The Adventures of Isabel* [2-3], **649**

Neumeier, Marty, and Byron Glaser. *Action Alphabet* [1-2], 758

Newman, Nanette. *There's a Bear in the Bath!* [1-2], **517**

Nolan, Dennis. *Dinosaur Dream* [1-2], **520**

Norworth, Jack. *Take Me Out to the Ballgame* [1-2], **521**

Paulsen, Gary. *Dogteam* [3-4], **738**

Pearson, Susan. *Lenore's Big Break* [1-2], **528**

Pilkey, Dav. *Dog Breath: The Horrible Trouble with Hally Tosis* [1-2], **530**

Dogzilla [2-3], **657**

Kat Kong [2-3], **658**

'Twas the Night Before Thanksgiving [1-2], **531**

When Cats Dream [1-2], **532**

Pinkwater, Daniel. *Author's Day* [2-3], **659**

Wempires [1-2], **535**

Polacco, Patricia. *Chicken Sunday* [2-3], **661**

Just Plain Fancy [2-3], **662**

My Rotten Redheaded Older Brother [1-2], **536**

Tikvah Means Hope [2-3], **664**

Provensen, Alice, and Martin Provensen. *The Glorious Flight: Across the Channel with Louis Blérot* [K-6], 2084

Rand, Gloria. *Salty Takes Off* [1-2], **540**

Rankin, Laura. *The Handmade Alphabet* [K-6], **1223**

Raschka, Chris. *Yo! Yes?* [1-2], **541**

Ringgold, Faith. *Aunt Harriet's Underground Railroad in the Sky* [2-3], **670**

Tar Beach [2-3], **671**

Rohmann, Eric. *Time Flies* [K-1], **350**

Roop, Peter, and Connie Roop. *One Earth, a Multitude of Creatures* [K-6], **1228**

Rosen, Michael. *Moving* [K-1], **352**

Roth, Roger. *The Sign Painter's Dream* [1-2], **545**

Ryder, Joanne. *Sea Elf* [K-3], **1231**

Winter Whale [K-3], **1232**

Rylant, Cynthia. *When I Was Young in the Mountains* [2-3], 989

Sanders, Scott Russell. *Warm as Wool* [1-2], **546**

Say, Allen. *Grandfather's Journey* [2-3], **674**

Schwartz, Amy. *Annabelle Swift, Kindergartner* [1-2], 794

Bea and Mr. Jones [1-2], 795

A Teeny Tiny Baby [K-1], **358**

Schwartz, David. *Supergrandpa* [2-3], **675**

Scieszka, Jon. *The Book That Jack Wrote* [1-2], **548**

The Frog Prince Continued [2-3], **676**

The Stinky Cheese Man and Other Fairly Stupid Tales [2-3], **677**

The True Story of the 3 Little Pigs [2-3], 993

Seligson, Susan. *Amos Camps Out: A Couch Adventure in the Woods* [1-2], **549**

Seligson, Susan, and Howie Schneider. *Amos: The Story of an Old Dog and His Couch* [K-1], 549

Shulevitz, Uri. *The Treasure* [2-3], 999

Siebert, Diane. *Mojave* [2-3], 1000

Plane Song [1-2], **552**

Train Song [1-2], **553**

Stevenson, James. *That Dreadful Day* [2-3], 1011

Swope, Sam. *The Araboolies of Liberty Street* [1-2], 829

Talbott, Hudson. *We're Back!* [2-3], 1013

Thaler, Mike. *The Teacher from the Black Lagoon* [2-3], **682**

Trivizas, Eugene. *The Three Little Wolves and the Big Bad Pig* [K-1], **378**

Tzannes, Robin. *Professor Puffendorf's Secret Potions* [1-2], **569**

Van Allsburg, Chris. *The Polar Express* [1-2], 835

The Stranger [3-4], 1124

The Widow's Broom [3-4], **752**

Viorst, Judith. *Alexander and the Terrible, Horrible, No Good, Very Bad Day* [1-2], 838

Wegman, William. *ABC* [1-2], **571**

Wells, Rosemary. *Max and Ruby's First Greek Myth: Pandora's Box* [1-2], **573**

Max's Chocolate Chicken [Pre-K], 286

Max's Christmas [Pre-K], 287

Wiesner, David. *June 29, 1999* [2-3], **690**

Tuesday [K-1], **385**

Williams, David. *Grandma Essie's Covered Wagon* [2-3], **691**

Wisniewski, David. *Rain Player* [2-3], **694**

Wood, Audrey. *King Bidgood's in the Bathtub* [1-2], 855

Wright, Kit. *Tigerella* [K-1], **389**

Yee, Paul. *Roses Sing on New Snow: A Delicious Tale* [2-3], **696**

Yolen, Jane. *Encounter* [3-4], **756**

Yorinks, Arthur. *Company's Coming* [2-3], 1034

Whitefish Will Rides Again! [1-2], **581**

Zolotow, Charlotte. *This Quiet Lady* [K-1], **393**

PIES

SEE ALSO Cookery; Food; Fruit

Johnston, Tony. *The Vanishing Pumpkin* [K-1], 443

Levitin, Sonia. *Nobody Stole the Pie* [1-2], 722

Matthews, Louise. *Gator Pie* [K-1], 506

Nixon, Joan Lowery. *Beats Me, Claude* [2-3], 971

Priceman, Marjorie. *How to Make an Apple Pie and See the World* [1-2], **538**

Schatell, Brian. *Farmer Goff and His Turkey Sam* [K-1], 543

PIGS

Ada, Alma Flor. *Dear Peter Rabbit* [1-2], **395**

Allard, Harry. *There's a Party at Mona's Tonight* [K-1], 319

Axelrod, Amy. *Pigs Will Be Pigs* [1-2], **403**

Boland, Janice. *Annabel* [Pre], **6**

Bond, Felicia. *Pointsettia and the Firefighters* [K-1], 338

Callen, Larry. *Pinch* [5-6], 1285

Carlson, Nancy L. *Louanne Pig in the Mysterious Valentine* [1-2], 637

Christelow, Eileen. *Mr. Murphy's Marvelous Invention* [1-2], 649

Cole, Brock. *Nothing but a Pig* [1-2], 651

Dyke, John. *Pigwig* [K-1], 379

Edwards, Frank B. *Mortimer Mooner Stopped Taking a Bath* [Pre-K], **94**

Flora, James. *Grandpa's Witched-Up Christmas* [2-3], 920

Gackenbach, Dick. *Harvey the Foolish Pig* [K-1], 397

Getz, Arthur. *Humphrey, the Dancing Pig* [K-1], 405

Gretz, Susanna. *It's Your Turn, Roger!* [K-1], 412

Grossman, Bill. *Tommy at the Grocery Store* [K-1], 414

Heller, Nicholas. *Woody* [Pre-K], **121**

Jeschke, Susan. *Perfect the Pig* [K-1], 438

Kasza, Keiko. *The Pig's Picnic* [Pre-K], 161

Keller, Holly. *Geraldine's Blanket* [Pre-K], 168

King-Smith, Dick. *Babe, the Gallant Pig* [5-6], 1319

Pigs Might Fly [5-6], 1320

Kirby, Susan. *Ike and Porker* [4-5], 1200

Lester, Helen. *Me First* [K-1], **304**

Lies, Brian. *Hamlet and the Enormous Chinese Dragon Kite* [1-2], **484**

Lobel, Arnold. *A Treeful of Pigs* [1-2], 729

McPhail, David. *Pig Pig and the Magic Photo Album* [K-1], 496

Pig Pig Gets a Job [K-1], **318**

Pig Pig Grows Up [Pre-K], 202

Pigs Aplenty, Pigs Galore! [K-1], **317**

Marshall, James. *Portly McSwine* [K-1], 503

Munsch, Robert. *Pigs* [K-1], **330**

Offen, Hilda. *Nice Work, Little Wolf!* [Pre-K], **173**

Peet, Bill. *Chester the Worldly Pig* [2-3], 975

Pinkwater, Daniel. *Three Big Hogs* [Pre-K], 229

Pomerantz, Charlotte. *The Piggy in the Puddle* [Pre-K], 231

Rayner, Mary. *Garth Pig and the Ice Cream Lady* [1-2], 781

Garth Pig Steals the Show [1-2], **543**

Mr. and Mrs. Pig's Evening Out [1-2], 782

Mrs. Pig's Bulk Buy [1-2], 783

Ten Pink Piglets: Garth Pig's Wall Song [Pre-K], **179**

Reddix, Valerie. *Millie and the Mud Hole* [Pre-K], **180**

Rodda, Emily. *The Pigs Are Flying* [4-5], 1231

Schwartz, Mary Ada. *Spiffen: A Tale of a Tidy Pig* [K-1], 547

Scieszka, Jon. *The True Story of the 3 Little Pigs* [2-3], 993

Steig, William. *The Amazing Bone* [2-3], 1006

Zeke Pippin [2-3], **678**

Stolz, Mary. *Quentin Corn* [5-6], 1365

Teague, Mark. *Pigsty* [1-2], **564**

Trivizas, Eugene. *The Three Little Wolves and the Big Bad Pig* [K-1], **378**

Vozar, David. *Yo, Hungry Wolf! A Nursery Rap* [1-2], **570**

Waddell, Martin. *The Pig in the Pond* [Pre], **50**

Wagner, Karen. *Silly Fred* [Pre-K], **203**

Watson, Pauline. *Wriggles the Little Wishing Pig* [K-1], 582

White, E. B. *Charlotte's Web* [2-3], 1027

Winthrop, Elizabeth. *Sloppy Kisses* [K-1], 595

Wood, Don, and Audrey Wood. *Piggies* [Pre], **59**

Zakhoder, Boris. *How a Piglet Crashed the Christmas Party* [1-2], 858

PIGS–Folklore

Cauley, Lorinda Bryan. *The Three Little Pigs* [Pre-2], 1420

Galdone, Paul. *The Amazing Pig* [2-4], 1457

The Three Little Pigs [Pre-1], 1474

Hooks, William H. *The Three Little Pigs and the Fox* [Pre-2], 1530

Kimmel, Eric A. *The Old Woman and Her Pig* [Pre-2], **956**

Lamont, Priscilla. *The Troublesome Pig: A Nursery Tale* [Pre-2], 1543

Litzinger, Rosanne. *The Old Woman and Her Pig: An Old English Tale* [Pre-1], **971**

Marshall, James. *The Three Little Pigs* [Pre-1], 1563

Pitre, Felix. *Juan Bobo and the Pig: A Puerto Rican Folktale* [K-2], **998**

PIGS–Folklore (cont.)

Rounds, Glen. *Three Little Pigs and the Big Bad Wolf* [Pre-2], **1010**

Zemach, Margot. *The Three Little Pigs: An Old Story* [Pre-2], 1639

PIGS–Poetry

Lobel, Arnold. *The Book of Pigericks* [2-6], 1861

PIGS–Riddles

Phillips, Louis. *Invisible Oink: Pig Jokes* [3-6], **1394**

PILGRIMS

Accorsi, William. *Friendship's First Thanksgiving* [K-1], **216**

Cohen, Barbara. *Molly's Pilgrim* [2-3], 893

Fritz, Jean. *Who's That Stepping on Plymouth Rock?* [3-6], 2035

George, Jean Craighead. *The First Thanksgiving* [1-4], **1147**

Harness, Cheryl. *Three Young Pilgrims* [2-3], **614**

Kroll, Steven. *Oh, What a Thanksgiving!* [1-2], 718

Sewall, Marcia. *The Pilgrims of Plimoth* [2-6], 2098

Waters, Kate. *Samuel Eaton's Day: A Day in the Life of a Pilgrim Boy* [2-4], **1250**

Sarah Morton's Day: A Day in the Life of a Pilgrim Girl [1-5], 2112

PILOTS

SEE Airplanes; Flight

PIONEERS

SEE Frontier and pioneer life

PIRATES

Cohen, Caron Lee. *Renata, Whizbrain and the Ghost* [2-3], 894

Faulkner, Matt. *The Amazing Voyage of Jackie Grace* [1-2], 666

Fleischman, Sid. *The Ghost in the Noonday Sun* [5-6], 1301

Haynes, Betsy. *The Ghost of the Gravestone Hearth* [4-5], 1185

McNaughton, Colin. *Anton B. Stanton and the Pirats* [1-2], 736

Peet, Bill. *Cyrus the Unsinkable Sea Serpent* [1-2], 767

Pinkwater, Daniel. *Ned Feldman, Space Pirate* [2-3], **660**

Strickland, Brad. *Dragon's Plunder* [5-6], **848**

PIZZA

SEE ALSO Cookery; Food

Kovalski, Maryanne. *Pizza for Breakfast* [1-2], **479**

Mahy, Margaret. *The Rattlebang Picnic* [1-2], **502**

PLAINS INDIANS

Goble, Paul. *Dream Wolf* [1-2], **443**

PLAINS INDIANS–Folklore

Love Flute [3-6], **916**

PLANETS

SEE Astronomy; Space flight

PLANTS

SEE ALSO Flowers; Gardens; Seeds; Trees; Vegetables

Back, Christine. *Bean and Plant* [Pre-3], 1989

Bash, Barbara. *Desert Giant: The World of the Saguaro Cactus* [2-5], 1994

Byars, Betsy. *McMummy* [4-5], **762**

Cowcher, Helen. *Whistling Thorn* [K-2], **1126**

Flora, James. *The Great Green Turkey Creek Monster* [2-3], 921

Gardiner, John Reynolds. *Top Secret* [5-6], 1303

Gibbons, Gail. *From Seed to Plant* [K-3], **1148**

Hall, Zoe. *It's Pumpkin Time!* [Pre], 18

Heller, Ruth. *The Reason for a Flower* [K-4], **1161**

Krauss, Ruth. *The Carrot Seed* [Pre-K], 178

Pulver, Robin. *Nobody's Mother Is in Second Grade* [K-1], **346**

Sadler, Marilyn. *Alistair and the Alien Invasion* [K-1], **356**

Zion, Gene. *The Plant Sitter* [K-1], 598

PLANTS–Folklore

Brusca, María Cristina, and Tona Wilson. *When Jaguars Ate the Moon: And Other Stories About Animals and Plants of the Americas* [2-6], 1061

PLAY

SEE ALSO Games

Heller, Nicholas. *An Adventure at Sea* [1-2], 685

Up the Wall [K-1], **281**

Henkes, Kevin. *A Weekend with Wendell* [K-1], 420

Kent, Jack. *Jim Jimmy James* [K-1], 454

McLerran, Alice. *Roxaboxen* [1-2], **499**

Phelan, Terry Wolfe. *The Week Mom Unplugged the TVs* [3-4], 1102

Pringle, Laurence. *Octopus Hug* [Pre-K], **178**

Waddell, Martin. *Squeak-a-Lot* [Pre], **52**

Wiesner, David. *Hurricane* [1-2], **574**

PLAY–Poetry

McMillan, Bruce. *Play Day: A Book of Terse Verse* [Pre-1], **1365**

PLAYS

Aardema, Verna. *Who's in Rabbit's House?* [2-4], 1385

Charlip, Remy, and Burton Supree. *Mother, Mother, I Feel Sick, Send for the Doctor Quick, Quick, Quick* [1-2], 646

Cohen, Miriam. *Starring First Grade* [K-1], 371

Freeman, Don. *Hattie the Backstage Bat* [K-1], 393

Gormley, Beatrice. *Fifth-Grade Magic* [4-5], 1181

Johnston, Johanna. *Speak Up, Edie* [K-1], 440

Lewison, Wendy Cheyette. *Shy Vi* [Pre-K], **151**

Nixon, Joan Lowery. *Gloria Chipmunk, Star!* [1-2], 760

Oppenheim, Joanne. *Mrs. Peloki's Class Play* [1-2], 763

Robinson, Barbara. *The Best Christmas Pageant Ever* [4-5], 1230

Stanley, Diane, and Peter Vennema. *Bard of Avon: The Story of William Shakespeare* [4-6], **1241**

Young, Ruth. *Starring Francine & Dave: Three One-Act Plays* [Pre-2], 2117

PLAYS–Collections

Giff, Patricia Reilly. *Show Time at the Polk Street School: Plays You Can Do Yourself or in the Classroom* [1-3], **1151**

Kline, Suzy. *The Herbie Jones Reader's Theater: Funny Scenes to Read Aloud* [2-4], **1170**

Shepard, Aaron. *Stories on Stage: Scripts for Reader's Theater* [2-6], **1237**

POETRY–Anthologies

Agard, John, and Grace Nichols. *A Caribbean Dozen: Poems from Caribbean Poets* [1-6], **1262**

Arbuthnot, Mary Hill. *Time for Poetry* [Pre-6], 1744

Bennett, Jill. *A Cup of Starshine: Poems and Pictures for Young Children* [Pre-2], **1268**

Booth, David. *'Til All the Stars Have Fallen: A Collection of Poems for Children* [3-5], **1273**

Brenner, Barbara. *The Earth Is Painted Green: A Garden of Poems About Our Planet* [1-5], **1274**

Cole, Joanna. *A New Treasury of Children's Poetry: Old Favorites and New Discoveries* [Pre-6], 1773

Cole, William. *A Zooful of Animals* [K-5], **1282**

Corrin, Sara, and Stephen Corrin. *Once Upon a Rhyme: 101 Poems for Young Children* [K-3], 1783

dePaola, Tomie. *Tomie dePaola's Book of Poems* [Pre-4], 1790

De Regniers, Beatrice Schenk. *Sing a Song of Popcorn: Every Child's Book of Poems* [Pre-4], 1792

Foster, John. *A First Poetry Book* [K-2], 1800

Let's Celebrate: Festival Poems [3-6], **1293**

Goldstein, Bobbye S. *Inner Chimes: Poems on Poetry* [2-6], **1298**

Hopkins, Lee Bennett. *More Surprises* [Pre-3], 1825

Side by Side: Poems to Read Together [K-2], 1827

Hopkins, Lee Bennett, and Misha Arenstein. *Thread One to a Star: A Book of Poems* [4-6], 1829

Janeczko, Paul B. *Poetry from A to Z: A Guide for Young Writers* [5-6], **1335**

Kennedy, Dorothy M., and X. J. Kennedy. *Talking Like the Rain: A First Book of Poems* [K-5], **1342**

Kennedy, X. J. *Knock at a Star: A Child's Introduction to Poetry* [4-6], 1847

Koch, Kenneth, and Kate Farrell. *Talking to the Sun* [Pre-6], 1849

Larrick, Nancy. *Piping Down the Valleys Wild* [2-6], 1852

Lewis, Richard. *Miracles: Poems by Children of the English-Speaking World* [1-6], 1856

Livingston, Myra Cohn. *Lots of Limericks* [4-6], **1359**

Moore, Lillian. *Go with the Poem* [3-6], 1874

Sunflakes: Poems for Children [Pre-3], **1375**

Panzer, Nora. *Celebrate America in Poetry and Art* [4-6], **1393**

Prelutsky, Jack. *For Laughing Out Loud: Poems to Tickle Your Funnybone* [K-5], **1397**

The Random House Book of Poetry for Children [1-5], 1916

Read-Aloud Rhymes for the Very Young [Pre-3], 1917

Rosen, Michael. *Poems for the Very Young* [Pre-2], **1405**

Saunders, Dennis. *Magic Lights and Streets of Shining Jet* [1-4], 1943

Sullivan, Charles. *Cowboys* [K-4], **1413**

Untermeyer, Louis. *The Golden Treasury of Poetry* [2-6], 1968

Westcott, Nadine Bernard. *Never Take a Pig to Lunch and Other Poems About the Fun of Eating* [1-4], **1421**

Whipple, Laura. *Celebrating America: A Collection of Poems and Images of the American Spirit* [3-6], **1422**

Eric Carle's Animals, Animals [K-4], 1974

POETRY–Anthologies (cont.)

Eric Carle's Dragons, Dragons & Other Creatures That Never Were [2-6], **1423**

Wilner, Isabel. *The Poetry Troupe: An Anthology of Poems to Read Aloud* [K-4], 1975

Yolen, Jane. *Alphabestiary: Animal Poems from A to Z* [1-4], **1426**

POETRY–Canadian

Booth, David. *'Til All the Stars Have Fallen: A Collection of Poems for Children* [3-5], **1273**

POETRY–Single Author

Adoff, Arnold. *Chocolate Dreams* [5-6], **1259**

Eats [2-6], 1742

In for Winter, Out for Spring [K-4], **1260**

Street Music: City Poems [2-6], **1261**

Benjamin, Alan. *A Nickel Buys a Rhyme* [Pre-2], **1267**

Bodecker, N. M. *Let's Marry Said the Cherry and Other Nonsense Poems* [K-5], 1751

A Person from Britain Whose Head was the Shape of a Mitten and Other Limericks [3-6], 1752

Water Pennies: And Other Poems [2-5], **1271**

Ciardi, John. *Doodle Soup* [1-4], 1769

Fast and Slow: Poems for Advanced Children and Beginning Parents [2-5], 1770

The Hopeful Trout and Other Limericks [3-6], 1771

You Read to Me, I'll Read to You [1-3], 1772

Dakos, Kalli. *If You're Not Here, Please Raise Your Hand: Poems about School* [2-6], **1283**

De Regniers, Beatrice Schenk. *This Big Cat and Other Cats I've Known* [Pre-2], 1793

Edwards, Richard. *Moon Frog: Animal Poems for Young Children* [K-3], **1285**

Eliot, T. S. *Mr. Mistoffelees with Mungojerrie and Rumpelteazer* [3-6], **1286**

Old Possum's Book of Practical Cats [4-6], 1795

Esbensen, Barbara Juster. *Cold Stars and Fireflies: Poems of the Four Seasons* [3-6], 1797

Who Shrank My Grandmother's House? Poems of Discovery [2-5], **1287**

Fatchen, Max. *The Country Mail Is Coming: Poems from Down Under* [3-6], **1289**

Florian, Douglas. *Beast Feast* [K-4], **1290**

Bing Bang Boing [1-6], **1291**

Monster Motel [K-3], **1292**

Graham, Joan Bransfield. *Splish Splash* [K-6], **1301**

Greenfield, Eloise. *Honey, I Love* [2-5], **1807**

Under the Sunday Tree [2-5], 1808

Grimes, Nikki. *Meet Danitra Brown* [3-5], **1302**

Harrison, David L. *Somebody Catch My Homework* [2-5], **1307**

Heide, Florence Parry. *Grim and Ghastly Goings-On* [1-4], **1309**

Hoban, Russell. *Egg Thoughts and Other Frances Songs* [K-2], 1813

Hoberman, Mary Ann. *Fathers, Mothers, Sisters, Brothers: A Collection of Family Poems* [K-4], **1314**

A Fine Fat Pig and Other Animal Poems [K-3], **1315**

Hughes, Langston. *Don't You Turn Back* [3-6], 1830

The Dream Keeper and Other Poems [4-6], **1332**

Jacobs, Leland B. *Just Around the Corner: Poems About the Seasons* [Pre-2], **1333**

Kennedy, Dorothy M. *I Thought I'd Take My Rat to School: Poems for September to June* [3-6], **1341**

Kennedy, X. J. *Drat These Brats* [4-6], **1343**

Ghastlies, Goops & Pincushions: Nonsense Verse [3-6], 1846

Klein, Robin. *Snakes and Ladders: Poems about the Ups and Downs of Life* [3-6], 1848

Lear, Edward. *Daffy Down Dillies: Silly Limericks* [3-6], **1348**

How Pleasant to Know Mr. Lear! [4-6], 1853

Of Pelicans and Pussycats: Poems and Limericks [K-5], **1349**

Lee, Dennis. *Alligator Pie* [Pre-4], 1854

The Ice Cream Store [Pre-3], **1350**

Jelly Belly: Original Nursery Rhymes [Pre-3], 1855

Lewis, J. Patrick. *Earth Verses and Water Rhymes* [2-4], **1352**

A Hippopotamustn't and Other Animal Verses [1-5], **1353**

Two-Legged, Four-Legged, No-Legged Rhymes [K-4], **1354**

Lillegard, Dee. *Do Not Feed the Table* [K-3], **1355**

Livingston, Myra Cohn. *Abraham Lincoln: A Man for All the People* [K-3], **1189**

A Song I Sang to You: A Selection of Poems [K-3], 1860

Lobel, Arnold. *The Book of Pigericks* [2-6], **1861**

Whiskers & Rhymes [Pre-3], 1862

Longfellow, Henry Wadsworth. *Paul Revere's Ride* [2-6], **1361**

McCord, David. *One at a Time* [K-4], 1864

McLoughland, Beverly. *A Hippo's a Heap: And Other Animal Poems* [K-3], **1364**

McNaughton, Colin. *Making Friends with Frankenstein: A Book of Monstrous Poems and Pictures* [2-6], **1366**

Margolis, Richard J. *Secrets of a Small Brother* [1-4], 1867

Merriam, Eve. *Blackberry Ink* [Pre-2], 1868
Chortles: New and Selected Wordplay Poems [3-6], 1869
Halloween ABC [3-6], **1372**
A Poem for a Pickle: Funnybone Verses [K-4], 1870
The Singing Green: New and Selected Poems for All Seasons [3-6], **1373**
You Be Good & I'll Be Night: Jump-on-the-Bed Poems [Pre-1], 1871

Milne, A. A. *Now We Are Six* [Pre-3], 1872

Mizamura, Kazue. *Flower Moon Snow: A Book of Haiku* [2-6], 1873

Moore, Lilian. *Adam Mouse's Book of Poems* [1-4], **1374**

Moss, Jeff. *The Butterfly Jar* [2-6], **1377**

Myers, Walter Dean. *Brown Angels: An Album of Pictures and Verse* [1-6], **1389**

Nash, Ogden. *Custard and Company* [3-6], 1893

Nims, Bonnie Larkin. *Just Beyond Reach and Other Riddle Poems* [K-3], **1390**

O'Neill, Mary L. *What Is That Sound!* [2-5], 1898

Peck, Robert Newton. *Bee Tree and Other Stuff* [4-6], 1899

Pomerantz, Charlotte. *If I Had a Paka* [K-4], 1902

Prelutsky, Jack. *The Baby Uggs Are Hatching* [K-4], 1904
The Dragons Are Singing Tonight [1-5], **1396**
The New Kid on the Block [K-5], 1911
Nightmares: Poems to Trouble Your Sleep [3-6], 1912
The Queen of Eene [2-4], 1914
Ride a Purple Pelican [Pre-2], 1918
The Sheriff of Rottenshot [2-4], 1920
The Snopp on the Sidewalk and Other Poems [K-3], 1921
Something Big Has Been Here [K-6], **1398**
Zoo Doings [K-4], 1924

Rylant, Cynthia. *Waiting to Waltz: A Childhood* [5-6], 1941

Sandburg, Carl. *Rainbows Are Made* [5-6], 1942

Schertle, Alice. *How Now, Brown Cow?* [1-6], **1406**

Silverstein, Shel. *Where the Sidewalk Ends* [Pre-6], 1952

Simmie, Lois. *Auntie's Knitting a Baby* [2-5], 1953

Singer, Marilyn. *It's Hard to Read a Map with a Beagle on Your Lap* [3-6], **1409**

Please Don't Squeeze Your Boa, Noah! [3-6], **1410**

Smith, William Jay. *Laughing Time: Nonsense Poems* [K-3], 1955

Springer, Nancy. *Music of Their Hooves: Poems About Horses* [3-6], **1411**

Starbird, Kaye. *The Covered Bridge House and Other Poems* [3-6], 1957

Viorst, Judith. *The Alphabet from Z to A: With Much Confusion on the Way* [3-6], **1416**
If I Were in Charge of the World and Other Worries: Poems for Children and Their Parents [2-5], 1969
Sad Underwear and Other Complications: More Poems for Children and Their Parents [2-6], **1417**

Watson, Clyde. *Father Fox's Pennyrhymes* [Pre-1], 1972

Weil, Zaro. *Mud, Moon and Me* [1-4], **1420**

Wong, Janet S. *Good Luck Gold and Other Poems* [4-6], **1424**

Worth, Valerie. *All the Small Poems and Fourteen More* [2-6], **1425**
Small Poems [2-6], 1979

Yolen, Jane. *Alphabestiary: Animal Poems from A to Z* [1-4], **1426**
Animal Fare [1-4], **1427**
Best Witches: Poems for Halloween [3-6], **1428**
Bird Watch: A Book of Poetry [3-6], **1429**
Raining Cats and Dogs [1-4], **1430**
The Three Bears Rhyme Book [Pre-2], 1981
What Rhymes with Moon? [1-5], **1431**

Zolotow, Charlotte. *Everything Glistens and Everything Sings* [K-4], 1984

POETS

Byars, Betsy. *Beans on the Roof* [2-3], 879

Clifford, Sandy. *The Roquefort Gang* [3-4], 1053

Corbett, Scott. *The Limerick Trick* [3-4], 1057

Janeczko, Paul B. *The Place My Words Are Looking For* [5-6], **1334**

Kalman, Maira. *Max Makes a Million* [2-3], **633**

Kamen, Gloria. *Edward Lear, King of Nonsense: A Biography* [4-6], **1169**

Lionni, Leo. *Frederick* [1-2], 727

Moore, Lilian. *I'll Meet You at the Cucumbers* [2-3], 967

Nikly, Michelle. *The Emperor's Plum Tree* [1-2], 759

Stanley, Diane, and Peter Vennema. *Bard of Avon: The Story of William Shakespeare* [4-6], **1241**

POINT OF VIEW

Duffey, Betsy. *A Boy in the Doghouse* [2-3], **605**

POINT OF VIEW (cont.)

Hall, Donald. *I Am the Dog, I Am the Cat* [1-2], **448**

Heckert, Connie. *Dribbles* [1-2], **452**

Moore, Lilian. *Adam Mouse's Book of Poems* [1-4], **1374**

Rosen, Michael. *Moving* [K-1], **352**

Schwartz, Amy. *A Teeny Tiny Baby* [K-1], **358**

Stevenson, James. *That's Exactly the Way It Wasn't* [1-2], **558**

POLICE

McCloskey, Robert. *Make Way for Ducklings* [1-2], 734

Sauer, Julie L. *Mike's House* [Pre-K], 252

POLISH AMERICANS

Leighton, Maxine Rhea. *An Ellis Island Christmas* [2-3], **638**

POLLUTION

Bunting, Eve. *Someday a Tree* [1-2], **416**

Cherry, Lynne. *A River Ran Wild: An Environmental History* [1-4], **1117**

Madden, Don. *The Wartville Wizard* [1-2], 738

Peet, Bill. *The Wump World* [2-3], 980

Rand, Gloria. *Prince William* [2-3], **668**

Seuss, Dr. *The Lorax* [2-3], 997

Shelby, Anne. *What to Do About Pollution* [Pre-2], **1236**

Temple, Lannis. *Dear World: How Children Around the World Feel About Our Environment* [2-6], **1247**

POND LIFE

Arnosky, Jim. *All Night Near the Water* [Pre-K], **67**

Fleming, Denise. *In the Small, Small Pond* [Pre-K], **104**

George, William T. *Box Turtle at Long Pond* [Pre-2], 2037

Pfeffer, Wendy. *From Tadpole to Frog* [Pre-1], **1219**

POP-UP BOOKS

SEE Toy and movable books

POPCORN

Asch, Frank. *Popcorn* [Pre-K], 15

dePaola, Tomie. *The Popcorn Book* [1-4], 2018

Thayer, Jane. *The Popcorn Dragon* [Pre-K], 273

POPULARITY

Hoffman, Mary. *Henry's Baby* [1-2], **454**

Honeycutt, Natalie. *Juliet Fisher and the Foolproof Plan* [2-3], **621**

Park, Barbara. *Rosie Swanson, Fourth-Grade Geek for President* [3-4], **737**

PORCUPINES

Carrick, Carol. *Ben and the Porcupine* [1-2], 640

Lester, Helen. *A Porcupine Named Fluffy* [K-1], 471

Lies, Brian. *Hamlet and the Enormous Chinese Dragon Kite* [1-2], **484**

Thomas, Patricia. *The One and Only Super-Duper Golly-Whopper Jim-Dandy Really-Handy Clock-Tock-Stopper* [1-2], **566**

POSTAL SERVICE

Skurzynski, Gloria. *Here Comes the Mail* [K-3], **1240**

POURQUOI TALES

Aardema, Verna. *Why Mosquitoes Buzz in People's Ears* [Pre-2], 1386

Bernhard, Emery. *How Snowshoe Hare Rescued the Sun: A Tale from the Arctic* [K-3], **866**

Bowden, Joan Chase. *Why the Tides Ebb and Flow* [1-6], 1406

Bruchac, Joseph. *The First Strawberries: A Cherokee Story* [K-3], **870**

The Great Ball Game: A Muskogee Story [K-3], **871**

Return of the Sun: Native American Tales from the Northeast Woodlands [3-6], **1060**

Climo, Shirley. *King of the Birds* [K-3], 1425

Crespo, George. *How the Sea Began: A Taino Myth* [1-6], **887**

Czernecki, Stefan, and Timothy Rhodes. *The Singing Snake* [K-2], **889**

French, Vivian. *Why the Sea Is Salt* [1-4], **906**

Garland, Sherry. *Why Ducks Sleep on One Leg* [1-4], **909**

Gates, Frieda. *Owl Eyes* [K-3], **911**

Gatti, Anne. *Tales from the African Plains* [3-6], **1066**

Gerson, Mary-Joan. *How Night Came from the Sea: A Story from Brazil* [K-4], **912**

Why the Sky Is Far Away: A Nigerian Folktale [K-4], **913**

Goble, Paul. *Crow Chief: A Plains Indian Story* [2-6], **915**

Iktomi and the Boulder: A Plains Indian Story [K-3], **1483**

Greene, Ellin. *The Legend of the Cranberry: A Paleo-Indian Tale* [1-4], **919**

Gregg, Andy. *Great Rabbit and the Long-Tailed Wildcat* [2-4], **921**

Hong, Lily Toy. *How the Ox Star Fell from Heaven* [1-4], **942**

Kennaway, Mwalimu. *Awful Aardvark* [Pre-K], **144**

Kipling, Rudyard. *The Elephant's Child* [2-3], 946
How the Camel Got His Hump [2-3], 947
How the Whale Got His Throat [1-2], 712
Just So Stories [3-4], **728**
Just So Stories [2-3], 948

Lester, Julius. *The Knee-High Man and Other Tales* [K-4], 1706

London, Jonathan, and Lanny Pinola. *Fire Race: A Karuk Coyote Tale About How Fire Came to the People* [K-3], **972**

Maddern, Eric. *The Fire Children: A West African Creation Tale* [K-3], **978**
Rainbow Bird: An Aboriginal Folktale from Northern Australia [K-3], **979**

Mollel, Tololwa M. *The Flying Tortoise: An Igbo Tale* [K-2], **987**

Mwenye Hadithi. *Greedy Zebra* [Pre-K], 125
Hungry Hyena [K-1], **331**

Ober, Hal. *How Music Came to the World* [1-4], **993**

Rodanas, Kristina. *Dragonfly's Tale* [K-3], **1005**

Rosen, Michael. *How the Giraffe Got Such a Long Neck . . . and Why Rhino Is So Grumpy* [Pre-2], **1007**

Ross, Gayle. *How Turtle's Back Was Cracked: A Traditional Cherokee Tale* [1-4], **1008**

Roth, Susan L. *Kanahena: A Cherokee Story* [Pre-2], 1587

Steptoe, John. *The Story of Jumping Mouse: A Native American Legend* [Pre-4], 1608

Temple, Frances. *Tiger Soup: An Anansi Story from Jamaica* [Pre-2], **1034**

Troughton, Joanna. *How the Birds Changed Their Feathers: A South American Indian Folk Tale* [Pre-3], 1616

Van de Wetering, Janwillem. *Hugh Pine* [3-4], 1127

Waldherr, Kris. *Persephone and the Pomegranate: A Myth from Greece* [2-6], **1041**

PRACTICAL JOKES

DeFelice, Cynthia. *Mule Eggs* [2-3], **604**

Naylor, Phyllis Reynolds. *The Boys Start the War* [3-4], **735**

Sheldon, Dyan. *My Brother Is a Visitor from Another Planet* [3-4], **746**

Wolkstein, Diane. *The Legend of Sleepy Hollow* [4-5], **795**

PRAYING MANTIS

SEE ALSO Insects

James, Betsy. *Mary Ann* [Pre-K], **133**

PREDICTABLE BOOKS

SEE Chantable refrain; Sequence stories

PREHISTORIC ANIMALS

SEE Animals, prehistoric; Dinosaurs

PREJUDICE

Bunting, Eve. *Smoky Night* [2-3], **593**

Estes, Eleanor. *The Hundred Dresses* [2-3], 914

Golenbock, Peter. *Teammates* [2-6], **1153**

Ikeda, Daisaku. *Over the Deep Blue Sea* [1-2], **460**

Livingston, Myra Cohn. *Keep on Singing: A Ballad of Marian Anderson* [1-4], **1190**
Let Freedom Ring: A Ballad of Martin Luther King, Jr. [1-6], **1191**

Marzollo, Jean. *Happy Birthday, Martin Luther King* [Pre-2], **1203**

Mazer, Anne. *The Oxboy* [5-6], **831**

Mitchell, Margaree King. *Uncle Jed's Barbershop* [2-3], **647**

Mochizuki, Ken. *Baseball Saved Us* [3-4], **733**

Nelson, Vaunda Micheaux. *Mayfield Crossing* [4-5], **784**

Ringgold, Faith. *Tar Beach* [2-3], **671**

Spinelli, Jerry. *Maniac Magee* [5-6], **847**

Taylor, Mildred D. *The Gold Cadillac* [4-5], 1248

Uchida, Yoshiko. *Journey Home* [5-6], 1370

Van Allsburg, Chris. *The Widow's Broom* [3-4], **752**

Yep, Laurence. *The Star Fisher* [5-6], **854**

PRESENTS

SEE Gifts

PRESIDENTS–U.S.

Brenner, Martha. *Abe Lincoln's Hat* [1-4], **1110**

Brown, Marc. *Arthur Meets the President* [1-2], **413**

Burns, Diane, and Clint Burns. *Hail to the Chief! Jokes about the Presidents* [2-6], **1276**

Cleveland, Will, and Mark Alvarez. *Yo, Millard Fillmore! (And All Those Other Presidents You Don't Know)* [4-6], **1119**

Freedman, Russell. *Lincoln: A Photobiography* [5-6], 2028

Giblin, James Cross. *George Washington: A Picture Book Biography* [1-4], **1150**

Griffin, Judith Berry. *Phoebe and the General* [2-5], 2042

Kunhardt, Edith. *Honest Abe* [K-3], **1179**

Osborne, Mary Pope. *George Washington: Leader of a New Nation* [5-6], **1214**

Rabin, Staton. *Casey Over There* [2-3], **666**

Seuling, Barbara. *The Last Cow on the White House Lawn & Other Little-Known Facts about the Presidency* [3-5], 2096

PRESIDENTS–U.S.–Poetry
Livingston, Myra Cohn. *Abraham Lincoln: A Man for All the People* [K-3], **1189**

PRIDE AND VANITY
Armstrong, Jennifer. *Chin Yu Min and the Ginger Cat* [2-3], **588**
Manson, Christopher. *The Marvelous Blue Mouse* [2-3], **641**
Pfister, Marcus. *The Rainbow Fish* [K-1], **337**
Polacco, Patricia. *Just Plain Fancy* [2-3], **662**

PRIDE AND VANITY–Folklore
Yolen, Jane. *Wings* [4-6], **1049**

PRINCES AND PRINCESSES
Andersen, Hans Christian. *The Princess and the Pea* [K-1], 322
Babbitt, Natalie. *Bub: Or, the Very Best Thing* [K-1], **224**
Duke, Kate. *Aunt Isabel Tells a Good One* [1-2], **436**
Elkin, Benjamin. *The Loudest Noise in the World* [K-1], 381
Fleischman, Sid. *The Whipping Boy* [4-5], 1172
Gwynne, Fred. *Pondlarker* [1-2], **447**
Houseman, Laurence. *Rocking-Horse Land* [1-2], 690
Jackson, Ellen. *Cinder Edna* [2-3], **626**
Kleven, Elisa. *The Paper Princess* [Pre-K], **146**
Laroche, Michel. *The Snow Rose* [3-4], 1086
Lewison, Wendy Cheyette. *The Princess and the Potty* [Pre], **29**
Napoli, Donna Jo. *The Prince of the Pond: Otherwise Known as De Fawg Pin* [4-5], **782**
Nesbit, E. *Melisande* [4-5], 1218
Pyle, Howard. *The Swan Maiden* [2-3], **665**
Scieszka, Jon. *The Frog Prince Continued* [2-3], **676**
Shields, Carol Diggory. *I Am Really a Princess* [1-2], **550**
Stanley, Diane. *Fortune* [3-4], 1117
Stanley, Fay. *The Last Princess: The Story of Princess Ka'iulani of Hawai'i* [4-6], **1243**
Thurber, James. *Many Moons* [2-3], 1015
Trivas, Irene. *Emma's Christmas* [2-3], **687**
Vande Velde, Vivian. *A Hidden Magic* [4-5], 1251
Vesey, A. *The Princess and the Frog* [1-2], 837
Wilsdorf, Anne. *Princess* [1-2], **577**
Wrede, Patricia. *Dealing with Dragons* [5-6], **853**
Yolen, Jane. *Sleeping Ugly* [2-3], 1033

PRINCES AND PRINCESSES–Folklore
Brown, Marcia. *Cinderella: Or, The Little Glass Slipper* [1-4], 1410

Carrick, Carol. *Aladdin and the Wonderful Lamp* [2-4], 1413
Demi. *The Firebird* [2-5], **893**
Early, Margaret. *Sleeping Beauty* [K-6], **899**
Gabler, Mirko. *Tall, Wide, and Sharp-Eye* [1-4], **907**
Gal, Laszlo. *Prince Ivan and the Firebird* [3-6], **908**
Galdone, Paul. *Cinderella* [1-4], 1458
Greene, Ellin. *Billy Beg and His Bull* [2-4], **918**
Grimm, Jacob. *Cinderella* [1-4], 1488
    The Donkey Prince [2-4], 1490
    The Frog Prince [K-3], 1493
    The Frog Prince: Or Iron Henry [1-4], **932**
    Iron John [2-6], **928**
    Rapunzel [2-4], **923**
    The Sleeping Beauty [2-5], 1505
    Snow White [2-5], 1506
    Thorn Rose: or, The Sleeping Beauty [1-4], 1508
    The Twelve Dancing Princesses [2-4], **930**
    The Twelve Dancing Princesses [1-4], 1509
    The Water of Life [3-6], 1511
Harris, Christie. *Mouse Woman and the Mischief-Makers* [4-6], 1691
Hastings, Selina. *The Firebird* [1-4], **938**
Huck, Charlotte. *Princess Furball* [1-4], 1531
Isele, Elizabeth. *The Frog Princess* [2-5], 1534
Karlin, Barbara. *Cinderella* [Pre-2], 1537
Kimmel, Eric A. *The Three Princes: A Tale from the Middle East* [1-4], **957**
    Three Sacks of Truth: A Story from France [2-5], **958**
Lang, Andrew. *Aladdin and the Wonderful Lamp* [2-5], 1544
Langton, Jane. *The Hedgehog Boy: A Latvian Folktale* [K-3], 1545
Lewis, J. Patrick. *The Frog Princess: A Russian Tale* [2-6], **969**
Martin, Claire. *Boots & the Glass Mountain* [2-6], **981**
Mayer, Marianna. *Aladdin and the Enchanted Lamp* [4-6], 1565
    The Spirit of the Blue Light [3-5], **986**
O'Brien, Anne Sibley. *The Princess and the Beggar: A Korean Folklore* [1-4], **994**
Pittman, Helena Clare. *A Grain of Rice* [2-4], 1580
Rayevsky, Inna. *The Talking Tree* [2-5], 1584
Reuter, Bjarne. *The Princess and the Sun, Moon and Stars* [1-4], 1585
San Souci, Robert D. *The Firebird* [3-5], **1012**
    The Tsar's Promise [3-6], **1018**
    The White Cat: An Old French Fairy Tale [2-5], **1019**
Scott, Sally. *The Magic Horse* [1-4], 1594

Sherman, Josepha. *Vassilisa the Wise: A Tale of Medieval Russia* [2-5], 1598

Steel, Flora Annie. *Tattercoats: An Old English Tale* [2-5], 1606

Thomson, Peggy. *The Brave Little Tailor* [1-4], **1035**

Wegman, William. *Cinderella* [1-4], **1042**

PRINCIPALS
SEE ALSO Schools; Teachers

Calmenson, Stephanie. *The Principal's New Clothes* [1-2], **420**

Kline, Suzy. *Horrible Harry and the Christmas Surprise* [1-2], **474**

Marshall, James. *The Cut-Ups* [1-2], 743

Schertle, Alice. *Jeremy Bean's St. Patrick's Day* [K-1], 544

Spinelli, Jerry. *Report to the Principal's Office* [4-5], 791

Udry, Janice May. *Angie* [2-3], 1017

PRINTING
Falwell, Cathryn. *The Letter Jesters* [2-4], **1140**

PROBLEM SOLVING
SEE ALSO Conflict resolution

Shannon, George. *More Stories to Solve: Fifteen Folktales from Around the World* [3-6], **1087**

PROCRASTINATION
Teague, Mark. *Frog Medicine* [2-3], **681**

PROJECT APOLLO
Fraser, Mary Ann. *One Giant Leap* [4-6], **1142**

PUBLIC SPEAKING
Brown, Marc. *Arthur Meets the President* [1-2], **413**

PUEBLO INDIANS–Folklore
Carey, Valerie Scho. *Quail Song: A Pueblo Indian Tale* [K-2], 876

Rodanas, Kristina. *Dragonfly's Tale* [K-3], **1005**

PUERTO RICO
Nodar, Carmen Santiago. *Abuelita's Paradise* [1-2], **519**

PUMPKINS
DeFelice, Cynthia. *Mule Eggs* [2-3], **604**

Hall, Zoe. *It's Pumpkin Time!* [Pre], **18**

McDonald, Megan. *The Great Pumpkin Switch* [1-2], **495**

Silverman, Erica. *Big Pumpkin* [K-1], **364**

Wolkstein, Diane. *The Legend of Sleepy Hollow* [4-5], **795**

PUNS
SEE Word games

PUPPETS
Izen, Marshall, and Jim West. *Why the Willow Weeps: A Story Told with Hands* [1-2], **461**

QUEENS
SEE Kings and rulers

QUESTIONS AND ANSWERS
Anholt, Catherine, and Laurence Anholt. *All About You* [Pre], **3**

Lasky, Kathryn. *The Librarian Who Measured the Earth* [3-6], **1180**

Miller, Margaret. *Can You Guess?* [Pre], **33**
Guess Who? [Pre-K], **165**
Where Does It Go? [Pre-K], **166**
Whose Shoe? [Pre-K], **168**

Torgersen, Don Arthur. *The Girl Who Tricked the Troll* [1-2], 832

Walton, Rick. *How Many, How Many, How Many* [Pre-K], **206**

Young, Ruth. *Who Says Moo?* [Pre], **61**

QUESTIONS AND ANSWERS–Poetry
Hopkins, Lee Bennett. *Questions* [1-3], **1324**

QUILTS
Flournoy, Valerie. *The Patchwork Quilt* [2-3], 925

Guback, Georgia. *Luka's Quilt* [K-1], **278**

Hopkinson, Deborah. *Sweet Clara and the Freedom Quilt* [2-3], **622**

Martin, Jacqueline Briggs. *Bizzy Bones and the Lost Quilt* [Pre-K], 206

RABBITS
Ada, Alma Flor. *Dear Peter Rabbit* [1-2], **395**

Anderson, Lonzo. *Two Hundred Rabbits* [1-2], 606

Bate, Lucy. *Little Rabbit's Loose Tooth* [K-1], 332

Brown, Margaret. *The Runaway Bunny* [Pre-K], 29

Cazet, Denys. *December 24th* [K-1], 359

Chadwick, Tim. *Cabbage Moon* [Pre-K], **81**

Christelow, Eileen. *Henry and the Dragon* [Pre-K], 49
Henry and the Red Stripes [K-1], 362

Cleveland, David. *The April Rabbits* [K-1], 366

Friedrich, Priscilla, and Otto Friedrich. *The Easter Bunny That Overslept* [K-1], 394

Gackenbach, Dick. *Hurray for Hattie Rabbit* [Pre-K], 99

Gregory, Valiska. *Babysitting for Benjamin* [K-1], **276**

Henkes, Kevin. *Bailey Goes Camping* [Pre-K], 131

Heyward, DuBose. *The Country Bunny and the Little Gold Shoes* [K-1], 423

RABBITS (cont.)

Howe, Deborah, and James Howe. *Bunnicula: A Rabbit-Tale of Mystery* [4-5], 1193

Howe, James. *Rabbit-Cadabra!* [1-2], **458**

Kraus, Robert. *Phil the Ventriloquist* [Pre-K], 176

Modesitt, Jeanne. *Vegetable Soup* [Pre-K], **170**

Potter, Beatrice. *The Tale of Peter Rabbit* [K-1], 528

Roberts, Bethany. *Waiting-for-Spring Stories* [K-1], 531

Shannon, George. *Dance Away* [Pre-K], 260

Steig, William. *Solomon the Rusty Nail* [2-3], 1008

Thomas, Patricia. *The One and Only Super-Duper Golly-Whopper Jim-Dandy Really-Handy Clock-Tock-Stopper* [1-2], **566**

Wells, Rosemary. *Max and Ruby's First Greek Myth: Pandora's Box* [1-2], **573**

Max's Chocolate Chicken [Pre-K], 286

Max's Christmas [Pre-K], 287

Voyage to the Bunny Planet books: First Tomato; The Island Light; Moss Pillows [K-1], **383**

Ziefert, Harriet. *Pete's Chicken* [K-1], **392**

Zolotow, Charlotte. *Mr. Rabbit and the Lovely Present* [Pre-K], 310

RABBITS–Folklore

Aardema, Verna. *Rabbit Makes a Monkey Out of Lion* [Pre-3], 1382

Aesop. *The Tortoise and the Hare: An Aesop Tale* [Pre-2], 1388

Gregg, Andy. *Great Rabbit and the Long-Tailed Wildcat* [2-4], **921**

Han, Suzanne Crowder. *The Rabbit's Escape* [1-5], **936**

The Rabbit's Judgment [1-5], **937**

Johnston, Tony. *The Tale of Rabbit and Coyote* [Pre-2], **947**

Kimmel, Eric A. *Three Sacks of Truth: A Story from France* [2-5], **958**

Lester, Julius. *Further Tales of Uncle Remus: The Misadventures of Brer Rabbit, Brer Fox, Brer Wolf, the Doodang, and Other Creatures* [2-5], **1075**

The Tales of Uncle Remus: The Adventures of Brer Rabbit [2-5], 1707

McDermott, Gerald. *Zomo the Rabbit: A Trickster Tale from West Africa* [Pre-1], **977**

Martin, Rafe. *Foolish Rabbit's Big Mistake* [Pre-2], 1564

Mayo, Gretchen Will. *Big Trouble for Tricky Rabbit!* [1-3], **1078**

Parks, Van Dyke, and Malcolm Jones. *Jump! The Adventures of Brer Rabbit* [2-5], 1714

Ross, Gayle. *How Rabbit Tricked Otter and Other Cherokee Trickster Stories* [1-4], **1084**

Tanaka, Béatrice. *The Chase: A Kutenai Indian Tale* [Pre-K], **1032**

Wildsmith, Brian. *The Hare and the Tortoise* [Pre-3], 1627

RACCOONS

North, Sterling. *Rascal: A Memoir of a Better Era* [4-6], 2079

Wells, Rosemary. *Timothy Goes to School* [K-1], 587

Whelan, Gloria. *A Week of Raccoons* [K-1], 589

RACE

Hamanaka, Sheila. *All the Colors of the Earth* [1-2], **449**

RACE–Folklore

Maddern, Eric. *The Fire Children: A West African Creation Tale* [K-3], **978**

RACE RELATIONS

Golenbock, Peter. *Teammates* [2-6], **1153**

Holland, Isabelle. *Behind the Lines* [5-6], **824**

Livingston, Myra Cohn. *Keep on Singing: A Ballad of Marian Anderson* [1-4], **1190**

Let Freedom Ring: A Ballad of Martin Luther King, Jr. [1-6], **1191**

Marzollo, Jean. *Happy Birthday, Martin Luther King* [Pre-2], **1203**

Nelson, Vaunda Micheaux. *Mayfield Crossing* [4-5], **784**

Polacco, Patricia. *Mrs. Katz and Tush* [2-3], **663**

Spinelli, Jerry. *Maniac Magee* [5-6], **847**

Yep, Laurence. *The Star Fisher* [5-6], **854**

RACING

Lewis, J. Patrick. *One Dog Day* [4-5], **774**

Seibert, Patricia. *Mush! Across Alaska in the World's Longest Sled-Dog Race* [1-4], **1235**

RAILROADS

SEE Trains

RAIN AND RAINFALL

SEE ALSO Clouds; Storms; Weather; Winter

Coombs, Patricia. *Dorrie and the Weather Box* [1-2], 653

Cooney, Nancy Evans. *The Umbrella Day* [Pre-K], 57

Ginsburg, Mirra. *Mushroom in the Rain* [Pre-K], 115

Harper, Jo. *Jalapeño Hal* [2-3], **615**

Martin, Bill, Jr., and John Archambault. *Listen to the Rain* [1-2], 746

Polacco, Patricia. *Thunder Cake* [K-1], 525

Stolz, Mary. *Storm in the Night* [1-2], 828

Wisniewski, David. *Rain Player* [2-3], **694**

Wood, Audrey. *The Napping House* [Pre-K], 301

RAIN AND RAINFALL–Folklore

Alexander, Ellen. *Llama and the Great Flood: A Folktale from Peru* [2-4], 1389

Bernhard, Emery. *The Tree That Rains: The Flood Myth of the Huichol Indians of Mexico* [1-4], **867**

Compton, Patricia A. *The Terrible Eek* [K-3], **885**

Yep, Laurence. *The Junior Thunder Lord* [1-4], **1046**

RAIN AND RAINFALL–Poetry

Prelutsky, Jack. *Rainy Rainy Saturday* [K-2], 1915

Radley, Gail. *Rainy Day Rhymes* [Pre-2], **1399**

RAIN FORESTS

SEE ALSO Jungles

Bodsworth, Nan. *A Nice Walk in the Jungle* [K-1], **233**

Cowcher, Helen. *Rain Forest* [K-1], **256**

Gilliland, Judith Heide. *River* [K-3], **1152**

Yolen, Jane. *Welcome to the Green House* [K-3], **1256**

RAINBOWS–Folklore

Shepard, Aaron. *The Legend of Slappy Hooper: An American Tall Tale* [1-3], **1023**

RANCH LIFE

Paulsen, Gary. *The Haymeadow* [5-6], **835**

RARE ANIMALS

SEE Endangered species

RATS

Jacques, Brian. *Redwall* [5-6], 1315

Kasza, Keiko. *The Rat and the Tiger* [Pre-K], 141

Kennedy, Richard. *Inside My Feet* [5-6], 1318

McNaughton, Colin. *Anton B. Stanton and the Pirats* [1-2], 736

O'Brien, Robert C. *Mrs. Frisby and the Rats of NIMH* [5-6], 1337

Skurzynski, Gloria. *What Happened to Hamelin* [5-6], 1358

RATS–Folklore

Cook, Joel. *The Rat's Daughter* [K-2], **886**

Corrin, Sara, and Stephen Corrin. *The Pied Piper of Hamelin* [2-6], 1431

Lemieux, Michèle. *Pied Piper of Hamelin* [2-5], **966**

Levine, Arthur A. *The Boy Who Drew Cats: A Japanese Folktale* [2-6], **968**

Wildsmith, Brian. *The Lion and the Rat* [Pre-3], 1628

RAVENS–Folklore

SEE ALSO Birds; Trickster tales

Dixon, Ann. *How Raven Brought Light to People* [K-4], **897**

McDermott, Gerald. *Raven: A Trickster Tale from the Pacific Northwest* [K-4], **976**

Shetterly, Susan Hand. *Raven's Light: A Myth from the People of the Northwest Coast* [2-5], **1024**

READER'S THEATER

Aliki. *Communication* [1-3], **1099**

Giff, Patricia Reilly. *Show Time at the Polk Street School: Plays You Can Do Yourself or in the Classroom* [1-3], **1151**

Kline, Suzy. *The Herbie Jones Reader's Theater: Funny Scenes to Read Aloud* [2-4], **1170**

Shepard, Aaron. *Stories on Stage: Scripts for Reader's Theater* [2-6], **1237**

Stevenson, James. *The Mud Flat Olympics* [1-2], **557**

Temple, Frances. *Tiger Soup: An Anansi Story from Jamaica* [Pre-2], **1034**

READING

SEE Books and reading

REBUSES

SEE Riddles

RECYCLING

Brown, Laurene Krasny, and Marc Brown. *Dinosaurs to the Rescue! A Guide to Protecting Our Planet* [Pre-3], **1112**

Earth Works Group. *50 Simple Things Kids Can Do to Save the Earth* [3-6], **1135**

Mills, Claudia. *Dinah for President* [4-5], **778**

REINDEER

Brett, Jan. *The Wild Christmas Reindeer* [K-1], **237**

Greenburg, Dan. *Young Santa* [4-5], **770**

Price, Moe. *The Reindeer Christmas* [K-1], **341**

REMARRIAGE

Lindbergh, Anne. *Travel Far, Pay No Fare* [5-6], **826**

REPTILES

SEE ALSO Chameleons; Frogs; Lizards; Salamanders; Snakes; Toads; Turtles

Carle, Eric. *The Mixed-Up Chameleon* [Pre-K], 38

Himmelman, John. *Talester the Lizard* [Pre-K], 134

Leedy, Loreen. *Tracks in the Sand* [K-2], **1183**

MacGregor, Ellen. *Theodore Turtle* [K-1], 491

Martin, James. *Chameleons: Dragons in the Trees* [2-5], **1201**

REPTILES (cont.)

Massie, Diane Redfield. *Chameleon Was a Spy* [2-3], 960

Mayer, Mercer. *There's an Alligator under My Bed* [Pre-K], 208

Nixon, Joan Lowery. *The Alligator under the Bed* [Pre-K], 218

Pinkwater, Daniel. *Lizard Music* [4-5], 1225

Ryder, Joanne. *Lizard in the Sun* [Pre-3], 2090

Shannon, George. *Lizard's Song* [Pre-K], 261

Waber, Bernard. *Lyle, Lyle Crocodile* [K-1], 578

Wolkoff, Judie. *Wally* [3-4], 1135

REPTILES–Riddles

Burns, Diane L. *Snakes Alive! Jokes about Snakes* [1-4], 1763

RESPONSIBILITY

Arnold, Tedd. *The Signmaker's Assistant* [1-2], **400**

Bauer, Marion Dane. *On My Honor* [5-6], 1273
A Question of Trust [5-6], **805**

Bunting, Eve. *A Day's Work* [2-3], **592**
Summer Wheels [2-3], **594**

Delton, Judy. *Angel in Charge* [3-4], 1061

Gardiner, John Reynolds. *Stone Fox* [3-4], 1067

Herzig, Alison Cragin. *The Big Deal* [2-3], **618**

Keller, Holly. *Island Baby* [K-1], **296**

Sachar, Louis. *Marvin Redpost: Alone in His Teacher's House* [2-3], **672**

Seuss, Dr. *Bartholomew and the Oobleck* [2-3], 994
Horton Hatches the Egg [1-2], 801

Ward, Lynd. *The Biggest Bear* [1-2], 844

RESTAURANTS

Axelrod, Amy. *Pigs Will Be Pigs* [1-2], **403**

Bang, Molly. *The Paper Crane* [1-2], 610

Calmenson, Stephanie. *Dinner at the Panda Palace* [Pre-K], **73**

Kovalski, Maryann. *Pizza for Breakfast* [1-2], **479**

Loomis, Christine. *In the Diner* [Pre-K], **154**

Shaw, Nancy. *Sheep Out to Eat* [K-1], **361**

Stadler, John. *Animal Cafe* [1-2], 819

Sun, Chying Feng. *Mama Bear* [1-2], **562**

REVERE, PAUL

Longfellow, Henry Wadsworth. *Paul Revere's Ride* [2-6], **1361**

REVOLUTIONARY WAR

SEE U.S.–History–Revolution

RHINOCEROS

Cowcher, Helen. *Whistling Thorn* [K-2], **1126**

Lester, Helen. *A Porcupine Named Fluffy* [K-1], 471

Lexai, Joan. *That's Good, That's Bad* [Pre-K], 187

Silverstein, Shel. *Who Wants a Cheap Rhinoceros?* [1-2], 812

RHINOCEROS–Folklore

Rosen, Michael. *How the Giraffe Got Such a Long Neck . . . and Why Rhino Is So Grumpy* [Pre-2], **1007**

RIDDLES

SEE ALSO Jokes; Knock-knock jokes

Adler, David A. *The Carsick Zebra and Other Animal Riddles* [K-3], 1739
Remember Betsy Floss: And Other Colonial American Riddles [2-6], 1740
Wild Pill Hickok and Other Old West Riddles [2-5], 1741

Barber, Antonia. *Catkin* [2-3], **590**

Bernstein, Joanne E., and Paul Cohen. *Creepy Crawly Critter Riddles* [2-5], 1748
What Was the Wicked Witch's Real Name? And Other Character Riddles [2-6], 1749

Brown, Marc. *Spooky Riddles* [K-3], 1761

Burns, Diane, and Clint Burns. *Hail to the Chief! Jokes about the Presidents* [2-6], **1276**

Burns, Diane L. *Snakes Alive! Jokes about Snakes* [1-4], 1763

Calmenson, Stephanie. *It Begins with an A* [Pre-K], **74**
What Am I? Very First Riddles [Pre-1], **1277**

Cerf, Bennett. *Bennett Cerf's Book of Riddles* [Pre-2], 1766

Churchill, E. Richard. *The Six-Million Dollar Cucumber: Riddles and Fun for Children* [Pre-6], 1768

Cole, Joanna, and Stephanie Calmenson. *Why Did the Chicken Cross the Road? And Other Riddles Old and New* [2-5], **1281**

Coletta, Irene, and Hallie Coletta. *From A to Z: The Collected Letters of Irene and Hallie Coletta* [2-3], 897

Cricket Magazine, editors of. *Cricket's Jokes, Riddles & Other Stuff* [K-5], 1785

De Regniers, Beatrice Schenk. *It Does Not Say Meow and Other Animal Riddle Rhymes* [Pre-1], 1791

Doty, Roy. *Tinkerbell Is a Ding-a-Ling* [4-6], 1794

Emrich, Duncan. *The Hodgepodge Book* [2-6], 1796

Gerberg, Mort. *Geographunny: A Book of Global Riddles* [3-6], **1295**

Gerler, William R. *A Pack of Riddles* [Pre-2], 1803

Gordon, Jeffie Ross. *Hide and Shriek: Riddles About Ghosts & Goblins* [2-5], **1300**

Gounaud, Karen Jo. *A Very Mice Joke Book* [1-5], 1806

Hall, Katy, and Lisa Eisenberg. *Batty Riddles* [1-4], **1304**

Buggy Riddles [Pre-2], 1809

Snakey Riddles [1-4], **1305**

Spacey Riddles [2-5], **1306**

Hartman, Victoria. *The Silliest Joke Book Ever* [3-5], **1308**

Hoff, Syd. *Syd Hoff's Animal Jokes* [K-2], 1815

Jones, Evelyn. *World's Wackiest Riddle Book* [2-6], 1833

Keller, Charles. *Alexander the Grape: Fruit and Vegetable Jokes* [2-6], 1834

Ballpoint Bananas and Other Jokes for Kids [2-6], 1835

Belly Laughs! Food Jokes & Riddles [2-6], **1337**

Count Draculations! Monsters Riddles [2-6], 1836

It's Raining Cats and Dogs: Cat and Dog Jokes [2-5], 1837

King Henry the Ape: Animal Jokes [2-6], **1338**

Llama Beans [1-4], 1838

The Nutty Joke Book [2-5], 1840

Remember the à la Mode! Riddles and Puns [2-6], 1841

Swine Lake: Music & Dance Riddles [3-6], 1843

Take Me to Your Liter: Science and Math Jokes [3-6], **1339**

Keller, Charles, and Richard Baker. *The Star-Spangled Banana and Other Revolutionary Riddles* [2-6], 1844

Koontz, Robin Michal. *I See Something You Don't See: A Riddle-Me Picture Book* [K-1], **301**

Levine, Caroline. *Riddles to Tell Your Cat* [3-6], **1351**

McMillan, Bruce, and Brett McMillan. *Puniddles* [2-3], 959

Maestro, Giulio. *More Halloween Howls: Riddles That Come Back to Haunt You* [2-5], **1367**

Razzle-Dazzle Riddles [Pre-3], 1866

Maestro, Marco, and Giulio Maestro. *Riddle City, USA! A Book of Geography Riddles* [3-6], **1368**

Mathews, Judith, and Fay Robinson. *Knock-Knock Knees and Funny Bones: Riddles for Every Body* [3-6], **1370**

Most, Bernard. *Can You Find It?* [K-1], **329**

Zoodles [1-2], **514**

Phillips, Louis. *Invisible Oink: Pig Jokes* [3-6], **1394**

The Upside Down Riddle Book [K-2], 1901

Rayner, Shoo. *My First Picture Joke Book* [K-2], **1401**

Rosenbloom, Joseph. *The Funniest Dinosaur Book Ever* [Pre-3], 1928

The Funniest Riddle Book Ever! [Pre-3], 1930

Giggles, Gags & Groaners [3-6], 1932

Monster Madness: Riddles, Jokes, Fun [3-6], 1935

Spooky Riddles and Jokes [2-6], 1937

The World's Best Sports Riddles and Jokes [2-6], 1939

Schwartz, Alvin. *The Cat's Elbow and Other Secret Languages* [2-6], 1945

Ten Copycats in a Boat and Other Riddles [Pre-2], 1948

Tomfoolery: Trickery and Foolery with Words [1-6], 1949

Swann, Brian. *A Basket Full of White Eggs* [K-3], 1960

Terban, Marvin. *The Dove Dove: Funny Homograph Riddles* [3-6], 1962

Funny You Should Ask: How to Make Up Jokes and Riddles with Wordplay [3-6], **1414**

Too Hot to Hoot: Funny Palindrome Riddles [2-6], 1965

Thaler, Mike. *The Chocolate Marshmelephant Sundae* [3-6], 1966

Walton, Rick, and Ann Walton. *Can You Match This? Jokes About Unlikely Pairs* [3-6], **1418**

What's Your Name, Again? More Jokes about Names [1-6], 1971

Withers, Carl. *A Rocket in My Pocket: The Rhymes and Chants of Young Americans* [K-4], 1977

Withers, Carl, and Sula Benet. *The American Riddle Book* [2-6], 1978

Young, Ed. *High on a Hill: A Book of Chinese Riddles* [2-4], 1982

Young, Frederica. *Super-Duper Jokes* [3-6], **1432**

Zimmerman, Andrea Griffing. *The Riddle Zoo* [K-2], 1983

RIDDLES–Folklore

Shannon, George. *More Stories to Solve: Fifteen Folktales from Around the World* [3-6], **1087**

Stories to Solve: Folktales from Aound the World [2-5], 1729

Vernon, Adele. *The Riddle* [3-6], 1622

RIDDLES–Poetry

Nims, Bonnie Larkin. *Just Beyond Reach and Other Riddle Poems* [K-3], **1390**

RIOTS

Bunting, Eve. *Smoky Night* [2-3], **593**

RIVERS

Bauer, Marion Dane. *On My Honor* [5-6], 1273

RIVERS (cont.)

Cherry, Lynne. *A River Ran Wild: An Environmental History* [1-4], **1117**

DeFelice, Cynthia. *Lostman's River* [5-6], **811**

Dorros, Arthur. *Follow the Water from Brook to Ocean* [K-3], **1133**

Flack, Marjorie. *The Story about Ping* [K-1], 387

Gilliland, Judith Heide. *River* [K-3], **1152**

Grahame, Kenneth. *The Wind in the Willows* [5-6], 1305

Kipling, Rudyard. *The Beginning of the Armadillos* [2-3], 945

Stevenson, James. *Monty* [K-1], 561

RIVERS–Folklore

Kellogg, Steven. *Mike Fink* [1-4], **948**

ROBBERS AND OUTLAWS

Brown, Jeff. *Flat Stanley* [1-2], 624

Christelow, Eileen. *Gertrude, the Bulldog Detective* [K-1], **252**

Coren, Alan. *Arthur the Kid* [2-3], 902

Cox, David. *Bossyboots* [1-2], 655

Dyke, John. *Pigwig* [K-1], 379

Fleischman, Paul. *The Half-a-Moon Inn* [5-6], 1299

Fleischman, Sid. *The Ghost on Saturday Night* [2-3], 918

The Whipping Boy [4-5], 1172

Flora, James. *Little Hatchy Hen* [2-3], 923

Gerrard, Roy. *Rosie and the Rustlers* [2-3], **610**

Greer, Gery, and Bob Ruddick. *Max and Me and the Wild West* [5-6], 1307

Kalan, Robert. *Stop, Thief!* [Pre-K], **138**

Kellogg, Steven. *Pinkerton, Behave* [1-2], 706

Kennedy, Richard. *The Contests at Cowlick* [1-2], 708

Kimmel, Eric A. *Four Dollars and Fifty Cents* [3-4], **721**

Kraus, Robert. *Phil the Ventriloquist* [Pre-K], 176

Lauber, Patricia. *Clarence and the Burglar* [1-2], 720

Lobel, Arnold. *How the Rooster Saved the Day* [Pre-K], 192

Macaulay, David. *Black and White* [1-2], **490**

Meddaugh, Susan. *Martha Speaks* [1-2], **506**

Mooser, Stephen. *Orphan Jeb at the Massacre* [4-5], 1215

Myller, Rolf. *A Very Noisy Day* [1-2], 755

Ross, Pat. *Gloria and the Super Soaper* [2-3], 987

Rounds, Glen. *Mr. Yowder and the Train Robbers* [4-5], 1232

Steig, William. *Caleb and Kate* [3-4], 1118

Zeke Pippin [2-3], **678**

Ungerer, Tomi. *Crictor* [K-1], 573

Yorinks, Arthur. *Whitefish Will Rides Again!* [1-2], **581**

Zimelman, Nathan. *How the Second Grade Got $8,205.50 to Visit the Statue of Liberty* [1-2], **583**

ROBBERS AND OUTLAWS–Folklore

Compton, Patricia A. *The Terrible Eek* [K-3], **885**

Grimm, Jacob. *The Bremen Town Musicians* [Pre-3], 1487

The Bremen Town Musicians [K-2], **925**, **931**

McVitty, Walter. *Ali Baba and the Forty Thieves* [3-6], 1557

ROBOTS

Mahy, Margaret. *Raging Robots and Unruly Uncles* [4-5], **777**

ROCKS

Baylor, Byrd. *Everybody Needs a Rock* [2-3], 873

Cole, Joanna. *The Magic School Bus Inside the Earth* [2-4], 2009

Fritz, Jean. *Who's That Stepping on Plymouth Rock?* [3-6], 2035

Hiscock, Bruce. *The Big Rock* [1-4], 2050

Lionni, Leo. *Alexander and the Wind-Up Mouse* [1-2], 726

Steig, William. *Sylvester and the Magic Pebble* [1-2], 821

ROCKS–Folklore

Goble, Paul. *Iktomi and the Boulder: A Plains Indian Story* [K-3], 1483

Stevens, Janet. *Coyote Steals the Blanket: A Ute Tale* [Pre-3], **1029**

ROLLER COASTERS

Duffey, Betsy. *Coaster* [4-5], **769**

ROMAN MYTHOLOGY

SEE Mythology

ROOSTERS

SEE ALSO Birds; Chickens; Ducks; Geese; Owls; Parrots

Kent, Jack. *Little Peep* [K-1], 455

Lobel, Arnold. *How the Rooster Saved the Day* [Pre-K], 192

ROOSTERS–Folklore

Ada, Alma Flor. *The Rooster Who Went to His Uncle's Wedding: A Latin American Folktale* [Pre-1], **858**

Ginsburg, Mirra. *The Magic Stove* [K-3], 1479

Gonzalez, Lucie M. *The Bossy Gallito: A Traditional Cuban Folktale* [K-2], **917**

RUNAWAYS

Annett, Cora. *How the Witch Got Alf* [2-3], 868

Avi. *Night Journeys* [5-6], 1268

Brown, Margaret. *The Runaway Bunny* [Pre-K], 29

Carlson, Natalie Savage. *Runaway Marie Louise* [Pre-K], 43

Cole, Brock. *No More Baths* [Pre-K], 52

Fleischman, Sid. *Jingo Django* [5-6], 1302

Fox, Paula. *Monkey Island* [5-6], **817**

Galbraith, Richard. *Reuben Runs Away* [Pre-K], 106

Garrett, Helen. *Angelo the Naughty One* [1-2], 676

Johnson, Jane. *Today I Thought I'd Run Away* [Pre-K], 154

Kent, Jack. *Joey Runs Away* [Pre-K], 169

Konigsburg, E. L. *From the Mixed-Up Files of Mrs. Basil E. Frankweiler* [4-5], 1201

Lasker, Joe. *The Do-Something Day* [K-1], 464

Mahy, Margaret. *Raging Robots and Unruly Uncles* [4-5], **777**

Radley, Gail. *The Golden Days* [5-6], **838**

Smith, Robert Kimmell. *Chocolate Fever* [2-3], 1003

Spinelli, Jerry. *Maniac Magee* [5-6], **847**

Warner, Gertrude Chandler. *The Boxcar Children* [2-3], 1025

RUSSIA

Kossman, Nina. *Behind the Border* [4-6], **1173**

Trivas, Irene. *Annie . . . Anya: A Month in Moscow* [K-1], **377**

RUSSIAN AMERICANS

Cohen, Barbara. *Make a Wish, Molly* [2-3], **598**

Kalman, Esther. *Tchaikovsky Discovers America* [2-3], **632**

RUSSIAN LANGUAGE

Trivas, Irene. *Annie . . . Anya: A Month in Moscow* [K-1], **377**

SAFETY

Brown, Marc, and Stephen Krensky. *Dinosaurs, Beware! A Safety Guide* [Pre-3], 2002

SAILING

Calhoun, Mary. *Henry the Sailor Cat* [1-2], **418**

Paxton, Tom. *Jennifer's Rabbit* [Pre-K], 224

Quinn-Harken, Janet. *Peter Penny's Dance* [1-2], 779

Van Allsburg, Chris. *The Wreck of the Zephyr* [3-4], 1126

SAILING–Poetry

Carryl, Charles E. *The Walloping Window-Blind* [2-3], **596**

ST. PATRICK'S DAY

SEE Holidays

SALAMANDERS

SEE ALSO Lizards; Reptiles

Walsh, Ellen Stoll. *Pip's Magic* [Pre-K], **205**

SALT–Folklore

French, Vivian. *Why the Sea Is Salt* [1-4], **906**

Langton, Jane. *Salt: A Russian Folktale* [2-5], **963**

SANTA CLAUS

Balian, Lorna. *Bah! Humbug?* [K-1], 328

Barracca, Debra, and Sal Barracca. *A Taxi Dog Christmas* [K-1], **229**

Brett, Jan. *The Wild Christmas Reindeer* [K-1], **237**

Burningham, John. *Harvey Slumfenburger's Christmas Present* [K-1], **244**

Flora, James. *Grandpa's Witched-Up Christmas* [2-3], 920

Friedrich, Priscilla, and Otto Friedrich. *The Easter Bunny That Overslept* [K-1], 394

Greenburg, Dan. *Young Santa* [4-5], **770**

Haywood, Carolyn. *A Christmas Fantasy* [K-1], 416

Howe, James. *The Fright before Christmas* [2-3], 935

Joyce, William. *Santa Calls* [2-3], **631**

McPhail, David. *Santa's Book of Names* [K-1], **319**

Moore, Clement C. *The Night before Christmas* [1-2], 753

Nixon, Joan Lowery. *That's the Spirit, Claude* [2-3], **650**

Paulsen, Gary. *A Christmas Sonata* [5-6], **833**

Price, Moe. *The Reindeer Christmas* [K-1], **341**

Prøysen, Alf. *Christmas Eve at Santa's* [K-1], **343**

Ross, Pat. *M & M and the Santa Secrets* [1-2], 785

Van Allsburg, Chris. *The Polar Express* [1-2], 835

Van Leeuwen, Jean. *The Great Christmas Kidnapping Caper* [3-4], 1128

Wells, Rosemary. *Max's Christmas* [Pre-K], 287

SANTA FE TRAIL

SEE ALSO Frontier and pioneer life; Oregon Trail

Russell, Marion. *Along the Santa Fe Trail: Marion Russell's Own Story* [2-5], **1230**

SCHOOLS

SEE ALSO Principals; Teachers

Adler, David A. *Eaton Stanley & the Mind Control Experiment* [4-5], 1137

Alexander, Martha. *Move Over, Twerp* [K-1], 315

Allard, Harry. *Miss Nelson Is Missing* [1-2], 601

Baer, Edith. *This Is the Way We Go to School: A Book About Children Around the World* [K-1], **226**

Bemelmans, Ludwig. *Madeline's Rescue* [K-1], 335

SCHOOLS (cont.)

Bennett, Anna Elizabeth. *Little Witch* [2-3], 874

Birdseye, Tom. *Just Call Me Stupid* [4-5], **759**

Blume, Judy. *Freckle Juice* [1-2], 618

Bourgeois, Paulette. *Too Many Chickens* [K-1], **235**

Boyd, Selma, and Pauline Boyd. *I Met a Polar Bear* [K-1], 340

Brandenberg, Franz. *No School Today* [K-1], 342

Brown, Marc. *Arthur Meets the President* [1-2], **413**

   Arthur's Teacher Trouble [1-2], 628

   Arthur's Tooth [1-2], 629

Bunting, Eve. *Our Teacher's Having a Baby* [K-1], **243**

Byars, Betsy. *The 18th Emergency* [4-5], 1155

Carlson, Nancy L. *Arnie and the New Kid* [1-2], **421**

Catling, Patrick Skene. *The Chocolate Touch* [2-3], 884

Caudill, Rebecca. *Did You Carry the Flag Today, Charlie?* [1-2], 643

Chapman, Carol. *Herbie's Troubles* [K-1], 361

Choi, Sook Nyul. *Halmoni and the Picnic* [1-2], **424**

Cleary, Beverly. *Henry Huggins* [2-3], 888

   Ralph S. Mouse [3-4], 1051

   Ramona Quimby, Age 8 [2-3], 889

   Ramona the Pest [2-3], 890

   Strider [5-6], **806**

Clifford, Eth. *Harvey's Horrible Snake Disaster* [3-4], 1052

Coerr, Eleanor. *Mieko and the Fifth Treasure* [3-4], **707**

Cohen, Barbara. *Molly's Pilgrim* [2-3], 893

Cohen, Miriam. *Jim Meets the Thing* [K-1], 367

   No Good in Art [K-1], 370

   Starring First Grade [K-1], 371

Cole, Joanna. *The Magic School Bus at the Waterworks* [2-4], 2008

   The Magic School Bus Inside the Human Body [2-4], 2010

Cone, Molly. *Come Back, Salmon: How a Group of Dedicated Kids Adopted Pigeon Creek and Brought It Back to Life* [4-6], **1125**

Conford, Ellen. *Lenny Kandell, Smart Aleck* [5-6], 1290

   Me and the Terrible Two [4-5], 1161

   Revenge of the Incredible Dr. Rancid and His Youthful Assistant, Jeffrey [4-5], 1162

   What's Cooking, Jenny Archer? [2-3], **601**

Cooney, Nancy Evans. *Chatterbox Jamie* [Pre-K], **87**

Coville, Bruce. *The Monster's Ring* [4-5], 1165

Crew, Linda. *Nekomah Creek* [3-4], **709**

Dahl, Roald. *Matilda* [5-6], 1292

Danziger, Paula. *Amber Brown Is Not a Crayon* [2-3], **603**

Davis, Gibbs. *Katy's First Haircut* [Pre-K], 63

DeJong, Meindert. *The Wheel on the School* [4-5], 1168

Doherty, Berlie. *Snowy* [K-1], **263**

Duffey, Betsy. *The Gadget War* [2-3], **606**

   The Math Whiz [2-3], **607**

Estes, Eleanor. *The Hundred Dresses* [2-3], 914

Fenner, Carol. *Randall's Wall* [5-6], **815**

Fitzhugh, Louise. *Harriet the Spy* [5-6], 1298

Flora, James. *Leopold the See-Through Crumbpicker* [1-2], 669

Gackenbach, Dick. *Tiny for a Day* [K-1], **273**

Gardiner, John Reynolds. *Top Secret* [5-6], 1303

Getz, David. *Almost Famous* [5-6], **818**

   Thin Air [5-6], **819**

Giff, Patricia Reilly. *Happy Birthday, Ronald Morgan!* [K-1], 406

   Show Time at the Polk Street School: Plays You Can Do Yourself or in the Classroom [1-3], **1151**

   Today Was a Terrible Day [1-2], 678

Gormley, Beatrice. *Fifth-Grade Magic* [4-5], 1181

Greenwald, Sheila. *Rosy Cole Discovers America!* [3-4], **711**

Haas, Dorothy F. *Tink in a Tangle* [2-3], 929

Hale, Sarah Josepha Buell. *Mary Had a Little Lamb* [Pre-K], **116**, **117**

Harding, William Harry. *Alvin's Famous No-Horse* [2-3], **613**

Harris, Dorothy Joan. *The School Mouse* [K-1], 415

Hayes, William. *Project: Genius* [5-6], 1308

Henkes, Kevin. *Chrysanthemum* [K-1], **282**

Hicks, Clifford B. *Peter Potts* [4-5], 1188

Hines, Anna Grossnickle. *What Joe Saw* [Pre-K], **123**

Hinton, S. E. *Big David, Little David* [K-1], **285**

Hoffman, Mary. *Amazing Grace* [K-1], **287**

Honeycutt, Natalie. *The All New Jonah Twist* [2-3], **934**

   Juliet Fisher and the Foolproof Plan [2-3], **621**

Howe, James. *The Day the Teacher Went Bananas* [Pre-K], 142

   Pinky and Rex and the Spelling Bee [1-2], **457**

Howlett, Bud. *I'm New Here* [2-5], **1166**

Hughes, Dean. *Nutty Knows All* [5-6], 1312

Hurwitz, Johanna. *Class Clown* [2-3], 936

   Class President [3-4], **715**

   Much Ado about Aldo [2-3], 937

Russell Sprouts [1-2], 695

School Spirit [3-4], **716**

Hutchins, Pat. *Three-Star Billy* [Pre-K], **130**

Johnson, Dolores. *What Will Mommy Do When I'm at School?* [Pre-K], **135**

Johnston, Johanna. *Speak Up, Edie* [K-1], 440

Kline, Suzy. *The Herbie Jones Reader's Theater: Funny Scenes to Read Aloud* [2-4], **1170**

Horrible Harry and the Christmas Surprise [1-2], **474**

Mary Marony and the Snake [1-2], **475**

Song Lee in Room 2B [1-2], **476**

What's the Matter with Herbie Jones? [2-3], 949

Korman, Gordon. *This Can't Be Happening at Macdonald Hall* [5-6], 1321

Leverich, Kathleen. *Best Enemies Again* [2-3], **639**

Levy, Elizabeth. *Keep Ms. Sugarman in the Fourth Grade* [3-4], **731**

Little, Jean. *From Anna* [4-5], **775**

Luttrell, Ida. *One Day at School* [1-2], 732

Lystad, Mary. *Jennifer Takes Over P.S. 94* [1-2], 733

McGovern, Ann. *Drop Everything, It's D.E.A.R. Time!* [1-2], **497**

McMillan, Bruce. *Mouse Views: What the Class Pet Saw* [K-1], **315**

McMullin, Kate. *The Great Ideas of Lila Fenwick* [4-5], 1209

Marshall, James. *The Cut-Ups* [1-2], 743

Martin, Ann. *Rachel Parker, Kindergarten Show-Off* [K-1], **321**

Maurer, Donna. *Annie, Bea, and Chi Chi Dolores: A School Day Alphabet* [Pre-K], **163**

Mills, Claudia. *After Fifth Grade, The World!* [4-5], 1214

Dinah for President [4-5], **778**

Mills, Lauren. *The Rag Coat* [2-3], **646**

Moore, Lilian. *The Snake That Went to School* [2-3], 968

Moss, Marissa. *Regina's Big Mistake* [K-1], **328**

Nabb, Magdalen. *Josie Smith at School* [1-2], **516**

Nelson, Vaunda Micheaux. *Mayfield Crossing* [4-5], **784**

Nixon, Joan Lowery. *Gloria Chipmunk, Star!* [1-2], 760

Oppenheim, Joanne. *Mrs. Peloki's Class Play* [1-2], 763

Park, Barbara. *Junie B. Jones and a Little Monkey Business* [2-3], **651**

Junie B. Jones and Some Sneaky Peeky Spying [2-3], **652**

Junie B. Jones and the Stupid Smelly Bus [2-3], **653**

Maxie, Rosie, and Earl—Partners in Grime [3-4], **736**

Rosie Swanson, Fourth-Grade Geek for President [3-4], **737**

Peck, Robert Newton. *Mr. Little* [5-6], 1343

Soup and Me [4-5], 1223

Petersen, P. J. *The Sub* [2-3], **656**

Peterson, Esther Allen. *Frederick's Alligator* [1-2], 773

Pfeffer, Susan Beth. *What Do You Do When Your Mouth Won't Open?* [5-6], 1344

Pinkwater, Daniel. *Author's Day* [2-3], **659**

Pulver, Robin. *Mrs. Toggle and the Dinosaur* [K-1], **344**

Mrs. Toggle's Beautiful Blue Shoe [K-1], **345**

Nobody's Mother Is in Second Grade [K-1], **346**

Rabe, Berniece. *The Balancing Girl* [K-1], 530

Regan, Dian Curtis. *The Curse of the Trouble Dolls* [2-3], **669**

Rinkoff, Barbara. *The Dragon's Handbooks* [2-3], 984

Robinson, Barbara. *The Best School Year Ever* [4-5], **788**

Robinson, Nancy K. *Just Plain Cat* [2-3], 986

Russo, Marisabina. *I Don't Want to Go Back to School* [K-1], **355**

Sachar, Louis. *Dogs Don't Tell Jokes* [5-6], **840**

Sideways Stories from Wayside School [3-4], 1110

Wayside School Is Falling Down [3-4], 1111

Sachs, Marilyn. *The Bears' House* [5-6], 1350

Say, Allen. *The Bicycle Man* [1-2], 791

Schertle, Alice. *Jeremy Bean's St. Patrick's Day* [K-1], 544

Schwartz, Amy. *Annabelle Swift, Kindergartner* [1-2], 794

Bea and Mr. Jones [1-2], 795

Scribner, Virginia. *Gopher Takes Heart* [3-4], **744**

Shreve, Susan. *Joshua T. Bates Takes Charge* [3-4], **747**

Smith, Janice Lee. *The Show-and-Tell War: And Other Stories about Adam Joshua* [1-2], 816

Snyder, Zilpha Keatley. *Libby on Wednesday* [5-6], **846**

Spinelli, Jerry. *Fourth Grade Rats* [3-4], **749**

Report to the Principal's Office [4-5], **791**

Stevenson, James. *That Dreadful Day* [2-3], 1011

Thayer, Jane. *Quiet on Account of Dinosaur* [K-1], 567

Tyler, Linda Wagner. *Waiting for Mom* [Pre-K], 276

Udry, Janice May. *Alfred* [K-1], 572

Angie [2-3], 1017

What Mary Jo Shared [Pre-K], 279

SCHOOLS (cont.)

Wardlaw, Lee. *Seventh-Grade Weirdo* [5-6], **850**

Wells, Rosemary. *Timothy Goes to School* [K-1], 587

Whitney, Alma Marshak. *Just Awful* [Pre-K], 293

Williams, Barbara. *The Author and Squinty Gritt* [1-2], **575**

Donna Jean's Disaster [1-2], 850

Williams, Jay, and Raymond Abrashkin. *Danny Dunn and the Homework Machine* [4-5], 1255

Willis, Val. *The Secret in the Matchbook* [K-1], 593

Wittman, Sally. *The Wonderful Mrs. Trumbly* [K-1], 596

Woodruff, Elvira. *The Magnificent Mummy Maker* [4-5], **799**

Show and Tell [K-1], **388**

Yashima, Taro. *Crow Boy* [2-3], 1032

Zimelman, Nathan. *How the Second Grade Got $8,205.50 to Visit the Statue of Liberty* [1-2], **583**

SCHOOLS–Poetry

Dakos, Kalli. *If You're Not Here, Please Raise Your Hand: Poems about School* [2-6], **1283**

Harrison, David L. *Somebody Catch My Homework* [2-5], **1307**

Kennedy, Dorothy M. *I Thought I'd Take My Rat to School: Poems for September to June* [3-6], **1341**

SCHOOLS–Riddles

Keller, Charles. *School Daze* [2-5], 1842

SCIENCE

Grillone, Lisa, and Joseph Gennaro. *Small Worlds Close Up* [4-6], 2043

Simon, Seymour. *The Dinosaur Is the Biggest Animal That Ever Lived and Other Wrong Ideas You Thought Were True* [2-5], 2100

SCIENCE–Experiments

Adler, David A. *Eaton Stanley & the Mind Control Experiment* [4-5], 1137

Brown, Bob. *How to Fool Your Friends* [3-5], 2000

Cobb, Vicki, and Kathy Darling. *Bet You Can! Science Possibilities to Fool You* [3-6], 2006

Cole, Joanna. *The Magic School Bus at the Waterworks* [2-4], 2008

The Magic School Bus Inside the Earth [2-4], 2009

Corbett, Scott. *The Lemonade Trick* [3-4], 1056

The Limerick Trick [3-4], 1057

Gardiner, John Reynolds. *Top Secret* [5-6], 1303

Hayes, William. *Project: Genius* [5-6], 1308

Hughes, Dean. *Nutty Knows All* [5-6], 1312

Lehane, M. S. *Science Tricks* [K-3], 2065

Simon, Seymour. *Einstein Anderson, Science Sleuth* [4-5], 1239

Wiesner, David. *June 29, 1999* [2-3], **690**

Williams, Jay, and Raymond Abrashkin. *Danny Dunn and the Homework Machine* [4-5], 1255

Woodruff, Elvira. *The Summer I Shrank My Grandmother* [4-5], **800**

SCIENCE–Riddles

Keller, Charles. *Take Me to Your Liter: Science and Math Jokes* [3-6], **1339**

SCIENCE FICTION

Alcock, Vivien. *The Monster Garden* [5-6], 1257

Ames, Mildred. *Is There Life on a Plastic Planet?* [5-6], 1263

Beatty, Jerome. *Matthew Looney's Invasion of the Earth* [4-5], 1142

Bradman, Tony. *It Came from Outer Space* [1-2], **410**

Brittain, Bill. *Shape-Changer* [4-5], **761**

Corbett, Scott. *The Donkey Planet* [4-5], 1163

Etra, Jonathan, and Stephanie Spinner. *Aliens for Breakfast* [2-3], 915

Fisk, Nicholas. *Grinny: A Novel of Science Fiction* [5-6], 1297

Harding, Lee. *The Fallen Spaceman* [3-4], 1070

L'Engle, Madeleine. *A Wrinkle in Time* [5-6], 1325

Lowry, Lois. *The Giver* [5-6], **828**

Marshall, Edward. *Space Case* [1-2], 742

Marshall, James. *Merry Christmas, Space Case* [1-2], 744

Paton Walsh, Jill. *The Green Book* [5-6], 1341

Pinkwater, Daniel. *Fat Men from Space* [3-4], 1103

Lizard Music [4-5], 1225

Ned Feldman, Space Pirate [2-3], **660**

The Slaves of Spiegel: A Magic Moscow Story [4-5], 1226

Roberts, Willo Davis. *The Girl with the Silver Eyes* [5-6], 1345

Ross, Tony. *I'm Coming to Get You* [K-1], 536

Sadler, Marilyn. *Alistair and the Alien Invasion* [K-1], **356**

Alistair in Outer Space [1-2], 787

Alistair's Time Machine [1-2], 789

Service, Pamela F. *Stinker from Space* [5-6], 1354

Sleator, William. *Into the Dream* [5-6], 1359

Slobodkin, Louis. *The Spaceship under the Apple Tree* [3-4], 1113

Slote, Alfred. *My Robot Buddy* [2-3], 1002

My Trip to Alpha I [3-4], 1114

Sterman, Betsy, and Samuel Sterman. *Too Much Magic* [3-4], 1119

Wiesner, David. *June 29, 1999* [2-3], **690**

Williams, Jay, and Raymond Abrashkin. *Danny Dunn, Time Traveler* [4-5], 1256

Woodruff, Elvira. *The Disappearing Bike Shop* [4-5], **797**

Yorinks, Arthur. *Company's Coming* [2-3], 1034

SCIENTISTS

Anderson, Margaret. *The Brain on Quartz Mountain* [3-4], 1041

Butterworth, Oliver. *The Enormous Egg* [4-5], 1154

Epstein, Sam, and Beryl Epstein. *Secret in a Sealed Bottle: Lazzaro Spallanzani's Work with Microbes* [5-6], 2022

Lasky, Kathryn. *The Librarian Who Measured the Earth* [3-6], **1180**

Ormondroyd, Edward. *David and the Phoenix* [3-4], 1100

Tzannes, Robin. *Professor Puffendorf's Secret Potions* [1-2], **569**

Ungerer, Tomi. *The Beast of Monsieur Racine* [2-3], 1018

Weiss, Ellen, and Mel Friedman. *The Poof Point* [5-6], **851**

The Tiny Parents [4-5], **794**

SCOTLAND

Hunter, Mollie. *Wicked One: A Story of Suspense* [5-6], 1313

Selden, George. *Sparrow Socks* [1-2], 799

SCULPTORS

Freeman, Don. *Norman the Doorman* [1-2], 671

Gardner, Jane Mylum. *Henry Moore: From Bones and Stones to Sketches and Sculptures* [2-5], **1146**

Schotter, Roni. *Captain Snap and the Children of Vinegar Lane* [1-2], 793

Stolz, Mary. *Zekmet, the Stone Carver* [4-5], 1244

SCULPTORS–Folklore

Yacowitz, Caryn. *The Jade Stone: A Chinese Folktale* [K-4], **1045**

SEA

SEE Ocean; Seashore

SEALS

Rand, Gloria. *Prince William* [2-3], **668**

SEALS–Folklore

Martin, Rafe. *The Boy Who Lived with the Seals* [2-4], **982**

SEASHORE

SEE ALSO Ocean

Bancroft, Catherine, and Hannah Coale Gruenberg. *Felix's Hat* [Pre-K], **70**

Cole, Joanna. *The Magic School Bus on the Ocean Floor* [2-4], **1122**

Haynes, Betsy. *The Ghost of the Gravestone Hearth* [4-5], 1185

Hughes, Shirley. *The Big Alfie Out of Doors Storybook* [Pre-K], **128**

Jonas, Ann. *Reflections* [1-2], 700

Levine, Evan. *Not the Piano, Mrs. Medley!* [1-2], **483**

McDonald, Megan. *Is This a House for Hermit Crab?* [K-1], **313**

McMillan, Bruce. *Beach Ball—Left, Right* [Pre-K], **158**

Ness, Evaline. *Sam, Bangs and Moonshine* [1-2], 757

O'Donnell, Elizabeth Lee. *The Twelve Days of Summer* [1-2], **523**

Peters, Lisa Westberg. *The Sun, the Wind and the Rain* [Pre-2], 2082

Robbins, Ken. *Beach Days* [Pre-K], 242

Samton, Sheila White. *Beside the Bay* [Pre-K], 250

Stevenson, James. *Clams Can't Sing* [K-1], 560

Tresselt, Alvin. *Hide and Seek Fog* [1-2], 833

Turkle, Brinton. *Do Not Open* [2-3], 1016

Weller, Frances Ward. *Riptide* [1-2], 848

Zion, Gene. *Harry by the Sea* [Pre-K], 307

Zoehfeld, Kathleen Weidner. *What Lives in a Shell?* [Pre-2], **1258**

SEASHORE–Folklore

Hodges, Margaret. *The Wave* [K-4], 1527

San Souci, Robert D. *Sukey and the Mermaid* [2-5], **1017**

SEASHORE–Poetry

McMillan, Bruce. *One Sun* [Pre-2], 1865

Shaw, Alison. *Until I Saw the Sea: A Collection of Seashore Poems* [K-4], **1408**

SEASONS

SEE ALSO Autumn; Months; Spring; Summer; Winter

Alexander, Sue. *There's More . . . Much More* [Pre-K], 3

Allen, Marjorie N., and Shelley Rotner. *Changes* [Pre-1], **1100**

Andersen, Janet S. *The Key into Winter* [2-3], **587**

Andrews, Jan. *Very Last First Time* [2-3], 867

Aylesworth, Jim. *One Crow: A Counting Rhyme* [Pre-K], 17

SEASONS (cont.)

Borden, Louise. *Caps, Hats, Socks, and Mittens: A Book about the Four Seasons* [Pre-K], 24

Burton, Virgina Lee. *Katy and the Big Snow* [Pre-K], 35

The Little House [1-2], 634

Clifton, Lucille. *The Boy Who Didn't Believe in Spring* [1-2], 650

Coleridge, Sara. *January Brings the Snow: A Book of Months* [Pre-K], 54

Emberley, Michael. *Welcome Back Sun* [1-2], **438**

Fowler, Susi Gregg. *When Summer Ends* [Pre-K], 90

Hall, Donald. *Ox-Cart Man* [2-3], 931

Johnson, Crockett. *Will Spring Be Early? or Will Spring Be Late?* [K-1], 439

Johnston, Tony. *Yonder* [2-3], 939

Kinsey-Warnock, Natalie. *When Spring Comes* [1-2], **469**

Laroche, Michel. *The Snow Rose* [3-4], 1086

Lemieux, Michele. *What's That Noise* [Pre-K], 184

Major, Beverly. *Playing Sardines* [1-2], 741

Minarik, Else Holmelund. *It's Spring!* [Pre-K], 213

Ryder, Joanne. *Chipmunk Song* [Pre-2], 2089

Sendak, Maurice. *Chicken Soup with Rice* [K-1], 551

Tejima, Keizaburo. *Fox's Dream* [K-1], 565

Udry, Janice May. *A Tree Is Nice* [Pre-K], 278

Van Allsburg, Chris. *The Stranger* [3-4], 1124

SEASONS–Folklore

Larry, Charles. *Peboan and Seegwun* [1-4], **964**

Proddow, Penelope. *Demeter and Persephone* [5-6], 1581

Waldherr, Kris. *Persephone and the Pomegranate: A Myth from Greece* [2-6], 1041

SEASONS–Poetry

Adoff, Arnold. *In for Winter, Out for Spring* [K-4], 1260

Bruchac, Joseph, and Jonathan London. *Thirteen Moons on Turtle's Back: A Native American Year of Moons* [2-6], **872**

Demi. *In the Eyes of the Cat: Japanese Poetry for All Seasons* [2-6], **1284**

Esbensen, Barbara Juster. *Cold Stars and Fireflies: Poems of the Four Seasons* [3-6], 1797

Frank, Josette. *Snow Toward Evening: A Year in a River Valley: Nature Poems* [3-6], **1294**

Higginson, William J. *Wind in the Long Grass: A Collection of Haiku* [2-6], **1313**

Hopkins, Lee Bennett. *Moments: Poems about the Seasons* [1-5], 1824

Ring Out, Wild Bells: Poems About Holidays and Seasons [K-5], **1326**

The Sky Is Full of Song [K-3], 1828

Small Talk: A Book of Short Poems [2-5], **1327**

Hughes, Shirley. *Out and About* [Pre-1], 1831

Jacobs, Leland B. *Just Around the Corner: Poems About the Seasons* [Pre-2], **1333**

Lewis, J. Patrick. *Earth Verses and Water Rhymes* [2-4], **1352**

Mizamura, Kazue. *Flower Moon Snow: A Book of Haiku* [2-6], 1873

Prelutsky, Jack. *It's Snowing! It's Snowing!* [Pre-3], 1907

What I Did Last Summer [K-3], 1923

Rogasky, Barbara. *Winter Poems* [3-6], **1403**

Singer, Marilyn. *Turtle in July* [1-4], 1954

SECRETARIES

Pearson, Susan. *Lenore's Big Break* [1-2], **528**

SECRETS

Heide, Florence Parry, and Judith Heide Gilliland. *The Day of Ahmed's Secret* [2-3], **616**

Park, Barbara. *Junie B. Jones and Some Sneaky Peeky Spying* [2-3], **652**

SEEDS

Garland, Sherry. *The Lotus Seed* [2-3], **609**

Gibbons, Gail. *From Seed to Plant* [K-3], **1148**

Heller, Ruth. *The Reason for a Flower* [K-4], **1161**

SEEDS–Folklore

Demi. *The Empty Pot* [K-3], **892**

SELF-ACCEPTANCE

SEE ALSO Self-concept; Self-esteem; Self-reliance

Gwynne, Fred. *Pondlarker* [1-2], **447**

Keller, Holly. *Horace* [Pre-K], **143**

Knowles, Sheena. *Edward the Emu* [K-1], **300**

SELF-CONCEPT

SEE ALSO Self-acceptance; Self-esteem; Self-reliance

Ames, Mildred. *Is There Life on a Plastic Planet?* [5-6], 1263

Andersen, Hans Christian. *The Ugly Duckling* [1-2], 603

Blume, Judy. *Freckle Juice* [1-2], 618

Byars, Betsy. *The Summer of the Swans* [5-6], 1282

Calmenson, Stephanie. *The Principal's New Clothes* [1-2], **420**

Caple, Kathy. *The Biggest Nose* [K-1], 356

Carle, Eric. *The Mixed-Up Chameleon* [Pre-K], 38

Chapman, Carol. *The Tale of Meshka the Kvetch* [2-3], 885

Cohen, Miriam. *No Good in Art* [K-1], 370

Conford, Ellen. *Impossible Possum* [1-2], 652
Revenge of the Incredible Dr. Rancid and His Youthful Assistant, Jeffrey [4-5], 1162

dePaola, Tomie. *Big Anthony and the Magic Ring* [2-3], 908

Holman, Felice. *The Blackmail Machine* [4-5], 1191

Howe, James. *I Wish I Were a Butterfly* [1-2], 692

Kasza, Keiko. *The Pig's Picnic* [Pre-K], 161

LeSieg, Theo. *I Wish That I Had Duck Feet* [K-1], 467

Lexai, Joan. *Benjie* [K-1], 472

Lionni, Leo. *Fish Is Fish* [K-1], 474

Lisle, Janet Taylor. *The Dancing Cats of Applesap* [4-5], 1205

Marshall, James. *Portly McSwine* [K-1], 503

Peet, Bill. *The Spooky Tail of Prewitt Peacock* [1-2], 771
The Whingdingdilly [2-3], 979

Pfeffer, Susan Beth. *What Do You Do When Your Mouth Won't Open?* [5-6], 1344

Rinkoff, Barbara. *The Remarkable Ramsey* [2-3], 985

Sachs, Marilyn. *Veronica Ganz* [4-5], 1236

Springstubb, Tricia. *The Magic Guinea Pig* [Pre-K], 270

Udry, Janice May. *What Mary Jo Shared* [Pre-K], 279

Waber, Bernard. *"You Look Ridiculous," Said the Rhinoceros to the Hippopotamus* [K-1], 580

Watson, Pauline. *Wriggles the Little Wishing Pig* [K-1], 582

Wells, Rosemary. *Shy Charles* [K-1], 586

Williams, Barbara. *Donna Jean's Disaster* [1-2], 850

Yashima, Taro. *Crow Boy* [2-3], 1032

Yorinks, Arthur. *It Happened in Pinsk* [2-3], 1035

SELF-ESTEEM

SEE ALSO Self-acceptance; Self-concept; Self-reliance

Birdseye, Tom. *Just Call Me Stupid* [4-5], **759**

Boland, Janice. *Annabel* [Pre], **6**

Coerr, Eleanor. *Mieko and the Fifth Treasure* [3-4], **707**

Coville, Bruce. *Jennifer Murdley's Toad* [4-5], **765**

Ernst, Lisa Campbell. *The Luckiest Kid on the Planet* [1-2], **439**

Harding, William Harry. *Alvin's Famous No-Horse* [2-3], **613**

Hoffman, Mary. *Amazing Grace* [K-1], **287**

Honeycutt, Natalie. *Juliet Fisher and the Foolproof Plan* [2-3], **621**

Johnston, Deborah. *Mathew Michael's Beastly Day* [K-1], **293**

Keller, Holly. *Horace* [Pre-K], **143**

Levy, Elizabeth. *Keep Ms. Sugarman in the Fourth Grade* [3-4], **731**

Lewison, Wendy Cheyette. *Shy Vi* [Pre-K], **151**

Mitchell, Rita Phillips. *Hue Boy* [K-1], **325**

Moss, Marissa. *Regina's Big Mistake* [K-1], **328**

Pearson, Susan. *Lenore's Big Break* [1-2], **528**

Scribner, Virginia. *Gopher Takes Heart* [3-4], **744**

SELF-RELIANCE

SEE ALSO Self-acceptance; Self-concept; Self-esteem

Bawden, Nina. *Humbug* [3-4], **703**

Benjamin, Saragail Katzman. *My Dog Ate It* [3-4], **704**

Getz, David. *Thin Air* [5-6], **819**

Hughes, Shirley. *Alfie Gets in First* [Pre-K], **143**

Paulsen, Gary. *The Haymeadow* [5-6], **835**

SELFISHNESS

Johnston, Tony. *Slither McCreep and His Brother Joe* [K-1], **294**

Lester, Helen. *Me First* [K-1], **304**

Mahy, Margaret. *The Great White Man-Eating Shark: A Cautionary Tale* [1-2], **501**

SENSES AND SENSATION

Gryski, Camilla. *Hands On, Thumbs Up: Secret Handshakes, Fingerprints, Sign Languages, and More Handy Ways to Have Fun with Hands* [3-6], **1154**

Hines, Anna Grossnickle. *What Joe Saw* [Pre-K], **123**

McMillan, Bruce. *Sense Suspense: A Guessing Game for the Five Senses* [Pre-K], **159**

Miller, Margaret. *My Five Senses* [Pre-K], **1207**

Otto, Carolyn. *I Can Tell by Touching* [Pre-1], **1215**

Pilkey, Dav. *Dog Breath: The Horrible Trouble with Hally Tosis* [1-2], **530**

Showers, Paul. *The Listening Walk* [Pre-K], **187**

SEPARATION ANXIETY

Bunting, Eve. *Our Teacher's Having a Baby* [K-1], **243**

Cooney, Nancy Evans. *Chatterbox Jamie* [Pre-K], **87**

Johnson, Dolores. *What Will Mommy Do When I'm at School?* [Pre-K], **135**

SEPARATION ANXIETY (cont.)
Waddell, Martin. *Owl Babies* [Pre], **49**

SEQUENCE STORIES
Arnold, Tedd. *Ollie Forgot* [1-2], 607
Barton, Byron. *Buzz Buzz Buzz* [Pre-K], 21
Birdseye, Tom. *Soap! Soap! Don't Forget the Soap! An Appalachian Folktale* [1-3], **869**
Bowden, Joan Chase. *The Bean Boy* [Pre-1], 1405
Carle, Eric. *Today Is Monday* [K-1], **248**
Cauley, Lorinda Bryan. *The Pancake Boy: An Old Norwegian Folk Tale* [1-3], 1418
Charlip, Remy. *Fortunately* [1-2], 645
Cook, Scott. *The Gingerbread Boy* [Pre-1], 1429
Dupré, Judith. *The Mouse Bride: A Mayan Folk Tale* [K-2], **898**
Emberley, Barbara. *Drummer Hoff* [Pre-K], 80
Esterl, Arnica. *The Fine Round Cake* [K-2], **903**
Fenton, Edward. *The Big Yellow Balloon* [1-2], 667
Flora, James. *Sherwood Walks Home* [Pre-K], 88
Galdone, Paul. *The Gingerbread Boy* [Pre-1], 1459
  Henny Penny [Pre-1], 1461
Goodsell, Jane. *Toby's Toe* [K-1], 407
Hobson, Sally. *Chicken Little* [Pre-K], **940**
Hogrogian, Nonny. *One Fine Day* [Pre-2], 1528
Hurlimann, Ruth. *The Proud White Cat* [Pre-2], 1532
Hutchins, Pat. *Rosie's Walk* [Pre-K], 149
Kalan, Robert. *Stop, Thief!* [Pre-K], **138**
Kimmel, Eric A. *The Gingerbread Man* [Pre-1], **953**
  The Greatest of All: A Japanese Folktale [K-2], **954**
Lester, Helen. *It Wasn't My Fault* [K-1], 469
Lexai, Joan. *That's Good, That's Bad* [Pre-K], 187
Martin, Bill, Jr. *Brown Bear, Brown Bear, What Do You See?* [Pre-K], 204
Mathews, Judith, and Fay Robinson. *Nathaniel Willy, Scared Silly* [Pre-2], **984**
Morgan, Pierr. *The Turnip: An Old Russian Folktale* [Pre-1], 1569
Moskin, Marietta. *Rosie's Birthday Present* [K-1], 510
Numeroff, Laura J. *If You Give a Moose a Muffin* [K-1], **334**
Paul, Anthony. *The Tiger Who Lost His Stripes* [1-2], 765
Roy, Ron. *Three Ducks Went Wandering* [Pre-K], 246
Schindel, John. *What's for Lunch?* [Pre-K], **185**
Simms, Laura. *The Squeaky Door* [Pre-2], **1026**
Troughton, Joanna. *Tortoise's Dream* [Pre-2], 1618

Tworkov, Jack. *The Camel Who Took a Walk* [K-1], 571
Westwood, Jennifer. *Going to Squintum's: A Foxy Folktale* [Pre-2], 1624
Zolotow, Charlotte. *The Quarreling Book* [1-2], 861

SHADOWS
Asch, Frank. *Bear Shadow* [Pre-K], 10
Christelow, Eileen. *Henry and the Dragon* [Pre-K], 49
Frascino, Edward. *My Cousin the King* [K-1], 390
Keats, Ezra Jack. *Dreams* [K-1], 448
Narahashi, Keiko. *I Have a Friend* [Pre-K], 215

SHADOWS–Poetry
Stevenson, Robert Louis. *My Shadow* [K-1], **374**

SHAKESPEARE, WILLIAM
Stanley, Diane, and Peter Vennema. *Bard of Avon: The Story of William Shakespeare* [4-6], **1241**

SHAPES
Carle, Eric. *The Secret Birthday Message* [Pre-K], 40
Charles, N. N. *What Am I? Looking Through Shapes at Apples and Grapes* [Pre-K], **84**
Crews, Donald. *Ten Black Dots* [Pre-K], 59
Ehlert, Lois. *Color Farm* [Pre-K], **96**
  Color Zoo [Pre-K], 76
Emberley, Ed. *The Wing on a Flea* [Pre-K], 81
Falwell, Cathryn. *Clowning Around* [K-1], **272**
MacDonald, Suse. *Sea Shapes* [Pre-K], **157**
Rogers, Paul. *The Shapes Game* [Pre-K], **181**
Sharratt, Nick. *My Mom and Dad Make Me Laugh* [Pre-K], **186**
Skofield, James. *'Round and Around* [Pre-K], **188**
Sundgaard, Arnold. *Meet Jack Appleknocker* [Pre-K], 272
Tompert, Ann. *Grandfather Tang's Story* [1-2], **567**

SHARING
SEE Generosity

SHARKS
Maestro, Betsy. *A Sea Full of Sharks* [1-3], **1196**
Mahy, Margaret. *The Great White Man-Eating Shark: A Cautionary Tale* [1-2], **501**

SHEEP
Beskow, Elsa. *Pelle's New Suit* [K-1], 336
dePaola, Tomie. *Charlie Needs a Cloak* [K-1], 376
Gordon, Jeffie Ross. *Six Sleepy Sheep* [Pre-K], **111**
Hale, Sarah Josepha Buell. *Mary Had a Little Lamb* [Pre-K], **116**, **117**, 127

Hughes, Shirley. *The Big Alfie Out of Doors Storybook* [Pre-K], **128**

Kiser, Kevin. *Sherman the Sheep* [K-1], **299**

McCully, Emily Arnold. *Speak Up, Blanche!* [1-2], **493**

Maestro, Betsy, and Giulio Maestro. *Lambs for Dinner* [K-1], 498

Paulsen, Gary. *The Haymeadow* [5-6], **835**

Sanders, Scott Russell. *Warm as Wool* [1-2], **546**

Shaw, Nancy. *Sheep in a Jeep* [K-1], 556
Sheep in a Shop [K-1], **360**
Sheep Out to Eat [K-1], **361**

Singer, Marilyn. *Chester the Out-of-Work Dog* [K-1], **366**

Ziefert, Harriet. *A New Coat for Anna* [K-1], 597

SHEEP–Folklore

Aardema, Verna. *Borreguita and the Coyote: A Tale from Ayutla, Mexico* [K-3], **856**

SHELLS

McDonald, Megan. *Is This a House for Hermit Crab?* [K-1], **313**

Zoehfeld, Kathleen Weidner. *What Lives in a Shell?* [Pre-2], **1258**

SHERIFFS

Yorinks, Arthur. *Whitefish Will Rides Again!* [1-2], **581**

SHIPS

SEE ALSO Boats and boating

Avi. *The True Confessions of Charlotte Doyle* [5-6], **803**

Ballard, Robert. *Exploring the Titanic* [4-6], **1102**

Fleischman, Sid. *The Ghost in the Noonday Sun* [5-6], 1301

Gerrard, Roy. *Sir Francis Drake: His Daring Deeds* [4-6], 2038

McCully, Emily Arnold. *The Amazing Felix* [1-2], **491**

Peet, Bill. *Cyrus the Unsinkable Sea Serpent* [1-2], 767

Strickland, Brad. *Dragon's Plunder* [5-6], **848**

Zhitkov, Boris. *How I Hunted the Little Fellows* [3-4], 1136

SHIPS–Folklore

Ransome, Arthur. *The Fool of the World and His Flying Ship* [2-4], 1583

SHOES

SEE ALSO Clothing and dress

Aiken, Joan. *The Moon's Revenge* [3-4], 1038

Banks, Kate. *Peter and the Talking Shoes* [K-1], **228**

Cleary, Beverly. *The Growing-Up Feet* [Pre-K], 50

Daly, Niki. *Not So Fast, Songololo* [Pre-K], 62

Fox, Mem. *Shoes from Grandpa* [Pre-K], **105**

Havill, Juanita. *Jamaica and Brianna* [Pre-K], **119**

Hughes, Shirley. *Alfie's Feet* [Pre-K], 145

Hurwitz, Johanna. *New Shoes for Sylvia* [Pre-K], **129**

Matsuno, Masako. *A Pair of Red Clogs* [1-2], 747

Miller, Margaret. *Whose Shoe?* [Pre-K], **168**

Patrick, Denise Lewis. *Red Dancing Shoes* [Pre-K], **175**

Pulver, Robin. *Mrs. Toggle's Beautiful Blue Shoe* [K-1], **345**

Schertle, Alice. *The April Fool* [2-3], **991**

Ungerer, Tomi. *One, Two, Where's My Shoe?* [Pre-K], 281

Winthrop, Elizabeth. *Shoes* [Pre-K], 300

SHOES–Folklore

Climo, Shirley. *The Korean Cinderella* [1-4], **878**

Grimm, Jacob. *The Elves and the Shoemaker* [Pre-2], 1491

SHOPPING

SEE ALSO Supermarkets

Allard, Harry. *I Will Not Go to a Market Today* [K-1], 316

Daly, Niki. *Not So Fast, Songololo* [Pre-K], 62

Falwell, Cathryn. *Feast for 10* [Pre], **11**

Grossman, Bill. *Tommy at the Grocery Store* [K-1], 414

Shaw, Nancy. *Sheep in a Shop* [K-1], **360**

SHORT STORIES

Ainsworth, Ruth. *The Phantom Carousel and Other Ghostly Tales* [4-5], 1138

Alexander, Lloyd. *The Town Cats and Other Tales* [5-6], **1261**

Babbitt, Natalie. *The Devil's Storybook* [5-6], **1270**

Banks, Lynne Reid. *The Magic Hare* [3-4], **702**

Bauer, Caroline Feller. *Thanksgiving: Stories and Poems* [2-4], **1266**
Windy Day: Stories and Poems [1-4], 1746

Blathwayt, Benedict. *Stories from Firefly Island* [1-2], **407**

Dahl, Roald. *The Wonderful Story of Henry Sugar and Six More* [5-6], 1293

Hunter, Mollie. *A Furl of Fairy Wind* [3-4], 1076

Jennings, Paul. *Unreal! Eight Surprising Stories* [5-6], **825**

Kipling, Rudyard. *Just So Stories* [3-4], **728**
Just So Stories [2-3], 948

Levitt, Paul M., Douglas A. Burger, and Elissa S. Guralnick. *The Weighty Word Book* [5-6], 1326

Lionni, Leo. *Frederick's Fables: A Leo Lionni Treasury of Favorite Stories* [1-2], 728

SHORT STORIES (cont.)

Low, Alice. *The Family Read-Aloud Holiday Treasury* [1-4], **1362**

Marshall, James. *Rats on the Roof and Other Stories* [2-3], **643**

Mendoza, George. *Gwot! Horribly Funny Hairticklers* [2-3], 962

Pepper, Dennis. *The Oxford Book of Scary Stories* [5-6], **836**

Pollack, Pamela. *The Random House Book of Humor for Children* [4-5], 1228

Rylant, Cynthia. *Children of Christmas: Stories for the Seasons* [5-6], 1349

Salway, Lance. *A Nasty Piece of Work and Other Ghost Stories* [5-6], 1351

Slote, Alfred. *The Devil Rides with Me and Other Fantastic Stories* [5-6], 1360

Waters, Fiona. *The Doubleday Book of Bedtime Stories* [K-1], **381**

SHYNESS

Cooney, Nancy Evans. *Chatterbox Jamie* [Pre-K], **87**

Lewison, Wendy Cheyette. *Shy Vi* [Pre-K], **151**

McCully, Emily Arnold. *Speak Up, Blanche!* [1-2], **493**

SIBLING RIVALRY

Blume, Judy. *The Pain and the Great One* [1-2], 619

Caseley, Judith. *Silly Baby* [Pre-K], 44

Cutler, Jane. *Darcy and Gran Don't Like Babies* [K-1], **259**

No Dogs Allowed [2-3], **602**

Dragonwagon, Crescent. *I Hate My Brother Harry* [1-2], 663

Hamilton, Morse. *Little Sister for Sale* [1-2], **450**

Henkes, Kevin. *Julius, the Baby of the World* [K-1], **283**

Hutchins, Pat. *Silly Billy!* [Pre], **24**

Johnston, Tony. *Slither McCreep and His Brother Joe* [K-1], **294**

Kellogg, Steven. *Much Bigger than Martin* [K-1], 453

Little, Jean. *Revenge of the Small Small* [1-2], **486**

Park, Barbara. *Operation: Dump the Chump* [3-4], 1101

Polacco, Patricia. *My Rotten Redheaded Older Brother* [1-2], **536**

Roche, P. K. *Good-Bye, Arnold* [K-1], 533

Root, Phyllis. *Moon Tiger* [K-1], 535

Russo, Marisabina. *Only Six More Days* [Pre-K], 248

Sheldon, Dyan. *My Brother Is a Visitor from Another Planet* [3-4], **746**

Stevenson, James. *Worse Than Willy!* [1-2], 827

Viorst, Judith. *I'll Fix Anthony* [K-1], 574

Woodruff, Elvira. *The Magnificent Mummy Maker* [4-5], **799**

Yaccarino, Dan. *Big Brother Mike* [K-1], **390**

Yorinks, Arthur. *Oh, Brother* [2-3], 1036

SIBLING RIVALRY–Poetry

Margolis, Richard J. *Secrets of a Small Brother* [1-2], 1867

SICK

Brandenberg, Franz. *I Wish I Was Sick, Too* [Pre-K], 26

Brown, Marc. *Arthur's Chicken Pox* [K-1], **239**

Charlip, Remy, and Burton Supree. *Mother, Mother, I Feel Sick, Send for the Doctor Quick, Quick, Quick* [1-2], 646

Cherry, Lynne. *Who's Sick Today?* [Pre-K], 47

Coerr, Eleanor. *Sadako* [2-5], **1120**

Sadako & the Thousand Paper Cranes [3-6], 2007

Gackenbach, Dick. *What's Claude Doing?* [Pre-K], 101

Gretz, Susanna. *Teddy Bears Cure a Cold* [K-1], 413

Jukes, Mavis. *I'll See You in My Dreams* [3-4], **718**

Le Guin, Ursula K. *A Visit from Dr. Katz* [Pre-K], 183

Little, Jean. *Revenge of the Small Small* [1-2], **486**

Loomis, Christine. *One Cow Coughs: A Counting Book for the Sick and Miserable* [Pre-K], **155**

Moutoussamy-Ashe, Jeanne. *Daddy and Me: A Photo Story of Arthur Ashe and His Daughter Camera* [K-6], **1213**

Paulsen, Gary. *A Christmas Sonata* [5-6], **833**

Schotter, Roni. *Captain Snap and the Children of Vinegar Lane* [1-2], 793

Slote, Alfred. *Hang Tough, Paul Mather* [4-5], 1241

Smith, Robert Kimmell. *Chocolate Fever* [2-3], 1003

Thurber, James. *Many Moons* [2-3], 1015

Wells, Rosemary. *Voyage to the Bunny Planet books: First Tomato; The Island Light; Moss Pillows* [K-1], **383**

Williams, Barbara. *Albert's Toothache* [Pre-K], 296

Woodruff, Elvira. *Dear Napoleon, I Know You're Dead, But . . .* [5-6], **852**

Zimmerman, Andrea, and David Clemesha. *The Cow Buzzed* [Pre-K], **215**

SIGN LANGUAGE

Gryski, Camilla. *Hands On, Thumbs Up: Secret Handshakes, Fingerprints, Sign Languages, and More Handy Ways to Have Fun with Hands* [3-6], **1154**

Michel, Anna. *The Story of Nim, the Chimp Who Learned Language* [3-6], 2076

Patterson, Francine. *Koko's Kitten* [2-6], 2080

Rankin, Laura. *The Handmade Alphabet* [K-6], **1223**

SIGNS AND SIGNBOARDS

Arnold, Tedd. *The Signmaker's Assistant* [1-2], **400**

Roth, Roger. *The Sign Painter's Dream* [1-2], **545**

SIGNS AND SIGNBOARDS–Folklore

Shepard, Aaron. *The Legend of Slappy Hooper: An American Tall Tale* [1-3], **1023**

SINGING–Folklore

Czernecki, Stefan, and Timothy Rhodes. *The Singing Snake* [K-2], **889**

SINGING GAMES

Glazer, Tom. *Eye Winker, Tom Tinker, Chin Chopper: Fifty Musical Fingerplays* [Pre-2], 1804

Langstaff, Nancy, and John Langstaff. *Jim Along Josie: A Collection of Folk Songs* [Pre-2], 1850

SINGLE-PARENT FAMILIES

Byars, Betsy. *McMummy* [4-5], **762**

Engel, Diana. *Fishing* [K-1], **268**

Polacco, Patricia. *Some Birthday!* [1-2], **537**

Quattlebaum, Mary. *Jackson Jones and the Puddle of Thorns* [4-5], **787**

Sun, Chying Feng. *Mama Bear* [1-2], **562**

SISTERS

SEE ALSO Brothers; Brothers and sisters

Cleary, Beverly. *Beezus and Ramona* [2-3], 887

Galbraith, Kathryn O. *Waiting for Jennifer* [K-1], 400

Hamilton, Morse. *Little Sister for Sale* [1-2], **450**

Henkes, Kevin. *Sheila Rae, the Brave* [Pre-K], 132

Howard, Ellen. *A Circle of Giving* [4-5], 1192

Minters, Frances. *Cinder-Elly* [1-2], **510**

Naylor, Phyllis Reynolds. *The Boys Start the War* [3-4], **735**

Witch's Sister [4-5], 1217

Polacco, Patricia. *Just Plain Fancy* [2-3], **662**

Samuels, Barbara. *Duncan & Dolores* [Pre-K], 251

Schwartz, Amy. *Annabelle Swift, Kindergartner* [1-2], 794

Seuling, Barbara. *The Triplets* [1-2], 800

Slepian, Jan. *Risk N' Roses* [5-6], 845

SISTERS–Folklore

Grimm, Jacob. *Mother Holly* [Pre-2], 1502

Martin, Rafe. *The Rough-Face Girl* [2-6], **983**

San Souci, Robert. *The Talking Eggs* [1-4], 1590

Steptoe, John. *Mufaro's Beautiful Daughters: An African Tale* [1-4], 1607

Young, Ed. *Lon Po Po: A Red-Riding Hood Story from China* [K-2], 1633

SIZE

Andersen, Hans Christian. *Thumbelina* [2-3], 864

Banks, Lynne Reid. *The Indian in the Cupboard* [5-6], 1272

Brenner, Barbara. *Mr. Tall and Mr. Small* [K-1], 343

Brown, Marc. *D.W. Thinks Big* [Pre-K], **71**

Chase, Mary. *Loretta Mason Potts* [4-5], 1157

Dahl, Roald. *Esio Trot* [3-4], **710**

Du Bois, William Pène. *The Giant* [5-6], 1294

Gackenbach, Dick. *Tiny for a Day* [K-1], **273**

Heide, Florence Parry. *The Shrinking of Treehorn* [3-4], 1071

Herzig, Alison Cragin. *The Big Deal* [2-3], **618**

Joyce, William. *George Shrinks* [K-1], 444

Lurie, Morris. *The Story of Imelda, Who Was Small* [K-1], **311**

McNaughton, Colin. *Anton B. Stanton and the Pirats* [1-2], 736

McPhail, David. *Great Cat* [K-1], 495

Melmed, Laura Krauss. *The Rainbabies* [1-2], **508**

Mitchell, Rita Phillips. *Hue Boy* [K-1], **325**

Most, Bernard. *How Big Were the Dinosaurs?* [K-2], **1212**

Mwenye Hadithi. *Crafty Chameleon* [Pre-K], 124
Tricky Tortoise [Pre-K], 126

Nesbit, E. *Melisande* [4-5], 1218

Norton, Mary. *The Borrowers* [5-6], 1336

Parish, Peggy. *No More Monsters for Me* [K-1], 517

Peet, Bill. *Big Bad Bruce* [1-2], 766

Pinkwater, Daniel. *The Wuggie Norple Story* [K-1], 524

Sleator, William. *Among the Dolls* [4-5], 1240

Tapp, Kathy Kennedy. *Moth-Kin Magic* [4-5], 1247

Weiss, Ellen, and Mel Friedman. *The Tiny Parents* [4-5], **794**

Wells, Robert E. *Is a Blue Whale the Biggest Thing There Is?* [2-5], **1251**

White, E. B. *Stuart Little* [3-4], 1131

Wiesner, David. *June 29, 1999* [2-3], **690**

Winthrop, Elizabeth. *The Castle in the Attic* [5-6], 1374

Woodruff, Elvira. *Show and Tell* [K-1], **388**

SIZE (cont.)
The Summer I Shrank My Grandmother [4-5], **800**

SIZE–Folklore
Brenner, Barbara. *Little One Inch* [K-4], 1407
Hughes, Monica. *Little Fingerling* [1-4], **945**
Renberg, Dalia Hardof. *King Solomon and the Bee* [K-3], **1001**

SKATEBOARDING
Barre, Shelley A. *Chive* [5-6], **804**
Kirk, Daniel. *Skateboard Monsters* [1-2], **472**

SKELETONS
SEE Bones

SKIING
Calhoun, Mary. *Cross-Country Cat* [1-2], 635
Fife, Dale. *North of Danger* [5-6], 1296

SKUNKS
Service, Pamela F. *Stinker from Space* [5-6], 1354

SKY
Cummings, Pat. *C.L.O.U.D.S.* [2-3], 903
Shaw, Charles G. *It Looked Like Spilt Milk* [Pre-K], 264

SKY–Folklore
Gerson, Mary-Joan. *Why the Sky Is Far Away: A Nigerian Folktale* [K-4], **913**
Shepard, Aaron. *The Legend of Slappy Hooper: An American Tall Tale* [1-3], **1023**

SLAPSTICK
Allard, Harry. *The Stupids Die* [K-1], 318
Noble, Trinka Hakes. *The Day Jimmy's Boa Ate the Wash* [1-2], 761
Meanwhile Back at the Ranch [2-3], 974
Rose, Anne. *The Triumphs of Fuzzy Fogtop* [1-2], 784
Silverstein, Shel. *A Giraffe and a Half* [1-2], 811

SLAVERY
Adler, David A. *A Picture Book of Harriet Tubman* [1-4], **1095**
A Picture Book of Sojourner Truth [2-4], **1096**
Chbosky, Stacey. *Who Owns the Sun?* [4-5], **1158**
Everett, Gwen. *John Brown: One Man Against Slavery* [5-6], **1138**
Ferris, Jeri. *Go Free or Die: A Story About Harriet Tubman* [3-5], **1141**
Hopkinson, Deborah. *Sweet Clara and the Freedom Quilt* [2-3], **622**
Hurmence, Belinda. *A Girl Called Boy* [5-6], 1314
Johnson, Dolores. *Now Let Me Fly: The Story of a Slave Family* [2-3], **629**

McGovern, Ann. *Runaway Slave: The Story of Harriet Tubman* [2-5], 2070
Monjo, F. N. *The Drinking Gourd* [2-3], 966
Polacco, Patricia. *Pink and Say* [4-5], **786**
Price, Leontyne. *Aïda* [5-6], **837**
Winter, Jeanette. *Follow the Drinking Gourd* [3-4], 1134

SLED DOG RACING
Paulsen, Gary. *Dogteam* [3-4], **738**
Seibert, Patricia. *Mush! Across Alaska in the World's Longest Sled-Dog Race* [1-4], **1235**

SLEDS
Chapman, Cheryl. *Snow on Snow on Snow* [Pre-K], **83**

SLEEP
SEE ALSO Bedtime stories
Cazet, Denys. *"I'm Not Sleepy"* [Pre-K], **80**
Gordon, Jeffie Ross. *Six Sleepy Sheep* [Pre-K], **111**
Hennessy, B. G. *Sleep Tight* [Pre], **21**
Himmelman, John. *Lights Out!* [1-2], **453**
Howard, Jane R. *When I'm Sleepy* [Pre-K], 141
Johnston, Johanna. *Edie Changes Her Mind* [Pre-K], 155
Kandoian, Ellen. *Under the Sun* [K-1], 445
Keats, Ezra Jack. *Dreams* [K-1], 448
Kennaway, Mwalimu. *Awful Aardvark* [Pre-K], **144**
Koide, Tan. *May We Sleep Here Tonight?* [Pre-K], 172
Kraus, Robert. *Milton the Early Riser* [Pre-K], 174
Lemieux, Michele. *What's That Noise* [Pre-K], 184
Lewison, Wendy Cheyette. *Going to Sleep on the Farm* [Pre], **28**
Murphy, Jill. *Peace at Last* [Pre-K], 214
Sharmat, Marjorie Weinman. *Go to Sleep, Nicholas Joe* [Pre-K], 263
Steig, William. *Zeke Pippin* [2-3], **678**
Stevenson, James. *What's Under My Bed?* [1-2], 826
Wood, Audrey. *The Napping House* [Pre-K], 301

SLEEP–Folklore
Day, David. *The Sleeper* [2-4], **891**
Garland, Sherry. *Why Ducks Sleep on One Leg* [1-4], **909**
Grimm, Jacob. *The Sleeping Beauty* [2-5], 1505
Thorn Rose: or, The Sleeping Beauty [1-4], 1508

SLEEP–Poetry
Prelutsky, Jack. *My Parents Think I'm Sleeping* [Pre-3], 1910

SNAILS

King-Smith, Dick. *Sophie's Snail* [1-2], 711
Marshall, James. *The Guest* [Pre-K], 203
Ryder, Joanne. *The Snail's Spell* [Pre-K], 249

SNAILS–Folklore

Wolkstein, Diane. *White Wave: A Chinese Tale* [2-6], 1631

SNAKES

SEE ALSO Reptiles

Asch, Frank. *Pearl's Promise* [3-4], **701**
Bodsworth, Nan. *A Nice Walk in the Jungle* [K-1], **233**
Byars, Betsy. *The Moon and I* [4-6], **1115**
Clifford, Eth. *Harvey's Horrible Snake Disaster* [3-4], 1052
Gray, Libba Moore. *Small Green Snake* [Pre-K], **113**
Johnston, Tony. *Slither McCreep and His Brother Joe* [K-1], **294**
Kastner, Jill. *Snake Hunt* [1-2], **465**
Kipling, Rudyard. *The Elephant's Child* [2-3], 946
Rikki-Tikki-Tavi [3-4], **729**
Kline, Suzy. *Mary Marony and the Snake* [1-2], **475**
Kudrna, C. Imbior. *To Bathe a Boa* [K-1], 463
Leydenfrost, Robert. *The Snake That Sneezed* [Pre-K], 188
McNulty, Faith. *A Snake in the House* [1-2], **500**
Maestro, Betsy. *Take a Look at Snakes* [1-4], **1198**
Moore, Lilian. *The Snake That Went to School* [2-3], 968
Noble, Trinka Hakes. *The Day Jimmy's Boa Ate the Wash* [1-2], 761
Rounds, Glen. *Mr. Yowder and the Train Robbers* [4-5], 1232
Ungerer, Tomi. *Crictor* [K-1], 573
Walsh, Ellen Stoll. *Mouse Count* [Pre], **54**

SNAKES–Folklore

Aardema, Verna. *What's So Funny, Ketu?* [1-4], 1384
Ata, Te. *Baby Rattlesnake* [Pre-1], **862**
Czernecki, Stefan, and Timothy Rhodes. *The Singing Snake* [K-2], **889**
Steptoe, John. *Mufaro's Beautiful Daughters: An African Tale* [1-4], 1607

SNAKES–Riddles

Burns, Diane L. *Snakes Alive! Jokes about Snakes* [1-4], 1763
Hall, Katy, and Lisa Eisenberg. *Snakey Riddles* [1-4], **1305**

SNOW

SEE ALSO Rain and rainfall; Storms; Weather; Winter

Brett, Jan. *Trouble with Trolls* [K-1], **236**
Burton, Virgina Lee. *Katy and the Big Snow* [Pre-K], 35
Calhoun, Mary. *Cross-Country Cat* [1-2], 635
The Night the Monster Came [2-3], 880
Chapman, Cheryl. *Snow on Snow on Snow* [Pre-K], **83**
Fleming, Susan. *Trapped on the Golden Flyer* [4-5], 1173
Keats, Ezra Jack. *The Snowy Day* [Pre-K], 165
Lindgren, Astrid. *The Tomten* [1-2], 725
London, Jonathan. *Froggy Gets Dressed* [Pre-K], **152**
Moskin, Marietta. *The Day of the Blizzard* [3-4], 1098
Nietzel, Shirley. *The Jacket I Wear in the Snow* [Pre-K], 217
Noble, Trinka Hakes. *Apple Tree Christmas* [2-3], 973
Rand, Gloria. *Salty Takes Off* [1-2], **540**
Sauer, Julie L. *Mike's House* [Pre-K], 252
Simon, Seymour. *Icebergs and Glaciers* [3-5], 2103
Slobodkin, Florence. *Too Many Mittens* [Pre-K], 268
Steig, William. *Brave Irene* [1-2], 820
Taylor, Mark. *Henry the Explorer* [K-1], 564
Ziefert, Harriet. *Snow Magic* [Pre-K], 306
Ziegler, Jack. *Mr. Knocky* [1-2], **582**
Zolotow, Charlotte. *Something Is Going to Happen* [Pre-K], 311

SNOW–Folklore

San Souci, Robert D. *The Snow Wife* [3-5], **1015**

SNOW–Poetry

Prelutsky, Jack. *It's Snowing! It's Snowing!* [Pre-3], 1907
Service, Robert W. *The Cremation of Sam McGee* [5-6], 1355

SOCCER

Foreman, Michael. *War Game* [5-6], **816**

SOCIAL ACTION

Cherry, Lynne. *A River Ran Wild: An Environmental History* [1-4], **1117**
Cone, Molly. *Come Back, Salmon: How a Group of Dedicated Kids Adopted Pigeon Creek and Brought It Back to Life* [4-6], **1125**
Hoose, Phillip. *It's Our World, Too! Stories of Young People Who Are Making a Difference* [5-6], **1163**

SOCIAL ACTION (cont.)

Shelby, Anne. *What to Do About Pollution* [Pre-2], **1236**

SOLAR SYSTEM

SEE Astronomy; Stars; Sun

SOLDIERS

Andersen, Hans Christian. *The Steadfast Tin Soldier* [2-3], **586**

McGovern, Ann. *The Secret Soldier: The Story of Deborah Sampson* [3-6], 2071

Rabin, Staton. *Casey Over There* [2-3], **666**

SOLDIERS–Folklore

Brown, Marcia. *Stone Soup* [1-4], 1412

Grimm, Jacob. *The Bearskinner* [2-4], 1486

Hutton, Warwick. *The Nose Tree* [2-5], 1533

McCurdy, Michael. *The Devils Who Learned to Be Good* [K-3], 1549

Reuter, Bjarne. *The Princess and the Sun, Moon and Stars* [1-4], 1585

SOLITUDE–Poetry

Huck, Charlotte. *Secret Places* [1-4], **1330**

SONGBOOKS

SEE ALSO Music; Songs; Stories with songs

Fox, Dan. *Go In and Out the Window: An Illustrated Songbook for Young People* [Pre-6], 1801

Garson, Eugenia. *The Laura Ingalls Wilder Songbook* [2-5], 1802

Glazer, Tom. *Eye Winker, Tom Tinker, Chin Chopper: Fifty Musical Fingerplays* [Pre-2], 1804

Tom Glazer's Treasury of Songs for Children [Pre-6], 1805

Hart, Jane. *Singing Bee! A Collection of Favorite Children's Songs* [K-2], 1810

Hoban, Russell. *Egg Thoughts and Other Frances Songs* [K-2], 1813

John, Timothy. *The Great Song Book* [Pre-5], 1832

Krull, Kathleen. *Gonna Sing My Head Off! American Folk Songs for Children* [K-5], **1344**

Langstaff, Nancy, and John Langstaff. *Jim Along Josie: A Collection of Folk Songs* [Pre-2], 1850

Mattox, Cheryl. *Shake It to the One That You Love the Best: Play Songs and Lullabies from Black Musical Traditions* [Pre-2], **1371**

Mother Goose. *Songs from Mother Goose: With the Traditional Melody for Each* [Pre-2], 1890

Nelson, Esther L. *The Funny Song Book* [Pre-6], 1894

Quackenbush, Robert. *The Holiday Songbook* [Pre-5], 1925

Raffi. *The Raffi Singable Songbook: A Collection of 51 Songs from Raffi's First Three Records for Young Children* [Pre-2], 1926

Seeger, Ruth Crawford. *American Folk Songs for Children* [Pre-4], 1951

Weiss, Nicki. *If You're Happy and You Know It: Eighteen Story Songs Set to Pictures* [Pre-2], 1973

Winn, Marie. *The Fireside Book of Fun and Game Songs* [Pre-6], 1976

Yolen, Jane. *The Fireside Song Book of Birds and Beasts* [Pre-6], 1980

SONGS

SEE ALSO Music; Songbooks; Stories with songs

Bates, Katharine Lee. *America the Beautiful* [Pre-6], **1265**

Brett, Jan. *The Twelve Days of Christmas* [Pre-6], 1755

Brown, Marc. *Hand Rhymes* [Pre-2], 1760

Carle, Eric. *Today Is Monday* [K-1], **248**

Cauley, Lorinda Bryan. *The Three Little Kittens* [Pre-K], 45

Child, Lydia Maria. *Over the River and Through the Wood: A Song for Thanksgiving* [K-1], **251**

Cole, Joanna, and Stephanie Calmenson. *The Eentsy, Weentsy Spider: Fingerplays and Action Rhymes* [Pre-2], **1279**

Duke, Kate. *Seven Froggies Went to School* [K-1], 377

Galdone, Paul. *Over in the Meadow: An Old Nursery Counting Rhyme* [Pre-K], 108

Glazer, Tom. *On Top of Spaghetti* [1-2], 679

Greene, Carol. *The Thirteen Days of Halloween* [1-2], 681

Guthrie, Woody, and Marjorie Mazia Guthrie. *Woody's 20 Grow Big Songs* [Pre-2], **1303**

Ivimey, John W. *The Complete Story of the Three Blind Mice* [Pre-K], 151

Complete Version of Ye Three Blind Mice [Pre-K], 152

Three Blind Mice: The Classic Nursery Rhyme [Pre-K], **131**

Jones, Carol. *Old MacDonald Had a Farm* [Pre-K], 157

This Old Man [Pre-K], **137**

Karas, G. Brian. *I Know an Old Lady* [K-1], **295**

King, Bob. *Sitting on the Farm* [Pre-K], **145**

Kovalski, Maryann. *The Wheels on the Bus* [Pre-K], 173

Lamont, Priscilla. *Ring-a-Round-a-Rosy: Nursery Rhymes, Action Rhymes and Lullabies* [Pre-1], **1345**

Langstaff, John. *Frog Went a-Courtin'* [Pre-K], 179

Over in the Meadow [Pre-K], 180

Leventhal, Debra. *What Is Your Language?* [Pre-K], **150**

Manushkin, Fran. *My Christmas Safari* [K-1], **320**

Mendoza, George. *A Wart Snake in a Fig Tree* [2-3], 963

Moss, Marissa. *Knick Knack Paddywack* [K-1], **327**

Mother Goose. *Jane Yolen's Mother Goose Songbook* [Pre-2], **1380**

The Mother Goose Songbook [Pre-2], **1387**

Niland, Kilmeny. *A Bellbird in a Flame Tree* [1-2], **518**

Norworth, Jack. *Take Me Out to the Ballgame* [1-2], **521**

O'Donnell, Elizabeth Lee. *The Twelve Days of Summer* [1-2], **523**

Parkinson, Kathy. *The Farmer in the Dell* [Pre-K], 223

Pearson, Tracey Campbell. *Old MacDonald Had a Farm* [Pre-K], 226

Peek, Merle. *Mary Wore Her Red Dress and Henry Wore His Green Sneakers* [Pre-K], 227

Rae, Mary Maki. *The Farmer in the Dell: A Singing Game* [Pre-K], 234

Raffi. *Down by the Bay* [1-2], 780

Five Little Ducks [Pre], **39**

The Raffi Christmas Treasury [Pre-2], **1400**

Spider on the Floor [K-1], **348**

Wheels on the Bus [Pre-K], 235

Rayner, Mary. *Ten Pink Piglets: Garth Pig's Wall Song* [Pre-K], **179**

Regan, Dian Curtis. *The Thirteen Hours of Halloween* [1-2], **544**

Rounds, Glen. *I Know an Old Lady Who Swallowed a Fly* [K-1], 537

Schwartz, Alvin. *And the Green Grass Grew All Around: Folk Poetry from Everyone* [2-6], **1407**

Slavin, Bill. *The Cat Came Back* [1-2], **555**

Sweet, Melissa. *Fiddle-I-Fee: A Farmyard Song for the Very Young* [Pre-K], **190**

Trivas, Irene. *Emma's Christmas* [2-3], **687**

Westcott, Nadine Bernard. *I Know an Old Lady Who Swallowed a Fly* [K-1], 588

Skip to My Lou [Pre-K], 292

Zelinsky, Paul O. *The Wheels on the Bus* [Pre-K], **214**

Zemach, Harve. *Mommy, Buy Me a China Doll* [Pre-K], 305

SONGS–Folklore

Aardema, Verna. *Bimwili and the Zimwi* [K-2], 1379

Wolkstein, Diane. *The Magic Orange Tree and Other Haitian Folktales* [2-6], 1737

SORCERERS

SEE Magicians; Wizards

SOUND

Showers, Paul. *The Listening Walk* [Pre-K], **187**

SOUND EFFECTS

Aliki. *At Mary Bloom's* [Pre-K], 4

Allen, Pamela. *Bertie and the Bear* [Pre-K], 7

Benjamin, Alan. *Rat-a-Tat, Pitter Pat* [Pre-K], 22

Bennett, David. *One Cow Moo Moo!* [Pre], **5**

Blake, Quentin. *All Join In* [Pre-2], **1270**

Burningham, John. *Mr. Gumpy's Outing* [Pre-K], 33

Carle, Eric. *The Very Busy Spider* [Pre-2], 41

The Very Quiet Cricket [Pre-K], **75**

Carlson, Bernice Wells. *Listen! And Help Tell the Story* [Pre-K], 1765

Carroll, Kathleen Sullivan. *One Red Rooster* [Pre], **7**

Cauley, Lorinda Bryan. *Old MacDonald Had a Farm* [Pre-K], **78**

Causley, Charles. *"Quack!" Said the Billy-Goat* [Pre-K], 46

Clarke, Gus. *EIEIO: The Story of Old MacDonald, Who Had a Farm* [Pre-K], **86**

Cuyler, Margery. *That's Good! That's Bad!* [Pre-K], **92**

De Zutter, Hank. *Who Says a Dog Goes Bow-Wow?* [Pre-2], **1131**

Dodds, Dayle Ann. *Do Bunnies Talk?* [K-1], **262**

Wheel Away! [Pre-K], 71

Duffy, Dee Dee. *Barnyard Tracks* [Pre], **10**

Flack, Marjorie. *Angus and the Ducks* [Pre-K], 85

Angus Lost [Pre-K], 86

Fleming, Denise. *Barnyard Banter* [Pre], **12**

Forrester, Victoria. *The Magnificent Moo* [Pre-K], 89

Fox, Mem. *Hattie and the Fox* [Pre-K], 91

Freeman, Don. *Quiet! There's a Canary in the Library* [Pre-K], 96

Gaeddert, Lou Ann. *Noisy Nancy Norris* [Pre-K], 102

Goodsell, Jane. *Toby's Toe* [K-1], 407

Gray, Libba Moore. *Small Green Snake* [Pre-K], **113**

Hellen, Nancy. *Old MacDonald Had a Farm* [Pre], **20**

Hutchins, Pat. *Good-Night, Owl* [Pre-K], 148

Jones, Carol. *Old MacDonald Had a Farm* [Pre-K], 157

SOUND EFFECTS (cont.)

Jones, Maurice. *I'm Going on a Dragon Hunt* [Pre-K], 158

Jorgensen, Gail. *Crocodile Beat* [Pre-K], 159

Kennaway, Mwalimu. *Awful Aardvark* [Pre-K], **144**

Kimmel, Eric A. *Charlie Drives the Stage* [2-3], 943

Koide, Tan. *May We Sleep Here Tonight?* [Pre-K], 172

Lester, Helen. *Cora Copycat* [K-1], 468

London, Jonathan. *Froggy Gets Dressed* [Pre-K], **152**

Let's Go, Froggy [Pre-K], **153**

Lyon, David. *The Biggest Truck* [Pre-K], 193

McGovern, Ann. *Too Much Noise* [Pre-2], 1556

Martin, Bill, Jr. *Polar Bear, Polar Bear, What Do You Hear?* [Pre-K], **160**

Modell, Frank. *Goodbye Old Year, Hello New Year* [K-1], 509

Mora, Pat. *Listen to the Desert / Oye al Desierto* [Pre-2], **1209**

Murphy, Jill. *Peace at Last* [Pre-K], 214

Myller, Rolf. *A Very Noisy Day* [1-2], 755

Pearson, Tracey Campbell. *Old MacDonald Had a Farm* [Pre-K], 226

Preston, Edna Mitchell. *Squawk to the Moon, Little Goose* [Pre-K], 233

Robinson, Marc. *Cock-a-Doodle-Doo! What Does It Sound Like to You?* [Pre-2], **1226**

Rounds, Glen. *Old MacDonald Had a Farm* [Pre-K], **182**

Rowe, John A. *Baby Crow* [Pre-K], **183**

Segal, Lore. *All the Way Home* [Pre-K], 253

Shapiro, Arnold L. *Who Says That?* [Pre], **43**

Sheppard, Jeff. *Splash, Splash* [Pre], **44**

Showers, Paul. *The Listening Walk* [Pre-K], **187**

Sivulich, Sandra Stroner. *I'm Going on a Bear Hunt* [Pre-K], 267

Stevenson, James. *Clams Can't Sing* [K-1], 560

That Terrible Halloween Night [1-2], 824

There's Nothing to Do! [1-2], 825

Yuck! [K-1], 562

Thomas, Patricia. *The One and Only Super-Duper Golly-Whopper Jim-Dandy Really-Handy Clock-Tock-Stopper* [1-2], **566**

Waddell, Martin. *The Happy Hedgehog Band* [Pre], **48**

The Pig in the Pond [Pre], **50**

Squeak-a-Lot [Pre], **52**

Whybrow, Ian. *Quacky Quack-Quack!* [Pre], **56**

Williams, Linda. *The Little Old Lady Who Was Not Afraid of Anything* [K-1], 591

Zimmerman, Andrea, and David Clemesha. *The Cow Buzzed* [Pre-K], **215**

SOUND EFFECTS–Folklore

Mathews, Judith, and Fay Robinson. *Nathaniel Willy, Scared Silly* [Pre-2], **984**

Roddy, Patricia. *Api and the Boy Stranger: A Village Creation Tale* [K-2], **1006**

Simms, Laura. *The Squeaky Door* [Pre-2], **1026**

SOUND EFFECTS–Poetry

O'Neill, Mary L. *What Is That Sound!* [2-5], 1898

SOUP

SEE ALSO Cookery; Food; Vegetables

Cushman, Doug. *Possum Stew* [Pre-K], **91**

DiSalvo-Ryan, DyAnne. *Uncle Willie and the Soup Kitchen* [1-2], **432**

Ehlert, Lois. *Growing Vegetable Soup* [Pre-K], 78

Everitt, Betsy. *Mean Soup* [Pre-K], **101**

Modesitt, Jeanne. *Vegetable Soup* [Pre-K], **170**

Patron, Susan. *Burgoo Stew* [1-2], **527**

SOUP–Folklore

Brown, Marcia. *Stone Soup* [1-4], 1412

McGovern, Ann. *Stone Soup* [Pre-2], 1555

Stewig, John Warren. *Stone Soup* [K-3], **1031**

Temple, Frances. *Tiger Soup: An Anansi Story from Jamaica* [Pre-2], **1034**

Zemach, Harve. *Nail Soup: A Swedish Folk Tale* [1-4], 1636

SPACE

SEE Astronomy; Moon; Space flight; Stars; Sun

SPACE AND TIME

SEE ALSO Time travel

Greer, Gery, and Bob Ruddick. *Max and Me and the Time Machine* [5-6], 1306

Max and Me and the Wild West [5-6], 1307

Hahn, Mary Downing. *Time for Andrew: A Ghost Story* [5-6], **820**

Hurmence, Belinda. *A Girl Called Boy* [5-6], 1314

L'Engle, Madeleine. *A Wrinkle in Time* [5-6], 1325

McMurtry, Stan. *The Bunjee Venture* [4-5], 1210

Pearce, Philippa. *Tom's Midnight Garden* [5-6], 1342

Rodda, Emily. *Finders Keepers* [4-5], **789**

Sadler, Marilyn. *Alistair's Time Machine* [1-2], 789

Sauer, Julie L. *Fog Magic* [5-6], 1353

Slepian, Jan. *Back to Before* [5-6], **843**

Tannen, Mary. *The Wizard Children of Finn* [5-6], 1367

Thomas, Jane Resh. *The Princess in the Pigpen* [5-6], 1369

Williams, Jay, and Raymond Abrashkin. *Danny Dunn, Time Traveler* [4-5], 1256

Wiseman, David. *Jeremy Visick* [5-6], 1375

Woodruff, Elvira. *George Washington's Socks* [4-5], **798**

SPACE FLIGHT

SEE ALSO Astronomy; Moon; Stars; Sun

Beatty, Jerome. *Matthew Looney's Invasion of the Earth* [4-5], 1142

Corbett, Scott. *The Donkey Planet* [4-5], 1163

Fraser, Mary Ann. *One Giant Leap* [4-6], **1142**

Harding, Lee. *The Fallen Spaceman* [3-4], 1070

Keats, Ezra Jack. *Regards to the Man in the Moon* [1-2], 703

Moss, Marissa. *Knick Knack Paddywack* [K-1], **327**

Pinkwater, Daniel. *Guys from Space* [K-1], 522

Ride, Sally, and Susan Okie. *To Space and Back* [3-6], 2086

Sadler, Marilyn. *Alistair and the Alien Invasion* [K-1], **356**

Alistair in Outer Space [1-2], 787

Slote, Alfred. *My Trip to Alpha I* [3-4], 1114

Teague, Mark. *Moog-Moog, Space Barber* [1-2], **563**

SPAIN

Kimmel, Eric A. *Bernal & Florinda: A Spanish Tale* [3-4], 720

SPANISH LANGUAGE

Dorros, Arthur. *Abuela* [1-2], **434**

Ehlert, Lois. *Moon Rope: Un Lazo a la Luna: A Peruvian Folktale* [Pre-2], **902**

Gonzalez, Lucie M. *The Bossy Gallito: A Traditional Cuban Folktale* [K-2], **917**

Lomas Garza, Carmen. *Family Pictures / Cuadros de Familia* [1-4], **1192**

McMillan, Bruce. *Sense Suspense: A Guessing Game for the Five Senses* [Pre-K], **159**

Mora, Pat. *Listen to the Desert / Oye al Desierto* [Pre-2], **1209**

Pitre, Felix. *Juan Bobo and the Pig: A Puerto Rican Folktale* [K-2], **998**

SPANISH LANGUAGE–Folklore

Baden, Robert. *And Sunday Makes Seven* [2-4], **864**

SPEECH

Meddaugh, Susan. *Martha Speaks* [1-2], **506**

SPEECH IMPAIRMENT

Kline, Suzy. *Mary Marony and the Snake* [1-2], **475**

SPIDERS

Cameron, Polly. *"I Can't," Said the Ant* [1-2], 636

Carle, Eric. *The Very Busy Spider* [Pre-K], 41

Kraus, Robert. *How Spider Saved Christmas* [K-1], 459

Raffi. *Spider on the Floor* [K-1], **348**

Trapani, Iza. *The Itsy Bitsy Spider* [Pre-K], **193**

White, E. B. *Charlotte's Web* [2-3], 1027

SPIDERS–Folklore

Appiah, Peggy. *Tales of an Ashanti Father* [3-6], 1653

Arkhurst, Joyce Cooper. *The Adventures of Spider: West African Folktales* [1-4], 1654

Climo, Shirley. *Someone Saw a Spider: Spider Facts and Folktales* [3-6], 1664

Courlander, Harold. *The Hat-Shaking Dance: And Other Tales from the Gold Coast* [2-6], 1668

Courlander, Harold, and George Herzog. *The Cow-Tail Switch and Other West African Stories* [2-6], 1670

Kimmel, Eric A. *Anansi and the Moss-Covered Rock* [Pre-2], 1541

Anansi and the Talking Melon [Pre-2], **949**

Anansi Goes Fishing [Pre-2], **950**

McDermott, Gerald. *Anansi the Spider: A Tale from the Ashanti* [Pre-3], 1550

SPIES

SEE ALSO Mystery and detective stories

Reit, Seymour. *Behind Rebel Lines: The Incredible Story of Emma Edmonds, Civil War Spy* [5-6], 2085

Wilson, Gahan. *Harry the Fat Bear Spy* [3-4], 1133

SPINA BIFIDA

Springer, Nancy. *Colt* [4-5], **792**

SPORTS

SEE Baseball; Football; Soccer; Sports–Biography; Sports–Poetry

SPORTS–Biography

Littlefield, Bill. *Champions: Stories of Ten Remarkable Athletes* [5-6], **1188**

SPORTS–Poetry

Hopkins, Lee Bennett. *Extra Innings: Baseball Poems* [4-6], **1318**

Morrison, Lillian. *At the Crack of the Bat: Baseball Poems* [4-6], **1376**

SPORTS–Riddles

Rosenbloom, Joseph. *The World's Best Sports Riddles and Jokes* [2-6], 1939

SPRING

SEE ALSO Seasons

Alexander, Sue. *There's More . . . Much More* [Pre-K], 3

Clifton, Lucille. *The Boy Who Didn't Believe in Spring* [1-2], 650

Emberley, Michael. *Welcome Back Sun* [1-2], **438**

Johnson, Crockett. *Will Spring Be Early? or Will Spring Be Late?* [K-1], 439

Kinsey-Warnock, Natalie. *When Spring Comes* [1-2], **469**

Minarik, Else Holmelund. *It's Spring!* [Pre-K], 213

Roberts, Bethany. *Waiting-for-Spring Stories* [K-1], 531

SPRING–Folklore

Wolkstein, Diane. *The Magic Wings: A Tale from China* [Pre-4], 1630

SQUIRRELS

Brown, Eileen. *Tick-Tock* [K-1], **238**

Drummond, V. H. *Phewtus the Squirrel* [Pre-K], 74

Ernst, Lisa Campbell. *Squirrel Park* [1-2], **440**

Kalan, Robert. *Stop, Thief!* [Pre-K], **138**

Kesey, Ken. *Little Tricker the Squirrel Meets Big Double the Bear* [2-3], **634**

Lisle, Janet Taylor. *Forest* [5-6], **827**

Shannon, George. *The Surprise* [Pre-K], 262

STARS

SEE ALSO Astronomy; Moon; Space flight; Sun

Hort, Lenny. *How Many Stars in the Sky?* [K-1], **288**

Moeri, Louise. *Star Mother's Youngest Child* [3-4], 1097

Sachs, Marilyn. *Matt's Mitt and Fleet-Footed Florence* [2-3], 990

Simon, Seymour. *Stars* [3-6], 2104

STARS–Folklore

Esbensen, Barbara Juster. *The Star Maiden: An Ojibway Tale* [2-5], 1451

Goble, Paul. *Her Seven Brothers* [3-6], 1482

Taylor, Harriet Peck. *Coyote Places the Stars* [1-3], **1033**

STATUE OF LIBERTY

Stevens, Carla. *Lily and Miss Liberty* [2-3], **679**

Zimelman, Nathan. *How the Second Grade Got $8,205.50 to Visit the Statue of Liberty* [1-2], **583**

STEALING

SEE ALSO Honesty

Bunting, Eve. *Summer Wheels* [2-3], **594**

Devlin, Harry, and Wende Devlin. *Cranberry Thanksgiving* [1-2], 660

King-Smith, Dick. *The Cuckoo Child* [3-4], **722**

Kroll, Steven. *Amanda and Giggling Ghost* [1-2], 715

Shyer, Marlene Fanta. *My Brother, the Thief* [5-6], 1356

Stroud, Virginia A. *Doesn't Fall Off His Horse* [2-3], **680**

STEPFAMILIES

Leach, Norman. *My Wicked Stepmother* [K-1], **302**

Lindbergh, Anne. *Travel Far, Pay No Fare* [5-6], **826**

Springer, Nancy. *Colt* [4-5], **792**

Woodruff, Elvira. *The Magnificent Mummy Maker* [4-5], **799**

STEPMOTHERS–Folklore

Climo, Shirley. *The Korean Cinderella* [1-4], **878**

Onyefulu, Obi. *Chinye: A West African Folk Tale* [K-3], **995**

Wilson, Barbara Ker. *Wishbones: A Folk Tale from China* [2-4], **1043**

Winthrop, Elizabeth. *Vasilissa the Beautiful: A Russian Folktale* [2-5], **1044**

STEPPARENTS

SEE Stepfamilies

STORES

SEE Shopping; Supermarkets

STORIES IN RHYME

SEE ALSO Narrative poetry; Poetry–Single author

Aardema, Verna. *Bringing the Rain to Kapiti Plain* [Pre-2], 1380

Aesop. *Aesop's Fables* [3-6], 1646

Belling the Cat and Other Aesop's Fables: Retold in Verse [3-6], **1056**

Alborough, Jez. *It's the Bear!* [Pre-K], **63**

Where's My Teddy? [Pre], **2**

Allen, Marjorie N., and Shelley Rotner. *Changes* [Pre-1], **1100**

Anholt, Catherine, and Laurence Anholt. *All About You* [Pre], **3**

Kids [Pre-K], **64**

What Makes Me Happy? [Pre-K], **65**

Aylesworth, Jim. *My Son John* [K-1], **222**

Old Black Fly [K-1], **223**

One Crow: A Counting Rhyme [Pre-K], 17

Baer, Edith. *This Is the Way We Go to School: A Book About Children Around the World* [K-1], **226**

Words are Like Faces [K-1], 324

Baker, Keith. *Big Fat Hen* [Pre], **4**

Barracca, Debra, and Sal Barracca. *The Adventures of Taxi Dog* [1-2], **404**

A Taxi Dog Christmas [K-1], **229**

Barrett, Judi. *Pickles Have Pimples: And Other Silly Statements* [1-2], 611

Baylor, Byrd. *Amigo* [1-2], 613

Behn, Harry. *Trees* [1-2], **406**

Bemelmans, Ludwig. *Madeline's Rescue* [K-1], 335

Brenner, Barbara. *Mr. Tall and Mr. Small* [K-1], 343

Brown, Paula. *Moon Jump: A Countdown* [K-1], **240**

Bunting, Eve. *Flower Garden* [Pre-K], **72**

Scary, Scary Halloween [K-1], 352

Calmenson, Stephanie. *Dinner at the Panda Palace* [Pre-K], **73**

It Begins with an A [Pre-K], **74**

Cameron, Polly. *"I Can't," Said the Ant* [1-2], 636

Carlstrom, Nancy White. *How Do You Say It Today, Jesse Bear?* [Pre-K], **76**

Carroll, Kathleen Sullivan. *One Red Rooster* [Pre], **7**

Carryl, Charles E. *The Walloping Window-Blind* [2-3], **596**

Cauley, Lorinda Bryan. *The Three Little Kittens* [Pre-K], 45

Treasure Hunt [Pre-K], **79**

Causley, Charles. *"Quack!" Said the Billy-Goat* [Pre-K], 46

Chapman, Cheryl. *Pass the Fritters, Critters* [Pre-K], **82**

Cherry, Lynne. *The Armadillo from Amarillo* [1-2], **423**

Who's Sick Today? [Pre-K], 47

Christelow, Eileen. *Five Little Monkeys Sitting in a Tree* [Pre-K], **85**

Cole, William. *Frances Face-Maker: A Going to Bed Book* [Pre-K], 53

Coleridge, Sara. *January Brings the Snow: A Book of Months* [Pre-K], 54

Coletta, Irene, and Hallie Coletta. *From A to Z: The Collected Letters of Irene and Hallie Coletta* [2-3], 897

Cooper, Melrose. *I Got a Family* [K-1], **255**

Crews, Donald. *Ten Black Dots* [Pre-K], 59

Cummings, Phil. *Goodness Gracious!* [Pre-K], **90**

Cushman, Doug. *The ABC Mystery* [1-2], **428**

Degen, Bruce. *Jamberry* [Pre-K], 64

dePaola, Tomie. *The Comic Adventures of Old Mother Hubbard and Her Dog* [Pre-1], 1438

De Regniers, Beatrice Schenk. *May I Bring a Friend?* [Pre-K], 69

Dodds, Dayle Ann. *Do Bunnies Talk?* [K-1], **262**

Wheel Away! [Pre-K], 71

Donaldson, Julia. *A Squash and a Squeeze* [K-1], **264**

Ehlert, Lois. *Feathers for Lunch* [K-1], **265**

Eichenberg, Fritz. *Ape in a Cape: An Alphabet of Odd Animals* [Pre-K], 79

Dancing in the Moon [K-1], 380

Emberley, Barbara. *Drummer Hoff* [Pre-K], 80

Emberley, Ed. *The Wing on a Flea* [Pre-K], 81

Evans, Katie. *Hunky Dory Ate It* [Pre-K], **100**

Falwell, Cathryn. *Feast for 10* [Pre], **11**

Field, Eugene. *The Gingham Dog and the Calico Cat* [Pre-K], **103**

Fleming, Denise. *Barnyard Banter* [Pre], **12**

In the Small, Small Pond [Pre-K], **104**

Fox, Mem. *Shoes from Grandpa* [Pre-K], **105**

Gag, Wanda. *Millions of Cats* [Pre-K], 104

Galdone, Joanna, and Paul Galdone. *Gertrude the Goose Who Forgot* [Pre-K], 107

Galdone, Paul. *The History of Mother Twaddle and the Marvelous Achievements of Her Son, Jack* [K-3], 1462

Old Mother Hubbard and Her Dog [Pre-1], 1468

Over in the Meadow: An Old Nursery Counting Rhyme [Pre-K], 108

Gelman, Rita Golden. *I Went to the Zoo* [K-1], **275**

Gerrard, Roy. *Rosie and the Rustlers* [2-3], **610**

Sir Francis Drake: His Daring Deeds [4-6], 2038

Goodspeed, Peter. *A Rhinoceros Wakes Me Up in the Morning* [Pre-K], 116

Grossman, Bill. *Tommy at the Grocery Store* [K-1], 414

Guarino, Deborah. *Is Your Mama a Llama?* [Pre-K], 123

Hale, Sarah Josepha Buell. *Mary Had a Little Lamb* [Pre-K], **116**, **117**, 127

Hamanaka, Sheila. *All the Colors of the Earth* [1-2], **449**

Harrison, David L. *When Cows Come Home* [Pre-K], **118**

Hayes, Sarah. *This Is the Bear* [Pre-K], **128**

This Is the Bear and the Scary Night [Pre], **19**

Heller, Ruth. *Animals Born Alive and Well* [K-4], **1159**

Chickens Aren't the Only Ones [K-4], **1160**

Kites Sail High: A Book about Verbs [3-5], 1812

STORIES IN RHYME (cont.)

Merry-Go-Round: A Book About Nouns [1-6], **1310**

Up, Up and Away: A Book About Adverbs [2-6], **1311**

Hellsing, Lennart. *Old Mother Hubbard and Her Dog* [Pre-K], 130

Hennessy, B. G. *The Missing Tarts* [Pre-K], 133

Sleep Tight [Pre], **21**

Hoberman, Mary Ann. *A House Is a House for Me* [K-1], 431

Huff, Barbara A. *Once Inside the Library* [1-2], **459**

Hulme, Joy N. *Sea Squares* [2-3], **624**

Hutchins, Pat. *Don't Forget the Bacon!* [K-1], 434

The Tale of Thomas Mead [1-2], 697

Where's the Baby? [K-1], 435

Ivimey, John W. *The Complete Story of the Three Blind Mice* [Pre-K], 151

Complete Version of Ye Three Blind Mice [Pre-K], 152

Three Blind Mice: The Classic Nursery Rhyme [Pre-K], **131**

Karas, G. Brian. *I Know an Old Lady* [K-1], **295**

King, Bob. *Sitting on the Farm* [Pre-K], **145**

Kirk, Daniel. *Skateboard Monsters* [1-2], **472**

Knowles, Sheena. *Edward the Emu* [K-1], **300**

Komaiko, Leah. *Earl's Too Cool for Me* [1-2], **477**

Koontz, Robin Michal. *I See Something You Don't See: A Riddle-Me Picture Book* [K-1], **301**

Kudrna, C. Imbior. *To Bathe a Boa* [K-1], 463

Langstaff, John. *Frog Went a-Courtin'* [Pre-K], 179

Over in the Meadow [Pre-K], 180

Lear, Edward. *The Owl and the Pussycat* [Pre-K], **148**, **149**, 181

The Quangle Wangle's Hat [K-1], 466

Leedy, Loreen. *A Number of Dragons* [Pre-K], 182

LeSieg, Theo. *I Wish That I Had Duck Feet* [K-1], 467

Lewison, Wendy Cheyette. *Going to Sleep on the Farm* [Pre], **28**

Lindbergh, Reeve. *The Day the Goose Got Loose* [K-1], **306**

There's a Cow in the Road! [K-1], **307**

Lindgren, Barbro. *The Wild Baby* [K-1], 473

Livingston, Myra Cohn. *Higgledy-Piggledy: Verses & Pictures* [2-3], 953

Lobel, Arnold. *The Ice Cream Cone Coot and Other Rare Birds* [2-3], 954

The Rose in My Garden [K-1], 485

Longfellow, Henry Wadsworth. *Paul Revere's Ride* [2-6], **1361**

Paul Revere's Ride [4-6], 1863

Loomis, Christine. *In the Diner* [Pre-K], **154**

One Cow Coughs: A Counting Book for the Sick and Miserable [Pre-K], **155**

Lord, John Vernon, and Janet Burroway. *The Giant Jam Sandwich* [1-2], 730

MacDonald, Amy. *Rachel Fister's Blister* [K-1], **312**

McMillan, Bruce. *Play Day: A Book of Terse Verse* [Pre-1], **1365**

McPhail, David. *Pigs Aplenty, Pigs Galore!* [K-1], **317**

Mahy, Margaret. *17 Kings and 42 Elephants* [K-1], 500

Marshall, James. *Old Mother Hubbard and Her Wonderful Dog* [Pre-1], **980**

Martin, Bill, Jr. *The Happy Hippopotami* [K-1], **322**

Martin, Bill, Jr., and John Archambault. *Barn Dance!* [K-1], 505

Chicka Chicka Boom Boom [Pre-K], 205

Marzollo, Jean. *In 1492* [K-3], **1204**

Pretend You're a Cat [Pre-K], **161**

Ten Cats Have Hats: A Counting Book [Pre-K], **162**

Medearis, Angela Shelf. *The Zebra-Riding Cowboy: A Folk Song from the Old West* [2-3], **645**

Minters, Frances. *Cinder-Elly* [1-2], **510**

Moore, Clement C. *The Night before Christmas* [1-2], 753

Morley, Diana. *Marms in the Marmalade* [1-4], 1876

Morrison, Bill. *Squeeze a Sneeze* [K-1], **326**

Moss, Lloyd. *Zin! Zin! Zin! A Violin* [1-2], **512**

Moss, Marissa. *Knick Knack Paddywack* [K-1], **327**

Nash, Ogden. *The Adventures of Isabel* [2-3], **649**

Nerlove, Miriam. *I Made a Mistake* [1-2], 756

Nietzel, Shirley. *The Jacket I Wear in the Snow* [Pre-K], 217

Nightingale, Sandy. *A Giraffe on the Moon* [Pre-K], **172**

Niland, Kilmeny. *A Bellbird in a Flame Tree* [1-2], **518**

Noll, Sally. *Jiggle Wiggle Prance* [K-1], 513

Numeroff, Laura J. *Dogs Don't Wear Sneakers* [K-1], **333**

O'Keefe, Susan Heyboer. *One Hungry Monster: A Counting Book in Rhyme* [Pre-K], **174**

Oppenheim, Joanne. *You Can't Catch Me!* [K-1], 516

Parkin, Rex. *The Red Carpet* [K-1], 519

Paxton, Tom. *Jennifer's Rabbit* [Pre-K], 224

Where's the Baby? [Pre], **38**

Peet, Bill. *Hubert's Hair-Raising Advenure* [1-2], 770

No Such Things [2-3], 978

Perkins, Al. *Hand, Hand, Fingers, Thumb* [Pre-K], 228

Pilkey, Dav. *'Twas the Night Before Thanksgiving* [1-2], **531**

Pinczes, Elinor J. *One Hundred Hungry Ants* [1-2], **533**

Prater, John. *"No!" Said Joe* [Pre-K], **177**

Prelutsky, Jack. *The Mean Old Mean Hyena* [2-3], 983

The Terrible Tiger [1-2], 778

Preston, Edna Mitchell. *Pop Corn & Ma Goodness* [K-1], 529

Raffi. *Down by the Bay* [1-2], 780

Reeves, Mona Rabun. *I Had a Cat* [Pre-K], 237

Riley, James Whitcomb. *The Gobble-Uns'll Git You Ef You Don't Watch Out* [3-4], 1108

Rogers, Paul. *The Shapes Game* [Pre-K], **181**

Rotner, Shelley, and Ken Kreisler. *Citybook* [K-1], **353**

Rounds, Glen. *I Know an Old Lady Who Swallowed a Fly* [K-1], 537

Samton, Sheila White. *Beside the Bay* [Pre-K], 250

Sendak, Maurice. *Chicken Soup with Rice* [K-1], 551

One Was Johnny: A Counting Book [Pre-K], 254

Pierre [K-1], 552

Serfozo, Mary. *Who Said Red?* [Pre-K], 256

Seuss, Dr. *The Cat in the Hat* [Pre-K], 258

Dr. Seuss' ABC [K-1], 553

Green Eggs and Ham [Pre-K], 259

Horton Hatches the Egg [1-2], 801

How the Grinch Stole Christmas [1-2], 802

If I Ran the Zoo [1-2], 803

The Lorax [2-3], 997

McElligot's Pool [1-2], 804

Marvin K. Mooney, Will You Please Go Now [K-1], 554

On Beyond Zebra [1-2], 805

Thidwick, the Big-Hearted Moose [1-2], 806

Shapiro, Arnold L. *Who Says That?* [Pre], **43**

Shaw, Nancy. *Sheep in a Jeep* [K-1], 556

Sheep in a Shop [K-1], **360**

Sheep Out to Eat [K-1], **361**

Sheppard, Jeff. *Splash, Splash* [Pre], **44**

Shute, Linda. *Halloween Party* [1-2], **551**

Siebert, Diane. *Plane Song* [1-2], **552**

Train Song [1-2], **553**

Truck Song [Pre-K], 266

Slavin, Bill. *The Cat Came Back* [1-2], **555**

Small, Terry. *The Legend of William Tell* [3-5], **1028**

Smath, Jerry. *A Hat So Simple* [K-1], **367**

Smith, William Jay. *Ho for a Hat!* [K-1], **368**

Stadler, John. *Cat Is Back at Bat* [K-1], **372**

Stevenson, Robert Louis. *Block City* [K-1], 563

My Shadow [K-1], **374**

Stickland, Henrietta. *Dinosaur Roar!* [Pre-K], **189**

Taylor, Livingston. *Can I Be Good?* [K-1], **375**

Thayer, Ernest Lawrence. *Casey at the Bat: A Ballad of the Republic, Sung in the Year 1888* [5-6], 1368

Thomas, Patricia. *The One and Only Super-Duper Golly-Whopper Jim-Dandy Really-Handy Clock-Tock-Stopper* [1-2], **566**

"Stand Back," Said the Elephant, "I'm Going to Sneeze!" [K-1], 568

Trapani, Iza. *The Itsy Bitsy Spider* [Pre-K], **193**

Turner, Gwenda. *Over on the Farm* [Pre-K], **195**

Van Laan, Nancy. *People, People, Everywhere!* [Pre-K], **196**

Viorst, Judith. *The Alphabet from Z to A: With Much Confusion on the Way* [3-6], **1416**

Voce, Louise. *Over in the Meadow: A Traditional Counting Rhyme* [Pre-K], **197**

Vozar, David. *Yo, Hungry Wolf! A Nursery Rap* [1-2], **570**

Wadsworth, Olive A. *Over in the Meadow: An Old Counting Rhyme* [Pre-K], **202**

Watson, Wendy. *Fox Went Out on a Chilly Night* [K-1], **382**

Weiss, Nicki. *An Egg Is an Egg* [Pre-K], **207**

Wells, Rosemary. *Shy Charles* [K-1], 586

Westcott, Nadine Bernard. *I Know an Old Lady Who Swallowed a Fly* [K-1], 588

The Lady with the Alligator Purse [Pre-K], 290

Skip to My Lou [Pre-K], 292

Williams, Sue. *I Went Walking* [Pre], **57**

Willis, Jeanne. *The Monster Bed* [K-1], 592

Winthrop, Elizabeth. *Shoes* [Pre-K], 300

Wise, William. *Ten Sly Piranhas: A Counting Story in Reverse (A Tale of Wickedness and Worse)* [1-2], **578**

Wood, Audrey. *Silly Sally* [Pre-K], **212**

Wright, Kit. *Tigerella* [K-1], **389**

Yee, Wong Herbert. *Big Black Bear* [Pre-K], **213**

Yektai, Niki. *Bears in Pairs* [Pre-K], 302

Young, Ruth. *Who Says Moo?* [Pre], **61**

Zelinsky, Paul O. *The Maid and the Mouse and the Odd-Shaped House* [1-2], 860

Zemach, Harve. *The Judge: An Untrue Tale* [2-3], 1037

STORIES TO TELL

Anderson, Leone Castell. *The Wonderful Shrinking Shirt* [1-2], 604

Ata, Te. *Baby Rattlesnake* [Pre-1], **862**

Aylesworth, Jim. *Hush Up!* [K-1], 323

Bauer, Caroline Feller. *Windy Day: Stories and Poems* [1-4], 1746

Baumgartner, Barbara. *Crocodile! Crocodile! Stories Told Around the World* [Pre-2], **1058**

Bennett, Jill. *Teeny Tiny* [Pre-2], 1403

Brown, Ruth A. *A Dark, Dark Tale* [K-1], 347

Cole, Joanna. *Golly Gump Swallowed a Fly* [K-1], 372

Flack, Marjorie. *Ask Mr. Bear* [Pre-K], 87

Forrester, Victoria. *The Magnificent Moo* [Pre-K], 89

Fox, Mem. *Hattie and the Fox* [Pre-K], 91

Freedman, Florence B. *It Happened in Chelm: A Story of the Legendary Town of Fools* [2-5], **905**

Gag, Wanda. *Millions of Cats* [Pre-K], 104

Galdone, Joanna. *The Tailypo: A Ghost Story* [2-4], 1456

Galdone, Paul. *The Teeny-Tiny Woman: A Ghost Story* [Pre-2], 1471

Johnson, Jane. *Today I Thought I'd Run Away* [Pre-K], 154

Jones, Maurice. *I'm Going on a Dragon Hunt* [Pre-K], 158

Kimmel, Eric A. *Anansi and the Moss-Covered Rock* [Pre-2], 1541

Little, Jean, and Maggie De Vries. *Once Upon a Golden Apple* [K-1], 478

Maestro, Giulio. *A Wise Monkey Tale* [K-1], 499

Martin, Bill, Jr. *Old Devil Wind* [K-1], **323**

Mendoza, George. *Gwot! Horribly Funny Hairticklers* [2-3], 962

Morgan, Pierr. *The Turnip: An Old Russian Folktale* [Pre-1], 1569

Munsch, Robert. *Pigs* [K-1], **330**

Patron, Susan. *Burgoo Stew* [1-2], **527**

Pinkwater, Daniel. *Tooth-Gnasher Superflash* [K-1], 523

Reddix, Valerie. *Millie and the Mud Hole* [Pre-K], **180**

Rosen, Michael. *We're Going on a Bear Hunt* [Pre-K], 245

Seeger, Pete. *Abiyoyo* [K-1], 548

Seeger, Pete, and Charles Seeger. *The Foolish Frog* [1-2], 797

Segal, Lore. *All the Way Home* [Pre-K], 253

Sherrow, Victoria. *There Goes the Ghost!* [K-1], 557

Shulevitz, Uri. *The Treasure* [2-3], 999

Shute, Linda. *Clever Tom and the Leprechaun* [Pre-3], 1599

Sivulich, Sandra Stroner. *I'm Going on a Bear Hunt* [Pre-K], 267

Van Laan, Nancy. *The Big Fat Worm* [Pre-K], 282

Vaughn, Marcia K. *Wombat Stew* [1-2], 836

Vipont, Elfrida. *The Elephant & the Bad Baby* [Pre-K], 283

Whybrow, Ian. *Quacky Quack-Quack!* [Pre], **56**

Williams, Linda. *The Little Old Lady Who Was Not Afraid of Anything* [K-1], 591

Withers, Carl. *I Saw a Rocket Walk a Mile: Nonsense Tales, Chants and Songs from Many Lands* [K-6], 1735

Tale of a Black Cat [1-2], 853

Wolkstein, Diane. *The Magic Wings: A Tale from China* [Pre-4], 1630

STORIES WITH SONGS

SEE ALSO Music; Songbooks; Songs

Harper, Wilhelmina. *The Gunniwolf* [Pre-1], 1519

Hoban, Russell. *A Baby Sister for Frances* [Pre-K], 137

Hurd, Thacher. *Mama Don't Allow* [K-1], 432

Kiser, Kevin. *Sherman the Sheep* [K-1], **299**

Kovalski, Maryann. *The Wheels on the Bus* [Pre-K], 173

McCloskey, Robert. *Lentil* [2-3], 956

San Souci, Robert D. *Sukey and the Mermaid* [2-5], **1017**

Seeger, Pete. *Abiyoyo* [K-1], 548

Seeger, Pete, and Charles Seeger. *The Foolish Frog* [1-2], 797

Shannon, George. *Lizard's Song* [Pre-K], 261

Vaughn, Marcia K. *Wombat Stew* [1-2], 836

Watson, Wendy. *Fox Went Out on a Chilly Night* [K-1], **382**

Winter, Jeanette. *Follow the Drinking Gourd* [3-4], 1134

Zelinsky, Paul O. *The Wheels on the Bus* [Pre-K], **214**

STORIES WITH SONGS–Folklore

Robinson, Adjai. *Singing Tales of Africa* [1-4], 1718

Wolkstein, Diane. *The Banza: A Haitian Story* [Pre-2], 1629

The Magic Orange Tree and Other Haitian Folktales [2-6], 1737

STORIES WITHOUT WORDS

Goffin, Josse. *Oh!* [Pre-K], **109**

McCully, Emily Arnold. *The Christmas Gift* [Pre-K], 195

Picnic [Pre-K], 196

Mariotti, Mario. *Hanimations* [K-6], **1199**
Rohmann, Eric. *Time Flies* [K-1], **350**
Turkle, Brinton. *Deep in the Forest* [K-1], 570
Ueno, Noriko. *Elephant Buttons* [Pre-K], 280
Ward, Lynd. *The Silver Pony* [2-3], 1024
Wiesner, David. *Tuesday* [K-1], **385**

STORMS

SEE ALSO Clouds; Rain and rainfall; Snow; Weather

Anderson, Lonzo. *The Ponies of Mykillengi* [2-3], 865
Fleming, Susan. *Trapped on the Golden Flyer* [4-5], 1173
McCloskey, Robert. *Time of Wonder* [2-3], 957
McPhail, David. *Great Cat* [K-1], 495
Moskin, Marietta. *The Day of the Blizzard* [3-4], 1098
Polacco, Patricia. *Thunder Cake* [K-1], 525
Simon, Seymour. *Storms* [4-6], 2105

STORMS–Folklore

Alexander, Ellen. *Llama and the Great Flood: A Folktale from Peru* [2-4], 1389

STORYTELLING

Alexander, Martha. *The Story Grandmother Told* [Pre-K], 2
Andersen, Hans Christian. *It's Perfectly True* [1-2], 602
Bess, Clayton. *The Truth about the Moon* [2-3], 875
Brown, Marc. *Arthur Babysits* [1-2], **412**
Carlson, Bernice Wells. *Listen! And Help Tell the Story* [Pre-2], 1765
Cazet, Denys. *"I'm Not Sleepy"* [Pre-K], **80**
Chase, Richard. *Grandfather Tales* [K-6], 1661
Jack Tales [4-6], 1662
Cleary, Beverly. *Petey's Bedtime Story* [K-1], **253**
Duke, Kate. *Aunt Isabel Tells a Good One* [1-2], **436**
Grifalconi, Ann. *The Village of Round and Square Houses* [K-4], 1485
Griffith, Helen V. *Grandaddy's Place* [1-2], 682
Haas, Dorothy F. *Tink in a Tangle* [2-3], 929
Haley, Gail E. *A Story, a Story* [K-3], 1517
Kalman, Maira. *Hey Willy, See the Pyramids* [2-3], 941
Kessler, Leonard. *Old Turtle's Baseball Stories* [1-2], 709
Kroll, Steven. *The Tyrannosaurus Game* [1-2], 719
Lindgren, Astrid. *The Ghost of Skinny Jack* [3-4], 1089
Long, Claudia. *Albert's Story* [K-1], 487
McCleery, William. *Wolf Story* [K-1], 489

Marshall, James. *Three Up a Tree* [K-1], 504
Ness, Evaline. *Sam, Bangs and Moonshine* [1-2], 757
Nixon, Joan Lowery. *The Gift* [3-4], 1099
Root, Phyllis. *Coyote and the Magic Words* [K-1], **351**
Segal, Lore. *Tell Me a Mitzi* [1-2], 798
Tashjian, Virginia. *Juba This and Juba That: Story Hour Stretches for Large or Small Groups* [Pre-4], 1961
Thurber, James. *The Great Quillow* [2-3], **684**
Tompert, Ann. *Grandfather Tang's Story* [1-2], **567**
Tunnell, Michael O. *Chinook!* [2-3], **688**
Turkle, Brinton. *The Adventures of Obadiah* [1-2], 834
Van Allsburg, Chris. *The Wreck of the Zephyr* [3-4], 1126
Ward, Lynd. *The Silver Pony* [2-3], 1024
Ziegler, Jack. *Mr. Knocky* [1-2], **582**

STUFFED ANIMALS

SEE ALSO Teddy bears; Toys

Dodds, Siobhan. *Grandpa Bud* [Pre], **9**
Drummond, V. H. *Phewtus the Squirrel* [Pre-K], 74
Field, Eugene. *The Gingham Dog and the Calico Cat* [Pre-K], **103**
Flora, James. *Sherwood Walks Home* [Pre-K], 88
Gackenbach, Dick. *Poppy, the Panda* [Pre-K], 100
Galbraith, Kathryn O. *Laura Charlotte* [Pre-K], 105
Goodspeed, Peter. *A Rhinoceros Wakes Me Up in the Morning* [Pre-K], 116
Hughes, Shirley. *Dogger* [Pre-K], 146
Smee, Nicola. *The Tusk Fairy* [Pre], **45**
Weiss, Nicki. *Hank and Oogie* [K-1], 584
Willard, Nancy. *Papa's Panda* [Pre-K], 295

STUTTERING

Kline, Suzy. *Mary Marony and the Snake* [1-2], **475**

SUBSTITUTE TEACHERS

Petersen, P. J. *The Sub* [2-3], **656**
Sachar, Louis. *Marvin Redpost: Alone in His Teacher's House* [2-3], **672**

SUBTRACTION

SEE ALSO Counting books; Mathematics

Brown, Paula. *Moon Jump: A Cowntdown* [K-1], **240**
Gordon, Jeffie Ross. *Six Sleepy Sheep* [Pre-K], **111**
Raffi. *Five Little Ducks* [Pre], **39**
Rayner, Mary. *Ten Pink Piglets: Garth Pig's Wall Song* [Pre-K], **179**

SUBTRACTION (cont.)

Wise, William. *Ten Sly Piranhas: A Counting Story in Reverse (A Tale of Wickedness and Worse)* [1-2], **578**

SUKKOTH

SEE ALSO Holidays; Jews

Polacco, Patricia. *Tikvah Means Hope* [2-3], **664**

SUMMER

SEE ALSO Seasons

McCloskey, Robert. *Time of Wonder* [2-3], 957

Major, Beverly. *Playing Sardines* [1-2], 741

Robbins, Ken. *Beach Days* [Pre-K], 242

SUMMER–Poetry

Prelutsky, Jack. *What I Did Last Summer* [K-3], 1923

SUN

SEE ALSO Astronomy; Moon; Stars

Emberley, Michael. *Welcome Back Sun* [1-2], **438**

Kandoian, Ellen. *Under the Sun* [K-1], 445

Kent, Jack. *Little Peep* [K-1], 455

Lobel, Arnold. *How the Rooster Saved the Day* [Pre-K], 192

SUN–Folklore

Aesop. *The Wind and the Sun* [K-2], **859**

Bernhard, Emery. *How Snowshoe Hare Rescued the Sun: A Tale from the Arctic* [K-3], **866**

Dayrell, Elphinstone. *Why the Sun and Moon Live in the Sky* [Pre-2], **1435**

Dixon, Ann. *How Raven Brought Light to People* [K-4], **897**

McDermott, Gerald. *Raven: A Trickster Tale from the Pacific Northwest* [K-4], **976**

Mollel, Tololwa M. *A Promise to the Sun: An African Story* [K-3], **990**

Shetterly, Susan Hand. *Raven's Light: A Myth from the People of the Northwest Coast* [2-5], **1024**

SUPERMARKETS

SEE ALSO Shopping

Park, Barbara. *Junie B. Jones and Some Sneaky Peeky Spying* [2-3], **652**

SUPERNATURAL

SEE ALSO Ghosts; Halloween; Witches; Wizards

Brittain, Bill. *Dr. Dredd's Wagon of Wonders* [5-6], 1277

Professor Popkin's Prodigious Polish: A Tale of Coven Tree [4-5], **760**

Slote, Alfred. *The Devil Rides with Me and Other Fantastic Stories* [5-6], 1360

SUPERNATURAL–Folklore

Bang, Molly. *The Goblins Giggle and Other Stories* [3-6], 1655

Carey, Valerie Scho. *Maggie Mab and the Bogey Beast* [2-4], **875**

Cecil, Laura. *Boo! Stories to Make You Jump* [1-4], **1062**

Climo, Shirley. *Piskies, Spriggans, and Other Magical Beings* [3-6], 1663

Goode, Diane. *Diane Goode's Book of Scary Stories & Songs* [2-4], **1068**

Harper, Wilhelmina. *Ghosts and Goblins: Stories for Halloween* [2-5], 1690

Harris, Christie. *Mouse Woman and the Mischief-Makers* [4-6], 1691

Leach, Maria. *The Thing at the Foot of the Bed and Other Scary Tales* [2-6], 1704

Schwartz, Alvin. *Scary Stories 3: More Tales to Chill Your Bones* [4-6], **1086**

SUPERNATURAL–Poetry

Bennett, Jill. *Spooky Poems* [K-4], **1269**

Brewton, John E., Lorraine A. Blackburn, and George M. Blackburn, III. *In the Witch's Kitchen: Poems for Halloween* [K-3], 1757

Brewton, Sara, and John E. Brewton. *Shrieks at Midnight: Macabre Poems, Eerie and Humorous* [4-6], 1758

Brown, Marc. *Scared Silly: A Book for the Brave* [1-3], **1275**

Hopkins, Lee Bennett. *Creatures* [2-5], 1820

Prelutsky, Jack. *Nightmares: Poems to Trouble Your Sleep* [3-6], 1912

SUPERNATURAL–Riddles

Brown, Marc. *Spooky Riddles* [K-3], 1761

Keller, Charles. *Count Draculations! Monsters Riddles* [2-6], 1836

Rosenbloom, Joseph. *Spooky Riddles and Jokes* [2-6], 1937

SUPERSTITIONS

Van Allsburg, Chris. *The Widow's Broom* [3-4], **752**

SUPERSTITIONS–Folklore

Perl, Lila. *Don't Sing before Breakfast, Don't Sleep in the Moonlight: Everyday Superstitions and How They Began* [4-6], 1715

Sarnoff, Jane. *Take Warning! A Book of Superstitions* [4-6], 1723

Schwartz, Alvin. *Cross Your Fingers, Spit in Your Hat: Superstitions and Other Beliefs* [3-6], 1724

SURVIVAL

Burnford, Sheila. *The Incredible Journey* [5-6], 1279

Farley, Walter. *The Black Stallion* [3-4], 1064

Fife, Dale. *North of Danger* [5-6], 1296

Fleming, Susan. *Trapped on the Golden Flyer* [4-5], 1173

George, Jean Craighead. *Julie of the Wolves* [5-6], 1304

My Side of the Mountain [4-5], 1176

Hill, Kirkpatrick. *Winter Camp* [5-6], **822**

Ho, Minfong. *The Clay Marble* [5-6], **823**

Kinsey-Warnock, Natalie. *The Bear That Heard Crying* [1-2], **468**

Landsman, Sandy. *Castaways on Chimp Island* [5-6], 1323

O'Dell, Scott. *Island of the Blue Dolphins* [5-6], 1339

Paton Walsh, Jill. *The Green Book* [5-6], 1341

Paulsen, Gary. *The Haymeadow* [5-6], **835**

Rand, Gloria. *Salty Takes Off* [1-2], **540**

Roy, Ron. *Nightmare Island* [4-5], 1234

Ruckman, Ivy. *Night of the Twisters* [4-5], 1235

Sperry, Armstrong. *Call It Courage* [4-5], 1242

Steig, William. *Abel's Island* [5-6], 1364

Stonely, Jack. *Scruffy* [4-5], 1245

Tapp, Kathy Kennedy. *Moth-Kin Magic* [4-5], 1247

Ullman, James Ramsay. *Banner in the Sky* [5-6], 1371

Williams, Gurney. *True Escape and Survival Stories* [4-6], 2115

Wuorio, Eva-Lis. *Code: Polonaise* [5-6], 1377

SUSPENSE

Arthur, Robert. *The Secret of Terror Castle* [5-6], 1265

Bellairs, John. *The House with a Clock in Its Walls* [4-5], 1143

Callen, Larry. *The Deadly Mandrake* [5-6], 1284

Fisk, Nicholas. *Grinny: A Novel of Science Fiction* [5-6], 1297

Fleischman, Paul. *The Half-a-Moon Inn* [5-6], 1299

Jennings, Paul. *Unreal! Eight Surprising Stories* [5-6], **825**

Kehret, Peg. *Deadly Stranger* [5-6], 1317

Kennedy, Richard. *Inside My Feet* [5-6], 1318

Lindgren, Astrid. *The Ghost of Skinny Jack* [3-4], 1089

Mendoza, George. *Gwot! Horribly Funny Hairticklers* [2-3], 962

Pepper, Dennis. *The Oxford Book of Scary Stories* [5-6], **836**

Roberts, Willo Davis. *The View from the Cherry Tree* [5-6], 1346

Sleator, William. *Among the Dolls* [4-5], 1240

York, Carol Beach. *I Will Make You Disappear* [5-6], 1378

SUSPENSE–Folklore

Bang, Molly. *The Goblins Giggle and Other Stories* [3-6], 1655

Cecil, Laura. *Boo! Stories to Make You Jump* [1-4], **1062**

Goode, Diane. *Diane Goode's Book of Scary Stories & Songs* [2-4], **1068**

Hodges, Margaret. *Hauntings: Ghosts and Ghouls from Around the World* [4-6], **1072**

Leach, Maria. *The Thing at the Foot of the Bed and Other Scary Tales* [2-6], 1704

Schwartz, Alvin. *Scary Stories 3: More Tales to Chill Your Bones* [4-6], **1086**

Scary Stories to Tell in the Dark [4-6], 1725

Young, Richard and Judy Dockrey Young. *Favorite Scary Stories of American Children* [3-6], **1093**

SUSPENSE–Poetry

Brewton, Sara, and John E. Brewton. *Shrieks at Midnight: Macabre Poems, Eerie and Humorous* [4-6], 1758

Brown, Marc. *Scared Silly: A Book for the Brave* [1-3], **1275**

Goode, Diane. *Diane Goode's Book of Scary Stories & Songs* [2-4], **1068**

Prelutsky, Jack. *Nightmares: Poems to Trouble Your Sleep* [3-6], 1912

SWANS

Andersen, Hans Christian. *The Wild Swans* [3-4], **700**

Pyle, Howard. *The Swan Maiden* [2-3], **665**

SWAZILAND

Leigh, Nila K. *Learning to Swim in Swaziland: A Child's-Eye View of a Southern African Country* [1-4], **1184**

SWEDEN

Schwartz, David. *Supergrandpa* [2-3], **675**

SWEDISH AMERICANS

Winter, Jeanette. *Klara's New World* [2-3], **693**

SWIMMING

Mahy, Margaret. *The Great White Man-Eating Shark: A Cautionary Tale* [1-2], **501**

Stott, Dorothy. *Too Much* [Pre], **47**

Waddell, Martin. *The Pig in the Pond* [Pre], **50**

SWINDLERS AND SWINDLING
Abolafia, Yossi. *Fox Tale* [1-2], **394**

SWINDLERS AND SWINDLING–Folklore
Han, Oki S., and Stephanie Haboush Plunkett. *Sir Whong and the Golden Pig* [2-5], **935**

TAILORS–Folklore
Galdone, Paul. *The Monster and the Tailor* [2-4], 1467
Grimm, Jacob. *The Valiant Little Tailor* [1-4], 1510
Thomson, Peggy. *The Brave Little Tailor* [1-4], **1035**

TAINO INDIANS–Folklore
Crespo, George. *How the Sea Began: A Taino Myth* [1-6], **887**

TALL TALES
Credle, Ellis. *Tall Tales from the High Hills and Other Stories* [4-6], 1672
Fleischman, Sid. *McBroom Tells the Truth* [3-4], 1066
Flora, James. *The Great Green Turkey Creek Monster* [2-3], 921
Harper, Jo. *Jalapeño Hal* [2-3], **615**
Isaacs, Anne. *Swamp Angel* [2-3], **625**
Keats, Ezra Jack. *John Henry: An American Legend* [1-4], 1538
Kellogg, Steven. *Johnny Appleseed* [1-4], 2058
Mike Fink [1-4], **948**
Lester, Julius. *John Henry* [1-4], **967**
McCormick, Dell J. *Paul Bunyan Swings His Axe* [3-6], 1709
Mahy, Margaret. *The Rattlebang Picnic* [1-2], **502**
Nixon, Joan Lowery. *Beats Me, Claude* [2-3], 971
Noble, Trinka Hakes. *Meanwhile Back at the Ranch* [2-3], 974
Osborne, Mary Pope. *American Tall Tales* [3-6], **1081**
Rounds, Glen. *Mr. Yowder and the Train Robbers* [4-5], 1232
Ol' Paul, the Mighty Logger [4-6], 1721
Sanfield, Steve. *A Natural Man: The True Story of John Henry* [4-6], 1588
San Souci, Robert D. *Larger Than Life: The Adventures of American Legendary Heroes* [3-6], **1085**
Schwartz, Alvin. *Chin Music: Tall Talk and Other Talk, Collected from American Folklore* [3-6], 1946
Whoppers: Tall Tales and Other Lies [3-6], 1726
Shepard, Aaron. *The Legend of Slappy Hooper: An American Tall Tale* [1-3], **1023**
Stevenson, James. *Could Be Worse* [1-2], 822
That's Exactly the Way It Wasn't [1-2], **558**

Tunnell, Michael O. *Chinook!* [2-3], **688**
Walker, Paul Robert. *Big Men, Big Country: A Collection of American Tall Tales* [4-6], **1090**

TATTLING
Park, Barbara. *Rosie Swanson, Fourth-Grade Geek for President* [3-4], **737**

TAXICABS
Barracca, Debra, and Sal Barracca. *A Taxi Dog Christmas* [K-1], **229**

TCHAIKOVSKY, PETER ILICH
Kalman, Esther. *Tchaikovsky Discovers America* [2-3], **632**

TEACHERS
SEE ALSO Principals; Schools
Adler, David A. *Eaton Stanley & the Mind Control Experiment* [4-5], 1137
Allard, Harry. *Miss Nelson Is Missing* [1-2], 601
Benjamin, Saragail Katzman. *My Dog Ate It* [3-4], **704**
Bodsworth, Nan. *A Nice Walk in the Jungle* [K-1], **233**
Bourgeois, Paulette. *Too Many Chickens* [K-1], **235**
Brown, Marc. *Arthur's Teacher Trouble* [1-2], 628
Bunting, Eve. *Our Teacher's Having a Baby* [K-1], **243**
Clymer, Eleanor. *My Brother Stevie* [3-4], 1054
Cole, Joanna. *The Magic School Bus at the Waterworks* [2-4], 2008
The Magic School Bus Inside the Earth [2-4], 2009
The Magic School Bus Inside the Human Body [2-4], 2010
The Magic School Bus Lost in the Solar System [1-4], **1121**
The Magic School Bus on the Ocean Floor [2-4], **1122**
Dahl, Roald. *Matilda* [5-6], 1292
Fenner, Carol. *Randall's Wall* [5-6], **815**
Flack, Marjorie. *Walter the Lazy Moose* [1-2], 668
Gardiner, John Reynolds. *Top Secret* [5-6], 1303
Giff, Patricia Reilly. *Today Was a Terrible Day* [1-2], 678
Harding, William Harry. *Alvin's Famous No-Horse* [2-3], **613**
Henkes, Kevin. *Chrysanthemum* [K-1], **282**
Houston, Gloria. *My Great Aunt Arizona* [1-6], **1165**
Howe, James. *The Day the Teacher Went Bananas* [Pre-K], 142
Kidd, Diana. *Onion Tears* [4-5], **772**
Kline, Suzy. *Horrible Harry and the Christmas Surprise* [1-2], **474**

Levy, Elizabeth. *Keep Ms. Sugarman in the Fourth Grade* [3-4], **731**

Luttrell, Ida. *One Day at School* [1-2], 732

McMullin, Kate. *The Great Ideas of Lila Fenwick* [4-5], 1209

Mills, Claudia. *After Fifth Grade, the World!* [4-5], 1214

Oppenheim, Joanne. *Mrs. Peloki's Class Play* [1-2], 763

Park, Barbara. *Junie B. Jones and Some Sneaky Peeky Spying* [2-3], **652**

Paterson, Katherine. *Bridge to Terabithia* [5-6], 1340

Peck, Robert Newton. *Mr. Little* [5-6], 1343

Petersen, P. J. *The Sub* [2-3], **656**

Pulver, Robin. *Mrs. Toggle and the Dinosaur* [K-1], **344**

Mrs. Toggle's Beautiful Blue Shoe [K-1], **345**

Russo, Marisabina. *I Don't Want to Go Back to School* [K-1], **355**

Sachar, Louis. *Marvin Redpost: Alone in His Teacher's House* [2-3], **672**

Sideways Stories from Wayside School [3-4], 1110

Wayside School Is Falling Down [3-4], 1111

Sachs, Marilyn. *The Bears' House* [5-6], 1350

Shreve, Susan. *The Gift of the Girl Who Couldn't Hear* [5-6], **841**

Stevenson, James. *That Dreadful Day* [2-3], 1011

Thaler, Mike. *The Teacher from the Black Lagoon* [2-3], **682**

Udry, Janice May. *Angie* [2-3], 1017

Whelan, Gloria. *Hannah* [2-3], **689**

Wittman, Sally. *The Wonderful Mrs. Trumbly* [K-1], 596

Wolkstein, Diane. *The Legend of Sleepy Hollow* [4-5], **795**

Woodruff, Elvira. *Show and Tell* [K-1], **388**

TEASING

Cole, Joanna. *Don't Call Me Names* [K-1], **254**

TEDDY BEARS

SEE ALSO Stuffed animals; Toys

Alborough, Jez. *It's the Bear!* [Pre-K], **63**

Where's My Teddy? [Pre], **2**

Bucknall, Caroline. *One Bear in the Picture* [Pre-K], 31

Dillon, Barbara. *The Teddy Bear Tree* [1-2], 662

Douglass, Barbara. *Good As New* [Pre-K], 72

Flora, James. *Sherwood Walks Home* [Pre-K], 88

Freeman, Don. *Beady Bear* [Pre-K], 92

Corduroy [Pre-K], 93

A Pocket for Corduroy [Pre-K], 95

Galbraith, Richard. *Reuben Runs Away* [Pre-K], 106

Gretz, Susanna. *Teddy Bears Cure a Cold* [Pre-K], 413

Hayes, Sarah. *This Is the Bear* [Pre-K], 128

This Is the Bear and the Scary Night [Pre], **19**

Hissey, Jane. *Little Bear's Trousers* [Pre-K], 135

Hoban, Lillian. *Arthur's Honey Bear* [Pre-K], 136

Keller, Holly. *A Bear for Christmas* [Pre-K], 167

Mansell, Dom. *My Old Teddy* [Pre], **32**

Milne, A. A. *Winnie-the-Pooh* [2-3], 964

Odgers, Sally Farrell. *Drummond: The Search for Sarah* [1-2], **522**

Sheldon, Dyan. *Love, Your Bear Pete* [K-1], **363**

Sun, Chying Feng. *Mama Bear* [1-2], **562**

Waber, Bernard. *Ira Sleeps Over* [1-2], 842

Wells, Rosemary. *Peabody* [Pre-K], 288

TEETH

Bate, Lucy. *Little Rabbit's Loose Tooth* [K-1], 332

Birdseye, Tom. *Air Mail to the Moon* [1-2], 616

Brown, Marc. *Arthur's Tooth* [1-2], 629

Cooney, Nancy Evans. *The Wobbly Tooth* [K-1], 374

Hoban, Lillian. *Arthur's Loose Tooth* [K-1], 427

Karlin, Nurit. *The Tooth Witch* [K-1], 447

Kellogg, Steven. *Prehistoric Pinkerton* [1-2], 707

McPhail, David. *The Bear's Toothache* [K-1], 493

Pinkwater, Daniel. *Fat Men from Space* [3-4], 1103

Steig, William. *Dr. DeSoto* [2-3], 1007

TELEPHONE

Allen, Jeffrey. *Mary Alice, Operator Number Nine* [K-1], 320

Dodds, Siobhan. *Grandpa Bud* [Pre], **9**

Wells, Rosemary. *Good Night, Fred* [Pre-K], 285

TELEVISION

Cohen, Miriam. *Jim Meets the Thing* [K-1], 367

Conford, Ellen. *Nibble, Nibble, Jenny Archer* [2-3], **600**

Heide, Florence Parry, and Roxanne Heide. *A Monster Is Coming! A Monster Is Coming!* [1-2], 684

Jones, Rebecca C. *Germy Blew It* [4-5], 1196

McPhail, David. *Fix-It* [K-1], 494

Miles, Betty. *The Secret Life of the Underwear Champ* [3-4], 1096

Phelan, Terry Wolfe. *The Week Mom Unplugged the TVs* [3-4], 1102

Rodda, Emily. *Finders Keepers* [4-5], **789**

TELL, WILLIAM

Early, Margaret. *William Tell* [2-6], **900**

Small, Terry. *The Legend of William Tell* [3-5], **1028**

TELLING TIME
SEE Time

TENNESSEE
Isaacs, Anne. *Swamp Angel* [2-3], **625**

TERMINALLY ILL
Jukes, Mavis. *I'll See You in My Dreams* [3-4], **718**

TEXAS
Beatty, Patricia. *That's One Ornery Orphan* [5-6], 1274
Cherry, Lynne. *The Armadillo from Amarillo* [1-2], **423**
Harper, Jo. *Jalapeño Hal* [2-3], **615**
Johnston, Tony. *The Cowboy and the Black-Eyed Pea* [3-4], **717**
Nixon, Joan Lowery. *Beats Me, Claude* [2-3], 971
That's the Spirit, Claude [2-3], **650**
Saunders, Susan. *Fish Fry* [1-2], 790

TEXAS–Folklore
dePaola, Tomie. *The Legend of the Bluebonnet: An Old Tale of Texas* [1-4], 1440

THANKSGIVING
Accorsi, William. *Friendship's First Thanksgiving* [K-1], **216**
Bauer, Caroline Feller. *Thanksgiving: Stories and Poems* [2-4], **1266**
Carlson, Nancy L. *A Visit to Grandma's* [K-1], **249**
Child, Lydia Maria. *Over the River and Through the Wood: A Song for Thanksgiving* [K-1], **251**
Cohen, Barbara. *Molly's Pilgrim* [2-3], 893
Devlin, Harry, and Wende Devlin. *Cranberry Thanksgiving* [1-2], 660
George, Jean Craighead. *The First Thanksgiving* [1-4], **1147**
Harness, Cheryl. *Three Young Pilgrims* [2-3], **614**
Johnston, Johanna. *Speak Up, Edie* [K-1], 440
Kroll, Steven. *Oh, What a Thanksgiving!* [1-2], 718
Pilkey, Dav. *'Twas the Night Before Thanksgiving* [1-2], **531**
Pinkwater, Daniel. *The Hoboken Chicken Emergency* [3-4], 1104
Schatell, Brian. *Farmer Goff and His Turkey Sam* [K-1], 543
Spinelli, Eileen. *Thanksgiving at the Tappletons'* [1-2], 818
Sterman, Betsy, and Samuel Sterman. *Backyard Dragon* [3-4], 750

THANKSGIVING–Folklore
Greene, Ellin. *The Legend of the Cranberry: A Paleo-Indian Tale* [1-4], **919**

THANKSGIVING–Poetry
Bauer, Caroline Feller. *Thanksgiving: Stories and Poems* [2-4], **1266**
Hopkins, Lee Bennett. *Merrily Comes Our Harvest In: Poems for Thanksgiving* [2-5], **1323**
Prelutsky, Jack. *It's Thanksgiving* [Pre-3], 1908

THIEVES
SEE Robbers and outlaws

TIGERS
Allen, Judy. *Tiger* [2-3], **585**
Blia, Xiong. *Nine-in-One, Grr! Grr! A Folktale from the Hmong People of Laos* [K-3], 1404
Kasza, Keiko. *The Rat and the Tiger* [Pre-K], **141**
Kraus, Robert. *Leo the Late Bloomer* [K-1], 460
Paul, Anthony. *The Tiger Who Lost His Stripes* [1-2], 765
Peet, Bill. *The Spooky Tail of Prewitt Peacock* [1-2], 771
Prelutsky, Jack. *The Terrible Tiger* [1-2], 778
Root, Phyllis. *Moon Tiger* [K-1], 535
Stanley, Diane. *Fortune* [3-4], 1117
Wright, Kit. *Tigerella* [K-1], **389**

TIGERS–Folklore
Compton, Patricia A. *The Terrible Eek* [K-3], **885**
Han, Suzanne Crowder. *The Rabbit's Escape* [1-5], **936**
The Rabbit's Judgment [1-5], **937**
Temple, Frances. *Tiger Soup: An Anansi Story from Jamaica* [Pre-2], **1034**
Wolkstein, Diane. *The Banza: A Haitian Story* [Pre-2], 1629

TIGHTROPE WALKING
McCully, Emily Arnold. *Mirette on the High Wire* [1-2], **492**

TIME
Allen, Jeffrey. *Mary Alice, Operator Number Nine* [K-1], 320
Brown, Eileen. *Tick-Tock* [K-1], **238**
Carle, Eric. *The Grouchy Ladybug* [Pre-K], 37
Hutchins, Pat. *Clocks and More Clocks* [K-1], 433
Krensky, Stephen. *Big Time Bears* [Pre-K], **147**
Lindbergh, Reeve. *There's a Cow in the Road!* [K-1], **307**
McGuire, Richard. *Night Becomes Day* [1-2], **498**
Singer, Marilyn. *Nine O'Clock Lullaby* [1-2], **554**

TIME AND SPACE
SEE Space and time

TIME–Poetry
Hopkins, Lee Bennett. *It's About Time!* [K-3], **1322**

TIME TRAVEL

SEE ALSO Space and time

Chetwin, Grace. *Friends in Time* [4-5], **764**

Cresswell, Helen. *Time Out* [3-4], **708**

Nolan, Dennis. *Dinosaur Dream* [1-2], **520**

Scieszka, Jon. *Your Mother Was a Neanderthal* [4-5], **790**

Weiss, Ellen, and Mel Friedman. *The Poof Point* [5-6], **851**

Woodruff, Elvira. *The Disappearing Bike Shop* [4-5], **797**

TIME ZONES

Kandoian, Ellen. *Is Anybody Up?* [Pre-K], **139**

Singer, Marilyn. *Nine O'Clock Lullaby* [1-2], **554**

TITANIC

Ballard, Robert. *Exploring the Titanic* [4-6], **1102**

TOADS

SEE ALSO Frogs; Reptiles

Coville, Bruce. *Jennifer Murdley's Toad* [4-5], **765**

Erickson, Russell E. *A Toad for Tuesday* [1-2], 665

Lobel, Arnold. *Frog and Toad Are Friends* [K-1], 479

TOADS–Folklore

Begay, Shonto. *Ma'ii and Cousin Horned Toad: A Traditional Navajo Story* [K-4], **865**

Lee, Jeanne M. *Toad Is the Uncle of Heaven* [Pre-2], 1546

TOILET TRAINING

Lewison, Wendy Cheyette. *The Princess and the Potty* [Pre], **29**

TONGUE TWISTERS

SEE ALSO Alliteration; Word games

Brandreth, Gyles. *The Biggest Tongue Twister Book in the World* [2-6], 1753

Brewton, Sara, John E. Brewton, and G. Meredith Blackburn, III. *My Tang's Tungled and Other Ridiculous Situations* [2-6], 1759

Brown, Marcia. *Peter Piper's Alphabet* [1-6], 1762

Cole, Joanna, and Stephanie Calmenson. *Six Sick Sheep: 101 Tongue Twisters* [2-5], **1280**

Cricket Magazine, editors of. *Cricket's Jokes, Riddles & Other Stuff* [K-5], 1785

Curtis, Foley. *The Little Book of Big Tongue Twisters* [1-4], 1786

Emrich, Duncan. *The Hodgepodge Book* [2-6], 1796

Gordon, Jeffie Ross. *Six Sleepy Sheep* [Pre-K], **111**

Keller, Charles. *Tongue Twisters* [K-3], **1340**

Rosenbloom, Joseph. *Twist These on Your Tongue* [3-6], 1938

Schwartz, Alvin. *Busy Buzzing Bumblebees and Other Tongue Twisters* [Pre-2], 1944

A Twister of Twists, a Tangler of Tongues [2-6], 1950

TOOTH FAIRY

Smee, Nicola. *The Tusk Fairy* [Pre], **45**

TORNADOES

SEE ALSO Storms; Weather; Wind

Branley, Franklyn M. *Tornado Alert* [1-4], 1998

Ruckman, Ivy. *Night of the Twisters* [4-5], 1235

TORTOISE

SEE Turtles

TOUCH

Gryski, Camilla. *Hands On, Thumbs Up: Secret Handshakes, Fingerprints, Sign Languages, and More Handy Ways to Have Fun with Hands* [3-6], **1154**

Otto, Carolyn. *I Can Tell by Touching* [Pre-1], **1215**

TOWNS

SEE Cities and towns

TOY AND MOVABLE BOOKS

Charles, N. N. *What Am I? Looking Through Shapes at Apples and Grapes* [Pre-K], **84**

Hellen, Nancy. *Old MacDonald Had a Farm* [Pre], **20**

Westcott, Nadine Bernard. *The Pop-Up, Pull-Tab Playtime House That Jack Built* [Pre-K], **208**

Zelinsky, Paul O. *The Wheels on the Bus* [Pre-K], **214**

TOYS

SEE ALSO Stuffed animals; Teddy bears

Andersen, Hans Christian. *The Steadfast Tin Soldier* [2-3], **586**

Banks, Lynne Reid. *The Indian in the Cupboard* [5-6], 1272

Galbraith, Kathryn O. *Laura Charlotte* [Pre-K], 105

Hissey, Jane. *Little Bear's Trousers* [Pre-K], 135

Hoban, Lillian. *Arthur's Honey Bear* [Pre-K], 136

Hutchins, Pat. *Silly Billy!* [Pre], **24**

Miller, Margaret. *Where Does It Go?* [Pre-K], **166**

Milne, A. A. *Winnie-the-Pooh* [2-3], 964

Ross, Pat. *Gloria and the Super Soaper* [2-3], 987

Stevenson, Robert Louis. *Block City* [K-1], 563

Weiss, Nicki. *Hank and Oogie* [K-1], 584

TOYS–Poetry

Field, Eugene. *The Gingham Dog and the Calico Cat* [Pre-K], **103**

TRAINS

Crews, Donald. *Freight Train* [Pre-K], 58

Fife, Dale. *Who's in Charge of Lincoln?* [2-3], 917

Fleming, Susan. *Trapped on the Golden Flyer* [4-5], 1173

Howard, Elizabeth Fitzgerald. *Mac & Marie & the Train Toss Surprise* [1-2], 455

Kirby, David, and Allen Woodman. *The Cows Are Going to Paris* [1-2], 471

London, Jonathan. *The Owl Who Became the Moon* [K-1], 310

Macaulay, David. *Black and White* [1-2], 490

Siebert, Diane. *Train Song* [1-2], 553

TRAINS–Folklore

Lester, Julius. *John Henry* [1-4], 967

TRANSFORMATIONS

Alexander, Lloyd. *The Cat Who Wished to Be a Man* [5-6], 1259

Andersen, Hans Christian. *The Wild Swans* [3-4], 700

Bacon, Peggy. *The Magic Touch* [3-4], 1043

Brittain, Bill. *Shape-Changer* [4-5], 761

Browne, Anthony. *Changes* [K-1], 241

Bunting, Eve. *Night of the Gargoyles* [3-4], 705

Cole, Brock. *Alpha and the Dirty Baby* [1-2], 426

Cole, Joanna. *Doctor Change* [2-3], 896

Corbett, Scott. *The Donkey Planet* [4-5], 1163

Coville, Bruce. *Jennifer Murdley's Toad* [4-5], 765

Dahl, Roald. *The Witches* [4-5], 1167

Gackenbach, Dick. *Tiny for a Day* [K-1], 273

Goffin, Josse. *Oh!* [Pre-K], 109

Hearn, Diane Dawson. *Dad's Dinosaur Day* [Pre-K], 120

Lionni, Leo. *Alexander and the Wind-Up Mouse* [1-2], 726

Moore, Inga. *The Sorcerer's Apprentice* [2-3], 648

Napoli, Donna Jo. *The Prince of the Pond: Otherwise Known as De Fawg Pin* [4-5], 782

Ogburn, Jacqueline K. *Scarlett Angelina Wolverton-Manning* [1-2], 524

Pyle, Howard. *The Swan Maiden* [2-3], 665

Rael, Elsa Okon. *Marushka's Egg* [2-3], 667

Ryder, Joanne. *Catching the Wind* [Pre-3], 2088
Lizard in the Sun [Pre-3], 2090
Sea Elf [K-3], 1231
White Bear, Ice Bear [Pre-3], 2091
Winter Whale [K-3], 1232

Stanley, Diane. *Fortune* [3-4], 1117

Steig, William. *Solomon the Rusty Nail* [2-3], 1008
Sylvester and the Magic Pebble [1-2], 821

Stolz, Mary. *Quentin Corn* [5-6], 1365

Tompert, Ann. *Grandfather Tang's Story* [1-2], 567

Tzannes, Robin. *Professor Puffendorf's Secret Potions* [1-2], 569

Van Allsburg, Chris. *The Sweetest Fig* [3-4], 751

Wright, Kit. *Tigerella* [K-1], 389

Yep, Laurence. *The Ghost Fox* [3-4], 755

TRANSFORMATIONS–Folklore

Bernhard, Emery. *The Tree That Rains: The Flood Myth of the Huichol Indians of Mexico* [1-4], 867

Carey, Valerie Scho. *Maggie Mab and the Bogey Beast* [2-4], 875

Dasent, George Webbe. *East o' the Sun and West o' the Moon* [3-6], 890

East o' the Sun & West o' the Moon: An Old Norse Tale [2-6], 1433

Gabler, Mirko. *Tall, Wide, and Sharp-Eye* [1-4], 907

Grimm, Jacob. *The Donkey Prince* [2-4], 1490
The Frog Prince [K-3], 1493
The Frog Prince: Or Iron Henry [1-4], 932
Jorinda and Joringel [2-4], 1498

Hague, Kathleen, and Michael Hague. *East of the Sun and West of the Moon* [3-5], 1513

Harris, Rosemary. *Beauty and the Beast* [2-5], 1520

Hughes, Monica. *Little Fingerling* [1-4], 945

Langton, Jane. *The Hedgehog Boy: A Latvian Folktale* [K-3], 1545

Lewis, J. Patrick. *The Frog Princess: A Russian Tale* [2-6], 969

Mayer, Marianna. *Beauty and the Beast* [2-5], 1566

Riggio, Anita. *Beware the Brindlebeast* [K-3], 1004

San Souci, Robert D. *The Snow Wife* [3-5], 1015
The Tsar's Promise [3-6], 1018
The White Cat: An Old French Fairy Tale [2-5], 1019

Yep, Laurence. *The Junior Thunder Lord* [1-4], 1046

Yolen, Jane. *Tam Lin* [3-6], 1048

TRANSPORTATION

SEE ALSO Airplanes; Automobiles; Bicycles; Buses; Taxicabs; Trains; Trucks

Baer, Edith. *This Is the Way We Go to School: A Book About Children Around the World* [K-1], 226

Barracca, Debra, and Sal Barracca. *The Adventures of Taxi Dog* [1-2], 404

Browne, Eileen. *No Problem* [1-2], 414

Burningham, John. *Harvey Slumfenburger's Christmas Present* [K-1], 244

Douglass, Barbara. *The Great Town and Country Bicycle Balloon Chase* [Pre-K], 73

Frank, John. *Odds 'N' Ends Alvy* [1-2], **441**

Kimmel, Eric A. *Charlie Drives the Stage* [2-3], 943

Kovalski, Maryann. *The Wheels on the Bus* [Pre-K], 173

Leventhal, Debra. *What Is Your Language?* [Pre-K], **150**

Merrill, Jean. *The Pushcart War* [5-6], 1331

Peterson, Esther Allen. *Penelope Gets Wheels* [1-2], 774

Pinkwater, Daniel. *Tooth-Gnasher Superflash* [K-1], 523

Seuss, Dr. *Marvin K. Mooney, Will You Please Go Now* [K-1], 554

Shaw, Nancy. *Sheep in a Jeep* [K-1], 556

Siebert, Diane. *Plane Song* [1-2], **552**
  Train Song [1-2], **553**
  Truck Song [Pre-K], 266

Zelinsky, Paul O. *The Wheels on the Bus* [Pre-K], **214**

TRAVEL
SEE Voyages and travels

TREASURE
SEE Buried treasure

TREES
SEE ALSO Flowers; Gardens; Plants; Vegetables

Bash, Barbara. *Tree of Life: The World of the African Baobab* [1-4], **1104**

Bunting, Eve. *Someday a Tree* [1-2], **416**

Cherry, Lynne. *The Great Kapok Tree: A Tale of the Amazon Rain Forest* [1-2], 647

Cowcher, Helen. *Rain Forest* [K-1], **256**

Ernst, Lisa Campbell. *Squirrel Park* [1-2], **440**

Gackenbach, Dick. *Mighty Tree* [Pre-2], **1145**

Hiscock, Bruce. *The Big Tree* [2-4], **1162**

Izen, Marshall, and Jim West. *Why the Willow Weeps: A Story Told with Hands* [1-2], **461**

Kellogg, Steven. *Johnny Appleseed* [1-4], 2058

Lyon, George Ella. *A B Cedar: An Alphabet of Trees* [Pre-6], 2068

Nikly, Michelle. *The Emperor's Plum Tree* [1-2], 759

Noble, Trinka Hakes. *Apple Tree Christmas* [2-3], 973

Seuss, Dr. *The Lorax* [2-3], 997

Silverstein, Shel. *The Giving Tree* [2-3], 1001

Udry, Janice May. *A Tree Is Nice* [Pre-K], 278

TREES–Folklore
Kimmel, Eric A. *Boots and His Brothers: A Norwegian Tale* [2-6], **952**

Lottridge, Celia Barker. *The Name of the Tree: A Bantu Folktale* [Pre-2], **973**

Say, Allen. *Once Under the Cherry Blossom Tree: An Old Japanese Tale* [1-4], 1592

Troughton, Joanna. *Tortoise's Dream* [Pre-2], 1618

TREES–Poetry
Behn, Harry. *Trees* [1-2], **406**

TRIALS
Alcock, Vivien. *The Trial of Anna Cotman* [5-6], **802**

Byars, Betsy. *Wanted . . . Mud Blossom* [4-5], **763**

TRICKS
SEE ALSO Magic

Baum, Arline, and Joseph Baum. *Opt: An Illusionary Tale* [3-4], 1044

Brandreth, Gyles. *Brain-Teasers and Mind-Benders* [3-6], 1997

Brown, Marc. *Arthur's April Fool* [1-2], 625

Churchill, E. Richard. *Devilish Bets to Trick Your Friends* [3-6], 2005

Eldin, Peter. *The Trickster's Handbook* [3-6], **1136**

Flora, James. *The Joking Man* [2-3], 922

McCully, Emily Arnold. *The Amazing Felix* [1-2], **491**

White, Laurence B., Jr., and Ray Broekel. *The Surprise Book* [2-6], 2114

TRICKSTER TALES
Aardema, Verna. *Anansi Finds a Fool* [1-5], **855**
  Borreguita and the Coyote: A Tale from Ayutla, Mexico [K-3], **856**
  Rabbit Makes a Monkey Out of Lion [Pre-3], 1382

Appiah, Peggy. *Tales of an Ashanti Father* [3-6], 1653

Arkhurst, Joyce Cooper. *The Adventures of Spider: West African Folktales* [1-4], 1654

Begay, Shonto. *Ma'ii and Cousin Horned Toad: A Traditional Navajo Story* [K-4], **865**

Climo, Shirley. *Stolen Thunder: A Norse Myth* [3-6], **880**

Coatsworth, Emerson, and David Coatsworth. *The Adventures of Nanabush: Ojibway Indian Stories* [2-5], **1665**

Courlander, Harold. *The Hat-Shaking Dance: And Other Tales from the Gold Coast* [2-6], **1668**
  The Piece of Fire and Other Haitian Tales [3-6], 1669

TRICKSTER TALES (cont.)

Courlander, Harold, and George Herzog. *The Cow-Tail Switch and Other West African Stories* [2-6], 1670

Cushman, Doug. *Possum Stew* [Pre-K], **91**

Goble, Paul. *Iktomi and the Boulder: A Plains Indian Story* [K-3], 1483

Greene, Jacqueline Dembar. *What His Father Did* [3-6], **920**

Gregg, Andy. *Great Rabbit and the Long-Tailed Wildcat* [2-4], **921**

Han, Suzanne Crowder. *The Rabbit's Escape* [1-5], **936**

Hastings, Selina. *Reynard the Fox* [3-6], **1071**

Johnston, Tony. *The Tale of Rabbit and Coyote* [Pre-2], **947**

Kesey, Ken. *Little Tricker the Squirrel Meets Big Double the Bear* [2-3], **634**

Kimmel, Eric A. *Anansi and the Moss-Covered Rock* [Pre-2], 1541

Anansi and the Talking Melon [Pre-2], **949**

Anansi Goes Fishing [Pre-2], **950**

Four Dollars and Fifty Cents [3-4], **721**

Knutson, Barbara. *Sungura and Leopard: A Swahili Trickster Tale* [K-3], **960**

Lester, Julius. *Further Tales of Uncle Remus: The Misadventures of Brer Rabbit, Brer Fox, Brer Wolf, the Doodang, and Other Creatures* [2-5], **1075**

The Tales of Uncle Remus: The Adventures of Brer Rabbit [2-5], 1707

McDermott, Gerald. *Coyote: A Trickster Tale from the American Southwest* [Pre-2], **975**

Raven: A Trickster Tale from the Pacific Northwest [K-4], **976**

Zomo the Rabbit: A Trickster Tale from West Africa [Pre-1], **977**

Mayo, Gretchen Will. *Big Trouble for Tricky Rabbit!* [1-3], **1078**

That Tricky Coyote! [K-2], **1079**

Mollel, Tololwa M. *The Flying Tortoise: An Igbo Tale* [K-2], **987**

Rhinos for Lunch and Elephants for Supper! [Pre-2], **991**

Mwenye Hadithi. *Baby Baboon* [Pre], **37**

Hungry Hyena [K-1], **331**

Parks, Van Dyke, and Malcolm Jones. *Jump! The Adventures of Brer Rabbit* [2-5], 1714

Robinson, Gail. *Raven the Trickster: Legends of the North American Indians* [4-6], 1719

Ross, Gayle. *How Rabbit Tricked Otter and Other Cherokee Trickster Stories* [1-4], **1084**

How Turtle's Back Was Cracked: A Traditional Cherokee Tale [1-4], **1008**

Roth, Susan L. *Kanahena: A Cherokee Story* [Pre-2], 1587

Stevens, Janet. *Coyote Steals the Blanket: A Ute Tale* [Pre-3], **1029**

Temple, Frances. *Tiger Soup: An Anansi Story from Jamaica* [Pre-2], **1034**

Yep, Laurence. *The Man Who Tricked a Ghost* [1-4], **1047**

TROJAN WAR

Sutcliff, Rosemary. *Black Ships Before Troy! The Story of the Iliad* [5-6], **1088**

TROLLS

SEE ALSO Fairies; Giants; Leprechauns; Monsters; Ogres

Brett, Jan. *Trouble with Trolls* [K-1], **236**

Langerlöf, Selma. *The Changeling* [2-3], **636**

LeGuin, Ursula K. *A Ride on the Red Mare's Back* [2-3], **637**

Marshall, Edward. *Troll Country* [K-1], 501

Torgersen, Don Arthur. *The Girl Who Tricked the Troll* [1-2], 832

TROLLS–Folklore

Asbjørnsen, P. C. *The Three Billy Goats Gruff* [Pre-2], 1396

Dasent, George Webbe. *The Cat on the Dovrefell: A Christmas Tale* [Pre-2], 1432

East o' the Sun and West o' the Moon [3-6], **890**

East o' the Sun & West o' the Moon: An Old Norse Tale [2-6], 1433

D'Aulaire, Ingri, and Edgar Parin D'Aulaire. *D'Aulaire's Trolls* [K-3], 1434

Galdone, Paul. *The Three Billy Goats Gruff* [Pre-1], 1473

Martin, Claire. *Boots & the Glass Mountain* [2-6], **981**

Rounds, Glen. *The Three Billy Goats Gruff* [Pre-2], **1009**

TRUCKS

SEE ALSO Automobiles; Buses; Transportation

Lyon, David. *The Biggest Truck* [Pre-K], 193

Merrill, Jean. *The Pushcart War* [5-6], 1331

Siebert, Diane. *Truck Song* [Pre-K], 266

Williams, Karen Lynn. *Tap-Tap* [1-2], **576**

TUBMAN, HARRIET

Ringgold, Faith. *Aunt Harriet's Underground Railroad in the Sky* [2-3], **670**

TURKEYS

Pilkey, Dav. *'Twas the Night Before Thanksgiving* [1-2], **531**

Schatell, Brian. *Farmer Goff and His Turkey Sam* [K-1], 543

TURKEYS–Folklore

Pollock, Penny. *The Turkey Girl: A Zuni Cinderella Story* [2-5], **1000**

TURTLES

SEE ALSO Reptiles

Asch, Frank. *Turtle Tale* [Pre-K], 16

Balian, Lorna. *The Animal* [K-1], 327

Berger, Terry. *The Turtle's Picnic: And Other Nonsense Stories* [1-2], 615

Blathwayt, Benedict. *Stories from Firefly Island* [1-2], **407**

Dahl, Roald. *Esio Trot* [3-4], **710**

George, William T. *Box Turtle at Long Pond* [Pre-2], 2037

Leedy, Loreen. *Tracks in the Sand* [K-2], **1183**

MacGregor, Ellen. *Theodore Turtle* [K-1], 491

Mwenye Hadithi. *Tricky Tortoise* [Pre-K], 126

Williams, Barbara. *Albert's Toothache* [Pre-K], 296

TURTLES–Folklore

Aesop. *The Tortoise and the Hare: An Aesop Tale* [Pre-2], 1388

Han, Suzanne Crowder. *The Rabbit's Escape* [1-5], **936**

Lottridge, Celia Barker. *The Name of the Tree: A Bantu Folktale* [Pre-2], **973**

Mollel, Tololwa M. *The Flying Tortoise: An Igbo Tale* [K-2], **987**

The King and the Tortoise [K-3], **988**

Ross, Gayle. *How Turtle's Back Was Cracked: A Traditional Cherokee Tale* [1-4], **1008**

Roth, Susan L. *Kanahena: A Cherokee Story* [Pre-2], 1587

Wildsmith, Brian. *The Hare and the Tortoise* [Pre-3], 1627

TWINS

Brown, Marc. *Arthur Babysits* [1-2], **412**

Cleary, Beverly. *The Growing-Up Feet* [Pre-K], 50

Conford, Ellen. *Me and the Terrible Two* [4-5], 1161

Crew, Linda. *Nekomah Creek* [3-4], **709**

McMillan, Bruce. *One, Two, One Pair!* [Pre], **31**

Seuling, Barbara. *The Triplets* [1-2], 800

Slobodkin, Florence. *Too Many Mittens* [Pre-K], 268

Wallace, Barbara Brooks. *The Twin in the Tavern* [5-6], **849**

Wisniewski, David. *The Warrior and the Wise Man* [2-3], 1031

UNCLES

Bellaits, John. *The House with a Clock in Its Walls* [4-5], 1143

Byars, Betsy. *The Winged Colt of Casa Mia* [3-4], 1048

DiSalvo-Ryan, DyAnne. *Uncle Willie and the Soup Kitchen* [1-2], **432**

Howard, Elizabeth Fitzgerald. *Mac & Marie & the Train Toss Surprise* [1-2], **455**

Jukes, Mavis. *I'll See You in My Dreams* [3-4], **718**

Lobel, Arnold. *Uncle Elephant* [K-1], 486

Martin, Jacqueline Briggs. *Bizzy Bones and the Lost Quilt* [Pre-K], 206

Mitchell, Margaree King. *Uncle Jed's Barbershop* [2-3], **647**

Pinkwater, Daniel. *Yobgorgle: Mystery Monster of Lake Ontario* [4-5], 1227

Schneider, Howie. *Uncle Lester's Hat* [K-1], **357**

Stevenson, James. *Worse Than the Worst* [1-2], **560**

Tripp, Wallace. *My Uncle Podger* [3-4], 1123

Wetterer, Margaret. *The Giant's Apprentice* [3-4], 1130

UNCLES–Folklore

French, Vivian. *Why the Sea Is Salt* [1-4], **906**

UNDERGROUND RAILROAD

SEE Slavery

UNICORNS–Folklore

Thomson, Peggy. *The Brave Little Tailor* [1-4], **1035**

U.S.–Constitutional History

Fritz, Jean. *Shh! We're Writing the Constitution* [4-6], 2032

Maestro, Betsy. *A More Perfect Union: The Story of Our Constitution* [2-5], 2073

U.S.–History

Cleveland, Will, and Mark Alvarez. *Yo, Millard Fillmore! (And All Those Other Presidents You Don't Know)* [4-6], **1119**

Freedman, Russell. *Immigrant Kids* [4-6], 2027

Hiscock, Bruce. *The Big Tree* [2-4], **1162**

Levine, Ellen. *If Your Name Was Changed at Ellis Island* [3-6], **1186**

Perl, Lila. *It Happened in America: True Stories from the Fifty States* [5-6], **1216**

U.S.–History–Civil War

Holland, Isabelle. *Behind the Lines* [5-6], **824**

Polacco, Patricia. *Pink and Say* [4-5], **786**

Reit, Seymour. *Behind Rebel Lines: The Incredible Story of Emma Edmonds, Civil War Spy* [5-6], 2085

U.S.–History–Colonial Period

Fritz, Jean. *The Double Life of Pocahontas* [4-6], 2031

Who's That Stepping on Plymouth Rock? [3-6], 2035

George, Jean Craighead. *The First Thanksgiving* [1-4], **1147**

McGovern, Ann. *If You Lived in Colonial Times* [2-5], 2069

Sewall, Marcia. *The Pilgrims of Plimoth* [2-6], 2098

Waters, Kate. *Samuel Eaton's Day: A Day in the Life of a Pilgrim Boy* [2-4], **1250**

Sarah Morton's Day: A Day in the Life of a Pilgrim Girl [1-5], 2112

U.S.–History–Colonial Period–Fiction

Avi. *Night Journeys* [5-6], 1268

Sauer, Julie L. *Fog Magic* [5-6], 1353

Speare, Elizabeth George. *The Sign of the Beaver* [5-6], 1363

U.S.–History–Revolution

Brown, Drollene P. *Sybil Rides for Independence* [2-4], 2001

D'Aulaire, Ingri, and Edgar Parin D'Aulaire. *Benjamin Franklin* [2-6], 2013

Fritz, Jean. *And Then What Happened, Paul Revere?* [3-6], 2029

Can't You Make Them Behave, King George? [3-6], 2030

What's the Big Idea, Ben Franklin? [3-6], 2033

Giblin, James Cross. *George Washington: A Picture Book Biography* [1-4], **1150**

Griffin, Judith Berry. *Phoebe and the General* [2-5], 2042

Longfellow, Henry Wadsworth. *Paul Revere's Ride* [4-6], 1863

McGovern, Ann. *The Secret Soldier: The Story of Deborah Sampson* [3-6], 2071

Osborne, Mary Pope. *George Washington: Leader of a New Nation* [5-6], **1214**

U.S.–History–Revolution–Fiction

Avi. *The Fighting Ground* [5-6], 1267

Brady, Esther Wood. *Toliver's Secret* [4-5], 1148

Collier, James Lincoln, and Christopher Collier. *My Brother Sam Is Dead* [5-6], 1288

Gauch, Patricia Lee. *This Time, Tempe Wick?* [2-3], 926

Lawson, Robert. *Ben and Me* [5-6], 1324

Woodruff, Elvira. *George Washington's Socks* [4-5], **798**

U.S.–History–Revolution–Poetry

Longfellow, Henry Wadsworth. *Paul Revere's Ride* [2-6], **1361**

U.S.–History–Riddles

Adler, David A. *Remember Betsy Floss: And Other Colonial American Riddles* [2-6], 1740

Wild Pill Hickok and Other Old West Riddles [2-5], 1741

Keller, Charles, and Richard Baker. *The Star-Spangled Banana and Other Revolutionary Riddles* [2-6], 1844

U.S.–History–1783-1865

Adler, David A. *A Picture Book of Harriet Tubman* [1-4], **1095**

A Picture Book of Sojourner Truth [2-4], **1096**

Blumberg, Rhoda. *The Incredible Journey of Lewis & Clark* [5-6], 1996

Ferris, Jeri. *Go Free or Die: A Story About Harriet Tubman* [3-5], **1141**

Freedman, Russell. *Lincoln: A Photobiography* [5-6], 2028

McGovern, Ann. *Runaway Slave: The Story of Harriet Tubman* [2-5], 2070

Russell, Marion. *Along the Santa Fe Trail: Marion Russell's Own Story* [2-5], **1230**

Winter, Jeanette. *Follow the Drinking Gourd* [3-4], 1134

U.S.–History–1783-1865–Fiction

Brink, Carol Ryrie. *Caddie Woodlawn* [4-5], 1151

Fleischman, Sid. *By the Great Horn Spoon* [5-6], 1300

Hopkinson, Deborah. *Sweet Clara and the Freedom Quilt* [2-3], **622**

Hurmence, Belinda. *A Girl Called Boy* [5-6], 1314

Johnson, Dolores. *Now Let Me Fly: The Story of a Slave Family* [2-3], **629**

Kirby, Susan. *Ike and Porker* [4-5], 1200

Monjo, F. N. *The Drinking Gourd* [2-3], 966

Mooser, Stephen. *Orphan Jeb at the Massacree* [4-5], 1215

Ringgold, Faith. *Aunt Harriet's Underground Railroad in the Sky* [2-3], **670**

Woodruff, Elvira. *Dear Levi: Letters from the Overland Trail* [4-5], **796**

U.S.–History–1865-1898

Freedman, Russell. *Buffalo Hunt* [5-6], 2025

Children of the Wild West [3-6], 2026

U.S.–History–1865-1898–Fiction

Andersen, Hans Christian. *The Tinderbox* [4-5], **757**

Beatty, Patricia. *That's One Ornery Orphan* [5-6], 1274

Van Leeuwen, Jean. *Bound for Oregon* [4-5], **793**

Wilder, Laura Ingalls. *Farmer Boy* [3-4], 1132
Little House in the Big Woods [2-3], 1028

U.S.–History–20th Century–Fiction

Brenner, Barbara. *A Year in the Life of Rosie Bernard* [4-5], 1149

Burch, Robert. *Ida Early Comes Over the Mountain* [4-5], 1153

Fitzgerald, John D. *The Great Brain* [4-5], 1171

U.S.–Poetry

Bates, Katharine Lee. *America the Beautiful* [Pre-6], **1265**

Panzer, Nora. *Celebrate America in Poetry and Art* [4-6], **1393**

Whipple, Laura. *Celebrating America: A Collection of Poems and Images of the American Spirit* [3-6], **1422**

U.S.–Riddles

Gerberg, Mort. *Geographunny: A Book of Global Riddles* [3-6], **1295**

Maestro, Marco, and Giulio Maestro. *Riddle City, USA! A Book of Geography Riddles* [3-6], **1368**

UNIVERSE

SEE ALSO Astronomy; Moon; Space flight; Stars; Sun

Mazer, Anne. *The Yellow Button* [1-2], **505**

Wells, Robert E. *Is a Blue Whale the Biggest Thing There Is?* [2-5], **1251**

UTE INDIANS–Folklore

Stevens, Janet. *Coyote Steals the Blanket: A Ute Tale* [Pre-3], **1029**

VACATIONS

Stanley, Diane. *Moe the Dog in Tropical Paradise* [1-2], **556**

VALENTINE'S DAY

Bunting, Eve. *The Valentine Bears* [K-1], 353

Carlson, Nancy L. *Louanne Pig in the Mysterious Valentine* [1-2], 637

Hoban, Lillian. *Arthur's Great Big Valentine* [K-1], 426

Modell, Frank. *One Zillion Valentines* [1-2], 751

Scribner, Virginia. *Gopher Takes Heart* [3-4], **744**

Sharmat, Marjorie Weinman. *The Best Valentine in the World* [1-2], 807

Spinelli, Eileen. *Somebody Loves You, Mr. Hatch* [K-1], **371**

Stevenson, James. *Happy Valentine's Day, Emma!* [1-2], 823

VALENTINE'S DAY–Poetry

Prelutsky, Jack. *It's Valentine's Day* [Pre-3], 1909

VAMPIRES

Howe, James. *Rabbit-Cadabra!* [1-2], **458**

Pinkwater, Daniel. *Wempires* [1-2], **535**

VANITY

SEE Pride and vanity

VEGETABLES

SEE ALSO Cookery; Flowers; Food; Fruit; Gardens; Plants; Soup

Ehlert, Lois. *Eating the Alphabet: Fruits and Vegetables from A to Z* [Pre-K], 77
Growing Vegetable Soup [Pre-K], 78

Hall, Zoe. *It's Pumpkin Time!* [Pre], **18**

Krauss, Ruth. *The Carrot Seed* [Pre-K], 178

McMillan, Bruce. *Growing Colors* [Pre-K], 197

Modesitt, Jeanne. *Vegetable Soup* [Pre-K], **170**

Nolan, Dennis. *Witch Bazooza* [1-2], 762

Wiesner, David. *June 29, 1999* [2-3], **690**

VEGETABLES–Folklore

Chocolate, Deborah M. Newton. *Talk, Talk: An Ashanti Legend* [1-5], **877**

dePaola, Tomie. *Jamie O'Rourke and the Big Potato: An Irish Folktale* [K-4], **895**

Domanska, Janina. *The Turnip* [Pre-1], 1448

Grimm, Jacob. *One Gift Deserves Another* [1-4], **927**

Morgan, Pierr. *The Turnip: An Old Russian Folktale* [Pre-1], 1569

Stevens, Janet. *Tops & Bottoms* [Pre-2], **1030**

Tolstoi, Alexie. *The Great Big Enormous Turnip* [Pre-1], 1614

VEGETABLES–Riddles

Keller, Charles. *Alexander the Grape: Fruit and Vegetable Jokes* [2-6], 1834

VENUS–Folklore

SEE ALSO Astronomy–Folklore

Mollel, Tololwa M. *The Orphan Boy: A Maasai Story* [1-4], **989**

VERBS

SEE English language–Grammar

VERMONT

Wells, Rosemary. *Waiting for the Evening Star* [3-4], **754**

VICTORIA, QUEEN OF GREAT BRITAIN, 1819-1901

King-Smith, Dick. *The Swoose* [3-4], **727**

VIETNAM

Keller, Holly. *Grandfather's Dream* [1-2], **466**

VIETNAM WAR

Garland, Sherry. *The Lotus Seed* [2-3], **609**
Kidd, Diana. *Onion Tears* [4-5], **772**

VIOLIN

Namioka, Lensey. *Yang the Youngest and His Terrible Ear* [4-5], **781**

VISUAL PERCEPTION

Bourke, Linda. *Eye Spy: A Mysterious Alphabet* [1-2], **409**
Brown, Ruth A. *If at First You Do Not See* [K-1], 348
Cauley, Lorinda Bryan. *Treasure Hunt* [Pre-K], **79**
Falwell, Cathryn. *Clowning Around* [K-1], **272**
Gardner, Beau. *Guess What?* [Pre-K], 110
    The Look Again . . . and Again, and Again, and Again Book [1-2], 675
Goffin, Josse. *Oh!* [Pre-K], **109**
Heller, Nicholas. *Up the Wall* [K-1], **281**
Hoban, Tana. *Look Again!* [1-2], 688
    Look! Look! Look! [K-1], **286**
Jonas, Ann. *The 13th Clue* [1-2], **464**
    Reflections [1-2], 700
    Round Trip [1-2], 701
Keller, Wallace. *The Wrong Side of the Bed* [K-1], **297**
MacDonald, Suse. *Alphabatics* [K-1], 490
MacDonald, Suse, and Bill Oakes. *Puzzlers* [K-1], **314**
McMillan, Bruce. *Beach Ball—Left, Right* [Pre-K], **158**
    Mouse Views: What the Class Pet Saw [K-1], **315**
Shaw, Charles G. *It Looked Like Spilt Milk* [Pre-K], 264
Ungerer, Tomi. *One, Two, Where's My Shoe?* [Pre-K], 281
Yektai, Niki. *What's Missing?* [Pre-K], 303
    What's Silly? [Pre-K], 304

VOCABULARY

SEE ALSO English language; Language; Word games
Anholt, Catherine, and Laurence Anholt. *All About You* [Pre], **3**
Appelt, Kathi. *Elephants Aloft* [Pre-K], **66**

Babbitt, Natalie. *The Search for Delicious* [4-5], 1139
Baer, Edith. *Words are Like Faces* [K-1], 324
Day, Alexandra. *Frank and Ernest* [2-3], 906
Dodds, Dayle Ann. *Do Bunnies Talk?* [K-1], **262**
Duke, Kate. *Guinea Pigs Far and Near* [Pre-K], 75
Falwell, Cathryn. *Clowning Around* [K-1], **272**
Hepworth, Cathi. *Antics! An Alphabetical Anthology* [2-6], **1312**
Hoban, Tana. *A Children's Zoo* [K-1], 430
Hughes, Shirley. *Giving* [Pre], **22**
Hunt, Bernice. *The Whatchmacallit Book* [3-6], 2052
Ipcar, Dahlov. *I Love My Anteater with an A* [3-4], 1078
Juster, Norton. *The Phantom Tollbooth* [5-6], 1316
Levitt, Paul M., Douglas A. Burger, and Elissa S. Guralnick. *The Weighty Word Book* [5-6], 1326
MacCarthy, Patricia. *Herds of Words* [K-6], **1363**
McMillan, Bruce. *Super Super Superwords* [Pre-K], 199
Merriam, Eve. *Chortles: New and Selected Wordplay Poems* [3-6], 1869
Miller, Margaret. *Can You Guess?* [Pre], **33**
Morley, Diana. *Marms in the Marmalade* [1-4], 1876
Nevins, Ann. *From the Horse's Mouth* [3-6], 1896
Roop, Peter, and Connie Roop. *One Earth, a Multitude of Creatures* [K-6], **1228**
Schwartz, Alvin. *Chin Music: Tall Talk and Other Talk, Collected from American Folklore* [3-6], 1946
Sperling, Susan Kelz. *Murflies and Wink-a-Peeps: Funny Old Words for Kids* [2-6], 1956
Steckler, Arthur. *101 More Words and How They Began* [3-6], 1958
Terban, Marvin. *In a Pickle and Other Funny Idioms* [3-6], 1964
Viorst, Judith. *The Alphabet from Z to A: With Much Confusion on the Way* [3-6], **1416**

VOCABULARY–Folklore

Gackenbach, Dick. *Arabella and Mr. Crack* [K-3], 1454
Sewall, Marcia. *Master of All Masters: An English Folktale* [K-3], 1597

VOICE

Kraus, Robert. *Phil the Ventriloquist* [Pre-K], 176
Porter, David Lord. *Help! Let Me Out* [2-3], 982

VOLCANOES

Anderson, Lonzo. *The Ponies of Mykillengi* [2-3], 865

Drury, Roger W. *The Finches' Fabulous Furnace* [4-5], 1170

Du Bois, William Pène. *The Twenty-One Balloons* [5-6], 1295

Lauber, Patricia. *Volcano: The Eruption and Healing of Mount St. Helens* [4-6], 2063

Lewis, Thomas P. *Hill of Fire* [1-2], 723

Mahy, Margaret. *The Rattlebang Picnic* [1-2], **502**

Simon, Seymour. *Volcanoes* [2-6], 2106

VOLCANOES–Folklore

Grifalconi, Ann. *The Village of Round and Square Houses* [K-4], 1485

Roddy, Patricia. *Api and the Boy Stranger: A Village Creation Tale* [K-2], **1006**

VOLES

Waddell, Martin. *Sam Vole and His Brothers* [Pre], **51**

VOYAGES AND TRAVELS

Avi. *The True Confessions of Charlotte Doyle* [5-6], **803**

Ball, Duncan. *Jeremy's Tail* [K-1], **227**

Brisson, Pat. *Magic Carpet* [1-2], **411**

Bursik, Rose. *Amelia's Fantastic Flight* [1-2], **417**

Conrad, Pam. *Pedro's Journal: A Voyage with Christopher Columbus, August 3, 1492–February 14, 1492* [5-6], **809**

Krupp, Robin Rector. *Let's Go Traveling* [3-5], **1177**

Leighton, Maxine Rhea. *An Ellis Island Christmas* [2-3], **638**

Lester, Alison. *The Journey Home* [K-1], **303**

Lobel, Anita. *Away from Home* [1-2], **487**

Priceman, Marjorie. *How to Make an Apple Pie and See the World* [1-2], **538**

Say, Allen. *Grandfather's Journey* [2-3], **674**

Schneider, Howie. *Uncle Lester's Hat* [K-1], **357**

Sheldon, Dyan. *Love, Your Bear Pete* [K-1], **363**

Winter, Jeanette. *Klara's New World* [2-3], **693**

WAMPANOAG INDIANS–Folklore

Manitonquat (Medicine Story). *Children of the Morning Light: Wampanoag Tales* [3-6], **1077**

WAR

SEE ALSO U.S.–History–Civil War; U.S.–History–Revolution; Vietnam War; World War, 1914-1918; World War, 1939-1945

Foreman, Michael. *War Game* [5-6], **816**

Garland, Sherry. *The Lotus Seed* [2-3], **609**

Heide, Florence Parry, and Judith Heide Gilliland. *Sami and the Time of the Troubles* [3-4], **713**

Ho, Minfong. *The Clay Marble* [5-6], **823**

Holland, Isabelle. *Behind the Lines* [5-6], **824**

Ikeda, Daisaku. *Over the Deep Blue Sea* [1-2], **460**

Kidd, Diana. *Onion Tears* [4-5], **772**

Lisle, Janet Taylor. *Forest* [5-6], **827**

Mellecker, Judith. *Randolph's Dream* [3-4], **732**

Morimoto, Junko. *My Hiroshima* [3-6], **1210**

Polacco, Patricia. *Pink and Say* [4-5], **786**

Price, Leontyne. *Aïda* [5-6], **837**

Rabin, Staton. *Casey Over There* [2-3], **666**

Stevenson, James. *Don't You Know There's a War On?* [2-6], **1245**

WAR–Folklore

Grimm, Jacob. *The Bear and the Bird King* [K-3], **929**

MacDonald, Margaret Read. *Peace Tales: World Folktales to Talk About* [1-6], **1076**

Sutcliff, Rosemary. *Black Ships Before Troy! The Story of the Iliad* [5-6], **1088**

WASCO INDIANS–Folklore

Taylor, Harriet Peck. *Coyote Places the Stars* [1-3], **1033**

WASHINGTON, D.C.

Brown, Marc. *Arthur Meets the President* [1-2], **413**

Bunting, Eve. *The Wall* [K-1], 354

Fife, Dale. *Who's in Charge of Lincoln?* [2-3], 917

WASHINGTON, GEORGE

Giblin, James Cross. *George Washington: A Picture Book Biography* [1-4], **1150**

Osborne, Mary Pope. *George Washington: Leader of a New Nation* [5-6], **1214**

Roth, Roger. *The Sign Painter's Dream* [1-2], **545**

Woodruff, Elvira. *George Washington's Socks* [4-5], **798**

WATER

Albert, Richard E. *Alejandro's Gift* [1-2], **397**

Cole, Joanna. *The Magic School Bus at the Waterworks* [2-4], 2008

Dorros, Arthur. *Follow the Water from Brook to Ocean* [K-3], **1133**

Hughes, Shirley. *An Evening at Alfie's* [Pre-K], 147

Peters, Lisa Westberg. *Water's Way* [K-3], **1218**

WATER–Folklore

Dayrell, Elphinstone. *Why the Sun and Moon Live in the Sky* [Pre-2], 1435

WATER–Poetry

Graham, Joan Bransfield. *Splish Splash* [K-6], **1301**

WATER POLLUTION
SEE Pollution

WEALTH
Armstrong, Jennifer. *Chin Yu Min and the Ginger Cat* [2-3], **588**

WEASELS
Ernst, Lisa Campbell. *Zinnia and Dot* [K-1], **271**

WEATHER
SEE ALSO Clouds; Rain and rainfall; Snow; Storms
Barrett, Judi. *Cloudy with a Chance of Meatballs* [2-3], 871
Branley, Franklyn M. *Tornado Alert* [1-4], 1998
Brittain, Bill. *Dr. Dredd's Wagon of Wonders* [5-6], 1277
Coombs, Patricia. *Dorrie and the Weather Box* [1-2], 653
Cooney, Nancy Evans. *The Umbrella Day* [Pre-K], 57
Cummings, Pat. *C.L.O.U.D.S.* [2-3], 903
Davis, Hubert. *A January Fog Will Freeze a Hog and Other Weather Folklore* [2-6], 2016
dePaola, Tomie. *The Cloud Book* [1-3], 2017
Ginsburg, Mirra. *Mushroom in the Rain* [Pre-K], 115
Harper, Jo. *Jalapeño Hal* [2-3], **615**
Keats, Ezra Jack. *The Snowy Day* [Pre-K], 165
McPhail, David. *Great Cat* [K-1], 495
Martin, Bill, Jr., and John Archambault. *Listen to the Rain* [1-2], 746
Moskin, Marietta. *The Day of the Blizzard* [3-4], 1098
Polacco, Patricia. *Thunder Cake* [K-1], 525
Rodda, Emily. *The Pigs Are Flying* [4-5], 1231
Ruckman, Ivy. *Night of the Twisters* [4-5], 1235
Seuss, Dr. *Bartholomew and the Oobleck* [2-3], 994
Simon, Seymour. *Storms* [4-6], 2105
Stevenson, James. *Brrr!* [K-1], **373**
Stolz, Mary. *Storm in the Night* [1-2], 828
Tresselt, Alvin. *Hide and Seek Fog* [1-2], 833
Tunnell, Michael O. *Chinook!* [2-3], **688**
Wiesner, David. *Hurricane* [1-2], **574**
Wisniewski, David. *Rain Player* [2-3], **694**
Wood, Audrey. *The Napping House* [Pre-K], 301

WEATHER–Folklore
Yep, Laurence. *The Junior Thunder Lord* [1-4], **1046**

WEATHER–Poetry
Bauer, Caroline Feller. *Windy Day: Stories and Poems* [1-4], 1746

Graham, Joan Bransfield. *Splish Splash* [K-6], **1301**
Hopkins, Lee Bennett. *Weather* [1-3], **1329**
Hughes, Shirley. *Out and About* [Pre-1], 1831
Lewis, J. Patrick. *Earth Verses and Water Rhymes* [2-4], **1352**
Prelutsky, Jack. *Rainy Rainy Saturday* [K-2], 1915
Radley, Gail. *Rainy Day Rhymes* [Pre-2], **1399**

WEDDINGS
Brown, Marc. *D.W. Thinks Big* [Pre-K], **71**

WEDDINGS–Folklore
Cook, Joel. *The Rat's Daughter* [K-2], **886**

WEIGHTS AND MEASURES
Tompert, Ann. *Just a Little Bit* [Pre-K], **192**

WEREWOLVES
Ogburn, Jacqueline K. *Scarlett Angelina Wolverton-Manning* [1-2], **524**
Rice, Bebe Faas. *The Year the Wolves Came* [5-6], **839**

WEST
Adler, David A. *Wild Bill Hickok and Other Old West Riddles* [2-5], 1741
Axelrod, Alan. *Songs of the Wild West* [1-6], **1264**
Beatty, Patricia. *That's One Ornery Orphan* [5-6], 1274
Blumberg, Rhoda. *The Incredible Journey of Lewis & Clark* [5-6], 1996
Coren, Alan. *Arthur the Kid* [2-3], 902
Fleischman, Sid. *By the Great Horn Spoon* [5-6], 1300
Freedman, Russell. *Buffalo Hunt* [5-6], 2025
Children of the Wild West [3-6], 2026
Gerrard, Roy. *Rosie and the Rustlers* [2-3], **610**
Gipson, Fred. *Old Yeller* [4-5], 1180
Greer, Gery, and Bob Ruddick. *Max and Me and the Wild West* [5-6], 1307
Harper, Jo. *Jalapeño Hal* [2-3], **615**
Johnston, Tony. *The Cowboy and the Black-Eyed Pea* [3-4], **717**
Kennedy, Richard. *The Contests at Cowlick* [1-2], 708
The Rise and Fall of Ben Gizzard [3-4], 1083
Kimmel, Eric A. *Charlie Drives the Stage* [2-3], 943
Four Dollars and Fifty Cents [3-4], **721**
Medearis, Angela Shelf. *The Zebra-Riding Cowboy: A Folk Song from the Old West* [2-3], **645**
Mooser, Stephen. *Orphan Jeb at the Massacree* [4-5], 1215

Sharmat, Marjorie Weinman. *Gila Monsters Meet You at the Airport* [1-2], 808

Sullivan, Charles. *Cowboys* [K-4], **1413**

Van Leeuwen, Jean. *Bound for Oregon* [4-5], **793**

Yorinks, Arthur. *Whitefish Will Rides Again!* [1-2], **581**

WEST VIRGINIA

Naylor, Phyllis Reynolds. *Shiloh* [5-6], **832**

Yep, Laurence. *The Star Fisher* [5-6], **854**

WHALES

Berger, Gilda. *Whales* [2-4], 1995

Kipling, Rudyard. *How the Whale Got His Throat* [1-2], 712

McCloskey, Robert. *Burt Dow, Deep-Water Man* [2-3], 955

McMillan, Bruce. *Going on a Whale Watch* [K-3], **1194**

Ryder, Joanne. *Winter Whale* [K-3], **1232**

Vollmer, Dennis. *Joshua Disobeys* [Pre-K], **198**

WHALES–Poetry

Livingston, Myra Cohn. *If You Ever Meet a Whale* [2-5], **1358**

WHEELCHAIRS

SEE ALSO Handicapped

Carlson, Nancy L. *Arnie and the New Kid* [1-2], **421**

Cowen-Fletcher, Jane. *Mama Zooms* [Pre-K], **89**

Damrell, Liz. *With the Wind* [1-2], **429**

Osofsky, Audrey. *My Buddy* [1-2], **526**

Russo, Marisabina. *Alex Is My Friend* [K-1], **354**

WILDCATS–Folklore

Gregg, Andy. *Great Rabbit and the Long-Tailed Wildcat* [2-4], **921**

WILDLIFE CONSERVATION

Facklam, Margery. *And Then There Was One: The Mysteries of Extinction* [3-6], **1139**

Koch, Michelle. *World Water Watch* [K-2], **1172**

Leslie-Melville, Betty. *Elephant Have the Right of Way: Life with the Wild Animals of Africa* [2-6], **1185**

WILDLIFE RESCUE

Heinrich, Bernd. *An Owl in the House: A Naturalist's Diary* [4-6], **1158**

Keller, Holly. *Island Baby* [K-1], **296**

Pfeffer, Wendy. *Popcorn Park Zoo: A Haven with a Heart* [3-5], **1220**

Rand, Gloria. *Prince William* [2-3], **668**

WIND

SEE ALSO Rain and rainfall; Storms; Tornadoes; Weather

Bauer, Caroline Feller. *Windy Day: Stories and Poems* [1-4], 1746

McKissack, Patricia C. *Mirandy and Brother Wind* [2-3], 958

Small, David. *Paper John* [1-2], 814

Tunnell, Michael O. *Chinook!* [2-3], **688**

WIND–Folklore

Aesop. *The Wind and the Sun* [K-2], **859**

Climo, Shirley. *The Match Between the Winds* [K-3], **879**

WINGS

Byars, Betsy. *The Winged Colt of Casa Mia* [3-4], 1048

Gormley, Beatrice. *Mail-Order Wings* [4-5], 1182

Le Guin, Ursula K. *Catwings* [2-3], 950

Lionni, Leo. *Tico and the Golden Wings* [2-3], 952

Woodruff, Elvira. *The Wing Shop* [1-2], **580**

WINGS–Folklore

Wolkstein, Diane. *The Magic Wings: A Tale from China* [Pre-4], 1630

WINTER

SEE ALSO Seasons; Snow

Anderson, Lonzo. *The Ponies of Mykillengi* [2-3], 865

Andrews, Jan. *Very Last First Time* [2-3], 867

Brett, Jan. *Trouble with Trolls* [K-1], **236**

Burton, Virgina Lee. *Katy and the Big Snow* [Pre-K], 35

Calhoun, Mary. *Cross-Country Cat* [1-2], 635

Chapman, Cheryl. *Snow on Snow on Snow* [Pre-K], **83**

Christelow, Eileen. *The Five-Dog Night* [1-2], **425**

Christiansen, Candace. *The Ice Horse* [2-3], **597**

Emberley, Michael. *Welcome Back Sun* [1-2], **438**

Fleming, Susan. *Trapped on the Golden Flyer* [4-5], 1173

Giff, Patricia Reilly. *The Winter Worm Business* [4-5], 1177

Hartley, Deborah. *Up North in Winter* [1-2], 683

Johnson, Crockett. *Will Spring Be Early? or Will Spring Be Late?* [K-1], 439

Keats, Ezra Jack. *The Snowy Day* [Pre-K], 165

Kinsey-Warnock, Natalie. *When Spring Comes* [1-2], **469**

Lewis, C. S. *The Lion, the Witch and the Wardrobe* [3-4], 1088

Lindgren, Astrid. *The Tomten* [1-2], 725

Lionni, Leo. *Frederick* [1-2], 727

Nietzel, Shirley. *The Jacket I Wear in the Snow* [Pre-K], 217

Paulsen, Gary. *Dogteam* [3-4], **738**

Rand, Gloria. *Salty Takes Off* [1-2], **540**

WINTER (cont.)

Rice, Bebe Faas. *The Year the Wolves Came* [5-6], **839**

Rice, Eve. *Oh, Lewis!* [Pre-K], 239

Rogers, Jean. *Runaway Mittens* [Pre-K], 244

Ryder, Joanne. *Chipmunk Song* [Pre-2], 2089

Seibert, Patricia. *Mush! Across Alaska in the World's Longest Sled-Dog Race* [1-4], **1235**

Selsam, Millicent, and Joyce Hunt. *Keep Looking!* [Pre-2], 2095

Slobodkin, Florence. *Too Many Mittens* [Pre-K], 268

Stanley, Diane. *Moe the Dog in Tropical Paradise* [1-2], **556**

Steig, William. *Brave Irene* [1-2], 820

Stevenson, James. *Brrr!* [K-1], **373**

Swan, Robert. *Destination: Antarctica* [4-6], 2108

Taylor, Mark. *Henry the Explorer* [K-1], 564

Tejima, Keizaburo. *Fox's Dream* [K-1], 565

Tunnell, Michael O. *Chinook!* [2-3], **688**

Waddell, Martin. *Let's Go Home, Little Bear* [Pre-K], **201**

Yolen, Jane. *Owl Moon* [1-2], 857

Ziefert, Harriet. *Snow Magic* [Pre-K], 306

Zolotow, Charlotte. *Something Is Going to Happen* [Pre-K], 311

WINTER–Folklore

Brett, Jan. *The Mitten* [Pre-2], 1409

De Regniers, Beatrice Schenk. *Little Sister and the Month Brothers* [K-3], 1445

Grimm, Jacob. *Mother Holly* [Pre-2], 1502

Larry, Charles. *Peboan and Seegwun* [1-4], **964**

Marshak, Samuel. *The Month Brothers: A Slavic Tale* [K-3], 1560

Proddow, Penelope. *Demeter and Persephone* [5-6], 1581

Tresselt, Alvin. *The Mitten: An Old Ukrainian Folktale* [Pre-2], 1615

WINTER–Poetry

Prelutsky, Jack. *It's Snowing! It's Snowing!* [Pre-3], 1907

Rogasky, Barbara. *Winter Poems* [3-6], **1403**

Service, Robert W. *The Cremation of Sam McGee* [5-6], 1355

WISCONSIN

Tews, Susan. *The Gingerbread Doll* [1-2], **565**

WISDOM–Folklore

McDermott, Gerald. *Zomo the Rabbit: A Trickster Tale from West Africa* [Pre-1], **977**

Uchida, Yoshiko. *The Wise Old Woman* [1-5], **1038**

Young, Ed. *Seven Blind Mice* [Pre-3], **1051**

WISHES

Aiken, Joan. *The Moon's Revenge* [3-4], 1038

Avi. *Bright Shadow* [5-6], 1266

Benton, Robert. *Don't Ever Wish for a 7-Foot Bear* [1-2], 614

Brittain, Bill. *All the Money in the World* [4-5], 1152

The Wish Giver: Three Tales of Coven Tree [5-6], 1278

Carle, Eric. *The Mixed-Up Chameleon* [Pre-K], 38

Chapman, Carol. *Barney Bipple's Magic Dandelions* [1-2], 644

Dillon, Barbara. *A Mom by Magic* [4-5], **767**

Gershator, Phillis. *Rata-Pata-Scata-Fata: A Caribbean Story* [Pre-K], **108**

Griffith, Helen V. *Emily and the Enchanted Frog* [1-2], **446**

Heller, Nicholas. *Woody* [Pre-K], **121**

Howe, James. *I Wish I Were a Butterfly* [1-2], 692

Hutchins, Hazel. *The Three and Many Wishes of Jason Reid* [3-4], 1077

King-Smith, Dick. *The Queen's Nose* [3-4], **726**

Kovalski, Maryann. *Pizza for Breakfast* [1-2], **479**

LeSieg, Theo. *I Wish That I Had Duck Feet* [K-1], 467

Lester, Helen. *Pookins Gets Her Way* [K-1], 470

Lionni, Leo. *Alexander and the Wind-Up Mouse* [1-2], 726

Pomerantz, Charlotte. *The Downtown Fairy Godmother* [2-3], 981

Steig, William. *Sylvester and the Magic Pebble* [1-2], 821

Sterman, Betsy, and Samuel Sterman. *Too Much Magic* [3-4], 1119

Tzannes, Robin. *Professor Puffendorf's Secret Potions* [1-2], **569**

Waber, Bernard. *"You Look Ridiculous," Said the Rhinoceros to the Hippopotamus* [K-1], 580

Watson, Pauline. *Wriggles the Little Wishing Pig* [K-1], 582

Williams, Jay. *One Big Wish* [2-3], 1030

Yolen, Jane. *Sleeping Ugly* [2-3], 1033

WISHES–Folklore

Brusca, María Cristina, and Tona Wilson. *The Blacksmith and the Devils* [3-6], **873**

Carrick, Carol. *Aladdin and the Wonderful Lamp* [2-4], 1413

Grimm, Jacob. *The Fisherman and His Wife* [2-4], 1492

Lang, Andrew. *Aladdin and the Wonderful Lamp* [2-5], 1544

Mayer, Marianna. *Aladdin and the Enchanted Lamp* [4-6], 1565
The Spirit of the Blue Light [3-5], **986**
Zemach, Margot. *The Three Wishes: An Old Story* [1-4], 1640

WIT AND HUMOR
SEE Humorous fiction; Humorous poetry; Humorous songs; Jokes; Knock-knock jokes; Riddles

WITCHES
SEE ALSO Ghosts; Halloween; Supernatural; Wizards
Adams, Adrienne. *A Woggle of Witches* [Pre-K], 1
Anderson, Lonzo. *The Halloween Party* [1-2], 605
Balian, Lorna. *Humbug Potion: An A B Cipher* [1-2], 608
Humbug Witch [Pre-K], 20
Banks, Lynne Reid. *The Adventures of King Midas* [4-5], **758**
Bennett, Anna Elizabeth. *Little Witch* [2-3], 874
Brittain, Bill. *Devil's Donkey* [5-6], 1276
Buehner, Caralyn. *A Job for Wittilda* [K-1], **242**
Carlson, Natalie Savage. *Spooky Night* [K-1], 357
Carris, Joan. *Witch-Cat* [3-4], **706**
Coombs, Patricia. *Dorrie and the Weather Box* [1-2], 653
Dahl, Roald. *The Witches* [4-5], 1167
dePaola, Tomie. *Big Anthony and the Magic Ring* [2-3], 908
Merry Christmas, Strega Nona [2-3], 909
Strega Nona Meets Her Match [1-2], **430**
Devlin, Harry, and Wende Devlin. *Old Witch Rescues Halloween* [1-2], 661
Dillon, Barbara. *Mrs. Tooey & the Terrible Toxic Tar* [3-4], 1062
What's Happened to Harry? [2-3], 910
Embry, Margaret. *The Blue-Nosed Witch* [2-3], 913
Flora, James. *Grandpa's Ghost Stories* [2-3], 919
Grandpa's Witched-Up Christmas [2-3], 920
Greene, Carol. *The Thirteen Days of Halloween* [1-2], 681
Howe, James. *Scared Silly: A Halloween Treat* [1-2], 693
Johnston, Tony. *The Witch's Hat* [Pre-K], 156
Karlin, Nurit. *The Tooth Witch* [K-1], 447
Kroll, Steven. *The Candy Witch* [K-1], 462
Lester, Helen. *Me First* [K-1], **304**
Lewis, C. S. *The Lion, the Witch and the Wardrobe* [3-4], 1088
The Magician's Nephew [4-5], 1204

Low, Alice. *The Witch Who Was Afraid of Witches* [1-2], 731
Mahy, Margaret. *The Boy Who Was Followed Home* [1-2], 739
Meddaugh, Susan. *The Witches' Supermarket* [1-2], **507**
Napoli, Donna Jo. *The Prince of the Pond: Otherwise Known as De Fawg Pin* [4-5], **782**
Naylor, Phyllis Reynolds. *Witch's Sister* [4-5], 1217
Nolan, Dennis. *Witch Bazooza* [1-2], 762
Peet, Bill. *Big Bad Bruce* [1-2], 766
The Whingdingdilly [2-3], 979
Pyle, Howard. *The Swan Maiden* [2-3], **665**
Rael, Elsa Okon. *Marushka's Egg* [2-3], **667**
Scieszka, Jon. *The Frog Prince Continued* [2-3], **676**
Sheldon, Dyan. *A Witch Got on at Paddington Station* [Pre-K], 265
Silverman, Erica. *Big Pumpkin* [K-1], **364**
Springstubb, Tricia. *The Magic Guinea Pig* [Pre-K], 270
Steig, William. *Caleb and Kate* [3-4], 1118
Stevenson, James. *Happy Valentine's Day, Emma!* [1-2], 823
Yuck! [K-1], 562
Van Allsburg, Chris. *The Widow's Broom* [3-4], **752**
Vande Velde, Vivian. *A Hidden Magic* [4-5], 1251
Wood, Audrey. *Heckedy Peg* [1-2], 854
York, Carol Beach. *I Will Make You Disappear* [5-6], 1378

WITCHES–Folklore
Arnold, Katya. *Baba Yaga: A Russian Folktale* [1-3], **860**
Baba Yaga & the Little Girl [K-3], **861**
Ayres, Becky Hickox. *Matreshka* [K-3], **863**
Baden, Robert. *And Sunday Makes Seven* [2-4], **864**
Cole, Joanna. *Bony-Legs* [K-2], 1426
Grimm, Jacob. *Hansel and Gretel* [K-2], **926**
Hansel and Gretel [2-4], 1496, 1497
Jorinda and Joringel [2-4], 1498
Little Brother and Little Sister [2-5], 1499
Rapunzel [2-4], 1503, **923**
Harper, Wilhelmina. *Ghosts and Goblins: Stories for Halloween* [2-5], 1690
Hirsch, Marilyn. *The Rabbi and the Twenty-Nine Witches* [K-2], 1524
Hoke, Helen. *Witches, Witches, Witches* [2-5], 1697

WITCHES–Folklore (cont.)

Hopkins, Lee Bennett. *Witching Time: Mischievous Stories and Poems* [2-4], 1698

Kimmel, Eric A. *Baba Yaga: A Russian Folktale* [K-2], **951**

Manning-Sanders, Ruth. *A Book of Witches* [2-6], 1710

Mayer, Marianna. *Baba Yaga and Vasilisa the Brave* [2-5], **985**

Nimmo, Jenny. *The Witches and the Singing Mice* [1-4], **992**

Rayevsky, Inna. *The Talking Tree* [2-5], 1584

Silverman, Maida. *Anna and the Seven Swans* [K-3], 1601

Small, Ernest. *Baba Yaga* [1-4], 1602

Walker, Barbara. *Teeny-Tiny and the Witch Woman* [2-4], 1623

Winthrop, Elizabeth. *Vasilissa the Beautiful: A Russian Folktale* [2-5], **1044**

WITCHES–Poetry

Hopkins, Lee Bennett. *Creatures* [2-5], 1820
Witching Time: Mischievous Stories and Poems [2-4], 1698

Yolen, Jane. *Best Witches: Poems for Halloween* [3-6], **1428**

WIZARDS

SEE ALSO Ghosts; Halloween; Magicians; Supernatural; Witches

Alexander, Lloyd. *The Wizard in the Tree* [5-6], 1262

Johnston, Tony. *The Vanishing Pumpkin* [K-1], 443

Lobel, Arnold. *The Great Blueness and Other Predicaments* [K-1], 480

McGraw, Eloise Jarvis. *Joel and the Great Merlini* [3-4], 1093

Madden, Don. *The Wartville Wizard* [1-2], 738

Mayer, Mercer. *Mrs. Beggs and the Wizard* [1-2], 749

Moore, Inga. *The Sorcerer's Apprentice* [2-3], **648**

Sterman, Betsy, and Samuel Sterman. *Backyard Dragon* [3-4], **750**

Wrede, Patricia. *Dealing with Dragons* [5-6], **853**

Yolen, Jane. *Wizard's Hall* [4-5], **801**

WIZARDS–Folklore

Gabler, Mirko. *Tall, Wide, and Sharp-Eye* [1-4], **907**

Grimm, Jacob. *The Donkey Prince* [2-4], 1490

WOLVES

Ada, Alma Flor. *Dear Peter Rabbit* [1-2], 395

Allard, Harry. *It's So Nice to Have a Wolf around the House* [K-1], 317

Blundell, Tony. *Beware of Boys* [K-1], **232**

Brandenberg, Jim. *To the Top of the World: Adventures with Arctic Wolves* [4-6], **1108**

Gay, Michael. *The Christmas Wolf* [K-1], 404

George, Jean Craighead. *Julie of the Wolves* [5-6], 1304

Gibbons, Gail. *Wolves* [1-3], **1149**

Goble, Paul. *Dream Wolf* [1-2], **443**

Kasza, Keiko. *The Wolf's Chicken Stew* [Pre-K], 162

London, Jonathan. *The Eyes of Gray Wolf* [1-2], **488**

McCleery, William. *Wolf Story* [K-1], 489

Maestro, Betsy, and Giulio Maestro. *Lambs for Dinner* [K-1], 498

Murphy, Jim. *The Call of the Wolves* [2-3], 969

Offen, Hilda. *Nice Work, Little Wolf!* [Pre-K], **173**

Rayner, Mary. *Garth Pig and the Ice Cream Lady* [1-2], 781
Garth Pig Steals the Show [1-2], **543**
Mr. and Mrs. Pig's Evening Out [1-2], 782
Ten Pink Piglets: Garth Pig's Wall Song [Pre-K], **179**

Rice, Bebe Faas. *The Year the Wolves Came* [5-6], **839**

Scieszka, Jon. *The True Story of the 3 Little Pigs* [2-3], 993

Storr, Catherine. *Clever Polly and the Stupid Wolf* [3-4], 1122

Trivizas, Eugene. *The Three Little Wolves and the Big Bad Pig* [K-1], **378**

Vozar, David. *Yo, Hungry Wolf! A Nursery Rap* [1-2], **570**

WOLVES–Folklore

Cauley, Lorinda Bryan. *The Three Little Pigs* [Pre-2], 1420

Compton, Patricia A. *The Terrible Eek* [K-3], **885**

Galdone, Paul. *The Three Little Pigs* [Pre-1], 1474

Grimm, Jacob. *Little Red Cap* [Pre-2], 1500
Little Red Riding Hood [Pre-2], 1501
Nanny Goat and the Seven Little Kids [K-2], **924**
The Wolf and the Seven Little Kids [Pre-1], 1512

Harper, Wilhelmina. *The Gunniwolf* [Pre-1], 1519

Marshall, James. *Red Riding Hood* [Pre-2], 1562
The Three Little Pigs [Pre-1], 1563

Ross, Gayle. *How Turtle's Back Was Cracked: A Traditional Cherokee Tale* [1-4], **1008**

Roth, Susan L. *Kanahena: A Cherokee Story* [Pre-2], 1587

Rounds, Glen. *Three Little Pigs and the Big Bad Wolf* [Pre-2], **1010**

Young, Ed. *Lon Po Po: A Red-Riding Hood Story from China* [K-2], 1633

Zemach, Margot. *The Three Little Pigs: An Old Story* [Pre-2], 1639

WOMEN–Biography

Adler, David A. *A Picture Book of Sojourner Truth* [2-4], **1096**

Brown, Don. *Ruth Law Thrills a Nation* [K-4], **1111**

Cole, Sheila. *The Dragon in the Cliff: A Novel Based on the Life of Mary Anning* [5-6], **807**

Houston, Gloria. *My Great Aunt Arizona* [1-6], **1165**

Lauber, Patricia. *Lost Star: The Story of Amelia Earhart* [5-6], 2061

Livingston, Myra Cohn. *Keep on Singing: A Ballad of Marian Anderson* [1-4], **1190**

McGovern, Ann. *The Secret Soldier: The Story of Deborah Sampson* [3-6], 2071

Polacco, Patricia. *Firetalking* [1-4], **1221**

Rappaport, Doreen. *Living Dangerously: American Women Who Risked Their Lives for Adventure* [4-6], **1224**

Reit, Seymour. *Behind Rebel Lines: The Incredible Story of Emma Edmonds, Civil War Spy* [5-6], 2085

Rylant, Cynthia. *Best Wishes* [1-5], **1233**

WOMEN–Folklore

Brusca, María Cristina, and Tona Wilson. *The Cook and the King* [2-4], **874**

Greene, Ellin. *Clever Cooks: A Concoction of Stories, Charms, Recipes and Riddles* [2-5], 1683

Lurie, Alison. *Clever Gretchen and Other Forgotten Folktales* [4-6], 1708

Minard, Rosemary. *Womenfolk and Fairy Tales* [3-6], 1712

Riordan, James. *The Woman in the Moon: And Other Tales of Forgotten Heroines* [4-6], 1717

Stamm, Claus. *Three Strong Women: A Tall Tale* [2-4], 1605

WOMEN–Poetry

Ness, Evaline. *Amelia Mixed the Mustard and Other Poems* [2-5], 1895

WORD GAMES

SEE ALSO Alliteration; English language; Tongue twisters; Vocabulary

Agee, Jon. *Go Hang a Salami! I'm a Lasagna Hog! And Other Palindromes* [2-6], **1263**

Barrol, Grady. *The Little Book of Anagrams* [3-6], 1745

Bourke, Linda. *Eye Spy: A Mysterious Alphabet* [1-2], **409**

Brandreth, Gyles. *Brain-Teasers and Mind-Benders* [3-6], 1997

Cauley, Lorinda Bryan. *Treasure Hunt* [Pre-K], **79**

Churchill, E. Richard. *Devilish Bets to Trick Your Friends* [3-6], 2005

Cricket Magazine, editors of. *Cricket's Jokes, Riddles & Other Stuff* [K-5], 1785

Doty, Roy. *Tinkerbell Is a Ding-a-Ling* [4-6], 1794

Emrich, Duncan. *The Hodgepodge Book* [2-6], 1796

Falwell, Cathryn. *Clowning Around* [K-1], **272**

Gerberg, Mort. *Geographunny: A Book of Global Riddles* [3-6], **1295**

Gordon, Jeffie Ross. *Hide and Shriek: Riddles About Ghosts & Goblins* [2-5], **1300**

Hartman, Victoria. *The Silliest Joke Book Ever* [3-5], **1308**

Hepworth, Cathi. *Antics! An Alphabetical Anthology* [2-6], **1312**

Hoguet, Susan. *I Unpacked My Grandmother's Trunk* [1-2], 689

Jonas, Ann. *The 13th Clue* [1-2], **464**

Keller, Charles. *Remember the à la Mode! Riddles and Puns* [2-6], 1841

Levitt, Paul M., Douglas A. Burger, and Elissa S. Guralnick. *The Weighty Word Book* [5-6], 1326

McMillan, Bruce, and Brett McMillan. *Puniddles* [2-3], 959

Maestro, Giulio. *Razzle-Dazzle Riddles* [Pre-3], 1866

Merriam, Eve. *Chortles: New and Selected Wordplay Poems* [3-6], 1869

The Singing Green: New and Selected Poems for All Seasons [3-6], **1373**

Most, Bernard. *Can You Find It?* [K-1], **329**

Hippopotamus Hunt [1-2], **513**

Zoodles [1-2], **514**

Phillips, Louis. *How Do You Get a Horse Out of the Bathtub? Profound Answers to Preposterous Questions* [5-6], 1900

263 Brain Busters: Just How Smart Are You, Anyway? [3-6], 2083

Rosenbloom, Joseph. *Daffy Definitions* [4-6], 1927

Schwartz, Alvin. *Tomfoolery: Trickery and Foolery with Words* [1-6], 1949

Steig, William. *CDB* [2-6], 1959

Terban, Marvin. *Funny You Should Ask: How to Make Up Jokes and Riddles with Wordplay* [3-6], **1414**

WORD GAMES (cont.)

Weil, Lisl. *Owl and Other Scrambles* [2-3], 1026

White, Laurence B., Jr., and Ray Broekel. *The Surprise Book* [2-6], 2114

Young, Frederica. *Super-Duper Jokes* [3-6], **1432**

WORDLESS BOOKS

SEE Stories without words

WORDS

SEE English language; Language; Vocabulary; Word games

WORK

Buehner, Caralyn. *A Job for Wittilda* [K-1], **242**

Bunting, Eve. *A Day's Work* [2-3], **592**

Demuth, Patricia Brennan. *The Ornery Morning* [K-1], **260**

Mitchell, Margaree King. *Uncle Jed's Barbershop* [2-3], **647**

Singer, Marilyn. *Chester the Out-of-Work Dog* [K-1], **366**

Waddell, Martin. *Farmer Duck* [Pre-K], **200**

Zimelman, Nathan. *How the Second Grade Got $8,205.50 to Visit the Statue of Liberty* [1-2], **583**

WORLD WAR, 1914-1918

Morpurgo, Michael. *War Horse* [5-6], 1334

WORLD WAR, 1914-1918–Fiction

Foreman, Michael. *War Game* [5-6], 816

Rabin, Staton. *Casey Over There* [2-3], **666**

Wells, Rosemary. *Waiting for the Evening Star* [3-4], **754**

WORLD WAR, 1939-1945

Abels, Chana Byers. *The Children We Remember* [4-6], 1985

Coerr, Eleanor. *Sadako* [2-5], **1120**

Sadako & the Thousand Paper Cranes [3-6], 2007

Isaacman, Clara, and Joan Adess Grossman. *Clara's Story* [5-6], 2054

Morimoto, Junko. *My Hiroshima* [3-6], **1210**

Stevenson, James. *Don't You Know There's a War On?* [2-6], **1245**

WORLD WAR, 1939-1945–Fiction

Coerr, Eleanor. *Mieko and the Fifth Treasure* [3-4], **707**

Fife, Dale. *North of Danger* [5-6], 1296

Lowry, Lois. *Number the Stars* [5-6], 1328

McSwigan, Marie. *Snow Treasure* [5-6], 1330

Mellecker, Judith. *Randolph's Dream* [3-4], **732**

Mochizuki, Ken. *Baseball Saved Us* [3-4], **733**

Paulsen, Gary. *A Christmas Sonata* [5-6], **833**

The Cookcamp [5-6], **834**

Streatfeild, Noel. *When the Sirens Wailed* [5-6], 1366

Uchida, Yoshiko. *Journey Home* [5-6], 1370

Wolitzer, Hilma. *Introducing Shirley Braverman* [5-6], 1376

Wuorio, Eva-Lis. *Code: Polonaise* [5-6], 1377

WORMS

Giff, Patricia Reilly. *The Winter Worm Business* [4-5], 1177

Lionni, Leo. *Inch by Inch* [K-1], 475

Rockwell, Thomas. *How to Eat Fried Worms* [3-4], 1109

Van Laan, Nancy. *The Big Fat Worm* [Pre-K], 282

WORRYING

Gackenbach, Dick. *Where Are Momma, Poppa, and Sister June?* [K-1], **274**

WOUNDS AND INJURIES

MacDonald, Amy. *Rachel Fister's Blister* [K-1], **312**

WRITERS

SEE Authors; Children's writing; Writing

WRITING

SEE ALSO Authors; Children's writing; Creative writing

Byars, Betsy. *The Moon and I* [4-6], **1115**

Conford, Ellen. *Jenny Archer, Author* [2-3], 898

Revenge of the Incredible Dr. Rancid and His Youthful Assistant, Jeffrey [4-5], 1162

Drescher, Henrik. *Simon's Book* [1-2], 664

Fitzhugh, Louise. *Harriet the Spy* [5-6], 1298

Goldstein, Bobbye S. *Inner Chimes: Poems on Poetry* [2-6], **1298**

Heide, Florence Parry. *Banana Twist* [5-6], 1310

Heide, Florence Parry, and Judith Heide Gilliland. *The Day of Ahmed's Secret* [2-3], **616**

Janeczko, Paul B. *Poetry from A to Z: A Guide for Young Writers* [5-6], **1335**

Johnston, Johanna. *That's Right, Edie* [K-1], 441

Krauss, Ruth. *Is This You?* [1-2], 714

Little, Jean. *Little by Little: A Writer's Education* [5-6], **1187**

Martin, Rafe. *A Storyteller's Story* [1-4], **1202**

Nixon, Joan Lowery. *If You Were a Writer* [2-3], 972

Polacco, Patricia. *Firetalking* [1-4], **1221**

Roop, Peter, and Connie Roop. *Ahyoka and the Talking Leaves* [3-4], **740**

Rylant, Cynthia. *Best Wishes* [1-5], **1233**

Snyder, Zilpha Keatley. *Libby on Wednesday* [5-6], **846**

Stanley, Diane. *The Good-Luck Pencil* [2-3], 1005

Williams, Vera B. *Cherries and Cherry Pits* [1-2], 852

WYOMING
Paulsen, Gary. *The Haymeadow* [5-6], **835**

YO-YOS
Dugan, Barbara. *Loop the Loop* [2-3], **608**

ZEBRAS
Mwenye Hadithi. *Greedy Zebra* [Pre-K], 125

ZOOS
Blumberg, Rhoda. *Jumbo* [2-5], **1107**
De Regniers, Beatrice Schenk. *May I Bring a Friend?* [Pre-K], 69
Gelman, Rita Golden. *I Went to the Zoo* [K-1], **275**
Jeschke, Susan. *Angela and Bear* [K-1], 437

Johnston, Ginny, and Judy Cutchins. *Andy Bear: A Polar Bear Cub Grows Up at the Zoo* [2-6], 2056
Knowles, Sheena. *Edward the Emu* [K-1], **300**
Martin, Bill, Jr. *Polar Bear, Polar Bear, What Do You Hear?* [Pre-K], **160**
Peet, Bill. *Encore for Eleanor* [1-2], 768
Pfeffer, Wendy. *Popcorn Park Zoo: A Haven with a Heart* [3-5], **1220**
Seuss, Dr. *If I Ran the Zoo* [1-2], 803

ZUNI INDIANS–Folklore
McDermott, Gerald. *Coyote: A Trickster Tale from the American Southwest* [Pre-2], **975**
Pollock, Penny. *The Turkey Girl: A Zuni Cinderella Story* [2-5], **1000**
Rodanas, Kristina. *Dragonfly's Tale* [K-3], **1005**

From KNIGHTS OF THE KITCHEN TABLE by Jon Scieszka, illustrated by
Lane Smith. Copyright © 1991 by Lane Smith on illustrations.
Used by permission of Viking Penguin, a division of Penguin Books USA Inc.

ABOUT THE AUTHOR

JUDY FREEMAN IS AN ELEMENTARY SCHOOL LIBRARIAN AT THE VAN Holten School in Bridgewater, New Jersey. Since 1981, as an adjunct staff member in the Professional Development Studies Department of the Rutgers University School of Communication, Information and Library Studies, she has developed and taught dozens of courses, workshops, and conferences in children's literature, booktalking, storytelling, creative dramatics, and library skills instruction. An acclaimed workshop presenter at seminars and in-service programs in both the United States and Canada, Freeman also writes the monthly "Learning with Literature" column for *Instructor* magazine and a yearly children's book feature for *Teacher* magazine. At home in Highland Park, New Jersey, she and her husband Izzy Feldman raise giant hibiscus, killer tomatoes, and two incorrigible, unrepentant cats.